Nineteenth-Century Literature Criticism

Guide to Gale Literary Criticism Series

When you need to review criticism of literary works, these are the Gale series to use:

If the author's death date is:	You should turn to:
After Dec. 31, 1959 (or author is still living)	***CONTEMPORARY LITERARY CRITICISM*** for example: Jorge Luis Borges, Anthony Burgess, William Faulkner, Mary Gordon, Ernest Hemingway, Iris Murdoch
1900 through 1959	***TWENTIETH-CENTURY LITERARY CRITICISM*** for example: Willa Cather, F. Scott Fitzgerald, Henry James, Mark Twain, Virginia Woolf
1800 through 1899	***NINETEENTH-CENTURY LITERATURE CRITICISM*** for example: Fedor Dostoevski, Nathaniel Hawthorne, George Sand, William Wordsworth
1400 through 1799	***LITERATURE CRITICISM FROM 1400 TO 1800 (excluding Shakespeare)*** for example: Anne Bradstreet, Daniel Defoe, Alexander Pope, François Rabelais, Jonathan Swift, Phillis Wheatley ***SHAKESPEAREAN CRITICISM*** Shakespeare's plays and poetry
Antiquity through 1399	***CLASSICAL AND MEDIEVAL LITERATURE CRITICISM*** for example: Dante, Homer, Plato, Sophocles, Vergil, the Beowulf Poet

---

Gale also publishes related criticism series:

CHILDREN'S LITERATURE REVIEW

This ongoing series covers authors of all eras. Presents criticism on authors and author/illustrators who write for the preschool through high school audience.

SHORT STORY CRITICISM

This series covers the major short fiction writers of all nationalities and periods of literary history.

ISSN 0732-1864

Volume 17

Nineteenth-Century Literature Criticism

Excerpts from Criticism of the
Works of Novelists, Poets, Playwrights,
Short Story Writers, Philosophers, and Other
Creative Writers Who Died between 1800
and 1899, from the First Published Critical
Appraisals to Current Evaluations

Janet Mullane
Editor

Robert Thomas Wilson
Associate Editor

Gale Research Company
Book Tower
Detroit, Michigan 48226

STAFF

Janet Mullane, *Editor*

Robert Thomas Wilson, *Associate Editor*

Gail Ann Schulte, *Senior Assistant Editor*

Rachel Carlson, Vivian L. Metcalf, Mary Nelson-Pulice, *Assistant Editors*

Cherie D. Abbey, Sheila Fitzgerald, Jelena Krstovic,
Phyllis Carmel Mendelson, Emily B. Tennyson, *Contributing Editors*
Denise Michlewicz Broderick, James P. Draper,
Melissa Reiff Hug, Debra A. Wells, *Contributing Assistant Editors*

Jeanne A. Gough, *Permissions & Production Manager*
Lizbeth A. Purdy, *Production Supervisor*
Kathleen M. Cook, *Assistant Production Coordinator*
Cathy Beranek, Suzanne Powers, Kristine E. Tipton,
Lee Ann Welsh, *Editorial Assistants*
Linda Marcella Pugliese, *Manuscript Coordinator*
Donna Craft, *Assistant Manuscript Coordinator*
Jennifer E. Gale, Maureen A. Puhl, Rosetta Irene Simms, *Manuscript Assistants*

Victoria B. Cariappa, *Research Supervisor*
Maureen R. Richards, *Research Coordinator*
Mary D. Wise, *Senior Research Assistant*
Joyce E. Doyle, Kevin B. Hillstrom, Karen O. Kaus, Eric Priehs,
Filomena Sgambati, Laura B. Standley, *Research Assistants*

Janice M. Mach, *Text Permissions Supervisor*
Kathy Grell, *Text Permissions Coordinator*
Mabel E. Gurney, Josephine M. Keene, *Senior Permissions Assistants*
Eileen H. Baehr, H. Diane Cooper, Anita L. Ransom,
Kimberly F. Smilay, *Permissions Assistants*
Melissa A. Kamuyu, Martha A. Mulder, Lisa M. Wimmer, *Permissions Clerks*

Patricia A. Seefelt, *Picture Permissions Supervisor*
Margaret A. Chamberlain, *Permissions Coordinator, Pictures*
Pamela A. Hayes, Lillian Tyus, *Permissions Clerks*

Copyright © 1988 by Gale Research Company

Library of Congress Catalog Card Number 81-6943
ISBN 0-8103-5817-4
ISSN 0732-1864

Computerized photocomposition by
Typographics, Incorporated
Kansas City, Missouri

Printed in the United States

Contents

Preface

The nineteenth century was a time of tremendous growth in human endeavor: in science, in social history, and particularly in literature. The era saw the development of the novel, witnessed radical changes from classicism to romanticism to realism, and fostered intellectual and artistic ideas that continue to inspire authors of our own century. The importance of the writers of the nineteenth century is twofold, for they provide insight into their own time as well as into the universal nature of human experience.

The literary criticism of an era can also give us insight into the moral and intellectual atmosphere of the past because the criteria by which a work of art is judged reflect current philosophical and social attitudes. Literary criticism takes many forms: the traditional essay, the book or play review, even the parodic poem. Criticism can also be of several types: normative, descriptive, interpretive, textual, appreciative, generic. Collectively, the range of critical response helps us to understand a work of art, an author, an era.

Scope of the Series

Nineteenth-Century Literature Criticism (NCLC) is designed to serve as an introduction for the student of nineteenth-century literature to the authors of that period and to the most significant commentators on these authors. Since the analysis of this literature spans almost two hundred years, a vast amount of critical material confronts the student. For that reason, *NCLC* presents significant passages from published criticism to aid students in the location and selection of commentaries on authors who died between 1800 and 1899. The need for *NCLC* was suggested by the usefulness of the Gale series *Twentieth-Century Literary Criticism (TCLC)* and *Contemporary Literary Criticism (CLC),* which excerpt criticism of creative writing of the twentieth century. For further information about *TCLC, CLC,* and Gale's other criticism series, users should consult the Guide to Gale Literary Criticism Series preceding the title page in this volume.

Each volume of *NCLC* is carefully compiled to include authors who represent a variety of genres and nationalities and who are currently regarded as the most important writers of their era. In addition to major authors who have attained worldwide renown, *NCLC* also presents criticism on lesser-known figures whose significant contributions to literary history are important to the study of nineteenth-century literature. These authors are important artists in their own right, and often enjoy such an immense popularity in their own countries that English-speaking readers should become more familiar with their work.

Author entries in *NCLC* are intended to be definitive overviews. In order to devote more attention to each writer, approximately ten to fifteen authors are included in each 600-page volume, compared with about forty authors in a *CLC* volume of similar size. The length of each author entry is intended to reflect the amount of attention the author has received from critics writing in English and from foreign critics in translation. Articles and books that have not been translated into English are excluded. However, since many of the major foreign studies have been translated into English and are excerpted in *NCLC,* author entries reflect the viewpoints of many nationalities. Each author entry represents a historical overview of critical reaction to the author's work: early criticism is presented to indicate initial responses, later selections represent any rise or decline in the author's literary reputation, and current analyses provide students with a modern perspective. In each entry, we have attempted to identify and include excerpts from all seminal essays of criticism.

An author may appear more than once in the series because of the great quantity of critical material available or because of a resurgence of criticism generated by events such as an author's centennial or anniversary celebration, the republication or posthumous publication of an author's works, or the publication of a newly translated work. Usually, one or more author entries in each volume of *NCLC* are devoted to individual works or groups of works by major authors who have appeared previously in the series. Only those works that have been the subjects of extensive criticism and are widely studied in literature courses are selected for this in-depth treatment. Nathaniel Hawthorne's *The Blithedale Romance* is the subject of such an entry in *NCLC,* Volume 17.

Organization of the Book

An author entry consists of the following elements: author heading, biographical and critical introduction, principal works, excerpts of criticism (each preceded by explanatory notes and followed by a bibliographical citation), and an additional bibliography for further reading.

- The *author heading* consists of the author's full name, followed by birth and death dates. The unbracketed portion of the name denotes the form under which the author most commonly wrote. If an author wrote consistently under a pseudonym, the pseudonym will be listed in the author heading and the real name given in parentheses on the first line of the biographical and critical introduction. Also located at the beginning of the introduction are any name variations under which an author wrote, including transliterated forms for authors whose languages use nonroman alphabets. Uncertainty as to a birth or death date is indicated by a question mark.

- A *portrait* of the author is included when available. Many entries also feature illustrations of materials pertinent to an author's career, including manuscript pages, letters, book illustrations, and representations of important people, places, and events in an author's life.

- The *biographical and critical introduction* contains background information that introduces the reader to an author and to the critical debate surrounding his or her work. When applicable, biographical and critical introductions are followed by references to additional entries on the author in other literary reference series published by Gale Research Company, including *Dictionary of Literary Biography, Children's Literature Review,* and *Something about the Author.*

- The list of *principal works* is chronological by date of first book publication and identifies the genre of each work. In those instances where the first publication was in other than the English language, the title and date of the first English-language edition are given in brackets. Unless otherwise indicated, dramas are dated by the first performance, rather than first publication.

- *Criticism* is arranged chronologically in each author entry to provide a useful perspective on changes in critical evaluation over the years. All titles by the author featured in the critical entry are printed in boldface type to enable the user to ascertain without difficulty the works being discussed. Also for purposes of easier identification, the critic's name and the publication date of the essay are given at the beginning of each piece of criticism. Unsigned criticism is preceded by the title of the journal in which it appeared. When an anonymous essay is later attributed to a critic, the critic's name appears in brackets at the beginning of the excerpt and in the bibliographical citation. Publication information (such as publisher names and book prices) and parenthetical numerical references (such as footnotes or page and line references to specific editions of works) have been deleted at the editor's discretion to provide smoother reading of the text.

- Critical essays are prefaced with *explanatory notes* as an additional aid to students using *NCLC*. The explanatory notes provide several types of useful information, including the reputation of the critic, the importance of a work of criticism, a synopsis of the essay, the specific approach of the critic (biographical, psychoanalytic, structuralist, etc.), and the growth of critical controversy or changes in critical trends regarding an author's work. In some cases, these notes include cross-references to related criticism in the author's entry or in the additional bibliography. Dates in parentheses within the explanatory notes refer to the dates of other essays in the author entry.

- A complete *bibliographical citation* designed to facilitate the location of the original essay or book follows each piece of criticism.

- The *additional bibliography* appearing at the end of each author entry suggests further reading on the author. In some cases it includes essays for which the editors could not obtain reprint rights.

An appendix lists the sources from which material in the volume is reprinted. It does not, however, list every book or periodical consulted for the volume.

Cumulative Indexes

Each volume of *NCLC* includes a cumulative index listing all the authors who have appeared in *Contemporary Literary Criticism, Twentieth-Century Literary Criticism, Nineteenth-Century Literature Criticism, Literature*

Criticism from 1400 to 1800, Classical and Medieval Literature Criticism, and *Short Story Criticism*, along with cross-references to the Gale series *Children's Literature Review, Authors in the News, Contemporary Authors, Contemporary Authors Autobiography Series, Dictionary of Literary Biography, Concise Dictionary of American Literary Biography, Something about the Author, Something about the Author Autobiography Series*, and *Yesterday's Authors of Books for Children*. Readers will welcome this cumulated author index as a useful tool for locating an author within the various series. The index, which lists birth and death dates when available, will be particularly valuable for those authors who are identified with a certain period but whose death dates cause them to be placed in another, or for those authors whose careers span two periods. For example, Fedor Dostoevski is found in *NCLC*, yet Leo Tolstoy, another major nineteenth-century Russian novelist, is found in *TCLC*.

Each volume of *NCLC* also includes a cumulative nationality index to authors. Authors are listed alphabetically by nationality, followed by the volume numbers in which they appear.

New Index

An important feature now appearing in *NCLC* is a cumulative title index, an alphabetical listing of the literary works discussed in the series since its inception. Each title listing includes the corresponding volume and page numbers where criticism may be located. Foreign language titles that have been translated are followed by the titles of the translations, for example: *Die Leiden des jungen Werthers (The Sorrows of Young Werther)*. Page numbers following these translated titles refer to all pages on which any form of the title, either foreign language or translated, appears. Titles of novels, dramas, nonfiction books, and poetry, short story, or essay collections are printed in italics, while all individual poems, short stories, and essays are printed in roman type within quotation marks. In cases where the same title is used by different authors, the author's surname is given in parentheses after the title, e.g., *Poems* (Wordsworth) and *Poems* (Coleridge).

Acknowledgments

No work of this scope can be accomplished without the cooperation of many people. The editors especially wish to thank the copyright holders of the excerpted criticism included in this volume, the permissions managers of many book and magazine publishing companies for assisting us in securing reprint rights, and Anthony Bogucki for assistance with copyright research. We are also grateful to the staffs of the Detroit Public Library, the Library of Congress, University of Michigan Library, and Wayne State University Library for making their resources available to us.

Suggestions Are Welcome

In response to various suggestions, several features have been added to *NCLC* since the series began, including: explanatory notes to excerpted criticism that provide important information regarding critics and their work; a cumulative author index listing authors in all Gale literary criticism series; entries devoted to criticism on a single work by a major author; more extensive illustrations; and a cumulative title index listing all the literary works discussed in the series.

The editors welcome additional comments and suggestions to expand the coverage and enhance the usefulness of the series.

Authors to Appear in Future Volumes

About, Edmond François 1828-1885
Aguilo I. Fuster, Maria 1825-1897
Aksakov, Konstantin 1817-1860
Aleardi, Aleardo 1812-1878
Alecsandri, Vasile 1821-1890
Alencar, José 1829-1877
Alfieri, Vittorio 1749-1803
Allingham, William 1824-1889
Almquist, Carl Jonas Love 1793-1866
Alorne, Leonor de Almeida 1750-1839
Alsop, Richard 1761-1815
Altimirano, Ignacio Manuel 1834-1893
Alvarenga, Manuel Inacio da Silva
    1749-1814
Alvares de Azevedo, Manuel Antonio
    1831-1852
Anzengruber, Ludwig 1839-1889
Arany, Janos 1817-1882
Arène, Paul 1843-1896
Aribau, Bonaventura Carlos 1798-1862
Arjona de Cubas, Manuel Maria de
    1771-1820
Arnault, Antoine Vincent 1766-1834
Arneth, Alfred von 1819-1897
Arnim, Bettina von 1785-1859
Arnold, Thomas 1795-1842
Arriaza y Superviela, Juan Bautista
    1770-1837
Asbjörnsen, Peter Christen 1812-1885
Ascasubi, Hilario 1807-1875
Atterbom, Per Daniel Amadeus
    1790-1855
Aubanel, Theodore 1829-1886
Auerbach, Berthold 1812-1882
Augier, Guillaume V.E. 1820-1889
Azeglio, Massimo D' 1798-1866
Azevedo, Guilherme de 1839-1882
Bakin (pseud. of Takizawa Okikani)
    1767-1848
Bakunin, Mikhail Aleksandrovich
    1814-1876
Baratynski, Jewgenij Abramovich
    1800-1844
Barnes, William 1801-1886
Batyushkov, Konstantin 1778-1855
Beattie, James 1735-1803
Becquer, Gustavo Adolfo 1836-1870
Bentham, Jeremy 1748-1832
Béranger, Jean-Pierre de 1780-1857
Berchet, Giovanni 1783-1851
Berzsenyi, Daniel 1776-1836
Black, William 1841-1898
Blair, Hugh 1718-1800
Blicher, Steen Steensen 1782-1848
Bocage, Manuel Maria Barbosa du
    1765-1805
Boratynsky, Yevgeny 1800-1844

Borel, Petrus 1809-1859
Boreman, Yokutiel 1825-1890
Borne, Ludwig 1786-1837
Botev, Hristo 1778-1842
Brinckman, John 1814-1870
Brown, Charles Brockden 1777-1810
Browning, Robert 1812-1889
Büchner, Georg 1813-1837
Campbell, James Edwin 1867-1895
Campbell, Thomas 1777-1844
Carlyle, Thomas 1795-1881
Castelo Branco, Camilo 1825-1890
Castro Alves, Antonio de 1847-1871
Chatterje, Bankin Chanda 1838-1894
Chivers, Thomas Holly 1807?-1858
Claudius, Matthias 1740-1815
Clough, Arthur Hugh 1819-1861
Cobbett, William 1762-1835
Colenso, John William 1814-1883
Coleridge, Hartley 1796-1849
Collett, Camilla 1813-1895
Comte, Auguste 1798-1857
Conrad, Robert T. 1810-1858
Conscience, Hendrik 1812-1883
Cooke, Philip Pendleton 1816-1850
Corbière, Edouard 1845-1875
Crabbe, George 1754-1832
Cruz E Sousa, João da 1861-1898
Desbordes-Valmore, Marceline
    1786-1859
Deschamps, Emile 1791-1871
Deus, João de 1830-1896
Dickinson, Emily 1830-1886
Dinis, Julio 1839-1871
Dinsmoor, Robert 1757-1836
Du Maurier, George 1834-1896
Echeverria, Esteban 1805-1851
Eminescy, Mihai 1850-1889
Engels, Friedrich 1820-1895
Espronceda, José 1808-1842
Ettinger, Solomon 1799-1855
Euchel, Issac 1756-1804
Ferguson, Samuel 1810-1886
Fernández de Lizardi, José Joaquín
    1776-1827
Fernández de Moratín, Leandro
    1760-1828
Fet, Afanasy 1820-1892
Feuillet, Octave 1821-1890
Fontane, Theodor 1819-1898
Freiligrath, Hermann Ferdinand
    1810-1876
Freytag, Gustav 1816-1895
Ganivet, Angel 1865-1898
Garrett, Almeida 1799-1854
Garshin, Vsevolod Mikhaylovich
    1855-1888

Gezelle, Guido 1830-1899
Ghalib, Asadullah Khan 1797-1869
Goldschmidt, Meir Aaron 1819-1887
Goncalves Dias, Antonio 1823-1864
Griboyedov, Aleksander Sergeyevich
    1795-1829
Grigor'yev, Appolon Aleksandrovich
    1822-1864
Groth, Klaus 1819-1899
Grun, Anastasius (pseud. of Anton
    Alexander Graf von Auersperg)
    1806-1876
Guerrazzi, Francesco Domenico
    1804-1873
Gutierrez Najera, Manuel 1859-1895
Gutzkow, Karl Ferdinand 1811-1878
Ha-Kohen, Shalom 1772-1845
Halleck, Fitz-Greene 1790-1867
Harris, George Washington 1814-1869
Hayne, Paul Hamilton 1830-1886
Hazlitt, William 1778-1830
Hebbel, Christian Friedrich 1813-1863
Hebel, Johann Peter 1760-1826
Hegel, Georg Wilhelm Friedrich
    1770-1831
Heiberg, Johann Ludvig 1813-1863
Herculano, Alexandre 1810-1866
Hertz, Henrik 1798-1870
Herwegh, Georg 1817-1875
Hoffman, Charles Fenno 1806-1884
Hooper, Johnson Jones 1815-1863
Horton, George Moses 1798-1880
Howitt, William 1792-1879
Hughes, Thomas 1822-1896
Imlay, Gilbert 1754?-1828?
Irwin, Thomas Caulfield 1823-1892
Isaacs, Jorge 1837-1895
Jacobsen, Jens Peter 1847-1885
Jippensha, Ikku 1765-1831
Kant, Immanuel 1724-1804
Karr, Jean Baptiste Alphonse
    1808-1890
Keble, John 1792-1866
Khomyakov, Alexey S. 1804-1860
Kierkegaard, Søren 1813-1855
Kinglake, Alexander W. 1809-1891
Kingsley, Charles 1819-1875
Kivi, Alexis 1834-1872
Koltsov, Alexey Vasilyevich 1809-1842
Kotzebue, August von 1761-1819
Kraszewski, Josef Ignacy 1812-1887
Kreutzwald, Friedrich Reinhold
    1803-1882
Krochmal, Nahman 1785-1840
Krudener, Valeria Barbara Julia de
    Wietinghoff 1766-1824
Lampman, Archibald 1861-1899

Lebensohn, Micah Joseph 1828-1852
Leconte de Lisle, Charles-Marie-René 1818-1894
Leontyev, Konstantin 1831-1891
Leopardi, Giacoma 1798-1837
Leskov, Nikolai 1831-1895
Lever, Charles James 1806-1872
Levisohn, Solomon 1789-1822
Lewes, George Henry 1817-1878
Leyden, John 1775-1811
Lobensohn, Micah Gregory 1775-1810
Longstreet, Augustus Baldwin 1790-1870
López de Ayola y Herrera, Adelardo 1819-1871
Lover, Samuel 1797-1868
Luzzato, Samuel David 1800-1865
Macedo, Joaquim Manuel de 1820-1882
Macha, Karel Hynek 1810-1836
Mackenzie, Henry 1745-1831
Malmon, Solomon 1754-1800
Mangan, James Clarence 1803-1849
Manzoni, Alessandro 1785-1873
Mapu, Abraham 1808-1868
Marii, Jose 1853-1895
Markovic, Svetozar 1846-1875
Martínez de La Rosa, Francisco 1787-1862
Mathews, Cornelius 1817-1889
McCulloch, Thomas 1776-1843
Merriman, Brian 1747-1805
Meyer, Conrad Ferdinand 1825-1898
Montgomery, James 1771-1854
Morton, Sarah Wentworth 1759-1846
Müller, Friedrich 1749-1825
Murger, Henri 1822-1861
Neruda, Jan 1834-1891
Nestroy, Johann 1801-1862
Newman, John Henry 1801-1890
Niccolini, Giambattista 1782-1861
Nievo, Ippolito 1831-1861
Nodier, Charles 1780-1844
Obradovic, Dositej 1742-1811
Oehlenschlager, Adam 1779-1850

O'Neddy, Philothee (pseud. of Theophile Dondey) 1811-1875
O'Shaughnessy, Arthur William Edgar 1844-1881
Ostrovsky, Alexander 1823-1886
Paine, Thomas 1737-1809
Peacock, Thomas Love 1785-1866
Perk, Jacques 1859-1881
Pisemsky, Alexey F. 1820-1881
Pompeia, Raul D'Avila 1863-1895
Popovic, Jovan Sterija 1806-1856
Praed, Winthrop Mackworth 1802-1839
Prati, Giovanni 1814-1884
Preseren, France 1800-1849
Pringle, Thomas 1789-1834
Procter, Adelaide Ann 1825-1864
Procter, Bryan Waller 1787-1874
Pye, Henry James 1745-1813
Quental, Antero Tarquinio de 1842-1891
Quinet, Edgar 1803-1875
Quintana, Manuel José 1772-1857
Radishchev, Aleksander 1749-1802
Raftery, Anthony 1784-1835
Raimund, Ferdinand 1790-1836
Reid, Mayne 1818-1883
Renan, Ernest 1823-1892
Reuter, Fritz 1810-1874
Rogers, Samuel 1763-1855
Ruckert, Friedrich 1788-1866
Runeberg, Johan 1804-1877
Rydberg, Viktor 1828-1895
Saavedra y Ramírez de Boquedano, Angel de 1791-1865
Sacher-Mosoch, Leopold von 1836-1895
Satanov, Isaac 1732-1805
Schiller, Johann Friedrich von 1759-1805
Schlegel, Karl 1772-1829
Sedgwick, Catherine Maria 1789-1867
Senoa, August 1838-1881
Shelley, Percy Bysshe 1792-1822
Shulman, Kalman 1819-1899

Sigourney, Lydia Howard Huntley 1791-1856
Silva, Jose Asuncion 1865-1896
Slaveykov, Petko 1828-1895
Smith, Richard Penn 1799-1854
Smolenskin, Peretz 1842-1885
Stagnelius, Erik Johan 1793-1823
Staring, Antonie Christiaan Wynand 1767-1840
Stendhal (pseud. of Henri Beyle) 1783-1842
Stifter, Adalbert 1805-1868
Stone, John Augustus 1801-1834
Taunay, Alfredo d'Ecragnole 1843-1899
Taylor, Bayard 1825-1878
Tennyson, Alfred, Lord 1809-1892
Terry, Lucy (Lucy Terry Prince) 1730-1821
Thompson, Daniel Pierce 1795-1868
Thompson, Samuel 1766-1816
Thomson, James 1834-1882
Tiedge, Christoph August 1752-1841
Timrod, Henry 1828-1867
Tommaseo, Nicolo 1802-1874
Tompa, Mihaly 1817-1888
Topelius, Zachris 1818-1898
Turgenev, Ivan 1818-1883
Tyutchev, Fedor I. 1803-1873
Uhland, Ludvig 1787-1862
Valaoritis, Aristotelis 1824-1879
Valles, Jules 1832-1885
Verde, Cesario 1855-1886
Villaverde, Cirilio 1812-1894
Vinje, Aasmund Olavsson 1818-1870
Vorosmarty, Mihaly 1800-1855
Weisse, Christian Felix 1726-1804
Welhaven, Johan S. 1807-1873
Werner, Zacharius 1768-1823
Wescott, Edward Noyes 1846-1898
Wessely, Nattali Herz 1725-1805
Whitman, Sarah Helen 1803-1878
Woolson, Constance Fenimore 1840-1894
Zhukovsky, Vasily 1783-1852

William Ellery Channing

1780-1842

American theologian, essayist, and critic.

A minister and theologian whose writings include sermons, essays, and pamphlets, Channing had a profound impact on nineteenth-century American religious thought. He is primarily remembered for championing the dignity of humankind and for articulately expressing his belief in religious and civic freedom. Although Channing opposed sectarianism, his espousal of the concept of God as one essential being and rejection of the doctrine of the Trinity have led historians to regard him as a major contributor to the development of the Unitarian movement in America. In addition, he has been credited with greatly influencing the American transcendentalists through his emphasis on reason in his theological works. Channing also gained a considerable reputation among his contemporaries as a literary and social critic; his most noted works include "Remarks on National Literature," an essay in which he calls for a genuine American literature, and *Slavery,* a pamphlet indicting slavery on moral grounds. In his own day, Channing was frequently censured for his refusal to align himself with any particular religious or social movement. Present-day scholars, however, view his nonpartisanship as consistent with his positive, if overly optimistic, belief in nonviolent reform.

Channing was born in Newport, Rhode Island, to William Channing, the state attorney general, and his wife, Lucy Ellery. At the age of twelve, Channing was sent to his uncle's home in New London, Connecticut, to prepare for college. In 1798, he graduated from Harvard with honors and later that same year acquired a tutorial position in Richmond, Virginia. In addition to fulfilling his tutorial obligations, Channing studied diligently to enter the ministry, often going without proper food, clothing, or rest, a practice that resulted in the permanent weakening of his health. He returned to Harvard in 1802 to complete his theological studies. The following year, Channing was ordained a Congregational minister and installed as pastor of the Federal Street Church in Boston, where he remained for the rest of his life.

Channing's most frequently discussed writings can be grouped into three categories: theological works, literary essays, and social criticism. The first group is composed of sermons, lectures, speeches, and theological essays published in Boston periodicals. While Channing's sermons pleased his congregation, they attracted little national attention until 1819, when he delivered "Unitarian Christianity" (also known as the "Baltimore Sermon") at the ordination of Jared Sparks, who later became a well-known historian. Written in response to the mounting dispute within the New England Congregational Church between its orthodox and liberal factions, the Calvinists and the anti-Calvinists, "Unitarian Christianity" outlined the liberal, or Unitarian, position. Refuting the Calvinist doctrines of the Trinity, predestination, and the elemental depravity of humanity, Channing stressed God's unity and beneficence, as well as humankind's resemblance to God and ability to rationally comprehend spiritual matters. Although Channing never formally aligned himself with the Unitarians, they adopted this sermon as an expression of their beliefs. In 1825, when the Unitarians separated from the Congregational Church, Chan-

ning was asked to serve as the first president of the American Unitarian Association, but declined because he felt that subscription to creeds restricted private intellectual and religious inquiry; he once remarked, "I wish to regard myself as belonging not to a sect, but to a community of free minds, of lovers of the truth, and followers of Christ, both on earth and in heaven." Among Channing's other important theological works are his sermons "The Moral Argument against Calvinism" and "Unitarian Christianity Most Favorable to Piety," both of which further explain the Unitarian theological position. "The Evidences of Revealed Religion," a lecture on supernatural revelation that Channing delivered at Harvard, and "Spiritual Freedom" (also known as the "Election Sermon"), an address to the Massachusetts state senate on the relationship between democracy and intellectual freedom, are also considered significant for their influence upon the American transcendentalist Ralph Waldo Emerson.

Channing's reputation as a literary critic rests on four essays, which were published in the Unitarian periodical the *Christian Examiner* between 1826 and 1830. In the first of these essays, "Remarks on the Character and Writings of John Milton," Channing cites Milton's works as evidence of the morally uplifting nature of poetry, which he terms the "divinest of all the arts." In "Remarks on the Life and Character of Napoleon," a review of Sir Walter Scott's biography of Napoleon

Bonaparte, Channing contends that there are three types of human greatness—moral, intellectual, and active—and assesses Napoleon's character in relation to them. Similarly, in the third essay, ''Remarks on the Character and Writings of Fénelon,'' Channing uses ethical standards as the basis for his judgment of the seventeenth-century French writer and mystic. Channing's final, and most important, literary essay, ''Remarks on National Literature,'' is a plea for an American literature free from British influence; in it, Channing argues that literature is ''among the most powerful methods of exalting the character of a nation, of forming a better race of men.'' Commentators often point out that this work, which Channing called a ''literary Declaration of Independence,'' anticipated by seven years Emerson's famous essay on the same subject, ''The American Scholar.'' In discussing Channing's four literary essays, critics generally note the consistency of his approach: in all of them, Channing evaluates the moral character of the authors discussed and emphasizes both the goodness of humankind and the ennobling qualities of literature. Modern scholars frequently praise the overall clarity of Channing's prose, but concede that it is occasionally repetitious, abstract, and overly dramatic—characteristics that are better suited for oration.

Beginning in the 1830s, Channing's writings increasingly focused on social issues, particularly slavery. His first important work on that subject, *Slavery*, was inspired by his trip in 1830 to the West Indies, where he had observed the English system of slave labor. In this pamphlet, which was published at a time when abolition was a subject of growing debate, Channing systematically argues that slavery is contrary to Christian principles. In addition to alienating the proslavery members of his congregation, *Slavery* provoked criticism from such abolitionist leaders as William Lloyd Garrison for Channing's hesitation to rebuke slaveholders or encourage antislavery violence. The pamphlet was, nevertheless, an articulate condemnation of slavery that strongly influenced public opinion. Channing's other antislavery writings include *The Abolitionists, Remarks on the Slavery Question, in a Letter to Jonathan Phillips, Esq., Emancipation*, and *A Letter to the Hon. Henry Clay, on the Annexation of Texas to the United States*, an open letter to the well-known statesman listing objections to the annexation of Texas as a slave state. Channing also addressed such issues as pacificism, temperance, education, and poverty in a number of other works, among them ''Self-Culture'' and *Lectures on the Elevation of the Laboring Portion of the Community*. Although he was praised for his humanitarian intentions, his proposal to bring about gradual social reform by appealing to people's innate goodness drew censure even from his admirers, many of whom believed that he was overly idealistic.

Channing is now remembered as one of the foremost theologians of his day. While his literary essays generally received favorable reviews, particularly in England, most modern commentators agree that Channing's contemporary reputation as a critic was inflated. Scholars today often note that Channing's literary criticism attracted the attention of early readers largely because of his stature as a religious leader. Yet despite the diminution of Channing's reputation as a literary critic, his immense theological and philosophical influence remains undisputed. Most religious historians trace the formation of the Unitarian denomination in America to Channing's introduction of the concepts of humankind's rationality and innate goodness into the New England Congregational Church. Although scholars continue to debate the extent to which Channing himself was a transcendentalist, they agree that such important mem-

bers of this school of thought as Emerson drew heavily upon his notions of God's unity and comprehensibility. Characterized by the critic George Edward Woodberry as a ''lover of truth unwilling to make proselytes,'' Channing, in his humanitarian quest for social justice and religious liberalism, helped shape the course of religious and philosophical thought in nineteenth-century America. For this contribution, Channing retains a distinguished place in the history of American letters.

(See also *Dictionary of Literary Biography*, Vol. 1: *The American Renaissance in New England*.)

*PRINCIPAL WORKS

''The Guest'' (fable) 1804; published in periodical *The Monthly Anthology*
''Unitarian Christianity: Discourse at the Ordination of the Rev. Jared Sparks'' (sermon) 1819
''The Moral Argument against Calvinism'' (sermon) 1820
''The Evidences of Revealed Religion: Discourse before the University in Cambridge'' (lecture) 1821
''Remarks on the Character and Writings of John Milton'' (essay) 1826; published in periodical *The Christian Examiner*
''Unitarian Christianity Most Favorable to Piety: Discourse at the Dedication of the Second Congregational Unitarian Church in New York'' (sermon) 1826
''Remarks on the Life and Character of Napoleon'' (essay) 1827-28; published in periodical *The Christian Examiner*
''Likeness to God: Discourse at the Ordination of the Rev. F. A. Farley'' (sermon) 1828
''Remarks on the Character and Writings of Fénelon'' (essay) 1829; published in periodical *The Christian Examiner*
Discourses, Reviews, and Miscellanies (sermons, lectures, and essays) 1830
''Remarks on National Literature'' (essay) 1830; published in periodical *The Christian Examiner*
''Spiritual Freedom: Discourse at the Annual Election, May 26, 1830'' (speech) 1830
Slavery (pamphlet) 1835
The Abolitionists (open letter) 1836
A Letter to the Hon. Henry Clay, on the Annexation of Texas to the United States (open letter) 1837
''Self-Culture'' (lecture) 1838
Remarks on the Slavery Question, in a Letter to Jonathan Phillips, Esq. (open letter) 1839
Emancipation (essay) 1840
Lectures on the Elevation of the Laboring Portion of the Community (pamphlet) 1840
The Works of William E. Channing, D.D. 6 vols. (sermons, lectures, speeches, open letters, and essays) 1841-43
''An Address Delivered at Lenox on the First of August, 1842, Being the Anniversary of Emancipation in the British West Indies'' (speech) 1842
Correspondence of William Ellery Channing and Lucy Aikin, from 1826 to 1842 (letters) 1874

*Individual lectures, sermons, and speeches listed here are chronologized by the date of delivery; these works are available in *The Works of William E. Channing, D.D.*

RALPH WALDO EMERSON   (journal date 1823)

[Emerson was one of the most influential figures of the nineteenth century. An American essayist and poet, he founded the transcendental movement and shaped a distinctly American philosophy that embraces optimism, individuality, and mysticism. His philosophy stresses the presence of ongoing creation and revelation by a god apparent in everything and everyone, as well as the essential unity of all thoughts, persons, and things in the divine whole. In the following excerpt from his journal, Emerson records his impressions of Channing's sermons. For additional commentary by Emerson, see the excerpt dated 1882(?).]

I heard Dr. Channing deliver a discourse upon Revelation as standing in comparison with Nature. I have heard no sermon approaching in excellence to this, since the Dudleian Lecture ["**The Evidences of Revealed Religion**," delivered by Dr. Channing in 1821]. The language was a transparent medium, conveying with the utmost distinctness the pictures in his mind to the mind of the hearers. He considered God's word to be the only expounder of his works, and that Nature had always been found insufficient to teach men the great doctrines which Revelation inculcated. Astronomy had in one or two ways an unhappy tendency. An universe of matter in which Deity would display his power and greatness must be of infinite extent and complicate relations, and, of course, too vast to be measured by the eye and understanding of man. Hence errors. Astronomy reveals to us [an] infinite number of worlds like our own, accommodated for the residence of such beings as we of gross matter. But to kindle our piety and urge our faith, we do not want such a world as this, but a purer, a world of morals and of spirits. La Place has written in the mountain album of Switzerland his avowal of Atheism. Newton had a better master than suns and stars. He heard of heaven ere he philosophized, and after travelling through mazes of the universe he returned to bow his laurelled head at the feet of Jesus of Nazareth. Dr. Channing regarded Revelation as much a part of the order of things as any other event. It would have been wise to have made an abstract of the Discourse immediately. (pp. 290-91)

> *Ralph Waldo Emerson, in a journal entry in October, 1823, in his* Journals of Ralph Waldo Emerson: 1820-1824, Vol. I, *edited by Edward Waldo Emerson and Waldo Emerson Forbes, Houghton Mifflin Company, 1909, pp. 290-93.*

[ROBERT FERGUSON]   (essay date 1825)

[In this excerpt from a favorable review of "The Evidences of Revealed Religion," Ferguson commends its brevity and intelligence and suggests that Channing write a popular, definitive work on Christianity.]

["**A Discourse on the Evidences of Revealed Religion**"] is an unassuming little work, of six-and-forty pages, thrown upon the world, unrecommended by any pompous display of deep learning or metaphysical subtlety. We had scarcely read half-a-dozen pages, however, before we were quite convinced that the author was a man of sound judgment and clear understanding, and the remainder of the work proved that he was equally correct in feeling, and refined in taste. We think that it unites all the requisites of a standard treatise on the Christian religion. In the first place, it is SHORT. In the next, there is much for the head, good plain common sense, intelligible to all; and, in the third place, there is very much for the heart.

Paley's *Evidences*, excellent as it is as a work, is much too long. Not one man in twenty thousand has a command over

his attention sufficient to sit down doggedly to understand his two propositions, each of which, if we remember right, requires eight or ten chapters to develop it entirely. The distance between the first and last links of the chain of reasoning, is too great to allow us to retain all the intermediate connexions. Then the style is as uninviting as it could be, at least to us. Addison is too diffuse. Grotius, which in our opinion is by far the most satisfactory work upon the subject, is too dry and learned for the generality. Christianity is preached to the peasant as well as to the philosopher. Its evidences, therefore, should be accessible to the one as well as to the other. There is nothing incompatible in the idea, the best works are those which are always most popular. . . .

A treatise on the evidences of Christianity should be deeply imbued with the spirit of Saint Paul. It should be, "All things to all men." The reasoning should be plain, manly, and profound, for the logician. The style should be elegant for the man of taste—and the man of feeling should be moved by the portraiture of the most exalted characters that ever sojourned on this earth. For our own part, we must own that our Saviour's character, considered as that of a man only, affords one of the strongest proofs of his being a God, that we can imagine. And yet how rarely is this view of the subject ever brought forward! (p. 160)

This view of our Saviour's character has many advantages, we were almost saying over every other—we are all of us capable of appreciating the social and kindred affections, of recognizing the sacrifices that one man makes for another. These touch the heart, and for them we have a *human sympathy*. But place before us a long train of intricate reasoning, to prove that there is a wonderful Being, at whose command the elements are congregated into form, and whose powers are illimitable—we may fear, we may wonder—but we shall rarely love. We, who are laymen, and who do not trouble ourselves much with controversial divinity, must confess that it was in the sublimity of its precepts, and in the loveliness of the conduct of its founder, that we felt the truth of the Christian religion. . . .

In a popular work on the evidences of Christianity . . . this view should not, in our opinion, be lost sight of,—Let all the overwhelming reasons, too, which the talent and industry of our divines have collected, be mingled with those deductions from Scripture, which, from their innate beauty, have furnished innumerable subjects for the poet and the painter, and we will venture to say, that such a work, so executed, will ensure the gratitude of all mankind. . . .

To write such a work requires a combination of excellencies which rarely co-exist. Dr Channing might probably attempt it himself; a very little enlargement of the plan, and a little more attention to the detail of his "lecture," would embrace all that we mean. (p. 161)

> *[Robert Ferguson], in a review of "A Discourse on the Evidences of Revealed Religion," in* Blackwood's Edinburgh Magazine, *Vol. XVIII, No. CIII, August, 1825, pp. 160-63.*

[WILLIAM HAZLITT]   (essay date 1829)

[An English essayist, Hazlitt was one of the most important critics of the Romantic age. He was a deft stylist, a master of the prose essay, and a leader of what was later termed "impressionist criticism"—a form of personal analysis directly opposed to the universal standards of critical judgment accepted by many eighteenth-century critics. In the following negative review of Chan-

ning's writings, Hazlitt focuses on his literary critiques, faulting them as derivative and biased.]

Dr Channing is a great tactician in reasoning; and reasoning has nothing to do with tactics. We do not like to see a writer constantly trying to steal a march upon opinion without having his retreat cut off—full of pretensions, and void of offence. It is as bad as the opposite extreme of outraging decorum at every step; and is only a more covert mode of attracting attention, and gaining surreptitious applause. We never saw any thing more guarded in this respect than Dr Channing's [*Sermons and Tracts*]—more completely suspended between heaven and earth. He keeps an eye on both worlds; kisses hands to the reading public all round; and does his best to stand well with different sects and parties. He is always in advance of the line, in an amiable and imposing attitude, but never far from succour. He is an Unitarian; but then he disclaims all connexion with Dr Priestley, as a materialist; he denounces Calvinism and the Church of England; but to show that this proceeds from no want of liberality, makes the *amende honorable* to Popery and Popish divines;—is an American Republican and a French Bourbonist—abuses Bonaparte, and observes a profound silence with respect to Ferdinand—likes wit, provided it is serious—and is zealous for the propagation of the Gospel and the honour of religion; but thinks it should form a coalition with reason, and be surrounded with a halo of modern lights. We cannot combine such a system of checks and saving clauses. We are dissatisfied with the want not only of originality of view, but of moral daring. (p. 132)

We like Dr Channing's Sermons best; his Criticisms less; his Politics least of all. We think several of his Discourses do great honour to himself and his profession, and are highly respectable models of pulpit-composition. We would instance more particularly, and recommend to the perusal of our readers, that **"On the Duties of Children."** The feeling, the justness of observation, the tenderness, and the severity, are deserving of all praise. The author here appears in a truly amiable and advantageous light. This composition alone makes us believe, that he is a good, and might, with proper direction and self-reliance, have been even a great man. (p. 133)

[Dr. Channing's] answer to Fenelon, on the subject of *self-annihilation*, [is] another favorable specimen of free enquiry, and of a higher or more philosophical cast. (p. 135)

There is a *primâ philosophiâ* view of the subject, which is, we think, above the ordinary level of polemical reasoning in our own country. In the line of argument adopted by our author, there is a strong reflection of the original and masterly views of the innate capacity of the soul for piety and goodness, insisted on in Bishop Butler's *Sermons*—a work which has fallen into neglect, partly because of the harshness and obscurity of its style, but more because it contains neither a libel on human nature, nor a burlesque upon religion. There is much in the above train of thought silently borrowed from this profound work. Dr Channing's argument is, we think, good and sound against the misanthropes in philosophy, and the cynics in religion, who alike maintain the absolute falsity of all human virtue; but the Bishop of Cambray might say, that, with respect to him, it was not a practical answer, so much as a verbal evasion; neither meeting his views nor removing the source of his complaints. Fenelon assuredly, in wishing to annihilate self, did not wish to extirpate charity and faith, but to crush the old serpent, the great enemy of these. There is no doubt of the capacity of the soul for good and evil; the only question is, which principle prevails and triumphs. The satirist and the man

of the world laugh at the pretension to superior sanctity and disinterestedness; the pious enthusiast may then be excused if he weeps at the want of them.

How far does that likeness to God, and sympathy with the whole human race, which Fenelon deprecates the want of, and Dr Channing boasts of, as the inseparable attribute and chief ornament of man, really take place or not in the present state of things, and as a preparation for another and infinitely more important one? If we regard the moral capacity of man, *self* is a unit that counts millions. Its essence and its glory, says our optimist, is to comprehend the whole human race in its benevolent regards. Does it do so? The understanding runs along the whole chain of being; the affections stop, for the most part, at the first link in the chain. Sense, appetite, pride, passion, engross the whole of this self, and leave it nearly indifferent, if not averse, to all other claims on its attention. In order that the moral attainments should keep pace with the vaunted capacity of man, knowledge should be identified with feeling. We know that there are a million of other beings of as much worth, of the same nature, made in the image of God like ourselves. Have we the same sympathy with every one of these? Do we feel a million times more for all of them put together, than for ourselves? The least pain in our little finger gives us more concern and uneasiness, than the destruction of millions of our fellow-beings. Fenelon laments bitterly and feelingly this disparity between duty and inclination, this want of charity, and eating of self into the soul. What is the consequence of the disproportionate ratios in which the head and the heart move? This paltry *self,* looking upon itself as of more importance than all the rest of the world, fancies itself the centre of the universe, and would have every one look upon it in the same light. Not being able to sympathize with others as it ought, it hates and envies them; is mad to think of its own insignificance in the general system; cannot bear a rival or a superior; despises and tramples on inferiors, and would crush and annihilate all pretensions but its own, that it might be *all in all*. The worm puts on the monarch, or the god, in thought and in secret; and it is only when it can do so in fact, and in public, and be the tyrant or idol of its fellows, that it is at ease or satisfied with itself. Fenelon was right in crying out (if it could have done any good) for the crucifying of this importunate self, and putting a better principle in its stead.

Dr Channing's [**"Remarks on the Character and Writings of John Milton"** and **"Remarks on the Life and Character of Napoleon"**] are both done upon the same false principle, of making out a case *for* or *against*. The one is full of commonplace eulogy, the other of common-place invective. They are pulpit-criticisms. An orator who is confined to expound the same texts and doctrines week after week, slides very naturally and laudably into a habit of monotony and paraphrase; is not allowed to be 'wise above what is written;' is grave from respect to his subject, and the authority attached to the truths he interprets; and if his style is tedious or his arguments trite, he is in no danger of being interrupted or taken to task by his audience. Such a person is unavoidably an advocate for certain received principles; often a dull one. He carries the professional license and character out of the pulpit into other things, and still fancies that he speaks 'with authority, and not as the scribes.' He may be prolix without suspecting it; may lay a solemn stress on the merest trifles; repeat truisms, and apologize for them as startling discoveries; may play the sophist, and conceive he is performing a sacred duty; and give what turn or gloss he pleases to any subject,—forgetting that the circumstances under which he declares himself, and the audience which he addresses, are entirely changed. If, as we readily allow, there are instances of preachers who have emancipated themselves from these professional habits, we can hardly add Dr Channing to the number.

His notice of Milton is elaborate and stately, but neither new nor discriminating. (pp. 138-40)

The bulk of the account of Milton, both as a poet and a prose-writer, is, we are constrained to say, mere imitation or amplification of what has been said by others. He observes, *ex cathedrâ*, and with due gravity, that the *forte* of Milton is sublimity—that the two first books of *Paradise Lost* are unrivalled examples of that quality. He then proceeds to show, that he is not without tenderness or beauty, though he has not the graphic minuteness of Cowper or of Crabbe; he next praises his versification in opposition to the critics—dwells on the freshness and innocence of the picture of Adam and Eve in Paradise—maintains that our sympathy with Satan is nothing but the admiration of moral strength of mind—acknowledges the harshness and virulence of Milton's controversial writings, but blames Dr Johnson for doing so. All this we have heard or said before. We are not edified at all, nor are we greatly flattered by it. It is as if we should convey a letter to a friend in America, and should find it transcribed and sent back to us with a heavy postage.

We do not, then, set much store by our author's criticisms, because they sometimes seem to be, in a great measure, borrowed from our own lucubrations. We set still less store by his politics, for they are borrowed from others. We have no objection to the most severe or caustic probing of the character of the late ruler of France; but we *do* object, in the name both of history and philosophy, to misrepresentations, and falsehoods, as the groundwork of such remarks. When England has exploded them, half in shame, and half in anger, the harpy echo lingers in America. The ugly mask has been taken off; but Dr Channing chooses to lecture on the mask in preference to the head. (p. 142)

[In his essay on Bonaparte,] Dr Channing very gravely divides greatness into different sorts, and places himself at the top among those who *talk* about things—commanders at the bottom among those who only *do* them. He finds fault with Bonaparte for not coming up to his standard of greatness; but in order that he may not, raises this standard too high for humanity. To put it in force would be to leave the ancient and modern world as bare of great names as the wilds of North America. To make common sense of it, any one great man must be all the others. Homer only sung of battles, and it was honour enough for Alexander to place his works in a golden cabinet. Dr Channing allows Bonaparte's supremacy in war; but disputes it in policy. How many persons, from the beginning of the world, have united the two in a greater degree, or wielded more power in consequence? If Bonaparte had not gained a single battle, or planned a single successful campaign; if he had not scattered Coalition after Coalition, but invited the Allies to march to Paris; if he had not quelled the factions, but left them to cut one another's throats and his own; if he had not ventured on the *Concordat*, or framed a Code of Laws for France; if he had encouraged no art or science or man of genius; if he had not humbled the pride of 'ancient thrones,' and risen from the ground of the people to an equal height with the Gods of the earth,—showing that the art and the right to reign is not confined to a particular race; if he had been any thing but what he was, and had done nothing, he would then have come up to Dr Channing's notions of greatness, and to his boasted stan-

dard of a hero! We in Europe, whether friends or foes, require something beyond this negative merit: we think that Caesar, Alexander, and Charlemagne, were 'no babies;' we think that to move the great masses of power and bind opinions in a spell, is as difficult as the turning a period or winding up a homily; and we are surprised that stanch republicans, who complain that the world bow to birth and rank alone, should turn with redoubled rage against intellect, the instant it became a match for pride and prejudice, and was the only thing that could be opposed to them with success, or could extort a moment's fear or awe for human genius or human nature.

Dr Channing's style is good, though in general too laboured, formal, and sustained. All is brought equally forward,—nothing is left to tell for itself. In the attempt to be copious, he is tautological; in striving to explain every thing, he overloads and obscures his meaning. The fault is the uniform desire to produce an effect, and the supposition that this is to be done by main force.

In one sermon, Dr Channing insists boldly and loudly on the necessity that American preachers should assume a loftier style, and put forth energies and pretensions to claim attention in proportion to the excited tone of public feeling, and the advances of modern literature and science. He reproaches them with their lukewarmness, and points out to them, as models, the novels of Scott and the poetry of Byron. If Dr Channing expects a grave preacher in a pulpit to excite the same interest as a tragedy hero on the stage, or a discourse on the meaning of a text of Scripture to enchain the feelings like one of the *Waverley Novels*, it will be a long time first. The mere proposal is *putting the will for the deed*, and an instance of that republican assurance and rejection of the idea of not being equal to any person or thing, which convinces pretenders of this stamp that there is no reason why they should not do all that others can, and a great deal more into the bargain. (pp. 143-44)

> [William Hazlitt], "American Literature—Dr Channing," in The Edinburgh Review, *Vol. L, No. XCIX, October, 1829, pp. 125-44.*

THE WESTMINSTER REVIEW   (essay date 1830)

> [*This anonymous critic hails Channing as "an incarnation of the intellectual spirit of Christianity" and offers a favorable assessment of his "Remarks on Associations" and his writings on Napoleon and Milton.*]

America has a right to be proud of Channing; and shame would it be for the criticism of England were he to be dismissed with affected contempt, "damned with faint praise," or only spoken of with that unmeaning generality of expression which would show that sufficient trouble had not been taken to understand him correctly, or sufficient candour not exercised to estimate him justly. (p. 476)

We consider Dr. Channing as an incarnation of the intellectual spirit of Christianity. He is the tenth Avatar of the principle of reformation; and come to complete the work. The shaking off the yoke of the Papacy; the abrogation of ceremonial and doctrinal corruptions; the republication, as in fact it was, of the Bible; the suppression of legal persecution; these were only preparatives to the noblest emancipation of all, the deliverance of the human mind into the "glorious liberty" of unshackled, active, and expatiating thought. That is the point towards which they tend; for the sake of which they are valuable; and whose accomplishment is their completion. Now the multitude of

Sermonizers, so far from labouring for the promotion of this object have not even eyes to see its beauty, or ears to hear its voice of inspiration. They want the very perception of its excellence. Not so our author. (p. 478)

Dr. Channing has taken the right course to make intelligent and true hearted men believe Christianity, and love Christianity. He deals with them in a frank and manly way. He exposes the real causes of their doubt, disgust, and alienation. He does not call names and fulminate judgments. He enters into no compromise with error, makes no appeal to prejudice, gives no quarter to imposition. He is a single-hearted man; and his sole aim is the glory of religion in elevating and blessing humanity. While he would rescue theology from the withering grasp of professional theologians; he also sees and censures the culpable neglect of it by those who should have interposed to preserve or rescue it from the debasement. (p. 480)

Dr. Channing considers freedom and independence of thought to be essentially connected with religion, . . . [and he also] regards the whole frame and structure of revelation, and indeed of nature, as put together on the principle of utility. That is to say, he regards whatever is external as framed and arranged for the purpose of ministering to the greatest ultimate good of the mind within us. There is, in his theology, no object ulterior to the happiness of man. He does not think the Deity like Jonathan Edwards, who, as Robert Hall once said, would have delighted in having the groans of the damned set to music and sung to him. All things in earth, heaven, and hell; all natural objects and all supernatural works; all history, science, and experience; everything seems to him to be created and ordained that it may minister to the developement of the faculties of the mind, and through that developement to the production of the noblest, the purest, the largest, and the most lasting happiness of humanity. On this principle he expounds all precepts and enforces all duties. There are no arbitrary obligations for the performance of useless and unprofitable acts, in his moral philosophy. He denies the validity of the sentence of divorce, pronounced by so many ecclesiastical courts, between religion and morality. He thinks that revelation has joined them with its blessing, and that the union is indissoluble. If this be as true as it is obviously good, and of that we cannot doubt, how much time, and labour, and money, and suffering, are wasted by almost every class of religionists.

There is a marvellous combination in Dr. Channing of the maximum of fearlessness with the minimum of offensiveness. No man can be more free from whatever indicates, or tends to excite, the Odium Theologicum. His boldness is often very startling, even to those who are not accustomed to be startled easily. We do not refer now to his doctrinal tenets, which are those of a not very numerous party, but to various positions for which he is personally responsible, and which seem likely to excite prejudice and animosity amongst all parties. An instance may be adduced from the last of his publications which has come to hand, the **"Remarks on Associations."** The design of this pamphlet is to check "the disposition which now prevails to form Associations and to accomplish all objects by organized masses." He points out, with great acuteness, the evils incidental to this popular mode of procedure, and the cases in which those evils overbalance the particular good which the cooperation is intended to accomplish. After discussing the philosophy of the subject, he investigates the merits of several of the most flourishing Associations in Boston and its neighbourhood; and amongst the rest, those formed for enforcing the observance of the Sabbath. Now if there be one subject on

which, more than another, the religionists of Great Britain and America are intolerantly superstitious, it is on this. A traveller who arrives in Edinburgh late on the Saturday night, and neglects the precaution of taking his trunk out of the office, must sanctify the sabbath in his dirty shirt; and the conscience of the Corporation will not (or did not, very recently) allow the removal of filth from the streets on the Sunday morning, however early the hour or noiseless the manner of that very needful operation. In London, the distresses of the nation have been ascribed to the profanation of the Sabbath, at a very numerous and respectable meeting, both of conformists and non-conformists; where, moreover, a zealous gentleman was greatly applauded for having attempted to prevail on his Majesty's Secretary of State for the Home Department to close the parks against the citizens on Sundays. Every sinner who goes to glory by the gallows, and truly it seems to be the King's highway to heaven, is made to confess to Sabbath-breaking as the origin of his crimes. In New England the popular feeling is strong and active on this matter. Various Associations have been formed aiming, amongst other things, not only to suppress all travelling on Sundays, but even to stop the mails. Now, considering his situation, we think it shews a high degree of moral courage in Dr. Channing to face, as he does, this sin-creating, idleness-promoting, comfort-destroying, conscience-perverting superstition. He has done so most manfully. To prevent mistake; which it will prevent, but not misrepresentation and calumny, as he must very well know; he condemns any idea of "the change of Sunday into a working day," and declares his conviction that "the first day of the week should be separated to the commemoration of Christ's resurrection, to public worship, to public Christian instruction, and in general to what are called the means of religion." (pp. 481-83)

One source of interest and power in Dr. Channing's productions is their strongly-marked individuality. They seem to bring us into intimate acquaintance with the man. They are like the private letters of a friend, relating indeed to topics of public nature and universal concern, but giving us his personal convictions, feelings, and wishes, in all their genuineness and fervency. He is no retailer of other men's phrases or other men's opinions. He uses words to express thoughts, his own thoughts. What his mouth utters, or his pen indites, his mind has first distinctly conceived, has elaborated, has arrived at the conviction of, by its own efforts, has wrought into itself, and surrounded with its own peculiar associations. If his language expresses emotion it is because he is moved. There are no rhetorical common-places, put in because their introduction is thought becoming. None of his sermons have the impersonality of too many homilies, which bear no marks of relation to time, place, or person. They are what he thinks, and what he feels; and as he thinks originally and feels nobly, they are read with an interest proportionably deep and vivid. . . . Open Dr. Channing's [volumes] almost any where, and you instantly feel as if in the presence of an extraordinary man, and one of whom you must know more. His mind comes into direct contact with your own. The fascination of genius is upon you; and in this instance, happily, the spell is a benignant one.

In the same spirit in which Dr. Channing invites the philosopher to enter the domains of theology, he has himself made sundry excursions into the fields of literature and politics; and he has erected an honourable trophy in each, by the articles on Scott's *Life of Napoleon*, and on the posthumous work of Milton recently discovered. (pp. 485-86)

["**Remarks on the Life and Character of Napoleon**"] consists of two parts; the first an analysis of his character, the second an estimate of ''the principle of action which governed him, and of which he was a remarkable manifestation;'' which principle Dr. Channing considers to be the love of power.

The general tendency of this essay is admirable. It shows how contemptible a thing a conqueror may be in one point of view, and how detestable he is in another. It proves how pitiful a modicum of intellect may suffice for a successful general. It exposes the folly of that idolatry of victory and splendour, to which the world has been so long addicted, and for which it has paid so dearly. He pursues a nefarious ambition from the field to the cabinet, and from the cabinet to the church, and allows it no right of sanctuary or benefit of clergy. He corrects the delusions by which the friends of freedom have suffered themselves to be blinded, and the practical mistakes into which they have too often fallen. And he announces, with subdued tone, yet prophetic dignity, the mode in which the enslaved nations of Europe may retrieve their liberties, and fix them on an everlasting foundation. (p. 486)

Entering, as we do most heartily, into the spirit of this Essay, we must yet express our regret that the author has not more severely scrutinized the alleged facts on which some of his censures are founded; that he has failed, as we think, to do justice to many qualities by which Napoleon was raised so immeasurably above the vulgar herd of kings, conquerors, and usurpers; and that he should not have perceived how much an antagonist power to legitimacy was worth to the world, even though that power was an imperial usurpation. (p. 488)

For doing justice to the character, and raising a not unworthy monument to the memory of John Milton, our author was eminently qualified, and the attempt [in **"Remarks on the Character and Writings of John Milton"**] is an eminently successful one. He had a theme completely after his own heart; and with all his heart did he apply himself to the task. Never has a writer been more completely ''filled, rapt, inspired'' by his subject than Dr. Channing was on this occasion. He did not sit down to indite a clever, sparkling, telling article, one in which, Milton's character and Milton's fame, should be subordinate objects to those of reviving the interest of a declining periodical, and making talk about the promising talent of the writer. The spirit of Milton was upon him, and possessed him, and he writes as one constrained to do so by thoughts too fervid, intense, and expansive, to be restrained. He speaks as a priest under the immediate influence of the god at whose altar he was ministering. So should genius be honoured.

There are none of the littlenesses of political party in this critique. He does not turn aside to have some dexterous fencing with the swordsmen of this or that faction. (pp. 488-89)

Dr. Channing is a republican; not merely by living under a republican form of government, but by clear conviction and strong affection. He thoroughly understands the true theory, practice, and tendency of republicanism. He perceives its real difference from despotism; for all governments are despotic or republican; its difference not only in form but in essence, not only in mode but in principle. He values it because it conducts man towards that self-government in which consists the perfection of his nature. Such are the men to speak freely and truly about Milton. Others come shackled to the subject. Their royalism, or their whiggism, or their toryism, lays them under a previous necessity for using the language of compromise or apology. They can only put forth a Jesuit's edition of Milton. (p. 489)

Those who care nothing about theology, can scarcely be said to care any thing about Milton. He is beyond the pale of their comprehension. But how few there are who, while they can appreciate the extent of his acquisitions, the beauties of his poetry, and the loftiness of his political principles, can also estimate the purity of his devotion, the freedom of his inquiries, the worth of his researches, and the amazing extent to which his criticisms and speculations anticipated the light and labour of succeeding generations.

Dr. Channing marvellously blends his fitness in this particular with that strong perception of the great, the good, and the beautiful, which is the essential requisite for poetical criticism. He is himself a poet; a creator of bright worlds, peopled with men who are as gods. He has himself explored the paths which lead to the fountain of tears, and to the sparkling waters of immortal life. He may never have made a verse in his life, but he knows the flavour of the true Hippocrene. When he tells us why a description is beautiful, we feel that he has first perceived and enjoyed its beauty. And his taste is especially for those images of power and of tenderness which so abound in Milton. Of these he has a deep feeling by which they are instantly appreciated, and which guides him to their true analysis. He has an instinct for these high qualities of the highest kind of poetry, as unerring as that fine tact by which Mr. Hazlitt, the first of our critics upon works of art, feels where a master's hand has touched the canvass, traces the original conception and mental prototype of the painting, and enshrines it in a rich and appropriate frame-work of poetical associations.

Dr. Channing is completely unrivalled in his display of the moral grandeur of Milton. And this is, after all, the noblest tribute. Nor does he, as a less skilful or a less benevolent critic might have done, depreciate mankind to exalt his hero. The fact of the existence of such a man is to him a pledge of the progress of humanity. . . .

> [We believe] that the sublime intelligence of Milton was imparted, not for his own sake only, but to awaken kindred virtue and greatness in other souls. Far from regarding him as standing alone and unapproachable, we believe that he is an illustration of what all who are true to their nature will become in the progress of their being; and we have held him forth not to excite an ineffectual admiration but to stir up our own and other's breasts to an exhilarating pursuit of high and ever-growing attainments of intellect and virtue.
>
> (pp. 490-91)

''Dr. Channing's Works,'' in The Westminster Review, *Vol. XII, No. XXIV, April, 1830, pp. 472-91.*

REV. LEONARD WITHINGTON   (essay date 1834)

[*After briefly discussing Channing's literary criticism and system of ethics, Withington analyzes in detail his theological beliefs as revealed in ''The Moral Argument against Calvinism.'' According to Withington, this sermon demonstrates ''how little form, substance and consistency his theological system possesses.''*]

Dr. Channing presents himself to us in [*Discourses, Reviews, and Miscellanies*], as a *critic*, an *ethical* writer, and a *theologian*.

As a *critic*, we cannot think very highly of his powers. His want of discrimination and analytic art, must forever disable him, if he can judge himself, from teaching others how to judge. Burke has said, "that men of strong sensibilities make poor judges of the works of taste," and possibly it may be so with our author. His ["**Remarks on the Character and Writings of John Milton**" and "**Remarks on the Character and Writings of Fenelon**"], though much praised, appear to us confused and indistinct, and made up of vague generalities. Our author tells us in his Review of Milton, that poetry is addressed to the immortal nature of man; that his relish for it is a *proof* of his immortality; that Milton is a very sublime poet; and very tender too. As to Milton's versification our critic remarks:

> His numbers have the prime charm of expressiveness. They vary with, and answer to, the depth or tenderness of his conceptions, and hold intimate alliance with the soul. Like Michael Angelo, in whose hands the marble was said to be flexible, he bends our language, which foreigners reproach with hardness, into whatever forms the subject demands. All the treasures of sweet and solemn sounds are at his command. Words, harsh and discordant in the writings of less gifted men, flow through his poetry in a full stream of harmony. This power over language is not to be ascribed to Milton's musical ear. It belongs to the soul.

Perhaps it may be superfluous to ask here, how the ear and soul are distinguished; and what the ear would be considered as apart from the soul.

As to Milton's *tenderness,* we must demur at our critic's conclusion. Certain we are, that the lines he has quoted from *Comus* are not an example of this quality. They have too much elaborate language,—too much fancy, to be eminently tender; and this defect in fact runs through most of Milton's efforts at the pathetic. The language of passion is always simple, and that of Milton is generally too gorgeous to move our hearts. (pp. 309-10)

In the vagueness and mysticism of the writings of Fenelon, Dr. Channing has a congenial theme. Fenelon had asserted, in the language of his school, that *self-crucifixion* is the great duty of Christians. Dr. Channing assents to this as substantially just, but thinks the proposition should be limited. We should not crucify our *intellectual powers,*—our "rational and moral existence." Fenelon is sufficiently dark, but the critic who would correct him, is still darker. There is nothing in all the volumes written on the Trinity, from the days of Abelard to those of Dr. Waterland, more vague and incomprehensible than this. . . .

Such is our author, considered as a critic. His great defect is his want of analytic power. He thinks with too little precision. His light is not a direct and simple ray from the noon-tide sun, but the broken and confused radiance which comes from a chandelier, which fatigues even the eye which admires it.

As an *ethical* writer, if it were possible to construct a system of ethics apart from religion, we should think more highly of Dr. Channing's powers, than in any other department. He is a warm friend of all the social virtues, and recommends them with glowing eloquence. But here again he is sometimes inclined to mysticism; and is more fond of deriving our duties from a *law within the mind,* than from the written law of revelation. (p. 311)

[Dr. Channing's ethical system] is not a practicable system: it is not clear; it is not derived, as ethics always should be, from the doctrines of the Christian system. Still our author dwells in a region very remote from the contagion of sense. You would hardly suppose that he ever felt the temptation of a mortal body. He is always chaste, pure, ethereal; and if his moral system evinced as entire a freedom from ambition, from the pride of genius, and the moody virtue of a contemplative recluse, as from the contamination of sensuality and vice, he would certainly be as pure a moralist as ever wrote.

But it is chiefly as a *theologian* that our concern with Dr. Channing lies. It is in this character, we conceive, that among superficial thinkers, his influence is most dangerous. We feel it important, therefore, to show how little form, substance, and consistency his theological system possesses, under all the gaudy robes of his eloquence. (pp. 312-13)

It is incumbent, we think, on every reformer, to *construct* as well as to *destroy;* to give us at least a protocol of the new treaty, before he tears the old parchment in pieces. It is quite a piece of vulgar wisdom, to pull down the pillars, and tear away the foundations of an old establishment; but to put up a new edifice, more elegant and convenient, is another affair. Let us suppose, for example, that an innovator in theology is dissatisfied with the doctrine of election, and proposes to remove it from his new system. It would certainly be incumbent on such an adventurer, not merely to evacuate his system of this doctrine, but to show also what were his views of the foreknowledge of God,—whether he believed in such foreknowledge, and how he would reconcile that foreknowledge with the non-existence of this doctrine, and likewise with the moral freedom of man. . . . In this way the reader is put in possession of the last results of the process consistently carried out; and he can judge of the harmony of the whole scheme.

This, it seems to me, every reformer is bound to do. But it is remarkable that Dr. Channing, amidst the most ample professions of reform, has left us in doubt as to what he believes, or what we should believe, respecting most of the great doctrines of revelation. He has torn away the foundations of the temple of truth, and left it in ruins. He has denied the Trinity, and of course the proper Deity of Christ; but *where,* in the rank of beings, he does place the Saviour, he has not told us. He abhors, with all the detestation of philosophical indignation, the common doctrine of the *atonement;* but he has left us utterly in the dark as to the precise influence which he supposes Christ's death to have on the pardon of a sinner. He declares that God would be a Draco, to govern frail creatures by a law, whose penalty is eternal punishment for every transgression; but how much sin would merit punishment, and whether future punishments are eternal,—on all this he preserves a profound silence. He has not told us whether Adam's transgression was personal or federal, whether it had any influence on the character of his posterity, what the purposes of Christ's death were, and what is the effect of his intercession; whether the influence of God's Spirit is the power of truth only, or something superinduced; what the limits of reason are, or what are the truths added to nature by the light of revelation. (pp. 313-14)

It was the glory of the Reformers, that they no sooner began to attack the errours of the Papal Church, than they published their own system, that the world might see the boundaries of their innovations, and compare the ancient darkness with the new sprung light. But this, we are sorry to say, is not the case with our author, or with modern Unitarians generally. In this respect they are even more inconsistent, than some of the wild-

est ancient heretics. Even Bassilides, who counfounded creation, and mixed the heavens and earth together, gave us nevertheless three hundred and sixty-five heavens, as a substitute
for the one he took away. The Unitarians tell us, the ground
on which we stand is hollow and unsafe; but they provide no
refuge to which we can fly. They disclaim Socinus; they disclaim Priestley; they disclaim each other; nor has one of them
attempted to construct a harmonious system of his own. It is
not enough to show that there are objections to the established
modes of thought; the question is, *are there less objections to
the new modes, which are proposed to be introduced?* The
truth is, there are objections to every thing. The most incon-
testible truths present their difficulties. The very existence of
matter has been disputed: and if our belief is to be governed
by objections, why do we not renounce the belief of a material
world, and embrace Berkley's doctrine of a world of ideas?

In a review of a work of Robert Fellows ["**The Moral Argument against Calvinism**"], our author gives us what he calls
the *moral argument* against Calvinism. In this, it seems to be
assumed, that there would be, and is, in man's nature, even
if not perverted by sin, a rising up of our moral sensibilities
against the Calvinistic views of the introduction and propagation of sin in our world, when these views are fairly explained;—that, as our hearts revolt at the character of Nero,
so they must at the government of God, when so developed to
the human mind; and that these instinctive sentiments are to
be trusted. What shocks the nature of man cannot belong to
the nature of God. "It is plain that a doctrine which contradicts
our best ideas of goodness and justice, cannot come from the
just and good God, or be a true representation of his character."
Dr. Channing declares that "this moral argument has always
been powerful to the pulling down of the strong holds of Calvinism." "Even in the dark period when this system was shaped
and finished at Geneva, its advocates often writhed under the
weight of it," and he thinks it is becoming more and more
troublesome to them every day. (pp. 314-15)

Dr. Channing then goes on to show, that we judge of God by
what we see in man; that as certain actions would be inconsistent with goodness in the creature, they must be equally
inconsistent with our views of goodness in the Creator; that
our limited knowledge is no proof, that we cannot see what is
just in God to a certain extent, and within a certain circle; that
though God is great, and we are ignorant, this does not prevent
us from seeing what we do see, and judging where he calls
upon us to judge. He makes a nice distinction between God's
being *incomprehensible* and *unintelligible;* affirms that he may
be incomprehensible, without being unintelligible; and that the
possibility of progression in knowledge should not destroy our
confidence in our present attainments. The sum of his whole
argument seems to be, that man should have such confidence
in his reasoning powers and moral sentiments, without the light
of revelation, as to say that the representations of the government of God made by Calvinism cannot be true. They shock
our nature, and therefore cannot belong to the Being who made
it.

In one sense, we must allow that Dr. Channing is the fairest
of all reasoners: for he not only states objections to his own
views strongly, but has thrown in some which he has not
attempted to answer. He has put into his adversary's argument
one little sentence which contains the pith of the whole matter:
*How inconsistent the miseries of life appear with the goodness
of the Creator!* Wrapt up in this short sentence are mines and
volcanos to explode the whole Unitarian system. We must

pause a little on this delicate ground, and hold our author to
his own objection.

The moral argument against Calvinism, (particularly that part
of it which treats of the introduction and propagation of moral
evil in our world,) is, that it shocks our best conceptions of
the justice and goodness of God. Two questions are to be here
asked and answered; before the validity of this argument can
be felt by any rational mind. FIRST, *What are our moral sentiments, and how are they to be distinguished from the sinful
partialities of the heart,* which Dr. Channing will allow to have
a being; and SECONDLY, *Is the subject*—i.e. the Calvinistic
representation—*within the circle within which our reason and
moral feelings are competent judges.* Both these questions are
vital to the subject; and on neither of them has Dr. Channing
attempted to shed a ray of light.

As to the first of these questions, every man knows that his
mind is a strange mixture, where the sentiments of justice and
the love of sin, blend, like the borders of the rainbow with the
blackness of the cloud. It is not easy for a man, especially
when interested, to trace the hair-width line which separates
these two feelings. "The heart is deceitful above all things and
desperately wicked;" and we often hear men object to the
goodness of God, when in fact they are only endeavouring to
escape the terrours of their own consciences. When our Saviour
told his disciples that the time should come, when he *that killeth
you shall think he doeth God service;* and when St. Paul says,
*I verily thought that I ought to do many things contrary to the
name of Jesus of Nazareth,* do they not both allow the fact,
that men may mistake the proudest and worst passions of the
heart, for just objections to the brightest doctrines of the best
system of religion? God is a king; his government is just and
holy; and submission belongs to man. But submission is not
congenial to proud hearts; and the whole of life is sometimes
nothing but an effort to obtain the approbation of conscience
in the practice of sin.

This moral argument, the Universalist pushes farther than Dr.
Channing, and the infidel still farther; and we cannot find that
our author draws any line to distinguish between *his* objections
to the severest systems, and the infidel's objections against his
own. That amiable man, Charles the II, according to Bishop
Burnet, had a moral argument against the seventh command-
ment. He did not think that God was going to damn a man for
taking a little pleasure in an irregular way. How exquisitely
natural! What a perfect picture is this speech of a voluptuous
heart! But the world is full of just such reasoners. It seems to
me, that it should be expected beforehand, that the government
of a just and holy God should not meet the approbation of
carnal, and sinful, and deeply interested creatures. It is perfectly natural, that they should sometimes mistake their sin-
engendered objections, for a moral argument against the holy
law, especially when these objections spring from the proudest
parts of our nature. The high aspirings of a lofty spirit, that
latent ambition, which I am afraid lies at the bottom of the
virtue taught in our author's glowing pages, incongenial as
they are with the humbling doctrines of the Gospel, are yet
among the most cherished feelings of the natural heart.

The wisest minds are sometimes most ingenious in imposing
on themselves. We would respectfully ask Dr. Channing, does
not the human mind sometimes mistake its prejudices and partialities for its moral judgement of what is befitting the justice
of God? Is not this possible, and even common? Before, then,
such an equivocal objection is put into the mouths of wicked
men, we earnestly entreat this writer, that some broad line may

be drawn, to prevent them from taking up objections, which shall cancel the whole word of God.

This moral argument by which Calvinism is to be overthrown, turns out to be as shadowy and variable as an objector's feelings. It may be stated thus: we disapprove of the Calvinistic system; this feeling we dignify by the name of moral disapprobation; and by this moral disapprobation the system is overthrown.

As to the second question, *whether this subject lies within the circle in which reason and moral approbation are competent judges*—we must remark, that if any point is beyond the reach of human investigation, and is one on which our moral sentiments should be exercised with peculiar caution, this is the very point,—how sin entered the world under the government of an all perfect God? The offensive doctrine of Calvinism is but one mode of answering this difficult question.

On this subject, as Dr. Channing has said, we judge of divine operations by earthly analogies. But does he not perceive, that in one or two points the analogy fails? We compare God with an earthly king; and we say such and such things would be wrong in an earthly king, and therefore they must be wrong in God. But do we reflect that his very perfections cast a mystery on this subject, which finite minds will scarcely ever be able to remove. God *made* his subjects, which an earthly king did not; God foreknows what his subjects will be and do, which earthly kings do not; God is *able* (so it would seem to us) to restrain or prevent the voluntary vices of his subjects; which earthly kings are not;—and hence comes the failure of all comparisons taken from earthly things.—Now we will not say that Calvinists have not spoken indiscreetly on these deep themes. But we do say, that no man has a right to declare, that *their* account is shocking to our moral sentiments, until he can devise some account which shall be less so.

The introduction of sin by the transgression of Adam; the hereditary propensity of all his posterity to evil; the assertion that men are sinners by nature;—all this has been objected to. It has been said, that such views represent God as acting in the most cruel and arbitrary manner; dooming a race to destruction for the fault of one, and giving men a nature from which they must sin, and then punishing them with everlasting destruction, because they follow it. How do you reconcile all this with the goodness of God? Alas! I know not; I am as ignorant as a child. But I suspect the real difficulty in all these objections is, *How can sin exist at all?* The *mode* of its introduction is of small importance. The great question is, Why was it ever permitted by an infinite God—infinite in power and benevolence—to enter the world he made? But this difficulty is not peculiar to the Bible or Calvinism. The great and astounding fact is, that sin exists. We see it,—we feel it,—we groan under it. It meets us in all our speculations, and humbles us in all our aspiring attempts to explain the mysteries of God.

We cannot but think, that Dr. Channing reposes too much confidence in the rectitude of man's moral feelings, and that too out of their appropriate circle,—in the most difficult sphere in which they can act, on the darkest subject about which the human mind can be employed. In the natural sciences, it is a maxim to disregard the conjectures of men, and to examine the works of God. Whenever man has substituted his own guesses for what *God has done,* he has almost invariably found himself in the wrong. Why should it not be so likewise, when he substitutes his own surmises and feelings for what *God has said?* It has long been a rule in philosophy, that we must come

to the examination of nature with the mind free, as ready to believe in one course of operation as another, whenever it is proved by experiments. This makes the true philosopher; and this is exactly equivalent in religion, to receiving the kingdom of heaven as a little child.

But there is one consideration, which makes the reason for implicit submission, more strong in religion than in science;—it is that there is no question which meets us in the threshold of science so baffling, as the origin of evil. All religion supposes pardon; and all pardon implies the existence of sin; and then comes the question, *how* its existence can be explained. The difficulty lies at the very porch of the temple. I have sometimes thought, that God placed this amazing mystery at the very door of our religious investigation, in order to show us, that in all our subsequent walkings, we must proceed by an implicit faith in his holy word.

Dr. Channing scouts the distinction between moral and natural ability; and says that an inability to do our duty which is *born* with us, is to all intents, and according to the established meaning of the word, *natural*. Whether the *words* moral and natural inability are the most happy to express the conception intended to be conveyed, we will not now say; and to affirm that there is such a distinction, and that we are compelled to make it in our intercourse with mankind, would be to do what has been done a thousand times already. But we cannot forbear to ask here, whether a *frailty* which is born with us, is not to all intents, and according to the established meaning of the word, *natural;* and whether it does not puzzle our reason, and shock our feelings as much to account for an inevitable frailty leading to sin, as for an inevitable sin itself? If it should be replied, that it is not quite so shocking to our established conceptions of his goodness, for God to allow the existence of such frailty, as of sin, why then it appears it is right for God to commit a little wrong, but not a great one.

On this subject it is important to be understood. The intention of these remarks is not to teach, that there are *no* cases in which our moral feelings may not be exercised on the works and ways of God; but that we should judge with caution; and that the question, which lies at the bottom of the offensive parts of Calvinism, is precisely the one on which a frail man should least trust the unregulated feelings of his own heart.

Dr. Channing objects to the Calvinist for reasoning so much from our ignorance, and for trusting so much to the developements of God's purposes in a future state, in order to reconcile his works with our views of his attributes.

> It is no slight objection to the mode of reasoning adopted by the Calvinists, that it renders the proof of the divine attributes impossible. When we object to his representations of the divine government, that they shock our clearest ideas of goodness and justice, he replies, that still they may be true, because we know very little of God, and what seems unjust to man, may be, in the Creator, the perfection of rectitude. Now this weapon has a double edge. If the strongest marks of injustice do not prove God unjust, then the strongest marks of the opposite character, do not prove him righteous. If the first do not deserve confidence because of our narrow views of God, neither do the last. If, when the more we know, the first may be found consistent with perfect rectitude, so, when more

shall be known, the last may be found consistent with perfect malignity and oppression. The reasoning of our opponents casts us on an ocean of awful uncertainty.

This is certainly very extraordinary reasoning.—Let us suppose a general, whose predominant character is that of a masterly tactician. He manœuvres in a manner incomprehensible to his soldiers, but the result is always victory. We will imagine, that many of his movements previous to the hour of success, appear very rash, and tending to the destruction of his soldiers. They can all see that some of his orders are wise; but some appear of a contrary character. Until the result explains them, they appear unworthy of his sagacity. Now would a soldier under such a general reason, as Dr. Channing teaches us to reason of God? If his captain should say to him, when he was disputing the wisdom of some dark order,—"We know but little about the plans of our commander as yet; he has always brought us out of every extremity; his prevailing ability should lead us to trust him, when we cannot see immediately the tendency of his plans;" would the soldier reply,—"Why, this is bad reasoning. This weapon has a double edge. If our general's foolish orders, do not prove him a fool, neither do his wise orders prove him wise," &c.? Would not such a subaltern be put under an arrest; unless indeed his miserable logic should lead them to suspect his brains rather than his heart? Certainly we should reason differently even concerning an intelligent man, much more concerning the infinite God. There are a thousand direct proofs of his benevolence, even on the principles of well understood Calvinism; and the seeming objections are but the clouds which his greatness, and our position on earth, draw before his great white throne. (pp. 316-22)

Dr. Channing brings three arguments to prove, that it is not presumptuous in man to judge of the government of God. The first is, that his attributes have been proved and explained, which supposes that we have some power of judging of these attributes. The second is, that divines have dwelt on the *internal* evidences of Christianity, which shows that its main doctrines meet our moral apprehensions. Lastly, that all Christians are accustomed to reason from God's attributes, and to use them as tests of doctrines. Now these arguments are very good, and would be worthy of the deepest attention, if his opponents had ever contended that our ignorance is such that we can *never* judge of God's ways. But they have always taken a middle and wiser ground. And in this case, they merely say, that as the Bible does teach some kind of derivation of sin from our fallen first parents, and that every man is by nature totally alienated from God; and as reason teaches us, that the introduction of moral evil is one of the darkest questions that ever exercised the human mind; considering these things it is presumptuous, in the last degree, to make our moral feelings, dark as they are by nature and corrupted by sin, a standard by which to reject a doctrine, than which, if we expunge it from revelation, reason, after all her independent efforts, can devise nothing more plausible. It is precisely the question, where failing in all our attempts to *unriddle,* we should learn to *trust.* And this we hold to be the purest rationalism.

There are many other passages in this piece which show the loose thinking of our eloquent author. For example, he says, that Calvinism owes its perpetuity to the influence of fear, in palsying the moral nature. Were we disposed to make a parody on this paragraph, it would be easy for us to say, that Unitarianism owes its existence (we could hardly say its *perpetuity,*) to presumption, throwing our moral nature into a delirious

fever. But we would soberly ask Dr. Channing, what sort of fear it is, which produces this moral paralysis? If he means the *fear of man,* this would be a very ungracious assertion for a son of New-England to utter respecting those Christian heroes, to whose boldness in resisting oppression, their degenerate sons are indebted for whatever of civil and religious freedom they now enjoy. Their whole life evinced an entire superiority to the fear of man. They even trampled on human authority. They took joyfully the spoiling of their goods, and despised at once the dictates of ancient authority, and the mandates of the star-chamber. It is one of the prominent characteristics of Calvin, in his Institutes and other writings, that he tramples on human authority, like so many rotten weeds, whenever it stands in his way, and it was one of the chief faults of that great but undervalued man. The same is true of our own Edwards, and many other eminent Calvinists. If he means the *fear of God,* why then we venture to ask, if there is any superabundance of this fear, which is likely to paralyze the mind. We have always supposed, that he is the wisest man, and most likely to find the truth, who *trembles* most at the word of God. This is a fear, which we humbly pray, may never depart from us in all our speculations.

Such are specimens (and many more might be added) of the loose and inaccurate reasoning by which this author has bewildered his readers, less than himself. (pp. 323-24)

We have spoken of the want of systematic views, and analytic power in Dr. Channing's mind. His thoughts are like those splendid clouds, which sometimes overhang the setting sun, rolled into beautiful shapes, reflecting the richest colours, filling the heavens which they adorn, with their crimson light; but at the same time, shifting while we view them; and composed of a vapoury texture which is soon to vanish, or increase the gloom of the approaching night. His mind rests on no foundation, and seems unable to build any superstructure. He is not one of those who, as Butler says, *write with simplicity and in earnest.* He invites us to follow him, and strews the gayest flowers in our path to lure us along; but he leads us only to the regions of negation. His grand aim and end is, to subvert a few obnoxious doctrines. And while this is true, there is no choiceness of diction, no elegance of style, no profusion of imagery, which can redeem his pages from the reproach of intellectual poverty.

Of his want of system he seems to be himself conscious, for he very ingenuously declares of his volume, that "very possibly it may seem to want perfect consistency. I have long been conscious, that we are more in danger of being enslaved to our own opinions, especially to such as we have expressed and defended, than to those of any other person; and I have accordingly desired to write, without any reference to any previous publications, or without any anxiety to accommodate my previous to my past views. In treatises prepared in this spirit and at distant intervals, some incongruities of thought and feeling can hardly fail to occur!" So much for progressive light! Dr. Channing wishes for a system of Unitarian divinity. But would there not be some danger before the author had finished the appendix, that the first chapters would be out of date? (pp. 327-28)

Rev. Leonard Withington, "Review of Channing's Works," in Literary and Theological Review, *Vol. I, No. II, June, 1834, pp. 304-35.*

FRASER'S MAGAZINE FOR TOWN & COUNTRY   (essay date 1838)

[*This anonymous commentator objects to Channing's religious and political beliefs but praises his style, calling him "unquestionably, the finest writer of the age."*]

Channing is, unquestionably, the finest writer of the age. His language is simple, nervous, and copious in Saxon. His periods are short, and constructed without any appearance of effort. His meaning does not require to be gathered, by dint of persevering investigation, from the heart of a cumbrous phraseology; it strikes at once. Nor is this its transparency the result of weakness, or want of compass; the very contrary is the case. From his writings, and especially from ["**Remarks on the Character and Writings of John Milton**"], there may be extracted some of the richest poetry and original conceptions, clothed in language, unfortunately for our literature, too little studied in the day in which we live. Channing appears to have imbued his mind with the spirit of the masters of our island tongue; their very tones seem to have filled his ear, and to have become key-notes to his finest compositions; their strong idiomatic English has evidently worked itself into the mind of our author, and taught him, that in the phraseology which weak minds pronounced to be *jejune* there was a versatility capable of becoming, in the hands of a master-mind, expressive of great and ennobling thought. We do not applaud or acquiesce in the meagre and unhappy creed of our author, nor have we any sympathy with his republican preferences. His Socinianism and democracy are occasionally rank enough to taint the fine thought and philosophic genius that pour out otherwise a refreshing fulness. We could have wished that he had retained his creed and his politics, and sent across the Atlantic to our literature all besides. The theologian and the politician we could in the present instance dispense with. The philosopher, the orator, the poet, the critic, we assign the very first rank; to these we award the tribute of unmingled praise. (p. 627)

"Channing's Literary and Political Essays: 'Remarks on Milton'," in Fraser's Magazine for Town & Country, *Vol. CI, No. XVII, May, 1838, pp. 627-35.*

[HENRY PETER BROUGHAM]   (essay date 1839)

[*In the following excerpt from a review of "Remarks on the Character and Writings of John Milton," Brougham condemns Channing's style as ornate, unintelligible, and prolix. In addition, Brougham contends that Channing's "false" conception of style caused him to misjudge Milton's talents as a writer.*]

As the name of Dr Channing stands high in American literature for several works which have shown much vigour of thinking, some talent for declamation, and generally considerable success in composition, we are bound to observe that, had nothing from his pen ever reached us but the tract now before us ["**Remarks on the Character and Writings of John Milton**"], we should have been at a loss to comprehend the grounds of the reputation which he enjoys to a certain degree on either side of the Atlantic. The taste which it displays is far from being correct; his diction is exceedingly affected; and the affectation is that of extreme vigour and refinement of thought, often when he is only unmeaning, contradictory, or obscure. His opinions on critical matters likewise indicate a very defective taste, and show that, in his own practice of writing, he goes wrong on a false theory; and in pursuit of the 'striking'—the 'grand'—the 'uncommon.' That his style should be perspicuous can, indeed, hardly be expected, when he avows the incredible

opinion, that a composition may be too easily understood, and complains of the recent efforts to make science intelligible to the bulk of mankind, that their tendency is to degrade philosophy under the show of seeking after usefulness. The tract before us is, indeed, less obscurely written than the ventilation of this absurd notion by its author might have led us to expect; but, if not so unintelligible, it is fully as shallow in most of its remarks as could well have been imagined of any writing that proceeded from a very respectable quarter. (p. 214)

We had hardly opened the tract, and not proceeded through the second page, when we found such writing as the following; a grievous sample of the havoc made in the works of able and eloquent writers by the determination to say what looks striking rather than what is just, and to strain after effect rather than truth. Not content with describing Milton as 'a profound scholar and a man of vast compass of thought, and imbued thoroughly with all ancient and modern learning'—(which is an exaggeration of the truth, for Milton had little or no scientific knowledge; but still it is like the truth which it exaggerates, and at all events it is quite intelligible)—Dr Channing must add for effect, and in order to say something out of the ordinary way, that he was 'able to master, to mould, to impregnate with his own intellectual power his great and varied acquisitions.' Now, this is saying not only something quite out of the ordinary way, but something beyond ordinary comprehension. A man may master, and he may mould by his intellectual power;—but what is he to master? Dr Channing says 'his own acquisitions'—as if he had said, 'this man is so wealthy that he is about to buy his own estate.' Nor is this the worst by a good deal. What meaning does the eloquent Doctor attach to the act of 'impregnating his acquisitions with his powers?' These are words—absolutely words only, and devoid of all, even the least meaning;—yet will we hold any one a wager that the author deems them a piece of fine writing; forgetting the sound old definition of 'that which is natural without being obvious,' and falling into the too common error of fancying that every thing not obvious is worth saying, however little natural or even intelligible. (p. 215)

Nor is it by any unaided efforts of our own that we have been enabled to infer from Dr Channing's practice, the account of his theory or principle of composition. . . . He has himself betrayed his own secret. The following passage, we verily do believe, stands unequalled among all the follies or affectations (for we can hardly conceive it to be seriously delivered) of all critics:—

> We know that simplicity and perspicuity are important qualities of style; but there are vastly nobler and more important ones;—such as energy and richness,—and in these Milton was not surpassed. The best style is not that which puts the reader most easily and in the shortest time in possession of a writer's naked thoughts; but that which is the truest image of a great intellect, which conveys fully and carries furthest into other souls the conceptions and feelings of a profound and lofty spirit. To be universally intelligible is not the highest merit. A great mind cannot, without injurious constraint, shrink itself to the grasp of common passive readers. Its natural movement is free, bold, and majestic, and it ought not to be required to part with these attributes that the multitude may keep pace with it. A full mind will naturally overflow

in long sentences; and in the moment of inspiration, when thick-coming thoughts and images crowd upon it, will often pour them forth in a splendid confusion, dazzling to common readers, but kindling to congenial spirits. There are writings which are clear through their shallowness. We must not expect in the ocean the transparency of the calm inland stream. For ourselves, we love what is called easy reading perhaps too well, especially in our hours of relaxation; but we love too to have our faculties tasked by master spirits. We delight in long sentences, in which a great truth, instead of being broken up into numerous periods, is spread out in its full proportions, is radiated with variety of illustration and imagery, is set forth in a splendid affluence of language, and flows like a full stream, with a majestic harmony which fills at once the ear and the soul. Such sentences are worthy and noble manifestations of a great and far-looking mind, which grasps at once vast fields of thought,—just as the natural eye takes in at a moment wide prospects of grandeur and beauty. We would not indeed have all compositions of this character. Let abundant provision be made for the common intellect. Let such writers as Addison (an honoured name) "bring down philosophy from heaven to earth." But let inspired genius fulfil its higher function of lifting the prepared mind from earth to heaven. Impose upon it no strict laws, for it is its own best law. Let it speak in its own language, in tones which suit its own ear. Let it not lay aside its natural port, or dwarf itself that it may be comprehended by the surrounding multitude. If not understood and relished now, let it place a generous confidence in other ages, and utter oracles, which futurity will expound. We are led to these remarks not merely for Milton's justification, but because our times seem to demand them. Literature, we fear, is becoming too popular. The whole community is now turned into readers, and in this we heartily rejoice; and we rejoice too that so much talent is employed in making knowledge accessible to all. We hail the general diffusion of intelligence as the brightest feature of the present age. But good and evil are never disjoined; and one bad consequence of the multitude of readers is, that men of genius are too anxious to please the multitude, and prefer a present shout of popularity to that less tumultuous, but deeper, more thrilling note of the trump of fame, which resounds and grows clearer and louder through all future ages.

First of all, though we can with difficulty suppose all this nonsense serious, and more than half imagine it is given as the means of showing what the author thinks his power of fine writing, yet, as he certainly acts upon the principles it contains, we are led to enter our early and decided protest against all and every portion of it. Any thing more pernicious, more hurtful to all good writing, and indeed more prejudicial to accurate thinking, cannot be imagined, than the propagation of such wild absurdities, under the authority of considerable names. For, absurd as such a theory is, it falls very easily in with the careless and loose habits in which shallow thinkers and loose reasoners are prone to indulge. Once persuade them that clearness and distinctness is not an essential requisite of diction, and there is no end to the propagation of flimsy trash, under the cover of sounding phrases; nor any limit to the prolixity of the ready and wearisome pen. All men beside Dr Channing have held that perspicuity is the first quality of style; that whatever of ornament it may have besides, shall only be taken cumulatively, and not substitutionally (to adopt in courts critical the language of the courts of law)—as an addition, not a substitute; and whoever would give us fine words for clear ones, the life and soul of composition, does a thing quite as fatal to good writing as the act of depriving a man of air (while you give him fine clothes and rich food), would be fatal to his natural life. All other critics, in all ages, have deemed the sense the principal object, and the language only accessory, or rather subsidiary and ancillary to the meaning it is intended to convey. Accordingly, a great writer or a great orator will not suffer us to think of the words he uses, and by which he effects his purpose. . . . All other men had supposed that words were used for the purpose of telling one person what another meant—all but Dr Channing—who conceives that the great object of authors is the same with that of riddle-makers,—to display their own skill in hiding their meaning, and exercise the ingenuity of others in finding it out. His favourite is the enigmatic style, not the lucid, not the perspicuous: his cry is 'riddle my riddle'; he stops you after a period with 'Ha! do you follow me? I'll warrant you can't tell what *that* means?' And certainly, in one particular, he differs from the old-fashioned riddle-monger, who always had a meaning, and only puzzled you to get at it; while the Doctor sometimes puzzles you when he has not much more meaning than the celebrated person of quality had in writing the well-known song recorded by Dean Swift.

As to the senseless, despicable trash about 'literature becoming too popular,' and writers now being in danger of sacrificing solid fame (what he is pleased to call very affectedly the 'deep, thrilling note of the trump of fame') to gratify the multitude and 'catch the present shout of popularity,' there never was any delirium more complete. Why, it is all the other way! Dr Channing is the person who is running after empty shouts and heedless multitudes; for he wraps up his meaning, which is often so successfully concealed that its existence is very questionable: he is trying to pass off tinsel for sterling metal—fine sounding phrases for distinct and valuable ideas—flimsy, vague, shadowy, half-formed, half-pursued ideas, for deep thoughts;— as if every thing that looks magnified in the mist he raises round it by his volume of long words were therefore larger than what we see clearly in the broad daylight;—and, having thus done, he gravely tells us that it is the attribute of a great genius to be above ordinary comprehensions, and conceal its meaning under such language, until, like the prophetic enigmas of the oracle, their meaning is discovered in some future age of the world.

When we find authors professing, and indeed laying down such absurd and at the same time dangerous principles of taste, we cannot wonder at their practice betraying the corruption of their doctrine. It is as little to be expected that their writings should be of the purity required by a just standard, as that men who hold and proclaim a profligate code of morality should lead virtuous lives. The natural temptations of passion are not more powerful allies of such a vicious system of ethics in seducing men to transgressions, than the natural indolence and carelessness which render labour irksome, and the natural self-complacency which makes severe revision and the 'sæpe stylum vertas' distasteful: or the natural impatience to appear before the world which shuts the ear to all advice about a 'nine years' suppression,' are incentives to sin against the rules of good taste, and fall into that rapid and slovenly style which pro-verbially makes easy writing hard reading.

To this rule of conduct we have already seen that Dr Channing's style affords no exception. In every page we trace its evil influence in most careless thinking and most faulty diction— a constant mistaking of strange things for strong ones—a per-petual striving after some half brought out notion, of which the mind had never formed to itself any distinct picture—a substitution of the glare of words for harmonious ideas; and, we are sorry to add, not rarely that worst vice of bad writers, the assuming to use words and phrases in a sense peculiar to themselves, partly in order to strike by novelty, partly in order to save the pains of more legitimate and more correct com-position. (pp. 216-19)

If Dr Channing were the only transgressor of sound critical rules—if he did not belong to a School which has of late years threatened the corruption of all correct taste, and even the subversion of our old and pure English language—we should hardly have dwelt at such length as we have done on his style; and should not have extended our reflections further than a protest against his respectable authority being used to propagate his vicious taste. But, though he is among the most distin-guished, he is yet but one of a pretty large class of writers, who, chiefly in affectedly written works of exaggerated sen-timent, dictated by a Narcissus-like love of their own fancied charms—in many departments of the periodical press, and still more recently in the Annuals written by ladies and gentlemen amateurs, are filling the republic of letters with productions all the more hurtful to the public taste, that these great faults of one class cannot be committed, any more than Dr Chan-ning's, without some talents, though of a showy and shining rather than a sterling kind; while the emptiness of the other is balanced and set off by the arts of the engraver. It is fair to add, that Dr Channing's language is generally free, as far as the words go, from the barbarisms with which so many of these writers, and chiefly of the periodical caste, are deforming our mother tongue. 'Tis true, his diction has nothing racy or id-iomatic to recommend it; it is heavy and pompous, and far enough from the pure Saxon phrase; but it is at least of the standard currency; whereas the others utter a base gibberish of their own coining, which bids fair to supplant all the good and lawful English of the realm. (p. 220)

How well does the admirable maxim of old Roger Ascham express the principle which we have been endeavouring to inculcate, and which the new school so habitually violates! 'We ought,' said he, 'to think like great minds, and speak like the common people.' The adepts of this new school cannot certainly be said to reverse while they break this rule; they speak unlike either ordinary or extraordinary men; and it would be far better if their thoughts more nearly resembled those of everyday mortals, than the kind of things which proceed from them; out of joint, discoloured in their hue, distorted in their proportions,—seemingly reconciled by no one thing but their being what never would have entered any mind in its ordinary and natural state. (pp. 221-22)

If any one thing can be more preposterous than another in all this, it is the notion taken up by Dr Channing that plainness and simplicity are inconsistent with force. He says in the pas-sage—the incredible passage above cited—that though 'sim-

plicity and perspicuity are important qualities of style, there are vastly nobler and more important ones,—such as energy and richness;' as if a man were to say, 'Air is good for health, but perfume is far better.' This is exactly the blunder our author has here fallen into. The perfume is useless to men who are stifled for want of air; and the access of the air, far from excluding the perfume, is required to waft it. Who ever heard before of clearness and simplicity being incompatible, of all things, with energy? Why, common parlance almost weds the two together. Thus, we say, 'simple energy'—'simple and energetic'—and did our critic ever hear of one Dante? or, per-adventure, of one Homer? Who ever thought that he was solv-ing a riddle, as far as the diction was concerned, when he read the energetic passages of those great masters of the sublime? Not only do the combinations of the words all present the correct solution of the meaning, but the plainest words are always employed in all the passages of greatest energy. To give instances would be endless. We are stating things of pro-verbial truth, and of every-day observation. A learned divine like Dr. Channing must have often made the same remark on the more powerful passages of the Scriptures. The writings of the Greek orators and Greek tragedians, as well as the finest passages of both Herodotus, Thucydides, and Livy are full of similar instances. (p. 224)

It remains that we say something respecting the substance of Dr Channing's tract; although we have already stated that it is the faulty style and the heterodox critical matter which induced us to undertake this discussion. Some, however, of the same errors also pervade the opinions which he delivers respecting Milton, although here we find far more that is valuable and deserving of unqualified commendation. He has a strong and lively sense (as who, indeed, in these days has not?) of the prodigious merits of that great man, both as a poet and a citizen; nor are these, as might be expected, lessened in his eyes, by the accident which makes the modern and the ancient repub-lican, the Unitarians of the nineteenth and the seventeenth century, the Independents who abhor church establishments on either side of the Atlantic, coincide in all their opinions, re-ligious as well as political. Our author's, however, is a dis-criminating and sober, not a blind admiration; he feels the beauties of the illustrious poet as a critic, not as a partizan; and if he sometimes misplaces his praise, and sometimes fan-cies he is discovering beauties long since well known and universally admired, we can pardon these little excesses, pro-ceeding, as they do, from a laudable fondness for so noble and so inspiring a theme.

Thus, after describing his almost unrivalled sublimity and im-mense power—though somewhat as if neither Homer nor Dante had ever lived—he adds, 'His sublimity is in every man's mouth: is it felt that his poetry breathes a sensibility and ten-derness hardly surpassed by its sublimity?' After some not very happy remarks, and, truth to say, not very intelligible, on 'great minds, being masters of their own enthusiasm,' and 'having a sensibility more intense and enduring,' and 'being more self-possessed and less perturbed than those of other men, and therefore less observed and felt, except by those who under-stand, through their own consciousness, the workings and ut-terance of genuine feelings'—he gives instances to prove that Milton could write with pathos and tenderness. Two are from *Comus*; and the discovery made by Dr Channing through this 'congenial feeling and consciousness' to other men denied, is the *unknown* passage beginning, 'Can any mortal mixture of earth's mould.' After this we are the less surprised at the other *unknown* passage of *Paradise Lost*, now brought to light, painting our first parents meeting in the morning, in which every other line is still as much the subject of constant quotations as Hamlet's soliloquy—*e.g.*, 'Heaven's last best gift,' the bee 'extracting liquid sweet,' 'temperate vapours bland,' &c. &c. But it is as well to note that he does not quote a far better instance, and one very much less hackneyed by the followers of Dr Pangloss, namely, Adam's address to Eve, beginning,

> 'Sweet is the breath of morn when she ascends
> With charm of earliest birds,' &c.

There is a great deal said, and certainly not too much, on the character of Satan; but of all the magical power displayed by the great bard, we believe there is none more transcendent, and none where his truly original genius more appears than in his picture of Death. . . . [It is singular that Channing] should make no allusion whatever to this extraordinary portion of *Paradise Lost.* (pp. 226-27)

From the poetry, Dr Channing turns to the prose writings of Milton; and he at once pronounces it to be a 'lesson long known to the initiated, and which the public are now learning, that they contain passages hardly inferior to his best poetry, and that they are marked throughout with the same vigorous mind which gave us *Paradise Lost.*' Now, as we are not amongst the initiated, we must take leave to pause upon this dictum, which prefaces the eulogy upon obscure composition already cited and discussed. We entirely deny the superlative merits of Milton's prose compositions; without, of course, doubting that they have great beauties of a certain kind, and contain occasionally fine passages. Nor is our denial grounded, as Dr Channing would suppose, from his defence of obscurity, upon that or upon their difficulty, for indeed we do not see any obscurity or difficulty in them; but they are written in a style the reverse of natural; the matter is always, or almost always, very inferior to the stilted diction; the author is ever labouring to look big; he is making a vast noise, and you cannot tell why; he is writing about it, and about it, without coming to the point. Nor is his diction, either in the arrangement, or the words, any thing like English. Does any one really believe that we should use a language such as the following—only remarkable for its involution, and for being pompous, whilst it says nothing? It is part of a passage cited by our author as exemplifying Milton's 'noble style.'—'Conceiving, therefore, this wayward subject against Prelaty, the touching whereof is

so distasteful and disquietous to a number of men, as by what hath been said I may deserve of my readers to be credited, that neither envy nor gall hath entered ever upon this controversy, but the enforcement of conscience only, and a preventive fear lest the omitting of this duty should be against me, when I would store up to myself the good provision of peaceful hours.' Nor do we much more admire the description of poetry ending with—'Whatsoever in religion is holy and sublime, in virtue amiable or grave; whatever hath passion or admiration in all the changes of that which is called fortune from without, or the wily subtilties or refluxes of man's thoughts; all these things, with a solid and treatable smoothness, to point out and describe.' . . . Now, when we humbly venture to reject this style altogether . . . , we have on our side no less than the high authority of Milton himself, to set against Dr Channing's. Who ever could trace the faintest resemblance to such diction in any of those divine compositions, where, being at home, he writes at his ease and naturally—walking without stilts, and thinking not of himself but of his great subject? What line in all the *Paradise Lost* ever approaches in the least degree to such turgid inflation? There all is simple, and easy, and light, and natural— even where the theme is most lofty, and would excuse, nay, almost demand, a swelling in the diction. The truth is, that Milton wrote Prose upon a False system, and Poetry on a True. He seems to have thought that a man must never write as he would speak. Whatever he had got to say must be delivered in an out of the way fashion. Not a sentence can be found in all the prose works which is easy or natural. Not an idea meets us which a person would have expressed in the same way had he followed the simple course of telling us plainly what he thought and meant. It is an eternal labour of language, very sonorous doubtless, but very often out comes nothing, or but little, from all the heavings of the mountain. (pp. 228-29)

In all the description of Death, there is not a word above the common standard of conversation—not a phrase out of the ordinary way of speaking. Does Dr Channing imagine it to be the less powerful because of this plainness? Indeed, even if many inflated passages should be shown in the poetry, what an account of a prose style is it to say, that it is always of the same inflation with certain passages of a poem undertaking to describe Heaven and Hell, and record the battles of devils with the Almighty and his seraphic host? But it is also to be added, that, find out inflated passages when you may, and in whatever numbers, the admiration of ages has been stamped upon the others, as the glory of Milton's name, and that these others are written in a style as plain, as perspicuous, as natural, as the prose diction is turgid and out of nature. (p. 230)

[*Henry Peter Brougham*], *"False Taste—Dr Channing," in* The Edinburgh Review, *Vol. LXIX, No. CXXXIX, April, 1839, pp. 214-30.*

THEODORE PARKER (journal date 1842)

[Parker was a prominent Unitarian clergyman who became widely known in the United States during the 1840s and 1850s for his espousal of transcendentalism and outspoken opposition to slavery. In the following excerpt from his journal, Parker mourns Channing's death.]

I have to-day heard of the death of Dr. Channing. He has fallen in the midst of his usefulness. His faculties grew brighter as age came on him. No man in America has left a sphere of such wide usefulness; no man since Washington has done so much to elevate his country. His life has been spent in the greatest

The house in Newport where Channing was born.

and best of works. A great man—and a good man—has gone home from the earth. Why, oh! my God, are so many left, when such are taken? Why could not I have died in his stead?

> *Theodore Parker, in a journal entry on October 5, 1842, in* Life and Correspondence of Theodore Parker, *Vol. I by John Weiss, 1863. Reprint by Bergman Publishers, 1969, p. 183.*

GEORGE BANCROFT   (essay date 1843)

[A leading nineteenth-century American historian, Bancroft was one of Channing's friends. In the following excerpt, he defends Channing's belief in nonviolent reform, which had been denounced by many contemporary abolitionists.]

Let us rejoice, that in our own day, the great principle of Free Inquiry has been renewed, upheld, and pursued to still wider applications than it had reached before, by the refined intelligence and genial benevolence of William Ellery Channing. Free Inquiry was the great rule which he inculcated, not for the maturity of age only, but for the ardent curiosity of youth: for he knew that freedom, far from leading to infidelity, strives for certainty, is restless in pursuit of a well-grounded conviction. Freedom of mind he claimed, therefore, for every pursuit of the human faculties; not for professors only, but for scholars; not for material science alone, but even there where authority had been most revered, in theology and in the church.

Nor did he confine the principle to theoretic speculations; he claimed it also in politics, and the affairs of social life. Not that he was a politician; Channing could be classed with no political party. He stood aloof from them all; and sought rather, behind the clouds of party strife, to discover the eternal principles that sway events and guide the centuries. His was the search for universal truth; he turned from men to the central light; he looked towards the region of absolute truth, of perfect justice. The laws of the moral world, the principles that come from the Eternal Mind, these were the objects of his pursuit; and he claimed for every man the right of calmly, fearlessly contemplating those truths, of seeking to apply them even to the affairs of life. (p. 524)

And yet, while we elevate our own minds to the capacity of receiving the sublime lessons which he uttered, if we look back upon his life, we shall find his love of reform balanced by a love of order, and the expansive energies of his benevolence restrained by a spirit of conservatism. He was not the mariner, who eagerly lifts the anchor and spreads his sail to the winds, and embarks on the ocean of experiment; he resembled rather the seer, who stands on the high cliff along the shore, and gazes to see what wind is rising, and gives his prayers, and his counsels, and benedictions to the more adventurous, who set sail. And sometimes he would call back the enterprising reformer: he would not attempt progress by methods of disorder and riot, or even of party organization; he would rather forego for a season the establishment of a right than seek to assert it by bloodshed and violence; like the Jewish mother who submitted to be withheld from her offspring for a season, through fear lest, otherwise, her child should be rent in twain.

And yet this abhorrence of violence hardly partook of timidity, certainly did not spring from a deficiency of decision. Did you consider his delicate organization, his light and frail frame, his sensitiveness to agreeable impressions, the exquisite culture of his taste, you might apprehend a want of firmness; but it was not so. Do you remember the fine lines in which Walter Scott describes the slender shafts of shapeless stone of Melrose Abbey, of which the foliaged tracery seemed woven of osier wreaths, and yet, as if changed by a fairy's spell, it proved to be of stone. So it was with Channing. He towered above the mediocrity of society, like the pinnacles of a Gothic minster, of which the tracery is infinitely delicate and airy, yet solid, durable, unyielding, and aspiring to the skies. Even sympathy, that which he loved most, he sacrificed readily to duty; and gave up the present applause of those by whom he was surrounded, rather than fail to win the world for his audience, and coming generations for his fame.

This firmness rested in an entire faith in moral power to reform the world. Not the union of men, not associations, not temperance societies nor abolition societies, not conventions: MORAL POWER was to him the Egeria that dictated, the energy that accomplished reform. Hence, while he objected to associations, he was ever ready to advocate the great moral purposes for which men come together. Was he not among the first to rebuke the international selfishness, that has so long held the commerce of the world in bonds? Was he not among the first in our midst to raise his voice against the horrors of war, the opprobrium of humanity? Who like him gathered the crowd to recognize the great lesson of temperance, carrying renovation to once desolated families; to the desponding and feeble of will? Who like him asserted the moral dignity of man, irrespective of wealth and rank? Indeed, one could hardly hear him on any public occasion, or even in private, but the great truth of man's equality, as a consequence of his divine birth, struggled for utterance. He knew that man was made in the image of God; that the gift of reason opened to him the path to the knowledge of creation, and to mastery over its powers. Having the highest reverence for genius, he yet recognized the image of the divine original everywhere, in every human form; and how often have his teachings repeated to many of us the doctrine so well expressed by one of kindred genius!

> Nor scour the seas, nor sift mankind,
> A poet or a friend to find;
> Behold, he watches at the door,
> Behold his shadow on the floor.
> *   *   *   the Pariah hind
> Admits thee to the Perfect Mind.

Hence Channing became the advocate of equality; recognized the power of the people as the great result of the modern centuries; and, knowing well that labor is the lot of man, that every mechanic art must be exercised, every service in life fulfilled, he sought to dignify labor, to exalt its character, not to lift the laborer out of his class, but to elevate that class into the highest regions of moral culture and enjoyment. (p. 525)

> *George Bancroft, "William Ellery Channing," in* The United States Magazine and Democratic Review, *Vol. XII, No. LIX, May, 1843, pp. 524-28.*

WILLIAM LLOYD GARRISON   (essay date 1848)

[A nationally recognized leader in the American abolitionist movement, Garrison founded the Liberator, *a weekly newspaper in which he vehemently denounced the institution of slavery. The excerpt below, drawn from a review of* Memoir of William Ellery Channing *(see the entry by William Henry Channing in the Additional Bibliography), was first published in the* Liberator *in 1848. Garrison discusses Channing's role as a reformer, focusing on his position regarding slavery.]*

My impressions of Dr. Channing were, that he was somewhat cold in temperament, timid in spirit, and oracular in feeling. But these have been greatly, if not entirely, removed by a perusal of [*Memoir of William Ellery Channing*]. I see him now in a new phase—in a better light. He certainly had no ardor of soul, but a mild and steady warmth of character appears to have been natural to him. I do not now think that he was timid, in a condemnatory sense; but his circumspection was almost excessive, his veneration large, and distrust of himself, rather than a fear of others, led him to appear to shrink from an uncompromising application of the principles he cherished. In the theological arena he exhibited more courage than elsewhere; yet, even there, he was far from being boldly aggressive, for controversy was not to his taste. In striving to be catholic and magnanimous, he was led to apologize for those who deserved severe condemnation. He was ever reluctant to believe that men sin wilfully, and, therefore, preferred to attack sin in the abstract than to deal with it personally. He was ready to condemn the fruit, but not the tree; for, by a strange moral discrimination, he could separate the one from the other. Hence, his testimonies were not very effective. In the abstract, the vilest of men are willing to admit that their conduct is reprehensible; but, practically, they demand exemption from condemnation.

In a pioneering sense, Dr. Channing was not a reformer; sympathetically, and through a conscientious conviction, he was. If he had lived in the days of the prophets or the apostles, he would have deplored their excessive zeal, their denunciatory spirit, their indiscriminate condemnation, their rash procedure, their lack of charity and gentleness; yet he would have had no hand in their persecution, but would have commended them as actuated by a sincere purpose, and as having a righteous object in view. He would have felt that the priests and rulers who were subjected to their terrible rebukes were dealt with far too roughly; and this would have moved him to say a word in their favor, in order to mitigate the severity of the punishment; yet he would have confessed, and wept over, the prevalent guilt in the land, and acknowledged that both priest and ruler were largely to blame for it. This, it seems to me, was a serious defect in his character, and greatly impaired his moral usefulness.

For example—he saw with great clearness, and deplored with much sincerity, the horrors of slavery and the injustice of slaveholding; but he did not like to hear slaveholders denounced, and regarded many of them as worthy of Christian recognition. He was for drawing out leviathan with a cord, or ensnaring him as a bird—forgetting that the monster regards iron as straw, and brass as rotten wood. No one ever seemed to be more deeply convinced of the iniquitous and desolating nature of war than himself; he was fervent in his pleas for peace; yet he held to the right of fighting in what is falsely called self-defence, and therefore failed to lay the axe at the root of the tree. It was so in his treatment of all other popular sins and sinners. He either lacked true moral discrimination, or stern integrity to principle.

I believe he was a sincere man, and true to his own convictions of duty. I think, as far as he saw the light, he was disposed to walk in the light, however great the peril or startling the consequences. He had in an eminent degree self-respect, which kept him from self-degradation by wilfully doing that which he knew to be wrong. His *Memoir* impresses me with a deep sense of his purity and uprightness. If he had given himself to any specific reform, without compromise, as a lecturing agent,

or in any other way that would have brought him in daily contact with the people of the land, I think his moral vision would have been purged, and his judgment of men and things rectified. In such a conflict, he had no practical experience whatever; and, without that experience, he was not qualified to sit in judgment on the language and measures of those who were valiantly contending for the right against a host of evil-doers. He was studious, contemplative, closet-bounded; it was impossible, therefore, for him to be in the stern battle of life, or to perceive in what quarter the assault was to be most vigorously made. Yet it is equally interesting and cheering, in reading his *Memoir,* to perceive his growing interest in reform and reformers. His voice of rebuke to a guilty nation was growing stronger, and his 'all hail' to the true-hearted more emphatic, continually.

We must judge him by the position that he occupied. . . . He was a clergyman—an office which it is scarcely possible for any man to fill without loss of independence, or spiritual detriment. In his case, it seems to have been merely technical, though he might have made it subservient to personal ambition and selfishness, as thousands of others have done. That he did not do so, is something to his credit. . . . His preëminence was not intellectual—for he had not an extraordinary intellect—but moral, religious, humane, in the largest and best use of those terms. He was utterly divorced from bigotry and sectarism. He believed in eternal progress, and therefore never stood still, but went onward—if not rapidly, without faltering. He changed his views and positions from time to time, but only to advance—never to retreat. Theologically, he is to be regarded as a prodigy on the score of independent investigation and free utterance. In this field, his labors cannot be over-estimated.

Again—he moved in a wealthy and an aristocratic circle, or rather was surrounded by those who are the last to sympathize with outcast humanity, or to believe that any good thing can come out of Nazareth. To write and speak on the subject of slavery as he did—unsatisfactory as it was to the abolitionists, who yearned to have him take still higher ground—was, in his position, an act of true heroism and of positive self-sacrifice; and, for a time—extending almost to the hour of his death—cost him the friendship of many whose good opinions nothing but a sense of duty could induce him to forfeit. The Unitarian denomination, as such, was deeply afflicted and mortified at his abolition tendencies; and, in spite of its almost idolatrous attachment to him, it could scarcely be at peace with him. Now that he is dead and the times have greatly changed, there is nothing to which that denomination (especially when charged with being still pro-slavery) more complacently points, in the illustrious career of Dr. Channing, than to his efforts to extirpate slavery in the land.

Much to my regret, I had no personal acquaintance with this remarkable man, though I longed for at least a single interview. But the *Liberator* was not to his taste, and my manner of conducting the anti-slavery enterprise seemed to him harsh, repulsive, and positively injurious. As he never expressed a wish to converse with me, I did not feel free to intrude myself upon his notice. For twelve years, he saw me struggling against all that was evil in the land—in a cause worthy of universal acclaim—with fidelity and an unfaltering spirit—but during all that time he never conveyed to me, directly or indirectly, a word of cheer, or a whisper of encouragement. Consequently, we never met for an interchange of sentiments. Had we done so, though there is no probability that we should have seen eye to eye in all things, we might have been mutually benefited.

I am sure that he misjudged my spirit, as well as misapprehended the philosophy of the anti-slavery reform; and I now think that I did not fully appreciate the difficulties of his situation or the peculiarities of his mind. His great mistake was—it amounted almost to infatuation—in supposing that a national evil like that of slavery, two centuries old, which had subdued to itself all the religious and political elements, and which held omnipotent sway over the land, could be overthrown without a mighty convulsion, or even much agitation, if wisely and carefully treated. He thought that it was the manner and the spirit of the abolitionists, and not the object they sought to accomplish, that so greatly excited the country, especially the Southern portion of it; and so, to set them a good example—to show them how easily they might propitiate the slaveholders while pleading for the emancipation of their slaves—he wrote his work on slavery, the circulation of which was deemed incendiary at the South, and the publication of which caused Gen. Waddy Thompson of South Carolina to exclaim, on the floor of Congress, that 'Dr. Channing was playing second fiddle to Garrison and Thompson.' This was an instructive experiment to the Doctor, and he did not fail to profit by it. (pp. 239-42)

> *William Lloyd Garrison, "The Anti-Sabbath Convention," in* William Lloyd Garrison, the Story of His Life: 1841-1860, Vol. III *by Wendell Phillips Garrison and Francis Jackson Garrison, The Century Co., 1889, pp. 218-43.*

JOHN CHAPMAN   (essay date 1848)

[*Chapman comments on the popular appeal of Channing's writings.*]

[Dr. Channing] is the first purely moral writer who has acquired a *popular* power, and found his way, not only into the boudoir of the professed reader, but into the pocket of the artisan. Essayists, never able to escape, as a class, the repute of dulness, have been content, from the time of Addison to that of Coleridge, to find acceptance in the library of the student, or at the breakfast-table of the man of letters; and even these have been glad to shelter themselves under the cover of some Review, which would secure them introduction to a political party of larger range than their own natural circulation. Channing, far from being dependent on such artificial extension of his audience, found all the customary media and methods of publication too narrow for his thought. His articles of review were snatched from the periodicals in which they first appeared, and, notwithstanding their grave and earnest character, spread with the rapidity of a revolutionary speech or an exciting fiction. His lectures and sermons, though perpetually trenching on the polemic ground of philosophy and divinity, could not be confined to the ordinary circle, but passed into the hands of thousands by whom the literature of the platform and the pulpit had been held in little respect. The numerous editions of his works, and the competition of popular publishers for their English sale, indicate a scope and direction of influence unexampled among writers of the same class. Channing could well afford to neglect the hostile criticisms with which he was occasionally assailed; whatever supercilious purists might say of his style, and scrupulous orthodoxy deplore in his theology, he was assuredly one of the *powers* of the passing age; made so, in part, by singular adaptation to its moral wants, in part by certain elements of intrinsic greatness. . . . (p. 318)

> *John Chapman, "Life of Channing," in* The Westminster and Foreign Quarterly Review, *Vol. L, No. I, October, 1848, pp. 317-48.*

ERNEST RENAN   (essay date 1854)

[*Renan was a noted French historian, philologist, and critic. In the following excerpt, he offers an overview of Channing as a man of impeccable virtue but mediocre intellect. Renan's remarks were originally published in the* Revue des deux mondes *in 1854.*]

It was without premeditation that Channing became a man of letters. His works show no literary ambition; not one displays the least pretension to art and style. Channing is an evangelical pastor and preacher: his works are but sermons, spiritual letters, articles for a religious journal. The notion of writing a book did not come to him until rather late, and happily it was not realized. The plan of this book was neither fresh nor original. It would have been an *essay* like so many others, on man and human nature, the incessant theme of the Anglo-Scotch philosophy. Channing would have been no exception to the tediousness of books of this sort, surely excellent for certain stages of intellectual culture, but teaching nothing, and of very little value now that history and our general ideas on the development of the human species have nearly forgotten that paltry philosophy.

No more was Channing a scholar or philosopher. His education was deficient; his historical learning is all at second and third hand. He did not have that delicate feeling for nuances which we call criticism, without which there is no understanding the past nor, consequently, any extensive grasp of human affairs. It is surprising to see at what point the Anglo-Saxon intelligence is dispossessed of that talent for historical insight so richly bestowed upon Germany—and so generously commanded in France by a few minds, provided that it is not a matter of too remote antiquity nor of a mentality too different from our own. For certain periods of political history, this middling acumen can produce estimable work, of sufficient truth; but for literary history, for religious history, for philosophical history—which are destined more and more to become the history that matters and to cast back into shadow whatever formerly went by that name—a wholly different power of divination is required; and such is the importance assumed in our time by such inquiries that it is no longer possible to be a thinker or a philosopher without possessing this power. Fortunately one can still, without it, perfectly well be a decent man. This is what Channing pre-eminently is; and this he is to a degree that approaches genius and is at least a thousand times more valuable than talent. Like all men who are born for the exercise of virtue rather than for contemplation, he has few ideas, and these are very simple. He believes in revelation, in the supernatural, in miracles, in prophets, in the Bible. He tries to prove the divineness of Christianity by arguments which are in no way different from those of the old school. This Puritan who contracts for his faith at so high a price, is at bottom hypercredulous in everything that belongs to history, for lack of training in the intellectual gymnastics that result from a long experience of the problems of the human mind.

Just as he lacks the method of criticism, Channing lacks also the instinct of high originality. When we compare this excellent soul, this saint of modern America, with those who, like him, have in the past been possessed by a zeal for the glory of God or for the welfare of their fellow men, a feeling of sadness, a chill, at once overtakes us. Instead of the splendid theology of ancient times, instead of that noble intoxication of a Francis of Assisi, which speaks so potently to the imagination, we find ourselves in the presence of an honest *gentleman*, upstanding, decorous, fervent and inspirational in manner, but without any aura of the marvelous; dedicated, but not grandly; noble and pure, but without poetry, unless it be a poetry wholly domestic and private. Far be it from us to prefer those paradox-ridden souls who, because they have apprehended the beauty of the past, would with an archaeologist's yearning reconstitute a vanished world—as though the first condition of serious homage were not to regard every object in its natural setting, in its own time. The dazzling fantasies of the ancient religions would in our day be chimerical. We cannot renew a dream by an act of will, and we cannot justly reproach men of the present age for lacking qualities which men of simpler times owed to ignorance and simplicity. It would be no less unjust to reproach Channing for the humbleness of his theology, since humbleness is, with regard to abstract thought, a precondition of reasonableness. His theology is at bottom all that theology can be in the nineteenth century and in America—dull, simple, seemly, practical; a Franklinesque theology, without metaphysical range or transcendental purpose. Those who value a religion for its simplicity and degree of transparency should be enchanted by this one. Surely if the modern temper is right in wishing a religion which, without excluding the supernatural, reduces the proportion of it as much as possible, Channing's religion is the most perfect, the most refined, that has yet appeared.

But is that, indeed, all there is to it? when the creed is reduced to belief in God and Christ, what shall we have gained? Will skepticism be appeased? Will the formula of Being be more complete, more clear? or the destiny of men and of mankind less unfathomable? Does Channing, with his antiseptic creed, avoid the objections of unbelief any better than Catholic theologians? Alas, no! He accepts the resurrection of Jesus Christ but not His divinity; he accepts the Bible but not hell. He deploys all the sensibility of a scholastic to establish, against the trinitarians, in what sense Christ is the son of God and in what sense he is not. But if one grants from beginning to end that there is a real miraculous existence, why not frankly call it divine? The one notion demands no greater effort of belief than the other. Indeed, along that road it is only the first step that is painful; we need not boggle at the supernatural; faith is all of a piece; the concession once made, it ill becomes us to demand the return of those rights which once and for all we have given away.

There to my mind is the pinched and contradictory aspect of Channing. What becomes of a rationalist who admits miracles, prophecies, and revelation? What good is it to tell me that this revelation must be measured by reason, and that in case of conflict reason should be preferred? With rationalism any halting point is arbitrary. The fact of this revelation, which is supposed at the outset to be self-evident, is after all the essential point which must be established; and, considering the severity of modern criticism, we cannot say that this is an easy matter. We are thus led into a diversity of opinion which is to be resolved by the hypothesis of a revelation. But if we assume that there is one absolute formula for truth, how are we to hope that it can be attained by the efforts of individuals? How can we trust our own judgments to the point of imputing infallibility to them, and of believing that we shall find the final truth which up to now no one has ever attained?

I know that I am directing at Channing the objection which Catholic theologians direct at Protestantism in general. Indeed the line of argument of Catholic apologists, an extremely weak if not worthless argument when aimed at that broad Protestantism which is nothing other than spiritualism attaching itself to the great Christian tradition, has always seemed to me unanswerable when aimed at that element in the Reformed Church

which aspires to the apparent strictness of Catholicism without putting on its shackles. When Protestantism does not lead to a purely rational religion, it seems to me illogical. That this illogic may be excusable and often honorable, I am the first to grant; but it must be said that if Protestantism aims only to replace one set of dogmatic beliefs with another, it no longer has any right to exist: Catholicism is then superior. Channing, on this point, never reached a perfectly clear formulation of his own thinking. If on the one hand he preaches the most complete freedom of belief, on the other he stops well short of a thorough-going criticism. If he comes out energetically against the established church, he by no means gives up hope of finding the one true form of Gospel teaching. In recommending that one seek for oneself, he does not dream that one may be carried by independent inquiry beyond Christianity. And yet, if we grant the reality of a revelation delivered at a certain moment in history, if we allow for divinely revealed truths, which consequently must impose themselves upon the conscience of whoever believes them to be revealed, where is the difficulty in accepting an outward establishment, a Church, informed by supernatural illumination? A miracle happening eighteen hundred years ago is neither more nor less easy to accept than a miracle that extends into our own time. The Catholic may rightly tell Channing: ''You are no more free than I, and you bow down to an authority much less intelligible: you obey the Bible, I obey the Church.'' I confess that for my part I should accept much more willingly the authority of the Church than the authority of the Bible. The Church is more human, more living; howsoever unalterable it may seem, it conforms better to the needs of each age. It is easier, if I may say so, to make the Church listen to reason than a book which has been sealed for eighteen hundred years.

. . . Moreover it is in the nature of an established religion to command belief less imperiously, precisely because it stands forth as an institution to which one can conform without having to bestow upon it an absolute belief, just as to obey the laws of the state it is not necessary to believe them the best in the world. . . . [Do] we observe that England and the United States, where everyone makes theology a personal concern, possess an intellectual culture superior to France's, where no one theologizes? Is habitual reading of the Bible, necessary consequence of the Protestant system, in itself so great a blessing? is the Catholic Church so guilty for having put the seal on this book and kept it hidden? Surely not: and I am tempted to say that the most magnificent act of statecraft of that great establishment is to have substituted itself, alive and active, for an authority that was voiceless. Hebrew literature is doubtless an admirable literature, but only for the scholar and critic, who can study it in the original and restore a true meaning to each of the curious fragments of which it is composed. As for those who trustingly worship it, they most often worship what simply is not there; the true original nature of the Old and New Testament books is lost to them. What are we to say of those semi-literates who plunge without preparation into a quite obscure antiquity? What may be imagined of the confusion of mind which habitual reading of a book like Revelations or even Kings will cause among these simple untutored people? We know the strange aberrations which, at the time of the English Civil War, issued from this unwholesome meditation. In America, the source of such extravagance is not yet dried up. Doubtless it may be much better to see a people reading the Bible than reading nothing, as in Catholic countries; but we must declare that the book could be better chosen. It is a sad spectacle—an intelligent nation spending its leisure on the monument of a bygone age and endlessly seeking its articles of belief in a book which contains none.

Channing's efforts to escape this tyranny of the Bible led him at times into curious struggles with received scripture. Hell, as orthodoxy conceives it, is repellent to his gentleness. For him hell exists only in the conscience, precisely as heaven knows nothing of locality and is simply union with God and with all great and good being. This I grant him; but how naïve to set himself to counting how many times hell is named in the Bible, and to observe with satisfaction that it appears only five or six times and that a *good* translation would find some way to be disencumbered of this disagreeable word! . . .

In general what is lacking in Channing is what up to now is lacking in America—high intellectual culture, and critical learning. He is not thoroughly informed on matters of the human understanding; he does not know all that may be known in his time. As a religion of the mind his religion is not equal to that of North Germany; as a great institution, it is not equal to Catholicism: it requires too great a sacrifice of critical judgment, and yet does not lay a sufficient demand on those who feel the need to believe. . . .

Channing's real mission was wholly moral. His theology, like all efforts to solve the unsolvable, is easily criticized; but his moral philosophy may be praised unreservedly: this is what makes him novel and original for us. Nothing indeed in our European settlement can give us any idea of such an apostle. To us the proselyting fervor which fashions the apostle or the missionary is inseparable from a definite and complex religion laden with dogma and ceremony. But here is a Vincent de Paul without the devoutness, a Cheverus minus the priesthood. . . . Channing's eminently Anglo-Saxon character, his gentlemanly refinements, his optimism, which made the vision of evil a real torment to him, rendered his ministry of benevolence that much more meritorious. . . . (pp. 80-6)

The problems which over here have disturbed the human mind, their solution not yet foreseen, are all settled for Channing by Christian love, by respect for man, by the conviction that human nature is good and that to unfold it is all to the good. Never has there been a firmer belief in progress, in the beneficent influence of enlightenment and civilization on all classes. Channing is a democrat, in the sense that he will admit no other kind of nobility than that of virtue and labor, and that he sees no salvation for humanity except in the intellectual cultivation of the common masses and in their introduction into the heart of the great family of civilization. "I am a leveller," he wrote in 1831; "but I would accomplish my object by elevating the low, by raising from a degrading indigence and brutal ignorance the laboring multitude. If I know what Christianity and philanthropy mean, they teach no plainer lesson than this."

. . . Here are noble feelings which it is well never to blush at. And yet are Channing's political and social ideas, so simple, so excellent, so pure, any more to be sheltered from criticism than his religious notions? Would a people which realized Channing's ideal be indeed a fulfilled people, according to our own image of high civilization? It may be doubted. It would be a virtuous and orderly people, made up of good, contented individuals; it would not be a great people. Human society is more complex than Channing supposes. In the face of calamities like those of the Middle Ages, we are led to feel that the essential thing is to make life as minimally wretched as possible; in the face of a moral slackening such as we are now

witnessing, we willingly believe that the work of social reform should be to bring into the world a little integrity; but these are narrow views, conceived under pressure of momentary necessity. Man is not on earth merely to be happy; he is not even merely to be virtuous; he is here to bring great things to pass through organized society, to attain nobility (or saintliness, as Christianity calls it), and to pass beyond the meanness in which the lives of nearly all individual men are dragged out. The past objection to Channing's world would be that we should perish of *ennui*; genius would be unprofitable in it, and great art impossible. Puritan Scotland, in the seventeenth century, shows us something very near the Unitarian dream, a kind of ideal commonwealth after the fashion of Israel, in which every one knew the Bible, argued out his faith, and debated public affairs, and in which drunkenness and profanity were unknown. But with what precious gift did seventeenth-century Scotland enrich the world? Would not God have been better venerated if, at the risk of a few discordant utterances, more lofty and noble things had been brought forth? Italy, on the other hand, is surely the country where Channing's ideal has been least realized: in the fifteenth and sixteenth centuries pagan, immoral, given over to all the transports of passion and genius; then beaten down, superstitious, beyond help; now dreary, fretful, bereft of wisdom. And yet if it were necessary that either Italy with her past or America with her future had to be swallowed up, which would leave the greater void in the heart of mankind? What is the whole of America in comparison with one ray of that immeasurable splendor with which, in Italy, a city of the second or third rank shines, Florence, Pisa, Siena, Perugia? Before taking a place comparable to those towns on the scale of human grandeur, New York and Boston have much to do, and I doubt whether it will be through vegetarian societies and the propagation of pure Unitarianism that they will begin to approach it. (pp. 86-8)

If the world's problems could be solved by rectitude, simplicity, temperateness of spirit, Channing would have solved them; but other qualifications are required, and Channing, who received from nature as many of these as nature grants, did not happen to live in an intellectual milieu which could develop them and bring them to fruition. Let it be said at once that nothing is worth more than integrity, goodness, true piety, these essential endowments of the noble soul. "When God created the human heart, he first put goodness there as the true stamp of the divine nature, to be the mark of that beneficent hand from which we all issue." But goodness alone is not sufficient to solve the riddle of things. Its role is fine enough: to sweeten life, but not to reveal life's secret. For that, learning and genius are as necessary as exaltation of heart and purity of soul. A world without learning and without genius is as incomplete as a world without righteousness. Channing scarcely understood anything except this last condition; and in this, too, he committed the sin of imagining things to be much simpler than they actually are. (p. 90)

Ernest Renan, "Channing and the Unitarian Movement in the United States," translated by Warner Berthoff, in The New England Quarterly, *Vol. XXXV, No. 1, March, 1932, pp. 75-92.*

G. REYNOLDS   (essay date 1880)

[*Reynolds discusses Channing's role as spokesperson for the Unitarian movement.*]

When one asks, What was Channing's relation to the Unitarian movement? the first answer right to be made is, He was not the *originator* of it. Not to insist now upon what every Unitarian devoutly believes, that the movement is as old as Christianity itself, that in all essentials it is the Christianity of Jesus Christ,— waiving all that, very evident it is that Unitarianism sends its roots far back into New England history. There are pretty clear intimations that in the first years of that history there were some serious doctrinal cleavages; that not even the men and women of the first generation were in all points quite agreed. Certainly, not less than one hundred years before Channing's time, here and there were men of so pronounced a type of divergence from the prevailing opinions, that they differed but little from modern Unitarianism of the conservative type. The ferment of the Revolution, its quickened life, the increasing freedom of mind as well as of body and estate which it secured, greatly promoted the change of theological position already begun. So nothing is more clear than that in the latter part of the eighteenth century, probably before, New England was full, if not of nominal, certainly of real, Unitarianism. (p. 353)

It would be a mistake, therefore, and an injustice, to attribute to [Channing] too large and too early a place in the Unitarian movement. There were *seen* workers, like the Wares, the Whitmans, Walker, Dewey; back of them, Priestley, Belsham, and many more; back of them, a great army of *unseen* workers, who scarcely knew what was their exact theological position, but who full well understood that their souls revolted against the cruel dogmas concerning God and the unworthy estimates of human nature then prevalent. (p. 354)

It would be equally far from the truth to describe Channing as the leader of a theological attack upon old dogmas, or as an organizer of a new sect. In the original structure of his mind, he was the opposite of all this. He had no fondness for truth in its controversial aspects. So it was always a sense of responsibility to deeply cherished conviction, and never any natural fondness for the task, which led him into theological discussions of any kind. You look in vain, too, in his writings for rigid and formulated creed statements. His style even, logical in substance, was not greatly logical in form. By nature a student, still more an independent thinker, and most of all an earnest searcher after truth, he had little taste and probably less capacity to be an organizer. That he did anything to make the Unitarian body a separate denomination was hardly of set purpose, but rather because truth clearly and earnestly stated has in it the tendency and the power to crystallize its own into some compact shape.

What is true to say is that every great movement of humanity, whether in thought or in affairs, in the fitting time, finds its best expression in an individual,—in one who holds in himself the finest qualities of that movement, and who has the gifts to make for it the noblest and the most adequate expression. (pp. 354-55)

Without underrating, then, the work of other men, what we have to affirm is that Channing gave the amplest, the loftiest, the most spiritual, and the most enduring expression to that liberal thought which, almost unperceived by those who held it, had grown to influence and power in New England, and whose time for more definite assertion had fully come. He had, too, in an eminent degree, the qualities which fitted him for the task. His intense conviction of the right and worth of spiritual freedom; that his soul loathed every chain imposed upon mind and conscience; the calmness and breadth of his nature, which lifted all topics above the atmosphere of mere party or

sect; his fine spirituality, which imparted glow and warmth and lofty meaning to convictions which in other hands had become dry and lifeless dogmas; his tender, subtle, uplifting power as a preacher, to be felt rather than described, and which gave him a personal hold on many of the purest, loftiest, and in all walks most influential men of his day; his literary gift, by which he was able to make his utterances not only full of the things he believed, but also readable and attractive,—all these qualities fitted him to express, with fulness, richness, and great moral elevation, the truth for which he stood. Men and women rejoiced to find what they themselves thought and felt most deeply and solemnly better told than they could tell it themselves. And surely it is mere truism to say that of that successful revolt against the cruelties and injustice of genuine Calvinism, which early Unitarianism was, the fullest record is to be found to-day in what never claimed to be a record at all,—Channing's works.

If now we accept this estimate of Channing,—as a man of great catholicity of temper and intellect, averse to controversy and divisions, yet full of intense convictions, endowed with the capacity to take into his deepest life the new truths which were stirring other minds, to stamp them with the impress of his own devout and spiritual nature, and to give them the most powerful and attractive expression of which they were capable,—then this other question arises, What influence did he exert on the convictions and life of the age? Too broad and full a question, too multiform in the lines of thought which it opens, to be answered except in the most fragmentary way!

You take down that single volume of his works, published by the American Unitarian Association: on the first page of the first discourse [**"Self-Culture"**], you read these words: "A man is great as a man, be he where or what he may. The grandeur of his nature turns to insignificance all outward distinctions. It is the image of God, the image even of His infinity; for no limit can be set to its unfolding." The inherent dignity of human nature! That no man, however low in hope and however mean and base in action, but has underneath all this an inalienable possibility of greatness and goodness! That no man so poor, so ignorant, so criminal, but through proper influences the native dignity may be brought back again! This conception of man seems almost the corner-stone of Channing's system, the sentiment, the conviction, the dogma, if you please to call it such, which constantly reappears in his works, and which greatly shaped the practical conduct and efforts of his life. And yet, when first uttered, what a heresy it was! How utterly it contradicted all that Calvinism meant! What an antipode it is to the doctrine of total or innate depravity, however stated and however limited! And yet this sentiment, this conviction, this affirmation, has burned itself into the real beliefs of our time. Quite powerless against it have been the nominal faiths of Christendom. Good men and women of every name and sect, holding quite likely the most rigid views of depravity, of election and reprobation, are feeling and acting as though every man was a child of God, capable of the most real salvation, if only we surround him with the saving conditions. Can we overestimate the influence which Channing has exerted in this direction? He was himself a practical and wise philanthropist. No interest of man was foreign to him. The care of the poor, the education of the ignorant, the rescue of the intemperate, the freeing of the slave, the resistance of war and the condemnation of its barbarities,—none of these things were forgotten or slighted by this refined student, by this man of a naturally recluse spirit. But this faithful, practical work was not his most important contribution to philanthropy. His doctrine of human nature was a far more wide-reaching one. By his indignant denial of all partial and derogatory statements regarding human nature, by his unceasing affirmation in every form of eloquent and convincing speech of its essential greatness, he has furnished the foundation, the moral background, for all philanthropies. (pp. 355-57)

Nor can we rate as less profound and impressive his influence on questions of purely theological and religious import. Particularly ought that influence to be noted as acting most powerfully outside the lines of the sect to which by denominational affiliation he belonged. For his own, all that Channing could do was to make a clear and attractive statement of great truths already cherished by them, and to give to those truths the hue and quality of his richly and tenderly endowed spiritual nature. And, no doubt, Unitarianism has inherited from that broad and catholic soul, not its anti-Calvinism,—for it had that from the beginning,—but its liberal conception of faith and duty, by which it refuses to confine its sympathies or its gifts within its own denominational limits,—a tendency well-nigh fatal to outward growth, but perhaps promotive of a real and ever widening, if unseen, influence. (p. 358)

What some might call the weakness of Channing's mind and character has also greatly helped to produce . . . results. That he was no organizer, that he was not much of a Unitarian in any narrow and limited sense, that he gave but little time or strength to enlarge the bounds or strengthen the walls of the sect, but that he was rather a simple and profound thinker, who sought for the truth as for hid treasures, and promulgated it sincerely and earnestly, and then left it to do its own work, without any machinery,—all this quality of character gave him admittance to minds which would have been closed and barred against him, had he come in another guise and with a different spirit. . . . It has been the fortune of Channing to attract the attention and to secure the respect and even admiration of persons of widely different opinions and tendencies. They have recognized the purity of his spirit, the breadth and elevation of his thoughts, and the deep spirituality of his teachings. These persons may not become, and indeed in most cases are not likely to become, in name or fact Unitarians. But they are baptized with a new spirit. They are different and higher believers in their own articles of faith. They bring into their communion the seeds of a more catholic hope and purpose.

It has been recently asserted that, whatever may have been Channing's theological influence in the past, to-day it is a declining and dying influence. In the face of the fact that his works are being translated into new languages, that both in England and America they are being circulated with a rapidity before unknown, the statement does not bear the stamp of veracity. Only in one sense is it correct; namely, that the truth he preached has fewer kingdoms of error and superstition to conquer. In that same sense, Luther, when he lived to see half his beloved Germany Protestant, may be said to have exercised a less striking and immediate influence than when he stood one for the truth, and all Christendom on the other side. In that same sense, Garrison, living to see American slavery ended, was not any longer that active influence he was when all the powers of Church and State were banded against him. And very likely, just here in New England, where the liberal faith has wrought most mightily, in a period of softened opinions, when the views which most offended the mind and insulted the conscience have been ordered to the rear, if not discharged as too badly wounded for good service, Channing is not, and is not likely to be, the seen and noticeable factor in the for-

mation of opinion that he once was. That is the penalty of success. Meanwhile, in the past he has worked, and his work abides. (pp. 360-62)

                    G. Reynolds, ''The Relation of Channing to the Uni-
                    tarian Movement, and His Influence upon the Moral
                    and Religious Convictions of the Age,'' in Unitarian
                    Review and Religious Magazine, *Vol. XIII, No. 4,
                    April, 1880, pp. 353-62.*

THOMAS HUGHES (essay date 1880)

[Hughes chronicles Channing's part in the American abolitionist movement.]

[Channing's] life and work were many-sided, and well worth study on all sides, but my purpose is to touch on one only, and to speak of him in his relations to that small band of men and women who, to my mind, have earned the highest place as benefactors of our race in this strange and eventful century— to whom the seeker for heroic and Christian lives, for the simplest, the truest, the bravest followers of the Son of Man, will find his highest examples—the Abolitionists of New England. I do not forget, I am proud always to remember, that Old England led the way, and that the struggle here too was one which tried men's hearts and reins. But honour to whom honour is due! And if we will try to think what our anti-slavery movement would have been, had our 800,000 slaves been scattered over the southern counties of England, instead of over islands thousands of miles away, and had belonged by law to the noblemen and squires in those counties more strictly than their rabbits and hares belong to them under our game laws, we shall have little hesitation, I think, in yielding freely the foremost place to the group of New Englanders amongst whom Channing stood out a noteworthy figure, in some respects undoubtedly the most noteworthy of all.

Yes, as Mr. Lowell sings—

All honour and praise to the women and men
Who spoke out for the dumb and the down-trodden then.
I need not to name them—already for each
I see history preparing the statue and niche.
They were harsh; but shall *you* be so shocked at hard words
Who have beaten your pruning-hooks up into swords? . . .
You needn't look shy at your sisters and brothers
Who stabbed with sharp words for the freedom of others—
No, a wreath, twine a wreath, for the loyal and true
Who, for sake of the many, dared stand with the few.

This defence, which he who was to become one of their most powerful voices here finds himself driven to make for the harshness of the abolitionists, was never needed for Channing; and it is for this reason that I have referred to him as perhaps the most noteworthy of them all. For in all the excitement of a controversy which he felt to be for the life itself, and to be going down to the roots of things; when the religious and respectable world shrank from the side of the teacher they had pretended to love and honour for thirty years; when the finger of hatred and scorn was pointed at him in the most influential journals as the fomenter of revolution and the associate of felons and fanatics—no word ever fell from his lips or pen which was not weighted with consideration for, and sympathy with, his enemies, and generous allowance for the difficulties of the Southern slave-owner. In his first great anti-slavery manifesto—[*A Letter to the Hon. Henry Clay, on the Annexation of Texas*]—he speaks of his own early residence in the South, and his life-long attachment to them in these words: ''There is something singularly captivating in the unbounded hospitality, the impulsive generosity, the carelessness for the future, the frank, open manners, the buoyant spirit and courage, which marks the people''; and from this attitude he never swerved in later years, when the contest had become most envenomed.

''Hitherto the Christian world has made very little progress in the divine art of assailing and overcoming evil,'' was one of his sayings; and it was with scrupulous care that he strove to set some example of the divine method in the great controversy of his own time.

Let me now, as briefly as possible, recall the position of the question in 1830. The struggle in England was drawing to an end. Those of us who are old enough will recollect those days—how children were brought up to use no sugar, and to give every penny they could call their own for the cause of the slave; when grown men and women were spending themselves freely for the same cause: how the time was one of bright hope and enthusiastic work! for the goal was full in view. On the 1st of August, 1834, the Act passed, and emancipation was a fact.

In the United States it was far otherwise. There year by year the prospect was growing darker, and the clouds were gathering. The Southern tone had changed under the strain of the immense development of the cotton trade. Instead of lamenting slavery as an evil inheritance from their fathers, which was to be curtailed by every prudent method, and finally extinguished, Calhoun and the other Southern leaders were now openly proclaiming it to be the true condition of the labourer, and the mainstay of Christian society. They were looking round eagerly for new slave states to balance the steady increase of free states in the North, and by savage word and savage act were challenging and trying to stamp out every attempt to interfere with their domestic institution.

Their challenge had been at last formally accepted, and the gauge of battle taken up in deadly earnest. It was in this winter of 1830-1 that Garrison, the immortal journeyman printer, by extraordinary self-denial and energy, got out the first number of the *Liberator,* declaring slavery to be a ''league with death and covenant with hell,'' and pledging himself and his friends to war with it to the bitter end. Their watchword was—uncompromising, immediate emancipation.

It was in this same winter that Channing went to spend some months at St. Croix. He had not been in a slave state since his boyhood, and he returned with all his old impressions confirmed and strengthened. Slavery he felt to be even a greater curse to the world than he had always proclaimed it, and so he preached on his return to New England. At the same time without joining them openly he showed much interest in the work of Garrison and the uncompromising party, pleading for them that ''deeply moved souls will speak strongly, and ought to speak, so as to move and shake nations.'' No wonder that they turned eagerly to him in the hope that he would come forward and lead their attack. But for the moment this could not be. The temper of the combatants, waxing fiercer day by day, was a barrier which he could not cross as yet, and no doubt the social ostracism—so formidable to one who for a generation had stood foremost amongst those whom his countrymen delighted to honour—weighed somewhat with him. He could defend the abolitionists as ''men moved by a passionate devotion to truth and freedom,'' which led them to speak ''with an indignant energy which ought not to be measured by the standard of ordinary times;'' but join them at once he could not.

And they in their disappointment were almost ready to denounce him as one of those New England recreants who are addressed in the first stirring appeal of Hosea Biglow to his Massachusetts fellow citizens:—

> Wall, go 'long to help 'em stealin',
>   Bigger pens to cram with slaves,
> Help the men that's ollers dealin'
>   Insults on your fathers' graves;
> Help the strong to grind the feeble,
>   Help the many agin the few;
> Help the men that call your people
>   White-washed slaves and peddlin' crew!

The question whether Channing would have done well to join the abolitionists in these early days will always remain fairly debateable, and will be settled by each of us according to the strength of his own fighting instinct. Those who blame him for delaying can at any rate call himself as a witness on their side. For when at the end of 1834 the Rev. Samuel May, general agent of the Boston Anti-Slavery Society, in answer to Channing's expostulations as to the harshness and violence of their language, and the heat and onesidedness of the abolitionist meetings, turned upon him with—''Why then have you left the movement in young and inexperienced hands? Why, sir, have you not moved—why have you not spoken before?'' Channing, after a pause, replied in his kindest tones, ''Brother May, I acknowledge the justice of your reproof. I have been silent too long.''

Looking, however, at the man's age and character, I cannot join in casting blame on Channing. Other men might have deserved reproach for not emphasising their convictions in this way; but not he. At school he had gained the name of the Peacemaker. He had been true to that character for half a century. While a gleam of hope remained that the South might even yet move in the direction of Abolition, a gentle firmness in remonstrance was the only weapon he could conscientiously sanction. And in 1830 there was still such a gleam of hope in the lurid clouds. As late as 1832 the question of Abolition was discussed in the Virginian legislature. Some few of the best Southern public men still held the old doctrine, and were ready to work for gradual emancipation. They were even doing so by a colonisation society and other stopgaps, the hollowness and worthlessness of which had not yet been proved. The Peacemaker therefore might still hope to prevail.

But now the time had indeed come when further hesitation would have left a stain on his armour. I have said that the South were on the look-out for new territories into which to carry their slaves, and the devil rarely fails to find what they are in search of for men on such a quest as that. In 1827 the Spanish American colonies had gained their independence. Mexico, the chief of them, and the nearest neighbour to the United States, had from the first looked up to the great Republic with hope and admiration. But from her elder sister no response came. Her goodwill was coldly put aside, for she had declared freedom to all slaves in her borders, and these borders, unhappily for her, comprised a magnificent territory called Texas, as large as any four states of the Union, and eminently fitted for cotton-growing, and therefore for slave labour.

The temptation of this Naboth's vineyard soon proved too strong for the slaveholders, and an immigration of planters and slaves set in. The Mexican government remonstrated, and high words ended in a declaration of independence by the new settlers, and fighting, which must soon have resulted in their defeat, for they scarcely amounted to 20,000 in all, but for the constant replenishment of their ranks by bands of filibusters from the other side of the Mississippi. By this means Texas maintained a precarious kind of independence, which she was bent on converting into annexation to the Union. For some time every American statesman scouted so shameless a proposal, but by degrees the value of the country began to impress the slave states more and more. Talk of "manifest destiny" began to be heard, not only in the *New Orleans Picayune,* and in the border ruffian country, but within the walls of Congress, till in 1835-6 it became clear that the question of annexation, involving almost certain war with Mexico, was about to be submitted to the great council of the nation.

Here then was a new departure, involving on the part of the nation a sanction of slavery such as had never yet been tolerated. Already Channing had begun to redeem his pledge. He had published a volume on slavery [*Slavery*], taking firm ground against the furious madness of the Southerners, who were calling for the suppression of anti-slavery publications, and setting prices on the heads of leading abolitionists; and against the more odious respectable Northern mobs, which even in Boston had broken up meetings, and in New York had dragged Garrison through the streets with a halter round his neck, intent on hanging him. Channing had also opened his pulpit to May, the general agent of the anti-slavery societies. Now he stepped forward as a leader, and stood frankly side by side with the abolitionists.

Selecting for his correspondent Henry Clay of Kentucky, the best and most moderate of Southern politicians, he addressed to him the most famous of his political writings, the letter on the annexation of Texas. I have already quoted from this work one of many passages which show his friendly temper towards the Southern slaveholders, but the most thoroughgoing abolitionist could take no exception to the firmness of the position taken, or the power with which it was held. Space will only allow me to give the briefest outline of this masterly paper.

> Congress . . . is about to be called on to decide whether Texas shall be annexed to the Union. Public questions have not been those on which my work has been spent; but no one speaks, the danger presses, and I cannot be silent. There are crimes which in their magnitude have a touch of the sublime, and this will be one of them. The current excuses only make it more odious. The annexationists talk of their zeal for freedom! what they really mean is their passion for unrighteous spoil—of manifest destiny! away with such vile sophistry; there can be no necessity for crime. Mexico came to us seven years ago, a sister republic just escaped from the yoke of a European tyranny; looking to us hopefully for goodwill and sympathy. Instead of these, in our unholy greed, we have sent them land speculators and ruffians who are waging war upon a nation to which we owed protection against such assaults. Is the time never to come when the neighbourhood of a more powerful and civilised people will prove a blessing and not a curse to an inferior community?

But the crime is aggravated by the real cause of it, which is the extension and perpetuation of the slave trade. What will other nations, what especially will England, say to it? We hope to prop up slavery by this filibustering, but the fall of slavery is as sure as the fall of your own Ohio to the sea. A nation provoking war by cupidity, by encroachment, and, above all, by efforts to spread slavery, is alike false to itself, to God, and to the human race. You are entering on a new and fatal path. Let the spread and perpetuation of slavery be once systematically proposed as a Southern policy, and a new feeling will burst forth in the North. Let Texas be once annexed, and there can be no more peace for us. We may not see the catastrophe of the tragedy, the first scene of which we seem so ready to enact; we who are enlarging the borders of slavery when all over Christendom there are signs of a growing elevation of the poor in every other country. We are sinking below the civilisation of our day; we are inviting the scorn, indignation, and abhorrence of the world. In short, this proposed measure will exert a disastrous influence on the moral sentiments and principles of this country, by sanctioning plunder, by inflaming cupidity, by encouraging lawless speculation, by bringing into the Confederacy a community whose whole history and circumstances are adverse to moral order and wholesome restraint, by violating national faith, by proposing immoral and inhuman ends, by placing us as a people in opposition to the efforts of philanthropy and the advancing movements of the civilised world. Freedom is fighting her battle in the world with long enough odds against her already. Let us not give new chances to her foes.

It is difficult in our space to give even a faint notion of the power of argument and beauty of style of this splendid protest, but I trust I may have induced some readers to go to the original. Texas was not annexed till after Channing's death, six years later, and there can be no doubt that the influence his letter to Mr. Clay exerted and the encouragement it brought to the minority in Congress helped materially to postpone the evil day.

Occasions for speech now crowded on him thick and fast. In July 1836 a mob sacked the office of the *Philanthropist* at Cincinnati, and drove Mr. Birney, its editor, from this city. Channing could not rest till he had written him the noble letter [*The Abolitionists*] . . . exhorting Birney and his friends to hold fast the right of free discussion, but to exercise it as Christians. "The Cross is the badge and standard of our religion. I honour all who bear it. I look with scorn on the selfish greatness of this world, and with pity upon the most gifted and prosperous in the struggle for office and power; but I look with reverence on the obscurest man who suffers for the right, who is true to a good but persecuted cause."

But his complete identification with the abolitionists did not come till the next year. In November 1837 the office of the *Alton Observer* in Illinois was attacked, sacked, and its owner and editor, Lovejoy, the friend and fellow-worker of Garrison, killed while defending his property. New England respectability was fairly startled at last. It was resolved by gentlemen of position, who had no dealings with abolitionists, that a meeting must be held in Faneuil Hall to protest against this and other acts of murderous violence, and to maintain the threatened right of free speech. A petition for the use of the hall was prepared, and the first signature was Channing's, above those of Sewall, Sturgis, and others of the best blood in Boston. The board of aldermen refused the hall, but the response from the whole Bay state to a temperate letter of Channing's in the *Daily Advertiser* soon convinced them that they had gone too far. The hall was granted, and the meeting held on December 8th, and Channing proposed resolutions in favour of freedom of speech and meeting prepared by himself. When these had been seconded, the attorney-general of Massachusetts rose, and in a speech in which he likened the Alton mob to the fathers of the revolution, opposed the resolutions. The meeting wavered, and they would probably have been lost but for the speech of an unknown youth, who has since proved himself the greatest of anti-slavery orators, Mr. Wendell Phillips. The resolutions were carried in the end by acclamation, and for the moment the cause of freedom triumphed in Boston. But too soon the clouds gathered again, swiftly and ominously, and from that time till his death, in 1842, Channing's soul was vexed, and his patience tried, by the blind fury and malignity with which the slave-owners' cause was pressed, and the frequent unwisdom and needless provocation with which the assault was met.

Within a few days of the Faneuil Hall meeting, when a weak or vain man would have been glorying in his triumph, he addressed a letter to the *Liberator* calling on the abolitionists to show their disapproval of Lovejoy's use of force at Alton. "You are a growing party, burning with righteous zeal," he urged; "but you are distrusted and hated by a multitude of your fellow-citizens. Here are the seeds of deadly strife, conflicts, bloodshed. Show your forbearance now, show that you will not meet force by force. Trust in the laws and the moral sympathy of the community. Try the power of suffering for truth. The first Christians tried it amongst communities more ferocious than ours, and prevailed."

And now he himself had to bear bitter humiliation for the truth's sake, such as the refusal of the committee of his own church to allow a service connected with the death of his friend Charles Follen, a leading abolitionist.

Yet he continued his work faithfully and even hopefully, speaking out at every dangerous turn in the conflict which was raging round him. His chief remaining works in connection with the slavery question are **"The Duty of the Free States,"** in which he defends the English Government for refusing to surrender a slave cargo, who had overpowered the officers and crew, and had carried the brig *Creole* into Nassau; and *Emancipation,* a tract on the great triumph in the West Indies. They should be read by all who desire to know the length and breadth of his strength and his charity.

As Englishmen, however, we may be allowed to refer with special pride to his last public utterance [**"An Address Delivered at Lenox"**]. In the summer of 1842 he was dying slowly in the lovely Berkshire hills, when the return of August 1st, the anniversary of emancipation in the West Indies, once more inspired him to lift up his voice for the outcast and the oppressed. To the men and women of Berkshire he spoke of the emancipation of the 800,000 British slaves. While giving full credit to the nation, and the men who had been the instruments of this change, he repeats once more—"Emancipation was the

fruit of Christian principle acting on the mind and head of a great people. The liberator of those slaves was Jesus Christ." And these are the last words he ever spoke in public:

> The song, "On earth, peace," will not always sound as a fiction. Oh, come, thou kingdom of God for which we daily pray! Come, friend and Saviour of the race who didst shed Thy blood on the cross to reconcile man to man and earth to Heaven! Come, ye predicted ages of righteousness and love for which the faithful have so long yearned! Come, Almighty Father, and crown with Thine omnipotence the humble strivings of Thy children to subvert oppression and wrong, to spread light and freedom, peace and joy, the truth and spirit of Thy Son through the whole earth.

(pp. 59-64)

Thomas Hughes, "Dr. Channing, the Abolitionist," in Macmillan's Magazine, *Vol. XLII, No. 247, May, 1880, pp. 59-64.*

RALPH WALDO EMERSON (essay date 1882?)

[*In the following excerpt, Emerson underscores Channing's powerful appeal to the American public. As the date of Emerson's composition is unknown, the year of his death has been used to date this excerpt. For additional commentary by Emerson, see the excerpt dated 1823.*]

I attribute much importance to two papers of Dr. Channing, one on Milton and one on Napoleon [**"Remarks on the Character and Writings of John Milton"** and **"Remarks on the Life and Character of Napoleon"**], which were the first specimens in this country of that large criticism which in England had given power and fame to the *Edinburgh Review.* They were widely read, and of course immediately fruitful in provoking emulation which lifted the style of Journalism. Dr. Channing, whilst he lived, was the star of the American Church, and we then thought, if we do not still think, that he left no successor in the pulpit. He could never be reported, for his eye and voice could not be printed, and his discourses lose their best in losing them. He was made for the public; his cold temperament made him the most unprofitable private companion; but all America would have been impoverished in wanting him. We could not then spare a single word he uttered in public, not so much as the reading a lesson in Scripture, or a hymn, and it is curious that his printed writings are almost a history of the times; as there was no great public interest, political, literary or even economical (for he wrote on the Tariff), on which he did not leave some printed record of his brave and thoughtful opinion. A poor little invalid all his life, he is yet one of those men who vindicate the power of the American race to produce greatness. (pp. 339-40)

Ralph Waldo Emerson, "Historic Notes of Life and Letters in New England," in his The Complete Works of Ralph Waldo Emerson: Lectures and Biographical Sketches, Vol. X, *1903-04. Reprint by AMS Press, 1979, pp. 323-70.*

W. M. SALTER (essay date 1888)

[*Salter discusses Channing's views on social reform, concentrating on his proposals for alleviating the poverty and suffering of the lower classes.*]

Channing was not a social reformer in the ordinary sense of the term. He looked on the world from the religious standpoint. He measured the actual by the ideal. His views as to the social problems were determined by his general philosophy. The seminal principle of religion he declared to be the aspiration towards that ideal which we express by the word perfection. "Religion," he said, "is not an exclusive impulse. It does not grow from an emotion that is centred wholly upon God, and seeks no other object. It springs from the same desire for whatever is more perfect than our own nature and our present life, which has impelled man towards all his great spiritual acquisitions and to all great improvements of society." The history of the development of this impulse towards perfection, of the forms it has assumed, of the objects to which it has gone out, of the intellectual conditions under which it has worked, constitutes the main moral and ideal significance of the history of humanity. (p. 207)

It was a part of his traditional faith that the wrongs of this world would be righted in another, that God had worked miracles and would again, that he answers prayer, and will establish his kingdom substantially as Jesus and the Church have expected. Channing was by no means a complete rationalist. But he uttered, for all that, just the method which the religion of the future must take. He had that fundamental view of man and his capacities which all ethics that aspires to be religion must presuppose. This view is that man is not only a creature, but a creator. He is moulded not merely by his environment, by heredity, or what he has been, but by himself, in obedience to an idea which perhaps never has been and is nowhere now realized. There is no kind of physical necessity about this idea: we have to choose it, and so man is free. Indeed, freedom and creative power are the same thing; and this it is that constitutes the dignity of man, and makes him a sacred being.

This creative dignity and mission belong to society as well as to the individual. "Bodily and mental forces," says Channing, "can be measured, but not the forces of the soul; nor can the results of increased mental energy be foretold. Such a community (as he has been describing) will tread down obstacles now deemed invincible, and turn them into helps. The inward moulds the outward. The power of a people lies in its mind; and this mind, if fortified and enlarged, will bring external things into harmony with itself. *It will create a new world* around it, corresponding to itself." I take this passage from the lecture *On the Elevation of the Laboring Classes,* than which there are few things more stirring in the whole literature of social reform. Think for a moment what the result might be if religion should come to mean creating such a new world, if the unnumbered prayers for the kingdom of God going up from the human heart were turned into prayers to men themselves, and they were summoned to create that kingdom which still, so far as this world is concerned, hangs in the air! I know it is said that prayer leads to deeds, but we do not pray at all to another for what we can do ourselves. There may be blessings beyond our control.

> We cannot kindle when we will
> The fire which in the heart resides.
> The spirit bloweth and is still,
> In mystery our soul abides.

But prayer for the accomplishment of justice in the world, prayer for the elevation of the poor and oppressed, prayer for that which Christianity pictures under "the kingdom of heaven,"—this should be to ourselves, and not to God. It is, in truth, a kind of pessimism, a kind of atheism, to say there

are any necessary limitations, any "cannot" of human power in this direction. (pp. 209-10)

Let not Channing be understood as a "leveller," in the ordinary sense of the word, though I am afraid there is a good deal of "cant" about this use of it. He says, indeed, "I am a leveller; but I would accomplish my object by elevating the low, by raising from a degrading indigence and brutal ignorance the laboring multitude." He allows that some inequalities of condition are natural and necessary. He even idealizes, sometimes, as to the possibilities of the poor, in and notwithstanding their poverty. But, in general, he is distinct as to its evil influences; and at one time he enumerates them at length. He says that poverty tends to impair self-respect, to hinder intellectual growth, to hurt family life, to make the poor envious and discontented, and that it leads to intemperance. In one or two passages, the ills of the present order of things are vividly portrayed:—

> We are accustomed to speak of the improvement of society; but its progress has been attended with one disastrous circumstance, which at times almost makes us doubt whether the good has not been too dearly bought. I refer to the fact that the elevation of one part of the community has been accompanied with the depression of another. Society has not gone forward, as a whole. By the side of splendid dwellings you descry the abodes of squalid poverty; and within the city walls, which enclose the educated and the refined, you may meet a half-civilized horde, given up to deeper degradation than the inhabitants of the wilderness
>
> • • • • •
>
> It is the unhappiness of most large cities that, instead of this union and sympathy, they consist of different ranks so widely separated as, indeed, to form different communities. In most large cities there may be said to be two nations, understanding as little of one another, having as little intercourse, as if they lived in different lands.

Dr. Channing distinctly recognized the fact that, under the present system of industry, the intellect of the laborer is "oppressed by drudging toil and urgent necessities of the animal nature." He spoke of the dreariness of factory life, in which a person's "employment is made up of a constant repetition of movements which require little thought," and said, with reference to the much boasted principle of the division of labor, that "by confining the mind to an unceasing round of petty operations it tends to break it into littleness; and hence we possess improved fabrics, but deteriorated men."

Let not the end of such considerations be called purely "material," over against which are to be set the spiritual aims of religion. This is a false antithesis. Material goods prepare the way to spiritual. Some freedom from material cares is necessary, that the powers of the spirit may unfold. "To me," says Channing, "the matter of complaint is, not that the laboring class want physical comforts,—though I wish these to be earned by fewer hours of labor,—but that they live only for their physical nature; . . . that labor is a badge of inferiority; that wealth forms a caste; that the multitudes are cut off from communications which would improve intellect, taste, and manners." It is the "degradation of mind and heart" too naturally going along with material degradation that most stirs his soul; and, while he pronounces "the means of comfort, of health, of neatness in food and apparel, and of occasional retirement and leisure" good in themselves, still more are they so, in his estimation, as means of the self-culture for which he so grandly pleads. The ends of life are spiritual. The ends of every man's life are spiritual,—not only of the artist or the poet or the philosopher, but of him or her who plies a loom, or digs in a mine, or toils in the kitchen or the street. So one be a man, one's ends are those of a man; and it is for the community to see that those ends are in some measure realized.

What makes the theme one of gravity, and not for curious discussion merely, the working classes have been rising to a consciousness of these higher ends of their being themselves. Dr. Channing had a profound and spiritual interpretation of some of the great movements of modern history. "I see . . . in the revolutionary spirit of our times," he said, "the promise of a freer and higher action of the human mind,—the pledge of a state of society more fit to perfect human beings. I regard the present state of the world in this moral light altogether." Again, "Men are now moved, not merely by physical wants and sufferings, but by ideas, by principles, by the conception of a better state of society, under which the rights of human nature will be recognized, and greater justice be done to the mind in all classes of the community." "The idea of human rights," he declares, "can never be stifled again." (pp. 212-14)

Channing saw in an ill-defined way the trouble which the social question might give us in the future. He says, "One thing seems plain, that there is no tendency in our present institutions and habits to bring relief. On the contrary, rich and poor seem to be more and more oppressed with incessant toil, exhausting forethought, anxious struggles, feverish competition." Further, he allows the necessity of revolutions in the past. He remarks of the process through which the Old World was passing in his time that "the strange illusion that a man, because he wears a garter or a riband, or was born to a title, belongs to another race, is fading away; and society must pass through a series of revolutions, silent or bloody, until a more natural order takes place of distinctions which grew originally out of force." Again: "Unfortunate as it may be, the people have begun to think, to ask reasons for what they do and suffer and believe, and to call the past to account. Old spells are broken, old reliances gone. . . . Allowing it to be best that society should rest on the depression of the multitude, the multitude will no longer be quiet when they are trodden under foot"; and so he adds: "Outward institutions cannot now secure us. Mightier powers than institutions have come into play among us,—the judgment, the opinions, the feelings of the many; and all hopes of stability which do not rest on the progress of the many must perish." Trouble seemed ahead to Channing in 1835. He wrote in that year, "The cry is, 'Property is insecure, law a rope of sand, and the mob sovereign.' The actual, present evil,—the evil of that worship of property which stifles all the nobler sentiments and makes men property,—this nobody sees: the appearances of approaching convulsions of property,—these shake the nerves of men, who are willing that our moral evils should be perpetuated to the end of time, provided their treasures be untouched. I have no fear of revolutions. We have conservative principles enough at work here. What exists troubles me more than what is to come." Now, when there is much more reason for apprehension than in Channing's time, we can imagine what he would say.

Yet Channing did not despair of a peaceful solution of the problem. There were, indeed, discouraging things. "How few," he laments, "understand that to raise the depressed by a wise culture to the dignity of men is the highest end of the social state!" The highest social art he declared to be yet in its infancy. "Great minds have nowhere solemnly, earnestly, undertaken to resolve the problem, how the multitudes of men may be elevated. The time is to come." He spoke at times with severity. For example: "The want of faith in improvement . . . is the darkest symptom. Much of this, I am sorry to say, is to be found here, but chiefly among what are called the 'better classes.' These are always selfishly timid, and never originate improvements worthy of the name." None the less is he hopeful. "How our present civilization," he wrote at the conclusion of the second lecture on the Elevation of the Laboring Classes, "is to be supplanted, I know not. I hope, however, that it is not doomed, like the old Roman civilization, to be quenched in blood. I trust that the works of ages are not to be laid low by violence, rapine, and the all-devouring sword. I trust that the existing social state contains in its bosom something better than it has yet unfolded. I trust that a brighter future is to come, not from the desolation, but from gradual, meliorating changes of the present." Again, "No man has seized the grand peculiarity of the present age who does not see in it the means and material of a vast and beneficent social change." He had, as every prophet must have, a faith in the possible. To him, "the signs of the times pointed to a great approaching modification of society. . . . The present selfish, dissocial system must give way." "A mighty revolution," started by Christianity, he says, "is not to stop until new ties shall have taken the place of those which have hitherto in the main connected the human race." "A better day is coming," he exclaims. "The kingdom of heaven is at hand. A purer Christianity, however slowly, is to take the place of that which bears but its name." (pp. 214-16)

I wish to speak, in closing, of one or two applications of his ideas which Dr. Channing made. He felt the need of an educational reform. He said: "The education of the mass of the people has consisted in giving them mechanical habits, in breaking them to current usages and modes of thinking, in teaching religion and morality as traditions. It is time that a rational culture should take the place of mechanical; that men should learn to act more from ideas and principles, and less from blind impulse and undiscerning imitation." He suggested "manual labor schools," which should combine the education of the body with that of the mind,—anticipating some of the most recent ideas on that subject. He declared one of his "dearest ideas" to be "the union of labor and culture." He said "the science of morals should form an important part of every child's instruction"; particularly should "the duty of the citizen to the State" be taught. Further, "the instructor should know intimately every child," which is, of course, in our public schools impossible, so long as one teacher is compelled to have anywhere from fifty to seventy-five or more pupils. Dr. Channing held that "there should be no economy in education, . . . no profession should receive so liberal remuneration"; and, in general, the ministry itself "must yield in importance to the office of training the young."

The evils of our industrial system Channing did not point out in detail, as a trained economist would have done; but, in general, he plainly saw them. He demanded that laborers should have a larger share in the fruits of their labor; and this the most thoughtful economists of the day declare can only be accomplished by a new system of industry, a cooperative, as opposed to the present competitive, system. In general, the idea of cooperation was attractive to Channing, if it was not to be the

Channing as a student.

central feature of the new social order which he believed would take the place of the one now existing.

Politics did not so much engage Dr. Channing, if, indeed, he did not have an inadequate view of the function of the State in social life. If the State is a mere police force, the religious teacher will have little to say of it. But, if it is society organized for this and other ends as well, the responsibility for the accomplishment of these higher ends must be fixed upon it, and an ideal and method of its action must be held up by the religious teacher. The responsibility, the duty of society with respect to its members, Channing did emphatically assert; and, if one hold the higher view of the State, the State will come to be one of the vehicles and instruments for the discharge of that responsibility and duty.

In relation to the churches, Dr. Channing gave most earnest suggestions. In a letter to a committee of the Unitarian Association, appointed to consider and report upon the Ministry at Large in Boston, he said, "It seems to me that we understand better than most Christians that it is the object of our religion to establish a fraternal union among all classes of society, to break down our present distinctions, and to direct all the energies of the cultivated and virtuous to the work of elevating the depressed classes to enlightened piety, to intellectual and moral dignity. To us, it seems to me, this great work peculiarly belongs." Moreover, the actual reformatory work, or at least the preliminary observation and study necessary to that work, was to be done by the Ministry at Large, supported by an association of Unitarian churches in Boston, known as the Benevolent Fraternity. A ministry was hardly ever started with more intelligent aims and purposes. The men ordained to its

work were not to be mere distributors of charity, nor to follow the ordinary lines of religious work among the poor, but to study in a scientific spirit the causes of poverty, and thus, in Dr. Channing's own language, "to give light to the legislator and philanthropist in the great work of its prevention and cure. To me," he continues, "this ministry is peculiarly interesting, regarded as the beginning of a series of operations for banishing from society its chief calamity and reproach, and for changing the face of the civilized and Christian world." From Dr. Tuckerman, the first member of this ministry, we have reports that are still valuable in the scientific sense. Yet Dr. Channing had to confess that the movement awakened little interest in the churches, and received little aid from them, though the greatest obstacle was the want of fit men for the work. (pp. 218-20)

Channing was ahead not only of his own time, but of ours. His theological opinions may have been transitional; but his views of man and society, his fundamental philosophy, his profound and earnest spirit, are for the future to appreciate duly. There are rich sources of mental and moral refreshment for any young man who will come into contact with him. Might his serious view of life and religion be more prevalent than it is! (p. 221)

W. M. Salter, "Channing as a Social Reformer," in Unitarian Review and Religious Magazine, *Vol. XXIX, No. 3, March, 1888, pp. 207-21.*

GEORGE EDWARD WOODBERRY (essay date 1891)

[Woodberry examines how three of Channing's character traits— "rectitude, sensibility, enthusiasm"—influenced his career and work. Woodberry's commentary was first published in 1891.]

Channing was the chief ornament of the American pulpit in his day. Like nearly all men illustrious in the religious life, he has won a kindlier and wider regard by his character than by his opinions, because the moods of devotion are simple and are universal in human nature, while opinion in theology is more variable and eccentric, and in some degree more accidental, than in any other branch of speculation. The deepest interest of his life lies not so much in the fruit of his genius as in the light of his spirit. Indeed, this acknowledgment is wrapped up in the indiscriminate eulogy by which his admirers have injured his fame, for they have presented him as a saint rather than as a thinker, as an example of ideal living rather than as a finder of truth. To put a man in the catalogue of saints is merely to write his epitaph; his life is the main thing, and Channing, although his biography records no great deeds in the world and no great crises of inner experience, is not alone in being far more interesting in his humanity than in his canonization. (pp. 289-90)

The most acute criticism ever passed upon Channing's character was by that unnamed critic who said, "He was kept from the highest goodness by his love of rectitude." The love of rectitude was his predominant trait; he was enslaved by it. He exacted more of himself, however, than of others. Right he must be, at all hazards, in motive, opinion, and action. It is melancholy to read page after page of his self-examination, so minute, intricate, and painful, so frequent and long continued. It almost awakens a doubt of the value of noble character to find it so unsure of itself, to see its possessor so absorbed in hunting his own shadow within the innermost retreats of thought and feeling. Channing seems to have preached more sermons to himself than to the world. His love of rectitude led him to this excessive conscientiousness, but it brought him great good in other directions. It gave him a respect for the opinions of other men as catholic as it was humble. He did not practice toleration toward them, for that expression implied to his mind a misplaced self-confidence; but he practiced charity, as toward men who felt equally with himself the binding force of the obligation to be right, and who had an equal chance of finding truth. His conviction of the universality of this obligation and his perception that it necessitates the independent exercise of individual powers encouraged in him a remarkable admiration for individuality, for the unhampered exercise of thought and unquestioned obedience to motive in which the richness of individual life consists.

His second great quality, as pervasive and controlling as his desire to be right, was sensibility. It was revealed in the sympathies and affections of private life, which are known to the world only by the report of friends; but it may be seen with equal clearness in the intensity of his delight in nature, and in the ardent feeling by which he realized ideal ends and gave them a living presence in his own life as objects of continuous effort. His sensitiveness to natural beauty was so keen that in moments of physical weakness it caused pain. "There are times," he wrote, "when I have been so feeble that a glance at the natural landscape, or even the sight of a beautiful flower, gave me a bodily pain from which I shrank." As life drew on to its end, the indestructible loveliness of nature became to him a source of joy and peace ever more prized. "The world grows younger with age!" he exclaimed more than once. In emotional susceptibility to ideas he resembled Shelley, and probably it was this likeness of feeling which led him to call Shelley, in ministerial language, but with extraordinary charity for that age, "a seraph gone astray." He retained through life the intellectual sympathies of his youth, and in his last days still had an inclination toward community of property as the solution of the social problem; like Wordsworth and Southey he recoiled from the excesses of the French, but he never gave up the tricolor for the white cockade. In his generation nearly all men were hopeful of the accomplishment of beneficent reforms; but Channing was filled with an enthusiasm of hope which was almost the fervor of conviction. He was without that practical enthusiasm which is aroused by the presence of great deeds immediately to be done; the objects for which he worked were far in the distance, scarcely discernible except from the mount of vision; but he was possessed by the enthusiasm which is kindled by the heat of thought and is wrapped in its own solitary flames, and he lived under the bright zenith of that mood of which Carlyle has shown the dark nadir and Teufelsdröch standing in its shadow gazing out over the sleeping city. These three principles—rectitude, sensibility, enthusiasm—were elemental in Channing's nature; and because they are moral, and not intellectual, he lived a spiritual rather than a mental life; he gained in depth rather than in breadth, and worked out his development by contemplation and prayer rather than by thought and act.

It appears strange, at first, that a man with these endowments should have been so conservative in opinion, and so little inclined to force upon the world what advanced opinions he did hold. A lover of truth unwilling to make proselytes, an enthusiast unwilling to act, seems an anomaly; but such was Channing's position. One cause of his aversion to pushing Unitarianism to its conclusion is found in the history of his own conversion and in the character of his attachment to the new faith; he was a revolter of the heart; he was liberalized by his feelings. "My inquiries," he said, "grew out of the shock given to my moral nature by the popular system of faith." He

was moved by sentiment in his rejection of Calvinism, and he was kept by sentiment from giving up the theory of the mysterious character and mission of Christ. The strength of his feelings operated to render him conservative, and the low estimate he apparently placed upon logical processes contributed to the same end. "It is a good plan," he wrote, "ever and anon to make a clean sweep of that to which we have arrived by logical thought, and take a new view; for the mind needs the baptism of wonder and hope to keep it vigorous and healthy for intuition." Either this distrust of the understanding working by logical processes, or else a native inaptitude for theological reasoning, prevented him from following out his principles to their conclusion. If he had framed a system, he would have held his views with greater certainty; as it was, he not only allowed the greatest liberty to individual opinion, but he distrusted himself. "You young thinkers," he said, "have the advantage of us in coming without superstitious preoccupation to the words of Scripture, and are more likely to get the obvious meaning. *We* shall walk in shadows to our graves." The strength of inbred sentiment could not be overpowered by such feeble intellectual conviction. He was a moral, not an intellectual, reformer; his work was not the destruction of a theology, but the spread of charity. He felt more than he reasoned, and hence his rationalism was bounded, not by the unknown, but by the mystical. He was satisfied with this, and does not seem to have wished to make a definite statement of his beliefs. The whole matter is summed up by Miss Peabody when she says, "The Christianity which Dr. Channing believed . . . was a spirit, not a form of thought." A spirit of devotion toward the divine, a spirit of love toward the human, Channing preached to the world and illustrated by his life; but a new form of thought which shows the intellectual advance that alone is fatal to conservatism,—this was no part of his gift to men.

In the antislavery cause his conservatism appears in a less pleasing light. Here he exhibited the scholar's reluctance to initiate reform, the scholar's perplexity before the practical barriers in the way of action. He was displeased by the rude voices about him, and frightened by the violence of determination which the reformers displayed. He looked to find the peace of the pulpit in the arena, and was bewildered by the alarms of the active strife. He did not choose his side until the last moment, and even then he delayed until he called down the just rebuke of May and the just defense that reformer made for his comrades: "The children of Abraham held their peace until at last the very stones have cried out, and you must expect them to cry out like the stones." Then, indeed, Channing showed that he was a Falkland on Cromwell's side, not acting without a doubt, but taking his place, nevertheless, openly and manfully beside the friend whom he had left alone too long. Yet he never lost, even in that stirring cause, the timidity of culture. He was of the generation of those cultivated men who earned for Boston the reputation for intellectual preëminence; but the political future of the country did not belong to him nor to his companions; it belonged to Garrison and Lincoln. Here it is that Father Taylor's keen criticism strikes home: "What a beautiful being Dr. Channing is! If he only had had any education!" Channing's education had been of the lamp, and not of the sword; it seemed to Father Taylor pitifully narrow and palsy-stricken beside his own experience of the world's misery. Channing's life affords one more illustration of the difficulty the cultivated man finds in understanding and forwarding reform in its beginning; but he deserves the credit of having rid himself of the prejudices and influences that marked the society in which he moved, to a greater degree, perhaps, than any other of his circle.

The value of Channing's work in religion and in reform will be differently rated by men, for his service was of a kind which is too apt to be forgotten. The intrinsic worth of his writings remains to be tested by time; but their historic worth, as a means of liberalizing the New England of his day, was great and memorable. He gave his right hand to Emerson and his left hand to Parker; and, although he could not accompany them on the way, he bade them Godspeed. It was, perhaps, mainly through his influence that they found the field prepared for them and the harvest ready, although he would not put his sickle in. It was largely due to him, also, that Boston became the philanthropic centre of the country. During his lifetime he won a remarkable respect and admiration. An exaggerated estimate of his eloquence, powers, and influence will continue to be held so long as any remain alive who heard his voice and remember its accents; in later times a truer judgment may be reached. Personally he was amiable, kindly, and courteous, notwithstanding the distance at which he seems to have kept all men. Dr. Walker said that conversation was always constrained in his study. In his nephew's narrative, it is said that the interview with him was "solemn as the visit to the shrine of an oracle" [see entry by William Henry Channing in the Additional Bibliography]. He himself told Miss Peabody after their friendship had lasted several years, that she had "the awe of the preacher" upon her. Finally, we read that no man ever freely laid his hand upon Channing's shoulder; and we wonder whether he ever remembered that St. John had "*handled* the Word made flesh." This self-seclusion, this isolation of sanctity, as it were, did not proceed from any value he set upon himself above his fellows; it was the natural failing of a man who lived much within himself, and who always meditated the loftiest of unworldly themes. He was a faithful and well-beloved friend; and if in this, as in other directions, he "failed of the highest goodness," there are few in the same walk of life who attain to equal sincerity, charity, and purity, or equal serviceableness to the world. (pp. 292-301)

> *George Edward Woodberry, "Three Men of Piety,"*
> *in his* Makers of Literature: Being Essays on Shelley,
> Landor, Browning, Byron, Arnold, Coleridge, Low-
> ell, Whittier, and Others, *The Macmillan Company,*
> *1900, pp. 271-301.*

JOHN GREENLEAF WHITTIER   (poem date 1892?)

[*A noted poet, abolitionist, journalist, and critic, Whittier is considered one of the most influential of nineteenth-century American figures. In the following poem, he pays tribute to Channing. As the date of the poem's composition is unknown, the year of Whittier's death has been used to date this entry.*]

Not vainly did old poets tell,
    Nor vainly did old genius paint
God's great and crowning miracle,
    The hero and the saint!

For even in a faithless day
    Can we our sainted ones discern;
And feel, while with them on the way,
    Our hearts within us burn.

And thus the common tongue and pen
    Which, world-wide, echo Channing's fame,
As one of Heaven's anointed men,
    Have sanctified his name.

In vain shall Rome her portals bar,
    And shut from him her saintly prize,
Whom, in the world's great calendar,
    All men shall canonize.

By Narragansett's sunny bay,
    Beneath his green embowering wood,
To me it seems but yesterday
    Since at his side I stood.

The slopes lay green with summer rains,
    The western wind blew fresh and free,
And glimmered down the orchard lanes
    The white surf of the sea.

With us was one, who, calm and true,
    Life's highest purpose understood,
And, like his blessed Master, knew
    The joy of doing good.

Unlearned, unknown to lettered fame,
    Yet on the lips of England's poor
And toiling millions dwelt his name,
    With blessings evermore.

Unknown to power or place, yet where
    The sun looks o'er the Carib sea,
It blended with the freeman's prayer
    And song of jubilee.

He told of England's sin and wrong,
    The ills her suffering children know,
The squalor of the city's throng,
    The green field's want and woe.

O'er Channing's face the tenderness
    Of sympathetic sorrow stole,
Like a still shadow, passionless,
    The sorrow of the soul.

But when the generous Briton told
    How hearts were answering to his own,
And Freedom's rising murmur rolled
    Up to the dull-eared throne,

I saw, methought, a glad surprise
    Thrill through that frail and pain-worn frame,
And, kindling in those deep, calm eyes,
    A still and earnest flame.

His few, brief words were such as move
    The human heart,—the Faith-sown seeds
Which ripen in the soil of love
    To high heroic deeds.

No bars of sect or clime were felt,
    The Babel strife of tongues had ceased,
And at one common altar knelt
    The Quaker and the priest.

And not in vain: with strength renewed,
    And zeal refreshed, and hope less dim,
For that brief meeting, each pursued
    The path allotted him.

How echoes yet each Western hill
    And vale with Channing's dying word!
How are the hearts of freemen still
    By that great warning stirred!

The stranger treads his native soil,
    And pleads, with zeal unfelt before,
The honest right of British toil,
    The claim of England's poor.

Before him time-wrought barriers fall,
    Old fears subside, old hatreds melt,
And, stretching o'er the sea's blue wall,
    The Saxon greets the Celt.

The yeoman on the Scottish lines,
    The Sheffield grinder, worn and grim,
The delver in the Cornwall mines,
    Look up with hope to him.

Swart smiters of the glowing steel,
    Dark feeders of the forge's flame,
Pale watchers at the loom and wheel,
    Repeat his honored name.

And thus the influence of that hour
    Of converse on Rhode Island's strand
Lives in the calm, resistless power
    Which moves our fatherland.

God blesses still the generous thought,
    And still the fitting word He speeds,
And Truth, at His requiring taught,
    He quickens into deeds.

Where is the victory of the grave?
    What dust upon the spirit lies?
God keeps the sacred life he gave,—
    The prophet never dies!

                                            (pp. 180-81)

John Greenleaf Whittier, "Personal Poems: Chan-
ning," in his The Complete Poetical Works of John
Greenleaf Whittier, *Houghton Mifflin Company, 1894,*
pp. 180-81.

DANIEL DULANY ADDISON   (essay date 1900)

[Addison outlines Channing's principal arguments in his literary
essays and in his writings on slavery and war.]

Channing's writings may be divided into three sections, political, religious, and philanthropic; while these divisions in a
measure are chronological they are not sharply defined. He
wrote on all three subjects in different proportions during the
whole of his productive life. In addition there are a few essays,
distinctly literary, notably, **"Remarks on the Character and**
Writings of John Milton," "Remarks on the Life and Char-
acter of Napoleon Bonaparte," "Remarks on the Character
and Writings of Fénelon," and **"Remarks on National**
Literature."

The literary essays were book-reviews in the *Christian Ex-*
aminer. In the one on Milton he shows his interest in poetry,
an interest that was fostered afterward by Wordsworth whom
he read more frequently than any other poet but Shakespeare.
To him poetry was the "divinest of all the arts," and of God's
gifts he considered "poetical genius the most transcendent."
Channing's thought of poetry was noble, for he believed its
greatness to lie in its interpretation of truth, and in its inspiration
toward the ideal. It had in it the germ of immortal life, for
through it, and by means of it, "the soul is perpetually stretching beyond what is present and visible, struggling against the
bounds of its earthly prison-house and seeking relief and joy

in imaginings of the unseen and ideal being." In answer to the
strange Puritanic objections to poetry, that it abounds in illusions and unrealities, his answer was that "the fictions of
genius are often vehicles of the sublimest verities." Though
Channing had this appreciation of poetry, and the poetic aspect
of nature stimulated him as when he roamed the seashore at
Newport, or crossed the ocean and travelled in Switzerland,
and visited Niagara, yet it was something above him which he
enjoyed without entering fully into its meaning. He could always have been an appreciative reader of poetry; never a producer of it. He had what in a vague way is called the poetic
temperament. He had none of the true poet's fire. His biographers speak of his poetic potentiality. It is a favorite way of
biographers when dealing with intense natures. There is no
evidence in his writings that he had the fancy of the born poet.
What appreciation he had was made. It never took vital hold
of him enough to lighten his orations and sermons with anything
above commonplace imagery. His interest was greatest in Milton's prose. This took hold of him because it expressed what
he believed in, the loftiness of virtue, the love of liberty and
contempt for "hereditary faith, servile reverence for established power." The theological Milton maintaining human
freedom and applying reason to Christian doctrines was a figure
of heroic proportions. The final joy of Channing when considering Milton was that he was an anti-Trinitarian, for it gave
him a new name with which to back up his own position:

> Our Trinitarian adversaries are perpetually
> ringing in our ears the names of the Fathers
> and Reformers. We take Milton, Locke, and
> Newton, and place them in our front, and want
> no others to oppose to the whole army of great
> names on the opposite side. Before these in-
> tellectual suns, the stars of self-named Ortho-
> doxy hide their diminished heads.

In the essays on Napoleon and Fénelon, Channing applies to
each the principle of his high conception of human character.
His judgment on both men is neither historical nor literary. It
is ethical. Napoleon, therefore, appears as the basest of men,
Fénelon as the noblest. In the general condemnation of the one
and the unrivalled praise of the other, there is a lack of analysis
and discrimination, the result of applying a general principle
to a particular case without an insight into motives and accomplishment. Napoleon's love of power and ambition, that led
him into cruelty and disregard of the rights of others, gave
Channing the chance to discuss the relations between the individual and government, Republicanism, Monarchy, Milita-
rism, and industrial prosperity. The main purpose of the essay
is set forth in the peroration:

> We have labored to show the superiority of
> moral power and influence to that sway, which
> has for ages been seized with bloody and eager
> hands. We have labored to hold up, to unmea-
> sured reprobation, him who would establish an
> Empire of brute force over rational beings. We
> have labored to hold forth, as the enemy of the
> race, the man who in any way would fetter the
> human mind, and subject other wills to his own.
> In a word, we have desired to awaken others
> and ourselves to a just reverence of our highest
> powers, and especially to that moral force, that
> energy of holy, virtuous purpose, without which
> we are slaves amidst the freest institutions.

One of Channing's best essays was the profound paper on **"National Literature."** With the growth of nationality and the development of a genuine Americanism, he foresaw the need and possibility of a native literature, to give expression to the thoughts that were seeking utterance, and to lead the people to ideals of patriotism and knowledge and religion. Coming just before the creative period in American literature, when it flowered forth in philosophy and poetry and fiction, the essay marks the transition from the meagreness of intellectual output, to the abundance that was so soon to come. Channing seemed, therefore, conscious of the impetus to letters that would result from the broader and freer use of the human intellect for which he contended. It was no accident that American literature grew up in the path of the movement for an unrestrained use of reason and investigation. His conception of the value of literature was not without an ethical content. He felt that it would produce nobler men. "The great distinction of a country," he wrote, "is that it produces superior men. Its natural advantages are not to be disdained; but they are of secondary importance. No matter what races of animals a country breeds, the great question is, Does it breed a noble race of men? No matter what its soil may be, the great question is, How far is it prolific of moral and intellectual power?" Again he asserted that "the true sovereigns of a country are those who determine its mind, its modes of thinking, tastes, its principles." He exposed two errors, which constantly found their way into print, one being that, since we had English literature to draw from, it was unnecessary for us to develop one of our own, and the other that what America needed was useful knowledge rather than what was termed "elegant literature." Of the first he said, we should not be confined to English literature, but the literatures of Continental Europe should also be ours, and this, instead of being a reason for making sterile the seed of self-expression, should rather fertilize it; and in dealing with the second, he enlarged the sphere of what was termed useful knowledge, by showing that any literature was useful which "calls forth the highest faculties, which expresses and communicates energy of thought, fruitfulness of invention, force of moral purpose, a thirst for the true, and a delight in the beautiful." He considered history revealing the causes and means of happiness, poetry touching the springs of the human soul, and philosophy treating of the foundations of knowledge and duty, to be as useful as mathematics. When the essayist dealt with the means of producing a native literature, he gave due credit to institutions of learning for which he pleaded, and the arousing of individual genius; but he argued for "a new action of the religious principle," asserting that our "chief hopes of an improved literature rest on our hopes of an improved religion." Channing saw that the idealism which inspired the noble deed, or the poem, was closely related to the idealism which inspired prayer and worship.

There was no interest of Channing's life of more vital concern to him than the history, the politics, and the statesmanship of America. The State to him was the guardian of the law and the upholder of moral principles. Whenever he saw partisan desire for gain propose and carry through schemes which he felt were wrong in motive and plan, he publicly stated his opinions in discourses, pamphlets, and books. Many of his most important publications, therefore, were of a political nature. They differ from many political writings of the clergy in that they are calm, reasoned out without excitement, full of a spirit of conciliation toward his opponents, but uncompromising when dealing with their principles. The War of 1812, the Seminole War, the questions arising out of the Hartford Convention, the annexation of Texas, and slavery in its many aspects, all deeply stirred him and brought forth characteristic utterances from his pen.

In Channing's attitude toward the War of 1812 he allied himself, as nearly as it was possible for him to become a member of a party, with the Federalists. He was in politics, as religion, an individualist. Though he feared the invasion of French influence as much as the most ardent Federalist, and regarded the war as unnecessary and unjust, he never for a moment considered the possibility of a secession from the Union because other states committed the nation to a policy of which he did not approve. In a review of the "Correspondence between John Quincy Adams and several citizens of Massachusetts, concerning the charge of a design to dissolve the union alleged to have existed in that state," he repelled the charge and took occasion to define what "the Union" should mean to a devoted citizen, not neglecting to point out the failures of the Federalists. Federalism, he said, "failed through despondence. Here was the rock on which Federalism split. Too many of its leading men wanted a just confidence in our free institutions, and in the moral ability of the people to uphold them." In Channing's idea of "the Union" there is none of the passionate regard of a later time. There is nothing sacred about it as there was to Webster. The highest function of the federal institutions which bound the states together was merely to avert evil, the highest political good, liberty, being negative; this he asserted over and over again. "We prize our bond of Union," he wrote, "as that which constitutes us one people; as preserving the different states from mutual jealousies and wars, and from separate alliances with foreign nations; as mitigating party spirit; in one word, as perpetuating our peace." The General Government should act as its name implied, not protecting certain branches of trade and neglecting others, and not making internal improvements a fountain of discord and bitterness through a palpable favoritism.

There was no subject upon which Channing wrote more vigorously than slavery. He never became an abolitionist, partly because of his calmness of view, and partly because he disliked to join with others in associations, believing firmly as he did in the importance of individual action. He rendered, however, important service in creating public sentiment; and his books were read where others were destroyed. The most noted of his anti-slavery writings were the treatise simply called *Slavery*, his letter to James G. Birney on *The Abolitionists*, the letter to Henry Clay *On the Annexation of Texas, Remarks on the Slavery Question, Emancipation*, and **"The Duty of the Free States."** Through all these different books and letters and pamphlets the same spirit is to be seen, the eagerness to point out to the slave owner and the Northern politician and capitalist, the moral facts that were involved, and how contrary the institution was to Christian principles. In the treatise *Slavery*, Channing really said almost all that was in his mind. The other writings are simply repetitions and elaborations of these first ideas. The book is divided into eight chapters, dealing with such questions as property rights, the evils of slavery, Scripture in relation to the institution, the means of removing slavery, and the duties of the hour. As to the contention that the slaves are property or as the South Carolina laws said, "chattels personal in the hands of their masters, and possessions to all intents and purposes whatsoever," Channing answered by taking the highest ground: "He cannot be property in the sight of God and justice because he is a rational, moral, immortal being." When told that governments decide what is property, he exclaimed, "What! is human legislation the measure of right? Are God's laws to be repealed by man's? Can governments do no wrong?" The evils of slavery were very fully set forth as destructive of intellectual life in the slave, the ignorance of the slave being necessary to the security of the master. The domestic influences of the institution were of the worst type: "The slave's home does not merit the name. To him it is no sanctuary. It is open to violation, insult, outrage. His children belong to another, are provided for by another, are disposed of by another.... His wife, son, and daughter may be lashed before his eyes, and not a finger must be lifted in their defence." The corresponding evil influences on the master's character and his conception of the purity of the home were unsparingly dealt with, as well as the influence on politics and on the nation. The analysis of Channing was keen. He allowed no argument to escape him, and when he approached the assertion that Scripture upheld slavery he could not keep his intensity in check. "Why may not Scripture be used," he said, "to stock our houses with wives as well as with slaves?" The true spirit of Christianity was shown to be the fulfilment of the law and the introduction of a life of freedom and brotherhood.

On the subject of the removal of slavery, Channing seems never to have got beyond the thought that such removal must be brought about by the slave-holding states themselves. Colonization, as well as gradual emancipation was suggested, but forcible interference by the North never became a possibility to him. "What is needed," he thought, "is that the slave-holding states should resolve conscientiously and in good faith to remove this greatest of moral evils and wrongs." Of the abolitionists Channing was outspoken; while he felt they were sincere he could not help deprecating their methods, and the perfectly futile cry of "Immediate Emancipation." The agitation of the abolitionists had done great harm in strengthening the sympathies of the free states with slavery and in alienating the South; "It made converts of a few individuals, but alienated multitudes. Its influence at the South has been wholly evil. It has stirred up bitter passions and a fierce fanaticism, which has shut every ear and every heart against its arguments and persuasions." In the letter to Birney, Channing deplores the physical violence used against the abolitionists, because he believed they should have the right of free speech, and he spares no words of condemnation against those who selfishly misrepresent the aims of those seeking to free the slaves. The influence of the judicious pleading of such men as Channing did more to educate the people of America in the moral way of dealing with the question than the boisterous opposition of hot-headed men who were fond of denunciation.

As an important state paper reflecting the sentiment of many, the letter to Henry Clay on *The Annexation of Texas to the United States* ranks high. It is written with dignity and force; and attracted general attention at the time of its publication in 1837. The motive for writing the letter is fully expressed in the words:

> Should Texas be annexed to our country, I feel that I could not forgive myself, if, with my deep, solemn impressions, I should do nothing to avert the evil.... The annexation of Texas, under existing circumstances, would be more than rashness; it would be madness.

The arguments against annexing Texas are put forth with rare skill. The criminality of the revolt which severed the country from Mexico, the unprincipled spirit of land speculation with the manufacture of land titles, the resolution to throw Texas open to slaveholders, are all treated from the highest ethical standpoint. Though the contention that "Texas is the first step

to Mexico" was not justified, yet the Mexican War showed the prophetical wisdom of the preacher in fearing bloodshed. He could not imagine that Mexico would be a passive prey or surrender without a struggle. The strongest argument found against the measure was that it would perpetuate slavery, and this would have an important bearing on the existence of the National Union. The South by an extension of territory would acquire disproportionate power and this would give new violence to the agitation of the slavery question.

> Let slavery be systematically proposed as the policy of these states, let it bind them together in efforts to establish political power, and a new feeling will burst forth through the whole North. It will be a concentration of moral, religious, political, and patriotic feelings. The fire, now smothered, will blaze out.

Channing in later life foresaw the possibility of the division of the Union, and should it be brought about he could not keep from himself the disaster that would ensue.

Though Channing recognized the dangers that were ahead he never counselled force. In the **"Duty of the Free States"** he expressed very fully his opinion on this subject:

> What is the duty of the North in regard to slavery? On this subject I will only say, I recommend no crusade against slavery, no use of physical or legislative power for its destruction, no irruption into the South to tamper with the slave, or to repeal or resist the laws. Our duties on this subject are plain. First, we must free ourselves, as I have said, from all constitutional or legal obligations to uphold slavery. In the next place we must give free and strong expression to our reprobation of slavery. The North has but one weapon, moral force, the utterance of moral judgment, moral feeling, and religious conviction.

Channing, by temperament, education, and contact with the vigorous minds of his time, was especially fitted for the position he took as a social reformer. Keenly alive to the trend of society in the direction of an enlarged democracy he felt the power that resided in the people when they were trained in the best arts of living and freed from the false restraints that had been put upon them by the ruling classes. He has a place therefore among those who, in the early portion of the nineteenth century, worked in the cause of the laboring man, and made possible in America the beneficial legislation, the numerous protections to life and limb, the establishment of libraries for the people, and the general excellence of the public schools.... Child-labor, American penal institutions, the education of the people, and the uplifting of the masses of the poor were continually in his mind; and by the use of his pen and his voice he worked so strenuously that he has the right to stand among those men of the century who have heard the cry of the multitudes;—prophetic enough to see that the advancement of human society can only come through the progress of the many as they cast aside the burdens and injustices of earlier times.

One of the first evils of modern society he attacked was war. He preached on many occasions in favor of arbitration and against the iniquity of settling disputes by the sword. His discourse on **"War,"** preached in 1816, prepared the way for the formation of the Peace Society of Massachusetts, the parent of similar societies in America. Dr. Channing prepared one of the first memorials to Congress on the subject of American coöperation with European governments in the "acknowledgment of those principles of peace and charity on which the prosperity of states and the happiness of families and individuals are alike suspended." The Seminole War was another opportunity for him to express his views on the cruelty and needlessness of war. In Channing's most noted address on the evils of war, he shows himself to be a careful observer of men as well as a student of history. After dealing with the obvious miseries caused by armed conflict such as disease, death, poverty, and the undermining of moral standards, he lays his finger on the causes that produce war which he ranks "among the most dreadful calamities which fall on a guilty world. . . . It tends to multiply and perpetuate itself without end. It feeds and grows on the blood which it sheds. The most luxuriant laurels grow from a root nourished with blood." The causes of war are classed as the love of excitement, of emotion, and of strong interest, the passion for superiority and for power, the admiration of the brilliant qualities displayed on the battlefield—"war being as we first see it decked with gay and splendid trappings"—and the early training of the people in the sentiments of barbarous ages. The line is drawn skilfully between moral courage and physical bravery, the latter being found in animals and among pirates and robbers "whose fearlessness is generally proportioned to the insensibility of their consciences." To the arguments in favor of war, that it kindles patriotism and sweeps off the idle and vicious members of the community, the answer is made, that the patriotism cherished by war is spurious, a vice not a virtue, for the genuine patriot knows that the welfare of his own country is conditioned upon the general progress of society, and that "war commonly generates as many profligates as it destroys." "There is another method," he urged, "not quite so summary as war, of ridding a country of unprofitable and injurious citizens, but vastly more effectual. . . . I refer to the exertions, which Christians have commenced, for the reformation and improvement of the ignorant and poor, and especially for the instruction and moral culture of indigent children." (pp. 206-26)

Dr. Channing through his long and busy career as the minister of the Federal Street Society in Boston, from 1803 until his death in 1842, was an intellectual and moral leader. In the midst of the Unitarian controversy he was foremost in contending for freedom of thought, and in the crises of American life, he always upheld what he considered to be the truth, urging a fearless application of Christian ethics to contemporary conditions. He was, in everything he engaged in, a pronounced individualist, not feeling responsibility to any association or organization, but giving utterance to his own ideas, believing firmly in their righteousness. Whether he is read much to-day matters not, he gave an impulse to the life about him, an impetus to fearless thought and to the freedom of the human soul. He was one of the spiritual forces of his time, and his watchwords are everywhere incorporated into life. (pp. 227-28)

Daniel Dulany Addison, "William Ellery Channing," in his The Clergy in American Life and Letters, *The Macmillan Company, 1900, pp. 191-228.*

VERNON LOUIS PARRINGTON   (essay date 1927)

[*Parrington, an American historian, critic, and educator, was awarded a Pulitzer Prize for the first two volumes of his influential* Main Currents in American Thought; *the third volume remained unfinished at the time of his death. In this series Parrington composed, according to Michael O'Brien, "not a study of Amer-*

ican literature so much as of American political thought refracted through literature." In the following excerpt from Main Currents, *Parrington traces the development of Channing's theology and social philosophy, arguing that both were ultimately based upon his concept of "man's excellence." Parrington also studies the two "master passions" of Channing's life—"respect for human nature and reverence for human liberty"—in relation to Federalism, Jeffersonianism, and French romantic philosophy.*]

Channing's heritage was drawn from the deepest wells of New England idealism; and filtered through his finely ethical mind it emerged pure and limpid, the living waters of the new faith. His noble preëminence was due to the simple spirituality of his nature. Intellectually, he was neither great nor original. In scholarship he was distinctly inferior to academic theologians like Andrews Norton and to omnivorous students like Theodore Parker. Almost wholly introspective he was influenced slowly by world-currents of thought, and such alien ideas as found lodgment in his mind took on a native form and color from his own convictions. Nevertheless though his meditations revolved about the pole-star of his own experience, his theology cautiously took shape under the pressure of two ideas that came to him from the latter years of the eighteenth century—the ideas of God's beneficence and of man's excellence. Once lodged in his mind, those ideas led to quite revolutionary consequences, not only in their disintegrating effect upon the Calvinistic dogmas in which he had been reared, but in the generous romanticism which they bequeathed to Unitarian theology. His intellectual development was late and halting, yet that he liberated himself at all was remarkable considering the world that bred him—Newport, frequented by wealthy planters and enriched by the slave trade, Cambridge and Boston then in the stagnancy of Federalist complacency. Of the same generation with Robert Treat Paine and Josiah Quincy, only a few years older than Rufus Choate and Edward Everett, as a boy sitting under the preaching of Samuel Hopkins—the rugged expounder of the Hopkinsian doctrine of willing to be damned for the glory of God, a doctrine so repugnant to the major tenets of Channing's theology—he belonged by temperament and training to the parochial world that accounted Fisher Ames a great orator, and looked with suspicion on the new century that was crowding in on its comfortable preserves.

From the deep New England ruts Channing pulled himself with incredible difficulty. His frequent reactions almost kept pace with his progress. For years he oscillated between freedom and dogma, now dominated by the Hopkinsian influence and thrown back upon a morbid Calvinism by ill health; then resolutely casting off the evil spell; until the year 1815, when the conservative wing declaring war upon the liberals, he was drawn into the controversy and took upon himself the burden of defending the liberal cause. He was then thirty-five, but it was not till four years later, in the celebrated Baltimore sermon at the ordination of Jared Sparks ["**Unitarian Christianity: Discourse at the Ordination of the Rev. Jared Sparks**"], that he offered a definitive statement of the new theology. The sermon brought him wide fame and fastened upon him the leadership of the Unitarian movement. Comment upon the new doctrines was widespread, and the circulation of the sermon in pamphlet form, according to a late biographer, "was not exceeded by any American publication until in 1830 Webster made his memorable reply to Hayne." The creative influence of that sermon in clarifying certain doctrines of Unitarianism and integrating the society should not blind us to the fact that it embodies only a portion of Channing's theology—the idea of God's beneficence. It is a reasoned attack upon Trinitarian Calvinism, upon those dogmas which reveal—in Channing's expressive phrase—

"how mournfully the human mind may misrepresent the Deity''; but it takes no account of the idea which later he came to place first—the idea of man's excellence.

Finer than the Baltimore sermon in its restrained eloquence—an eloquence that burns with an intensity rare in Channing—and in its dramatic exposition of the doctrine of the atonement, is the sermon entitled **"Unitarian Christianity most Favorable to Piety,"** delivered in 1826 at the dedication of the second Unitarian church in New York City. In this sermon Channing made use of a daring comparison which startled his friends and gave mortal offense to orthodox Calvinists. It is probably the most dramatic passage to be found in his writings, and it so well exemplifies the temper of the controversy that it deserves quotation. After discussing the Edwardean philosophy of infinite punishment and the nature of atonement, he proceeded:

> Let me, then, set it before you, in new terms, and by a new illustration; and if in so doing, I may wound the feelings of some who hear me, I beg them to believe, that I do it with pain, and from no impulse but a desire to serve the cause of truth.—Suppose, then, that a teacher should come among you, and should tell you, that the Creator, in order to pardon his own children, had erected a gallows in the centre of the universe, and had publicly executed upon it, in room of the offenders, an Infinite Being, the partaker of his own Supreme Divinity; suppose him to declare, that this execution was appointed, as a most conspicuous and terrible manifestation of God's justice, and of the infinite woe denounced by his law; and suppose him to add, that all beings in heaven and earth are required to fix their eyes on this fearful sight, as the most powerful enforcement of obedience and virtue. Would you not tell him, that he calumniated his Maker? Would you not say to him, that this central gallows threw gloom over the universe; that the spirit of a government, whose very acts of pardon were written in such blood, was terror, not paternal love; and that the obedience which needed to be upheld by this horrid spectacle, was nothing worth? Would you not say to him, that even you, in this infancy and imperfection of your being, were capable of being wrought upon by nobler motives, and of hating sin through more generous views; and that much more the angels, those pure flames of love, need not the gallows and an executed God to confirm their loyalty? You would all so feel, at such teaching as I have supposed; and yet how does this differ from the popular doctrine of atonement?

In seeking an explanation of Channing's break with New England orthodoxy—a breach that widened greatly with years, coming to embrace politics and economics as well as theology, alienating many of its own congregation and bringing acute grief to him—one can scarcely over-emphasize the influence of his Virginia experience. During the twenty-one months that he spent on the southern plantation, painfully isolated and lonely, he grappled seriously with a body of thought from which the environment of his youth had pretty much shut him away. Virginia in 1798 was ardently Jeffersonian, and French romantic philosophy was a commonplace in Virginia libraries.

While Channing never went over wholly to Jeffersonianism, but retained certain Federalist prejudices after the old foundations had turned to quicksand under his feet, he there began a long process of speculative brooding that was to carry him far from the political principles of Boston. French revolutionary thought provided his chief intellectual stimulus during the critical Virginia period. Rousseau he read with profound interest, together with Godwin's *Political Justice* and Mary Wollstonecraft's *Rights of Woman*. The Physiocratic economics that sanctioned the agrarian bias of Jeffersonian democracy seems to have made no appeal to a mind primarily ethical in outlook, yet he went so far as to dabble in communistic theory, and for a time contemplated joining a communistic community. From France, moreover, he derived the idea of the excellence of human nature and the perfectibility of man, ideas which became the mainspring of his later thinking, creative determining both his theology and his social philosophy, and transforming his whole intellectual world.

In July, 1800, eight months before it took formal possession of the White House, "French infidel philosophy" made its appearance in New England in the person of a slight, health-broken youth, who returned to his quiet theological studies, quite unmindful of the gunpowder he had brought back in his intellectual luggage. It was long before a spark was to strike home, but the powder was there and would do its work eventually. In passing through Channing's mind, the contributions of French romanticism merged with the native heritage of New England idealism, and supplemented by contributions from English Arian thought, slowly assumed definite form that came to issue in three dominating ideas, namely: God is love, man is potentially noble, religion is an excellent life. Enveloping these master ideas, in which they were carried as in a medium, was a pervasive ethical spirit that colored all his thinking and eventually took form in that striking phrase into which all of Channing is compressed, "the adoration of goodness—this is religion." This constituted his reply to the Edwardean theology that debased man to the sole end of exalting a monstrous God—the doctrine of "sweetness and light" was set over against the dogmas of reprobation and election.

With his profound sense of justice, Channing could not follow "the adoration of goodness" into an aloof and mystical pietism. The temptation was strong, for his finely aristocratic and hesitant nature prompted him to stand apart from all turmoil and partisan struggle. He disliked controversy and distrusted all dogmatists. The world of economics and politics was exceedingly distasteful to him; he would gladly stop his ears against the clamor of organized groups and strident parties. The Abolitionists, with whose purpose he deeply sympathized, seemed to him intolerant and their tactics vulgar. There is a measure of justice in Garrison's comment after Channing's death: "His nerves were delicately strung. The sound of a ram's horn was painfully distressing to him. He was firmly persuaded that nothing but a silver trumpet was needed to cause the walls of Jericho to fall; and he did his best upon his own." And yet, however unwillingly, he was drawn inevitably into an agitation that touched both his religion and his humanity; and between 1835 and 1837 he issued three notable contributions to the controversy: *Slavery*, a reply to the Southern apologists; *The Abolitionists*, an open letter to James Birney, whose Abolition press had been wrecked by an Ohio mob; and a noble appeal to Henry Clay against the annexation of Texas [*On the Annexation of Texas*]. In the latter year he spoke in Faneuil Hall at a turbulent meeting called to protest against the murder of

Lovejoy, the meeting at which Wendell Phillips made his dramatic first appearance on the Abolition platform.

The point of view from which Channing approached the problem of slavery is clearly set forth in his "Introductory Remarks," written in 1841 for a collected edition of his works, and which constitutes his *apologia pro vita sua.* In this extraordinarily lucid and just statement he reduces the master passions of his life to two—respect for human nature, and reverence for human liberty—passions which were inseparable in all his thinking. Of the first he says, "The following writings will be found to be distinguished by nothing more than by the high estimate which they express of human nature. A respect for the human soul breathes through them." This attitude he elaborates at length:

> An enlightened, disinterested human being, morally strong, and exerting a wide influence by the power of virtue, is the clearest reflection of the divine splendour on earth. . . . The glory of the Maker lies in his work. . . . Those men glorify God most, who look with keen eye and loving heart on his works, who catch in all some glimpses of beauty and power, who have a spiritual sense for good in its dimmest manifestations, and who can so interpret the world, that it becomes a bright witness to the Divinity.
>
> I have also felt and continually insisted, that a new reverence for man was essential to the cause of social reform. . . . There can be no spirit of brotherhood, no true peace, any farther than men come to understand their affinity with and relation to God and the infinite purpose for which he gave them life.

(pp. 321-26)

Out of this reverence for human nature flowed his "reverence for Liberty, for human rights; a sentiment which has grown with my growth, which is striking deeper root in my age, which seems to me a chief element of true love for mankind, and which alone fits a man for intercourse with his fellow-creatures."

> It is because I have learned the essential equality of men before the common Father, that I cannot endure to see one man establishing his arbitrary will over another by fraud, or force, or wealth, or rank, or superstitious claims. It is because the human being has moral powers, because he carries a law in his own breast and was made to govern himself, that I cannot endure to see him taken out of his own hands and fashioned into a tool by another's avarice or pride. It is because I see in him a great nature, the divine image, and vast capacities, that I demand for him means of self-development, spheres for free action—that I call society not to fetter, but to aid his growth.

In such humanitarian idealism did French romantic philosophy come to flower in the generous mind of this son of New England. He was no longer narrowly Unitarian; he had become a social revolutionary with Utopian dreams. The minister's wealthy parishioners might worship the common Father complacently under the shadow of slavery, black or white, but the minister could not; he had caught a glimpse of the Promised Land and would lead his flock towards it. Unhappily, the vast abyss of Negro slavery lay between, and Channing considered it with growing concern. In his examination of the problem he was broadly philosophical rather than narrowly partisan. He rested his case against slavery on an ethical adaptation of the natural-rights theory. Since man is both rational and moral, he argued, he cannot be deprived by law or custom of the essential prerogatives of personality. The inalienable rights of man are in essence no other than the rights of personality—the right to exercise his reason, to seek light of his conscience, to enjoy the fruits of his labor, to enter into domestic relations, in short to be free to live as a man in a state of civilization. To treat man as property is the grossest denial and violation of that which by its nature is inviolable and inalienable. Channing pushed his argument further and asserted that the institution of slavery was not only irrational and immoral, but a fundamental denial of democracy. It must end in perverting the political state to its own evil. The southern conception of a Greek democracy resting on black slavery he looked upon as the final prostitution of the democratic ideal. "Those who tell us that slavery is a necessary condition of a republic, do not justify the former, but pronounce a sentence of reprobation on the latter." For those text-mongerers who professed to justify slavery by Scripture, he had only scorn. By such methods polygamy might as readily be justified.

Inquiry into the nature and scope of individual rights brought Channing face to face with the problem of the political state and the duties of citizenship. Here his break with Boston Federalism was final and complete. He judged men and institutions by ethical standards; State Street judged them by economic standards. By his own path he went back to the eighteenth century, and interpreting the functions and province of government in the light of Godwin's *Political Justice,* he arrived at the conception of a constantly diminishing political state that should eventually disappear. The dogma of political sovereignty he denied: "The state is equally restrained with individuals by the Moral Law" (*Slavery*). The expediency of some restraint upon individual action he accepted, but with the proviso that it be exercised only to the end of the common wellbeing. "The authority of the state to impose laws on its members I cheerfully allow; but this has limits, which are found to be more and more narrow in proportion to the progress of moral science" (*Ibid.*). "That government is most perfect, in which Policy is most entirely subjected to Justice, or in which the supreme and constant aim is to secure the rights of every human being" (*Ibid.*). To such a government loyalty will be given gladly; but in the event that expediency should prevail over justice, and the state should prostitute its power by exploiting one class for the benefit of another, then must loyalty be transferred from the state to the higher law. "Justice is a greater good than property, not greater in degree, but in kind" (*Ibid.*). "The good of the individual is more important than the outward prosperity of the State" (*Ibid.*). In such doctrines Channing paid his respects to the political philosophy of Webster.

The final outcome of his political thinking was a close approximation to the position of Jefferson. His distrust of power grew more apprehensive as he reflected on the common abuse of power, and the cheap and paltry appeals by which the unthinking are swayed. Before the organized power of the mass, the individual is helpless. In the "Introductory Remarks" he went further than he had done in earlier writings in analysis of the state, and such a passage as this might have been penned by John Taylor of Caroline County. It is pure Jeffersonianism.

> So fearful is the principle of which I have spoken, that I have thought it right to recommend

restrictions on power and a simplicity in government beyond what most approve. Power, I apprehend, should not be suffered to run into great masses. No more of it should be confided to rulers than is absolutely necessary to repress crime and preserve public order. A purer age may warrant larger trusts; but the less of government now the better, if society be kept in peace.There should exist, if possible, no office to madden ambition. . . . One of the tremendous evils of the world, is the monstrous accumulation of power in a few hands. . . . Is any man pure enough to be trusted with it? Ought such a prize as this to be held out to ambition? Can we wonder at the shameless profligacy, intrigue, and the base sacrifices of public interests by which it is sought, and, when gained, held fast? Undoubtedly, great social changes are required to heal this evil, to diminish this accumulation of power. National spirit, which is virtual hostility to all countries but our own, must yield to a growing humanity, to a new knowledge of the spirit of Christ. Another important step is, a better comprehension by communities that government is at best a rude machinery, which can accomplish but very limited good, and which, when strained to accomplish what individuals should do for themselves, is sure to be perverted by selfishness to narrow purposes, or to defeat through ignorance its own ends. Man is too ignorant to govern much, to form vast plans for states and empires. Human policy has almost always been in conflict with the great laws of social well-being, and the less we rely on it the better. The less of power given to man over man the better.

Channing had evidently read his *Political Justice* to good effect, for the spirit of eighteenth-century liberalism had passed into his thought and given shape to his political philosophy. In his hatred of war, his pacifism, his humanitarian concern, his social-mindedness, his repudiation of all coercive centralizing power, he proved himself a child of Godwin. He would have no tyranny, whether by the organized state or by the unorganized mass. He extended to all men the right of free thought and free speech. In no other cause did he speak more vehemently than in defense of this democratic right. When the Abolitionists were mobbed and their presses broken he rejoiced in their refusal to be silenced. "From my heart I thank them," he wrote. "I am myself their debtor. I am not sure, that I should this moment write in safety, had they shrunk from the conflict, had they shut their lips, imposed silence on their presses, and hid themselves before their ferocious assailants. . . . I thank the Abolitionists, that in this evil day, they were true to the rights which the multitude were ready to betray." (pp. 326-29)

High-minded and generous was this child of Puritan idealism who had gone to school to French infidel philosophy—never untrue to the principle of free inquiry which in demanding for himself he willingly granted others. He calmly accepted the fact of disintegration which is implicit in all liberalism—the denial of traditional authority and ancient custom—partly because he believed the old ways were bad, but in part also because he held strongly to his faith in human nature. Despite failure and discouragement he clung to his cardinal belief—

"My one sublime idea, which has given me unity of mind, the greatness, the divinity of the soul." He broke the more willingly with an ungenerous past because he envisaged a nobler future. An intuitive individualist, he was a forerunner of transcendental individualism, and he found himself in hearty accord with Emerson's doctrines in the Divinity School address. With the later rationalistic phase of Unitarianism which began with Theodore Parker's memorable South Boston sermon *On the Transient and Permanent in Christianity,* in May, 1841, he found himself only partly in intellectual sympathy. He remained a supernaturalist after the younger generation had rejected supernaturalism; but his sturdy adherence to the principle of liberalism would not suffer him to join in the Unitarian hue and cry raised against the young radical. Unitarianism turned orthodox, and bent on erecting new dogmas, seemed to him treasonable to every liberal hope. "As to Mr. Parker," he wrote, "I wish him to preach what he thoroughly believes and feels. I trust the account you received of attempts to *put him down* was in the main a fiction. Let the full heart pour itself forth!" Sixteen months after he penned those words Channing was dead, but the spirit of his life was embodied in the great ferment that was rising about him when he died. "Let the full heart pour itself forth"—to many sober Bostonians it seemed that New England had taken that injunction quite too literally and was pouring forth disturbant and gusty heresies, but Channing would scarcely have disapproved. (p. 330)

> *Vernon Louis Parrington, "The Rise of Liberalism: Liberalism and Calvinism," in his* Main Currents in American Thought, an Interpretation of American Literature from the Beginnings to 1920: The Romantic Revolution in America, 1800-1860, Vol. 2, *Harcourt Brace Jovanovich, 1927, pp. 313-30.*

ROBERT E. SPILLER (essay date 1930)

[Spiller contends that literary historians have underestimated the significance of Channing's writings.]

The revision of a literary reputation is a dangerous, and often futile, enterprise. Especially is this true when the name in question has been almost entirely erased from literary history. "We meet to-day to celebrate a great preacher," said Charles W. Eliot in introducing his lecture on the elder Channing [see Additional Bibliography]. There is no record of a dissenting voice. No one in that audience remembered that the great preacher had once been greeted as "the finest writer of our age" [see excerpt from *Fraser's Magazine* dated 1838], and had been thought worthy of serious, though not altogether friendly, consideration from the caustic pens of Hazlitt and Brougham [see excerpts dated 1829 and 1839]. Channing as an author has been dismissed and forgotten.

As long as the element of fashion influences literary judgments it will never be safe to leave such ominous silences undisturbed. No such widespread opinions are ever wholly in error. The eighteenth century greeted the romantic revival with hostility and scorn, and the romantic writers fought bitterly and successfully against these attacks. The present age finds much real justice in both positions. Similarly, American literary judgments deferred with too great a solicitude to the English critics of the early nineteenth century, and the wholesome self-assertions of Fenimore Cooper, Emerson and others which resulted, established a degree of mental independence which made a national literature possible. It is time for an objective view of this controversy, also.

Channing was caught in both these conflicts and the subsequent estimate of him has, as a result, been colored. Philosophically akin to Wordsworth, Coleridge, and Carlyle, he was also accepted by the reviewers as one of themselves. Recognized by English critics as a writer of note, he was also among the first to declare the need for American intellectual independence.

During the years from 1823 to 1849, when his reputation in England was being formed and developed, he occupied a position only below Irving and Cooper in the English estimate of American literary excellences. This opinion aroused criticism in America, not because Channing was included, but because Bryant, Halleck, and many others were not. There is no doubt that Channing's historical position in American literary history, with special reference to its relations with English influences, is usually underestimated to-day.

But the explanation that his foreign reputation was merely an aspect of America's early mental servility, is inadequate. Even a casual examination of the six volumes of his collected works shows how superficial and unsound such a judgment would be. Channing not only was among the first American writers to win British critical consideration; he anticipated, by almost a generation in his thought and by seven years in his public pronouncement, the independence of mind which was proclaimed by Emerson in "The American Scholar." Channing's essay ["**Remarks on National Literature**"] is inferior in literary quality to the more famous address on the same topic, but it contains the outlines of the same philosophical position and a statement of an identical demand for American mental self-reliance which was attained by the Emersonian methods of study and meditation. There is reason now to regard Emerson's essay as a declaration of New England's rather than America's self-consciousness. The frontier, agrarian, and industrial movements have given to American literature ideals and forms which are not included within the metaphysical limits of that document. But in so far as Emerson's work represents a mile-stone in the progress of our national thought, Channing's assumes, by priority, an importance great enough to compensate for its somewhat lower philosophical and literary value.

Finally, if we pass beyond the table of contents and examine the body of Channing's essays, lectures, and sermons, we find at least a larger proportion of non-theological work than the customary literary estimate of the man would lead us to anticipate. This work shows that Channing not only mastered the critical essay, which was recognized in his day as one of the most worthy means of literary expression, but that his thought, in its range as well as its form, spread far beyond the limits of controversial Unitarian dogma and the rhetorical restrictions of the pulpit. His tendency to moralize, which is usually pointed to as a restriction upon his literary worth, was in reality his means of escape from the more rigid mental limitations of his predecessors in New England prose. Deriving from his forefathers, from the idealists of Germany, and the rationalists of France, his mind followed the path which he himself so urgently recommended, and he applied his principles to the state and being of man in theory and fact, as well as to the idea of God. He thus linked Coleridge and Wordsworth with Carlyle and Ruskin. Emerson substituted a deistic conception of nature for Channing's Unitarian God, following the path of Wordsworth, whereas Channing's thought was more akin to that of Coleridge; Emerson approached a democratic ideal of human relationships in his *Representative Men,* whereas Channing, in his ["**Remarks on the Character and Writings of John Milton**" and "**Remarks on the Life and Character of Napoleon**"], stated

and illustrated the theory of heroism which Carlyle later elaborated; finally, the conception of the dignity of manual labor, which, in the lectures and experiments of Carlyle, Ruskin, and William Morris, proclaimed the transition to a new social order, finds a full and adequate expression in the writings of this New England clergyman, of one generation, at least, earlier than any of these men.

The fact that Channing's work was recognized as worthy of considered thought by both English and American critics in his own day is, therefore, not so unaccountable as it might at first seem. The comparison of his present-day literary position with that accorded to him by his British contemporaries, and even a casual reexamination of those of his essays and sermons which are least dogmatic in aim and method, should be worth the undertaking, even though a revision of judgment as to his absolute importance must await further and more exhaustive study. (pp. 55-9)

> *Robert E. Spiller, "A Case for W. E. Channing,"
> in* The New England Quarterly, *Vol. III, January,
> 1930, pp. 55-81.*

ARTHUR I. LADU   (essay date 1939)

[Ladu argues that Channing was not a transcendentalist.]

Although writers on American literature do not agree upon the relation of the elder William Ellery Channing to transcendentalism, it appears that most of them consider him to have been a transcendentalist before transcendentalism had become full-fledged, or at least to have been a forerunner of the transcendentalist movement. Thus, one historian says that with regard to his emphasis on the sanctity of the individual conscience, Channing was "the direct intellectual precursor of Emerson and the Transcendentalists." H. C. Goddard calls Channing "the bridge between Unitarianism and transcendentalism," and thinks that Channing "shows a development in the transcendental direction," adding that

> all those distinctive doctrines which gave his
> preaching uniqueness and significance in his
> own day and which give him historical impor-
> tance now, flowed from the transcendental ele-
> ments in his belief [see Additional Bibliography].

Professor Parrington, in like manner, refers to Channing as "a forerunner of transcendental individualism" [see excerpt dated 1927]. O. B. Frothingham, however, thinks that Channing was not essentially a transcendentalist, but that he came nearer to being a liberal Unitarian, while another writer puts Channing and Emerson casually together as formulators of the positive creed of Unitarianism. Not only do historians fail to agree as to Channing's relation to transcendentalism, but they appear rather vague; to call a man a bridge between two movements is not to indicate clearly his relation to either. (p. 129)

Part of the misunderstanding regarding Channing's position evidently results from the fact that, at least during his last years, he expressed dissatisfaction with Unitarianism. This is one of the reasons for Goddard's conclusion that Channing showed increasing sympathy with transcendentalism. But Channing's dissatisfaction did not reflect a change on his part; the change was in Unitarianism, not in him.

In his famous 1819 sermon Channing defined the position of the Unitarians, and apparently felt himself in genuine sympathy with them. With them he rejected Calvinism, and proclaimed the unity of God, the dignity of man, the significance of Jesus as divinely sent to be an example for humanity, and the love of God for man. With them, too—and this was perhaps most important of all—he welcomed the spirit of free inquiry, the untrammeled activity of the human spirit in its attempt to establish its proper relationship with God and man. To accomplish this end, Channing desired for men complete freedom from authority that they might ''give themselves to deliberate, devout, fearless study of God's word in connection with his works and providence''; as long as he thought the Unitarians had the same desire, he felt himself one of them. He thought they still had that desire in 1826 when he preached his sermon **"Unitarian Christianity Most Favorable to Piety."** He thought so in 1831 when he wrote of the Unitarian faith: ''It has no established creed or symbol. Its friends think each for himself, and differ much from each other.'' But during the decade that followed, Channing felt that Unitarianism had developed a creed of its own, by which he could no more be bound than he could by the creed of Calvinism. At length he thought himself forced to condemn the Unitarian creed decisively. In 1841 he wrote to James Martineau:

> Old Unitarianism must undergo important modification or developments. . . . It began as a protest against the rejection of reason. . . . It pledged itself to progress, as its life and end; but it has gradually grown stationary, and now we have a *Unitarian Orthodoxy*.

In another letter written in the same year he said:

> I do not speak as a Unitarian, but an independent Christian. I have little or no interest in Unitarians *as a sect*. . . . With Dr. Priestley . . . who had most to do in producing the late Unitarian movement, I have less sympathy than with many of the ''Orthodox.''

Again in 1841 he wrote to W. Trevilcock:

> I am little of a Unitarian, have little sympathy with the system of Priestley and Belsham, and stand aloof from all but those . . . who look for a purer and more effectual manifestation of Christian truth.

It seems plain that it was not Channing that changed, but Unitarianism. Consequently, that his opinion of Unitarianism in 1841 was different from that which he had held a decade earlier does not mean that he moved, as did Emerson, in the direction of transcendentalism.

Insistence upon the validity of immediate intuition, independent of any external experience or teaching, is an important tenet in the transcendental philosophy. In fact, it gives to transcendentalism its most significant characteristic; namely, its striking faith in the infallibility of the individual conscience. (pp. 130-32)

This cardinal point of transcendentalism Channing rejected. Particularly he disagreed with the transcendental attitude toward Christ and the miracles, and toward the Christian virtues of humility and meekness in which throughout his life he firmly believed. In a letter to George Bush in 1841 he wrote:

> I might adopt much of the Trinitarian language, not only on the Trinity, but the Atonement. I could say, that Christ died to magnify the law, to satisfy Divine justice, and that God cannot

forgive without manifesting his displeasure at sin.

At another time he said:

> Christian truth coming to me from the living soul of Jesus, with his living faith and love, and brought out in his grand and beautiful life, is a very, very different thing from an abstract system.

How far Channing's religious philosophy separated him from the transcendentalists he was well aware. Concerning their interpretation of Jesus he wrote:

> Any speculations which throw mists or doubts over his history, and diminish the conviction of his grandeur and importance, are poor and must come to naught. . . . I do fear a tendency in the present movement, to loosen the tie which binds the soul to its great Friend and Deliverer.

In 1841 he wrote to James Martineau concerning the transcendentalists:

> They are anxious to defend the soul's immediate connection with God. They fear lest Christ be made a barrier between the soul and the Supreme, and are in danger of substituting private inspiration for Christianity. Should they go thus far, my hopes from them will cease wholly.

This comment Channing follows with an exhaustive defense of the validity and value of faith in miracles. To Miss Peabody he writes:

> I am also grieved to find you insensible to the clear, bright distinction between Jesus Christ and ourselves. To me, and I should think to every reader of the New Testament, he stands apart, alone. . . . He is a being of moral perfection, unstained by sin.

Channing's belief in the divine nature of Jesus and the New Testament, and his conception of sin, clearly indicate a fundamental distinction between his thought and transcendentalism. ''I am somewhat disappointed that this new movement is to do so little for the spiritual regeneration of society,'' he reflects, and later adds: ''I have little hope in this new movement, except as it indicates deep wants of the soul. . . .'' Again he writes to Miss Peabody:

> It would seem as if our experience had shown you human nature developing its highest sentiments without help and confirmation from abroad. To me, history and observation and experience read very different lessons, and the consequences of overlooking them are not doubtful.

How completely does this contradict the vital transcendentalist idea that intuitive knowledge is supremely valid, and that history and experience are of comparatively little worth. Furthermore, it is apparent that Channing was not hazy about transcendentalism. He understood its essential nature, and expressly repudiated it.

But perhaps the difference between Channing's philosophy and that of the transcendentalists is nowhere better indicated than in his criticism of Theodore Parker's sermon, ''The Transient and the Permanent in Christianity.'' Writing to Miss Peabody in 1841, a year before his death, Channing says of it:

> I grieved that he did not give some clear, direct expression of his belief in the Christian miracles. His silence under such circumstances makes me fear that he does not believe them. I see not how the rejection of these can be separated from the rejection of Jesus Christ. . . . There is not a trace of a time when he existed in men's minds without them. . . . Without miracles the historical Christ is gone. . . . Reduce Christianity to a set of abstract ideas, sever it from its teacher, and it ceases to be ''the power of God unto salvation.''

It has been advanced as evidence of Channing's sympathy with transcendentalism that he pleaded for toleration of Parker's views, and for his right to express himself fully. Naturally Channing would have done so, for belief in religious and intellectual liberty, in the untrammeled expression of ideas, was a vital part of his creed. But it is evident from the above passage that he did not agree with Parker's ideas. (pp. 132-34)

Arthur I. Ladu, ''Channing and Transcendentalism,'' in American Literature, *Vol. 11, No. 2, May, 1939, pp. 129-37.*

ROBERT LEET PATTERSON   (essay date 1952)

[*Patterson points out the connection between Channing's theological doctrine of the* ''essential sameness *of divine and human attributes'' and his concepts of free will and moral responsibility.*]

As it is impossible, according to Channing, to think of God aright except in terms of man, so the converse holds good, that it is impossible to think of man aright except in terms of God. . . . As God is man in the large, so is man, as it were, God in the little. He is a form of divinity. This is a thought which one encounters again and again, expressed in varied phraseology, in Channing's writings. But we must be careful not to read into it the pantheistic implications attributed to it by certain varieties of Transcendentalism. The finite consciousness is not included within the absolute mind, nor is it destined to final absorption into the divine essence. Such a view is wholly incompatible with Channing's robust personalism. Man is definitely a creature, and a creature he will forever remain. Moreover he is a creature capable, not only of progress, but also of retrogression. In language of the deepest feeling Channing warns his auditors against the ''folly'' of ''thinking lightly of sin.'' To be conquered by it is the worst evil that can befall one, an evil so horrible that it may, indeed, culminate in irretrievable ruin.

This sombre possibility however, is but the inevitable consequence of man's capacity for spiritual progress, a progress to which no limits can be set. It is an advance which can continue without end. The limitless capacities of the human spirit constitute the ''impress'' of God's infinity. ''The soul,'' Channing insists, ''viewed in these lights, should fill us with awe. It is an immortal germ, which may be said to contain now within itself what endless ages are to unfold. It is truly an image of the infinity of God, and no words can do justice to its grandeur.''

Thus to stress the greatness and worth of human nature is, Channing recognizes, to lay oneself open to the charge of propagating a doctrine which is apt to impress the hearer as strange and heterodox. As a matter of fact he is sounding a chord which has perpetually vibrated throughout the history of Christian thought, but only to produce perpetual discord. Frequently the teachings of the mystics, and occasionally even the utterances of orthodox theologians, strike the same note. Nevertheless Channing is quite right in asserting that the characteristic tendency of the theological mind has been ''to establish striking contrasts between man and God, and not to see and rejoice in the likeness between them.'' . . . It is, Channing thinks, a natural tendency. The habitual contemplation of the infinity and power of the Deity has led men to prostrate themselves in abject, and even slavish, adoration. But, though a natural tendency, it is an unfortunate one, and has resulted in the serious error of underestimating the potentialities of man and of acquiescing in his present imperfections. The pressing task of theology, he maintains, is to reconcile the finite and the infinite, man's free will and the boundlessness of divine power, human rights and God's sovereignty.

To accomplish this, Channing concedes, is ''no very easy work.'' ''But,'' he urges, ''it must be done. Man's free activity is as important to religion as God's infinity. In the Kingdom of Heaven, the moral power of the subject is as essential as the omnipotence of the sovereign. The rights of both have the same sacredness. To rob man of his dignity is as truly to subvert religion as to strip God of his perfection. We must believe in man's agency as truly as in the Divine, in his freedom as truly as in his dependence, in his individual being as truly as in the great doctrine of living in God. Just as far as the desire of exalting the Divinity obscures these conceptions, our religion is sublimated into mysticism or degraded into servility.''

In the Orient, Channing believes, a monistic philosophy which denies the reality of the individual soul has been the seed of political despotism. (pp. 97-8)

In the case of the Greeks and Romans, Channing continues, their extremely anthropomorphic polytheism was unfavorable to religious reverence; yet, on the other hand, their assertion of individual independence and responsibility was highly beneficial. Turning next to the Christian Church, he observes that among Roman Catholics the mystical impulse has perpetually manifested itself; and its effect, he believes, has been the encouragement of a point of view approximating that of the Oriental pantheists. Fenelon's quietism, he observes, amounted to a ''disease.'' The Quakers, too, in their effort to bring the soul into a state of concentrated attention in which it could hear the voice of God, have tended in the same direction. Lastly, Calvinism, with its denial of free will, has also trodden this well-worn path.

The Calvinist, Channing recognizes, does not intentionally associate himself with the pantheist. On the contrary, he explicitly affirms the distinction between the divine and the human consciousness; yet, by his refusal to concede genuine efficacy to human will, he has landed himself in a position which is to all intents and purposes identical with the pantheist's. The motive which has stimulated this unfortunate development has been the Calvinist's loyalty to his fundamental principle, *Soli Deo Gloria.* In itself this loyalty is highly commendable. Where the Calvinist has gone astray has been in his identification of God's glory with unlimited and arbitrary power. He has failed to see that in the creation of free, morally responsible agents, capable of voluntary obedience and of genuine progress toward perfection, consists the true glory of God. The fear that, by acknowledging the freedom of the creature, one minimizes or denies his dependence upon God is groundless. ''On the contrary, the greater the creature, the more extensive is his de-

The Federal Street Church in Boston, where Channing was ordained.

pendence; the more he has to give thanks for, the more he owes to the free gift of his Creator.''

Moreover the notion that absolute dependence is the root of religion and the basic doctrine of Christianity is erroneous. The fundamental question, Channing contends, is, What kind of universe did God create, and for what purpose did he create it? To answer this question we must approach it from the side of creation. To begin with the idea of an Absolute and Indefinite Being is to go about it the wrong way.

> What but a vague shadow, a sounding name, is the metaphysical Deity, the substance without modes, the being without properties, the naked unity, which performs such a part in some of our philosophical systems? The only God whom our thoughts can rest on, and our hearts can cling to, and our consciences can recognize, is the God whose image dwells in our own souls. The grand ideas of Power, Reason, Wisdom, Love, Rectitude, Holiness, Blessedness, that is, of all God's attributes, come from within, from the action of our spiritual nature. Many indeed think they learn God from the works of design and skill in the outward world; but our ideas of design and skill,

of a determining cause, of an end or purpose, are derived from consciousness, from our own souls. Thus the soul is the spring of the knowledge of God.

Here again, we have the re-assertion of the doctrine of *essential sameness* of divine and human attributes so fundamental in Channing's thought. The idea of God which he so emphatically repudiates is that of scholastic philosophy; and this repudiation carries with it that of the *analogia entis* by the aid of which the idea in question is developed. It is because God is in reality a being like man, a person in the full sense of the word, that we can revere his character, discern, admire, and approve his purposes, and endeavor to cooperate with those purposes.

We must not suppose, however, because Channing affirms with such vehemence and conviction the freedom of the human will, that he feels that no difficulties are involved in the assertion, or believes that he himself has said the last word upon the problem which it raises. On the contrary, we find him, in his essay upon Milton [**"Remarks on the Character and Writings of John Milton"**], clamoring for more light. What he is concerned to insist upon is that the consciousness of free choice and of moral responsibility is not something which can be explained away, but a hard, indubitable fact which must be recognized, and the implications of which must be examined by, and incorporated within, any philosophy which professes to offer a coherent and integrated world view.

From what has been said it is clear that the status of man in the universe is a relatively exalted one. For Channing, as for the Psalmist, he is ''a little lower than the angels.'' And from this follow conclusions of the greatest import, not only in the spheres of religion and ethics, but also in those of politics and the social sciences. For it is precisely because man is a creature of divine origin and potentialities that each individual of the species can make upon his fellows claims of the most sacred character. ''The spiritual principle in man,'' says Channing, ''is what entitles him to our brotherly regard.'' What he is justified in expecting of us above all else is interest in him as an intellectual, moral, and religious being. Upon this point Channing is most explicit and emphatic, and his emphasis merits our attention; for nowhere do we find him at a farther remove from those twentieth century ''humanists'' who invoke the *aegis* of his memory with an enthusiasm equal to that wherewith they repudiate his basic teachings.

The issue comes out clearly in Channing's lecture *On the Elevation of the Laboring Classes* when he tells us wherein the desired elevation consists.

> It is not an outward change of condition. It is not release from labor. It is not struggling for another rank. It is not political power. I understand something deeper. I know but one elevation of a human being, and that is elevation of soul. Without this it matters nothing where a man stands or what he possesses; and with it, he towers, he is one of God's nobility, no matter what place he holds in the social scale. There is but one elevation for a laborer and for all other men. There are not different kinds of dignity for different orders of men, but one and the same to all.

Such elevation, he fully concedes, can be greatly assisted by the betterment of the external environment, and will itself in turn stimulate such a process of amelioration; nevertheless we find this devoted philanthropist asserting with regard to such material development that "supposing it to exist in separation from inward growth and life, it would be nothing worth, nor would I raise a finger to promote it."

Moral worth, then, is the only source of human dignity, and the only ultimate end to be striven for. From this it does not follow that material goods are unimportant, but that they are instrumental, and that their importance is therefore secondary. Moral perfection, Channing tells us, is man's "only true and enduring good." Were we to take these words in their literal sense, we should be forced to conclude that virtue is the only intrinsic value. Yet can they be so taken? The frequent references to what seem obviously to be other intrinsic values suggest that the phrase "moral perfection" is to be equated with the Good, that it is a general term intended to apply not only to virtue but also to these other intrinsic values.

Beauty, for instance, is the recipient of an enthusiastic homage; and, although we are left in some uncertainty as to its precise relationship to the Good, there can be no question that it is an intrinsic, and not an instrumental, value. God himself is the All-Beautiful, and the beauty of the created universe is a revelation of him.

Truth, again, is accorded an almost unbounded reverence. It is "the light of the Infinite Mind, and the image of God in his creatures. Nothing endures but truth.... The love of truth, a deep thirst for it, a deliberate purpose to seek it and hold it fast, may be considered as the very foundation of human culture and dignity." Was not moral worth, we may ask, allotted this high place? There is no inconsistency here, Channing would reply, for the general tendency to distinguish between intellect and conscience, thought and virtue, is, he holds, a mistaken one. The ego cannot be thus divided into separate faculties. "We mutilate our nature," he asserts with an earnestness which would enlist the sympathy of a twentieth-century psychologist, "by thus drawing lines between actions or energies of the soul, which are intimately, indissolubly, bound together. The head and the heart are not more vitally connected than thought and virtue. Does not conscience include, as a part of itself, the noblest action of intellect or reason? Do we not degrade it by making it a mere feeling? Is it not something more? Is it not a wise discernment of the right, the holy, the good? Take away thought from virtue, and what remains worthy of a man? Is not high virtue more than blind instinct? Is it not founded on, and does it not include clear, bright perceptions of what is lovely and grand in character and action?" By denying the rational character of moral judgment, he insists, we should deliver conscience over to become the prey of fanaticism and delusion. (pp. 99-102)

In his possession of reason ... lies man's true greatness, and the development of his intellectual capacity is his first duty. But while all knowledge is good, Channing insists in language reminiscent of St. Augustine, of Calvin, and of Descartes, that what is of greatest import to man is the knowledge of himself and of his relation to God.

The emotions of benevolence, love, reverence, too are good; but what is true of reason is true of emotion also, that it finds its highest object and its chief end in God. And, last of all, happiness is a value, which in the most exalted form accompanies the attainment of the other intrinsic values, and which reaches its highest degree of intensity in the experience of fellowship with the Divine.

The "supreme good" and the "chief end" of man, Channing tells us, "is to bring out, cultivate, and perfect our highest powers, to become wise, holy, disinterested, noble beings, to unite ourselves to God by love and adoration, and to revere his image in his children." It is evident, therefore, that his ethical position is practically identical with that of the school which today we term eudaemonist, or perfectionist. (pp. 102-03)

Robert Leet Patterson, in his The Philosophy of William Ellery Channing, *Bookman Associates, 1952, 298 p.*

DAVID P. EDGELL   (essay date 1955)

[In addition to examining Channing's informal literary crticism, Edgell delineates the strengths and weaknesses of his style.]

[Four] essays—on Milton, Napoleon, Fénelon and National Literature—comprise Channing's title to fame as a literary figure. They are his only formal excursions into criticism. Yet they do not cover the whole of his views, and before we try to make up our minds on his significance, we should think about his informal criticism—his opinions of the books he read and his recommendations to others. The most remarkable aspect of this informal criticism is the narrowness of Channing's range of intellectual sympathy, for with all his generosity in public toward the personality of others and with all his attempts to give every devil his due, he was entirely capable of letting a preconception about a man's moral character interfere with a just appreciation of the man's works. Joseph Blanco White noticed this defect in Channing before they had started to correspond, and mentioned it in a letter to a friend: "I have lately read Channing's Sermons.... They are admirable; and yet Channing himself does not seem totally free from theological intolerance. Witness what he says against the English Unitarians."

As early as 1815, Channing had repudiated identification wth English Unitarian materialists like Priestley; sixteen years later he was arguing with Lucy Aikin about Priestley, still, apparently, without having given much attention to the study of his works: "I know little of his works, and probably shall not read them, for I have little sympathy with his ethical and metaphysical doctrines, and seldom turn my thoughts to the religious controversies on which he spent so much of his zeal." Channing's real reason for not reading Priestley seems to have been his intense distrust of the Englishman's morality. He admitted, by way of faint praise, that Priestley was probably a good man personally, but continued, "I have had many doubts of his moral greatness. It is not a good sign when a man carries out his speculations without the least fear or hesitation, when they seem to shock the highest moral principles." Strange words from one who had spent the last fifteen years of his life writing to "shock the highest moral principles" of the Calvinists!

Channing's dislike of men and books whose heretical tendencies were different from his own extended to historians as well as philosophers. He was anxious to protect his young friend Eloise Payne from the ravages of infidelity, and wrote to her in 1809 apropos of historians:

> I can tell you whom I do not like. Hume and Gibbon are names which, I hope, excite in me no unchristian asperity, but I cannot pronounce them without feelings of strong displeasure. I view them as enemies of the virtue, hopes, consolations and best interests of mankind. They

have labored to extinguish in us every fear of death, to blot out from creation every trace of divine wisdom and love, and to wrap futurity in hopeless darkness.

As if this indictment were not sufficient, he added, "I think his [Gibbon's] forced, affected stile [*sic*] a serious objection to his work." And then, with typical caution, Channing appended a postscript: "I have spoken with too little limitation on infidel writers. When they write on subjects which have no connection with religion and morality, my remarks will not apply."

If the Doctor was insistent on a canon of correct moral feeling in historical and philosophical writing, he was even stricter in his demands on fiction. Elizabeth Peabody reported that he "expressed the fear that to lose oneself in imaginative sympathy and beautiful heroes and heroines, sympathizing as we always do with the noble, and gratified by the poetic justice which was dealt all the characters, satisfied us with ourselves, though our own life was of a lower tone." And in a letter to Miss Peabody, written some time after she had started her bookshop and lending library in Boston, he remonstrated with her about the type of books she was buying: "You sent me some volumes of Balzac—I have feared, the French novels could not be circulated without putting some readers in peril—and ought not to be in your library."

All of Channing's literary perceptions were not so starkly moral in nature. Novelty in itself had no fears for him; he had been among the first in Boston to welcome Wordsworth as a great poet, and remained an ardent admirer for the rest of his life. Fifty years after the event, Bronson Alcott remembered that Channing had been the first to mention the name of Wordsworth to him, and added that he questioned "whether a single townsman of mine had ever heard of Wordsworth at that time." And near the end of his own life Channing still remembered his short interview with the poet and some of the comments that had been made about Wordsworth's growing conservatism. He wrote of these matters to Felicia Hemans, revealing a loyalty that was perhaps only the obverse of his prejudice against infidels:

> I grieve at the privation of sight which you think him [Wordsworth] doomed to suffer. . . . I was told, when in England, after I had seen him, that he had been injured by the notice of the great, that he had forgotten the nobility of genius and lofty sentiment in the presence of the *artificial* aristocracy of this world, that he had sunk into a position, that even that low passion, the love of money, had settled upon him. I could not and would not believe that a man, to whom my heart and mind owed so large a debt, was so fallen—and yet I could not escape an uneasy suspicion, that prosperity had found some weak part in him. Your letter did much to give me back the sentiment with which I used to contemplate him.

Coleridge was another whom the Doctor admired, and the admiration was apparently reciprocated. Coleridge, in a letter to Washington Allston, wrote that though he had known Channing in part before his visit, it was a "gratification" to converse with him and to find that he was "amiable" and "discriminating," and possessed the "love of wisdom and the wisdom of love." Some years later, when the letter was recalled to

Channing's mind, he reminisced: "I was amused . . . on my return to America, to read in a letter he [Coleridge] had written to Mr. Allston, that he had seldom met a person so interested in conversation as Mr. Channing; for my part was simply interrogative: I made not a single original remark!" Later in the same conversation he defended Coleridge's turn toward conservatism, holding that though he repudiated Unitarianism, he spared the personality of the Unitarians and that he remained more liberal than either Wordsworth or Southey.

Paradoxically enough, considering his distaste for novels because they tended to make the reader satisfied with his low lot, Channing was fond—with reservations—of Scott:

> He was anything but a philosopher. But in *extent* of observation, in the quick perception of the endless varieties of human character, in the discovery of their signs and manifestations . . . where will you find his equal? . . . I do not say he ever touches the highest springs within me, but he had bound me by new sympathies to my race.

Goethe, too, Channing liked in the same way, and in the same way found him lacking in high moral purpose. Miss Peabody reports that it took the Doctor a whole winter to get through *Wilhelm Meister*. He appreciated "its artistic merit and meaning," she tells us, but he would often turn from it to one of his old favorites, Miss Mitford.

He thought Mrs. Hemans a great poet, if somewhat too inclined to gloom. His view of Byron is what might be expected:

> That a mind so gifted should have been left to devote its energies to the cause of impiety and vice, and should be so soon and suddenly taken, without making reparation to insulted truth and virtue,—that such a mind is to live for ages in its writings only to degrade and corrupt,—in all this we see the mysterious character of God's providence.

The one unexpected note in Channing's approach to literature was his acceptance, patronizing as it was, of Shelley. He had read some of Shelley's work and had heard something of his life from Southey, who, the Doctor thought, "did not interpret him profoundly." Channing suggested, anticipating Arnold, that "Shelley was a seraph gone astray, who needed friends that he never found in this world." In view of Shelley's opinion of Christianity, Channing's tolerance seems strange, for he had condemned Godwin out of hand: "There are some errors which show such a strange obliquity of intellect as to destroy my confidence in the judgment of those who adopt them. Godwin does not believe in a god, and such a mind must be as unsound as one which should not believe in the existence of the sun."

Taken all in all, Channing's literary judgments show the same eclecticism (stiffened by a high sense of the individual's moral importance) that . . . [is evident] in his philosophical, religious, and social views. The difficulties of applying such a congeries of feelings, concepts, and prejudices are sufficiently obvious to the twentieth-century reader; one may almost say that Channing succeeded in being an impressive figure in spite of his theories. And in literary criticism these difficulties are fatal.

In short, Channing was a moralist rather than a critic, and only men infused with the same religious intensity—in an age like the nineteenth century—could have confused the two. Besides Hazlitt, only two major critical figures of the nineteenth century had anything to say about Channing: Coleridge was agreeably impressed by the Doctor in his capacity as listener and moralist; Matthew Arnold . . . dismissed Channing as "the flower of moral and intelligent mediocrity." And with this judgment, as applied to Channing's criticism, we shall have to concur.

A word or two remains to be said concerning Channing as a writer. Organization was not his strong point, though he was at times capable of arranging his writing into more or less logical divisions—as in his slavery pamphlets. He wrote easily, and seldom (as his manuscripts testify) felt the need for extensive revision. In light of his writing habits and method of composition, this is to be wondered at. Harriet Martineau, an indefatigable writer herself, was amazed to find that he thought only two hours in twenty-four could be profitably expended in composition for publication. She wrote in her autobiography that Channing's practice, when he was in Rhode Island, was "to saunter round the garden once every hour, and then come back to the desk; and when in Boston, he went to the drawingroom instead, or walked about in his library. . . . I wondered how he could ever get or keep his ideas in train, under such frequent interruption."

The virtues of Channing's style are those of oratory. First and most important, he was almost invariably clear. At times . . . his clarity was achieved perhaps as the result of a somewhat dubious oversimplification; but in the main his writing is entirely lucid. It boasts, as well, an occasional epigrammatic touch, though he was never so successful at epigram as Emerson. Yet Channing could, on occasion, produce a striking phrase, as in his description of Jonathan Phillips as one who hung the universe in crape; or a striking image, as in his famous likening of Calvinism's insistence on the redemptive power of the blood of Christ to a religion which placed a gallows in the center of the world and bade men worship it. He was able also to build a fine oratorical climax, as in his addresses on Napoleon.

Renan's contention that Channing became a writer without premeditation is only partly true, and his statement that Channing's "works do not bear witness to any literary ambition. There is not in them a single passage where the least pretension to art or style is to be remarked" [see excerpt dated 1854] is simply not true at all. Even though Channing did eschew florid ornamentation and did not search out literature for apposite references, he was deeply concerned with delivering his message as effectively as possible. Plainness, however, he thought a virtue; consequently he seldom made use of literary tropes to adorn his thought.

On the other side of the ledger, we must account as unfortunate his habit of using abstractions. Far better, if, like Emerson, he could have made use of the meal in the firkin and the milk in the pan to give his ideas point and relevancy. And his constant repetition, however desirable a device it may have been in making sure that a listening audience understood his sermon, is thoroughly vexatious to the modern reader.

With these objections in mind, we may well wonder at the opinion of the *North American Review* writer that Channing was the stylistic equal of Irving. Channing's style, he wrote, "is equally elegant, and a little more pure, correct and pointed than that of Mr. Irving." But worse was to come: the writer went on to announce that Channing was superior to everyone in this country, and to Coleridge and "Carlile" in England.

We are likely to regard such an opinion as pure extravagance, and to agree with Emerson when he wrote:

I cannot help seeing that Doctor Channing would have been a much greater writer had he found a strict tribunal of writers, a graduated intellectual empire established in the land, and knew that bad logic would not pass, and that the most severe exaction was to be made on all who enter these lists. . . . It is very easy to reach the degree of culture that prevails around us; very hard to pass it, and Doctor Channing, had he found Wordsworth, Southey, Coleridge, and Lamb around him, would as easily have been severe with himself and risen a degree higher as he has stood where he is.

These words, hard though they are, sum up Channing's position in American literary culture. He lived at a time when good writers were few. Both his stylistic virtues and his sincerity stood him in good stead, and he achieved a literary reputation greater, perhaps, than would have been his in any other period of our country's history. (pp. 216-24)

> *David P. Edgell, in his* William Ellery Channing:
> An Intellectual Portrait, *The Beacon Press, 1955,
> 264 p.*

ARTHUR W. BROWN   (essay date 1962)

[*Brown comments upon the completed portion of Channing's unfinished treatise on human nature and briefly discusses the influences that shaped his style and method of writing.*]

Like Milton, Channing believed there was a high correlation between what one was as a person and how one wrote. So he filled his library with the best authors (*morally* best) in order to build up a reverence for virtue and to strengthen himself in his battle against human imperfection. And like Milton again, he wanted to write a great work that would demonstrate man's potential for freedom and perfection.

Apparently the idea for such a work came early in his career as a minister although he did not mention it until after his return from England in 1823. Then scattered references to it, increasing in frequency of appearance as time went on, recur in his private papers and in his correspondence. Apparently it was to have been an examination of human nature "to determine its central law, and the end for which all religious and political institutions should be established."

To accomplish his lofty purpose, Channing had planned a work consisting of three parts: the first to deal with man; the second, with God; and the third, with the duties resulting from man's relationship to God. The eight chapters of the first part which were composed—a rather pitiful fragment of accomplishment to represent the plans and aspirations of nearly an entire lifetime—are only first sketches; and they lack clarity and organization. Various threads of influence are discernible; but there is no pattern to indicate a rationale behind the material that had been collected.

The general background of the fragment is eighteenth century. It begins in true Lockean fashion with a discussion of sensation; but it follows up the Lockean lead with ideas borrowed from the Scotch School which came after Locke. Sensations are described as "occasions" rather than "causes" of intellectual activity, and the mind is cited as furnishing the universe from its own store instead of deriving its riches from it.

The idealism of the piece is incontestable, but Channing's eclectic method makes identification of specific sources virtually impossible. He had drawn from Plato and Price, Wordsworth and Coleridge, Cousin and Jouffroy, Kant and Carlyle; but a lack of critical acumen prevented his welding these materials into a coherent system. Gifted with the mind of neither an Edwards nor a Hume, he was as incapable of erecting a logical edifice like the *Freedom of the Will* or the *Treatise of Human Nature* as he was of arguing in behalf of human depravity and a blood atonement. Channing's talent was not to devise systems of logic but to drive home—through the dense barriers of stale custom and habit and in spite of human inertia—a few great ideas by force of example and by constant reiteration in conversation, sermon, and pamphlet.

Naturally Channing was disappointed by his lack of progress on his *magnum opus,* but he was accustomed to temporizing with circumstances. He counted his time well spent because he could remember that his sermons and discourses had been enriched by his study. Besides he had written much more on account of it. Writing, he believed, was one of the great means of giving precision, clearness, consistency, and energy to thought; and for a long time he had attempted to sharpen his powers of concentration by increasing his efforts in composition. "One of the great laws of our nature, and a law singularly important to social beings," he said, "is, that the intellect enlarges and strengthens itself by expressing worthily its best views. . . . Superior minds are formed, not merely by solitary thought, but almost as much by communication."

In his emphasis upon clarity and precision and upon the power of the written word to improve the mind, Channing followed in the steps of those eighteenth-century arbiters of taste, Lord Kames and Hugh Blair, both of whom he had studied at Harvard and whom his brother, Edward Tyrell, taught, along with Archibald Alison and Thomas Brown of the Scotch School, to Harvard undergraduates like Emerson, Holmes, and Thoreau. Moreover, when Dr. Channing declared that "the laborious distribution of a great subject, so as to assign to each part or topic its just position and due proportion, is singularly fitted to give compass and persevering force of thought," he was not only following the pattern of discourse established in New England by the early Puritan ministers but also proving himself a good disciple of Addison by using the standard idiom of neoclassic decorum. Aesthetically, he looked both backward and forward; he acknowledged as late as 1837 his humility before "the spontaneous graces" of Addison and Goldsmith, yet he wrote almost simultaneously in his projected treatise that beauty was in the mind, as the Scotch School argued, and not in the objects perceived by the mind.

Up to the very close of his writing career, therefore, Channing was an exponent of eighteenth-century methods of writing as well as of the more mechanical and technical aspects of its rules on style. Perspicuity, force, and precision are spelled out in his sermons and critical articles; and his purism in language is demonstrated by the avidity with which he seized upon neologisms in the letters of his correspondents. . . . To the larger and less cut-and-dried features of style he devoted much attention; and he seldom neglected, especially in his ordination sermons, to emphasize the importance of developing a personal style in both written and spoken communication. It was, he believed, the primary factor in determining the creative power of a writer; and it depended very little upon the structure of sentences and size of vocabulary, but chiefly upon the mind of the person writing. He was asserting, therefore, the power

of the mind (or soul) to invigorate art. By so doing, he was putting aside the cold and mechanical standards of Kames and Blair for the warm and organic principles of the romantics. He was still a "judicious" critic of literature; but his moralism was rather the dynamic doctrine of Wordsworth and Coleridge than the negative didacticism of Addison and Steele. Insofar as he emphasized the spiritual relationship between man and nature, he was giving expression to the idealism of his age in much the same way as the English romantics. (pp. 106-09)

> *Arthur W. Brown, in his* William Ellery Channing, *Twayne Publishers, Inc., 1962, 172 p.*

HARMON L. SMITH (essay date 1964)

[*Smith outlines the fundamentals of Channing's theological beliefs, analyzing, among other topics, Channing's concepts of God and Christ, his theory of reason, and his ideas concerning the relationship between nature and grace.*]

The basic theological conviction of orthodox Protestant Christianity since Calvin has been that the infinite essence of God's being cannot be grasped by the powers of the human intellect. The insight of empirical epistemology in Locke, and before him in Descartes, is ardently maintained by the orthodox theologian who holds no room for any general or natural revelation, at least to the extent that man has no innate, positive awareness of God. Original sin has seen to that. Instead, human concepts are formed as a consequence of experience, in which our ideas are abstracted from the objects which we encounter. While the existence of these objects is not necessary but contingent, it is, however, impossible for us to conceive that God, in whom essence and existence are united, should not exist. So, the divine Essence lies beyond the limits of our experience and evades all of the categories of human thought. We can rationally know *that* God is but not *what* he is. God, for Locke, is more the conclusion of a theory than an object encountering its subject. So, too, with the orthodox estimate of man's natural powers. The only assertions we can make about God are therefore negative: he is immutable, immaterial, invisible, etc.

Classical Christian orthodoxy, however, has not been able to stop here. It has felt, and rightly, that this variety of the Kantian *Ding an sich* defies conceptual description. If God is to be more than a word in man's religious vocabulary, knowledge of him, however meager, must be available. How is this knowledge available? The most frequently given answer asserts that such knowledge is available by use of the principle of analogy. By involving the principle of analogy we can thereby arrive at a positive, affirmative knowledge of God.

It is of significant contemporary interest that many Roman Catholic and Protestant theologians alike continue to agree with the Roman Catholic and Calvinist theologians of Channing's era that this general principle of asserting negative and affirmative is basically sound as the foundation of man's positive knowledge about God. It was this particular orthodox epistemology which drew Channing's direct fire. He understood well enough the fundamental basis upon which it rested and devoted himself with tireless zeal and rare intellectual acumen to describing and discrediting what he took to be an error; namely, the assertion of the total incapacity of the human mind to attain to any definite knowledge of the divine attributes. For Channing,

> errors relating to God seem to us among the most pernicious that can grow up among Christians; for they darken, and, in the strong lan-

guage of Scripture, "turn to blood" the Sun of the Spiritual Universe. Around just views of the Divine character all truths and all virtues naturally gather; and although some minds of native irrepressible vigor may rise to greatness in spite of dishonorable conceptions of God, yet, as a general rule, human nature cannot spread to its just and full proportions under their appalling, enslaving, heart-withering control.

Confronted by the threats of such a dishonorable view, Channing expressed his views, notably in his essay **"The Moral Argument Against Calvinism,"** and in his sermon at the ordination of F. A. Farley in 1828 entitled **"Likeness to God."** A cursory examination of these works reveals the following sequence of ideas: (1) The very essence of religion lies in man's growth in likeness to God. (2) There are no degrees of truth. Our knowledge is subject to quantitative, not qualitative, limitation. (3) We enjoy an essential sameness with God. (4) Knowledge of this identity is within man. (5) The Christian's vocation is to honor God in becoming like him.

Channing's fundamental convictions rest upon three basic presuppositions: (1) that man's true blessedness consists in the love of God; (2) that God can be loved as Person only if he is conceived of as Person; and (3) that if he is so conceived as Person, an essential likeness with respect to God and man must be possible.

Regarding Christ, Channing is disposed to insist upon his unique authority and lordship. He is also concerned to emphasize that the Christian's commitment to Christ does not, in any way, involve mental or moral servility nor any restraint of intellectual freedom. Christ is the great Liberator from bondage of every kind. If one would be free, he must follow Christ; for to follow him is to become truly free.

In the Scriptures, Jesus continually spoke of God. Jesus himself is continually spoken of as the Son of God, who receives power, works miracles, and judges justly by God's appointment. Moreover, "the inferiority of Christ pervades the New Testament." From these references Channing concludes and establishes his view of the subordination of the Son to the Father.

But Channing was also obliged to establish his view rationally. And this he undertook, with a will, in terms of establishing the essential unity and integrity of Christ's person. We need only mention the intellectual *scandalon* of Christianity, the hypostatic union of the human and divine will and of the human and divine nature which yet constitute but a single person, to indicate the offense Channing felt in the doctrines of the Incarnation and the Trinity. In contemporary psychological language, Channing was insisting upon the "whole person" of Jesus. For Channing's complaint was not only with orthodoxy's tritheism, but also with its Nestorianism. The point of his entire inquiry at this juncture is thus twofold: positively, that the doctrine of the Incarnation is first of all a statement about the character and identity of God; negatively, that one cannot love and give allegiance to what he does not understand.

The quest for the "whole person" of Christ has its fruition in Channing's premise that it is the personality of Christ, rather than any attributes human or divine, that is of greatest significance. It is in this, his personality, that Christ's perfection is to be found. It is likewise in Channing's commitment to Christ's moral perfection that the question of his ontological status is largely excluded as a point of compelling interest. Christ is, then, to borrow another phrase from modern psychology, the

perfectly "integrated person." He was, in a word, "very man." Christ became what we are in order that we might become as he is. But Christ is not merely human. He is at once very man and more than man, divine but not God.

One further point must be made here. Without the ability and freedom to strive and achieve by effort, there can be no genuinely moral life. To posit an omnipotent will, of which man's will in every jot and tittle is but the expression, is an utterly incredible position for Channing. What virtue is there in the mechanical movement of automatons directed inexorably to some predetermined destiny by a celestial monad? For Channing, there is none. Moreover, every man, Christ included, must be able to achieve his moral character and perfection by the exertion of his own willing and achieving. Virtue cannot properly be said to be constituted by divine fiat.

These are fundamental convictions for Channing, and Robert Patterson is essentially correct in stating that Channing's Arianism rests on these two principles: the moral perfection of Christ and freedom of the will. Historically these two principles alone serve well to indicate how much the unique spirit of the eighteenth century is expressed in Channing. One sees here not only a keen insistence on the dignity of man, but also the responsibility impinging upon him for obedience to, and the realization of, a set of moral standards which man himself had no part in creating but which, nonetheless, he must reverence and serve.

What, then, is the unique work of this person, Christ? The most cogent answer developed by Channing is found in chapter nine of *The Perfect Life*. Here Jesus is described as the "great emancipator" who sets at liberty man's intellect, his conscience, his "imprisoned energy of love," and most of all his love for the perfect. For Channing, this emancipation pervaded Jesus' life and is wholly confirmed by his death. One would expect Channing to deny any substitutionary theory of the atonement, and he does. There is, for Channing, no infinite guilt requiring infinite satisfaction by an infinite being. Rather,

> by Christ's blood I understand his spirit, his entire devotion to the cause of human virtue and to the will of God. By his cross I mean his celestial love, I mean the great principles of piety and righteousness, in asserting which he died. To be redeemed by his blood is to be redeemed by his goodness.... According to these views, moral purity, Christian virtue, spiritual perfection, is the supreme good to be bestowed by the blood and cross of Christ.

The death of Christ is, in the main, the culmination of the perfectly free and obedient and, therefore, perfectly virtuous life.

> We earnestly maintain that Jesus, instead of calling forth, in any way or degree, the mercy of the Father, was sent by that mercy to be our Saviour; that he is nothing to the human race but what he is by God's appointment; that he communicates nothing but what God empowers him to bestow; that our Father in heaven is originally, essentially, and eternally placable, and disposed to forgive; and that his unborrowed, underived, and unchangeable love is the only fountain of what flows to us through his Son.

A crucial underlying premise of all that has been said thus far rests upon the firm conviction that intelligibility is a mark of God's great wisdom in the creation of man and the universe. Revelation itself rests upon the authority of reason in the sense that reason, likewise a gift from God, proves the evidences of revelation's truth and thus binds man to receive and obey it. Reason, in fact, interprets revelation; and nothing contrary to reason has a right to faith. Reason is, for Channing, natural revelation by which man receives truth through his natural faculties. Revelation, on the other hand, is conditioned by miracle and prophecy. To that extent revelation is natural reason enlarged, the validity of which is vouched for by reason. To this point, Channing follows Locke. Hence he affirms:

> I glory in Christianity because it enlarges, invigorates, exalts my rational nature. If I could not be a Christian without ceasing to be rational, I should not hesitate as to my choice. I feel myself bound to sacrifice to Christianity property, reputation, life; but I ought not to sacrifice to any religion that reason which lifts me above the brute and constitutes me a man. I can conceive no sacrilege greater than to prostrate or renounce the highest faculty which we have derived from God.

Channing is now immediately in a position diametrically opposite to that of the orthodox. It would be unfair to Channing to suggest that he was unaware either of his opposition to the orthodox position or of the orthodox position to which he was opposed. He himself gives an excellent and succinct summary of Samuel Hopkins' and the Calvinists' argument in his 1836 sermon on Christian worship ["**Christian Worship**"]. Channing's quarrel with the Calvinists is, in a word, that both rationally and morally they have severed the Creator from the creature.

In order to appreciate Channing's argument, one must notice again his conviction of the supremacy of reason and its competence to ideal with every question, including revelation.

> No miraculous voice from heaven assures me that it is God's word, nor does any mysterious voice within my soul command me to believe the supernatural works of Christ. . . . I must examine it by the same rational faculties by which other subjects are tried. I must ask what are its evidences, and I must lay them before reason, the only power by which evidence can be weighed.

The importance of this insistence becomes clearer when the essential characteristics of reason are explicated.

> First, it belongs to reason to comprehend universal truths. . . . But it does not stop here. Reason is also exercised in applying these universal truths to particular cases, beings, and events. . . . Reason is [secondly] the power which tends and is perpetually striving to reduce our various thoughts to unity or consistency. Perhaps the most fundamental conviction of reason is, that all truths agree together.

Here one discerns the Neoplatonic element in Channing's thought. For it is from these characteristics that Channing can proceed to argue that there is a rational continuity between Creator and creature, that the gospel offers itself to the creature's reason, and that to sever this relationship is to make communication between God and man impossible. It is relevant to note at this point that Channing's theory of the dignity of man rests upon this predicate of rational continuity.

It is now proper to ask how one may know that the ideas fashioned in the mind correspond with objective truth and reality. Locke's empiricism had not been able to offer a satisfactory answer to this question, maintaining as it did that natural knowledge has a more certain foundation for knowing than revelation. It may be objected that Channing, following Lockean influence, did not hew to the logical line any better than did Locke himself; but that under the influence of Richard Price, who had followed the Cambridge Platonists of the Cudworth stripe, he proceeded to a Platonic-Augustinian development of his soteriology and anthropology. It was for David Hume to push the Lockean skepticism to its logical extreme, but Channing could not. Channing was therefore obliged to diverge from Locke, at this juncture, in an attempt to relate these two kinds of knowledge by introducing a supplement to the logical understanding; namely, the capacity of the human mind for God.

> God's wisdom is a pledge that whatever is necessary for *us,* and necessary for salvation, is revealed too plainly to be mistaken, and too consistently to be questioned, by a sound and upright mind. It is not the mark of wisdom to use an unintelligible phraseology, to communicate what is above our capacities, to confuse and unsettle the intellect by appearances of contradiction. . . . A revelation is a gift of light. It cannot thicken our darkness and multiply our perplexities.

It would, of course, require little imagination to move from this to an assertion that the human mind is capable of apprehending God independently, that is, without the qualification of any divine assistance. It is to this further step that the Calvinists would raise particular objections. Arguing from the *analogia entis,* the Calvinists of the Edwardean and Hopkinsian school could maintain that man, in neither reason nor moral judgment, is capable of passing upon the content of revelation. But to take this step would be to misinterpret Channing, for there is within this man and his thought a strain of evangelical piety very much unlike strict, cold, naked rationalism.

If Channing seems to presume on the divine and sovereign God, it is only because he cannot comprehend any such infinitely qualitative abyss as the Calvinists claim between the human and the divine. There is, rather, for him a profound awareness of man's responsibility as a moral being to know and be governed by the wisdom and will of God. So sure is Channing that God would not divorce himself from the moral awareness of man that he urges: "It is plain that a doctrine which contradicts our best ideas of goodness and justice cannot come from the just and good God, or be a true representation of his character." It is expressly true that for Channing equality with God, in the Pauline sense, is not a thing to be grasped. Far from being pagan, this way of perceiving the relation between nature and grace is distinctly in the Augustinian tradition.

It remains now to state Channing's understanding of grace. And if grace be a favorable disposition on the part of God without reference to any merit or desert in the object of his favor, Channing's seeming imbalance with reference to reason can be misleading and misunderstood. A more accurate estimate is to be found in Channing's confession that "it is my faith in this perfection of the Divine Mind that inspires me with reverence for the human, for they are intimately connected, the latter being a derivation from the former. . . . Severed from God, reason would lose its grandeur.'' Such is the inadequacy of man's reason if it be divorced from God that

> at the introduction of Christianity, the human family were plunged into gross and debasing error, and the light of nature had not served for ages to guide them back to truth. Philosophy had done its best, and failed. A new element, a new power, seems to have been wanting to the progress of the race. That in such an exigence miraculous aid should be imparted accords with our best views of God.

Moreover, natural reason alone would founder in its attempt to discover God *only in nature.* One may, and in fact should, develop and use every faculty to discern the truth in nature. Nevertheless, for the man of genuine piety, something lacks. ''I see, in this fixed order, his care of the race, but not his constant, boundless concern for myself. Nature speaks of a general divinity, not of the friend and benefactor of each living soul.'' In a word:

> Nature alone does not meet our wants. . . . Every man must feel that, left to nature as his only guide, he must wander in doubt as to the life to come. Where but from God himself can I learn my destination? . . . I see not how He can do it but by supernatural teaching—by a miraculous revelation. Miracles are the appropriate, and would seem to be the only mode of placing beyond doubt man's future and immortal being.

One need not become bogged down here in an exegesis of ''miracle'' and ''revelation'' in Channing's thought. It is sufficient to say that to the extent that miracle reveals the divine intention, it is revelation, and that to the extent that revelation proceeds from a power above nature, it is miracle. It is therefore a serious error ever to confound nature and supernature in Channing's thought. While both concepts proceed from the same source, they are nonetheless distinguishable by their own peculiar constitution.

Again, although religion may be said to be in the nature of man, Channing is on no account a pantheist. God is, at all costs, the ultimate referent; and man's dignity is derivative in that, in spite of the Fall, he has not lost his essential likeness to God. ''Its [religion's] germs exist in us all. We have, each of us, the spiritual eye to see, the mind to know, the heart to love, the will to obey God. We have a spiritual nature that may bear the image of divine perfection.'' Moreover:

> He [Christ] creates no new truth; for truth is eternal. And what is still more important, he does not teach truth *wholly new* to men. The great principles of religion belong to human nature; and they are manifested in all God's works and in his providence. We live in darkness, not because there is no sun of truth. . . . The cause of our not seeing is in ourselves. The inward eye is diseased or shut.

How shall this be overcome? Channing is able to speak for himself:

The wants of the sinner may be expressed almost in one word. He wants assurances of mercy in his Creator. He wants pledges that God is love in its purest form, that is, that He has a goodness so disinterested, free, full, strong, and immutable, that the ingratitude and disobedience of his creatures cannot overcome it. This unconquerable love, which in Scripture is denominated grace, and *which waits not for merit to call it forth,* but flows out to the most guilty, is the sinner's only hope, and it is fitted to call forth the most devoted gratitude.

Is this the same Channing who proclaimed that ''Christianity is a rational religion. Were it not so I should be ashamed to profess it''; that ''if religion be the shipwreck of understanding, we cannot keep too far from it''? It is, indeed, the same Channing. A cursory reading of Channing perhaps always leaves one reflecting upon the fact that this man is unquestionably a thoroughgoing rationalist, the product of the (especially British) Enlightenment. But a more detailed study of Channing's works suffices to impress one with the truth of the position that Channing is, in rare dimensions, the product of a combination of influences: the Enlightenment, Neoplatonism, and pietism.

It is correct to say that Channing certainly may give the impression of imbalance in the favor of reason in most of his writing. But it needs also to be remembered that his own effort was largely precipitated by others . . . , that the harbinger of a new era is not unlikely to exaggerate and caricature, and that the Calvinist position against which he directed his polemic required something of a frontal assault. In many ways it is remarkable that he was able to restrain the limits of the new liberal Christianity. That he did proceed at a deliberate pace is to his credit. Moreover, that he understood grace to be a favorable disposition on the part of God without reference to any merit or desert in man is attested to in the following paragraphs, the first of which was written at the outset of Channing's prominence as the titular head of the liberal Christians (1819) and the second only two months before his death (1842):

> Our system teaches that God's mercy is not an instinctive tenderness, which cannot inflict pain, but an all-wise love, which desires the true and lasting good of its object, and consequently desires first for the sinner that restoration to purity without which shame, and suffering, and exile from God and heaven are of necessity and unalterably his doom. Thus Unitarianism holds forth God's grace and forgiving goodness most resplendently; and, by this manifestation of him, it tends to . . . an ingenuous aversion to sin, not because sin brings punishment, but because it separates the mind from this merciful Father.

• • • • •

The doctrine of the ''Word made flesh'' shows us God uniting himself most intimately with our nature, manifesting himself in a human form, for the very end of making us partakers of his own perfection. The doctrine of grace, as it is termed, reveals the Infinite Father imparting his Holy Spirit—the best gift he can impart—to the humblest human being who implores it. Thus love and reverence for human nature—a love for man stronger than death—is the very spirit of Christianity.

Certainly Channing's theology differs considerably from that of those theologians whose forte is grace alone: Channing's estimate of man is more optimistic; his grasp of the solidarity of the race in social and personal sin is less realistic; and the impartation of grace assumes a more gradual character than one finds in the Calvinists. Nevertheless, it may be claimed as not only fair to Channing, but as a tenable conclusion on the basis of his own writings, that in spite of accusations to the contrary the notion of grace as man's undeserving receipt of God's blessing is the foundation of the gospel he preached.

> We indeed attach great importance to Christian works, or Christian obedience, believing that a practice or life conformed to the precepts and example of Jesus is the great end for which faith in him is required, and is the great condition on which everlasting life is bestowed.... Still, we always and earnestly maintain that no human virtue, no human obedience, can give a legal claim, a right by merit, to the life and immortality brought to light by Christ. We see and mourn over the deficiencies, broken resolutions, and mixed motives of the best men. We always affirm that God's grace, benignity, free kindness, is needed by the most advanced Christians, and that to this alone we owe the promise in the gospel, of full remission and everlasting happiness to the penitent.

(pp. 397-406)

> *Harmon L. Smith, "Nature and Grace: Their Significance for William Ellery Channing," in* Religion in Life, *Vol. XXXIII, No. 3, Summer, 1964, pp. 395-406.*

ROBERT S. WARD (essay date 1965)

> [*Ward discusses Channing's and Joseph Story's efforts to promote a genuine American literature.*]

During the first period of the literary history of the United States, the half century following the Revolution, two men did much to further our national literature whose prowess in other professions tends to make us forget their literary achievements. Second only to Mr. Justice Marshall in the legal profession of the time was Joseph Story, and second to none in theology was William Ellery Channing.... [Both Channing and Story] belonged to the "Age of Jackson," the age of Webster, Calhoun, and Clay. Indeed, each in his unique way embellished Henry Clay's American System in its cultural aspects, not only in law and theology, where Story's constitutional theory and adaptations of the Common Law and Channing's Unitarian theology were the leading achievements of the age, but in literature, which each believed to be a crucial expression of the national mind. (p. 363)

On August 31, 1826, Mr. Justice Joseph Story of the United States Supreme Court delivered the Phi Beta Kappa Oration at Harvard taking for his topic "Characteristics of the Age."... Himself an amateur poet, his love of letters led him to devote the body of his oration to an account of "the department of general and miscellaneous literature" where "the genius of the age has displayed itself in innumerable varieties of form and beauty, from the humble page, which presumes to teach the infant mind the first lines of thought, to the lofty works, which discourse of history, and philosophy, and ethics, and government."... (p. 364)

[Story also] addressed himself to the importance of a national literature:

> To us, Americans, nothing, indeed, can, or ought to be indifferent, that respects the cause of science and literature. We have taken a stand among the nations of the earth, and have successfully asserted our claim to political equality.... We assert an equality of voice and vote in the republic of letters, and assume for ourselves the right to decide on the merits of others, as well as to vindicate our own.... We contend for prizes with nations whose intellectual glory has received the homage of centuries.... It is not by a few vain boasts, or vainer self-complacency, or rash daring, that we are to win our war to the first literary distinction....

He concluded his pleas for a national literature with a note of optimism based on the roots already planted for which "we have no reason to blush" and an admonition that Americans "should hold nothing, which human genius or human enterprise has yet attained as beyond their reach." (p. 367)

During the same year, 1826, Judge Story's distinguished classmate, William Ellery Channing, also struck a blow for literature. It was Emerson who reminisced: "I attribute much importance to two papers of Dr. Channing, one on Milton and one on Napoleon, which were the first specimens in this country of that large criticism which in England had given power and fame to the *Edinburgh Review*" [see excerpt dated 1882(?)]. In the **"Remarks on the Character and Writings of John Milton,"** Dr. Channing joined Story in attacking facile virtuosity, "... the superficial doctrine of a later day that poetry flourishes most in an uncultivated soil, and that imagination shapes its brightest visions from the mists of a superstitious age; and he [Milton] had no dread of accumulating knowledge, lest it should oppress and smother his genius." He too desired no parochial nationalism, felt universality to mark "the highest order of intellect," and believed in the benefits broad and classical learning could bestow upon literature. He cited "... Milton as a practical example of the benefits of that universal culture of intellect which forms the distinction of our times, but which some dread as unfriendly to original thought. Let such remember that mind is in its own nature diffusive." And he agreed in disdain of those who regarded "poetry as light reading.... We agree with Milton in his estimate of poetry. It seems to us the divinest of all the arts." Like Story he abhorred the fact that "... poetry has been made the instrument of vice, the pander of bad passions...." And he too castigated "that whining sensibility and exaggeration of morbid feeling which makes so much of modern poetry effeminating." But just as Story brought many of his legal principles, possibly too many, to bear upon the subject of literature so did Channing bring theology into his literary theory and thereby out of agreement with his more mundane classmates. His spiritual bias led him to a less realistic, idealized view of poetry:

> ... for it is the breathing or expression of that principle or sentiment which is deepest and sublimest in human nature,—we mean, of that thirst or aspiration to which no mind is wholly a stranger, for something purer and lovelier,

something more powerful, lofty, and thrilling, than ordinary and real life affords. No doctrine is more common among Christians than that of man's immortality; but it is not so generally understood that the germs or principles of his whole future being are *now* wrapped up in his soul, as the rudiments of the future plant in the seed. . . . In an intellectual nature, framed for progress and for higher modes of being, there must be creative energies, powers of original and ever-growing thought; and poetry is the form in which these energies are deeply manifested. It is the glorious prerogative of this art, that it ''makes all things new'' for the gratification of a divine instinct.

This is Unitarian theology in its literary manifestation and toward the idealistic end of the spectrum bordering on Transcendentalism. Story was near the other, the realistic end of the same spectrum and therefore probably read with slight misgiving that poetry ''depicts the soul in those modes of repose or agitation, of tenderness or sublime emotion, which manifest its thirst for a more powerful and joyful existence. To a man of a literal and prosaic character, the mind may seem lawless in these workings; but it observes higher laws than it transgresses. . . .'' His theology accounts for Channing's disdain for the naturalistic realism which Story extolled. ''It [poetry] lifts the mind above ordinary life, gives it a respite from depressing cares, and awakens the consciousness of its affinity with what is pure and noble.'' Never the Democrat that Story was, his religion also led him to have less concern for the common reader. In defending Milton against the charge that his prose style was ''difficult and obscure,'' he lamented ''the fastidiousness and effeminacy of modern readers. . . .'' He would ''let inspired genius fulfil its higher function of lifting the prepared mind from earth to heaven. . . . Let it not lay aside its natural port, or dwarf itself that it may be comprehended by the surrounding multitude.''

It was not until four years later in the *Christian Examiner* for January, 1830, that Dr. Channing issued his **''Remarks on a National Literature''** in which he began by defining ''National Literature'' as ''the expression of a nation's mind in writing . . . the production among a people of important works in philosophy, and in the departments of imagination and taste . . . the contributions of new truths to the stock of human knowledge . . . the thoughts of profound and original minds, elaborated by the toil of composition, and fixed and made immortal in books.'' It was to him ''the distinction which a nation should most earnestly covet.'' Then he fitted it into the American System: ''There is a harmony between all our great interests, between inward and outward improvements; and by establishing among them a wise order, all will be secured.'' But again his nationalism was, like that of Story's, subordinated to universality: ''We love our country much, but mankind more. . . . In all nations we recognize one great family, and our chief wish for our native land is, that it may take the first rank among the lights and benefactors of the human race.'' His theology of moral progress led him to value a national literature as bringing to bear the highest minds upon the lowest masses; ''Literature is the concentration of intellect for the purpose of spreading itself abroad and multiplying its energy.''

Asking whether we could now be said to have a national literature, he regretted that ''the few standard works which we have produced, and which promise to live, can hardly, by any

A painting of Channing by Washington Allston.

courtesy, be denominated a national literature.'' Nor could he find solace in the breadth of our elementary education. ''A dead level of intellect, even if it should rise above what is common in other nations, would not answer our wishes and hopes for our country. We want the human intellect to do its utmost here.'' ''Whilst clamoring against dependence on European manufactures, we contentedly rely on Europe for the nobler and more important fabrics of the intellect. . . . We believe that it [our liberty] does open to us an indefinite intellectual progress.'' The failure so far to create a national literature has attributed to ''the common doctrine that we need, in this country, useful knowledge, rather than profound, extensive, and elegant literature, and that this last, if we covet it, may be imported from abroad in such variety and abundance as to save us the necessity of producing it among ourselves.''

Channing was pragmatist enough not only to affirm the desirability of useful knowledge but to assert the utility of beauty; ''. . .the idea of beauty is an indestructible principle of our nature, and this single truth is enough to put us on our guard against vulgar notions of utility. . . . Poetry is useful by touching deep springs in the human soul; by giving voice to its more delicate feelings; by breathing out, and making more intelligible, the sympathy which subsists between the mind and the outward universe. . . .'' Here he was approaching functional expressionism and Transcendental naturalism.

As for letting Europe do our intellectual work for us, he objected that any people of advancement must ''promote within itself every variety of intellectual exertion.'' He argued the need of gifted Americans for institutions to develop their genius, the unintelligibility of foreign intellect to us unless we develop our own intellect, the special need of a republic for men of distinguished intellect because of the free communication between the gifted few and the many, and the need for an original literature to establish resistance to foreign influence: "There is a great stir to secure to ourselves the manufacturing of our own clothing. We say, let others spin and weave for us, but let them not think for us. A people whose government and laws are nothing but the embodying of public opinion, should jealously guard this opinion against foreign dictation. We need a literature to counteract, and to use wisely the literature which we import." Thus Dr. Channing sought to modify the American System, exchanging cotton mills for books.

Having pointed out that no foreign literature "sprung from the soul of another people" could express our unique "character and feelings" and that literature "creates, as well as manifests intellectual power, and, without it, the highest minds will never be summoned to the most invigorating action," he went on to show that "the same creative energy is manifested in the production of a noble style as in abstracting beautiful forms from lifeless stone. How unfaithful then is a nation to its own intellect, in which graceand force of style receive no culture!" And in support of this thesis he shows awareness of the correspondence between the artist's originality of style and his uniqueness of intellect.

It was, however, in his final appeal that the Doctor rose to new heights of awareness of the function of literature in a democratic culture. In supporting the proposition that "man is the great subject of literature, and juster and profounder views of man may be expected here than elsewhere," he pointed out that in Europe, instead of men, we meet "Kings, nobles, priests, peasants," people who value themselves for their blood, their rank, or other artificial distinction. "The institutions of the Old World all tend to throw obscurity over what we most need to know, and that is, the worth and claims of a human being." Nowhere has the Puritan focus on psychological values rather than external posturing been more forcefully asserted. Howells was a true son of the good Doctor when he reacted to his friend Henry James's lament over the poverty of Hawthorne's New England materials, the lack of aristocracy, established church, picturesque peasantry, with the ironic explosion "Nothing but the whole of life itself." And Channing was optimistic over the future of our literature which should surpass that of Europe because of our freedom for inquiry."We want a literature, in which genius will pay supreme if not undivided homage to truth and virtue; in which the childish admiration of what has been called greatness will give place to a wise moral judgment. . . ."

In closing he suggested the means for creating this kind of literature with particular emphasis upon the social motivation for it. "Literature has been originated and modified by a variety of principles; by patriotism and national feeling, by reverence for antiquity, by the spirit of innovation, by enthusiasm, by scepticism, by the passion for fame, by romantic love, and by political and religious convulsions." His suggestion for a new and higher motivating principle was of course "the religious principle."

These earlier efforts to inject literary infusions into the blood of the American System are interesting as harbingers of what was to follow.

Nowhere was Dr. Channing more the precursor of Emerson than here. In the "American Scholar" we hear echoed the voices of Story and Channing calling for work: "Our anniversary is one of hope, and, perhaps, not enough of labor." Like them he is unwilling to admit that we have as yet evidenced anything more than "a friendly sign of the survival of the love of letters amongst a people too busy to give to letters any more." No more than Channing does he believe that we can live on "the sere remains of foreign harvests." We may doubt that either Story or Channing was happy to hear him relegate books to a place after nature among the influences on the mind of the scholar, but Channing would certainly have applauded the assertion that "books are the best of things, well used; abused, among the worst" and that "the one thing in the world of value, is the active soul." Certainly Story more than Channing would sympathize as Emerson read with joy an auspicious sign "the fact that the same movement which effected the elevation of what was called the lowest class in the state, assumed in literature a very marked and as benign an aspect. Instead of the sublime and beautiful, the near, the low, the common, was explored and poetized." Both could applaud, "we will walk on our own feet; we will work with our own hands; we will speak our own minds," and Channing, if not Story could approve, "A nation of men will for the first time exist, because each believes himself inspired by the Divine Soul which also inspires all men." It was to take nearly a hundred more years for this dream to come to pass, but when the time came, after two world wars, for the American System to come of age practical idealism in thought and in art had come to be its crown. (pp. 368-74)

Robert S. Ward, "The American System in Literature," in The New England Quarterly, *Vol. XXXVIII, No. 3, September, 1965, pp. 363-74.*

DAVID ROBINSON (essay date 1981)

[Robinson analyzes Channing's idea of self-culture, focusing on his interpretation and use of Samuel Hopkins's doctrine of "disinterested benevolence."]

In assessing the importance of William Ellery Channing to his generation, Ralph Waldo Emerson pronounced him "our Bishop" and put in sharp focus what was for him an intellectual problem, and what has remained for us a historical one. It is not the word "bishop" that is problematic, for almost no one disputed the leadership of Channing in the first decades of the nineteenth century, that crucially formative period for our culture. . . . The problem with Emerson's phrase "our Bishop" is rather with the word "our," for Emerson's use of it as the leader of the transcendentalist movement presumably implied a claim by that movement on the influence of Channing for their own party. As for the justice of that claim, one can only observe that it has been debated within every generation since Channing's death, and shows no signs of being settled now. What is important is that not only did Emerson and his compatriots make a concerted effort to claim Channing as their own, but their intellectual opposition did also, and by midcentury the term "Channing Unitarianism" became a shorthand for traditional, Christological, conservative, and denominationally oriented Unitarianism.

That both these groups could look back to Channing not only as founder but as a continuing source of moral inspiration is a good example of what Ahlstrom has called "the mystery of Channing," a puzzling but undeniable influence that continues to render him a "spiritual guide" for a very diverse group of followers. . . . I hope to contribute to the solution of the mystery by pointing to what is not, strictly speaking, a theological doctrine of Channing, but rather an imaginative construct that is as much symbol or image as logical affirmation, and was probably more evocative to his followers than any doctrine he ever preached. It was Channing's repeated insistence that the soul could grow—that it was a living thing not unlike a plant or animal, and that, like a plant, with careful culture it could be nurtured to develop a certain potentiality of its nature. Parched New England simply drank this notion in, for it transformed the dead weight of Puritan moral discipline into a process of patient nurture, and threw a new and softer light on the ingrained habit of introspection. (pp. 221-23)

The origin of anything so complex as an idea or intellectual construct is virtually impossible to pinpoint, but in the case of Channing's idea of self-culture, we can come as close as we are ever likely to get in such an attempt. To do so we have to return to a certain clump of willows in Cambridge in the late 1790s, where Channing found himself in a state of mystical transport while reading the works of the moral philosopher, Francis Hutcheson. "I longed to die, and felt as if heaven alone could give room for the exercise of such emotion," Channing remembered, and he dated his spiritual progress from that moment of inspiration. Hutcheson was a popular thinker in those days, but not known ordinarily to produce such effects, so it is evident that the young Channing was fertile ground for his speculations. The nature of those speculations centered around Hutcheson's concept of the "moral sense," an innate power for discriminating between right and wrong that he posed against prevalent theories of virtue as self-interest. This concept was the core of Hutcheson's writings, and closely related to it was a concept of *"disinterested affection,"* a capacity for acting wholly apart from, or even in opposition to, one's personal advantage, in deference to a worthier goal. Such an emotion established in Hutcheson's view "a *universal determination* to *benevolence* in mankind." Although he recognized the possibility of the degeneration of the moral sense, like any other sense, he also argued for its universal availability to mankind, and commented that its presence in human nature "is one of the strongest evidences of goodness in the Author of nature." Such a vision of human capacity and Divine benevolence triggered Channing's rapture, and offered him the fundamentals of a theological program which he eventually elaborated as leader of New England's liberal movement in theology. (pp. 223-24)

Channing was not the first New Englander to seize upon the idea of disinterestedness as a theological tool of some value. The term "disinterested benevolence" became the central concept in the system of the great Calvinist and heir to Jonathan Edwards, Samuel Hopkins.

Hopkins holds the distinction of being at once the most distinguished Calvinist thinker of his day, and also the man most responsible, unintentionally of course, for Calvinism's loss of its hold on the American popular mind. In a further irony, the term most clearly responsible for the alienation of many readers from Hopkins is also the term which in many ways accounts for Channing's appeal: disinterestedness. The vast difference lies in the use to which the two men put the idea. Hopkins bases his major work, *The System of Doctrines,* on the proposition "that holiness consists in disinterested benevolence, which is in the nature of it, and in all its exercises, wholly contrary and opposed to self love." This was not a startling, nor even a particularly controversial doctrine when it was published in 1793, but with a remorseless logic, Hopkins wrung from it a corollary which stirred even those New Englanders

who were not theologically inclined. The corollary was that the supreme test of disinterested benevolence was the willingness to sacrifice oneself, even to the point of suffering eternal damnation, for the greater glory of God. This notion made Hopkins, as Lawrence Buell has aptly put it, "the bogeyman of late Puritan theology," and with the possible exception of the doctrine of infant damnation, it caused more sheer terror, and eventually more disgust, than any theological idea in American history. John White Chadwick, a later biographer of Channing, could not resist a bit of sarcasm respecting that doctrine when he tried to explain just how Hopkins's system was an advance over that of his Calvinist predecessors:

> We think of him as the teacher of a horrible theology, but in his day he was a radical, and his theology was more human than that from which it appealed. Even his favorite proposition was an advance. Jonathan Edwards had got no further than that we should be willing to see our friends and near relations damned for the glory of God.

Obviously, such a doctrine gave the liberal Unitarians who rebelled against it a powerful polemical position: And what kind of God, they asked, could be glorified by such a sacrifice?

It was Channing who was most responsible for articulating that response, even though he later listed Hopkins along with Hutcheson as a major influence, citing specifically Hopkins's "theory of disinterestedness." That two minds as different as Hopkins and Channing could find common ground in this concept illustrates the influence of emotion and sensibility, as well as logic, in intellectual history. Despite the similarities in their superficially austere demeanor, Channing was turned not toward the eighteenth century, but toward Wordsworth and the new romanticism, a disposition which allowed him to embrace the idea of disinterestedness, and then make far different use of it than Hopkins did. Disinterested benevolence was not a yardstick with which to measure human depravity, as Hopkins would have it, but rather a suggestion of a divine principle within human nature which could be infinitely cultivated. For Hopkins disinterestedness was an impossible standard; for Channing it was a living and growing principle.

Even though there was no one who detested sectarian controversy more, Channing molded his philosophy during the Unitarian controversy with Calvinism, a long-simmering dispute which broke into the open when Boston liberals were accused not only of holding heretical positions, but of hiding them. Channing led the liberal response, which was partly self-defense, but which also included a frontal assault on Calvinism, the nature of which is suggested by one of Channing's pieces entitled **"The Moral Argument Against Calvinism."** The point was that aside from any questions of logical truth or consistency, Calvinism fostered moral degeneracy by inculcating corrupt views of God and man, thereby stunting the initiative and aspiration that were essential for moral development. To the adherents of Calvinism, who had made acute moral sensitivity a hallmark of their system, this must have been a painful attack. Never one to pull his punches, Channing flatly argued that "Calvinism owes its perpetuity to the influence of fear in palsying the moral nature." Its major weakness is its "inconsistency . . . with the divine perfections" which renders it contradictory to "our ideas of goodness and justice." He went on in this piece to describe the Calvinist God as one who creates men in corruption, "withholds the grace which is necessary to their recovery, and condemns them to 'most grievous torments in soul and body without intermission in hell-fire for ever'.'' Such a deity, he suggests, in perhaps his most daring insult, can only be regarded as ''heathen.'' As he put it, ''A man of plain sense, whose spirit had not been broken to this creed by education or terror, will think that it is not necessary for us to travel to heathen countries to learn how mournfully the human mind may misrepresent the Deity.''

These are fiery polemics indeed, but Channing felt that he undertook such an attack out of necessity rather than choice, and dreaded the personal rancor that theological debate often spawned. He also recognized that the denial of a doctrine did not in itself constitute intellectual progress. Calvinism, he argued, ''has passed its meridian, and is sinking to rise no more,'' a victim of ''the progress of the human mind, and . . . the progress of the spirit of the gospel.'' ''Progress,'' and any of a number of other words that signified growth and development, were central to Channing, and in almost all of his polemical writings he returned to a core of affirmation that he hoped would overshadow the disputation. In **''The Moral Argument Against Calvinism,''** the text that has concerned us so far, that affirmative core is Channing's appeal to the conscience, which he terms ''the primary law of our nature'' and ''our sole capacity for religion.''

What Channing here calls conscience was a version of the moral sense or the moral faculty, very close to that propounded by Hutcheson and others in the eighteenth century. But in Channing's hands, and also in those of Emerson, the moral sense signified more than what Channing here calls ''the power of perceiving moral distinctions,'' and took on dynamic qualities that link it closely with that central faculty in romantic thought, the imagination. It meant not only the ability to judge, but the power to aspire. An entry from Emerson's journal in the 1820s argued that the function of moral sense is ''to point to a faultless and unattainable perfection,'' or further, ''to be an index of the Creator's character . . . in . . . illustration of the command—'Be Ye perfect as He is perfect'.'' In his treatise against Calvinism, Channing had argued in a similar vein that the moral sense alone gives man the ability to make judgments about God, providing the power to recognize attributes of Deity such as ''benevolence, equity, and righteousness.'' This was a point which he would expand during the 1820s, giving it particular emphasis in his well-known sermon of 1828, **''Likeness to God.''** There he boldly turned ordinary Christian perceptions around by arguing that our perception of God was completely dependent on conscience, rather than conscience being dependent upon God, and asserted that it was rightly called ''the Divinity within us.'' The extreme importance of conscience reflected the fact that ''the glory of the Supreme Being is eminently moral.'' Thus, the fine line that separated the created being from the Creator was obscured by Channing, who insisted on the one hand on the fatherhood of God and the necessity of our filial relationship with him, but emphasized on the other that ''the idea of God, sublime and awful as it is, is the idea of our own spiritual nature, purified and enlarged to infinity.'' It was not Channing's intention to call into question the ontological status of God, though his statement can be inferred to have certain affinities with the modernist vision of God as the imaginative creation of man. He hoped to emphasize instead that ''in ourselves are the elements of the Divinity,'' a point that did not call into question God's origin, but rather attempted to heal the split between God and humanity that he felt Calvinism had created. The essence of religion as Channing defines it is ''a growing likeness to the Supreme Being'' made possible by the ''traces of infinity in the human mind.'' Re-

ligion thus becomes a process of cultivation, of bringing this infinite potential into ever-increasing reality in the moral and spiritual life. If the notion of ''traces of infinity'' begins to sound vague, Channing specifies them primarily in terms of the intellectual and artistic life—''original thought, . . . the creations of genius, . . . the soarings of imagination, . . . its love of beauty and grandeur''—but he adds that the most important sign of the mind's infinity is a moral one, ''disinterestedness.'' Samuel Hopkins quite probably turned in his grave to hear his category put to such a use, but if Channing so much as paused before pronouncing the mind both infinite and perfectible, there is no indication of it.

It is easy to take the notion of self-culture that I have been describing here as a program of self-aggrandizement with disturbingly asocial and egotistical overtones. And in fact, as the doctrine was watered down and divorced from its theological roots during the course of the nineteenth century, it gradually lent itself to the various popular theories of the ''self-made man,'' becoming a kind of ideology for the robber baron. Although in its context it seems much less harsh, the following quotation from Emerson's ''Self-Reliance'' can strike one as a kind of invitation to irresponsibility:

> Then, again, do not tell me, as a good man did to-day, of my obligation to put all poor men in good situations. Are they *my* poor? I tell thee, thou foolish philanthropist, that I grudge the dollar, the dime, the cent I give to such men as do not belong to me and to whom I do not belong . . .though I confess with shame I sometimes succumb and give the dollar it is a wicked dollar, which by and by I shall have the manhood to withhold.

It is therefore essential to keep the metaphysical basis of Channing's idea in mind, and to remember the importance of its historical context. In his recent indictment of contemporary America, *The Culture of Narcissism,* Christopher Lasch was careful to distinguish the modern ''narcissist'' from various species of nineteenth-century American individualism. Lasch's discrimination is an important one, and although he himself does not make this point, I would argue that the conception of self based on the theological and metaphysical assumptions that we can see working in Channing accounts in part for this distinction. Channing's religious assumptions not only placed the emphasis on the self, but when rightly seen, served to prevent a slide into pure self-absorption that was a potential threat.

The doctrine of God's immanence is the most salient characteristic of those assumptions, best expressed in Channing's dictum from **''Likeness to God'':** ''The creation is a birth and shining forth of the Divine Mind.'' While God's immanence is usually linked with a theology of nature and even theories of pantheism, the important realization for Channing was that God, as mind, manifested himself in the human mind. So close was the connection between the Divine and human mind that he at one point asserted that ''God is another name for human intelligence raised above all error and imperfection, and extended to all possible truth.'' This of course did not rule out for Channing the presence of God in nature—an idea that the transcendentalists of a generation later would seize upon more avidly—but he did emphasize that ''we see God around us because He dwells within us'' and almost always returned his discourses to a devotional emphasis on this fact of the God within. In a vein that followed romantic thinking generally, he argued that "the beauty of the outward creation is . . . the emblem or expression" of the soul.

Out of this doctrine of the God within, Channing was able to fashion a definition of religion as progressive moral activity, a process of "growing likeness to the Supreme Being" that at its best held the elements of devotionalism and moralism in a fine balance. There is a potential problem, however, which emerges when we hold the ideas of the divine presence and human progress side by side, for the idea of divine presence, of God immanent within the soul, seems to undercut the imperative for progress and growth which is so persistent in Channing's writings. If Channing seriously meant that the mind was infinite, what room did that claim leave for progress? We can see this problem at its acutest in an 1815 sermon, **"Indications of Immortality."** In elaborating a theory of human nature, Channing rises to a pair of rhetorical questions, each of which grasps one pole of the paradox: "Is not *perfection*, then, the end of his being? Is he not made to advance, to ascend, forever?" Perfection, in the ordinary sense of the word, would exclude advancement, since the very possibility of advancement or progress implies that a state of perfection has not yet been reached. Yet Channing poses these questions with no apparent sense of difficulty, reminding us that he is indeed the spiritual father of Emerson, who claimed that "a foolish consistency is the hobgoblin of little minds." (pp. 225-30)

It was neither naiveté nor an Emersonian disdain for consistency that accounts for Channing's apparent contradiction, however, but instead a rather special conception of "the perfect" as it applied to mind and spirit. What distinguished mind from matter, and established the immortal nature of mind, was an infinite capacity for expansion. Channing pursues this point at length in a sermon on **"Immortality,"** in which the analogy of the growth of a tree, as a material entity, is used to indicate the unique qualities of mind. After reaching a certain stage of growth, bearing "leaves, flowers, and fruit," the tree's design is fulfilled, and "the principle of life within it can effect no more." But the mind, he argues, never seems to reach such a stage at which we pronounce its design fulfilled. For the mind,

> perfection consists not in fixed, prescribed effects, not in exact and defined attainments, but in an original, creative, unconfinable energy, which yields new products, which carries it into new fields of thought and new efforts for religion and humanity.

Channing's striking insight is that mental and spiritual growth—and these two terms are almost interchangeable in this instance—leads to further mental and spiritual growth. Mental progress creates further mental capacity, and that in turn leads to further mental progress. It was for this reason that Channing could hazard the potential contradiction between progress and perfection, eluding the entire issue by defining perfection as progress. This he did, in fact, as early as 1810: "Do you ask in what this perfection [of mind] consists? I answer, in *knowledge*, in *love*, and in *activity*." This activity was a constant reaching out to stages of growth which always revealed another stage beyond. (pp. 230-31)

By positing a concept of continual growth and self-culture, Channing had solved for himself some vexing problems about the nature and availability of perfection for the soul. But while his conception of progress on the one hand explicitly denied an end to it, on the other hand it implied in fact that there was an end, the achievement of a nature identical to that of God.

That which distinguishes progress from mere motion is a goal or an end, and in Channing's discussions of the progress of the soul, God is always implied as the goal of culture. The fact that progress toward that goal is continual suggests that Channing was on the verge of a conception of God as himself growing, a God of process that we now think of in terms of the work of Alfred North Whitehead and Charles Hartshorne. But Channing never made such an idea explicit, and his work stands as a point of emergence, retaining some elements of the older world of fixed and permanent entities, while it strained at the bounds of that world through its doctrine of perpetual progress. (p. 233)

> *David Robinson, "The Legacy of Channing: Culture as a Religious Category in New England Thought," in* Harvard Theological Review, *Vol. 74, No. 2, April, 1981, pp. 221-39.*

ADDITIONAL BIBLIOGRAPHY

Bartlett, Irving H. Introduction to *William Ellery Channing: Unitarian Christianity and Other Essays,* by William Ellery Channing, edited by Irving H. Bartlett, pp. vii-xxx. American Heritage Series, edited by Oskar Piest, no. 21. New York: Liberal Arts Press, 1957.
> An overview of Channing's theological beliefs that incorporates biographical details.

Bratton, Fred Gladstone. "New England Unitarianism." In his *The Legacy of the Liberal Spirit: Men and Movements in the Making of Modern Thought*, pp. 183-200. New York: Charles Scribner's Sons, 1943.
> Examines the lives of Emerson, Thoreau, and Channing and compares their contributions to New England Unitarianism. Bratton states that, of the three, Channing "perhaps deserves the most important niche in the history of American liberalism."

Brooks, Van Wyck. "The New Age in Boston and Cambridge." In his *The Flowering of New England, 1815-1865*, pp. 89-110. New York: E. P. Dutton & Co., 1936.
> Portrays Channing as the "great religious figure" among the circle of Bostonians that included Daniel Webster, George Ticknor, and other luminaries.

Brown, Arthur W. *Always Young for Liberty: A Biography of William Ellery Channing.* Syracuse, N.Y.: Syracuse University Press, 1956, 268 p.
> A biography that focuses on Channing's position of leadership in nineteenth-century America.

Chadwick, John White. *William Ellery Channing: Minister of Religion*. Cambridge: Houghton, Mifflin and Co., Riverside Press, 1903, 463 p.
> A highly regarded early biography, written by a Unitarian minister.

[Channing, William Henry.] *Memoir of William Ellery Channing, with Extracts from His Correspondence and Manuscripts.* 3 vols. Boston: American Unitarian Association, 1848.
> An early biography written by Channing's nephew. Critics generally agree that although this work provides insight into Channing's character, it is factually inaccurate at times.

Delbanco, Andrew. *William Ellery Channing: An Essay on the Liberal Spirit in America.* Cambridge: Harvard University Press, 1981, 203 p.
> Examines Channing's philosophical views Delbanco claims that Channing lived a life of "unresolved uncertainty," dissatisfied with the religious orthodoxy of his day, yet unwilling to embrace transcendentalism.

Doubleday, Neal F. "Channing on the Nature of Man." *The Journal of Religion* XXIII, No. 4 (October 1943): 245-57.

Discusses Channing's teachings on the goodness of humanity and their influence on American literature.

Downs, Lenthiel H. "Emerson and Dr. Channing: Two Men from Boston." *The New England Quarterly* XX, No. 4 (December 1947): 516-34.
Compares the philosophical beliefs of Channing and Emerson.

Eliot, Charles W. "Channing." In his *Four American Leaders,* pp. 59-71. Boston: Beacon Press, 1906.
The text of a commemorative speech Eliot delivered in 1903 at the unveiling of the Channing statue in Boston.

Fabian, Bernhard. "The Channing Revival: Remarks on Recent Publications." *Jahrbuch für Amerikastudien* 2 (1957): 197-212.
Reviews the modern reassessment of Channing's work.

Frothingham, Paul Revere. *William Ellery Channing: His Messages from the Spirit.* Cambridge: Houghton, Mifflin and Co., Riverside Press, 1903, 52 p.
An anecdotal account of Channing's life and beliefs.

Goddard, Harold Clarke. "Transcendentalism." In *The Cambridge History of American Literature,* Vol. I, edited by William Peterfield Trent and others, pp. 326-48. New York: Macmillan Co., 1933.
A historical survey of transcendentalism in which Channing is presented as "the bridge between Unitarianism and transcendentalism."

Gray, Joseph M. M. "William Ellery Channing: A Theological Hamlet." In his *Prophets of the Soul,* pp. 113-37. New York: Abingdon Press, 1936.
Surveys Channing's life and thought. Gray views Channing as a Hamlet-like character because his "progress . . . was always by advance and recession, so that before he ever came to an unqualified position, he was generally considered to be now on one side and now on the other."

Haroutunian, Joseph. "The Unitarian Revolt." In his *Piety versus Moralism: The Passing of the New England Theology,* pp. 177-219. New York: Henry Holt and Co., 1932.
Recounts the history of the Unitarian movement, briefly examining Channing's role in its development.

Hastings, Hester. *William Ellery Channing and l'Académie des sciences morales et politiques 1870: "L'etude sur Channing" and the "Lost" Prize Essay.* Providence, R.I.: Brown University Press, 1959, 61 p.
Analyzes two nineteenth-century French-language essays on Channing. Hastings also gives an account of Channing's favorable critical reception in nineteenth-century France.

Higginson, Thomas Wentworth. "Two New England Heretics: Channing and Parker." *The Independent* LIV, No. 2790 (22 May 1902): 1234-36.
Contends that Channing eventually came to share Parker's belief in the "simple humanity" of Christ.

Hochmuth, Marie. "William Ellery Channing, New England Conversationalist." *The Quarterly Journal of Speech* XXX, No. 4 (December 1944): 429-39.
Examines Channing's development as a conversationalist. Hochmuth asserts that "Channing as a conversationalist in America shares the reputation that Coleridge enjoyed in England."

Lyons, Nathan. "The Figure of William Ellery Channing." *The Michigan Quarterly Review* VII, No. 2 (Spring 1968): 120-26.
A biographical portrait that includes a positive assessment of Channing's literary and philosophical accomplishments.

Martineau, Harriet. "Channing." In her *Retrospect of Western Travel,* Vol. II, pp. 117-28. London: Saunders and Otley, 1838.
An anecdotal account of Channing's abolitionist activities.

Mead, Edwin D. Introduction to *Discourses on War,* by William Ellery Channing, pp. v-lxi. Boston: For the International Union by Ginn & Co., 1903.

A biographical sketch that focuses on Channing's position regarding war and democracy.

Mendelsohn, Jack. *Channing: The Reluctant Radical.* Boston: Little, Brown and Co., 1971, 308 p.
A critical biography emphasizing the complexity of Channing's personality and his broad-mindedness as a theologian.

Meyer, Donald H. "William Ellery Channing and the Inward Enlightenment." In his *The Democratic Enlightenment,* pp. 199-209. New York: G. P. Putnam's Sons, Capricorn Books, 1976.
Presents Channing as a post-Enlightenment intellectual who used philosophical inquiry "not to eradicate error or clarify thought" but rather to defend his already existing religious beliefs.

Peabody, Elizabeth Palmer. *Reminiscences of Rev. Wm. Ellery Channing, D.D.* Boston: Roberts Brothers, 1880, 459 p.
Recollections of Channing by his personal secretary. Peabody includes some of Channing's letters along with her reminiscences.

Pearson, Samuel C., Jr. "All Things New: Images of Man in Early Nineteenth Century America." *Encounter: Creative Theological Scholarship* 35, No. 1 (Winter 1974): 1-13.
Describes the philosophical contributions that Channing, Alexander Campbell, and Horace Bushnell made to nineteenth-century ideas concerning the state of humanity. Pearson underscores the emphasis Channing placed upon humankind's reasoning abilities and potential greatness.

Puknat, Siegfried B. "Channing and German Thought." *Proceedings of the American Philosophical Society* 101, No. 2 (19 April 1957): 195-203.
Discusses Channing's familiarity with German philosophy and literature.

Reinhardt, John E. "The Evolution of William Ellery Channing's Sociopolitical Ideas." *American Literature* XXVI, No. 2 (May 1954): 154-65.
Examines the development of Channing's sociopolitical beliefs as evidenced in his writings. Reinhardt argues that Channing suffered "personal disillusionment because of his unsuccessful efforts to juxtapose the principle of coercive sovereignty and that of benevolent social action."

Rice, Madeleine Hooke. "William Ellery Channing: The Making of a Social Gospel." *Proceedings of the American Philosophical Society* 97, No. 1 (14 February 1953): 31-43.
Describes Channing's life as a Boston minister.

———. *Federal Street Pastor: The Life of William Ellery Channing.* New York: Bookman Associates, 1961, 360 p.
A detailed introductory study of Channing's life and works.

Robison, Lois R. "William Ellery Channing." In *Founders of Christian Movements,* edited by Philip Henry Lotz, pp. 134-42. Creative Personalities Series, edited by Philip Henry Lotz, vol. III. New York: Association Press, 1941.
A brief account of Channing's life, works, and beliefs.

Rowe, Henry Kalloch. "William Ellery Channing." In his *Modern Pathfinders of Christianity: The Lives and Deeds of Seven Centuries of Christian Leaders,* pp. 172-83. 1928. Reprint. Essay Index Reprint Series. Freeport, N.Y.: Books for Libraries Press, 1968.
Outlines the basic tenets of Unitarianism and Channing's reaction to them.

Rusterholtz, Wallace P. "William Ellery Channing: Gentleman Reformer." In his *American Heretics and Saints,* pp. 145-76. Boston: Manthorne & Burack, 1938.
Divides Channing's career as a minister into three periods. According to Rusterholtz, during the first period Channing "de-Calvinized theology and then emphasized ethics at the expense of theology; in his second period, he reformed his theology to fit his ethics; and in his final period he fused the new ethics and theology into a humanitarian philosophy of life."

Schneider, Herbert Wallace. ''The Intellectual Background of William Ellery Channing.'' *Church History* VII (March 1938): 3-23.

A chronological study of Channing's intellectual development as revealed in his writings. Schneider attempts to show that Channing's thought represented the culmination of the ideals of the American Enlightenment.

Schuster, Eunice Minette. *Native American Anarchism: A Study of Left-Wing American Individualism.* Smith College Studies in History, edited by John C. Hildt, William Dodge Gray, and Harold Underwood Faulkner, vol. XVII, nos. 1-4 (October 1931-July 1932). Northampton, Mass.: Department of History of Smith College, 1932, 202 p.

Presents Channing as a religious anarchist who challenged Calvinistic doctrines through his emphasis on ''positive individualism.''

Stephenson, George M. ''The Unitarian Movement.'' In his *The Puritan Heritage*, pp. 114-28. New York: Macmillan Co., 1952.

Explains Channing's role in the development of Unitarianism.

Sweet, William Warren. ''Leaders of Christian Thought.'' In his *Makers of Christianity: From John Cotton to Lyman Abbott*, pp. 279-333. New York: Henry Holt and Co., 1937.

Includes a brief treatment of Channing's place in nineteenth-century religious history.

Thurston, Charles Rawson. ''The Homes and Haunts of Channing.'' *The New England Magazine* n.s. XV, No. 4 (December 1896): 417-31.

A description of Channing's residences that incorporates biographical details.

Tiffany, Nina Moore. ''William Ellery Channing.'' In her *Pathbreakers*, pp. 3-30. Boston: Beacon Press, 1949.

An introductory sketch of Channing's life.

Virtanen, Reino. ''Tocqueville and William Ellery Channing.'' *The New England Quarterly* 22, No. 1 (March 1950): 21-8.

Suggests that Channing's ''Remarks on National Literature'' may have influenced the French writer Alexis de Tocqueville's evaluation of American literature.

Wagenknecht, Edward. ''William Ellery Channing: Messages from the Spirit.'' In his *Ambassadors for Christ: Seven American Preachers*, pp. 40-67. New York: Oxford University Press, 1972.

A biographical account that includes a description of Channing's reputation among his contemporaries.

Joseph Arthur (Comte) de Gobineau

1816-1882

French essayist, historian, novelist, short story writer, poet, biographer, and critic.

Gobineau was an influential nineteenth-century French man of letters who was one of the first writers to propound the idea of Aryan superiority as a scientific theory. He is chiefly remembered as the author of *Essai sur l'inégalité des races humaines* (commonly known as *Essay on the Inequality of the Human Races)*, a controversial social and political history in which race is held to be the motivating factor behind world events. In contrast to previous historians who believed that the past had been shaped by a series of military battles, political struggles, and the actions of great individuals, he argued that the course of civilizations depends only upon blood race and that the unchecked assimilation of races, especially the mixing of so-called ''inferior'' blood with that of ''superior'' Aryans, leads to cultural decay. While the *Essay* remains his most well-known work, Gobineau also wrote novels and short stories, which are generally considered minor today.

Gobineau was born at Ville d'Avray, near Paris, into a family of the lesser nobility, whose aristocratic heritage greatly influenced many of his writings. Educated by private tutors at home and at the College of Bienne in Switzerland, he early developed an enduring interest in literature and languages, intensively studying German, Latin, and Persian. He went to Paris in the mid-1830s to seek his fortune in the business world, but soon turned to writing. He worked steadily through the 1840s, contributing literary and political articles to respected journals and publishing his first full-length work, a three-act play entitled *Les adieux de Don Juan,* as well as several novels. His income from writing did not satisfy him, however, and Gobineau considered diplomacy as a career. His chance came in 1849 when his close friend Alexis de Tocqueville, the celebrated author of *Democracy in America,* was appointed French foreign minister and made Gobineau the head of his cabinet. Although the ministry lasted only a few months, it enabled Gobineau to join the French diplomatic service. From 1849, when he became first secretary to the French legation at Berne, to almost the end of his life, Gobineau held a succession of diplomatic posts in different parts of the world, including Switzerland, Germany, Newfoundland, Persia, Greece, Brazil, and Sweden. His impressions of these places served as the basis for many of his works. Shortly after the publication of the final part of the *Essay* in 1855, Gobineau went to Tehran, and his experiences there proved especially influential: upon his return to France, he wrote a fictional account of his Eastern sojourn, *Trois ans en Asie,* and several other works relating to Persian history and culture. The following years saw more travel and writing: Gobineau wrote three of his best-known works of fiction, *Souvenirs de voyage (The Crimson Handkerchief and Other Stories), Les pléiades (The Pleiads),* and *Nouvelles asiatiques (Romances of the East),* and completed a study of the Italian Renaissance. He retired from diplomatic service in 1877 and settled in Italy, where he devoted his time to sculpture and writing. He continued to travel, returning often to France, but his health gradually worsened. He died of apoplexy at Turin in 1882.

Gobineau is primarily known as a racial theorist, but he wrote in a wide variety of genres with varying degrees of success. He began by composing historical and romantic adventure novels. Although most of these early works were not favorably noticed by contemporary reviewers and are now usually passed over as inferior to his later productions, modern critics have noted his idealization of romantic love, a theme that was to interest Gobineau throughout his writing career. Following the publication of the *Essay* and his residence in Persia, Gobineau devoted himself to Eastern subjects. He composed several nonfiction works over a period of about ten years, notably *Les religions et les philosophies dans l'Asie centrale* and *Histoire des perses (The World of the Persians),* the former a close study of Asian culture, the latter a comprehensive history of Persia. Gobineau's Asian experiences also provided the foundation for two collections, *The Crimson Handkerchief* and *Romances of the East,* both of which contain stories of sentimental love set against exotic backgrounds. According to critics, these tales, like his other imaginative works, reveal his gift for storytelling, irony, humor, and acute psychological perception. Some scholars have argued that these stories also show his preoccupation with individualism and with an aristocracy of spirit displayed by superior members of society. These concerns are evident in all his works written after the *Essay* and especially prominent in his novel *The Pleiads:* ''the book of an aristocrat,'' Gobineau wrote, ''which opposes the conversation of exceptional beings to the confused clamor of the masses.'' In this work, he again depicts idealized love, through which his heroes and heroines achieve nobility. Indeed, Gobineau's concern with an aristocracy of spirit characterizes two other late works, *La renaissance (The Renaissance)* and *L'histoire d'Ottar Jarl*. In *The Renaissance,* a set of historical portraits of Renaissance figures written in dialogue form, Gobineau extols the individual, demonstrating his appreciation for an age in which the most intelligent, capable, daring, energetic, and brave people were able to flourish. In *Ottar Jarl,* he pursued a different approach; in this family history, Gobineau traces his ancestry back to Ottar Jarl, a famous Norwegian pirate and member of a royal race descended from the god Odin. Gobineau's imaginative writings were, for the most part, reviewed when first published and then largely ignored in the late nineteenth and early twentieth centuries. In recent years, however, some scholars have attempted to deflect critical attention away from the *Essay,* arguing that Gobineau's imaginative works form the basis of his enduring reputation.

Essay on the Inequality of the Human Races is Gobineau's most closely studied work, as well as his most controversial one. The author set out to determine why civilizations rise and fall, constructing a comprehensive philosophy of history founded on the systematic description and classification of races. Gobineau divided human beings into a hierarchy of three distinct races: the black race, the lowest in the hierarchy, which is characterized by limited intellect, unpredictable mood shifts, sensuality, and disdain for human life and suffering, but also strong artistic instincts as well as great energy and will; the yellow race, which represents mediocrity, is stubborn and apathetic, but ordered and practical; and the white race, which is marked by superior intelligence, physical strength, respect for life and liberty, and a strong sense of self-preservation. The white race, according to Gobineau, is composed of Chamites, Semites, and Japhetides, the latter branch including Aryans, the pinnacle of civilization. This branch, he further theorized, spread from the central Asian plateau and formed the Hindu, Iranian, Hellenic, Celtic, Slavonic, and Germanic peoples. The concept underlying Gobineau's racist doctrine is that of racial determinism, the belief that permanent intellectual and physiological qualities belong to races, are passed on genetically, and are unaffected by education or environment. Gobineau argued that civilizations decay through the mixing of races, but he also maintained that limited crossbreeding is sometimes beneficial, especially when the merging of compatible temperaments takes place. As an example, Gobineau indicated that the mixing of the blood of blacks and whites may yield an artistic temperament governed by reason—an advantageous result that may temporarily lead to cultural advancement. He emphasized, however, that the mixing of races inevitably leads to cultural and political degeneration and the collapse of civilization. Gobineau was thus profoundly pessimistic about the future of civilization—''We do not come from the ape but we are rapidly getting there,'' he once claimed.

Gobineau's *Essay* is important not only as a historical and theoretical document, but also for its influence on later thinkers. The work was not initially well received in France: it languished in the bookshops and was largely overlooked by the press and the learned reviews. In private correspondence with Gobineau, Tocqueville commented: ''[I] think your book is fated to return to France from abroad, especially from Germany. Alone in Europe, the Germans possess the particular talent of becoming impassioned with what they take as abstract truths, without considering their practical consequences.'' Indeed it was outside France, principally in Germany, that the *Essay* enjoyed its greatest early success, and it was briefly popular among American anti-abolitionists, whose selective reading of the work supported their proslavery stance. In Germany, the English-born racial theorist Houston Stewart Chamberlain took the essay as the starting point for his 1899 study, *Grundlagen des neunzehnten Jahrhunderts,* in which he eagerly promoted Aryanism and strongly condemned Jews as evil. Chamberlain, like many of Gobineau's intellectual heirs, failed to acknowledge his debt to Gobineau and in fact stated his opposition to him on many issues, but critics challenge his claims of originality. By the early twentieth century, the *Essay* had, as Tocqueville predicted, returned to France: the work was embraced by a host of French admirers who styled themselves ''Gobineans,'' and clubs were formed for the study of Gobineau's thought. The *Essay* enjoyed great popularity among the Nazis, who used it selectively as a political instrument of racism, ignoring Gobineau's original intent of illustrating the irrevocable decline of society. Many critics agree that Adolf Hitler, for example, strongly echoed the pro-Aryan passages of the work in several sections of *Mein Kampf,* and others note that Nazi writer Alfred Rosenberg relied heavily on the *Essay* for many of his racist tracts and studies. By World War II, the work had been misread and interpolated to the point where it was rarely represented fairly or without ulterior motive. Since that time, scholars have attempted to approach the work objectively, exposing what they see as the discrete fallacies and shortcomings of its thesis, rather than condemning or praising it outright. Gobineau's literary style has also been examined closely in recent years, with commentators—especially in France and Germany—agreeing that the author's treatment of his subject was direct and clear. Today, Gobineau is widely considered a capable writer and a gifted and sincere, if misguided, thinker.

''You consider yourself a man of the past,'' wrote Princess Carolyn von Sayn-Wittgenstein to Gobineau; ''I am firmly convinced you are a man of the Future.'' Gobineau did not anticipate the legacy and impact of his *Essay,* nor is it likely he would have encouraged it. Rather, critics note that he planned his best-known work as a historical study of the rise and fall of civilizations, not as a racist diatribe directed against non-Aryans, and never advocated action based on his conclusions. Over the years, however, the *Essay* has been alternately revered, denounced, and misrepresented, and commentators remain at odds about the value of the work. Critics also disagree about the importance of Gobineau's imaginative writings, while praising his psychological acuity, descriptive powers, and narrative skill. Yet despite the controversy generated by his writings, Gobineau's *Essay* remains one of the most influential historical works ever written.

PRINCIPAL WORKS

Les adieux de Don Juan [first publication]   (drama)   1844
La chronique rimée de Jean Chouan et de ses compagnons
     (poetry)   1846
*Le prisonnier chanceux; ou, Les aventures de Jean de la
     Tour-Miracle*   (novel)   1846; published in periodical
     La quotidienne
[*The Lucky Prisoner,* 1926]
L'abbaye de Typhaines   (novel)   1847; published in
     periodical *Le conservateur*
     [*Typhaines Abbey: A Tale of the Twelfth Century,* 1869;
     also published as *The Rose of Typhaines: A Tale of the
     Communes in the Twelfth Century,* 1872]

Les aventures de Nicolas Belavoir (novel) 1847;
    published in periodical *L'union monarchique*
Mademoiselle Irnois (novel) 1847; published in periodical
    Le national
Octave et Marguerite (novel) 1847; published in
    periodical *Le journal des debats;* also published as
    Ternove, 1848
Essai sur l'inégalité des races humaines. 4 vols. (essay)
    1853-55
    [*The Moral and Intellectual Diversity of Races, with
    Particular Reference to Their Respective Influence in
    the Civil and Political History of Mankind* (partial
    translation), 1856; also published as *The Inequality of
    Human Races* (partial translation), 1915]
Lectures des textes cunéiformes (essays) 1858
Trois ans en Asie (short stories) 1859
Voyage à Terre-Neuve (sketches) 1861
Traité des écritures cunéiformes (essay) 1864
Les religions et les philosophies dans l'Asie centrale
    (essay) 1865
*Histoire des perses, d'après les auteurs orientaux, grecs, et
    latins, et particulièrement d'après les manuscrits
    orientaux inédits* (history) 1869
    [*The World of the Persians*, 1971]
*Souvenirs de voyage (short stories) 1872
    [*The Crimson Handkerchief and Other Stories*, 1927]
Les pléiades (novel) 1874
    [*The Pleiads*, 1928; also published as *Sons of Kings*,
    1966]
Nouvelles asiatiques (short stories) 1876
    [*Romances of the East*, 1878; also published as *Five
    Oriental Tales*, 1925; *The Dancing Girl of Shamakha,
    and Other Asiatic Tales*, 1926; and *Tales of Asia*, 1947]
*La renaissance: Savonarole, César Borgia, Jules II, Léon X,
    Michel-Ange; Scènes historiques* (biographical
    sketches) 1877
    [*The Renaissance: Savonarola, Cesare Borgia, Julius II,
    Leo X, Michael Angelo*, 1913]
*L'histoire d'Ottar Jarl, pirate norvégien, conquérant du
    pays de Bray, en Normandie, et de sa descendance*
    (history) 1879
***Correspondance entre Alexis de Tocqueville et Arthur de
    Gobineau, 1843-1859* (letters) 1908
La fleur d'or (essays) 1917
    [*The Golden Flower*, 1924]
*Études critiques (1844-1848): Balzac, Alfred de Musset,
    Théophile Gautier, Henri Heine, Jules Janin, Sainte-
    Beuve* (criticism) 1927
***Ce qui est arrivé à la France en 1870 (essay) 1970
Gobineau: Selected Political Writings (essays, novel
    extracts, and letters) 1970

*This work contains "Le mouchoir rouge," "Akrivie Phrangopoulo,"
and "La chasse au caribou."

**These letters were translated and published in 1959 in *"The Eu-
ropean Revolution" and Correspondence with Gobineau*, by Alexis
de Tocqueville.

***This work was written during the early 1870s.

JOSEPH ARTHUR GOBINEAU (essay date 1853)

[*In the following excerpt from Gobineau's dedication to the* Essay,
addressed to George V, King of Hanover, Gobineau describes the
*origin and objective of the work. His remarks were first published
in 1853. For additional commentary by Gobineau, see the excerpt
dated 1876.*]

The great events—the bloody wars, the revolutions and the
breaking up of laws—which have been rife for so many years
in the states of Europe, are apt to turn men's minds to the
study of political problems. While the vulgar consider merely
immediate results, and heap all their praise and blame on the
little electric spark that marks the contact with their own interests, the more serious thinker will seek to discover the hidden
causes of these terrible upheavals. He will descend, lamp in
hand, by the obscure paths of philosophy and history; and in
the analysis of the human heart or the careful search among
the annals of the past he will try to gain the master-key to the
enigma which has so long baffled the imagination of man.

Like everyone else, I have felt all the prickings of curiosity to
which our restless modern world gives rise. But when I tried
to study, as completely as I could, the forces underlying this
world, I found the horizon of my inquiry growing wider and
wider. I had to push further and further into the past, and,
forced by analogy almost in spite of myself, to lift my eyes
further and further into the future. It seemed that I should aspire
to know not merely the immediate causes of the plagues that
are supposed to chasten us, but also to trace the more remote
reasons for those social evils which the most meagre knowledge
of history will show to have prevailed, in exactly the same
form, among all the nations that ever lived, as well as those
which survive today—evils that in all likelihood will exist
among nations yet unborn.

Further, the present age, I thought, offered peculiar facilities
for such an inquiry. While its very restlessness urges us on to
a kind of historical chemistry, it also makes our labours easier.
The thick mists, the profound darkness that from time immemorial veiled the beginnings of civilizations different from
our own, now lift and dissolve under the sun of science. An
analytic method of marvellous delicacy has made a Rome,
unknown to Livy, rise before us under the hands of Niebuhr,
and has unravelled for us the truths that lay hid among the
legendary tales of early Greece. In another quarter of the world,
the Germanic peoples, so long misunderstood, appear to us
now as great and majestic as they were thought barbarous by
the writers of the Later Empire. Egypt opens its subterranean
tombs, translates its hieroglyphs, and reveals the age of its
pyramids. Assyria lays bare its palaces with their endless inscriptions, which had till yesterday been buried beneath their
own ruins. The Iran of Zoroaster has held no secrets from the
searching eyes of Burnouf, and the Vedas of early India take
us back to events not far from the dawn of creation. From all
these conquests together, so important in themselves, we gain
a larger and truer understanding of Homer, Herodotus, and
especially of the first chapters of the Bible, that deep well of
truth, whose riches we can only begin to appreciate when we
go down into it with a fully enlightened mind.

These sudden and unexpected discoveries are naturally not
always beyond the reach of criticism. They are far from giving
us complete lists of dynasties, or an unbroken sequence of
reigns and events. In spite, however, of the fragmentary nature
of their results, many of them are admirable for my present
purpose, and far more fruitful than the most accurate chronological tables would be. I welcome, most of all, the revelation of manners and customs, of the very portraits and costumes of vanished peoples. We know the condition of their
art. Their whole life, public and private, physical and moral,

is unrolled before us, and it becomes possible to reconstruct, with the aid of the most authentic materials, that which constitutes the personality of races and mainly determines their value.

With such a treasury of knowledge, new or newly understood, to draw upon, no one can claim any longer to explain the complicated play of social forces, the causes of the rise and decay of nations, in the light of the purely abstract and hypothetical arguments supplied by a sceptical philosophy. Since we have now an abundance of postitive facts crowding upon us from all sides, rising from every sepulchre, and lying ready to every seeker's hand, we may no longer, like the theorists of the Revolution, form a collection of imaginary beings out of clouds, and amuse ourselves by moving these chimeras about like marionettes, in a political environment manufactured to suit them. The reality is now too pressing, too well known; and it forbids games like these, which are always unseasonable, and sometimes impious. There is only one tribunal competent to decide rationally upon the general characteristics of man, and that is history—a severe judge, I confess, and one to whom we may well fear to appeal in an age so wretched as our own.

Not that the past is itself without stain. It includes everything, and so may well have many faults, and more than one shameful dereliction of duty, to confess. The men of today might even be justified in flourishing in its face some new merits of their own. But suppose, as an answer to their charges, that the past suddenly called up the gigantic shades of the heroic ages, what would they say then? If it reproached them with having compromised the names of religious faith, political honour and moral duty, what would they answer? If it told them that they are no longer fit for anything but to work out the knowledge of which the principles had already been recognized and laid down by itself; that the virtue of the ancients has become a laughing-stock, that energy has passed from man to steam, that the light of poetry is out, that its great prophets are no more, and that what men call their interests are confined to the most pitiful tasks of daily life;—how could they defend themselves?

They could merely reply that not every beautiful thing is dead which has been swallowed up in silence; it may be only sleeping. All ages, they might say, have beheld periods of transition, when life grapples with suffering and in the end arises victorious and splendid. Just as Chaldaea in its dotage was succeeded by the young and vigorous Persia, tottering Greece by virile Rome, and the degenerate rule of Augustulus by the kingdoms of the noble Teutonic princes, so the races of modern times will regain their lost youth.

This was a hope I myself cherished for a brief moment, and I should like to have at once flung back in the teeth of History its accusations and gloomy forebodings, had I not been suddenly struck with the devastating thought, that in my hurry I was putting forward something that was absolutely without proof. I began to look about for proofs, and so, in my sympathy for the living, was more and more driven to plumb to their depths the secrets of the dead.

Then, passing from one induction to another, I was gradually penetrated by the conviction that the racial question overshadows all other problems of history, that it holds the key to them all, and that the inequality of the races from whose fusion a people is formed is enough to explain the whole course of its destiny. Everyone must have had some inkling of this colossal truth, for everyone must have seen how certain agglomerations of men have descended on some country, and utterly

transformed its way of life; how they have shown themselves able to strike out a new vein of activity where, before their coming, all had been sunk in torpor. Thus, to take an example, a new era of power was opened for Great Britain by the Anglo-Saxon invasion, thanks to a decree of Providence, which by sending to this island some of the peoples governed by the sword of Your Majesty's illustrious ancestors, was to bring two branches of the same nation under the sceptre of a single house—a house that can trace its glorious title to the dim sources of the heroic nation itself.

Recognizing that both strong and weak races exist, I preferred to examine the former, to analyse their qualities, and especially to follow them back to their origins. By this method I convinced myself at last that everything great, noble and fruitful in the works of man on this earth, in science, art and civilization, derives from a single starting-point, is the development of a single germ and the result of a single thought; it belongs to one family alone, the different branches of which have reigned in all the civilized countries of the universe.

The present work [*Essai sur l'inégalité des races humaines*], which I now lay humbly at the feet of Your Majesty, embodies an account of this thesis. I have not thought it fitting to forsake the elevated and pure spheres of scientific discussion in order to descend to the level of contemporary polemic. I have not sought to shed light upon what the future holds, either for tomorrow or for the years to come. The periods I cover are vast and broad. My researches begin with the first people that existed and continue even as far as those which are yet to come. My calculations are in terms of centuries. I am creating, in short, a work of moral geology. I rarely mention man and still more rarely do I talk of him as citizen or subject. Often, indeed always, I am speaking of different ethnic groupings. For, at the level I have adopted, I am concerned neither with the accidents of nationality nor even with the existence of states, but rather with the diversity of races, societies and civilizations. (pp. 37-42)

> *Joseph Arthur Gobineau, "Essay on the Inequality of the Human Races," translated by Adrian Collins, in* Gobineau: Selected Political Writings, *edited by Michael D. Biddiss, Jonathan Cape, 1970, pp. 37-176.*

ALEXIS DE TOCQUEVILLE   (letter dates 1853-57)

[*Tocqueville is considered one of the greatest literary and political figures of nineteenth-century France. He is best known for* La démocratie en Amérique *and* L'ancien régime et la révolution, *the former a classic study of the nineteenth-century American political scene, the latter a painstaking survey of social and political life in pre-Revolution France. An ardent letter writer, Tocqueville carried on a sixteen-year correspondence with Gobineau, who was a close friend and confidant and who served briefly as Tocqueville's secretary and diplomatic assistant. In the following excerpts from six letters to Gobineau dated 1853, 1856, and 1857, Tocqueville strongly censures Gobineau's racial, religious, and political views, but expresses admiration and personal affection for the author.*]

[17 November 1853]

[My criticisms of the first volume of your *Essai sur l'inégalité des races humaines*] relate directly to your principal idea. I must frankly tell you that you have not convinced me. Every one of my objections persists. You may, nonetheless, be right in defending yourself from the charge of materialism. Your doctrine is rather a sort of fatalism, of predestination if you wish but, at any rate, very different from that of St. Augustine, from the Jansenists, and from the Calvinists (the very last are closest to your doctrines), since you tie predestination and matter closely together. You continually speak about races regenerating or degenerating, losing or acquiring through an infusion of new blood social capacities which they have not previously had. (I think these are your own words.) I must frankly say that, to me, this sort of predestation is a close relative of the purest materialism.

And be assured that should the masses, whose reasoning always follows the most beaten tracks, accept your doctrines, it would lead them straight from races to individuals and from social capacities to all sorts of potentialities.

Whether the element of fatality should be introduced into the material order of things, or whether God willed to make different kinds of men so that He imposed special burdens of race on some, withholding from them a capacity for certain feelings, for certain thoughts, for certain habits, for certain qualities— all this has nothing to do with my own concern with the practical consequences of these philosophical doctrines. The consequence of both theories is that of a vast limitation, if not a complete abolition, of human liberty. Thus I confess that after having read your book I remain, as before, opposed in the extreme to your doctrines. I believe that they are probably quite false; I know that they are certtainly very pernicious.

Surely among the different families which compose the human race there exist certain tendencies, certain proper aptitudes resulting from thousands of different causes. But that these tendencies, that these capacities should be insuperable has not only never been proved but no one will ever be able to prove it since to do so one would need to know not only the past but also the future. I am sure that Julius Caesar, had he had the time, would have willingly written a book to prove that the savages he had met in Britain did not belong to the same race as the Romans, and that the latter were destined thus by nature to rule the world while the former were destined to vegetate in one of its corners. *Tu regere imperio populos, Romane, memento,* said our old acquaintance Virgil. If your doctrine were to relate merely to the *externally* recognizable differences of human families and through these enduring characteristics assign them to differences in creation, it would still be far from convincing to me but at least it would be less fantastic and easier to understand. But when one applies it within one of these great families, for example, within the white race, then the thread of reasoning becomes entangled and loses itself. What, in this whole world, is more difficult to find than the place, the time, and the composite elements that produced men who by now possess no visible traces of their mixed origins? Those events took place in remote and barbaric times, leaving us nothing but vague myths or written fragments.

Do you really believe that by tracing the destiny of peoples along these lines you can truly clarify history? And that our knowledge about humans becomes more certain as we abandon the practice followed since the beginning of time by the many great minds who have searched to find the cause of human events in the influence of certain men, of certain emotions, of certain thoughts, and of certain beliefs?

If only your doctrine, without being better established than theirs, could serve mankind better! But evidently the contrary is true. What purpose does it serve to persuade lesser peoples living in abject conditions of barbarism or slavery that, such

being their racial nature, they can do nothing to better themselves, to change their habits, or to ameliorate their status? Don't you see how inherent in your doctrine are all the evils produced by permanent inequality: pride, violence, the scorn of one's fellow men, tyranny and abjection in every one of their forms? How can you speak to me, my dear friend, about distinctions between *the qualities that make moral truths operative* and what you call *social aptitude?* What difference is there between the two? After, for some time, one has observed the way in which public affairs are conducted, do you think one can avoid the impression that their effects are the results of the same causes which make for success in private life; that courage, energy, honesty, farsightedness, and common sense are the real reasons behind the prosperity of empires as well as behind the prosperity of private families; and that, in one word, the destiny of men, whether of individuals or of nations, depends on what they want to be?

I stop here: let me, please, rest at this point. There is an entire world between our beliefs. I much prefer to turn to what I may praise without reserve. Though I am no less vividly impressed with this than with what I expressed earlier, I must unfortunately be much shorter here as I cannot enter in detail into everything that I do approve in your book. Briefly I shall say that this book is far the most remarkable of your writings; that, to me at least, very great erudition is manifested by your researches and that there is great talent and extraordinary insight in the way you have employed their results. Those who approve your fundamental thesis or those who wish it to be true (and, in our days, after the wear and tear of sixty years of revolution, there are many in France who may want to believe in something similar) must read it with great enthusiasm since your book is well constructed; it proceeds straight to its conclusion, and it is argued most intelligently. I proved my sincerity in my strictures; please believe equally in the sincerity of my praises. Your work has real and great value, and it certainly establishes you at the head of those who have proposed similar doctrines. (pp. 227-30)

• • • • •

[20 December 1853]

[I do not wish to discuss the potential dangers of your thesis with you] except in person. If, as they say, discussion so often only confirms previous prejudices, what then results from a written debate? It is waste or, at least, poor use made of time. You may perhaps be right, but you chose precisely the thesis which, to me, has always seemed the most dangerous one for our times. That, in addition, I persist in believing how false your principle is in its extreme applications should convince you that you will not be able to convert me, and certainly not from a distance. The last century had an exaggerated and somewhat childish trust in the control which men and peoples were supposed to have of their own destinies. It was the error of those times; a noble error, after all; it may have led to many follies, but it also produced great things, compared to which we shall seem quite small in the eyes of posterity. The weary aftermath of revolutions, the weakening of passions, the miscarriage of so many generous ideas and of so many great hopes have now led us to the opposite extreme. After having felt ourselves capable of transforming ourselves, we now feel incapable of reforming ourselves; after having had excessive pride, we have now fallen into excessive self-pity; we thought we could do everything, and now we think we can do nothing; we like to think that struggle and effort are henceforth useless and that our blood, muscles, and nerves will always be stronger than our will power and courage. This is really the great sickness of our age; it is very different from that of our parents. Irrespective of your argument, your book supports these tendencies: despite yourself, it promotes the spiritual lassitude of your already weakening contemporaries. All this does not keep me from seeing what is truly remarkable in your book, and even to be greatly interested in it, as one is in those bad children whose parents are one's best friends and who, as it often happens with bad children, are talented enough to please. However, by studying German I have not yet become enough of a German to be captivated so much by the novelty or by the philosophical merits of an idea as to overlook its moral or political effects. I still would require your *spoken* eloquence to convince me. (pp. 231-32)

· · · · ·

[8 January 1856]

[I received the last two volumes of your *Essai sur l'inégalité des races humaines*], though I have not yet read them. . . . Thus I cannot send you the expected censure which you seem so much to desire. Otherwise I continue having divided feelings about your work; I dislike the book, and I like the author; and I have trouble, at times, in balancing such opposite sentiments. What I disapprove of in the book I told you before: it is less the work itself than its tendency, which I consider dangerous. If we were to suffer from excessive enthusiasm and self-confidence, as did our ancestors of 1789, I would consider your book a salutary *cold shower*. But we have disgracefully come to the opposite extreme. We have no regard for anything, beginning with ourselves; we have no faith in anything, including ourselves. A book which tries to prove that men in this world are merely obeying their physical *constitutions* and that their will power can do almost nothing to influence their destinies is like opium given to a patient whose blood has already weakened. So much for the book. About the author I must say that he is a man of many talents and that he is a great friend of mine, whom I should like to have as my colleague, which, in turn, forces me to praise the product in order to help its producer. (pp. 269-70)

· · · · ·

[30 July 1856]

You know that I cannot reconcile myself to your theses in any way and my thoughts are so much *obsessed* on this point that the very reasons with which you are trying to make them more acceptable tend to confirm my opposition even more, an opposition which remains *latent* only because of my personal affection for you. In your penultimate letter you compare yourself to a physician who announces to his patient that he is mortally ill. You ask: What is immoral in that? My answer is that even though this act in itself may not be immoral, its consequences assuredly are most immoral and pernicious. If one of these mornings my doctor were to say to me: "My dear sir, I have the honor to announce that you are mortally ill and, inasmuch as all of your vital organs are affected, I must add that there is absolutely no chance for you to recover," my first temptation would be to knock that doctor down. Thereafter I should think I would have no choice but either to pull the covers over myself and wait for the announced end or, if I possessed the temper which animated the circle of Boccaccio during the Florentine plague, to think of nothing else but to sample all the possible pleasures before this inevitable end, to burn, as they say, the candle at both ends. Or again, I could profit from this doctor's sentence by preparing myself for eter-

nal life. But societies do not have eternal lives. Thus your doctor will certainly not number me among his clients. I must add that physicians, like philosophers, are often greatly mistaken in their prognostications; I have seen more than one person condemned by physicians who nevertheless became quite well subsequently and who angrily criticized the doctor for having uselessly frightened and discouraged him. Thus you will see, my dear friend, that though I am much disposed to admit the talents of the author I cannot uphold the validity of his ideas. (pp. 291-92)

· · · · ·

[14 January 1857]

[I cannot] believe how you could fail to see the difficulty of reconciling your scientific theories with the letter and with the spirit of Christianity. About the letter: what is clearer in Genesis than the unity of the human race and the descent of all men from the same ancestor? About the spirit: is it not its unique trait to have abolished those racial distinctions which the Jewish religion still retained and to have made therefrom but one human race, all of whose members are equally capable of improving and uniting themselves? How can this spirit—and I am trying to use plain common sense—be reconciled with a doctrine that makes races distinct and unequal, with differing capacities of understanding, of judgment, of action, due to some original and immutable disposition which invisibly denies the possibility of improvement for certain peoples? Evidently Christianity wishes to make all men brothers and equals. Your doctrine makes them cousins at best whose common father is very far away in the heavens; to you down here there are only victors and vanquished, masters and slaves, due to their different birthrights. This is obvious, since your doctrines are being approved, cited, commented upon by whom? by slave-owners and by those who favor the perpetuation of slavery on the basis of radical differences of race. I well know that right now there are in the south of the United States Christian pastors and perhaps even good priests (though they are slaveowners) who preach from their pulpit doctrines which are undoubtedly analogous with yours. But be assured that the majority of Christians, consisting of those whose interests do not subconsciously incline them toward your ideas—be assured, I say, that the majority of Christians of this world cannot have the least sympathy for your doctrines. (pp. 305-06)

· · · · ·

[24 January 1857]

I ask you to permit me, my dear friend, to discuss your political theories no longer. Not being able to maintain the liberties which existed five hundred years ago, you prefer that we maintain none: good. Afraid of submitting to the despotism of parties under which it was possible at least to defend, in speech and in the press, one's own dignity and one's own freedom, you prefer to be oppressed directly by one single individual at a time, but so absolutely that no one, yourself no more than anyone else, could say a single word. Good again. Different tastes ought not to be disputed. Rather than to witness the intrigues of parliaments, you prefer a regime in which the greatest events may be overshadowed by a stock exchange speculation or by the outcome of an industrial enterprise. Even better. I must admit that I am not very successful with you. Since I have known you, your temperament has always seemed independent (you see that I regard you incapable of hypocrisy). It must be in our present state of affairs that I finally find you satisfied with things and with people as they now are! But, seriously, where can our political discussions lead us? We belong to two diametrically opposed orbits. Thus we cannot hope to convince each other. Now when one deals with grave questions and with new ideas one should not discuss them with one's friends when one has no hope of persuading them. Each of us is perfectly logical in his mode of thinking. You consider people today as if they were overgrown children, very degenerate and very ill-educated. And, consequently, it seems proper to you that they should be led with blinds, through noise, with a great clangor of bells, in nicely embroidered uniforms, which are often but liveries of servants. I, too, believe that our contemporaries have been badly brought up and that this is a prime cause of their miseries and of their weakness, but I believe that a better upbringing could repair the wrongs done by their miseducation; I believe that it is not permissible to renounce such an effort. I believe that one could still achieve something with our contemporaries, as with all men, through an able appeal to their natural decency and common sense. In brief, I wish to treat them like human beings. Maybe I am wrong. But I am merely following the consequences of my principles and, moreover, I find a deep and inspiring pleasure in following them. You profoundly distrust mankind, at least *our* kind; you believe that it is not only decadent but incapable of ever lifting itself up again. Our very physical constitution, according to you, condemns us to servitude. It is, then, very logical that, to maintain at least some order in such a mob, government of the sword and even of the whip seem to have some merit in your eyes. Still I do not think that you would offer your own bare back in order to render personal confirmation of your principles. For myself, I do not think that I have either the right or the inclination to entertain such opinions about my race and my country. I believe that one should not despair of them. To me, human societies, like persons, become something worth while only through their use of liberty. I have always said that it is more difficult to stabilize and to maintain liberty in our new democratic societies than in certain aristocratic societies of the past. But I shall never dare to think it impossible. And I pray to God lest He inspire me with the idea that one might as well despair of trying. No, I shall not believe that this human race, which is at the head of all visible creation, has become that bastardized flock of sheep which you say it is, and that nothing remains but to deliver it without future and without hope to a small number of shepherds who, after all, are not better animals than are we, the human sheep, and who indeed are often worse. You will forgive me when I have less confidence in you than in the goodness and in the justice of God. (pp. 308-10)

> *Alexis de Tocqueville, in extracts from six of his letters to Joseph Arthur de Gobineau from November 17, 1853 to January 24, 1857, in his "The European Revolution" & Correspondence with Gobineau, edited and translated by John Lukacs, Doubleday & Company, Inc., 1959, pp. 226-30, 231-33, 268-71, 290-95, 303-07, 308-10.*

H. HOTZ (essay date 1855)

[*Hotz was a nineteenth-century American anti-abolitionist. In the following excerpt from the 1855 introduction to his partial translation of the* Essay, *he favorably analyzes and builds upon Gobineau's conception of the division of races, yet argues that he overlooked the importance of the intellect.*]

Civilization, says Mr. Gobineau [in ***Essay on the Inequality of the Human Races***] arises from the combined action and mutual reaction of man's moral aspirations, and the pressure of his material wants. This, in a general sense, is obviously true. But let us see the practical application. I shall endeavor to give a concise abstract of his views, and then to point out where and why he errs.

In some races, says he, the spiritual aspirations predominate over their physical desires, in others it is the reverse. In none are either entirely wanting. According to the relative proportion and intensity of either of these influences, which counteract and yet assist each other, the tendency of the civilization varies. If either is possessed in but a feeble degree, or if one of them so greatly outweighs the other as to completely neutralize its effects, there is no civilization, and never can be one until the race is modified by intermixture with one of higher endowments. But if both prevail to a sufficient extent, the preponderance of either one determines the character of the civilization. In the Chinese, it is the material tendency that prevails, in the Hindoo the other. Consequently we find that in China, civilization is principally directed towards the gratification of physical wants, the perfection of material well-being. In other words, it is of an eminently utilitarian character, which discourages all speculation not susceptible of immediate practical application. (pp. 82-3)

Hindoo culture, on the contrary, displays a very opposite tendency. Among that nation, everything is speculative, nothing practical. The toils of human intellect are in the regions of the abstract where the mind often loses itself in depths beyond its sounding. The material wants are few and easily supplied. If great works are undertaken, it is in honor of the gods, so that even their physical labor bears homage to the invisible rather than the visible world. (pp. 84-5)

[Mr. Gobineau] therefore divides all races into these two categories, taking the Chinese as the type of the one and the Hindoos as that of the other. According to him, the yellow races belong pre-eminently to the former, the black to the latter, while the white are distinguished by a greater intensity and better proportion of the qualities of both. But this division, and no other is consistent with the author's proposition, by assuming that in the black races the moral preponderates over the physical tendency, comes in direct conflict not only with the plain teachings of anatomy, but with all we know of the history of those races. I shall attempt to show wherein Mr. Gobineau's error lies, an error from the consequences of which I see no possibility for him to escape, and suggest an emendation which, so far from invalidating his general position, tends rather to confirm and strengthen it. (p. 85)

The error, it seems to me, lies in the . . . confusion of distinct ideas. . . . In ordinary language, we speak of the physical and moral nature of man, terming physical whatever relates to his material, and moral what relates to his immaterial being. Again, we speak of *mind,* and though in theory we consider it as a synonyme of soul, in practical application it has a very different signification. A person may cultivate his mind without benefiting his soul, and the term *a superior mind,* does not necessarily imply moral excellency. . . . [Mental] qualifications or acquisitions are in no way connected with sound morality or true piety. . . . [The] greatest monsters that blot the page of history, have been, for the most part, men of what are called superior minds, of great intellectual attainments. Indeed, wickedness is seldom very dangerous, unless joined to intellect, as the common sense of mankind has expressed in the adage that a fool is seldom a knave. We daily see men perverting the highest mental gifts to the basest purposes, a fact which ought to be carefully weighed by those who believe that education consists in the cultivation of the intellect only. I therefore consider the moral endowments of man as practically different from the mental or intellectual, at least in their manifestations, if not in their essence. To define my idea more clearly, let me attempt to explain the difference between what I term the moral and the intellectual nature of man. (pp. 86-7)

The former is what leads man to look beyond his earthly existence, and gives even the most brutish savage some vague idea of a Deity. I am making no rash or unfounded assertion when I declare, Mr. Locke's weighty opinion to the contrary notwithstanding, that no tribe has ever been discovered in which some notion of this kind, however rude, was wanting, and I consider it innate—a yearning, as it were, of the soul towards the regions to which it belongs. The feeling of religion is implanted in our breast; it is not a production of the intellect, and this the Christian church confirms when it declares that *faith* we owe to the grace of God.

Intellect is that faculty of soul by which it takes cognizance of, classes and compares the facts of the *material* world. As all perceptions are derived through the senses, it follows that upon the nicety of these its powers must in a great measure depend. The vigor and delicacy of the nerves, and the size and texture of the brain in which they all centre, form what we call native intellectual gifts. Hence, when the body is impaired, the mind suffers; "mens sana in corpore sano;" hence, a fever prostrates, and may forever destroy, the most powerful intellect; a glass of wine may dim and distort it. Here, then, is the grand distinction between soul and mind. The latter, human wickedness may annihilate; the former, man killeth not. (pp. 87-8)

The strictly moral attributes of man . . . , those attributes which enable him to communicate with his Maker, are common—probably in equal degree—to all men, and to all races of men. But his communications with the external world depend on his physical conformation. The body is the connecting link between the spirit and the material world, and, by its intimate relations to both, specially adapted to be the means of communication between them. There seems to me nothing irrational or irreligious in the doctrine that, according to the perfectness of this means of communication, must be the intercourse between the two. A person with dull auditory organs can never appreciate music, and whatever his talents otherwise may be, can never become a Meyerbeer or a Mozart. Upon quickness of perception, power of analysis and combination, perseverance and endurance, depend our intellectual faculties, both in their degree and their kind; and are not they blunted or otherwise modified in a morbid state of the body? I consider it therefore established beyond dispute, that a certain general physical conformation is productive of corresponding mental characteristics. A human being, whom God has created with a negro's skull and general *physique,* can never equal one with a Newton's or a Humboldt's cranial development, though the soul of both is equally precious in the eyes of the Lord, and should be in the eyes of all his followers. There is no tendency to materialism in this idea; I have no sympathy with those who deny the existence of the soul, because they cannot find it under the scalpel, and I consider the body not the mental agent, but the servant, the tool.

It is true that science has not discovered, and perhaps never will discover, what physical differences correspond to the differences in individual minds. Phrenology, starting with brilliant promises, and bringing to the task powers of no mean order,

has failed. But there is a vast difference between the characteristics by which we distinguish individuals of the same race, and those by which we distinguish races themselves. The former are not strictly—at least not immediately—hereditary, for the child most often differs from both parents in body and mind, because no two individuals, as no two leaves of one tree, are precisely alike. But, although every oak-leaf differs from its fellow, we know the leaf of the oak-tree from that of the beech, or every other; and, in the same manner, races are distinguished by peculiarities which are hereditary and permanent. Thus, every negro differs from every other negro, else we could not tell them apart; yet all, if pure blood, have the same characteristics in common that distinguish them from the white. I have been prolix, but intentionally so, in my discrimination between individual distinction and those of race, because of the latter, comparative anatomy takes cognizance; the former are left to phrenology, and I wished to remove any suspicion that in the investigation of moral and intellectual diversities of races, recourse must be had to the ill-authenticated speculations of a dubious science. But, from the data of comparative anatomy, attained by a slow and cautious progress, we deduce that races are distinguished by certain permanent physical characteristics; and, if these physical characteristics correspond to the mental, it follows as an obvious conclusion that the latter are permanent also. History ratifies the conclusion, and the common sense of mankind practically acquiesces in it.

To return, then, to our author. I would add to his two elements of civilization a third—intellect *per se;* or rather, to speak more correctly, I would subdivide one of his elements into two, of which one is probably dependent on physical conformation. The combinations will then be more complex, but will remove every difficulty.

I remarked that although we may consider all races as possessed of equal moral endowments, we yet may speak of moral diversities; because, without the light of revelation, man has nothing but his intellect whereby to compass the immaterial world, and the manifestation of his moral faculties must therefore be in proportion to the clearness of his intellectual, and their preponderance over the animal tendencies. (pp. 90-3)

[The] races comprised in each [of Mr. Gobineau's three groups, the black, yellow, and white races,] vary among themselves, if not with regard to the relative proportion in which they possess the elements of civilization, at least in their intensity. The following formulas will, I think, apply to the majority of cases, and, at the same time, bring out my idea in a clearer light:—

If the animal propensities are strongly developed, and not tempered by the intellectual faculties, the moral conceptions must be exceedingly low, because they necessarily depend on the clearness, refinement, and comprehensiveness of the ideas derived from the material world through the senses. The religious cravings will, therefore, be contented with a gross worship of material objects, and the moral sense degenerate into a grovelling superstition. The utmost elevation which a population, so constituted, can reach, will be an unconscious impersonation of the good aspirations and the evil tendencies of their nature under the form of a good and an evil spirit, to the latter of which absurd and often bloody homage is paid. Government there can be no other than the right which force gives to the strong, and its forms will be slavery among themselves, and submissiveness of all to a tyrannical absolutism.

When the same animal propensities are combined with intellect of a higher order, the moral faculties have more room for action. The penetration of intellect will not be long in discovering that the gratification of physical desires is easiest and safest in a state of order and stability. Hence a more complex system of legislation both social and political. The conceptions of the Deity will be more elevated and refined, though the idea of a future state will probably be connected with visions of material enjoyment, as in the paradise of the Mohammedans.

Where the animal propensities are weak and the intellect feeble, a vegetating national life results. No political organization, or of the very simplest kind. Few laws, for what need of restraining passions which do not exist. The moral sense content with the vague recognition of a superior being, to whom few or no rites are rendered.

But when the animal propensities are so moderate as to be subordinate to an intellect more or less vigorous, the moral aspirations will yearn towards the regions of the abstract. Religion becomes a system of metaphysics, and often loses itself in the mazes of its own subtlety. The political organization and civil legislation will be simple, for there are few passions to restrain; but the laws which regulate social intercourse will be many and various, and supposed to emanate directly from the Deity.

Strong animal passions, joined to an intellect equally strong, allow the greatest expanse for the moral sense. Political organizations the most complex and varied, social and civil laws the most studied, will be the outward character of a society composed of such elements. Internally we shall perceive the greatest contrasts of individual goodness and wickedness. Religion will be a symbolism of human passions and the natural elements for the many, an ingenious fabric of moral speculations for the few.

I have here rapidly sketched a series of pictures from nature, which the historian and ethnographer will not fail to recognize. Whether the features thus cursorily delineated are owing to the causes to which I ascribe them, I must leave for the reader to decide. My space is too limited to allow of my entering into an elaborate argumentation. But I would observe that, by taking this view of the subject, we can understand why all human—and therefore false—religions are so intimately connected with the social and political organization of the peoples which profess them, and why they are so plainly mapped out on the globe as belonging to certain races, to whom alone they are applicable, and beyond whose area they cannot extend: while Christianity knows no political or social forms, no geographical or ethnological limits. The former, being the productions of human intellect, must vary with its variation, and perish in its decay, while revelation is universal and immutable, like the Intelligence of which it is the emanation. (pp. 94-7)

> *H. Hotz, "Analytical Introduction," in* The Moral and Intellectual Diversity of Races *by Count A. de Gobineau, 1856. Reprint by Garland Publishing, Inc., 1984, pp. 2-103.*

[F. W. NEWMAN]   (essay date 1865)

[*A nineteenth-century English classical scholar, Newman made important contributions to linguistics and mathematics and wrote often on social, political, and religious issues. In the following excerpt from a review of Gobineau's* Traité des écritures cunéiforms, *he unfavorably compares Gobineau's essay on*

cuneiform writing with Sir Henry Rawlinson's work on the same subject.]

The contrast of Gobineau and Rawlinson is certainly great. The arrow which divides *words* in Rawlinson, divides *sentences* in Gobineau. The characters which in Rawlinson mean letters, in Gobineau generally mean words. In Rawlinson we find five textual vowels, in Gobineau none at all. In Gobineau we have a series of incredible monosyllables, in Rawlinson organized inflected words. In Rawlinson we have a reasonable variety of sound, in Gobineau a portentous monotony. In [Rawlinson] . . . one modern character is an equivalent for one cuneiform; in Gobineau there are many characters with one sound, and many sounds with one character. In Rawlinson we find sentences with compact syntax, and with full grammatical apparatus; in Gobineau we have scarcely a verb or a pronoun, no adverbs, no prepositions, no cases, no structure, nothing like human language. In Rawlinson we have continuous thought, narrative or argument, with consistent allusions to history and geography; in Gobineau we have an idiotic blank, or fanatical absurdity. In Rawlinson we find abundant relation in words and forms, as also in the composition of sentences, with Zend, Sanscrit, Greek, Latin; yet the Achæmenian has marked peculiarities of its own in its syntax, in the possessive and locative cases, and in its article, neither wholly Greek, nor wholly Latin. But the jargon exhibited by Gobineau has nothing of form or development admitting of comparison; and by his own account has no definite meaning. Now whence comes this wonderful contrast? Evidently from the mode of origination and research. The alphabet of Rawlinson was developed by forty years' perseverance in research after proper names, which conserve, as they originated, phonetic symbols: but the alphabet of Count Gobineau is developed by ambitious abstract phantasies, which affect to be independent of proper names, of history, and even of linguistic knowledge; for he pretends to determine the power of the letters before he has the least idea of the sense beneath them.

Under the circumstances, we might blame ourselves for having bestowed so much time and paper on [*Traité des écritures cunéiformes*]. But he is a forcible and brilliant writer: he is Minister of France in Persia; he has written a big, an elegant, and a learned book: and many in England are liable to be led by such outward pretensions. We have therefore thought it not a waste of time to enter thus minutely into the subject. (p. 613)

> [*F. W. Newman*], "Cuneiform Inscriptions—Gobineau versus Rawlinson," in Fraser's Magazine for Town & Country, Vol. LXXII, No. CCCCXXXI, November, 1865, pp. 589-613.

E. ROBERT LYTTON   (essay date 1874)

[*Best known by his pseudonym Owen Meredith, Lytton was a nineteenth-century English statesman and man of letters who achieved particular literary success with his long verse romance,* Lucile. *Like Gobineau, he was keenly interested in race and miscegenation, attributing English decadence to race degeneration resulting from the mixture of Irish and German blood. In the following excerpt from a positive review of* The Pleiads, *Lytton comments on its subject, narrative structure, and characters.*]

[*The Pleiades*] is in many respects, and from many points of view, a remarkable book. . . . It cannot be called a novel, and must not be regarded as a novel. It belongs to that class of compositions of which *Wilhelm Meister* is the greatest. It gives plastic form to the impressions made upon its author's mind by the social and political aspects of his age. He is a cosmopolitan and highly cultivated Frenchman, with a long experience of official life, and uncommon faculties, as well as opportunities, for the comparative study of character in his own and other countries. The book itself is published subsequent to events which must have profoundly impressed the mind of every thoughtful Frenchman; and therefore in so far as it reveals to us the impressions of such a mind, it deserves, and will reward, attention.

But it is, first of all, a work of art that I wish to speak of this book. The perusal of it has left me wondering how it happens that the genius of its author has so long been diverted from a form wherein it finds such effective expression. Count Gobineau's erudition is, here, always apparent, but never obtrusive. He writes in the style of a man of the world who is not only ''well-read,'' but also ''well-bred.'' As a diplomatist he must have been a keen observer of mankind. As a story-teller, he somewhat resembles Balzac, who was less a novelist than a psychologist. For Balzac studied human sensations scientifically, and explained their mysteries by a method which artfully substituted for the human heart in analogous creation of his own.

The Pleiades is a study of character, not made *in animâ vili.* It constructs certain types which ideally combine qualities, not perhaps combined in any living individual, but certainly common to the life of the whole species. Such a licence is incontestably legitimate to the poet; but his legitimate exercise of it is subject to stringent conditions. The logic of the imagination is as severe as that of the reason. The poet presents to us the world in its ideal proportions; but, in so doing, he must preserve the ideal harmony of such proportions. So long as he does this, his abstractions are as strictly true as those of the mathematician, which have no material counterparts. They only cease to be true when they present incongruous images to the imagination. The ideal artist must not marry the brows of Jove to the lips of the Hermaphrodite, nor set the head of Phœbus on the shoulders of Hercules. This is a danger from which the writers of vulgar fiction are exempt. Count Gobineau has not entirely escaped it. But it would be ungracious to dwell upon occasional failures in so high an order of effort. It behoves us to consider the method, in reference only to the purpose, of this singular fiction, which enunciates truths, if it does not always embody truth. Here, in short, is a microscopic study of considerable interest. But it is the optic, rather than the object, that is interesting. (pp. 293-94)

Count Gobineau has constructed, in the form of a romance, a magnificent psychologic microscope, and he exhibits its dissolvant powers by means of a series of *artificial test-objects.* His Theodores and Candeuils, his Tonskas and Auroras, are neither diatoms nor naviculæ, but systems of microscopic lines engraved with rare skill on the slides of his instrument; and the high and uncommon powers of that instrument are admirably displayed in the analysis of them.

The story opens with a felicitous fancy, the meeting of ''The Three Calenders;'' and, if the book contained only the pages in which the underlying idea of this fancy is developed and explained by the first Calender, Wilfred Nore, it should suffice for a durable monument of its author's genius. A literature, free from accident, would not willingly lose possession of such excellent writing.

Three young men, previously unknown to each other, meet in the course of their respective travels at Airolo. One is a French-man, the other an Englishman, the third a German. They are the ''Three Calenders, sons of kings;'' and the story of each Calender is very naturally and pleasantly introduced by a friendly discussion between them, in which each sets forth and defends his own way of looking at life. These three representatives of different nationalities are brought together again at a small German court, and their separate antecedents and characters are then woven into a single thread of destiny. (p. 295)

I shall venture to find fault with Count Gobineau's first sentence. ''Il était six heures du soir à peu près, *peut-être six et demie.* La malle-poste filait, &c.'' Why this precision of detail? Nothing in the story depends upon it. What can it possibly matter to the reader whether the *malle-poste* arrived at six o'clock or at half-past six? This pedantry of detail, tiresome enough in the ordinary realistic novel, seems to me wholly out of place in the higher order of romance, and unworthy of the genius of such a writer as Count Gobineau. In the descriptions of scenery and travel which, judiciously restricted and never inappropriate, greatly enhance the charm of *The Pleiades,* the author's lively imagination and intimate knowledge of what he describes are always agreeably tempered by his good taste as a man of the world. These passages are effective without being affected. The sentiment of them never degenerates into sentimentality, for Count Gobineau has not only poetic fancy but wit, in a happy equipoise which saves both qualities from the faults of exaggeration. In the delineation of his characters he has known how to harmonize freshness and force of colouring with the delicate outlines appropriate to youth. In the three characters of Laudon, Lanze, and Wilfred Nore, these graceful outlines are charmingly preserved from the defect which, if the delineation of those characters were less masterly, might have been a sceptical frivolity in Laudon, a heavy earnestness in Lanze, and a moral pedantry in Wilfred Nore.

Nevertheless, Count Gobineau is not altogether free from the common defect of those artists who excel as colourists rather than as draughtsmen. The reflections and remarks which he puts into the mouth of his characters are always original, suggestive, and full of interest. But many of them are too obviously his own, and some of them might as naturally be uttered by any other character in the story, as by the particular character to whom they are assigned. The heat of the author's fancy or feelings sometimes carries him beyond the lines within which his characters should be confined. Perfect plastic precision is rare even among writers of the highest order. Shakespeare had it, and so had Goethe. In *Faust* and *Hamlet* every word is a portrait. But in almost all the dramas of Schiller there are occasionally verses which might be spoken as well by any one, as by any other, of his *dramatis personæ.* In *Wallenstein,* for instance, whether it be the ambitious Duke of Friedland, the heroic Max Piccolomini, or the resentful Butler that is before us, we see but one and the same personality. It is sublime, sympathetic, profound, noble, gentle, wise; but, under whatever mask be on it, we immediately recognise it as the personality of Schiller.

If this be a defect in art, however, it is one, not to be pardoned, but gratefully and reverently welcomed, whenever it admits us to direct intercourse with a noble nature or a vigorous intellect; and this it does in the present case. An author may know much, know how to express what he knows, and know how to express it well; but there is an indescribable way of expressing it, whereby alone the author can impress the reader with a conviction that he not only knows much, but also loves what he knows. This indescribable characteristic of style, rare even among the most celebrated writers, constitutes the pervading charm of *The Pleiades*. (pp. 299-300)

[The book] is an enunciation of truths rather than a representation of truth. At every step over the purely fictitious ground of it, one is startled and arrested by the presence of some truth so vital and so forcibly presented, as to suggest to the mind of any speculative reader a question whether the full expression of truth be not entirely dependent on the employment of fiction.

Take, for instance, the sentiment of love. The embodiment of true love is a girl who flings herself over Waterloo Bridge because her sweetheart has enlisted. But in this form love cannot tell us what love is. . . . Love, indeed, is unfitted for intellectual life. The love that can only express itself by a silent embrace is more eloquent than the love which knows how to say "I love" in a thousand different ways. Intellect, on the contrary, craves after speech. It is fond of refining, too, and would fain uplift into its own lofty region all it deigns to deal with. Poor love—is ill at ease up there in the cold with intellect; and all our love romances, lived or written, are but the contortions of the sufferer. If intellect could find a more generally interesting subject for analysis, it would probably reject this gross passion from humanity. But so universal is the interest which humanity feels even in imaginary love affairs, that, were there no love left in the world, we should still go on talking and writing about love just as if it really existed. However fatiguing the passion may be to its victim, it never fatigues the public; whereas, the less an author seems fatigued by the superiority of his intellect, the more he is likely to fatigue the attention of his readers. I do not say that this is the case with the *Pleiades*. On the contrary, the book, far from being fatiguing, is full of charm and full of interest. But the charm and the interest belong to the author's genius rather than to his story; to what his characters say, rather than to what they do. That a man should love a woman, and end by marrying her, is not sufficient to constitute a romance. The romance, or prose-fiction, though epic in form, should be dramatic in structure. That is to say, the novelist or romance-writer should omit all details which do not affect the action of his story. It is quite conceivable that, in his leisure hours, Macbeth painted in water-colours, or bred short-horns, or played backgammon. But in the drama all he has to do is to murder Duncan, and fight with fate for his stolen throne.

The *dramatis personæ* of the *Pleiades* do all sorts of things, which it is quite natural that they should do, but not at all necessary that they should do in reference to the story. They move about the book like the persons who walk about at a German watering-place, having nothing in common, except to drink the waters and feel all the worse for it. After swallowing a certain number of little goblets, and walking a certain number of miles up and down the promenade, those persons separate. Or, strictly speaking, they do not separate, for they never combined. Each goes his own way. Yet all these personages are extremely interesting. They are sovereigns, statesmen, diplomatists, authors, artists, men of science, fine ladies, grand seigneurs. Never again, or elsewhere, are we likely to see all at once so many distinguished people. The personages we meet there are interesting to everybody; but what they do there is interesting to nobody. Generally speaking, Count Gobineau's characters want plasticity. It is difficult for the reader's imagination to put a distinct physiognomy to them. They are too much like dissolving views, in which different images succeed each other and mingle together within the same frame. From this observation, however, it would be necessary to except

those two masterly creations in female character, Harriet Coxe, and the Countess Tonska, if the story of the Countess did not terminate, and that of Harriet commence, in a manner very difficult to reconcile with what is imaginable of the temperaments they represent.

A more beautiful conception than Harriet is hardly to be found in fiction. Rare, indeed, must be the genius of a writer who could conceive so exquisite an ideal of female character. It is thoroughly noble, and exceedingly touching in its heroic strength and tenderness, its delicate purity, and sustained refinement; yet withal perfectly human and natural. Moreover, excepting the one defect (as it seems to me) which I have mentioned, this conception is admirably worked out. But I think it an error in the author's judgment to introduce us to this beautiful soul under a mystification which allows us to mistake Harriet, till we know her better, for a crafty old maid. The opera of *Fidelio* should not be preceded by the overture of Figaro's marriage; though each is a masterpiece. A similar objection applies to the *finale* of the Countess Tonska. This character is the author's most elaborate creation. He has drawn it with all the vigour of fresco, and all the careful delicacy and high finish of miniature. It is at once both a type and a portrait; and, but for the last touch, would be a masterpiece unsurpassed by anything which Balzac has created in the same type: a type which may perhaps have no counterpart in England, but which will at once be recognised by every one who is familiar with Continental society. I have known three or four Countess Tonskas, and can testify to the astonishing accuracy of the portrait by Count Gobineau. He could not have understood them better if he had lived for years in that cavity which, in other women is occupied by the heart, and in women of this type, by the restless and desperate efforts of the head to imagine the emotions of a heart that is missing. But the Countess Tonska of real life does not end by marrying, beneath her rank, a little German sculptor of mediocre genius, because he is pulingly devoted to her. At least, she may make such a marriage—for she is capable of every absurdity under heaven—but, having made it, she is sure to repent it next day, and to be as miserable as before. Count Gobineau would perhaps reply to this objection that he has known a case in point. Probably. But if you undertake to draw a perfect circle and fail, it is beside the point to say that there are imperfect circles in nature. The Countess Tonskas who end as loving wives to men of humble station, and second-rate talent, are not perfect Countess Tonskas. This objection may perhaps be otherwise opposed upon higher ground, by pleading the author's obligation to his moral purpose, which is apparently to prove that *amor omnia vincit;* and the chapter in which Harriet enforces that moral, and illustrates it by the story of Don Juan, is charmingly written. But still, the moral purpose of even the most didactic romance should grow naturally out of the moral character of its hero and heroines. (pp. 300-02)

Count Gobineau's Madame Tonska, not only sees clearly all the defects of her adorers, but she *foresees* the end of their passion; and at last she deliberately, and in cold blood, bandages her own eyes that she may not see the man she marries. In this she acts sensibly enough, but not consistently. One final objection I must make to some details in Count Gobineau's picture of the "Residence." It is open to every novelist to turn into ridicule those poor little departed German courts, notwithstanding the maxim of *de mortuis nil nisi bonum.* Thackeray has made the most of such opportunities. But I am surprised that an experienced diplomatist and man of the world like Count Gobineau, should seriously ask us to imagine the possibility of a German prince being aide-de-camp to his brother, the reigning sovereign, or of that sovereign immediately inviting to dinner two perfect strangers who have left cards with one of his chamberlains. Again, there is nothing in the law at any time applicable to such cases which could have prevented Count Gobineau's Prince William from resigning the throne immediately on his accession to it, if he wished to do so; nothing whatever which could have obliged him to obtain permission from his father during the lifetime of the latter. Nor, on the other hand, would it have been possible for any real German prince in the position of Prince Theodore to abdicate in favour of his son-in-law when he had brothers living. These technical inaccuracies affect one like a door that creaks and will not shut properly. One's sense of discomfort is increased by the thought of how easily the cause of it might have been remedied.

The character of Laudon is somewhat undecided. For a *bon enfant*, as he is, the episode of Olimpe Berbier seems to me singularly harsh, and Laudon's portrait of his father is, I think, unnecessarily painful.

But in all these minor defects of the story lies the secret of the rare and great merit of the book. Had the author strictly subordinated his genius to the laws and limitations aesthetically imposed upon the representation of actual life and real character, he could not possibly hence have given full vent to those pregnant reflections, and suggestive trains of thought, which abound in his pages; nor yet could he have made as exhaustive and profound as it is, his analysis of the sentiments and passions which he investigates as a geometer investigates lines and figures, by first reducing them to abstractions. If the *dramatis personæ* of the **Pleiades** never said anything not perfectly appropriate to their characters, many pages of this book would have remained unwritten; and those pages are perhaps the liveliest and most entertaining. The book is saturated with ideas. It is eloquent, witty, wise. Nor is it possible to praise too highly the variety, the flexibility, the perfect good taste and idiomatic force of Count Gobineau's style as a romance writer. (pp. 303-04)

Here I must end a very imperfect and inadequate notice of a very remarkable book. To all who value genuine books I venture to recommend the perusal of it. It is no doubt a fierce denunciation of all the social and political creeds which are just now most in favour. But it is not the cry of a revivalist. It advocates no attempt to rehabilitate worn-out symbols, or re-establish fallen powers. Count Gobineau keenly recognises, and unsparingly ridicules, the futile frivolity of all such attempts; and it may be said that its purpose in this book is to illustrate a conviction, which he has elsewhere expressed, that human races and societies are subject to decay from natural and inevitable causes, which cannot be removed by the application of social, political, or theological nostrums to the body politic. In the present condition of France, and indeed of Europe generally, Count Gobineau seems to see only the beginning of the end. Those who value intellectual and moral independence he exhorts to extricate themselves as much as possible from the social and political agitations of a world incurably disordered; and the philosophy of the **Pleiades** is indeed much the same as that which induced Candide to devote himself to the cultivation of his cabbages. Count Gobineau is not likely to make many converts to such a philosophy; but even its most strenuous opponents may find a charm in the eloquence, the fancy, and the wit with which it is proclaimed and illustrated in this singular romance. (p. 307)

E. Robert Lytton, "A Novelty in French Fiction," in The Fortnightly Review, *n.s. Vol. XVI, No. XCIII, September 1, 1874, pp. 293-307.*

JOSEPH ARTHUR GOBINEAU   (essay date 1876)

[*In the following excerpt from his 1876 introduction to* Romances of the East, *Gobineau states the purpose of the work and presents his view of his subject, the Asiatics. For additional commentary by Gobineau, see the excerpt dated 1853.*]

The best book which has been written on the Asiatic national temperament is decidedly Morier's romance entitled *Hadji-Baba.* It is, of course, understood that the *Thousand and One Nights* is not in question; this remains incomparable, and will never be equaled. This masterpiece being excepted, *Hadji-Baba* takes the highest rank. Its author was secretary of the British legation at Teheran at an era when everything appertaining to the East India Company's service reflected a splendor which recalled the Golden Age. Morier has thoroughly seen, known, and penetrated, all that he has described, and in his pictures the colors are perfectly harmonious; but his charming book occupies a single point of view. What he depicts is the levity, the mental inconsistency, and the poverty of moral ideas, among the Persians. He has admirably developed and treated his subject. He has taken a physiognomy under one aspect, and what this aspect presents he has rendered perfectly without omitting a feature; but he has not gone beyond the lines traced by the position of his model. He has not done this, and he should not be blamed for it. Only the result is, that he has not shown everything. For this cause, and since there was no reason for copying anew the form in which he has succeeded so well, I have desired to produce, not a book, but a series of tales, which method has enabled me to express what I wished to reproduce under a varied and large number of aspects.

[In *Nouvelles asiatiques,*] I have not simply aimed at presenting, after Morier, the more or less conscious immorality of Asiatics, and the spirit of falsehood which rules them; I have kept this in view, however, but that was not enough for me. It has seemed to me proper not to omit the bravery of some, the sincerely romantic spirit of others; the natural goodness of these, the thorough probity of those; among some, the passion of patriotism carried to excess; among others, perfect generosity, devotion, and affection; among all, an incomparable ease, and the absolute tyranny of the first impulse, whether good or bad. I have not sought, moreover, to paint a single country, and this is why I have transported the reader sometimes to the hamlets of Circassians, sometimes into Turkish or Persian or Afghan towns, sometimes to the bosom of fertile valleys, often to the midst of arid and dusty plains; but, despite the care I have taken to depict different types under the sway of various pursuits and in the heart of very dissimilar regions, I am far from thinking that I have exhausted the treasures in which I have dipped.

Among the number of absurdities that we owe to certain philosophers, there is none more marked than the axiom, "Man is everywhere the same." We should write the reverse of this and teach, "Men are in no place the same." One can see without trouble that a Chinaman possesses two arms and two legs, two eyes and a nose, like a Hottentot or a Paris citizen; but it is needless to talk an hour with each of these individuals in order to perceive and conclude that no intellectual and moral bond exists between them, save it be the conviction that each must eat when he is hungry, and sleep when slumber overcomes him. On all other subjects the method of collecting ideas, the nature and junction of these ideas, their hatching, their efflorescence, their colors, all differ. For the negro belonging to the country south of Lake Tehad it is rational, indispensable, praiseworthy, pious, to massacre the foreigner as soon as he can seize him, and if the last breath of his body can be extorted by means of torture, delicately applied and graduated, so much the better, and the conscience of the operator feels uncommonly well. Let the same foreigner fall into the hands of an Egyptian Arab: the latter would have neither peace nor truce, rest or contentment, except, by one means or another, he had extorted the last penny from him, and, if possible, taken even his shirt. The negro and the Arab do not certainly coincide in the method of dealing with humanity. But imagine both in conversation with St. Vincent de Paul. What would be the common ground between these three natures? Introduce a philosopher as judge of the conversation: do you think he would be right in maintaining that men are everywhere the same? It is because men are everywhere essentially different—their passions, their vices, their method of looking on themselves and on others, their beliefs, interests, the problems in which they are engaged— that the study of them affords so varied and lively an interest, and hence it is important to indulge in this study to account for the *rôle* that men fill in the midst of creation. This is what gives history its value, poetry a part of its worth, romance all its *raison d'être*. (pp. 7-10)

> *Joseph Arthur Gobineau, in an introduction to* Romances of the East, *1878. Reprint by Arno Press Inc., 1973, pp. 7-10.*

HENRY JAMES (essay date 1876)

[*James was an American-born English novelist, short story writer, critic, and essayist of the late nineteenth and early twentieth centuries. He is regarded as one of the greatest novelists of the English language and is also admired as a lucid and insightful critic. As a young man, he traveled extensively throughout Great Britain and Europe, and his criticism is informed by his sensitivity to European culture, particularly English and French literature of the late nineteenth century. In the following excerpt from a review of* Romances of the East, *James praises Gobineau's depiction of Eastern life.*]

It is not too much to say of M. de Gobineau that he is a fascinating writer. His merit is not the usual French merit of form; he does not present that hard, smooth surface, as flawless as that of the delicate white porcelain manufactured in France and known as *biscuit*—as flawless and about as individual— which is offered us by the usual French story-teller; his charm is much more that of substance. He is a man of thought, of deep observation, of a taste for general truths, and he is intellectually less after the French pattern than any Frenchman of his day. To Oriental studies M. de Gobineau has devoted much of his life, and his excellent work entitled *Les Religions de l'Asie* is probably much better known than any of his attempts in the line of fiction. In this collection of tales [*Nouvelles asiatiques*] he sums up some of his personal impressions of the Oriental character. (p. 344)

The author has endeavored to be as characteristic as possible, and to select types and cases which shall be intensely illustrative. The local color of the East in its material sense has probably been overdone during the last thirty years. What M. de Gobineau has tried to reproduce is the local color of the Oriental mind and soul. He is a very acute psychologist, and he handles the subtle threads of the Eastern character with singularly uner-

ring fingers. He puts himself as far as possible into the Asiatic skin, looks at things from his heroes' and heroines' point of view, never comments nor protests, but contents himself with relating exactly how his characters felt and acted in the circumstances which he has devised for them. His tales are six in number, and they are perhaps of unequal merit; two, at least, of which the scene is laid in Persia—**"The Story of Gamber-Ali"** and **"The War of the Turcomans"**—are genuine masterpieces. **"The Dancing-Girl of Shamakha"** is a story of the Russian Caucasus, and is a very curious and touching study of the female character in regions where the aspirations of the softer sex have not that elevated tone which they have attained among ourselves. The figure of Omm-Djéhâne is indeed an admirable portrait of a formidable but doubtless very possible original. The word "Tartar" has passed into English speech with a very invidious meaning, which, it must be confessed, is completely justified by M. de Gobineau's vivid representation of a passionate Tartar maiden. And, in speaking of this tale, we may note the singular fact that M. Gobineau, when he has occasion to introduce a European hero, never selects one of his own countrymen. In *Les Pléiades* the two heroes were English and German; the heroines were English, German, and Russian. In **"La Danseuse de Shamakha"** the interesting young European whom he makes the object of the hopeless passion of his fascinating Calmuck is a Spaniard; and in the last tale in the book, the **"Vie de Voyage,"** desiring to represent the emotions of a civilized young couple who undertake to travel in an immense caravan, he selects two Italians. It may almost be said that with M. de Gobineau any reference to his native land is conspicuous by its absence. This, however, is a detail. The second story, **"L'illustre Magicien,"** is perhaps the least interesting, though it doubtless touches a very characteristic point, being the history of a most exemplary and amiable young Persian, married to a wife in every way worthy of him, and enjoying the fullest domestic bliss and prosperity, who leaves his happy home to follow a squalid Dervish and learn the great secret of truth.

"Gamber-Ali," as we have said, is admirable, and, as a sympathetic and irresponsible picture of unconscious rascality, is hardly inferior to one of Browning's dramatic monologues. (It should be noted that the author always tells his story exactly as a fellow-townsman of his hero would tell it—with the same moral tone.) Gamber-Ali is a young man about town at Shiraz, remarkable for his personal beauty and his love of amusement, whose entrance into active life the author relates in detail. The details are taken, as the French say, *sur le vif*, and afford an interesting picture of the state of manners and morals in the land of Firdousi and of the jewelled monarch whom the kingdoms of Europe outstrove each other three years since to entertain. Gamber-Ali is the child of epicurean parents, and the Bohemian ménage of the shiftless painter Hassan-Kahn and his terrible wife, Bibi-Djanem, is very happily touched off. Their dissipated son, in a drunken scrimmage in a tavern, has the good fortune to pass for having diverted a few blows from the portly person of one of the hangers-on of the palace of the governor, and the gratitude of this flurried functionary proves the stepping-stone of the young man's fortunes. He becomes a sort of Persian Gil-Blas, obtains a place in the governor's suite, learns all the tricks of the trade, lies and steals triumphantly, and lines his pocket with the bribes of all applicants for justice or favor. But his avidity proves his ruin, or nearly so, inasmuch as he fails to share his booty with his employers, to whom, properly, a handsome percentage of all profits is due. This brings him into contempt and disgrace, and finally, having stabbed to death one of his fellow-servants, he is obliged to flee for his life, and takes refuge in a mosque erected over the tomb of an eminent saint. The account of his sojourn in this inviolable asylum is the best part of the story. He is represented as being in an insurmountable agony of fear as to what will be done to him if he is taken, and the picture of his frank, expansive, absorbing terror completes admirably the whole portrait of his smoothness, softness, impudence, luxuriousness, and, as it were, feminine rascality. The most solemn assurances that he will be allowed to escape in safety cannot induce him to budge. He becomes an object of extreme interest to all the faithful who frequent the mosque, and who cover him with admiration and sympathy. The ladies of the locality "go on" about him as if he were a handsome tenor or light comedian in New York, and a perpetual chorus of feminine lamentation and adulation surrounds his resting-place. At last the King of Kings, in person, comes to visit the mosque, and the terror of Gamber-Ali, lest the mighty monarch should detach him by force from his refuge, becomes such that he clings to the walls of the monument (the tomb of the saint) as a drowning man to a spar. He is pointed out to the king, who condescends to converse with him, tries to persuade him that he may go in peace, and finally gives his royal word that not a hair of his head shall be touched. But Gamber-Ali, stupid with terror, only clings the closer and trembles the harder, and the monarch marches off in disgust. Then the chorus of admiration from the ladies deepens, and the young refugee is almost mobbed by the fair spectators. At last the sentiment of the assemblage finds expression in the energetic conduct of a great lady, who makes her way into the sacred enclosure and fairly kidnaps Gamber-Ali, now too exhausted with inanition to resist, having been afraid to touch the cakes and sweetmeats offered him by his admirers lest they should poison him. The lady in question carries him off in her coach-and-four, comforts and consoles him, and makes him her chief steward; in which character he may now be seen riding about in state, more beautiful than ever, supremely happy, covered with jewels, and adored by all observers.

"La Guerre des Turcomans" is a picture of Persian optimism, or, at least, of the amiable serenity with which persons of that enviable race may endure the most odious tribulations. Ghoulam-Hussein relates his own adventures, and his tone is a wonderful mixture of patience and humility in the individual, and complacency and impudence in the race. There is an extraordinary air of truth in his wife's repeated experiments in matrimony—for in offering facilities for such experiments Persia appears almost to compete with certain sections of our own country—and in his easily-accepted miseries and easily-enjoyed mitigations during his life in the army and his captivity by the foe. **"Les Amants de Kandahar"** is striking, but it is more romantic, less ironical, and less entertaining than its companions. **"La Vie de Voyage"** is hardly a tale; it is a sketch of homesickness, of what a young European woman feels when she is launched in a great caravan with a two months' journey before her; of the oppressive strangeness and isolation, amounting almost to terror, which finally forces her to persuade her husband to retreat in the first caravan they encounter bound for Europe. We had marked for quotation from these pages an admirable description of the aspect, march, and movement of a great promiscuous caravan, but we have exceeded our space. All M. de Gobineau's pages, moreover, are worth reading; they are the work of a rich and serious mind, of a really philosophic observer. (pp. 344-45)

Henry James, "Gobineau's 'Nouvelles asiatiques'," in The Nation, New York, Vol. XXIII, No. 597, December 7, 1876, pp. 344-45.

HOUSTON STEWART CHAMBERLAIN (essay date 1899)

[*Chamberlain was an English-born German historian, philosopher, and political writer. In his* Grundlagen des neunzehnten Jahrhunderts *(published in 1899 and excerpted below), a broad pro-German survey of European culture, he promoted Aryan supremacy and helped inspire Nazi racist theory. A virulent anti-Semite who saw the entrance of the Jews into European history as "an element foreign to everything that Europe had hitherto been, and achieved, and had a call to achieve," he denied that Jesus Christ was a Jew, praised the ancient Romans for throwing off Semitic influence, and, in an especially pro-German paean, claimed Dante Alighieri, William Shakespeare, John Milton, René Descartes, John Locke, and Sir Isaac Newton as legitimate Teutons. Chamberlain found widespread support for his claims in Germany, but elsewhere he was generally criticized for his narrow nationalism and insensitive application of historical method. Here, he evaluates Gobineau's racist theory, challenging his claim that crossbreeding leads irrevocably to the decline of the human race.*]

Certain historians of the nineteenth century, even men so intellectually pre-eminent as Count Gobineau, have supported the view that Judaism has always had merely a disintegrating influence upon all peoples. I cannot share this conviction. In truth, where the Jews become very numerous in a strange land, they may make it their object to fulfil the promises of their Prophets and with the best will and conscience to "consume the strange peoples"; did they not say of themselves, even in the lifetime of Moses, that they were "like locusts"? However, we must distinguish between Judaism and the Jews and admit that Judaism as an idea is one of the most conservative ideas in the world. The idea of physical race-unity and race-purity, which is the very essence of Judaism, signifies the recognition of a fundamental physiological fact of life; wherever we observe life, from the hyphomycetes to the noble horse, we see the importance of "race"; Judaism made this law of nature sacred. And this is the reason why it triumphantly prevailed at that critical moment in the history of the world, when a rich legacy was waiting in vain for worthy heirs. It did not further, but rather put a stop to, universal disintegration. The Jewish dogma was like a sharp acid which is poured into a liquid which is being decomposed in order to clear it and keep it from further decomposition. Though this acid may not be to the taste of every one, yet it has played so decisive a part in the history of the epoch of culture to which we belong that we ought to be grateful to the giver. . . . (pp. 254-55)

If the men who should be the most competent to pronounce an opinion on the essence and significance of Race show . . . an incredible lack of judgment—if in dealing with a subject where wide experience is necessary for sure perception, they bring to bear upon it nothing but hollow political phrases—how can we wonder that the unlearned should talk nonsense even when their instinct points out the true path? For the subject has in these days aroused interest in widely various strata of society, and where the learned refuse to teach, the unlearned must shift for themselves. When in the fifties Count Gobineau published his brilliant work [*Essai sur l'inégalité des races humaines*], it passed unnoticed: no one seemed to know what it all meant. Like poor Virchow men stood puzzled before a riddle. Now that the Century has come to an end things have changed: the more passionate, more impulsive element in the nations pays great and direct attention to this question. But in what a maze of contradiction, errors and delusions public opinion moves! Notice how Gobineau bases his account—so astonishingly rich in intuitive ideas which have later been verified and in historical knowledge—upon the dogmatic supposition that the world was peopled by Shem, Ham and Japhet. Such a gaping void in capacity of judgment in the author suffices, in spite of all his documentary support, to relegate his work to the hybrid class of scientific phantasmagorias. With this is connected Gobineau's further fantastic idea, that the originally ''pure'' noble races crossed with each other in the course of history, and with every crossing became irrevocably less pure and less noble. From this we must of necessity derive a hopelessly pessimistic view of the future of the human race. But this supposition rests upon total ignorance of the physiological importance of what we have to understand by ''race.'' A noble race does not fall from Heaven, it becomes noble gradually, just like fruit-trees, and this gradual process can begin anew at any moment, as soon as accident of geography and history or a fixed plan (as in the case of the Jews) creates the conditions. We meet similar absurdities at every step. We have, for example, a powerful Anti-Semitic movement: are we to consider the Jews as identical with the rest of the Semites? Have not the Jews by their very development made themselves a peculiar, pure race profoundly different from the others? Is it certain that an important crossing did not precede the birth of this people? And what is an Aryan? We hear so many and so definite pronouncements on this head. We contrast the Aryan with the ''Semite,'' by whom we ordinarily understand ''the Jew'' and nothing more, and that is at least a thoroughly concrete conception based upon experience. But what kind of man is the Aryan? What concrete conception does he correspond to? Only he who knows nothing of ethnography can give a definite answer to this question. (pp. 262-64)

To beget sons, sons of the right kind, is without question the most sacred duty of the individual towards society; whatever else he may achieve, nothing will have such a lasting and indelible influence as the contribution to the increasing ennoblement of the race. From the limited, false standpoint of Gobineau it certainly does not much matter, for we can only decline and fall sooner or later; still less correct are they who appear to contradict him, but adopt the same hypothetical acceptation of aboriginal pure nations; but any one who understands how noble races are in reality produced, knows that they can arise again at any moment; that depends on us; here nature has clearly pointed out to us a great duty. Those men of the chaos therefore, who considered begetting a sin, and complete abstinence therefrom the highest of all virtues, committed a crime against the most sacred law of nature, they tried to prevent all good, noble men and women from leaving descendants, thus promoting the increase of the evil only, which meant of course that they did their best to bring about the deterioration of the human race. (pp. 315-16)

> *Houston Stewart Chamberlain, in his* Foundations of the Nineteenth Century, *Vol. I, translated by John Lees, 1910. Reprint by Howard Fertig, 1968, 578 p.*

GEORGES CHATTERTON-HILL (essay date 1913)

[*Chatterton-Hill describes and defends the thesis of the* Essay—*that ''race is the primordial element in social evolution.''*]

It is as the author of the *Essai sur l'Inégalité des Races humaines* that Gobineau will live in the history of thought. True, he wrote other books, some of them exceedingly charming, such as *Trois Ans en Asie* and *Religions et Philosophies de l'Asie centrale*; true, also, he was many things during his lifetime— diplomatist, historian, ethnologist, anthropologist, man of letters, philosopher, besides being a brilliant conversationalist. But all these many accomplishments do but subserve one great

end. Gobineau was an aristocrat, by birth, by education, by taste, by conviction; and if he was an historian and an ethnologist, an anthropologist and a man of letters, all his vast stores of erudition, all his deep and searching historical insight, all the resources of his knowledge, were employed and called into use in order to justify the existence of the aristocracy. Such was the aim of the *Essai sur l'Inégalité des Races humaines*. All Gobineau is contained in the *Essai*. His subsequent works are but concrete applications to a particular case of the teaching contained in the *Essai*—as in the case of his *Histoire des Perses*; or else they refer you back to the *Essai* at every opportunity—as in *Trois Ans en Asie* or *Religions et Philosophies*. (p. 1088)

The thesis which Gobineau set out to defend in the *Essai* was this: the *race* is the primordial element in social evolution. The chief factor governing the development of the human species is the *hierarchy of the different races*. 'The strongest [he wrote] play in the tragedy of the world the part of the kings and masters. The weaker content themselves with lesser activities.' As against the supremacy attributed by Comte to ideas, by Taine to the environment, by Marx to the forms of economic production, Gobineau maintains that social evolution is determined mainly, if not exclusively, by the struggle for survival and domination between the various races that compose humanity. It is here that the key to human history is to be found.

Such being his thesis, Gobineau sought to classify the chief racial divisions of humanity. He admitted three principal divisions, classed by him according to color—namely, the white race, the yellow race, and the black race. Of these, the white race is the first, being superior alike in its biological qualities, in its social organisation, and in its intellectual development, to the other two races; the yellow race is inferior to the white, but superior to the black, which latter represents the lowest scale of human evolution. But the white race is itself not a homogeneous entity; it is divided up into two main 'ethnies,' or, as Gobineau calls them, *genres*—the Aryan and the Semitic. The Aryan constitutes the culminating point attained by organic and social evolution, the Aryan 'ethnie' is the purest and finest stock ever bred. Everything great, everything noble, is derived from this unique Aryan source.

Unfortunately, the purity of the Aryan stock has not been maintained. If we consider the real 'progress' of humanity as being in direct ratio to the predominance, at a given epoch, of a race containing the greatest amount of pure Aryan blood, then, indeed, must it be feared that degeneracy, not progress, be the result of the present trend of social evolution. For what is degeneracy? (pp. 1089-90)

[For Gobineau, degeneracy is] synonymous with intermingling. The race which, ethnically speaking, is pure, is also the strong race. Unfortunately is purity of race nowhere to be found. It may be admitted—and, in Gobineau's thesis, it must be admitted—as an hypothesis, as a necessary hypothesis perhaps; but it is only an hypothesis. As a matter of fact, each one of us, at the twentieth generation, owes his origin to more than one million ancestors, and inherits less than one-millionth part from each; thus must everyone necessarily have more or less mixed blood in his veins. Gobineau expressly recognised that complete purity of race is a chimera; but what is not a chimera, what is certainly possible, and what is indeed necessary in the highest interests of mankind, is relative purity. That which seems, however, especially noticeable in the evolution of the human races is their constant intermingling, and this process of intermingling does not tend to diminish with the advance of civilisation. On the contrary, with the increased facilities for communication, with the levelling of the barriers that separate the classes, with the democratising influence exercised by modern science, the intermingling of the various peoples and races goes on ever increasing.

We seem to arrive, therefore, at a paradoxical conclusion. On the one hand, the strength of a race depends on its purity of blood, and the well-being of mankind as a whole depends on the strength of its composite races. It is the strong race, the race of the masters, on which the destinies of mankind depend. On the other hand, the whole mechanism of our modern civilisation tends to develop just those very conditions in which even relative purity of race is rendered impossible. Is, therefore, Western civilisation hostile to the veritable well-being of mankind, prejudicial to the real progress of the human race? Gobineau, anticipating Darwin and Nietzsche, had no hesitation in answering this question with an emphatic affirmative. (pp. 1090-91)

Gobineau took as his starting-point the fact, postulated by him *a priori,* that the racial factor dominates all the others in social evolution; religion, the environment, economic conditions, are all subordinated by Gobineau to the race. The race creates the religion adapted to its needs, it likewise modifies the environment according to its wants, and the economic conditions do but reflect its innate moral characteristics—such as its energy, its tenacity, its sense of justice. Those who attribute the greatness of a nation to its geographical position are, says Gobineau, much mistaken. Greece and Portugal, Genoa and Venice, enjoy a geographical and maritime situation similar to that of Great Britain. Why is it that Greece and Portugal, Genoa and Venice have lost their former greatness, while Great Britain has maintained her supremacy? The explanation must be sought in the fact that the dominating race in the former countries and cities, that race which was their mainstay and the *raison d'être* of their greatness, has disappeared. Thus was Gobineau led to reject all those explanations of national degeneracy which tend to substitute secondary causes for the primary one. The second chapter of the *Essai* is entitled: 'Fanaticism, luxury, immorality, and irreligion do not necessarily bring about the fall of nations.' True to his theory concerning the predominance of the race in social evolution, Gobineau was bound to seek the real cause of the fall of nations in the degeneracy of the upper classes in such nations—degeneracy caused by intermingling with inferior classes.

One of the most remarkable phenomena in history, which could not fail to strike Gobineau, as it must strike even a superficial observer, is that of the rise and fall of nations. The history of the world is as a vast stage, on which the curtain rises periodically, showing us the brilliant and wondrous spectacle of India and Persia, of Greece and Egypt, of Rome and Carthage, of Mexico and Peru, of the empires of the Turks and of the Mongols, of other empires which have shed the light of their glory on the world; and all these have fallen and disappeared, leaving in many cases scarcely any material trace of their former greatness. Gobineau, in his *Essai,* has dwelt upon the tragic fate of many of these great civilisations—of India, of Egypt, of Assyria, of Greece, of China, of Rome. What lesson, according to him, does the history of these civilisations teach us? First and foremost the fact strikes us that all the civilisations considered by Gobineau were founded by the Aryan race. This (maintains Gobineau) is no theory, but an historical fact. The yellow and black races have shown themselves incapable of founding a durable civilisation. Chinese civilisation is itself

due to the invasion of an Aryan colony from India, which subsequently intermingled with the Malay and other populations. There is no single instance of a great civilisation due to a race of Mongol or negro origin. As for hybrid races, they are likewise capable only of being civilised—not of civilising. And everywhere we find stagnation once the Aryan blood in a nation is exhausted.

Seen in the light of Gobineau's theories, history resolves itself, as M. Robert Dreyfus says [in *La Vie et les Prophéties du Comte de Gobineau* (1905)], 'into a fresque on which each race leaves the trace of its blood and of its colour.' However far backward the eye of the historical investigator may penetrate, no trace of an entirely pure race can be found. Purity of race is thus solely an hypothesis, but it is an hypothesis on which the whole doctrine of Gobineau is founded. Intermingling is the fate of every race; but, necessary as it seems to be, intermingling is none the less in the highest degree pernicious. Gobineau is pessimistic. The superior races are contaminated by crossing, and the result of this contamination is the advent of the democratic movement, with its doctrine of equality. In the measure that democracy advances, it destroys those select races, that *élite,* which formerly governed the world and rendered humanity valuable. (pp. 1092-94)

[Gobineau's doctrine] concerning the inequality of human races, concerning the growing decadence of humanity as the result of 'hybridisation' and crossings carried to excess, reminds us of one who, coming after Gobineau, has been destined to rise to the heights of fame—namely, of Friedrich Nietzsche. (p. 1095)

[Just] as Gobineau sought to show that he was the descendant of Ottar Jarl, who was in turn the emanation of Odin, so did Nietzsche endeavour to make us believe that he descended from a long line of Polish Counts of the name of Nietzky. This aristocratism pervades the works of both, constitutes the foundation of the theories of both. It was as an aristocrat that Gobineau sought to justify the position of the aristocracy in the world, in his *Essai sur l'Inégalité;* and it was his aristocratic temperament that caused Nietzsche to endeavour to separate completely the 'morals of the Masters' from the 'morals of the slaves.' The aristocrat Nietzsche did not loathe the French Revolution, and the democratic movement which has resulted from it, more intensely than did the aristocrat Gobineau. The efforts of both were concentrated on the justification of the aristocracy. The scientific apparatus brought into play by Gobineau, the magnificent historical survey of the *Essai,* the resources of anthropological, psychological, philosophical erudition from which the great Frenchman was able to draw so freely: all this is replaced, with Nietzsche, by the lyrical effusions of *Zarathustra,* by the infuriated and violent invective, beautiful by its very violence, which we find in *Jenseits,* in *Der Antichrist,* in *Götzendämmerung.* Nietzsche put Gobineau's theories into poetry. And Nietzsche was able to complete Gobineau, by making the ideas dear to the latter known throughout the world. The austere and erudite ***Essai sur l'Inégalité des Races humaines*** has remained the exclusive property of a limited number. Few people, perhaps, have read Nietzsche, and fewer have understood him. But great has been the echo of *Zarathustra* in Europe. The aphorism, convenient in form, has been conveyed from mouth to mouth, and people who have never dreamed of reading Nietzsche in the original have caught hold of certain famous aphorisms, and think they know Nietzsche. (pp. 1098-99)

Such a work as the ***Essai sur l'Inégalité*** deserves to form part of the intellectual patrimony of humanity for all times. In writing it, Gobineau raised a monument to his genius which is imperishable. And the best judgment on Gobineau, the one which most perfectly sums up the man and his work, is pronounced by a young diplomatist with more money than intellect: 'The conversation of M. de Gobineau,' said this gentleman, 'is really fatiguing; it compels one to think too much.'

In an age of superficiality, this is perhaps the highest tribute that could be paid to the Comte de Gobineau. (p. 1101)

> *Georges Chatterton-Hill, "Gobineau, Nietzsche, Wagner," in* The Nineteenth Century and After, *Vol. 73, No. 435, May, 1913, pp. 1088-1101.*

OSCAR LEVY   (essay date 1913)

[*Levy was an English physician, translator, and essayist who wrote extensively on Gobineau's life and works. In the following excerpt, he considers the strengths and weaknesses of Gobineau's racist theory and briefly surveys* Les religions et les philosophies dans l'Asie centrale *and* The Renaissance.]

When Gobineau was an old man, his *Essay on the Inequality of Human Races* went into a second edition, to which he prefixed a new introduction. In this he declares: "I leave these pages just as I wrote them many years ago, when the doctrine they contain sprang out of my mind just like a bird that puts its head out of its nest and then seeks its way in illimitable space." This poetical sentence alone gives the reader a hint of the great value of the book, a value which at first sight might not seem so obvious. For there is no doubt that the *Essay* is not free from faults. It is very long, it is rather chaotic, and it is dry reading in places. It suffers from great prejudices and from some omissions. Neither its facts, nor its theories, nor its judgments are wholly admirable or even true. But what is wholly admirable is the spirit in which the book is written. It is one of the few books that had to be written—the author's heart, one feels, would have burst in the fulness of its ecstasy, if it had not found an outlet on paper. The book is full of inward fire, of fire only half hidden and breaking out again and again from underneath the grey ashes of scientific, archæological, historic, linguistic and other facts. It is a rebellious book, but the rebel in this case is a creative rebel, a rebel from above, a rebel against the rebels of his time, and, let me add, of our own time. He is an aristocratic rebel, who has deduced and proves from history a terrible truth which he throws like a bomb into the faces of the victorious heretics, reformers, radicals, socialists, and other Philistines and Pharisees of revolution. This truth discovered by Gobineau is the all-importance of race. This truth is the neglect of the principle of race under democratic conditions. This truth is the refutation of the democratic idea that by means of an improvement in environment a healthy and noble people could be produced out of a rotten stock. (pp. xiv-xv)

History, philology, archæology, anthropology, are called in by the author to support his thesis, or rather his cry of alarm. For the poet again and again peeps out from behind his pedantic, dry, and scientific mask, and this long epic, which might fitly be called "The Twilight of the Aryan," rings out in a noble and passionate complaint, worthy of a great author and laying bare the bleeding heart of a Jewish prophet:

> Not death, but the certainty of dying in degradation, is the gloomy prospect in store for us; and perhaps this disgrace that is doomed to fall upon our posterity might leave us cold, did we

not feel, with a hidden thrill of terror, that the clawing hands of destiny are already upon our shoulders.

If we wish to gauge the importance and novelty of this idea, we must go back to the nineteenth century and remember the two main currents of thought regarding men, currents which we shall understand all the better as they are still flowing, though with diminished strength, through the thought of our own day. One of these is the spiritualistic current of Christianity, the Christianity that wishes to save every soul because it thinks everyone perfectible and possibly, if converted to the eternal truth, equal to everybody else. In opposition to this trend of thought stands the materialistic school of the natural scientist, a school based upon the ideas of Montesquieu, Herder, and Hegel, or in this country, of Buckle and John Stuart Mill, according to which a human being is an unstable entity dependent upon outside circumstances and changing with them—a creature, in short, of chance and environment. In opposition to both these schools, the spiritualistic and the materialistic, Count Gobineau had the courage to declare, in the midst of his dark age, that the environment scarcely mattered, that the "eternal truth" was an impotent assumption, and that everything, perfectibility as well as history, depended upon the blood, upon the race. His conclusions were the same as Disraeli's, who probably had never heard of him: "All is race, there is no other truth."

From this little glimpse at the *Essay* alone we may perceive that we have to do with an author of the aristocratic school, that is to say, of a school that heartily despises the values of modern morality. Gobineau . . . belongs to the same school as Nietzsche, and thus he not only despises our current opinions on "good and evil," but he fears and loathes them on account of their deleterious effect upon humanity. For Gobineau as well as Nietzsche had noticed fifty years ago what the most cultured people of to-day are only beginning to suspect, that our moral values, the values of Democracy, Socialism, Liberalism, Christianity, lead to the survival of a type of man who has no right to survive, or who ought only to survive on an inferior plane. Gobineau as well as Nietzsche knew that "good" under the present values and in our time only means "tame, adaptable, conventional," at best "industrious, persevering, efficient and businesslike." Both could never forget, and again and again they emphasize the fact, that goodness in non-vulgar times meant something quite different from to-day, that goodness once upon a time signified "energy, bravery, daring, strength of character, power of endurance, power of attacking, power of overcoming," that it did *not* mean "harmlessness, absence of faults and vices, negative virtue, female virtue, commercial sharpness and cleverness, mediocrity."

True, Gobineau did not, like Nietzsche, hold Christianity openly responsible for this transvaluation of noble values into coward's values, but he nevertheless agrees with him as to the source of this evil by pointing with great emphasis to the influence of the later Semitic race. To the earlier Semite, the warrior-Semite, the Semite under his kings, he seems to have given full approval. This *Sémite-blanc primitif* as he is called in the *Essay* is, according to the author, even a near relation to his hero, the Aryan, and his actions, as those of unbroken conqueror tribes, found in Gobineau a natural and willing admirer. Unfortunately these early white Semites mixed their blood with lower races and thus degenerated. Through this mixture, the race of Shem fell for ever from the high position it held in the ancient world; nay, it even became *le fond corrupteur* of this ancient world, and by its intermarriage with the pure and noble Aryan blood it ruined the race of Rome. Here it will be seen, we come across one of those deductions of Gobineau's which he—to satisfy his theory that every degeneration arises from the crossing of races—had to make, but which is nevertheless only a partial truth. For how, we may ask, could these insignificant Semitic tribes spoil the noble blood of a whole mighty empire, even supposing that some of them did intermarry with the Romans, which the Jews, as far as we know, never did to a great extent? And what, it might be asked, led the proud Romans to intermarry with such inferior beings?

This is, no doubt, a weak point in Gobineau's system: he overrates the physical effects of a race and neglects its spiritual influence; he overlooks the influence of ideas and values. Surely a race may influence the world directly by its blood; but yet more frequent and much more powerful is the indirect influence, the influence of ideas, and this is the influence which the Jews have exercised. It was by means of their ideas, not by means of their blood, that the Semitic race broke the Roman Empire. It was Christianity, that popular accentuation of Judaism, which among the slaves, women, and weaklings of Rome found such a ready acceptance, that slowly but surely undermined that unique and flourishing empire. It was Christianity that made the slaves equal to their masters, that, helped by decadent Pagan philosophy, poisoned the good conscience and healthy instincts of these masters, and finally led them to intermarry with slaves and barbarians. It was intermarriage with the non-race, with the people, that led to the ruin of Rome: it was the mixture of different classes . . . much more than the mixtures of different races that produced that decadent and servile chaos of the later Roman Empire.

But apart from these minor shortcomings there are startling flashes of wisdom in the *Essay,* flashes which attest the unprejudiced and pagan attitude of Gobineau's mind, and further prove that Gobineau was a Nietzschean before Nietzsche. Gobineau sees the connection between later Semitism and Democracy, he sees that Democracy is the enemy of all government and all society: "All civilisations that assume democratic forms are speedily ruined," he says. In the question of slavery, he is likewise in agreement with Nietzsche:

> Slavery, [says our author] like all human institutions, rests not only upon constraint but upon other conditions as well. . . . There is no doubt that slavery sometimes has a legitimate basis, and we are almost justified in laying down that in this case it results quite as much from the consent of the slave as from the moral and physical predominance of the master.

But the real genius of Gobineau, the clear thought, flashes out—just as that of Schopenhauer in his *Parerga and Paralipomena*—when he forgets his system and speaks of what he has seen and felt.

Gobineau's "Philosophy of History," as we have seen, is to some extent forced and questionable, and even in its truer and indisputable parts it has been more lucidly developed by Friedrich Nietzsche; but when the theory of the *Essay* leaves Gobineau he becomes a true pioneer of thought. I am referring here to a science—or rather an art, which, after the collapse of wiredrawn metaphysics and idealist tomfooleries, will play the principal part in any further philosophy: the art of psychology, that is to say, the insight into the character of human beings and the subsequent valuation of this character.

Gobineau at twenty-two years of age.

It is in this that Gobineau, as a poet, excels. His psychology of the yellow race is a masterpiece. His description of the purest and the noblest Aryan organisation, that of the Brahmins, is of the greatest value even to-day. . . . (pp. xvi-xix)

In Oriental towns, towards evening, when the talk and the bustle of the market is at its loudest, a voice from above is suddenly heard, ringing out into the crystal air over housetops and bazaars, over gardens and fountains, over rivers and coffee-houses, a voice that drowns with its clear and metallic force the noisy talk of the vulgar crowd in the market place below. It is the voice of the Muezzin who from the top of the minaret calls the faithful to prayer. Let us listen to him. Let us forget the literary market place below with its Jewish and Christian, French and German dealers in modern ideas, let us no longer heed that loud, crowded, and alas! so empty shopland, where the honest merchants are not intelligent, where the intelligent merchants are not honest, and where the crowds of sellers and buyers are neither one nor the other. Let us listen to the voice from above, let us listen to the Muezzin, let us listen to Gobineau's own words and ideas.

In light, sweet, and joyful tones this voice rings out of the pages of Gobineau's *Les Religions et les Philosophies dans l'Asie Centrale.* The first chapter of this book on the moral and religious character of the Asiatics, has justly become famous, and, with its lucid power of argument, will come as a surprise to many intelligent Europeans, accustomed as they are to look down upon all Asiatics as inferior beings. Gobineau is able to undermine many of their prejudices, for some of the so-called Asiatic vices are only vices in the eyes of the simple-minded European, and really turn out to be virtues, if only seen in the proper light. Thus, that dreaded Asiatic hypocrisy (a practice so common in Central Asia that it has received the special name of *Ketman*) is, according to our exploring ambassador, only a mask put on by the more profound Oriental mind in order to keep truth away from inferior or vulgar souls. Gobineau compares this behaviour of the modern Asiatic with that of the Greek philosophers, who likewise taught that all truth of a superior kind should be enveloped in mystery, for it was not reasonable to throw higher wisdom before inferior and unworthy beings. But while thus paying a high compliment to the intelligence and profundity of the Asiatic, Gobineau does not forget that drawback which every high development of the poetical and psychological faculties must bring in its train. It is this superabundance of thought which makes the Asiatic as much of a fantastic dreamer as a superabundance of common sense makes his European brother a dry matter-of-fact creature. And it is this crowd of ideas and theories, which constantly chase and supplant each other in the mind of the Asiatic, that are the cause and source of his political weakness. This over-intelligence, as it might be called, isolates our Asiatic from his fellows to such an extent that collective action (based as it always must be upon uniformity of sentiment in a large number of people) becomes almost an impossibility among the gifted Asiatic races. As a consolation it might be conceded to the Asiatic that fools find it much easier to combine, first because they are obliged to do so on account of their weakness, and then because no individuality of their own makes them shrink from too close a contact with their brethren. In Asia, Count Gobineau tells us, with an ironical side-glance at Europe, fools are the greatest exception.

But the best part of the book, and the greater part of it, is dedicated to the history of the Babists, a Persian sect founded shortly before Gobineau came to Persia, by a young and spirited Persian who was called "The Bab." It is a strange tale that our author has here to tell, a story which seems to us more than familiar, reminding us as it does of the common religious bonds of Asia and Europe, of the holy tales of our own gospel. Was it the intention of Count Gobineau—and this is a question that will easily occur to a critic who is accustomed to look for the meaning between the lines—to write a parody on the ancient document of the Christian faith? I do not think so for a moment, for Gobineau had, like many Catholics, even free-thinking Catholics, a sort of shyness about touching upon religion in too outspoken a manner. If there is parody, it is entirely unconscious, but parody undoubtedly there is. There is the Saviour, the "Bab," that is to say, "the only door by which one can reach the knowledge of God," a quiet, studious, patient, and somewhat mystical youth, *une âme douce et un peu rêveuse,* as Gobineau describes him. (pp. l-liii)

[The story of the "Bab"] is related in a cold and sceptical manner, very accurately to be sure, but not without touches of irony and Voltairian wit, by a man who decidedly has some doubts about all Saviours and all enthusiasts, by a man who knows from his own experience that it is more difficult to live for truth than to die for it, by a man who has a silent smile even for self-sacrifice; for he knows that self-sacrifice comes most easily to those whose self does not matter much, to those who sacrifice little with their "selves." A *grand seigneur* is relating this extraordinary story, a man who is freethinking without being unprincipled, gay without being foolish, warm-hearted without being gushing, and cool without being phlegmatic or platitudinarian. It is an important contribution to literature: the first narrative of a holy movement, by an unholy

and sober pen. It is a decided improvement upon a very holy book: it is a gospel written by a gentleman.

But let no one believe that this refined gentleman always preserves his refinement of manner. True, the tenor of the Count's literary work cannot be compared to that of the more passionate Nietzsche, whose mighty curses on civilisation run into eighteen volumes and whose only prototypes in literature—prototypes standing, though, for the opposite ideal—are the ancient Jewish prophets. But let no one be mistaken by this outward appearance of more grace, repose, and restraint: at bottom, it must be repeated again and again, Gobineau and Nietzsche are men of the same stamp, and the French Count can raise his voice to the same dangerous pitch as the German, or rather anti-German philosopher. And on these rare occasions, we entirely miss that "Greek Harmony," that "golden mean," which is so dear to the Philistine worshippers of classical antiquity, we look absolutely in vain for that "sweetness and light," which a gifted, though Victorian, author once so urgently recommended to his public; true, there is light, but only for those who can see; true, there is sweetness, but only for people with healthy and not over-fastidious tongues. (pp. liv-lv)

• • • • •

It was only natural that the artistic imagination of a Gobineau willingly turned back to that golden time of the post-Christian era, to that only time of the Christian era which was no longer Christian, to that time when Christianity lay vanquished and broken in the very heart of Christianity, in Rome itself; to the time of the Renaissance. In his predilection for the Italian Revival, Gobineau only proved once more his intimate and genuine relationship to that best school of European thought, to those few eminent poets and critics, who had all hated the Semitic infection around them, who had all abhorred the Christian revolutionary spirit, who had all turned their backs upon the slaves and their clamorous desires for liberty and equality. In the age of the Renaissance it had been—so they all saw with deep envy—*their* turn; it was the age of liberty for them, for the best, the intelligent, the daring, the brave, the proud, the beautiful—the age for an enlightened aristocracy of birth and spirit. There was liberty then, because there was no equality, for where there is liberty there can be no equality, and where there is equality there can be no liberty. Liberty is the requirement of the few, equality the wish of the many—and Gobineau's age, having declared for the many, had driven its most valuable, its only useful members into despair, madness, suicide, or at least into isolation. No wonder, those few isolated beings—a Goethe, a Stendhal, a Nietzsche, a Gobineau, and even a Heine—turned their saddened eyes back to the opposite age, to the age of freedom for them, the generous, loving, free-spirited and brave; to the age, when Kings, Popes and Statesmen were not yet servants of the mob and of the State, but masters of the State, of their own individualities, of their own wishes, and above all had wishes and desires, that corresponded to those of the great artists and writers of their time. Noble Renaissance, to what depth of despair and darkness has the world "progressed" since then!

It was left to this late-born son of the Renaissance, this pagan by heart and intelligence, this super-Christian *gentilhomme*— it was left to Gobineau to give us in [*The Renaissance*] a true historical and poetical picture of the Renaissance, such as none of his or our own contemporaries have been able to present to the world. Himself a scholar, a poet, a sculptor, and likewise an ambassador, he was so nearly related to that glorious Italian age and its versatile genius, to a Michael Angelo and a Leonardo da Vinci, that an insight into the period and into the character of its leading spirits came to him naturally and instinctively. And thus here, over the head of four centuries, one lonely but kindred spirit speaks to his equals, to his true and only, but alas, departed brethren. He understands them, with their fears and their hopes, their loves and their hatreds, their virtues and their vices—he rightly diagnoses what ruined them, he rightly divines what had elevated them. Justice itself speaks out of the pages of the book, and that highest kind of justice, an innocent, childlike, a poet's justice, a justice that is high above moral prejudices. The clear and benevolent sun of Gobineau's thought shines upon weak and strong, upon Christians and Nobles, upon Protestants and Catholics, upon populace and artists, upon saints and criminals alike, and wherever its rays fall, they warm, they adorn, and they enlighten. A man like Luther, with whom Gobineau could hardly have had any sympathy, is brought nearer to our understanding, nay, to our heart; he too, that great destructive spirit, that great unconscious evildoer, could not have acted otherwise. A man like Savonarola, that monster of morality, that Puritan of the renascence, that "Bab" translated into European and Nazarene, is appreciated by our poet, a little too much, one would even think, especially when this moralist is said to have influenced the great Michael Angelo, whose morality was certainly of a different and higher order. And not only the moral and revolutionary heroes, the rebels and the Protestants, open their hearts to the magical key of the Count's genius, but likewise their enemies, the Catholics, the faithful sons of the ancient Church, the opponents and repressors of the Reformation. There is Charles V. and his son, Philip II., stern and unbending both, typical representatives of law and order, men, who, though rightly considering the "Calvinistic and Lutheran abomination as a cancer in the flank of the Church," proceed to cure that cancer with fire and iron; favouring the Jesuitical order, re-establishing the mediæval inquisition, re-introducing the Christian faith upon the Papal chair, and thus committing more murders and atrocities than that "monster" Cæsar Borgia himself.

And murders and atrocities, which Gobineau in his innermost heart utterly condemns, for, as he is careful to inform us, these crimes of the Reformation and the counter-Reformation were, compared with those of Cæsar Borgia, absolutely senseless, because they were religious crimes. There is not the slightest doubt that Count Gobineau's sympathies, in spite of his great tolerance and his poetical benevolence towards even the religious people of the period, are entirely on the side of the pagans, of the Popes and their artists, on the side of a Julius II. and Cæsar Borgia, of a Machiavelli, and Michael Angelo. Nor is the reason for this far to seek: his book is written in favour of the Master-Morality, and Gobineau's secret endeavour is to throw suspicion upon the prevailing and all-powerful Morality of his good and brave, though neurotic, feminine, and prosaic contemporaries. (pp. lxii-lxv)

> We are bequeathing [thus run the last words of the aged Michael Angelo], We are bequeathing a great legacy, great examples.... The earth is richer than it was before our coming. What is to disappear will not disappear altogether.... The fields can rest and remain fallow for awhile: the seed is in the clods. The fog may spread and the grey and watery sky become covered with mist and rain, but the sun is above.... Who knows what will come again?

I know it—and know it for a certainty—a new Renascence. The dawn of this age is upon us: soon the sun of reason will rise again and his first rays will dissipate the fog of superstition and the nightmare of democracy. May the first translation of this truly great book help to prepare the Anglo-Saxon world for this coming new age! May it find readers worthy of its great ideals! May it give light and strength to those upon whose shoulders the heavy task of leadership may be destined to fall! (p. lxvi)

> *Oscar Levy, in an introduction to* The Renascence: Savonarola, Cesare Borgia, Julius II, Leo X, Michael Angelo *by Arthur, Count Gobineau, edited by Oscar Levy, translated by Paul V. Cohn, G. P. Putnam's Sons, 1913, pp. iii-lxvi.*

THOMAS SECCOMBE   (essay date 1916)

[*A turn-of-the-century English man of letters, Seccombe is remembered chiefly for his* Age of Johnson, *a careful study of late eighteenth-century English literary life. In the following excerpt from a review of a new translation of the* Essay, *he briefly describes and attacks Gobineau's racial theory.*]

[The] vast generalisations of Gobineau . . . [in *Essay on the Inequality of the Human Races*] furnished the stock-in-trade of Nietzsche and the champions of the superman. They express the belief arrived at already in 1853 by the author that Race and Aristocracy are the prime conditions of civilisation. Already he distrusted the influence of environment, and the efficacy of religion and morality. The great thing was to be an Indo-European or Aryan. The Aryan, or Nordic, stock was the sole guarantee of progress, and the good of mankind needed that it should rule and annihilate "slave-values." The great human types are fixed, hereditary and permanent. Climate and lapse of time cannot fundamentally alter these distinctions. Each race is shut up in its own individuality, and can issue from its idiosyncrasy only, and that with difficulty, by a mixture of blood. Of the multitude of peoples which live, or have lived, on the earth, ten alone have risen to the position of complete societies: the Indo-Aryans, the Egyptians, the Assyrians, the Greeks, the Chinese, the Roman, the Germanic, the Alleghanic, the Mexican, and the Peruvian. The remainder gravitate round these more or less independently, like planets round their suns. If there is any element of life in these ten civilisations that is not due to the impulse of the white races, any seed of death that does not come from the inferior stocks that mingled with them, then the whole theory of this book is false. The central doctrine is that there is no true civilisation possible among European peoples where the Aryan type is not predominant. No spontaneous civilisation can be found among black or yellow races. When the Aryan blood is exhausted stagnation supervenes. Historical generalisation of this frantic kind reminds us of Buckle and Disraeli. He resembles Buckle in his profound and persistent religious scepticism, Disraeli in his rejection of Darwinism. Gobineau appeals to one of the strongest prejudices of the modern world—the prejudice of race. Such an appeal strikes us as an extremely dismal one, unconvincing, grossly exaggerated, opposed to the highest interests of humanity. It represents, no doubt, the German point of view as to the exploitation of the world by the ablest and fiercest, the iron organisation of a supreme pack of whippers-in, and the devil take the hindmost. It is the negation of Christianity. (pp. 135-36)

Thomas Seccombe, "Past and Present," in The
Bookman, *London, Vol. 49, No. 292, January, 1916,
pp. 135-36.*

ALFRED RAHILLY (essay date 1916)

*[Rahilly challenges what he calls Gobineau's "blood-stock theory
of culture."]*

The real interest of Gobineau's views [in ***Essay on the Inequality
of the Human Races***] . . . lies in the fact that they were not
only incorporated into the new philosophy of the superman,
but were in unison with the eugenist preoccupations of post-
Darwinian sociology, and were compacted into the politico-
racial consciousness of at least one great European Power. Just
now there is a poignant relevancy too in his attempts to descry
the deeper causes of the development and conflict of races.
For him "the racial question over-shadows all other problems
of history, it holds the key to them all" [see excerpt dated
1853]. The fall of civilisations appeared to Gobineau to be the
most striking and also the most obscure phenomenon of history.
The spectres of dead empires—Assyria, Egypt, Greece, Rome—
haunted his imagination, and awoke in his mind the horrible
suspicion that the present world-fabric, which seems (or seemed)
so stable and secure, was destined to dissolve and leave not a
wrack behind. (p. 126)

"Every assemblage of men," [Gobineau writes] in words
prophetic of Nietzsche's Eternal Recurrence, "every assemblage of men, together with the kind of culture it produces, is
doomed to perish." No doubt, the various historic types of
culture have disappeared amid widely different circumstances.
But, if we pierce below the surface, we soon find that

> this very necessity of coming to an end, that
> weighs imperiously on all societies without ex-
> ception, presupposes a general cause, which,
> though hidden, cannot be explained away.

Such is the rather pessimistic conclusion of the Count's historical researches; and to some it has seemed that his gloomy
foreboding is finding its fulfilment. "The catastrophe," writes
Dr. Oscar Levy, "which Gobineau prophesied to an Aristocracy which had forgotten its tradition, to a Democracy which
had no root in reality, to a Christianity which he thought entirely inefficient, is now upon us." But before coming to this
conclusion it is necessary to examine carefully Gobineau's own
analysis of racial degenerescence, and to realise how there
could be built on it not only the mystical redemption of Wagner
(which is intelligible enough), but also the somewhat forced
and boisterous optimism of Nietzsche and his congeners. What
then, in Gobineau's opinion, is the general cause so fatally
provocative of the progress and decay of peoples?

He scornfully rejects the theory of the milieu, introduced into
historical science by Montesquieu and destined within a few
years to be ably vindicated by Buckle. He refuses to have
recourse to "the blessed phrase: the influence of environment."
"The brutish fellah," he urges, "is tanned by the same sun
as scorched the powerful priest of Memphis; the learned professor of Berlin lectures under the same inclement sky that
once beheld the wretched existence of the Finnish savage."
And if the physical or geographical factor cannot be accepted
as the primary moulding force of a race, the social environment
is equally incapable of creating its creator. Social institutions
preserve and promote the special genius and innate qualities

of a nation, but "they fail miserably whenever they attempt to
alter these or to extend them beyond their natural limits."

Gobineau is equally emphatic in denying the action of moral
forces. He has a chapter to prove that "fanaticism, luxury,
corruption of morals, and irreligion do not necessarily lead to
the fall of societies," and in another he maintains that "Christianity neither creates nor changes the capacity for civilisation." "The curious idea," he remarks, "that the early Romans had all the virtues has now been rightly given up by most
people." The idea that Imperial Rome had no virtue and no
religion is much more persistent, but this too Gobineau rejects.
"I believe," he says,

> that there has never been a real breach of con-
> tinuity in the religious beliefs of any nation on
> earth. . . . The theories of the men of culture
> mattered nothing; the mass of the people neither
> would nor could give up one belief before they
> had been provided with another.

We cannot, then, admit either that corruption and unbelief
shattered the pagan civilisation of Rome or that Christianity is
the source whence modern nations and cultures have taken their
rise. This rather surprising conclusion from the pen of a Catholic deserves to be given in the author's own words:

> Christianity is a civilising force in so far as it
> makes a man better minded and better man-
> nered; yet it is only indirectly so, for it has no
> idea of applying the improvement in morals and
> intelligence to the perishable things of this world,
> and it is always content with the social con-
> ditions in which it finds its neophytes, however
> imperfect the conditions may be. . . . It leaves
> all men as it finds them—the Chinese in his
> robes, the Eskimo in his furs, the first eating
> rice, and the second eating whale-blubber. . . .
> It uses all civilisations and is above all. . . . I
> have never understood the ultra-modern doc-
> trine which identifies the law of Christ and the
> interests of this world in such a way that it
> creates from their union a fictitious social order
> which it calls "Christian civilisation."

There is exaggeration in this up-to-date version of the fact that
in Christ's Church there is neither Jew nor Gentile, neither
freeman nor slave. But it is a healthy exaggeration in an age
of widespread Erastianism when the Church is regarded and
justified merely as an institution for social reform, and at a
moment when the economic and political structure of Christian
Europe has been rent asunder. The Church as an institution
does not depend on its civic or cultural utility; it owes its
existence to an act of God. "She would rather save the soul
of one single wild bandit of Calabria or whining beggar of
Palermo," writes Cardinal Newman, "than draw a hundred
lines of railroad through the length and breadth of Italy, or
carry out a sanitary reform in its fullest details in every city
of Sicily, except so far as these great national works tended
to some spiritual good beyond them."

If, then, the destiny of a people is to be explained neither by
its environment nor by its ideals, where are we to look for the
key to its history? Gobineau's answer can be put in a single
sentence: "The inequality of the races from whose fusion a
people is formed is enough to explain the whole course of its
destiny." This view implies, firstly, that any historic people
is derived from genetically different stocks; secondly, that these

stocks contribute different characters; thirdly, that these characters are permanent. In other words, Gobinism is simply eugenics writ large, or rather—if we also adopt the author's pessimistic conclusions—it is racial dysgenics. . . . [For Gobineau degeneration is] the result of miscegenation; a people dies only if it loses its aggregate of racial elements. If the empire of Darius had, at the battle of Arbela, been able to fill its ranks with Persians—that is to say, with real Aryans; if the Romans of the later Empire had had a Senate and an army of the same stock as that which existed at the time of the Fabii, their dominion would never have come to an end. As a State indeed they might have succumbed to the fortunes of war, but not as a civilisation or as a social organism; for the State is based on force, while culture is determined by breed. In Gobineau's view, society, like a multicellular animal, has its youth, maturity, old age and death; while simple organisms, such as a pure race or a protozoan, are eternal.

This, then, is what he terms his main thesis—namely, that "peoples degenerate only in consequence of the various admixtures of blood which they undergo." And he undertakes to prove this by showing that every great civilisation owed its origin and continuance to the white race, and furthermore that among these civilisations the specifically European is dependent on Aryan blood and decays when its Aryan or Germanic stock becomes enfeebled. No spontaneous civilisation is to be found among the black or yellow races; when their share of Aryan blood is exhausted, stagnation supervenes. Similarly almost the whole of Europe is at present inhabited by groups whose basis, though white, is non-Aryan; but "there is no true civilisation among the European peoples where the Aryan branch is not predominant." In fact, "where the Germanic element has never penetrated, our special kind of civilisation does not exist"; it was "the Germanic races which in the fifth century transformed the Western mind." If we confine ourselves to Europe, we may therefore express Gobineau's theory as Aristocratism plus Aryanism. He holds that all progress of European nations in art, literature and politics is due to a "race of princes," and that this aristocratic race is of Germanic blood. It is necessary to distinguish these two theses, because, while Nietzsche adopted only the first, publicists and popular ethnologists have advocated the second.

The blood-stock theory of culture naturally appealed to an aristocratic imperialist such as Gobineau and to a megalomaniac would-be-aristocrat like Nietzsche. To both of them democracy was the culminating crime of humanity, it was the sin against the race-spirit; salvation could be had only by preserving the power and purity of the ruling caste. (pp. 127-31)

If Gobineau's historic Aryanism . . . proves to be scientifically untenable, what is left of his general theory of the inequality of human races? His suggestive analysis of the decadence of peoples is undoubtedly of permanent value, for it is really based on the existence of different hereditary strains in a people or nation. It is easy to imagine several ways in which a differential social selection acting on these stocks may produce national degeneration. Such a military differentiation of blood occurred both in ancient Greece and in republican Rome. We read of seven hundred families being exiled at one time from Athens and a thousand leading citizens executed at Mitylene; Rome witnessed the wholesale massacres of Marius, Cinna, Sulla, and the Triumvirs. In both cases history selected the best stock for extinction and committed the future to the progeny of the mediocre and the unfit. A modern war does the same, and the present differential birth-rate is a similar form of race-murder.

But Gobineau's further identification of these strains with definite historic races or prehistoric ethnic types is a much more doubtful assumption. All that we really know of such races are a few cranial measurements and colour observations; beyond these nothing else can be definitely predicated of any European race. There certainly is not the slightest proof that we can correlate all the complex incommensurable qualities which go to constitute greatness and nobility, with two or three simple physical characteristics such as blondness, tallness, and long-headedness. Gobineau's Aryan is as unreal and unscientific as Lombroso's criminal.

Furthermore, the admission of comparatively stable strains in a people has no parity with the supposition of intrinsically immutable races. When we speak of these strains as nature in opposition to nurture, we merely mean those qualities which are relatively permanent under the small range of variation of the external conditions which prevails in practice. It is merely implied that the ordinary environmental changes subject to municipal or individual control have only a limited direct influence on racial progress. There is absolutely no implication that the relatively impervious nucleus which we call nature or strain would not be susceptible to other or more prolonged variations of environment. Indeed, this latter suggestion is verified in the case of animals and plants; witness the experience of British pedigree stock in Argentina and of American cotton in Egypt. In the case of human races there is ample evidence that under certain conditions they are capable of large physical and mental changes. The Teutons, who are now exalted as the ideal of development, must have appeared irredeemable savages to the ancient Romans, just as the yellow and black races appeared to Gobineau. The great cultural advance of Fijians, Hindus, Maoris, and Japanese is also quite contrary to his anticipations and predictions. We have no right to assume a final blood inferiority of these "backward" races. If racial variety is the result of environmental changes such as climatic control, then similar changes must still be capable of producing such variety. The distinctive blondness and stature of the Teuton can only be accounted for on the supposition that they are due to the influence of the northern environment and artificial selection acting on a branch of the neolithic Europeans. Indeed, there is contemporary evidence that a race does not remain permanently true to type except under the conditions of its race-home. For instance, the negro of North America has already begun to show approximation to the white in facial outline, skull-shape, and intellectual development, this last probably due to greater elasticity of cranium allowing its contents to expand. Similarly it has been found that the American-born Jew is taller and more long-headed than the European-born.

When from physical environment we turn to social and economic influences we find ample evidence that the inequality is largely artificial. For example, we have often heard of the incurable laziness of the negro; we now know that it is due to hookworm. (pp. 138-40)

[We] may fitly conclude that, before attributing to some mysterious and inherent inequality of race the diversities of character and capacity of mankind, we should first exhaust the possible influence of physical, social, and economic environment. And, as this has not yet been done, the thesis of Gobineau remains unproved. (p. 140)

Alfred Rahilly, "Race and Super-Race," in The Dublin Review, *Vol. 159, No. 318, July, 1916, pp. 125-40.*

THE TIMES LITERARY SUPPLEMENT (essay date 1922)

[*This anonymous critic favorably discusses the artistry of three of Gobineau's imaginative works,* L'abbaye de Typhaines *(Typhaines Abbey),* Ternove, *and* The Crimson Handkerchief.]

For most readers of French literature Gobineau is a man of two books—*La Renaissance* and *L'Essai sur l'Inégalité des Races Humaines.* These two works, so suggestive of more recent ideas, have alone kept Gobineau some reputation among the general public. He has always had a few enthusiasts who have admired and collected his almost unobtainable works. Now an effort is being made to republish a number of his works which have lain forgotten for nearly half a century, while others which had never been published at all are now being issued for the first time. . . . If the three books reviewed here [*L'Abbaye de Typhaines, Ternove* and *Souvenirs de Voyage*] are typical of Gobineau's talent, it is rather surprising that the bulk of his work should have fallen into such complete oblivion. They have obvious limitations, but also quite obvious merits. There is something a little factitious in the novel convention Gobineau adopts, but, on the other hand, there is nothing merely freakish or purely opportunist in it. In each case Gobineau was aiming at the creation of a work of art. Except for two stories in *Souvenirs de Voyage* he seems to have just failed to achieve the big things he planned for himself. And the reader is bound to be worried by the inevitable comparisons; *L'Abbaye de Typhaines* might be simply an attempt to write a Scott novel more intelligently and less conventionally than Scott; *Ternove* might be merely a re-working of a typically Stendhalien theme. There precisely is the trouble; there are obvious faults in both Scott and Stendhal as novelists, and yet no one, even a man of genius, can write a better Scott novel than Scott merely by avoiding his faults.

Look for a minute at *L'Abbaye de Typhaines.* Gobineau clearly intended to give a less romantic, more accurate panorama of medieval life than Scott, with his temperament, prejudices, and purely conventional idea of the novel, ever attempted. Gobineau has carefully avoided any such threadbare device as that of the missing heir so over-worked by Scott; he has also dropped the happy family ending, whose absence in the *Bride of Lammermoor* only makes the exception more startling. This is no disparagement of Scott's genius; it is simply a *constatation* one cannot honestly avoid. And yet, though Gobineau must be allowed great power of evocation, thorough knowledge of his period, skill in characterization, and great ability in linking up a number of rapid adventures, *L'Abbaye de Typhaines* is distinctly inferior to *Ivanhoe,* for example. And this is all the more odd because Gobineau's main theme is an excellent one and really far more interesting that the factitious chivalry of *Ivanhoe.* Perhaps the difference lies in a certain lack of humour and "human nature"; Gobineau's women, Damerones and Mahaut, are certainly more life-like than Rebecca and the fair Rowena, but he has no scene with half the zest and movement and enjoyment of the carouse of Friar Tuck and the Black Knight. *L'Abbaye de Typhaines* is a little too political, not quite enough of a novel. Avowedly it was written with the purpose of showing the similarity between the Revolution of 1789 and the uprising of the medieval communes. The history of the rebellion of the tenants of Typhaines against their feudal lord, the abbot, is the central motive of the story.

Where Gobineau excels is in his typically French talent of character "portraits." In the course of his narrative he attempts most of the salient characters of medieval France, and it must be admitted that he "renders" them amazingly well. Philippe de Cornehaut represents the medieval ideal of the good knight, a Crusader, a born fighter, though not quarrelsome, true to his lady, honest, rather stupid, proud of his rank and birth, perfectly ready to sacrifice himself for the only social order he understands—that of the Church and the feudal overlord. In Simon we have the opposite type of the revolutionary, the fanatical lover of liberty, who spends his energy and the force of his strong character in urging the townspeople to rebel against their feudal lord and set up a commune. Abbot Anselm, a carefully described character, is the typical Church landlord of the best kind, disinterested, self-sacrificing, charitable but utterly inflexible when it comes to yielding a fraction of the power and land which the Church has entrusted to him; a Churchman with a military sense of duty. The Bishop of Châlons is the more learned, egotistical, and fussy Churchman; Saint Norbert, the wandering preacher, represents the mixture of energy, abilities, and mysticism which made up the medieval saint, like Bernard. We get portraits of Louis le Gros, a mere soldier, inferior in splendour to many of his powerful vassals; the Comte de Nevers, the small sovereign vassal; Baudouin, the merely unscrupulous baron; the Abbé de Saint-Denis, the born administrator, working to reduce the strength of the vassals and to make France a real kingdom—a work not achieved until the reign of Louis XI. Then there are Cornehaut's squire, Foulkes, a sort of faithful Gurth; Rigauld, superstitious and servile; Payeu, rather like the smith in the *Fair Maid of Perth;* Joslin, the merely stupid and brutal serf; Mahaut, the jealous and petulant *châtelaine;* Damerones, the *bourgeoise,* capable of passion and devotion, who naturally becomes a nun. All this gallery is exceedingly animated and moves through Gobineau's pages in a lively way. If some of the characters are conventional, that is simply because the remoteness of time causes us to see the people of those distant centuries as types rather than as individuals. It is inevitable that an attempt to recreate the whole life of a period should result in a mere panorama; Scott instinctively limits the extent of his canvas and avoids these gigantic historical themes.

Ternove is a very different and perhaps rather more successful book. It was an early work . . . , and its First Empire setting, as well as the character of Octave de Ternove, give it an oddly Stendhalien appearance. The description of the Hundred Days is particularly lively and vivid; it is perhaps worth mentioning that Gobineau got his facts from his father, who was an aide-de-camp in the small remnant of the army which remained loyal to Louis XVIII. All this part of the novel is worth comparing with Stendhal's celebrated description of Waterloo, and Chateaubriand's no less celebrated description of the flight to Ghent. There are some admirable touches in Gobineau's description, like that where he describes the disorder in the Royal Army, except for one regiment, which happened to have been recruited from Napoleon's Guard. In this novel Gobineau has abandoned the panoramic method and historical events are strictly subordinated to the main action, which centres about Octave de Ternove. This typically Stendhalien young man is tossed between love and ambition; trying to gratify both passions he naturally comes to grief.

Gobineau is a cynic about love; he appears to think it a misfortune whatever happens. Thus in *L'Abbaye de Typhaines,* the knight does not get Mahaut, and goes off in despair to die as a Templar; in *Ternove* Octave gets Marguerite and is completely bored in consequence. Gobineau has admirably drawn the character which is bound to be miserable because it desires incompatible goods from life. To be happily married is a career so exacting as to leave no room for other ambitions.

Souvenirs de Voyage shows that the short story was Gobineau's real *forte*. "La Chasse au Caribou" is negligible, a mere *boutade,* a caricature of American extravagance; but both "**Le Mouchoir Rouge**" and "**Akrivie Phrangopoulo**" are admirable, something between a Balzac and a Conrad story. Under the discipline of this form Gobineau had no chance to run into his faults of diffuseness and a crowded stage. He is forced to keep the main episode, and he does it triumphantly. He is very sharp at noticing the idiosyncrasies of Levantine morals, the curious mixture of primitive and subtle motives. "**Le Mouchoir Rouge**" makes one think of a Casanova adventure described by Balzac; it is one of those calmly arranged assassinations which seem revolting to us, but which are the simplest things in the world to a couple of Mediterranean lovers. But the story of the lady with the long Greek name is the masterpiece. The English naval officer, the two solemnly old-fashioned Greek dignitaries, Akrivie herself, are all perfect. And how Gobineau enjoys his irony! We have seen him deny happiness in other love affairs; here he makes a perfectly happy marriage between an English aristocrat and a Greek girl as primitive as Nausicaa. According to Gobineau, the marriage was successful merely because of this primitive quality in Akrivie; she had not the slightest pretension to a life of her own. When Captain Scott asks her to marry him she is merely hurt; but when he sees his mistake and "arranges" the matter with her father she is perfectly contented. She is magnificent physically, a sort of Homeric heroine; but completely undeveloped mentally, an obedient daughter, an obedient wife. After she is married Akrivie has no interest in the world except her husband and possible children. A pleasant slap at Romanticism and Feminism! The descriptions of Mediterranean islands, the sea, the volcano, in these two stories are truly admirable. They carry one's mind at once to the magnificent descriptive gift of Mr. Conrad. They are certainly well above Gobineau's other work and ought to remain permanently in French literature. It is truly amazing that they should have been overlooked so long. Perhaps in the excitement of discovery one tends to overestimate an author, yet, making every allowance for the rosy views of enthusiasm, one can certainly claim that Gobineau is an author who deserves to be read for more than *La Renaissance* and the *Essai sur l'Inégalité des Races Humaines.* Even a literature so rich as French cannot afford to disdain him.

"The Revival of Gobineau," in The Times Literary Supplement, *No. 1082, October 12, 1922, p. 642.*

ERNEST R. TRATTNER   (essay date 1938)

[*Trattner was an American author and rabbi who wrote widely on the history of ideas. In the following excerpt, taken from a chapter on the evolution of racism in his* Architects of Ideas, *Trattner remonstrates against Gobineau's theory of Aryan supremacy, attributing to his influence the rise of twentieth-century German nationalism.*]

Of the many people who have passionately believed in the superiority of the white race none has exerted as profound an influence, or has played as important a role among the *idées-forces* of our modern world, as the French journalist and diplomat, Count Arthur de Gobineau. . . . Perhaps no other book on race has had such a tremendous influence, as did his *Essai sur l'inégalité des races humaines* (*Essay on the Inequality of Human Races*). What Karl Marx's *Das Kapital* has meant to communists, Gobineau's *Essai* has meant to race-dogmatists. (p. 356)

Gobineau was unquestionably an able and many-sided man—poet, artist, novelist, diplomat, politician, journalist, sculptor, traveler—but his mind was pervaded with a disgust for democracy and a hatred of humanity which can be traced in the forty volumes he has left us. The *Essai,* however, was inspired by Gobineau's researches begun on his own family tree; and by his own admission it was written in part to prove the superiority of his own race. Simply put, Gobineau argued that the white race—the Aryan—is superior to all other races, and of the Aryans (of which Gobineau passionately believed he was a member) the Germans are the purest modern representatives. He was among the first to call the Latin races decadent. Of the population of his own country, Gobineau declared that the vast masses were racially a Gallo-Roman mob "whose chief instinct is envy and revolution." He deplored the fact that France has only a few Aryan Nordics.

The foundation of Gobineau's system is the classification and characterization of the races. He divides mankind into three races: the *black,* which represents passion, is animal-like and capricious, yet possessed of lyricism and the artistic temperament; the *yellow* which represents mediocrity, is stubborn and apathetic, but is gifted with a sense of order and a sense of practicality; the *white,* which possesses godlike reason and honor, excels in all things. Particularly does it excel in physical beauty. "The peoples who are not of white blood approach beauty but do not attain it." As regards physical strength Gobineau said, "We shall have to give the palm to those who belong to the white race." (p. 357)

Gobineau's racial theory furnished a simple explanatory key whereby one could construct a grand and sweeping philosophy of history. "I have become convinced," declared Gobineau with strong dogmatic emphasis, "that everything in the way of human creation, science, art, civilization, all that is great and noble and fruitful on earth, points to a single source, is sprung from one and the same root, belongs only to one family, the various branches of which have dominated every civilized region of the world" [see excerpt dated 1853]. This one family, Gobineau revealed, is none other than the Aryan race. All civilization originally sprang from the virile qualities of Aryans, and wherever civilization declines it is because Aryan blood has been bastardized by intermarriage. With the admixture of bloods Aryans always lose their sense of aristocracy and also their high consciousness of race superiority. This then opens the way for decadence and degeneracy which insist on equality—that is, democracy. Although "the white race originally possessed the monopoly of beauty, intelligence and strength, by its union with other varieties hybrids were created, which were beautiful without strength, strong without intelligence, or, if intelligent, both weak and ugly." Thus Gobineau's explanation is simplicity itself. Why do civilizations rise? Because of Aryan blood. Why do they fall? Because that blood is contaminated by foreign elements. Hitler has taken these chapters to heart.

There is a platitude in logic that a man can prove anything if he selects his evidence and uses it to bolster his theory. Take the case, for example, of the good bishop who stood for the first time on Mount Sinai and solemnly ejaculated: "Now I know that Moses wrote the Pentateuch." Patient investigation and dependable evidence had nothing to do with his ecstatic outburst. In a sweep of ecstasy akin to that of the bishop, Gobineau stood one day on an islet in the North Sea, one of the Skaeren, and felt a "mystic conviction" that his remote ancestors originated on this tiny pine-fringed rock. Although the Count was brown-haired with golden brown eyes, this did not prevent him from actually believing that he was a Nordic-Aryan descended from Ottar Jarl, a Viking hero.

Thus Gobineau could not only quote Scripture for his purposes but he was extraordinarily facile in inventing his own passages. He stretched, warped, distorted and created evidence to his own liking, and then permeated the whole with the mysticism of pseudo science which the Germans hungrily absorbed. That the supreme race is the Aryan and the Teutons are its modern wonder-working representatives was most palatable to the Germans embarking upon an ambitious career of exploitation and conquest. The fact that nothing was known scientifically of an Aryan race, that its supposed existence was a purely hypothetical construction, apparently never troubled these dogmatists.

Among those who are without knowledge of the merits and demerits of opposing theories, the one which is understood with the least effort is the one most likely to gain acceptance. Gobineau's contribution in elaborating these Aryan concepts into the Teutonic myth was a considerable factor in the growth of Germany's race vanity, chiming in beautifully with the aspirations of the leaders of Pan-Germanism. It is amusing to note, however, that Gobineau on numerous occasions denied the identity of the heroic Germans or Teutons (*les Germains*) with the modern Germans (*les Allemands*). He even placed the German people below the French in racial value because he thought them more mixed. To the many contradictions in Gobineau's writings the Germans paid slight heed. The Gobineau societies flourished. (pp. 358-59)

> *Ernest R. Trattner, "Boas . . . Theory of Man," in his* Architects of Ideas: The Story of the Great Theories of Mankind, *Carrick & Evans, Inc., 1938, pp. 351-74.*

ARNOLD H. ROWBOTHAM (essay date 1939)

[*In this detailed description of Gobinist Aryanism, Rowbotham exposes what he considers its weaknesses and links it to contemporary events.*]

As an ethnological theory, "Aryanism" has been examined and rejected by experts but it has persisted as a social and political theory and in recent times it is being used to give moral support to a new type of nationalism in which the State takes over those functions of government slowly developed by the democracies of the West during the last two hundred years. As a social and political philosophy, "Aryanism" is the expression of the conviction that the moral excellencies of our civilization are derived from a single race, the Aryans, who are supposed to have sprung into being somewhere in the plateaux of Central Asia.

Aryanism, in theory, is the expression of an aristocratic ideal, an essential belief in pure racial stock as a necessary basis of leadership in human affairs. It is not surprising, therefore, that it should have found its first most active theoretical expositor in a Frenchman whose whole life and thought breathed the spirit of aristocracy. This man [was] Joseph-Arthur, Comte de Gobineau. . . . For the greater part of . . . thirty years, Gobineau served his country at Frankfort, Berne, Athens, Stockholm, and in Newfoundland, Brazil, and Persia. His diplomatic career gave him the opportunity to study the life and customs of the countries to which he was accredited. He was enormously interested in the traces of the past which he found there. In each country he used his brilliant powers of observation and

his undoubted erudition to evoke the historical background of the place, to evaluate the heritage of tradition which was to be found there and to place that country within the framework of the ethnological system which he has already created. In Athens he immersed himself in the glories of ancient Greece and tried with his own hands to reproduce a little of the beauty of Hellenic sculpture. In Stockholm he lived again the heroic days of the Northern sagas. His years at Teheran gave him material for several volumes, notably his *History of the Persians,* a brilliant though somewhat fantastic story of the Iranian people, and two small volumes on the *Religions and Philosophies of Central Asia,* filled with extraordinarily acute observations on oriental psychology. For the young diplomat the study of history and race *mores* was a fascinating, almost a mystical, experience. He had the faculty of re-living, in his own mind, the ancient life of the country and of vitalizing the emergence of that past in the life of the present. (pp. 152-53)

[Gobineau's] life and philosophy remained true, to the very last, to the principles expounded in the masterpiece which he had written at the early age of thirty-five, the *Essay on the Inequality of Human Races.* In each place that he lived he saw in everything around him the proofs of his aristocracy. This conviction grew, rather than diminished, as he advanced in age. When he was sixty-three, he put his ideas regarding his racial heritage in a work entitled *The History of Ottar Jarl, Norwegian Pirate . . . and of his Descendants.* This, one of the most remarkable family histories ever written, is his *apologia pro vita sua.* "I descend from Odin" is his text as he attempts to trace the history of his divine origin. It is said of Gobineau that one day visiting the Nordic ruins near Djursholm, he exclaimed to his companion "This is the city of Ottar Jarl. This is the place of my origin. I feel it." The work is permeated with this mystical conviction. There are, perforce, lacunae in the story where the records are lacking, (the author particularly bemoans a gap of a hundred years, from 1453 to 1550) but on the whole the author can trace, to his satisfaction, the course of the Viking blood down through the centuries until it reached him, Arthur Joseph de Gobineau, a French nobleman of the nineteenth century. He gloried in this rôle of nobleman when, in 1857, he purchased the château of Trye in Normandy, the country of his ancestors, where he lived with aristocratic dignity and the keenest satisfaction the life of a feudal nobleman.

But if the motive force of his life is to be found in his unfailing sense of aristocracy the center of his thought lies in his conception of the Race and its importance in human history. For Gobineau the question of Race in the development of civilization outweighed all others. The reason for the rise and fall of nations is to be found not in the effects of luxury, of fanaticism, of evil manners or irreligion but in the nature of their blood mixture. The persistence of a culture is determined by the degree of purity of the stock. But history has been proved that racial purity is hard to maintain. There is in man a dual urge of repulsion and attraction and the relation of these two elements working in the race explains its subsequent history. The strength of a people is determined only by the permanence of its stock, but this is difficult to maintain. Political conquest does not save a race. The conqueror, by his superior energy, may be predominant for a time but by the infiltration of the blood of the conquered, he finally falls a victim of the deadly process of miscegenation. So the course of all history is to be explained by this element of blood mixture. (pp. 154-55)

The purpose of Gobineau's *Essay,* according to the author, was "to fix and determine the principle of death in all societies and to trace its effects on the lives of the nations of whom history has left us a record''. The book falls in the class of those works, such as Bossuet's *Discourse on Universal History,* which attempt to explain the story of civilization in terms of a single, and often predetermined, thesis. It substitutes for Boussuet's Divine Providence the idea of a Chosen People, the Aryans, and the work is the story of the latter's dissemination and gradual corruption. The author first establishes a hierarchy of the races. At the bottom is the negro, whose determining characteristics are blind appetite, predominance of the senses, and an instability of desires. On the middle level is the yellow race with the tendencies toward mediocrity (a damning characteristic in the eyes of the author), a love of the practical and a respect for custom. At the top of this hierarchy is the white race and for them Gobineau (borrowing perhaps from Montesquieu) chooses Honor as the motive of conduct. Having determined the anthropological basis for his system he then proceeds to historical considerations. Here, strangely enough, he falls back on the Biblical legend of the sons of Noah. This furnishes interesting evidence of his fundamental conservatism. Throughout his work, Gobineau pays lip service to the Christian faith, even while the logical course of his ideas leads him to a rejection of religion as a vital influence in human culture. The lord of the manor of Trye, who attended religious services every Sunday out of a feeling of *noblesse oblige,* accepted organized religion as an ally of tradition and therefore of aristocracy. He saw no inconsistency, therefore, in basing his system on the ancient legend of Shem, Ham, and Japheth.

The Aryans were, then, a branch of the family of Japheth who, in the course of its migrations, had come to rest somewhere on the plateaux of Central Asia. As he describes this ideal race the language of the writer forsakes the calm precision of the scientist and adopts the lyrical accents of the poet. ''Everything great, noble and fruitful on this earth which the mind of man has devised'', he proclaims, ''science, art, civilization, brings the observer to a single point, comes from a single germ, results from a single thought, belongs to only one family the different branches of which have reigned in all civilized countries of the universe'' [see excerpt dated 1853]. In other words: The history of civilization is the history of the Aryan.

This race of heroes in due time migrated from the Central Asian plateaux. One branch went southward in the direction of Assyria where they mingled with the yellow sons of Ham. Another branch met the sons of Shem who introduced the black strain into their blood. By these mixture of the sons of Shem and Ham became responsible for all the corrupting influences in subsequent racial development. The Semitic mixture then turned on the Hamitic and, subduing them, produced the Mediterranean peoples and started the movement whereby the principle of authority seeped gradually from the topmost stratum of society downward until it permeated the whole, producing a vast mediocrity and creating modern democracy. Gobineau, while admitting certain good effects of the Semitic invasion of Europe, sees in the movement a vast degrading force, the chief implement of disaster in the West.

In this semitizing of Europe the Hebrews imitated their racial brothers (to use the words of the Baron de Seillière) ''as the French provincial imitates the Parisian''. Gobineau's attitude towards the Jew is not entirely consistent. As a believer in the supreme virtue of the persistence of racial stock, he is forced to praise this quality in the Hebrew people but he includes them in his condemnation of the Semitic races and, in general, he sees in them only a disturbing factor on all peoples, which has

led critics to believe that his theories imply anti-semiticism, in the modern implication of the term.

While the Semitic peoples were being established in south eastern Asia, a wandering group of Aryans had reached the valley of the Nile, imposed themselves on the black race there, and founded the Egyptian race. Below the Pamir plateau the Aryans had become the Aryas of India. Here the caste system (the definite social distinction between the élite and the pariah) enabled the Aryan to retain for a time the purity of his blood but finally Buddhism was introduced and, dealing a vital blow to Brahmanism, hastened the decadence of the Hindu Aryan.

So, several centuries before Christ, there were signs everywhere of the growing corruption of the god-like Aryan stock. The subsequent history of the race is the story of the persistence of this purity, in a modified degree, in certain ''oases'' of culture: the Aryas of India, the Iranians of Persia, the Hellenic Greeks and the Sarmates (fathers of the Germanic tribes). The problem of China caused the author some difficulty, since he maintained that no great nation could exist without the presence of Aryan blood. He solved the problem by asserting that, in the earliest times, a band of Aryan Hindu warriors had invaded the country and imposed their strain on the natives. How this mixture resulted in customs of universal mediocrity, the exact opposite to the characteristics of the conquerors, Gobineau never satisfactorily explained. Problems of this kind, which seem to present insuperable difficulties, are inherent in a system based on such sweeping generalizations. The author never allowed himself to be worried by contradictions of detail but the number of the contradictions, as Houston Chamberlain says, ''relegates the work to the hybrid class of scientific phantasmagoria''.

Having followed the god-like Aryans through Asia and Northern Africa, we are now brought to Europe where Gobineau finds striking support of his theories. It was Greece which was first in the path of the flood of Semitic corruption sweeping northward from Asia; Greece, who in the legends of the Titans retained for centuries the story of the Aryan protagonists of the race. Gobineau asserts that the first stages of miscegenation produced only good. Theseus was a real Aryan, a cousin of the Vikings. Ulysses, on the other hand, was a fine type of the Semitized Aryan. The Homeric age represents the period when the effect of decadence through blood mixture had not begun to show its effects.

Two aspects of Greek culture, in particular, received the author's attention. The first was Greek art and philosophy which Gobineau admired so profoundly (even while, he significantly adds, he ''reserves his respect for more essential things''). It is not surprising, in view of his idea of the Aryan, to find him asserting that the ''glory of Greece'' owed its source to the infiltration of the Semitic blood, just as had been the case with Assyria and Egypt. The pure Aryan was a man of action, a devotee of the cult of energy. He lived in an atmosphere of strife. His baptism was of blood; his career that of the sword. He was a doer and not a thinker. There is in this glorification of energy an implied contempt for the intellect and the artistry of man. The Aryan rose to his pre-eminent place as a leader through his physical gifts, and his moral superiority lay in certain essential characteristics which Gobineau never clearly explained. Herein lies the glaring weakness of his system. It is apparent, if we follow the author's ideas, to their logical conclusion, that the life of thought, the products of art and philosophy, become a kind of inferior substitute for energy, on a lower moral level. Thus we arrive almost at the Rousseauist conclusion that the products of human skill and intelligence are a sign, if not a source, of decadence. In its moral implication the theory leads to the dictum that Might makes Right which is, indeed, the conclusion of the contemporary cult of Aryanism in Germany.

The other element which interested the author in Greece was its rôle in the development of the democratic state. Democracy, whether in its ancient Greek form or in the modern conception, was to Gobineau anathema. It was the antithesis of that individualism which was the outstanding characteristic of the Aryan hero. It was the triumph of the "mud" (la boue) over the "élite". In his epic poem *Amadis* (written late in life and published posthumously) it is Ahriman, the arch-spirit of evil, who proudly boasts that he invented the rabble. In the same poem, Theophrastus, a Gobinian Lucifer who is making war on the heroes, asserts that he is in alliance with the disbelievers in God, the traitors and the Masses. . . . The poet attributes to the people the spirit of the iconoclast. . . . He condemns in the masses an inability to choose their rulers, making them the prey of the demagogue. He pours his scorn on their unthinking restlessness and their tendency to "love and hate according to the newspapers". For Gobineau, the true course of history had been diverted by the revolution of 1789 which had opened the door "to violence and all the democratic atrocities". This feeling that he was living in the Dark Ages undoubtedly colored his whole pessimistic philosophy. It certainly caused him to minimize the importance of Greek culture.

Greece, then, had well reached the first stages of decay when it passed on its culture to Rome. In spite of its virility and energy, Gobineau sees little to admire in Roman civilization. He sees in the descendants of Romulus no real race. They were a mixed breed already enervated by miscegenation and fell an easy prey to the deadly effects of luxury introduced by the Semitic blood from the south. He scornfully condemns their culture as the product of the vilest plebeian and the humble bourgeois. This defilement became more widespread through the Roman system of colonization which encouraged intermarriage with native women throughout the empire. This had the effect of bringing about the "chaos of the nations" and the hastening of the final catastrophe. In some of the most eloquent pages of the *Essay* Gobineau graphically describes this universal decadence.

This gradual deterioration of racial stock produced by Semitic blood flooding in from the south was met by a similar movement from the north where the Aryan Celts and Gauls had already been tainted with the "frivolous", pacific yellow race and were rapidly losing the high seriousness of their Aryan character (and, incidentally, developing a genius for commerce). The Celts had at first enslaved their Mongolian visitors. This gives the author a chance to explain his views on slavery. He asserts that the tendency towards racial mixture often produces a condition whereby the inferior race places itself more or less willingly in a position of serfdom, as a social and economic necessity. He implies that the abuses of the slave system are not sufficient excuse to deny its social necessity. This championship of slavery is not surprising in a man who looked upon society as being divided into two classes, masters and servants. The term which Gobineau uses for the masses in *Amadis:* "la boue" is indicative of his attitude towards the great majority of his fellow beings. The humanitarian theories started by Montesquieu and his fellow philosophers a hundred years earlier had in no way modified his aristocracy and as he saw in human affairs no movement of progress, but rather the

contrary, he did not concern himself with the problem of the progressive amelioration of the lot of the common man.

The Aryan-Celts, then, were rendered decadent by the blood of the yellow race and, even in his own time, Gobineau thought he could see, in the faces of the Breton peasants around him, the traces of this Mongolian defilement. As for the Slavs, the other branch of the Aryans which produced the Celts, he concurs in the contempt shown in the Russophobia of his time. He finds them "a stagnant marsh in which all superior ethnic strains, after a few hours of triumph find themselves engulfed".

So, by the end of the empire, the deadly work of miscegenation had brought complete disaster to almost the whole of Europe. Then, on this universal European decadence, burst the godlike Nordics, the Germanic and Scandinavian Aryans from the north. The newcomers belonged to two separate branches of the Aryan race. The one, the Sarmates, had descended from the Scythians who, intermarrying with the Amazons, had dwelt for a time in the Caucasus until, swinging north, they founded the people of the Alans or Roxolans in central Russia, where in their city of Asgard, they already resembled the Germanic heroes of the sagas. Travelling still north and west, they split into two streams: the one occupying Pomerania and Southern Sweden as the Goths; and the other, under the name of the Sakas, going to Norway. These are the Aryans of the modern theories. With that restlessness characteristic of all the Aryans (for Gobineau's Chosen People have throughout history been nomads) they aryanized the Celtic mixture to the south and gave them vigor to oppose the first wave of the Germanic invasion. Meantime in the east the Aryan blood had become defiled by mixture with the Huns. In the West and North-west, away from danger of contact with other races, the divine stock remained pure. Even among these Germanic tribes however, the degree of racial purity differed, in direct relation to their geographical situation. The ascending order of this racial hierarchy is as follows: the Goths, the Vandals, the Lombards, the Burgundians, the Franks and the Anglo-Saxons, the latter being of the purest racial stock. These were the tribes who swept south to overwhelm the decadent Roman empire. That they were not able to revive the glories of Rome is due to the fact that they themselves were infected by the virus of miscegenation. The subsequent history of Europe is the story of this degeneration. All that is noble, all that is worth while in this history is explained by the persistence, or rather emergence in a certain group, of the original Aryan characteristics, producing what the author calls "golden flowers" (*fleurs d'or*) of culture such as the Italian Renaissance, or in the isolated individual, producing the "hero" of the Carlyle tradition.

We may pause here to ask: What were the characteristics of these god-like Nordics? Gobineau has left us no doubt as to their nature. Of noble stature, handsome appearance, and warlike disposition, the Aryan is superior to all others in the measure of his intelligence and his energy. These two elements dominate his character and determine his morality, good or bad. "Thus placed on a pedestal", says the author of the *Essay,* "standing out against the background which he dominates, the Germanic Aryan is a powerful creature. His superiority over his *milieu* gives to everything he does or says a major importance." In politics he is an individualist. With him "man is everything and the nation nothing". When he associates with his fellows of other racial stock it is the association of master and servant, for the nobility of his features, the vigor and majesty of his tall stature and his muscular strength make of him a super-man. His whole life is regulated by the cult of freedom. Even the sacred terms "patriotism" and "home" have little meaning for him, being, in effect, restrictions on his personal liberty. He is his own judge of morality and ethics, committing his share of reprehensible acts (Gobineau will not deny him the "virility" of lawlessness) with a kind of godlike superiority over good and evil. For religion his imagination builds for him a pantheon where the gods are only dimly distinguished from the heroes of his race. His paradise is a Valhalla where wine and blood flow freely.

Under the stress of blood mixture with the Celts and the Slavs these characteristics are modified. He finally accepts the gods of his defilers and becomes an idolator. He adopts also the institution of priesthood, giving to the priest the task of civil administration. The criminal is given over to the latter for punishment, a living sacrifice not to the vengeance of man but to the anger of the gods. The center of the social law is the *odel*, the incontestable property of the chief, where he remains undisputed master. Political disintegration and corruption comes when the *odel* as the unit of society is displaced by the rule of the *konungr* or king and, in the act of homage of the feudal system, the original freedom of the original Aryan is destroyed. Under the feudal system the Nordic hero starts down the long descent to ruin. Slowly, inevitably the race becomes corrupt and the end, universal ruin, is the pessimistic conclusion of the Gobinist philosophy.

The significant element in this system of Gobineau is the peculiar nature of the Aryan's superiority. It is an amoral superiority based on energy, power and an innate, arrogant sense of natural leadership. Stripped of its racial mysticism it makes of force a virtue and even a necessity. Carried to its logical conclusion, it would mean a return to barbarism, for Gobineau at least implies that all the arts of civilization are non-Aryan or, at best, the result of race mixture. Drawing up a balance sheet between the "pure" and the "impure" races, we have on the side of the latter the creation of music and art, the development of commerce, the evolution of social and political institutions and, on the side of the Aryan, merely a sense of divine origin and of the gifts of leadership and the upholding of the doctrines of Force. To follow the argument to its natural conclusions, then, it would seem that non-Aryan means civilization while Aryan means primitivism or even barbarism.

In its political aspects, Gobinist Aryanism denies all the progress of the last two hundred years. It returns the worker to serfdom; the bourgeois to the tyranny of the overlord. It takes from the masses any ability to raise themselves to higher levels or to maintain those higher standards. It makes the voice of the people the cry of the beast. It makes democracy ridiculous. It makes of social progress a hollow sham.

The importance of "Race" was beginning to be doubted even in Renan's time. In view of the greatness of the "mongrel" nations of the West today, the conception of a "pure Race" is absurd. But this has not prevented the use of the Aryan myth in recent times. In modern Germany, however, it is the application of the theory, and not the theory itself, which is dangerous. It is the conclusion that the modern Aryans, pure or impure, are above the Law. In this most recent exposition of Aryanism, the element of efficiency has displaced that of energy. The State, as a unit, has taken the place of the individual (which is certainly not what Gobineau preached) but the psychology is the same. The system implies: Firstly the doctrine of power and force, involving a contempt for the transcendental in man, religion and philosophy and the subordination of the intellectual products of man to the demands of

the leader (that is, to political exigency) resulting in the death of free effort in art and *belles lettres,* if not in science; Secondly, a distrust and contempt of the ability of the ordinary human being to govern his own affairs; to choose his rulers sanely or to make his laws wisely; a denial, in short, of the efficacy of modern democracy as a competent political system; Lastly, that the Aryan, being unique, is at odds with the rest of the world and that for his own salvation he must be constantly on guard against this hostility, thus making war an ever-present possibility.

So, after nearly a hundred years, the fantastic pessimistic philosophy of the brilliant French diplomat is seized upon and twisted to the use of a mystic demagogue who finds in the idea of the pure Aryan an excuse for thrusting civilization back dangerously near to the age of barbarism. (pp. 156-65)

> *Arnold H. Rowbotham, "Gobineau and the Aryan Terror," in* The Sewanee Review, *Vol. XLVII, No. 2, April, 1939, pp. 152-65.*

WILLIAM MONTGOMERY McGOVERN   (essay date 1941)

[*McGovern outlines the major tenets of Gobineau's racist view of history.*]

Count Arthur de Gobineau . . . may be regarded as the founder of the modern racialist school. He was primarily a diplomat, an artist, and a poet, but he also wrote a number of books on historical and ethnological problems, of which the most important and the most influential was *The Inequality of Human Races.* Gobineau was far more a man of letters than a scientist, and he put forth many ideas which later on even his most ardent disciples have been forced to disavow. Nevertheless in the course of his long and rather rambling work Gobineau developed a number of cardinal doctrines or theses which in some form or other have been adopted by practically all the advocates of racialism. Among these, four are of especial importance.

The first of these cardinal doctrines is that mankind is divided into a number of separate races, each with its own physical, emotional, and mental characteristics. The obvious differences between the black skin of the Negro, the yellow skin of the Chinese, and the white skin of the European is no greater than the invisible, but none the less real, differences between the emotional and mental characteristics of the members of these three races. These differences are, of course, considered hereditary, and are in no way affected by education or environment. Just as a Negro invariably transmits his kinky hair and his black skin to his children, so he likewise invariably transmits the emotional and mental features characteristic of the black race. All pure-blooded blacks will therefore inevitably inherit the same general emotional and mental characteristics. In the case of intermarriage between races, the children will continue to have the emotional and mental characteristics of both parents, but in a diluted form. A white father and a black mother produce children which are neither white nor black but chocolate-colored. In like manner mulatto children will inherit some but not all of the intelligence and imagination characteristic of the white races, and some but not all of the artistic and musical sense which (according to Gobineau) is especially characteristic of the Negro race.

The second cardinal doctrine of Gobineau's creed is that as races radically and innately differ from one another, it follows that some races are invariably and inevitably superior to others. Among the pure-blooded races the Negroes rank the lowest of all (at least as regards their intellectual ability), then come the members of the yellow race, and then the members of the white race. The black race represents passion, is animal-like, with highly developed senses but poor reasoning power. The Negroes are carefree, capricious, and gluttonous, yet have a strongly marked musical and artistic capacity. The Negroes tend towards extreme individualism, even anarchy, and the only way in which they can be ruled is by despotism. The yellow race, though clearly superior to the Negroes, is still not the highest, as its essential characteristic is mediocrity. The members of this race are stubborn, apathetic, and practical. They have a pronounced leaning to law and order, but are uninventive and incapable of producing great leaders or great geniuses. The whites, on the other hand, excel in most physical, mental, and moral qualities. They are neither as sensuous and passionate as the blacks nor as apathetic and unemotional as the yellows. They are rich in reason, energy, resourcefulness, and creativeness. But even among the white peoples, there are notable differences. The Semites, for example, are somewhat inferior to the other white groups, as they are really a combination of white and black races. The Slavs are also somewhat inferior, as they represent a combination of the white and yellow races. The greatest of the white races is the Aryan race, to which belonged the Germanic peoples of antiquity, but which is now to be found in greater purity among the aristocrats of France and England than in Germany proper.

The third cardinal doctrine of Gobineau's creed is that a slight mixture of races is usually productive of much good, and at times has been the cause of a great advance in civilization. In Gobineau's opinion, mankind has produced ten great civilizations in times past. All of these civilizations were created by the white races, more especially by the Aryans, but only after the white races had conquered and partially mixed with other peoples. The Indian civilization was produced by the Aryan conquest of and partial mingling with the native Dravidians. The Egyptian civilization was created by an Aryan colony from India which settled in the Nile Valley at an early period and intermarried, to a certain extent, with non-Aryan aborigines. Chinese civilization began with an invasion of the Yellow River Basin by different branches of the Aryan race. To Gobineau, if the three great races had remained strictly separate, supremacy would always have remained in the hands of the pure white race, but the world would have missed certain advantages which have followed from the admixture of blood. Thus, for example, artistic genius, which is foreign to each of the three main races, arose only after the mingling, in certain proportions, of the whites and the blacks. In Egypt the admixture of Negro blood was too great, but Greece had the exact dosage of Negro blood to make it supreme in artistic endeavor.

The fourth cardinal doctrine in Gobineau's creed is that while a small admixture of alien blood improves races—even improves the noble Aryan race—yet a large or constant admixture of such alien blood inevitably produces racial degeneration, which in turn leads to cultural and even to political degeneration. In other words, civilization is created by the right amount of race mixture and is destroyed by too much. Gobineau was thoroughly pessimistic with regard to the modern world. Everywhere he saw evidence that the noble Aryan race is becoming polluted by the lesser breeds, with the result that the future of world civilization appeared very gloomy. To take but a single example of his reasoning along this point: Originally the Aryans in India were a small conquering and governing aristocracy. A small admixture of Dravidian blood permitted this little group to produce the great civilization of Vedic antiquity. As time

went on, however, the Aryan aristocracy absorbed more and more Dravidian blood (in spite of would-be strict caste laws) with the result that the governing group lost its racial identity. In consequence India began to degenerate. She became a prey to new invaders. Not only did she lose her political independence, but even her artistic and literary life became stagnant. To Gobineau, the story of India is but a prototype of racial history in other parts of the world.

To Gobineau, even Europe, the modern homeland of the white races, presents us with a similar picture. The great civilizations of Greece and Rome were founded by Aryan invaders who intermarried only to a slight extent with the aboriginal populations. As time went on, however, the invaders lost their racial purity, and the more racial amalgamation progressed, the more the governing aristocracies (the creators of civilization) lost their precious qualities. As a result both Greece and Rome eventually collapsed, more from racial degeneration than from any other cause. Modern Europe shows us another vivid and tragic picture of racial amalgamation—and cultural decay. The members of the old aristocracy of France were descended in large measure from the Frankish invaders of the early Middle Ages, while the lower classes in France were the descendants of the Latinized Celts. To Gobineau there was a *racial* difference between these two groups, as the Franks were far closer to the original Aryan type than were the Celts. As long as the French aristocracy remained relatively pure, it was able to create and preserve a characteristic French civilization. But with the relaxing of the social distinctions and the consequent intermarriage between the various classes in modern times, the French aristocracy has steadily degenerated. To Gobineau, the French Revolution was especially disastrous to French civilization, as it resulted in the killing of large numbers of the upper classes (with their higher proportion of pure Aryan blood) and the political and social triumph of the lower classes in which Aryan blood was greatly diluted.

With Gobineau's glorification of the Germanic-Franks it might appear, at first sight, as if his doctrine meant the glorification of everything German. But Gobineau was too good a Frenchman to permit this interpretation of his doctrine to gain ground. He sharply distinguished between the glorious *Germains* of former times and the degenerate *Allemands* of modern times. To him, the modern Germans were racially even more mixed and hence more impure than the French, or, at least, than the French upper class. To Gobineau the purest Aryan blood in the present time is to be found in England and in America, a fact which accounts for the much talked-of Anglo-Saxon supremacy in world affairs. But even here racial amalgamation is rapidly taking place—the English with the Celts, the Americans with Negroes and South European immigrants—with the result that both England and America are faced with inevitable decay in the not distant future. (pp. 500-04)

William Montgomery McGovern, "The Social Darwinists and Their Allies," in his From Luther to Hitler: The History of Fascist-Nazi Political Philosophy, *Houghton Mifflin Company, 1941, pp. 453-527.*

ERNST CASSIRER   (essay date 1945)

[*Cassirer was a German-born philosopher and historian who is recognized as a leading twentieth-century authority on the works of Gottfried Wilhelm von Leibniz, Jean Jacques Rousseau, and Immanuel Kant. In the following excerpt, he considers the weaknesses of Gobineau's historical and philosophical method in the*

Essay. *This was completed shortly before the critic's death in 1945.*]

In the political struggles of the past decades hero worship and race worship have been in such a close alliance that, in all their interests and tendencies, they seemed to be almost one and the same thing. . . . In a theoretical analysis, however, we should not allow ourselves to be deceived by this league between the two forces. They are by no means identical—neither genetically nor systematically. Their psychological motives, their historical origin, their meaning and purpose are not the same. To understand them we must separate them.

We can easily convince ourselves of this difference by studying the authors who, in the second half of the nineteenth century, became the chief representatives of the two trends of thought. There was scarcely anything that these authors had in common, for Carlyle's lectures on hero worship and Gobineau's *Essai sur l'inégalité des races humaines* are, in a sense, incommensurable. The two books are dissimilar in ideas and intellectual tendency and in style. Between the Scotch puritan and the French aristocrat there could be no real solidarity of interests. They stood for widely divergent moral, political, and social ideals. The fact that their ideas could be used later for a common end does not obliterate this discrepancy. It was a new step, and a step of the greatest consequence, when hero worship lost its original meaning and blended with a race worship and when both of them became integral parts of the same political program.

In order to grasp the purport of Gobineau's book . . . we must not read into it these later political tendencies. They are quite alien to the meaning of the author. Gobineau did not intend to write a political pamphlet but rather a historical and philosophical treatise. He never thought of applying his principles to a reconstruction or revolution of the political and social order. His was not an active philosophy. His view of history was fatalistic. History follows a definite and inexorable law. We cannot hope to change the course of events; all we can do is to understand and accept it. Gobineau's book is filled with a strong *amor fati*. The destiny of the human race is predetermined from the very beginning. No effort of man can avert it. Man cannot change his fate. But, on the other hand, he cannot refrain from asking over and over again the same question. If he cannot master his destiny, he wants at least to know where he comes from and whither he goes. This desire is one of fundamental and ineradicable human instincts.

Gobineau was not only convinced that he had found a new approach to the problem but also that he was the first who had really succeeded in solving the old riddle. All the former religious and metaphysical answers are declared by him to be inadequate. For all of them missed the principal point, the essential factor in human history. Without an insight into this factor history remains a sealed book. But now the seal is broken and the mystery of human life and human civilization is revealed. For the *fact* of the moral and intellectual diversity of races is obvious. Nobody can deny or neglect it. But what has been entirely unknown is the significance and the vital importance of this fact. Until this importance is clearly understood all historians of human civilization are groping in the dark.

History is no science; it is only a conglomerate of subjective thoughts; a wishful thinking rather than a coherent and systematic theory. Gobineau boasted of having made an end to this state of affairs. "It is a question of making history join the family of the natural sciences, of giving it . . . all the pre-

cision of this kind of knowledge, finally of removing it from the biased jurisdiction whose arbitrariness the political factions impose upon it up to this day." Gobineau did not speak as an advocate of a definite political program but as a scientist, and he thought his deductions were infallible. He was convinced that history, after innumerable vain efforts, had at last come to its maturity and virility in his work. He looked upon himself as a second Copernicus, the Copernicus of the historical world. Once we have found the true center of this world, everything is changed. We are no longer concerned with mere opinions about things, we will live and move in the things themselves; our eyes are able to see, our ears to hear, our hands to touch.

But no reader of Gobineau's work can help feeling deep disappointment when comparing this magnificent and gigantic plan with its execution. In the history of science there is perhaps no other example where so high a purpose was pursued with such insufficient means. It is true that Gobineau had amassed vast material taken from the most various sources. He spoke not only as a historian but also as a linguist, anthropologist, and ethnologist. Yet when we begin to analyze his arguments we find them, in most cases, extremely weak. A high and proud edifice is erected upon a very small and fragile basis. The first French critics of Gobineau's book immediately saw the fundamental defects of his historical method. Even Gobineau's partisans and followers had frankly to admit the lacunae and the obvious fallacies in his pretended "scientific" demonstration. Houston Stewart Chamberlain spoke of Gobineau's "childish omniscience." As a matter of fact he does seem to know everything. To him history has no secret. He knows not only its general course; he knows all its details, he feels himself able to answer the most intricate questions. He penetrates into the remotest origin of things; and he sees everything under its true conditions and in its right place. But as soon as it comes to the crucial point, the empirical proofs of his thesis, the weakness of Gobineau's *Essai* becomes palpable and unmistakable. He deals with the facts in the most arbitrary way. Everything that seems to support his thesis is readily admitted. On the other hand the negative instances are completely ignored or, at least, minimized. He shows a complete lack of that critical method which had been taught by the great historians of the nineteenth century.

Let us take a few concrete examples of his way of arguing and reasoning. One of his firmest convictions was that the white race is the only one that had the will and power to build up a cultural life. This principle became the cornerstone of his theory of the radical diversity of human races. The black and yellow races have no life, no will, no energy of their own. They are nothing but dead stuff in the hands of their masters— the inert mass that has to be moved by the higher races. On the other hand Gobineau could not entirely overlook the fact that there are definite traces of human civilization in some regions of the world in which the influence of the white race is highly improbable. How did he overcome this obstacle? His answer is very simple. The dogma itself is firmly established. It admits of no doubt and no exception. If our evidence is too scanty to confirm the dogma, or if it seems to be in open contradiction to it, it is for the historian to complete and correct the evidence. He must stretch the facts to make them fit into the preconceived scheme.

Gobineau never feels the slightest scruples about filling in the lacks of our historical knowledge by the boldest assumptions. China, for instance, shows in very ancient times a highly developed cultural life. But since, on the other hand, it is quite certain that the two inferior varieties of the human race, the Negroes and the yellow race, are only the gross canvas, the cotton and wool, upon which the white race has spun their own delicate and silky threads, the conclusion is unavoidable that Chinese culture was not the work of the Chinese people. We have to regard it as a product of foreign tribes which immigrated from India, of those Kschattryas who invaded and conquered China and laid the foundations for the central kingdom and the celestial empire. The same holds for those traces of a very old culture that we find in the Western hemisphere. It is impossible to assume that the American aboriginal tribes could, by their own efforts, find the way to civilization. According to Gobineau the Indians of the American continent form no separate race. They are only an amalgam, a mixture of the black and yellow races. How should these poor bastards ever have been able to govern and organize themselves? No history and no development were possible as long as the black races only struggled among themselves and the yellow races moved in their own narrow circle. The results of these conflicts were entirely unproductive; they could leave no trace in human history. Such was the case in America, in the greatest part of Africa, and in a considerable part of Asia. But whenever and wherever we find history and culture we must be on the lookout for the white man. We are sure of finding him; for his presence and his activity may be inferred, by a mere process of deductive reasoning, from the first principle of Gobineau's theory: "History springs only from contact of the white races."

Gobineau admits that there is no evidence of a contact between the white races and the aboriginal tribes of America before the discovery of the Western hemisphere. But the fact can be affirmed on the strength of general a priori principles.

> Of the multitude of peoples which live or have lived on the earth, ten alone have arisen to the position of complete societies. The remainder have gravitated round these more or less independently, like planets round their suns. If there is any element of life in these ten civilizations that is not due to the impulse of the white races, any seed of death that does not come from the inferior stocks that mingled with them, then the whole theory on which this book rests is false.

Gobineau was absolutely sure of his results. His self-confidence was unlimited. He declared that his proofs were "incorruptible as a diamond." The viperine tooth of the demagogic idea, he exclaimed, will never be able to bite upon these incontrovertible proofs. But it is easy to see the true character of these so-called adamantine and incontrovertible proofs. They are nothing but a *petitio principii*. If in a logical textbook we were in need of a striking example of this fallacy we could do no better than to choose the work of Gobineau. His facts are always in agreement with his principles; for, if the historical facts are missing, they are framed and forged according to his theories. And the same facts are used again for proving the truth of the theory. Assuredly Gobineau did not mean to deceive his readers, but he constantly deceived himself. He was quite sincere and quite naïve. He never was aware of the vicious circle, on which his whole theory depends. He spoke as a scholar and as a philosopher; but he never claimed to have found his principles by rational methods.

To him personal feelings were always better and more convincing than logical or historical arguments. And these feelings were very clear and outspoken. He belonged to an old aris-

tocratic family and was filled with an immoderate pride, which was constantly humiliated. He, the member of a noble race, had to live under the petty conditions of a bourgeois system for which he felt a deep disgust. To him it was not only natural, it was in a sense a moral duty to think in terms of his caste. The caste was to him a much higher and nobler reality than the nation or the individual man. In his book he praised the Aryan Brahmans for having first understood and firmly established the value and the paramount importance of the caste. Theirs was a real stroke of genius, a profound and original idea that showed an entirely new way for the progress of the human race. In order to prove the claims of the French nobility Gobineau went back to a doctrine that had been propounded and defended in the eighteenth century by Boulainvilliers and that had become the basis of the theory of French feudalism. In his analysis of Boulainvilliers' book Montesquieu described it as a "conspiracy against the third estate." Boulainvilliers had emphatically denied that France is a homogeneous whole. The nation is divided into two races that have at bottom nothing in common. They speak a common language; but they have neither common rights nor a common origin. The French nobility draws its origin from the Franks, the German invaders and conquerors; the mass of the people belongs to the subjugated, to the serfs who have lost every claim to an independent life. "The true French," wrote one of the advocates of this theory, "incarnated in our day in the nobility and its partisans, are the sons of free men; the former slaves and all races alike employed primarily in labor by their masters are the fathers of the Third Estate."

All this was eagerly accepted by Gobineau. But he had set himself a greater and much more difficult task. He spoke of human civilization as a philosopher who could not confine himself within the narrow limit of French history. What we see in the French nation is only an example and a symptom of a much more general process. French history is, as it were, a portrait in miniature. It shows the image of the whole cultural process on a small and reduced scale. That conflict between patricians and plebeians, between the conquerors and the serfs, is the eternal theme of human history. He who understands the nature and the reasons of this conflict has found the clue to man's historical life.

This starting point of Gobineau's theory shows at once the deep difference between hero worship and race worship. They express widely divergent and even opposite conceptions of human history. "Is not the whole purport of history," asked Carlyle, "biographic?" And he did not hesitate to answer this question in the affirmative. This interest in the individuals is entirely absent in Gobineau's work. His whole exposition was, indeed, given without even mentioning proper names. When reading Carlyle we have the impression that with every new great man, with every religious, philosophical, literary, political genius, there begins a new chapter in human history. The whole character of the religious world was completely changed, for example, by the appearance of Mahomet or Luther; the political world and the world of poetry were revolutionized by Cromwell or by Dante and Shakespeare. Every new hero is a new incarnation of one and the same great invisible power of the "Divine Idea." In Gobineau's description of the historical and cultural world this divine Idea has vanished. He too is a romantic and a mystic; but his mysticism is of a much more realistic type. The great men do not fall from the heavens. Their whole force originates in the earth; in the native soil in which they have their roots. The best qualities of the great men are the qualities of their races. By themselves they could do nothing; they are only the embodiments of the deepest powers of the race to which they belong.

In this sense Gobineau could have subscribed to Hegel's words that the individuals are only "the agents of the world-spirit." But when Gobineau wrote his book the times had changed. Gobineau and his generation no longer believed in lofty metaphysical principles. They were in need of something more palpable: of something that "our eyes are able to see, our ears to hear, our hands to touch." The new theory seemed to satisfy all these conditions.

Practically speaking this was a great and obvious advantage. Here was something that could fill a lack which, in the second half of the nineteenth century, was felt everywhere. Man is, after all, a metaphysical animal. His "metaphysical need" is ineradicable. But the great metaphysical systems of the nineteenth century were no longer able to give a clear and understandable answer to these questions. They had become so intricate and sophisticated that they were almost unintelligible. With Gobineau's book it was quite different. To be sure, his own theory of the race as the fundamental and predominant power in human history was still thoroughly metaphysical. But Gobineau's metaphysics claimed to be a natural science and seemed to be based upon an experience of the simplest kind. Not everyone is able to follow a long chain of metaphysical deductions; not everyone can study Hegel's *Phenomenology of Mind* or his *Philosophy of History*. But anybody understands the language of his race and his blood—or believes he understands it. Since its first beginnings metaphysics had sought for an undoubtable, unshakable, universal principle but was constantly frustrated in its hopes. According to Gobineau this was unavoidable as long as metaphysics persisted in its traditional intellectualistic attitude. The problem of the so-called "universals" and their reality has been discussed throughout the whole history of philosophy. But what philosophers never realized was the fact that the real "universals" are not to be sought in the thoughts of men but in these substantial forces that determine his destiny. Of all these forces the race is the strongest and the most unquestionable. Here we have a fact, not a mere idea.

Newton had found a fundamental fact of the physical world through which he was able to explain the whole material universe. He had discovered the law of gravitation. But in the human world the common center toward which all things gravitate was still unknown. Gobineau was convinced that he had found the solution of this problem. And he imposed the same feeling upon the minds of his readers. Here was a new type of theory that, from the outset, had a strong and strange fascination. It is foolish in a man to deny or to resist the power of his race, just as foolish as if a material particle should attempt to resist the force of gravitation.

That race is an important factor in human history; that different races have built up different forms of culture; that these forms are not on the same level; that they vary both in their character and in their value—all this was a generally acknowledged fact. Since Montesquieu's *Esprit des Lois* even the physical conditions of these variations had been carefully studied. It was not, however, this well-known problem with which Gobineau was concerned. His was a much more general and difficult task. He had to prove that race is the *only* master and ruler of the historical world; that all the other forces are its underlings and satellites. Our modern idea of the totalitarian state was entirely unfamiliar to Gobineau. If he had known it he would have vehemently protested against it. Even patriotism was to

him a mere idol and prejudice. Yet, however opposed to all nationalistic ideals, Gobineau belongs to those writers who, in an indirect way, have done most to prepare the ideology of the totalitarian state. It was the totalitarianism of race that marked the road to the later conceptions of the totalitarian state. (pp. 224-32)

[This] is one of the most important and interesting features in Gobineau's theory. But, so far as I see, this point has not yet had its due in the literature on the subject. Gobineau's doctrine has been analyzed and criticized from every possible angle and philosophers, sociologists, politicians, historians, anthropologists have had their share in these discussions. But to my mind it is not the glorification of the race as such that is the most important element in Gobineau's theory. To be proud of his ancestors, of his birth and descent, is a natural character of man. If it is a prejudice it is a very common prejudice. It need not necessarily endanger or undermine man's social and ethical life. But what we find in Gobineau is something quite different. It is *an attempt to destroy all other values*. The god of the race, as he was proclaimed by Gobineau, is a jealous god. He does not allow other gods to be adored beside himself. Race is everything; all the other forces are nothing. They have no independent meaning or value. If they have any power this power is not an autonomous one. It is only delegated to them by their superior and sovereign: the omnipotent race. This fact appears in all forms of cultural life, in religion, in morality, in philosophy and art, in the nation and in the state. (p. 232-33)

What was left after [the *Essai*], this systematic work of destruction? What remained for Gobineau himself, and what could he promise his followers and believers? We find the answer to the first question in Gobineau's last book. In 1879 he published his *Histoire d'Ottar Jarl, pirate norvégien, conquérant du pays de Bray en Normandie, et de sa descendance.* This book is perhaps one of the most curious in the whole history of literature. Here Gobineau is no longer concerned with the history of human civilization. His interest has shifted. All he wishes to know is his *own* descent and the descent of his family. He believes himself to be in possession of definite proofs that his family is directly descended from Ottar Jarl, a famous Norwegian pirate, a member of the royal race of the Ynglings who traced back their own origin to Odin, the highest god. And what a narrow-minded view of human life and human history we find in this book! If Gobineau, at the time of its publication, had not been a well-known author, the author of the *Essai* and *Renaissance,* nobody would have taken it seriously. He had always spoken with an immoderate and extravagant aristocratic pride. But this time his pride became absurd and ridiculous and bordered on megalomania. The philosopher of universal history has become the philosopher of the history of his own family. Instead of studying the genealogy of culture he is only engrossed in his own genealogy. That was a sad issue of so great an enterprise. Gobineau had begun with a great promise of making history an exact science and freeing us from all subjective illusions and preconceived opinions about its course. But at the end of his literary career this horizon has dwindled away. His feelings and thoughts are fixed upon one point— his own pedigree! "Parturiunt montes, nascetur ridiculus mus."

All this reveals to us a general feature of Gobineau's thought. The impoverishment of his personal life and the narrowing of his mental horizon was in a sense the necessary outcome of his theory. His discovery of the excellence and the incomparable value of the Aryan race had filled him with the greatest

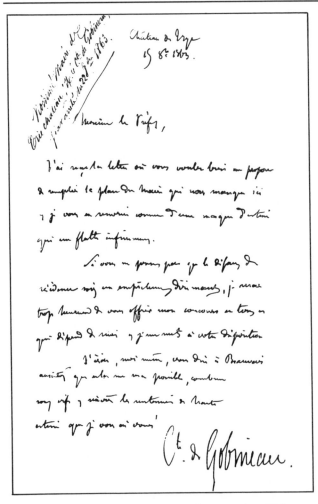

A letter in which Gobineau accepts the mayoralty of Trie.

enthusiasm. If he speaks of the moment in which this race made its first appearance in human history he can hardly find words that are strong enough to describe its vital importance. This was not only an earthly, but also a cosmic moment—a spectacle not only for men, but for the gods and the heavens. This seemed to be an ecstatic view of human history, a beginning filled with the greatest expectations and promises. If the Aryan family, the noblest, the most intelligent and most energetic race, is the real actor in the great historical drama, what unlimited hopes can we not entertain for the progress of human civilization! Gobineau's work thus begins with a sort of intoxication, an intoxication of race worship and self worship.

But this feeling is superseded by a deep disillusionment. By a sort of dialectic in reverse the first optimistic view suddenly turns into a deep and incurable pessimism. The higher races, in fulfilling their historical mission, necessarily and inevitably destroy themselves. They cannot rule and organize the world without being in close contact with the world. But to them contact is a dangerous thing, the permanent and eternal source of infection. The result could not be but disastrous for the higher races. Cooperation between different races means cohabitation, cohabitation means blood mixture, and blood mixture means decay and degeneration. It is always the beginning of the end. With the passing of the purity of the race its strength goes and its organizing power. The higher races become the victims of their own work, the slaves of their slaves.

At the end of his book Gobineau drew the general conclusions from the principles of this theory. In his imagination he conjures the image of the last men who shall live on earth. At this time the degeneration of the nobler races will be complete and all race distinctions will be extinct. Then the vivifying principle in human history will have ceased to exist. To be sure people will live peacefully together. There will be no contest between them but, on the other hand, there will be no energy, no sense of enterprise, no will to power and conquest. The equalitarian ideals of our modern demagogues will be fulfilled. But human life will have lost everything that made it worth living. Men will live in a state of happiness like a flock of sheep or a herd of buffaloes. This period of great and content somnolence will be followed by a period of stupor, and, at last, of complete lethargy. Gobineau even undertook to estimate the length of these different periods. His verdict is that the period of strength, of real life, has long ago faded away. We are now living in a state of decrepitude and exhaustion. The human race can perhaps drag along its petty and miserable existence for some more hundred years; but its fate is sealed; its death is inevitable.

That is the last word of Gobineau's theory; and it is, indeed, the quintessence of his whole work. In the first sentences of his book he had already foreshadowed this end. Race worship was to Gobineau the highest form of worship, the worship of the highest god. But his god is by no means invincible and immortal. On the contrary he is extremely vulnerable. Even in the moments of highest exaltation Gobineau could never forget the coming fate: the fate of the "twilight of the gods." Les dieux s'en vont—the gods must die.

> The fall of civilizations is the most striking, and, at the same time, the most obscure of all the phenomena of history. It is a calamity that strikes fear into the soul, and yet has always something so mysterious and so vast in reserve, that the thinker is never weary of looking at it, of studying it, of groping for its secrets . . . we are forced to affirm that every assemblage of men, however ingenious the network of social relations that protects it, acquires on the very day of its birth, hidden among the elements of its life, the seed of an inevitable death. But what is this seed, this principle of death? Is it uniform, as its results are, and do all civilizations perish from the same cause?

Now we see the solution before our very eyes. The result is not only a deep pessimism but also a complete negativism and nihilism. Gobineau had made a clean sweep of all human values. He had decided to offer them to the new god, to the Moloch of the race. But this god was a dying god, and his death sealed the fate of human history and human civilization: it entangled them in his own ruin. (pp. 244-47)

> *Ernst Cassirer, "From Hero Worship to Race Worship," in his* The Myth of the State, *Yale University Press, 1946, pp. 224-47.*

HANNAH ARENDT (essay date 1951)

[*A German-born American political philosopher and literary essayist, Arendt ranks among the most important political thinkers of the twentieth century. In her many works she considered the central issues of the times—war, revolution, political power, violence, anti-Semitism—with original, and at times controversial, insight. In her seminal* The Origins of Totalitarianism (*published in 1951 and excerpted below) and the controversial* Eichmann in Jerusalem, *she examined the phenomenon of totalitarianism, illuminating the factors that permitted its ascendance. Here, she considers the nature and purpose of the* Essay.]

In 1853, Count Arthur de Gobineau published his *Essai sur l'Inégalité des Races Humaines* which, only some fifty years later, at the turn of the century, was to become a kind of standard work for race theories in history. The first sentence of the four-volume work—"The fall of civilization is the most striking and, at the same time, the most obscure of all phenomena of history"—indicates clearly the essentially new and modern interest of its author, the new pessimistic mood which pervades his work and which is the ideological force that was capable of uniting all previous factors and conflicting opinions. True, from time immemorial, mankind has wanted to know as much as possible about past cultures, fallen empires, extinct peoples; but nobody before Gobineau thought of finding one single reason, one single force according to which civilization always and everywhere rises and falls. Doctrines of decay seem to have some very intimate connection with race-thinking. It certainly is no coincidence that another early "believer in race," Benjamin Disraeli, was equally fascinated by the fall of cultures, while on the other hand Hegel, whose philosophy was concerned in great part with the dialectical law of development in history, was never interested in the rise and fall of cultures as such or in any law which would explain the death of nations: Gobineau demonstrated precisely such a law. Without Darwinism or any other evolutionist theory to influence him, this historian boasted of having introduced history into the family of natural sciences, detected the natural law of all courses of events, reduced all spiritual utterances or cultural phenomena to something "that by virtue of exact science our eyes can see, our ears can hear, our hands can touch."

The most surprising aspect of the theory, set forth in the midst of the optimistic nineteenth century, is the fact that the author is fascinated by the fall and hardly interested in the rise of civilizations. At the time of writing the *Essai* Gobineau gave but little thought to the possible use of his theory as a weapon in actual politics, and therefore had the courage to draw the inherent sinister consequences of his law of decay. In contrast to Spengler, who predicts only the fall of Western culture, Gobineau foresees with "scientific" precision nothing less than the definite disappearance of Man—or, in his words, of the human race—from the face of the earth. After four volumes of rewriting human history, he concludes: "One might be tempted to assign a total duration of 12 to 14 thousand years to human rule over the earth, which era is divided into two periods: the first has passed away and possessed the youth . . . the second has begun and will witness the declining course down toward decrepitude."

It has rightly been observed [by Robert Dreyfus] that Gobineau, thirty years before Nietzsche, was concerned with the problem of *"décadence."* There is, however, this difference, that Nietzsche possessed the basic experience of European decadence, writing as he did during the climax of this movement with Baudelaire in France, Swinburne in England, and Wagner in Germany, whereas Gobineau was hardly aware of the variety of the modern *taedium vitae,* and must be regarded as the last heir of Boulainvilliers and the French exiled nobility who, without psychological complications, simply (and rightly) feared for the fate of aristocracy as a caste. With a certain naïveté he accepted almost literally the eighteenth-century doctrines about the origin of the French people: the bourgeois are the descendants of Gallic-Roman slaves, noblemen are Germanic.

The same is true for his insistence on the international character of nobility. A more modern aspect of his theories is revealed in the fact that he possibly was an impostor (his French title being more than dubious), that he exaggerated and overstrained the older doctrines until they became frankly ridiculous—he claimed for himself a genealogy which led over a Scandinavian pirate to Odin: "I, too, am of the race of Gods." But his real importance is that in the midst of progress-ideologies he prophesied doom, the end of mankind in a slow natural catastrophe. When Gobineau started his work, in the days of the bourgeois king, Louis Philippe, the fate of nobility appeared sealed. Nobility no longer needed to fear the victory of the *Tiers Etat,* it had already occurred and they could only complain. Their distress, as expressed by Gobineau, sometimes comes very near to the great despair of the poets of decadence who, a few decades later, sang the frailty of all things human—*les neiges d'antan,* the snows of yesteryear. As far as Gobineau himself was concerned, this affinity is rather incidental; but it is interesting to note that once this affinity was established, nothing could prevent very respectable intellectuals at the turn of the century, like Robert Dreyfus in France or Thomas Mann in Germany, from taking this descendant of Odin seriously. Long before the horrible and the ridiculous had merged into the humanly incomprehensible mixture that is the hallmark of our century, the ridiculous had lost its power to kill.

It is also to the peculiar pessimistic mood, to the active despair of the last decades of the century that Gobineau owed his belated fame. This, however, does not necessarily mean that he himself was a forerunner of the generation of "the merry dance of death and trade" (Joseph Conrad). He was neither a statesman who believed in business nor a poet who praised death. He was only a curious mixture of frustrated nobleman and romantic intellectual who invented racism almost by accident. This was when he saw that he could not simply accept the old doctrines of the two peoples within France and that, in view of changed circumstances, he had to revise the old line that the best men necessarily are at the top of society. In sad contrast to his teachers, he had to explain why the best men, noblemen, could not even hope to regain their former position. Step by step, he identified the fall of his caste with the fall of France, then of western civilization, and then of the whole of mankind. Thus he made that discovery, for which he was so much admired by later writers and biographers, that the fall of civilizations is due to a degeneration of race and the decay of race is due to a mixture of blood. This implies that in every mixture the lower race is always dominant. This kind of argumentation, almost commonplace after the turn of the century, did not fit in with the progress-doctrines of Gobineau's contemporaries, who soon acquired another *idée fixe,* the "survival of the fittest." The liberal optimism of the victorious bourgeoisie wanted a new edition of the might-right theory, not the key to history or the proof of inevitable decay. Gobineau tried in vain to get a wider audience by taking a side in the American slave issue and by conveniently building his whole system on the basic conflict between white and black. He had to wait almost fifty years to become a success among the elite, and not until the first World War with its wave of death-philosophies could his works claim wide popularity.

What Gobineau was actually looking for in politics was the definition and creation of an "elite" to replace the aristocracy. Instead of princes, he proposed a "race of princes," the Aryans, who he said were in danger of being submerged by the lower non-Aryan classes through democracy. The concept of race made it possible to organize the "innate personalities" of

German romanticism, to define them as members of a natural aristocracy destined to rule over all others. If race and mixture of races are the all-determining factors for the individual—and Gobineau did not assume the existence of "pure" breeds—it is possible to pretend that physical superiorities might evolve in every individual no matter what his present social situation, that every exceptional man belongs to the "true surviving sons of . . . the Merovings," the "sons of kings." Thanks to race, an "elite" would be formed which could lay claim to the old prerogatives of feudal families, and this only by asserting that they felt like noblemen; the acceptance of the race ideology as such would become conclusive proof that an individual was "well-bred," that "blue blood" ran through his veins and that a superior origin implied superior rights. From one political event, therefore, the decline of the nobility, the Count drew two contradictory consequences—the decay of the human race and the formation of a new natural aristocracy. But he did not live to see the practical application of his teachings which resolved their inherent contradictions—the new race-aristocracy actually began to effect the "inevitable" decay of mankind in a supreme effort to destroy it.

Following the example of his forerunners, the exiled French noblemen, Gobineau saw in his race-elite not only a bulwark against democracy but also against the "Canaan monstrosity" of patriotism. And since France still happened to be the *"patrie" par excellence,* for her government—whether kingdom or Empire or Republic—was still based upon the essential equality of men, and since, worst of all, she was the only country of his time in which even people with black skin could enjoy civil rights, it was natural for Gobineau to give allegiance not to the French people, but to the English, and later, after the French defeat of 1871, to the Germans. Nor can this lack of dignity be called accidental and his opportunism an unhappy coincidence. The old saying that nothing succeeds like success reckons with people who are used to various and arbitrary opinions. Ideologists who pretend to possess the key to reality are forced to change and twist their opinions about single cases according to the latest events and can never afford to come into conflict with their ever-changing deity, reality. It would be absurd to ask people to be reliable who by their very convictions must justify any given situation.

It must be conceded that up to the time when the Nazis, in establishing themselves as a race-elite, frankly bestowed their contempt on all peoples, including the German, French racism was the most consistent, for it never fell into the weakness of patriotism. (This attitude did not change even during the last war; true, the *"essence aryenne"* no longer was a monopoly of the Germans but rather of the Anglo-Saxons, the Swedes, and the Normans, but nation, patriotism, and law were still considered to be "prejudices, fictitious and nominal values.") Even Taine believed firmly in the superior genius of the "Germanic nation," and Ernest Renan was probably the first to oppose the "Semites" to the "Aryans" in a decisive *"division du genre humain,"* although he held civilization to be the great superior force which destroys local originalities as well as original race differences. All the loose race talk that is so characteristic of French writers after 1870, even if they are not racists in any strict sense of the word, follows antinational, pro-Germanic lines.

If the consistent antinational trend of Gobinism served to equip the enemies of French democracy and, later, of the Third Republic, with real or fictitious allies beyond the frontiers of their country, the specific amalgamation of the race and "elite"

concepts equipped the international intelligentsia with new and exciting psychological toys to play with on the great playground of history. Gobineau's *"fils des rois"* were close relatives of the romantic heroes, saints, geniuses and supermen of the late nineteenth century, all of whom can hardly hide their German romantic origin. The inherent irresponsibility of romantic opinions received a new stimulant from Gobineau's mixture of races, because this mixture showed a historical event of the past which could be traced in the depths of one's own self. This meant that inner experiences could be given historical significance, that one's own self had become the battlefield of history. [According to Elie Faure], "Since I read the *Essai,* every time some conflict stirred up the hidden sources of my being, I have felt that a relentless battle went on in my soul, the battle between the black, the yellow, the Semite and the Aryans." Significant as this and similar confessions may be of the state of mind of modern intellectuals, who are the true heirs of romanticism whatever opinion they happen to hold, they nevertheless indicate the essential harmlessness and political innocence of people who probably could have been forced into line by each and every ideology. (pp. 170-75)

*Hannah Arendt, "Race-Thinking Before Racism,"
in her* The Origins of Totalitarianism, *new edition,
Harcourt Brace Jovanovich, 1966, pp. 158-84.*

LOUIS TENENBAUM (essay date 1957)

[Tenenbaum examines the portrayal of love and sentiment in Gobineau's imaginative works, comparing them with the writings of Stendhal and Prosper Mérimée.]

Gobineau has justly been recognized as the successor to Stendhal and Mérimée, the outstanding representatives of *la tradition sèche* in nineteenth-century prose fiction. In all three writers a literary technique of extreme sobriety and economy overlays a romanticism of varied depth and extent, but having in common an admiration for moral aristocracy as it is expressed in energy and power of the will. All three have, accordingly, been considered in some measure as precursors of Nietzsche. Love as a manifestation of energetic individualism has an important role in Stendhal and Gobineau, but Mérimée's pessimism prevented his treatment of the theme with the implicit idealism of the other two. Stendhal and Gobineau, on the other hand, were quite capable of leaving aside their idealism to depict, like Mérimée, the ridicule and dishonesty of insincere sentimental relationships. Unlike Stendhal, however, Gobineau had an emotional rather than rational attitude toward politics and political man, and for his fiction, therefore, love has come to have a primary function.

Gobineau realized this, perhaps unconsciously, for his most important work of fiction, *Les Pléiades,* which was conceived as a politico-philosophical novel and whose early chapters illustrate this conception, changes emphasis, in midstream as it were, and becomes a lyrical apotheosis of love. Gobineau's idealization of love, most cogently depicted in *Les Pléiades,* published in 1874, can be traced back as far as 1847, the date of the *nouvelle Mademoiselle Irnois.* Already in that work the concept that true passion does not demand reciprocity, that it can exist in unnourished purity with no hope of fulfillment, makes valid the heroine's love for the unsuspecting *ébéniste.* . . . *Mademoiselle Irnois* is an extraordinary work when considered in the light of Gobineau's later stories; the ennobling influence of a true passion is granted to a creature possessing none of the aristocracy of spirit which he was so careful to insist upon after the publication of *Essai sur l'Inégalité des Races humaines.* It is an indication that in 1847 he was closer to the influence of the Stendhal who had once declared that the energy he admired could be found in an ant, as well as in an elephant. Even in 1847 Gobineau could not resist injecting a reflection of his die-hard legitimistic sentiments into a work of fiction; thus the satirical references to the bourgeois king and the *aperçus* of the corrupt favoritism which extinguishes the single flame in Emmelina Irnois' life.

This *nouvelle,* had it been delineated with somewhat more impassiveness, and less idealism, would fit well into a volume of Mérimée's stories; the subject and the ironic treatment are distinctly characteristic of the latter. *Mademoiselle Irnois* is the only *nouvelle* which Gobineau set against a Parisian background. He was never to return to a French setting in his short stories, and there is only a fleeting satirical treatment of some Parisian scenes glimpsed in **"La Chasse au Caribou"** and in *Les Pléiades.* This later refusal to portray his compatriots against a native setting symbolizes Gobineau's sense of isolation from his country and his times. Like their creator, his French heroes are spiritual or physical exiles. The arbitrary rejection of the vitiating Parisian or French atmosphere distinguishes him sharply from both Stendhal and Mérimée, who in *Le Rouge et le Noir, Lucien Leuwen,* "La Vase Étrusque," and "La Double Méprise," respectively, made literary capital out of the essential disparities between their heroes or heroines and the superficiality and decadence of the environment.

There is a sentimental naïveté which Stendhal would have found antipathetic in Gobineau's concept of love as a means to moral grandeur. This belief informs **"La Danseuse de Shamakha"** and **"Les Amants de Kandahar"** in the collection *Nouvelles Asiatiques* and figures importantly in *Les Pléiades.* It offers the idealistic elements of **"Akrivie Phrangopoulo"** but has a weaker function in that story; its importance in *Mademoiselle Irnois* has already been pointed out. Gobineau was driven to his romantic idealization of *la grande passion* by his uncompromising perfectionism. In literature Mérimée was satisfied with pessimism; Stendhal rejected sentimentality. Gobineau, like Kassem, the hero of **"L'Illustre Magicien,"** was in search of the Absolute, and like Kassem, he found that the Absolute was Love. It was indeed all that he could oppose to his pessimistic historical conclusions concerning the inescapable disintegration of Western civilization by the corruption of Aryan racial purity.

The energy which the Stendhalian hero or heroine may manifest in the satisfaction of personal or political ambition, as well as in the life of the sentiments, can only be channeled into the latter for the Gobineau personage. With the possible exception of Fabrice del Dongo, the struggle with society is important to the development of the Stendhalian hero; Gobineau's heroes never enter into this conflict. Their innate qualities as *fils de rois* make this unnecessary; they are above the sordid bourgeois struggles of "decaying" nineteenth-century European civilization. Ideally their energies and wills must be tested by the yardstick of a grand passion. The heroes and heroines of *Les Pléiades* successfully pass this test, achieving varying degrees of happiness, or even, as in the case of Casimir Bullet, failing to achieve it; yet all reach heights of grandeur and nobility in the course of sentimental experience, maintaining undefiled a purity of soul which Stendhal, in spite of Rousseauistic temptations, was temperamentally unfitted to accept. Even Fabrice del Dongo, in a sense the purest of Stendhalian heroes, can be accused of Machiavellism. Gobineau did not escape some of

his century's sentimental romanticism, which both Stendhal and Mérimée had rejected.

Part of this romanticism can be distinguished in Gobineau's conviction of the fatality of passion, *l'amour-fatalité,* which is discernible in his idealistic love stories, from *Mademoiselle Irnois* to *Les Pléiades.* In the light of this concept Gobineau heroes or heroines are shown to be attracted and held fast in their passionate bonds by sentimental lines of force, often but not always explicable by the corresponding moral worth of the being loved. In the *nouvelles* **"Akrivie Phrangopoulo,"** **"Les Amants de Kandahar,"** and **"La Danseuse de Shamakha"** the first encounter of the principals is enough to convince the lover of the inevitability and totality of the sentimental attachment. The dancing girl, Omm-Djéhâne, of the last-named story, struggles unsuccessfully to fight against her feeling for the Spanish officer, and achieves moral stature as she is physically destroyed. In this narrative the primitive energy and ferocity of spirit with which Gobineau endows the Asiatic heroine is suggestive of Carmen and Lamiel. The Polish countess Sophie Tonska of *Les Pléiades* shares with Omm-Djéhâne these qualities of *la femme fatale,* a type which Gobineau uses antiromantically, considering the ironic destiny of the Caucasian *lesghy* and the final surrender of Sophie to the love of the sculptor Conrad Lanze. True passion in Gobineau's view, then, is the means of redemption of *la femme fatale.* We have here the paradox of one romantic concept being used to destroy another.

The use by Gobineau of *l'amour-fatalité* is perhaps most strongly marked in the love affairs of Sophie Tonska, in *Les Pléiades,* who inspires in turn four passions, none of which Gobineau justifies with psychological validity. He offers only her extraordinary physical attraction to account for the mysterious power of the Polish countess, her aura of fatal fascination. This weakness in Sophie's portrait is compensated for by the originality of her presentation as a woman tragically incapable of love. Since Gobineau's purpose was to indicate in Sophie the ironic contrast of a woman with every qualification for inspiring a great love but unable to reciprocate, the reader is obliged to reject as a sentimental weakness in the author her final, gratuitous acceptance of the faithful and impassioned Conrad Lanze.

Gobineau insists on the importance of suffering as a concomitant of *la grande passion;* in this romantic concept he was not far from Stendhal, whose theory of crystallization comported torments of uncertainty and rejection for his *passionés.* In Stendhal's fiction, however, this suffering was generally a spur to energetic action. Gobineau's ideal lovers tend to suffer passively and to reveal grandeur of soul in a type of renunciation which is in itself a form of energy. In *Les Pléiades* the loves of Wilfred Nore and Harriet Coxe, of Conrad Lanze, of Casimir Bullet, and of Prince Jean-Théodore present examples of this strength granted to the lover to accept the perverse dictates of Fate.

In all these love stories suffering and renunciation are the purifying agents which emphasize the high moral integrity of the participants. Even the "racially inferior" Omm-Djéhâne, of **"La Danseuse de Shamakha,"** exemplifies this concept. In the allegorical fantasy **"L'Illustre Magicien,"** Kassem's pursuit of the Absolute, with its cruel demands of abandonment and asceticism, is fittingly rewarded. In two of Gobineau's Stendhalian stories, **"Le Mouchoir Rouge"** and **"Adélaïde,"** the respective heroines, Sophie Lanze and Adélaïde, do possess the amoral energies which characterize the women in *Chroniques Italiennes.* However, neither woman represents the

Gobineau ideal except in her determined struggle to overcome the obstacle of family in the pursuit of love. Here they join Mohsèn and Djemylèh of **"Les Amants de Kandahar,"** Gobineau's Asiatic interpretation of the Romeo and Juliet theme treated by Stendhal in "L'Abbesse de Castro."

Gobineau's disdain of sensuality is in accord with the ennobling role of love in his aesthetic. While his strong attraction for the exotic is reflected in his powers of sensuous evocation, which are at their best in the stories of the *Nouvelles Asiatiques,* the erotic aspects of Oriental civilization are muted and restrained in that work. His characters skillfully walk the sometimes thin line between sensuousness and sensuality; the lack of deviation is significant. Instead of following Stendhal's example of the chaste presentation of erotic passion, Gobineau rigorously excluded the suggestion of physical love in his fiction. Even when closest to abandoning intellectual lucidity, his heroes and heroines do not lose control; it is an essential mark of their "superiority." This *chevaleresque* concept contributes to the impression of naïveté which some portions of *Les Pléiades* make on the modern reader. The Gobineau knight-errant vanquishes temptation and preserves his purity for his lady fair, and for a relationship sanctioned by society.

Coexistent with this semi-courtly idealism, however, are certain insights into sexual psychology not unworthy of Freud. The portrait of Sophie Tonska is a perceptive foreshadowing of a sublimated emotional-sexual maladjustment commonly diagnosed by present-day psychologists. Sophie's self-knowledge and her attempts at compensation which form the basis of her fictional personality pertain more to our own age of psychoanalysis than to the late nineteenth-century world. *Les Pléiades* offers another unusual sentimental relationship in Harriet Coxe's self-effacing love for the melancholy, illusionless Wilfred Nore. In at least two other instances, in the *nouvelles* **"Adélaïde"** and **"Le Mouchoir Rouge,"** the attraction of an older woman for a younger man was used by Gobineau. Those stories make ironic use of the discrepancy in ages, whereas the love of Harriet and Nore is conceived in a sentimental, almost tragic way. The romanticism of Gobineau's fictive invention in this attachment is acceptable to the twentieth-century reader only because of the delicate analysis of sentiment which redeems it throughout the entire length of the narrative. The author, indeed, flirted with a kind of literary naturalism in having the Englishman test his love for the older, less physically charming Harriet by indulging his momentary attraction to the young, brilliant Liliane Lanze. It is typical of Gobineau that Nore should justify intellectually his eventual rejection of Harriet's rival.

Gobineau must join Stendhal in the latter's quasi deification of love-passion, although the former's depiction of love is considerably attenuated in confrontation with the intense, realistic cruelty of the Stendhalian heroes and heroines. Where Stendhal was supremely true to nature in his psychological analysis of amorous sentiment, Gobineau permits his romanesque conception to place itself between himself and his personages. The result is not a lack of truth; it is instead a blurring of the contours and a preference for certain slight sentimentalities which caress the imagination, where Stendhal's incisive comments stimulate and prod the intellect.

Both Stendhal and Gobineau are opposed in their glorification of love to Mérimée, whose fiction expresses a cynical disillusionment and a sense of the futility of amorous attachments. "Arsène Guillot," with its thematic suggestion of the prostitute's redemption through love, seems to represent Mérimée's

closest approach to his confreres. Orso della Rebbia—conceived as a center of the conflict between primitive Mediterranean energies and enervating Continental cultural influences—is perhaps the nearest to a Gobineau character in Mérimée's fiction. But the weakness of the love story in "Colomba" is notable, and Gobineau, with his marked admiration for the English, could not have approved of the thinly drawn, superficial Lydia Nevil. Gobineau was as capable as Mérimée of depicting perverse women (viz., Omm-Djéhâne, Sophie Lanze, Sophie Tonska, Adélaïde), but it is hard to imagine Mérimée, or Stendhal for that matter, creating such innocents as Emmelina Irnois, Akrivie Phrangopoulo, Harriet Coxe, and Aurora Pamina. For Gobineau's ideal lovers are psychologically uncomplex, without reserve and of a total generosity. (pp. 107-11)

Gobineau most resembles Stendhal and Mérimée when he treats with comic satire a corollary of his aesthetic of love, the ridicule of personages incapable of or prevented from the exercise of sincerity and generosity in their emotional or sentimental relationships. In stories such as **"Adélaïde," "Le Mouchoir Rouge," "La Chasse au Caribou,"** and in several episodes of *Les Pléiades,* Stendhalian and Mériméean flavors abound, as his incisive eighteenth-century clarity illuminates the weakness of the ungenerous ego with an all-comprehending, uninsistent irony. The brunt of the satire is borne by those individuals who are unable to see clearly into their own hearts, or who cannot or will not analyze their motivations and actions. The comic relief in these portraits often endows the narratives in which they appear with a greater dimension than the stories where Gobineau's idealism is more directly manifested. This accounts for the superiority of the irony laden **"Le Mouchoir Rouge"** and **"La Chasse au Caribou"** over the purely idealistic **"Akrivie Phrangopoulo."**

The men and women who best embody Gobineau's sentimental and emotional beliefs tend to lack depth and complexity because their superiority, as he conceived it, lay precisely in a straightforward and willed knowledge of themselves. This accounts, conversely, for the present-day reader's disappointment in the incompleteness of the portraits of Sophie Tonska and Lucie and Henri de Gennevilliers in *Les Pléiades,* for one senses that these essentially satirical characters represent a rich mine which Gobineau failed to exploit. We may attribute the success of Stendhal's best character creations to his ability to see both their comic and their tragic sides. Gobineau's sense of humor failed him, however, when he sought to portray the individuals who best represented his concept of moral elite. Fortunately for his fiction, he was attracted by the civilizations and regions which did not fit into his ethnological concepts of superiority. To the resulting contrast in his mind we owe the inspiration for his two most successful collections of shorter fiction, *Souvenirs de Voyage* and *Nouvelles Asiatiques.*

In thus extolling the talents of Gobineau, *ironiste et satirique,* we must not be unjust to the merits of his idealized love stories. Their tendencies to oversimplification and weaknesses in dramatic intensity are a seemingly necessary consequence of the clear-sighted honesty and strength of will which his "aristocrats" possess. The resulting quality of *romanesque,* conditioned by Gobineau's forceful critical intelligence, has a freshness and emotional appeal which assure to his *nouvelles* and to his last novel, *Les Pléiades,* a secure place among the works of second rank in French literature. (pp. 111-12)

Louis Tenenbaum, "Love in the Prose Fiction of Gobineau," in Modern Language Quarterly, *Vol. 18, No. 2, June, 1957, pp. 107-12.*

JACQUES BARZUN   (essay date 1965)

[*Barzun is a French-born American educator and writer whose wide range of learning has produced distinguished works in several fields, including history, culture, musicology, literary criticism, and biography. In the following excerpt from the 1965 revision of an essay first published in 1937, he describes what he considers myths generated by misreadings of the* Essay, *praising Gobineau's intellect and maintaining that, while responsible for certain race beliefs, the author should not be held culpable for all later racist thinking.*]

Writers who have taken a stand against German racism have usually looked for a villain as the head and fount of the evil and they have had little trouble in finding one. The Germans themselves have pointed to Arthur de Gobineau as their master and inspirer. Unfortunately, Gobineau's famous *Essay on the Inequality of Races*, published in the middle of the nineteenth century, is one of those books, like Marx's *Capital* and Montesquieu's *Spirit of the Laws,* that everybody talks about but no one ever reads. It is the common fate of two-volume works of erudition, but it does not seem to prevent their influence from working, from spreading, and from generating powerful myths. Gobineau's *Essay* has unquestionably done these things, yet it is a grave mistake to regard him on that account as a narrow-minded snob or a fanatical theorist. He must answer for much, but he is not the villain sought for by his indignant accusers.

The Count, in fact, is not only personally charming, but he is without doubt a first-rate intellect. Granted that he furnished a host of lesser writers with race-ideas and convenient clichés, he himself was superior to his own doctrine and he applied it with the playfulness of a genius fascinated by ideas. Before the end of his life Gobineau had supplemented, if not actually supplanted, his race-theory of history with the notion of an intellectual aristocracy, and his race-prejudice with a utopian desire that Plato or Jefferson might not have disavowed. . . . (pp. 50-1)

[Gobineau] felt born out of his time; but it would be an error to think that his passion for the past, the future, and the elsewhere was an escape or a retreat from the present. He belongs in that regard with the Romanticists. Perhaps no generation of men since the Renaissance has lived so intensely and perceptively, nor made so much poetry and truth out of a present that was out of joint. Like them a poet at heart, despite his wretched versification, Gobineau's literary output was born of conviction. His critical and political articles, his novels and tales, his travel books and Oriental studies, his letters and his sculpture, his diplomatic work, his friendships and his life, must command the respect of anyone acquainted with them, who is not also blinded by partisanship or bewildered by the versatility of a genuine artist.

It is entirely true that this versatility leads Gobineau to contradict himself on important points in the course of the forty volumes he has left us. But those contradictions, as with greater dialecticians than he, always have their explanation in circumstance. They must be held signs of honesty, rather than weakness, of mind. Gobineau had the realist's eye and he was uttering no more than the truth when he said that in studying a new people he "repudiated any true or false idea he might have had of their superiority." If inconsistency resulted, the fault lies with an unmanageable race-doctrine, not with the man observing history or life.

Now, what is Gobineau's race-theory? It boils down to three ideas: special race-characteristics, blood-mixture, and decadence. As to race Gobineau starts with the threefold division of mankind into white, yellow, and black. To the first he ascribes all the noble qualities of manhood, leadership, energy, superiority. The yellow races have stability and fertility. The black are endowed with sensuality and the artistic impulse. At this point Gobineau's scheme shows a novel feature which is unique in race-theorizing. It is only when two races mix, he says, that civilization occurs. Art and government are the signs of civilization and no single race can produce these by itself. But civilization leads to more and more mixing of "inferior blood" with that of the ruling caste, so that the "great race" is inevitably bastardized and decadence follows.

What Gobineau is really doing is to offer an answer to the ever-fascinating question of why civilizations rise and fall. Race is for him the answer, and one is forced to admit that Gobineau is so far a good historian that he sees all the European nations as products of the interpenetration of cultures. As a prophet he is again sound in thinking that nothing is going to stop the process of "mixing." It is when *races,* rather than peoples or cultures, are discovered as the elements in the mixture that the historian must take issue with Gobineau. Pessimist and fatalist as he is because of the "inevitability of race," he deserves a certain respect for rejecting the hope of a "pure race" preserving its "blood" intact. For him—and this is the result of Aryan philology in the manner of Prichard or Max Müller—the primitive *Aryas,* who were the progenitors of the great white race, have left very few pure specimens in our midst. What happened to the great majority was contamination by yellow and Negro blood. The Semites are Negroid and the Semites have infected the whole Mediterranean basin with their "nigridity." That is why the so-called Latin nations—France, Italy, Spain, Portugal—are a decadent, slavish, and worthless stock: they are thoroughly semitized, melanized. . . . Gobineau paints us the portrait of these unfortunates with the colors of his own disgust for democracy, servility, corruption, and mediocrity.

Obviously, Gobineau, reversing the usual process, starts with a desire for the truth about a great historical question, and ends by finding a confirmation of his hypothesis in the contemporary scene. At his narrowest, Gobineau is actuated by defensible motives—a genuine passion for art, for selectivity, for energy and devotion to causes transcending self or national interest. The vehemence of his racial denunciations is never ignorant fanaticism, and one comes to feel about him what Swift said of himself—that he hated the human race as a whole, but "heartily loved John, Peter, Thomas, and the rest."

The proof of this comparison is that when Gobineau was sent as minister to Persia in 1856, after the publication of the *Essay,* he acclimatized himself readily and conceived a love for the "semitized" and "melanized" Persians inconsistent with his written profession of faith. His work on the history and religion of the Persians breathes sympathy and understanding in a measure that few writers wholly innocent of racial bias could achieve. His next diplomatic post took him to Greece, for whose people and art he had conceived an aversion ever since becoming aware of their semitization in Macedonian and Hellenistic times. But, once on the spot, Gobineau observes, absorbs, and grows enthusiastic.

In Newfoundland and Sweden, despite some frankly acknowledged disappointments of his racial forecasts, he found himself completely in tune with his surroundings. Only in Brazil did he show intractability. He hated the "nigridized race," even though he became a close friend and confidant of the Emperor

Pedro, hardly a pure Aryan. But one suspects that Gobineau's distaste for Brazil was due to the climate, which made him suffer, and to the political rebuke of his appointment there, which made his proud and clear conscience suffer even more.

Gobineau's ideas on France itself have made a number of his biographers justly call him a continuator of Boulainvilliers and Montesquieu. He is a Nordicist like them, wielding the added power that, since their day, belonged to the new adjective Aryan. Racially, says Gobineau, France has only a few Aryan Nordics left; the rest are a Gallo-Roman mob whose chief instinct is envy and revolution, and whose highest taste in politics or in art is the circus. Using the word ''race'' in an honorific sense, Gobineau declares that these Latins are anything but a race. What has happened is of course the hopeless semitization of the breed, with the result that mediocrity is everywhere in power. Their political mismanagement, their moral corruption, was at no time more evident to the Count than during the war of 1870. On the conduct of that war he wrote a harsh but convincing pamphlet [*Ce qui est arrivé à la France en 1870*] which he himself considered his best work, the fruit of twenty-one years' observation and reflection. The severity of its strictures . . . has prevented many French racists, otherwise in agreement with Gobineau, from avowing his influence; it is precisely this brand of unintelligent patriotism which Gobineau most abhorred. He had traveled too far and knew Germany too well to believe, much less to be willing to repeat, the absurdities about the Germans current during the Franco-Prussian War. He thought patriotism a tyrannical invention of the Semitic race. That conclusion, if true, would greatly embarrass those French nationalists who combine rabid patriotism with anti-Semitism. Shortly before his death Gobineau further qualified his opinion. ''One must love one's country soberly, to be able to forgive it much. One must love everything in the world in the same way for the same reason, that everything needs great indulgence.''. . . This is not the utterance of an anti-patriot, but of a stoical moralist.

Whether motivated by pessimism or by stoicism, Gobineau was among the first to term the Latin races decadent and to sound a warning against the yellow peril. Already in the *Essay*, the hordes of silent yellow men are pictured as bound to engulf the decreasing race of whites precariously perched on the peninsular tip of the Asiatic continent we call Europe. The Count was perhaps not so much inconsistent about the East as fascinated and frightened by it. As an early orientalist and philologian, he had translated cuneiform inscriptions, but he also wrote articles against the Asiatic menace. He was attracted by magic and talismans, by fatalism and the ascetic life, so much so that during his own lifetime theosophic circles gave his works ready circulation and quiet renown. But he had moments of revulsion. In Scandinavia, swayed by the associations of the language and the surroundings, his orientalism fell away from him and he returned with zest to the Norse mythology admired in the *Essay*. His new acquaintance with Richard Wagner made this rediscovery doubly fresh and attractive. He sculptured a Walküre; yet there was a Buddha nearby swathed in damp cloths.

Behind this mixed love and fear on the philosophical plane, Gobineau was moved by practical considerations. In 1867 he writes to his friend Adalbert von Keller: ''The Orient is our great enemy: the danger began with the death of Alexander.'' He had seen in Persia the process of religious and racial mixture bringing about urban democracy, and he thought he saw a close parallel between the progress of Proudhon's philosophical an-

archism in Europe and the spread of the economic-evangelical movement known as Bab-ism in the Middle East. The East, history suggested to him, always kills the civilizations that conquer it—hence the grave danger of European imperialism in Asia. As the struggle of the powers shifted more and more to the East, awareness of the yellow peril grew in Gobineau's mind, and in an article dated 1880-81 that did not reach the public until after his death, he reviewed the gradual encroachment of ''Semitic blood'' in Europe from Greece to Scandinavia, analyzed with much insight the Anglo-Russian conflict in Asia, and predicted a world upheaval as the result of imperialism. Imperialism spelled danger to him because it augmented race-mixture, and race-mixture ''having gone so far in the modern world can only accelerate the evil to the final extremity.'' The panicky doctrine of the early 1900's clarioned forth by the newspapers and the German Emperor is here in more than embryonic form, as is also the chief point of modern prophecies like Henri Massis' *Defense de l'Occident*.

To reconcile the Count's writings with his tolerant behavior needs really no legerdemain. Gobineau was first and foremost a cosmopolitan spirit curious about the world. He belonged to that small but permanent class of Frenchmen who travel and who, doing it with their eyes and minds open, never make the mistake of supposing that the Alps, the Channel, and the Pyrenees are the outer edges of civilization. . . . (pp. 53-8)

To understand a man's mind in its strength and weakness is one thing; to measure the effects and distortions of his thought is another, far more difficult task. Gobineau himself is a sympathetic character, but there is no doubt that he is responsible for a particular set of influential race-beliefs. Aryan, Germanic, inferior and superior races, race-mixture, degenerescence, semitization, and nigridization are ideas or at least words that he dinned into the minds of his contemporaries and descendants. The habit of quotation-picking among scholars and the echolalia of publicists have done the rest. To make Gobineau solely responsible, as certain detractors have done, or entirely uninfluential, as some French critics still persist in doing, is to go against the facts. . . . (p. 61)

[The words Gobineau] used have become familiar throughout Western civilization. He did not invent them, he did not make a tight system of the things they stood for, he charged them with no relentless animus, and he did not propagate their use by his own powers alone. But it was something new and pregnant to have combined in however loose a scheme the earlier traditions of racial prejudice and theory. Before the *Essay* most race-theorizing had fallen into two categories—the anthropological racism of Retzius, Quatrefages, and Blumenbach; and the cultural or historical racism of Thierry, Niebuhr, Klemm, Guizot, or Stubbs. The attempted grafting of one upon the other branch of learning by Edwards was too specialized to succeed with the general public. Gobineau had a larger scope and did better. He was scientific and utilized Blumenbach, Prichard, Carus, Retzius, and Morton. He observed in races not only their physical characters in the manner of the old anthropology; but, keeping pace with the new, noted their skull-shapes and stature. He was a political historian and his whole *Essay* was designed to solve the problem of the rise and fall of civilizations. He was a social historian who revivified the thesis of Boulainvilliers, Montesquieu, and Guizot. He was a philologist who appropriated the data of Celtic research, oriental mythology, and Sanskrit literature. Add to these his pitiless reiteration of the term ''Aryan-Germanic,'' and the conviction is inescapable that he is the most comprehensive expounder of a great modern myth. *Omne concipiendum vivit; whatever must be conceived, exists.* This motto, taken from Gobineau, is the essence of race-belief. But for posterity perhaps his most novel contribution is his belief that art results only from the contact of two diverse races. (pp. 76-7)

Jacques Barzun, "Gobineau," in his Race: A Study in Superstition, *revised edition, Harper & Row, Publishers, 1965, pp. 50-77.*

DOUGLAS PARMÉE (essay date 1966)

[*Parmée examines the aesthetic characteristics of* The Pleiads, *here referred to as* Sons of Kings.]

For many, Gobineau's work has been spoilt—unread—by his reputation as father of modern racialism, and its inevitable associations. Indeed, although Gobineau's friendship with Wagner and influence on Nietzsche may be considered tolerably respectable, to have your name linked with the work of Houston Steward Chamberlain is much more dubious and to have influenced Rosenberg and Hitler downright discreditable. The fact is that Gobineau, an impulsive thinker who was all too ready to build a grain of brilliantly intuited truth into a mountain of half truths, has been the victim of tendentious interpretation which makes him appear as the prophet of the German *Herrenvolk*. We are, fortunately, not here concerned with these theories, seemingly based on the dubious hypothesis of the existence of a pure, primitive white Aryan stock whose priceless virtue has been and is being corrupted by dilution with other baser (e.g. Celtic!) blood; but in judging such garbled interpretations, it is worth remembering that Gobineau himself considered that in Germany, too, this process of degeneracy had advanced beyond recall; and although, by the time Gobineau was composing *Sons of Kings,* he seems to have written off many of his more fanciful racial theories (even if his historical prognosis for Europe remained gloomy enough), the picture of the Burbach court, based possibly on his experience as a diplomat at Hanover and Frankfurt on the Main in 1851 and 1854, contains few intimations of a master-race. (p. vii)

'It is . . . because men are basically different . . . that the study of them presents such a lively and varied interest and that it is important . . . to remember the part which men as individuals and not as mere abstractions play in the universe surrounding them. This is the sole justification of the novel.' These words from Gobineau's preface to *Les Nouvelles asiatiques*, first published in 1876 [see excerpt above], well sum up his views. The *Nouvelles* themselves, however, vivid and amusing as they are, rely too much on a rather facile exoticism to be in the first rank, as compared with the two major full-length works of Gobineau's maturity, *Les Pléiades* and *La Renaissance*. Both similarly extol the individual, the first in novel form, the second in a vast dramatic fresco in dialogue, a paen of praise as much to the energetic dedicated artist as to the ruthlessly amoral man of action, but it is set, alas, in the dangerous abstraction of a turbulent past far too close to Gobineau's own stormy longings, and too likely to appeal to his besetting vice of impulsive generalization: Gobineau always had a suspect weakness for the *condottiere*. In *Les Pléiades,* on the other hand, we are in a recognizably modern world, idealized though it is, and it is Gobineau, himself a man of the world and shrewd observer, who remains in charge as the narrator. Above all, in *Les Pléiades,* Gobineau makes constant use of that most valuable corrective to excessive fantasy and emotion, irony.

In a letter of 1874, Gobineau wrote of *Sons of Kings:* 'c'est de mes livres celui qui m'est le plus cher, parce que j'y ai dit le plus de choses qui me tiennent à cœur' ('it is my favourite amongst my books, because I said in it more of the things that are close to my heart'). He brought to it his own enthusiastic beliefs but was clever enough to realize that the novel form enabled him to distribute among various characters certain excessive opinions and qualities which, combined in one person, would have formed an extravagant, contradictory, and improbable character. As a result, no one character can be identified as himself and all of them, not excluding the lovable Wilfrid, are the subject, on occasion, of criticism or even satire, sometimes gently humorous, at others mordant.

A further corrective to excessive involvement in personal emotions is achieved by the deliberately artificial, although completely convincing establishment of the story-teller's conventions. Except for the rather contrived meeting of the three *calenders* on Lake Maggiore, we accept without question the intricate intertwining of plots which, through the continual switching of scene, maintain the reader in constant dramatic suspense. Such expert narration is certainly not unrelated to the *Thousand and One Nights,* and, indeed, in the first section of *Sons of Kings,* Gobineau deliberately invites the comparison by the device of making the three chief heroes tell their tales in the way of the calenders or dervishes of the *Arabian Nights.*

Originality of temperament and ideas, narrative skill: to these Gobineau adds his knowledge of men and women, which, if seeming sometimes more intuited, is often clearly and earthily pragmatic; sometimes, it is borrowed. Stendhal in particular was a source of information and a reader of *De l'Amour* will have no difficulty in recognizing Stendhal's hand in, for example, the comments on love among the Italians [in] *Sons of Kings*. It may well be argued that the very motive force behind the actions of the *Sons of Kings* (which includes, of course, Kings' daughters as well) is the Stendhalian *chasse au bonheur.* But Gobineau is far from being purely derivative; he looks forward as well as backwards and we are not surprised to find Proust writing in a letter to his friend Robert Dreyfus: 'I've become a *gobinien;* I can think only of him' [see Additional Bibliography]. Certainly many of Gobineau's analyses are Proustian in emphasis if not in expression as, for example, his comments on the role of jealousy in love.

Like Proust, Gobineau shows a distrust of mere intelligence, although his preference for the virtues of honesty towards oneself and towards others, of courage in self-examination and of energy to act accordingly is not specifically Proustian. Both take a somewhat gloomy view of mankind in general, however much Gobineau himself may pin his hopes on the existence of an *élite*. In this connexion the reader may well be justified in raising his eyebrows when he finds Gobineau, in *Sons of Kings,* prepared to resolve all the difficulties of love in a final chord of harmony. In the work of someone who once described mankind as 'L'animal méchant par excellence', the various happy endings and particularly the *deus ex machina* of the death of John Theodore's wife seem difficult to accept; they surely constitute an artistic flaw which must be attributed to Gobineau's euphoria springing from his happiness with the Comtesse de la Tour.

Such flaws are rare. In this long work, Gobineau has, on the whole, achieved a miraculous blend of lyricism and satire, imagination and analysis, in a word, of passionate belief in the existence of absolutes and a realization of the temporality of the human condition; and in an age when social pressures towards conformity may increase, it is refreshing to read about men and women who, albeit in favoured circumstances, dare to be themselves. It would, indeed, be strange if a novelist admired by, among many others, two such different writers as Jean Cocteau and Albert Camus, should not have much to offer every reader. (pp. x-xiii)

Douglas Parmée, in an introduction to Sons of Kings *by Joseph-Arthur Gobineau, translated by Douglas Parmée, Oxford University Press, London, 1966, pp. vii-xiii.*

MICHAEL D. BIDDISS (essay date 1970)

[*Biddiss is an English historian of European racism and an authority on Gobineau's life and thought. In the following excerpt, he considers the intellectual background of Gobineau's racist writings, chiefly as it bears on the development of the author's philosophical and political pessimism.*]

[Under what influences did Gobineau's] brand of pessimism come to be expressed in racial form? In the first place, the history of the French nation had been discussed often before in terms of links between Race and Class. The ancient rivalries of Gauls, Romans and Franks—all readily endowed with racial vices and virtues—and the relationship between their conflicts and the class structure of contemporary France had long been central themes of French historiography. Such an ethnic interpretation is hinted in the accounts of Caesar and Tacitus but the theme was certainly developed explicitly from the sixteenth century onwards. In the eighteenth century Henri de Boulainviller provided the classic exposition of the aristocratic version of this argument. He maintained that the Franks, having conquered the Roman rulers of the already vanquished Gauls, had come to form the French nobility and to hold their property and superior position by right of conquest. At the Revolution the Abbé Sieyès had been happy to stand Boulainviller on his head by maintaining that the recent triumph of the oppressed masses was the hitherto delayed manifestation of their Gallic superiority over the Frankish aristocracy. In the early nineteenth century such popular historians as Augustin Thierry continued to make the association of Class and Race. It was therefore scarcely surprising that Gobineau, the self-styled aristocrat viewing the nobility under siege, found inspiration in these sources of racial historiography and drew on Boulainviller in particular.

There were other more generalized influences. The Romantic Movement manifested increasing concern with the primitive origins and purity of peoples as embodied in myth, saga and legend. There was also a renaissance of interest in the Orient that prompted Gobineau's generation to draw comparisons and contrasts between the civilizations of East and West. When Michelet considered India he was confirmed in his conviction as to the identity of all mankind. For men such as Gobineau these wider horizons testified primarily to the differences and inequalities among men. Orientalism, in its philological form, made a further and specific contribution to that branch of race thinking which concerned the putative triumphs and virtues of an Aryan race. After Sir William Jones had established in the 1780s a connection between the Sanskrit, Greek, Latin, Persian, Celtic and Germanic languages and their common indebtedness to an 'Aryan' mother tongue, it was a short (though illogical) step to the supposition that a single race must correspond to this linguistic family. Thus the Aryan and his myth were born, and it was not long before scholars were devoting lengthy theses to the discussion of his birthplace, his migrations

and settlements, and his triumphs and culture-bearing activities throughout history. Such learned endeavours were especially popular in Germany where the romantics gave the idea eloquent expression in the form of Aryan-Teutonism.

These speculations on the Aryans were closely connected with more general attempts at classifying mankind in relation to the natural order. From the late eighteenth century the sciences of anthropology, ethnology and pre-historical archaeology, aided by zoology and geology, devoted much of their energy to divining the racial groupings of man. One of Gobineau's boldest pretensions was indeed that of synthesizing all their discoveries with those of more conventional history, and this was one of the major objectives of the [*Essay on the Inequality of the Human Races*].

This work . . . owes much to the intellectual context of that period which the cultural historian Jacques Barzun has characterized as the age of Darwin, Marx and Wagner. Racism, with its concern for the physical aspects of man, was a natural part of the environment of speculation which culminated in 1859 with the publication of Darwin's *Origin of Species*. Between Wagner and Gobineau there was later a personal friendship but, even in 1850, the composer was not only already inspired by the Teutonic past but had also asserted that Race was the key to artistic creation and had produced his antisemitic polemic *Judaism in Music* to explain certain aspects of cultural degradation.

Like Marx, Gobineau had become obsessed with deterministic historical explanation in terms of a single idea. What class conflict was to one the mixture of races had become to the other—the fundamental key to social interpretation. Again we see connections between Race and Class, here associated in their identical function as secular symbols of group loyalty in an age when political theory had lost almost completely its earlier role as the servant of the city state or of the Church or of a dynasty. The major works of Marx and Gobineau, directing loyalty to Class on the one hand and Race on the other, are in essence responses to the same crisis—that of alienation from the social, economic and cultural state of contemporary Europe. But the detailed causes of their resentment and the content of their responses certainly differ. By 1850 Gobineau had come to associate urbanization and industrialization not only with the ideas of materialism, equality, democracy and socialism, but also with a growing cosmopolitanism and movement towards human unity encouraged by miscegenation. The rejection of such ideas is part of his hostility to what Oswald Spengler came to call 'Megalopolis', the devouring world-city. This embodies the destruction of classes and states—indeed of all conventional social and political barriers. But what to Marx was an ideal was to Gobineau a prospect of unmitigated disaster. For Marx such destruction was the necessary precondition of true social harmony. But Gobineau, throughout his search for social order and the true freedom which a racial elite alone could appreciate, maintained, like Shakespeare's Ulysses and like those who adhered to the idea of a Great Chain of Being, that such harmony was possible only through the preservation of degree and hierarchy. The caste system of the Brahmins, not the classless society of Marx, was to him harmonious.

Gobineau has in common with many later racists this concern with the defence of social status and economic interest. He experienced a significant disjunction between desire and gratification, between his present moderate existence and his assessment of the previous situation of his class and family. It was within this context that Gobineau suffered from the humiliation of non-recognition. He experienced a form of bastardization complex—combining pride in himself in defiance of accepted values with the desire for conventional legitimation and recognition. Such a complex is especially relevant to a justification in terms of race, since this is necessarily connected with denouncing blood-mixture, regarded literally or figuratively, as the outcome of illicit or undesirable union. Although he never formulated his position in these precise terms, Gobineau strove, in a society that progressively refused recognition to himself and his caste, for self-legitimation by stressing that it was not he but the bulk of his contemporaries who were debased. This is the essence of the class-consciousness which Gobineau came to express in racist form. (pp. 18-22)

Gobineau's philosophy of history is founded on the belief that there are innate inequalities among the races of men. He devotes much versatility and many a convoluted argument to the hoary topic of Genesis and the unity or multiplicity of the original human Creation. In effect, conveniently ignoring primal man as beyond the reach of our knowledge, he settles for an emphasis upon the physical differences—and the intellectual and cultural inequalities illogically deduced therefrom—among all men that have been known to history. But in his discussion of this 'Separation of Races' inconsistency abounds. Perhaps most flagrantly of all he regards the 'Hamite', one of the basic types alleged as knowable, sometimes as essentially negroid and sometimes as not.

The fundamental racist doctrine of the *Essay* was voiced by Gobineau in his Dedication: 'I was gradually penetrated by the conviction that the racial question overshadows all other problems of history, that it holds the key to them all, and that the inequality of the races from whose fusion a people is formed is enough to explain the whole course of its destiny . . . I convinced myself at last that everything great, noble and fruitful in the works of man on this earth, in science, art and civilization, derives from a single starting-point, is the development of a single germ and the result of a single thought; it belongs to one family alone, the different branches of which have reigned in all the civilized countries of the universe' [see excerpt dated 1853]. These were sentiments which were eventually echoed in almost identical terms in *Mein Kampf.* Both there and in the *Essay,* despite the occasional pious references to the divine hand, it is racial dynamics which control human destiny. Long before Spengler and Toynbee, Gobineau saw historical movement in terms of the cyclical rise and fall of those quasi-organic civilizations which he lists at the conclusion of the first Book of the *Essay.* Yet his account of their development does not amount to any simple plea for blood-purity. The tragic element of Nemesis in his historical drama is that civilization can be created only by a combination of Aryan with alien blood. Thus the mixture of blood is both the life-giver and the death-bringer to civilization, and death is inherent in life. Alienated from the modern world and appalled by the sheer human fluidity of its migrations and social mobility, Gobineau was convinced that, after centuries of the miscegenation which led to the debasement of the higher stocks, civilization had reached its ultimate crisis. What makes him almost unique among race theorists is his total paralysis of response to that crisis.

In so far as the paralysis is firstly a moral one Gobineau is not outstandingly different from other racists, all of whom must finally fail to reconcile the conflict between historical determinism and free will. Some racists, in completely denying the humanity of certain portions of mankind, thereby deny these groups any capacity for moral judgment. Gobineau, it is true, never attains the extremes of depersonalization and dehumanization finally reached by the Nazis in their death camps. In the *Essay* he is prompt to castigate, for instance, the total lack of human consideration given by the now debased Anglo-Saxons of North America to the Negroes and indigenous Indians whom they persecute. He affirms explicitly that even the lowest of mankind have elements of conscience and judgment which mark them off decisively from the beast. On the other hand, Gobineau does suggest that in its levels of innate capacity for development and improvement mankind shows immense variation. And here, like the Nazis, he indulges in the crudest typologies of human groupings. Even if he avoids the ultimate in depersonalization he can still declare that 'I will not discuss the moral and intellectual worth of individuals taken one by one.' Such an anti-individualistic approach considers morality and intellect not as personal matters but within the context of race alone, establishing a hierarchy of group typologies within each of which the myriad human variations are annihilated. The ethical superiority of the white peoples is based upon tautology, being implicit in the very definition. In Gobineau's account man is unable to change the essence which controls the actions susceptible to moral judgment, and his theory eliminates any proper notion of individual responsibility. Such a race theory is in implication morally totalitarian, leading to the annihilation of all other value-systems and of traditional religious morality in particular. Gobineau develops instead an ethic of predestination and justification by blood which takes man beyond all conventional ideas of good and evil. In . . . *The Pleiads* and *The Renaissance* all these facets of his philosophy, and of race thinking generally, are further strikingly epitomized.

Gobineau's virtual uniqueness among racists stems, however, from the fact that to this moral paralysis there is added a paralysis of political exhortation. . . . [His] correspondence with Tocqueville vividly illustrates the horrific conjunction between his ethical nihilism and his total lack of pragmatic concern. In the Conclusion of the *Essay* Gobineau reveals his relentlessly pessimistic prognosis. The Aryan blood, now almost exhausted, is no longer capable of continuing its task of creating civilizations. Mediocrity and decay abound. Reliant upon the reification of his physical metaphors, Gobineau sees in the organism that is civilization a corruption and degeneration beyond all cure. His hatred of human migrations and intermixture often seems to approach a plea for social stagnation, even perhaps for the abolition of social life itself. Long before the threat of universal racial confrontation was obvious, at a time when racial rivalries were not primarily those of colour and still three-quarters of a century before the term 'racism' was coined, Gobineau turned towards the yellow hordes in the East and vividly depicted his view of the unavoidable crisis of the West. Beyond the most temporary and ineffectual makeshifts, beyond a flight from the world into stoicism by the few men of worth remaining, Gobineau has no political programme of racial and cultural regeneration to offer. Like Gibbon amidst the ruins of the Capitol, Gobineau begins his great work pondering upon the decline and fall of civilizations. Unlike Gibbon, there alone his thoughts remain. (pp. 24-8)

Between the pessimism of Gobineau and the regenerative optimism of those who, in preaching 'Gobinism', came to make use of his doctrines there is of course a vast gulf. But it is not altogether unbridgeable. Though in his own lifetime Gobineau's *Essay* met with negligible success, the history of Gobinism proper does begin in his very last years. It was his friendship with Richard Wagner, dating from 1876, that proved decisive, for Gobineau and Gobinism first reached fame and infamy as part of the Wagnerian movement. The Master had found in Gobineau's views on ethnic chaos a systematic treatment of elements in his own theory of cultural decay, but, unlike the Frenchman, he complemented these with ideas of regeneration. After the death of the two men within months of each other, the Bayreuth circle continued to cultivate the memory of Gobineau and a more optimistic version of his ideas. Into Gobinism was infused an anti-Jewish element that had not been prominent in the *Essay.* Modern Germans conveniently forgot that its praise was not for themselves but for the Teutons who had emerged from fifth-century forests before losing their identity and their vigour somewhere in the Middle Ages. They neglected Gobineau's assaults upon vulgar nationalism and upon the imperialistic expansion which so encouraged blood-mixture. Despite his disavowal of any regenerative programme, least of all the sort that would in fact only hasten miscegenation, his name became posthumously linked with ideas of Pan-Germanic expansion. By the time that the Gobineau Society was founded in 1894 its hero's work had suffered a not too subtle metamorphosis. In that new form it was to provide inspiration for such twentieth-century magicians of the Myth of Blood as Houston Stewart Chamberlain, Alfred Rosenberg and Adolf Hitler himself. In the Führer's Reich the *Essay,* suitably adjusted, became a popular school reader. Whatever lack of explicit acknowledgment Gobineau may have received, over and over again in the political literature of Nazism there are phrases and conceptions profoundly echoing his work of the 1850s. Above all, there is in the *mode* of thinking every similarity. Despite all the optimism, all the activism, all the messianism so foreign to Gobineau, such a link could not be concealed.

Just as Hegel might not have recognized much of Hegelianism, or Marx much of Marxism, so Gobineau might fairly have denied the accuracy of much that was preached in his name. His writings are a major root of the Right not so much on account of their detailed content as because of the mode of thinking that they embody. In content the doctrines of European racism—such as Celticism, Slavism, Teutonism and Anglo-Saxonism—have revealed great variety. But in the mode of thought in the endless repetition of the same errors of method, their similarities have been equally marked. To all of them may be applied John Stuart Mill's retort that 'Of all vulgar modes of escaping from the consideration of the effect of social and moral influences on the human mind, the most vulgar is that of attributing the diversities of conduct and character to inherent natural differences.' The later progress of both genetic and sociological knowledge has done nothing to invalidate Mill's fundamental contention that human differences are due to a much more complex interaction of hereditary and environmental factors than racists allow. In September 1967 a UNESCO Statement on Race, prepared by an international panel of leading biologists, geneticists, physical anthropologists and sociologists, declared that 'Current biological knowledge does not permit us to impute cultural achievements to differences in genetic potential.' Many contemporary geneticists indeed cast doubt upon the validity of viewing races as discrete units, and seriously question the whole practice of racial classification itself. Yet the fundamental objection to the political ideas of racism must always be moral rather than scientific. Could any biological revolution justify to us a mode of thinking which, like Gobineau's, denies us the right to judge human beings essentially as individuals?

It is true that, in some senses, Gobineau's *Essay* is not so much a 'black book' as one that was blackened by distortions through time. But in, for instance, his illogicality, his inconsistency, his tendency to moral nihilism and racial determinism, he left negligently so many hostages to fortune that he has less of a defence than some against the charges upon which he is indicted for the posthumous uses of his work. With the premise of equal human rights and dignity once denied, with that of racial inequality once accepted, a perilous journey begins and it is a foolish man who believes that it will be easy to halt short of the horrific terminus. For racism is too much a matter of absolutes. Eventually it must destroy all those who, like Gobineau, strive for an element of benevolence, because in benevolence there is compromise. Eventually racism must pose directly the uncompromising question as to who shall be killer and who victim—the ultimate political question beyond which further questions, even if they exist, are certainly not political in nature. (pp. 29-32)

It would be dangerously wrong to suppose that European race feeling and race thinking are dead. The Nazi experience undoubtedly brought an emotional revulsion against them—but it is one that may easily be disregarded under the threat from the coloured hordes of Africa and Asia. It would be wrong to suppose that a mode of thinking which flourished in the age of European world domination cannot survive in the period of comparative decline. Indeed, it is this very decline, and the prospect of its continuance as Afro-Asia takes a larger position in the world, that may create the environment for renewed European racism. In that context no amount of refutation by biologists and geneticists can guarantee against the possibility of the phoenix-like re-emergence of such a potent political myth. The post-war neo-fascists have not hesitated to purvey doctrines of Pan-Europeanism as a response to the crisis of colour confrontation. We must beware the complacent view that racism stands outside the mainstream of the Western tradition of political thought and that, being an aberration into foreign fields, it is unlikely to regain its influence. Unfortunately, in its intolerance, its denial of human dignity, its moral authoritarianism, and in much else, it is a very real part of any tradition that we have. In his convictions as to the coloured peril, in his expressions of fear, in his alienation, Gobineau can still strike sympathetic chords in the hearts of many of our contemporaries. Racism is a bogus mode of thought, but one which retains a certain cheap plausibility, particularly when the coloured peoples are developing their own ideas of racial supremacy. The fear of Western decline, central to Gobineau's thinking, is in the great tradition of European continental paranoia. Today the potential enemy for his successors is not Islam, nor even the Jews, but is regarded as being the Afro-Asian world, the bulk of whose states agree upon denouncing the West over racial issues, if upon little else.

Despite his originality and his remarkable prescience as to the kind of issue which would increasingly dominate world affairs, Gobineau's mode of thinking would have vitiated any advice that he might have given. In the event, he himself felt simply unable to offer any political wisdom for improving the situation. It is a sobering thought that he would probably have dismissed our quest for more positive and purposeful ideas and actions with the rebuke that it is an elementary error to suppose that every social and political problem must be automatically susceptible to some kind of effective solution. It would certainly be dangerous for us to agree with the view that the racial problems of the modern world are already beyond solution. But, as they loom even larger, it would be no less perilous to believe that they will cure themselves without our commitment to their solution or that they will be cured by racist theories.

Despite all his errors of analysis and method, it is unfortunately necessary to admit that, as the situation worsens year by year, Gobineau's conclusions, at least, take on renewed significance. How much longer shall we be able to maintain that he was wrong in seeing racial crisis as an insoluble problem? For the present, even while striving to find solutions, it seems wise to recognize reluctantly that there is no aspect of social and political affairs more deserving of some of the pessimism which marked Gobineau's thought than that which concerns the races of the world, their growing rivalries and conflicts. This is the sense in which present trends may yet bear out his remark that 'I shall only come to be appreciated a hundred years after my death.' (pp. 33-5)

> Michael D. Biddiss, "Introduction: Human Inequality and Racial Crisis," in Gobineau: Selected Political Writings by Joseph Arthur Gobineau, edited by Michael D. Biddiss, Jonathan Cape, 1970, pp. 13-35.

D. C. J. LEE (essay date 1979)

[Lee compares Gobineau's historical method with that of two of his contemporaries, Tocqueville and Ernest Renan.]

Gobineau is a writer one approaches with caution, both out of respect for his genuine stature and from an inescapable sense of unease. Even now, close on a century after his death, no claim to critical or historical detachment can fully obliterate the memory of the reverence or anger that his ideas once inspired, nor dissociate his name from the blood shed in the cause of an ideology of race to which he gave—if nothing else—a coherent framework. It may be that since the end of the Second World War we have begun to achieve some more balanced and rounded view of the author of the *Essai sur l'inégalité des races humaines.* The stylistic analysis of *Les Pléiades* conducted in 1957 by Michael Riffaterre, the establishment in 1966 of the *Etudes Gobiniennes,* the important recent studies that have appeared, all point to a desirably calmer evaluation. Yet the very scrupulousness of the scholarship that has made the Gobineau review a model of its kind attests to the lingering sensitivity of the subject. And this is perhaps as it should be. For Gobineau retains, in the words of [Michael Biddiss], a profound contemporary relevance in illuminating 'problems still posed by a mode of thought that uses race as an instrument of social explanation and often of political effort too.' There is at once a case for reassessment but also for frank awareness. While the Gobineau legend demands to be dispelled and with it the over-simplifications that do gross injustice to a refined and challenging mind, the impact of this legend itself requires recognition as do the fundamental social and political issues that Gobineau's writings have brought to light.

The presence of so many different facets and associations is only the first of the considerable problems facing the modern critic and biographer. A recent study [by Jean Gaulmier] suggests Gobineau is a spectre, a phantom, out of reach and yet disturbingly present. The serious gaps that remain in our knowledge of the man, particularly during the crucial formative years, give Gobineau the appearance of emerging, a mentality fully formed, like a meteor in the sky of nineteenth-century thought. Central by reputation as is the *Essai sur l'inégalité des races humaines,* a study devoted to Gobineau's political or sociological ideas must attempt to set the race work in the context of his related, if less spectacular, contributions in other areas: his farsighted views on decentralisation developed in the short-lived *Revue provinciale,* his gloomy yet penetrating diagnosis

of the causes of French defeat in the 1870 war. What were his achievements and his reputation in his profession as ambassador of France? What were his relations with women other than the stormy ones with his wife and his belated attachment to the Comtesse de La Tour? The information that might reveal a different side to his character remains obscure. Nor may we, in the end, forget that Gobineau was also a poet, novelist, sculptor and that, like his contemporary Renan, the artist in him, as much as the philosopher, played a significant part in determining the structure and range of his thought. These are, in some measure, issues of fact, but also issues of classification and here perhaps is the central difficulty impinging even on our use of such terms as 'racist', 'racism' which we can too readily apply in retrospect with all their modern connotations. Gobineau was a racist in the sense defined by Michael Biddiss of one who relies uniquely on a racial system for an explanation of history and society. Yet to the extent that these words now possess clear associations of anti-semitism or colour prejudice they misrepresent the immediate character of Gobineau's race theory which is more concerned with the identification of a process than with its aggressive application. In Gobineau's radically determinist scheme of things, all effort to change by action the direction of history whose fatal course has long been set must appear puny and vain. Just as he was uncomprehendingly scornful of those who, after the publication of the *Essai,* used it to justify the oppression of the American negro, his 'guilt by association' for the atrocities of the Nazi death camps is in one respect that of the naïve confidence of a whole century which came to establish scientific truth—or speculation in the name of science—as morally self-justifying and not open to examination within any other frame of reference but its own. If Sartre can now claim that to speak is to act and in those terms condemn the nineteenth-century *bourgeois* writer for his hypocritical attachment to pure art or pure knowledge, it is because an intellectual revolution to which we are perhaps too close fully to appreciate, separates our own age from the age of Gobineau. The interwar years translated the theory of race into political action. That experience itself has created a modern convention that makes discussion of racial difference a taboo. In the nineteenth-century, only the deeply perceptive such as Tocqueville were in a position to anticipate the impact of an argument that, in its own terms and context, was no more than a single stone in the vast edifice of Positivist knowledge. In each case, it is history itself which has made Gobineau its own mirror.

Initially indeed, the phenomenon of Gobineau is explained by his having been quintessentially a man of his time, even to the extent of his protest against it. The central question raised by Gobineau is that of race but more fundamentally it is one of a state of mind which he shared with a whole generation and which, in his case, found expression in a racial doctrine which thus becomes effect and not cause. What makes him unique is the critical intensity of the combination, the potential for transmission into political action of an analysis of contemporary values which, in others, by reason of temperament or upbringing, took less protean or explosive forms. Two instances among Gobineau's contemporaries may be taken to illustrate the point. Gobineau's relations with Alexis de Tocqueville and their correspondence between 1843 and 1859 [see excerpt dated 1853-57], constitute a remarkable record of the moral and political divergence of two minds with a common point of departure. The case of Ernest Renan, whose intellectual interests constantly intermesh with those of Gobineau to the point where the author of the *Essai* will begin to suspect Renan of plagiarism, is likewise that of a different cast of mind giving rise to

Le château de Trie in Normandy, Gobineau's principal residence during most of his diplomatic career.

an entirely different view of the state and future of European society.

The common ground is that of a sense of lost identity and spiritual and moral security shared by a whole generation of French thinkers in the face of the destruction of political and religious norms at the hands of eighteenth-century analysis and the culminating moment of the French Revolution. Tocqueville and Renan, like Gobineau, confront a post-aristocratic and post-Christian society in which the threat of anonymity posed by the rise of the mass democratic state is the secular mirror of the erosion of the ordered world of Biblical authority. In each case too, the Revolution of 1848 and its aftermath provide a confirmation of tendencies already sensed and act as a catalyst to declarations of principle. All three men betray the desire for a new analysis, political or historical, to satisfy their own instincts of uniqueness and absolute value. Yet this state of mind can find an outlet in many forms whether it is rank nostalgia and pessimism towards modern society, some type of substitute creed fulfilling the psychological needs previously met by former faith, or a description of history which explains or justifies the present condition of *malaise.*

Tocqueville, possibly be being less susceptible than either Renan or Gobineau to the influence of German thought, offers the least systematic and most pragmatic view of post-revolutionary Western democracy. He shared Gobineau's love of nobility and in fact enjoyed an ancestry considerably more distinguished than that which the author of ***Ottar Jarl*** sought constantly to manufacture for himself. Like Gobineau, Tocqueville feared that democracy would lead to mediocrity; yet his love of liberty is the overriding force so that here, as in his abiding respect for the ethics of Christianity as a declared unbeliever, it is Tocqueville's ability to separate value from dogma and thus remain free of his own prejudices that marks him as a temperament apart from his energetic disciple. It was Tocqueville who formulated the most penetrating critique of the ***Essai sur l'inégalité des races humaines*** at the time of the book's publication, identifying it as a work which would find a more ready response in Germany than in France and one which, in the rigour of its determinism, represented an invitation to despair. . . . Janine Buenzod rightly discerns that what ultimately separates Tocqueville from Gobineau is a cultural tradition: Tocqueville's values, Graeco-Roman in origin, represent those of Western democracy in their emphasis on law, justice and freedom. The values of Gobineau are essentially tribal and, contrary to the spirit of subsequent efforts to assimilate his thinking to German or even French nationalism, reflect a rejection of the structures of nation states evolved by history for the primitive ties of kinship and blood. For Gobineau, the rootlessness which he experienced is transmuted into the virtue of the stateless barbarian and into a condemnation of Hellenic civilisation.

It is not perhaps surprising that Renan, while sharing Gobineau's fascination for the cultural origins of Western society, should remain a stranger to such a view. Renan's essay *L'Avenir de la science* which he began in 1848 is, even more than the ***Essai sur l'inégalité des races humaines,*** a direct response to the events of that year in the form of a profession of faith. Yet unlike Gobineau and Tocqueville, Renan came from a humble background so that his elitism and search for new absolutes of value reflect his personal academic achievements and are, as a result, more strongly orientated towards the future, more fundamentally optimistic and redemptive than those of either of his contemporaries. In Renan, the fear of anonymity is finely balanced by his sense of participation in a positive historical advance just as the characteristic orientation of his thought towards dialogue or drama is a reflection of an ideal of truth which is inclusive rather than reductive, and of a conception of history as unfulfilled rather than fatally decadent. It is significant therefore that Renan's frequently expressed views on racial difference, if they stand comparison with those of Gobineau in the isolation and praise of the Aryan, are nevertheless centred on cultural achievements and involve the parallel recognition of the poetic and moral contribution of the Semitic races. In 1890, when Renan finally published *L'Avenir de la science,* his greater pessimism is reflected in his admission of the reality of Gobineau's thesis: 'L'inégalité des races est constatée'. In 1856, however, Renan's response to Gobineau's essay on race was to envisage the transcendence of such distinctions in the march of humanity towards ecumenical consciousness. . . .

Gobineau's two contemporaries clearly illustrate the fundamental difference between the academic and the political mind. Renan's systematic analysis of the polarities of Western culture reveals the methods and attitudes of the intellectual theorist of history and is consistent with a conception of truth which can only be expressed as a potential or tendency. Tocqueville's emphasis on self-determination and considered action is that of a political consciousness which views history and society in terms of life situations and remains aware of the historical uniqueness of any given moment. Yet what they have in common is no less important: namely the heritage of the Christian belief in values which transcend immediate material circumstances, whether this is expressed in the form of Renan's historical idealism or Tocqueville's practical ethics. And in these two aspects is to be found, perhaps, the central issue uncovered by Gobineau's manner of thought. It has been rightly pointed out that the ***Essai sur l'inégalité des races humaines*** was never intended as a work of political prescription. Indeed, we have seen that its rigid determinism is in contradiction with the spirit of political activity. Yet in his work as an academic Gobineau brings to the analysis of history that instinct for simplification which is the mark of a man of action and which reveals itself likewise in his nostalgia for an age of individual responsibility. In this respect, the *Essai* exemplifies that process of 'psychological compensation' identified in Gobineau's thought by M. Jean-Jacques Chevallier. Yet the machinery of this displacement is a complex one. Simultaneously political and a-political, Gobineau's reaction to the problems of his age has the form of an academic exploration of what are seen as inevitable tendencies, but constitutes nonetheless an uncompromising act of political aversion. Equally, his radical materialism may be seen as at once a total renunciation of Christian values and as an assumption of the doctrinal intensity of religious dogma: the race theory is both secular and sectarian.

Here the character of Gobineau's thought begins to approach that of Marx. As Professor Biddiss argues, the similarity between the two writers extends to their readiness to offer an explanation of history in terms of a single determining agent, as well as to their fundamental materialism and to their analysis of society by means of a 'group' theory: in one case that of race, in the other that of class. Marx's analysis is economic and Gobineau's is ethnological but in both is found the awareness of man's alienation at the hands of modern society from his true identity as a species being. The strength of their dual influence on European ideas is, however, to be found in the association of political conviction with a demonstration of historical necessity and in the substitution of a cult of the secular for the tenets of Christian belief. Much has been written about the surrogate religions of the nineteenth century but, in a recent study, Professor Owen Chadwick has suggested that we should be wrong to regard Marxism simply as a form of Christian heresy: the thought of Marx is a classic case of the assimilation to the secular, 'the most powerful philosophy of secularization in the nineteenth century'. His assessment could well have included Gobineau. For what is created in each case is an entirely new value system embracing individual conduct as well as historical purpose, having no reference to the spiritually transcendent but offering the potential for simplification demanded of cultural myth. Marx, as he said himself, was no Marxist. Gobineau was no Gobiniste. But by carrying their sense of history only as far as their own beliefs and thus overlooking the historicity of their own positions both thinkers present their ideas as possessing an absolute claim on reality and invite absolute attachment. There can certainly be no coincidence in the fact that the two most powerful political movements of our own time, Fascism and Communism, the politics of race and those of class, are both born of a parallel response to the plight of nineteenth-century man and have evolved in different circumstances through similar passionate distortion at the hands of uninformed or uncritical disciples.

D. C. J. Lee, in an introduction to Gobineau, *by Ludwig Schemann, Arno Press, 1979.*

PETER FAWCETT   (essay date 1984)

[*Fawcett examines Gobineau's principal fiction, chiefly* The Pleiads, Romances of the East, *and* The Crimson Handkerchief, *maintaining that these are the works for which he will be remembered.*]

Gobineau prophesied once; ''Je ne serai donc apprécié de mes contemporains [*sic*] que cent ans après ma mort''. He had the misfortune to be little read during his lifetime and to be championed after his death by a German disciple of Wagner's at a time when French distrust of anything that found favour *outre-Rhin* was at its height. Despite one or two surges of popularity—Proust declared himself ''engobinisé'' in 1904—his reputation as the father of modern racism and the identification of his views with some of the most obnoxious theories of National Socialism mean that he has remained, in Jean Mistler's well-known phrase, ''le plus grand méconnu du XIXᵉ siècle''. (p. 323)

Was Gobineau a racist? The answer is clearly no. In common with much of the best anthropological thinking of his day he merely regarded the degeneracy of mankind, as attributable to the evils of miscegenation. What he described to his English friend Robert Lytton as the only idea he had ever had in his life, ''l'idée du sang et de ses conséquences'', underlies all his work. But he saw no hope of either halting or reversing the process. His vision was unrelievedly pessimistic. Mankind was, as far as he was concerned, irretrievably doomed.

However, once some of his less palatable opinions are set aside, he emerges as a man of absorbing intellectual passions who must have been a delightful companion and who was far more capable than most members of his generation of entering with generosity into the spirit of whatever seemed strange and unfamiliar. He once told his daughter "il n'y a réellement au monde que les romans de chevalerie", and "l'amour des romans de chevalerie", was, he claimed, "un trait de famille". His most recent biographer has characterized him as a tragic Don Quixote. The major enterprise of his life, of which the [*Essai sur l'inégalité des races humaines*] was only a part, was to trace his own genealogy back to the Viking pirate, Ottar Jarl, who settled in France in 843. It is as a writer of fiction, at odds with the realist tradition of the nineteenth-century novel, that he seems in the long run most likely to survive.

He began his literary career as a journalist in the 1840s. By the time of his marriage in 1846, he had turned his hand to the production of *romans-feuilletons* to make ends meet. The only one of his works of this period, and the only one prior to the *Essai,* to have successfully stood the test of time is the Balzacian short story, *Mademoiselle Irnois,* which . . . may have been inspired by the plight of his younger sister Caroline, whom a spinal malady forced to spend most of her life lying down. It is told with a verve and delicacy which make it extremely readable.

For twenty years, while pursuing the diplomatic career to which he was introduced by Tocqueville, Gobineau wrote no more fiction. He returned to the genre in 1868 under the influence of his love for the two Dragoumis sisters, Marika and Zoë, daughters of a former minister to the deposed King Otho, whom he met during his mission to Athens. He began to develop a highly personal style of *nouvelle,* based on his acknowledged skill as a raconteur, in which a loose fictional framework would allow him to give free rein to his views and opinions on a wide range of topics.

The first such story was **"Le Mouchoir rouge",** a sombre tale of murder and revenge set in Cephalonia, which had probably been told to Gobineau by one of his Greek friends or learnt by him on the spot, and which belies its opening sentence: "Céphalonie est une île charmante". Gobineau never found it so, and did not like its inhabitants, whom he regarded as the products of a mixture of bloods.

This was followed by **"La Chasse au caribou",** in which Gobineau drew on his visit to Newfoundland as a member of a fisheries commission in 1859. Here he tells the story of a naïve young Frenchman who goes to the island in search of adventures worth the retelling and ends up engaged in error to an American Grace Darling. It is a kind of *L'Ingénu* in reverse, and, while mocking the stupidity of his compatriot, Gobineau makes plain his admiration for the island's inhabitants, "ces natures brutales", each one of them a formidable colossus.

But nothing in the New World can possibly equal the delights of Naxos, recalled from Rio de Janeiro in September 1869, in **"Akrivie Phrangopoulo".** This story is based on Gobineau's own voyage to the Cyclades two years earlier on an English corvette captained by Lindsay Brine and on "les rêveries que Brine et moi avons faites sur le bonheur de vivre dans une pareille île sans avoir plus rien de commun avec le monde". Its hero, Henry Norton, modelled on Brine, falls in love with the beautiful Naxiot girl whose name appears in the title and who is described as "la femme des temps homériques", his "belle au bois dormant", the precious flower of this island

paradise where nothing has changed since the Crusades. By virtue of his Englishness—"cette race normande, la plus agissante, la plus ambitieuse, la plus turbulente, la plus intéressée de toutes les races du globe, est en même temps la plus portée à reconnaître et à pratiquer le renoncement aux choses"— Norton has the courage to relinquish his command and settle down with his bride, becoming one of those rare "déserteurs du beau monde". Gobineau claimed to have encountered in every quarter of the globe. First, however, he takes his hosts on a pleasure-trip to the neighboring islands, which becomes the occasion for an entertaining digression, relating to a descent into the great cave on Antiparos, about the worthlessness of subterranean tourism where one ends up, after risking life and limb, unable to see "quoi que ce soit qui vaille la peine d'être cherché à trois pas", as well as for a magnificent Wagnerian description of continued volcanic activity on Santorini following the eruption of 1866.

These three stories, written primarily to amuse the Dragoumis sisters, were gathered together and with **"Akrivie Phrangopoulo"** as the centre-piece, published in 1872 under the title *Souvenirs de voyage.* There should perhaps have been a fourth story in the shape of **"Adélaïde",** written in a single day in December 1869, but it referred to persons still living and did not, therefore, appear during Gobineau's lifetime. When it was eventually published in the *Nouvelle Revue Française* in 1913, it was immediately recognized as one of his masterpieces and Gide would have done better to mention it, rather than *Les Pléiades,* when he spoke of Radiguet's debt to Gobineau, as it prefigures *Les Bal du comte d'Orgel* to a remarkable degree.

Also originally intended for *Souvenirs de voyage,* but too late to be included, was **"La Danseuse de Shamakha",** which became instead the first of the *Nouvelles asiatiques,* based on Gobineau's missions to Persia in 1855-58 and 1861-63. In September 1872 he wrote to Marika Dragoumis from Stockholm: "J'ai inventé à Athènes cette manière de nouvelles que j'ai la prétention de donner pour originales et bien à moi; mais c'est ici que je l'ai perfectionnée". The new stories he regarded as superior to those he had already written, and their purpose, as stated in the preface to the published volume in 1876, was to show "ce que sont devenus aujourd'hui les premiers civilisateurs du monde, les premiers conquérants, les premiers savants, les premiers théologiens que la planète ait connus", so as to invite the reader to reflect "sur certains signes qui se produisent actuellement en Europe, et qui ne sont pas sans présenter des analogies avec la même décrépitude". In point of fact, only three out of the six stories are set wholly or mainly in Persia and, though they have been highly praised for the understanding they show of Asian character, the viewpoint throughout remains distinctly European.

"La Danseuse de Shamakha" itself, which is comparable in style and structure to **"Akrivie Phrangopoulo",** turns out to be the story of a Caucasian Electra, whose Orestes has been corrupted by contact with Western civilization since the Lezgian village in which they were brought up, perched like an eyrie on top of a mountain peak, was destroyed by the Russian invaders. Similarly, **"Les Amants de Kandahar",** a complex tale of love and honour, stands out as an Afghan version of *Romeo and Juliet,* which, although frequently regarded as one of Gobineau's most ordinary stories, can equally be seen as one of his best for its raciness and the beautiful descriptions of love it contains. Of the stories set in Persia, **"Histoire de Gambér-Aly"** and **"La Guerre des Turcomans"** portray in a picaresque vein the system of patronage and extortion on which the modern state survived, notably in **"La Guerre des Tur- comans"** where the account of military incompetence fore- shadows Céline's hilarious depiction of the First World War; whereas **"L'Illustre Magicien"** is acknowledged to be an *Ara- bian Nights*-style transposition of Gobineau's last great love, for Mathilde de la Tour, the young wife of the Italian ambas- sador in Stockholm, with whom he formed a pact of everlasting friendship at the Norwegian king's coronation in 1873.

The last of the stories, fittingly entitled **"La Vie de voyage"**, tells of a journey, undertaken by Gobineau in the opposite direction, by a newly married Italian couple between Erzerum and Tabriz. The great caravan of two thousand people is seen as a town on the move, ruled over by the Moses-like figure of the chief muleteer, "le plus despotique et le plus inflexible des législateurs", and its life of "vagabondage organisé," as the most natural expression of "le caractère et l'esprit des Asiatiques". It all proves too much for the Europeans (as it had done for Mme Gobineau), and, having had their fill of mystery and adventure, they end up by cutting their journey short.

Gobineau possessed the inestimable gift as a traveller of being tirelessly curious about variations in human behaviour, and this he imparts to his reader in the lively portraits of individuals of different nationalities and creeds which litter his work. Before he died he had started a further collection of *Nouvelles féodales*. However, in 1871, in the aftermath of the Franco-Prussian War, he had begun writing his "grand roman" of *Les Pléiades,* which he saw as "le point culminant" of the form he had invented and in which he had intended to abandon himself completely to his "sentiment vrai sur la société moderne". *Les Pléiades* is the product of the Commune in the same way as the *Essai* had been of the 1848 revolution. The theme of the novel is stated in a letter to Count Prokesch-Osten, one-time Austrian ambassador in Constaninople, to whom he wrote: "Je fais aussi un roman très développé intitulé *Les Pléiades* ayant pour base cette idée, qu'il n'y a plus de peuples, mais seule- ment, dans toute l'Europe, quelques individualités surnageant comme des débris sur un déluge".

Les Pléiades is undoubtedly one of the strangest pieces of fiction ever written. It is a cross between a romance of chivalry and Goethe's *Wilhelm Meister* and *Elective Affinities*. It begins superbly with a descent into Italy by stage-coach along the shores of Lake Maggiore and the encounter of three young men of differing nationalities, "poissons de la même espèce", on their way to Isola Bella. The most articulate of the three is the Englishman, Wilfrid Nore, and it is he who defines them as "trois calenders, fils de Rois", and defends the right of those "êtres lumineux", who in each generation stand apart from the crowd, to "se qualifier de Pléiade." Each of them proceeds to tell his life-story, but it is only the Frenchman, Louis Lau- don, modelled on Acaste in *Le Misanthrope,* who at this stage is willing to reveal to the others his amorous affairs, showing a lack of "réserve" for which he is sharply rebuked by Nore. They then split up, having agreed to meet again in the autumn in the home town of the third member of the trio, Conrad Lanze, a German.

It is around this tiny principality of Burbach that much of the rest of the novel is centred. It is governed by the melancholy Jean-Théodore, who, like most modern rulers, is reduced to the level of a puppet in his public functions. One by one, each of the "Pléiades", to whom must be added the colourful and eccentric Countess Tonska and Conrad's younger sister Liliane, achieves a form of happiness, mostly through love, but only

after a great deal of suffering. Jean-Théodore himself, who gradually emerges as the book's major character, abdicates his throne and almost dies of a broken heart, before the providential death of his estranged first wife allows him to set up home with his uncle's stepdaughter in a secluded chalet far from the haunts of civilization. There can be no doubt that wishful think- ing about the outcome of his own affair with Mathilde de la Tour made Gobineau—who was not above wanting his own wife dead—profoundly change the course of the novel during the process of composition. To Prokesch-Osten, who was shocked by the amount of love it contained, he replied: "Vous pron- oncez le mot de *maladie*; c'est parfaitement exact; un amour comme ceux-là est une maladie . . . mais c'est la maladie des âmes fortes. . . . Je l'ai donnée aux Pléiades; ai-je eu tort?" Within the book itself, love is defined as a "maladie sacrée, mais horrible et confinant à la folie". It is an ordeal by which each of the characters, like a medieval knight, is put to the test. One of the key images of the novel, present from its opening pages, is that of a turbulent mountain stream which creates havoc and destruction in its wake and only opens out into a broad and expansive river when it reaches the plain. It is as though each of the "Pléiades" must ride the rapids of uncontrolled passion before attaining the serenity that is their ultimate reward.

Although *Les Pléiades* turns out eventually to be mainly about love, it contains some astringent pages about the nature of modern society, notably in Nore's opening monologue where he divides the mass of human beings, with a Célinian vigour, into the three categories of "les imbéciles", "les drôles" and "les brutes". Elsewhere it is suggested that more than ever it is the duty of "l'honnête homme, l'homme qui se sent une âme" to "se replier sur lui-même, et, ne pouvant sauver les autres, de travailler à s'améliorer", and, in a lapidary phrase which sums up the whole of Gobineau's philosophy, "l'en- semble est petit, misérable, honteux, répugnant. L'être isolé s'élève". What Mérimée termed his "bosse de l'observation comique" is apparent in the description of the results of dis- tribution by the English Bible societies in Asia: "Les Chinois s'en servent en guise de tuiles pour les maisons; les Persans, plus littéraires, appliquent les reliures à l'habillement de leurs propres livres". But his skills of character-creation are rudi- mentary and nearly all the inhabitants of the world of *Les Pléiades* emerge as interchangeable, the men being based on himself and the women either on his wife and daughters or on Madame de la Tour, according to whether they are meant to be unpleasant or pleasant.

The novel is basically, like the *Essai* and all Gobineau's other works, an attempt at personal mythologization. This is what gives it its appearance of a magnificent, but flawed, epic. One suspects that Gobineau might have chosen as its epitaph the lines he wrote in what may be a fragment of its lost sequel, *Les Voiles noirs,* intended to be "le superlatif des *Pléiades*", concerning the nineteenth-century Swedish epic, *Frithiofs saga*, which he described as:

> un de ces livres comme tous les peuples n'en possèdent pas et qui par leurs défauts, par leurs lacunes, par leurs faiblesses même, par leurs prétentions plutôt que par ce qu'ils peuvent réellement donner, se sont acquis une popular- ité profonde et durable auprès des imaginations pour lesquelles elles ont été créées et il n'est rien plus heureux dans la destinée d'un livre.

As Remy de Gourmont is reported to have said, "Gobineau est quelqu'un. Il compte". (pp. 323-24)

> *Peter Fawcett, "Blood and Its Consequences," in* The Times Literary Supplement, *March 30, 1984, pp. 323-24.*

ADDITIONAL BIBLIOGRAPHY

Banton, Michael. "Racial Thought before Darwin: Racism at Its Zenith." In his *Race Relations*, pp. 28-33. London: Tavistock Publications, 1967.
　　Contains a short study of the *Essay* that emphasizes the originality and complexity of the work.

Biddiss, Michael D. "Gobineau and the Origins of European Racism." *Race: Journal of the Institute of Race Relations* 7, No. 3 (January 1966): 255-70.
　　Studies Gobineau's racist beliefs in relation to those of Nazi and Fascist philosophers, contrasting Gobineau's extreme pessimism with the twentieth-century thinkers' optimistic trust in regeneration.

———. "Gobineau and the Aryan Myth." *History Today* 16, No. 8 (August 1966): 572-78.
　　Characterizes Gobineau as one of the chief originators of modern racist doctrine, noting especially his contribution to the development of Aryan racism.

———. *Father of Racist Ideology: The Social and Political Thought of Count Gobineau.* New York: Weybright and Talley, 1970, 314 p.
　　A study of Gobineau's historical philosophy, focusing on the development of his ethnological ideas.

Boyd, Ernest. Preface to *Five Oriental Tales,* by Comte de Gobineau, pp. 5-9. New York: Viking Press, 1925.
　　Discusses the merits of Gobineau's imaginative writings, especially *Romances of the East*.

Duclaux, Mary [A. Mary F. Robinson]. "Gobineau, Prophet." In her *The French Procession: A Pageant of Great Writers*, pp. 221-30. London: T. Fisher Unwin, 1909.
　　A brief overview of Gobineau's literary and diplomatic career. Duclaux argues that the author's genius and originality "lay less in his general ideas than in his mythopoetic faculty."

Ellwood, Charles A. "Racial Social Philosophers." In his *The Story of Social Philosophy*, pp. 304-11. New York: Prentice-Hall, 1938.
　　Cites biological, historical, and experiential evidence to demonstrate that Gobineau was wrong in believing in the "all-might of racial heredity."

Études gobiniennes. Paris: Klincksiek, 1966-78.
　　A French periodical devoted to Gobineau studies.

Fortier, Paul A. "Gobineau and German Racism." *Comparative Literature* XIX, No. 4 (Fall 1967): 341-50.
　　Compares Nazi race theory with Gobineau's beliefs.

Gribble, Francis. "Gobineau and the Nordic Races." *The Fortnightly Review* n.s. CXVIII, No. DCCVIII (1 December 1925): 792-801.
　　Briefly surveys Gobineau's life and thought.

Herbert, Arthur S. "Count de Gobineau's Ethnological Theory." *The Nineteenth Century* 70, No. 413 (July 1911): 115-34.
　　Commends the style and structure of the *Essay* and praises the erudition of the author.

Hone, J. M. "Count Arthur of Gobineau: Race-Mystic." *The Contemporary Review* CIV (July 1913): 94-103.
　　Concludes that the *Essay* may be read as an indictment of nineteenth-century utilitarianism, as pure symbolism, or as "a supreme expression of that race-mysticism which has always affected . . . human action."

Layard, G. S. "A Nietzsche before the Fact." *The Bookman* (London) 45, No. 265 (October 1913): 46-7.
　　A review of *The Renaissance* in which the critic compares Gobineau's conception of aristocracy with that of Friedrich Nietzsche.

Lehrmann, Charles C. "Gobineau's Theory." In his *The Jewish Element in French Literature*, translated by George Klin, pp. 174-77. Rutherford, N.J.: Fairleigh Dickinson University Press, 1971.
　　Examines why the *Essay* was coolly received by Gobineau's French contemporaries.

Lukacs, John. "A Note on Gobineau." In *"The European Revolution" and Correspondence with Gobineau,* by Alexis de Tocqueville, edited and translated by John Lukacs, pp. 179-87. Garden City, N.Y.: Doubleday & Co., Doubleday Anchor Books, 1959.
　　A summary treatment of Gobineau's life and ideas in which the critic argues that Gobineau was not a precursor of German National Socialism.

Morse, J. Mitchell. "Gobineau and Thomas Mann." In *Helen Adolf Festschrift,* edited by Sheema Z. Buehne, James L. Hodge, and Lucille B. Pinto, pp. 252-67. New York: Frederick Ungar Publishing Co., 1968.
　　Detects the "unpleasant odor" of Gobineau's ideas in the writings of Thomas Mann.

Nef, John. "Truth, Belief, and Civilization: Tocqueville and Gobineau." *The Review of Politics* 25, No. 4 (October 1963): 460-82.
　　Contrasts Gobineau's scientific approach to racial doctrines with Tocqueville's religious approach.

La nouvelle revue française (1 February 1934).
　　A single number dedicated to Gobineau and Gobinism.

Park, Robert Ezra. "Human Migration and the Marginal Man." In his *Race and Culture*, pp. 345-56. New York: Free Press, 1950.
　　Maintains that Gobineau conceived civilization to be strictly the result of evolutionary processes, not of changing relations between people.

Proust, Marcel. Letter to Émile Straus. In his *Letters of Marcel Proust,* edited and translated by Mina Curtiss, pp. 267-68. New York: Random House, 1949.
　　A 1914 letter in which Proust claims in passing, "France, indeed, spent many years near Gobineau without suspecting that he had genius."

Redman, Ben Ray. Introduction to *The Golden Flower,* by Arthur, Count Gobineau, translated by Ben Ray Redman, pp. iii-xxx. New York: G. P. Putnam's Sons, 1924.
　　A brief survey of Gobineau's life and literary career, emphasizing the evolution of the form and content of *The Renaissance*.

Revue Europe (1 October 1923).
　　A special issue on Gobineau and his works.

Richter, Melvin. "A Debate on Race: The Tocqueville-Gobineau Correspondence." *Commentary* 25, No. 2 (February 1958): 151-60.
　　Discusses Gobineau's correspondence with Tocqueville and suggests ways in which the *Essay* influenced later race theorists.

Rowbotham, Arnold H. *The Literary Works of Count de Gobineau.* Paris: Librarie Ancienne Honoré Champion, 1929, 171 p.
　　Approaches Gobineau as primarily a literary artist, with chapters on his novels and short stories, oriental and historical works, and poetry.

Souday, Paul. "Increasing Fame of Gobineau." *The New York Times* LXXIV, No. 24,494 (15 February 1925): sec. 3, p. 11.
　　Notes the reprinting of a selection of Gobineau's novels, maintaining that the author surpassed the elder Alexandre Dumas as a writer of romance.

Spring, Gerald M. *The Vitalism of Count de Gobineau.* New York: Publications of the Institute of French Studies, 1932, 303 p.
　　A general survey focusing on Gobineau and self-determinism.

Stanton, Theodore. "Literary Affairs in Paris." *The Dial* (Chicago) LX, No. 710 (20 January 1916): 52-5.

　　Argues that contemporary French attacks on Gobineau's reputed promotion of Germany are an example of French nationalism "gone mad."

Thibaudet, Albert. "The Reactionaries: Gobineau." In his *French Literature from 1795 to Our Era,* translated by Charles Lam Markmann, p. 339. New York: Funk & Wagnalls, 1967.

　　A brief assessment of Gobineau in which the critic asserts that *Romances of the East* and *Trois ans en Asie* constitute "perhaps the truest view of the Orient that there has ever been in French fiction."

"Decomposition of France." *The Times Literary Supplement,* no. 4,226 (30 March 1984): 323-24.

　　Examines *Ce qui est arrivé à la France en 1870.*

Valette, Rebecca M. *Arthur de Gobineau and the Short Story.* University of North Carolina Studies in the Romance Languages and Literatures, no. 79. Chapel Hill: University of North Carolina Press, 1969, 187 p.

　　A close analysis of Gobineau's short fiction that includes discussions of the author's picaresque narrative style, his treatment of the theme of love, and his interest in the confrontation of cultures.

Nathaniel Hawthorne

1804-1864

(Born Nathaniel Hathorne) American novelist, short story writer, and essayist.

The following entry presents criticism of Hawthorne's novel *The Blithedale Romance* (1852). For additional information on Hawthorne's career and *The Blithedale Romance,* see *NCLC,* Vols. 2 and 10.

The Blithedale Romance is regarded as an important part of Hawthorne's contribution to American literature. Although critics generally agree that *Blithedale* lacks the sustained excellence of Hawthorne's masterpiece, *The Scarlet Letter,* they often concur in awarding it a high place among his works. *Blithedale* is valued not only for its commentary on nineteenth-century American utopianism but also for what it reveals, through its autobiographical content, about the personality and artistic stance of one of America's greatest writers.

The fourth of Hawthorne's five completed novels, *Blithedale* was written in the winter of 1851-52 while he was living in West Newton, Massachusetts. The experiences upon which Hawthorne based much of the novel, however, took place during his stay in 1841 at Brook Farm, an experimental utopian community in West Roxbury, nine miles outside of Boston. Launched in the spring of 1841, Brook Farm was intended to be an agricultural cooperative that would provide its members—through the principle of shared labor—with a living while at the same time allowing them leisure for artistic and literary pursuits. The community was founded by the literary critic and social reformer George Ripley, and various prominent authors expressed interest in the scheme, including Margaret Fuller, Ralph Waldo Emerson, Theodore Parker, and Orestes Brownson. According to biographers, Hawthorne saw in Brook Farm a means of providing for himself and his fiancée, Sophia Peabody, that would not interfere with his writing. After joining the community, however, Hawthorne's enthusiasm for the venture quickly wore off. He left in November of 1841, convinced that intellectual endeavor was incompatible with hard physical exertion. Although his literary efforts at Brook Farm proved a failure, Hawthorne kept careful records of his time there in his journals and letters; these later bore fruit in the plot, physical settings, and characters of *Blithedale.* Indeed, a comparison of passages from his letters and notebooks with portions of the novel shows that he transferred many of his thoughts and descriptions of Brook Farm almost verbatim.

By the time he wrote *Blithedale,* Hawthorne was already established as perhaps the leading American author of his day. The widespread success of his novel *The Scarlet Letter* upon its publication in 1850 had rendered thoroughly inaccurate his previous description of himself as "the obscurest man of letters in America," and the appearance of *The House of the Seven Gables* in the following year further enhanced his reputation. In July of 1851, while unsure about which direction to take after completing *The House of the Seven Gables,* Hawthorne wrote to a friend, "I don't know what I shall write next. Should it be a romance, I mean to put an extra touch of the devil in it, for I doubt whether the public will stand two quiet books in succession without my losing ground." The following No-

vember, Hawthorne began *Blithedale,* completing the manuscript in April of 1852; the new novel was then published in July.

The story of *Blithedale* is narrated by Miles Coverdale, a detached and coldly analytical minor New England poet who travels from Boston to the Brook Farm-like community of Blithedale in search of brotherhood and a life congenial to his art. There, he becomes caught up in the lives of three people: Hollingsworth, a former blacksmith who is obsessed with a monomaniacal scheme for the reform of criminals; Zenobia, a wealthy, beautiful, and passionate woman who has taken up the cause of women's rights; and Priscilla, a frail young seamstress about whom there is an air of mystery. In the course of the story, both Zenobia and Priscilla fall in love with Hollingsworth while Coverdale looks on with seemingly dispassionate curiosity, unwilling or unable to express the attraction that he feels for both women. Eventually Coverdale, like Hawthorne, becomes disenchanted with communal life and returns to the city, where he is surprised to encounter Zenobia and Priscilla, the latter of whom has fallen under the control of a mesmerist named Westervelt. The two women are subsequently revealed to be half sisters, and Hollingsworth rescues Priscilla from Westervelt by breaking his mesmeric hold over her. The three return to Blithedale, where Zenobia drowns herself after Hollingsworth informs her that he loves Priscilla and that his earlier courtship of Zenobia had been in pursuit of money for his rehabilitation scheme. Years later, Coverdale meets Hollingsworth who—plagued by guilt over Zenobia's death—has abandoned his plan for reforming criminals and is now a broken man, wholly reliant on Priscilla. The novel ends with Coverdale's startling admission that he, too, loves Priscilla.

Blithedale was for the most part well received by its contemporary critics, both in England and in the United States. Despite Hawthorne's insistence in the preface that the novel ought not to be read as a commentary on Brook Farm, the relationship between Blithedale and its model occupied a prominent place in early reviews. Numerous critics speculated on possible real-life counterparts for the major figures in the novel, many of them interpreting Coverdale's critique of the community as Hawthorne's own judgment of Brook Farm. Although most early reviewers welcomed *Blithedale* as further evidence of Hawthorne's literary genius, some were disturbed by the melancholy strain of the story. George Eliot, for example, complained that Hawthorne's ''moral faculty [was] morbid as well as weak; all his characters partake of the same infirmity.'' Furthermore, a large number of writers warned that Hawthorne's analytical approach to his characters, like that of his inquisitive narrator, bordered on the inhumane. During the remainder of the nineteenth century, critics—with such notable exceptions as Henry James—often found *Blithedale* Hawthorne's least successful novel, arguing that it lacked the purposeful execution of such works as *The Scarlet Letter,* a viewpoint that continued to be widespread through the first half of the twentieth century.

Although as late as 1949 Mark Van Doren could still dismiss it as Hawthorne's weakest novel, critics in the 1950s began to display a gradually increasing interest in *Blithedale* that continues today. By 1968, critical attention to the novel had grown to such an extent that Seymour Gross and Rosalie Murphy stated that, with the exception of *The Scarlet Letter,* studies of *Blithedale* ''outstripped those of any of Hawthorne's other longer works.'' In analyzing the novel, modern scholars have focused on several major areas of discussion, including its narrative technique and autobiographical content. One of the principal concerns of critics has been the relationship between Coverdale's personality, his function as narrator, and the novel's point of view. Scholars have been unable to agree about the implications of Coverdale's attitudes toward his fellow characters and the extent to which his views represent Hawthorne's own. Thus, the ambiguous nature of the novel's moral message has been frequently discussed, with commentators debating the significance of the fates of the various characters. The implications of Hawthorne's autobiographical self-portrait as Coverdale have also been widely analyzed by critics and biographers, many of whom have sought for clues to the author's own artistic makeup in the personality of his narrator. Several studies of Coverdale have examined how his character reflects not only Hawthorne's conception of the role of the artist in society but also his own experience of the danger in being an observer of life rather than a participant. Critics have extensively explored the cultural perspective of *Blithedale* as well, particularly as it reflects both Hawthorne's Puritan heritage and his attitude toward utopianism as a social phenomenon of American society; numerous studies have sought to resolve the apparent conflict between the author's fascination with utopian communities and his cynicism about the possibility for change through group endeavor rather than individual growth. In addition, *Blithedale* remains the subject of numerous specialized investigations into its structure, imagery, symbol-

ism, source materials, and influence on subsequent writers. For the wide range of critical scrutiny it has attracted, therefore, as well as for its lasting biographical interest, *Blithedale* seems destined to endure as a work essential to Hawthorne's distinguished place in American letters.

(See also *Dictionary of Literary Biography,* Vol. 1: *The American Renaissance in New England* and *Yesterday's Authors of Books for Children,* Vol. 2.)

NATHANIEL HAWTHORNE (letter date 1841)

[*In the following excerpt from a letter written to his fiancée while he was living at Brook Farm, Hawthorne expresses his doubts concerning the compatibility of intellectual activity and strenuous physical labor. Coverdale offers a similar opinion in* Blithedale *about the effect of hard work upon his ability to write. Hawthorne's reference to the ''gold mine'' has been identified as a euphemism for the manure pile. For additional commentary by Hawthorne, see the excerpts dated 1841 and 1852.*]

I have been too busy to write thee a long letter by this opportunity; for I think this present life of mine gives me an antipathy to pen and ink, even more than my Custom-House experience did. I could not live without the idea of thee, nor without spiritual communion with thee; but, in the midst of toil, or after a hard day's work in the gold mine, my soul obstinately refuses to be poured out on paper. That abominable gold mine! Thank God, we anticipate getting rid of its treasures, in the course of two or three days. Of all hateful places, that is the worst; and I shall never comfort myself for having spent so many days of blessed sunshine there. It is my opinion, dearest, that a man's soul may be buried and perish under a dung-heap or in a furrow of the field, just as well as under a pile of money. (p. 20)

> *Nathaniel Hawthorne, in a letter to Sophia A. Peabody on June 2, 1841, in his* Love Letters of Nathaniel Hawthorne: 1839-1863, *1907. Reprint by NCR Microcard Editions, 1972, pp. 20-1.*

NATHANIEL HAWTHORNE (letter date 1841)

[*In this excerpt from a letter written to his fiancée while he was visiting Salem, Hawthorne speculates on the illusory quality of his life at Brook Farm, where he was still residing at the time. Critics and biographers have seen in this and similar passages in Hawthorne's correspondence the source of many of Coverdale's expressions of doubt about his stay at Blithedale. For additional commentary by Hawthorne, see the excerpts dated 1841 and 1852.*]

Sweetest, it seems very long already since I saw thee; but thou hast been all the time in my thoughts; so that my being has been continuous. Therefore, in one sense, it does not seem as if we had parted at all. But really I should judge it to be twenty years since I left Brook Farm; and I take this to be one proof that my life there was an unnatural and unsuitable, and therefore an unreal one. It already looks like a dream behind me. The real Me was never an associate of the community; there has been a spectral Appearance there, sounding the horn at daybreak, and milking the cows, and hoeing potatoes, and raking hay, toiling and sweating in the sun, and doing me the honor to assume my name. But be thou not deceived, Dove, of my heart. This Spectre was not thy husband. Nevertheless, it is somewhat remarkable that thy husband's hands have, during the past summer, grown very brown and rough; insomuch that many people persist in believing that he, after all, was the aforesaid spectral horn-sounder, cow-milker, potatoe-hoer, and hay-raker. But such people do not know a reality from a shadow. (pp. 36-7)

> *Nathaniel Hawthorne, in a letter to Sophia A. Pea-*
> *body on September 3, 1841, in his* Love Letters of
> Nathaniel Hawthorne: 1839-1863, *1907. Reprint by*
> *NCR Microcard Editions, 1972, pp. 34-7.*

NATHANIEL HAWTHORNE   (essay date 1852)

[*In the following excerpt from the preface to the first edition of* Blithedale, *Hawthorne discusses his use of Brook Farm as a model for the Blithedale community. For additional commentary by Hawthorne, see the excerpts dated 1841.*]

In the 'Blithedale' of this volume, many readers will probably suspect a faint and not very faithful shadowing of Brook Farm, in Roxbury, which (now a little more than ten years ago) was occupied and cultivated by a company of socialists. The Author does not wish to deny, that he had this Community in his mind, and that (having had the good fortune, for a time, to be personally connected with it) he has occasionally availed himself of his actual reminiscences, in the hope of giving a more lifelike tint to the fancy-sketch in the following pages. He begs it to be understood, however, that he has considered the Institution itself as not less fairly the subject of fictitious handling, than the imaginary personages whom he has introduced there. His whole treatment of the affair is altogether incidental to the main purpose of the Romance; nor does he put forward the slightest pretensions to illustrate a theory, or elicit a conclusion, favorable or otherwise, in respect to Socialism.

In short, his present concern with the Socialist Community is merely to establish a theatre, a little removed from the highway of ordinary travel, where the creatures of his brain may play their phantasmagorical antics, without exposing them to too close a comparison with the actual events of real lives. In the old countries, with which Fiction has long been conversant, a certain conventional privilege seems to be awarded to the romancer; his work is not put exactly side by side with nature; and he is allowed a license with regard to every-day Probability, in view of the improved effects which he is bound to produce thereby. Among ourselves, on the contrary, there is as yet no such Faery Land, so like the real world, that, in a suitable remoteness, one cannot well tell the difference, but with an atmosphere of strange enchantment, beheld through which the inhabitants have a propriety of their own. This atmosphere is what the American romancer needs. In its absence, the beings of imagination are compelled to show themselves in the same category as actually living mortals; a necessity that generally renders the paint and pasteboard of their composition but too painfully discernible. With the idea of partially obviating this difficulty, (the sense of which has always pressed very heavily upon him,) the Author has ventured to make free with his old, and affectionately remembered home, at Brook Farm, as being, certainly, the most romantic episode of his own life—essentially a daydream, and yet a fact—and thus offering an available foothold between fiction and reality. Furthermore, the scene was in good keeping with the personages whom he desired to introduce.

These characters, he feels it right to say, are entirely fictitious. It would, indeed, (considering how few amiable qualities he

distributes among his imaginary progeny,) be a most grievous wrong to his former excellent associates, were the Author to allow it to be supposed that he has been sketching any of their likenesses. Had he attempted it, they would at least have recognized the touches of a friendly pencil. But he has done nothing of the kind. The self-concentrated Philanthropist; the high-spirited Woman, bruising herself against the narrow limitations of her sex; the weakly Maiden, whose tremulous nerves endow her with Sibylline attributes; the Minor Poet, beginning life with strenuous aspirations, which die out with his youthful fervor—all these might have been looked for, at Brook Farm, but, by some accident, never made their appearance there. (pp. 1-3)

> *Nathaniel Hawthorne, in a preface to his* The Blithe-
> dale Romance, *edited by Seymour Gross and Rosalie*
> *Murphy, W. W. Norton & Company, Inc., 1978, pp.*
> *1-3.*

[HENRY F. CHORLEY]   (essay date 1852)

[*Chorley, who was one of Hawthorne's most enthusiastic supporters among contemporary English critics, offers a positive evaluation of* Blithedale, *emphasizing the peculiarly American character of the novel.*]

[*The Blithedale Romance*] is eminently an American book;—not, however, a book showing the America of *Sam Slick* and *Leather-Stocking*,—the home of the money-making droll rich in mother-wit, or of the dweller in the wilderness rich in mother-poetry.—Mr. Hawthorne's America is a vast new country, the inhabitants of which have neither materially nor intellectually as yet found their boundaries,—a land heaving with restless impatience, on the part of some among its best spirits, to exemplify new ideas in new forms of civilized life. But Mr. Hawthorne knows that in America, as well as in worlds worn more threadbare, poets, philosophers and philanthropists however vehemently seized on by such fever of vain-longing, are forced to break themselves against the barriers of Mortality and Time—to allow for inevitable exceptions—to abide unforeseen checks,—in short, to re-commence their dream and their work with each fresh generation, in a manner tantalizing to enthusiasts who would grasp perfection for themselves and mankind, and that instantaneously.—The author's sermon is none the less a sermon because he did not mean it as such. He must be fully believed when he tells us that, while placing the scene of his third tale in a Socialist community he had no intention of pronouncing upon Socialism, either in principle or in practice [see excerpt dated 1852]. Mr. Hawthorne's preface assures us that he conjured up his vision of Brook Farm, Roxbury, merely as a befitting scene for the action of certain beings of his mind, without thought of lesson or decision on a question so grave and complex. This, however, makes him all the more valuable as a witness. The thoughtful reader will hardly fail to draw some morals for himself from a tale which, though made up of exceptional personages, is yet true to human characteristics and human feelings, and pregnant with universal emotion as well as with deep special meaning. (p. 741)

> [*Henry F. Chorley*], *in a review of "The Blithedale*
> *Romance," in* The Athenaeum, *No. 1289, July 10,*
> *1852, pp. 741-43.*

THE CHRISTIAN EXAMINER AND RELIGIOUS MISCELLANY (essay date 1852)

[*In the following excerpt from an anonymous review of* Blithedale, *the critic focuses primarily on Hawthorne's use of Brook Farm and its inhabitants for fictional purposes, criticizing him for mis-representing "the facts and characters of assured history."*]

The preface to this captivating volume is by no means the least important part of it. And yet we would advise all readers who wish to peruse [*The Blithedale Romance*] under an illusion which will add an intense interest to its pages, to postpone the preface [see excerpt dated 1852] till they have gone through the book. Certainly one has reason to believe that Mr. Hawthorne is presenting in these pages a story, which, however it may depend for its decorative and fanciful details upon his rich imagination, is essentially a delineation of life and character as presented at "Brook Farm." It is well known that he was a member of that community of amiable men and women, who undertook there to realize their ideas of a better system of social relations. He fixes there the scene of his story, with frequent reference to the localities around, keeping up a close connection with the neighboring city of Boston; and the volume owes very much of its lifelike fidelity of representation to the reader's supposition that the characters are as real as the theory and the institution in which they have their parts. Yet in the preface Mr. Hawthorne, with a charming frankness which neutralizes much of the charm of his story, repudiates altogether the matter-of-fact view so far as regards his associates at "Brook Farm," and pleads necessity as his reason for confounding fact and fiction.

We cannot but regard the license which Mr. Hawthorne allows himself in this respect as open to grave objection. Seeing that many readers obtain all their knowledge of historical facts from the incidental implications of history which are involved in a well-drawn romance, we maintain that a novelist has no right to tamper with actual verities. His obligation to adhere strictly to historic truth is all the more to be exacted whenever the character and good repute of any real person are involved. Now Mr. Hawthorne is a daring offender in this respect. It is the only drawback upon our high admiration of him. We trust he will take no offence at this our free expression of opinion, when, while offering to him a respectful and grateful homage for all the spiritual glow and all the human wisdom which we find on his pages, we venture to question his right to misrepresent the facts and characters of assured history. If he shaded and clouded his incidents somewhat more obscurely, if he removed them farther back or farther off from the region of our actual sight and knowledge, he would be safer in using the privileges of the romancer. But he gives us such distinct and sharp boundary lines, and deals so boldly with matters and persons, the truth of whose prose life repels the poetry of his fiction, that we are induced to confide in him as a chronicler, rather than to indulge him as a romancer. Thus in his *Scarlet Letter* he assures us in his preface that he has historical papers which authenticate the story that follows. That story involves the gross and slanderous imputation that the colleague pastor of the First Church in Boston, who preached the Election Sermon the year after the death of Governor Winthrop, was a mean and hypocritical adulterer, and went from the pulpit to the pillory to confess to that character in presence of those who had just been hanging reverently upon his lips. How would this outrageous fiction, which is utterly without foundation, deceive a reader who had no exact knowledge of our history! We can pardon the anachronism, in the same work, by which the little children in Boston are represented as practising for the game of annoying Quakers half a score of years before such a thing as a Quaker had been heard of even in Old England. But we cannot admit the license of a novelist to go the length of a vile and infamous imputation upon a Boston minister of

a spotless character. In his *Blithedale Romance,* Mr. Hawthorne ventures upon a similar freedom, though by no means so gross a one, in confounding fact and fiction. So vividly does he present to us the scheme at Brook Farm, to which some of our acquaintance were parties, so sharply and accurately does he portray some of the incidents of life there, that we are irresistibly impelled to fix the real names of men and women to the characters of his book. We cannot help doing this. We pay a tribute to Mr. Hawthorne's power when we confess that we cannot believe that he is drawing upon his imagination. We ask, Whom does he mean to describe as Zenobia? Is it Mrs.—, or Miss—? Then, as we know that no one of the excellent women who formed the community at "Brook Farm" was driven to suicide by disappointed love, we find ourselves constructing the whole character from a combination of some half a dozen of the women whose talents or peculiarities have made them prominent in this neighborhood. We can gather up in this way all the elements of his Zenobia, except the comparatively unimportant one of queenly beauty which he ascribes to her. We leave to the help-meet of the author to settle with him the issue that may arise from his description of himself as a bachelor.

Having thus relieved our minds of the disagreeable part of a critic's duty, we are the more free to express our delight and gratitude, after the perusal of the book before us. Mr. Hawthorne is a writer of marvellous power, a most wise and genial philosopher, a true poet, and a skilful painter. We have gained instruction from his pages, of the most difficult kind to obtain, of the most valuable sort for use. The quiet humor, the good-tempered satire, which has no element of cynicism, the analysis of character, with the tracing of the deeper motives which fashion its outer workings and its inner growth, the clear vision for truth, and, above all, the sagacity which distinguishes between the really spiritual in thought and life and the morbid phenomena which so often propose themselves as spiritualities,—these are the tokens of a master-mind in our author. We thank him most heartily for this book, and gratefully acknowledge that it has offered to us wise and good lessons which ought to make us strong for faith and duty. (pp. 292-94)

A review of "The Blithedale Romance," in The Christian Examiner and Religious Miscellany, *Vol. 53, No. 173, September, 1852, pp. 292-94.*

[EDWIN PERCY WHIPPLE]   (essay date 1852)

[*Whipple, who read the manuscript of the novel prior to its publication, offers a highly favorable evaluation of* Blithedale, *praising—among other qualities—its unity, intellectual depth, and narrative technique. For additional criticism by Whipple, see* NCLC, *Vol. 2.*]

[*The Blithedale Romance*] seems to us the most perfect in execution of any of Hawthorne's works, and as a work of art, hardly equaled by any thing else which the country has produced. It is a real organism of the mind, with the strict unity of one of Nature's own creations. It seems to have grown up in the author's nature, as a tree or plant grows from the earth, in obedience to the law of its germ. This unity cannot be made clear by analysis; it is felt in the oneness of impression it makes on the reader's imagination. The author's hold on the central principle is never relaxed; it never slips from his grasp; and yet every thing is developed with a victorious ease which adds a new charm to the interest of the materials. The romance, also, has more thought in it than either of its predecessors; it is literally crammed with the results of most delicate and searching observations of life, manners and character, and of the most piercing imaginative analysis of motives and tendencies; yet nothing seems labored, but the profoundest reflections glide unobtrusively into the free flow of the narration and description, equally valuable from their felicitous relation to the events and persons of the story, and for their detached depth and power. The work is not without a certain morbid tint in the general coloring of the mood whence it proceeds; but this peculiarity is fainter than is usual with Hawthorne.

The scene of the story is laid in Blithedale, an imaginary community on the model of the celebrated Brook Farm, of Roxbury, of which Hawthorne himself was a member. The practical difficulties in the way of combining intellectual and manual labor on socialist principles constitutes the humor of the book; but the interest centres in three characters, Hollingsworth, Zenobia, and Priscilla. These are represented as they appear through the medium of an imagined mind, that of Miles Coverdale, the narrator of the story, a person indolent of will, but of an apprehensive, penetrating, and inquisitive intellect. This discerner of spirits only tells us his own discoveries; and there is a wonderful originality and power displayed in thus representing the characters. What is lost by this mode, on definite views, is more than made up in the stimulus given both to our acuteness and curiosity, and its manifold suggestiveness. We are joint watchers with Miles himself, and sometimes find ourselves disagreeing with him in his interpretation of an act or expression of the persons he is observing. The events are purely mental, the changes and crises of moods of mind. Three persons of essentially different characters and purposes, are placed together; the law of spiritual influence, the magnetism of soul on soul begins to operate; and the processes of thought and emotion are then presented in perfect logical order to their inevitable catastrophe. These characters are Hollingsworth, a reformer, whose whole nature becomes ruthless under the dominion of one absorbing idea—Zenobia, a beautiful, imperious, impassioned, self-willed woman, superbly endowed in person and intellect, but with something provokingly equivocal in her character—and Priscilla, an embodiment of feminine affection in its simplest type. Westervelt, an elegant piece of earthliness, "not so much born as damned into the world," plays a Mephistophelian part in this mental drama; and is so skillfully represented that the reader joins at the end, with the author, in praying that Heaven may annihilate him. "May his pernicious soul rot half a grain a day."

With all the delicate sharpness of insight into the most elusive movements of Consciousness, by which the romance is characterized, the drapery cast over the whole representation, is rich and flowing, and there is no parade of metaphysical acuteness. All the profound and penetrating observation seems the result of a certain careless felicity of aim, which hits the mark in the white without any preliminary posturing or elaborate preparation. The stronger, and harsher passions are represented with the same ease as the evanescent shades of thought and emotion. The humorous and descriptive scenes are in Hawthorne's best style. The peculiarities of New England life at the present day are admirably caught and permanently embodied; Silas Foster and Hollingsworth being both genuine Yankees and representative men. The great passage of the volume is Zenobia's death, which is not so much tragic as tragedy itself. In short, whether we consider *The Blithedale Romance* as a study in that philosophy of the human mind which peers into the inmost recesses and first principles of mind and character, or a highly colored and fascinating story, it does not yield in interest or value to any of Hawthorne's preceding

works, while it is removed from a comparison with them by essential differences in its purpose and mode of treatment, and is perhaps their superior in affluence and fineness of thought, and masterly perception of the first remote workings of great and absorbing passions. (p. 334)

> *[Edwin Percy Whipple], in a review of "The Blithedale Romance," in* Graham's Magazine, *Vol. XLI, No. 3, September, 1852, pp. 333-34.*

THE AMERICAN WHIG REVIEW   (essay date 1852)

> [*This anonymous critic discusses various aspects of* Blithedale, *reproaching Hawthorne for his often "unsubstantial" portrayal of the novel's major characters and the melancholy nature of the story.*]

When it was publicly understood that Mr. Hawthorne was engaged in the composition of a romance, having for its origin, if not its subject, a community which once had a brief existence at Brook Farm, speculation was awakened, anticipations grew vivid, and the reading public awaited anxiously the issue of a book which it was hoped would combine in itself the palatable spices of novelty and personality. A portion of these expectations were doomed to disappointment. In the preface to the *Blithedale Romance,* Mr. Hawthorne distinctly disavowed any intention of painting portraits [see excerpt dated 1852]. To his sojourn at Brook Farm he attributes his inspiration, but that is all. Blithedale is no caligraph of Brook Farm. Zenobia first sprang into actual existence from the printing press of Ticknor, Reed and Fields, and the quiet Priscilla is nothing more than one of those pretty phantoms with which Mr. Hawthorne occasionally adorns his romances.

We believe that if Mr. Hawthorne had intended to give a faithful portrait of Brook Farm and its inmates, he would have signally failed. He has no genius for realities, save in inanimate nature. Between his characters and the reader falls a gauze-like veil of imagination, on which their shadows flit and move, and play strange dramas replete with second-hand life. An air of unreality enshrouds all his creations. They are either dead, or have never lived, and when they pass away they leave behind them an oppressive and unwholesome chill. (p. 417)

Mr. Hawthorne deals artistically with shadows. There is a strange, unearthly fascination about the fair spectres that throng his works, and we know no man who can distort nature, or idealize abortions more cleverly than the author of the *Scarlet Letter.* But we question much, if we strip Mr. Hawthorne's works of a certain beauty and originality of style which they are always sure to possess, whether the path which he has chosen is a healthy one. To us it does not seem as if the fresh wind of morning blew across his track; we do not feel the strong pulse of nature throbbing beneath the turf he treads upon. When an author sits down to make a book, he should not alone consult the inclinations of his own genius regarding its purpose or its construction. If he should happen to be imbued with strange, saturnine doctrines, or be haunted by a morbid suspicion of human nature, in God's name let him not write one word. Better that all the beautiful, wild thoughts with which his brain is teeming should moulder for ever in neglect and darkness, than that one soul was overshadowed by stern, uncongenial dogmas, which should have died with their Puritan fathers. It is not alone necessary to produce a work of art. The soul of beauty is Truth, and Truth is ever progressive. The true artist therefore endeavors to make the world better. He does not look behind him, and dig out of the graves of past centuries skeletons to serve as models for his pictures; but looks onward for more perfect shapes, and though sometimes obliged to design from the defective forms around him, he infuses, as it were, some of the divine spirit of the future into them, and lo! we love them with all their faults. But Mr. Hawthorne discards all idea of successful human progress. All his characters seem so weighed down with their own evilness of nature, that they can scarcely keep their balance, much less take their places in the universal march. Like the lord mentioned in Scripture, he issues an invitation to the halt, the blind, and the lame of soul, to gather around his board, and then asks us to feast at the same table. It is a pity that Mr. Hawthorne should not have been originally imbued with more universal tenderness. It is a pity that he displays nature to us so shrouded and secluded, and that he should be afflicted with such a melancholy craving for human curiosities. His men are either vicious, crazed, or misanthropical, and his women are either unwomanly, unearthly, or unhappy. His books have no sunny side to them. They are unripe to the very core.

We are more struck with the want of this living tenderness in the *Blithedale Romance* than in any of Mr. Hawthorne's previous novels. In the *Scarlet Letter* and the *House of the Seven Gables,* a certain gloominess of thought suited the antiquity of the subjects; but in his last performance, the date of the events, and the nature of the story, entitle us to expect something brighter and less unhealthy. The efforts of any set of hopeful, well-meaning people to shame society into better ways, are deserving of respect, as long as they do not attempt to interfere with those sacred foundation-stones of morality on which all society rests. It was a pure fresh thought, that of flying from the turmoil of the city, and toiling in common upon the broad fields for bread. With all their fallacies, there is much that is good and noble about the American communists. It is a sad mistake to suppose them stern exponents of the gross and absurd system laid down by Fourier. They are not, at least as far as our knowledge goes, either dishonest or sensual. They do not mock at rational rights, or try to overturn the constitution of society. We believe their ruling idea to be that of isolating themselves from all that is corrupt in the congregations of mankind called cities, and seek in open country and healthy toil the sweets and triumphs of a purer life. One would imagine that dealing with a subject like this would in some degree counteract Mr. Hawthorne's ascetic humor. One would have thought that, in narrating a course of events which, acted on as they were by the surrounding circumstances, must have been somewhat buoyant and fresh, he would have burst that icy chain of puritanical gloom, and for once made a holiday with Nature. No such thing! From the beginning to the end, the *Blithedale Romance* is a melancholy chronicle, less repulsive, it is true, than its predecessors, but still sad and inexpressibly mournful. Not that the author has intended it to be uniformly pathetic. It is very evident that he sat down with the intention of writing a strong, vigorous book upon a strong, vigorous subject; but his own baneful spirit hovered over the pages, and turned the ink into bitterness and tears.

Let us review his characters, and see if we can find any thing genial among them. Hollingsworth in importance comes first. A rude fragment of a great man. Unyielding as granite in any matters on which he has decided, yet possessing a latent tenderness of nature that, if he had been the creature of other hands than Mr. Hawthorne's, would have been his redemption. But our author is deeply read in human imperfection, and lets no opportunity slip of thrusting it before his readers. A horrid hump of unappeasable egotism is stuck between Hollings-

worth's shoulders. He is depicted as a sort of human Maël-strom, engulfing all natures that come within his range, and relentlessly absorbing them in his own vast necessities. He is selfish, dogmatic, and inhumanly proud, and all these frightful attributes are tacked on to a character that, in the hands of a Dickens or a Fielding, would have loomed out from the canvas with sufficient imperfection to make it human, but with enough of heart and goodness to compel us to love it.

Readers will perchance say that Mr. Hawthorne has a right to deal with his characters according to his pleasure, and that we are not authorized to quarrel with the length of their noses, or the angularities of their natures. No doubt. But, on the other hand, Mr. Hawthorne has no right to blacken and defame humanity, by animating his shadowy people with worse passions and more imperfect souls than we meet with in the world.

Miles Coverdale, the narrator of the tale, is to us a most repulsive being. A poet, but yet no poetry in his deeds. A sneering, suspicious, inquisitive, and disappointed man, who rejects Hollingsworth's advances because he fears that a connection between them may lead to some ulterior peril; who allows Zenobia to dominate over his nature, because she launches at him a few wild words, and who forsakes the rough, healthy life of Blithedale, because he pines for Turkey carpets and a sea-coal fire. Such is the man upon whose dictum Mr. Hawthorne would endeavor covertly to show the futility of the enterprise in whose favor he was once enlisted.

Zenobia, the character on which he has probably bestowed the most pains, is no doubt true to nature. Women that thrust themselves out of their sphere must inevitably lose many of those graces which constitute their peculiar charm. Looked upon by their own sex with dismay, and by ours with certain mingled feelings of jealousy and pity, they voluntarily isolate themselves from the generality of the world, and fancy themselves martyrs. They are punished with contempt, and to reformers of their fiery nature, contempt is worse than death. They blaspheme God by stepping beyond the limits He has assigned to them through all ages, and seem to fancy that they can better laws which are eternal and immutable.

The Zenobia of our author does not command our interest. Her character, though poetically colored, is not sufficiently powerful for a woman that has so far outstridden the even pace of society. She has a certain amount of courage and passion, but no philosophy. Her impulses start off in the wrong direction, nor does she seem to possess the earnestness necessary to induce a woman to defy public opinion. She is a mere fierce, wild wind, blowing hither and thither, with no fixity of purpose, and making us shrink closer every moment from the contact.

In truth, with the exception of Priscilla, who is faint and shadowy, the dramatis personae at Blithedale are not to our taste. There is a bad purpose in every one of them—a purpose, too, which is neither finally redeemed nor condemned.

Notwithstanding the faults which we have alluded to, and which cling to Mr. Hawthorne tenaciously in all his works, there is much to be admired in the *Blithedale Romance.* If our author takes a dark view of society, he takes a bright one of nature. He paints truthfully and poetically, and possesses a Herrick-like fashion of deducing morals from flowers, rocks, and herbage, or any other little feature in his visionary landscape. (pp. 417-19)

On the socialist theory Mr. Hawthorne says little in the *Blithedale Romance*. That he is no longer a convert is evident, but he does not attempt to discuss the matter philosophically. Judging from many passages in the book, we should say that he had been sadly disappointed in the experiment made at Brook Farm, and sought thus covertly and incidentally to record his opinion. One of the most curious characteristics of the book is, that not one of the persons assembled at Blithedale treat the institution as if they were in earnest. Zenobia sneers at it— Coverdale grumbles at it—Hollingsworth condemns—Priscilla alone endures it. We know not if this is a feature drawn from realities. If it is not, Mr. Hawthorne is immediately placed in the position of having created a group of fictitious hypocrites, not true to human nature, merely for the sake of placing them in a novel position and surrounding them with fresh scenery. (p. 420)

In Priscilla, Mr. Hawthorne has essayed a delicate character, but in his portraiture he has availed himself of an ingenious expedient, which we know not whether to rank as intentional or accidental. In drawing a portrait, there are two ways of attaining delicacy of outline. One is by making the outline itself so faint and indistinct that it appears as it were to mingle with the surrounding shadow; the other and more difficult one is, to paint, and paint detail after detail, until the whole becomes so finished a work of art, so harmoniously colored, that one feature does not strike us more forcibly than another; so homogeneous in its aspect that outline, background and detail are all painted perfectly on our perceptions in a manner that defies analysis. Now, there is no question that the man who employs the first means has infinitely easier work than the last. He has nothing to do but conjure you up a pretty-looking ghost, and lo! the work is done. Mr. Hawthorne is fond of these ghosts. Priscilla is a ghost; we do not realize her, even to the end. Her connection with Westervelt is shadowy and ill-defined. Zenobia's influence over her nature is only indistinctly intimated. Her own mental construction is left almost an open question; and even when, in the crowning of the drama, we find her the support, the crutch of the rugged Hollingsworth, there is no satisfactory happiness wreathed about her destiny. This is not artistic or wholesome. We all know that a certain fascination springs up in every breast when the undefined is presented. The love of spectral stories, and superhuman exhibitions, all have their root in this, and Mr. Hawthorne appears to know well how to play upon this secret chord with his fantastic shadows. We do not look upon his treatment of character as fair. He does not give it to us in its entirety, but puts us off with a pleasant phantasmagoria. We should attribute this to inability in any other man, but we feel too well convinced of Mr. Hawthorne's genius to doubt his capability for an instant to furnish us with a perfect picture. But we doubt his will. This sketchy painting is easy and rapid. A very few lines will indicate a spectre, when it would take an entire month to paint a woman; and Mr. Hawthorne finds this unsubstantial picture-making suit his own dreamy and sometimes morbid fancy. For Heaven's sake, Mr. Hawthorne, do not continue to give us shadows, even if they be as sweet and loveable as Priscilla! Recollect that you have earned a great name as a writer of romance, and will necessarily have many followers. Cease then, good sir: for if you continue to give us shadows, in another year your imitators will inundate their books with skeletons!

That Mr. Hawthorne can paint vividly when he likes it, few who have read his novels can doubt. He possesses all the requisites for the task—power of language, felicity of collateral

incident, and a certain subdued richness of style which is one of his greatest charms. The . . . uescription of the death of Zenobia is exquisitely managed. (pp. 420-21)

[It] is powerful—sadness and strength mingled into a most poetical and vivid death-scene. A thought crosses us, whether Mr. Hawthorne would paint a wedding as well as a death; whether he could conjure as distinctly before our vision the bridal flowers, as he has done the black, damp weeds that waved around the grave of Zenobia. We fear not. His genius has a church-yard beauty about it, and revels amid graves, and executions, and all the sad leavings of mortality. We know no man whom we would sooner ask to write our epitaph. We feel assured that it would be poetical, and suitable in the highest degree. (p. 423)

A review of "The Blithedale Romance," in The American Whig Review, *Vol. XVI, No. V, November, 1852, pp. 417-24.*

[FRANCIS JACOX] (essay date 1853)

[*Jacox lauds* Blithedale *as the finest of Hawthorne's works and emphasizes its artistry, particularly its fascinating character studies.*]

The Blithedale Romance we esteem . . . the highest and best of Mr. Hawthorne's works. The tale is narrated with more ingenuity and ease [than his previous writings]; the characters are at least equal to their predecessors, and the style is at once richer and more robust—more mellowed, and yet more pointed and distinct. A true artist has planned and has filled up the plot, ordering each conjunction of incidents, and interweaving the cross threads of design and destiny with masterly tact; skilled in the by-play of suggestion, hint, and pregnant passing intimation—in the provocative spell of suspense—in the harmonious development of once scattered and seemingly unrelated forces. His humour is fresher in quality, and his tragic power is exercised with almost oppressive effect—at times making the boldest, oldest romance-reader

Hold his breath
For a while;

at others, making all *but* him lose the dimmed line in blinding tears. There are scenes that rivet themselves on the memory— such as Coverdale's interview with Westervelt in the woodland solitude, followed by his observation of another rencontre from his leafy hermitage in the vine-entangled pine-tree; and the dramatic recital of Zenobia's Legend; and the rendezvous at Eliot's Pulpit; and above all, the dreadful errand by midnight in quest of the Dead—intensified in its grim horror by the contrasted temperaments of the three searchers, especially Silas Foster's rude matter-of-fact hardness, probing with coarse unconscious finger the wounds of a proud and sensitive soul. There are touches of exquisite pathos in the evolution of the tale of sorrow, mingled with shrewd "interludes" of irony and humour which only deepen the distress. Antiperistasis, Sir Thomas Browne would call it.

Upon the bearing of the romance on Socialism we need not descant, the author explicitly disclaiming all intent of pronouncing *pro* or *con* on the theories in question. As to the characters, too, he as explicitly repudiates the idea, which in the teeth of such disclaimer, and of internal evidence also, has been attributed to him, of portraying in the Blithedale actors the actual companions of his Brook Farm career—or other American celebrities (as though Margaret Fuller were Zenobia, because both living on "Rights of Woman" excitement, and both dying by drowning!). The characters are few; but each forms a study. The gorgeous Zenobia—from out whose imposing nature was felt to breathe an influence "such as we might suppose to come from Eve, when she was just made, and her Creator brought her to Adam, saying, 'Behold! here is a Woman!'"—not an influence merely fraught with especial gentleness, grace, modesty, and shyness, but a "certain warm and rich characteristic, which seems, for the most part, to have been refined away out of the feminine system." Hollingsworth—by nature deeply and warmly benevolent, but restricting his benevolence exclusively to one channel, and having nothing to spare for other great manifestations of love to man, nor scarcely for the nutriment of individual attachments, unless they minister, in some way, to the terrible egotism which he mistakes for an angel of God:—with something of the woman moulded into his great stalwart frame, and a spirit of prayer abiding and working in his heart;—but himself grown to be the bond-slave of his philanthropic theory, which has become to him in effect a cold spectral monster of his own conjuring; persuading himself that the importance of his public ends renders it allowable to throw aside his private conscience; embodying himself in a project, which the disenchanted Zenobia reprobates with hissing defiance as "self, self, self!" Priscilla, again: a weakly bud that blossoms into health and hope under the fostering clime of Blithedale, where she seems a butterfly at play in a flickering bit of sunshine, and mistaking it for a broad and eternal summer—though her gaiety reveals at times how delicate an instrument she is, and what fragile harp-strings are her nerves—a being of slender and shadowy grace, whose mysterious qualities make her seem diaphanous with spiritual light. Silas Foster, too: "lank, stalwart, uncouth, and grisly-bearded;" the prose element, and very dense prose, too, in the poetry of the Communists; with his palm of sole-leather and his joints of rusty iron, and his brain (as Zenobia pronounces it) of Savoy cabbage. And old Moodie, or Fauntleroy—that finished picture of a skulking outcast—shy and serpentine—with a queer appearance of hiding himself behind the patch of his left eye—a deplorable grey shadow—mysterious, but not mad; his mind only needing to be screwed up, like an instrument long out of tune, the strings of which have ceased to vibrate smartly and sharply—"a subdued, undemonstrative old man, who would doubtless drink a glass of liquor, now and then, and probably more than was good for him; not, however, with a purpose of undue exhilaration, but in the hope of bringing his spirits up to the ordinary level of the world's cheerfulness." Miles Coverdale himself is no lay figure in the group of actors. His character is replete with interest, whether as a partial presentment of the author's own person, or as a type of no uncommon individuality in this age of "yeast." We have in him a strange but most true "coincidence" of warm feeling and freezing reflection, of the kind deep heart and the vexed and vacillating brain, of a natural tendency to faith and a constitutional taint of scepticism, of the sensuous, indolent epicurean and the habitual cynic, of the idealist—all hope, and the realist—all disappointment. It is this fusion of opposite, not contradictory qualities, which gives so much piquancy and flavour to Coverdale's character, and his author's writings in general.

To become a member of the Blithedale socialistic institute, at which the world laughed as it *will* laugh at castles in the air—and all the while, evidently all the while, to be convinced at heart that the scheme is impracticable—this is quite *au naturel* with the Blithedale romancer. When he retires, and former acquaintances show themselves inclined to ridicule his heroic

devotion to the cause of human welfare, he sanctions the jest, and explains that really he had but been experimentalising, and with no valuable amount of hope or fear at stake, and that the thing had enabled him to pass the summer in a novel and agreeable way, had afforded him some grotesque specimens of artificial simplicity, and could not, therefore, *quoad* himself, be reckoned a failure. Miles gives us the best insight into his mind in its distinctive features, by such a passing reflection as this—where he is recording the invigorating tone of Blithedale air to the new converts from faded conventional life: "We had thrown off that sweet, bewitching, enervating indolence, which is better, after all, than most of the enjoyments within mortal grasp." His deficiency in the *excelsior* aspiration of the sanguine temperament stands revealed in every chapter. A little exaggerated, but that not much, in his language to Priscilla: "My past life has been a tiresome one enough; yet I would rather look backward ten times than forward once. For, little as we know of our life to come, we may be very sure, for one thing, that the good we aim at will not be attained. People never do get just the good they seek. If it come at all, it is something else, which they never dreamed of, and did not particularly want." And the conflicting influences of which we have spoken are notably illustrated when he describes his antipathy to, heightened by his very sympathy with, the odious Westervelt: "The professor's tone represented that of worldly society at large, where a cold scepticism smothers what it can of our spiritual aspirations, and makes the rest ridiculous. I detested this kind of man; and all the more because a part of my own nature showed itself responsive to him." An admirable bit of psychology, and eminently *like* Nathaniel Hawthorne.

But for our restricted limits, fain would we string together a few of those pithy reflections with which the romance abounds—many of them, indeed, questionable, but nearly all worth transcription, and stamped with the quaint die of the romancer's *esprit*. Differ from him as you may, you are all along interested in him, and are apt to find more in his crotchets than in a dullard's "exquisite reasons." (pp. 207-09)

[Francis Jacox], "American Authorship: Nathaniel Hawthorne," in The New Monthly Magazine, *Vol. XCVIII, No. CCCXC, June, 1853, pp. 202-12.*

[MARGARET OLIPHANT] (essay date 1855)

[*Oliphant was a prolific nineteenth-century Scottish novelist, critic, biographer, and historian. A regular contributor to* Blackwood's Magazine, *she published nearly one hundred novels, many of them popular tales of English and Scottish provincial life, including her best-known work, the series of novels known as the* Chronicles of Carlingford. *Here, Oliphant takes issue with the intellectuality and subject matter of* Blithedale.]

In the **Blithedale Romance** we have . . . less of natural character, and more of a diseased and morbid conventional life [than in **The Scarlet Letter** and **The House of Seven Gables**]. American patriots ought to have no quarrel with our saucy tourists and wandering notabilities, in comparison with the due and just quarrel they have with writers of their own. What extraordinary specimens of womankind are Zenobia and Priscilla, the heroines of this tale! What a meddling, curious, impertinent rogue, a psychological Paul Pry, is Miles Coverdale, the teller of the story! How thoroughly worn out and *blasé* must that young world be, which gets up excitements in its languid life, only by means of veiled ladies, mysterious clairvoyants, rapping spirits, or, in a milder fashion, by sherry-cobbler and something cocktails for the men, and lectures on the rights of women for

A painting of Brook Farm in 1844.

the ladies. We enter this strange existence with a sort of wondering inquiry whether any *events* ever take place there, or if, instead, there is nothing to be done but for everybody to observe everybody else, and for all society to act on the universal impulse of getting up a tragedy somewhere, for the pleasure of looking at it; or if that may not be, of setting up supernatural intercourse one way or another, and warming up with occult and forbidden influences the cold and waveless tide of life. We do not believe in Zenobia drowning herself. It is a piece of sham entirely, and never impresses us with the slightest idea of reality. Nor are we moved with any single emotion throughout the entire course of the tale. There is nothing touching in the mystery of old Moodie; nothing attractive in the pale clairvoyant Priscilla—the victim, as we are led to suppose, of Mesmerism and its handsome diabolical professor. We are equally indifferent to the imperious and splendid Zenobia, and to the weak sketchy outline of Hollingsworth, whose ''stern'' features are washed in with the faintest water-colours, and who does not seem capable of anything but of making these two women fall in love with him. The sole thing that looks true, and seems to have blood in its veins, is Silas Foster, the farmer and manager of practical matters for the Utopian community, which proposes to reform the world by making ploughmen of themselves. Could they have done it honestly, we cannot fancy any better plan for the visionary inhabitants of the farm and the romance of Blithedale. Honest work might do a great deal for these languid philosophers; and Mr. Hawthorne himself, we should suppose, could scarcely be in great condition for dissecting his neighbours and their ''inner nature'' after a day's ploughing or reaping; but mystery, Mesmerism, love, and jealousy, are too many for the placid angel of agriculture, and

young America by no means makes a success in its experiment, either by reforming others or itself.

After all, we are not ethereal people. We are neither fairies nor angels. Even to make our conversation—and, still more to make our life—we want more than thoughts and fancies—we want *things*. You may sneer at the commonplace necessity, yet it *is* one; and it is precisely your Zenobias and Hollingsworths, your middle-aged people, who have broken loose from family and kindred and have no *events* in their life, who do all the mischief, and make all the sentimentalisms and false philosophies in the world. When we come to have no duties, except those we ''owe to ourselves'' or ''to society,'' woe to us! Wise were the novelists of old, who ended their story with the youthful marriage, which left the hero and the heroine on the threshold of the maturer dangers of life, when fiction would not greatly aid them, but when the battle-ground, the real conflict, enemies not to be chased away, and sorrows unforgettable, remained. The trials of youth are safe ground; and so, to a considerable extent, are the trials of husbands and wives, when they struggle with the world, and not with each other; but the solitary maturer men and women, who have nothing happening to them, who are limited by no particular duties, and have not even the blessed necessity of working for their daily bread—these are the problem of the world; and the novelist had need to be wary who tries to deal with it. (pp. 564-65)

Mr. Hawthorne, we are afraid, is one of those writers who aim at an intellectual audience, and address themselves mainly to such. We are greatly of opinion that this is a mistake and a delusion, and that nothing good comes of it. The novelist's true audience is the common people—the people of ordinary comprehension and everyday sympathies, whatever their rank may be. (p. 565)

[Margaret Oliphant], "Modern Novelists: Great and Small," in Blackwood's Edinburgh Magazine, Vol. LXXVII, No. CCCCLXXV, May, 1855, pp. 554-68.

GEORGE PARSONS LATHROP (essay date 1876)

[Lathrop identifies the distinctive qualities of Blithedale that separate it from Hawthorne's other novels.]

The special characteristic of **The Blithedale Romance** seems to me to be its appearance of unlabored ease, and a consequent breeziness of effect distinguishing its atmosphere from that of any of the other romances. The style is admirably finished, and yet there is no part of the book that gives the same impression of almost unnecessary polish which occasionally intervenes between one's admiration and the **Seven Gables**. On this score, **Blithedale** is certainly the most consummate of the four completed romances. And as Hawthorne has nowhere given us more robust and splendid characterization than that of Zenobia and Hollingsworth, the work also takes high rank on this ground. The shadows, which seemed partly dispersed in the **Seven Gables**, gather again in this succeeding story; but, on the other hand, it is not so jarringly terrible as **The Scarlet Letter.** From this it is saved partly by the sylvan surrounding and the pleasant changes of scene. In comparing it with the other works, I find that it lets itself be best defined as a mean between extremes; so that it ought to have the credit of being the most evenly attempered of all. The theme is certainly as deep as that of the earlier ones, and more tangible to the general reader than that of **The Marble Faun;** it is also more novel than that of **The Scarlet Letter** or even the **Seven Gables,** and has an attractive air of growing simply and naturally out of a phenomenon extremely common in New England, namely, the man who is dominated and blinded by a theory. And the way in which Hollingsworth, through this very prepossession and absorption, is brought to the ruin of his own scheme, and has to concentrate his charity for criminals upon himself as the first criminal needing reformation, is very masterly. Yet, in discussing the relative positions of these four works, I am not sure that we can reach any decision more stable than that of mere preference. (pp. 241-42)

George Parsons Lathrop, in his A Study of Hawthorne, J. R. Osgood and Company, 1876, 350 p.

HENRY JAMES (essay date 1896)

[James was an American-born English novelist, short story writer, critic, and essayist of the late nineteenth and early twentieth centuries. He is regarded as one of the greatest novelists of the English language and is also admired as a lucid and insightful critic. In the following excerpt from an 1896 introduction to Hawthorne's works, James comments briefly on Blithedale as a reflection of Hawthorne's experience at Brook Farm. For additional commentary on Blithedale by James, see NCLC, Vol. 2.]

[In **The Blithedale Romance,** Hawthorne] made the most, for the food of fancy, of what came under his hand,—happy in an appetite that could often find a feast in meagre materials. The third of his novels is an echo, delightfully poetized, of his residence at Brook Farm. "Transcendentalism" was in those days in New England much in the air; and the most comprehensive account of the partakers of this quaint experiment appears to have been held to be that they were Transcendentalists.

More simply stated, they were young, candid radicals, reformers, philanthropists. The fact that it sprang—all irresponsibly indeed—from the observation of a known episode, gives **The Blithedale Romance** also a certain value as a picture of manners; the place portrayed, however, opens quickly enough into the pleasantest and idlest dream-world. Hawthorne, we gather, dreamed there more than he worked; he has traced his attitude delightfully in that of the fitful and ironical Coverdale, as to whom we wonder why he chose to rub shoulders quite so much. We think of him as drowsing on a hillside with his hat pulled over his eyes, and the neighboring hum of reform turning in his ears, to a refrain as vague as an old song. One thing is certain: that if he failed his companions as a laborer in the field, it was only that he might associate them with another sort of success.

We feel, however, that he lets them off easily, when we think of some of the queer figures and queer nostrums then abroad in the land, and which his mild satire—incurring none the less some mild reproach—fails to grind in its mill. The idea that he most tangibly presents is that of the unconscious way in which the search for the common good may cover a hundred interested impulses and personal motives; the suggestion that such a company could only be bound together more by its delusions, its mutual suspicions and frictions, than by any successful surrender of self. The book contains two images of large and admirable intention: that of Hollingsworth the heavy-handed radical, selfish and sincere, with no sense for jokes, for forms, or for shades; and that of Zenobia the woman of "sympathies," the passionate patroness of "causes," who plays as it were with revolution, and only encounters embarrassment. Zenobia is the most graceful of all portraits of the strong-minded of her sex; borrowing something of her grace, moreover, from the fate that was not to allow her to grow old and shrill, and not least touching from the air we attribute to her of looking, with her fine imagination, for adventures that were hardly, under the circumstances, to be met. We fill out the figure, perhaps, and even lend to the vision something more than Hawthorne intended. Zenobia was, like Coverdale himself, a subject of dreams that were not to find form at Roxbury; but Coverdale had other resources, while she had none but her final failure. Hawthorne indicates no more interesting aspect of the matter than her baffled effort to make a hero of Hollingsworth, who proves, to her misfortune, so much too inelastic for the part. All this, as we read it to-day, has a soft, shy glamour, a touch of the poetry of far-off things. Nothing of the author's is a happier expression of . . . his sense of the romance of New England. (pp. 463-65)

Henry James, "American Writers: Nathaniel Hawthorne (1804-1864)," in his Literary Criticism, The Library of America, 1984, pp. 458-68.

GEORGE E. WOODBERRY (essay date 1902)

[Woodberry was an American critic, poet, and educator. In the following excerpt, he offers a negative assessment of Blithedale, faulting its structure, characters, and subject matter.]

[**The Blithedale Romance**] is the least substantial of any of [Hawthorne's] longer works. It lacks the intensity of power that distinguishes **The Scarlet Letter,** and the accumulated richness of surface that belongs to **The House of the Seven Gables,** due to the overlaying of story on story in that epitome of a New England family history. **The Blithedale Romance,** on the contrary, has both less depth and less inclusiveness; and much of its vogue springs from the fact of its being a reflection of the life of Brook Farm, which possesses an interest in its own right. Hawthorne used his material in the direct way that was his custom, and transferred bodily to his novel, to make its background and atmosphere, what he had preserved in his note-books or memory from the period of his residence with the reformers. The April snowstorm in which he arrived at the farm, his illness there, the vine-hung tree that he made his autumnal arbor, the costume and habits, the fancy-dress party, the Dutch realism of the figure of Silas Foster, and many another detail occur at once to the mind as from this origin; his own attitude is sketched frankly in Miles Coverdale, and the germs of others of the characters, notably Priscilla, are to be found in the same experience. The life of the farmhouse, however, is not of sufficient interest in itself to hold attention very closely, and the socialistic experiment, after all, is not the theme of the story; these things merely afford a convenient and appropriate ground on which to develop a study of the typical reformer, as Hawthorne conceived him, the nature, trials, temptations, and indwelling fate of such a man; and to this task the author addressed himself. In the way in which he worked out the problem, he revealed his own judgment on the moral type brought so variously and persistently under his observation by the wave of reform that was so strongly characteristic of his times.

The characters are, as usual, few, and they have that special trait of isolation which is the birthmark of Hawthorne's creations. Zenobia, Priscilla, and Hollingsworth are the trio, who, each in an environment of solitude, make the essence of the plot by their mutual relations. Zenobia is set apart by her secret history and physical nature, and Priscilla by her magnetic powers and enslavement to the mesmerist; Hollingsworth is absorbed in his mission. It is unlikely that Hawthorne intended any of these as a portrait of any real person, though as the seamstress of Brook Farm gave the external figure of Priscilla, it may well be that certain suggestions of temperament were found for the other two characters among his impressions of persons whom he met. Neither Zenobia nor Priscilla, notwithstanding the latter's name, are essentially New England characters; in each of them there is something alien to the soil, and they are represented as coming from a different stock. Hollingsworth, on the other hand, is meant as a native type. The unfolding of the story, and the treatment of the characters, are not managed with any great skill. Hawthorne harks back to his old habits, and does so in a feebler way than would have been anticipated. He interjects the short story of The Veiled Lady, for example, in the middle of the narrative, as he had placed the tale of Alice in *The House of the Seven Gables,* but very ineffectively; it is a pale narrative and does not count visibly in the progress of the novel, but only inferentially. He uses also the exotic flower, which Zenobia wears, as a physical symbol, but it plays no part and is only a relic of his old manner. The description of the performance in the country hall seems like an extract from one of the old annuals of the same calibre as the Story-Teller's Exhibition. Mesmerism is the feebler substitute for the old witchcraft element. In a word, the work is not well knit together, and the various methods of old are weakly combined. One comes back to the moral situation as the centre of interest; and in it he exhibits the reformer as failing in the same ways in which other egotists fail, for he perceives in the enthusiasm of the humanitarian only selfishness, arrogance, intolerance in another form. Hollingsworth, with the best of motives apparently, since his cause is his motive, as he believes, is faithless to his associates and willing to wreck their enterprise because it stands in his way and he

is out of sympathy with it; he is faithless to Priscilla in so far as he accepts Zenobia because she can aid him with her wealth, and on her losing her wealth he is faithless to her in returning to Priscilla; he has lost the power to be true, in the other relations of life, through his devotion to his cause. One feels that Hollingsworth is the victim of Hawthorne's moral theory about him. It is true that at the end Hawthorne has secured in the character that tragic reversal which is always effective, in the point that Hollingsworth, who set out to be the friend and uplifter and saviour of the criminal classes, sees at last in himself the murderer of Zenobia; but this is shown almost by a side-light, and not as the climax of the plot, perhaps because the reader does not hold him guilty in any true sense of the disaster which overtakes Zenobia. In its main situation, therefore, the plot, while it suggests and illustrates the temptations and failures of a nature such as Hollingsworth's, does not carry conviction. Description takes the place of action; much of Zenobia's life and of Hollingsworth's, also, is left untold in the time after Coverdale left them; as in the case of Judge Pyncheon, the wrong-doing is left much in the shadow, suggested, hinted at, narrated finally, but not shown in the life; and such wrong-doing loses the edge of villainy. It might be believed that Hollingsworth as a man failed; but as a typical man, as that reformer who is only another shape of the selfish and heartless egotist sacrificing everything wrongfully to his philanthropic end, it is not so easily believed that he must have failed; it is the absence of this logical necessity that discredits him as a type, and takes out of his character and career the universal quality. This, however, may be only a personal impression. The truth of the novel, on the ethical side, may be plainer to others; it presents some aspects of moral truth, carefully studied and probably observed, but they seem very partial aspects, and too incomplete to allow them, taken all together, to be called typical. The power of the story lies rather in its external realism, and especially in that last scene, which was taken from Hawthorne's experience at Concord on the night when he took part in rescuing the body of the young woman who had drowned herself; but with the exception of this last scene, and of some of the sketches that reproduce most faithfully the life and circumstances of Brook Farm, the novel does not equal its predecessors in the ethical or imaginative value of its material, in romantic vividness, or in the literary skill of its construction. The elements of the story are themselves inferior; and perhaps Hawthorne made the most of them that they were capable of; but his mind was antipathetic to his main theme. His representation of the New England reformer is as partial as that of the Puritan minister; both are depraved types, and in the former there is not that vivid truth to general human nature which makes the latter so powerful a revelation of the sinful heart. (pp. 227-32)

George E. Woodberry, in his Nathaniel Hawthorne, *1902. Reprint by Gale Research Company, 1967, 302 p.*

D. H. LAWRENCE (essay date 1923)

[*Lawrence was an English novelist, poet, and essayist who is noted for his introduction of modern psychological themes into English fiction. Here, he offers an impressionistic interpretation of the intention, meaning, and significance of* Blithedale.]

Hawthorne came nearest to actuality in the *Blithedale Romance.* This novel is a sort of picture of the notorious Brook Farm experiment. There the famous idealists and transcendentalists of America met to till the soil and hew the timber in the sweat of their own brows, thinking high thoughts the while, and breathing an atmosphere of communal love, and tingling in tune with the Oversoul, like so many strings of a super-celestial harp. An old twang of the Crèvecoeur instrument.

Of course they fell out like cats and dogs. Couldn't stand one another. And all the music they made was the music of their quarrelling.

You *can't* idealize hard work. Which is why America invents so many machines and contrivances of all sort: so that they need do no physical work.

And that's why the idealists left off brookfarming, and took to bookfarming.

You *can't* idealize the essential brute blood-activity, the brute blood desires, the basic, sardonic blood-knowledge.

That you *can't* idealize.

And you can't eliminate it.

So there's the end of ideal man.

Man is made up of a dual consciousness, of which the two halves are most of the time in opposition to one another—and will be so as long as time lasts.

You've got to learn to change from one consciousness to the other, turn and about. Not to try to make either absolute, or dominant. The Holy Ghost tells you the how and when.

Never did Nathaniel feel himself more spectral—of course he went brookfarming—than when he was winding the horn in the morning to summon the transcendental labourers to their tasks, or than when marching off with a hoe ideally to hoe the turnips, "Never did I feel more spectral," says Nathaniel.

Never did I feel such a fool, would have been more to the point.

Farcical fools, trying to idealize labour. You'll never succeed in idealizing hard work. Before you can dig mother earth you've got to take off your ideal jacket. The harder a man works, at brute labour, the thinner becomes his idealism, the darker his mind. And the harder a man works, at mental labour, at idealism, at transcendental occupations, the thinner becomes his blood, and the more brittle his nerves.

Oh, the brittle-nerved brookfarmers!

You've got to be able to do both: the mental work, and the brute work. But be prepared to step from one pair of shoes into another. Don't try and make it all one pair of shoes.

The attempt to idealize the blood!

Nathaniel knew he was a fool, attempting it.

He went home to his amiable spouse and his sanctum sanctorum of a study.

Nathaniel!

But the **Blithedale Romance**. It has a beautiful, wintry-evening farm-kitchen sort of opening.

Dramatis Personae:

1. *I.*—The narrator: whom we will call Nathaniel. A wisp of a sensitive, withal deep, literary young man no longer so very young.

2. *Zenobia:* a dark, proudly voluptuous clever woman with a tropical flower in her hair. Said to be sketched from Margaret

Fuller, in whom Hawthorne saw some "evil nature". Nathaniel was more aware of Zenobia's voluptuousness than of her "mind".

3. *Hollingsworth:* a black-bearded blacksmith with a deep-voiced lust for saving criminals. Wants to build a great Home for these unfortunates.

4. *Priscilla:* a sort of White Lily, a clinging little mediumistic sempstress who has been made use of in public seances. A sort of prostitute soul.

5. *Zenobia's Husband:* an unpleasant decayed person with magnetic powers and teeth full of gold—or set in gold. It is he who has given public spiritualist demonstrations, with Priscilla for the medium. He is of the dark, sensual, decayed-handsome sort, and comes in unexpectedly by the back door.

Plot I.—I, Nathaniel, at once catch cold, and have to be put to bed. Am nursed with inordinate tenderness by the blacksmith, whose great hands are gentler than a woman's, etc.

The two men love one another with a love surpassing the love of women, so long as the healing-and-salvation business lasts. When Nathaniel wants to get well and have a soul of his own, he turns with hate to this black-bearded, booming salvationist, Hephaestos of the underworld. Hates him for tyrannous monomaniac.

Plot II.—Zenobia, that clever lustrous woman, is fascinated by the criminal-saving blacksmith, and would have him at any price. Meanwhile she has the subtlest current of understanding with the frail but deep Nathaniel. And she takes the White Lily half-pityingly, half contemptuously under a rich and glossy dark wing.

Plot III.—The blacksmith is after Zenobia, to get her money for his criminal asylum: of which, of course, he will be the first inmate.

Plot IV.—Nathaniel also feels his mouth watering for the dark-luscious Zenobia.

Plot V.—The White Lily, Priscilla, vaporously festering, turns out to be the famous Veiled Lady of public spiritualist shows: she whom the undesirable Husband, called the Professor, has used as a medium. Also she is Zenobia's half-sister.

Débâcle

Nobody wants Zenobia in the end. She goes off without her flower. The blacksmith marries Priscilla. Nathaniel dribblingly confesses that he, too, has loved Prissy all the while. Boo-hoo!

Conclusion

A few years after, Nathaniel meets the blacksmith in a country lane near a humble cottage, leaning totteringly on the arm of the frail but fervent Priscilla. Gone are all dreams of asylums, and the saviour of criminals can't even save himself from his own Veiled Lady.

There you have a nice little bunch of idealists, transcendentalists, brookfarmers, and disintegrated gentry. All going slightly rotten.

Two Pearls: a white Pearl and a black Pearl: the latter more expensive, lurid with money.

The white Pearl, the little medium, Priscilla, the imitation pearl, has truly some "supernormal" powers. She could drain the blacksmith of his blackness and his smith-strength.

Priscilla, the little psychic prostitute. The degenerate descendant of Ligeia. The absolutely yielding, ''loving'' woman, who abandons herself utterly to her lover. Or even to a gold-toothed ''professor'' of spiritualism.

Is it all bunkum, this spiritualism? Is it just rot, this Veiled Lady?

Not quite. Apart even from telepathy, the apparatus of human consciousness is the most wonderful message-receiver in existence. Beats a wireless station to nothing.

Put Prissy under the tablecloth then. Miaow!

What happens? Prissy under the tablecloth, like a canary when you cover his cage, goes into a ''sleep'', a trance.

A trance, not a sleep. A trance means that all her *individual*, personal intelligence goes to sleep, like a hen with her head under her wing. But the *apparatus* of consciousness remains working. Without a soul in it.

And what can this apparatus of consciousness do, when it works? Why, surely something. A wireless apparatus goes tick-tick-tick, taking down messages. So does your human apparatus. All kinds of messages. Only the soul, or the under-consciousness, deals with these messages in the dark, in the under-conscious. Which is the natural course of events.

But what sorts of messages? All sorts. Vibrations from the stars, vibrations from unknown magnetos, vibrations from unknown people, unknown passions. The human apparatus receives them all and they are all dealt with in the under-conscious.

There are also vibrations of thought, many, many. Necessary to get the two human instruments in key.

There may even be vibrations of ghosts in the air. Ghosts being dead *wills*, mind you, not dead souls. The soul has nothing to do with these dodges.

But some unit of force may persist for a time, after the death of an individual—some associations of vibrations may linger like little clouds in the etheric atmosphere after the death of a human being, or an animal. And these little clots of vibration may transfer themselves to the conscious-apparatus of the medium. So that the dead son of a disconsolate widow may send a message to his mourning mother to tell her that he owes Bill Jackson seven dollars: or that Uncle Sam's will is in the back of the bureau: and cheer up, Mother, I'm all right.

There is never much worth in these ''messages'', because they are never more than fragmentary items of dead, disintegrated consciousness. And the medium has, and always will have, a hopeless job, trying to disentangle the muddle of messages.

Again, coming events *may* cast their shadow before. The oracle may receive on her conscious-apparatus material vibrations to say that the next great war will break out in 1925. And in so far as the realm of cause-and-effect is master of the living soul, in so far as events are mechanically maturing, the forecast may be true.

But the living souls of men may upset the *mechanical* march of events at any moment.

Rien de certain.

Vibrations of subtlest matter. Concatenations of vibrations and shocks! Spiritualism.

And what then? It is all just materialistic, and a good deal is, and always will be, charlatanry.

Because the real human soul, the Holy Ghost, has its own deep prescience, which will not be put into figures, but flows on dark, a stream of prescience.

And the real human soul is too proud, and too sincere in its belief in the Holy Ghost that is within, to stoop to the practices of these spiritualist and other psychic tricks of material vibrations.

Because the first part of reverence is the acceptance of the fact that the Holy Ghost will never materialize: will never be anything but a ghost.

And the second part of reverence is the watchful observance of the motions, the comings and goings within us, of the Holy Ghost, and of the many gods that make up the Holy Ghost.

The Father had his day, and fell.

The Son has had his day, and fell.

It is the day of the Holy Ghost.

But when souls fall corrupt, into disintegration, they have no more day. They have sinned against the Holy Ghost.

These people in **Blithedale Romance** have sinned against the Holy Ghost, and corruption has set in.

All, perhaps, except the I, Nathaniel. He is still a sad, integral consciousness.

But not excepting Zenobia. The Black Pearl is rotting down. Fast. The cleverer she is, the faster she rots.

And they are all disintegrating, so they take to psychic tricks. It is a certain sign of the disintegration of the psyche in a man, and much more so in a woman, when she takes to spiritualism, and table-rapping, and occult messages, or witchcraft and supernatural powers of that sort. When men want to be supernatural, be sure that something has gone wrong in their natural stuff. More so, even, with a woman.

And yet the soul has its own profound subtleties of knowing. And the blood has its strange omniscience.

But this isn't impudent and materialistic, like spiritualism and magic and all that range of pretentious supernaturalism. (pp. 104-10)

D. H. Lawrence, ''Hawthorne's 'Blithedale Romance','' in his Studies in Classic American Literature, *1923. Reprint by The Viking Press, 1964, pp. 101-10.*

MARK VAN DOREN   (essay date 1949)

[*Van Doren was one of the most prolific men of letters in twentieth-century American writing. His work includes poetry, novels, short stories, drama, criticism, social commentary, and the editing of a number of popular anthologies. Van Doren's criticism is aimed at the general reader, rather than the scholar or specialist, and is noted for its lively perceptiveness and wide interest. Here, Van Doren dismisses* Blithedale *as a poor novel, attributing its failure to Hawthorne's inability to mine his experience.*]

The Blithedale Romance has no outstanding virtue of any kind. What stands out everywhere in it is Hawthorne's doubt, which has returned in full force after three years of rapid and confident composition, that he knows what he is doing. Few poorer novels have been produced by a first-rate talent. Only Hawthorne's talent is here, and it is apologetic. This shows in the distressingly pale character of the narrator, who is Hawthorne himself if anybody in his work ever was. Miles Coverdale not only tells his story badly—so badly that when he is not forcing scenes he is suppressing them altogether, with the result that we do not know what the story is—but sports and luxuriates in the role of spectator until we lose patience with him much as Zenobia does when she catches him spying on her in her Boston hotel. To be sure it is Hawthorne who writes her denunciation of Coverdale on that occasion; but this does not save him from the charge of incompetence we bring. It is indeed his way of accepting the charge: a laudable piece of candor, but it comes too late.

The Blithedale Romance owes more to Hawthorne's experience, and to his note-books, than does any other narrative he published. This is precisely why it fails. He did not know how to use his experience. He knew only how to use his imagination, and in this case his imagination was absent or tired. The subject is Brook Farm, and the heroine is perhaps Margaret Fuller. Hawthorne always denied this, pointing to a passage in which Priscilla, not her more splendid sister, was said in so many words to resemble that intellectual lady. But Priscilla does not resemble Margaret Fuller; and if Zenobia in some aspects does—being eloquent, lofty, and proud—it still remains doubtful whether as a person in the book she lives. It is difficult to see why James thought she did [see *NCLC*, Vol. 2]. She is as much like Hester Prynne as waxworks are like women. Her beauty, so much insisted upon, is never felt; the flower in her hair is ineffective; and her tragedy is trash. Neither the villain Westervelt with his false teeth—a singular degradation of Hawthorne's symbol of deformity in devils—nor the near-villain Hollingsworth with his cold reformer's heart is put into tragic relation with her; and the wispy Priscilla, whom she in turn victimizes in some fashion never clear, is as feeble a foil as Cleopatra would desire. But Zenobia is as little like Cleopatra as like Hester. The circumstances of her suicide, copied wth few changes from a remarkable passage of the note-book Hawthorne kept at the Old Manse—he had witnessed there the drowned body of Martha Hunt, and recorded the experience with grotesque, relentless power—are not made relevant here, because nothing in Zenobia's death seems necessary. Certainly there is nothing morally terrible in it. So the mesmerism with which Hawthorne dabbles, though it is the best modern equivalent he can find for witchcraft or original sin, has none of "the devil" in it. Hawthorne loathed the spiritualist antics of his time, and more than once warned Sophia against them; but this does not mean that he has made them sinister in *Blithedale Romance*. They are not so, just as Brook Farm refuses to realize itself out of the note-book he kept there. He was doing his best with the world he lived in, but so far it bewildered rather than reinforced his art. If some of the amusement he felt at West Roxbury creeps into this romance, and gives it a beguiling lightness here and there, this very lightness becomes a fault when we remember that we are supposed to be assisting at a tragedy. Coverdale keeps recommending the tragedy, and proving that it is real. But Coverdale is an ass, and tragedy needs no proof. In the same year with *The Blithedale Romance* appeared *Uncle Tom's Cabin*, a work supposedly more crude. The elegant crudities of Hawthorne are less forgivable than the forthright ones of Mrs. Stowe. (pp. 188-91)

> *Mark Van Doren, in his* Nathaniel Hawthorne, *1949.*
> *Reprint by The Viking Press, 1957, 279 p.*

ROY R. MALE   (essay date 1957)

[*In the following excerpt, Male asserts that* Blithedale *represents Hawthorne's response to the ongoing attempts of Americans to* achieve dramatic social change through hard work, utopian planning, and new technology rather than through individual moral growth. According to the critic, Hawthorne felt that suffering and tragedy were the necessary ingredients of spiritual transformation without which genuine social reform could not occur.*]

In *The Blithedale Romance* Hawthorne arrived at his definitive criticism of the recurring American efforts at transformation without tragedy. While his ever optimistic contemporaries were busy converting trees into lumber, whales into oil, and water into power, Hawthorne adhered to his "one idea": that moral conversion, which is the only kind that really matters, cannot be achieved through intellectual schemes, incessant industry, or technological progress. A spiritual sea change must be *suffered;* this is unfortunate, but there is no other way. "There is no instance in all history," he wrote in his life of Pierce, "of the human will and intellect having perfected any great moral reform by methods which it adapted to that end."

With this central idea in mind, Hawthorne composed *The Blithedale Romance* by selecting and manipulating his observations and experiences of a decade: the gruesome suicide of a woman in the prime of life; the contemporary delusion of mesmerism; the Brook Farm experiment; the quiet, determined drinkers at Parker's grogshop; the gulf between the intellectual and the yeoman; his interest in the dangerously sterile but fascinating role of the withdrawn observer. In 1842 he set down one hint of the story to come when he wrote in his notebook: "To allegorize life with a masquerade, and represent mankind generally as masquers. Here and there a natural face may appear." The vision of life that emerged ten years later, though it lacks the tense conflict of *The Scarlet Letter,* is far richer than one usually realizes upon first reading. The book seems to me to be perfectly achieved and just as relevant in the age of extrasensory perception and atomic conversion as it was in the era of mesmerism. Until recently, criticism of *The Blithedale Romance* so often dwelled upon such peripheral matters as whether or not Zenobia resembled Margaret Fuller that it remains one of the most underrated works in American fiction.

Now that the demands for a prosaic realism in fiction have receded, it is unnecessary to labor the point that *The Blithedale Romance* is not an ineffectual effort at a documentary of Brook Farm, nor is it merely Hawthorne's satirical comment on philanthropists and reform movements. As he stated in the preface and in a letter to G. W. Curtis, the real subject of the book is neither Brook Farm nor socialism. His work presents, as Henry James would say, "experience liberated, so to speak; experience disengaged, disembroiled, disencumbered, exempt from the conditions which usually attach to it," so that its deepest implications may be explored. The implications in this instance are not pleasant to contemplate, but to a generation educated by D. H. Lawrence, T. S. Eliot, Thomas Mann, and Robert Penn Warren they probably seem more real than they did in 1852. The Blithedale community stands as the type of all those efforts in the Western world to ignore Solomon's wisdom about the seasons, to purify by escaping from time into space, to achieve rebirth by putting on a mask. The comic masquerade, as Hawthorne viewed it, is the mode of changing our minds, and as such it is vitally necessary. The mischief comes when we expect it to change our hearts.

Blithedale, then, turns out to be an ironic name, thinly veiling what ultimately emerges as a pastoral wasteland. The inhabitants of the community debate over a name for their utopia; some favor calling it "The Oasis," but "others insisted on a proviso for reconsidering the matter at a twelve-month's end, when a final decision might be had, whether to name it 'The Oasis,' or 'Sahara'.'' By the end of the book it is obvious that Blithedale, far from being ''the one green spot in the moral sand-waste of the world,'' has instead simply revealed its own barrenness. What the inhabitants hope will be a May Day—a warm, ''hearty'' purification—turns out to be a winter's tale told in retrospect by a frosty bachelor.

Hawthorne deliberately wrote, I suspect, toward the ''big scene'' that he felt to be securely within his grasp—the midnight discovery of Zenobia's suicide. Soon after the story opens, to cite but one instance, Zenobia prophesies her fate with ''the entrance of the sable knight Hollingsworth and this shadowy snow-maiden, who, precisely at the stroke of midnight, shall melt away at my feet in a pool of ice-cold water and give me my death with a pair of wet slippers.'' Coverdale's dream, in which he foresees ''a dim shadow'' of the catastrophe, thus provides an explicit comment on Hawthorne's method of subtly anticipating later events.

The Blithedale experiment is, first, an attempt to avoid the embrace of time. Coverdale and his friends ride ''far beyond the strike of city clocks'' into pure, snow-covered space. Theirs is an effort to blur the distinction between seasons, to overcome the desolation of winter by the warmth of their reforming zeal. ''We can never call ourselves regenerated men,'' says one of Coverdale's companions, ''till a February northeaster shall be as grateful to us as the softest breeze of June.'' They declare May Day a ''movable festival,'' and it is only the ineffectual Coverdale who gradually senses the blank unreality of their ''spick-and-span novelty.'' By the time he decides to leave the community, he has finally attained a wisdom that, though commonplace elsewhere, seems downright orphic after life at Blithedale: ''Times change, and people change,'' he tells Priscilla; ''and if our hearts do not change as readily, so much the worse for us.''

Acting as a measure of the community's failure, therefore, is the temporal structure of the book. Narrated by one who has withdrawn from life, the story unfolds against the background of the seasons. Viewed against the fundamental rhythms of nature, the various human efforts at rebirth without roots become even more frustrating. Recalling the firelight, which at the beginning of the Blithedale experiment had made the men look ''full of youth, warm blood, and hope,'' Coverdale ruefully remarks that its genial glow has now dwindled to the ''phosphoric glimmer . . . which exudes . . . from the damp fragments of decayed trees.'' He explicitly proclaims his own rebirth in May: having passed through a kind of death, he is ''quite another man,'' ''clothed anew.'' And later he finds a ''hermitage'' in the weeds that suggests the perfect shelter of the womb. It is ''a hollow chamber of rare seclusion'' in which his individuality is ''inviolate.'' Sitting there, Coverdale prophesies a rebirth in October: ''I . . . fore-reckoned the abundance of my vintage. It gladdened me to anticipate the surprise of the Community when, like an allegorical figure of rich October, I should make my appearance, with shoulders bent beneath the burden of ripe grapes and some of the crushed ones crimsoning my brows with a blood-stain.'' But this fruitful October never comes for him, and in the end he is forced to acknowledge that his life has been ''all an emptiness.''

There are other futile attempts at regeneration. The drinkers in the saloon achieve ''renewed youth and vigor, the brisk, cheerful sense of things present and to come''—a feeling that lasts ''for about a quarter of an hour.'' The fate of these people is typified in the picture of a drunkard that hangs on the wall.

''The death-in-life was too well portrayed. . . . Your only comfort lay in the forced reflection, that real as he looked, the poor caitiff was but imaginary—a bit of painted canvas.'' The mesmerist, Westervelt, also offers a new life. He speaks of ''a new era that was dawning upon the world; an era that would link soul to soul with a closeness that should finally convert both worlds into one great, mutually conscious brotherhood.'' The ''cold and dead materialism'' of this brotherhood is matched by the mechanical method of conversion advocated by Fourier. Drain the salt from the sea, as he had proposed, transform the water to lemonade, and all the savor is gone. *The Blithedale Romance* is thus a kind of *Walden* in reverse. (Zenobia, coincidentally, anticipates Thoreau's exact words when she says of her experience in the community: ''It was good; but there are other lives as good or better.'') The story begins in the spring and ends with the fall; the whole progression is condensed in the exhilaration of the brisk September day that makes Coverdale buoyant at first but later only emphasizes his ''sickness of the spirits.''

The effort to reform the spirit externally, then, leads to disintegration. Sharply contrasted to the dynamic wholeness of nature are the images of rigidity, mutilation, and decay that lead inexorably to the discovery of Zenobia's horribly rigid and mutilated corpse. It is ''the marble image of a death-agony,'' the catastrophe that Coverdale dimly foresaw when he awakened from his dream after the first evening in Blithedale and saw the moon shining on the snowy landscape, which looked ''like a lifeless copy of the world in marble.'' Zenobia is cast aside like ''a broken tool'' by the inflexible Hollingsworth; and Coverdale's cool analysis of Hollingsworth is, as he himself admits, a kind of dissection. ''If we take the freedom to put a friend under our microscope,'' he says, ''we inevitably tear him into bits.'' The Blithedale group is ''gentility in tatters,'' while the visitors from town, the ratlike Moodie and the infamous Westervelt, embody a decadent materialism. The mesmerist's discourse is like ''a current of chill air issuing out of a sepulchral vault, and bringing the smell of corruption along with it.''

The second major pattern of images is one of withdrawal and concealment. As Frank Davidson has pointed out, everyone in the book except Silas Foster and his pigs is veiled in one form or another [see Additional Bibliography]. Priscilla, the Veiled Lady, is ''insulated'' from time and space; the pseudonym of Zenobia is a ''sort of mask in which she comes from the world, retaining all the privileges of privacy—a contrivance, in short, like the white drapery of the Veiled Lady.'' Old Moodie hides behind his alias and his patch; Westervelt's gold teeth reveal him to Coverdale as a humbug whose ''face, for aught I knew, might be removable like a mask.'' Hollingsworth's mask is his philanthropic project: ''You are a better masquerader than the witches and gypsies yonder,'' Zenobia tells him, ''for your disguise is a self-deception.'' The whole community has, of course, withdrawn from life into a kind of masquerade, but Coverdale finds it necessary to retreat even further into the hermitage. His typical stance finds him ''a little withdrawn from the window.''

The failure of Blithedale may be summed up as a misplaced faith in the comic vision of life as a mode of emotional conversion. The essence of the comic vision, as Hawthorne considered it, lay in the breaking of bonds—links with the past, ties with social classes. As Melville's mentor Solomon said, there is ''a time to embrace, and a time to refrain from embracing,'' and the communitarians have confused the tragic usefulness of the one with the comic purpose of the other. (pp. 139-45)

As in *The Scarlet Letter,* [an] understanding of what Hawthorne is doing in this book hinges in part upon accurate identification of the characters and the allegorical personifications. Once again we find the woman (Zenobia) and the man (Hollingsworth), their guilt (Westervelt), and their possible redemption (Priscilla). But here the woman is attempting to evade the "one event" of womanhood; the man has welded an intellectual shield over his heart; the redemptive agent is the medium of both truth and falsehood; and the story is narrated in the first person by an observer.

The most vital character in the book is Zenobia. The very essence of womanhood, she is the "first comer," she is the Amazon queen, she is Eve. "One felt an influence breathing out of her," says Coverdale, "such as we might suppose to come from Eve, when she was first made, and her creator brought her to Adam, saying, 'Behold! here is a woman!'" And he cannot resist summoning up a vision of her, clad in "Eve's earliest garment."

Zenobia's present attire expresses her contempt for the traditional role of women. As Newton Arvin observed some years ago, her exotic flower indicates her pride in competing with men. She desires to go afield, to speculate; just as she has no scruples about rifling a cherry tree of its blossoms, so her full flowering will be cut off by her attempt to be "stump-oratress." She despises the traditional feminine occupation of investment; this sympathetic function has been split off and concentrated in the seamstress, Priscilla. Like all Hawthorne's women (as opposed to his feminine personifications), Zenobia's character has "good and evil in it." Redundant with life, she makes all the other characters seem pale. But in this pastoral wasteland, her vitality is doomed. The others are bent upon destroying it: Coverdale by his incessant probing, his cool dissection, and Hollingsworth by making her a tool in his conspiracy. But it is Zenobia herself who is chiefly responsible for her self-destruction. She is quite willing to subvert the most gracious aspects of her womanhood (Priscilla) in order to have Hollingsworth on her own terms.

When man attempts to purify himself through psychiatry, intellectual schemes, and material progress, the burden of guilt tends to assume the very forms by which he seeks to erase it. Thus Zenobia's guilt is embodied in Westervelt, who, as his name implies, speaks with "the tone of worldly society at large." The "moral deterioration attendant on a false and shallow life" that results from Zenobia's "marriage" to the values of the Western world inevitably leads to her death beneath the dark mask of the river. When Coverdale sees her in the luxurious boardinghouse, she has taken on a glittering luster that, like her flower, is artificial. Even her death has something affected about it: Coverdale observes that "we cannot even put ourselves to death in whole-hearted simplicity."

The gradual destruction of Zenobia is reinforced, as we have noted, by images that shift from life to death. The death images are combined in the personification of her guilt. Westervelt's appearance at the lyceum is the nadir in a series of morbid exhibitions; he is preceded by the physiologist with his "real skeletons" and by the museum of wax figures. But what makes Westervelt completely repulsive is that he typifies a ghastly life-in-death. In his grim correlation of gold with mesmerism, Hawthorne anticipated Lionel Trilling's observation that money is like a spook in having a life of its own that properly it should

not have. Like the stones in the house of Usher, Westervelt has an indecent, clammy existence. Coverdale's reaction to him is "a creeping of the flesh, as when feeling about in a dark place, one touches something cold and slimy." Westervelt's discourse at the lyceum reminds one of the metallic clanking as Madeline Usher rises from her underground vault.

As Zenobia says in her own defense, the major reason for her dissatisfaction with womanhood lies in the reduced stature of the man. "Let man be but manly and godlike," she tells Hollingsworth, "and woman is only too ready to become to him what you say." Originally warmhearted, close to the center of humanity, he has become the false priest of this "apostolic society." Unexpectedly tender in caring for the invalid Coverdale and unique in the community in possessing a strong religious faith, Hollingsworth can manage everyone but himself. He preaches eloquently from Eliot's pulpit to his three "disciples," but his abstract desire to root out all evil becomes merely a shield to protect himself from healthy emotion. The dangers of his abstraction appear most clearly in his "visionary edifice." Instead of planning a home with roots, a house that would be "time-worn, and full of storied love, and joy, and sorrow," he tries to seduce the woman into inhabiting a purely intellectual prison for "the reform and mental culture of our criminal brethren." In masquerading as a reformer, Hollingsworth deceives not only his friends but also himself. When he finally attains self-knowledge, it is too late for any fruitful union with the woman. Recognizing his fatal error in rejecting the vitality of Zenobia and his part in her death, he condemns himself to an agony of self-accusation. His final outcome cannot be fully understood, however, until we grasp Priscilla's identity.

As Hawthorne's opening introduction of the Veiled Lady would indicate, Priscilla is a key figure in the story, though as a personification her chief importance proceeds from her relationships to other characters. Various clues help to establish her allegorical identity. An orphan in worldly society, linked only to the woman as stepsister and handmaiden, Priscilla is like Pearl in being the providential "first-fruits of the world." In commercial life she has been like a flower faintly blooming in the crack of a sidewalk. She has the gift of hearing the Miltonic "airy tongues that syllable forth men's names." No one from the town calls for her. Like Puck, she ruins the milk and spoils the dinner. Priscilla, in short, is spritelike Fancy, the "medium" of truth and falsehood. Coverdale clearly identifies her during his illness. "There is a species of intuition," he says, "either a spiritual life, or the subtle recognition of a fact" that comes to us during sickness. "Vapors then rise up to the brain, and take shapes that often image falsehood, but sometimes truth." A few pages later, he remarks of Priscilla's visit to his bedside: "My weakly condition, I suppose, supplied a medium in which she could approach me." As the medium, Priscilla's charm is not "positive" or "material"; she is blown about like a leaf. "I never have any free will," she exclaims plaintively to Coverdale. Unable to stand on her own legs, she draws her potential life from Zenobia and Hollingsworth. As the artistic medium, her province lies "somewhere between disease and beauty." We see now why Hawthorne begins with the Veiled Lady. For the book's action may be summed up in the efforts of each character to manipulate, corrupt, or achieve the medium of truth.

Incidentally, Hawthorne uses Priscilla as his own medium for what I take to be a covert but devastating thrust at Margaret Fuller. Priscilla brings a "sealed letter" to Coverdale's bedside. When he does not immediately offer to take it, Priscilla draws back and holds the letter "against her bosom, with both hands clasped over it." As she holds this pose, Miles is struck by a remarkable parallel. Though her figure and facial features differ, Priscilla's air and general expression remind him of "a friend of mine, one of the most gifted women of the age." A woman with a letter clasped to her bosom? Surely this is a veiled reference to Hester Prynne—an old friend of Hawthorne's and one of the most gifted women of any age. When Coverdale goes on to say that Priscilla reminds him of Margaret Fuller, we see that this is more than mild coincidence. The Transcendentalist authoress is being compared to the lady with the scarlet A; but where Hester's letter was "open," Margaret Fuller's is sealed. Whether this is simply Hawthorne's implied criticism of Miss Fuller's feminist activities or whether it is a more pointed comment on her personal life must be left to conjecture. All that he will say is that the comparison is "a singular anomaly of likeness coexisting with perfect dissimilitude."

Less important allegorically but more interesting as a person than Priscilla is Miles Coverdale, the middle-aged bachelor who tells the story in retrospect. He represents Hawthorne's sole full-length effort at rigorously limiting the point of view to a first-person narrator. A minor poet of the Transcendental school, Coverdale is a fictive ancestor of the cynical narrator, Jack Burden, in Robert Penn Warren's *All the King's Men*. A perceptive observer, he functions like Burden as the equivalent of a Greek chorus. It used to be argued that he was not sufficiently dissociated from the author; many of his experiences stem from those Hawthorne recorded in his notebook, and at times the narrator expresses views that we know to be those of his creator. But, as Matthiessen has cautioned in his *American Renaissance*, "We must remember that Coverdale is not Hawthorne any more than Prufrock is Eliot, that in each case the author has exorcized a dangerous part of his experience by treating it with irony." The simplest way to state the relationship is to say that Coverdale is what Hawthorne feared he might have become had he not given himself in love and marriage. But further modifications will have to be made as we examine Coverdale's role more closely.

His name, like the names Westervelt and Zenobia, was not chosen idly. It would be interesting to know Hawthorne's source of information about the sixteenth-century translator of the Bible, Miles Coverdale. It seems to have been fairly common knowledge that Coverdale was "somewhat weak and timorous, and all through his life leaned on a more powerful nature. In the hour of trouble he was content to remain in obscurity and left the crown of martyrdom to be earned by men of tougher stripe." One could hardly ask for a better brief description of Hawthorne's minor poet.

Though Coverdale owes his name to the early sixteenth century, his predicament is eminently modern. Hawthorne himself knew only too well the dangers of retreating from life and the difficulty of opening up an intercourse with the world. In this book he objectified his experience by means of technique; that is, he discovered in the one major hazard of first-person narration a means for dramatizing the plight of his artist. As Percy Lubbock said in his classic study of the subject, when the point of view is limited, "the man or woman who acts as the vessel of sensation is always in danger of seeming a light, uncertain weight compared with the other people in the book—simply because the other people are objective images, plainly outlined, while the seer in the midst is precluded from that advantage,

and must see without being directly seen. He, who doubtless ought to bulk in the story more massively than anyone, tends to remain the least recognizable of the company, and even to dissolve in a kind of impalpable blur." Coverdale ultimately admits that his life is "colorless," that he is but a "dim figure." The subject of *The Blithedale Romance* is thus inseparable from its form: the images of withdrawal and the traits of the narrator coincide with the way the story is told.

Coverdale's great fault, of course, is that he tries to live by proxy. (This may be the relevance of Priscilla's name; in New England's legendary history, the classic attempt to make love by proxy is associated with the names Miles and Priscilla.) He tries to know himself by probing the selves of others, and he accepts nothing on faith. Zenobia emphasizes this failing in her legend of the Veiled Lady. The Theodore of her story, like Coverdale, has "a natural tendency toward scepticism," and he conceals himself behind a screen. He will not take the Veiled Lady on faith; he prefers "to lift the veil first," just as Coverdale does with all his friends.

A bachelor with a taste for wine and a good cigar, Coverdale would be willing to die for a good cause—"provided, however, the effort did not involve an unreasonable amount of trouble. If Kossuth, for example, would pitch the battlefield of Hungarian rights within an easy ride of my abode, and choose a mild, sunny morning, after breakfast, for the conflict, Miles Coverdale would be his man, for one brave rush upon the levelled bayonets." It is not surprising that he finds it relatively easy to see the world through the eyes of the former hedonist, Moodie, and the cynical materialist, Westervelt. Like the painted old man who confronts Gustav von Aschenbach in Thomas Mann's *Death in Venice,* old Moodie is an image of Coverdale's future self. "I tried to identify my mind with the old fellow's," he says, "and take his view of the world, as if looking through a smoke-blackened glass at the sun. It robbed the landscape of all its life. . . . When my eyes are dimmer than they have yet come to be, I will go thither again, and see . . . if the cold and lifeless tint of his perceptions be not then repeated in my own." The colorless Moodie, who lives solely in his daughters, provides the book's most notable example of life by proxy and is thus Hawthorne's most incisive comment on Coverdale's weakness.

We sympathize with Coverdale partly because he resembles the modern intellectual cut off from ancient certitudes, longing to submerge himself in a group yet fearful that in doing so he will lose his individuality. Hollingsworth offers him a chance to submit to authority in an effort to benefit humanity. His appeal is very similar to that of the Communist party when it attracted numerous intellectuals in the nineteen thirties, or to that of the Church in earlier centuries: "It [Hollingsworth's project] offers you (what you have told me, over and over again, that you most need) a purpose in life, worthy of the extremest self-devotion,—worthy of martyrdom, should God so order it! In this view, I present it to you. You can greatly benefit mankind. Your peculiar faculties, as I shall direct them, are capable of being so wrought into this enterprise that not one of them need lie idle." This impulse toward authoritarianism, when coupled with the intimate personal bond between the two men, makes Hollingsworth's proposal almost irresistible. "Be with me . . . or be against me," he says, with the either-or logic of the demagogue. "There is no third choice for you." Despite this pressure, Coverdale retains his integrity; for once he reserves the right to look "through his own optics." But even this, his one great moral triumph, is, typically, an act of rejection.

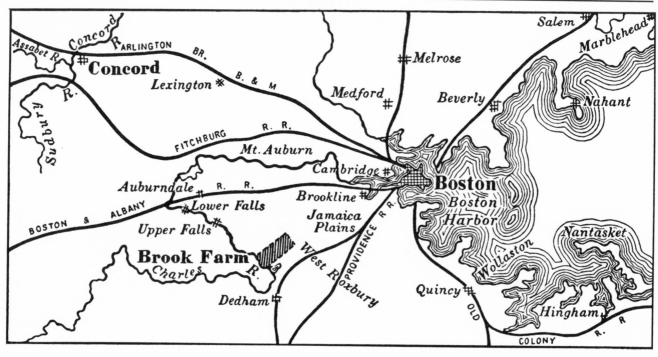

A map of Brook Farm and the surrounding area.

Miles Coverdale ought to be a translator, like his sixteenth-century prototype. But one of the book's recurrent ironies is that during the empty religious experience of this small army of ''saints and martyrs'' no translation—moral or artistic—occurs. Priscilla knits her silk purses, and Silas Foster tends his swine; but she is remarkably inefficient in the farm routine, and he is simply bored with intellectual or artistic endeavors. Thus the book demonstrates the impossibility of making a silk purse out of a sow's ear. Coverdale recognizes that his poetry is thin and bodiless, but he is so exhausted by his raw experience that he is unable to convert it into art. This, we know, was often Hawthorne's view of his own artistic predicament, both in America at the customhouse and later in England at the consulate. But he was never driven to Coverdale's final position of proclaiming an acutely self-conscious art for art's sake. Coverdale has earlier remarked that he cared for Priscilla—not for her realities but for ''the fancy-work with which I have idly decked her out.'' With no vital content in his art, he becomes solipsistically obsessed with its form. Thus at the end of the book he feebly confesses his love for his medium.

Priscilla, as we know, has been wedded to Hollingsworth. He is united with the medium of truth only after he has been educated by Zenobia's death. As Hawthorne put it a few years later, ''Woman must strike through her own heart to reach a human life.'' In *The Scarlet Letter* and *The Marble Faun* this tragic awareness proceeds from a passionate union between man and woman. But in *The Blithedale Romance* there is no redemption through tragedy—only an abortive catastrophe. In their quest for reformation and refinement, the man and woman of the Western world have sacrificed their normal emotions, including sexual passion. Coverdale hints at the sexless outcome of their relationship when he anticipates a ''sufficiently tragic catastrophe, though the dagger and the bowl should go for nothing in it.'' The sexual imagery is fully developed in the gruesome midnight search for Zenobia's body, when Hollingsworth with ''a nervous jerky movement'' begins to plunge

his hooked pole into the blackness and eventually penetrates Zenobia's heart. The implication seems to be that once the normal rhythms of time, the seasons, and love are rejected, they will reassert themselves in ugly distorted forms. Coverdale had earlier remarked that Blithedale ''seemed to authorize any individual, of either sex, to fall in love with any other, regardless of what would elsewhere be judged suitable and prudent.'' What begins as pastoral love play ends in what might almost be called necrophilia.

The Blithedale Romance is thus Hawthorne's most pessimistic book. It is pessimistic precisely because the characters attain no tragic vision. Between the routine, mechanized time of the city clocks and the dynamic, natural seasons lies Blithedale—''an epoch of annihilated space.'' Between ''the conservatives, the writers of *The North American Review,* the merchants, the politicians, the Cambridge men, and all those respectable old blockheads, who still . . . kept a death-grip on one or two ideas which had not come into vogue since yesterday morning'' and the unsubstantial globe of Blithedale lies a vacuum for Coverdale, a dark watery grave for Zenobia, and an eternity of agonizing reappraisal for Hollingsworth. As D. H. Lawrence perceived, Hawthorne knew ''disagreeable things in his inner soul'' [see *NCLC,* Vol. 2]. Many of these things have been rediscovered in this century. But we have produced few novelists who can write of them not only with Hawthorne's unflinching courage but with his warm, deep sympathy. (pp. 146-56)

> Roy R. Male, ''The Pastoral Wasteland: 'The Blithedale Romance','' *in his* Hawthorne's Tragic Vision, *1957. Reprint by W. W. Norton & Company, Inc., 1964, pp. 139-56.*

IRVING HOWE (essay date 1957)

[*A longtime editor of the magazine* Dissent *and a regular contributor to the* New Republic, *Howe is one of America's most highly respected literary critics and social historians. In the following excerpt, Howe explores how* Blithedale *reflects Hawthorne's perception of the relationship between ideology, sexuality, and politics.*]

No portrait of Hawthorne, wrote Henry James, "is at all exact which fails to insist upon the constant struggle which must have gone on between his shyness and his desire to know something of life; between what may be called his evasive and inquisitive tendencies." This remark provides a clue not merely to Hawthorne but to a good many other American writers, including James himself, for it focuses on the dualities of moral attitude and literary approach that cut through so much of our literature. In the work of Hawthorne, and especially in *The Blithedale Romance,* they are particularly severe: his outer moral conventionality (the "blue-eyed Nathaniel") as against his suppressed recalcitrance, which sometimes breaks out as an extreme boldness of moral speech; the frequent Augustan deadness of his prose as against its occasional release into pure and passionate lucidity; the mild and almost somnolent surface of his mind, so utterly unimpressive in its own right, as against the vital emotional strength beneath.

Throughout his life Hawthorne was caught up in what we would now call a crisis of religious belief. His acute moral sense had been largely detached from the traditional context of orthodox faith, but it had found little else in which to thrive, certainly no buoying social vision—which may explain why he turned so often to allegory, the one literary mode in which it might be possible to represent the moral sense as an independent force. Estranged from the dominant progressivist thought of his time, Hawthorne could summon no large enthusiasms nor pledge himself to any social movement; his prevalent temper was skeptical, though a powerful impulse within him worked to assault and deride his skepticism. But what is so curiously "modern" about Hawthorne's crisis of belief is that he seems to have been drawn less to belief itself—he was quite free from the mania for certainty—than to the enlargements of feeling that might come with belief, the passions it might release and regulate. In its assumptions this attitude toward religious belief might almost be called "pragmatic," odd as that word seems in relation to Hawthorne.

As a 19th century American he could not acquiesce in Puritan dogma, but as a man who had neither the enthusiasm nor the fatuousness of Transcendental optimism he could not break free from the Puritan mode of vision. He did not see *what* the Puritans had seen, he saw *as* they had seen. He felt that no matter how questionable the notion of "original sin" might be as doctrine or how distasteful if allowed to become the substance of a practical morality, it nonetheless touched upon a fundamental truth concerning human beings. This truth he reduced from a dogma to an insight, defending it on empirical grounds rather than as revelation.

Similar problems of belief troubled him, though far less acutely, in politics. A democrat by hesitation rather than by conviction, he disliked reformers, distrusted the Abolitionists, and sympathized with that wing of the Democratic Party, a mediocre small-souled wing, which hoped to patch up a truce of expediency with the slave-owning South. In an age blazing with certainty, he had to make his way on doubt. The breakdown of faith in God, human capacity and social progress that would later shake the world, was foreshadowed in his life, and though he seldom made these opinions explicit, they form the buried foundations of his visible work.

Yet one cannot read his novels without seeing that in addition to the skeptic there is a man so eager for experiment in personal life that at times the "inquisitive tendency" becomes sheer hunger. This Hawthorne finds himself drawn, against his will and sometimes without his conscious knowledge, to moral outlaws who dare what he himself never even desired to dare. This Hawthorne yearns for some great liberating transformation which will bring him, for the first time, into full vibrant life. His mind was sluggish, mild, rationalistic; his creative self was passionate, warmly receptive, sometimes even sensual. It would be oversimplifying to see these two strands as always in opposition, for that would have made his life unendurable; but the two strands are there.

The quiet of Hawthorne's life was interrupted by a few adventures, a few raids on experience, of which the most interesting was perhaps his brief participation in Brook Farm, the utopian community of the 1840's. Most of Hawthorne's biographers, refusing to reach beneath the surface of his reminiscence, have assumed that since he did not agree with the ideas of the reformers he entered the Brook Farm community simply to find a way of supporting his future wife. But that hardly seems a sufficient reason, for it is unlikely that so hardheaded a man as Hawthorne would have thought Brook Farm a good financial investment, or would have thought of it primarily as a good investment. More plausible, though admittedly speculative, is the assumption that Hawthorne, apart from motives of convenience and perhaps without fully realizing it himself, was seeking in Brook Farm another kind of investment, an investment in shared life. What may have tempted him was not the ideas of the reformers, but their large enthusiasm, their animating idealism, their implicit faith in the possibility of human communication.

And despite its antipathy to the reformers, despite the tone of aggressive mockery it generally takes toward them, *The Blithedale Romance* makes it abundantly clear that Brook Farm had struck deeply and forever into Hawthorne's consciousness. In his own secretive way he had come up against many of the problems that would dominate the 20th century novel: the relation between ideology and utopia, the meeting between politics and sex.

The dualism that controls almost everything in *The Blithedale Romance* is that between subject and object, narrator and event. At the several points where the novel breaks down, the trouble is not merely one of literary structure, it also involves a radical uncertainty as to the possibilities of knowledge. Everything is seen through the eyes of Coverdale, a timid "minor poet" recalling his stay at Blithedale, the utopian community modelled after Brook Farm; and so methodical is the evasiveness and mystification with which he presents the action that one begins to suspect the book is hampered less by literary clumsiness than by some psychological block of which he is merely the symptom.

Coverdale is a self-portrait of Hawthorne, but a highly distorted and mocking self-portrait, as if Hawthorne were trying to isolate and thereby exorcise everything within him that impedes full participation in life. The tendency to withdrawal that is so noticeable in Coverdale represents not merely a New Englander's fear of involvement in the dangers of society; it is also a moony narcissism by means of which an habitual observer, unable to validate his sense of the external world, tries magically to deny its reality. This symbolic annihilation of whatever resists control of the will reaches its climax when Hawthorne destroys, physically and psychologically, the two main characters who threaten Coverdale, though nothing in the logic of the plot requires so violent or extreme a conclusion.

As against the ineffectual Coverdale—who, by the way, lacks neither intelligence nor shrewdness—Hawthorne sets up several centers of anxiety. Blithedale itself, a place of idealism and effort; Zenobia, a sexually magnificent and intellectually daring woman who is shown as the central figure of the community; Hollingsworth, a reformer who has come to Blithedale to "bore from within" in behalf of a monomaniacal scheme for salvaging convicts; and finally Priscilla, a sweet priss of a girl who represents the feminine principle in its most conservative aspect (that which makes the family go round)—all these challenge Coverdale, for all tempt him to break out of the circle of selfhood. His problem then becomes, how can he drain off some of their energy and power without himself taking the risks of commitment? Emotional parasitism is an obvious course, but with obvious limitations; in the end Hawthorne simply "rescues" Coverdale by suppressing the conflicts that threaten to liberate him—and thereby, it might be added, destroying the novel.

Coverdale's relation to the utopian community is one of the first but still among the best treatments in American writing of what happens when a hesitant intellectual attaches himself to a political enterprise. Looking back from his withered bachelorhood Coverdale is proud that at least once in his life he dared to plunge: "Whatever else I repent of, let it be reckoned neither among my sins nor my follies that I once had force and faith enough to form generous hopes of the world's destiny. . . ." And throughout the book Hawthorne retains a qualified affection for that side of New England utopianism which would later prompt Parrington to speak of Brook Farm as "a social poem fashioned out of Yankee homespun."

When Coverdale finally leaves Blithedale, he does so from a feeling—it will reappear in many American novels—that he is inadequate to public life, incapable of the monolithic enthusiasms a utopian politics demands. ("The greatest obstacle to being heroic," he shrewdly notes, "is the doubt whether one may not be going to prove one's self a fool.") Partly, too, he "sees through" the utopian impulse, discovering what would hardly surprise or shock a more realistic and experienced man: that behind its ideal claims it often shelters personal inadequacy and ideological fanaticism. And finally he grows weary of that constant depreciation of the present in the name of an ideal future which seems so necessary to utopian radicalism: "I was beginning to lose the sense of what kind of world it was, among innumerable schemes of what it might or ought to be."

Yet all of this, though pointed enough, is not very far from the usual criticism of utopian politics or, for that matter, from the usual attack upon 19th century ideas of progress; and what really distinguishes *The Blithedale Romance* is another kind of criticism, double-edged, subtle and generally unnoticed. Hawthorne saw that, motives apart, the formation of isolated utopian communities is seldom a threat to society; he understood that no matter how pure its inner moral aspirations might be, the utopian community could not avoid functioning as part of the materialistic world it detested.

> I very soon became sensible [says Coverdale] that, as regarded society at large, we stood in a position of new hostility, rather than new brotherhood . . . Constituting so pitiful a minority as now, we were inevitably estranged from the rest of mankind in pretty fair propor-

tion with the strictness of our mutual bond among ourselves.

And at another point:

> The peril of our new way of life was not lest we should fail to become practical agriculturists, but that we should probably cease to be anything else.

It is interesting, and a little amusing, to note how closely these caustic observations approach the Marxist criticism of utopian communities. For if Hawthorne's sentences are transposed into economic terms, what he is saying is that by virtue of being subject to the demands and pressures of the market, the utopian community becomes a competitive unit in a competitive society ("we stood in a position of new hostility") and must therefore be infected with its mores. The utopian who would cut himself off from the ugly world must, to preserve his utopia, become a "practical agriculturist"—which means to model his utopia upon the society he rejects.

This criticism, which strikes so hard a blow at the political fancies of many 19th century American intellectuals, is advanced by Hawthorne with a cruel and almost joyous insistence, but that does not make it any the less true. Hawthorne, of course, was as far from the Marxist imagination as anyone could be, but almost any criticism of utopian politics from a point of view committed to struggle within the world would have to render a similar judgment.

If Hawthorne criticizes the utopian impulse on the ground that it does not really succeed in avoiding the evil of the great world, he also implies that another trouble with utopianism is that it does not bring its followers into a sufficiently close relation with the evil of the great world. And in the context of the novel these two ideas are not as incompatible as they might seem.

For the whole utopian venture at Blithedale, with its effort to transform the impulse of political idealism into a pastoral retreat, bears a thoroughly innocent air. It is an innocence peculiar to many 19th century American intellectuals, who believed that politics, when it was not simply a vulgarity to be avoided, could be engaged in by proclaiming a series of moral precepts. (Though Emerson shied away from the utopian communities, they were actually founded on his principle that individual regeneration must precede social politics—the only difference being that in the utopian communities a number of individuals came together to seek their regeneration in common.) This innocence—or perhaps one should speak of a willed search for innocence—was of course related to the hopelessly crude and corrupt nature of our "ordinary" national politics, and it showed itself in no more endearing form than its assumption that "ordinary" politics could be gotten away from, or supplanted, by the politics of pastoral retreat. America itself having in some sense gone astray, utopianism would remake it in the small.

The characters in *The Blithedale Romance,* even those who are meant as figures of worldliness, also partake of this New England innocence. For while Zenobia and Hollingsworth, the one a radical in behavior and the other a radical in ideology, are treated as figures of enviable passion and experience, there is a tacit recognition throughout the book that it is only by Coverdale's standards that they can seem so rich in passion and experience. Hollingsworth, writes Hawthorne, "ought to have commenced his investigation of [the reform of criminals] by perpetrating some huge sin in his proper person, and examining the conditions of his conscience afterwards.'' To be sure, this trenchant observation is put into the mouth of Coverdale, who is frequently envious of Hollingsworth's political passion; but there is surely nothing unfamiliar, or at odds with our sense of psychological realism, in Coverdale's need to depreciate that which he most admires. It is as if Hawthorne, soon to punish Zenobia and Hollingsworth for their putative boldness, can accept his desire to punish them only through a half-suppressed feeling that, in reality, they are not bold enough.

The uneasy mixture of skepticism and yearning that complicates Hawthorne's treatment of the utopian community can also be seen in his approach to Zenobia and Hollingsworth as individuals. Zenobia rules the book. ''Passionate, luxurious, lacking simplicity, not deeply refined,'' she is the frankest embodiment of sensuality in Hawthorne's work. Except for Hollingsworth, whose appetite runs to political notions rather than human flesh, everyone in the book is drawn to her. For she alone is really alive, she alone is open in her sexuality. As if to cover up the freedom of his characterization, Hawthorne also endows her with a somewhat operatic manner, but this does not seriously detract from Zenobia's power and when one remembers how difficult and damaging the role of feminine reformer must have been in 19th century New England it even has a certain appropriateness. Throughout the book Zenobia is celebrated in rhapsodic outbursts:

> Zenobia had a rich, though varying color. It was, most of the while, a flame, and anon a sudden paleness. Her eyes glowed.... Her gestures were free, and strikingly impressive. The whole woman was alive with a passionate intensity, which I now perceived to be the phase in which her beauty culminated. Any passion would have become her well; and passionate love, perhaps, the best of all.

In her opulent, inaccessible sexuality Zenobia becomes a kind of New England earth goddess—though, given Hawthorne's estimate of New England women, a very intellectual goddess too. Both ways, she is the name of his desire.

Hawthorne quickly penetrates to the source and nature of Zenobia's sexuality; he relates it, both in its power and its limitations, to her political boldness. He understands that in her person is realized the threat to traditional modes of life which the others merely talk about. And he sees how, in turn, her political boldness contributes to and sanctions her personal freedom:

> She made no scruple of over-setting all human institutions, and scattering them as with a breeze from her fan. A female reformer, in her attacks upon society, has an instinctive sense of where the life lies, and is inclined to aim directly at that spot. Especially the relation between the sexes is naturally among the earliest to attract her attention.

This powerful insight Hawthorne puts to two uses, making Zenobia into a vibrant woman who challenges established social norms but also showing how this very challenge twists and depletes her life. For as Zenobia ruefully admits, ''the whole universe, her own sex and yours, and Providence, and Destiny, to boot, make common cause against the woman who swerves one hair's-breadth out of the beaten track.''

But if Zenobia's intellectual and political audacity makes possible a new kind of personal freedom, it also involves the danger of a confusion of sexual roles. Zenobia's unconventionality as a woman allows her a certain masculine energy and arrogance, and while this brings her public satisfactions it also prevents her from winning Hollingsworth's love; for he is one of those reformers who prefers that his own wife be tame and submissive. In a brilliant little passage Hawthorne hints at the tragicomic difficulties of Zenobia's position. Asked at the beginning of the book whether she knows Hollingsworth, Zenobia replies, ''No, only as an auditor—auditress, I mean—of some of his lectures.''

Can Zenobia, however, be both the personification of forbidden sexuality and a woman capable of so revealing a slip as the one I have just quoted? Is Hawthorne ''cheating'' when he portrays Zenobia as a richly feminine figure yet particularly open to the dangers of subverting the feminine role?

Whatever the difficulty may be with Zenobia, it is not in Hawthorne's initial conception of her, which is marvellously deep and subtle; in fact, it is one of his major intuitive strokes that he notices how the political atmosphere which encourages a freer sexuality also threatens the feminine role. The trouble lies in Hawthorne's presentation, his unwillingness or incapacity to live up to the promise of his opening pages. For, like everything else in the book, Zenobia comes through only in flickers; we do not see her in a developed action that would call upon the intelligence she undoubtedly has; the speculative insights into the relation between her public and private selves appear mainly as occasional remarks that do not affect the bulk of the novel. Either because he draws back from his subject, fearful of his own boldness, or because he could not work up an action by which to sustain his subject, Hawthorne does not show us Zenobia in the motions and gestures of life. And that, of course, is one reason he can imply that she is not so thoroughly a figure of passion and experience as Coverdale supposes. The more she is to be shown as a temptress, the more must her temptations be called into question.

What is true for Zenobia as a projection of desire is truer still for Hollingsworth as a warning against the dangers of ideology. A number of recent critics have praised Hawthorne's presentation of Hollingsworth as a prophetic anticipation of the reformer who is cold to everything but his own scheme. Were Hollingsworth ''there,'' were he endowed with a certain contingency and thickness and color of presentation, this point might well be true. For it is clearly Hawthorne's intention to show in Hollingsworth the utopian impulse as it has hardened into an inhumane ideology. But in the novel as Hawthorne wrote it, Hollingsworth is a dismal failure. He never *does* anything, he seldom displays any emotional fluidity or complexity, he is rarely given one of those saving human touches which, by their very presence, would make more credible his essential inhumanity.

There are, of course, a few passages in which Hawthorne breathes a little life into him—as when Hollingsworth, with that single-minded sincerity which is a form of blindness, asks Coverdale, ''How can you be my life-long friend, except you strive with me toward the great object of my life?'' or when Zenobia bursts out that Hollingsworth's political dedication ''is all self!... Nothing else; nothing but self, self, self!''

Such passages, however, do little but suggest how great was Hawthorne's opportunity and how seldom he seized it, for Hollingsworth conforms so neatly to Hawthorne's skepticism concerning reformers that he cannot have much reality of his own. Nothing is granted any scope in the book that would allow Hollingsworth to resist or complicate the point he is meant to illustrate. Presumably a warning against the terrible consequences of a fanatic ideology, he is seldom allowed any vitality as a character because Hawthorne's sense of him is itself so thoroughly ideological. What Hawthorne had wished to warn against in his portrait of Hollingsworth becomes a crucial deficiency of the portrait itself.

Any critic who cares enough to write about *The Blithedale Romance* runs the risk of suggesting that it is a better book than it actually is, for its themes would appear so close to our current preoccupations that they need merely be stated in order to arouse interest. And with a novel so abundant in potentiality and so limited in realization there is the further danger of writing about the book it might have been—a very great book, indeed!—rather than the one it is. Yet by any serious reckoning *The Blithedale Romance* must be called a remarkable failure of a very remarkable writer.

One way of testing this judgment is to consider how difficult it is to specify the novel's controlling significance. It is possible to trace the assumptions behind Hawthorne's treatment of utopian radicalism; to observe the partial success with which he has drawn figures appropriate to the utopian community and has noticed the relationship between politics and sex, ideology and utopia as they take shape in such an environment. But none of this is yet to see the book as a coherent work of art, a disciplined whole that is informed by a serious moral interest—and that, I think, is precisely what cannot be done.

One can, to be sure, offer a number of generalized thematic statements. But it is not possible closely to relate Hawthorne's serious thematic intentions with most of the happenings in the book, which consist of mistaken identities belatedly discovered, secret marriages long repented of, spiritual exercises and hypnotic experiments, melodramatic suicides and Gothic flim-flam. Between the serious matter, confined mostly to the first fifty pages, and a tedious gim-crack plot there is seldom any vital relation.

How then are we to account for this radical incoherence?

In a recent essay on Hawthorne, Philip Rahv has written that "the emotional economy" of *The Blithedale Romance* "is throughout one of displacement . . . the only genuine relationship is that of Coverdale to Zenobia: the rest is mystification. But the whole point of Coverdale's behavior is to avoid involvement" [see Additional Bibliography]. The remark is keen, though I would qualify it by adding that there does seem to be one other relationship which for Coverdale has elements of risk and involvement: his aborted discipleship to Hollingsworth. He draws back from Zenobia's personal freedom, he draws back from Hollingsworth's political commitment, and in both cases he finds reasons, often good enough in their own right, with which to rationalize his timidity. Zenobia and Hollingsworth together stand for "the world," the dangerous beckoning world of experience and liberation. To cheat Coverdale of these temptations, Hawthorne must end the novel by drowning Zenobia and breaking Hollingsworth's spirit.

And yet . . . one feels drawn to the book, to its sudden sparks of perception, its underground passions. Henry James saw enough possibilities in its subject to base one of his major novels upon it: *The Bostonians*, in many ways, is the masterpiece that Hawthorne's book might have been. But even James did not exhaust its possibilities, and if ever a novel is written that dives beneath

the surface of political life in 20th century America its author may find a storehouse of hidden reserves in Hawthorne's great failure *The Blithedale Romance*. (pp. 163-75)

Irving Howe, "Some American Novelists: The Politics of Isolation," in his Politics and the Novel, *Horizon Press, 1957, pp. 159-202.*

A. N. KAUL   (essay date 1963)

[*Kaul suggests that* Blithedale *is to some extent an attempt by Hawthorne to come to terms with the Puritan tradition of his ancestors. In Kaul's words, the subject of the novel was for Hawthorne "an embodiment of the archetypal American experience: withdrawal from a corrupt society to form a regenerate community."*]

In *The Scarlet Letter* Hawthorne had noted the utopian aspect of the Puritan migration to New England. In *The Blithedale Romance* he presents the utopian experiment of Brook Farm as an extension of the Puritan tradition. The backward glance of comparison runs like a rich thread through the pattern of the latter novel, making explicit the significance which the American romancer saw in this otherwise quixotic enterprise.

The day on which the visionaries assemble at Blithedale—to begin "the life of Paradise anew"—is bleaker and less encouraging than the day of the Pilgrims' landing as described by William Bradford. How conscious Hawthorne's narrator is of the suggested parallel we notice when, seated by the blazing hearth of the farmhouse at the end of the tempestuous journey, he reflects that "the old Pilgrims might have swung their kettle over precisely such a fire as this" and that, though Blithedale was hardly a day's walk from the old city, "we had transported ourselves a world-wide distance from the system of society that shackled us at breakfast-time." The Blithedalers are careful to distinguish the moral idealism of their motivation from the guiding principles of other contemporary communitarians. When Miles Coverdale reads the works of Fourier during his convalescence, he concludes that the world was mistaken in equating Blithedale with Fourierism "inasmuch as the two theories differed, as widely as the zenith from the nadir, in their main principles." Hollingsworth, to whom Coverdale puts the case, dismisses the Frenchman in an impassioned speech which is a curious amalgam of Hawthorne and the elder James. Fourier, Hollingsworth declares,

> has committed the unpardonable sin; for what more monstrous iniquity could the Devil himself contrive than to choose the selfish principle,—the principle of all human wrong, the very blackness of man's heart, the portion of ourselves which we shudder at, and which it is the whole aim of spiritual discipline to eradicate,—to choose it as the master-workman of his system? To seize upon and foster whatever vile, petty, sordid, filthy, bestial, and abominable corruptions have cankered into our nature, to be the efficient instruments of his infernal regeneration!

Since "the selfish principle" at the base of organized society is also the chief reason for the Blithedalers' withdrawal from it, in denouncing Fourier, Hollingsworth is stating by implication their own different purpose. The irony here, however, lies in the fact—which will be noted more fully later—that this criticism of Fourier remains the ultimate comment on Hollingsworth himself. The true importance of the Blithedale experiment, as Hawthorne presents it, is that it embodies the visionary hope for mankind which was coeval with the American settlement itself. Miles Coverdale puts the claim for it explicitly when he opens a later chapter, "Eliot's Pulpit," by saying: "Our Sundays at Blithedale were not ordinarily kept with such rigid observance as might have befitted the descendants of the Pilgrims, whose high enterprise, as we sometimes flattered ourselves, we had taken up, and were carrying it onward and aloft, to a point which they never dreamed of attaining."

In many ways Hawthorne was, as Mrs. Q. D. Leavis says, the unwilling heir of the Puritans. But this is far from being true with regard to the tradition of idealism which was a part of his inheritance. On the contrary, he affirmed it in the only serious way in which an artist can affirm tradition: by becoming its critic. It must be said in passing that as far as the actual experiment of Brook Farm is concerned, Hawthorne's motives in joining it were as mixed as those of his ancestors in coming to America. On the one hand, there was the practical expectation of a comfortable livelihood for himself and Sophia. On the other, there was a good deal of simple faith in the theory behind the venture—enough faith, at any rate, to induce him to stake a thousand dollars from his meager resources on its success. Brook Farm, as he says in the preface to the novel, was "essentially a day-dream, and yet a fact" [see excerpt dated 1852], and indeed, in the curious episode of his association with it, one finds it difficult to separate the hard-headed Yankee from the wild-eyed dreamer. Perhaps, like Coverdale, he hoped that in the long run "between theory and practice, a true and available mode of life might be struck out."

However, be his personal motivation what it may, the important thing to realize is that Brook Farm presented Hawthorne with an appropriate subject for his theme. In **"Earth's Holocaust,"** the fantasy which describes an attempted regeneration, he had observed that it mattered little whether the attempt was made in the time past or time to come. The contours of the action were indeed hidden in the whole history of America. *The Scarlet Letter* had dealt with it at its very source in the seventeenth century. In *Blithedale* Hawthorne brought the action up to date. Here again was an embodiment of the archetypal American experience: withdrawal from a corrupt society to form a regenerate community. The basis for regeneration had of course shifted from theological to economic theory; social morality was no longer embedded in metaphysics. In this sense Hawthorne was marking realistically enough the shift in tradition that had occurred over the centuries. . . . [Although] in America, unlike Europe, the communitarian tradition developed in unbroken continuity from its chiliastic source in the seventeenth century, the experimenters of the nineteenth century were communitarians first and sectarians only in the second place—or not at all. Moreover, it was no longer confined to alien groups. Ripley's community was both native in composition and secular in purpose.

It is to emphasize the action of withdrawal and to underline the exercise of that radical choice which America was supposed to have made permanently available to mankind that the novel opens in society, with Coverdale about to take the plunge which he later compares to the Pilgrims' worldwide leap across the Atlantic. In the temporary movement of the story back to society, which occurs in the middle of the novel, we get some richly evoked scenes of Boston life. This is the most detailed body of social description in Hawthorne, and it comes very close to the best manner of European fiction. Hawthorne is not, however, a "social" novelist, and this presentation is the background rather than the milieu of the action, which explores not a social problem but the possibility of repudiating organized society in its entirety. The subject is not Boston life but rather the drama of Boston and Blithedale, or the American dialectic between actual society and ideal community. The theme is not reform but social regeneration.

While the Blithedalean visionaries acknowledge their kinship with the American Puritans of the seventeenth century, their own enterprise arises primarily from a repugnance to the principle of economic individualism, from the fact that society has come to be organized exclusively on the basis of the force which had caused the failure of Bradford's communitarian experiment but which Bradford had accepted as an inevitable factor of God's dispensation for the New World. Of course the Blithedale community has other avowed objectives, like the belief in agriculture as the true foundation of the good life. This, however, constitutes the ridiculous part of their venture, and is treated uniformly as such by Hawthorne. It is indeed the chief target of the mild but persistent comedy in which Silas Foster, together with the pigs and the manure dump, serves to point out the reality behind the masquerade, while Miles Coverdale, like Shakespeare's Touchstone, performs the function of more articulate comic exposure. Hawthorne, as much as Melville, faced but overcame the nineteenth-century temptation toward the Arcadian relapse. It is true that outdoor life helps both Priscilla and Coverdale to add sunburn to their cheeks. But, as Coverdale observes:

> The peril of our new way of life was not lest we should fail in becoming practical agriculturists, but that we should probably cease to be anything else. . . . The clods of earth, which we so constantly belabored and turned over and over, were never etherealized into thought. Our thoughts, on the contrary, were fast becoming cloddish. Our labor symbolized nothing, and left us mentally sluggish in the dusk of the evening. Intellectual activity is incompatible with any large amount of bodily exercise. The yeoman and the scholar—the yeoman and the man of finest moral culture, though not the man of sturdiest sense and integrity—are two distinct individuals, and can never be melted or welded into one substance.

Hawthorne is exposing here again the fallacy of the virgin scene: the assumption that a new and regenerated life demands the total repudiation of man's accumulated moral and material achievement, and that, as soon as the heritage of the past is abandoned, regeneration begins of its own accord. In a later chapter, while describing the exciting bustle of city life, Coverdale goes on to say how all this "was just as valuable, in its way, as the sighing of the breeze among the birch-trees that overshadowed Eliot's pulpit." When in the same chapter he observes a scene of simple domestic affection, being fresh from the discords he has witnessed at Blithedale, he reflects that he had not "seen a prettier bit of nature" during his summer in the country than the actors in that scene had shown him here "in a rather stylish boarding-house."

One should be careful, however, not to divert the ridicule that Hawthorne reserves for the Arcadia to other aspects of the community idea. As a matter of fact, though he presents Blithedale in its single corporate image, he clearly distinguishes between the different values involved in its broad spectrum. For instance, he does not debunk the issue of the equality of the sexes as he does the cult of agriculture. His attitude toward it is ambiguous in the sense that he accords to it the dignity of a serious though not one-sided argument. It is true that even the ardent feminist Zenobia gives in to Hollingsworth's view that should women ever dream of straying from their natural subservience to man, the male sex must "use its physical force, that unmistakable evidence of sovereignty, to scourge them back within their proper bounds!" But as Coverdale reflects a moment later, is such submission to male egotism a token of woman's true nature or is it "the result of ages of compelled degradation?" Together with this goes the further reflection that "women, however intellectually superior, so seldom disquiet themselves about the rights or wrongs of their sex, unless their own individual affections chance to lie in idleness, or to be ill at ease." Thus, while Zenobia's side of the case is presented as unquestionably superior to Hollingsworth's Nietzschean bombast, the whole issue of feminist reform is seen as a secondary question—an unfortunate consequence of the general distortion of human relations in society. With regard to the primary cause of such dislocations—which is indeed the cause of the Blithedalean withdrawal—Hawthorne leaves us in no doubt. Early in the novel, while commenting on the first day's assembly at Blithedale, Coverdale observes:

> If ever men might lawfully dream awake, and give utterance to their wildest visions without dread of laughter or scorn on the part of the audience,—yes, and speak of earthly happiness, for themselves and mankind, as an object to be hopefully striven for, and probably attained,—we who made that little semicircle round the blazing fire were those very men. We had left the rusty iron framework of society behind us; we had broken through many hindrances that are powerful enough to keep most people on the weary tread-mill of the established system, even while they feel its irksomeness almost as intolerable as we did. We had stepped down from the pulpit; we had flung aside the pen; we had shut up the ledger . . . It was our purpose . . . [to show] mankind the example of a life governed by other than the false and cruel principles on which human society has all along been based.

> And, first of all, we had divorced ourselves from pride, and were striving to supply its place with familiar love. . . . We sought our profit by mutual aid, instead of wresting it by the strong hand from an enemy, or filching it craftily from those less shrewd than ourselves (if, indeed, there were any such in New England), or winning it by selfish competition with a neighbor; in one or another of which fashions every son of woman both perpetrates and suffers his share of the common evil, whether he chooses it or no.

Whatever one may say of Blithedale and its members as things eventually turn out, there is no question about the force with which the vision of an ideal community is presented here. Nor is there any ambiguity about the distribution of sympathies as between the values avowed by Coverdale and those which govern the "iron framework of society." The visionaries stand—in theory at least—upon the principle of human brotherhood as against the predatory competitiveness of the established system. Blithedale itself, as we shall see, is finally judged in terms of its own professed values and not by the standards and norms of society. It is only when, and insofar as, the visionaries themselves turn out to be men of iron masquerading in Arcadian costume, that Blithedale is dismissed as a humbug—as false as society but more hypocritical. But this process of criticism—of exposing the same basic drives twice over and of showing the corrupted rebel as more reprehensible than the original villain—does not lead to a reversal of values involved in the challenge. It makes for a more clear-sighted affirmation. Nor does the novelist, as distinct from the characters who are all more or less ironically presented, abandon his position with regard to "the common evil" of exploitative individualism which every person in society either suffers from or perpetrates. Hawthorne's attitude, it must be said, does not involve the repudiation of individual freedom and choice. On the contrary, like the elder James, he insists on the primacy of the moral person in all social arrangements. But the individualism he champions is not incompatible with, but rather tends toward and finds its richest fulfillment in, the human community.

Since the story is mainly concerned with the fortunes of the Blithedale community, the image of the surrounding society occupies of necessity a marginal position. Yet this is strictly true only in a physical sense. In reality, the main characters of the story, who are all communitarians, carry with themselves, more or less visibly, the outwardly repudiated social values and attitudes—like old earth clinging to tufts of transplanted grass. It is this fact which makes *Blithedale* an exploration of the dialectical rather than simply the oppositional relation between actual society and the aspiration toward a better community life. But, apart from this, one of the most remarkable feats of the novel is the manner in which the two peripheral characters—old Moodie and Westervelt—are made to suggest concretely certain sinister forces working in the depths of the social world. Although one would at first sight suppose them to belong wholly to the machinery of romance, even their connection with the central theme of *Blithedale* is close enough for one to conclude that Hawthorne's apologia in the preface with regard to the introduction of the communitarian experiment into the romance [see excerpt dated 1852] should be treated in the same light as Mark Twain's celebrated warning against finding a moral in *Huckleberry Finn*. Where Hawthorne maintains cautiously that the whole treatment of Brook Farm is "altogether incidental to the main purpose of the romance," one feels the whole romance is in reality a characteristically modulated projection of the main society-community theme.

In *The Seven Gables* Hawthorne had observed that in nineteenth-century America, "amid the fluctuating waves of our social life, somebody is always at the drowning-point." This process and the consequent sense of insecurity are exemplified in *Blithedale*—more starkly and less sentimentally than in the case of Hepzibah Pyncheon—by old Moodie: the grandee of yesterday become the pauper of today; Fauntleroy turned into "a gray kennel-rat." This is a motif which recurs in a good deal of later American fiction, the career of George Hurstwood in *Sister Carrie* being a case which readily comes to mind. Hawthorne's method, however, is one of poetic, or "romantic," evocation rather than the "realistic" accumulation of minute detail, and his purpose is not so much to show the impassable gulf between classes as to point out the morally untenable nature of those distinctions which separate man from man in society. It is only in this sense that the fact of the relation between Zenobia and Priscilla becomes more meaningful than a mere contrivance of romantic plotting, for the sisterhood that is avowed at Blithedale but denied in society is not a playful masquerade as Zenobia seems to think; it is a reflection of the true nature of things.

In Westervelt, who is also connected with Zenobia and Priscilla, the projected force is one of secret power. The relation between him and the poor seamstress Priscilla is not unlike that between Ethan Brand and Esther, and mesmerism is to that extent presented as a peculiarly sinister variation of exploitative science. It makes "a delusive show of spirituality" but is "really imbued throughout with a cold and dead materialism." Westervelt represents in this sense the final degradation of the Puritan tradition. However, just as Hawthorne had explored the social implications of Puritan theology, he uses here the new psychic phenomenon to embody a sociological insight. These subtle transferences and suggested correlations are characteristic of Hawthorne's complex fictional method. Westervelt is in many ways the polished gentleman, a representative of the social type in which Coverdale sees a partial reflection of his own pre-Blithedale existence. But he is also a wizard the gold band around whose false teeth reveals him somehow as a "moral and physical humbug." Yet his power, though exerted invisibly, is real enough. In its remote control it suggests the exploitative power which technology was putting into the hands of men: the power to bring individuals into total bondage while leaving them outwardly free and untouched. Westervelt's human shape is thus "a necromantic, or perhaps a mechanical contrivance, in which a demon walked about." He, too, affirms faith in a golden future and speaks publicly of the dawning era "that would link soul to soul" in "mutually conscious brotherhood," but he speaks of it "as if it were a matter of chemical discovery." As against the brotherhood of voluntary love, which is based upon the magnetic chain of human sympathy, Westervelt's mesmeric union is enforced bondage, destructive of true individuality as well as true community.

The brotherhood of love and mutual sympathy, which is lacking or perverted in an individualist social system, is precisely what the Blithedale community has taken for the foundation of its life. It is likewise the basis of Hawthorne's criticism of Blithedale itself. What the novel finally calls in doubt is not the values avowed by the visionaries but their means, materials, and ultimately the depth and sincerity of their professions. Zenobia is a dilettante who, until she meets Hollingsworth, expects from Blithedale nothing worse than a naughty frolic and hardly anything better than a pleasant interlude in rusticity. She takes the experiment as a stage set for an unaccustomed personal role, and a curious theatricality accompanies her doings at Blithedale right up to the manner of her suicide. Coverdale is at heart a well-meaning sybarite who has joined the community out of boredom with an aimless life, although the sense of direction and purpose he develops while there is a different matter. He and Zenobia share between themselves the accusation that the Veiled Lady levels at Theodore in Zenobia's own legend: "Dost thou come hither, not in holy faith, nor with a pure and generous purpose, but in scornful scepticism and idle curiosity?" For his detachment and lack of faith Coverdale indeed suffers the same fate as Theodore does for not saving from her bondage the girl he eventually loves: he relapses into a purposeless life haunted by his lost dream. Zenobia pays for her scorn and impure motives by a gruesome death.

The one person at Blithedale who lacks neither faith nor energy is Hollingsworth. But his faith is not the faith in a regenerate community, and his energy, like that of the Puritan magistrates with whom he is explicitly compared, drives him into a moral blindness of unique opacity. Unlike the dilettantish triflers, he is in deadly earnest, and he is a true builder rather than a dreamer of schemes. What he seeks to build, however, is not a regenerate community but an enduring edifice for the treatment of criminals. His monomaniacal preoccupation with crime is the nineteenth-century equivalent of the Puritan absorption with sin. If Coverdale testifies to the ineffectuality of nineteenth-century American idealism, Hollingsworth remains a permanently frightening symbol of what happens to a visionary scheme when it is geared to an individual's ruthless egotism and overwhelming energy. As Hawthorne insists in several places, Hollingsworth's plan of criminal reform was motivated by an initially noble impulse. But he has fallen into the reformer's occupational disease of monomania—a danger which Emerson noted in "New England Reformers": "Do not be so vain of your one objection. Do you think there is only one? Alas! my good friend, there is no part of society or of life better than any other part." Hawthorne, a true visionary of the hopeful American years, had the same objection to reformist zeal; and Hollingsworth's scheme becomes truly criminal when, in pursuit of its success, he subverts the nobler purpose of total regeneration embodied in the Blithedale community, destroying in the process also the faith and happiness of its other members. The key chapter for understanding the developments which lead eventually to the failure of the community, is the one appropriately entitled "A Crisis." It is here that Hollingsworth repudiates the communitarian idea, and we realize how he has used the experiment as a covert base for his own operations. He has made arrangements with Zenobia, on morally dubious grounds, for the financial support of his reformist enterprise. Nor is he prepared to accept Coverdale's suggestion that he reveal his design to the other members of the community. On the contrary, he invites Coverdale, too, to become his collaborator and join in the subversion of the Blithedale experiment. "And have you no regrets," Coverdale inquires,

> in overthrowing this fair system of our new life, which has been planned so deeply, and is now beginning to flourish so hopefully around us? How beautiful it is, and, so far as we can yet see, how practicable! The ages have waited for us, and here we are, the very first that have essayed to carry on our mortal existence in love and mutual help! Hollingsworth, I would be loath to take the ruin of this enterprise upon my conscience.

To which the indomitable man replies: "Then let it rest wholly upon mine!" When Coverdale refuses to join him finally, rather than tolerate a friend who does not share his own fanatical purpose Hollingsworth repudiates the bond of personal friendship too.

This man of iron thus possesses all those attributes that Hawthorne had enumerated in *The Seven Gables* as constituting the essential moral continuity between the Puritan of the seventeenth century and his descendant of the nineteenth. Like the members of that persistent clan, he is brutal in personal relations and dishonest in public ones, "laying his purposes deep, and following them out with an inveteracy of pursuit that knew neither rest nor conscience; trampling on the weak, and, when essential to his ends, doing his utmost to beat down the strong." His altruistic professions notwithstanding, Hollingsworth reveals in himself finally the same egotism, selfish principle, or

The costume worn by women at Brook Farm from 1841 to 1847.

ruthless individualism which the Blithedalean visionaries identified as the "common evil" of the established system. In *The Seven Gables* Hawthorne had said that the truth about a public man is often best discovered in a woman's view of him, and in *Blithedale* it is indeed a disillusioned Zenobia who gives utterance to the moral obliquity of Hollingsworth's character. "It is all self!" she declares in one of the climaxial scenes of the novel. "Nothing else; nothing but self, self, self! The fiend, I doubt not, has made his choicest mirth of you these seven years past, and especially in the mad summer which we have spent together. I see it now! I am awake, disenchanted, disinthralled! Self, self, self!"

Thus at Blithedale, too, instead of brotherhood there is selfhood, instead of faith there is skepticism, and instead of love there is fresh antagonism. It is not that, as Coverdale puts it, the Blithedaleans stand in a position of "new hostility, rather than new brotherhood" with regard to the society at large; because, as Coverdale himself adds, this could not fail to be the case so long as they were in "so pitiful a minority." Their estrangement from society is inevitable in "proportion with the strictness of our mutual bond among ourselves." The criticism of the Blithedale community therefore lies not in its hostile relation to the surrounding social system but rather in the absence of the promised bond within itself and in the divergence between its theory of mutual sympathy on the one

hand and its reality of fresh antagonisms and mutual suspicions on the other. When Coverdale returns to Blithedale toward the end of the novel it has become a grim battlefield, with Hollingsworth resembling a Puritan magistrate holding an inquest of life and death in a case of witchcraft. The succeeding scenes enact Zenobia's tragedy, which, as Mark Van Doren says, is trash [see excerpt dated 1949]. But it seems to me that Van Doren misses the whole force of this calculated vulgarity, for the point is precisely that the community, built on a premise of high idealism, should resolve itself finally into the same old story of love, jealousy, and sensational suicide. Zenobia's fate only illustrates the true tragedy of Blithedale.

The great test of the experiment's human worth is of course Priscilla. It is not for nothing that Coverdale is made to put the question of Blithedale's success or failure to her avatar as the Veiled Lady in the opening chapter. Unless the visionaries can save this daughter of poverty from her bondage, their enterprise will be a mockery of their principles. It is, indeed, Hollingsworth who declares: "As we do by this friendless girl, so shall we prosper." After vanishing from her enslavement to Westervelt, she has arisen, as Zenobia says in her legend, among this knot of visionary people to await her new destiny. What volumes of meaning this conveys with regard to the hope that was associated with the whole experiment of America! But the visionaries deliver Priscilla back to Westervelt, Zenobia being the chief instrument of her renewed bondage. A long line of critics has taken Hawthorne to task for not revealing the precise nature of Zenobia's relation with Westervelt. To me it seems that the ambiguity with which he surrounds their connection detracts nothing from, but rather adds to, the intended effect of obscure but intimate collusion. It is a collusion in which Hollingsworth is somewhat vaguely but quite unquestionably implicated, for, when Coverdale asks Priscilla in town if Hollingsworth knows where she is, the girl replies that she has come at his bidding. Coverdale himself, though honest, plays the limited role that befits his self-appointed position as chorus to the action.

Blithedale is thus not the regenerate community it professes to be. It is a company bound together, as the younger Henry James said in words that might have come from his father, rather by "its mutual suspicions and frictions, than by any successful surrender of self" [see excerpt dated 1896]. It has repeated rather than eliminated the cardinal sin of the outwardly repudiated society. "Alas," the narrator says at the end of the novel, "what faith is requisite to bear up against such results of generous effort!" Hawthorne had taken for his theme the exploration of such generous effort over the whole field of American history. Faced with the corruption which inevitably overtook the visionary schemes, it is not surprising that, like Cooper, he seems to conclude that nothing like social perfection is possible upon this earth. But, like Cooper again, he knew that it was foolish to expect perfection before its time. Because his faith was matched by his historical understanding, he did not become cynical. He realized that the nineteenth century belonged to gold-toothed wizards and narrow-minded reformers, and, what is more, the visionaries were themselves imbued with the spirit of their age. Blithedale was accordingly doomed from the outset, not only to failure, but to unreality. As Coverdale says of the experiment from the perspective of his retreat to Boston: "But, considered in a profounder relation, it was part of another age, a different state of society, a segment of an existence peculiar in its aims and methods, a leaf of some mysterious volume interpolated into the current history which time was writing off."

Set out of its time and place, the community remains thus only a noble and anticipatory gesture of hope. There is, however, no unreality about the values it affirms even in failure. The true measure of these values is neither Hollingsworth nor Zenobia. They constitute the destructive element. One must look elsewhere—to Priscilla and Coverdale—for their tragic affirmation. Whatever her ultimate destiny, it is only at Blithedale that Priscilla comes into her proper heritage of freedom, happiness, dignity, and even love—such as it is. With regard to Coverdale, though his end is not very different from his beginning, we must not overlook the development that lies in between. After he sheds the more frivolous part of his skepticism together with his illness, he is reborn into a new existence. He is not, it is true, converted to the Arcadia of pigs and masquerades. Nor does he by any means abandon the serious part of his critical attitude toward the enterprise. The important change lies in the new sense of community which he acquires and which gives meaning to his otherwise empty life. He returns to Boston only because of the break with Hollingsworth and the consequent feeling of excommunication. How much he still belongs inwardly to Blithedale, however, we see from the tumultuous excitement with which he returns to it and the deep response with which he greets its distant glimpse: "In the sweat of my brow I had there earned bread and eaten it, and so established my claim to be on earth, and my fellowship with all the sons of labor. I could have knelt down, and have laid my breast against that soil. The red clay of which my frame was moulded seemed nearer akin to those crumbling furrows than to any other portion of the world's dust. There was my home, and there might be my grave." Years later the middle-aged Coverdale voices the same sentiment: "Often, however, in these years that are darkening around me, I remember our beautiful scheme of a noble and unselfish life; and how fair, in that first summer, appeared the prospect that it might endure for generations, and be perfected, as the ages rolled away, into the system of a people and a world! Were my former associates now there,—were there only three or four of those true-hearted men still laboring in the sun,—I sometimes fancy that I should direct my world-weary footsteps thitherward, and entreat them to receive me, for old friendship's sake."

To seek an affirmation of visionary hope, Cooper had read American history backward. Hawthorne, who started with the past, had moved up to his own time, and from there referred the faith in a sane community life to some possible future age. "More and more I feel that we had struck upon what ought to be a truth," as Coverdale says. "Posterity may dig it up, and profit by it." (pp. 196-213)

> *A. N. Kaul, "Nathaniel Hawthorne: Heir and Critic of the Puritan Tradition," in his* The American Vision: Actual and Ideal Society in Nineteenth-Century Fiction, *Yale University Press, 1963, pp. 139-213.*

KELLEY GRIFFITH, JR. (essay date 1968)

[*Griffith theorizes that the structure of* Blithedale *derives from Hawthorne's focus on dreams and dream imagery within the narrative.*]

Critics who have seen *The Blithedale Romance* as a work of art and tried to pacify skeptical readers by explicating it have found it an enigma wrapped in a riddle. Certainly attempting to find form in it—aside from consistent themes, tone, and meaning—has been unrewarding.

Plot, which gives form to most narratives, is a paramount problem in *Blithedale*. What is the reader to do with Old Moodie, the interpolated legends, the Veiled Lady, and Coverdale's confession of love for Priscilla at the end of the book? Central focus is another problem of form. The narrator is biased, unreliable, unlikable, and he distorts his characters. Hawthorne compounds these problems by building into the book obvious structural features. He clearly divides the book into halves; he threads the book with irony, satire, and recurrent motifs.

Most of the unfavorable criticism of *Blithedale* has centered on these problems of form. This criticism usually sees Blithedale as a "satire" of Brook Farm and holds that because Hawthorne could not maintain the satiric point of view, the book fails structurally. Other critics, however, take an approach that helps make the form of *Blithedale* a unified whole. Their understanding is that Coverdale is central to the meaning and form of the book—that the actions and opinions of the characters (including Coverdale) must be seen as reflected off Coverdale's mind and not Hawthorne's. . . . Granted, Hawthorne puts some of his Brook Farm notes into Coverdale's mind, but Coverdale is a fully drawn character apart from the author. At most, Coverdale is an objectified "part" of Hawthorne's psyche. He is what Hawthorne "might have become" had he not done this or that, but he is not the complete Hawthorne.

Understanding Coverdale's character makes possible a new view of the form of *Blithedale*. Just as Hawthorne is not Coverdale, the erratic structure of Coverdale's narrative relates to Coverdale's personality, not Hawthorne's. In other words, Hawthorne purposely distorts the narrative in order to indicate Coverdale's state of mind. In this way, he works through the mind of a highly sensitive, ironical, intelligent, though disturbed mind much the way in which James works through Lambert Strether's or Sterne through Tristram Shandy's. (pp. 15-16)

The form Hawthorne uses for the book, consequently, cannot be defined in traditional structural terms. The plot does not proceed logically simply because Hawthorne did not intend for it to do so. The form of *Blithedale*, rather, is like that of an interior monologue, which represents the narrator's illogical thought processes and his attempts to shift events in his mind until he can settle on an arrangement satisfactory to himself.

An author may use many devices to give form to an interior monologue. Hawthorne's most consistent device—the device that gives form to the entire book—is dream. Daniel Hoffman has already noted Hawthorne's connection of dream with a stream-of-consciousness quality in *Blithedale* [see Additional Bibliography]. "We can never be certain," he says, "whether Miles Coverdale is reporting what he has actually seen and heard, or what he has dreamed. Parts of the book indeed seem to rely on, to create, a stream-of-consciousness narration." He further notes Hawthorne's own comment in the Preface that the Brook Farm experience seemed like a "day-dream, and yet a fact" to him [see excerpt dated 1852]: "In his romance," Hoffman says, "he has Miles Coverdale treat Blithedale as though it were both. . . . The facts and the dreams appear inextricably intertwined."

Crucial in the form that Coverdale's dreams give *Blithedale* is the division of the book into halves. In the first half (up to Chapter XV), the narrative moves logically. Except for the Veiled Lady legend and the sporadic appearances of Old Moodie, the reader can accept the events as reasonable enough. The second half, however, is extraordinary for its chaotic ordering of incidents and its refusal to fructify many of the crucial developments of the first half. The reason for this difference between the halves lies in Hawthorne's use of Coverdale's dreams. The first half we can accept for the most part as real; the second half we may see for the most part as dream—as a mirror of what Coverdale has seen and thought in the first half and of what he *in fact* learns after he leaves Blithedale.

Hawthorne's treatment of dream in *Blithedale* is complex and entangled with his major themes. He presents at least three types of dreams, all of which contain elements of one another, all of which represent the unreal or an imaginative reworking of the real. First, there is the "dream" of bringing about a utopia (Chapter III is named "A Knot of Dreamers"). This "dream" Hawthorne connects with the Puritan "dream" of establishing an ideal Christian society in the New World. Second, there is the "dream" created by the imagination and memory, which solidifies in the work of art, itself a "dream." The work of art seems equivalent to the stocking Mrs. Foster knits in Chapter V: she sits asleep yet keeps her needles moving; thus she foots the stocking "out of the texture of a dream." Finally, there is the dream one has when asleep. Coverdale has several vivid dreams of this sort. All of these dreams integrate with the veil and mask imagery that recur in the book and with the basic questions in Coverdale's mind as to what is real and unreal, how to get at the real, and how to represent the real (life) and the unreal (art).

The dreams Coverdale has when asleep and the "dreams" of his imagination figure prominently in the structure of the book. In them, Hawthorne creates the stream-of-consciousness narration that throws the second half out of phase with the first. All of the dream references in the first half, however, make the second half plausible. Following Hawthorne's own statement in the Preface that Brook Farm was "essentially a daydream" [see excerpt dated 1852], Coverdale at the beginning pictures the Blithedale utopians as daydreamers. Through the dimness of his memory he creates dream-like characters: Zenobia appears "like a ghost, a little wanner than the life" and Priscilla is otherworldly. Coverdale's imagination is hyperactive. He constantly changes reality to something else. His imaginative gift he protects and nurtures and equates with his individuality: "Unless renewed," he says, "by a yet farther withdrawal [than Blithedale] towards the inner circle of self-communion, I lost the better part of my individuality." At his hermitage, which symbolizes withdrawal within himself, he decks Priscilla out with "fancy-work" and flings her an imaginary message. Hawthorne equates Coverdale's fits of imagination with a dream state. The reader may justifiably wonder how much of Coverdale's version of meeting Westervelt in the woods can be trusted. Coverdale goes into the woods to enjoy one of his self-contemplative moods "with my heart full of a drowsy pleasure." While walking, Coverdale fails to notice Westervelt, who manages to pass him by "almost without impressing either the sound or sight upon my consciousness." When they do meet, Westervelt has "almost the effect of an apparition," is a "spectral character." Later, at Eliot's Pulpit, Coverdale wonders if Westervelt were a goblin, "a vision that I had witnessed in the wood." Hawthorne also in the first half establishes the fact that Coverdale can dream fantastically when asleep. The night he falls ill, he has "half-waking dreams" that in his belief "would have anticipated several of the chief incidents of this narrative, including a dim shadow of its catastrophe." He views life through a "mist of fever" and sees Zenobia as an enchantress, whose "flower in her hair is a talisman": "if you were to snatch it away, she would vanish, or be transformed into something else." Zenobia calls this an "idea worthy of a feverish poet."

The first half of *Blithedale,* then, is a fairly accurate telling of what Coverdale experiences at Blithedale Farm, but Hawthorne strews it with references to dream, and he establishes the fancifulness of Coverdale's mind and Coverdale's ability to dream psychic dreams. The second half, on the other hand, is literally a different story. The key chapter, the one that sets up the dream, stream-of-consciousness method, is Chapter XVI, "Leave-Takings." Hawthorne first indicates Coverdale's state of mind. Coverdale says that his change of attitude toward Blithedale was "dreamlike and miserable." He explains that at Blithedale he had lost a sense of the "existing state of the world." Of late he has felt that "everything in nature and human existence was fluid, or fast becoming so; that the crust of the Earth, in many places, was broken, and its whole surface portentously upheaving; that it was a day of crisis, and that we ourselves were in the critical vortex. Our great globe floated in the atmosphere of infinite space like an unsubstantial bubble." He wants to go back for a while to "the settled system of things." Zenobia in telling him goodbye refuses his help and says: "It needs a wild steersman when we voyage through Chaos! The anchor is up! Farewell!" Coverdale in turn tells Priscilla that he has a "foreboding that, were I to return even so soon as tomorrow morning, I should find everything changed." Of the principal characters, therefore, Zenobia and Coverdale are in a frenzied state of mind. The world for them has turned topsy-turvy. The second half of *Blithedale* will indeed be a voyage through chaos—*mental* chaos. And from this point on, the anchor is up.

Hawthorne next, in the last incident of the chapter, hints how he will take the reader on this voyage through chaos. Coverdale visits Silas Foster's four pigs and describes them as "the very symbols of slothful ease and sensual comfort." These "greasy citizens" "stifled, and buried alive" as they were in "their own corporeal substance," were "sensible of the ponderous and fat satisfaction of their existence": "Peeping at me, an instant, out of their small, red, hardly perceptible eyes, they dropt asleep again; yet not so far asleep but that their unctuous bliss was still present to them, betwixt dream and reality." In the following chapter, this piglike state is exactly the state that Miles Coverdale falls into when he settles in his hotel room. He orders a coal fire (in summer) and is "glad to find myself growing a little too warm with an artificial temperature." He begins to lose perspective: "At one moment, the very circumstances now surrounding me—my coal fire, and the dingy room in the bustling hotel—appeared far off and intangible. The next instant, Blithedale looked vague, as if it were at a distance both in time and space, and so shadowy, that a question might be raised whether the whole affair had been anything more than the thoughts of a speculative man. I had never before experienced a mood that so robbed the actual world of its solidity." Nonetheless, he will "enjoy the moral sillabub [of the mood] until quite dissolved away," just as the pigs might enjoy their evening meal.

Coverdale says that he spent the next few days in this mood, "in the laziest manner possible," reading a book that had a "sort of sluggish flow, like that of a stream in which your boat is as often aground as afloat." After visiting the theater one night, he sleeps and dreams about Hollingsworth, Zenobia, and Priscilla: "It was not till I had quitted my three friends that they first began to encroach upon my dreams." Supposedly he wakens from his dream, but the same dream mood, "one of those unreasonable sadnesses that you know not how to deal with, because it involves nothing for common-sense to clutch," lingers in his mind. His feelings of guilt well up within him that he left Blithedale too soon and resigned his friends "to their fate." Looking out the window, he sees Zenobia and Priscilla in the boarding house across from his hotel. The description of this discovery coincides with his mood. Coverdale says that he saw "with no positive surprise, but as if I had all along expected the incident" that the girl was Zenobia. Such expectancy and lack of surprise would be probable in a dream but hardly so in real life. Also, he sees Zenobia "like a full-length picture," as if she were appearing in the cinemascope of his mind rather than in a real boarding-house window.

This dream mood of Coverdale's, which, like the pigs', is between dream and reality, between sleeping and waking, pervades the entire sequence of events from his discovery of Zenobia in the boarding house to his falling asleep at Eliot's Pulpit after Zenobia's confrontation with Hollingsworth, near the end of the book. Much, if not all, of what Coverdale reports between these chapters may be seen as dream or half-dream. This dream sequence proceeds in episodes.

The first episode begins with Coverdale's discovery of Zenobia and Priscilla in the boarding house. When Zenobia pulls down the curtain to cut off Coverdale's view, he reviews the moral question of his voyeurism, and suggests that if he had to be judge as well as witness to the events of Zenobia's and Hollingsworth's lives, he would pass down a just sentence yet would be mindful of his love for them and their good qualities. This prefigures the sequence at Eliot's Pulpit when Zenobia calls him "Judge Coverdale" and asks him to pass sentence on her and Hollingsworth. When Coverdale visits Zenobia's drawing room, the event is dream-like. The brilliancy of the room dazzles him: "it struck me that here was the fulfilment of every fantasy of an imagination, revelling in various methods of costly self-indulgence and splendid ease. Pictures, marbles, vases . . . and the whole repeated and doubled by the reflection of a great mirror, which showed me Zenobia's proud figure, likewise, and my own." Ironically, he tells Zenobia that the Blithedale days seem to him "like a dream," and Zenobia chides him for converting the past into a dream. He describes Priscilla as a dream-like figure, whose pure white dress "seems to be floating about her like a mist." To complete the dream aura, Coverdale tells Priscilla, "everything that I meet with, now-a-days, makes me wonder whether I am awake. You, especially, have always seemed like a figure in a dream—and now more than ever." Priscilla counters with the comment that Zenobia is much more like a dream than she is. Westervelt, the "spectral figure" of the first half, appears and takes the two "dreams" away. The title of the chapter is aptly "They Vanish."

The next episode in the dream sequence is Coverdale's meeting with Old Moodie. The saloon contains art works which either idealize reality or overemphasize it. It contains topers who seek rejuvenation through the dream state brought on by alcohol. The most unreal aspect of the saloon is the fountain, whose coral and rock-work and fishes are "like the fanciful thoughts that coquet with a poet in his dream." Old Moodie glides "like a spirit, assuming visibility close to your elbow." "His existence," says Coverdale, "looked so colorless and torpid—so very faintly shadowed on the canvass of reality—that I was half afraid lest he should altogether disappear, even while my eyes were fixed full upon his figure." Old Moodie tells his story, with which Coverdale admits taking "romantic

and legendary license," while both he and Coverdale are slightly inebriated. The legend elaborates both on Fauntleroy's shadowy character, pointing out that as "from one dream into another, Fauntleroy looked forth out of his present grimy environment, into that past magnificence," and on Priscilla's ghostly quality. Zenobia's diamonds produce the same sort of dream effect in Old Moodie's room that the fountain does in the saloon. Coverdale ends the episode by admitting fabricating both Old Moodie's meeting with Zenobia and his thoughts about his two daughters after Zenobia leaves.

The third event in Coverdale's dream sequence occurs in a lyceum several weeks after his meeting with Old Moodie. He reflects on how he has spent hours deliberating on his friends, "and rendering them more misty and unsubstantial than at first, by the quantity of speculative musing, thus kneaded in with them. Hollingsworth, Zenobia, Priscilla! These three had absorbed my life into themselves." He then tells of finding Hollingsworth at the lyceum awaiting the appearance of the Veiled Lady. The incidents that Coverdale describes and his own actions are strange. He puts his mouth close to Hollingsworth's ear, addresses him in a "sepulchral, melodramatic whisper," and asks where Zenobia is. Skeptic though Coverdale is when awake, he finds himself believing horrible things about what one can do to another's soul. Hollingsworth gives a "convulsive start" when Coverdale asks what he has done with Priscilla. The Veiled Lady, that legendary figure from the first half of the book, appears like a "disembodied spirit." Finally, Hollingsworth calls Priscilla away, who gives a shriek, "like one escaping from her deadliest enemy."

The fourth episode in Coverdale's dream sequence contains the most dream-like chapter of all, "The Masqueraders," and sets the scene for Zenobia's death. It begins with Coverdale's going back to Blithedale and, again, brooding about his three friends: "Hollingsworth, Zenobia, Priscilla! They glided mistily before me, as I walked." And, again, he feels guilty about his role in their affairs. He cannot, as he walks, believe that Blithedale and the events of the summer have been real, and he asks the question that constantly plays on his mind, What is reality? He begins to catch glimpses of Blithedale Farm, saying, "That, surely, was something real." He reviews the "ominous impressions" that he has had since the end of the first half: "For, still, at every turn of my shifting fantasies, the thought stared me in the face, that some evil thing had befallen us, or was ready to befall." As he passes on in his trip back to Blithedale, he reviews meaningful places and things. He comes to the place in the river where Zenobia will drown. He rests for a moment in his hermitage. He gets angry at cows he has milked, who refuse to recognize him. And he comes on all of the Blithedale utopians, who are nightmarish in their attire and actions: "I saw a concourse of strange figures beneath the overshadowing branches; they appeared, and vanished, and came again, confusedly, with the streaks of sunlight glimmering down upon them." Instead of acting as his friends, they dance to "the devil's tune" and chase Coverdale: "The whole fantastic rabble forthwith streamed off in pursuit of me, so that I was like a mad poet hunted by chimaeras." As he runs from them, he stumbled over some dead logs and conjures up the "long-dead woodman, and his long-dead wife and children, coming out of their chill graves, and essaying to make a fire with this heap of mossy fuel!" He wanders from this spot "quite lost in reverie," neither knowing nor caring where he is going, when "a low, soft, well-remembered voice" calls to him. Another voice speaks and seems almost the voice of judgment, calling Coverdale to the Final Reckoning: "Miles Coverdale!. . . . Let him come forward, then!"

Finally, in the last episode of the dream sequence, Coverdale finds himself confronted with his three friends at Eliot's Pulpit. There Zenobia taunts him about "following up" on his game, "groping for human emotions in the dark corners of the heart." He witnesses Zenobia's judgment of Hollingsworth, which is a repetition of his own opinions formed in the first half of the book, and the revelation of Zenobia's undefined offense against Priscilla, also which he has suspected since the first half. Zenobia calls Blithedale a "foolish dream," and after she leaves the spot Coverdale is "affected with a fantasy that Zenobia had not actually gone, but was still hovering about the spot, and haunting it." In a state of mental exhaustion, Coverdale sleeps and has a dream that "converged to some tragical catastrophe." His awakening confronts him face to face with the event that, far from being dream, is stark, brutal reality— Zenobia's death and the discovery of her body in the river.

All of these dream episodes, with the exception in part of the meeting with Old Moodie and with the Fauntleroy legend, follow a pattern that evolves from the first half of the book. The pattern begins first with Coverdale brooding, even "dreaming" about Hollingsworth, Zenobia, and Priscilla, something he did from the early chapters of the first half. Second, as he works them up in his imagination, he brings in his own guilt resulting from his moral obligation to them (he leaves them to their fate at the end of the first half) or from the questions relating to his art (he is a voyeur from the first). Third, he questions the value of Blithedale utopianism (often satirizing it, as in the lyceum incident, where Westervelt offers his version of utopia), and wonders what is reality—whether the events of the past, if not the present, are all dream. Both of these he does throughout the first half. Finally, he reiterates his judgment of Zenobia and Hollingsworth for taking advantage of Priscilla. This judgment brings on his sense of foreboding, a foreboding that he began to have when he first suspected Hollingsworth's character.

The episodes in the dream sequence, therefore, are a stream-of-consciousness, dream mirror of the events in the first half of the book. But because they bring the Priscilla-Hollingsworth-Zenobia relationship to a crisis, they are also reflections of facts that Coverdale has found out in "waking moments" since the first half, facts that Coverdale chooses to leave hazy but which have enough significance to bring on the catastrophe that ends the book. The reader, of course, can never know specifically what these facts are because we see them only through the distorted medium of Coverdale's dreams.

Seeing how dream molds the form of *The Blithedale Romance* introduces numerous new possibilities in interpreting this enigmatic novel of Hawthorne's. It possibly brings the book into another genre, the dream allegory. *The Blithedale Romance* resembles Bunyan's *Pilgrim's Progress,* the one dream allegory that Hawthorne knew best, more than it resembles any other book. The pilgrim imagery throughout the book, like the dream imagery, is manifest, and just like the narrator of *Pilgrim's Progress,* Coverdale seems to "dream a dream" of allegorical significance. Although as the central "pilgrim" of the book he has not reached the Celestial City, he at least can face his moral problems, write them out for all to see, and admit the one thing that will throw light on the most morally agonizing event in his life. *Blithedale,* in fact, is Coverdale's attempt to purge through art, through allegory, the guilt and suffering from his soul. His confession of love for Priscilla is

not a confession of love for a human being (for Coverdale is most obviously drawn physically and emotionally to Zenobia) but love for the way of life and art that she allegorizes in his imagination.

But more important, Hawthorne's use of dream in *Blithedale* makes the book—and thus Hawthorne—more meaningful for us today. Lionel Trilling's strictures that Hawthorne does not, like Kafka, set the reader free from the restrictions of reality appear invalid. Kafka, Trilling says, is aesthetically successful because his imagination deals only with subjective reality: "Like the dream, it confronts subjective fact only, and there are no aesthetically unsuccessful dreams, no failed nightmares." On the other hand, Hawthorne's "too limited faith in the imagination" makes him insist "that the world is there, that we are dependent upon it": "At his very most powerful, Hawthorne does not interpose his imagination between us and the world; however successfully he may project illusion, he must point beyond it to the irrefrangible solidity."

Yet the second half of *Blithedale* is dream. In it Hawthorne does "interpose his imagination between us and the world"; he sets the reader free from objective reality and sends him floating down the stream of Coverdale's chaotic conscious. As Zenobia says, the anchor is up!

Dream, consequently, does more than harmonize the disparate structural elements of *The Blithedale Romance* into one unified whole; it makes the book relevant in a century influenced by Kafka, Joyce, and Eliot. (pp. 16-26)

Kelley Griffith, Jr., "Form in 'The Blithedale Romance'," in American Literature, *Vol. XL, No. 1, March, 1968, pp. 15-26.*

NINA BAYM   (essay date 1968)

[*Baym argues that* Blithedale *"embodies a radical romanticism" centered on Coverdale's character and his inability to feel passion. The novel suggests, Baym points out, that utopias are doomed to failure because their members are ultimately unable to free themselves of the social constraints from which they seek to escape.*]

The shelf of books written about Nathaniel Hawthorne in the last few decades presents a remarkably consistent interpretation of the author as a humanist, continually reminding a democratically progressive, romantically self-assertive era about the reality of human imperfection. . . . *The Blithedale Romance,* for example, is universally taken to be the study of a Utopia that fails because original sin, the heart's inclination toward evil, accompanies the reformers into their New Eden and there, unleashed by their naïve self-trust, destroys all.

This interpretation, elegantly varied from book to book and article to article, has flourished despite its acknowledged inability to cope with large segments of the action. Of Westervelt and the Veiled Lady nothing more edifying can be found in standard criticism than that "the 'mysterious' aspects of Hawthorne's plot are certainly not likely to hold our attention long today!" [see entry by Hyatt H. Waggoner in the Additional Bibliography]. It is generally agreed that Hawthorne did not successfully blend the realistic details drawn from his participation in the Brook Farm community with the melodramatic plot; the book is too leadenly realistic for a romance, but too fantastic for a novel. Some critics deplore Hawthorne's misguided ambition to chronicle the real, while others regret the waste of first-rate social material. The narrator, though recognized as a familiar Hawthorne "type," is regarded as unwisely chosen for the circumstances: his coldness keeps him too remote from the action to convey its life, his prying makes him unpleasant company for the reader, and his ignorance almost suggests the possibility of an unreliable narrative. Until recently, most critics have maintained that while Priscilla is unquestionably Hawthorne's favored feminine character, he failed to surmount the problem of rendering goodness; consequently, the book does not effectively realize its moral position against the contrastingly sinful Zenobia.

No doubt there have been novels as ineptly written as this catalogue of faults implies, even by major novelists. Yet one cannot help noticing that the overwhelming intent of the criticism has been to maintain the view of Hawthorne as cautionary moralist, even if artistry and coherence must be discarded in the process. Irving Howe, for example, speaks of the book's "radical incoherence," its almost total failure to realize its intentions [see excerpt dated 1957]. But what, then, *has* Blithedale realized? Suppose one were to assume that the novel contains a coherent action; what sense would one then find in it? The following interpretation results from such an approach. It discovers that **The Blithedale Romance** embodies a radical romanticism. Blithedale Farm is a subverted Utopia, but its downfall is not original sin. The community is destroyed by the lingering pressures and effects of the repressive social organization it has tried to escape. In human experience, the self is born into a society, and has never known freedom. Hawthorne is concerned with those evils in the soul that are "the result of ages of compelled degradation." The attempt to liberate reveals that man carries his cage around inside him and will, when left alone, recreate his oppression.

We begin by accepting Hawthorne's prefatory statement that **Blithedale** is, regardless of its sources, a romance and not a novel. It does not try to imitate appearances, surfaces, and probabilities, though it reserves the right to use fact for its own purposes. Brook Farm was most apt for his intentions, Hawthorne says, because it permitted him to "establish a theatre, a little removed from the highway of ordinary travel, where the creatures of his brain may play their phantasmagorical antics, without exposing them to too close a comparison with the actual events of real lives." **The Blithedale Romance** is the literary realization of an imagined world, just as Brook Farm itself was an attempt to realize an imagined world. Moreover, as is often the case in Hawthorne's fiction (e.g., **"Rappaccini's Daughter," "Young Goodman Brown," "My Kinsman, Major Molyneux"**), the work realizes a particular character's imagined world. What Blithedale "is" is inseparable from what it is to Coverdale, for nothing is known in the book but what is known by him. To ask whether there could be a more accurate rendering of the story than Coverdale's, is—given the absence of corrective devices in the narrative—a meaningless question. The book's reality is Coverdale's world; ultimately he is its only character, and everything that happens in the novel must be understood in reference to him. (pp. 545-47)

Such reality is, of course, the stuff of much, or most, modern literature. The hero's adventures occur on the stage of his own psyche, and through them we comprehend that psyche.

It cannot be said of Coverdale that he adventures, since he is a notably passive character. He takes the role of the dreaming mind, a passive consciousness, observing the figures of his own "conscious sleep" (I borrow the phrase from Hawthorne's early story **"Alice Doane's Appeal"**). Much of the story is puzzling and obscure to the dreamer who, even as he imagines it, is trying to understand it. The story contains its own ex-

planation, and yet its meaning is exasperatingly elusive. (pp. 547-48)

Of Coverdale's ineffectiveness there can be no doubt. His many attempts to control, influence, even involve himself with the characters, are rebuffed. Where at first he is a kind of steady center in their circle, he is gradually pushed aside; as he becomes superfluous, he finds himself strangely drained of energy. A parasitism is implied precisely opposite to that commonly assumed to exist in the novel. We do not find Coverdale drawing his life from the characters, but find him losing it to them. In Chapter XXIII the abandoned Coverdale complains that he has been wandering like an "exorcised spirit that has been driven from its old haunts, after a mighty struggle." The three had "absorbed my life into themselves. . . . The more I consider myself, as I then was, the more do I recognize how deeply my connection with those three had affected all my being." Earlier he has spoken of his life as having been "attenuated of much of its proper substance" through his involvement with these characters. His passivity and their energy are two aspects of a single event, the dream in which the dreaming mind is possessed by its images.

The gradual drift of the characters, over the novel's course, away from harmonious relations toward polarization and eventual violent confrontation represents a process of split and struggle within the personality. Imagery of masks and veils, much noted in the criticism, contributes to the dreamlike atmosphere of uncertain identities, and figures the indirect, misleading, and elusive ways in which truth is at once embodied and muffled in fantasy. The carnival or pageant during which Zenobia is repudiated by Hollingsworth represents a moment of truth when the characters cease to pose as people and appear as the imaginary or mythical figures they *really* are—Zenobia as the soul's queen, Hollingsworth as its wrathful judge. And the catastrophic conclusion leaves Coverdale forever psychically inert, never able to achieve that unity of being which would have enabled him to have a purpose in life.

The trip to Blithedale Farm is Coverdale's attempt to find a purpose. The narration chronicles the failure of his inner exploration. In the opening chapters he undertakes the familiar journey into the self in search of one's inner core, the struggle to make contact with the sources of life and energy within and to return to the surface, refreshed and rejuvenated. In Boston Coverdale enjoys the "sweet, bewitching, enervating indolence" of a genteel bachelorhood, parcelling out the social days among "my pleasant bachelor-parlor, sunny and shadowy . . . ; my centre-table, strewn with books and periodicals; my writing-desk, with a half-finished poem in a stanza of my own contrivance; my morning lounge at the reading-room or picture-gallery; my noontide walk along the cheery pavement, with the suggestive succession of human faces, and the brisk throb of human life, in which I shared; my dinner at the Albion . . . ; my evening at the billiard-club, the concert, the theatre, or at somebody's party, if I pleased." This pleasant life lacks vigor; in its atmosphere of tepid hedonism, art is but another languid pastime. Coverdale leaves it behind to liberate and test his talent. He wants to become a poet, "to produce something that shall really deserve to be called poetry—true, strong, natural, and sweet."

The withdrawal and search are symbolized in two parallel ways, which may be distinguished as the public and private, or outer and inner dimensions of Coverdale's quest. The movement from Boston to Blithedale supplies an outer form for the journey, which is paralleled on the inner stage by a movement from Priscilla, the Veiled Lady (the Spiritual Ideal: Love and Art in genteel society), to Zenobia. Boston represents the prison of institutions and conformity. Leaving the city with other members of the community, Coverdale notes "how the buildings, on either side, seemed to press too closely upon us, insomuch that our mighty hearts found barely room enough to throb between them. The snowfall, too, looked inexpressibly dreary, (I had almost called it dingy,) coming down through an atmosphere of city-smoke, and alighting on the sidewalk, only to be moulded into the impress of somebody's patched boot or over-shoe." And Coverdale draws a fine transcendental moral from his observations: "thus, the track of an old conventionalism was visible on what was freshest from the sky."

Blithedale, in contrast, is a radical community which aims, in an atmosphere of informality and innovation, to establish forms of labor and of love which will express and liberate, rather than inhibit and distort, the human spirit. It hopes to restructure human relationships around the principle of "familiar love" and to "lessen the laboring man's great burthen of toil." Life is to be "governed by other than the false and cruel principles, on which human society has all along been based." Coverdale is not deeply interested in the community's economic aims, for as a man of means he feels little tie to the working classes. Yet he recognizes a common interest, since work and leisure are both socially controlled activities. As for the aim of more natural and loving relationships between human beings, Coverdale has his version of that goal as well. The springtime in which Coverdale leaves for Blithedale symbolizes (as has often been noted) the rejuvenating and regenerating purposes of his withdrawal from society, as well as the optimism implicit in his quest. The severe snow he encounters represents the necessary death of the social self prior to spiritual rebirth. He contracts a bad cold, and points out that its severity is directly due to the "hot-house warmth of a town-residence and the luxurious life in which I indulged myself." Recovering, he rejoins the community on May Day, exulting in the belief that he has been reborn." (pp. 549-51)

Coverdale thinks his struggle is over. In truth it is about to begin. Recognizing only external obstacles, Coverdale has naïvely imagined that removal from society would be sufficient to liberate the powers of self. He is as yet unaware that inhibiting forces exist within as well as without. His innocence is paralleled by the community's here, for it believes in the possibility of reform without revolution.

The true, deep aim of Coverdale's quest is private; he wants to tap the soul's reservoir of energy, to make contact with its passionate, creative, active principle. This principle underlies, or animates, all forms of human self-expression whether in work, love, or play. It is the source of all impulsive, creative, and passionate activity; hence sexual and poetic energy are but varying forms of the same drive and, consequently, Zenobia, who unites in her person sex, art, and nature, is its perfect symbol. Of course, in addition, she is politically radical. Though the life-principle is not inherently or originally political, it inevitably comes in conflict with society because it is continually asserting the primacy of self and activity over institutions and stability. Society, whose necessary goals are permanence and control, forces this romantic energy into the mold of rebellion. Zenobia, from society's point of view, is morally suspect, as is the energetic and passionate principle she represents. She is the real aim of Coverdale's search, and that is why she is waiting to greet him at Blithedale, and why in comparison to her the rest of the enterprise pales and looks unreal, becomes

"a masquerade, a pastoral, a counterfeit Arcadia." She, and not the community, represents the reality Coverdale is seeking.

In this symbolic function, Zenobia is the creative energy both of nature and the self; without committing himself quite to a transcendental view of the unity of all things Hawthorne does at least imply a relation between nature and the creative self. But Zenobia's role is not by any means encompassed in this dual function; she is also, most impressively and concretely, a woman, and Hawthorne outperforms the feminists in the decisive way in which he links the liberation and fulfilment of the male to his understanding of and relation to woman. Not the threatening dark lady of the post-Victorians, nor even the ambivalently conceived symbol of experience, both fascinating and frightening, in Philip Rahv's famous formulation, Zenobia is simply, as Coverdale says, "a magnificent woman" [see Additional Bibliography]. She is a depiction of the eternal feminine as earthy, maternal, domestic, natural, sensual, brilliant, loving, and demanding, and is described mainly in images of softness, radiance, warmth, and health, none of which are even slightly ambivalent or ambiguous in their emotional import. (pp. 552-53)

Two aspects of Zenobia do not fit the unambiguous picture I am presenting here: first, her feminism and, second, the exotic flower, daily renewed, which she wears in her hair. Unquestionably Hawthorne does not think much of Zenobia *as a feminist*. "Her poor little stories and tracts never half did justice to her intellect," he says, praising the intellect even as he deprecates the form it has found to express itself. "I recognized no severe culture in Zenobia; her mind was full of weeds. It startled me sometimes, in my state of moral, as well as bodily faint-heartedness, to observe the hardihood of her philosophy; she made no scruple of oversetting all human institutions, and scattering them as with a breeze from her fan." Zenobia is uncultured because culture is a matter of society, institutions, and the past. True original energy is, by its nature, somewhat barbaric: Walt Whitman was shortly to dramatize this point. Under the pressure of historical circumstances, Zenobia has become a female pamphleteer. The role is inherently unworthy of her (her true place is in a timeless natural setting such as Blithedale aspires to be), but it is the best she can do in a society that offers woman no worthy roles at all. Lastly, Coverdale's references to his own faint-heartedness make clear that Zenobia's "hardihood" is not being criticized; on the contrary, she illuminates Coverdale's feebleness.

For that hothouse flower Zenobia has had to suffer a great deal of critical abuse. But when one reads that it was "so fit, indeed, that Nature had evidently created this floral gem, in a happy exuberance, for the one purpose of worthily adorning Zenobia's head," it is difficult to assert that it symbolizes sensual evil, or something unnatural. It *is* sensual, but neither evil nor unnatural. That is its point: it proclaims that Zenobia's nature is passionate as well as pastoral. It may frighten the sexually morbid, but in itself it is innocent. One may hazard that what Hawthorne is trying to do here is precisely to reinstate sexuality as a legitimate and natural element of femininity—and, by implication, of maleness. It will be a sign of Coverdale's "recovery" when his feelings about Zenobia no longer embarrass him. And because, in Zenobia, all kinds of passionate and creative energies have united in a fundamental Eros, we can say that Coverdale's freedom depends on his ability to accept woman in her totality. The major block to Coverdale's release of energies is—because these energies are passionate—his inability to acknowledge passion as an element of human character. It is about Zenobia, and not Priscilla, that he ought to be writing poems; then he would be doing something more than contriving stanzas. Art is passionate and it celebrates passion; rejecting this truth, Coverdale is incapable of mature artistry and must remain a childish man, an ineffectual "poetling" (to borrow Whitman's phrase). Until man becomes able to accept the fact that the source of his strength is "erotic" (in the large sense of the term) he will be unable to draw on it. The narrative of **The Blithedale Romance** demonstrates Coverdale's incapacity. The ability freely to accept the woman is frequently the test of a man in Hawthorne's writings—one which he invariably fails.

The relation between Coverdale and Zenobia begins auspiciously, as they sit together beside the blazing kitchen fire. But the fire is only of brush-wood; its energy will not endure. Were Coverdale the man so easily to solve his problems, he would not have needed to go to Blithedale to confront them. Silas Foster (the story's chorus) predicts the fire's imminent death, and then a knock on the door announces the arrival of Hollingsworth and Priscilla, who will put out Blithedale's fires permanently by killing Zenobia. Zenobia is soon laughingly to forecast her own doom when she calls Hollingsworth the "sable knight" and Priscilla the "shadowy snow maiden who . . . shall melt away at my feet, in a pool of ice-water, and give me my death with a pair of wet slippers." Priscilla and Hollingsworth are heavily veiled, and the veiling both obscures and yet displays the hidden beings beneath. Priscilla's cloak hides everything of her person except its all-important insubstantiality; Hollingsworth in his snow-covered coat looks like a polar bear. Hollingsworth is continually portrayed in images amalgamating fire and ice. He is a polar animal, an iron savage. The imagery of iron and of cold is clear enough, defining Hollingsworth as severe, rigid, and, except on his one topic, unpassionate. The iron metaphors foreshadow his eventual appearance as a Puritan judge, for Hawthorne's Puritans are always iron men. In **The Blithedale Romance** we also find iron imagery applied to society. The point of the animal imagery is that Hollingsworth, although he does not know it, derives his energies from the savage core of his nature just like everyone else. The high morality of his philanthropy encourages a fatal delusion, fatal because when in his ignorance he repudiates Zenobia he destroys himself. (pp. 554-56)

In relation to Coverdale, Hollingsworth's role is very complicated. He is an alter ego, an admired version of the self, energetic, forceful, attractive, and purposeful to an extreme. He is also a father figure, rival and judge of the self. Perhaps we may infer from this coincidence of roles that Coverdale's weaknesses derive from the simple fact that he has too much respect for authority. Thus the alter ego is authoritarian. Coverdale supposes that the father within the self will rejoice at the son's maturity; he supposes that the father is an admirable model, a great emancipator. He assumes that his admiration for Hollingsworth as an individual will be reciprocated in kind. But Hollingsworth is a jailor who admires nothing in individuals, and desires nothing but their submission. He must dominate, and his morality serves his tyranny. His pretensions to being a romantic are "hollow" (Hollingsworth—Hollowworth?). His nature does not change in the course of the novel, but Coverdale's perception of him alters. More accurately, Coverdale comes to accept what he has already perceived but refused to credit. (p. 557)

Hollingsworth wants the Blithedale property as the ground for his reform school. The contrast with Blithedale's purposes could

not be more complete, and indeed his plans require dispossessing the Blithedalers as a preliminary. Far from envisioning a free relation between man and nature, Hollingsworth's scheme involves shutting man away from nature in an institution—a building—which conforms not to the spirit of the individuals within it, but to *his* spirit. Forever busy planning his structure to the last detail, his goal of a solid material edifice represents a negation of the organic ideal, in which shape flows from within and is never perfected, remaining sensitive to inner flux. While the Blithedalers are programmatic nonconformists who tolerate all styles of life—"whoso would be a man, must be a nonconformist"—Hollingsworth would impose, through his institution, a conforming sameness on individuals. He would not encourage people to grow in their ways, but force them to grow his way. Thus, he is not a romantic gone wrong, but a false reformer. . . . Hollingsworth's vision denies the human freedom on which Blithedale is based and rejects the fundamental transcendental tenet, belief that man is divine and that therefore all men must treat each other as gods. Lastly, accepting as it does social judgments of morality and guilt, Hollingsworth's scheme to reform criminals perpetuates the social definitions of human nature that the romantic soul rejects. In sum, Hollingsworth does not represent a corrupted extreme of romantic libertarianism. He is the opposite principle, the spirit of authoritarian domination. (p. 558)

The plot of the novel shows how Hollingsworth uses the power which has been granted to him by the other characters, to destroy. The crux of the plot is his choice between two women; the surface reason for his choice is money. Having no sense of the women as people, he is unaware of the meanings of his choice in terms of the book's larger logic. One might ask, indeed, whether Hawthorne's plotting is not irrelevant and mechanical here. Of course it says something about Hollingsworth, that he makes his choice solely on economic grounds. It points up his lack of passion, reinforces his image as a man of institutions, concerned with things, substances, mass, power, money. Too, the disparity between the reason for his choice and the line of moral righteousness with which he dismisses Zenobia—his complete failure to see that in manipulating human passions he has done something deeply wrong—makes an acerbic comment on society's moralism. Hollingsworth's sanctimonious morality is no more than rationalization; yet, like society, Hollingsworth has the power to make his moral judgments stick.

The rerouting of the fortune from Zenobia to Priscilla is also of significance. Though Zenobia, for most of the book, is the wealthy sister, the depiction of her does not utilize money for its effect. Her richness is all of body and spirit. She dresses in homely, dateless rustic garb and is continually portrayed in natural images—even the hothouse flower is real. She operates in a frame independent of money. This is not true of Priscilla, who has been deformed by poverty. Whether one thinks of her as the seamstress or as the Veiled Lady, one finds her intimately connected with economic questions, servant to an environment that demands artifice. As a seamstress she makes one highly specialized luxury item, a finely wrought silk purse. Whether this product has sartorial or sexual meaning, it is created for a jaded market. As the Veiled Lady, Priscilla herself is artifice: Hawthorne brings this out quite clearly in the Boston scenes of the novel, where the two women undergo striking transformations. Zenobia, though beautiful as ever, seems curiously artificial and dead despite the amazing luxury of her dress, perhaps because of it. The hothouse flower has been replaced by a jewel, and this metamorphosis signifies the way, in an artificial context, her attractions seem unnatural. Coverdale, talking to her, cannot rid himself of the sensation that she is acting a part.

In contrast, pallid Priscilla comes to life. In the city she is in her element. Although Coverdale asserts that her beauty is so delicate that "it was safest, in her case, to attempt no art of dress," he declares in the next breath that her marvellous perfection is due to consummate art. "I wondered what Zenobia meant by evolving so much loveliness out of this poor girl." As a result of this art, Priscilla has become a symbol of matchless purity and innocence. But it takes the city to bring her meaning out. "Ever since she came among us, I have been dimly sensible of just this charm which you have brought out. But it was never absolutely visible till now." And Coverdale then expresses the book's most bitter paradox. "She is as lovely," he proclaims, "as a flower." In other words, Priscilla is the true artificial flower of the book, the flower that appears natural in the city, the domain of repression and artificial pleasures. Zenobia's flower, in the distorting glass of civilization, looks fake. She does not belong here, but Priscilla fits in.

The point of this is that, as money is intricately and intimately bound into the fabric of society, and as Priscilla is a creature of society and Zenobia is in revolt against it, the money *belongs* with Priscilla. . . . Moodie's decision to redirect the fortune, appropriately enough, stems from Zenobia's failure properly to treat Priscilla as a sister. There is every indication that he has insinuated Priscilla into Blithedale just *as* a test of Zenobia. To accept Priscilla is, for Zenobia, to accept the very shape of womanhood she is in rebellion against, society's version of the feminine. She loses her fortune, then, because she refuses to surrender on society's terms. The wrath of society, relayed to her by Hollingsworth, who acts (as he acted in bringing Priscilla to Blithedale) as Moodie's surrogate, is inevitable. (pp. 559-61)

As Zenobia is the natural and eternal woman, Priscilla is the woman in history, distorted by her social role and misrepresented by the ideals derived from her. She is considered an inferior being, subjected, exploited, and yet idealized. The ideal is pernicious because it derives from woman's subjected state and ultimately ennobles the condition of slavery. As seamstress Priscilla represents the whole range of exploited feminine roles in society, all of which, from wife to prostitute, were viewed by feminists as examples of economic subjection of woman to man. As the Veiled Lady, Priscilla stands for the feminine ideal. Just as Zenobia projects a part of Coverdale's personality, Priscilla too represents part of Coverdale, but here there is a divergence in the parallel because Priscilla is less an active force than a channel for forces. The true opposition, in terms of Coverdale's psyche, is between Zenobia and Hollingsworth, but Priscilla *plays the role* of Zenobia's anti-self. This is entirely appropriate to Priscilla's status as a medium. "I am blown about like a leaf. . . . I never have any free will."

The various meanings of Priscilla are centered on her role as woman in the city. This presentation has always struck readers as the most "incoherent" part of the book; first, because it is hard to grasp the interrelatedness of her two incarnations, let alone to interpret the obscured meanings of the Veiled Lady. Second, according to whether Priscilla is viewed as herself the most abject victim of social tyranny, or as an agent in the service of that tyranny, the point of view toward her changes radically. In the first instance she is an object of almost bathetic compassion, but as an agent she is regarded with fear, distrust, and repugnance. (pp. 561-62)

A portrait of Hawthorne in 1846.

Coverdale's imagination is much taken up with the spectacle of her frailty, but, as he himself has to admit, Priscilla is mostly a shadowy background for his own fantasizing, a void for the poet to decorate. She is, in fact, a fine subject for the kind of poetry Coverdale writes. The poetic impulse to idealize the vapid leads, inevitably, to vapid poetry. Moreover, the celebration of feebleness and frailty turns these qualities into admired attributes, and thus the genteel poet does his part in maintaining the status quo by praising it. It is hard to shake the appealing image of Priscilla out of the heart, but there is no hope for man or woman unless she is dislodged. The condition of woman in the nineteenth century, in a word, is slavery. Hollingsworth's response to the idea of an alteration in her status is appropriately ferocious.

> Her place is at man's side. Her office, that of the Sympathizer; the unreserved, unquestioning Believer . . . the Echo of God's own voice, pronouncing, "It is well done!" All the separate action of woman is, and ever has been, and always shall be, false, foolish, vain, destructive of her own best and holiest qualities, void of every good effect, and productive of intolerable mischiefs! Man is a wretch without woman; but woman is a monster . . . without man, as her acknowledged principal! As true as I had once a mother, whom I loved . . . if there were a chance of their attaining the end which these petticoated monstrosities have in view, I would call upon my own sex to use its physical force, that unmistakable evidence of sovereignty, to scourge them back within their proper bounds!

The reference to physical force as evidence of sovereignty reveals Hollingsworth more clearly than ever, and indicates as well how true it is that woman is a slave in his system, rhetoric notwithstanding. His words strike Coverdale as "outrageous," the "very intensity of masculine egotism," which "deprived woman of her very soul, her inexpressible and unfathomable all, to make it a mere incident in the great sum of man." Coverdale does not recognize in his own alternate version of the ideal relations between woman and man an equal, if less savage, egotism, and he is piqued by the indifference with which his declamation in favor of women is received by Zenobia and Priscilla. And he is wrong when he interprets Zenobia's words, "Let man be but manly and god-like and woman is only too ready to become to him what you say," as her submission to Hollingsworth's views, for her qualification is vital. Except as man takes woman as a free spirit, equal to his own and with the same rights, he is not manly or godlike.

Priscilla, the "gentle parasite," the "type of womanhood, such as man has spent centuries in making it," rewards Hollingsworth for his defense of slavery with a "glance of . . . entire acquiescence and unquestioning faith." In her approbation it is clear that she and Hollingsworth belong together, and as they entered the novel together so they will leave it. Though she adores him, Priscilla can never be Hollingsworth's wife or friend. In the beginning she is his child, and at the end she is his nurse. And she is fulfilled in her role as caretaker and guardian to the broken Hollingsworth, thus literally realizing the idea that a degrading conception of woman implies a degradation of man. If man idolizes a crippled spirit, he will cripple his own. Man "is never content," Zenobia comments, "unless he can degrade himself by stooping towards what he loves. In denying us our rights, he betrays even more blindness to his own interests, than profligate disregard of ours." Expanded to cover all the meanings of Zenobia's presence in the book, her remark can stand as the novel's epigraph; yet even she does not fathom the depths of that blindness.

These matters are recapitulated on a much more intimate and—given the temper of the times—dangerous level in the story of the Veiled Lady. When Priscilla is not making purses she is performing on the stage as the subject of Westervelt's mesmeric powers. In these appearances she wears a many-layered, gauzy white veil. The Veiled Lady is the Victorian ideal of womanhood as a spiritual (noncorporeal) being, carried to an extreme and implicating in its extremity the basest kinds of human emotions. Though she is proclaimed as a being almost entirely spiritual, she is in fact a "possessed" creature owned and exploited by Westervelt. She is in a position which denies her spiritual nature even while pretending to demonstrate it. The particular being in whose service she performs is a cosmopolitan devil, his name implying his worldliness. Like Moodie, another urban figure, he lives off the proceeds of his exploitation; but where the one employs her physical talents, the other employs her very soul. As a cosmopolitan charlatan, he caters to a curious set of prurient and voyeuristic tastes in the audience, which comes to see purity violated, modesty exhibited. F. O. Matthiessen spoke of Hawthorne's Hilda as performing a kind of spiritual strip-tease—the phrase is even more aptly applied to Priscilla, for the veil functions largely to excite the viewers' interest in what it conceals. The Veiled Lady titillates even as she appeals to an ideal of feminine purity. On the one hand, talk of purity "veils" what is actually taking place; on the other, the purity itself contributes to the excitement of the display.

The veil, along with the references to Priscilla's insubstantial frame, and metaphors of shadows and melting snows, and

contrasts to Zenobia's ample proportions, goes far to suggest that in this ideal of spirituality a crude equation has been made with lack of body. As woman is *literally* less and less physical, she is more spiritual, as though these were quantitative matters. To deny the flesh is to deny the emotions flesh arouses, and this ideal indeed denies the normality of sex. Zenobia's flower becomes a jewel in Boston because society considers sex unnatural. Westervelt's game inhibits the acceptance of sex as normal by holding up a flesh-denying ideal of purity. Simultaneously he controls his audience's emotions through participation in an act of ritual violation of that very ideal. Yet, the denial of sex is not Westervelt's ultimate goal; he is aiming to suppress the radical Eros itself, in its totality. Ideally, he would use Zenobia to deny herself; failing that, he seeks to blot her image out of the hearts of men by polluting it. The Veiled Lady's exhibitions are cathartic spectacles to draw off and channel threatening emotions; they are rituals of socialization.

Westervelt is a hideous creation, and he exists somewhere in the deepest layers of Coverdale's mind. Coverdale meets him in the forest, always Hawthorne's locale for the soul's profundities. In Coverdale's mind he operates as the demon of sexual cynicism and fear, the internalization of society's life-denying strategies. "The Professor's tone represented that of worldly society at large, where a cold scepticism smothers what it can of our spiritual aspirations, and makes the rest ridiculous. I detested this kind of man, and all the more, because a part of my own nature showed itself responsive to him." Westervelt within the psyche tarnishes the images of all women; he is the principle of "dirty-mindedness." Zenobia, too, has been in bondage to him, and in a sense always will be so; but at the same time she has fundamentally escaped him. The two seem to occupy separate spheres. They cannot touch. In the forest Coverdale notices that "as they passed among the trees . . . she took good heed that even the hem of her garment should not brush against the stranger's person." Watching them again at the boarding house, he observes that "it still seemed to me, as on the former occasion, that Zenobia repelled him—that, perchance, they mutually repelled each other—by some incompatibility of their spheres. A key contrast between the two is made in terms of heat and coldness, so that Westervelt's deviltry is linked to all the other images of rigidness and coldness in the book, to the rigid, passion-repressing, "puritanical" part of the personality.

Finally, the combination of Veil and Devil suggests that the Lady may even be a delusion, conjured up to deflect men from true ideals, such as (perhaps) those embodied in Blithedale and its resident goddess. This delusory ideal, though it promises fulfillment, in fact means incompleteness for man and woman. So we have seen, and so Zenobia tries to imply in her "Legend of the Silvery Veil" (Chapter XII, the middle of the book). Theodore, sneaking into the Veiled Lady's dressing room for a peep, is asked for a kiss by the shadowy figure. The idea repels him; he imagines all kinds of horrors beneath the veil, and refuses the request. Failing to accept the physical side of relations between the sexes, he forfeits his opportunity to set the Veiled Lady free. She sorrowfully disappears, but not before Theodore has seen her lovely face, the memory of which is to haunt him for the rest of his life and make his existence seem unsubstantial. In this story, Zenobia is actually assimilating the Veiled Lady to herself: insofar as the Veiled Lady is a girl or woman, she must be treated as a being of flesh and blood. Life is "realized" only in the flesh. Priscilla is imprisoned in the "ideal" which men like Theodore and Coverdale have imposed on her. The ideal keeps people dead, keeps them forever unrealized, makes a society of phantoms no more real than the Lady herself.

Priscilla in Blithedale, then, is enormously dangerous, but only Zenobia sees it. From the beginning her energies are absorbed in attempting to detach Priscilla from Hollingsworth, so that there may be a longed-for union of the forces of passion and control, a union that might make a whole, vigorous self. Zenobia's strategy, since she is incapable of artifice, consists largely in contrasting Priscilla's physical meagerness to her own full womanhood. The tactic is self-defeating, for the more Zenobia demonstrates the nature of her rival, the more she calls up the prior socio-moral commitments of the men. However pathetic Priscilla, in the fragility of her physical frame, may appear to be, and however she is an exploited slave in her relation to men, she is not helpless in a battle against Zenobia. Men will fight to the death to defend her as a slave. In this sense, both the men in the story are on her side, and Zenobia succeeds only in aligning the men against her. Increasingly she defines the conventional polarity of pit and pedestal and puts herself in the pit. The more the contrast between the Boston and Blithedale women is clarified, the more uncomfortable Coverdale becomes and the more angry Hollingsworth. In the long run, Hollingsworth is immune to Zenobia because she stands for the romantic individualism and freedom he so abhors. In the long run, too, Coverdale cannot overcome his attachment to genteel poetry and the genteel way of life to serve the romantic muse.

Thus, in full season, the adventure at Blithedale leads to a polarization of forces so extreme that even the earlier anxious moments at the farm can be remembered as harmonious. Acting under a confluence of forces, Hollingsworth takes on his core identity as Puritan judge and condemns Zenobia. His action signifies, on all levels of her meaning, her death. As the life force, she has been put down; as woman, she has been denied a place in a world administered by men. She kills herself, as she must, but the marble imagery of the scene by the rock shows that she is, before her suicide, already dead. With her death Blithedale, too, dies for Coverdale; his chance is finished. He returns to Boston in desolation, looking ahead to an empty future, from the vantage point of which only these months at the farm will appear to him to have been "real." He leaves Blithedale not a new man but a mutilated one. His inner quest has ended in catastrophe because he has proven too weak to become free.

The destruction of Hollingsworth is particularly interesting. From the social vantage point, he has triumphed, but as an aspect of Coverdale he must go down to destruction with the rest of the personality. It has been his supreme folly to imagine that he has acted as an "inspired" man; acted, that is, on energy supplied from higher sources. But it seems as if he too has ultimately derived his powers from Zenobia, as though she were the book's true sun, its sole source of energy. Casting out Zenobia, Hollingsworth inadvertently casts out his own vitality and thus ruins himself. He makes himself into a fit mate for Priscilla, and is seen some years later showing a "childlike, or childish, tendency to press close, and closer still, to the side of the slender woman whose arm was within his."

His act demonstrates that it is necessary, for the life of the organism, that the punishing tendencies of the soul be checked, for if left free they will crush it. The controlling forces within must themselves be controlled, because they will not control themselves; on the contrary, interpreting themselves as trans-

mitters of the divine, they will brook no restraint. The goal, presumably, is in some kind of harmony in the consciousness between energy and restraint, but such a mediating force as is required Coverdale cannot supply. Agonizedly, he watches the drama of his fragmenting psyche, but cannot impress himself on the warring forces. Eventually he witnesses his own collapse.

Undoubtedly books have been written on the complementary theme, the dangers to the personality when the passionate energies are given free rein, rather than when the punishing and repressive capacities are released unhindered. But *The Blithedale Romance* is not such a book. We cannot even hypothesize, after reading it, what Hawthorne would "do" with the theme of complete self-expression, because this novel is about the murder (and suicide) of self-expressive energies in the soul. Utopias do not work because they never succeed in freeing themselves from the many subtle pressures of the society they think to leave behind. Indeed, the judging core of the personality, an anarchic and intemperate concentration of inhibiting forces, is far more severe when it is not muffled by the easygoing life of Boston which, if it inhibits the passions, also inhibits their punishment. We cannot see *Blithedale* as a book saying that society does well insofar as it controls the passions, on the assumption that without control the soul is a passionate and evil anarchy. We have to see Hawthorne saying, rather, that insofar as society seeks to eliminate the passions altogether it seeks its own eventual suicide: there is no society without people, and there are no people without passion. What Hawthorne's hero might do if he were free, one does not know, because he cannot free himself. (pp. 562-69)

> Nina Baym, "'The Blithedale Romance': A Radical Reading," in The Journal of English and Germanic Philology, *Vol. LXVII, No. 4, October, 1968, pp. 545-69.*

JAMES H. JUSTUS (essay date 1975)

[*Justus provides an extended analysis of Coverdale's character and his role as the narrator of* Blithedale.]

As a document, *The Blithedale Romance* directly confronts the question, livelier perhaps in antebellum Massachusetts than elsewhere, of "How shall a man live?" It exploits the competing claims for saying how, from such pseudo-sciences as mesmerism and spiritualism to such serious concerns as social theory and humanitarianism. Indeed, it touches upon choices demanded by a reformist culture: material grubbing or spiritual transformation? labor or leisure? commerce or art? urban or rural values? patchwork revision or radical reform? dilettantism or ideology? The generating energies in this narrative emerge from what Hawthorne's Concord neighbor Emerson referred to variously as "The Present Age," "The Times," or "The Mind and Manners of the XIX Century." Here, the truths of the human heart are tested by the explicitly social and cultural ferment of reform, the most characteristic signature of American life in the 1840's and 1850's. In no other of his fictions does Hawthorne encompass such a remarkable spectrum of lifestyles of his time; *Blithedale* is his "Mind and Manners of the XIX Century," his one romance that at least aspires to the form of the novel.

The pivot in this romance-novel is Coverdale. The bits and pieces of the story of the Blithedale brotherhood form the substance of Coverdale's story; these same bits and pieces, augmented by the ramifying implications of the urban past and the conflict of influences both personal and ideological in Coverdale, form the substance of Hawthorne's story. If Coverdale is an embarrassingly peripheral actor in the romance of Blithedale, Hawthorne makes him the leading performer in *The Blithedale Romance*. That Coverdale, as narrator, is not entirely to be trusted in the tale he tells is by now generally accepted, but Coverdale's limitations follow from the contextual fact that the elusive and disjointed events which Coverdale relates are totemistic events whose importance lies in the valuations he puts on them. The character of this narrator finally cannot be abstracted from the form which he encloses (the story he tells), but, more crucially, he cannot be abstracted from the form which encloses him (the story which Hawthorne tells).

Whereas this minor New England poet writes of a failed communal enterprise, Hawthorne writes of a failed human being—and does so both as romancer and novelist. Coverdale explores the weaknesses of egotists, faithless lovers, proud businessmen brought low, females both liberated and parasitic, grubby Yankee farmers, and spiritualist charlatans, all of whom undercut the high purposes of Blithedale; Hawthorne explores the process by which a man who shrinks from the taint of human imperfection dooms himself irrevocably to a life of sterile complacency. (pp. 22-4)

Miles Coverdale begins his last chapter with a conventional tack: "It remains only to say a few words about myself." What follows, however, is gratuitous, since the entire story has been more a self-dramatization than an account of a failed communal experiment. What the reader learns of the founding and disbanding of Blithedale is thin, curiously inert, generalized; any sense of a thickly textured life comes primarily from the minutely recorded stages of the narrator's personal relationships.

Amiable as he is, Coverdale displays revealing deficiencies both as a man and as an artist, and those deficiencies matter. While Hawthorne was always too ambivalent about the artist ever to equate the good man and good artist, both kinds of flaws in Coverdale coincide in such a way that they not merely round out the portrait of one character but also signal Hawthorne's abiding interest in both the implications of the cold heart in human affairs and in the possibilities and limitations of art. From his own account, two aspects of Coverdale can be isolated for analysis without damaging the overall texture of his narrative: his attitude toward Hollingsworth (which suggests his frailty as a man) and his use of Zenobia as symbol (which establishes the aesthetic boundaries of his art). Coverdale's judgment that he has made "but a poor and dim figure in [his] own narrative," like so many evaluations which he makes earlier, is untrue. Though the springs of action for most of the principals in the story remain hidden, those of Coverdale do not. For all his flaws he is the most familiar, the most knowable character in the book.

Coverdale's declaration of love for Priscilla at the end of his narrative may not be as jejune as earlier readers took it to be, but it indicates a spiritual impoverishment more profound than some readers now are willing to grant. Prior to his "Confession," Coverdale gives no indications that he looks upon the seamstress as anything more than a vacuous encumbrance, a patronizing attitude betraying a social and intellectual snobbery. Throughout the narrative, however, he has been attracted to both Zenobia—for her sexuality, her intelligence and passion, and her "mystery"—and Hollingsworth—for his masculine authoritativeness and his magnetism; he has even been drawn briefly, Coverdale admits, to the despicable Westervelt. But all are finally irrelevant in the matter. "Miles Coverdale's Confession" covertly acknowledges an inability to love, a radically disabling flaw which cripples him both as man and artist. His unimpressive substitutes for love, on which he expends considerable energy, are a peevish antipathy for masculine power and an exaggerated emphasis on feminine passion. Those substitutes are a direct outgrowth of his disappointing relationships with Hollingsworth and Zenobia.

Critics usually take Hollingsworth's scheme to rehabilitate criminals at face value (which is to say at Coverdale's valuation)—at best a single-minded, abstract, "partial" reform of the kind which both Emerson and Hawthorne distrusted, and at worst one that is grandiose, self-serving, dishonest, and possibly illegal. Although Hollingsworth's language in Chapter 15 is egocentric and absolutist, as befitting the radical reformer, much of the extremist tone is a result of Coverdale's mediating consciousness. After Hollingsworth rejects Coverdale's proposal to put some of Fourier's principles to work at Blithedale, Coverdale uses the incident to charge his friend with a lack of "real sympathy with our feelings and our hopes"; and he characterizes Hollingsworth's philanthropic reform with such terms as "one channel," "prolonged fiddling upon one string," and "his lonely and exclusive object in life." But Hollingsworth rejects the Fourieristic system because he believes it to be based on "the selfish principle—the principle of all human wrong, the very blackness of man's heart, the portion of ourselves which we shudder at, and which it is the whole aim of spiritual discipline to eradicate."

And though his own scheme may be overly sanguine, its principle is unselfishness. It concerned, Coverdale reports, "the reformation of the wicked by methods moral, intellectual, and industrial, by the sympathy of pure, humble, and yet exalted minds, and by opening to his pupils the possibility of a worthier life than that which had become their fate." Since even in the narrator's paraphrase the project sounds more admirable than heinous, to discredit it Coverdale falls back on what "most people thought": that it was "impracticable." But Hollingsworth rightly assesses the impracticableness of Blithedale, which is, he says, "a wretched, unsubstantial scheme . . . on which we have wasted a precious summer of our lives." As reforms go, Hollingsworth's is considerably more tangible and less self-serving than the Blithedale experiment, which Coverdale defends in language that betrays an unsupportable position even as it reveals the abstraction of his commitment.

The man who in April calls Blithedale a "counterfeit Arcadia" and who with his "customary levity" admits that he has little purpose in life other than to "make pretty verses, and play a part, with . . . the rest of the amateurs, in our pastoral," is the same man who in August exclaims that the community is now "beginning to flourish." Hollingsworth disagrees: "It is full of defects—irremediable and damning ones!—from first to last, there is nothing else! I grasp it in my hand, and find no substance whatever. There is not human nature in it!" Coverdale's adherence to the idealism of Blithedale is escapist, and Hollingsworth's invitation to "strike hands" with him promises this minor poet no more "languor and vague wretchedness" but "strength, courage, immitigable will—everything that a manly and generous nature should desire!" From Coverdale's perspective, the temptation is evil, but from the reader's it has all the marks of a healthy alternative for "an indolent or half-occupied man."

What Hollingsworth offers to Coverdale is what Coverdale, given his coldness and abstraction, cannot accept: a tangible brotherhood, disinterested devotion, generous cooperation, purpose, and above all, love. Coverdale admits, "I stood aloof."

It is the stance that damns. Blithedale is a sham, but as long as it is detached from what Hollingsworth calls "human nature," as long, that is, as it is safely idealized, Coverdale can pretend to a new life of courage and purpose. A few days after the "crisis" in the potato patch, Coverdale, with "intolerable discontent and irksomeness," lays down his hoe, says farewell to the pigs, and takes his first leave of Blithedale.

If Coverdale's failure as a man is crystallized in his "tragic passage-at-arms" with Hollingsworth, his failure as an artist is confirmed by his last meeting with Zenobia, a scene marked by his inability to redeem his superficial and derivative art with insight and charity. After Hollingsworth's rejection of Zenobia, only Coverdale witnesses her convulsive weeping. Regaining her composure, she adopts what is by this time her usual brittle and deflating attitude toward him: "Ah, I perceive what you are about! You are turning this whole affair into a ballad. Pray let me hear as many stanzas as you happen to have ready!" The words are an echo of her remark to Coverdale on their first evening, when he surmises that Priscilla has come to join the community to pay homage to the well-known feminist. "Since you see the young woman in so poetical a light," Zenobia says, "you had better turn the affair into a ballad." After projecting a romantic literary ballad, which becomes a fanciful condensation of the narrative of *Blithedale,* Zenobia turns from fanciful chatter to a more down-to-earth explanation. By "tokens that escape the obtuseness of masculine perceptions," she declares Priscilla not a death-dealing snow-maiden but a poor seamstress from the city come for "no more transcendental purpose" than to do Zenobia's miscellaneous sewing. The "affair" which might be turned into a ballad is not one of thwarted sexual love between an exotic woman and a rugged philanthropist, but a sisterly love that carries with it moral responsibility. If it is a kind of love which lies beyond Coverdale's "obtuse" perceptions, its violation of course lies even further. By her betrayal of Priscilla, Zenobia sins against the human heart in ways far more serious than her frustrated passion for Hollingsworth could ever do. That remorse over her betrayal of Priscilla for her own gain (love, money, or both) might have impelled her to take her own life never occurs to Coverdale.

The repartee between Zenobia and Coverdale on her final evening is a grim replay of this earlier scene, and her manner is an intensified version of her earlier bantering and edged wit. She utters a "sharp, light laugh." She ranges from mild irony to scornful sarcasm to haughty solemnity to calm security; but throughout the exchange, Coverdale notes that she is also "laughing" or "smiling" and remarks on the strange way in which her mind seemed "to vibrate from the deepest earnest to mere levity." It is clearly the portrait of a woman only partly in control of her emotions; but it is also a glimpse of a woman sufficiently alert to her confidant's limitations to allow him (indeed, to encourage him) to interpret her grief as simplistically as he, with his "obtuseness," is inclined to do. Thus, Zenobia collaborates with Coverdale on a little ballad about herself, the point of which is the way the world conspires against the woman "who swerves one hair's breadth out of the beaten track." Coverdale interprets this specifically as Zenobia's love for Hollingsworth and generally as the dangers of the passions which overcome the intellectual, liberated woman. Though he protests that her interpretation has "too stern a moral," it is nevertheless the one he adopts.

If the moral is "too stern," it is also irrelevant. *The Blithedale Romance* is remarkably free of evidence that the world punishes this feminist for her activities. As in other works of Hawthorne, the source and means of punishment here are more profoundly spiritual than those at the service of the world. (The same is true for Hollingsworth, whose public scheme for the reformation of criminals must be painfully internalized to cope "with a single murderer.") Though we hear much of Zenobia's activism in the cause of women's rights—which would presumably distort her humanity just as Hollingsworth's philanthropy is said to distort his—what Hawthorne dramatizes is feminine spirit, not ideological advocacy. And in the most explicitly "feminist" chapter in the book, "Eliot's Pulpit," Zenobia's statements on women's rights pale into vagueness when set beside Coverdale's own conciliating, extravagant vision of a matriarchy in which the submissive male "would kneel before a woman-ruler!"

Coverdale's limited understanding of both friends is betrayed by his language. Hollingsworth's challenge provokes Coverdale to self-torturing envy. Whereas in the earlier chapters the narrator speaks merely patronizingly of his friend, after "A Crisis" he drops even the pretense of good will. The diction grows excessive, even virulent: *odious, loathsomeness; great, black ugliness of sin; trample on considerations; squalid.* After Zenobia's death, his conduct toward Hollingsworth is dictated by what Coverdale believes to be "all the evil" of which the philanthropist is guilty; his taunts are those of a harpy. Coverdale's "ballad" about Zenobia, the kind which might have reclaimed a genteel, minor Romantic, turns out to be simply another work about the passionate heroine who, "defeated on the broad battlefield of life," falls on "her own sword, merely because Love had gone against her." Even Westervelt, at her grave, knows better than this. The world, concludes Coverdale, should throw open "all its avenues to the passport of a woman's bleeding heart." The vision is derivative just as the language which describes it is shabby. But Coverdale's failure of perception here, antecedent to his failure as artist, should come as no surprise. Much earlier, with his narrator's arrival at Blithedale, Hawthorne has prepared the reader for this moment. His new friends, particularly Zenobia, understand that Coverdale will be poet in residence, which means a continuation of his role as romantic poet now put to the service of the brotherhood; Coverdale, however, apparently expects that his new life will be the source for an art that will be qualitatively different from his previous work. Perhaps now, he says to Zenobia, he will write something deserving the name of poetry—"true, strong, natural, and sweet, as is the life which we are going to lead—something that shall have the notes of wild-birds twittering through it, or a strain like the wind-anthems in the woods." If this remark does nothing else, it establishes Coverdale as a thoroughly undistinguished talent of Mainstream Romantic. Although Hawthorne protects his readers from knowing at first hand any of his protagonist's productions, the implications are clear. The new experience should result in work more ambitious and more significant than the mechanical competence which finally attracts the attention of Rufus W. Griswold. Now to be tested are the depth and breadth of Coverdale's artistic powers, and the crucial question has implications both personal and aesthetic. Can this creator of trivial art show himself to be more than trivial? Can he in fact create something better than trivial art? The results are not promising. If there is tragedy attendant upon Zenobia's fate, it takes shape, outside and beyond the range of Coverdale's perceptions. If there is tragedy attendant upon Hollingsworth's abortive scheme for the reformation of criminals, its resonances are heard despite Coverdale's assessment of the man.

Coverdale's "romance," then, is one of the thinner kinds. It is compounded of soaring passions—most of them misdirected and coming to grim fruition. Two linked ironies emerge—that a self-confessed idler whose lack of purpose has rendered his life "all an emptiness" should denounce and hound someone else whose errors have dried up his "rich juices," and that the rich potentialities of artistic renewal should wither to the point where Coverdale can divert the tragedy of Zenobia into conventional nineteenth-century melodrama.

The Blithedale Romance stands as its own critique of Coverdale. As a memoir, it contains the testing of himself as a man; the memoir itself is the test of Coverdale the artist. He fails the first test, and only ironically does he pass the second. A bittersweet narrative, not wind-anthems or onomatopoetic songs about twittering birds, is Coverdale's ultimate response.

If Coverdale's focus in his narrative is blurred by a multiplicity of subjects (Hollingsworth, Zenobia, Old Moodie, his own routine urban life as well as his one ambivalent adventure in communal living), Hawthorne's focus on Coverdale is as sharp, intense, and composed a bit of portraiture as that provided by other first-person narratives of the nineteenth century. One of the remarkable accomplishments of *Blithedale* is Hawthorne's novelistic exploration of a theme most commonly seen in those tales written as romances, allegories, or exampla. Coverdale, a man whose emotional deficiency isolates him from the human mainstream, joins the ranks of Wakefield, Ethan Brand, Roger Chillingworth, Aylmer ("**The Birthmark**"), and Giovanni ("**Rappaccini's Daughter**"); but unlike them, he seems to exist in an actual and multidimensional society which asserts its own claims beyond the rather rigid ones he chooses to acknowledge. Hawthorne allows his protagonist entry into a wide area of contemporary life, the pleasing urbanities of society in the city, the not-so-pleasing physical demands of life in the country, the low-powered lyceum entertainments in the villages. Though in writing his memoir Coverdale thinks and acts as the romancer, Hawthorne renders the context in which Coverdale moves with the kind of circumstantial detail, the observations of commonplace reality, which occur more often in Hawthorne's notebooks than in his fiction.

Readers find Coverdale as unsatisfactory as do most of his fellow participants in the Blithedale brotherhood, and for much the same reasons: his reticence to commit himself humanly to others and his dilettantish curiosity. Both his reticence and his curiosity are expressions of a man whose frustrated search for meaning leads him to the dubious comfort of "conjectured" reconstructions of events and their significance.

Coverdale's insufficiency as man or artist cannot be justified or wished away, but lurking about this narrator is something more than mere obtuseness or inexcusable behavior. Many of Hawthorne's protagonists—saints and sinners alike—suffer from spiritual rigidity, obsessiveness, isolation, and the cold heart which threatens their moral survival; but unlike most of them, Coverdale displays a sense of humor, a tonic irony directed toward himself as well as others, a distancing perspective which permits disclosure of those ambivalences pulling him from one inadequate footing to another. With these characteristics Hawthorne extends the complexities only suggested by his customary quasi-allegorical figures into a narrator more fictively realistic. The gain is substantial. For this character whose dilemma is neither so domestic as Wakefield's nor so apocalyptic as Ethan Brand's, Hawthorne succeeds in projecting a situation that is understated, bland, and modern in its horror onto a consciousness singularly unequipped to perceive the horror.

That very disparity allows Hawthorne to lavish his full creative attention on a character who, despite an irritating and acerbic ineffectuality, stands revealed as pathetic.

For all the annoying complacency in which he cloaks himself, Coverdale still possesses a certain frail honesty which makes his failures humanly, even poignantly, understandable. The reader is not surprised, for example, when he asserts, on practically the last page of his narrative, that he would still be willing to die for a just cause provided "the effort did not involve an unreasonable amount of trouble," because this is precisely the attitude he reveals in Chapter I, when he expresses a willingness to do Old Moodie a favor if it involves "no special trouble" to himself. Early or late, Coverdale never disguises his arid emotions. What gives this account both its chill and its pathos is the realization that at its end nothing has changed. Even more pathetic, however, is the realization that Coverdale fails to understand his limited nature; his experiences, though traumatic, contribute nothing to his potential self-knowledge. It is a horrifying self-portrait of a man whose divided sensibilities are never harmonized, whose purposelessness is never replaced by purpose, and whose inability to love continues to be trivialized by fantasy.

Except for the final chapter, Coverdale seems not to see his narrative as a confession. But in its larger perspective, Hawthorne surely means for his readers to see it as such. This protagonist is not an Underground or Superfluous Man. Those Russian figures, alive as they are to every suggestion of suffering, grope messily and blatantly for some meaning to their separated lives. Coverdale, however, covers his tracks, throwing off pursuit by the civility of his personality, and presumes that sickness is to be found in souls other than his own. His document, for all its veneer of control and self-sufficiency, is confessional, and its complexity comes not from Coverdale's bland exposition but from Hawthorne's manipulation of his narrator's character.

The key to that character is Coverdale's idealism. Behind the aloofness, behind the witty and abrasive language, stands the man of good will who insists that the ideal represented by the Blithedale experiment is one to which he once genuinely subscribed. Moreover, at the end of the narrative he strongly suggests that of that little band of reformers, only he has remained faithful to its high undertaking. The adventure is a crucial one for Coverdale; and both the substance and the style of his account bespeak the poignant efforts of a man struggling to redeem himself morally and aesthetically. Alone of the major characters, including even the frail and ill-used Priscilla, Coverdale engages in no real deceptions, has no past worthy of concealing, offers no covert reformist schemes as alternatives to the community; but despite those admirable, if negative, virtues, he is concerned exclusively with ideal relationships. He is unprepared to accept, or at first even to acknowledge, the imperfect human context in which the ideal must realize itself if it is to realize itself at all. The idea of brotherhood, like a high and certainly cloudy romance, continues to attract him more than a decade after the collapse of Blithedale. As Hawthorne makes clear, however, the *idea* of brotherhood is not sufficient for redemption. Hollingsworth and Zenobia come to experience the full human implications when idealism and factuality clash, which is another way of saying that they attain a tragic self-awareness denied Coverdale.

Coverdale's very inability to do full justice to his Blithedale fellows ironically allows a self-concentration—the disclosure of character broader and richer than is possible in the portrayal of Hollingsworth, Zenobia, and Priscilla. Hawthorne's choice of a first-person narrator provides an obvious but functional hiatus of information at several crucial moments throughout the narrative. Zenobia, for example, tells Coverdale that he has returned to Blithedale "half an hour too late" to witness a climactic scene between her and Hollingsworth, and Coverdale with some chagrin admits the missed opportunity:

> And what subjects had been discussed here? All, no doubt, that, for so many months past, had kept my heart and my imagination idly feverish. Zenobia's whole character and history; the true nature of her mysterious connection with Westervelt; her later purposes towards Hollingsworth, and, reciprocally, his in reference to her; and, finally, the degree in which Zenobia had been cognizant of the plot against Priscilla, and what, at last, had been the real object of that scheme. On these points, as before, I was left to my own conjectures.

Considering the consummate effectiveness of the final scaffold scene in *The Scarlet Letter,* it is somewhat surprising that Hawthorne should pass up an opportunity to dramatize what would normally have been its counterpart in this work. Technically, of course, Hawthorne limits himself: to supply information unavailable to Coverdale would violate point of view, even with the latitude generally enjoyed by the romancer. He as well as his narrator must remain content with Coverdale's "conjectures." But why should Hawthorne deliberately delay his narrator's arrival for the key scene thirty minutes too late? Dramatized or not, this is the climactic moment in the action, the moment from which Zenobia's death and funeral and Hollingsworth's remorse inevitably follow. A simple adjustment, coming so late in the narrative, would have necessitated no radical changes in plot progression or character development. The answer lies in consistency of characterization. If Hawthorne had finally given his narrator full access to those subjects about which he had been "feverish" for several months, a vital aspect of Coverdale's character—mischievous curiosity—would have been mitigated. By keeping Coverdale in ignorance Hawthorne maintains the careful ambivalence with which he imbues his narrator from the beginning. Disallowing him the final and most important revelations is a deft tactic. It not only sustains the too-little-too-late aspect of Coverdale with which the reader has come to be so familiar; it also marks an innovative imagination at work—in its tidy culmination, the romance form is in this case skewed just enough to deprive both narrator and reader of full gratification. Both must be content with the "conjectures" of one limited man whose partial view is not only self-evident but also self-admitted.

It is tempting to sympathize with Hollingsworth's impatience with Coverdale's fashionable airs or with Zenobia's exasperation when she accuses him of "Bigotry; self-conceit; an insolent curiosity; a meddlesome temper; a cold-blooded criticism . . . ; a monstrous scepticism." But the reader knows Coverdale better than his friends know him, and for all his flaws, he is not quite a monster. He is, to be sure, a "frosty bachelor" who takes too keen an interest in indulging his curiosity; and coupled to his ineffectual and rigid idealism is a mannered style which paradoxically establishes him as a frivolous dabbler among solemn socialists. When he is not being the abrasive wit, he is the moralistic meddler. His customary moral posture is a little silly, but, more important, it is also sad. It dooms him from any further emotional growth, either

in or out of Blithedale. The personal renewal promised by the new life is aborted, and with it goes the chance for artistic renewal. Thus, Coverdale will recast his Blithedale experiences according to both what he knows (which is limited enough) and what he feels—pity and exasperation in dangerous proportions.

What Hawthorne achieves in this work is a sense of the human costs of failure, the pathos of weakness, without any diminishment of his own tough-minded standards for the conduct of life. In no other work does he succeed so well in dramatizing emptiness and purposelessness; in no other work does he sacrifice so many of the comfortable conventions of allegory or moral apologue or legend for the more difficult challenges of the realistic memoir, exchanging (in currently fashionable terms) telling for showing. Coverdale looks forward to James's emotional cripples (Marcher of "The Beast in the Jungle," Winterbourne of *Daisy Miller,* or Acton of *The Europeans*) and beyond them—to the desperate expatriates of Fitzgerald's and Hemingway's fiction and to the hollow men of Eliot's earlier poems. In permitting Coverdale virtually to construct his self, his voice, his configuring nuances, Hawthorne releases the ironic possibilities of a narrating intelligence who unconsciously steps beyond the limits which, as a romancer, he consciously observes. (pp. 25-36)

> *James H. Justus, "Hawthorne's Coverdale: Character and Art in 'The Blithedale Romance',"* in American Literature, *Vol. XLVII, No. 1, March, 1975, pp. 21-36.*

ROY HARVEY PEARCE (essay date 1975)

[*Pearce suggests that* Blithedale *can be interpreted as a reflection of Hawthorne's skepticism about the possibility of escaping from the real world into an Arcadian utopia.*]

Much of the difficulty we have with *The Blithedale Romance* inevitably derives from the fact of its matrix in Hawthorne's participation in the Brook Farm venture. Granting even his prefatory disclaimers about the relationship of the romance to its "origins" in his experience, we still must insist that the book is an "anti-utopia" and consequently feel obliged to demand of it that it should have qualities of exact and exacting socio-cultural observations appropriate to that "genre"; that it should be less melodramatic and more satirical; that its first-person narrator must be either altogether in control of his narrative or altogether its victim—not, as is the actual case, somewhere between the two postures. Anti-utopian writing, we conclude, should not be all *that* ambiguous. And in our interpretations of *The Blithedale Romance* we tend on the one hand to second-guess Hawthorne and to demonstrate how much better the book would be were it not so ambiguous in its anti-utopianism, or, on the other, to strain to make a case out for it not as an anti-utopia but as an almost perfected romance of protest against things as they were and are—with Coverdale, not Zenobia, the real suicide in the whole affair.

Surely it is crucial for *The Blithedale Romance* that it grows out of Hawthorne's Brook Farm experience. What is centrally at issue—or should be—is his particular interpretation of that experience and his rendering of the interpretation, his sense of the "utopianism" he was doubting, not ours. (p. 49)

The preface [is] . . . a critical point of entry—or commencement—for an approach to *The Blithedale Romance* [see excerpt dated 1852]. Claiming that his recollections of Brook Farm are but incidental to his story, Hawthorne is explicit as to his intentions:

> In short, his present concern with the Socialist Community is merely to establish a theatre, a little removed from the highway of ordinary travel, where the creatures of his brain may play their phantasmagorical antics, without exposing them to too close a comparison with the actual events of real lives.

He would claim the privileges of the romancer who needs a "Faery Land, so like the real world, that, in a suitable remoteness, one cannot well tell the difference, but with an atmosphere of strange enchantment, beheld through which the inhabitants have a propriety of their own." It follows that his characters are not to be understood as real Brook Farmers but as types entirely appropriate to a romance: "The self-concentrated Philanthropist; the high-spirited Woman, bruising herself against the narrow limitations of her sex; the weakly Maiden, whose tremulous nerves endow her with Sibylline attributes; the Minor Poet, beginning life with strenuous aspirations which die out with his youthful fervor. . . ."

These sentiments and these claims are of course analogous to those in the preface to *The House of the Seven Gables*. And they derive from a problem common to the two romances—indeed, to virtually all of Hawthorne's work after *The Scarlet Letter*: that he set himself increasingly to treating of contemporaneous life and so found himself increasingly concerned with the sort of materials which the novel as a literary form had been evolved to comprehend: the experience of life as interesting, demanding, and valuable precisely as it could be conceived of in terms lived through day-to-day. The romancer's problem was in effect to get such perspective on that experience as would free him of the novelist's regular commitment to evoke it in its own terms, so to be in some ultimate sense at least a "realist." Hawthorne's means to this end in *The House of the Seven Gables* had been to conceive of himself as a historian whose special knowledge of the history of the Pyncheons gave him a power of psychological perception such that he could function as romancer.

The problem in *The Blithedale Romance,* granting its matrix in Hawthorne's Brook Farm experience, granting his dubiety about that experience (itself quite evident in opinions expressed when he was actually at Brook Farm), is a particularly difficult one. For it is immanently necessary in anti-utopian writings—as in the utopian writings which call them forth—that there be a strong quality of novelistic treatment. This derives from the nature of the utopian enterprise itself, in which revolutionary fantasies are rendered as though realizable in quite concrete, particular, immediate, and realistic terms.

Henry James's contrast of the real and the romantic—especially because it comes in the midst of his lucubrations on Hawthorne—is useful here:

> The real represents to my perception the things we cannot possibly *not* know, sooner or late, in one way or another; it being but one of the accidents of our hampered state, and one of the incidents of their quantity and number, that particular instances have not yet come our way. The romantic stands, on the other hand, for the things that, with all the facilities in the world, all the wealth and all the courage and all the wit and the adventure, we never *can* directly

know; the things that can reach us only through the beautiful circuit and subterfuge of our thought and our desire.

Hope for a utopian society may well be rooted in the romantic impulse as James defines it. But its realization, ironically enough, depends upon a bringing into full play the realistic impulse. As it were, "particular instances" must not be just generally, exotically, or allegorically desiderated, but rather forced to "come our way"—forced into being in concrete and particular "quantity and number." And when what is in question is anti-utopian writing, the burden of the novelistic is all the greater. For then there is a further formal problem, that of satire. (And as it has recently been demonstrated, utopia, anti-utopia, and satire are, as literary modes, in their origin and development, as well as in their form and function, integrally related one with another.) Behind James's discomfort with *The Blithedale Romance* in his little book on Hawthorne [see *NCLC,* Vol. 2] lie the problems he sets for himself in his later preface to the New York edition version of *The American.* And James's discomfort has of course been that of many critics who have come after him. That discomfort is at the root of our difficulty with *The Blithedale Romance.*

The primary intention of Hawthorne's Preface to *The Blithedale Romance,* then, is to assuage that discomfort and to find a way around that difficulty. Hawthorne is insisting not that we forget about the "real" Brook Farm but rather that we should let ourselves be guided into an acceptance of what he has made out of his experience there:

> This ["Faery Land"] atmosphere is what the American romancer needs. In its absence, the beings of imagination are compelled to show themselves in the same category as actually living mortals; a necessity that generally renders the paint and pasteboard of their composition but too painfully discernible. With the idea of partially obviating this difficulty (the sense of which has always pressed very heavily upon him), the author has ventured to make free with his old, and affectionately remembered home, at BROOK FARM, as being, certainly, the most romantic episode of his own life—essentially a day-dream, and yet a fact—and thus offering an available foothold between fiction and reality. Furthermore, the scene was in good keeping with the personages whom he desired to introduce.

The principal personage so introduced is Miles Coverdale. Hawthorne compounds his formal problem and complicates our comprehending his point-of-view by introducing Coverdale as a first-person narrator—sometimes unreliable—in whose vocabulary, as Hawthorne creates it for him, terms like "daydream" and its analogues are prime instruments of understanding and interpretation. Hawthorne's critique of Brook Farm, one concludes, is a critique of a day-dream made out to be rendered by a day-dreamer, a recollection of a fantasy by a compulsive fantast, an anti-utopia told by a failed utopian.

The task accordingly set for the interpreter of *The Blithedale Romance* is to ascertain the particular utopian quality of Blithedale, not of Brook Farm. That quality, in a word, is Arcadian: a version of what A. O. Lovejoy long ago analyzed as Western Man's overwhelming yearning to return to what he was sure must have been an earlier, simpler state of affairs, "soft primitivism''; what we can describe, in psychological terms, as a compulsion to idyllic regression. Hawthorne does have Coverdale and the others—when they are brought to confront this state of affairs—speak ironically, though most often their irony is directed not at themselves but at their fellows, as though each thinks that the other, not himself, is guilty of Arcadianism. Moreover, in the particular case of Coverdale (and the particular case is integral with his being a first-person narrator whose style as thinker is perilously close to that of his creator as it is set forth in the Preface), there is evidence of what we might best call a manifest and a latent Arcadianism. In the first instance, Coverdale habitually mocks the utopian aspirations of those at Blithedale, often including himself. In the second instance, however, Hawthorne makes him, all-unknowing, reveal his own regressive qualities; herein he is—especially in the last third of the romance—the arch peeping-tom, the voyeur who, hoping to find a means of simplifying his life to the uttermost, longs for an Arcadia beyond the ken of that his fellows are trying to create, an Arcadia of the solitary. It might well be that in creating Coverdale Hawthorne is trying to exorcise out of himself a fundamental drive in his own character, as in creating Blithedale and its special society, he is trying to come to see as ''fact'' a long-gone ''day-dream,'' and so come to grips with a vital portion of his own history. At any rate, what is centrally at issue in *The Blithedale Romance*—what is central to its import—is utopianism as Arcadianism.

This motif is sharply delineated early in the narrative, in Chapter VIII—''A Modern Arcadia.'' Coverdale emerges from his sick-room on May-Day, and, as the narrative progresses, for the first time begins to see the relationship which obtains among Zenobia, Priscilla, and Hollingsworth. He finds Zenobia and Priscilla ''a Maying together,'' and, as Hollingsworth appears, realizes how Priscilla is torn between her devotion to the other two. He sees the whole scene as somehow vitalizing and now senses that at Blithedale he can undergo a kind of rebirth:

> My fit of illness had been an avenue between two existences; the low-arched and darksome doorway, through which I had crept out of a life of old conventionalisms, on my hands and knees, as it were, and gained admittance into the freer region that lay beyond. In this respect, it was like death. And, as with death, too, it was good to have gone through it. Not otherwise could I have rid myself of a thousand follies, fripperies, prejudices, habits, and other such worldly dust as inevitably settles upon the crowd along the broad highway, giving them all one sordid aspect, before noon-time, however freshly they may have begun their pilgrimage, in the dewy morning. The very substance upon my bones had not been fit to live with, in any better, truer, or more energetic mode than that to which I was accustomed. So it was taken off me and flung aside, like any other worn out or unseasonable garment; and, after shivering a little while in my skeleton, I began to be clothed anew, and much more satisfactorily than in my previous suit. In literal and physical truth, I was quite another man.

And so he is led to meditate upon the forces which make Blithedale operative. Above all, he decides, his life and that of his fellows is now no longer artificially ordered, its conventions now being set by the fundamental laws of ''Nature.''

The title page of the first edition of Blithedale.

The rationale is the traditional one in Arcadian-primitivistic thought. As ''Arcadians,'' he writes, those at Blithedale—individualists all—are nonetheless not ''the pastoral people of poetry and the stage.'' Rather, they live a ''yeoman life.'' And at this point he can afford to be ironic—this time concerning the difficulties confronting Arcadians when they would set themselves to physical labor. The irony, so it develops as the narrative continues, is also sensed by Zenobia and Hollingsworth, whom he reports as being amused at the sight of a minor poet turned yeoman. Hollingsworth at least approves. Coverdale reports him as commenting: ''There is at least this good in a life of toil, that it takes the nonsense and fancy-work out of a man, and leaves nothing but what truly belongs to him.'' At this point, Zenobia accepts Hollingsworth's truth as her own, and Coverdale—now with them a committed Arcadian—does not gainsay them.

Chapter VIII serves as an initial focal point for the Arcadian motifs in *The Blithedale Romance*. The motifs, however, are highlighted throughout the romance. In Chapter III, Coverdale recalls his proclaiming his intention to begin writing a new kind of poetry—''true, strong, natural, and sweet, as is the life we are going to lead. . . .'' In this chapter too he remembers his discovering that Zenobia can be another Eve, as life at Blithedale will not be ''artificial.'' In Chapter IV there is the record of Hollingsworth's declaration that the coming of Priscilla indeed marks a new beginning of things, and in Chapter

V of his insistence that his utopia, his "socialist scheme," will be wholly altruistic. In Chapter V too there is reported the discussion of the search for a name for the colony; "Utopia," presumably because it calls to mind "artificial" arrangements, is "unanimously scouted down" and Blithedale is agreed upon—all this on an evening when Coverdale must report, with an irony whose full implications he cannot foresee, "How cold an Arcadia was this!" In Chapter IX Coverdale comments that it was in the nature of Blithedale to incline all "to the soft affections of the Golden Age" and later Zenobia is reported as describing events at Blithedale (here again there is an irony whose eventual implications are not foreseen) as the playing out of a "pastoral." In Chapter X Coverdale says that in the view of visitors to Blithedale, "we were as poetical as Arcadians, besides being as practical as the hardest-fisted husbandmen in Massachusetts." And so it goes—until toward the end, when in Chapter XX, Zenobia, in town, annoyed at Coverdale's spying on her, is reported as speaking of "such Arcadian freedom of falling in love as we lately have enjoyed . . . ," and when in Chapter XXIII Coverdale, looking back, can say only of his earlier Arcadian hopes for his time at Blithedale, ". . . it had enabled me to pass the summer in a novel and agreeable way, had afforded me some grotesque specimens of artificial simplicity. . . ."

The movement, as regards the Arcadian motifs, is from naive commitment to amused irony to disillusionment. But there is a degree of ambiguity at all points—an ambiguity deriving in good part from Coverdale's being continually caught between the realms of day-dream and fact. The turning-point, if it can justifiably be called that, perhaps comes toward the middle of the narrative, in Chapter XV, after Coverdale has at long last begun to realize the terrible complications of the relationships among Zenobia, Priscilla, and Hollingsworth. It is in this chapter that Hollingsworth first manifests himself for what he is—single-mindedly devoted to his version of utopia, altogether careless of the aspirations of others. In the course of their conversation Coverdale begins to have his doubts about the perdurability of Blithedale and all that it stands for. He sees that death must inevitably come to someone in this Arcadia:

> "I wonder, Hollingsworth, who, of all these strong men, and fair women and maidens, is doomed the first to die. Would it not be well, even before we have the absolute need of it, to fix upon a spot for a cemetery? Let us choose the rudest, roughest, most uncultivable spot, for Death's garden-ground; and Death shall teach us to beautify it, grave by grave."

There is portrayed here a crisis (and the chapter is called "A Crisis") not only in Hollingsworth's relationships with his fellows but in Coverdale's sense of the whole Arcadian enterprise that is Blithedale. But here again, Hawthorne is writing according to the Arcadian tradition. For this episode derives—whether or not consciously on Hawthorne's part, it is impossible to say—from the traditional "Et in Arcadia ego" topos, in which the presence of death is found to be ineluctable in the Arcadian scheme of things. And the "Et in Arcadia ego" topos is affirmed, at almost the very end, in Chapter XXVII, when Coverdale must meditate on the "ugly circumstances" of Zenobia's suicide and of the injury to her body done in the process of recovering it. He somehow cannot believe that Zenobia would have drowned herself if she had realized how indecorous she would have looked in death. For, he writes, "in Zenobia's case there was some tint of the Arcadian affectation that had been visible enough in all our lives, for a few months past."

The Arcadian mode was indeed an affectation in Hawthorne's view of things. He has Coverdale, in exhausted retrospect, write of Blithedale in the last "confessional" chapter: "The experiment, so far as its original projectors were concerned, proved, long ago a failure; first lapsing into Fourierism, and dying, as it well deserved, for this infidelity to its own higher spirit." Hawthorne, indeed, believed whole-heartedly in that "higher spirit," but could nonetheless find it, for people like Coverdale and the rest, an affectation. It was an affectation for such as them, because it was a "higher spirit" appropriate only to children. And what is centrally involved in *The Blithedale Romance*—what gives it its special import—is Hawthorne's conviction that willy-nilly Coverdale and the rest are acting like children, trying to reduce—or to return—life to terms impossible for adults. Surely Coverdale's voyeurism, including its sexual aspects as his attitude toward Zenobia reveals them, has something to do with his failure to grow up.

At this point some historical considerations are . . . worth noting. *The Blithedale Romance* is a project Hawthorne undertook at that point in his life when at long last he was doing what he had committed himself to do as early as 1838, retelling Greek myths in a style appropriate to children. The chronology is important. On January 1, 1851, Hawthorne finished *The House of the Seven Gables*. On April 7, 1851, he reported to a correspondent that he was planning *A Wonder-Book*. On May 3, 1851, he reported that *A Wonder-Book* was in fact designed. On July 15, 1851, *A Wonder-Book* was in his publisher Fields's hands. On July 24, 1851, he reported that he had decided to write a book based on his Brook Farm experiences. On November 8, 1851, *A Wonder-Book* was published. Around November 23, 1851, he reported that he had begun to write the book which became *The Blithedale Romance*. On May 2, 1852, he sent the manuscript of *The Blithedale Romance* to Whipple. On June 8, 1852, he reported that he was thinking about writing a continuation of *A Wonder-Book* (this became *Tanglewood Tales*). He was stalled in this enterprise subsequently, because he agreed to write Franklin Pierce's campaign biography and then involved himself in the campaign itself. In November, 1852, with Pierce elected, he knew that he would get the consulship at Liverpool; and on March 15, 1853, he could report that he was working on the continuation of *A Wonder-Book*. *Tanglewood Tales* was published in England and the United States in August 1853.

The point of the chronologizing is to emphasize the fact that *The Blithedale Romance* was written at a time when Hawthorne was most deeply concerned to demonstrate that Arcadianism was quite properly a stage in the development of the child's life. Both *A Wonder-Book* and *Tanglewood Tales* center on that notion. Hawthorne has a young collegian, Eustace Bright, retell Greek myths from a child's perspective. More important to the present argument, he is persuaded that the myths, as he has them retold, are pure not only from the child's point-of-view but from an historical point-of-view. Hawthorne went to standard learned sources, took the myths as they had come down to him, but felt bound to take into account the fact that over the ages they had accreted to themselves the complications and corruptions of adult life—complications and corruptions which he made clear were inevitable but nonetheless were not integral to the myths in their "pure" state. This is yet another version of his obsession with *felix culpa*.

The best summary of his view occurs in the preface to *Tanglewood Tales,* in which he speaks in his own person:

> . . . Eustace told me that these myths were the most singular things in the world, and that he was invariably astonished, whenever he began to relate one, by the readiness with which it adapted itself to the childish purity of his auditors. The objectionable characteristics seem to be a parasitical growth, having no essential connection with the original fable. . . . When the first poet or romancer told these marvellous legends (such was Eustace Bright's opinion), it was still the Golden Age. Evil had never yet existed; and sorrow, misfortune, crime, were mere shadows which the mind fancifully created for itself, as a shelter against too sunny realities; or, at most, but prophetic dreams, to which the dreamer himself did not yield a waking credence. Children are now the only representatives of the men and women of that happy era; and therefore it is that we must raise the intellect and the fancy to the levels of childhood, in order to re-create the original myths.

Hawthorne is here eulogizing the sort of world which he perforce treated dyslogistically in *The Blithedale Romance.* For the Arcadian world of Blithedale is essentially—and for Hawthorne's purposes, inappropriately—a child's world—not the sort of utopia of which Emerson wrote so cheerfully in "New England Reformers" (1844): "What a fertility of projects for the salvation of the world!" Rather the world of Blithedale is one to which all concerned willy-nilly regress in their desperate attempt to find a place where what they take to be their gifts and commitments can be realized. It is a Land of Cockaigne in which the Identity Crisis (the critic needs the concepts of ego psychology if he is to be a proper literary historian) can be forever postponed.

Early in the romance, Hawthorne writes: "As for Zenobia, there was a glow in her cheeks that made me think of Pandora, fresh from Vulcan's workshop, and full of the celestial warmth by dint of which he had tempered and moulded her." In *A Wonder-Book* Hawthorne retells the Pandora myth in a story called **"The Paradise of Children."** Pandora, in this piece, is a child, as is Epithemeus, her husband in traditional versions of the story. She fusses at length over the mysterious box which Mercury has left, does not realize that her existence is idyllic, and finally opens the box, releasing a multitude of evils on the world, but also releasing Hope. In the middle of the story, Hawthorne comments thus on his Pandora:

> It might have been better for Pandora if she had a little work to do, or anything to employ her mind upon, so as not to be so constantly thinking of [opening the box]. But children led so easy a life, before any Troubles came into the world, that they really had a great deal too much leisure. . . . When life is all sport, toil is the real play. . . .

Those in residence at Blithedale, it will be recalled, do in fact "toil, but, once they discover that toil is in fact not play, not enthusiastically." What they *really* wish, Hawthorne is suggesting, is that regressive state of life wherein they will be free to realize themselves in a way the conditions of life lived day-to-day in society will not allow. With the exception of Zen-

obia—and this is what makes her, as James first pointed out, Hawthorne's most realized woman—they have rejected the option of adjusting their fantasies to the exigencies of life lived in the world proper. She is the exception, because such an option does not altogether exist for her. But she is nonetheless not quite right, since she could have changed her name and her life-style to that, not of Margaret Fuller, but of Elizabeth or Mary Peabody. She remains, however, a passionate *Sophia* Peabody. And that is her tragedy, the only one in *The Blithedale Romance.* The rest is pathos.

It could have been more. Hawthorne, I believe, did not have sufficient perspective on his own commitment to the notion that childhood, however Arcadian, was also a stage in growing up and into the world, a world which could not be that of the romance. Still, I think the tone of the book—mocking in its irony, not satirical—is justified by its intention and its import. My own historical fantasy as regards the place of *The Blithedale Romance* in Hawthorne's *oeuvre* is that the young collegian, Eustace Bright, who tells the stories in *A Wonder-Book* and *Tanglewood Tales,* finished college, tried his hand at literature, could not bring himself to face the practicalities of the life of the writer as his friend Nathaniel Hawthorne had done, with Hawthorne went to Brook Farm, and never recovered from the experience, precisely because the experience was for him, as it was not for Hawthorne, an abiding fact rather than a kind of day-dream. Later—as I reconstruct the inside story of *The Blithedale Romance*—he recounted his adventures, hopes, and aspirations to Hawthorne and agreed that his friend might tell them, if only his name were changed. From Bright to Coverdale. Any literary historian—with some etymological training—would understand. (pp. 51-63)

> *Roy Harvey Pearce, "Day-Dream and Fact: The Import of 'The Blithedale Romance'," in* Individual and Community: Variations on a Theme in American Fiction, *edited by Kenneth H. Baldwin and David K. Kirby, Duke University Press, 1975, pp. 49-63.*

MICHAEL DAVITT BELL   (essay date 1980)

[Bell contends that "the failure of American Romanticism is the great subject of The Blithedale Romance." *According to the critic, Coverdale and the other characters in the novel are frustrated in their attempts to achieve spiritual regeneration because they are unwilling to confront the psychological and social realities operating within themselves and their community.]*

The main theme of *The Blithedale Romance* is . . . renewal—the revival of empty forms into spiritual youth and warmth. This theme operates on many levels: not only social or cultural but also personal, aesthetic, and perhaps even religious. The Utopian experiment, like the love of Holgrave and Phoebe in *The House of the Seven Gables,* is a "scheme for beginning the life of Paradise anew." It is a return to lost origins—to a fresh air, as Coverdale puts it, that has "not been spoken into words of falsehood, formality, and error." Coverdale himself moves to Blithedale in search of a renewal at once personal—the discovery of a new purpose in life—and aesthetic—the connection of his poetry with something "real" or "substantial." Priscilla, too, like Coverdale's insubstantial fancies, is revived by being "mingled" with substantial reality. Even the drinking of the old topers, in the saloon where Coverdale seeks out Old Moodie, is tied to the general theme of renewal—in terms that again recall Holgrave's appeal to Phoebe. "The true purpose of their drinking," Coverdale explains, "—and one that will induce men to drink, or do something equivalent, as long as this weary world shall endure—was the renewed youth and vigor, the brisk, cheerful sense of things present and to come, with which, for about a quarter-of-an-hour, the dram permeated their systems.''

Coverdale's ''for about a quarter-of-an-hour'' is ominous. All the efforts at renewal in *The Blithedale Romance,* including the Utopian experiment itself, are equally, if not always so rapidly, evanescent, and Coverdale implies a historical development more enervating, even, than the displacement of original spirit into empty formalism. For the saloon images a Utopian impulse that has moved from ''spirit'' to ''spirits''—from genuine inspiration to artificial stimulants. The account of Westervelt's spiritualism reveals how fully, in the nineteenth-century America of *The Blithedale Romance,* even the antiformal impulse of spiritual regeneration has become a species of formal, mechanical artifice. It is in this sense that America, as a culture, has literalized the direst implications of the romance. Westervelt promises spiritual rebirth, but it is to be sought, apparently, through chemical means.

Coverdale is careful to distance himself from Westervelt's bogus spiritualism, yet he has earlier admitted to a sense of kinship with the professor. The night before setting out for Blithedale, we learn in the book's first sentence, Coverdale had attended ''the wonderful exhibition of the Veiled Lady,'' and he returns to it toward the close; he is, in fact, well on his way to becoming a regular customer. There are more than a few suggestive similarities between Westervelt's spurious art and the art of Miles Coverdale, as romancer, and the account of Westervelt's plans for the regeneration of the world sounds a good deal like the project of the Blithedale Utopians. ''He spoke,'' writes Coverdale, ''of a new era that was dawning upon the world; an era that would link soul to soul, and the present life to what we call futurity, with a closeness that should finally convert both worlds into one great, mutually conscious brotherhood.''

Of course, the community's failure—its betrayal of its ideals—is to some extent a result of practical political or social problems. The bond of the community is, as Coverdale puts it, ''not affirmative, but negative.'' Theirs is a rebellion without a positive program. The one bond or ideal they do espouse in common, ''familiar love,'' is difficult to implement. They eschew competition only to find themselves in commercial competition with the outside world, and, internally, the ideal of ''familiar love'' soon gives way to the nasty reality of sexual competition among Zenobia, Priscilla, Hollingsworth, and Coverdale. As with the ''Utopia of human virtue and happiness,'' described at the outset of *The Scarlet Letter,* so, at Blithedale, ''practical necessities'' soon overwhelm the ideals of the ''original project.''

Coverdale's artistic ideals also succumb, in his view, to a tyranny of inevitable circumstance. He sets out, through immersion in the ''reality'' of farming, to produce verse at once ''poetic'' and ''real.'' His is the ideal of the conservative romancer: he will ''mingle'' the Imaginary and the Actual. But actuality overwhelms his poetry as surely as it overwhelms the idealism of the Utopians. ''Our labor,'' Coverdale laments, ''symbolized nothing, and left us mentally sluggish in the dusk of the evening. Intellectual activity is incompatible with any large amount of bodily exercise.''

There is something disingenuous, however, in this explanation. The real failure, of the Blithedale experiment and of Coverdale's art, is not a triumph of actual over ideal. It is, rather,

a prior failure of idealism—a failure of the artist and his society to confront the true nature of the originating spirit of literary and social order. What Coverdale and his cohorts call an appeal to imagination or spirit is in fact an evasion of both. Several cultural historians have recently described what they see as a failure of Romanticism in nineteenth-century America, namely, the refusal of accepted cultural spokesmen and spokeswomen to acknowledge the reality of social and psychological disrelation, the dark night of the soul, confronted by their great European and British contemporaries. (pp. 185-87)

In this sense, and nowhere more clearly than in Coverdale's musings on his purpose as an artist, the failure of American Romanticism is the great subject of *The Blithedale Romance;* for in Coverdale's theory and practice of literary art we see the ultimate extension of his society's corruption of regenerative ''spirit.'' Zenobia, he writes,

> should have made it a point of duty . . . to sit endlessly to painters and sculptors, and preferably to the latter; because the cold decorum of the marble would consist with the utmost scantiness of drapery, so that the eye might chastely be gladdened with her material perfection, in its entirety.

The duplicity of this appeal to artistic etherealization—the tension between ''chastely'' and ''gladdened''—is suggested even more forcefully in Coverdale's account of the realistic paintings of roast beef, sirloins and the like, that he encounters later in the saloon. In these paintings, he insists ''you seemed to have the genuine article before you, and yet with an indescribable, ideal charm.'' Earlier, however, he has speculated: ''Some very hungry painter, I suppose, had wrought these subjects of still life, heightening his imagination with his appetite, and earning, it is to be hoped, the privilege of a daily dinner off whichever of his pictorial viands he liked best.'' It is interesting to read this idea back to the passage about being ''chastely . . . gladdened,'' through art, by Zenobia's ''material perfection.'' Coverdale's ''aesthetic'' prurience, his sublimation of ''appetite'' into ''ideal charm,'' suggests at the very least that Hawthorne understood a good deal about what went on beneath the ''chaste'' surface of his culture's bogus ''idealism.'' Like Washington Irving, Coverdale displaces his guilty fantasies into the safer realms of ''spiritual'' or ''aesthetic'' platitude, and Hawthorne is fully aware of the operation of this displacement.

Coverdale's unacknowledged prurience, moreover, provides a kind of paradigm for the general failure of Blithedale. Of the Utopians we meet, only Zenobia comes anywhere near to trusting the community's alleged ''spirit.'' She is the only one whose love is open and passionate, untinged by opportunism, and the community suppresses her sincerity and sexuality, her frank awareness that ''familiar love'' may have something to do with sex, as thoroughly as does the romancer, Miles Coverdale. Like Coverdale's art, the community's treatment of Zenobia forces upon her precisely the fate that Aylmer, in his refusal to face and acknowledge the ''truth'' obscured by his scientific ''self-deception,'' forces upon Georgiana [in **''The Birthmark''**]. As a result of Aylmer's experiment, Georgiana's cheek assumes a ''marble paleness''; in death she becomes literally a statue. Coverdale wishes ''chastely'' to indulge his repressed sexual fantasies about Zenobia by displacing her into ''the cold decorum of . . . marble.'' Zenobia, at the close of *The Blithedale Romance,* becomes ''the marble image of a death-agony.'' Zenobia, to be sure, has her faults and excesses, but it is in the community's refusal to acknowledge in her the truths masked by its "idealism" that we see the strong parallel between Blithedale and Coverdale's romance about it—in the repressiveness and shallowness of that "ideal" toward which both strive.

The ideal's fullest incarnation, if one may use so strong a term, is Priscilla. She is *already* "ideal." She is already, in Coverdale's terms, "artistically" safe. Indeed, she is a literalization of a fictional stereotype, the sexless, "girlish" woman, and the community, at Hollingsworth's suggestion, happily accepts its treatment of her as the test of its adherence to its ideals. But the ideal represented by Priscilla is highly suspect. Her initial appearance of ethereality is just that, an appearance. It has more in common with the emaciation of Poe's "spiritual" vampires than with any true spiritual quality. And Priscilla, we must not forget, *is* the Veiled Lady, the star of Westervelt's spurious show. Finally, Priscilla's actions and apparent motives, whatever her appearance, are hardly admirable. She comes to Blithedale to test Zenobia's sisterly love, but she conceals from Zenobia the fact that they are sisters. As a result, Old Moodie takes his money from Zenobia and transfers it to Priscilla, who then, apparently as a consequence, gets Zenobia's man.

If this is "ideality," it is ideality of a peculiarly acquisitive and ultimately prosperous sort. It reminds one of Arthur Mervyn's equally successful pursuit of sincerity [in Charles Brockden Brown's *Arthur Mervyn*]; and Priscilla's success, like Arthur's, involves the deliberate sublimation of "desperate suggestions" into "better thoughts." With Priscilla an "artistic" ideal enters directly into the action of *The Blithedale Romance,* but hers is an "art," not of expression, but of repression. She is "ideal" largely in appearing sexless. She exists and prospers entirely as an evasive sublimation of all those fantasies Coverdale can indulge only "chastely." Coverdale's evasion of Zenobia, his turning instead to the "ideality" of art or of Priscilla, is ultimately an evasion of himself, of the impulses he cannot face openly without guilt. It is an evasion of true Romanticism, of truly imaginative self-discovery. His confession of "love" for Priscilla, on the other hand, is a capitulation to bogus Romanticism, to sentimentality. Passion is made safe by being surrounded with all the trappings of spiritual religion. But this rhetoric, Hawthorne's irony makes clear, still has as its basis the very guilty fantasy it is meant to repress; and sentimentality, as Priscilla's prosperity reveals, is the rhetoric not only of Coverdale's repressed imagination but of his culture.

What has been sentimentalized most fully, in *The Blithedale Romance,* is the very impulse toward regeneration that lay at the heart of the Puritan migration and that supposedly lies at the heart of Blithedale. The faith of the founders, Hawthorne writes in **"Main Street,"** was in itself a genuine "spiritual mystery." At Blithedale, a community that has retreated in guilty fear from *true* "spirit" and "mystery," such terms are used in a curious fashion. The "freedom" of Zenobia's "deportment" leads a nervous Coverdale to surmise that she is "a woman to whom wedlock had thrown wide the gates of mystery." "What are you seeking to discover in me?" asks Zenobia. "The mystery of your life," answers Coverdale. Earlier, he meditates on the peculiarities of the little purses Priscilla manufactures, which Old Moodie, we learn later, is in the habit of "quietly insinuating under the notice" of young gentlemen in the saloon:

> Their peculiar excellence, besides the great delicacy and beauty of the manufacture, lay in the almost impossibility that any uninitiated person should discover the aperture; although, to a practised touch, they would open as wide as charity or prodigality might wish. I wondered if it were not a symbol of Priscilla's own mystery.

Worst of all is Coverdale's grisly account of the search for Zenobia's body:

> Hollingsworth at first sat motionless, with the hooked-pole elevated in the air. But, by-and-by, with a nervous and jerky movement, he began to plunge it into the blackness that upbore us, setting his teeth, and making precisely such thrusts, methought, as if he were stabbing at a deadly enemy. I bent over the side of the boat. So obscure, however, so awfully mysterious, was that dark stream, that—and the thought made me shiver like a leaf—I might as well have tried to look into the enigma of the eternal world, to discover what had become of Zenobia's soul, as into the river's depths, to find her body.

For all its sentimental rhetoric, this passage, like Aylmer's gruesome dream or the *Mad Trist* of Poe's Lancelot Canning, transforms sexual fantasy into guilty aggression. Such is the course of the "love" that Blithedale has set out to embody as a social ideal. It fails not so much because of the counterforce of individual selfishness as because it is itself no "ideal" but a hollow abstraction, a denial or evasion of its own most central reality.

The obscene *double-entendres* in these passages are clearly not deliberate on Coverdale's part, but they are just as surely deliberate on Hawthorne's and may thus suggest what "dale" it is the narrator wishes to "cover." The point is that a culture that has sublimated sexuality into a quasi-religious vocabulary of "spirit" and "mystery," a sentimentalized displacement of the truths of imagination or fantasy, is inevitably going to slip into unintended *double-entendre* in its "spiritual" discourse. For this discourse and the culture that sustains it no longer *have* any genuine basis in "spiritual" experience; they have sacrificed that relation. What drives them is the unacknowledgable force of their evasion, of their sacrifice. Characters in *The Scarlet Letter* . . . have a habit of silencing those who hint at their own deepest impulses with an admonitory "Hush." In the spiritual "ideality" of Blithedale, this "Hush" has become an aesthetic and social principle.

We must be very clear about what happens in *The Blithedale Romance.* In a sense we might say that the suppression or repression of Zenobia is simply a nineteenth-century version of what happens to Hester in *The Scarlet Letter.* The Puritan fathers, however, are quite open about what they are doing: they suppress Hester's rebellious passion because it threatens their civil system. While they may imprison and punish her, they do not sentimentalize either her motives or their own. Her ideals, whatever their connection to the community's "first stir of spirit," are not their ideals. The Utopians at Blithedale, on the other hand, claim to espouse the very individualism for which Zenobia stands. Hester at least had the support of coherent opposition. Zenobia confronts a world, by contrast, in which a sentimentalized language of social and spiritual "idealism" has become a medium of psychological repression and social control. In the allegorical social drama of *The Scarlet Letter*, the Beadle and the scaffold may also be forces of social control, but this control is overt. The Beadle and the scaffold, in this sense, mean what they say. In the "ideal" social drama of Blithedale, things mean precisely what they do not say.

Blithedale's sentimental language of social control finds its objective correlative in Priscilla and does so with a straight face. The irony of this language, as it functions to conceal the guilty fears and fantasies at its heart, is never openly acknowledged. The whole culture has taken on the quality of one of Poe's "arabesques." If Zenobia behaves at times melodramatically or theatrically, as in the mode of her suicide, we can hardly blame her. Hester was forced to play a part in a drama that, for all its allegorical coerciveness, was rooted in "practical necessities," but Zenobia acts in a world in which such necessities, and the regenerative impulse that stands against them, have taken on the character of fiction.

"A veil may be needful," Hawthorne wrote in his *American Notebooks* in the mid-1830s, "but never a mask." Coverdale accuses Zenobia of using her name as "a sort of mask"; he prefers the spurious spirituality of Priscilla, the Veiled Lady. But it is Coverdale and his community who, in their refusal to confront the full implications of the imaginative regeneration they claim to espouse, turn the veil of symbolic expression into a mask of evasion. They thus turn their social life—quite literally, when Coverdale returns to Blithedale—into a masquerade. It is in this sense that Coverdale's guilty obfuscation becomes symptomatic of a more general social obfuscation. Seventeenth-century New England, in Hawthorne's view, displaced sentiments into words. Their nineteenth-century descendants at Blithedale have lost sight of the distinction. For sentiments they have substituted sentimentality.

It was against precisely such sentimental evasion that Melville spent the bulk of his career protesting. Zenobia strikes the Melvillean note in her final speech to Coverdale, before his first departure from Blithedale: "It needs a wild steersman when we voyage through Chaos! The anchor is up! Farewell!" But no one at Blithedale is willing to cast off all cables. At their next meeting Coverdale accuses Zenobia, in his mind, of turning herself into "a work of art," but she has no choice in a society whose only surviving values are, in the worst sense, "artistic." Even in asserting that he "malevolently beheld the true character of the woman" beneath her outward style, Coverdale can describe this character only in "aesthetic" terms: "passionate, luxurious, lacking simplicity, not deeply refined, incapable of pure and perfect taste." It is small wonder that in Zenobia's gestures Coverdale sees "something like the illusion which a great actress flings around her," for the world in which she acts is less a community than an audience. In such a world, as the one-legged cynic puts it in Melville's *Confidence-Man*, "to do, is to act; so all doers are actors." (pp. 187-93)

> *Michael Davitt Bell, "The Death of the Spirit: Nathaniel Hawthorne," in his* The Development of American Romance: The Sacrifice of Relation, *The University of Chicago Press, 1980, pp. 168-93.*

KEITH CARABINE   (essay date 1982)

[*Exploring his assertion that* Blithedale "*is, in part, about the education of Coverdale, into an acceptance of the role of the artist as sympathetic observer who misses out on life," Carabine offers a detailed study of Coverdale's character, his function as the narrator of* Blithedale, *and the implications of his unreliability as a source of information about himself and the other characters in the novel.*]

It is characteristic of Hawthorne's craft in *The Blithedale Romance* that the opening chapter hints how we are to read the narrative, and alerts us to the extraordinary relation of Coverdale to his own narrative, and why that relation is significant. Also, in retrospect, we see how Hawthorne has worked for suggestive analogies in 'The Veiled Lady', and in the association of both her exhibitor and his victim, with the exhibitor of the romance itself.

The wonderful exhibition of the veiled lady 'under such skilfully contrived circumstances of stage effect, . . . which at once mystified and illuminated' her 'remarkable performances' is a triple image: of the very form of the story—a 'skilfully contrived' masquerade; of the reader's position—'mystified' and awaiting 'illumination'; and of a judgement upon the Blithedale experiment itself as another form of 'mock life'.

Westervelt as the 'exhibitor' of Priscilla works both as an analogy with and a contrast to Coverdale who is himself an 'exhibitor' of 'three characters who figure so largely on my own private theatre'. Unlike Westervelt we are continually made aware that Coverdale is not in charge of affairs. He is obliged for much of his narrative, as with Moodie in the first chapter, to 'arrive' 'only through subsequent events', 'at a plausible conjecture as to what his business could have been'. In fact, his stance is extraordinary: writing twelve years after the events he describes he still 'conjectures' as to 'Zenobia's whole character and history; . . . her later purposes towards Hollingsworth'. He confesses he is 'a secondary or tertiary personage' in his own narrative, and, characteristically, he is either a distant observer of the action, or he stumbles upon an event, such as Zenobia's 'trial', thirty minutes after it is over. Moreover, unlike Westervelt, the manager of 'the phenomenon in the mesmeric line' who keeps Priscilla under a spell 'enshrouded with the misty drapery of the veil' insulated from 'the material world, from time and space', Coverdale does not *possess* the 'subjects' of his theatre. In fact, it is precisely because Coverdale's characters are not puppets, and can, like Moodie, continually interrupt and surprise his bewildered speculations, that Coverdale avoids 'the cold tendency' which is truly embodied in the 'unhumanized' heart of Westervelt.

Coverdale's remarkable position in relation to his own narrative, and the consequences of that relation with regard to how his story will be told, are captured in his response to 'the Veiled Lady's' 'Sibylline' prophecy: he is left 'turning' a 'riddle in my mind, and trying to catch its slippery purport by the tail'. Unlike Westervelt who deals in spells, Coverdale is still, at the time of writing, probing a mystery. And we are invited to share both the process of his discoveries and his struggle to establish his authority over the 'slippery' meanings and the consequences of the tale he has to tell.

It is the analogy with Priscilla which establishes that, though Coverdale may not be the artist as mesmerist, he *is* the artist as clairvoyant or medium, flickeringly aware of the future, and responsive, like Priscilla to Westervelt, to the moods and demands, to the *influence* of his characters. Thus during his first night at Blithedale, Coverdale's 'half-waking dreams . . . anticipated several of the chief incidents of this narrative including a dim shadow of its catastrophe'. As Coverdale recognizes, he is, willy-nilly, 'something like a mesmerical clairvoyant' who operates through 'a species of intuition' which renders him subject to being taken over, like Priscilla, by forces he cannot control. I take this to be the meaning of the curious moment when Coverdale, high in his hermitage, is visited by 'a mood of disbelief in moral beauty or heroism, and a conviction of the folly of attempting to benefit the world'. It is only when Westervelt hoves into view that Coverdale recognizes it was 'chiefly . . . this man's influence' that had sponsored the sceptical and sneering view which '. . . had filled my mental vision in regard to all life's better purposes'.

It is surely apt that Coverdale first meets the woman he loves under the 'management' of a mesmerist. That it is his fate to love a woman who is always free to be someone else's possession, who is always a medium for others' designs, ironically mirrors the position of the artist in relation to his own creations, of man in relation to his fellows, and of his fellows in association with each other. These issues are illuminated in the sequel to the first chapter, namely Coverdale's second visit to see 'the Veiled Lady' in 'A Village Hall'.

Coverdale's involuntary intuition in his 'hermitage' prepares us for his 'horror and disgust' as he realizes that if the mesmerist's claims 'of the miraculous power of one human being over the will and passions of another' are true, then 'the individual soul was annihilated . . . and . . . the idea of man's eternal responsibility was made ridiculous, and immortality rendered at once, impossible, and not worth acceptance'. Furthermore that Westervelt imbues Coverdale with 'a sneering view' ensures that Coverdale can recognize 'the smell of corruption' in the latter's talk of 'a new era that . . . would link soul to soul, and the present life to what we call futurity' and 'finally convert both worlds into the great mutually conscious brotherhood'.

The implications of Coverdale's noble judgement are threefold. Firstly, as Coverdale is aware, for the artist to mimic the mesmerist is both to annihilate the individual soul of his creations, to deny his 'responsibility', and, therefore, to damn himself. The consequence is that his characters must be 'free' to decide their own fates; thus ensuring the writer's authority is provisional. Secondly, if the author as man responds similarly to the integrity of his fellows, and does not act (as Hollingsworth does in this scene when he takes Priscilla away from Westervelt) he must remain a perennial observer experiencing life, like Coverdale, as both alienation and loss. Coverdale suffers the mortification of watching Priscilla's rescue from Westervelt, 'her deadliest enemy', to land 'safe forever!'—in the equally possessive arms of Hollingsworth. Thirdly, and even more importantly, Coverdale's recognition that Westervelt's aims express a 'cold and dead materialism', masquerading as brotherhood, enables Hawthorne to establish the authority of his narrator. After all in losing Priscilla 'forever' he learns the hard way that Westervelt's ideal 'brotherhood' operates as a black parody of Blithedale's aims for a better world. Both systems indeed are not 'new sciences' but the revival of 'old humbugs' which deny the possibility of new sympathetic forms of human relations.

Coverdale's responsiveness as medium, his perceptions as clairvoyant, and his doubts about both, are essential, initially, to an understanding of his function. Even his 'hermitage' which he ironically confesses 'was my one exclusive possession, while I counted myself a brother of the socialists', and which is commonly regarded as proof of his fundamental disaffection from the aims of Blithedale is less self-serving and defensive than it appears. His 'hermitage' is in fact at once an embodiment and an outcome of a series of devastating perceptions. Indeed, he only retreats to it after recognizing 'the presence

of Zenobia caused our heroic enterprise to show like an illusion, a masquerade, a posture, a counterfeit Arcadia'; after he discerns that Hollingsworth 'had come among us, actuated by no real sympathy with our feelings and hopes'; after he grimly divines that 'for a girl like Priscilla and a woman like Zenobia to jostle one another in their love of a man like Hollingsworth, was likely to be no child's play'; and still more importantly, after he recognizes 'my own part in these transactions was singularly subordinate. It resembled that of Chorus in a classic play'.

Coverdale's retreat is also a necessary step because unlike his fellow medium, Priscilla, he questions his 'species of intuition' and lives in terror that the source and consequences of his clairvoyance may be demonic—thus rendering him susceptible to confusing 'a spiritual lie' and 'a subtle recognition of a fact'. Coverdale's wise awareness of this danger saves him not only from Westervelt's demonism, but, too, from 'the spiritual lie' which Hollingsworth unwittingly lives. Thus, whereas the latter wastes 'all the warmth of his heart' on his 'philanthropic theory!' which turns into 'a cold spectral monster which he had himself conjured up', Coverdale recognizes that too exclusive a devotion 'to the study of men and women' risks fashioning 'a monster' which 'after all . . . may be said to have been created mainly by ourselves'. Coverdale, therefore, withdraws from Hollingsworth not because of 'his reticence to commit himself humanly to others' but because his friend's 'spiritual discipline' masks egotistic designs like Westervelt's which violate the very spirit of Blithedale and enslave the wills of Priscilla and Zenobia. Hollingsworth in his treatment of Priscilla fails therefore the victim figure who, as he recognizes, will prove *a test case of Blithedale values:* 'as we do by this friendless girl so shall we prosper'.

As refractions of the artist's problems, then, Westervelt and Hollingsworth establish that it is to Coverdale's credit that he is aware of the risks of 'demonism' and of self-conjured 'spectral monsters'. It is however, Priscilla, who is oblivious to such dangers, who is the major key to Coverdale's authenticity as an artist and his limitations as a man. As Priscilla is not free of Westervelt when she is brought to Blithedale, and experiences only another form of possession (which she accepts unquestioningly), so Coverdale discovers that he cannot, either in his hermitage or in Boston, avoid the responsibilities of his 'sympathies'—root meaning 'having a fellow feeling'—sponsored by his commitment, no matter how consciously ambivalent, towards the Blithedale experiment, or, more importantly, by his 'species of intuition', which ties him, irrevocably, in ways he had not anticipated, to his friends. Thus even though he leaves Blithedale for Boston after 'the tragic passage-at-arms' with Hollingsworth, and after Zenobia's stagy rejection of his counsel ('It needs a wild steersman when we voyage through chaos! The anchor is up! Farewell!'), 'they first' begin to 'encroach upon' his 'dreams' and then, again, press back into his life as he looks out of the back window of his hotel only to see Priscilla, Westervelt and Zenobia together in 'a rather stylish boarding house'. In one of the central passages in the romance he reflects:

> There now needed only Hollingsworth and old
> Moodie to complete the knot of characters, whom
> a real intricacy of events, greatly assisted by
> my method of insulating them from other re-
> lations, had kept so long upon my mental stage,
> as actors in a drama. In itself, perhaps, it was
> no very remarkable event that they should thus

A photograph of Hawthorne thought to have been taken in about 1863.

come across me, at the moment when I imagined myself free. Nevertheless, there seemed something fatal in the coincidence that had borne me to this one spot . . . and transfixed me there, and compelled me again to waste my already wearied sympathies on affairs which were none of mine, and persons who cared little for me. . . . After the effort which it cost me to fling them off—after consummating my escape, as I thought, from these goblins of flesh and blood and pausing to revive myself with a breath or two of an atmosphere in which they should have no share—it was a positive despair, to find the same figures arraying themselves before me, and presenting their old problem in a shape that made it more insoluble than ever.

I began to long for a catastrophe. If the noble temper of Hollingsworth's soul were doomed to be utterly corrupted by the too powerful purpose, which had grown out of what was noblest in him; if the rich and generous qualities of Zenobia's womanhood might not save her; if Priscilla must perish by her tenderness and faith, so simple and so devout;—then be it so! Let it all come! . . . I would look on, as it seemed my part to do, understandingly, if my intellect could fathom the meaning and the moral, and, at all events, reverently and sadly. The curtain fallen,

I would pass onward with my poor individual life, which was now attenuated of much of its proper substance, and diffused among many alien interests.

It is Priscilla's fate to be pursued by two figures she never recognizes as 'goblins of flesh and blood'. Westervelt exploits her for her clairvoyance and Hollingsworth for her money. Her 'faith, so simple and so devout' ensures she does not realize at the end that the 'vindictive shadow' of Zenobia—another 'goblin of flesh and blood'—'dogs the side' of Hollingsworth 'where' she 'is not'. Yet as Coverdale ruefully acknowledges her 'fine heart' has found in the broken, 'child like' Hollingsworth 'its proper substance', whereas his own 'life' is indeed 'attenuated'. His fate, as a human being, in contrast to Priscilla's, as he now courageously and honestly acknowledges, is to be an onlooker, wasting 'his weary sympathies on affairs which were none of mine and persons who cared little for me'. Coverdale's 'let it all come' is not, as Crews argues, 'a vengeful daydream', nor is it merely fatalism; he is beginning to learn that he cannot change the role he must, ineluctably, play of 'Chorus in a classic play'. In fact *The Blithedale Romance* is, in part, about the education of Coverdale, into an acceptance of the role of the artist as sympathetic observer who misses out on life.

The 'goblins of flesh and blood' who will not be flung off and who present 'their old problem in a shape . . . more insoluble than ever' tempt him as an artist in ways Priscilla can never know. Zenobia, Hollingsworth and Priscilla are, to paraphrase Pirandello, 'three characters in search of an author'. Their search, as Coverdale recognizes, involves the artist in a paradox. An attempt to understand and solve 'their old problem' involves the artist both as medium and as diagnostician: and both functions involve the artist's recognition that his characters are 'goblins of flesh and blood'. They are 'goblins' in the precise meaning of the term: 'ugly and mischievous demons' who fly about the world deceiving folk. Their need to have their story told and their 'old problem' understood tempts Coverdale to commit the unpardonable Hawthorneian sin of violating their 'flesh and blood' by restricting them to his 'mental stage' and thus surrendering like Westervelt to 'the miraculous powers' of demonism. Furthermore the artist cannot refuse them because they are, too, 'of flesh and blood', they are his friends, able at once to 'encroach' upon his 'dreams' and to solicit his essentially unwearying sympathies. Yet, simultaneously, as goblins, eager to damn him, they unavoidably stimulate the arrogance resident even in sympathy and proceed to induce Coverdale and Hawthorne to produce yet another version of 'mock life' masquerading this time as sympathy and accordance.

The paradox heightens, because as the passage I have quoted illustrates, as Coverdale must distance himself to understand the problem of his characters, so Hawthorne must distance himself in order to use and to understand his chosen narrator, Coverdale. Hence both the coolness and the comedy in Hawthorne's relation to Coverdale. The latter's rather calculating remarks at the beginning of the passage reflect Hawthorne's typical self-referentiality: the 'method', the use of 'the knot of characters' is *his* way of ensuring that the inherent duplicity of his romance works. Hawthorne's 'theatre', his masquerade, is not as much of 'a fancy-sketch' as he would have us believe in his Preface. Nor clearly is his 'whole treatment of the affair' of Brook Farm 'incidental to the main purpose of the romance' [see excerpt dated 1852]. The 'old problem' which Coverdale accepts as his business to solve involves an estimation of why the oldest story of all—unrequited love—seems to embody the reasons for the failure of the Blithedale experiment. Coverdale's analysis reveals that 'their old problem' like the Blithedale community's efforts to change the relation between the sexes, to strive for brotherhood and to escape from individualism and ego, stumble inexorably against the stubborn fact of 'the self'.

That Hawthorne distances himself from Coverdale who feels estranged from his own narrative is entirely unsurprising. As Mark Kinkead-Weekes [has remarked] . . . , even in *The Scarlet Letter,* 'an authorial *persona,* persistently interposing a highly artificial style between us and what we see'—and, one might add, receive. Of course Hawthorne treats Coverdale on occasion as a comic figure. Coverdale's earnest protestations that he thought he had escaped these 'goblins of flesh and blood' involve a ludicrous, even surrealistic aspect (never entirely missing in Hawthorne's fiction) which will wax larger when Coverdale is chased by 'chimeras'. Further, Coverdale's sober projection of an anticipated stance ('The curtain fallen, I would pass onward, with my poor, individual life') is slightly in excess of its occasion, and thus again works ironically at his expense. Again Hawthorne is quite capable of burlesquing his narrator's 'curiosity' (and incidentally the conventions of the first person novel) when he places his narrator in his hermitage straining to hear what Westervelt and Zenobia have to say. Coverdale is obliged to confess mournfully (and therefore comically), 'I could hardly make out an intelligible sentence on either side'.

I think it is a mistake, however, to think that, because Coverdale is treated in part as a comic figure, who is reluctant even to tell the story, and who doubts his fitness for the task, that therefore he is not to be taken seriously. Rather I would stress that Hawthorne has also invested in Coverdale (in his only novel which grew out of a shared experience with friends and associates) his deepest feelings and perceptions concerning the place and responsibility of the artist in relation to his fellow men and to society at large. Through Coverdale he ponders the right of the artist to treat and remould communal human experiences. (pp. 111-19)

The last third of the romance confirms that Coverdale's quest for artistic authority involves him in a continual struggle to balance the competing claims and dangers of both his analytic detachment and his sympathetic involvement.

Early in Chapter 19 Coverdale honestly and painfully acknowledges his 'keen, revengeful sense of the insult inflicted by Zenobia's scornful recognition, and more particularly by her letting down the curtain' but he asserts nonetheless his fitness as 'chorus'.

> She should have been able to appreciate that quality of the intellect and the heart, which impelled me (often against my own will, and to the detriment of my own comfort) to live in other lives, and to endeavour—by generous sympathies . . . and by bringing my human spirit into manifold accordance with the companions whom God assigned me—to learn the secret which was hidden even from themselves.

Hawthorne is dramatizing here his own, as well as Coverdale's, sense of the arrogance of the artist who wishes 'to learn the secrets . . . hidden even from themselves'. Both author and narrator escape demonism on the one hand and loss of self on

the other, because they struggle to bring their 'human spirit into manifold accordance' (root meaning 'to bring heart to heart') 'with the companions . . . God assigned' them. *They both strive in their art to fulfil the aims of Blithedale.* The quest for 'accordance' is in diametrical opposition to Westervelt's 'cold and dead materialism', to Hollingsworth's divisive, self-deceiving philanthropic system, and to Zenobia's display of self. Even more crucially Coverdale's 'accordance', though stimulated by Priscilla's 'tender faith', involves an effort to understand (with all the risks involved) which 'a character so simply constituted as hers', and which 'has room only for a single predominant affection', can never face. Priscilla's love then is, paradoxically, the opposite of the Hawthorneian artist's understanding.

Once Hawthorne has established that an effort to bring about a 'manifold accordance' sustains both Coverdale's authority—and his own—it is not surprising that the following sequence clarifies both Coverdale's awakening sense of the shape his narrative will take and the kind of response he expects to develop in his reader. Confident now of his fitness for 'the office' of 'observer' he continues in Chapter XIX:

> True; I might have condemned them. Had I been judge, as well as witness, my sentence might have been stern as that of Destiny itself. But still, no trait of original nobility of character; no struggle against temptation; no iron necessity of will, on the one hand, nor extenuating circumstance to be derived from passion and despair, on the other; no remorse that might co-exist with error, even if powerless to prevent it; no proud repentance that should claim retribution as a meed—would go unappreciated. True, again, I might give my full assent to the punishment which was sure to follow. But it would be given mournfully, and with undiminished love. And, after all was finished, I would come, as if to gather up the white ashes of those who had perished at the stake, and to tell the world—the wrong being now atoned for—how much had perished there, which it had never yet known how to praise.

Leo B. Levy detects in such passages 'the sternness of the Puritan age . . . [persisting] in Coverdale's fantasy of condemning to the stake those who have failed to confide in him' [see Additional Bibliography]. He fails to recognize that at such moments Coverdale is less concerned with judgement than with appreciation and with tragic waste. Coverdale's terms may serve as a summary of the great themes and attitudes of Shakespearean tragedy. Hawthorne's aim, no less, is to write a tragic romance which will mould and measure the human loss, the tragic waste, at the heart of the love quartet and of the Blithedale experiment in 'accordance'.

We miss both the distinction and the oddity of *The Blithedale Romance* if we do not realize that Hawthorne deliberately trusts such solemn business to a narrator who 'exaggerates' his 'own defects', who is, as we have seen, both bewildered and clairvoyant, both eagerly curious and painfully shy, both intuitive and distrustful of his intuitions. In the world of Hawthorne's fictions such opposing responses are just. As Coverdale brilliantly realises, 'a man cannot always decide for himself whether his own heart is cold or warm'. In Hawthorne the human heart never knows itself well enough to set up the kingdom of heaven on earth (as the Blithedalians wish)—let alone to securely anticipate the kingdom of heaven itself, as his 'good . . . just and sage' Puritans do.

That Hawthorne trusts his narrative to a narrator who 'exaggerates' his 'own defects' as surely as Hawthorne reveals them and that he so remorselessly pressurizes his narrator and ensures he is accused of every failing and every danger the Hawthorneian artist is prone to, means inevitably that Coverdale struggles to establish his authority. As readers, we are obliged to share Coverdale's ambivalent responses to 'the goblins of flesh and blood' who haunt, oppose, and finally in the figure of Zenobia, solicit him 'to turn the affair into a ballad'. In the closing chapters it is not Coverdale who is 'witless'. Rather his and our pain is that we watch his friends, witless of their fate, accuse him of meddling. Thus in Chapter XX Zenobia anticipates Coverdale's desire to rescue Priscilla from Westervelt: 'With all your fancied acuteness, you step blindfold into these affairs. For any mischief that may follow your interference, I hold you responsible!' Zenobia's blind outrage at the only person who is aware of the impending 'mischief' is outrageous. She knows better at the close.

Priscilla confesses to Coverdale that 'I am blown about like a leaf. . . . I never have any free will' and Coverdale too, discovers—try as he might—that he, too, cannot 'resume an exclusive sway over' himself. He confesses: 'Hollingsworth, Zenobia, Priscilla! These three had absorbed my life into themselves. Together with an inexpressible longing to know their fortunes, there was likewise a morbid resentment of my own pain, and a stubborn reluctance to come again within their sphere'. Coverdale, however, is inextricably bound to them; apart from them his life is 'a restless activity to no purpose'. Both his sympathy as a medium and his analytic desire to understand their 'old problem' ensure that he cannot escape 'the goblins of flesh and blood' who want their story told.

'Two nights' after accidentally seeing Hollingsworth rescue Priscilla from Westervelt in 'A Village Hall' he returns to Blithedale 'with a yearning interest to learn the upshot of all my story'. As usual, he fears that his 'sickness of spirits' alone, has engendered 'the spectral throng so apt to steal out of an unquiet heart', and thus render him vulnerable to 'a spiritual lie'; but his intuition that 'some evil thing had befallen us or was ready to befall' is confirmed by the 'fantastic rabble' of 'the Masqueraders'. The masqueraders, like Zenobia, confirm 'our heroic enterprise' to be 'an illusion, a masquerade, a counterfeit Arcadia'—a kind of extended **"Maypole of Merrymount"**—and when they pursue him he is indeed 'a mad poet haunted by chimeras'. The fate he has tried to avoid suddenly overtakes him. The moment is surreal. Coverdale is here intensely comic; yet the cry of the masquerader dressed like the devil—'he is always ready to dance to the devil's tune'—expresses both his deepest fear and that of his creator, of the artist's potential doom. 'Quite lost in reverie' he stumbles on (note he does not seek out) 'the goblins of flesh and blood' who have absorbed him into themselves and will not let him rest. Respectful of their passion, awed and fearful, Coverdale says:

'I will retire'.

'This place is free to you', answered Hollingsworth.

'As free as to ourselves', added Zenobia. 'This long while past, you have been following up your game, groping for human emotions in the dark corners of the heart. Had you been here

a little sooner, you might have seen them dragged into the daylight. I could even wish to have my trial over again, with you standing by, to see fair-play! Do you know, Mr. Coverdale, I have been on trial for my life'.

She laughed while speaking thus. But, in truth, as my eyes wandered from one of the group to another, I saw in Hollingsworth all that an artist could desire for the grim portrait of a Puritan magistrate, holding inquest of life and death in a case of witchcraft;—in Zenobia, the sorceress herself, not aged, wrinkled, and decrepit, but fair enough to tempt Satan with a force reciprocal to his own;—and in Priscilla, the pale victim, whose soul and body had been wasted by her spells. Had a pile of faggots been heaped against the rock, this hint of impending doom would have completed the suggestive picture.

'It was too hard upon me', continued Zenobia, addressing Hollingsworth, 'that judge, jury, and accuser should all be comprehended in one man!'

On trial here is not merely Zenobia before Hollingsworth, or Coverdale before Zenobia, but the Hawthorneian artist before his characters: which is to say Hawthorne before his conscience or what James calls his 'morality'. Hollingsworth 'as puritan magistrate' is a reincarnation of iron Puritans such as Endicott and Governor Bellingham and Hawthorne's own great, great grandfather John Hathorne, who, as Hawthorne wrote in 'The Custom-House Sketch', 'made himself so conspicuous in the martyrdom of the witches that their blood may fairly be said to have left a stain upon him'. Hollingsworth is the very representative of 'a goblin of flesh and blood' piping the devil's tune, holding like the puritan magistrates, the power of life and death over helpless so-called sorceresses like Zenobia or innocent victims such as Priscilla. The magistrates in *The Scarlet Letter* are self-righteously certain that they can use the letter A as 'a living sermon against sin, until the ignominious letter be engraved upon her tombstone', but the omniscient narrator states 'out of the whole human family, it would not have been easy to select the same number of wise and virtuous persons who should be less capable of . . . judgement on an erring woman's heart'. In contrast to the certainty of judgement embodied in Hollingsworth and the long line of Puritans behind him, we have the Hawthorneian artist desperate once again to emphasize the secretiveness, the mystery and the freedom of his characters: they have not faced 'judge, jury and accuser comprehended in the *one man of the artist*'! Rather the countermovement, as we have seen, is that the characters *demand* their story be told.

Zenobia is crucial to this thrust. As early as Chapter 5 she teases Coverdale about his fascination for Priscilla: 'Since you see the young woman in so poetical a light . . . you'd better turn the affair into a ballad. It is a grand subject and worthy of supernatural machinery'. The culminating moment of this theme occurs after the trial scene when Zenobia and Coverdale are left alone in perhaps the most moving and powerful moment in the whole of Hawthorne's fiction:

Zenobia had entirely forgotten me. She fancied herself alone with her great grief. And had it been only a common pity that I felt for her . . . the sacredness and awfulness of the crisis might have impelled me to steal away silently . . .

But ... I never once dreamed of questioning my right to be there, now, as I had questioned it just before, when I came so suddenly upon Hollingsworth and herself ... It suits me not to explain what was the analogy that I saw, or imagined, between Zenobia's situation and mine; nor, I believe, will the reader detect this one secret, hidden beneath many a revelation which perhaps concerned me less. In simple truth, however, as Zenobia leaned her forehead against the rock ... it seemed to me that the self-same pang, with hardly mitigated torment, leaped thrilling from her heart-strings to my own. Was it wrong, therefore, if I felt myself consecrated to the priesthood by sympathy like this, and called upon to minister to this woman's affliction, so far as mortal could?

But, indeed, what could mortal do for her? Nothing! The attempt would be a mockery and an anguish ...

'Is it you, Miles Coverdale?' said she, smiling. 'Ah, I perceive what you are about! You are turning this whole affair into a ballad. Pray let me hear as many stanzas as you happen to have ready!'

'Oh, hush, Zenobia!' I answered. 'Heaven knows what an ache is in my soul!'

'It is genuine tragedy, is it not?' rejoined Zenobia, with a sharp, light laugh. 'And you are willing to allow, perhaps that I have had hard measure. But it is a woman's doom ... But, Mr. Coverdale, by all means write this ballad, and put your soul's ache into it, and turn your sympathy to good account as other poets do, and as poets must, unless they choose to give us glittering icicles instead of lines of fire. As for the moral, it shall be distilled into the final stanza, in a drop of bitter honey'.

Coverdale does not question his 'right to be there, now', as he shares with Zenobia the finest moment of accordance in the romance. The secret analogy with Zenobia contains a deeply felt paradox: Coverdale with Priscilla, and Zenobia with Hollingsworth, experience the torment of loss of self to the other without hope of togetherness; but because their hearts have been touched they are both at this moment 'beings of reality', united in their anguish and grief.

Zenobia the self-appointed 'tragedy queen' of the story thinks 'It is a genuine tragedy' because it tells of 'a woman's doom'. But though Coverdale, after her suicide, accepts her judgement ('the world should throw open all its avenues to the passport of a woman's bleeding heart') the tragedy has wider implications. These are embodied in Coverdale's final reflections on Hollingsworth's 'perilous', 'exclusive' philanthropy: 'I see in Hollingsworth an exemplification of the most awful truth in Bunyan's book of such;—from the very gate of Heaven, there is a by-way to the pit!' That 'by-way' is a broad path in the actual slough of this world, in which the road to hell is paved with good intentions—the good intentions of the original pilgrims to whom Coverdale compares the Blithedalians; of the latter in their effort 'to establish the one true system'; of Hollingsworth for prison reform; of Zenobia for women's rights;

of Coverdale for a better world. All prove in Zenobia's words 'varieties of mock life'.

Hawthorne's vision of mankind anticipates Conrad's and T. S. Eliot's. The Congo to Marlow like the Blithedale world to Hawthorne is 'a dream sensation' and 'what redeems' both ventures 'is the idea only'. But in Eliot's words in 'The Hollow Men':

> Between the idea
> And the reality
> Between the motion
> And the act
> Falls the Shadow

'The shadow' in Hawthorne, as Zenobia tells Hollingsworth, is 'Self, self, self!', which is inexorably embodied in any project, and which threatens to turn all human plans and ambitions into masquerades. Not least the writing of tales. As Coverdale realizes Zenobia's version of her 'genuine tragedy' is the *romantic tragedy,* of the ballad of 'village maidens ... wronged in their first love ... seeking peace in the bosom of the old, familiar stream'. The 'drop of bitter honey' 'distilled into the final stanza' of her version, and of her life, is the old story of the woman who dies for love. It is a grim irony that in completing *that* pattern Zenobia confirms that the shadow of 'the self' was with her until the very end, because her postured romantic death embodies, as Coverdale gloomily realizes, 'some tint of the Arcadian affectation'.

Whereas Zenobia takes her 'soul's ache' to a watery grave which hideously rigidifies her, the shy, frail, self-mocking Coverdale puts 'his soul's ache' into a *tragic romance* which truly ends with a 'moral' and 'a drop of bitter honey'. Thus Coverdale's final disclosure confirms that the projected 'life of love and free-heartedness' which Zenobia has looked to as the goal of Blithedale is an impossibility. 'Love and free-heartedness', as the romance demonstrates, are at odds. And that bitter-sweet recognition has profound implications for Coverdale. Early in the romance the minor poetaster has enthusiastically explained to Zenobia that he means 'to produce ... poetry—true, strong, natural and sweet, as is the life we are going to lead'. By the close he knows better: 'As for poetry, I have given it up'. But, most importantly, Coverdale's last revelation, which in turn reveals that Hawthorne has deliberately thrown a 'veil' over his narrative, draws our attention to the novel as 'a masquerade', one that has deliberately mystified and deceived us so that we *realize* the consecrating power of the artist, the fakes and ploys of whose masquerade serve to ensure that Coverdale truly fulfils his role:

> It resembled that of the Chorus in a classic play, which seems to be set aloof from the possibility of personal concernment, and bestows the whole measure of its hope or fear, its exultation or sorrow, on the fortunes of others, between whom and itself this sympathy is the only bond. Destiny ... chooses ... the presence of at least one calm observer. It is his office ... to detect the final fitness of incident to character, and distil, in his long-brooding thought, the whole morality of the performance.

One of the great distinctions of *The Blithedale Romance* is that it captures what it costs in human terms for an author to be 'a calm observer'. It is at once to live off and in 'the fortunes of others'. As both Coverdale and his creator know, keen perceptive and analytic powers lead to a deficiency in feeling and the risk of the artist's estrangement from his fellows. On the other hand, the romance captures the consecrating powers of the artist. The artist is 'sacra-re' that is 'made sacred' because he is 'set apart' (*O.E.D.*); but he works also for accordance (con = together). The Hawthorneian artist strives to give us 'the whole morality' and the whole cost.

Thus 'the final passage' is indeed 'bitter honey'. The oxymoron is precise. Coverdale's life has been *bitter* honey. He cannot understand why Zenobia and Priscilla should be under the sway of such a monster of selfishness as Westervelt and such a distinctively egoistic spirit as Hollingsworth. We come to realize, however, that the very ego and purpose of these figures have seemingly conferred meaning upon the lives of the women who surround them. '*Bitter* honey', too, because Coverdale's analytic curiosity ensures his divorce from the woman he loves. The artist as man pays a high price for his scepticism. Like Theodore in Zenobia's legend he is left to pine 'for ever and ever for another sight of that dim mournful face—which might have been his life—long, household, fireside joy—to desire, and waste life in a feverish quest, and never meet it more'.

Yet, too, both as a man and an artist he has experienced 'bitter *honey*'; he has been haunted by three characters in search of him who, though they have sought definition from him, they have provided, too, the only definition and 'proper substance' he himself is ever to know in life. Hence his attenuation whenever he is apart from them, and Blithedale is over. But truly 'bitter honey' because, as an artist Coverdale gives shape and purpose to their lives in the tragic romance he has written. It is surely satisfying to the reader to know that at least one person has loved that test case of Blithedale values, Priscilla. Moreover, because Coverdale's heart is and was touched; because he once did have hopes for Blithedale which he still remembers as 'our beautiful scheme of a noble and unselfish life'; because he can attest even at the end 'I feel we had struck upon what ought to have been a truth' he has *earned* the 'consecrated' right to turn 'his sympathy to good account' and to write if not Zenobia's romantic tragedy, his own tragic romance. That is **The Blithedale Romance** in which, for once in his artistic career, he is able 'to detect the final fitness of incident to character, and distil, in his long-brooding thought, the whole morality of the performance'. (pp. 120-28)

> *Keith Carabine, "'Bitter Honey': Miles Coverdale as Narrator in 'The Blithedale Romance',"* in Nathaniel Hawthorne: New Critical Essays, *edited by A. Robert Lee, Barnes and Noble, 1982, pp. 110-30.*

ADDITIONAL BIBLIOGRAPHY

Auchincloss, Louis. "*The Blithedale Romance:* A Study of Form and Point of View." *The Nathaniel Hawthorne Journal* 2 (1972): 53-8.
    Examines the structure and authorial viewpoint of *Blithedale*.

Bales, Kent. "The Allegory and the Radical Romantic Ethic of *The Blithedale Romance*." *American Literature* XLVI, No. 1 (March 1974): 41-53.
    Argues that *Blithedale* is "an allegory that defines radical romantic values in relation to Miles Coverdale and to the entire Blithedale experiment in community building."

Bewley, Marius. "*The Blithedale Romance* and *The Bostonians*." In his *The Complex Fate: Hawthorne, Henry James and Some Other American Writers*, pp. 11-30. New York: Grove Press, 1954.
    Explores the influence of *Blithedale* on Henry James's novel *The Bostonians*.

"*The Blithedale Romance* (1852)." In *Hawthorne: The Critical Heritage*, edited by J. Donald Crowley, pp. 241-71. Critical Heritage Series, edited by B. C. Southam. New York: Barnes & Noble, 1970.
    Reprints selected early reviews of *Blithedale*.

Boswell, Jeanetta. *Nathaniel Hawthorne and the Critics: A Checklist of Criticism, 1900-1978*. Scarecrow Author Bibliographies, no. 57. Metuchen, N.J.: Scarecrow Press, 1982, 273 p.
    A bibliography of twentieth-century commentary on Hawthorne and his works published through 1978.

Byers, John R., Jr., and Owen, James J. *A Concordance to the Five Novels of Nathaniel Hawthorne*. 2 vols. Garland Reference Library of the Humanities, vol. 182. New York: Garland Publishing, 1979.
    A computer generated concordance to the texts of Hawthorne's novels, including *Blithedale*.

Crews, Frederick C. "A New Reading of *The Blithedale Romance*." *American Literature* 29, No. 2 (May 1957): 147-70.
    Posits that previous critics of *Blithedale* have misinterpreted the novel by not recognizing that the shortcomings of the narrative are Coverdale's fault rather than Hawthorne's.

———. "Turning the Affair into a Ballad." In his *The Sins of the Fathers: Hawthorne's Psychological Themes*, pp. 194-212. New York: Oxford University Press, 1966.
    Maintains that in *Blithedale* Hawthorne, "finding his literal plot hopelessly distorted by irrational fantasy, turned the book into a self-critical comedy by attributing that distortion to his narrator."

Davidson, Frank. "Toward a Re-evaluation of *The Blithedale Romance*." *The New England Quarterly* XXV, No. 3 (September 1952): 374-83.
    Suggests that a critical reassessment of *Blithedale* is in order and outlines important areas for discussion.

Fogle, Richard Harter. "*The Blithedale Romance*." In his *Hawthorne's Fiction: The Light and the Dark*, rev. ed., pp. 168-89. Norman: University of Oklahoma Press, 1964.
    Identifies two principal themes in *Blithedale*: the tragedy of the human heart in isolation and the Utopian aspirations of the Blithedale community.

———. "Priscilla's Veil: A Study of Hawthorne's Veil-Imagery in *The Blithedale Romance*." *The Nathaniel Hawthorne Journal* 2 (1972): 59-65.
    Investigates Hawthorne's use of the veil as a key image in *Blithedale*.

Gollin, Rita K. "'Dream-Work' in *The Blithedale Romance*." *ESQ* 19, No. 2 (1973): 74-83.
    Argues that *Blithedale* is primarily concerned with dreaming and daydreaming.

Gross, Seymour, and Murphy, Rosalie, eds. *The Blithedale Romance: An Authoritative Text, Backgrounds and Sources, Criticism*, by Nathaniel Hawthorne and others. A Norton Critical Edition. New York: W. W. Norton & Co., 1978, 418 p.
    A standard text of the novel, including background information and source material for the work, as well as a selection of important nineteenth- and twentieth-century criticism.

Hoffman, Daniel. "*The Blithedale Romance*: May-Day in a Cold Arcadia." In his *Form and Fable in American Fiction*, pp. 202-18. New York: Oxford University Press, 1961.
    Asserts that beneath the surface of its seemingly tentative and awkward plot, *Blithedale* is a well-organized and sophisticated novel.

Howard, David. "*The Blithedale Romance* and a Sense of Revolution." In *Tradition and Tolerance in Nineteenth-Century Fiction: Critical Essays on Some English and American Novels*, edited by David Howard, John Lucas, and John Goode, pp. 55-97. London: Routledge and Kegan Paul, 1966.
    Contends that *Blithedale* is a novel whose central concern is social and personal change.

Johnson, Claudia D. "'Shapes That Often Mirror Falsehood, but Sometimes Truth': *The Blithedale Romance.*" In her *The Productive Tension of Hawthorne's Art,* pp. 83-102. University: University of Alabama Press, 1981.

    Theorizes that in *Blithedale,* Hawthorne criticizes the tendency in nineteenth-century Romantic art to glorify the self-centered individual and artist.

Lang, Hans-Joachim. "*The Blithedale Romance:* A History of Ideas Approach." In *Literatur und Sprache der Vereinigten Staaten: Aufsätze zu Ehren von Hans Galinsky,* edited by Hans Helmcke, Klaus Lubbers, and Renate Schmidt-v. Bardeleben, pp. 88-106. Heidelberg: Carl Winter Universitätsverlag, 1969.

    Examines the cultural, political, and philosophical milieu in which *Blithedale* was conceived and written.

Lefcowitz, Allan, and Lefcowitz, Barbara. "Some Rents in the Veil: New Light on Priscilla and Zenobia in *The Blithedale Romance.*" *Nineteenth-Century Fiction* 21, No. 3 (December 1966): 263-75.

    Proposes that the ambiguous nature of Zenobia and Priscilla as characters reflects Hawthorne's ambivalent feelings about their roles as sexual beings, a factor which in turn contributed to *Blithedale*'s structural collapse.

Levy, Leo B. "*The Blithedale Romance:* Hawthorne's 'Voyage through Chaos'." *Studies in Romanticism* VIII, No. I (Autumn 1968): 1-15.

    Maintains that *Blithedale* can be seen as a manifestation of Hawthorne's concern with the conflicting elements of a rapidly changing American society.

Long, Robert Emmet. "Transformations: *The Blithedale Romance* to Howells and James." *American Literature* XLVII, No. 4 (January 1976): 552-71.

    Explores the influence of *Blithedale* on the works of Henry James and William Dean Howells.

Matheson, Terence J. "Feminism and Femininity in *The Blithedale Romance.*" *The Nathaniel Hawthorne Journal* 6 (1976): 215-26.

    A study of Hawthorne's portrayal in *Blithedale* of the place of women in society.

Murray, Peter B. "Mythopoesis in *The Blithedale Romance.*" *PMLA* 75, Pt. 2, No. 5 (December 1960): 591-96.

    An analysis of the "symbolic and structural aspects of the *Romance* through which Coverdale's ideas on human interdependence and human perfectibility as related to mortality are expressed."

Ragan, James F. "The Irony in Hawthorne's *Blithedale.*" *The New England Quarterly* XXXV, No. 2 (June 1962): 239-46.

    A study of Hawthorne's use of irony in the novel.

Rahv, Philip. "The Dark Lady of Salem." *Partisan Review* VIII, No. 5 (September-October 1941): 362-81.

    A discussion of Hawthorne's apparent fascination with dark and seductive heroines that includes commentary on Zenobia in *Blithedale.*

Ross, Donald. "Dreams and Sexual Repression in *The Blithedale Romance.*" *PMLA* 86, No. 5 (October 1971): 1014-17.

    Explores the psychosexual significance of Coverdale's dreams in *Blithedale.*

Smith, Allan Gardner Lloyd. "The Fourth Side: *The Blithedale Romance.*" In his *Eve Tempted: Writing and Sexuality in Hawthorne's Fiction,* pp. 73-90. London: Croom Helm, 1984.

    Investigates the sexual implications of the theatrical motifs in *Blithedale.*

Waggoner, Hyatt H. "*The Blithedale Romance.*" In his *Hawthorne: A Critical Study,* rev. ed., pp. 188-208. Cambridge: Harvard University Press, Belknap Press, 1963.

    A close analysis of *Blithedale.*

José Hernández

1834-1886

Argentine poet and journalist.

Hernández is known for his epic poem *Martin Fierro*, which is recognized as a classic in South American literature for its representation of the gaucho. Comprised of two parts—*El gaucho Martín Fierro (The Departure of Martin Fierro)* and *La vuelta de Martín Fierro (The Return of Martin Fierro)*—this work tells the story of Martin Fierro, whose struggles epitomize the problems faced by the Argentine gauchos during the nineteenth century, when political and economic forces combined to destroy their way of life. Consistently praised for its sympathetic and realistic depiction of the gauchos' solitary existence on the pampas, *Martin Fierro* met with enormous success and remains popular today.

Hernández grew up on his parents' ranch near Buenos Aires. There, he was in close contact with gauchos who worked as ranch hands, and he eventually came to sympathize with their way of life. Although he failed to complete his formal education because of respiratory problems, he studied on his own and read extensively. Hernández's early adulthood was troubled by political turmoil: following the overthrow of dictator Juan Manuel de Rosas in 1852, Argentina entered a decade of civil strife between Buenos Aires and the other provinces. In 1853 Hernández joined the army, fighting for the provinces until they met with defeat at Pavón in 1861, an event that led to the establishment of a central government in Buenos Aires. Upon leaving the army, Hernández lived in Corientes and later in Rosario, working as a journalist and government official. He married Carolina González de Solar in 1863 and in the same year published his first book, *Vida del chacho: Rasgos biográficos del general D. Andel V. Peñaloza*, a biography of a noted gaucho military leader. In 1868 Hernández moved back to Buenos Aires, where he founded *Rio de la Plata*, a newspaper in which he denounced the government's unfair treatment of the gauchos, particularly protesting their widespread conscription into the army to fight against the Indians. After a year, however, this publication was suppressed. Nevertheless, Hernández persisted in seeking better treatment for the gauchos, and in 1872 he published *The Departure of Martin Fierro* in the hope that this realistic description of life on the pampas would help their cause. Immediately popular, *The Departure of Martin Fierro* was soon stocked in the rural stores where the gauchos bought their supplies, and legends spread among them that Fierro actually lived across the border and would someday return. The success of the poem was so great, in fact, that Hernández became known to the people of Buenos Aires as "Don Martín." Heartened by the acceptance of this work, Hernández published a continuation of the tale in 1879, *The Return of Martin Fierro*, which was also well received. Hernández's only subsequent lengthy work, *Instrucción del estanciero*, was a handbook advocating the adoption of progressive farming and breeding techniques. He continued, however, to publish political essays and eventually became a senator under a new administration. He served in congress in Buenos Aires until his death from a heart attack at the age of fifty-two.

Martin Fierro is frequently praised for its realistic depiction of both the gauchos' vices and redeeming qualities; indeed,

critics agree that Hernández was one of the first writers to avoid sentimentality and condescension in portraying the gaucho. The first part of the work, *The Departure of Martin Fierro*, is a 2,325-line poem in which Fierro, a *payador*, or gaucho bard, mournfully sings of his conscription into the army, the abuse he receives there, his subsequent desertion and lawless existence, and his ultimate decision to live among his enemies, the Indians. Hernández had intended *The Departure of Martin Fierro* for an urban audience, hoping to make the public aware that the injustices suffered by the gauchos contributed to their unruliness. However, it was more warmly received by the gauchos themselves, and Hernández addressed the second part of the poem, *The Return of Martin Fierro*, directly to them, stressing the importance of hard work and religion. In this poem, which is twice the length of *The Departure of Martin Fierro*, Fierro returns to society and searches for his lost wife and sons.

Commentary on Hernández's work focuses almost entirely on *Martin Fierro*. His newspaper articles and books have been generally overlooked by critics and are now considered of historical value only. Contemporary response to *Martin Fierro* was slight, but a few reviewers discussed such aspects of the poem as its idiomatic language and the accuracy of its description of gaucho life. In the late nineteenth century, critical interest in *Martin Fierro* was stimulated by two Spanish scholars,

Miguel de Unamuno, who wrote an essay on the Hispanic roots of the work, and Marcelino Menéndez y Pelayo, who published a portion of it in an anthology of Latin American poetry, thus insuring its wide circulation. The poem's critical reputation was further enhanced in 1913, when the distinguished Argentine writer Leopoldo Lugones delivered a series of lectures in which he hailed *Martín Fierro* as a national epic comparable to the *Iliad* and the *Odyssey*. Since that time, *Martín Fierro* has been the subject of increasing critical attention. In addition, it has been translated into numerous languages, reissued many times, and adapted for the Argentine screen. Although most of the commentary on *Martín Fierro* is in Spanish, several English-language studies have been published, with critics examining, among other topics, the epic characteristics of the poem, its didactic purpose, and its biblical motifs. Today, *Martín Fierro* is still widely read in Argentina, and Hernández is remembered for capturing and immortalizing the life of the nineteenth-century gaucho.

PRINCIPAL WORKS

Vida del chacho: Rasgos biográficos del general D. Andel V. Peñaloza (biography) 1863
El gaucho Martín Fierro (poetry) 1872
  [*The Departure of Martin Fierro* published in *The Gaucho Martin Fierro*, 1935]
La vuelta de Martín Fierro (poetry) 1879
  [*The Return of Martin Fierro* published in *The Gaucho Martin Fierro*, 1935]
Instrucción del estanciero: Tratado completo para la planteación y manejo de un establecimiento de campo destinado a la cria de hacienda vacuna, lanar y caballar (handbook) 1881
The Gaucho Martin Fierro (poetry) 1935

LA PRENSA (essay date 1873)

[*This anonymous critic heralds the publication of* The Departure of Martin Fierro. *This excerpt was drawn from a review first published in* La prensa *on 16 January 1873.*]

Yesterday a book began circulating, written in gaucho-style verse by José Hernández, former publisher of *El Río de la Plata*, and former government official of Corrientes Province. This book is entitled [*El gaucho Martín Fierro*]. It is not a simple story adorned in literary forms; it is the palpitating story of those who up to a short time ago inhabited the countryside, pursued daily by invading Indians and recruiters of army troops.

> *In an extract from "La prensa," in* The Gaucho Martín Fierro *by José Hernández, translated by Frank G. Carrino, Alberto J. Carlos, and Norman Mangouni, State University of New York Press, 1974, p. 2.*

MARIANO A. PELLIZA (letter date 1873)

[*In the following excerpt from a letter to Hernández, Pelliza compares* The Departure of Martin Fierro *with Harriet Beecher Stowe's* Uncle Tom's Cabin.]

If here [Argentina] we had people capable of vindicating the rights of man and of the citizen, the native inhabitant of the

countryside, your [*El gaucho Martín Fierro*] would have produced the marvellous effect obtained in North America by *Uncle Tom's Cabin*, because both are the product of a sublime good will toward man. The lifting of a fallen race, reinstating civil and political conditions that were daringly snatched away through abuse, is the aim of both books. There, an attack was made on a legal institution; nevertheless, the cry of natural law triumphed, whereas here, the gaucho is scourged unjustifiably through the simple abuse of power.

> *Mariano A. Pelliza, in an extract from a letter to José Hernández on March 27, 1873, in* The Gaucho Martín Fierro *by José Hernández, translated by Frank G. Carrino, Alberto J. Carlos, and Norman Mangouni, State University of New York Press, 1974, p. 2.*

HENRY A. HOLMES (essay date 1923)

[*Holmes analyzes numerous aspects of* Martin Fierro, *including its epic, didactic, satiric, and lyrical qualities; its rhyme scheme; and the function of the gaucho dialect in the poem. Holmes also praises* Martin Fierro *for its terse descriptions, rapid movement, and straightforwardness. For additional commentary by Holmes, see the excerpt dated 1948.*]

The two Parts of *Martín Fierro* present a variety of literary forms. [*El gaucho Martín Fierro*] is practically all epic material. Likewise, in *La Vuelta,* the first ten cantos may be conveniently accepted *en bloc* as epic, for even where the single lines do not justify the use of this term, as for instance the elegiac strains at the death of Cruz, the underlying principle exists always. Cantos XI and XII of *La Vuelta* may be regarded as a not specially inspired but quite necessary appendix to the chief epic portion.

In Canto XX appears a new personage, Picardía, who is later discovered to be the son of Cruz. His adventures are those of a full-sized *pícaro,* but like the hero of the great Spanish picaresque novel *Lazarillo de Tormes,* he was not born so. Taking into consideration the expansiveness of his schemes of deception, intrigue, and brutality, ranging all the way from the individual to the universal; the broad interests, actual as well as potential, which are involved; and the vastness of the poetic stage—all this, on the one hand, and on the other the fact that Picardía reveals himself to be the son of Cruz—we are clearly conscious of an epic flavor in Cantos XX-XXVIII, and a more than casual relation to the epic of Part I. Canto XXXI is a transitional narrative, and Canto XXX contains that precious episode, the . . . *payada de contrapunto* between the negro and Fierro. It is a lyric gem in an epic setting. It cannot be dissociated from the stress and strain of the hero's life in Part I. (pp. 145-46)

The objection may be raised, that this analysis omits, in both parts, certain cantos which for the sake of consistency ought to be included in the epic section. These cantos, moreover, are intimately connected with the main characters and threads of the story. I admit the force of this objection, and should be rather pleased than otherwise to hear it advanced, for I have felt at times a keen inclination to place the cantos in question on a par with those sections classed as particularly epic; and have been forced to conclude that it is impossible, in any canto of the entire poem, to get wholly away from the atmosphere of the epic. But in [*El gaucho Martín Fierro*], I note in Canto VI the elegy on "the abandoned home;" in IV, V, and XII, satiric verse; in IX, some purest lyric—in fact, two entire pages of it form a piquant contrast to the fight that follows.

Cantos XIII-XIX of *La Vuelta,* narrate young Fierro's life with an old rascal named Viscacha. The latter reminds us strongly of one of Espronceda's characters, the old convict in *El Diablo Mundo* who gave such picturesque advice to Fabio. These cantos are epic "asides;" they are a set of little novels or impressions done in quick glaring colors. The cynical satire of Viscacha is unforgettable. He pillories well-nigh all mankind.

It were well, also, not to overlook the very palpable dramatic tendency in Cantos XXIV and XXV. We may assume that in this section Picardía impersonated freely the characters of whom he was singing.

Cantos XXXI-XXXIII are mainly didactic. Martín gives fatherly advice to his sons and Picardía. The poet, too, has his little word. The epic thrills of the earlier cantos having subsided, action gives place to moralizing, and the poem closes on a serious but not exalted or dramatic plane. Retrospective calm follows the former agonizing struggles of Fierro, as a peaceful sunset may succeed a storm-racked day. But the veiled threat of the negro must not be overlooked. Other storms may arise. Fierro's antagonists may come again to grips with him, for all his change of name (XXXIII). An observation of Gummere applies to this truly epic feature: "primitve ballads, however inadequate they would seem for our own needs, come from men who knew life at its hardest, faced it, accepted it, well aware that a losing fight is at the end of every march."

The vast majority of the strophes in both [*El gaucho Martín Fierro*] and *La Vuelta* show the following rhyme sequence, which is used for all purposes, elegy, narration, satire, lyric: [ABBCCB].

It is understood that this scheme refers to individual strophes merely. The rhymes themselves vary from stanza to stanza. In both Part I and Part II, the first canto, and most of the following cantos, begin with this arrangement, which is employed two hundred and seventy-eight times in [*El gaucho Martín Fierro*] and six hundred and thirty-two in *La Vuelta.* Without reckoning sporadic verse-combinations differing from the above, we find in *Martín Fierro* three other sequences interspersed, with consequent prevention of monotony.

The first and most frequent of these alternations runs thus: [ABBCBC].

This too is used in narration and in all the other poetic types. There seems to be no other reason for its introduction than the desire to avoid monotony. In [*El gaucho Martín Fierro*], sixty-eight strophes of this class are found; in *La Vuelta,* sixty-seven. But *La Vuelta* is more than twice as long as [*El gaucho Martín Fierro*].

Cuartetas are employed rather more often in Part II than in Part I; Cf. [*El gaucho Martín Fierro*], VII and VIII, and [*La Vuelta*], XXVII and XXVIII. Here narrative predominates, though with an occasional satiric or elegiac touch.

The third variant is the *romance* form, occurring in Cantos XI, XX, XXIX, and XXXI of *La Vuelta.*

Hernández seems to value it chiefly for interludes or transitional passages. Thus in [*La Vuelta*], XI, Fierro, after ending his own story, introduces his sons; in XX, appears Picardía; in XXIX, the negro, and in XXXI, the company breaks up after the *payada,* and we are prepared for Fierro's last verses of counsel.

These short *romances* are at once interludes and introductions. (pp. 146-49)

Many of the verses [in *Martín Fierro*] thrill with music. One of the commonplaces which the reader is apt to forget, is that the entire poem is, theoretically, to be sung. In [*El gaucho Martín Fierro*], VII and VIII, the singer passes from one form to another, as varying moods possess him, and in [*El gaucho Martín Fierro*], XI, to enhance the grace of that famous gaucho dance, the *pericón, seguidillas* are sung by the guitarist:

> Las mujeres son todas
> Como las mulas, etc.

Were we to ignore the "elegant voluptuousness" of the dance which gives occasion to these verses, we should be at a loss to account for their presence. Songs were a feature of the old gaucho *pericón,* says Rojas, and the *payadores* often introduced lyric novelties.

The value of the lyric form in *Martín Fierro* is precisely that it aids in maintaining fresh the heritage of all the old *payadores,* of whom Fierro is a specimen and Santos Vega the archetype. Had Hernández chosen another form for his defense of the gauchos—had he cast it, for instance, in the mold of *La Araucana*—it would not have been in keeping with either the theme or the setting. . . . Our author keeps faith with [the gauchos'] nature, using their music as well as their speech, and the epic qualities in his subject make an impressive narration inevitable, despite the guitar and the popular meter.

The custom of the gaucho singer is to prolong indefinitely the ultimate syllable of the verse. It has been suggested that this curiously mournful prolongation is inherited from old Spain, and that perhaps the church hymns, with their many accented *últimas,* are particularly responsible for this.

Let us now consider the gaucho vocabulary with regard to its literary function. In its use, Hernández is quite consistent. Few of his verses fail to spring directly from the gauchos' own lips. Mitre criticised him for this. In his *Armonías,* Mitre could have made use of the same racy language, but he believed that a sense of art proscribed it. The results speak for themselves. We are not thrilled by Mitre—nor indeed by Echeverría—and we *are* thrilled by Hernández, who lost consciousness of himself in his heroes. One does not object to the occasional roughness of the *Cantar del Cid.* Shakespeare and Cervantes are now and then "vulgar", that is, true to life. The gaucho manner of speech is one of the chief components of the local color, one which Hernández felt deeply and used effectively. Such employment is an art. And regarding the use of local color, it is here in place to state the following thesis, which may be found in slightly different form in Rojas: *Martín Fierro* does not abound in narrowly specific details, because it is dealing with universals on an epic canvas. You may place the hero's rancho at Pergamino or at Dolores: the essential elements of gaucho life are the same. And it was these elements, faithfully and sympathetically reproduced, which assured for the poem an instantaneous success. The *rancho,* the *fogón* (or fireside), the rough, hearty dishes prepared by the *china,* the gaucho's horse and his outfit, his life, his pleasures, his service and suffering: all these things you may have on your lips and in your heart, if you will read *Martín Fierro.* It is a gaucho dictionary; or shall we say, the gaucho's Bible? (pp. 150-53)

For those who demand proof that [*Martín Fierro*] is artistic and universal, the following paragraphs are submitted.

Burdensome description is lacking. This is true of the Bible, of Homer, of Shakespeare. The reader will recall Homer's descriptive tag, "swift-footed," "loud-sounding," and the like, whose value we do not need to discuss. I cull at random from *Martín Fierro*: *en mi moro ensarciando* (on my mane-tossing black horse), *el de ollín* (soot-faced negro), *peligrosa inquietud* (dread born of threatening dangers), *la tierra en donde crece el ombú* (the land of the *ombú*) —what a host of associations this carries!—*un güey corneta* (troublesome steer or person). The conclusion will be that in regard to terse, epigrammatic characterization, Hernández is a true follower of Homer. Surely one forceful, luminous phrase of Hernández is worth all the disquisitions of Sarmiento. Give us Fierro, one gaucho, at the ruins of his one and only home, with all his family scattered, and we can visualize a thousand gauchos in like evil case.

The hand that pens the slightly coarse epithet, the rude phrase not meant for the drawingroom, can in the next instant give us so emotional a verse as this:

> Por suerte en aquel momento
> Venía coloriando el alba, etc.

Bear in mind that this Hector of horsemen has just been hewing and stabbing, and then—he catches a glimpse of dawn off in the east! He is transformed, and he invokes the Virgin as his protectress in the fearful battle with these cruel pursuers. There is a rich psychology in this passage: "By good luck . . . at that instant—The dawn came lighting up the sky." Wordsworth's was a strong emotion as he cried: "My heart leaps up when I behold a rainbow," but he is more wordy. The charm of Hernández' verse is to feel, as the gaucho feels, deeply but silently. His is in general a noble style.

Also, the poem is a poem of realities. How can a poem claim to be epic and deal with any other realm than that of realities? "I sing of arms"—true, oh Virgil! and Fierro too sings of arms, and of horses, of vast lands for chasing and racing, and of fiendish enemies to fight. 'Tis all primitive, and rude, and popular, and (possibly) brutal, but epics are frequently so, for they deal with very rough and apparently formless masses, through which darts a living flame, that spurs men on to action!

Likewise—and more especially is this true in the more decidedly epic portions—*Martín Fierro* is rapid in its movement. I challenge the reader not to be caught swaying in his chair in an inescapable participation, as he sees Fierro in the *mêlée* of Indians and conscripts. One asks oneself how the action can be so rapid if the verse used in that description is the usual octosyllabic. Well, to appreciate the happy selection of the details is to give the answer. The ground trembles—Fierro's mount is slow—they flee like doves from hawks. Vivid is the present tense in *si no traigo bolas,* and *si me alcanza,* etc. Under the hands of genius we see the theme bursting all the hampering bonds of the rhetoricians and hurtling along with such speed as that which ever and anon stirs us in the *Poema del mío Cid.*

Another quality is directness. There is no complicated intrigue. Tremendous, undeviating gallops across-country were a daily habit. Gauchos followed their leader, not his politics. Their platform, slogans, principles, were all direct. So is the story. The great primitive epics are shining examples of directness. There must be no tricks: bedazzlement and uncertainty do not become the epic. So Fierro's fellows speak out "straight." If Martín will be an outlaw, he resolves to be worse than a wild animal. Throughout the work, one observes that a salient feature is the inexorable progress. When, in Picardía's story, the *Comandante* levies recruits for the frontier, the faces of the hapless victims flit by as do faces in the cinematograph. Direct progress; direct speech. Ready epithets are hurled by the official at each man, and he is gone, without argument or irrelevant observations.

Some admirers of so stirring a narrative are inclined to wish that it had been made, as it were, an out-and-out epic: that all the pure lyric, and satirical, and didactic portions, had been excised. "Would not the essence of Part I," they say, "together with the first cantos of *La Vuelta* and the central thought of the Picardía story, constitute a fine, foursquare, pampa epic?" Yes—and no. A certain consistency might be attained, but at the expense of the poem's humanity. Let us remember the words of Victor Hugo: *Il y a tout dans tout.* The instantaneous popular response to the criticised portions is their permanent justification. We may well believe that the writer whose heart was so aflame over gaucho wrongs, was the only writer who could thrill us with the *gesta* of the gauchos. Surely *Paradise Lost* is didactic, and the *Divine Comedy* is a series of fearsome fustigations. Let *Martín Fierro* follow these, if it be only from afar.

Of course to say the foregoing is to say that *Martín Fierro* is not a primitive or popular epic. That, at least, should be immediately apparent. For though Hernández really lost himself amazingly in the ensemble of his gauchos, nevertheless he was "there," and we know it. Every earnest plea for his protégés makes it more apparent. There remains one classification, and one alone, for *Martín Fierro.*

It is a popularized narration, epic in spirit, and epic in most essentials, but generally lyric in verse-form.

Voltaire says an epic is a recital in verse of heroic adventures. *Martín Fierro* fulfils this condition, if in no other passage than the narrative of the crossing of the perilous desert. Martín is a hero, for, as representative, he defends as best he can, the inherent liberties of his *pago* (district), class, and race. That he is only a pawn in the game, does not deter him. He is great, because he has a great ideal, viz., refusal, in the name of liberty, to submit. He is the Argentine Robin Hood.

"The marvellous" should be in the heart of the epic hero, says Larousse. In Chapters I and VI, we have looked into the gaucho's heart. What did we find there if not lively imagination, profound superstitions, intimate communion with nature, and a vast capacity for heroism and suffering?

"To have an epic character, an event must bear the stamp of the absolute," pronounces the *Diccionario Hispano-Americano.* The disappearance of the gaucho,

> "When for a moment, like a drop of rain,
> He sinks into the yeast of"

social waves, is fated, absolutely.

I mentioned Voltaire. In that same definition, the author of *La Henriade* allows the broadest possible scope to the action. But amplitude inheres in the epic, by or without the grace of Voltaire. Addison said that Aristotle's rules for the epic cannot be supposed to quadrate exactly with the heroic poems written since his time. In other words, besides ample scope, the genre has demanded and will continue to demand, the right to evolve.

Surely enough has been said to confirm our poem in the right to be exactly what it is: not an anonymous work, but very successfully popularized, with stirring epic characteristics, in a lyric dress. (pp. 154-59)

Martín Fierro is the culmination of all the gaucho literary production: the supreme expression of a life which, like Troy, "was." No other work of the class claims so much for itself, nor has any other as complete justification. An *a fortiori* is useful here. *Martín Fierro* is more serious than either *Santos Vega* or *Fausto*. But these two were the best of all the considerable gaucho narrations up to and including their year of publication. Hence *Martín Fierro* is, beyond doubt, the work to be reckoned with. Gutiérrez and other prominent writers coming after Hernández, betook themselves to the novel and the drama, as to fields not completely worked. Obligado is the only notable exception to the abandonment of lyric, and his *Santos Vega* is worked-over folklore, not firmly knit relation.

This poem of *Martín Fierro,* though aesthetically satisfying and historically true, though written by one whose mastery of the language must, I think, be admitted, has not yet been universally recognized. *Martín Fierro* has received great praise in all the South American countries, probably all that could be expected where jealousy and self-aggrandizement are common. It is much appreciated in Spain. That it has not conquered the rest of the western world is because of the comparative inconspicuousness of its scene, and the comparative ignorance of Spanish in nations outside the Hispanic group, until recent days. I roundly affirm that its value is great. . . . (pp. 164-65)

> *Henry A. Holmes, in his* "Martin Fierro": An Epic of the Argentine, *Instituto de las Españas en los Estados Unidos, 1923, 183 p.*

ARTURO TORRES-RÍOSECO (essay date 1942)

[*Torres-Ríoseco discusses the epic characteristics of* Martin Fierro *and notes the poem's immense popularity.*]

In [*Martín Fierro*] (1872), by José Hernández (1834-86), the gauchesque epic reached its climax, and produced one of the classics of Spanish American literature. Hernández himself was something of an epic figure: 'His luxuriant, Jove-like beard, immense frame, and benign countenance were imposing, while certain details of his costume, such as the gaucho hat and sometimes the top boots, were in no wise ridiculous.' An ardent politician, he was a member of the Federalist party—and a constant opponent of Mitre (the first constitutional President of a united Argentina) and of Sarmiento (the great educator), against whom he conspired, establishing himself in a Buenos Aires hostel and soliciting men and money for a rebellion. Indeed, Hernández took an active part in the uprising of the last gaucho insurrectionist, López Jordán. For in politics as in his famous epic, Hernández was on the side of the gaucho and the gaucho *caudillo* against the forces of 'civilization.'

It is perhaps this siding with the gaucho that gives *Martín Fierro* its epic proportions, and lends the protagonist heroic stature. Martín is a gaucho persecuted by the Argentine authorities because his views of life do not agree with those of modern society. He recognizes no rights of property. The pampa land, like the sky and the air, has no owner; the only tribunal capable of rendering justice—Martín Fierro's justice—is his own knife, his *facón*. Judges, mayors, army officers, police corrupt to the core, these are the mortal enemies of the gaucho. Martín Fierro fights this society that tries to displace the old order of things, and he becomes a moral force in Argentine history—the champion of liberty, a truly epic character. Speaking of this quality, Leopoldo Lugones says:

Like all epic poems, *Martín Fierro* represents the heroic life of the race: it fights for liberty against adversity and injustice. Martín Fierro is a champion of that right which they have taken away from him; he is the Cid Campeador of that heroic cycle made immortal eight centuries before by the Spanish legends; he is a typical knight-errant helping fair maidens in distress. Another characteristic is his flight to the enemy's land when he is persecuted in his own!

This kinship to the Spanish *epopeya* has been noted by other critics. As a matter of fact, *Martín Fierro* does have two distinctly Spanish antecedents—the *Romancero* and the picaresque novel. In the case of the former, the Spanish *romances* or popular ballads were of course the forerunners of the gaucho *romances,* and Martín the *payador* is their legitimate inheritor. In the case of the latter, Martín has at times some of the qualities of the rogue, but it is in two characters, in 'old man Vizcacha' and in Picardía that one finds 'all the tricks and philosophy' of the Spanish *pícaros*. But over and above all this, the purpose of *Martín Fierro* was the creation of an epic hero who embodies a national—that is, an Argentine—ideal. Hernández succeeded amply in this aim. All the other aspects of his work—description, narration, landscape—are subordinate to the fundamental one: the personality of his hero. To be sure, this gaucho poem lacks the robustness, the unity, the poetic loftiness, the philosophical import, and the grandeur of the *Iliad* or the *Chanson de Roland;* but in its own right, in the personality of Martín and what he stands for, it is a representative national epic.

Hernández has indeed created a very human hero—perhaps too human to be fully heroic—in the person of Martín Fierro, minstrel ·and outlaw. Martín, like a true *payador,* tunes his guitar and begins to sing his own story:

> I sit me here to sing my song
> To the beat of my old guitar;
> For the man whose life is a bitter cup,
> With a song may yet his heart lift up,
> As the lonely bird on the leafless tree
> That sings 'neath the gloaming star . . .

As a good gaucho, Martín rejoices in his liberty and his solitude on the pampas:

> And this is my pride: to live as free
> As the bird that cleaves the sky;
> I build no nest in this careworn earth,
> Where sorrow is long, and short is mirth;
> And when I am gone none will grieve for me,
> And none care where I lie.

Martín begins his history by recalling his happy early days in the *estancias:* the gauchos setting out to work with the dawn, buckling on their spurs and taking their soft saddle-skins; the day's tasks of breaking horses or guiding flocks on the plain; and finally, with nightfall, the merry gathering after supper by the kitchen fire.

But that golden age soon ceased, and the peace of the gaucho's hearth was succeeded by military persecution and frontier garrison duty. Martín goes on to tell of his miseries in the army, Indian fights, corporal punishment, delayed pay, and so on. At length he deserts and returns home to find that:

> Only a few bare poles were left.
> And the thatch and nothing more;
> Christ knows it was a mournful sight,

It withered my heart up like a blight,
And there in the wreck of my ruined home,
To be revenged I swore.

From then on, Martín is an outlaw. The following stanzas give a picture of his existence as a runaway, in *pulperías* and dance-halls; his first crime, which he considers a 'legal fight' for his honor; his wandering over the pampas:

They call him a drunken gaucho beast
If he takes a spot of gin;
If he goes to a dance he's an upstart boor;
If he plays at cards he's a sharper sure;
He's a brawler if he defends himself;
If he doesn't—they do him in.

A hunted man now, Martín passes solitary nights on the desert, tracked by police riders. At length, the constabulary catches up and sets upon him, ten to one. But Martín triumphs in the fight, thanks to the help of Cruz, a former gaucho outlaw turned sergeant. Cruz and Martín become fast friends, companions in misfortune, and finally resolve to go beyond the frontier and join the Indians:

And one day when the sun's first ray
Made the plain like a sheet of gold,
Cruz pointed back where the eye scarce caught
The last ranch stand like a tiny dot.
And as he looked, two burning tears
Down the cheeks of Fierro rolled.

Such was the original poem of *Martín Fierro*. Seven years later, encouraged by the reception of his work, Hernández published a sequel entitled *The Return of Martín Fierro* (1879). In this second part, Fierro and Cruz pass several years in an Indian village, until Cruz dies of the small-pox. Fierro then decides to return to civilization, and—after killing a cruel Indian chieftain and rescuing a captive white woman—he makes his way back across the desert. Returned to the settlements, Martín goes from ranch to ranch, seeking his old friends, and learning that the Law is no longer hunting him. Finally, at a gaucho gathering he meets two of his sons, and the boys tell their own stories—the older boy relating his unjust imprisonment, the younger telling of his association with the rascally old Vizcacha. Still another new arrival is then introduced, the young gaucho Picardía, who is none other than the son of Martín's late friend Cruz. By this time, the story has lost its vigor and intensity and Hernández repeats himself. He introduces episodes that have nothing to do with the story, and finally the returned gaucho and the three boys part—the four could never earn a living together—and Martín ends the poem on this sentimental note:

And if life fails me, this I know,
When the news of my death is spread,
The roaming gaucho, far away
In the desert lands, will be sad that day,
And a sudden ache in his heart will wake,
When he knows that I am dead.

Martín Fierro was right. All the gauchos know his story and weep his death, the death of a whole race of gauchos of his type, destroyed by the machinery and wealth that is called 'civilization.' His name is even today a symbol of that virile life of the plains in which a gaucho was a free man, not a cog in an economic and social system; and with all his defects, he is a better representative of Americanism than the modern farm-hand or the Syrian peddler who crosses the pampas that Martín

used to roam. *Martín Fierro* is well known nowadays not only in the Argentine, but in all of Spanish America and in the Peninsula as well. Even the great Spanish intellectual, Miguel de Unamuno, used to recite the *Martín Fierro* to his students in the University of Salamanca, along with the *Iliad* and the *Odyssey*. The poem has been translated into several languages, and scholars all over the world have shown interest in its gaucho idiom and literary technique.

But perhaps the soundest estimate of its worth is to be found in the humbler homage rendered Hernández by his own compatriots of the Argentine pampas, as it is recorded in this typical scene related by Cunninghame Graham in his *A Vanishing Race*:

In the long evenings, seated around the fire, passing the maté around, the adventures of Martín were sure to be discussed. The gauchos seemed to take him as the embodiment of themselves and all their troubles, and talked of him as if at any moment he might lift the mare's hide which acted as door and walk into the hut. Those of the company who could read (not the majority) were wont to read aloud to the unlettered from a well-worn, greasy book, printed on flimsy paper in thin and broken type, after extracting the precious book from the recesses of their saddle-bags or from their riding boots. The others got it by heart and then repeated it as a sort of litany.

This, rather than the estimate of any university critic, would seem to be the true measure of *Martín Fierro:* Deriving from the folk-songs of the *payador*, this epic has succeeded so thoroughly in creating an embodiment of the gaucho and his struggle, that it is welcomed back by the gauchos themselves into a sort of folk literature. (pp. 146-51)

Arturo Torres-Ríoseco, "Gaucho Literature," in his The Epic of Latin American Literature, *Oxford University Press, 1942, pp. 133-67.*

HENRY ALFRED HOLMES   (essay date 1948)

[Holmes argues that the gauchos in Martin Fierro *are identified with the land, the heavens, and humanity. For additional commentary by Holmes, see the excerpt dated 1923.]*

Nothing has been more inevitable than that commentators should dwell on the obviously Spanish inheritance that stamps every page of *Martín Fierro*. Unamuno, Salaverría, Onís, and many another have rendered this valuable service. Equally natural is the zeal of those who, impressed by the regional and national threads running through its fabric, have set themselves to showing how Hernández has interpreted an Argentine era and the *genius loci*, even the spirit of present-day Argentina. Theirs has been a creditable purpose, and they have fulfilled it well. Our generation is deeply indebted to Rojas, Lugones, Gálvez, Tiscornia, and a host of others whose loving devotion has sought out the literary ancestors of *Martín Fierro,* described the pampa, that majestic stage whereon its drama is enacted, and evaluated the lesser works which have succeeded it. Nobody has given the poem more ringing praise than the recent winner of the Nobel prize in literature, Gabriela Mistral. In her thinking, "*Martín Fierro* assumes a certain character as of a sacred work; gives the effect of a tutelary divinity in print:

a power that would save us and defend us if we kept in closer touch with it than we do.''

These, then, have noted in the epic the Spanish romanticism and ''point of honor,'' together with a fatalism reminding us of the Moors; the squalor and chicanery of an epoch when the immature Argentine republic was striving to develop, and was expending the gauchos in frontier warfare against the Indians; the picturesque gaucho speech and customs; and above all, the glory and mystery of the pampa.

It remains to point out three fundamental and universal identifications. In this New World epic, Fierro and his fellows are identified with the land, with the heavens, and with man.

The inextinguishable longing of man to identify himself with land, with the earth which nurtures him, to occupy it and be possessed by it, has alike the sanctions of earliest religion (''that thy days may be long on the land which the Lord thy God giveth thee'') and the stimulating example of millions in our own times. Consider the implications of this longing— land and liberty, land and life, land and posterity to enjoy it. They are all implict in Fierro's lofty declaration:

> Soy gaucho, y entiéndanló
> como mi lengua lo esplica:
> para mí la tierra es chica
> y pudiera ser mayor;
> ni la víbora me pica
> ni quema mi frente el sol.
>
> Nací como nace el peje
> en el fondo de la mar;
> naides me puede quitar
> aquello que Dios me dió:
> lo que al mundo truje yo
> del mundo lo he de llevar.

[I am a gaucho, and you must take this as I explain it: I feel this earth too small for me. Even were it bigger, it would still be too small. The viper does not bite me, nor does the sun burn my brow. My birth was as natural as the birth of fishes in the sea's vast depths. None can wrest from me what God gave me. What I brought into the world, from the world I'll carry away.]

Consider further that this identification in *Martín Fierro* is timeless. Thus to the inevitability of the earth and man's attachment to it is added the aspect of—one is tempted to say, limitless duration. The passionate devotion which is voiced in the opening cantos is reiterated steadily through the whole poem. ''Remain in the spot where your life began,'' advises old Vizcacha. To indicate unswerving approval of the customs and ideals of Fierro, which of course must include a plot of earth to abide in and endlessly cherish, the final Canto asserts: ''No, such evil rainstorms (i.e., of greed) will never bring down the hut that gives proper shelter to this story.'' The true gaucho, *integer vitae scelerisque purus,* will dwell in a storm-resisting abode. Though he may be forced to leave it, he will long for it and, if possible, return to it.

To these aspects of inevitability and timeless consistency must be added a third, true wisdom. He who loves and clings to the land is imbued with a telluric wisdom born of experience. His life is not only normal and forever consistent, but it possesses

a lore never to be found in books. Martín Fierro, deeply versed in that lore, may be excused for saying proudly:

> Aquí no valen dotores:
> sólo vale la esperencia;
> aquí verán su inocencia
> esos que todo lo saben,
> porque esto tiene otra llave
> y el gaucho tiene su cencia.

[Here ''doctors'' are worth nothing; experience is all that counts. Here the city know-it-alls would feel their ignorance, for these mysteries have another key and the gaucho has his own learning.]

No shallow Pierian spring is the source of that shrewd and steady intelligence; all Nature, a boundless ocean, has compassed it about.

But our gaucho hero is also identified with the heavens: not the skies whose smiles and frowns, fecundating warmth and chilling tempests, are all intimately known to such a frontiersman as Fierro, but the heavens that reasoning men feel impelled to *consider.* Such a man was the Psalmist who worshipfully said: ''When I consider thy heavens, the work of thy fingers, the moon and the stars, which thou hast ordained; what is man, that thou art mindful of him?'' and was forced to conclude that God had made man but little lower than the angels. Hear how Martín Fierro considered the heavens:

> Ansí me hallaba una noche
> contemplando las estrellas,
> que le parecen más bellas
> cuando uno es más desgraciao
> y que Dios las haga criao
> para consolarse en ellas.
>
> Les tiene el hombre cariño . . .

[Thus I was gazing one night at the stars. The more one is in trouble, the lovelier they seem, as if God made them perhaps for us to take comfort from them. A man feels affection for them . . .]

Quaint but staggering wisdom of the unlettered plainsman! Worlds beyond worlds there may be, of which our learning speaks nothing as yet; while of those planets with which we are most familiar, how scant is the sum of our knowledge! Martín Fierro may have spoken more wisely than the wisest of our astronomers, when he said that God may have created them for man's consolation. And so, man loves them; he is theirs, and they are his.

It is small wonder that this identification is found among the lyric gems clustering thickly in Canto XXX of *La Vuelta de Martín Fierro,* which is the story of the contest in song between Martín and the Negro minstrel. The latter, a genuine if unlettered bard, sings:

> Los cielos lloran y cantan
> hasta en el mayor silencio;
> lloran al cáir el rocío,
> cantan al silbar los vientos,
> lloran cuando cain las aguas
> cantan cuando brama el trueno.

[The heavens weep and sing even when it is quietest. They weep in the dew; they sing when

the winds blow; they weep in the falling rains,
and sing when the thunder crashes.]

Here is the representative of a social class that had less to hope for than Fierro's; whose ancestors came from the jungle, not from civilized Spain; nevertheless, the Negro like Fierro is at ease when treating the sublimest themes. Like Fierro, he finds in the heavens that which is mysterious and divine, but he also finds a human note when "the heavens weep and sing." He touches with poetic awe on the voices of the night: those secrets hidden in the darkness, echoing infinite laments, only to be vanquished by the puissance of the sun, whose joyous rising sends men about the business of life, absorbed till the shadows lengthen, the night returns, and again the souls of the dead plead for their prayers through the night watches.

So vital and ever-present is this identification of man's living with the sun and the stars above him, visible signs of that divine grace in which "we live and move and have our being," that the moment you remove a character in this poem from their beneficent influence, he begins to suffer the torments of the damned. Fierro's older son knows from unhappy experience what the inside of a penitentiary is like. He says, "There the day has no sun, the night no stars." In a gush of utter longing he cries, "What would I not give to have a horse to mount and a plain to ride over!" God's good earth beneath him, and God's heaven arching blue overhead—to enjoy this, were to be again a man!

Martín Fierro and his fellow-gauchos are identified with man. This does not mean their adherence to a village, a party, or a nation. Nor does it signify the throwing of an exclusive light in the story upon men's whimsies, frailties, or passions. A long roll of human characteristics is called in *Martín Fierro,* but they are not the core of the poem. When we say that our hero is identified with man, we mean that his lot is that of all men, always, everywhere. And the lot of mankind is to suffer and sorrow. Here again, as in so many other important features, the poem is Biblical, and commonplace (which is high praise), and universal. No comedy is this, but pages stained with blood, and sweat, and tears, and its epic quality is determined, at least in part, by the way Fierro bears his sufferings. Concluding the reading, one is astonished to see how one has moved out from a tiny "district," hidden away in South America, to the vast stage of all humanity, where Fierro is Everyman who, having done all, can still stand the slings and arrows of outrageous fortune.

It is totally beside the point that before he was pressed for militia service he was a happy man, pleased with himself and with his lot. So, at one time, was Job. The question is, what is Fierro forced to endure? How does he "take it?" What is the conclusion of the whole matter, that verdict which each of us will instinctively feel summoned to pronounce as the gauchos' advocate closes his account of their tragic lot, their essential humanity?

If we have listened to it as Fierro says the *paisanos* will hear him, we shall not be at a loss for the answers! (pp. xxix-xxxvi)

> *Henry Alfred Holmes, "Fundamental Identifications in 'Martín Fierro'," in* "Martín Fierro": The Argentine Gaucho Epic *by José Hernández, translated by Henry Alfred Holmes, Hispanic Institute in the United States, 1948, pp. xxix-xxxvi.*

DONALD G. CASTANIEN   (essay date 1953)

[*Castanien examines how Hernández's intended audience affects his depiction of gauchos in* The Departure of Martin Fierro *and* The Return of Martin Fierro.]

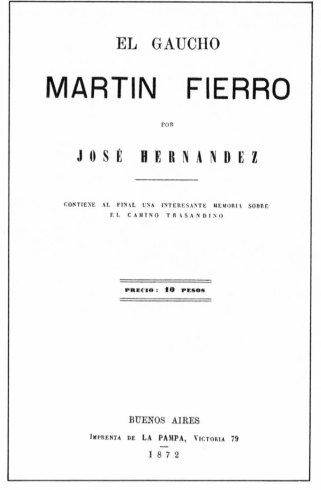

EL GAUCHO

MARTIN FIERRO

POR

JOSÉ HERNANDEZ

CONTIENE AL FINAL UNA INTERESANTE MEMORIA SOBRE
EL CAMINO TRASANDINO

PRECIO: **10** PESOS

BUENOS AIRES

IMPRENTA DE LA PAMPA, VICTORIA 79

1872

The title page of the first edition of The Departure of Martin Fierro.

By 1872, when José Hernández published the first part of *Martín Fierro,* the gaucho was a well-established figure in Argentine literature; he appeared in many roles, not all of them flattering. None of the writers of gauchesque literature took any cognizance of the plight of the gaucho. Nor was it the literary men alone who were unaware of, or ignored, the fact that the gaucho was doomed. Civilization, represented by the cities and the national government, showed no interest in alleviating the hard conditions under which the gaucho existed.

Such lack of concern aroused Hernández to write his poem in an effort to awaken public opinion so that something might be done to save the gaucho. He indicates in the letter to Don José Zoilo Miguens, prefixed as a prologue to [*El gaucho Martín Fierro*], that a more sympathetic portrayal of the gaucho was needed: "Quizá la empresa habría sido para mí más fácil y de mejor éxito, si sólo me hubiera propuesto hacer reír a costa de su ignorancia, como se halla autorizado por el uso, en este género de composiciones. . . ." Later he speaks again of the distorted picture given by other writers and places the blame for the gaucho's ruin on the advances of civilization: ". . . tan poco conocido por lo mismo que es difícil estudiarlo, tan erróneamente juzgado muchas veces, que al paso que avanzan las conquistas de la civilización, va perdiéndose casi por completo."

There can be little doubt that Hernández intended the first part of *Martín Fierro* for a city audience, an audience that represented that civilization which, in the opinion of the author, was destroying the gaucho. In the letter mentioned above he says, ''Me he esforzado, sin presumir haberlo conseguido, en presentar un tipo que personificara el carácter de nuestros gauchos . . .'' and ''. . . mi objeto ha sido dibujar a grandes rasgos, aunque fielmente, sus costumbres, sus trabajos, sus hábitos de vida, su índole, sus vicios y sus virtudes. . . .''

These statements indicate that Hernández was not writing about the gaucho for the entertainment and edification of the gaucho. Rather he directed his description of the gaucho's condition to a public unacquainted with it. That public was the city and the government responsible, through neglect, for the ruin of the gaucho. He further states in the letter, ''Al fin me he decidido a que mi pobre Martín Fierro . . . salga a conocer el mundo. . . .'' If Martín Fierro is going to meet the world, the world is going to meet Martín Fierro.

The gaucho represented by Martín Fierro is not a charming figure; he is, in truth, semibarbarian. Hernández exerts himself to explain the causes of this state of semi-barbarianism and to show that in the gaucho there is an innate moral and social conscience which under other conditions could grow. His plan, then, was to present to the ''civilized'' public a true, if not pretty picture of the gaucho and his condition. How successful the portrayal was is evident in the fact that the poem was enthusiastically received by the gauchos themselves, and the legend grew among them that Martín Fierro truly existed. Hernández, the author, was lost from sight.

It was not until seven years later that Hernández published the *Vuelta de Martín Fierro*. If [*El gaucho Martín Fierro*] was intended for a city audience, the *Vuelta* was directed to the gauchos who had received [*El gaucho Martín Fierro*] so warmly. By addressing his new poem directly to the gauchos, Hernández hoped to inculcate in them the social and moral virtues which they must cultivate in order to survive as citizens of the Argentine republic.

In the ''Cuatro palabras de conversación con los lectores'' which serves as a prologue to the *Vuelta,* Hernández remarks that a book proposing to awaken intelligence and love of reading in an uneducated public must reflect faithfully the customs, ideas, sentiments and language of such a group. He adds,

> Ojalá hubiera un libro que gozara del dichoso
> privilegio de circular incesantemente de mano
> en mano en esa inmensa población diseminada
> en nuestras vastas campañas, y que bajo una
> forma que lo hiciera agradable, que asegurara
> su popularidad, sirviera de ameno pasatiempo
> a sus lectores, pero. . . .

Then follows a list of the aims for such a book: to teach respect for honest work, to exalt the moral virtues, to teach the love of God, to combat superstition, to teach respect for self and for others, to point out the duties of the father to his son and those of the son to his father, to foster mutual love and respect between husband and wife, to encourage the love of liberty, to teach the value of charity, friendship, gratitude, tolerance, justice and prudence.

Here Hernández has described his own work without mentioning it directly. The success of the first part of *Martín Fierro* brought him such prestige among the gauchos that it was possible for him to attain the desired circulation of his new work.

He thus had at hand the means to continue his campaign to save the gaucho.

[*El gaucho Martín Fierro*], in order to make an urban public aware of its responsibility toward the gaucho, contains two principal ideas. First, the gaucho, left to himself, is a peaceful and useful member of society, and second, the government is responsible for the gaucho's turning aside from society.

Martín Fierro describes his life before being forced to enter the army and draws a portrait of a faithful husband and father:

> Sosegao vivía en mi rancho
> Como el pájaro en su nido—
> Allí mis hijos queridos
> Iban creciendo a mi lado—

Again, when he returns to his home after deserting from the army and finds it destroyed and his family scattered, his concern is not so much for himself as for those who must go suffering through the world with no one to protect them. Demonstrating noble charity toward his wife, he forgives her when he finds out she ''. . . se voló / Con no sé qué gavilán,'' because he realizes that she needed the protection the other could give her. This certainly is not the reaction of a brute, but rather that of a rational being. At heart, Fierro is a peaceful man who by choice neither fights nor kills: ''Que nunca peleo ni mato / Sinó por necesidá.'' Before becoming an outlaw, he was forced to kill an Indian in battle and justified the killing saying that it was done in self-defense and in war. Fierro indicates that he knows how to work: ''Dende chiquito gané / La vida con mi trabajo.'' He also expresses respect for established authority: ''Es güeno vivir en paz / Con quien nos ha de mandar.''

These virtues are not strong enough to withstand the cruel and unjust treatment that he receives at the hands of the military authorities. It is, in fact, the manner of forcing the gaucho into military service and the mistreatment he receives that evoke the criticism of Hernández; to these causes he attributes the change of the peaceful gaucho into the outlaw gaucho.

The only justifiable reason for forcing the gaucho to enter military service was to protect the frontier communities against the attacks of the Indians. Presumably, then, the army was maintained on the frontier for the protection of the nation. But the gaucho, on reaching his post, discovered that fighting the Indians was only a part of his service. He was called upon to perform tasks which had nothing to do with military service:

> Allí tuito va al revés:
> Los milicos se hacen piones,
> Y andan en las poblaciones
> Emprestaos pa trabajar—
> Los rejuntan pa peliar
> Cuando entran Indios ladrones.

As if that were not enough, the gaucho saw himself treated as a criminal: ''. . . si nos trataban / Como se trata a malevos.'' Besides, because the gauchos in the army received their pay irregularly, if they received it at all, they lacked the necessities of life. They wore rags which hardly covered their nakedness and had no money to buy adequate clothing: ''Yo no tenía ni camisa / Ni cosa que se parezca.''

It is not strange, then, that Martín Fierro decided to desert and become an outlaw. He returned to his home and found no trace either of his family or his property; his anger was so bitter that ''Yo juré en esa ocasión / Ser más malo que una fiera.'' Hernández does not trouble himself with the question of whether the resolution of Fierro should be condoned. For him the important thing is that the gaucho was so harshly treated during his military service that he became a serious problem for the preservation of peace and order in the republic.

Now that Martín Fierro has become an outlaw, the poet describes his crimes just as he had previously described his original propensity for a peaceful life. The gaucho has now adopted an antisocial attitude. The murder of the negro here serves as an example. Fierro, drunk when the negro and negress arrived at the dance, insulted the woman and provoked a quarrel with her escort. The killing was the result. The murder was not justified; it was simply the act of a quarrelsome, bitter man.

The outcome of all this was the complete demoralization of the gaucho and society's loss of the gaucho as a valuable member, for he imagines that life among the Indians will be more pleasant:

> Allá habrá siguridá
> Ya que aquí no la tenemos—
> Menos males pasaremos,
> Y ha de haber grande alegría
> El día que nos descolguemos
> En alguna toldería.

The fact that Fierro and Cruz preferred to risk their lives among the Indians rather than endure life in the army was another indirect condemnation of the government, especially since the poet had previously described the Indians as barbarians without pity and other human qualities. The final result of the demoralization and persecution of the gaucho can be nothing less than his complete destruction:

> Pero si siguen las cosas
> Como van hasta el presente,
> Puede ser que redepente
> Veamos el campo desierto,
> Y blanquiando solamente
> Los güesos de los que han muerto.

Cruz ends his story with the following words:

> Y se hacen los que no aciertan
> A dar con la coyontura—
> Mientras al gaucho lo apura
> Con rigor la autoridá
> Ellos a la enfermedá
> Le están errando la cura.

The problem of the gaucho remains in the hands of the authorities.

At the end of the first part, Fierro appeared as an outlaw, an antisocial being, who showed no respect for law and order, who believed that he owed no obedience to the laws of a society that had mistreated him. How different is the Martín Fierro of the second part. If Fierro is to serve as an example for the Argentine gauchos, an example who will encourage them to cultivate the qualities mentioned in the "Cuatro palabras," he must necessarily undergo some change of character. He announces his new attitude in the following verses:

> He visto rodar la bola
> Y no se quiere parar,
> Al fin de tanto rodar
> Me he decidido a venir
> A ver si puedo vivir
> Y me dejan trabajar.

He had departed a murderer but now he feels that he must justify the killings. Concerning the slaying of the negro, he excuses himself saying that the negro was the aggressor and that he killed him in self-defense. He uses the same pretext to justify the killing in the *pulpería*. Here the surprising thing is that in the first part there was no indication of aggression on the part of the victims. Now that he no longer bears the guilt of the two crimes, the way is open for Fierro to return to the society of man. Hernández is now writing from the point of view of the society he previously condemned.

In his new character we find Martín Fierro preaching stoic patience in misfortune, a strong contrast to his resolution to become an outlaw in the first part:

> Mas todo varón prudente
> Sufre tranquilo sus males—
> . . . . .
> Al fin la misericordia
> De Dios nos quiso amparar—
> Es preciso soportar
> Los trabajos con costancia—
> Alcanzamos a una Estancia
> Después de tanto penar.

When he attempts to justify resisting arrest, he shows respect for established authority, likewise a very surprising attitude compared with the ideas he expressed as an outlaw:

> Y no era el Gefe el que hablaba,
> Sinó un cualquiera de entre ellos.
> Y ese, me parece a mí
> No es modo de hacer arreglos,
> Ni con el que es inocente,
> Ni con el culpable menos.

giving us to understand that if the *jefe* had given the order to surrender, he would have obeyed.

He shows respect for religion when he expresses his regret at not knowing a prayer at Cruz's death and when he tries to give his friend a Christian burial. In aphoristic phrases he extols the virtues of gratitude and justice: "Quien recibe beneficios / Jamás los debe olvidar," "La justicia es un deber, / Y sus méritos no callo."

The description of the life of the Indians may be considered as an example for the gauchos. The moral defects of the Indians are very similar to those of the outlaw gaucho: laziness, lack of pity and kindness, robbery, drunkenness, fighting and murder. The lesson to be drawn is that just as the Indian tribes were finally broken up and the Indians destroyed as a result of their evil ways, so will the gaucho suffer if he does not reform. Here Hernández is teaching by the "medios hábilmente escondidos" of which he speaks in the "Cuatro palabras."

With the story of the elder son, Hernández returns to his criticism of society in its relations with the gaucho. The evil conditions in the prisons are the theme of this section of the poem. The prisoner is treated with criminal negligence—once lodged in jail he is forgotten and never knows when he may be set free. Denied companionship and deprived of the privilege of using the gift of speech, the prisoner becomes little better than an animal. Added to the criticism of the administration of the prisons is a warning to the gaucho, for the elder son advises his listeners to take his words seriously and to conduct themselves honorably in order to avoid prison. In this section occurs one of the few allusions to education: "Allí lamenté mil veces / No haber aprendido a ler."

The didactic element in the story of the younger son is contained, for the most part, in the words of Vizcacha. Sometimes the moral lesson is expressed directly, at others it is inferred. The whole sordid life of Vizcacha serves as an object lesson for the gaucho. He lived in incredibly filthy surroundings, he stole and he was accused of having murdered his wife. His blasphemy and heresy just before his death horrified the younger son. The hand that appeared from his grave may be interpreted as a sign to the gaucho that an evil life brings torment in death.

At one point in his story, the younger son indulges in self-criticism:

> Llora el hombre ingratitudes
> Sin tener un jundamento,
> Acusa sin miramiento
> A la que el mal le ocasiona,
> Y tal vez en su persona
> No hay ningún merecimiento.

It is true that here he is speaking of the trouble the widow caused him, but it is significant that a gaucho had the moral judgment to examine his own blameworthiness as a cause of his misfortunes. Considering the laments of Martín Fierro and Cruz in the first part, this is rather remarkable.

Picardía takes up again the theme of criticism of the government and the treatment that the gaucho receives in the army. His complaints are those of all the others: the unjust method of selecting soldiers, the corruption of the officers and the dissolution of the family when the father enters military service. Picardía expresses admiration for many social and moral values, among them, the value of a good name:

> Aquel que tiene buen nombre
> Muchos disgustos ahorra—
> Y entre tanta mazamorra
> Lo olviden esta alvertencia:
> Aprendí por esperencia
> Que el mal nombre no se borra.

respect of children for their parents:

> El que sabe ser buen hijo
> A los suyos se parece—
> Y aquel que a su lado crece
> Y a su padre no hace honor,
> Como castigo merece
> De la desdicha el rigor.

the evils of gambling and the virtue of work:

> Y esto digo claramente
> Porque he dejao de jugar—
> Y les puedo asigurar,
> Como que fuí del oficio—
> Más cuesta aprender un vicio
> Que aprender a trabajar.

respect for self and for others:

> "En las carpetas de juego
> Y en la mesa eletoral,
> A todo hombre soy igual—
> Respeto al que me respeta
> Pero el naipe y la boleta
> Naides me lo ha de tocar."

Fierro's words of farewell to his two sons and to Picardía sum up the virtues which Hernández catalogued in the "Cuatro palabras" and which he expressed in the preceding cantos. He recommends that they exercise the virtues of honest work, love of God, faithfulness to friends, tolerance, family love, prudence, respect for the aged, respect for authority, and honesty. Likewise he warns them they should shun the evils of fear, covetousness, murder and drunkenness.

In canto XXXIII the poet takes his leave and uses the occasion to sum up his ideas on the future of the gaucho:

> Es el pobre en su orfandá
> De la fortuna el desecho—
> Porque naides toma a pecho
> El defender a su raza—
> Debe el gaucho tener casa,
> Escuela, iglesia y derechos.

Hernández leaves us with no doubt that the rehabilitation of the gaucho is his goal. At first, he apparently felt that the forces of civilization, responsible for the downfall of the gaucho, must provide the means for his continued existence by fulfilling its duty of just and impartial treatment of all citizens. Later, having accepted as a *fait accompli* the establishment of a more or less stable society in the pampas, he became aware of the fact that the gaucho also had to change and to accept the responsibilities of a citizen. Society owed the gaucho consideration and the gaucho owed society respect for the moral virtues necessary to the preservation of society. [*El gaucho Martín Fierro*] and the *Vuelta* are complementary and although Hernández offers no practical plan for realizing his ideal, he does suggest a broad outline for such a plan. While it is often unsatisfactory to assign motives for the creation of a work of art, Hernández makes it clear that at least one of his purposes was didactic and that the accusations and criticisms made were intended to strengthen the nation:

> No es para mal de ninguno
> Sino para bien de todos.

(pp. 28-32)

Donald G. Castanien, "Hernández's Didactic Purpose in 'Martín Fierro'," in The Modern Language Journal, *Vol. XXXVII, No. 1, January, 1953, pp. 28-32.*

EDWARD LAROCQUE TINKER (essay date 1961)

[*Tinker praises* Martin Fierro *as a great Argentine epic.*]

Hernández, in his classic [*Martín Fierro*], . . . chose the octosyllabic line of the ancient Spanish *romance,* and wrote in the racy jargon of the gaucho—a mixture of New World with the Old, of archaic Spanish and Indian accretions. This makes the book a philological legacy of the utmost importance, for its author was a past master in the tangy talk that had rung in his ears since childhood.

Martín Fierro was published in two parts, their appearance separated by seven years. The first came out in 1872 and describes the hero's wandering life among the *Christianos,* his unmerited persecution by the authorities, and his enforced service in the army. This became so unbearable that he deserted with his friend Cruz and crossed the frontier to take refuge among the Indians.

All through the poem one feels the author's deep resentment of the many injustices visited on the gaucho, a resentment he epitomizes in a few pregnant lines:

> The wretched gaucho's a waif and stray,
> Cast out in the wilds to roam;
> His wrongs never stir a single heart,
> To take up the outcast gaucho's part,
> And give him his rights as a citizen—
> A church, and schools, and a home.

The poem met with an immediate success, but, in spite of this, Hernández did not publish the last portion—*La Vuelta—The Return of Martín Fierro*—until 1879.

It was longer that the first, and gave an account of Fierro's life among the Indians after he and Cruz had deserted from the army, into which they had been inducted by force. There were excellent descriptions of aboriginal customs in war and peace, and it told how Martín Fierro, after the death of Cruz, returned to civilization only to find his rancho in ruins and his family dispersed. On the way he encountered an Indian chief who had killed the child of a white captive under her eyes and was in the act of beating her unmercifully. Martín attacked the Indian, who defended himself with *bolas,* a wicked weapon consisting of two round stones attached to either end of a rawhide thong. Then ensued a battle that was Homeric—one of the best descriptions of a fight ever written. (pp. 21-2)

The poem was at once authentic folklore, an important sociological document, and the most beloved of Argentine classics; for the people of the pampa saw their lives reflected in Martín Fierro as in a mirror, and in his sufferings and wrongs they read their own. Wherever gauchos gathered or lounged in rancho or *pulpería,* they were bound, eventually, to discuss Martín's adventures, and they talked of him, Cunninghame Graham said, "as if at any moment he might lift the mare's hide which acted as a door and walk in" [see excerpt by Torres-Ríoseco dated 1942].

Not only did the countryfolk endow the book's character with life, but they went even further; for Hernández, heavily bearded and built like a circus strongman, with his deep resonant voice that earned him the nickname of the "wooden rattle," was so close to their mental picture of what Martín Fierro looked like that the two were merged in the mind of the public, and passersby in the street often addressed Hernández as "Don Martín." This led him to remark ruefully that he was a father christened with his son's name.

This great gaucho classic has sold more copies than any other Latin-American book—even Rodó's *Ariel,* Jorge Isaac's *Maria,* or Sarmiento's *Facundo.* It has been serialized in newspapers, and repeatedly pirated. For the rich it has been published in luxurious formats, and innumerable artists of note have tried their hands at illustrating it. For the poor it has been printed on the backs of calendars, or in pulp-paper pamphlets decorated with crude woodcuts, which, like any necessity—cotton goods, sardines, or the cheap rum called *caña*—were kept on the shelves of every *pulpería.*

This was not surprising, for here, at last, was the complete and definitive portrait of the gaucho, heroic in size, painted against his pampa backdrop. It sang his virtues and explained his faults with added poignancy because it was the story of the last stand of a vanishing class. Hernández may have idealized him, but he created from his essence a national figure and an

indigenous epic. The history of the gaucho was the history of his country.

Ricardo Rojas summed it all up when he said that *Martín Fierro,* in its unity and subject matter, is for Argentina's literature what *La Chanson de Roland* is for the French or *El Cantar de mio Cid* for the Spanish.

Hernández' masterpiece was the apogee of poetry in the true tradition of the *payador*—a genre that was vital and alive as long as it was written by men who had lived the life of the pampas. (pp. 24-6)

> *Edward Larocque Tinker, "The Gaucho in Verse,"*
> *in his* Life and Literature of the Pampas, *University*
> *of Florida Press, 1961, pp. 9-26.*

LEWIS H. RUBMAN   (essay date 1967)

[*Rubman interprets Fierro as an Orpheus figure and his friend Cruz as a Christ figure.*]

At the very moment when the *payador* Martín Fierro claims to be an unlettered troubador, he affirms his position in the tradition of divinely inspired poetry that can be traced at least as far back as the Delphic oracles and the poems on which the Orphic rites were based:

> Yo no soy cantor letrao,
> mas si me pongo a cantar
> no tengo cuando acabar
> y me envejezco cantando;
> las coplas me van brotando
> como agua de manantial.

That is, the words come to Fierro from underground and surge through him, just as the voice of the gods was heard in the well at Delphos. The poet's source, like that of the spring, is underground, and we shall see that it is of a descent to the underworld that he, like Orpheus, has experienced that he must sing. By singing of his harrowing of Hell, the narrator fulfills a divine function and will thus gain Paradise:

> El cantar mi gloria labra,
> y poniéndome a cantar,
> cantando me han de encontrar
> aunque la tierra se abra.

As we shall see, the earth has, in poetic fact, opened for Fierro. In this connection, it is significant that some of the features that differentiate Orphism from Homeric religion are, in the words of Sir William Smith, "a sense of sin and the need for personal atonement; [and] the idea of the suffering and death of a good-man. . . ." That is, the Orphic tradition fits easily into a Christian context. Thus it is proper for Fierro to pray:

> Vengan Santos
> milagrosos,
> vengan todos en mi ayuda,
> · · · · · ·
> pido a mi Dios que me asista
> en una ocasión tan ruda.

In expressing the suffering and metaphorical death of the poet-narrator, [*El Gaucho Martín Fierro*] passes briefly through what Northrup Frye calls "the zenith, summer, and marriage or triumph phase" of the universal mythic cycle of poetry to "the sunset, autumn and death" and "the darkness, winter, and dissolution" phases. The traitor, instrumental to myths of fall (sunset, autumn, death) is, ironically, the government. The ogre of "the darkness, winter and dissolution phase" is the Negro, who, as we shall see, is the Devil and whose *milonga* is a threat to Fierro's traditional *payada*. After defeating the Devil, Fierro still must escape from Hell. He manages to do this when Cruz miraculously takes pity on him. His salvation by the intercession of Christ (Cruz = Cross) is poetically logical since both Christ and the poet are heroes of descent and resurrection myths. At the end of the poem we can intuit the "dawn, spring and birth phase [which includes] revival and resurrection . . . and (because the four phases are a cycle) . . . the defeat of the powers of darkness, winter and death."

The process of fall and rise is adumbrated very early in the poem:

> Cantando me he de morir,
> cantando me han de enterrar,
> y cantando me he de llegar
> al pie del Eterno Padre.

These lines indicate Fierro's dual nature. Like all souls, his is potentially sinless. But he is human, and so his song begins with his fall "Dende el vientre de mi madre." This song, however, will redeem him, will raise him.

The singing which Fierro claims to have done at his birth foreshadows the song of his second fall, the journey to Hell, and his second birth, his salvation. That song, the [*El Gaucho Martín Fierro*], will accompany him through death and bring him to God. Only then will it cease. Thus, Fierro's poem is, in large part, about his singing, his fulfillment of his divine role.

In fact, the gaucho's wanderings are part of a divine process. Like Christ, he is ordained to suffer on earth, which in [*El Gaucho Martín Fierro*] is presented in infernal terms, and then to rise to Heaven: he will come "al pie del Eterno Padre."

Yet Christ, who was God, was also a man. So Martín Fierro, who is not God but only divinely inspired, is very human. So much so that even a writer as given to abstractions as Jorge Luis Borges has considered Fierro's humanity the outstanding achievement of Hernández's poem. Every reference to Fierro's inspiration affirms his humanity. This is inherent in the very nature of language, which, in order to express the ineffable, names the immediate. Thus, the *payador*'s divine function must be expressed in earthly terms, just as God had to express Himself in the immediate language of the Old Testament and ultimately in the metaphor of Christ, who—like any metaphor—was at once immediate (human) and transcendent (divine). Indeed, this fusion can be a principle of literary order. As Ursula Brumm has pointed out: "The symbol is an exact reference to something indefinite, to a suggested line of thought and feeling which defies precise statement and thus points toward the infinite, while the Christ figure is employed to give a definite, though transcendent meaning to the profusion and often chaotic complexity of life, which otherwise would be incomprehensible, or in danger of a nihilistic interpretation."

Accordingly, what we are about to encounter in the [*El Gaucho Martín Fierro*] in no way detracts from the humanity of its narrator; rather, it provides a new perspective that makes all the more miraculous the immediate reality of the characterization.

After a poem filled with complaints—Fierro is one of the most self-pitying narrators in all of literature—the *payador* recounts his halcyon days of "zenith, summer, and marriage or triumph." At dawn, "el lucero / brillaba en el cielo santo" and everything "era un encanto." Both "cielo santo" and "encanto" are ordinary expressions that can be used in reference to the most mundane circumstances. Yet, it is the task of the poet to enchant us, and his spell, his *encanto,* gives words their maximum meaning. We already have suggested that, in the poem's terms, Fierro is inspired. Now, if a work is inspired, it is what Borges has called "un texto absoluto, donde la colaboración del azar es calculable en cero."

The daily tasks of the gaucho take on a ritual air after Fierro's description of the dawn. He remembers how

> . . . con el buche bien lleno
> era cosa superior
> irse en brazos del amor
> a dormir como la gente,
> pa empezar al día siguiente
> las fainas del día anterior.

The cyclical impression we get from these lines is reenforced by the observation that this work "no era trabajo, / más bien era junción." The gaucho's success in his chores is an indication of his divine inspiration, since "el hombre muestra en la vida / la astucia que Dios le dió."

But Fierro is doomed to fall from this idyllic state through the evil of the government:

> Pues si usté pisa en su rancho
> y si el alcalde lo sabe,
> lo caza lo mesmo que ave.

Earlier . . . Fierro has claimed that "Mi gloria es vivir tan libre / como el pájaro del Cielo." The bird of Heaven is the Holy Ghost, the inspiration of [*El Gaucho Martín Fierro*].

It could be objected that a literal translation would render "Cielo" as "sky." This would ignore, however, the fact that the last line reads "como *el* pájaro *del* Cielo" and not "como pájaro en el cielo." Furthermore, "gloria," too, has heavenly associations, although we should by no means dismiss its more mundane meanings. (pp. 454-55)

The hell-like nature of Fierro's exile is adumbrated before he begins the narrative of his experiences on the frontier:

> Áhi comienzan sus desgracias,
> áhi principia el perción;
> porque ya no hay salvación
> Ansí empezaron mis males
> lo mesmo que los de tantos;
> · · · · ·
> Después que uno está perdido
> no lo salvan ni los santos.

The terms in which the frontier is described leave little doubt about its infernal nature: "Las cosas que aquí se ven / ni los diablos las pensaron." The hellishness of the frontier garrison is not merely metaphorical:

> De los pobres que allá había
> a ninguno lo largaron;
> los más viejos rezongaron,
> pero a uno que se quejó
> en seguida lo estaquiaron
> y la cosa se acabó.

The Indians, like petty demons, have the run of the place:

> . . . los indios, le asiguro,
> dentraban cuando querían;
> como no los perseguían
> siempre andaban sin apuro.

Fierro contradicts himself . . . when he says "salíamos muy apuraos / a perseguirlos [a los indios]." Nonetheless, it is clear that he considers them devils. In deed, their function is to torment:

> se llevaban las cautivas,
> y nos contaban que a veces
> les descarnaban los pieses,
> a las pobrecitas, vivas.

The frontier transforms the appearance of Fierro and his companions, making them look like condemned souls:

> Y andábamos de mugrientos
> que el mirarnos daba horror;
> ¡les juro que era un dolor
> ver esos hombres, por Cristo!

Their misery is so great that "Yaguané [piojo] que allí [su manta] ganaba [entraba] / no salía . . . ni con indulto."

While the activities of the summer phase were ritual, each day passing through the same stations as the preceding one, in Hell, the winter phase,

> . . . pasaron los meses,
> y vino el año siguiente,
> y las cosas igualmente
> siguieron del mesmo modo.
> Adrede parece todo
> para aburrir a la gente.

That is, ritual has been replaced by an eternal attrition.

The possibility that Fierro, like Christ, has descended to Hell to expiate the sins of others is presented: "Y ansí sufrí ese castigo / tal vez por culpas ajenas." After his run-in with the Gringo sentry, Fierro calls himself "el pavo de la boba," a phrase which Francisco I. Castro defines as "[una] persona . . . que carga con las culpas ajenas . . ."

Here our interpretation runs parallel to the one that Hernández and most critics have given the poem. Martín Fierro suffers archetypically the fate of the disappearing gaucho. However, we go a little further, maintaining that the nature of Fierro's suffering makes him an Orpheus figure, like Christ except that he is not divine although both his poetry and suffering are divinely ordained and inspired.

The treachery of the government officials is described humorously in terms that nonetheless suggest the religious nature of their betrayal: "Al mandarnos nos hicieron / más promesas que a un altar."

The three crucial moments after Fierro's arrival in Hell are his escape from the garrison, the fight with the Negro, and his rescue by Cruz. The first of these begins Fierro's upward movement although he is not liberated from Hell until he and Cruz cross the desert (whose significance we shall discuss later) together.

Fierro decides to escape in a moment of complete despair. When he abandons all hope, he can rise since it is impossible for him to fall any further. At this point, he exclaims:

> Dende chiquito gané
> la vida con mi trabajo,
> y aunque siempre estuve abajo
> y no sé lo que es subir,
> también el mucho sufrir
> suele cansarnos. ¡barajo!

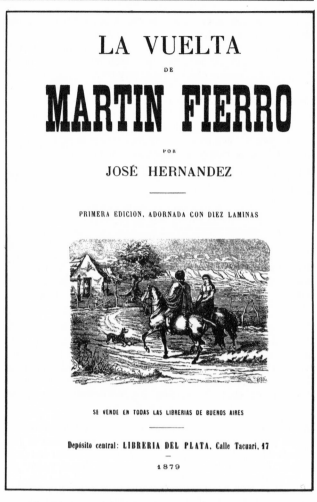

LA VUELTA

DE

MARTIN FIERRO

POR

JOSÉ HERNANDEZ

PRIMERA EDICION, ADORNADA CON DIEZ LAMINAS

SE VENDE EN TODAS LAS LIBRERIAS DE BUENOS AIRES

Depósito central: LIBRERIA DEL PLATA, Calle Tacuari, 17

1879

The title page of the first edition of The Return of Martin Fierro.

Fierro's desperate rebellion ought not to come as a surprise since, when he arrived at the garrison, he proclaimed the impossibility of a free man remaining there: "¡Quién aguanta aquel infierno!" His escape is due to the poetic necessity of the plot which, ironically, reveals the narrator's equally necessary freedom. Fierro is a poet with a divine mission: he cannot forever be imprisoned by the forces of darkness.

After deserting the army he had been forced to join by the treachery of the government, Fierro returns home and finds "ni rastro del rancho," wife, or children. When Orpheus turned to look at Eurydice just before reaching the Earth's surface, she was pulled back into the Underworld. When Fierro looks for his wife, she too is gone, lost to the poet. But unlike Orpheus, the *payador* remains in Hell. His escape from the frontier was only the beginning of his upward motion since at the site of his old home, Fierro tells us, "me quedé / más triste que Jueves Santo."

The reference to the death of Christ is reenforced by the fight with the Negro, whose diabolic role we shall try to establish in three ways. First, we shall investigate the relationship in the narrative structure between the circumstances of the fight and the two *pulperías* mentioned earlier in the text. Next, we shall refer to the role of the Negro in both popular and cultured demonology. Finally, we shall examine the language with which Fierro refers to his adversary.

Early in the poem, Fierro recalled how, during the triumphal phase of his epic,

> Mi gala en las pulperías
> era, cuando había más gente,
> ponerme medio caliente,
> pues cuando puntiao me encuentro,
> me salen coplas de adentro
> como agua de la vertiente.

That is, before his fall, liquor was the agent of his inspiration: the higher he got, the more easily his verses came to him. This is described in an image that resembles very closely the one with which Fierro established the Orphic nature of his poem, "Las coplas me van brotando / como agua de manantial." It was while under this bacchic inspiration that Fierro was pressed into service:

> Cantando estaba una vez
> en una gran diversión,
> y aprovechó la ocasión
> como quiso el Juez de Paz . . .
> se presentó, y ay no más
> hizo una arriada en montón.

Fierro's fall from grace can be seen in the irony with which the *pulpería* he patronized while at the frontier is called "El boliche de virtú." In the lowest circle of Hell, the proprietor "Nos tenía apuntaos a todos / con más cuentas que un rosario. . . ." This humorous reference to the rosary makes all the more evident the depths to which Fierro and his companions have fallen. Even more important is the fact that Fierro did not sing at "El boliche de virtú." Instead,

> Yo me arrecosté a un horcón
> dando tiempo a que pagaran,
> y poniendo güena cara
> estuve haciéndome el pollo,
> a esperar que me llamaran
> para recebir mi bollo.
> Pero áhi me pude quedar
> pegao pa siempre al horcón;
> ya era casi la oración
> y ninguno me llamba.

When he is denied his pay—when no one calls him—in a *pulpería*—once the scene of his fall—Fierro's very existence is denied: "¡Y qué querés recebir," the Major demands, "si no has dentrao en la lista!"

When Fierro fights the Negro, he has not yet recovered his poetic voice, symbolically lost at "El boliche de virtú." He will recover it by defeating the Negro, the singer of the *milonga*, thereby reaffirming the traditional *payada*.

While feeling "medio desesperao," Fierro hears of a party and "a ver la milonga fuí." The relevance of this to Fierro's poetic tradition can be seen in Vicente Rossi's finding that "En la banda oriental del Plata se llamaron 'milongas' a las reuniones de los aficionados a payar en los suburbios ciudadanos, dispensándoles en consecuencia el título de 'milongueros,' porque se reservaba el de 'payadores' para los genuinos improvisadores camperos, por quienes el pueblo tenía sincera admiración y respeto. Por derivación forzosa se llamaron 'milongas' los versos que en esos torneos se estilaban." In the [*El Gaucho Martín Fierro*], the *milonga* (social gathering) is essentially a *pulpería* where the tradition of the *payador* is to be tested since the *milonga* (song) implies a battle: "Distingue por lo tanto a la versada milonguera su especial carácter de polemista y orillera,

por eso se le agregó, muy acertadamente, el calificativo de 'canto de contrapunto,' que denota bien el hecho de choque de cantores," so that *milonga* came to mean *embrollo*. As Rossi has pointed out, it is in this sense that Fierro uses the word when he says,

> Yo he visto en esa milonga
> muchos Jefes con estancia,
> y piones en abundancia,
> y majadas y rodeos;
> he visto negocios feos
> a pesar de mi inorancia.

Thus it is altogether fitting—necessary, in fact—for Fierro to engage in a singing battle with the Negro and his girl friend and then to convert the rivalry into mortal enmity. The *payador*—the Orphic singer, divinely inspired—would have to consider the *milonguero*—whose song is a degeneration of the *payada* and demands violence—a member of the Devil's party. When this *milonguero* is black, he becomes the Devil himself. This interpretation is strengthened by the fact that there is but one Negro (implicitly the Devil) and many Indians (implicitly demons) in the [*El Gaucho Martín Fierro*].

We shall consider the diabolic role Fierro assigns his enemy in a moment, but first we want to refer briefly to the traditional association of the Negro with the Devil.

When the Honorable Elijah Muhammed proclaimed that the white man was the Devil, he merely inverted an ancient white tradition. Blackness has been interpreted as the mark of Cain, and the Negro race has been said to be variously the children of Ham and of Hagar (it is on this latter tradition that the Black Muslim movement is based). In addition, the Devil often is pictured as black. One of the demons that tormented Saint Anthony took the form of a Negro boy. The ambivalence of the medieval attitude towards the Devil can be seen in his two predominant images: angel and blackamoor. Black, in western culture, is the color of evil (as in the Black Mass and innumerable popular expressions). More specifically, the place of the Negro in the Argentine folk tradition can be seen in the quatrain with which Fierro insults the Negro woman:

> "A los blancos hizo Dios,
> a los mulatos San Pedro,
> a los negros hizo el diablo
> para tizón del infierno."

When Fierro kills the Negro, he does it by "dándole de punta y hacha / pa dejar un diablo menos." Indeed, the Negro's appearance had been diabolic: "En lo escuro le brillaban / los ojos como linterna," and "me atropelló / como a quererme comer. . . ."

Commentators such as Martínez Estrada have noted that Fierro starts the fight. Yet, if we are correct in considering the Negro's *milonga* a threat to Fierro's poetic tradition, reenforced by the *milonguero*'s blackness, then the Negro's existence must be considered a mortal danger to Fierro and his poem. Besides, as we have seen, the *milonga* implies a fight. Thus Fierro, in challenging the Negro, accepts combat on his terms. Moreover, the Negro is a super-human enemy. He is not just a man, not even just a demon, but the Devil that Fierro must defeat in order to escape from Hell. Although on a literal level, Fierro kills the Negro, on a symbolic plane, the Devil continues to live and torment other souls:

> Después supe que al finao
> ni siquiera lo velaron,
> y retobao en un cuero
> sin rezarle lo enterraon.

Y dicen que dende entonces
cuando es la noche serena
suele verse una luz mala
como de alma que anda en pena.

But Fierro, having left "un diablo menos," is immune and can treat the Negro with charity:

Yo tengo intención a veces,
para que no pene tanto,
de sacar de allí los güesos
y echarlos al campo santo.

Once he has defeated the Devil, Fierro "dentra a cruzar el mundo / como burro con la carga" until Christ, in the person of Cruz, intercedes to save him. This intercession is completely unexpected and, thus, miraculous. While "contemplando en sus carreras / las estrellas que Dios cría," he is surrounded by soldiers. When it looks as if his death is inevitable, Fierro vows,

. . . "Si me salva
la Virgen en este apuro
en adelante le juro
ser más güeno que una malva."

He then assumes a foetal position ("hecho ovillo me quedé") that symbolizes his rebirth. Minutes later, Cruz rescues him.

Two of our statements remain to be proved. First, we must show that Cruz is a Christ figure, that he is significantly more divine than Fierro. Then we must indicate our reasons for believing that *El Gaucho Martín Fierro* implies the salvation of its protagonist. The two points are, of course, interrelated.

After saving Fierro's life, Cruz tells us something of his own. In its sufferings, it is remarkably similar to Fierro's. Two circumstances, however, differentiate the two gauchos. The more obvious is that of their names. "Fierro" is hard and is used in the poem to mean "knife": "le hice sentir el fierro." This is not a man to take pity on his enemies until after he has killed them. Cruz, whose name patently is a Christian reference, does forgive his enemies and risks his life to save Fierro, whose courage he admires. Fierro symbolically recognizes Cruz's role when, immediately after his rescue,

Yo junté las osamentas,
me hinqué y les recé un bendito,
hice una cruz de un palito,
y pedí a mi Dios clemente
me perdonara el delito
de haber muerto tanta gente.

That is, Fierro symbolizes his conversion in an act that makes visible the Christian significance inherent in his savior's name.

Less obvious but perhaps more important is the difference in how the two express the source of their inspiration. Fierro, as we have seen, feels his verse surge through him like water from a spring, a pagan image. Cruz, however, announces that

A otros les brotan las coplas
como agua de manantial;
pues a mí me pasa igual
aunque las mías nada valen,
de la boca se me salen
como ovejas del corral.

Cruz's modesty is in striking contrast with Fierro's artistic pride. Moreover, Christ is the Lamb of God as well as the Shepherd of His flock. The two metaphors might be inconsis-

tent, just as Cruz's imagery is rather startling, but they certainly associate Christ with sheep. Thus Cruz's song is specifically Christian, and, considering his role in saving Fierro's life, Cruz can be considered a Christ figure.

Of course there is a great difference between saving a man's life and saving his soul, but we hope to show that Cruz does not limit himself to Fierro's physical salvation.

At the end of the poem, after Fierro and Cruz have finished their narratives, Hernández adds that "por la frontera cruzaron." This, in itself, would not justify a comparison between the *frontera* (which means both "frontier territory" and "border") and the gates of Heaven. Nonetheless, [from] what we have seen so far such an interpretation is not unthinkable. Furthermore, it soon becomes evident that Cruz is taking Fierro to Paradise: "Y siguiendo el fiel del rumbo / se entraron en el desierto. . . ." They follow *el fiel del rumbo* through the desert, loaded with associations of Moses (who, according to the allegorical exegesis of the Old Testament, prefigures Christ) leading the Jews to the Promised Land and of the hermit saints of the third and fourth centuries who went to the desert to purge their sins and earn salvation.

Thus Hernández is being overly coy when he says,

no sé si los habrán muerto
en alguna correría,
pero espero que algún día
sabré de ellos algo cierto.

The poem's structure, reenforced by the religious nature of much of its vocabulary, demands that, after his fall, Fierro be raised. Cruz's Christ-like qualities make him the poetically logical agent of Fierro's salvation. And so, based on what Fierro and Cruz tell us—both directly and indirectly—, we can assume that the *payador* has reached the "dawn, spring and birth phase" of his cycle. After all, Martín Fierro, not José Hernández, is the inspired singer of his poem. (pp. 456-60)

Lewis H. Rubman, " 'Martín Fierro' as Orphic Poetry," in Hispania, *Vol. L, No. 3, September, 1967, pp. 454-60.*

ENRIQUE ANDERSON-IMBERT   (essay date 1969)

[*Anderson-Imbert contends that* Martín Fierro *is not an epic poem, but rather a popular poem in which Hernández expresses his personal beliefs.*]

[José Hernández] was a man of letters who sympathized with the cause of the gauchos and distrusted the Europeanist spirit of the statesmen of his day. He must have been fed up with hearing the same remarks: gaucho literature did not have literary merit, it was only enjoyable in works like *Fausto*. And he probably felt resentful since his own preferences had no place in the scale of values of his time. What is certain is that he decided to join the gaucho series by writing a poem also: *Martín Fierro*. . . . His intentions were serious. In the depths of his verses there is a muted polemic against the Europeanist group that is indifferent to the gaucho world, or against Europeanists who believed that *Fausto* was the measure of what gaucho literature could produce. Hernández breaks out in song, fully aware of his sober mission, and above all, quite cognizant that there are those who do not believe in him or in the gaucho literature of which he is capable. He reproaches the gauchesque poets for a task half done. Hernández realizes that he himself is bringing something new and more complete. And in order to record it, he imitates with more talent than the others the authentic voice of the gaucho. *Martín Fierro* then, has a twofold public—cultured readers and gauchos. With the same words he offers two distinct messages. From the cultured readers, he demands justice for the gaucho. As for the gauchos, he attempts to give them moral lessons to better their condition. In other words, *Martín Fierro* was a political poem when read in the city and a pedagogical poem when read in the country. However, in miming the gauchos with the intention of bettering them morally, Hernández achieved something ingenious: an emotional and imaginative identification with the world of the gaucho. His *Martín Fierro* became an outstanding example of an individual poet who allies himself with popular poetry, re-elaborates its material, exalts it poetically, and allows the profound voice of an entire society to be heard in his own voice. *Martín Fierro* is not an epic poem. It is a popular poem in which the poet, with all deliberation, puts his song in the service of an oral tradition. The impulse is individual; the source is popular. Hernández does not adapt the poems of others—he invents everything, but in the spiritual attitude of a legendary *payador* or gaucho balladeer. For this reason, his *Martín Fierro* seems to derive from an anonymous people. For this reason the gauchos read it as their own. For this reason the traditional elements are not brought from the outside, but felt and conceived by an Hernández transformed into an ordinary inhabitant of the pampas.

He was, then, a cultured poet with a traditional manner. The cultured poet is easily recognized in the skilled construction of the poem and in his intentions toward social reform which give coherence of plot to the adventures and value to the protagonist as a type and as a symbol. The traditional manner is that of improvisation. Hernández had observed the country men with keen attention. He had lived with them and imitated them. Saturated with the gaucho spirit, Hernández makes believe he is improvising: "the couplets spring from me / like water from a fountain." It's not true—the emendation of the manuscripts and the study of the systematic lines in *Martín Fierro* reveal the arduous task involved in its composition. One of *Martín Fierro's* stylistic traits is that Hernández writes with self-constraint, attuning his voice to that of the gaucho he carries in him. He knows that his cultured voice would cripple the poem, that it is the voice of the gaucho that will give it its quality. He does not write in a prevalent gaucho dialect, but rather in a normal Spanish language which he fashions from within with a gaucho's outlook on life. It is an individual, energetic, creative language, rich in folklore but with no frontiers between what he gathered and what he invented.

The seven years between the *Departure* and the *Return* accentuate the poem's intention to promote reform. The conduct of the gaucho Fierro is motivated by different reasons. In the *Departure* Hernández raises a series of sociological situations within which he moves the anarchic, proud, and maltreated figure of the gaucho. The point of departure, then, is logical and constructive, and belongs to one who has studied social reality and proposes to disseminate his political message. There are allusions to the doctors of Buenos Aires, to Sarmiento's politics, to the government's abuses. Allegorically, Fierro flees with no other hope than that offered by the Indians who live beyond the pale of civilization. In the *Return,* Fierro reappears, but with a European and progressivist vision of work: "for the land gives no fruit / if not watered by sweat." "Vandalism is ended." Now he avoids fights and explains why earlier he had killed; they are legal justifications which show that Hernández, down deep, was a conservative who respected the law, the

reason being that, by 1879—Avellaneda is the new president, Sarmiento no longer holding the reins—Hernández recognizes "society" as legitimate, which earlier he had condemned in the *Departure*. There are two moralities in the *Return:* the one that Hernández proposes and one that the cynicism of the old man Vizcacha documents as a reality, the first morality having ideal goals and the second, opportunistic ones. Hernández' idealism and Vizcacha's realism. An Argentina with a program and an Argentina without morals. Lights and shadows. Civilization versus barbarism: here is where Hernández, the enemy of Sarmiento, in the end agrees with him. *Martín Fierro* is one of the most original poems emanating from Hispanic romanticism. Its strophe, keeping within romantic metrics, indicated an effort to avoid classical rigor without being dragged under by traditional currents: octosyllabic verses organized in sextets, with the initial verse free of rhyme, the four following lines in rhymed couplets, and the last one rhyming with the second and third (abbccb). The poem had the traits of the "romantic school": literature as an expression of society; local color; nationalism; sympathy for the people; the exotic theme of Indian customs; the exiled and doleful hero as the victim of society; Fierro's noble friendship with Cruz; the novelistic episodes of violent contrasts as in the death of Vizcacha, the fight between the Indian and Fierro in front of the woman, the child whose throat is cut, and the happy meetings of Fierro with his children and with those of Cruz. (pp. 266-69)

> Enrique Anderson-Imbert, *"1860-1880: José Hernández,"* in his Spanish-American Literature: A History, Vol. I, *edited and translated by Elaine Malley, revised edition, Wayne State University Press, 1969, pp. 266-69.*

NANCY VOGELEY (essay date 1982)

[*Vogeley argues that, just as Fierro signifies the extinction of the gauchos, the black* payador *in* The Return of Martin Fierro *represents the disappearance of blacks in Argentina.*]

When the *Moreno* challenges Martín Fierro to a *payada* or song contest in the Argentine gauchesque poem *Martín Fierro,* the *contrapunto* that results is an outstanding dramatic moment. José Hernández wrote the second part of the poem, the *Vuelta,* in which the episode occurs, to respond to the great popularity of the first part, [*El gaucho Martín Fierro*]. Literary scholars generally see the mock battle as a structural link between the two parts because the *Moreno* proclaims he has come to avenge the senseless murder of his brother at the hands of Martín Fierro—an injustice which has occurred in the earlier book. But scholars fail to attach much importance to the challenger's color beyond this ready means of showing adversary status. Yet the use of a black man for such a role can be shown to be more significant than has hitherto been established.

Blacks were a much more obvious presence in Argentina in the colonial period than they are today. . . . Blacks had been brought to Argentina in great numbers to provide a labor force, and generally they were employed in Buenos Aires and in the towns in domestic service and as artisans and tradesmen. It is estimated that in 1810 blacks and mulattoes comprised some 60,000 chiefly in the urban population and that by 1895 this number had shrunk to 5,000. This loss is made even more critical by the disproportion such a figure represents to the total population, which in 1895 had seen the addition of large numbers of European immigrants. The loss is treated with what may be more apparent than real puzzlement. Undoubtedly, miscegenation and diseases such as tuberculosis diminished their numbers. But the main reason seems to be that many of the newly freed black slaves were immediately absorbed as soldiers into the various military campaigns of the nineteenth century and thus were exterminated. . . . European immigration, which only began intensively in 1860, was just beginning to show its force in displacing population at the time Hernández published the two parts of his poem. Consequently, Hernández had the evidence he needed to proclaim the end of an age. The black had already disappeared, in effect, with the abolition of slavery, and the gaucho was on his way to extinction as organized agriculture and the growth of cattle-related industries made his way of life obsolete. So the death of two formerly important social groups is associated with the changeover in economic institutions. However, Hernández's poem is mostly backward looking without offering any note of optimism for the future. Critics have remarked on the dreamlike quality of the *payada* in which the disembodied voices speak, and this effect helps to deny the two singers' historical vitality. Undoubtedly, Hernández's focus in the poem is on the gaucho and his disappearance from society, but the use of a comparable historical figure as his song partner underscores their mutual tragedy.

The tragedy makes a villainous or a destructive force responsible for the death of these two sympathetically portrayed social types. Society's institutions are personified in such morally corrupt figures as the judge who unjustly sentenced Martín Fierro in [*El gaucho Martín Fierro*], the various army officials who cheated him of his pay and then punished him cruelly, and the military commander who appropriated Cruz's wife. The historical process is represented in terms of a border war with the Indians in which the gaucho is made to fight for the government. However, the government does not pay the gaucho for his services and, indeed, withholds any sense of belonging. So the gaucho moves in a no-man's-land, literally and psychically uprooted and deprived of any property or family ties he may have had. Society has created a situation from which there is no escape.

Hernández's "Carta-Prólogo" to the *Vuelta* states the author's intention that the literary work be so like the gaucho's world, particularly with regard to the mode of expression, that the uncivilized gaucho may feel the book is an extension of his own world. Ostensibly, Hernández as the father figure is writing the poem for the instruction of his untutored gaucho son. But the plan for social improvement given in the Introduction is not anything the gaucho can implement; it becomes obvious that Hernández has written the *Vuelta* for the educated city dweller, the source of political and economic power and the only possibility for moral leadership. The gaucho is justified as a worthy candidate for society's efforts by the suggestion that he is the natural man Romanticism has endowed with intelligence in all areas of the world where man has lived in close contact with Nature. Thus, Argentina is made to reevaluate this *mestizo* creation she has scorned in light of an international attitude her cultivated classes admire.

E. Martínez Estrada and J. M. Salaverría share in the opinion that Hernández did not realize he had created a picture of hell. Martínez Estrada says that Hernández incorporated into his poem the proverbs and sayings of the gaucho so as to capture his folk wisdom, without understanding the awful irony that the inhabitants of this world have no freedom to form their own actions—whether prudently or not. I would suggest that Hernández did understand the discrepancy between the Intro-

duction's list of ideals the book should accomplish and the message of hopelessness in the text. It is up to society to reform its institutions so that "Enseñando que el trabajo honrado es la fuente principal de toda mejora y bienestar," for example, may be more than an empty slogan. However, the reader senses that any such reform would come too late to save the gaucho, who at the end of the poem sets out, as it were, on a diaspora. The gaucho—father and sons—will try to find a place in society using other names, thus bringing to an end the noble race. (pp. 34-7)

The *payada* was an episode composed apart from the planned structure of the *Vuelta*. C. A. Leumann, who has consulted the notebooks in which it was drafted, hypothesizes that Hernández needed a strong counterbalancing episode after the fight with the Indian and Vizcacha's long and powerful testament. Thus, Leumann treats it as a separate composition if not an afterthought, though a fortuitous one which allows the gaucho to display his singing prowess in a form already established in popular, oral poetry. The singing contest effectively channeled the gaucho's aggressive spirits into a verbal struggle for supremacy and had become a standard of gaucho entertainment. Santos Vega, the legendary gaucho *payador*, who roamed the countryside conquering all challengers until one day he met with the devil disguised as a black, had already been borrowed from popular tradition by the literary adaptation of Hilario Ascasubi. Ascasubi's work was published in 1872, though fragments of it had appeared as early as 1851, so it is conceivable that Hernández's casting for the *payada* in *Martín Fierro* is influenced by the Ascasubi poem, as well as folk beliefs.

Although the knowledge the black possesses and his wit in answering do suggest infernal wisdom, Hernández is, nevertheless, rejecting the well-known interpretations of the black singer as the devil. He is explicit in this sextina:

> Pinta el blanco negro al diablo,
> Y el negro, blanco lo pinta;
> Blanca la cara o retinta
> No habla en contra ni en favor:
> De los hombres el Criador
> No hizo dos clases distintas.

However, he appears to be playing off this expectation by showing the black's special knowledge of the universe. In explaining the song of the night, for example, the black's knowledge is indirectly described as mysteriously knowing secrets: "Son los secretos misterios / Que las tinieblas esconden." But the devilish ability to penetrate the secrets of the universe fails completely in answering a simple, practical question about work. Here Hernández may be underscoring the essential difference between these two kinds of knowledge. Although the knowledge each has is partial, each is destined to fail. The black is excluded from one kind of knowledge—city knowledge—because of his class, and the gaucho is excluded from the other kind—the exercise of practical knowledge—because society forces him into the noneconomic occupation of fighting its wars.

The reader recognizes their equally pathetic underdog condition and agonizes that their hostile energies are directed against one another rather than at the society whose injustice has brought about their destruction. Jorge Luis Borges has indirectly hit on an important link between the black and the gaucho when he says:

An illustration of Fierro and the black payador, from The Return of Martin Fierro.

Esta ausencia de lo épico tiene su explicación. Hernández quería ejecutar lo que hoy llamaríamos un trabajo antimilitarista y esto lo forzó a escamotear o a mitigar lo heroico, para que los rigores padecidos por el protagonista no se contaminaran de gloria.

The two figures placed as warriors displaying their power at this dramatically strategic point in the poem can be plainly seen as fellow victims of Argentina's wars in the nineteenth century. And the *payada* can be seen as the last, commemorative gasp of their manhood.

Whether Hernández intended this meaning for the *Vuelta* is, perhaps, a secondary concern. Certainly Leumann and Martínez Estrada both point to the manuscript information and the textual differences of assonanted rhyme in the *payada* to establish its independent creation and thus its independent nature. Yet the *montage* technique of changing stanzas from one place to another, and of adding and subtracting which Hernández used, allows for this antimilitarist evolution from the original portion, which is Picardía's speech. The bulk of Picardía's narrative deals with his military service in the frontier war—how he was drafted because of a grudge and the inhuman treatment he received as a soldier. A gaucho's protest of an exploitative government, seen in terms of the military, may thus be identified as the heart of the poem. The *Ñato* or flat-nosed official responsible for having Picardía sentenced to army service may also be the inspiration for the *Moreno* who sings in the *payada* later. At one point the *Ñato* is called *mulato*, which, however, may only be an insult. But the *Ñato* has developed his grudge in part because Picardía has dared to steal his girl friend, an incident which recalls a similar situation in [*El gaucho Martín Fierro*] when Martín Fierro dared to intrude between a *Negro* and a *Negra* who had caught his eye. In addition, the *Ñato* is known as a guitar player who also makes up songs. So this enemy figure from Picardía's tale can be shown to combine the structural elements for both of the black episodes in [*El gaucho Martín Fierro*] and the *Vuelta*.

An additional bit of evidence giving value to the historical role of the blacks and joining their fate to that of the gauchos is a letter written by Juan María Torres, dated in Montevideo on February 18, 1874, to Hernández in which he comments on Part I of *Martín Fierro:*

> Martín Fierro pertenece a esa clase desventurada, que en la República Argentina ha sustituído a la negra, extinguida ya, en los trabajos y sacrificios de sangre y de vida, en beneficio exclusivo de las clases más elevadas o más ambiciosas de la sociedad . . . ¿Es digno para un pueblo culto, es honroso para un gobierno que se dice ilustrado, que esto suceda?

Relations between blacks and gauchos must have been both friendly and antagonistic during those years of the nineteenth century. Rejected as they were by the *criollo* population of the cities and by the Indians on the extremities of the nation, the two groups faced a common lot. Both represented a low social class rather than a clearly defined racial grouping. Although the blacks had mainly been found in Buenos Aires and in the towns, in later years they became a part of the rural scene, though there their work still seemed to be domestic service on *estancias*. . . . Martínez Estrada seems to feel that contacts between the two groups were not very frequent and uses the evidence of the poem to adjudge the gaucho's feelings of racial superiority toward blacks. Indeed, it is true that in the *payada* the *Moreno* is servile and apologizes for his color. Yet the way he belittles himself as the vehicle of expression recalls the way that the rabbi Sem Tob asked that his Jewish religion not detract from his moral sayings in fourteenth-century Castile. So how much of this racial consciousness is due to the ritual nature of poetry pretending to wisdom and how much is owing to authentic feelings of differences is open to question. The black of the *payada* obviously feels himself to be different by virtue of his education with the *fraile;* and he also mentions the race's loving nature which, in contradistinction to the gaucho's situation, has meant he was part of a large family presided over by a loving mother. The inference, then, is that his emotional nature is more sensitive than the gaucho's, and this may account for his ability to interpret the sounds of nature, which is one test, and to define how love begins as another. His experience of slavery, too, peculiarly prepares him for a question on the law which he answers so as to show its inequities. His questions to Martín Fierro, on the other hand, put the gaucho in the position of explaining that seemingly God-ordained categories are really man-made. Additionally, each of the tests is usually accompanied by some personal message or attack which must be answered. The gaucho's words to the *Moreno* focus on the *Moreno*'s inferior race and station, his passionate nature, etc., whereas the *Moreno* has to content himself, in return, with defending himself and trying to elevate his worth. He abstains from mentioning Martín Fierro's person directly. Even his desire to avenge his brother's death and accuse Martín Fierro is cloaked in generalities. So the whole pattern of the questioning, rather than haphazard, may be shown to derive from the protagonists' unique social character. Both conclude their songs with almost the same disclaimer—they are not *adivinos* or fortune-tellers; their knowledge does not extend to the future. The care they take to announce their obedience to Destiny's law sounds like the traditional superstitious concern of the artistic work which makes a display of knowledge not be taken to challenge the gods. Yet the identical phraseology may also point to a sad awareness of their similar historical fate. (pp. 40-5)

Nancy Vogeley, "The Figure of the Black 'Payador' in 'Martín Fierro'," in CLA Journal, Vol. XXVI, No. 1, September, 1982, pp. 34-48.

ADDITIONAL BIBLIOGRAPHY

Astiz, Carlos Alberto. Introduction to *The Gaucho Martín Fierro*, rev. ed., by José Hernández, translated by C. E. Ward, pp. xiii, xv, xvii. Albany: State University of New York Press, 1967.
    Suggests that Argentina's current political situation is similar to the one that Hernández depicted.

Benson, Nettie Lee. "*Martín Fierro:* Best Seller." *Americas* 25, No. 2 (February 1973): 8-12.
    Summarizes the plot, publication history, and critical reception of *The Departure of Martin Fierro* and *The Return of Martin Fierro*.

———, ed. *Catalogue of "Martín Fierro" Materials in The University of Texas Library.* Guides and Bibliographies Series, no. 6. Austin: The Institute of Latin American Studies, The University of Texas at Austin, 1973, 135 p.
    Gives the publication history of Hernández's works and describes the extensive Hernández collection at The University of Texas at Austin.

Carrino, Frank G. Introduction to *The Gaucho Martín Fierro,* by José Hernández, translated by Frank G. Carrino, Alberto J. Carlos, and Norman Mangouni, pp. 1-10. UNESCO Collection of Representative Works: Latin American Series. Albany: State University of New York Press, 1974.
    Outlines early critical reaction to *The Departure of Martin Fierro.*

Kaye, Frances W. "Cooper, Sarmiento, Wister, and Hernández: The Search for a New World Literary Hero." *CLA Journal* XIX, No. 3 (March 1976): 404-11.
    A comparative study of the works of Hernández, James Fenimore Cooper, Domingo F. Sarmiento, and Owen Wister that focuses on their depictions of heroes.

Owen, Walter. Introduction to *The Gaucho Martin Fierro,* by José Hernández, translated by Walter Owen, pp. xi-xxiv. New York: Farrar & Rinehart, 1936.
    Provides a brief sketch of Hernández's life and background on his works.

Sava, Walter. "Literary Criticism of *Martín Fierro* from 1873 to 1915." *Hispanofila* 25, No. 75 (May 1982): 51-68.
    Chronicles the critical reaction to *Martín Fierro* from 1873 to 1915.

Scroggins, Daniel C. *A Concordance of José Hernández' "Martín Fierro."* University of Missouri Studies, vol. LIII. Columbia: University of Missouri Press, 1971, 251 p.
    A Spanish-language concordance that includes a brief English introduction to Hernández's works.

Gerard Manley Hopkins

1844-1889

English poet.

Hopkins is considered a major English poet. Although his mature poems number less than fifty, they have elicited extensive study and appreciative criticism from a wide spectrum of scholars in the twentieth century. Frequently dealing with religious themes and evoking imagery from nature, Hopkins's poems are distinguished by stylistic innovations, most notably his striking diction and pioneering use of a meter he termed "sprung rhythm." Hopkins's radical departures from poetic traditions, coupled with his reluctance to publish his writings, caused his works to be almost completely unknown in the nineteenth century. However, critics today agree that Hopkins wrote some of the finest and most complex poems in the English language, and he is now firmly established as an outstanding innovator and a major force in the development of modern poetry.

The oldest of Manley and Kate Hopkins's nine children, Hopkins was born in Stratford, Essex, and raised in a prosperous and cultured environment. As a youth he received lessons in music and sketching, was exposed to art and literature, and traveled in Europe with his family. Beginning in 1854, he attended the Cholmeley Grammar School in Highgate, where he excelled in his courses and won a school poetry competition. In 1863 he obtained a scholarship to the prestigious Balliol College at Oxford University. His experiences at Oxford were to have a profound influence on his life: there he pursued his interests in poetry, music, sketching, and art criticism, established important friendships, and, most importantly, came under the influence of the teachings of John Henry Newman, a leading figure in the Oxford Movement and an important Catholic apologist and educator. In 1866, after months of soul-searching, Hopkins resolved to leave the Church of England and become a Catholic. The following year he graduated from Oxford with high academic honors and accepted a teaching position in Birmingham. Then, in the spring of 1868, he decided to become a Jesuit priest. He burned all his early poems, vowing to give up writing and dedicate himself fully to his religious calling. He entered Manresa House in Roehampton in the fall of 1868 to undergo the rigorous training of the Jesuit novitiate, and in the following years went on to study philosophy at St. Mary's Hall, Stonyhurst, and theology at St. Bueno's College, Wales. After his ordination in 1877, Hopkins served as a priest in London, Oxford, Liverpool, and Glasgow parishes and taught classics at the Jesuit Stonyhurst College. In 1884 he was appointed a fellow in classics at the Royal University of Ireland and professor of Greek at the University College in Dublin, positions he retained until his death from typhoid in 1889.

Although he was a dedicated priest and teacher, Hopkins was not, most biographers agree, temperamentally suited to his work assignments. As time passed, he became progressively more isolated and depressed, and he was plagued with ill-health and spiritual doubts, particularly during his years in Ireland. Many writers on Hopkins have suggested that a major source of his unhappiness was his difficulty reconciling his priestly duties with his poetic impulse. For several years after destroying his early poems, Hopkins wrote no poetry except for a few

minor occasional pieces on religious themes. But in 1876, with the approval of his superior, he returned to writing verse, although he strictly limited the time he spent on composition.

The first work Hopkins produced after he began writing again, "The Wreck of the Deutschland," was an account of the widely publicized loss at sea of the German ship the *Deutschland,* in which he also examines his spiritual struggles. In this poem, Hopkins introduced the revolutionary sprung rhythm he is credited with originating. Unlike conventional poetic meter in which the rhythm is based on regular alternation of stressed and unstressed syllables, the meter of sprung rhythm is determined by the number of stressed syllables alone. Thus, in a line where few unstressed syllables are used, the movement is slow and heavy, while the use of many unstressed syllables creates a rapid, light effect. Hopkins claimed that this irregular meter appears in classical literature, Old English and Welsh poetry, nursery rhymes, and the works of William Shakespeare and John Milton. Moreover, he valued it as "nearest to the rhythm of prose, that is the native and natural rhythm of speech." "The Wreck of the Deutschland" is generally considered to be the first English work written primarily in sprung rhythm. As well as experimenting with meter in this poem, Hopkins first employed several other poetic techniques for which he has become known. His diction is characterized by unusual compound words, coined phrases, and terms borrowed from dialect, further complicated by intentional ambiguities and multiple meanings. In addition, he frequently utilizes elliptical phrasing, compression, internal rhyme, assonance, alliteration, and metaphor. "The Wreck of the Deutschland" also introduced what were to be the central philosophical concerns of Hopkins's mature poetry. The poem reflects both Hopkins's belief in the doctrine that humans are created to praise God and his commitment to the Jesuit practices of meditation and spiritual self-examination. The teachings of the thirteenth-century Franciscan scholar John Duns Scotus likewise influenced his works. From Duns Scotus's teaching of "haecceitas," or the "thisness" of all things, Hopkins developed the concepts of "inscape," a term he coined to describe the inward, distinctive, essential quality of a thing, and "instress," which refers to the force that gives a natural object its inscape and allows that inscape to be seen and expressed by the viewer.

After completing "The Wreck of the Deutschland," Hopkins continued to experiment with style, language, and meter. He is perhaps most widely known for his shorter poems on nature, many of which were written in the early years of his priesthood. In such celebrations of natural beauty as "Spring," "Inversnaid," "Pied Beauty," "God's Grandeur," "The Starlight Night," and his best-known sonnet, "The Windhover," Hopkins strove to capture the inscape of creation as a means of knowing and praising God. In other poems, including "Felix Randal," "Tom's Garland," and "Harry Ploughman," he examines the inscape of common working people, while in his unfinished poem on Margaret Clitheroe and his drama fragment on St. Winefred he deals with Christian martyrs. Hopkins's last works, known as the "terrible sonnets," express spiritual struggle. In "No Worst, There Is None," "Carrion Comfort," "I Wake and Feel the Fell of Dark, Not Day," and "Thou Art Indeed Just, Lord," Hopkins chronicles the sense of sterility, isolation, and despair he experienced toward the end of his life. In the sonnets "Spelt from Sibyl's Leaves" and "That Nature Is a Heraclitean Fire," he works toward a resolution of his spiritual questionings. Although Hopkins feared that his poetic power was declining in his final years, the terrible sonnets are nonetheless highly regarded by critics for Hopkins's unguarded self-revelation and mastery of the sonnet form.

In addition to his poetry, Hopkins left behind a diverse collection of prose writings, including sermons, devotional readings, lectures, and class notes, as well as a journal in which he recorded his observations of nature and detailed his spiritual life. He also maintained an extensive correspondence, particularly with three other poets: Robert Bridges, a friend from Oxford, Richard Watson Dixon, who had been his grammar school tutor, and Coventry Patmore, a fellow Catholic. Bridges, Dixon, and Patmore were, almost without exception, Hopkins's only contemporaries to see his poems, and though they frequently failed to understand his works, they valued his friendship and critical judgments of their poems. Hopkins's prose writings have proved invaluable to students of his works, providing insights into his character and clues to important influences on his thought, as well as commentaries and explanatory notes on his poems. His letters to Bridges are considered especially significant because Hopkins thought highly of Bridges's judgment and sent most of his poems to him for safekeeping and evaluation.

None of Hopkins's major works were published in his lifetime. He submitted "The Wreck of the Deutschland" to the Jesuit periodical the *Month* in 1876, but it was refused, as was his next offering, a simpler poem on a similar theme, "The Loss

of the Eurydice." After the rejections of the "two wrecks," as he referred to them, Hopkins submitted a selection of his sonnets to an anthology but once again was refused. Despite the urgings of his friends, he was unwilling to make any further attempts to have his poems printed. Following Hopkins's death, Bridges, his literary executor, arranged for a few of his simpler works to appear in verse anthologies. The selections by Hopkins in these works received little notice, however, except in Catholic circles where "Heaven Haven" and "The Habit of Perfection" were praised for their religious content.

In 1918 Bridges compiled and published *Poems of Gerard Manley Hopkins,* the first collection of the poet's works. Early critical response to the volume generally echoed Bridges's explanatory notes in which he condemned the "obscurities," "oddities," and "faults of taste" in Hopkins's verse. A few reviewers of the collection praised Hopkins's expression of religious feeling, but the predominant response was one of bewildered incomprehension. In the 1920s, the poems found a small but select following among such literary figures as Laura Riding, Robert Graves, I. A. Richards, and William Empson. Early proponents of a close reading of the poetic text, these critics valued the complexity of Hopkins's works and his stylistic originality. The 1930s saw an enormous growth of interest in Hopkins's works. In that decade his letters and personal papers were first published, together with a second, enlarged edition of the poems. Among the young poets of the 1930s, Hopkins was revered as a model; his influence is evident in the works of writers as diverse as Dylan Thomas, W. H. Auden, Cecil Day Lewis, and Robert Lowell. With the centenary of Hopkins's birth, numerous critical essays and appreciations appeared, and since that time his works have continued to attract extensive analysis. Hopkins's writings have proved highly suited to New Critical approaches emphasizing explanation and interpretation of individual poems with particular attention to their style, rhythm, and imagery. His poems have also received the scrutiny of poststructuralist and deconstructionist critics, who consider his use of deliberately ambiguous language of profound interest.

Hopkins has been the subject of numerous studies undertaken from a wide range of critical perspectives, and though a few commentators maintain that he is essentially a minor author because of the narrowness of his experience, he is now regarded as one of the greatest poets of the Victorian era. Acclaimed for his powerful influence on modern poetry, Hopkins continues to be praised as an innovative and revolutionary stylist who wrote some of the most challenging poems in the English language on the subjects of the self, nature, and religion.

PRINCIPAL WORKS

Poems of Gerard Manley Hopkins   (poetry)   1918; also
     published as *Poems of Gerard Manley Hopkins*
     [enlarged editions], 1930, 1948, 1967
*The Correspondence of Gerard Manley Hopkins and Richard
     Watson Dixon*   (letters)   1935
The Letters of Gerard Manley Hopkins to Robert Bridges
     (letters)   1935
The Notebooks and Papers of Gerard Manley Hopkins
     (diary, journal, and notes)   1937
Further Letters of Gerard Manley Hopkins   (letters)   1938
The Journals and Papers of Gerard Manley Hopkins
     (diary, journal, and notes)   1959
*The Sermons and Devotional Writings of Gerard Manley
     Hopkins*   (sermons, journals, and notes)   1959

GERARD MANLEY HOPKINS   (letter date 1877)

[*Hopkins and Bridges met while at Oxford, establishing a friendship that was to be an important source of encouragement and constructive criticism for both men. Bridges, trained as a physician, retired from his practice in 1882 to devote himself to writing poetry and dramas. Though he was appointed poet laureate in 1913, Bridges is now primarily known for his important friendship with Hopkins and his role in the publication of Hopkins's poems. An extensive correspondence between the two poets began in 1865 and continued with few interruptions until Hopkins's death. Considering Bridges his "audience," Hopkins frequently sent his only copies of manuscript poems to Bridges, who compiled them in a notebook. After Hopkins's death, Bridges destroyed his own letters and deleted portions of Hopkins's, but critics have found even this one-sided correspondence to be an invaluable aid in understanding Hopkins's life and poetry. In this excerpt from a letter to Bridges, Hopkins responds to Bridges's negative appraisal and parody of "The Wreck of the Deutschland" with a defense of his rhymes and a detailed explanation of the innovative sprung rhythm he first used in this work. He urges Bridges to reread his poem and give him considered criticism.*]

Your parody reassures me about your understanding the metre. Only remark, as you say that there is no conceivable license I shd. not be able to justify, that with all my licenses, or rather laws, I am stricter than you and I might say than anybody I know. With the exception of the *Bremen* stanza, which was, I think, the first written after 10 years' interval of silence, and before I had fixed my principles, my rhymes are rigidly good—to the ear—and such rhymes as *love* and *prove* I scout utterly. And my quantity is not like 'Fĭftў/twō Bĕdfŏrd Squāre', where *fĭftў* might pass but *Bĕdfŏrd* I should never admit. Not only so but Swinburne's dactyls and anapaests are halting to my ear: I never allow e.g. *I* or *my* (that is diphthongs, for *I = a + i* and *my = ma + i*) in the short or weak syllables of those feet, excepting before vowels, semi-vowels, or *r,* and rarely then, or when the measure becomes (what is the word?) molossic [amphibrachic] . . . , for then the first short is almost long. If you look again you will see. So that I may say my apparent licences are counterbalanced, and more, by my strictness. In fact all English verse, except Milton's, almost, offends me as 'licentious'. Remember this.

I do not of course claim to have invented *sprung rhythms* but only *sprung rhythm;* I mean that single lines and single instances of it are not uncommon in English and I have pointed them out in lecturing—e.g. 'why should this: desert be?'—which the editors have variously amended; 'There to meet: with Macbeth' or 'There to meet with Mac: beth'; Campbell has some throughout the "Battle of the Baltic"—and their fleet along the deep: proudly shone'—and "Ye Mariners"—'as ye sweep: through the deep' etc; Moore has some which I cannot recall; there is one in *Grongar Hilll;* and, not to speak of *Pom pom,* in Nursery Rhymes, Weather Saws, and Refrains they are very common—but what I do in the **"Deutschland"** etc is to enfranchise them as a regular and permanent principle of scansion.

There are no outriding feet in the **"Deutschland."** An outriding foot is, by a sort of contradiction, a recognized extra-metrical effect; it is and it is not part of the metre; not part of it, not being counted, but part of it by producing a calculated effect which tells in the general success. But the long, e.g. seven-syllabled, feet of the **"Deutschland"** are strictly metrical. Outriding feet belong to counterpointed verse, which supposes a well-known and unmistakable or unforgetable standard rhythm: the **"Deutschland"** is not counterpointed; counterpoint is excluded by sprung rhythm. But in some of my sonnets I have

mingled the two systems: this is the most delicate and difficult business of all. (pp. 44-5)

Why do I employ sprung rhythm at all? Because it is the nearest to the rhythm of prose, that is the native and natural rhythm of speech, the least forced, the most rhetorical and emphatic of all possible rhythms, combining, as it seems to me, opposite and, one wd. have thought, incompatible excellences, markedness of rhythm—that is rhythm's self—and naturalness of expression—for why, if it is forcible in prose to say 'lashed: rod', am I obliged to weaken this in verse, which ought to be stronger, not weaker, into 'láshed birch-ród' or something?

My verse is less to be read than heard, as I have told you before; it is oratorical, that is the rhythm is so. I think if you will study what I have here said you will be much more pleased with it and may I say? converted to it.

You ask may you call it 'presumptious jugglery'. No, but only for this reason, that *presumptious* is not English.

I cannot think of altering anything. Why shd. I? I do not write for the public. You are my public and I hope to convert you.

You say you wd. not for any money read my poem again. Nevertheless I beg you will. Besides money, you know, there is love. If it is obscure do not bother yourself with the meaning but pay attention to the best and most intelligible stanzas, as the two last of each part and the narrative of the wreck. If you had done this you wd. have liked it better and sent me some serviceable criticisms, but now your criticism is of no use, being only a protest memorialising me against my whole policy and proceedings.

I may add for your greater interest and edification that what refers to myself in the poem is all strictly and literally true and did all occur; nothing is added for poetical padding. (pp. 46-7)

> *Gerard Manley Hopkins, in a letter to Robert Bridges on April 21, 1877, in his* The Letters of Gerard Manley Hopkins to Robert Bridges, *edited by Claude Colleer Abbott, Oxford University Press, London, 1935, pp. 44-7.*

GERARD MANLEY HOPKINS   (letter date 1878)

[*In this excerpt from a letter accompanying his manuscript of "The Loss of the Eurydice," Hopkins again responds to Bridges's attack on "The Wreck of the Deutschland."*]

I enclosed you my **"Eurydice,"** which the *Month* refused. It is my only copy. Write no bilgewater about it: I will presently tell you what that is and till then excuse the term. I must tell you I am sorry you never read the **"Deutschland"** again.

Granted that it needs study and is obscure, for indeed I was not over-desirous that the meaning of all should be quite clear, at least unmistakable, you might, without the effort that to make it all out would seem to have required, have nevertheless read it so that lines and stanzas should be left in the memory and superficial impressions deepened, and have liked some without exhausting all. I am sure I have read and enjoyed pages of poetry that way. Why, sometimes one enjoys and admires the very lines one cannot understand, as for instance 'If it were done when 'tis done' sqq., which is all obscure and disputed, though how fine it is everybody sees and nobody disputes. And so of many more passages in Shakspere and others. Besides you would have got more weathered to the style and its features—not really odd. Now they say that vessels sailing from the port of London will take (perhaps it should be / used once to take) Thames water for the voyage: it was foul and stunk at first as the ship worked but by degrees casting its filth was in a few days very pure and sweet and wholesomer and better than any water in the world. However that maybe, it is true to my purpose. When a new thing, such as my ventures in the **"Deutschland"** are, is presented us our first criticisms are not our truest, best, most homefelt, or most lasting but what come easiest on the instant. They are barbarous and like what the ignorant and the ruck say. This was so with you. The **"Deutsch-land"** on her first run worked very much and unsettled you, thickening and clouding your mind with vulgar mudbottom and common sewage (I see that I am going it with the image) and just then unhappily you *drew off* your criticisms all stinking (a necessity now of the image) and bilgy, whereas if you had let your thoughts cast themselves they would have been clearer in themselves and more to my taste too. I did not heed them therefore, perceiving they were a first drawing-off. Same of the **"Eurydice"**—which being short and easy please read more than once. (pp. 50-1)

> *Gerard Manley Hopkins, in a letter to Robert Bridges on May 13, 1878, in his* The Letters of Gerard Manley Hopkins to Robert Bridges, *edited by Claude Colleer Abbott, Oxford University Press, London, 1935, pp. 49-51.*

GERARD MANLEY HOPKINS   (letter date 1878)

[*Here, Hopkins emphasizes the importance of metrical stress to an effective reading of "The Loss of the Eurydice."*]

To do the **"Eurydice"** any kind of justice you must not slovenly read it with the eyes but with your ears, as if the paper were declaiming it at you. For instance the line 'she had come from a cruise training seamen' read without stress and declaim is mere Lloyd's Shipping Intelligence; properly read it is quite a different thing. Stress is the life of it. (pp. 51-2)

> *Gerard Manley Hopkins, in a letter to Robert Bridges on May 21, 1878, in his* The Letters of Gerard Manley Hopkins to Robert Bridges, *edited by Claude Colleer Abbott, Oxford University Press, London, 1935, pp. 51-2.*

GERARD MANLEY HOPKINS   (letter date 1878)

[*The following excerpt is drawn from one of Hopkins's letters to Richard Watson Dixon, a minor poet and the author of a scholarly six volume* History of the Church of England from the Abolition of the Roman Jurisdiction. *The publication of his striking and unusual poetry in* Historical Odes and Other Poems, *though unheralded by critics, led to a renewed friendship with Hopkins, a former pupil, and the two poets offered one another encouragement and critical advice. Here, Hopkins describes the circumstances that led to his writing "The Wreck of the Deutschland" and explains the metrical system he employed.*]

You ask, do I write verse myself. What I had written I burnt before I became a Jesuit and resolved to write no more, as not belonging to my profession, unless it were by the wish of my superiors; so for seven years I wrote nothing but two or three little presentation pieces which occasion called for. But when in the winter of '75 the Deutschland was wrecked in the mouth of the Thames and five Franciscan nuns, exiles from Germany by the Falck Laws, aboard of her were drowned I was affected by the account and happening to say so to my rector he said that he wished someone would write a poem on the subject.

On this hint I set to work and, though my hand was out at first, produced one. I had long had haunting my ear the echo of a new rhythm which now I realised on paper. To speak shortly, it consists in scanning by accents or stresses alone, without any account of the number of syllables, so that a foot may be one strong syllable or it may be many light and one strong. I do not say the idea is altogether new; there are hints of it in music, in nursery rhymes and popular jingles, in the poets themselves, and, since then, I have seen it talked about as a thing possible in critics. Here are instances—'Díng, dóng, béll; Pússy's in the wéll; Whó pút her ín? Líttle Jóhnny Thín. Whó púlled her óut? Líttle Jóhnny Stóut.' For if each line has three stresses or three feet it follows that some of the feet are of one syllable only. So too 'Óne, twó, Búckle my shóe' *passim.* In Campbell you have 'Ánd their fléet alóng the *deep próudly* shóne'—'Ít was tén of Ápril *mórn bý* the chíme' etc; in Shakespeare 'Whý shd. *this* désert bé?' corrected wrongly by the editors; in Moore a little melody I cannot quote; etc. But no one has professedly used it and made it the principle throughout, that I know of. Nevertheless to me it appears, I own, to be a better and more natural principle than the ordinary system, much more flexible, and capable of much greater effects. However I had to mark the stresses in blue chalk, and this and my rhymes carried on from one line into another and certain chimes suggested by the Welsh poetry I had been reading (what they call *cynghanedd*) and a great many more oddnesses could not but dismay an editor's eye, so that when I offered it to our magazine the *Month*, though at first they accepted it, after a time they withdrew and dared not print it. After writing this I held myself free to compose, but cannot find it in my conscience to spend time upon it; so I have done little and shall do less. But I wrote a shorter piece on the Eurydice, also in 'sprung rhythm', as I call it, but simpler, shorter, and without marks, and offered the *Month* that too, but they did not like it either. Also I have written some sonnets and a few other little things; some in sprung rhythm, with various other experiments—as 'outriding feet', that is parts of which do not count in the scanning (such as you find in Shakespeare's later plays, but as a license, whereas mine are rather calculated effects); others in the ordinary scanning *counterpointed* (this is counterpoint: 'Hóme to his móther's hóuse *private* retúrned' and 'Bút to vánquish by wísdom héllish wíles' etc); others, one or two, in common uncounterpointed rhythm. But even the impulse to write is wanting, for I have no thought of publishing. (pp. 14-15)

> *Gerard Manley Hopkins, in a letter to Richard Watson Dixon on October 5, 1878, in* The Correspondence of Gerard Manley Hopkins and Richard Watson Dixon, *edited by Claude Colleer Abbott, Oxford University Press, London, 1935, pp. 12-16.*

GERARD MANLEY HOPKINS   (letter date 1879)

[*Here, Hopkins describes the barriers to his writing career and responds to Bridges's charge that his verse is stylistically odd with an explication of a phrase from his poem "The Lantern Out of Doors."*]

All . . . that I think of doing is to keep my verses together in one place—at present I have not even correct copies—, that, if anyone shd. like, they might be published after my death. And that again is unlikely, as well as remote. I could add other considerations, as that if I meant to publish at all it ought to be more or ought at least to be followed up, and how can that be? I cannot in conscience spend time on poetry, neither have

I the inducements and inspirations that make others compose. Feeling, love in particular, is the great moving power and spring of verse and the only person that I am in love with seldom, especially now, stirs my heart sensibly and when he does I cannot always 'make capital' of it, it would be a sacrilege to do so. Then again I have of myself made verse so laborious.

No doubt my poetry errs on the side of oddness. I hope in time to have a more balanced and Miltonic style. But as air, melody, is what strikes me most of all in music and design in painting, so design, pattern or what I am in the habit of calling 'inscape' is what I above all aim at in poetry. Now it is the virtue of design, pattern, or inscape to be distinctive and it is the vice of distinctiveness to become queer. This vice I cannot have escaped. However 'winding the eyes' [from **"The Lantern Out of Doors"**] is queer only if looked at from the wrong point of view: looked at as a motion in and of the eyeballs it is what you say, but I mean that the eye winds only in the sense that its focus or point of sight winds and that coincides with a point of the object and winds with that. For the object, a lantern passing further and further away and bearing now east, now west of one right line, is truly and properly described as winding. That is how it should be taken then. (pp. 66-7)

> *Gerard Manley Hopkins, in a letter to Robert Bridges on February 15, 1879, in his* The Letters of Gerard Manley Hopkins to Robert Bridges, *edited by Claude Colleer Abbott, Oxford University Press, London, 1935, pp. 65-7.*

GERARD MANLEY HOPKINS   (letter date 1879)

[In this excerpt, Hopkins recommends reading his poems ''with the ears'' rather than ''with the eyes.'']

Everybody cannot be expected to like my pieces. Moreover the oddness may make them repulsive at first and yet Lang might have liked them on a second reading. Indeed when, on somebody returning me the **"Eurydice,"** I opened and read some lines, reading, as one commonly reads whether prose or verse, with the eyes, so to say, only, it struck me aghast with a kind of raw nakedness and unmitigated violence I was unprepared for: but take breath and read it with the ears, as I always wish to be read, and my verse becomes all right. (p. 79)

> *Gerard Manley Hopkins, in a letter to Robert Bridges on April 22, 1879, in his* The Letters of Gerard Manley Hopkins to Robert Bridges, *edited by Claude Colleer Abbott, Oxford University Press, London, 1935, pp. 77-81.*

GERARD MANLEY HOPKINS   (letter date 1879)

[Hopkins explains his use of inverted word order and his preference for the language of contemporary speech.]

I do avoid [inversions], because they weaken and because they destroy the earnestness or in-earnestness of the utterance. Nevertheless in prose I use them more than other people, because there they have great advantages of another sort. Now these advantages they should have in verse too, but they must not seem to be due to the verse: that is what is so enfeebling (for instance the finest of your sonnets to my mind has a line enfeebled by inversion plainly due to the verse, as I said once before ''Tis joy the falling of her fold to view'—but how it should be mended I do not see). As it is, I feel my way to their use. However in a nearly finished piece I have a very

bold one indeed. So also I cut myself off from the use of *ere, o'er, wellnigh, what time, say not* (for *do not say*), because, though dignified, they neither belong to nor ever cd. arise from, or be the elevation of, ordinary modern speech. For it seems to me that the poetical language of an age shd. be the current language heightened, to any degree heightened and unlike itself, but not (I mean normally: passing freaks and graces are another thing) an obsolete one. This is Shakespeare's and Milton's practice and the want of it will be fatal to Tennyson's Idylls and plays, to Swinburne, and perhaps to Morris. (p. 89)

> *Gerard Manley Hopkins, in a letter to Robert Bridges on August 14, 1879, in his* The Letters of Gerard Manley Hopkins to Robert Bridges, *edited by Claude Colleer Abbott, Oxford University Press, London, 1935, pp. 85-9.*

GERARD MANLEY HOPKINS   (letter date 1879)

[In this excerpt, Hopkins describes his progress in writing his dramatic tragedies based on the martyrdoms of St. Winefred and Margaret Clitheroe.]

I have a greater undertaking on hand than any yet, a tragedy on St. Winefred's Martyrdom and then one on Margaret Clitheroe's. The first has made some way and, since it will no doubt be long before it is finished, if ever, I can only send you some sample scenes. But I hope to be able to send you the murder scene and some more not very long hence. I mean them to be short, say in 3 or even 2 acts; the characters few. I have been writing **"St. Winefred"** in alexandrines, and am, I hope, getting a certain control of them, and in sprung rhythm, which lends itself to expressing passion. I seem to find myself, after some experiment, equal to the more stirring and critical parts of the action, which are in themselves the more important, but about the filling in and minor parts I am not sure how far my powers will go. I have for one thing so little varied experience. In reading Shakespeare one feels with despair the scope and richness of his gifts, equal to everything; he had besides sufficient experience of life and, of course, practical knowledge of the theatre. (pp. 92-3)

> *Gerard Manley Hopkins, in a letter to Robert Bridges on October 8, 1879, in his* The Letters of Gerard Manley Hopkins to Robert Bridges, *edited by Claude Colleer Abbott, Oxford University Press, London, 1935, pp. 90-3.*

R. W. DIXON   (letter date 1880)

[In the excerpt below, Dixon enthusiastically praises the emotional power of Hopkins's poetry.]

I return your Poems at last, having copied some, but not so many as I wished. . . . I have read them many times with the greatest admiration: in the power of forcibly & delicately giving the essence of things in nature, & of carrying one out of one's self with healing, these poems are unmatched. The **"Eurydice"** no one could read without the deepest & most ennobling emotion. The Sonnets are all truly wonderful: of them my best favourites are the **"Starlight Night,"** the **"Skylark,"** **"Duns Scotus Oxford"**: and the **"Windhover."**

I am haunted by the lines—

> And you were a liar, o blue March day,
> Bright, sunlanced fire of the heavenly bay.

which seem to me more English-Greek than Milton, or as much so, & with more passion. The **"Deutschland"** is enormously powerful: it has however such elements of deep distress in it that one reads it with less excited delight though not with less interest than the others. I hope that you will accept the tribute of my deep and intense admiration. You spoke of sending me some more. I cannot in truth say what I think of your work. (pp. 32-3)

> *R. W. Dixon, in a letter to Gerard Manley Hopkins on March 1, 1880, in* The Correspondence of Gerard Manley Hopkins and Richard Watson Dixon, *edited by Claude Colleer Abbott, Oxford University Press, London, 1935, pp. 32-3.*

GERARD MANLEY HOPKINS   (letter date 1882)

[*In this excerpt, Hopkins responds to Bridges's suggestion that "The Leaden Echo and the Golden Echo" was influenced by Walt Whitman's works.*]

[What I have to read of Whitman's], though very little, is quite enough to give a strong impression of his marked and original manner and way of thought and in particular of his rhythm. It might be even enough, I shall not deny, to originate or, much more, influence another's style: they say the French trace their whole modern school of landscape to a single piece of Constable's exhibited at the Salon early this century.

The question then is only about the fact. But first I may as well say what I should not otherwise have said, that I always knew in my heart Walt Whitman's mind to be more like my own than any other man's living. As he is a very great scoundrel this is not a pleasant confession. And this also makes me the more desirous to read him and the more determined that I will not.

Nevertheless I believe that you are quite mistaken about [**"The Leaden Echo and the Golden Echo"**] and that on second thoughts you will find the fancied resemblance diminish and the imitation disappear.

And first of the rhythm. Of course I saw that there was to the eye something in my long lines like his, that the one would remind people of the other. And both are in irregular rhythms. There the likeness ends. The pieces of his I read were mostly in an irregular rhythmic prose: that is what they are thought to be meant for and what they seemed to me to be. . . . Here then I must make the answer which will apply here and to all like cases and to the examples which may be found up and down the poets of the use of sprung rhythm—*if they could have done it they would:* sprung rhythm, once you hear it, is so eminently natural a thing and so effective a thing that if they had known of it they would have used it. Many people, as we say, have been 'burning', but they all missed it; they took it up and mislaid it again. So far as I know—I am enquiring and presently I shall be able to speak more decidedly—it existed in full force in Anglo saxon verse and in great beauty; in a degraded and doggrel shape in *Piers Ploughman* (I am reading that famous poem and am coming to the conclusion that it is not worth reading); Greene was the last who employed it at all consciously and he never continuously; then it disappeared—for one cadence in it here and there is not sprung rhythm and one swallow does not make a spring. (I put aside Milton's case, for it is altogether singular.) In a matter like this a thing does not exist, is not *done* unless it is wittingly and willingly done; to recognise the form you are employing

and to mean it is everything. To apply this: there is (I suppose, but you will know) no sign that Whitman means to use paeons or outriding feet where these breaks in rhythm occur; it seems to me a mere extravagance to think he means people to understand of themselves what they are slow to understand even when marked or pointed out. If he does not mean it then he does not do it; or in short what he means to write—and writes—is rhythmic prose and that only. And after all, you probably grant this.

Good. Now prose rhythm in English is always one of two things (allowing my convention about scanning upwards or from slack to stress and not from stress to slack)—either iambic or anapaestic. You may make a third measure (let us call it) by intermixing them. One of these three simple measures then, all iambic or all anapaestic or mingled iambic and anapaestic, is what he in every case means to write. He dreams of no other and he *means* a rugged or, as he calls it in that very piece 'Spirit that formed this scene' (which is very instructive and should be read on this very subject), a 'savage' art and rhythm.

Extremes meet, and (I must for truth's sake say what sounds pride) this savagery of his art, this rhythm in its last ruggedness and decomposition into common prose, comes near the last elaboration of mine. For that piece of mine is very highly wrought. The long lines are not rhythm run to seed: everything is weighed and timed in them. Wait till they have taken hold of your ear and you will find it so. No, but what it *is* like is the rhythm of Greek tragic choruses or of Pindar: which is pure sprung rhythm. And that has the same changes of cadence from point to point as this piece. If you want to try it, read one till you have settled the true places of the stress, mark these, then read it aloud, and you will see. Without this these choruses are prose bewitched; with it they are sprung rhythm like that piece of mine.

Besides, why did you not say **"Binsey Poplars"** was like Whitman? The present piece is in the same kind and vein, but developed, an advance. The lines and the stanzas (of which there are two in each poem and having much the same relation to one another) are both longer, but the two pieces are greatly alike: just look. If so how is this a being untrue to myself? I am sure it is no such thing.

The above remarks are not meant to run down Whitman. His 'savage' style has advantages, and he has chosen it; he says so. But you cannot eat your cake and keep it: he eats his offhand, I keep mine. It makes a very great difference. Neither do I deny all resemblance. In particular I noticed in 'Spirit that formed this scene' a preference for the alexandrine. I have the same preference: I came to it by degrees, I did not take it from him.

About diction the matter does not allow me so clearly to point out my independence as about rhythm. I cannot think that the present piece owes anything to him. I hope not, here especially, for it is not even spoken in my own person but in that of St. Winefred's maidens. It ought to sound like the thoughts of a good but lively girl and not at all like—not at all like Walt Whitman. But perhaps your mind may have changed by this.

I wish I had not spent so much time in defending the piece. (pp.154-58)

> *Gerard Manley Hopkins, in a letter to Roberet Bridges on October 18, 1882, in his* The Letters of Gerard Manley Hopkins to Robert Bridges, *edited by Claude Colleer Abbott, Oxford University Press, London, 1935, pp. 154-58.*

GERARD MANLEY HOPKINS   (essay date 1883?)

[The following excerpt is drawn from a preface Hopkins wrote to accompany the manuscript book of his poems collected and later published by Bridges. In his remarks, tentatively dated by Bridges, Hopkins focuses on the history, features, and use of sprung rhythm.]

The poems in this book are written some in Running Rhythm, the common rhythm in English use, some in Sprung Rhythm, and some in a mixture of the two. And those in the common rhythm are some counterpointed, some not.

Common English rhythm, called Running Rhythm above, is measured by feet of either two or three syllables and (putting aside the imperfect feet at the beginning and end of lines and also some unusual measures in which feet seem to be paired together and double or composite feet to arise) never more nor less.

Every foot has one principal stress or accent, and this or the syllable it falls on may be called the Stress of the foot and the other part, the one or two unaccented syllables, the Slack. Feet (and the rhythms made out of them) in which the Stress comes first are called Falling Feet and Falling Rhythms, feet and rhythm in which the Slack comes first are called Rising Feet and Rhythms, and if the Stress is between two Slacks there will be Rocking Feet and Rhythms. These distinctions are real and true to nature; but for purposes of scanning it is a great convenience to follow the example of music and take the stress always first, as the accent or the chief accent always come first in a musical bar. If this is done there will be in common English verse only two possible feet—the so-called accentual Trochee and Dactyl, and correspondingly only two possible uniform rhythms, the so-called Trochaic and Dactylic. But they may be mixed and then what the Greeks called a Logaoedic Rhythm arises. These are the facts and according to these the scanning of ordinary regularly-written English verse is very simple indeed and to bring in other principles is here unnecessary.

But because verse written strictly in these feet and by these principles will become same and tame the poets have brought in licences and departures from rule to give variety, and especially when the natural rhythm is rising, as in the common ten-syllable or five-foot verse, rhymed or blank. These irregularities are chiefly Reversed Feet and Reversed or Counterpoint Rhythm, which two things are two steps or degrees of licence in the same kind. By a reversed foot I mean the putting the stress where, to judge by the rest of the measure, the slack should be and the slack where the stress, and this is done freely at the beginning of a line and, in the course of a line, after a pause; only scarcely ever in the second foot or place and never in the last, unless when the poet designs some extraordinary effect; for these places are characteristic and sensitive and cannot well be touched. But the reversal of the first foot and of some middle foot after a strong pause is a thing so natural that our poets have generally done it, from Chaucer down, without remark and it commonly passes unnoticed and cannot be said to amount to a formal change of rhythm, but rather is that irregularity which all natural growth and motion shews. If however the reversal is repeated in two feet running, especially so as to include the sensitive second foot, it must be due either to great want of ear or else is a calculated effect, the superinducing or *mounting* of a new rhythm upon the old; and since the new or mounted rhythm is actually heard and at the same time the mind naturaly supplies the natural or standard foregoing rhythm, for we do not forget what the rhythm is that by rights we should be hearing, two rhythms are in some manner running at once and we have something answerable to coun-

terpoint in music, which is two or more strains of tune going on together, and this is Counterpoint Rhythm. Of this kind of verse Milton is the great master and the choruses of *Samson Agonistes* are written throughout in it—but with the disadvantage that he does not let the reader clearly know what the ground-rhythm is meant to be and so they have struck most readers as merely irregular. And in fact if you counterpoint throughout, since one only of the counter rhythms is actually heard, the other is really destroyed or cannot come to exist and what is written is one rhythm only and probably Sprung Rhythm, of which I now speak.

Sprung Rhythm, as used in this book, is measured by feet of from one to four syllables, regularly, and for particular effects any number of weak or slack syllables may be used. It has one stress, which falls on the only syllable, if there is only one, or, if there are more, then scanning as above, on the first, and so gives rise to four sorts of feet, a monosyllable and the so-called accentual Trochee, Dactyl, and the First Paeon. And there will be four corresponding natural rhythms; but nominally the feet are mixed and any one may follow any other. And hence Sprung Rhythm differs from Running Rhythm in having or being only one nominal rhythm, a mixed or 'logaoedic' one, instead of three, but on the other hand in having twice the flexibility of foot, so that any two stresses may either follow one another running or be divided by one, two, or three slack syllables. But strict Sprung Rhythm cannot be counterpointed. In Sprung Rhythm, as in logaoedic rhythm generally, the feet are assumed to be equally long or strong and their seeming inequality is made up by pause or stressing.

Remark also that it is natural in Sprung Rhythm for the lines to be *rove over,* that is for the scanning of each line immediately to take up that of the one before, so that if the first has one or more syllables at its end the other must have so many the less at its beginning; and in fact the scanning runs on without break from the beginning, say, of a stanza to the end and all the stanza is one long strain, though written in lines asunder.

Two licences are natural to Sprung Rhythm. The one is rests, as in music; but of this an example is scarcely to be found in this book, unless in the "Echos," second line. The other is *hangers* or *outrides,* that is one, two, or three slack syllables added to a foot and not counting in the nominal scanning. They are so called because they seem to hang below the line or ride forward or backward from it in another dimension than the line itself, according to a principle needless to explain here. These outriding half feet or hangers are marked by a loop underneath them, and plenty of them will be found.

The other marks are easily understood, namely accents, where the reader might be in doubt which syllable should have the stress; slurs, that is loops *over* syllables, to tie them together into the time of one; little loops at the end of a line to shew that the rhyme goes on to the first letter of the next line; what in music are called pauses . . . , to shew that the syllable should be dwelt on; and twirls . . . , to mark reversed or counterpointed rhythm.

Note on the nature and history of Sprung Rhythm—Sprung Rhythm is the most natural of things. For (1) it is the rhythm of common speech and of written prose, when rhythm is perceived in them. (2) It is the rhythm of all but the most monotonously regular music, so that in the words of choruses and refrains and in songs written closely to music it arises. (3) It is found in nursery rhymes, weather saws, and so on; because, however these may have been once made in running rhythm, the terminations having dropped off by the change of language, the stresses come together and so the rhythm is sprung, (4) It arises in common verse when reversed or counterpointed, for the same reason.

But nevertheless in spite of all this and though Greek and Latin lyric verse, which is well known, and the old English verse seen in *Pierce Ploughman* are in sprung rhythm, it has in fact ceased to be used since the Elizabethan age, Greene being the last writer who can be said to have recognized it. For perhaps there was not, down to our days, a single, even short, poem in English in which sprung rhythm is employed—not for single effects or in fixed places—but as the governing principle of the scansion. I say this because the contrary has been asserted: if it is otherwise the poem should be cited. (pp. 45-9)

> *Gerard Manley Hopkins, in a preface to his* The Poems of Gerard Manley Hopkins, *edited by W. H. Gardner and N. H. MacKenzie, fourth edition, Oxford University Press, Oxford, 1970, pp. 45-9.*

COVENTRY PATMORE   (letter date 1884)

[*Patmore is known as the Victorian poet of married and mystical love, a theme developed in his major works,* The Angel in the House *and* The Unknown Eros. *Additionally, he wrote numerous essays in which he promulgated his individualistic and often extremely conservative views on social and religious issues. Although he enjoyed considerable popularity in the 1850s, his reputation thereafter declined markedly, due in part, perhaps, to his conversion to Catholicism in 1864. Here, Patmore complains that Hopkins's obscurity of thought is further complicated by an overabundance of technical experiments that make his poems strange and difficult to understand. For additional commentary by Patmore, see the excerpt dated May 2, 1884.*]

I have read your poems—most of them several times—and find my first impression confirmed with each reading. It seems to me that the thought and feeling of these poems, if expressed without any obscuring novelty of mode, are such as often to require the whole attention to apprehend and digest them; and are therefore of a kind to appeal only to the few. But to the already sufficiently arduous character of such poetry you seem to me to have added the difficulty of following *several* entirely novel and simultaneous experiments in versification and construction, together with an altogether unprecedented system of alliteration and compound words;—any one of which novelties would be startling and productive of distraction from the poetic matter to be expressed.

System and learned theory are manifest in all these experiments; but they seem to me to be *too* manifest. To me they often darken the thought and feeling which all arts and artifices of language should only illustrate; and I often find it as hard to follow you as I have found it to follow the darkest parts of Browning—who, however, has not an equal excuse of philosophic system. 'Thoughts that *voluntary* move harmonious numbers' is, I suppose, the best definition of poetry that ever was spoken. Whenever your thoughts forget their theories they do so move, and no one who knows what poetry is can mistake them for anything but poetry. **"The Blessed Virgin Compared to the Air We Breathe"** and a few other pieces are exquisite to my mind, but, in these, you have attained to move almost unconsciously in your self-imposed shackles, and consequently the ear follows you without much interruption from the surprise of such novelties; and I can conceive that, after awhile, they would become additional delights. But I do not think that I could ever become sufficiently accustomed to your favourite

Poem, **"The Wreck of the Deutschland"** to reconcile me to its strangenesses.

I do not think that your musical signs . . . help at all. I fancy I should always read the passages in which they occur as you intend them to be read, without any such aid; and people who would not do so would not be *practically* helped by the notation. (pp. 352-53)

I might very likely be wrong, for I see that Bridges goes along with you where I cannot, & where I do not believe that I ever could and I deliberately recognise in . . . [him] a sounder and more delicate taste than my own. You remember I only claimed to be a God among the *Gallery* Gods—i.e. the common run of *Nineteenth Century, Fortnightly* & such critics. I feel *absolutely* sure that you would never conciliate *them*—but Bridges' appreciation is a fact that I cannot get over. I cannot understand his not seeing defects in your system wh. I seem to see so clearly; and when I do not understand a man's ignorance, I obey the Philosopher and think myself ignorant of his understanding. So please do not rely upon impressions which I distrust myself. (pp. 353-54)

> *Coventry Patmore, in a letter to Gerard Manley Hopkins on March 20, 1884, in* Further Letters of Gerard Manley Hopkins: Including His Correspondence with Coventry Patmore *by Gerard Manley Hopkins, edited by Claude Colleer Abbott, revised edition, Oxford University Press, London, 1956, pp. 352-54.*

COVENTRY PATMORE   (letter date 1884)

[*In this excerpt from a letter to Bridges, Patmore confesses that he cannot understand Hopkins's works. For additional commentary by Patmore, see the excerpt dated March 20, 1884.*]

To me [Hopkins's] poetry has the effect of veins of pure gold embedded in masses of unpracticable quartz. He assures me that his 'thoughts involuntarily moved' in such numbers, and that he did not write them from preconceived theories. I cannot understand it. His genius is however unmistakable, and is lovely and unique in its effects whenever he approximates to the ordinary rules of composition. (pp. 36-7)

> *Coventry Patmore, in a letter to Robert Bridges on May 2, 1884, in* Gerard Manley Hopkins, 'Poems': A Casebook, *edited by Margaret Bottrall, The Macmillan Press Ltd., 1975, pp. 36-8.*

GERARD MANLEY HOPKINS   (letter date 1887)

[*In this brief excerpt, Hopkins speaks of a critical study that he believed to be his most important work. The manuscript to which he refers was not found among his papers, and it is speculated that he destroyed the book in an unfinished state.*]

I have done some part of a book on Pindar's metres and Greek metres in general and metre in general and almost on art in general and wider still, but that I shall ever get far on with it or, if I do, sail through all the rocks and shoals that lie before me I scarcely dare to hope and yet I do greatly desire, since the thoughts are well worth preserving: they are a solid foundation for criticism. What becomes of my verses I care little, but about things like this, what I write or could write on philosophical matters, I do; and the reason of the difference is that the verses stand or fall by their simple selves and, though by being read they might do good, by being unread they do no harm; but if the other things are unsaid right they will be said by somebody else wrong, and that is what will not let me rest. (p. 150)

Gerard Manley Hopkins, in a letter to Richard Watson Dixon on January 27, 1887, in The Correspondence of Gerard Manley Hopkins and Richard Watson Dixon, *edited by Claude Colleer Abbott, Oxford University Press, London, 1935, pp. 149-51.*

GERARD MANLEY HOPKINS (letter date 1887)

[In the following excerpt, Hopkins discusses his syntax.]

I want Harry Ploughman to be a vivid figure before the mind's eye; if he is not that the sonnet ["**Harry Ploughman**"] fails. The difficulties are of syntax no doubt. Dividing a compound word by a clause sandwiched into it was a desperate deed, I feel, and I do not feel that it was an unquestionable success. But which is the line you do not understand? I do myself think, I may say, that it would be an immense advance in notation (so to call it) in writing as the record of speech, to distinguish the subject, verb, object, and in general to express the construction to the eye; as is done already partly in punctuation by everybody, partly in capitals by the Germans, more fully in accentuation by the Hebrews. And I daresay it will come. But it would, I think, not do for me: it seems a confession of unintelligibility. And yet I don't know. At all events there is a difference. My meaning surely *ought* to appear of itself; but in a language like English, and in an age of it like the present, written words are really matter open and indifferent to the receiving of different and alternative verse-forms, some of which the reader cannot possibly be sure are meant unless they are marked for him. Besides metrical marks are for the performer and such marks are proper in every art. Though indeed one might say syntactical marks are for the performer too. But however that reminds me that one thing I am now resolved on, it is to prefix short prose *arguments* to some of my pieces. These too will expose me to carping, but I do not mind. Epic and drama and ballad and many, most, things should be at once intelligible; but everything need not and cannot be. Plainly if it is possible to express a sub[t]le and recondite thought on a subtle and recondite subject in a subtle and recondite way and with great felicity and perfection, in the end, something must be sacrificed, with so trying a task, in the process, and this may be the being at once, nay perhaps even the being without explanation at all, intelligible. Neither, in the same light, does it seem to be me a real objection (though this one I hope not to lay myself open to) that the argument should be even longer than the piece; for the merit of the work may lie for one thing in its terseness. It is like a mate which may be given, one way only, in three moves; otherwise, various ways, in many. (p. 266)

Gerard Manley Hopkins, in a letter to Robert Bridges on November 6, 1887, in his The Letters of Gerard Manley Hopkins to Robert Bridges, *edited by Claude Colleer Abbott, Oxford University Press, London, 1935, pp. 264-67.*

GERARD MANLEY HOPKINS (letter date 1888)

[Hopkins here provides a detailed explication of "Tom's Garland," which neither Bridges nor Dixon was able to understand. Their failure to comprehend Hopkins's self-described "highly wrought" style in this poem, many critics believe, led to his decision to adopt a simpler, more "Miltonic" mode in his future works.]

I laughed outright and often, but very sardonically, to think you and the Canon could not construe my last sonnet ["**Tom's Garland**"]; that he had to write to you for a crib. It is plain I must go no farther on this road: if you and he cannot understand me who will? Yet, declaimed, the strange constructions would be dramatic and effective. Must I interpret it? It means then that, as St. Paul and Plato and Hobbes and everybody says, the commonwealth or well ordered human society is like one man; a body with many members and each its function; some higher, some lower, but all honourable, from the honour which belongs to the whole. The head is the sovereign, who has no superior but God and from heaven receives his or her authority: we must then imagine this head as bare (see St. Paul much on this) and covered, so to say, only with the sun and stars, of which the crown is a symbol, which is an ornament but not a covering; it has an enormous hat or skull cap, the vault of heaven. The foot is the day labourer, and this is armed with hobnail boots, because it has to wear and be worn by the ground; which again is symbolical; for it is navvies or day labourers who, on the great scale or in gangs and millions, mainly trench, tunnel, blast, and in others ways disfigure, 'mammock' the earth and, on a small scale, singly, and superficially stamp it with their footprints. And the 'garlands' of nails they wear are therefore the visible badge of the place they fill, the lowest in the commonwealth. But this place still shares the common honour, and if it wants one advantage, glory or public fame, makes up for it by another, ease of mind, absence of care; and these things are symbolized by the gold and the iron garlands. (O, once explained, how clear it all is!) Therefore the scene of the poem is laid at evening, when they are giving over work and one after another pile their picks, with which they earn their living, and swing off home, knocking sparks out of mother earth not now by labour and of choice but by the mere footing, being strongshod and making no hardship of hardness, taking all easy. And so to supper and bed. Here comes a violent but effective hyperbaton or suspension, in which the action of the mind mimics that of the labourer—surveys his lot, low but free from care; then by a sudden strong act throws it over the shoulder or tosses it away as a light matter. The witnessing of which lightheartednesss makes me indignant with the fools of Radical Levellers. But presently I remember that this is all very well for those who are in, however low in, the Commonwealth and share in any way the Common weal; but that the curse of our times is that many do not share it, that they are outcasts from it and have neither security nor splendour; that they share care with the high and obscurity with the low, but wealth or comfort with neither. And this state of things, I say, is the origin of Loafers, Tramps, Cornerboys, Roughs, Socialists and other pests of society. And I think that it is a very pregnant sonnet and in point of execution very highly wrought. Too much so, I am afraid. (pp. 272-74)

Gerard Manley Hopkins, in a letter to Robert Bridges on February 10, 1888, in his The Letters of Gerard Manley Hopkins to Robert Bridges, *edited by Claude Colleer Abbott, Oxford University Press, London, 1935, pp. 272-74.*

GERARD MANLEY HOPKINS (letter date 1888)

[In the following excerpt from a letter to Bridges, Hopkins comments on differences in their literary tastes.]

I am sorry to hear of our differing so much in taste: I was hardly aware of it. (It is not nearly so sad as differing in religion). I feel how great the loss is of not reading, as you say; but if I did read I do not much think the effect of it would be what you seem to expect, on either my compositions or my judgments.

I *must* read something of Greek and Latin letters and lately I sent you a sonnet, on the **"Heraclitean Fire,"** in which a great deal of early Greek philosophical thought was distilled; but the liquor of the distillation did not taste very Greek, did it? The effect of studying masterpieces is to make me admire and do otherwise. So it must be on every original artist to some degree, on me to a marked degree. Perhaps then more reading would only *refine my singularity*, which is not what you want. . . . (pp. 290-91)

Wide reading does two things—it extends knowledge and it adjusts the judgment. Now it is mostly found that learned judgment is less singular than an unlearned one and oftener agrees with the common and popular judgment, with which it coincides as a fine balance or other measure does with the rule of thumb. But, so far as I see, where we differ in judgment, my judgments are less singular than yours; I agree more than you do with the mob and with the *communis criticorum*. Presumably I shd. agree with these still more if I read more and so differ still more from you than now. . . .

To return to composition for a moment: what I want there, to be more intelligible, smoother, and less singular, is an audience. I think the fragments I wrote of **"St. Winefred,"** which was meant to be played, were not hard to understand. My prose I am sure is clear and even flowing. (p. 291)

Gerard Manley Hopkins, in a letter to Robert Bridges on September 25, 1888, in his The Letters of Gerard Manley Hopkins to Robert Bridges, *edited by Claude Colleer Abbott, Oxford University Press, London, 1935, pp. 290-92.*

ROBERT BRIDGES   (essay date 1894)

[*The following excerpt is from a brief introductory note to a selection of Hopkins's poems published in the 1894 anthology* The Poets and Poems of the Century. *For additional criticism by Bridges, see the excerpt dated 1918.*]

Hopkins's early verse shows a mastery of Keatsian sweetnesses, but he soon developed a very different sort of style of his own, so full of experiments in rhythm and diction that, were his poems collected into one volume, they would appear as a unique effort in English literature. Most of his poems are religious, and marked with Catholic theology, and almost all are injured by a natural eccentricity, a love for sublety and uncommonness. . . . And this quality of mind hampered their author through life; for though to a fine intellect and varied accomplishments (he was both a draughtsman and a musician) he united humour, great personal charm, and the most attractive virtues of a tender and sympathetic nature,—which won him love wherever he went, and gave him zeal for his work—yet he was not considered publicly successful in his profession. . . . (p. 41)

Poems so far removed as his came to be from the ordinary simplicity of grammar and metre, had they no other drawback, could never be popular; but they will interest poets; and they may perhaps prove welcome to the critic, for they have this plain fault, that, aiming at an unattainable perfection of language (as if words—each with its two-fold value in sense and in sound—could be arranged like so many separate gems to compose a whole expression of thought, in which the force of

grammar and the beauty of rhythm absolutely correspond), they not only sacrifice simplicity, but very often, among verses of the rarest beauty, show a neglect of those canons of taste which seem common to all poetry. (pp. 41-2)

Robert Bridges, in an extract in Gerard Manley Hopkins, Poems: A Casebook, *edited by Margaret Bottrall, The Macmillan Press Ltd., 1975, pp. 41-2.*

KATHERINE BRÉGY   (essay date 1909)

[*Brégy examines Hopkins's religious themes and literary innovations in the few poems anthologized prior to the publication of his collected works in 1918.*]

[Hopkins is] a poet who, when he shall come into his just inheritance of human praise, may well be known as the Crashaw of the Oxford Movement. Very early the imperious obediences of the religious life took him from a purely literary career; and early, too, came the great Silencer. Yet to examine his few and scattered poems is to be convinced that the divine fire burned upon his brow, once and until the end, albeit in curious and unwonted arabesques. (p. 433)

[The] wood of Gerard Hopkins' cross lay just beyond his doorsill. But in the wise and sweet economy of life the cross for most of us is pilgrim-staff as well. Our poet's pathway was not destined to lead beside the pleasant ways of garden or hearthstone; it was to know conflict from without and from within; but his consolations, more especially in youth, were notable. By nature—that is to say God—he had been rarely dowered. . . . [His] was the awakened soul; and something of his absorbtion in spiritual things may be guessed from the opening stanzas of a little undated Hymn:

> Thee, God, I come from, to Thee go;
> All day long I like fountain flow
> From Thy hand out, swayed about
> Mote-like in Thy mighty glow.
>
> (pp. 434-35)

Gerard Hopkins had written poetry as a boy. . . . [The lyric sweetness of his early **"Vision of Mermaids"**] has a momentary suggestion of Tennyson—but in its sensuous love of beauty there is an abiding affinity to the poet of "Endymion." Here is a picture of early summer, charming in its blithe and sunny abandonment:

> Soon—as when Summer of her sister Spring
> Crushes and tears the rare enjewelling,
> And boasting "I have fairer things than these,"
> Plashes amid the billowy apple-trees
> His lusty hands, in gusts of scented wind
> Swirling out bloom till all the air is blind
> With rosy foam and pelting blossom and mists
> Of driving vermeil rain; and, as he lists,
> The dainty onyx-coronals deflowers,
> A glorious wanton;—all the wrecks in showers
> Crowd down upon a stream, and jostling thick
> With bubbles bugle-eyed, struggle and stick
> On tangled shoals that bar the brook—a crowd
> Of filmy globes and rosy floating cloud.

The prodigal melodiousness, the simplicity of meter, and the colorful word-painting of this early poem are all notable; but still, it is manifestly an *early* poem! One feels that it lacks distinction, individuality—that the poet whose touch was most indubitably here had yet to "find himself."

"The Habit of Perfection" . . . was written four years later. It is in all ways more significant. For, while, retaining that delicate and exquisite sweetness, it bears distinct prophecy of those characteristics which were to mark our poet's maturer work; the subjectivity and intensity of feeling, the eccentricity of expression and preoccupation with spiritual ideas, are all here foreshadowed. It is, indeed, one of the most interesting and revealing of his poems—the *Abrenuntio* of a pure and cloistral spirit. But it came periously near being a valedictory as well. For almost ten years after entering the Jesuit novitiate, Gerard Hopkins' poetic labors ceased, and his lips seem literally to have "shaped nothing" but the mighty offices of his calling. When the young levite turned once more to the world, her immemorial face held manifold and mysterious meanings for him. With the poet's sensuous appreciation of the outer life was to mingle henceforth a vein of ethical and divine interpretation. *Omnia creata*—had he not weighed and sounded this world of shadow and symbol and enigma? But two realities abode steadfast: God and the struggling soul of man!

We will admit that all this is emphatically Ignatian—but it is also emphatically catholic; it is the story of every illumined soul. Nature is first a pageant to us, and then a process; and at last we perceive it to be, in Carlyle's words, the "garment of God"—and, withal, enveloping mantle of man. This deepening of vision is noticeable throughout Father Hopkins' work, as it has been in the work of many another authentic poet. And always was the world fresh to him, as it is fresh to children and to the very mature. At every turn, and by sheer force of his own vivid individuality, he was finding that "something of the unexplored," that "grain of the unknown," which Flaubert so sagely counselled de Maupassant to seek in all things; but which none of us may ever hope to find until we cease looking upon life through the traditional lenses of other eyes. Therefore was Father Hopkins Ignatian in his own very personal way. Few men have loved nature more rapturously than he; fewer still with such a youthful and perennial curiosity. There is a tender excitement in his attitude toward natural beauty (whether treated incidentally or as a a parable) that is very contagious, and the exultation of that early and earthly **"Vision"** clung to the young monk almost with life itself. Nature, indeed, was his one secular inspiration; and that even she was not wholly secular is evinced by the characteristic music of his spring song [**"Spring"**]:

> Nothing is so beautiful as spring—
> When weeds, in wheels, shoot long and lovely and
> 　　lush:
> Thrush's eggs look little low heavens, and thrush
> Through the echoing timber does so rinse and ring
> The ear, it strikes like lightnings to hear him sing;
> The glassy pear-tree leaves and blooms, they brush
> The descending blue; that blue is all in a rush
> With richness; the racing lambs, too, have fair their
> 　　fling.
> What is all this juice and all this joy?
> A strain of the earth's sweet being in the beginning
> In Eden garden.—Have, get before it cloy,
> Before it cloud, Christ, lord, and sour with sinning,
> Innocent mind and Mayday in girl and boy,
> Most, O Maid's Child, thy choice and worthy the
> 　　winning.

Here at last, in one of the most hackneyed of poetic subjects, we are come upon an original vein of poetry; a spiritual motivation, a vigor of word-painting, and a metrical proficiency of very real distinction. (pp. 436-38)

Another sonnet of the same year, **"The Starlight Night,"** is almost equally striking in music and in metaphor. But it must be acknowledged that both of these poems bear traces of that eccentricity and occasional ambiguity which point forward to Father Hopkins' eventual excesses. Lucidity was the chief grace he sacrificed as years wore on; and his fondness for uncommon words—at one moment academic and literate, at another provincial—did not help matters. **"Inversnaid"** is an extreme instance of his later manner: there is a certain bounding and prancing charm about it, but in truth, the stream's highroad is sadly obstructed by Anglo-Saxon and other archaic undergrowth. *Wiry heathpacks—flitches of fern*—and the *groins of the braes that the brook treads through,* send the reader's mind back with some ruefulness to that lovely random line from the **"Vision of Mermaids"**:

> To know the dusk depths of the ponderous sea!

We are not born original in these latter days of literature, it would seem; we must achieve originality—and often at the cost of so much complexity! . . . But there is one ineradicable simplicity about religious men—they are always coming back upon God. To Him they reach out, and peradventure attain, through the mysteries of nature, through the mazes of science and abstract speculation, even through the fundamental intricacies of their own temperament. His Spirit they perceive brooding above the patient earth, glorifying and illumining her travail. And so we find Father Hopkins' ultimate message, clarion-clear, in [his] very direct and characteristic sonnet upon **"God's Grandeur."** (p. 439)

The vital and arresting quality of [**"God's Grandeur"**] distinguishes all of Gerard Hopkins' religious poetry; and it is in his religious quality, after all, that he attained most unequivocally. There is an invariable quickness and reality in his work—although at moments it may also be a bit fantastic—at the very point where the tendency of so many other poets is to become a little cold or a little sweet. We may search for many a long day among the treasures of English Catholic verse before we shall find such a powerful and poetic meditation upon the Holy Eucharist as he has left us in [**"Barnfloor and Winepress"**]. (p. 440)

In quite other vein, and of real lyric charm, is **"Rosa Mystica."** Father Hopkins has contrived to throw a glamour of simplicity and ingenuousness over thoughts by no means simple; while the use of assonance and alliteration (frequent and nearly always felicitous throughout his work) and of the refrain, provide a very rhythmic vehicle. (pp. 440-41)

Our well-loved Francis Thompson was, in life and in death, often hailed as the successor of Crashaw. But the mantle of that mystic dreamer and songster fell far more truly upon the shoulders of Gerard Hopkins. *His* was not merely the exuberant fancy ever bursting into curious and striking analogies, but the intimate and childlike tenderness, the metrical cunning, and the almost impeccable ear for lyric music which characterized the older poet. His was the same wistful pathos and resolute detachment from life's more passional aspects. In both men was a similar tragic sensitiveness—an inevitable recoil from the inconsistency and ugliness and corruption which are a part of human existence. (p. 441)

Thinking about heaven makes all of us wistful; but it is pondering on the tear-stains and blood-stains of earth that crushes out the joy of life. Father Gerard had, seemingly from boyhood, a dangerous realization of this omnipresent sorrow of living; his own experience did not tend to lighten the burden, and

Hopkins at age eighteen.

throughout his later years the weight was well-nigh intolerable. Sanely enough he gauged the cause of so much bitterness; it was the "blight man was born for" if he happened to be an idealist—it was the consciousness of his own too twisted nature! "It is Margaret you mourn for," he told one little Margaret when she was grieving over the falling glory of autumn: but, none the less, outer conditions will all along furnish the occasion of Margaret's grief. . . . One of the sonnets of [his final, sorrowful years in Dublin] (all of which are colored by an ominous and leaden gray!) reveals his sense of exile—**"To Seem the Stranger Lies My Lot—My Life among Strangers"**—and expresses his human and priestly sorrow that

> Father and mother dear,
> Brothers and sisters are in Christ not near.

But another indicates that the cause of Father Hopkins' darkness lay deeper down than loneliness (too familiar to the sons of St. Ignatius!) or than any normal weariness of the day's work. Few lines of such haunting sadness have come to us from the hand of any Christian poet:

> Thou art indeed just, Lord, if I contend
> With Thee; but, sir, so what I plead is just,
> Why do sinners' ways prosper? and why must
> Disappointment all I endeavour end?
> Wert Thou my enemy, O Thou my Friend,
> How couldst thou worse, I wonder, than Thou dost
> Defeat, thwart me? . . .

We must surmise a great part of this last struggle; but it would seem to illustrate that spiritual phenomenon of *desolation* which has immersed so many a chosen soul. (pp. 444-45)

[The poems] speak for themselves, and if their faults are conspicuous enough, so too is their unique and magnetic attraction. No doubt this is in the nature of an acquired taste. They were not written for the public (during their maker's lifetime not one of them was put into print!) they were written for the consolation of the poet and a few chosen friends. And to such readers no concessions need be made. Father Hopkins' very delicate craftsmanship—and not less the singularity of his mental processes—might produce on some minds an impressioon of artificiality. Yet nothing could be further from the fact, for in all the poems of his manhood there is a poignant, even a passionate sincerity. It is quite true that his elliptical and involved expression mars more than one poem of rare and vital imagining. It is true also, and of the nature of the case, that our poet was to a certain degree self-centered in his dream of life. He was not an egoist; but it must be obvious that from first to last he was an individualist. And in our human reckonings the individualist pays, and then he pays again; and after that, in Wilde's phrase, he keeps on paying! Yet in the final count his chances of survival are excellent. Outside of the poets, Father Hopkins' work has had no recognition and no understanding; but his somewhat exotic influence might easily be pointed out in one or two of the foremost Catholic songsters of to-day. And for all its aloofness, the young priest's work struck root in the poetic past. Its subtle and complex fancifulness and its white heat of spirituality go back in direct line to that earlier Jesuit, Father Southwell; while one would wager that Hopkins knew and loved other seventeenth-century lyrists beside the very manifest Crashaw. (pp. 446-47)

Merely great poetry is, of course, seldom popular; although the greatest of all poetry—that of Homer and Dante and Shakespeare—strikes a universal echo in the hearts of men. It is inclusive, and it is written not as an escape from life but as the inevitable and impassioned expression of life itself. Gerard Hopkins' artistry was not of this supreme sort. He was essentially a minor poet: he wrote incredibly little and he interpreted few phases of human experience. But, with the minor poet's distinctive merit, he worked his narrow field with completeness and intensity. And who can deny that the very quality which seemed, at worst, an eccentric and literate mannerism, proved itself in the finer passages a strikingly original and authentic inspiration? (p. 447)

> *Katherine Brégy, "Gerard Hopkins: An Epitaph and an Appreciation," in* The Catholic World, *Vol. LXXXVIII, No. 526, January, 1909, pp. 433-47.*

JOYCE KILMER (essay date 1914)

[*A noted American poet of the early twentieth century, Kilmer discusses Hopkins's language and finds the "lavishness of his method" suited to "the overwhelming greatness of his theme."*]

> The world is charged with the grandeur of God.
> It will flame out like shining from shook foil.

These opening lines of ["**God's Grandeur**"] illustrate clearly Gerard Hopkins' spirit and method. Like that other Jesuit, Robert Southwell, he was a Catholic poet: for him to write a poem on a secular theme was difficult, almost impossible. He sang "the grandeur of God," and for his song he used a language which in its curious perfection is exclusively his own.

One may search his writings in vain for a figure that is not novel and true. He took from his own experience those comparisons that are the material of poetry, and rejected, it seems, such of them as already bore marks of use. For him, the grandeur of God flames out from the world not like light from stars, but like "shining from shook foil." He writes not of soft hands, not of velvety hands, but of "feel-of-primrose hands." He writes not that thrush's eggs are blue as the sky, but that they "look little low heavens." The starry skies of a winter night are "the dim woods quick with diamond wells," or "the gray lawns cold where quaking gold-dew lies." In Spring "the blue is all in a rush with richness," and Summer "plashes amid the billowy apple-trees his lusty hands."

Now, it may be that these exquisite figures would not entitle their maker to high praise if they were isolated bits of splendor, if (like the economical verse-makers of our own day) he had made each one the excuse for a poem. But they come in bewildering profusion. Gerard Hopkins' poems are successions of lovely images, each a poem in itself.

This statement may give its reader the idea that of Gerard Hopkins' poetry may be said, as Charles Ricketts said of Charles Conder's pictures, "There are too many roses." No one who reads his poems, however, will make this criticism. The roses are there of right—all of them. They are, it may be said, necessary roses. They are the cunningly placed elements of an elaborate pattern, a pattern of which roses are the appropriate material. And the red and white of their petals come from the blood and tears that nourished their roots.

It is the overwhelming greatness of his theme that justifies the lavishness of his method. The word "mystic" is nowadays applied so wantonly to every gossiper about things supernatural that it is to most people meaningless. . . . Gerard Hopkins was more nearly a true mystic than either Francis Thompson or Lionel Johnson. The desire, at any rate, for the mystical union with God is evident in every line he wrote, and even more than his friend Coventry Patmore he knew the "dark night of the soul."

This being the case, his theme being God and his writing being an act of adoration, it is profitless to criticise him, as Mr. Robert Bridges has done, for "sacrificing simplicity" and violating those mysterious things, the "canons of taste" [see excerpt dated 1894]. (pp. 242-44)

[Walter Pater] had no keener sensitivity to the color and music of language. Gerard Hopkins' purpose—a purpose impossible of fulfilment but not therefore less worth the effort—was "to arrange words like so many separate gems to compose a whole expression of thought, in which the force of grammar and the beauty of rhythm absolutely correspond."

There will always be those who dislike the wealth of imagery which characterizes Gerard Hopkins' poetry, because they do not understand his mental and spiritual attitude. Perhaps for some critics an altar cloth may be too richly embroidered and a chalice too golden. Ointment of spikenard is "very costly." (p. 245)

Joyce Kilmer, "The Poetry of Gerard Hopkins," in Poetry, Vol. IV, No. 4, September, 1914, pp. 241-45.

ROBERT BRIDGES (essay date 1918)

[*The following commentary is drawn from the preface to the explanatory notes included in Bridges's 1918 edition of Hopkins's Poems and from Bridges's note on "The Wreck of the Deutschland," included in the same work. Bridges's observations have played a controversial role in Hopkins criticism. Many early reviewers echoed his complaints against what he considered stylistic blemishes, obscurity, oddity, and freakish effects in Hopkins's works. Most later commentators, however, dispute the validity of these appraisals, some even accusing Bridges of jealously sabotaging his friend's superior poems. Others speculate that his harsh comments were an attempt to forestall the ridicule he expected the poems to elicit. It is generally agreed that Bridges's understanding of Hopkins's works was imperfect and prejudiced by his anti-religious, specifically anti-Catholic, outlook; however, scholars concede that his feat of compiling and publishing Hopkins's poems was a major contribution to English literature. For additional commentary by Bridges, see the excerpt dated 1894.*]

Apart from questions of taste—and if [Hopkins's] poems were to be arraigned for errors of what may be called taste, they might be convicted of occasional affectation in metaphor, as where the hills are 'as a stallion stalwart, very-violet-sweet', or of some perversion of human feeling, as, for instance, the nostrils' relish of incense 'along the sanctuary side', or 'the Holy Ghost with warm breast and with ah! bright wings', these and a few such examples are mostly efforts to force emotion into theological or sectarian channels, as in 'the comfortless unconfessed' and the unpoetic line 'His mystery must be instressed stressed', or, again, the exaggerated Marianism of some pieces, or the naked encounter of sensualism and asceticism which hurts **"The Leaden Echo and the Golden Echo"**.

Apart, I say, from such faults of taste, which few as they numerically are yet affect my liking and more repel my sympathy than do all the rude shocks of his purely artistic wantonness—apart from these there are definite faults of style which a reader must have courage to face, and must in some measure condone before he can discover the great beauties. For these blemishes in the poet's style are of such quality and magnitude as to deny him even a hearing from those who love a continuous literary decorum and are grown to be intolerant of its absence. And it is well to be clear that there is no pretence to reverse the condemnation of those faults, for which the poet has duly suffered. The extravagances are and will remain what they were. Nor can credit be gained from pointing them out: yet, to put readers at their ease, I will here define them: they may be called Oddity and Obscurity; and since the first may provoke laughter when a writer is serious (and this poet is always serious), while the latter must prevent him from being understood (and this poet has always something to say), it may be assumed that they were not a part of his intention. (p. 43)

As regards Oddity . . . , it is plain that the poet was himself fully alive to it, but he was not sufficiently aware of his obscurity, and he could not understand why his friends found his sentences so difficult: he would never have believed that, among all the ellipses and liberties of his grammar, the one chief cause is his habitual omission of the relative pronoun; and yet this is so, and the examination of a simple example or two may serve a general purpose.

This grammatical liberty, though it is a common convenience in conversation and has therefore its proper place in good writing, is apt to confuse the parts of speech, and to reduce a normal sequence of words to mere jargon. Writers who carelessly rely on their elliptical speech-forms to govern the elaborate sentences of their literary composition little know what a conscious effort of interpretation they often impose on their readers. But it was not carelessness in Gerard Hopkins: he had full skill and practice and scholarship in conventional forms, and it is easy to see that he banished these purely constructional syllables from his verse because they took up room which he thought he could not afford them: he needed in his scheme all his space for his poetical words, and he wished those to crowd out every merely grammatical colourless or toneless element; and so when he had got into the habit of doing without these relative pronouns—though he must, I suppose, have supplied them in his thought,—he abuses the license beyond precedent, as when he writes [in **"The Loss of the Eurydice"**] 'O Hero savest!' for 'O Hero that savest!'.

Another example of this [from the 5th stanza of **"The Bugler's First Communion"**] will discover another cause of obscurity: the line 'Squander the hell-rook ranks sally to molest him' means 'Scatter the ranks that sally to molest him': but since the words *squander* and *sally* occupy similar positions in the two sections of the verse, and are enforced by a similar accentuation, the second verb deprived of its pronoun will follow the first and appear as an imperative; and there is nothing to prevent its being so taken but the contradiction that it makes in the meaning; whereas the grammar should expose and enforce the meaning, not have to be determined by the meaning. Moreover, there is no way of enunciating this line which will avoid the confusion; because if, knowing that *sally* should not have the same intonation as *squander,* the reader mitigates the accent, and in doing so lessens or obliterates the caesural pause which exposes its accent, then *ranks* becomes a genitive and *sally* a substantive.

Here, then, is another source of the poet's obscurity; that in aiming at condensation he neglects the need that there is for care in the placing of words that are grammatically ambiguous. English swarms with words that have one identical form for substantive, adjective, and verb; and such a word should never be so placed as to allow of any doubt as to what part of speech it is used for; because such ambiguity or momentary uncertainty destroys the force of the sentence. Now our author not only neglects this essential propriety but he would seem even to welcome and seek artistic effect in the consequent confusion; and he will sometimes so arrange such words that a reader looking for a verb may find that he has two or three ambiguous monosyllables from which to select, and must be in doubt as to which promises best to give any meaning that he can welcome; and then, after his choice is made, he may be left with some homeless monosyllable still on his hands. Nor is our author apparently sensitive to the irrelevant suggestions that our numerous homophones cause; and he will provoke further ambiguities or obscurities by straining the meaning of these unfortunate words.

Finally, the rhymes where they are peculiar are often repellent, and so far from adding charm to the verse that they appear as obstacles. This must not blind one from recognizing that Gerard Hopkins, where he is simple and straightforward in his rhyme is a master of it—there are many instances—but when he indulges in freaks, his childishness is incredible. His intention in such places is that the verses should be recited as running on without pause, and the rhyme occurring in their midst should be like a phonetic accident, merely satisfying the prescribed form. But his phonetic rhymes are often indefensible on his own principle. The rhyme to *communion* in **"The Bugler"** is hideous, and the suspicion that the poet thought it ingenious is appalling; *eternal,* in **"The Loss of the Eurydice"**, does not correspond with *burn all,* and in **"Felix Randal"** *and some* and *handsome* is as truly an eye-rhyme as the *love* and *prove* which he despised and abjured;—and it is more distressing,

because the old-fashioned conventional eye-rhymes are accepted as such without speech-adaptation, and to many ears are a pleasant relief from the fixed jingle of the perfect rhyme; whereas his false ear-rhymes ask to have their slight but indispensable differences obliterated in the reading, and thus they expose their defect, which is of a disagreeable and vulgar or even comic quality. He did not escape full criticism and ample ridicule for such things in his lifetime; and in '83 he wrote: 'Some of my rhymes I regret, but they are past changing, grubs in amber: there are only a few of these; others are unassailable; some others again there are which malignity may munch at but the Muses love'.

Now these are bad faults, and, as I said, a reader, if he is to get any enjoyment from the author's genius, must be somewhat tolerant of them; and they have a real relation to the means whereby the very forcible and original effects of beauty are produced. There is nothing stranger in these poems than the mixture of passages of extreme delicacy and exquisite diction with passages where, in a jungle of rough root-words, emphasis seems to oust euphony; and both these qualities, emphasis and euphony, appear in their extreme forms. It was an idiosyncrasy of this student's mind to push everything to its logical extreme, and take pleasure in a paradoxical result; as may be seen in his prosody where a simple theory seems to be used only as a basis for unexampled liberty. He was flattered when I called him [prodigiously excessive], and saw the humour of it—and one would expect to find in his work the force of emphatic condensation and the magic of melodious expression, both in their extreme forms. Now since those who study style in itself must allow a proper place to the emphatic expression, this experiment, which supplies as novel examples of success as of failure, should be full of interest; and such interest will promote tolerance.

The fragment [**"On a Piece of Music"**] is the draft of what appears to be an attempt to explain how an artist has not free-will in his creation. He works out his own nature instinctively as he happens to be made, and is irresponsible for the result. It is lamentable that Gerard Hopkins died when, to judge by his latest work, he was beginning to concentrate the force of all his luxuriant experiments in rhythm and diction, and castigate his art into a more reserved style. Few will read the terrible posthumous sonnets without such high admiration and respect for his poetical powers as must lead them to search out the rare masterly beauties that distingush his work. (pp. 44-7)

• • • • •

The labour spent on the great metrical experiment [**"The Wreck of the Deutschland"**] must have served to establish the poet's prosody and perhaps his diction: therefore the poem stands logically as well as chronologically in the front of his book, like a great dragon folded in the gate to forbid all entrance, and confident in his strength from past success. This editor advises the reader to circumvent him and attack him later in the rear, for he was himself shamefully worsted in a brave frontal assault, the more easily perhaps because both subject and treatment were distasteful to him. A good method of approach is to read stanza 16 aloud to a chance company. To the metrist and rhythmist the poem will be of interest from the first, and throughout. (pp. 47-8)

Robert Bridges, "Early Criticism," in Gerard Manley Hopkins, Poems: A Casebook, *edited by Margaret Bottrall, The Macmillan Press Ltd., 1975, pp. 41-80.*

E. BRETT YOUNG (essay date 1918)

[*In this excerpt, Young offers a mixed review of* Poems of Gerard Manley Hopkins.]

[Hopkins's] elaborately wrought verse, with its devices of rhythm and assonance, invites applause no more than the curious decoration of a missal. But these poems have a subtlety of workmanship which makes it certain that they will not be forgotten; for their value as adventures in technique—if they were nothing more—cannot be ignored by the poets who will seek hereafter for new forms of expression. (p. 191)

When Gerard Hopkins renounced the "natural man," burning his poems, he reined in a poetic fancy that was almost riotous in its exuberance. His muse took, as it were, the veil. (p. 192)

[Between "**A Vision of Mermaids**," written in his boyhood, and "**The Candle Indoors**," written seventeen years later, there] is a difference not of style only, but of orientation. There is a gulf fixed between the early verse, with what Doctor Bridges calls its Keatsian sweetnesses [see excerpt dated 1894], and the austere accents of [his later writings]. His work, developing naturally from such a beginning, would never have been without sensuous beauty. A young poet whose talent was bearing such fruit, might well have been content to linger a little longer with the Hesperides. I conclude that Hopkins deliberately abandoned this easy sweetness. If he had merely carried the repressive part of his code into his verse, he might have been silenced altogether. But he was ascetic in the original sense of the word; he became ascetic in his poetry as in his life, devoting himself to the pursuit of a new technique by tireless trial and experiment in the art which he loved too well to abandon.

Crabbed and cryptic, sometimes harsh and even ugly this later and better verse undoubtedly is. Hopkins was both draughtsman and poet, and I think his few critics have failed to realize how far the verbal complexity is the outcome of a collision between the two arts. He lavished his genius in trying to translate the delight of a quick eye into terms that would please a subtle ear. Phrases like "blear-all black," "mealed-with-yellow sallows," "a wind-puff bonnet of fawn-froth," show his impatience with a language that will not fit itself to niceties of colour and movement. He reversed Scriabine's experiment of the colour-organ by trying to paint with sounds, and . . . he nearly achieves the impossible end. . . . (pp. 193-94)

Hopkins is most like Keats in his passion for the shows of nature. But he likes the little pageants best—the tiny, meticulous shifts of the kaleidoscope—and seen melodies are sweetest to him. His genius was in danger of being quite snared in a network of small lights and shadows. We find this delight in things seen—I am tempted to call it a lust of the eye—in the lovely sonnet in which "the self-remembring soul sweetly recovers its kindred with the stars . . ." and again in the picture of the stream in "**Inversnaid**." . . . (pp. 194-95)

He invades, too, in his restlessness, the realm of pure music. Alliteration and assonance are not for him, as for Swinburne, a means of emphasizing the rhythm of the verse. Often they run counter to it, and he blends two melodies in one line. It is not easy to deduce, from his one-sided correspondence with Conventry Patmore, precisely what theories of metre he evolved. But the ear is, after all, the only arbiter in these matters, and Hopkins's counterpoint, which impressed Patmore as "lovely and unique," should not alarm a generation far more alert to the attraction of subtle rhythms. The machinery of English verse is not equal to the triple strain of sound, sense, and colour

which Hopkins tried to place upon it, and his effects are often won at the expense of a baffling disregard of grammar. But many even of his crabbedest lines, in which the words have been jolted out of all natural relationship, and the sense seems buried under the ruins, haunt the memory with an echo of rare loveliness.

It may be that the blossom for which he waited was only budding when his life came to an end. The unrest of mind which darkened his later years creeps everywhere into his verse. Its beauty gleams against a background of melancholy. He turns constantly—as in "**The Candle Indoors**" and the "**Starlit Night**"—from the poetic aspect of things, with their lovely and sad gestures, to the religious import which he conceives to lie behind them. He interprets beauty in terms of death, regeneration and resurrection. (pp. 195-96)

Pope said of Herbert that he wrote "like a gentleman, for his own amusement." Hopkins wrote like a devotee offering a sacrifice. Sometimes he is stung by "the fine delight that fathers thought" and poetry. But in the midst of his song, he seems to turn aside with a sigh, confessing, like an older poet and mystic,

There is no dealing with Thee in this art.

(p. 196)

*E. Brett Young, "The Poetry of Gerard Hopkins,"
in* To-day, *Vol. II, No. 11, January, 1918, pp. 191-96.*

THE TIMES LITERARY SUPPLEMENT (essay date 1919)

[*This critic comments on the unique qualities of Hopkins's poetry.*]

["**The Wreck of the Deutschland**"] is still more novel than the most novel poems of to-day. Mr. Bridges calls it a great dragon folded in the gate to forbid all entrance [see excerpt dated 1918]; and, indeed, it is difficult. For Hopkins poetry meant difficulty; he wrote it to say more than could be said otherwise; it was for him a packing of words with sense, both emotional and intellectual. The defect of the newest English poetry is that it says too little. Our young poets seem determined to make their art too easy, at least for themselves, to reduce it to expletives. But Hopkins went further than any other poet known to us from common speech. In all his more difficult poems there are several ordinary poems assumed, both their ideas and their metre; and on these assumptions, which the reader is expected to make, he builds his own poem. It is like that modern music which assumes the conventions of older music and departs from them, still using them as the basis of departure. But Hopkins's verse is more difficult even than that music because it assumes that the reader grasps the sense of what is unsaid. He begins where most poets leave off, not out of affectation, but because he wishes to go further. Sometimes even the grammar is implied; its skeleton is not there, you have to imagine it there. The words succeed each other without it, each one bringing a new inrush of sense into the sentence, which hardly exists; and each inrush would in ordinary prose, or even verse, need a whole sentence to itself. Here is an example, not the most extreme, from "**The Wreck of the Deutschland**." The subject is Christ:—

I admire thee, master of the tides.
Of the Yore-flood, of the year's fall;
The recurb and the recovery of the gulf's sides.

The girth of it and the wharf of it and the wall;
Stanching, quenching ocean of a motionable mind;
Ground of being, and granite of it; past all
    Grasp God, throned behind
Death with a sovereignty that heeds but hides,
    bodes but abides.

In Hopkins's poetry words become independent, as if they were whole sentences; they bang in one after another; and this independence affects the metre. The sense emphasis of the single word is in the sound also. But the verse survives the great test of verse; it is best read aloud; then the very sense becomes clearer and anyone with an ear can hear that the method is not affectation but eagerness to find an expression for the depths of the mind, for things hardly yet consciously thought or felt. Hopkins was exploring not merely the instrument of verse, but the undiscovered regions of his own, and the universal, soul. And in this exploration he has the audacity and the good faith of the religious poet. He is like Crashaw in his extravagance and the manner in which he redeems it by good faith. His worst trick is that of passing from one word to another like the Jewish admirer of Mr. Jaggers in *Great Expectations,* merely because they are alike in sound. This, at its worst, produces the effect almost of idiocy, of speech without sense and prolonged merely by echoes. It seems to be a bad habit, like stuttering, except that he did not strive against it. Perhaps he sought words that way, took shots at them, so to speak, and enjoyed the process; but we cannot enjoy it; and yet we forgive him all such faults and brush hastily through them in search of the beauties that he makes us expect. . . .

[*Poems of Gerard Manley Hopkins*] thrills with spirit, a spirit that does not disdain sense but heightens it. The poems are crowded with objects sharply cut, and with sounds no less sharp and clashing; you fight your way through the verses, yet they draw you on. There is beauty everywhere without luxury, the beauty that seems to come of painful intense watching, the utter, disinterested delight of one who sees another world, not through, but in this one. It is as if he heard everywhere a music too difficult, because too beautiful, for our ears and noted down what he could catch of it; authentic fragments that we trust even when they bewilder us.

> *"Gerard Hopkins," in* The Times Literary Supple-
> ment, *No. 886, January 9, 1919, p. 19.*

EDWARD SAPIR (essay date 1921)

[*The following excerpt is taken from an appreciative review of* Poems of Gerard Manley Hopkins. *Later scholars point to Sapir's comments as a turning point in the critical assessment and understanding of Hopkins's works.*]

Hopkins is long in coming into his own; but it is not too much to say that his own will be secure, among the few that know, if not among the crowd, when many of Georgian name that completely overshadows him for the moment shall have become food for the curious.

For Hopkins' poetry is of the most precious. His voice is easily one of the half dozen most individual voices in the whole course of English nineteenth-century poetry. One may be repelled by his mannerisms, but he cannot be denied that overwhelming authenticity, that almost terrible immediacy of utterance, that distinguishes the genius from the man of talent. I would compare him to D. H. Lawrence but for his far greater sensitiveness to the music of words, to the rhythms and ever-changing speeds

of syllables. . . . Joyce Kilmer [see excerpt dated 1914] speaks of his mysticism and of his gloriously original imagery. This mysticism of the Jesuit poet is not a poetic manner, it is the very breath of his soul. Hopkins simply could not help comparing the Holy Virgin to the air we breathe; he was magnificently in earnest about the Holy Ghost that

>   over the bent
> World broods with warm breast and with ah! bright wings.

As for imagery, there is hardly a line . . . that does not glow with some strange new flower, divinely picked from his imagination.

Undeniably this poet is difficult. He strives for no innocuous Victorian smoothness. I have referred to his mannerisms, which are numerous and not always readily assimilable. They have an obsessive, turbulent quality about them—these repeated and trebly repeated words, the poignantly or rapturously interrupting *oh*'s and *ah*'s, the headlong omission of articles and relatives, the sometimes violent word order, the strange yet how often so lovely compounds, the plays on words, and, most of all, his wild joy in the sheer sound of words. This phonetic passion of Hopkins rushes him into a perfect maze of rhymes, half-rhymes, assonances, alliterations:

> Tatter-tassle-tangled and dingle-a-dangled
> Dandy-hung dainty head.

These clangs are not like the nicely calculated jingling loveliness of Poe or Swinburne. They, no less than the impatient ruggednesses of his diction, are the foam-flakes and eddies of a passionate, swift-streaming expression. To a certain extent Hopkins undoubtedly loved difficulty, even obscurity, for its own sake. He may have found in it a symbolic reflection of the tumult that raged in his soul. Yet we must beware of exaggerating the external difficulties; they yield with unexpected ease to the modicum of good will that Hopkins has a right to expect of us.

Hopkins' prosody, concerning which he has something to say in his preface [see excerpt dated 1883(?)] is worthy of careful study. In his most distinctive pieces he abandons the "running" verse of traditional English poetry and substitutes for it his own "sprung" rhythms. This new verse of his is not based on the smooth flow of regularly recurring stresses. The stresses are carefully grouped into line and stanza patterns, but the movement of the verse is wholly free. The iambic or trochaic foot yields at any moment to a spondee or a dactyl or a foot of one stressed and three or more unstressed syllables. There is, however, no blind groping in this irregular movement. It is nicely adjusted to the constantly shifting speed of the verse. Hopkins' effects, with a few exceptions, are in the highest degree successful. Read with the ear, never with the eye, his verse flows with an entirely new vigor and lightness, while the stanzaic form gives it a powerful compactness and drive. It is doubtful if the freest verse of our day is more sensitive in its rhythmic pulsations than the "sprung" verse of Hopkins. (pp. 330-32)

Yet neither mannerisms of diction and style nor prosody define the essential Hopkins. The real Hopkins is a passionate soul unendingly in conflict. The consuming mysticism, the intense religious faith are unreconciled with a basic sensuality that leaves the poet no peace. He is longing to give up the loveliness of the world for that greater loveliness of the spirit that all but descends to envelop him like a mother; but he is too poignantly aware of all sensuous beauty, too insistently haunted by the allurements of the flesh. A Freudian psychologist might call him an imperfectly sex-sublimated mystic. Girlish tenderness is masked by ruggedness. And his fuming self-torment is exteriorized by a diction that strains, and by a rhythmic flow that leaps or runs or stamps but never walks. (p. 334)

Edward Sapir, "Gerard Hopkins," in Poetry, *Vol. XVIII, No. VI, September, 1921, pp. 330-36.*

ALAN PORTER (essay date 1923)

[*Porter, advocating close study of Hopkins's poems, provides an explication of "To What Serves Mortal Beauty" to demonstrate the approach required by Hopkins's characteristically complex and elliptical style.*]

Readers who meet [Hopkins's poems] for the first time and attempt them casually often make neither head nor tail of them; here and there they may be astounded by some audacious phrase—"the dappled-with-damson east," "a dare-gale skylark scanted in a dull cage," or, of the stars, "O look at all the fire-folk sitting in the air!"—but, without persistence, they may dismiss most of the poems as quaint and perverse or account it disproportionate to spend much labour on one poet, a poet not cannonized among the great. Indeed, Gerard Hopkins may well be taken as a test-case in obscurity.

His poems repay study. He was, like all true poets, "the first poet in the world for some things." And his difficulties are necessary: they are the impress of himself. He was a man of heightened, almost hysterical, acuteness of sense. To him, the thrush:—

> Through the echoing timber does so rinse and wring
> The ear, it strikes like lightnings to hear him sing;

and, when a cuckoo calls:—

> The whole landscape flushes on a sudden at a sound.

Coincident with this quickening of sense was a fierce variability of mood. He was subject often to the "carrion comfort, despair," and he spoke truly when he described himself as:—

> this tormented mind
> With this tormented mind tormenting yet.

Like most other true poets he had little of that sense of humour which makes our humanity half laughable, that minor blasphemy through which we alleviate the stress of life. And, naturally with such a temperament, what most affected him in fact and art, his ideal beauty, was a moodlessness, a suddenly-seized, abrupt finality, a flash off an architypical perfection. His torment came from the conflict between his belief in this absolute and the acknowledged rarity in the world of evidence for belief. His quickened sense gave him also an original pattern of music for his verse and original theories in metric. It was a music sometimes too sweet:—

> In coop and in comb the fleece of his foam
> Flutes and low to the lake falls home.—

but more generally nerved by clash and resolved inconsonance, knit close and made virile. He never betrayed it for the sake of meaning; but he was fastidious, too, to match sense with music. For this reason he was compelled often to use obscure words or curious new coinages. And in his determination to have sense and music at one, to reconcile emphasis and euphony, he took other liberties with language. He refused to give prominence to words that are not visual and dynamic, to

stress articles, pronouns, or conjunctions. He would tuck them away in unheard-of places or entirely omit them, and his scholarship in Latin made him forget that an uninflected language has need of such words. He wrote for no public, he hoped for no fame, he made no compromise. His qualities had thus the fullest room for development. . . .

These are the causes of his obscurity: briefly, he created an idiom of his own. The poems are not so hard of comprehension as at first sight they seem. Read slowly and, as it were, tonelessly, but with alert intelligence, they will soon shape themselves and cohere. I have chosen one for comment, part paraphrase, part explanation, not because it seemed more beautiful than others, but because it illustrates his phraseology and cast of thought, and because it seems to me that a reader, once master of such a poem as this, will be able to find his way with ease among most of the others:—

"To What Serves Mortal Beauty"

> To what serves Mortal Beauty—dangerous; does set
>   dancing blood—the O-seal-that-so feature, flung
>   prouder form
> Than Purcell tune lets tread to? See: it does this: keeps
>   warm
> Men's wits to the things that are; what good means—
>   where a glance
> Master may more than gaze, gaze out of countenance.
> Those lovely lads once, wet-fresh windfalls of war's
>   storm,
> How then should Gregory, a father, have gleanèd else
>   from swarmed Rome. But God to a nation dealt that
>   day's dear chance.
>
> To man, that needs would worship block or barren
>   stone,
> Our law says: Love what are love's worthiest, were all
>   known;
> World's loveliest—men's selves. Self flashes off frame
>   and face.
> What do then? how meet beauty? Merely meet it; own,
> Home at heart, heaven's sweet gift; then leave, let that
>   alone.
> Yea, wish that though, wish all, God's better beauty,
>   grace.

What is the purpose of a sudden, transitory beauty (when such beauty is dangerous, quickens our pulses so), a feature, appearance, turn of body that makes us cry out to have it kept eternally as it is, a form that is thrown from its object more sheerly, with more assured finality, than the forms even a tune of Purcell's creates without effort for our spirits to dance to? It keeps men with an alert affection for reality. What an excellent means of achieving this it is, when a quick glance may bring out and secure more beauty than a prolonged stare. How otherwise, if there weren't this sudden beauty, could Gregory, in crowded Rome, have found out the Angle slaves? Gregory's chance-seeing of their loveliness was God's doing, to bless a whole nation. Man naturally would concentrate his affection on the static things of earth, but Christ has told us to love what, if we could see thoroughly, is the worthiest thing to love, the souls, selves, of men, the real being and make of men. We see it sometimes in a flash from their attitude or countenance. What are we to do when we meet it? Merely take it, recognize it, in our deepest heart, as the gift of heaven; and then have done, draw no morals, pursue it no further. But yes, one thing there is: wish that and everything else a better beauty than beauty, a linking-up with God's purposes.

My explanation is clumsy and spoils the poem; perhaps it will help with the syntax and show that Gerard Hopkins writes, in fact, with perfect clarity.

> Alan Porter, "Difficult Beauty," in The Spectator, Vol. 130, No. 4933, January 13, 1923, p. 66.

I. A. RICHARDS   (essay date 1926)

[*Richards is considered a forerunner of New Criticism, a critical movement that emphasizes close reading and explication of a text rather than stressing the biographical, historical, or moral vision of the artist. Because of his status in critical circles, Richards's predominately positive criticism of Hopkins's works was important in drawing scholarly attention to the poems. In the excerpt below, he offers close readings of "The Windhover" and "Spelt from Sibyl's Leaves."*]

[Hopkins] may be described, without opposition, as the most obscure of English verse writers. (p. 195)

[Possibly the obscurity of his works] may explain the fact that these poems are not yet widely known. But their originality and the audacity of their experimentation have much to do with the delay. Even their editor found himself compelled to apologize at length for what he termed "blemishes in the poet's style" [see excerpt by Bridges dated 1918]. "It is well to be clear that there is no pretence to reverse the condemnation of these faults, for which the poet has duly suffered. The extravagances are and will remain what they were . . . it may be assumed that they were not a part of his intention." But too many other experiments have been made recently, especially in the last eight years, for this lofty tone and confident assumption to be maintained. The more the poems are studied, the clearer it becomes that their oddities are always deliberate. They may be aberrations, they are not blemishes. It is easier to see this to-day since some of his most daring innovations have been, in part, attempted independently by later poets.

I propose to examine a few of his best poems from this angle, choosing those which are both most suggestive technically and most indicative of his temper and mould as a poet. It is an important fact that he is so often most himself when he is most experimental. (p. 196)

Hopkins was always ready to disturb the usual word order of prose to gain an improvement in rhythm or an increased emotional poignancy, *To own my heart* = to my own heart; *reaving* = taking away. He uses words always as tools, an attitude toward them which the purist and grammarian can never understand. He was clear, too, that his poetry was for the ear, not for the eye, a point that should be noted before we proceed to **"The Windhover,"** which, unless we begin by listening to it, may *only* bewilder us. To quote from a letter: . . . [Take] breath and read it with the ears, as I always wish to be read, and my verse becomes all right" [see excerpt dated April 22, 1879]. I have to confess that **"The Windhover"** only became all right for me, in the sense of perfectly clear and explicit, intellectually satisfying as well as emotionally moving, after many readings and several days of reflection. (p. 197)

The dedication [to **"The Windhover"**] at first sight is puzzling. Hopkins said of this poem that it was the best thing he ever wrote, which is to me in part the explanation. It sounds like an echo of the offering made eleven years ago when his early poems were burnt. For a while I thought that the apostrophe,

"O my chevalier!" (it is perhaps superfluous to mention that this word rhymes strictly with "here" and has only three syllables) had reference to Christ. I take it now to refer only to the poet, though the moral ideal, embodied of course for Hopkins in Christ, is before the mind.

Some further suggestions towards elucidation may save the reader trouble. If he does not need them I crave his forgiveness. *Kingdom of daylight's dauphin*—I see (unnecessarily) the falcon as a minature sun, flashing so high up. *Rung upon the rein*—a term from the *manège*, ringing a horse = causing it to circle round one on a long rein. *My heart in hiding*—as with other good poets I have come to expect that when Hopkins leaves something which looks at first glance as though it were a concession to rhyme or a mere pleasing jingle of words, some really important point is involved. Why in hiding? Hiding from what? Does this link up with "a billion times told lovelier, more dangerous, O my chevalier!"? What is the greater danger and what the less? I should say that the poet's heart is in hiding from Life, has chosen a safer way, and that the greater danger is the greater exposure to temptation and error than a more adventurous, less sheltered course (sheltered by Faith?) brings with it. Another, equally plausible reading would be this: Renouncing the glamour of the outer life of adventure the poet transfers its qualities of audacity to the inner life. (*Here* is the bosom, the inner consciousness.) The greater danger is that to which the moral hero is exposed. Both readings may be combined, but pages of prose would be required for a paraphrase of the result. The last three lines carry the thought of the achievement possible through renunciation further, and explain, with the image of the ash-covered fire, why the dangers of the inner life are greater. So much for the sense; but the close has a strange, weary, almost exhausted, rhythm, and the word "gall" has an extraordinary force, bringing out painfully the shock with which the sight of the soaring bird has jarred the poet into an unappeased discontent.

If we compare those poems and passages of poems which were conceived definitely within the circle of Hopkins' theology with those which transcend it, we shall find difficulty in resisting the conclusion that the poet in him was often oppressed and stifled by the priest. In this case the conflict which seems to lie behind and prompt all Hopkins' better poems is temporarily resolved through a stoic acceptance of sacrifice. An asceticism which fails to reach ecstasy and accepts the failure. All Hopkins' poems are in this sense poems of defeat. (pp. 198-99)

Elucidations are perhaps less needed [in **"Spelt from Sibyl's Leaves."**] The heart speaks after "Heart you round me right" to the end, applying in the moral sphere the parable of the passing away of all the delights, accidents, nuances, the "dapple" of existence, to give place to the awful dichotomy of right and wrong. It is characteristic of this poet that there is no repose for him in the night of traditional morality. As the terrible last line shows, the renunciation of all the myriad temptations of life brought no gain. It was all loss. The present order of "black, white; right, wrong" was an afterthought and an intentional rearrangement; the original order was more orthodox. *Let life, waned*—the imperative mood carries through to the end; let life part, pen, pack, let life be aware of. *All throughther* = each through the other.

I cannot refrain from pointing to the marvelous third and fourth lines. They seem to me to anticipate the descriptions we hope our younger contemporary poets will soon write. Such synaesthesis has tempted several of them, but this is, I believe, the supreme example. Hopkins' technical innovations reach out, however, into many fields. As a means of rendering self-consciousness, for example, consider this:

> Only what word
> Wisest my heart breeds dark heaven's baffling ban
> Bars or hell's spell thwarts. This to hoard unheard,
> Heard unheeded, leaves me a lonely began.

(pp. 200-01)

Few writers have dealt more directly with their experience or been more candid [than Hopkins in the sonnets representing his inner conflict]. Perhaps to do this must invite the charge of oddity, of playfulness, of whimsical eccentricity and wantonness. To some of his slighter pieces these charges do apply. Like other writers he had to practise and perfect his craft. The little that has been written about him has already said too much about this aspect. His work as a pioneer has not been equally insisted upon. It is true that Gerard Hopkins did not fully realize what he was doing to the technique of poetry. For example, while retaining rhyme, he gave himself complete rhythmical freedom, but disguised this freedom as a system of what he called Sprung Rhythm, employing four sorts of feet. . . . Since what he called *hangers* or *outrides* (one, two, or three slack syllables added to a foot and not counting in the nominal scanning) were also permitted, it will be plain that he had nothing to fear from the absurdities of prosodists. A curious way, however, of eluding a mischievous tradition and a spurious question, to give them a mock observance and an equally unreal answer! (pp. 202-03)

Meanwhile the lamentable fact must be admitted that many people just ripe to read Hopkins have been and will be too busy asking "does he scan?" to notice that he has anything to say to them. And of those that escape this trap that our teachers so assiduously set, many will be still too troubled by beliefs and disbeliefs to understand him. His is a poetry of divided and equal passions—which very nearly makes a new thing out of a new fusion of them both. But Hopkins' intelligence, though its subtlety with details was extraordinary, failed to remould its materials sufficiently in attacking his central problem. He solved it emotionally, at a cost which amounted to martyrdom; intellectually he was too stiff, too "cogged and cumbered" with beliefs, those bundles of invested emotional capital, to escape except through appalling tension. The analysis of his poetry is hardly possible, however, without the use of technical langauge; the terms "intellectual" and "emotional" are too loose. His stature as a poet will not be recognized until the importance of the Belief problem from which his poetry sprang has been noticed. He did not need other beliefs than those he held. Like the rest of us, whatever our beliefs, he needed a change in belief, the mental attitude, itself. (p. 203)

I. A. Richards, "Gerard Hopkins," in The Dial, *Vol. 81, No. 3, September, 1926, pp. 195-203.*

ISIDOR SCHNEIDER (essay date 1930)

[*This excerpt is taken from a review anticipating the publication of a second, enlarged edition of Hopkins's poems. With its assertion that "Hopkins belongs among the great poets of English literature," Schneider's evaluation represents the growing critical approval afforded Hopkins's poems in the 1930s.*]

With the publication of the forthcoming new edition of the poems it will probably be observed that in some recent poetry influences attributed to other poets are in reality Hopkins's. The Poet Laureate's work owns it, and Hart Crane's "The Bridge," unquestionably a great poem and one of the few of our generation, shows the present benefits of Hopkins's liberating and enriching experiments.

This influence cannot, I think, be attributed mainly to his many and extraordinary contributions to English versification, although they are the first to be noticed and both in quality and in quantity constitute probably the greatest addition made by a single poet. Today we are inclined rather to imitate an attitude of mind than a form; and for that reason a T. S. Eliot exerts more authority than an E. E. Cummings. In Hopkins, however, it is not so much an attitude of mind—else we should all seek some individual form of asceticism—as the virtue of an example. Here is a poet who was not afraid to write exactly as he wished, who dared to take the risk of a crabbed and queer appearance, of obscurities into which readers would not follow him.

Such independence has always been rare in literature. Few poets seem to have been so indifferent to or disciplined against the pleasure of publication. It is the only form of his asceticism that it would be profitable for us to imitate, though devout Catholics may think differently. . . .

He wrote, as he said. . ., to satisfy a love of design; but he wrote, too, out of a love and understanding of words, of their sound and of their sense, that is unrivaled in our literature. He played almost boisterously with them, running them out in delightful repetitions, in transformations and substitutions. This freedom with words is even more characteristic than his rhythms or his marvelous imagery. This and the exigencies of his bold rhythmic scheme led to the oddities for which Bridges apologizes too much [see excerpt dated 1918], and of which the author was fully conscious. . . . (p. 456)

The elements of Hopkins's originality are bewildering. He is astonishingly bold with words and with forms of speech; he is free with ellipses, coins new words, breaks them in two, transfers the parts of combined words, as when "brimful in a flash" becomes brim in a flashful"; rhymes internally, alliterates, omits that's and which's to have every word dynamic, and displaces prepositions so that their very movement in the sentence adds to their force; combines words to sharpen their rhythm, quicken their meaning, and harmonize their sound.

Such a procedure is inimitable; it is his poetic personality, which will certainly stimulate and encourage other poets along the paths of their own individuality, but which it would be very dangerous to copy. It is his prosody that is his main contribution.

"For purpose of scanning," he writes, "it is a great convenience to follow the example of music and take the stress always first. . . . If this is done there will be in common English verse only two possible feet—the so-called accentual trochee and dactyl" [see excerpt dated 1883(?)]. This may seem to conflict with the admitted fact that English verse is largely iambic; and his own use of trochaic and dactylic rhythms gives his poetry its oddness. In developing his rhythm he substitutes good English words for the Latin and Greek terms. Thesis he calls "stress"; arsis, "slack." The iambic he calls "rising"; trochaic, "falling" rhythm; where the stress falls in the middle he calls it "rocking" rhythm. "Mixed" (logaoedic) rhythm results where these are mingled for variety. Again taking example from music (in which he was adept enough to compose fugues) he contrasts rhythms for counterpoint and achieves striking effects. However, his most important contribution to versification is what he names "sprung" rhythm, which is counterpointed throughout. Each stanza is scanned continuously so that the lines merge together. It may have "hangers" or "outrides," a series of unaccented syllables which contribute pauses and variety. The feet have from one to four syllables, the accent falling always on the first. Hopkins makes remarkable use of the one-syllable foot, which gives concentrated and intense effects. . . .

If the innovations strike us first we must remember that it is the major poetry heightened by them that is his real contribution. Beyond question Hopkins belongs among the great poets of English literature. The experiments may be taken as evidence of the subtlety and diversity of one of the greatest minds to express itself in poetry in his generation. (p. 458)

> Isidor Schneider, "A Great Poet," in The Nation, New York, Vol. CXXX, No. 3380, April 16, 1930, pp. 456, 458.

HERBERT READ   (essay date 1933)

[*Read was a prolific English poet, critic, and novelist. In the general comments on Hopkins's poetry excerpted here, Read counters the critical reservations expressed by Bridges (see the excerpts dated 1894 and 1918) and examines such central aspects of Hopkins's poetic philosophy as his metrical theory, vocabulary, imagery, and subject matter.*]

Hopkins is only just emerging from the darkness to which his original genius condemned him. It is a familiar story; nothing could have made Hopkins's poetry popular in his day: it was necessary that it should first be absorbed by the sensibility of a new generation of poets, and by them masticated to a suitable pulp for less sympathetic minds. That process is going on apace now, and when the history of the last decade of English poetry comes to be written by a dispassionate critic, no influence will rank in importance with that of Gerard Manley Hopkins.

Hopkins himself was aware of the quality of his genius, and therefore knew what to expect from his contemporaries. (pp. 45-6)

Probably the only one of his small circle who understood him fully was his fellow-poet, Richard Watson Dixon. Dixon, writing to Hopkins to urge him to write more poems, refers to their quality as "something that I cannot describe, but know to myself by the inadequate word *terrible pathos*—something of what you call temper in poetry: a right temper which goes to the point of the terrible: the terrible crystal. Milton is the only one else who has anything like it, and he has it in a totally different way; he has it through indignation, through injured majesty, which is an inferior thing. . . ." Here is a full understanding which we do not find in the published letters and writings of others who knew Hopkins—not in Coventry Patmore, who floundered in deep astonishment, and not in his closest friend and final editor, the late Poet Laureate. To contend that Dr. Bridges did not understand the poetry of Hopkins would not be quite fair; he understood the craftsmanship of it, and was sensible to the beauty. But there seems to have been an essential lack of sympathy—not of personal sympathy, but of sympathy in poetic ideals. The Preface to the notes which Dr. Bridges contributed to the first edition of the poems . . . [see excerpt dated 1918] is marked by a pedantic velleity which would be excusable only on the assumption that we are dealing with a poet of minor interest. That is, indeed, the attitude: "Please look at this odd fellow whom for friendship's sake I have rescued from oblivion." The emphasis on oddity and obscurity is quite extraordinary, and in the end all we are

expected to have is a certain technical interest, leading to tolerance, and the discovery of "rare masterly beauties." Hopkins is convicted of affectation in metaphor, perversion of human feeling, exaggerated Marianism, the "naked encounter of sensualism and asceticism which hurts the **'Golden Echo'**," purely artistic wantonness, definite faults of style, incredible childishness in rhyming—at times disagreeable and vulgar and even comic; and generally of deliberate and unnecessary obscurity. Everything, in such an indictment, must depend on the judge's set of laws, and in criticising Dr. Bridge's treatment of Hopkins, I am wishing to say no more than that the Poet Laureate applied a code which was not that of the indicted. The lack of sympathy is shown precisely in this fact. Hopkins was a revolutionary; that is to say, his values were so fundamentally opposed to current practices that only by an effort of the imagination could they be comprehended. Once they are comprehended, many apparent faults are justified, and there is no reason to dwell on any of them.

Hopkins was serene and modest in his self-confidence. He could admit the criticism of his friends, and yet quietly persist in his perverseness. (pp. 46-8)

A full exposition of Hopkins's theories would take us far into a discussion of the historical development of poetry. Let me briefly indicate their main features. There is in the first place a metrical theory, of the greatest importance. Hopkins's poems are written in a mixture of what he called Running Rhythm and Sprung Rhythm. Running rhythm, or common English rhythm, is measured in feet of either two or three syllables, and each foot has one principal stress or accent. Hopkins preferred to take the stress always first, for purposes of scanning; but obviously that is only a question of convenience. To vary this running rhythm, poets have introduced various licences, of which the chief are reversed feet and reversed rhythm. If you pursue these variations far enough, the original measure will seem to disappear, and you will have the measure called by Hopkins sprung rhythm. In this measure each foot has one stress, which falls on the only syllable, if there is only one, or on the first if there are more than one. Normally there should not be more than four syllables to a foot, and the feet are regular measured in time. Their seeming inequality is made up by pause and stressing.

In general, sprung rhythm, as Hopkins claimed, is the most natural of things. He tabulated the reasons:

(1) It is the rhythm of common speech and of written prose, when rhythm is perceived in them.

(2) It is the rhythm of all but the most monotonously regular music, so that in the words of choruses and refrains and in song closely written to music it arises.

(3) It is found in nursery rhymes, weather saws, and so on; because, however these may have been once made in running rhythm, the terminations having dropped off by the change of language, the stresses come together and so the rhythm is sprung.

(4) It arises in common verse when reversed or counterpointed, for the same reason.

These reasons need no further comment; but there are two historical considerations to note. Sprung rhythm is not an innovation; it is the rhythm natural to English verse before the Renaissance. It is the rhythm of *Piers Ploughman* and of Skelton. Greene was the last writer to use it, and since the Elizabethan age, as Hopkins claimed, there is not a single, even short poem, in which sprung rhythm is employed as a principle of scansion. The other observation Hopkins could not make, because it is part of our history since his time. It is that the principles contended for by Hopkins on the basis of scholarship and original tradition (but only *contended* for on that basis: he actually wrote as he felt, and then went to history to justify himself) are in many essentials identical with the principles contended for by those modern poets already mentioned (whose advocacy and practice of 'free verse' is also based on feeling and intuition rather than historical analysis.)

A second characteristic of Hopkins's poetry which while not so original, is yet a cause of strangeness, may be found in his vocabulary. No true poet hesitates to invent words when his sensibility finds no satisfaction in current phrases. Words like 'shive-light' and 'firedint' are probably such inventions. But most of Hopkins's innovations are in the nature of new combinations of existing words, sometimes contracted similes, or metaphors, and in this respect his vocabulary has a surface similarity to that of James Joyce. Examples of such phrases are to be found in almost every poem: 'the beadbonny ash,' 'fallowbootfellow,' 'windlaced,' 'churlsgrace,' 'footfretted,' 'clammyish lashtender combs,' 'wildworth,' and so on. Commoner phrases like 'beetle-browed' or 'star-eyed' are of the same kind, made in the same way, and freely used by him. Here again an explanation would take us far beyond the immediate subject; for it concerns the original nature of poetry itself—the emotional sound-complex uttered in primitive self-expression. . . . Poetry can be renewed only by discovering the original sense of word formation: the words do not come pat in great poetry, but are torn out of the context of experience; they are not in the poet's mind, but in the nature of things he describes. (pp. 49-52)

Of Hopkins's imagery, there is not much in general to be said, but that 'not much' is all. He had that acute and sharp sensuous awareness essential to all great poets. He was physically aware of textures, surfaces, colours, patterns of every kind; aware acutely of earth's diurnal course, or growth and decay of animality in man and of vitality in all things. Everywhere there is passionate apprehension, passionate expression and equally that passion for form without which these other passions are spendthrift. But the form is inherent in the passion. For, as Emerson remarked with his occasional deep insight, ''it is not metres, but a metre-making argument, that makes a poem—a thought so passionate and alive, that, like the spirit of a plant or an animal, it has an architecture of its own, and adorns nature with a new thing''.

The thought in Hopkins's poetry tends to be overlaid by the surface beauty. But the thought is very real there, and as the idiom becomes more accepted, will emerge in its variety and strength. There is no explicit system, nor need there be in great poetry. Perhaps the only essential quality is a sense of values, and this Hopkins had in a fervid degree. He was a convert to Roman Catholicism, and might have ranged widely in intellectual curiosity had he not preferred to submit to authority. One of his contemporaries at St. Beuno's Theological College wrote of him:

> I have rarely known anyone who sacrificed so much in undertaking the yoke of religion. If I had known him outside, I should have said that his love of speculation and originality of thought would make it almost impossible for him to submit his intellect to authority.

Perhaps in actual intensity his poetry gained more than it lost by this step, but one cannot help regretting the curtailment it suffered in range and quantity. After joining the Church, he applied to himself a strict ascetic censorship, and apart from what he may have destroyed, deliberately refrained from writing under every wayward inspiration. (pp. 52-4)

> *Herbert Read, in a chapter in his* Form in Modern
> Poetry, *Sheed & Ward, 1933, pp. 35-55.*

EDITH SITWELL   (essay date 1934)

[*An English poet, biographer, and critic, Sitwell first received public attention in 1916 as the editor of* Wheels, *a series of anthologies of contemporary poetry that offered readers an alternative to the sentimental work of the popular poets of the era. Colored with idiosyncratic imagery and highly personal allusion, her own works reflect her belief that sound and rhythm should take precedence over meaning in poetry. In the excerpt below, Sitwell centers on the intrinsic unity of form and meaning that she discovers in Hopkins's poetry.*]

It is a fact that Hopkins should never be regarded as a model, since he worked his own discoveries to the uttermost point; there is no room for advancement, for development, along his lines. But leaving this truth aside it is a melancholy fact that his imitators have misunderstood his examples, and, ignorant that his rhythmical impetus, his magnificence of texture, are the results, at once natural and cultivated, of the properties of his material acted upon by the impact of his personality, they have produced poems with superimposed rhythms instead of rhythms inherent in the properties of the material. . . . Imitations of Hopkins have resulted . . . in a complete loss of melody, arising from falsified, clumsy, or too-thick vowel-schemes, clumsy and huddled-up assonance patterns, useless alliterations, and a meaningless accumulation of knotted consonants.

Yet great (though incapable of further development) are the technical wonders from which these imitations have sprung—these slandered originals are full of significance. Not, perhaps, since Dryden and Pope have we had such mountains and gulfs, such raging waves, such deserts of the eternal cold, and these are produced not by a succession of images alone, but by the movement of the lines, by the texture, and by Hopkins' supreme gift of rhetoric. It should be realized that rhetoric is not an incrustation, a foreign body which has somehow transformed the exterior surface of a poem, distracting the mind from the main line; it is, instead, an immense fire breaking from the poem as from a volcano. Sometimes it is smooth, sometimes it is fierce; but the manner in which it is born is the same. ''Decoration'' in poetry does not exist; either the physical beauty has arisen from the properties of the material, or the poem is a bad poem. (pp. 51-2)

Many of Hopkins' poems appear at first sight strange; and this is due in part to his acute and strange visual sense, a sense which pierces down to the essence of the thing seen, and which, heightening the truth of it, by endowing it with attributes which at first seem alien, with colours that are sharper, clearer, more piercing than those that are seen by the common eye, succeeds in producing its inherent spirit. He does not obscure the thing seen by loading it with useless details, he produces the essence by giving one sharp visual impression, performing miracles by using comparisons which seem very remote, as when, for instance, in the lovely fragment that I am about to quote, he compares the fair hair of a youth to a sheaf of bluebells. This, to me, gives the fairness of the hair, and shows the straightness of it, and the way in which it flaps, for, of all flowers, only a sheaf of bluebells has this particular limpness. The fragment is one of an unfinished poem, and how innocent and gay and rustic is the movement of it.

> The furl of fresh-leaved dogrose down
> His cheeks the forth-and-flaunting sun
> Had swarthed about with lion-brown
> Before the Spring was done.
>
> His locks like all a ravel-rope's end,
> With hempen strands in spray—
> Fallow, foam-fallow, hanks—fall'n off their ranks,
> Swung down at a disarray.
>
> Or like a juicy and jostling shock
> Of bluebells sheaved in May
> Or wind-long fleeces on the flock
> A day off shearing day.
>
> Then over his turnèd temples—here—
> Was a rose, or, failing that,
> Rough-Robin or five-lipped campion clear
> For a beauty-bow to his hat,
> And the sunlight sidled, like dewdrops, like dandled
>   diamonds,
> Through the sieve of the straw of the plait.

Here we have a youth, in the midst of his walk, suddenly leaping into the air and dancing for a step or two, because of the fun of being alive on this lovely and unfading summer morning. The innocent and sweet movement of this very lovely fragment is due, partly, to the skilful interposition of an extra syllable from time to time, and an occasional rare internal rhyme; and the clearness and poignant colours of the morning are conveyed by the sounds of "juicy," "bluebells," "sheaved," with their varying degrees of deep and piercing colour.

This acute and piercing visual apprehension, this sharpening and heightening of the thing seen, so as to obtain its essential spirit, is found again in these lines from **"The May Magnificat"**:

> Ask of her, the mighty mother:
> Her reply puts this other
> Question: what is Spring?
> Growth in everything—
>
> Flesh and fleece, fur and feather,
> Grass and greenworld all together,
> Star-eyed strawberry-breasted
> Throstle above her nested
>
> Cluster of bugle blue eggs thin
> Forms and warms the life within;
> And bird and blossom swell
> In sod or sheath or shell.
>
>   .   .   .   .   .   .
>
> When drop-of-blood and foam-dapple
> Bloom lights the orchard apple
> And thicket and thorp are merry
> With silver-surfèd cherry.
>
> And azuring-over greybell makes
> Wood banks and brakes wash wet like lakes
> And magic cuckoocall
> Caps, clears, and clinches all.

This ecstasy all through mothering earth
Tells Mary her mirth till Christ's birth
To remember and exultation
In God who was her salvation.

In the sharply-seen image of the "star-eyed strawberry-breasted" thrush—strawberry-breasted because of the freckles on her breast—in the enhanced and deepened colour of the "bugle blue eggs," in which the sharp U of "bugle" melting to the softer U of "blue" gives the reflection and the sisterhood of the deep blue heaven, the flower, and the egg, shifting and changing in the clear light, in the acutely-seen "greybells," we have the same piercing, truth-finding vision that produced for us the fair hair of the country youth.

But now we must turn from this exquisite and youthful happiness, this unfading spring weather, to the "terrible" poems. Let us take, to begin with, the first verse of that great poem, **"The Wreck of the Deutschland"**:

> Thou mastering me
> God! giver of breath and bread;
> World's strand, sway of the sea;
> Lord of living and dead;
> Thou hast bound bones and veins in me,
>   fastened me flesh,
> And after it almost unmade, what with dread,
> Thy doing: and dost thou touch me afresh?
> Over again I feel thy finger and find thee.

In this passage we have the huge primeval swell of the sea, with its mountain-heights and its hell-depths, we have the movement before life began, conveyed by technical means.

In the slow and majestic first line, the long and strongly-swelling vowels, and the alliterative M's, produce the sensation of an immense wave gathering itself up, rising slowly, ever increasing in its huge power, till we come to the pause that follows the long vowel of "me." Then the wave falls, only to rush forward again.

After this majestic line comes the heaving line

> God! giver of breath and bread,

ending with the ship poised on the top of the wave. This last effect is caused by the assonances of "breath and bread." The sound of "breath" is slightly longer, has slightly more of a swell beneath the surface than "bread," because of the "th." This pause on the top of the wave is followed by the gigantic straining forward of the waves in the line

> World's strand, sway of the sea,

an effect that has been produced by the strong alliterative S's, reinforced by the internal R's of "World's strand," followed by the internal W of "sway." This line, after the huge tossing up and down from the dulled A of "strand" to the higher dissonantal A of "sway," ends by sweeping forward still further with the long vowel-sound of "sea," a sound that is more peaceful than that of "strand" and "sway" because of the absence of consonants.

The whole poem is inhabited by a gigantic and overwhelming power, like that of the element that inspired it. The huge force produced by the alliteration in the lines I have analysed above, and in such a line as

> Thou hast bound bones and veins in me,
>   fastened me flesh,

Hopkins's headpiece for his early poem "A Vision of the Mermaids."

has rarely been exceeded, even by Dryden and by Pope, those masters of the effects that can be produced by alliteration. It is true that the last line I have quoted from Hopkins is necessarily, because of its subject, more static than most of the more magnificent lines of Dryden and of Pope, yet Hopkins' line is of nearly an equally giant stature. At the end of this verse, the huge primeval power, splendour and terror which inhabit it change to the softness and tenderness of

> Over again I feel thy finger and find thee,

a line which is equalled in gentleness and sweetness by the lovely line in the ninth verse:

> Thou art lightning and love, I found it, a winter and
> warm.

How huge is the contrast between this and the black coldness and opaqueness, like that of savage waters, of the line

> And the sea flint-flake, black-backed in the regular
> blow,

The opaqueness of this is caused by the flat assonances, the thick consonants, of "black-backed" and "blow."

In the same verse, we find this line:

> Wiry and white-fiery and whirlwind-swivelled snow.

I cannot recall any other English poet who has produced such a feeling of huge and elemental cold as Hopkins, a cold that is sometimes devouring, sometimes dulled. In the line quoted above, Hopkins produces the sensation of watching a wave receding and then plunging forward, by rhyming the first and the fourth word. A higher and more piercing dissonantal I precedes the second rhyme, and this feeling of the wave plunging forward is the result, too, of the internal R's, which always either lengthen a word or else make it flutter. In this case (as in the line

> World's strand, sway of the sea,

they lengthen it, or rather give the feeling of an immeasurable force driving forward.

This relentless and inevitable wave-stretch, this driving forward, contained in the sound of "whirl" is followed immediately by the shrinking sound of "wind," the I's in "wind" and "swivelled" being dull with cold.

We find an equally world-huge, overwhelming coldness in this quotation from **"The Loss of the Eurydice"**:

> A beetling baldbright cloud through England
> Riding: there did storms not mingle? and
> Hailropes hustle and grind their
> Heavengravel? Wolfsnow, worlds of it, wind there?

In this, our very bones seem ground and beaten by the ropes of the harsh hail. The effect may, or may not, be partly due to the grinding harshness of the ''grind'' ''heavengravel'' sounds, and to the long-sustained high internal rhymes ''grind'' and ''wind.'' The imagery is, however, mainly responsible for the magnificence of the verse—the huge imagination, the deep consciousness that inspired the phrase ''Wolfsnow, worlds of it, wind there.''

How tremendous is the difference between this overwhelming universe of the cold, and the ripeness, the fullness, the flooding of the whole being, conveyed by this passage about a heart filled with the contemplation of Christ's Passion.

After the passage:

> The dense and the driven Passion, and frightful sweat;
> Thence the discharge of it, there it's swelling to be,
> Though felt before, though in high flood yet—
> What none would have known of it, only the heart,
>   being hard at bay,

comes these lines:

>   Is out with it! Oh,
> We lash with the best or worst
> Word last! How a lush-kept plush-capped sloe
> Will, mouthed to flesh-burst
> Gush!—flush the man, the being with it, sour or sweet,
> Brim, in a flash, full!—Hither then, last or first,
> To hero of Calvary, Christ's feet—
> Never ask if meaning it, wanting it, warned of it—men
>   go.

I do not care, personally, for these lines, because I find the substance too rich, too thick, for my taste. But the richness is deliberate: the thick gushing of the ripe blood is intentional.

A lovely movement, a sense that all is well, that all creation is part of a controlled and gigantic design, is given by the internal rhymes and assonances of:

> For, how to the heart's cheering
> The down-dugged ground-hugged grey
> Hovers off, the jay-blue heavens appearing
> Of pied and peeled May!
> Blue-beating and hoary glow-height; or night, still
>   higher,
> With belled fire and the moth-soft Milky Way,
> What by your measure is the heaven of desire,
> The treasure never eyesight got, nor was ever guessed
>   what for the hearing?

The movement of this is like that of a bird flying through the bright air, swooping downward to its nest, then up again, through the holy and peaceful light. (pp. 56-62)

[In ''Binsey Poplars''] again the texture and movement are born from the needs of the subject. This suitability is particularly exquisite in the first verse:

> My aspens dear, whose airy cages quelled,
> Quelled or quenched in leaves the leaping sun,
> All felled, felled, are all felled;
>
> Of a fresh and following folded rank
>   That spared, not one,
>   That dandled a sandalled
> Shadow that swam or sank
> On meadow and river and wind-wandering weed-
>   winding bank.

A lovely air blows through these lines, produced by the wandering and fluctuating length of the lines, and by the fact that ''weed-winding'' is a higher, and slightly slower, echo of ''wind-wandering.'' The alliterative Qu sounds give us the feeling of dew-laden leaves. (pp. 65-6)

If we compare the exquisite lightness and airiness and subtlety of **''Binsey Poplars''** with the terror and huge strength of **''Carrion Comfort''**—perhaps the greatest of Hopkins' sonnets— we . . . see the variety of which he is capable. (p. 66)

The great strangeness of [**''Carrion Comfort''**] is almost entirely a matter of texture. He recognized this strangeness in nearly all his poems, for we find him writing to a friend in a letter dated 1879: . . . ''[As] air, melody, is what strikes me most of all in music, and design in painting, so design, pattern or what I call inscape is what I, above all, aim at in poetry. Now it is the virtue of design, pattern, or inscape to be distinctive, and it is the vice of distinctiveness to become queer. This vice I cannot have escaped'' [see excerpt dated February 15, 1879]. Later we find him explaining . . . ''[On] somebody returning me the **''Eurydice,''** I opened and read some lines, as one commonly reads whether prose or verse, with the eyes, so to say only, it struck me aghast with a kind of raw nakedness and unmitigated violence I was unprepared for: but take breath and read it with the ears, as I always wish to read, and my verse becomes all right'' [see excerpt dated April 22, 1879].

It is exactly in this raw nakedness and unmitigated violence, in a sort of leonine majesty, that Hopkins' greatness was shown. (pp. 67-8)

> *Edith Sitwell, ''Gerard Manley Hopkins,'' in her* Aspects of Modern Poetry, *1934. Reprint by Books for Libraries Press, 1970; distributed by Arno Press, Inc., pp. 51-72.*

C. DAY LEWIS   (essay date 1934)

[*Lewis, an English man of letters, is linked with W. H. Auden, Stephen Spender, and Louis MacNeice as one of the leftist Oxford poets of the 1930s. Eventually named poet laureate of England, he is today generally regarded as a minor figure in modern English poetry. Here, Lewis classifies Hopkins as a ''naïf'' poet who was uninfluenced by any previous school of literature and discusses his revolutionary uses of sprung rhythm, alliteration, and assonance. Lewis's commentary was first published in 1934.*]

Hopkins as a poet seems to have entered the world by a kind of partheno-genesis. The author of such lines as these—

> I caught this morning morning's minion, king—
> Dom of daylight's Dauphin, dapple-dawn-drawn Falcon,
>   in his riding.

or this—

>   Or to-fro tender tram beams truckle at the eye—

is difficult to connect with anything in the past. Attempts have been made to trace his derivation back to Milton. Except for Hopkins's own statement that Milton's counterpoint rhythmm, particularly as used in the choruses of *Samson Agonistes*, is apt to become identical with the 'sprung rhythm' which Hopkins himself used, I can see no warrant for such a derivation. The nearest approach to his verse texture I can find is in the Greek choruses, more especially those of Æschylus: we may note in his work something of the same fluidity of line, the same architectural massiveness and decorated verbal accumulation.

Leaving aside verse-texture, and considering what I must call, rather vaguely, poetic merit, I find eminent in Hopkins that quality which made Shakespeare supreme. Eliot, in a recent work, has expressed it as follows: 'The re-creation of word and image which happens fitfully in the poetry of such a poet as Coleridge happens almost incessantly with Shakespeare. Again and again, in his use of a word, he will give a new meaning or extract a latent one. . . .' That 're-creation of word and image' is the last secret of poetic technique, and the extent to which Hopkins achieved it may be gauged by the excerpts printed below: the sensitive reader may discover in them, also, something of the quality and 'feel' of Shakespeare's own poetry.

> Look at the stars! look, look up at the skies!
> O look at all the fire-folk sitting in the air!
> The bright boroughs, the circle-citadels there! . . .

(Juliet might be speaking there.)

> As a dare-gale skylark scanted in a dull cage . . .

> are you that liar
> And, cast by conscience out, spendsavour salt?

But, for all this, Hopkins remains without affinities. Poets may be divided into two classes; those who assimilate a number of influences and construct an original speech from them, and those whose voice seems to come out of the blue, reminding us of nothing we have heard before. (pp. 167-68)

Though one or two of Hopkins's mature poems come into the first class (**"The Blessed Virgin Compared to the Air We Breathe,"** for instance, which, except for a line here and there, might have been written by one of the metaphysical school), he is predominantly . . . a 'naïf' poet. (Since writing this section, I have discovered in one of Hopkins's letters the following passage: 'The effect of studying masterpieces is to make me admire and do otherwise . . .') It is, therefore, all the more remarkable to find him exerting such an influence on modern verse; for poets of this type do not belong to any 'school' of poetry and are apt not to found one. We admire Blake or Housman from a distance: any closer approach to their technique would lead us into pastiche. This is, perhaps, because their technique springs more immediately and purely from their experience than is the case with the 'sophisticated' writer. Up to a point this is true of Hopkins's also: one is frequently coming across undigested fragments of his style imbedded in post-war verse. But he has had a much more real influence than this mere bequeathing of echoes: and it is due, I think, to the fact that, unlike most naïf poets, he was a technical innovator. Such poets (Blake, Housman, Emily Dickinson) are usually content to work within conventional forms: their dæmon does the rest. It may seem contradictory to assert that a technical innovator can be a naïf poet, but I do not believe it is necessarily so. I should even go so far as to call Hopkins an unconscious revolutionary: in other words, his innovations are not due to a deliberate rebelling against the conventional technique of the time, as were those of Wordsworth, but spring from a kind of innocent experimenting with words, as a child of genius might invent a new style of architecture while playing with bricks.

One of Hopkins's most striking innovations is his frequent use of what he calls 'sprung rhythm.' It is not perhaps quite accurate to term it an innovation, for it approximates to the rhythm of *Piers Plowman* and the old nursery rhymes. But to all intents and purposes it is revolutionary. Wordsworth aimed at simplifying poetry, bringing it nearer to common speech: he ef-

fected this by a radical change in the use of words, not by radical changes in prosody. Hopkins was not working on any such theory of communication, but he produced in fact a result the opposite of Wordsworth's: by him the language of poetry was removed almost as far as possible from ordinary language—it becomes incantation again; while his prosody swings to the other extreme, for it is based on the rhythm of common speech. (pp. 169-71)

Till Hopkins, almost all English verse since Langland had been written in metres divisible into feet of two or three syllables, iambic or dactylic-anapæstic in effect. It is therefore syllabically quantitative verse. Any variations, such as the substition of trochee for iamb, had been variations on a metre of not less than two syllables per foot, and the beat—except in a few strictly dactylic poems, 'Take her up tenderly'—had the effect of coming on the last syllable of the foot. Sprung rhythm differs from this quantitative metre in the following ways. It is based on one syllable stressed in each foot: this syllable may stand alone in its foot or it may be accompanied by a number of unstressed syllables, usually not more than four. (p. 171)

The stress, where there is more than one syllable in the foot, comes as a rule on its first syllable: but a uniformly trochaic-dactylic effect is avoided by the use of what Hopkins called 'out-rides,' unstressed syllables occasionally placed before the stressed ones at the beginning of the foot. Thus in his metres the stress is the foundation, whereas in English verse as a whole, quantity—i.e. two or three syllables to a foot—is the foundation. And since stress is the basis of common speech rhythm, we may say that this sprung rhythm approximates to the rhythm of common speech.

In its favour as a poetical instrument we can put forward a greater freedom for rhythmical effects than is afforded by syllabically-quantitative metre with all its possible licences. No such lively representation of the hover and swoop of a kestrel could be achieved within the limits of the latter as we find in the first of the lines quoted above. And in the second, the heavy determination of 'sheer plod,' with its successive stresses accentuated by the three unstressed syllables before them, is again an effect which could not be procured within a conventional metre. On the other hand, the metrical foundation of sprung rhythm is so shifting and elastic that in employing it we are almost bound to lose that most desirable of rhythmical effects, the counterpoint of the line spoken according to the natural rhythm of the words working in contrast to the strict beat of the metre. (p. 172)

Another objection to sprung rhythm as used by Hopkins is that it often does not conform closely enough to common speech rhythm: we find ourselves compelled to run over a number of heavy syllables, which would certainly be stressed in ordinary speech, before we come to the intended stress. The intended stress, indeed, is often difficult to find. (p. 173)

Less questionably successful than Hopkins's use of sprung rhythm is his use of alliteration and internal assonance. He employs both constantly, yet, like all successful technical tricks, they are indistinguishable from the pattern which they help to create. These devices are seen to best advantage in **"The Leaden Echo and the Golden Echo,"** a poem which is coupled in my mind with Tennyson's "Ballad of the Revenge" as representing the most remarkable technical achievement of Victorian poetry. It begins—

> How to keep—is there any any, is there none such,
> nowhere known some, bow or brooch or braid or brace,
> lace, latch or catch or key to keep

Back Beauty, keep it, beauty, beauty, beauty, . . .
　　from vanishing away? . . .

Notice how cunningly alliteration and assonance are contrived
to modulate from one vowel key into another. Yet there is
nothing forced, no flavour of artifice. The poem must be read
aloud, and with an unprejudiced intellect, for it is a sustained
sensual rhapsody; something for which our acquaintance with
civilized poetry leaves us unprepared. It is the measure of
Hopkins's poetical stature that, though a man of great intellectual ability, he was capable of writing this kind of rhapsody
without ever degenerating into rhetoric.

　　. . . Only not within seeing of the sun,
　　Not within the singeing of the strong sun,
　　Tall sun's tingeing, or treacherous the tainting of the
　　　　earth's air . . .

Alliteration, internal assonance and repetition are the chief
instruments used by Hopkins in creating a poetry of rare concentration. . . . The flight of his imagination is very swift: the
following of it often a breathless business. What obscurity we
may find when first we read him is due, not to a clouded
imagination or an unsettled intellect, but to his lightning dashes
from image to image, so quick that we are unable at first to
perceive the points of contact. He is a true revolutionary poet,
for his imagination was always breaking up and melting down
the inherited forms of language, fusing them into new possibilities, hammering them into new shapes. His intense faith
and his violent spiritual agonies are experiences which few of
us to-day—happily or unhappily—are able to share: they caused
some of his most magnificent poems. . . . (pp. 173-75)

　　　　C. Day Lewis, "A Hope for Poetry," in his Collected
　　　　Poems: 1929-1933 & A Hope for Poetry, *Random
　　　　House, 1935, pp. 161-256.*

BERNARD KELLY　(essay date 1935)

　　[*Writing from a firmly Roman Catholic perspective, Kelly offers
　　close readings of "The Windhover" and "The Wreck of the
　　Deutschland" in the excerpt below.*]

["**The Windhover**"] is the masterpiece of [Hopkins's] metrical
revision of the sonnet form. It has all the power and velocity
of his mental creation. It wears the character of that joy of the
senses which is the unmistakable Hopkins. Those students of
poetry who find the analysis of metre dull must remember that
in Hopkins each metrical discovery has the value of a formal
excitement allied to his creative mind. The names he gives to
his particular inventions are evidence of this. The donnish
metrician does not call a handful of syllables flung against the
metre of a line to give pause and echo to its movement *Outrides;*
and *Paeans,* accepted from the Greek, is a loud and lovely
word. A dead measure was of no use to Hopkins. His scansion
is alive with values in movement. But what is more important
to the less technical reader is his use of the senses by sound
and image, and the life they receive in the poem by its driving
intellectual force.

Returning to . . . ["**The Windhover**"], patient of accidental
obscurities, (accidental because we read the printed word and
do not hear the poem spoken aloud as it was meant to be) we
clear the ground by another reading. We find the rush of glorious words 'kingdom of daylight's dauphin' to mean 'dauphin
of the kingdom of daylight', and move more securely in its
rhythm as its grammar discloses itself. The juxtaposition of
'skate' and 'bow-bend' loses its absurd suggestion (our fault,

our own absurdity) of an angler landing a fish on a rod bent
double, and yields of its own accord the bending flight of the
skater and the smooth skim of the ice. But the first lines of
the sestet present a real difficulty, the difficulty of intense
thought alive and aloud in words that clamour disturbingly on
every joy of the senses. What is 'here', what is 'Buckle', what
is 'fire', and why the emphasis of 'and', so small a word?

Firstly 'here' is not an exclamatory to attract attention, as the
more vulgar 'hi' or 'oy'. It is there in the poem with work to
do, and in the most important position of the line. It is a
directive. To explain it will partly explain the word which
follows. The poem opened with the poet in the act of seeing
the windhover. Behind the masterly achievements of the bird
on the wing the poet was watching unseen until he appeared
at the end of the octet. 'My heart in hiding Stirred for a bird, . . .'
and the poet, grasping the valiant beauty of the bird in his
mind, exclaimed, 'the achieve of, the mastery of the thing!'
'Here', then, is in the poet's mind. He clutched at the beauty
of the bird, crying aloud at its mastery. But now he commands,

　　　Brute beauty and valour and act, oh, air,
　　　　pride, plume, here Buckle!

Buckle, loud, bright, impetuous word, bidding the union closer.
It was the poet first, in the act of sensation, who seized the
bird. It is the bird now, present in the senses, who is commanded to lock in the embrace of the mind; the bird itself in
its own power and act present in the image of it.

. . . *and* the fire that breaks from thee then, a billion Times
told lovelier, more dangerous, O my chevalier!

The intellect in its act of knowing is at once active and passive.
The intelligence is informed by its object, receiving by the
ministry of the *intellectus agens* the intelligible form, the real
nature of the thing to be known. The intelligence is rendered
fecund, receiving in a union more intimate and subtle than that
of form and matter the nature of the real. It becomes the thing,
moving from perfect receptivity to perfect act; act in which the
mind is become a universe of stars, of movement, of the peril
of hawks on the wing. But for consummation of the act of
knowledge, Logos, childbirth of the glory it has conceived;
and the cry of the poet marshals the senses to be ministers of
the joy of utterance.

The peril and the beauty of the windhover inform, are one
with, the peril and the beauty of the poet's mind, who sees
and knows the bird in the dapple-dawn of daylight's kingdom.
A billion times told lovelier, more dangerous, O my chevalier!
The incalculable splendours of the mind meeting beauty are to
be found again in Hopkins, and 'more dangerous' will be seen
to be no mere epithet for valiant movement.

There it is. You may accept less from the poem, but behind
it will always be the knowledge (unimaginable knowledge,
almost claiming the title of mystery) of the mind in its act of
knowing; knowledge itself shining in the act of poetic creation,
that shone before abstractly in the delicate precisions of Aristotle, of St Thomas, of Scotus, of the theologians he knew.

No wonder of it. . . .

The theologian which is the poet in him, here as everywhere
one and the same person, explains as St Thomas might have
explained, saving their differences of manner, that the intelligibility of things is in their act. It is from the act of ploughing
that we know the plough. Embers blue-bleak, things dead,
things bleak for lack of life, fall shining into the mind, gall

themselves, expending a splendour in the act of change (act in which the world, perpetually losing its being, shines to the mind in dying) that, lost now to the thing, lives in the beholder's mind for ever. The beauty and dismay loud in the sound of those last two lines are the dismay of men in the brittle beauty of this world, that, being beauty still, lives chiefly in Christ and no one else, but in this world yields its joy only in *articulo mortis.*

· · · · ·

It is useless to read **"The Wreck of the Deutschland"** with a mind unprepared for the profound power of its spiritual movement. Meditate first for a fortnight on the Passion of our Lord. The exercise will not guarantee an understanding of the poem, but will put you in touch with it. The meaning, the movement, the poetic depth (always in Hopkins the same thing with the spiritual depth of mind searched, probed, made lucid by the august theology of the Church) of this, the longest and most powerful of his poems, is Christianity integral and absolute, Christianity splendid and entire in its accepted sacrifice. Its place is beside and among the liturgies of Holy Week that culminate in the Host's return to the altars made bare for His Passion.

I propose to treat separately as two movements of the poem what are in fact two sides or aspects of the same movement, a movement which is the substance, the form, the force, the maker of life in the poem itself. This I propose to do on account of the difficulty of the speculative thought which, though it deepens and quickens the significance of the poem, is far from explicit in the text, whereas the main act is explicit as far as will suffice for an adequate poetic understanding of it. By the *act* I do not mean the mere physical fact of shipwreck, but a more profound spiritual act to which the shipwreck is material or fuel only, and of which the poem is utterance.

A first part of ten stanzas is prefixed not as a prologue in the sense of a thing apart introducing the theme but not entering into the turmoil; it is a flying start, a beginning of the movement itself in its full force which overtakes the shipwreck, the so-called merely narrative part, carrying that forward with its own velocity. (pp. xviii-xxiv)

Powerfully, in the fullness of his mastery of an itself masterful rhythm, Hopkins uncovers the depths like the bed of the sea in which the poem is to move; the swell of a North Sea storm. And 'sprung rhythm' is the rhythm of a deep-sea swell. Stanzas 2 and 3 overshadow in the mind of the poet what is to be enacted later on deck, when

> . . . the inboard seas run swirling and hawling;
> 　　The rash smart sloggering brine
> Blinds her; but she that whether sees one thing, one;
> Has one fetch in her: she rears herself to divine
> 　　Ears, and the call of the tall nun
> To the men in the tops and the tackle rode over the
> 　　storm's brawling.

They overshadow too, in a way marvellously complete, the later spiritual life of the poet himself, a life of stress and terror and the rare dear joy of consolation, that we understand clumsily, but the saints know perfectly and with great gladness.

Into the threatened storm, storm of the spiritual life that now takes up the action of the hurricane and the storm at sea, travel

five Franciscan nuns to their drowning, exiles by the Falk laws aboard the Deutschland.

> And the sea flint-flake, black-backed in the regular
> 　　blow,
> Sitting Eastnortheast, in cursed quarter, the wind;
> 　　Wiry and white-fiery and whirlwind-swivelled snow
> Spins to the widow-making unchilding unfathering deeps.

The merciless winter sea is in these four lines, that are more merciless even than the sea. Into this bitterness the Deutschland sweeps to meet the ruin that is prepared for her,

> 　　She struck— . . . .
> And frightful a nightfall folded rueful a day
> Nor rescue, only rocket and lightship, shone,
> 　　And lives at last were washing away:
> 　　. . . . .
> 　　They fought with God's cold—
> And they could not and fell to the deck
> (Crushed them) or water (and drowned them) or rolled
> 　　With the sea-romp over the wreck.

What mastery, what superb rhythm! The wreckage, the helplessness, the hurl and the romp of a murderous sea: they are here, in these four lines. Never was the there such a poet. And the pity of it, and the piercing of that pity in the heroic figure of the tall nun, touch the heart of the poet, and he calls aloud to his own heart,

> 　　Ah, touched in your bower of bone
> 　　Are you! turned for an exquisite smart,
> Have you! make words break from me here all
> 　　alone,
> 　　Do you!—mother of being in me, heart.
> O unteachably after evil, but uttering truth,
> Why, tears! is it? tears; such a melting, a madrigal
> 　　start!
> 　　Never-eldering revel and river of youth,
> What can it be, this glee? the good you have there of
> 　　your own?

Here and throughout the poem, in the first three stanzas . . . and in the end, the poet is the celebrant. It is he who offers through the vehicle of his hands, of his mind, a sacrifice of which the victim, other than he, is he also by participation. Hopkins is the priest of poetry; he is also the poet of the priesthood. The sufferings of shipwreck, terrible in the words, profound in the feeling of the poem, are an offering, an oblation, and an oblation received.

> . . . but thou art above, thou Orion of light;
> Thy unchancelling poising palms were weighing the
> 　　worth,
> 　　Thou martyr-master: in thy sight
> Storm flakes were scroll-leaved flowers, lily showers—
> 　　sweet heaven was astrew in them.

If the shipwreck had been merely narrative, the poem merely pictorial in its narration, then these lines have turned it inside out like an old coat lined with incredible jewels. Suffering, the cruelest torment, becomes sacrifice, becomes in that perfect act of oblation sweet heaven astrew in flowers. (pp. xxvi-xxix)

The first thing, admirable always, terrifying in [Hopkins], is his directness. All that would have softened the poem to timid ears he gloriously refuses. If we are to have our joy, we who dare to wear the insignia of Christ, we are to have it in the majesty of its conquest, in the shattering beauty of the crucified

Incarnate God. Comfort he flings aside. We are dazed, dazzled, wonderfully elated in the high heart of the tall nun.

He was to cure the extremity where he had cast her. For Christ was that extremity. He in the storm met joy for His joy of the harvest. Reason, breathless, lagging, big with stupendous truths, is consumed in vision. Pain has become sacrifice, has become joy. Christ the priest; Christ the victim; Christ the joy of the accepted sacrifice. Everywhere one face only. Behind, exact, a glacial pregnant monument, the mystery of the Immaculate Conception dominates the last four lines of the 30th stanza. Read the lovely poem, **"The Blessed Virgin Compared to the Air We Breathe"**, and come back for the significance of these lines. In this climax the 'problem of human suffering' receives its only tolerable solution. (pp. xxxii-xxxiii)

What I propose to deal with as a second movement of the poem is an intellectual probing, that everywhere searches out the first movement, and is itself sometimes so vitally the form of that movement that the distinction I have made will often seem a violent one. I made it in order to separate what is very difficult indeed from what is intellectually less difficult, in such a way that the poem in both its aspects could be considered entire. To this second enquiry must be prefaced the fact of Hopkins' discipleship of Duns Scotus. The task of criticism is made more arduous still by the practical inaccessibility of an authentic text of Scotus, and that of this essay by my own inability to possess a text, for without possession I cannot study.

Much of what follows will therefore be guesswork aided by significant quotation, and in this respect hardly anything that Hopkins ever did or said was insignificant. Even the type of adjective he so loved, *rash-fresh,* has a peculiar importance to the admiration of Scotus that was so constant in his mind. Of his first enthusiasm he wrote "It may come to nothing, or it may be a gift from God. But just then when I took in any inscape of the sky or sea I thought of Scotus." It did not come to nothing. He wrote in his diary later, "I do not think I have ever seen anything more beautiful than the blue-bell I have been looking at. I know the beauty of Our Lord by it. Its inscape is mixed of strength and grace like an ash-tree." There is enough here to let us know that Scotus would explain more. A further significant (?diary) extract from Father Lahey's book [see Additional Bibliography], "God's utterance of Himself in Himself is God the Word, outside Himself is this world. This world is then word, expression, news of God. Therefore its end, its purpose, its purport, its meaning, is God, and its life or work to name and praise Him", links in a surprising way with the note on the Purcell sonnet, "Sake is a word I find it convenient to use.... I mean by it the being a thing has out of itself, as a voice by its echo, a face by its reflection, a body by its shadow, a man by his name, fame or memory, *and also* that in the thing by virtue of which it has this being abroad, and that is something distinctive, marked, ... as for voice and echo clearness ...." *Inscape* too, lovely delicate indefinable word, denotes with him a character of distinctiveness, and a man's mind is much revealed in his favourite words, especially if he invents them himself.

The Scotist *v* Thomist debate engaged on one of its battle-fronts upon the perfections of created things, and how these are verified in God; and in what way the attributes we properly predicate of Him are distinct from the Divine Essence. (The nature of the identity here determines the nature of the distinction.) On the Scotist side, *distinctio realis formalis,* (the rash-fresh character of the Scotist mind); on the Thomist, *distinctio virtualis eminenter æquivalens* (justice and prudence of

Saint Thomas). On both sides subtlety, for *eminentia* itself is among the most beautiful and revealing conquests of Thomist metaphysics, but on the side of Scotus, rash-freshness, an excitement in dialectic ingenuity, a passion for close intellectual, almost physical, encounter. The value of this attitude of mind may be guessed from later Scotism, but must be sought originally in Duns Scotus himself; the effect of it on Hopkins' thought is evident and profound. (pp. xxxiv-xxxvii)

There is a passionate mysteriousness of thought [in stanzas 5-8 of **"The Wreck of the Deutschland"**] of which the poet has taken care to give his warnings; but it is important thought, for in it the intimacy of Christ's appealing in the beauty of this world is vitally apprehended by the mind in the white-hot clarity of its creative excitement. And this clarity, subjectively speaking, is one which the purely metaphysical mind will not easily understand; one too which many modern theorists of poetry tend to stultify.

The apprehension of beauty (I mean of the tangible beauty of this world) means in the mind of the beholder a simultaneous delight of the intelligence and the senses. Not two delights at once, but one, a delight in which the senses and the mind are integral in one act. This is the delight towards which Hopkins' poetry moves, and in the pursuit of it he does not refine away to nothing the sensible and emotional qualities of beauty. Rather he renders them more fecund, more vitally themselves, than any poetry can which rests in emotion and the senses alone. He tends to a fusion of all that words can utter; of their intelligibility, of their sound, of the power they have on emotion, of the meaning they have to desire. And this fusion is living and intimate, a fusion made in the pain of poetic creation, lit by the clarity of a rare mind. But more than this. He is not content to rest delightfully in the objects of poetic experience. The whole force of his mind and of his nature drives him further. As in the conclusion of the Sonnet **"Ash-boughs"** he says

> .... it is old earth's groping toward the steep
> Heaven whom she childs us by.

opening, as it were, a window in created beauty to look through on the Uncreated, so again and sometimes by the neat structure of the verse as in **"Pied Beauty"**, but often by the direct drive and grappling of the mind into the very object of his poetic experience, he seeks from the heart of things that secret word of praise which is their link with their Creator. (pp. xxxix-xl)

[The] appealing of natural beauty is not for nothing. It is to bring man "To hero of Calvary, Christ's feet". How can this be if the beautiful "has the nature of an end in itself"? Hopkins has already said "This world is then word, expression, news of God." *News* says more than to indicate the formal proofs of metaphysics, for to them the world is only evidence. It says in fact, that the being and substance of the world is God's meaning, God's external utterance, God's information. And the world is not an Encyclopædia Britannica, nor yet a Daily Mail. It is a telegram, reply prepaid, addressed to a particular person, man.

> I kiss my hand
> To the stars, lovely-asunder
> Starlight, wafting him out of it....

Upon the lines here quoted these further lines from the sonnet, **"Hurrahing in Harvest"**, are a significant comment.

> I walk, I lift up, I lift up heart, eyes,
> Down all that glory in the heavens to glean
> our Saviour;

Our Saviour precisely, since through Him only can our senses be lifted to the supernatural; since it is He, the Eternal Word, whose meaning lies under the beauties of the world.

> These things, these things were here and but the
>   beholder
>   Wanting; which two when they once meet,
> The heart rears wings bold and bolder
>   And hurls for him, O half hurls earth for him off
>   under his feet.

The poet's meaning, in [stanzas 5-8] . . . would seem to be that the Incarnation and Redemption, which have gladdened the destiny of man, have also profoundly affected his relation to the beauty of this world. For if the world is news of God it is also news from an Incarnate God; not that the truths of Christian faith are revealed by the world, rather that a message of divine love becomes loaded with divine sacrifice. . . . Beauty is signed with the cross, and is an invitation to the cross. And this is not an intellectual or devotional construction put on the world by the faithful, but is of the very nature of the world and of beauty, for the world is news of God.

>   "Nor first from heaven (and few know this)
>   Swings the stroke dealt—"

Perhaps even now we had better be content, with the rest of the faithful, to *"waver and miss."* Certainly he does mean that.

The call of Christ in the beauty of this world is a call from the cross; and this is a key to the intellectual vitality of very nearly all the mature poetry of Gerard Hopkins; a vitality not going at a cross purpose to his 'pure poetry', but making that poetry; not crushing the life of the emotions and the senses, but giving them the very juice and life and direction of their own nature.

Word, that heard and kept thee and uttered thee outright.

Giving them, over and above, a motion they would not have dared to claim. The priest's offering is Christ, bearing with and within Him, *quem totus non capit orbis,* humanity and the world, His creation. The offering of the poet is that same world, but through human senses, a human mind, bearing because of them its meaning to humanity, which is Christ; because of the marks of his humanity, Christ crucified. (pp. xli-xliv)

> *Bernard Kelly, in his* The Mind & Poetry of Gerard Manley Hopkins, S. J., *1935. Reprint by The Folcroft Press, Inc., 1969, 46 p.*

DAVID DAICHES   (essay date 1936)

[*Daiches is a prominent English scholar and critic who has written extensively on English and American literature. His criticism has been characterized as appreciative in content and attached to no single methodology. Here, he discusses the "explosive" quality of Hopkins's language before examining his influence on contemporary poetic technique.*]

[A] discussion of the influence of Hopkins [on contemporary poetry] must confine itself to the technical aspect only. And perhaps the best way of beginning such a discussion is to pose the simple question: Why is Hopkins involved at all?

The answer to this question the critics have been inclined to take too much for granted. A poet who sought out new paths as Hopkins did was bound, they assume, to be immediately influential as soon as he became known. But is this true? If Hopkins had published in his own lifetime would he have

influenced the poetry of his contemporaries as he has that of our own generation? It is very improbable; but even if we grant that there would have been such influence, the further question remains, which, put in its most extreme form, is just this: Why should a post-war Communist seek inspiration from a nineteenth century Jesuit? The conditions under which poetry is written to-day are so totally different in every respect from those which prevailed at the time when Hopkins wrote, that the terrific force of the impact of Hopkins' verse on post-war poetry demands an explanation. There is little in the poet's life, in his beliefs, or in his sympathies, to find a response in such a poet as, say, Cecil Day Lewis or Stephen Spender. The answer to our question is not, however, difficult to find: it is simply that the post-war poets, for differing reasons, came to adopt an attitude to the poetic medium which Hopkins, for reasons of his own, had adopted and exploited.

This is the point of contact. Hopkins' use of language in verse was similar to what the modern poets were demanding and attempting. . . . [In Hopkins they found] one whose attitude to the medium of poetry seemed to be identical with theirs; and how splendidly he had justified that attitude in practice! (pp. 24-5)

What, then, was it in Hopkins' attitude to the poetic medium that appealed so immediately to the post-war poets? We have only to listen to the first two verses of the first of his mature poems ["**The Wreck of the Deutschland**"] to get a large part of the answer to this question.

>   Thou mastering me
>   God! giver of breath and bread;
> World's strand, sway of the sea;
>   Lord of living and dead;
> Thou hast bound bones and veins in me, fastened me
>   flesh,
> And after it almost unmade, what with dread,
>   Thy doing: and dost thou touch me afresh?
> Over again I feel thy finger and find thee.
>
>   I did say yes
>   O at lightning and lashed rod;
> Thou heardst me truer than tongue confess
>   Thy terror, O Christ, O God;
> Thou knowest the walls, altar and hour and night;
> The swoon of a heart that the sweep and hurl of thee
>   trod
>   Hard down with a horror of height:
> And the midriff astrain with leaning of, laced with fire
>   of stress.

We can see here as well as anywhere in Hopkins that *straining after a directness beyond that allowed by the formal syntactic use of language* which was such a feature of his poetry and which has so appealed to the poets of our own day. Such poetry is as far removed from Mallarmé's poetry of suggestion as it is from Dryden's poetry of statement. There is here a different directness than that attained by the directness of "sound-echoing-sense"—even in its most highly developed form—or of symbolism. Here was a new way of getting rid of the barrier that the formal modes of language opposed to the immediacy of union between subject and object, between the manner of expression and the thing expressed. How much more immediate was the phrase "thou mastering me God!" than the more conventionally poetic "God who art my master." The poet had leapt at his thought directly, irresistibly, and allowed the form of his expression to be dictated by an emotional rather than a logical sequence. It was this sense of directness that impressed the poets as it impresses any sensitive reader—this and the new rhythms which Hopkins employed. These were the two objects towards which the poets were striving: a new directness and an escape from the normal rhythms of English verse. (pp. 25-7)

[The poems of Hopkins] helped to give direction to the revolt against the later Romantic tradition in English poetry.

For what were the chief features of late Romantic poetry? Were they not a desire to use language for the sake of language, a denial of the right of the objective world to influence the medium which described it, the glorification of the means of expression as an end in itself? Was not this implicit in the work of Tennyson, of Swinburne, and of the poets of the 'nineties? And it was against this that the poetry of Hopkins was an implied protest. The exploitation of language was no worthy aim in itself: it was the wresting of words to meet fact that mattered. Embroidery was obfuscation—it merely got in the way. Donne and Hopkins were surely agreed on that point, and in that they appealed to the moderns. Donne's method of achieving his aim was—if one may be allowed the phrase—to intellectualise his passion; Hopkins' way was to evolve a practice (and, after the event, a theory) which enabled him to present his feeling and his thought in a progression of highly wrought images and ideas set down in words deliberately chosen for their intensity, their concentration, their approximation, as it were, to the naked fact itself. Is there any poem in the language where the words are so deliberately harnessed to the service of expression as **"The Leaden Echo and the Golden Echo"**? . . . Here is a use of language at the opposite pole from, say, that of Swinburne. With Swinburne language nearly always came first, and effective language for its own sake was the aim. With Hopkins language was a servant, to be bullied and coerced into as immediate contact with the thought as was possible. The rules of grammar and of syntax were not allowed to stand in the way; if they affected the immediacy of the expression they were ignored. Thus Hopkins sacrificed an obvious intelligibility to a directness which was not even intelligible—far less direct—until the meaning had, to use Hopkins' own term, "exploded." His obscurity is due to the fact that his meaning "explodes" far more rarely than he anticipated. Naturally as he knew from the beginning what he wanted to say, he could not put himself in the place of the reader, who approached the meaning from the other end. A reliance on the eventual "explosion" of the meaning, rather than on logical exposition combined with the resources of sound and suggestion, is dangerous, but if it is effective it is much more direct and powerful and immediate in its communication than the more normal way. (pp. 28-30)

The trouble, of course, is that Hopkins very often does not achieve that explosive clarity at second reading that he aimed at and to which he sacrificed the "meaning to be felt without effort." And his imitators, not perhaps grasping his principle of explosive meaning at all, fail even more frequently to achieve any kind of intelligibility. . . . The poetry of Hopkins is highly disciplined—over-disciplined, some may maintain, but no one can deny that his finest poems are due to a wrestling with language which did not come easily however spontaneous the effect may be to the reader.

It was, then, his impatience with the poetic medium as generally accepted in the nineteenth century that brought Hopkins into immediate contact with the modern poets. The practice in which such impatience resulted was rationalised in his theory of "Sprung Rhythm," a theory highly important in its liberating effect on English metre since 1918. (pp. 31-2)

A gnarled oak stump sketched by Hopkins in Hampstead, dated 1862.

We come across [explanations of sprung rhythm] frequently throughout the letters of Hopkins to Bridges and R. W. Dixon, and they show what an indefatigable metrical theorist he was. All his life Hopkins was interested in the theory of metre, classical even more than English, and it is important to bear this in mind when comparing his work with that of his modern imitators. The difference in quality as regards metrical achievement is often explained by the fact that Hopkins had studied the subject carefully in all its aspects and came to the writing of poetry with a technical knowledge which none of the modern poets possesses. This does not, however, prevent us from realising that Hopkins' elaborate theory of sprung rhythm . . . was a rationalisation of an instinctive desire to achieve more direct methods of expression in more spontaneous-sounding rhthyms.

Hopkins had other peculiarities. His use of tmesis, enjambement, and coined words are three of the more important. He made frequent and often subtle use of alliteration, too, and a less frequent though equally noticeable use of peculiar rhymes, rhymes which often strike the reader as ludicrous, such as "crew in" with "ruin," "boon he on" with "communion," and "Irish" with "sire he sh(ares)," "shares" being the first word of the third line, and the line being "rove over." All these features sprang from the same cause—impatience with the syntactical division of language into ordered components and a desire to get behind syntax to a more cogent logic. Perhaps in less than half of his work can he be called successful in this effort, but had he lived he would probably have achieved a more uniformly successful method of attaining his aims— aims which, let it be repeated, he so largely shares with the modern poets.

When Hopkins is successful he attains a rhythmic and musical effect which is integral to the verse in a peculiar degree; it is not in any way superimposed on the meaning. The **"Echoes"** song is a fine example of this, as is also the famous **"Wind-hover."** . . . But the dangers of this method are easily shown:

> To what serves mortal beauty—dangerous; does set
>   dancing blood—the O-seal-that-so feature, flung
>   prouder form
> Than Purcell turn lets tread to?

Here there is no white-hot welding of form and content, but only a painful stuttering. When a passion which is single struggles with a medium that consists of separate words a fusion must take place or the words scatter to the ground ineffective. At his best Hopkins does achieve this fusion. Perhaps no poet after Shakespeare shows such a sense of the infinite gap between emotion which is single and unified, and the medium of language which has to be assembled in time before the emotion can be expressed. Other poets showed no concern when faced with this fact, accepting the medium as it was and making the best of it. Only Shakespeare, with a technique that in the last resort defies analysis, was able to bridge that gap consistently. It is Hopkins' greatness that, in his own way, he also did so—occasionally. It would be idle to maintain that he did so often.

The publication of Hopkins, and the discovery by the modern poets that he had had a problem similar to their own resulting in an attitude to the poetic medium similar to their own, led at once to imitation of every kind. The imitation, which consisted in superimposing crude Hopkinsesque fragments on to an alien style, was of no value and only did harm, but the influence was also felt in a more valuable way than that. The poets absorbed the rhythms of Hopkins and these helped to loosen up their style, to redeem it on the one hand from sloppy poetic prose and on the other from congested and unpoetic "wit-writing." The use a poet made of the example of Hopkins was a very good test of his understanding of Hopkins' achievement. The poet who made the example an excuse to write insensitively and obscurely was modelling his verse on Hopkins' failures.

Once we see Hopkins as a rallying point after years of experiment with the poetic medium we can attempt to consider his influence on the moderns. . . . (pp. 34-7)

[But for all the influence which Hopkins] has had on the modern poets, there is a fundamental difference between his work and that of his imitators—even technically. In the first place, none of the moderns have the tactual and visual sense that Hopkins had; their verse is more purely intellectual. Hopkins' imagination was to a very high degree sensuous, and the difficulty of his poems is often due less to intellectual subtlety than to the welding of different kinds of sensuous experience in a struggle for complete expression. Edith Sitwell does the same sort of thing much more blatantly when she talks of the "purring sound of fires," the "dark songs of birds," the "blue wind," the "creaking light," etc. Hopkins' confusion of the senses is less obvious and based more on a preternatural sensitivity than on a desire to be effective. In his sonnet **"Duns Scotus's Oxford"** we see how the senses of sight and hearing determine the vocabulary:

> Towering city and branchy between towers;
> Cuckoo-echoing, bell-swarmed, lark-charmed, rook-
>   raked, river-rounded;
> The dapple-eared lily below thee; that country and town
>   did
> Once encounter in, here coped and poised powers.

None of the moderns have this sensuous awareness. Spender, for example, writes:

> My parents kept me from children who were rough
> And who threw words like stones and who wore torn
>   clothes.
> Their thighs showed through rags. They ran in the street
> And climbed cliffs and stripped by the country streams.

There is a purely intellectual quality here that Hopkins, for all the "cerebration" in his verse, would never have allowed. The meaning is conveyed by verbs which convey nothing to the senses. "Their thighs *showed* through rags." "Who wore torn clothes." Hopkins would never have been satisfied with the abstract verb "showed" or the general phrase "wore torn clothes": he would have made you see them instead of merely talking about them. Hopkins stands alone in the intensity of his perceptions, and this involves an important difference in his use of the poetic medium.

Hopkins, too, had a gift for naturalising words in foreign contexts which the modern poets have only partly inherited. In a phrase like "What lovely behaviour of silk-sack clouds" (from **"Hurrahing in Harvest"**) the word "behaviour" is surprising and effective. This device, when it is found in modern poetry, has none of the subtlety with which Hopkins used it.

But there are more important differences than these between the poetry of Hopkins and that of contemporary poets. The main one is this. Hopkins was sure of the content, the matter, of his verse; he had no problem there—he took it for granted that the kind of subject he wished to write about was a fit subject for poetry and he wrote only when the inspiration came. All his conscious attention was devoted to form. His experiments and innovations were all due to a striving after new means of expression, not after new matter to express. The new matter he may have had, but it came without striving, and his desire to justify his themes theologically had no relevance to his poetic activity. As a poet he was concerned with originating a new technique, and it was to this that all his conscious experimentation was directed. But his modern imitators are even more preoccupied with content than with form. Indeed it may be questioned whether they are fundamentally concerned about form at all. . . . Many of them have adopted sprung rhythm ready-made without any understanding of its organic nature or appreciation of . . . its peculiar pleasure. In technique their only concern seems to be towards a looseness *ad infinitum*, counterbalanced, when they remember, with a stiffening of intricacy by some such method as the Wilfred Owen type of assonance. And all the while they grow more and more concerned about their subject, what they are to write about. This was not Hopkins' attitude, and it puts a big gulf between his poetry and that of his modern imitators.

So while Hopkins and the modern poets have similar attitudes to the poetic medium, they differ in their more fundamental attitudes to poetry. To Hopkins, an attitude to the medium was identified with a complete theory of poetry—at least the other elements in the theory were obvious and taken as a matter of course. If you had something to put into poetry and came seriously to your subject, that was all that mattered. "A kind of touchstone of the highest or most living art," he wrote Bridges in 1886, "is seriousness; not gravity but the being in earnest with your subject—reality." He was not worried about what the poet *ought* to say—as long as he meant what he did say. The matter for poetry was not itself poetry: the way the matter was used was what made poetry. (pp. 41-5)

A less fundamental but equally interesting point of difference is that Hopkins did not allow his preoccupation with technique to interfere with his lyrical faculty—he retained the ability to *sing*, which the modern poets have lost through over much self-consciousness. The self-consciousness of the modern poet is twofold: he has too much knowledge of the psychology of poetic creation, of his own mental processes, to be comfortable in creation, and, secondly, an undue social sensitiveness makes him worried and apologetic in his artistic activity. Hopkins suffered from neither of these ills, and that was his good fortune rather than his merit: had he lived to-day he could hardly have avoided the influence of modern psychology or the effects of an altered social atmosphere. But as things were he retained a remarkably fresh lyrical vein.

> Look at the stars! look, look up at the skies!
> O look at all the fire-folk sitting in the air!

There is nothing like this in contemporary poetry—nothing, either, like the more meditative mood of **"God's Grandeur"** and **"The Sea and the Skylark,"** which show a restrained lyrical quality rare in any poet. This lyrical faculty of Hopkins is akin to that startling directness of approach which produces some of his most effective lines:

> The Eurydice—it concerned thee, O Lord,

or

> And you were a liar, O blue March day.

The verse of the contemporary poets is technically much simpler and more elementary than that of Hopkins. Auden and Spender, for example, though they show considerable Hopkins influence, generally use loose iambic feet with simple counterpoint and equivalence which gives something of the effect of sprung rhythm without being so technically accomplished or so highly wrought. This is the third major difference between Hopkins and his imitators. (pp. 45-7)

Tracing the disintegration of the traditional English poetic medium through Whitman, Pound and Eliot, we can readily see how Hopkins stepped in to play at once a constructive and destructive rôle—constructive in that he did achieve a valuable new metric (not altogether new, but at least revived), destructive, in that his impatience with the formal limitations of language coincided with a similar impatience on the part of the post-war poets and encouraged them to go to strange lengths in their desire for immediacy of expression. His total influence on modern poetry cannot yet be estimated. It is still difficult to see clearly into the tangle of influences which have been working on English poetry during the last decade, and which are still potent. What is due to Donne and Eliot, what to Pound, what to Hopkins, what to Whitman, what to Yeats, and what to the French poets at the end of the last century and later—to mention only some of the forces at work—cannot yet be decided. But however we may apportion the influence, we cannot doubt that Hopkins did do much, and for the reason that he represented a definite step in the disintegration of the traditional medium. (pp. 50-1)

> David Daiches, *"Gerard Manley Hopkins and the Modern Poets,"* in his New Literary Values: Studies in Modern Literature, *1936. Reprint by Books for Libraries Press, 1968; distributed by Arno Press, Inc., pp. 23-51.*

PHILIP HENDERSON (essay date 1939)

[*Henderson was an English man of letters known for his studies of Christopher Marlowe and other English literary figures. Henderson here compares Hopkins—a "passionate and frustrated nature struggling with self-imposed shackles"—to the American poet Walt Whitman and suggests that Hopkins's religious asceticism, which led to a preoccupation with suffering and martyrdom in his work, ultimately killed him.*]

'I always knew in my heart Walt Whitman's mind to be more like my own than any other man's living,' Hopkins wrote to Robert Bridges in 1882. 'As he is a very great scoundrel this is not a pleasant confession. And this also makes me the more desirous to read him and the more determined that I will not' [see excerpt dated 1882]. Why Hopkins, a Jesuit, thought of Whitman as a very great scoundrel, and why, in spite of that, he had such an attraction for him, was not due only to the inherent contrariety of his nature. Whitman represented all that side of himself which he had vainly tried to suppress in the name of religion; he found in Whitman that same overmastering virile energy and turbulence, that luxuriant sensuality, that devouring love of the physical beauty of men and the world which even the 'particular examinen' of St. Ignatius had failed to stifle.

Bridges had written to say that **"The Leaden Echo and the Golden Echo"** was written in imitation of Whitman, and this had deeply disturbed both the Jesuit and the poet in Hopkins. 'I cannot think that the present piece owes anything to him,' he replies, 'I hope not, here especially, for it is not even spoken in my own person, but in that of St. Winefred's maidens. It ought to sound like the thoughts of a good but lively girl and not at all like—not at all like Walt Whitman.' It would be interesting to know what Hopkins' first thought was when he broke off. Certainly the proximity of that very great scoundrel and St. Winefred's 'good but lively' maidens must have been a disturbing thought, especially as he knew very well that the rank healthy male in Whitman was quite capable of giving this lamenting girl a short and practical answer to all her nostalgic regrets for the golden echo of passing beauty. Hopkins was also disturbed as a craftsman by Bridges' suggestion, because his own minutely careful and considered execution was the very opposite of the spontaneous and unselected gush of words in *Leaves of Grass*—'the Word *En-Masse*.' Yet he was forced to recognize that extremes—and not only extremes of asceticism and sensuality—sometimes meet. 'I must for truth's sake say what sounds like pride,' he admits, 'this savagery of his art, this rhythm in its last ruggedness and decomposition into common prose, comes near the last elaboration of mine.' (pp. 103-05)

[Whitman] was determined to give the password primeval, to sing the bed-fellow's song. He would reject nothing, neither 'bellies press'd and glued together with love' nor 'The curious sympathy one feels when feeling with the hand the naked meat of the body.' He was determined to send his barbaric yawp over the roofs of the world. 'I had,' he said, 'great trouble in leaving out the stock poetical touches but succeeded at last.'

It is not difficult to understand the dangerous attraction of this kind of thing to the exquisite and over-disciplined sensibilities of Father Hopkins. The same impulses of self-denial and self-torture that kept him from publishing his work in his lifetime, and that made him decide that he was being self-indulgent in writing poetry at all, made him elaborate a prosody that imposed rules of the utmost difficulty and rigour. His natural affinity was with the conversational ease of Whitman: so while claiming the right to use colloquial rhythms and diction, he elaborated an art that, in its concentration and strange, twisted constructions, is the very opposite of Whitman. He aimed not only, as Robert Bridges said of him, at 'an unattainable perfection of language,' he aimed at an unattainable perfection of living. In everything he was fascinated by what was difficult and yet more difficult, by all that made the greatest possible demands upon his strength and integrity. Just as in life he struggled incessantly towards self-conquest, the subdual of his nature to 'the Will of God,' so each poem presented itself to him as another opportunity for the conquest of language and rhythm and its subdual to his own exacting demands. If syntax cracked under the strain, if rhythm sometimes staggered, so did his own endurance under the strain he almost daily imposed upon it. He packs his lines so full that they can hardly hold their teeming wealth. His poems have a breathless quality as though he were anxious that not the minutest subtlety of thought or sensation shall escape him, that everything down to the last shred and overtone of an experience shall be concentrated and distilled. And all this is done with such a nervous haste and intensity, and the simultaneous use of many of the devices of prosody, such as stress, alliteration, assonance, internal and end rhyme, that do not usually appear packed together in this way, that we are reminded of Time that with a robber's haste crams his rich thievery up, he knows not how. Except, of course, that Hopkins always knows very well what he is doing.

The only outlet for this self-consuming passion he allowed himself was in his love of nature, though even here he did not permit himself to love nature for its own sake—everything had to be made, as far as possible, to illustrate some point of doctrine in order to 'give beauty back to God—beauty's self and beauty's giver.' Often the doctrine is tacked on to the end of a poem merely to excuse the riot of his senses, for in spite of himself, Hopkins' appreciation of nature was often dangerously pagan. But frustration brought its own reward in sadism and a preoccupation with torture and suffering. His sensuality, consistently inhibited, gave rise in his poems to recurrent images of mutilation—'gash,' in the sense of cut flesh, is one of his most-used words. Apple-blossom appears to him as 'drop-of-blood-and-foam dapple,' poppies are described as 'blood-gush blade-gash.' In the fragment on archery we read of the arrow 'Right rooting in the bare butt's wincing navel.' As we should expect, he was much preoccupied with the Catholic martyrs. He has a poem on Margaret Clitheroe, pressed to death at York in 1586, 'while within her womb the child was quick'; in the unfinished tragedy on St. Winefred's martyrdom occurs the line 'I all my being hacked in half with her neck.' He began poems on Campion, Sherwin, and Bryant, but these were either never finished or destroyed, perhaps because he had begun to suspect that his interest in martyrdom was not entirely what it should be. (pp. 107-10)

[All] that we know of Hopkins's life and work gives the impression of a passionate and frustrated nature struggling with self-imposed shackles. But even so he always seems to have been haunted and oppressed by his failure to live up to the standards he had set himself. This is shown also by the fact that he never found the kind of work for which he was fitted even inside his own Order, as may be judged from the constant changes in his appointments—Roehampton, London, Oxford, Liverpool, Stonyhurst, and finally Dublin, where he seems to have been more wretched than anywhere else. 'Never was a squarer man in a rounder hole,' one of his Dublin contemporaries said of him. But the question is: would a man of his peculiarly difficult nature have ever found satisfaction in any walk of life? One can hardly imagine him, for instance, as happily married; still less as a business man, politician or civil servant. In fact, one can only think of him as wrestling with his soul in solitude, though his nature seems to have craved an outer discipline, some mould within which to work, for he was afraid, as well he might be, of his own potentialities for emotion. In a different kind of society the subjective problems he had to solve would have been different, indeed, they may even have been solved for him in advance; but as it was his Christian faith, or perhaps it would be truer to say his passionate desire for faith, does not seem to have solved anything. His mind was too honest, too rebellious, too genuinely experimental and adventurous to be satisfied with a dogma, though he did his best to tame it with the spiritual exercises of St. Ignatius.

On the other hand, his mind was essentially religious: the keen-fastidious and super-subtle sensations that he demanded from life could only have found satisfaction in denial, for in any attempt to fulfilment they would inevitably have lost their edge, their ecstasy. So that his self-denial was in itself a form of voluptuousness, but a voluptuousness grown so fine that physical indulgence would have meant vulgarization of its pure essence. 'This is that chastity of mind which seems to lie at the very heart and to be the parent of all other good, the seeing at once what is best, the holding to that, and the not allowing anything else to be even heard pleading to the contrary.' And yet this severe epicurean had to admit towards the end of his life that Whitman's mind was more like his own than any other man's living!

In an industrial age of continually increasing complexity like our own, when 'all is seared with trade; bleared, smeared, with toil; And wears man's smudge and shares man's smell,' the need for the healing, refreshing power of the earth, and the large, tranquil harmony of its seasons, for that 'dearest freshness deep down things,' becomes a need ever-recurrent and more intense. This appears not only in Hopkins's passionate, eager way of looking at clouds, sunsets, waters, trees, and birds, but in his hungry observation of their smallest detail. This kind of feeling for nature is first evident in the Romantic Movement that began about the time of the Industrial Revolution in the eighteenth century; with Wordsworth and Shelley it grew into a need to identify themselves with nature; with Whitman and Hopkins it is a fever to be in actual physical contact with 'earthworld, airworld, waterworld.' 'I am in love with it,' cries Whitman:

> I will go to the bank by the wood and become
>   undisguised and naked,
> I am mad for it to be in contact with me.

Hopkins's passion of eagerness is all the more intense for being so long held in check: when at last he allows it to find expression, it leaps and flings itself through his lines like a bird released from the hand. It is nature in all its richness, fecundity, and careless abundance that assaults his starved senses and challenges his spirit pent up in an ascetic regimen. It is 'a juice rides rich through bluebells,' weeds 'long and lovely and lush,' 'March-bloom, like on mealed-with-yellow sallows,' 'rose-moles all in stipple upon trout,' thrush's eggs like 'little low heavens,' 'a stallion stalwart, very-violet-sweet,' aspens in summer 'whose airy cages quelled, Quelled or quenched in leaves the leaping sun.'—'What is all this juice and all this joy?' As Charles Madge has noted both Whitman's and Hopkins's images frequently make their appeal straight to the salivary glands, 'those tell-tale sources of moisture which have been so fruitful a subject for Pavlov and physiological psychology.'

It is hardly necessary to observe that the religious sublimation of the exalted physical states produced in Hopkins by nature, or thrilling proximity to 'lovely manly mould,' was far from complete, although we do find him noting in his *Journal:* 'I do not think I have ever seen anything more beautiful than the bluebell I have been looking at. I know the beauty of Our Lord by it.' It is still more curious in the poems to find all this spontaneous and purely sensual joy in wild things twisted into a religious dogma, for in spite of himself, Hopkins was drawn to

> All things counter, original, spare, strange;
> Whatever is fickle, freckled (who knows how?)

Still more revealing is his undisguisedly voluptuous appreciation of the little bugler in his scarlet coat 'Breathing bloom of a chastity in mansex fine,' who came to him for his first communion:

> When limber liquid youth, that to all I teach
> Yields tender as a pushed peach.

Indeed, as Professor Abbott guardedly remarks [in his introduction to [*The Letters of Gerard Manley Hopkins to Robert Bridges*]: 'There is something not altogether subdued to the Christian purpose in this side of the poet's work.'

As he grew older this contrast between the juicy ripeness, the luxuriant abundance of nature, and his own self-imposed sterility became more and more acute in Hopkins's mind. The cry 'O thou lord of life, send my roots rain,' recalls that same thirst for fertility that dominates *The Waste Land*. The insistence in the winter world of the last sonnets is always upon the ascetic sacrifice that he has made and the terrible thought that he, a man of unusual vigour and great creative powers, had become an eunuch, even though it was 'for the Kingdom of Heaven's sake.' There is an ever-growing note of resentment and rebellion. Nowhere is this more evident than in that last sonnet written in the year of his death and directed accusingly at God.

> Thou art indeed just, Lord, if I contend
> With thee; but, sir, so what I plead is just.
> Why do sinners' ways prosper? and why must
> Disappointment all I endeavour end?
>   Wert thou my enemy, O thou my friend,
> How wouldst thou worse, I wonder, than thou dost
> Defeat, thwart me? Oh, the sots and thralls of lust
> Do in spare hours more thrive than I that spend,
> Sir, life upon thy cause. See, banks and brakes
> Now, leavèd how thick! lacèd they are again
> With fretty chervil, look, and fresh wind shakes
> Them; birds build—but not I build; no, but strain,
> Time's eunuch, and not breed one work that wakes.
> Mine, O thou lord of life, send my roots rain.

But the only rain that came to him was the sweat of his own agony. He is shut up in the prison of himself with a terrible sterile conflict in the dark air of the mind, the fine delight 'live and lancing as a blowpipe flame' gone for ever. (pp. 121-27)

According to Hopkins's biographer, Father Lahey [see Additional Bibliography], 'the celebrated "terrible sonnets" are only terrible in the same way that the beauty of Jesus Christ is terrible. Only the strong pinions of an eagle can realize the cherished happiness of such suffering.' Here speaks the mas-

ochistic spirit of the Christian religion. One wonders if Father Lahey himself was ever fortunate enough to partake of such cherished happiness. Certainly the grandeur of these sonnets derives from the intensity of their suffering. But it is (as Hopkins knew—and what could he have known worse?) a sterile, self-defeating suffering. Their torment is the torment of frustration, lost conviction, unbearable heartache. They are poetry on the rack. One can almost hear the sinews of the mind cracking in their rending, wrenching anguish,

> Not, I'll not, carrion comfort, Despair, not feast on
>   thee;
> Not untwist—slack they may be—these last strands of
>   man
> In me or, most weary, cry *I can no more*. I can;
> Can something, hope, wish day come, not choose not to
>   be.
> But ah, but O thou terrible, why wouldst thou rude on
>   me
> Thy wring-world right foot rock? lay a lionlimb against
>   me? scan
> With darksome devouring eyes my bruisèd bones? and
>   fan,
> O in turns of tempest, me heaped there; me frantic to
>   avoid thee and flee?
> Why? That my chaff might fly; my grain lie, sheer and
>   clear.

Certainly these poems have the purging effect of great tragedy, and Hopkins tried to think that he was purified in this 'heaven-handling' as he lay 'wrestling with (my God!) my God.' At times, he tells us, that even in his blackest hour his heart stole joy, would laugh and cheer. Cheer whom, he suddenly asks: God or he that fought him? But neither the cheering nor the desperate laughter was to last very much longer, for by the age of forty-five he was dead.

> We hear our hearts grate on themselves: it kills
> To bruise them dearer.

Hopkins may have been purified by his suffering; it may, indeed, as Father Lahey remarks, have been 'the greatest and most cherished *gift* from One Who has accepted literally His servant's oblation.' But it was a gift that killed him.

'Natural heart's ivy, Patience, masks Our ruins of wrecked past purpose.' But perhaps he had succeeded only too well in his imitation of Christ, for he remarks in one of his letters that Christ 'was doomed to succeed by failure. . . . However much he understood all this, it was an intolerable grief to submit to it. He left the example: it is very strengthening, but except in that sense it is not consoling.' Strengthening, was it? It seems that Hopkins had to sustain his faith by a continual act of will. For a man of such a powerful, subtle mind the strain was, as we know, often intolerable. There is something altogether over-ecstatic in all his stated beliefs to ring quite true—yet, if they were not true, all the suffering he had voluntarily imposed upon himself was in vain. Nowhere does this appear so clearly, perhaps, as in the sonnet **"That Nature Is a Heraclitean Fire and of the Comfort of the Resurrection."**

> Million-fuelèd, nature's bonfire burns on.
> But quenched her bonniest, dearest to her, her clearest-
>   selvèd spark
> Man, how fast his firedint, his mark on mind, is gone!
> Both are in an unfathomable, all is in an enormous dark
> Drowned. O pity and indignation! Manshape, that shone

Sheer off, disseveral, a star, death blots black out; nor
  mark
    Is any of him at all so stark
But vastness blurs and time beats level. Enough! the
  Resurrection,
A heart's-clarion! Away grief's gasping, joyless days,
  dejection.
      Across my foundering deck shone
A beacon, an eternal beam. Flesh fade, and mortal trash
Fall to the residuary worm; world's wildfire, leave but
  ash:
    In a flash, at a trumpet crash,
I am all at once what Christ is, since he was what I am,
  and
This Jack, joke, poor potsherd, patch, matchwood,
  immortal diamond
    Is immortal diamond.

Is this a triumph of faith or the desperation of despair? Had Hopkins lived in the sixteenth century, he would almost certainly have faced martyrdom for his faith, had not his life been, as it was, one long protracted martyrdom. For a man of his passionate temperament, for a poet of his genius to suppress deliberately his own abounding powers in the name of religion, it could have been no less. If we doubt this, there is the testimony of his last sonnets, where 'Hope has grown grey hairs.' The regimen of St. Ignatius gradually pressed him to death, like Margaret Clitheroe. But his dying lasted a lifetime. (pp. 127-31)

> *Philip Henderson, "Gerard Manley Hopkins," in his* The Poet and Society, *Secker & Warburg, 1939, pp. 103-31.*

JOHN PICK (essay date 1942)

[*Pick's book-length biographical and critical study centers on the thesis that for Hopkins the vocations of priest and poet were inseparable. In the following discussion of some of Hopkins's best-known poems, Pick interprets the works as religious celebrations of God's creation and cites the influence upon Hopkins of the spiritual exercises of St. Ignatius of Loyola.*]

[Ten of Hopkins's] most delightful and exuberant religious poems were written in the months just preceding his ordination (23rd September, 1877) and in those immediately after he had become a Jesuit priest. 1878 added three more poems to his body of religious verse.

These poems of 1877-8, like **"The Wreck of the Deutschland"**, were the fruit of his broken silence, but they have a smoother flow than the ode of 1875. Yet the recurrent motifs of these compositions are implicitly contained in the earlier poem. The same sacramental view of nature is expressed, the same realization that God must win His creatures to Him. The same technical devices, now not so obviously new, are further elaborated and developed.

A religious experience of beauty is the central theme that runs through most of these poems—an experience of created things moulded and directed by the Spiritual Exercises. We must recall once more—for its echo is found all through the poems of this period—Hopkins' own succinct statement of the meaning and purpose of all things—his précis of the "Principle and Foundation":

> God's utterance of himself in himself is God the Word, outside himself is this world. This

world then is word, expression, news, of God. Therefore its ends, its purpose, its purport, its meaning, is God, and its life or work to name and praise Him.

Here is stated that sacramental view of nature which sees all things as avenues to the supreme Being. Man may rise from an experience of particular things, of "inscapes", to God; he may find in the many the One. Natural beauty can bring man to higher Beauty. Indeed did not Scotus contend that the world existed for the very purpose of bridging the gap between finite man and the Infinite?

The poems of 1877-8 show how the world expresses God and praises Him. But Hopkins' growing concern is with man. Does he perceive the world as a constant call to perfection? Does he use created things to pursue his own end which is also God? The contrast between the beauty of created things as a message from God, and man, his blindness and waywardness, give to many of Hopkins' poems their peculiar vitality and beauty.

The poems of these two years are full of joyous wonder at the beauty of the world, of a joy enhanced because creation is seen sacramentally and because he himself is using beauty to praise his Maker. No longer do we find the versifying of unrealized abstractions as in his Oxford poems. Nor are the poems surfeited with the lushness and luxuriance of his **"Vision of the Mermaids"**. The senses are not suppressed, but they are directed. They become instruments and means with which to praise God. There is an integration of sense, intellect, and emotion in one act in which the whole man seeks God. Hopkins had attained that essential integrity which correlates all perceptions and thoughts, the spiritual and material, in one universal pattern of which God is the design.

The joy in the variegated and transient "inscapes" of the world is Franciscan in its eagerness in **"Pied Beauty"**. A wimpling rhythm of sound and colour, this curtal-sonnet sees in the variety of nature participations in God; but not until the last lines does the poet pull all together and touch the spark which gives the whole its direction and aim:

> Glory be to God for dappled things—
>   For skies of couple-colour as a brinded cow;
>   For rose-moles all in stipple upon trout that swim;
> Fresh-firecoal chestnut-falls; finches' wings;
>   Landscape plotted and pieced—fold, fallow, and
>   plough;
>   And áll trádes, their gear and tackle and trim.
> All things counter, original, spare, strange;
>   Whatever is fickle, freckled (who knows how?)
>   With swift, slow; sweet, sour; adazzle, dim;
> He fathers-forth whose beauty is past change:
>   Praise him.

In the last line all the preceding Scotist "inscapes" raise the poet to "Immutable Beauty". They have particularized beauty, but God is Beauty in Itself. Yet it is by knowing transient beauty, the many, that the heart mounts up to the unchanging One. Hopkins shares the Pauline vision: "For the invisible things of Him, from the creation of the world, are clearly seen, being understood by the things that are made." St. Thomas had emphasized that "as all the perfections of creatures descend in order from God, who is the highest of perfection, man should begin from the lower creatures and ascend by degrees, and so advance to the knowledge of God". And St. Bonaventure had pointed out the same road: "The creatures of this visible world signify the invisible attributes of God, because God is the source, model and last end of every creature, and because every effect points to its cause, every image to its model, every road to its goal.''

The ''inscapes'' which Hopkins poured into **''Pied Beauty''**, itself an ''inscape'' of delicate variety and pattern, lifted him to a higher and more exalted Beauty—but the sacramental world remained to be enjoyed, yet not to be worshipped as Beauty Absolute. Yet this is a thing that is often misunderstood. Plato himself had said that ''the true order of going . . . is to use the beauties of earth as steps along which he mounts upwards for the sake of that other Beauty''. But the whole Platonist tradition tended to despise created beauty for the sake of Uncreated Beauty. The Christian tradition was essentially different, in spite of the frequent ''contempt of creatures'' which one finds; for, as Maritain has written,

> This phrase, which primary exhibits the weakness of human language, must not be misunderstood. The saint sees in practical fact the nothingness of creatures with regard to the Being he loves and the End he has chosen. It is a loving contempt of all things other than that beloved. And the more he despises creatures in the degree to which they might be rivals of God, or objects of a possible choice to the exclusion of God, the more he cherishes them as loved by God, and made by Him as fair and worthy of our love. . . . So we understand the paradox whereby in the end the saint includes in a universal love of kinship and of piety—incomparably more free, but also more tender and more happy, than any selfish love of the voluptuary or the miser—all the weakness and the beauty of things, all he had left behind him on his journey.

And in the very Constitutions of his Order Hopkins was taught to place his affection in the Creator of all things, ''loving Him in all creatures and them all in Him, according to His most holy and divine Will''. (Rule 17)

True, in these poems there is greater intensity than in Walt Whitman, that poet so like and yet so unlike Hopkins. Yet it is a misunderstanding of a religious position to speak, as does Robert Bridges, of ''the naked encounter of sensualism and asceticism'' in the poetry of Hopkins [see excerpt dated 1918]. The critics of the Jesuit have gone very wide of the mark in their failure to understand the attitude behind these poems. Frances Winwar has written that ''something which he could not altogether confine to Christian purpose betrayed itself in his work, containing more of Pater's concentration of feeling in a single verse than Wilde's whole volume''. Herbert Read has said that such a poem as **''The Windhover''** is completely objective in its senseful catalogue, but that Hopkins got over his scruples by declaring the poem ''To Christ Our Lord''. And very recently Philip Henderson has contended that in spite of himself Hopkins' appreciation of nature was dangerously pagan.

All these critics are amazed to find a Jesuit who can communicate the loveliness of God's world with such haunting appreciation. They, rather than Hopkins, may be said to be the victims of that puritanism which Monsignor Ronald Knox refers to as the Englishman's substitute for asceticism.

''Pied Beauty'' and the other poems of this group—indeed all that Hopkins ever wrote—are the poet's *Laudate Dominum* in which he calls on all creation to praise their Creator; for, as Peter the Venerable said, when the world ceases to offer sacrifice to God, it will cease to be God's. The secret behind these poems is expressed tersely in two lines from **''Ash-Boughs''**:

> It is old earth's groping towards the steep
> Heaven whom she childs us by.

Thus another priest has recently reminded us: ''Art has as its ultimate object the playing of a priestly role, to sanctify nature, and lead it back to God. The Christian artist gives to silent creation a voice and the wherewithal to satisfy its deepest desire: praise.'' (pp. 52-6)

Thus it is that a Jesuit like Hopkins can be at the same time a priest true to heaven and a poet true to earth.

More delicately fanciful than **''Pied Beauty''** is **''The Starlight Night''**, in which the beauty about him is conceived as the outer wall of heaven, a midpoint at which the world touches the periphery of Beauty, Christ. In the octet, the mind in white heat captures the ''inscapes'' of the sky in a series of exclamatory images:

> Look at the stars! look, look up at the skies!
>   O look at all the fire-folk sitting in the air!
>   The bright boroughs, the circle-citadels there!
> Down in dim woods the diamond delves! the elves'-eyes!
> The grey lawns cold where gold, where quickgold lies!
>   Wind-beat whitebeam! airy abeles set on a flare!
>   Flake-doves sent floating forth at a farmyard scare!—
> Ah well! it is all a purchase, all is a prize.

The last line has made the theme explicit: by a disciplined and directed use of created beauty all may rise to Beauty even higher. The sestet continues:

> Buy then! bid then!—What?—Prayer, patience, alms,
>   vows.
> Look, look: a May-mess, like on orchard boughs!
>   Look! March-bloom, like on mealed-with-yellow
>   sallows!
> These are indeed the barn; withindoors house
> The shocks. This piece-bright paling shuts the spouse
>   Christ home, Christ and his mother and all his
>   hallows.

One is inevitably reminded of an experience Hopkins had recorded in his Journal, where he told how one August evening in 1874 ''as we drove home the stars came out thick: I leant back to look at them and my heart opening more than usual praised our Lord to and in whom all that beauty comes home''. His Ignatian training had indeed opened his heart very wide when he came to write such poems as **''The Starlight Night''**.

In **''The May Magnificat''** the tremulous beauty of Spring symbolizes the purity and beauty of Mary. The poem abounds with joy in the appeal of the growing world.

> When drop-of-blood-and-foam-dapple
> Bloom lights the orchard-apple
>   And thicket and thorp are merry
>   With silver-surfèd cherry
>
> And azuring-over greybell makes
> Wood banks and brakes wash wet like lakes
>   And magic cuckoocall
>   Caps, clears, and clinches all.

But the lines are not merely a collection of attractive sensuous images, of "inscapes" flung together in verse form. Rather, all the senses are employed as instruments to praise Mary:

> This ecstasy all through mothering earth
> Tells Mary her mirth till Christ's birth
> To remember and exultation
> In God who was her salvation.

The whole poem was written as an occasional piece to be hung, anonymously, before the Lady Statue at Stònyhurst during May, when it was the custom to compose verses to Mary. Obviously it is not in his characteristic manner, for it was an attempt to appeal to the popular taste and Hopkins admitted that in such writing he usually felt himself "to come short". But I see no indication that Hopkins was dissatisfied for the reason that, as Claude Colleer Abbott suggests, "the lush, yet fresh, beauty of the descriptive writing, which conveys the very 'feel' of Maytime, clashes inevitably with praise of the Virgin Mary". That is utterly to misunderstand the function of the senses and of created beauty.

But the poem of this group that is born of his greatest exuberance, bringing to an emotional crescendo his experience of beauty, is **"Hurrahing in Harvest"**. It bears the stamp of an almost ecstatic experience of the sacramental operation of nature upon him. Indeed Hopkins himself told Bridges that it was "the outcome of half an hour of extreme enthusiasm as I walked home alone one day from fishing in the Elwy". Three years later he was attempting to express in another art form that memorable half hour's "spontaneous overflow of powerful feeling", for he was trying to set the piece to music.

The poem opens with his declaration of the "inscapes" he had experienced in lines charged with joyous wonder at the beauty of created things:

> Summer ends now; now, barbarous in beauty, the
>   stooks arise
>   Around; up above, what wind-walks! what lovely
>   behaviour
> Of silk-sack clouds! has wilder, wilful-wavier
> Meal-drift moulded ever and melted across skies?

But the lines that follow have even greater vigour and delight—a delight born of rare spiritual joy. Confronted with created beauty, the heart flushed with it experiences it as news of God:

> I walk, I lift up, I lift up heart, eyes,
>   Down all that glory in the heavens to glean our
>   Saviour;
>   And, èyes, heárt, what looks, what lips yet gave you
>   a
> Rapturous love's greeting of realer, of rounder replies?

Here is an experimental "instress" of a "rapturous love's greeting"—an infusion of the being with beauty and its message of divine love. It is testimony that Hopkins' arduous practice of the Spiritual Exercises culminated in the final "Contemplation to Obtain Love".

The next lines firmly and powerfully praise God as the very "ground of being, and granite of it":

> And the azurous hung hills are his world-wielding
>   shoulder
>   Majestic—as a stallion stalwart, very-violet-sweet!

Then comes the consummation in ecstatic desire for union:

> These things, these things were here and but the
>   beholder
>   Wanting; which two when they once meet,
> The heart rears wings bold and bolder
>   And hurls for him, O half hurls earth for him off
>   under his feet.

Such a climax, an experience of earthly beauty as powerfully pulling man to God and of man co-operating by rapturously flying to Divine Love, is analogous to the religious experience of **"The Wreck of the Deutschland"**. Even some of the imagery is the same:

> I whirled out wings that spell
> And fled with a fling of the heart to the heart of the
>   Host.
> My heart, but you were dovewinged, I can tell,
>   Carrier-witted, I am bold to boast,
> To flash from the flame to the flame then, tower from
>   the grace to the grace.

And again he reads aright the message in the world:

> Wording it how but by him that present and past,
> Heaven and earth are word of, worded by?

The whole tradition of Catholic thought was a force in moulding such an attitude. St. Augustine had written:

> Thy whole creation ceaseth not, nor is silent in
> Thy praise: neither the spirit of man directed
> unto Thee, nor creation animate or inanimate,
> by the voice of those who meditate thereon:
> that so our souls may from their weariness arise
> towards Thee, leaning on those things which
> Thou hast created, and passing on to Thyself,
> who madest them wonderfully; and there is re-
> freshment and true strength.

(pp. 56-9)

But throughout it was especially the Spiritual Exercises which were the primary force behind his poems. This is very clearly seen if we examine the notes that Hopkins wrote for an address based on the "Principle and Foundation". We do not know the date of these jottings, nor do we know their occasion. But we do know that they parallel closely—even to very phrases—the poems of 1877-8. And they reinforce, once more, our testimony of the extent to which Hopkins' new vision sprang from his spiritual life as a Jesuit.

These notes consider first the meaning of creation and its end; then Hopkins asks: do created things fulfil their purpose? Especially does man?

With an abundance of homely figures—some of the most delightful prose Hopkins ever wrote—the address unfolds the implications of St. Ignatius' teaching:

> Why did God create? . . . He meant the world
> to give him praise, reverence, and service; *to
> give him glory*. It is like a garden, a field he
> sows: what should it bear him? praise, rever-
> ence, and service; it should yield him glory. It
> is an estate he farms: what should it bring him
> in? Praise, reverence and service; it should re-
> pay him glory. It is a leasehold he lets out:
> what should its rent be? Praise, reverence, and
> service; its rent is his glory. It is a bird he
> teaches to sing, a pipe, a harp he plays on: what
> should it sing to him? etc. It is a glass he looks

in: what should it shew him? With praise, reverence, and service it should shew him his own glory. It is a book he has written, of the riches of his knowledge, teaching endless truths, full lessons of wisdom, a poem of beauty: what is it about? His praise, the reverence due to him, the way to serve him; it tells him of his glory. It is a censer fuming: what is the sweet incense? His praise, his reverence, his service; it rises to his glory. It is an altar and a victim lying in his sight: why is it offered? To his praise, honour, and service: it is a sacrifice to his glory.

In the next section Hopkins looks about him at created things, exclusive of man, to see whether they fulfil this purpose of expressing and praising God; his answer is:

> The sun and stars shining glorify God. They stand where he placed them, they move where he bid them. ''The heavens declare the glory of God.''

Then come important distinctions and qualifications:

> They glorify God, *but they do not know it.* The birds sing to him, the thunder speaks of his terror, the lion is like his strength, the sea is like his greatness, the honey like his sweetness; they are something like him, they make him known, they tell of him, they give him glory, but they do not know they do, they do not know him. . . . This then is poor praise, faint reverence, slight service, dull glory. Nevertheless what they can *they always do.*

Pied and dappled things, ''lovely-asunder starlight'', ''the dappled-with-damson west'', ''skies of couple-colour'', ''March-bloom'', May-time's ''drop-of-blood-and-foam-dapple'', the ''silk-sack clouds''—all these created things are news of God and praise Him though they do not know they do. Yet only through man is their beauty really sacramental.

Then Hopkins turns to consider man whom he calls ''life's pride and cared-for-crown'' in the hierarchy of beings. St. Thomas had called him the noblest thing in nature and the Psalmist put him just after the angels. If man uses nature sacramentally he is fulfilling his purpose; if he employs created beauty to raise him to Beauty he is pursuing his end.

> But amidst them all is man, man and the angels: we will speak of man. Man was created. Like the rest then to praise, reverence, and serve God; to give him glory. He does so, even by his being, beyond all visible creatures: ''What a piece of work is man!'' (Expand by ''Domine, Dominus, quam admirabile, etc. . . . Quid est homo. . . . Minuisti eum paulo minus ab angelis.'') But man can know God, *can mean to give him glory.* This then was why he was made, to give God glory and to mean to give it; to praise God freely, willingly to reverence him, gladly to serve him. Man was made to give, and mean to give, God glory.

Then he asks whether man actually does pursue his end and purpose and give God glory. Again the images pour forth in abundant variation upon the same theme:

Does man then do it? Never mind others now nor the race of man: Do I do it?—If I sin I do not: how can I dishonour God and honour him? wilfully dishonour him and yet be meaning to honour him? . . . No, we have not answered God's purpose, we have not reached the end of our being. Are we God's orchard or God's vineyard? we have yielded rotten fruit, sour grapes, or none. Are we his cornfield sown? we have not come to ear or are mildewed in the ear. Are we his farm? it is a losing one to him. Are we his tenants? we have refused him rent. Are we his singing bird? we will not learn to sing. Are we his pipe or harp? we are out of tune, we grate upon his ear. Are we his glass to look in? we are deep in dust or our silver gone or we are broken or, worst of all, we misshape his face and make God's image hideous. Are we his book? we are blotted, we are scribbled over with foulness and blasphemy. Are we his censer? we breathe stench and not sweetness. Are we his sacrifice? we are like the sacrifice of Balac, or Core, and of Cain. If we have sinned we are all this.

The contrast expressed in these notes between nature as instinctively and automatically yet unconsciously praising or expressing God and man as wayward and sinful, failing to use nature sacramentally—this contrast becomes the hinge on which several of the 1877-8 poems turn.

''God's Grandeur'' opens with an explosive metaphor expressing the immanence of God. The poet's awareness of created beauty as a reflection of God is so intense that he cannot understand why it is not obvious to all men.

> The world is charged with the grandeur of God.
>   It will flame out, like shining from shook foil;
>   It gathers to a greatness, like the ooze of oil
> Crushed. Why do men then now not reck his rod?

The next quatrain sets in contrast man's use of nature, his failure to recognize it as news and praise and grandeur of God, his failure to use created things to pursue his own end. The lines are also a summary of the particular sins of the nineteenth century:

> Generations have trod, have trod, have trod;
>   And all is seared with trade; bleared, smeared with toil;
>   And wears man's smudge and shares man's smell: the soil
> Is bare now, nor can foot feel, being shod.

Then the sestet rounds out the contrast by stressing the constant renewal and renascence of natural beauty. Why?—because God continues to express Himself in the world:

> And for all this, nature is never spent;
>   There lives the dearest freshness deep down things;
> And though the last lights off the black West went
>   Oh, morning, at the brown brink eastward, springs—
> Because the Holy Ghost over the bent
>   World broods with warm breast and with ah! bright wings.

This last is no mere fanciful image. This recognition of ''dearest freshness deep down things'' is more than a cold intellectual perception that by his Presence, Essence, and Power, God is in all things. It is an experience, rather, of one flushed by the intuition that the world brings to the sensitive heart, a message loaded with divine love. That this is no mere subjective reading of the poem we can see from a study of Hopkins' notes on the joyful climax to the Spiritual Exercises, the "Contemplation to Obtain Love". There St. Ignatius urges man to look on the created world about him as an effort of God to communicate His love to man, as a vision of God's love. Hopkins' notations in his Commentary are fragmentary, and the thought is theologically difficult. He wrote:

> This contemplation . . . is the contemplation of the Holy Ghost sent to us through creatures. Observe then it is on love and the Holy Ghost is called Love . . . shown "in operibus", the works of God's finger; . . . consisting "in communicatione" etc., and the Holy Ghost as he is the bond and mutual love of Father and Son, so of God and man; that the Holy Ghost is uncreated grace and the sharing by man of the divine nature and the bestowal of himself by God on man.

That Hopkins was experiencing the physical universe as a bond between God and man, as a message from the Divine Goodness, as "news, word, expression" of the Eternal Lover, is further emphasized by three lines he added to the above passage: "All things therefore are charged with love, are charged with God and if we know how to touch them give off sparks and take fire, yield drops and flow, ring and tell of him"—words which have their poetical counterpart in

> The world is charged with the grandeur of God.
> It will flame out, like shining from shook foil.

In such expressions—as in all sacramentalism—there is the danger of pantheistic language. There are few theologians who have expressed more clearly the immanence and transcendence of God than Hopkins when he wrote in his Commentary:

> God is so deeply present to everything ("Tu autem, O bone omnipotens, eras superior summo meo et interior intimo meo") that it would be impossible for him but for his infinity not to be identified with them or, from the other side, impossible but for his infinity so to be present to them. This is oddly expressed, I see; I mean—a being so intimately present as God is to other things would be identified with them were it not for God's infinity or were it not for God's infinity he could not be so intimately present to things.

The antithesis between the beauty of nature and man and his use of created things is calmer and less "charged with God" in a poem Hopkins wrote soon after going to Oxford to take up his duties at St. Aloysius' Church in 1878. That he had an affection for the landscape around Oxford is clear from his own undergraduate diary; that his love for it continued is evident in a letter which he wrote to Canon Dixon when he returned there as a Jesuit priest:

> You will see that I have again changed my abode and am returned to my Alma Mater and need not go far to have before my eyes "the little-headed willows two and two" and that landscape, the charm of Oxford, green shoul-

A sketch by Hopkins titled "Manor Farm, Shanklin, July 8, 1863."

dering grey, which is already abridged and soured and perhaps will soon be put out altogether.

In this prose passage he also indicates his disapproval of nineteenth-century mercantilism which had "seared with trade, bleared, smeared" the beauty which was meant to bring man to God.

The first quatrain of **"Duns Scotus's Oxford"** captures the charm and appeal of the university town:

> Towery city and branchy between towers;
> Cuckoo-echoing, bell-swarmèd, lark-charmèd, rook-racked, river-rounded;
> The dapple-eared lily below thee; that country and town did
> Once encounter in, here coped and poisèd powers.

The next lines sketch the effect of man's use of created things—as in **"God's Grandeur"**, except that they are not as direct in their judgment

> Thou hast a base and brickish skirt there, sours
> That neighbour-nature thy grey beauty is grounded
> Best in; graceless growth, thou hast confounded
> Rural rural keeping—folk, flocks, and flowers.

Yet in the sestet of this poem, Hopkins finds some consolation in the beauties which remain, in the memory of the great mediaeval Franciscan who had shown him how to direct his experience of "inscapes" to God:

> Yet ah! this air I gather and I release
> He lived on; these weeds and waters, these walls are
>   what
> He haunted who of all men most sways my spirits to
>   peace;
> Of reality the rarest-veined unraveller; a not
> Rivalled insight, be rival Italy or Greece;
> Who fired France for Mary without spot.

The contrast between natural beauty, ever renewing its hymn to God, and man, wayward and silent, is far more explicit and direct in **"The Sea and the Skylark"**:

> On ear and ear two noises too old to end
> Trench—right, the tide that ramps against the shore;
>   With a flood or a fall, low lull-off or all roar,
> Frequenting there while moon shall wear and wend.

In vibrant contrast to "the tide that ramps against the shore", comes the exquisitely beautiful image of the song of the skylark as the unskeining of a rolled ribbon swirling and fluttering to the earth:

> Left hand, off land, I hear the lark ascend,
>   His rash-fresh re-winded new-skeinèd score
>   In crisps of curl off wild winch whirl, and pour
> And pelt music, till none's to spill nor spend.

In opposition to the shimmering beauty of the skylark's song and "the low lull-off or all roar" of the sea is man, created also to sing his hymn of praise, reverence, and service to God. But does he? The entire sestet is devoted to the answer:

> How these two shame this shallow and frail town!
>   How ring right out our sordid turbid time,
> Being pure! We, life's pride and cared-for crown,
>   Have lost that cheer and charm of earth's past prime:
> Our make and making break, are breaking, down
>   To man's last dust, drain fast towards man's first
>   slime.

Our race and civilization are fast draining towards the slime from which we were created—our materialism is leading us literally back to matter instead of raising us through matter to Heaven. We have forgotten our duty to God. "Are we his singing birds?" Hopkins asks in his notes on the "Principle and Foundation"; he shakes his head, "We will not learn to sing".

Thus in several poems of this period, the poet prays that God may send to man the grace that will complete him so that he will be enabled "to give God glory and to mean to give it; to praise God freely, willingly to reverence him, gladly to serve Him".

"In the Valley of the Elwy" contrasts the beauty of Wales with man who fails to see in this beauty a call to God. The Welsh landscape had attracted Hopkins from the time when as a seminarian he first entered St. Beuno's; it operated on him with a religious impact. "Looking all around but most in looking far up the valley", he entered into his Journal a week after he arrived there in 1874, "I felt an instress and charm of Wales. Indeed in coming here I began to feel a desire to do something for the conversion of Wales". The same desire is in the sonnet he wrote three years later. He referred to Wales as "always

to me a mother of Muses". The mother of muses was with him when he wrote **"In the Valley of the Elwy"**:

> Lovely the woods, waters, meadows, combes, vales,
> All the air things wear that build this world of Wales;
>   Only the inmate does not correspond:
> God, lover of souls, swaying considerate scales,
> Complete thy creature dear O where it fails,
>   Being mighty a master, being a father and fond.

This is essentially the same prayer as he had uttered in **"The Wreck of the Deutschland"** ("Father and fondler of heart thou hast wrung . . . melt him but master him still").

The culmination of **"The Loss of the Eurydice"** is another variation on this theme. Most of the elegy is a pictorial description and narration of the wreck of the boat and the loss of lives. But at the close the poet cannot restrain himself and he bursts out:

> O well wept, mother have lost son;
> Wept, wife; wept, sweetheart would be one:
>   Though grief yield them no good
> Yet shed what tears sad truelove should.
>
> But to Christ lord of thunder
> Crouch: lay knee by earth low under:
>   "Holiest, loveliest, bravest,
> Save my hero, O Hero savest.
>
> And the prayer thou hearst me making
> Have, at the awful overtaking,
>   Heard; have heard and granted,
> Grace that day grace was wanted."

For Robert Bridges, apparently disturbed by the elliptical compression of these lines, the poet wrote an exegesis which makes the prayer essentially the same as that of **"In the Valley of the Elwy"**:

> The words are put into the mouth of a mother, wife, or sweetheart who has lost a son, husband, or lover respectively by the disaster and who prays Christ, whom she addresses "Hero, savest", that is, "Hero that savest", that is, Hero of a Saviour, to save (that is, have saved) her hero, that is, her son, husband, or lover: "Hero of a Saviour" (the line means) "be the saviour of my hero".

There is the same hope expressed in **"The Wreck of the Deutschland"** that grace will have saved the souls which often seem to reject it:

> Yet did the dark side of the bay of thy blessing
> Not vault them, the millions of rounds of thy mercy not
>   reeve even them in?

Such too is the burden of **"The Lantern Oút of Doors"**, written contemporaneously with **"The Loss of the Éurydice"** and **"In the Valley of the Elwy"**.

> Christ minds; Christ's interest, what to avow or amend
>   There, éyes them, heart wánts, care háunts, foot
>   fóllows kind,
> Their ránsom, thèir rescue, ánd first, fást, last friend.

"In the Valley of the Elwy" had spoken of the beauty of Wales; "only the inmate does not correspond". The contrast between nature as symbolic of innocence and man's tendency to sin is the basis of a further poem, **"Spring"**. Into the octet of this sonnet Hopkins poured all his keen sensibility, sketching the natural beauty and freshness of Spring:

> Nothing is so beautiful as spring—
>   When weed, in wheels, shoot long and lovely and lush;
>   Thrush's eggs look little low heavens, and thrush
> Through the echoing timber does so rinse and wring
> The ear, it strikes like lightnings to hear him sing;
>   The glassy peartree leaves and blooms, they brush
>   The descending blue; that blue is all in a rush
> With richness; the racing lambs too have fair their fling.

This becomes reminiscent of an earlier sinless world, of Eden, when natural beauty and moral beauty existed side by side, when all created things, creatures and man, were praising God and giving Him glory:

> What is all this juice and all this joy?
>   A strain of the earth's sweet being in the beginning
> In Eden garden.

Then comes the closing prayer or admonition to win innocent and sinless youth, Christ's choice, before it "sour with sinning"—while it still has moral beauty:

>   Have, get, before it cloy,
>   Before it cloud, Christ, lord, and sour with sinning,
> Innocent mind and Mayday in girl and boy.
>   Most, O maid's child, thy choice and worthy the
>   winning.

It is just because—and this is to be remembered all through these poems—man is free that he can sin; it is just because he is free that he can refuse to use nature sacramentally, can turn his back on the call to the Cross, can refuse to follow Christ. And Hopkins wrote a magnificent poem on the nature of man, **"The Caged Skylark"**.

Constituted by a substantial union of body and soul, man must use his will, which distinguishes him from the rest of creation, to mould himself to perfection, a perfection in which body and soul cooperate according to the nature of their union. He is not soul alone, with the body a mere instrument, as Plato would have it. Man is not man without the body. That body is not a prison which only hampers the soul. Man is not to try, in a false sort of spirituality, to throw off the body, the senses. St. Thomas contended that the soul, being an integral part of the human composition, is constituted in its full natural perfection only by its union with the body. Indeed, he taught that "even after death, when the soul attains its beatitude in the vision of God, 'its desire is not fully set at rest': it longs for reunion with the body as partner in its glory".

Man himself is a hierarchy of powers, each important, yet to be subordinated one to another. Man, since the fall in the Garden of Eden, has had to practise asceticism, "to make sensuality", as St. Ignatius expressed it in the Spiritual Exercises, "obey reason and all inferior parts be more subject to the superior". The life of the senses, however, must not be suppressed or killed; it must be controlled and dedicated.

These are the ideas which Hopkins endeavoured to communicate in **"The Caged Skylark"**, which deals with the nature of man, on the scholastic theory of the substantial union of body and the spirit according to which the body and the senses cannot be rejected but must be disciplined, because "Man's spirit will be flesh-bound when found at best, But uncumbered".

The major part of the poem expresses the difficulties of living in the body, of obtaining the perfect equipoise:

> As a dare-gale skylark scanted in a dull cage
>   Man's mounting spirit in his bone-house, mean
>   house, dwells—
>   That bird beyond the remembering his free fells;
> This is drudgery, day-labouring-out life's age.
>
> Though aloft on turf or perch or poor low stage,
>   Both sing sometimes the sweetest, sweetest spells,
>   Yet both droop deadly sometimes in their cells
> Or wring their barriers in bursts of fear or rage.
>
> Not that the sweet-fowl, song-fowl, needs no rest—
> Why, hear him, hear him, babble and drop down to his
>   nest,
>   But his own nest, wild nest, no prison.

Such lines would seem to consider the flesh as a cage, a prison for the soul, the spirit anxious to find freedom from its bondage. But the final lines make clear that this is true only until the ideal relationship (when the cage is no cage, the prison no prison) is attained:

> Man's spirit will be flesh-bound when found at best,
> But uncumbered: meadow-down is not distressed
>   For a rainbow footing it nor he for his bones risen.

And the dogmas of the Incarnation, the Resurrection, as well as the whole liturgical worship of the Church, have constantly reasserted the sanctity of the body, the holiness of the senses.

"The Windhover: To Christ Our Lord" is the greatest of Hopkins' poems of this period, greatest in the implications of its subject, greatest in its metrical accomplishment. Hopkins himself referred to it as "the best thing I ever wrote". It is indeed "the achieve of, the mastery of the thing".

The octet is an onomatopoeic and emphatic recreation of the flight of the windhover in its magnificent and triumphant career. Instrumental in its music, it moves with the rhythm of flight: it starts with a swirl, soars, whirls again, and then banks with the wind:

> I caught this morning morning's minion, kingdom of
>   daylight's dauphin, dapple-dawn-drawn Falcon,
>   in his riding
>   Of the rolling level underneath him steady air,
>   and striding
> High there, how he rung upon the rein of a wimpling
>   wing
> In his ecstasy! then off, off forth on swing,
>   As a skate's heel sweeps smooth on a bow-bend:
>   the hurl and gliding
>   Rebuffed the big wind. My heart in hiding
> Stirred for a bird,—the achieve of, the mastery of
>   the thing!

From the opening "I caught this morning morning's minion" to "the achieve of, the mastery of the thing" the poet is in an ecstasy of amazement at the mastery of brilliant success of the windhover—a beauty so great that it is difficult to imagine any that has its equal.

But there is a beauty far, far greater. And the sestet is devoted to a revelation of a beauty beyond this beauty, a beauty which is "a billion times told lovelier, more dangerous" than the purely natural and triumphant flight. And whence comes this achievement which is more than achievement, this mastery which is more than mastery?

It is in the act of "buckling" when the windhover swoops down, when its flight is crumpled, when "brute beauty and valour and act, oh, air, pride, plume" in an act of self-sacrifice, or self-destruction, of mystical self-immolation send off a fire far greater than any natural beauty:

> Brute beauty and valour and act,
> oh, air, pride, plume, here
> Buckle! And the fire that breaks from thee then, a billion
> Times told lovelier, more dangerous, O my chevalier!

Nor is this to be wondered at, for this is true even in humble little things—is true of everything: the sheen of common earth shines out when the plough breaks it into furrows; and fire breaks from fire only in the moment of its own destruction:

> No wonder of it: shéer plód makes plough down
>   sillion
> Shine, and blue-bleak embers, ah my dear,
> Fall, gall themselves, and gash gold-vermilion.

Here is Christ upon the Cross and Hopkins the *alter Christus.* Beautiful was Christ's public life, but "a billion times told lovelier" was His self-immolation on the Cross, His sacrifice transmuted by the Fire of Love into something far greater than any mere natural beauty. More beautiful than any natural achievement was Hopkins' own humble and plodding continuance of the ethic of redemption through his own mystical self-destruction, his own humble following of Christ to the very Cross of Calvary. And the beauty of Christ and the beauty of the Jesuit to eyes that see more than this world is the beauty of their dying to live. "Here the faithful waver, the faithless fable and miss." But always

> thou art above, thou Orion of light;
> Thy unchancelling poising palms were weighing the
>   worth,
> Thou martyr-master: in thy sight
> Storm flakes were scroll-leaved flowers, lily showers—
>   sweet heaven was astrew in them.

This is the story of Christ and it is the story of Gerard Manley Hopkins: The Folly of the Cross. (pp. 60-71)

> *John Pick, in his* Gerard Manley Hopkins: Priest and Poet, *Oxford University Press, London, 1942, 169 p.*

F. R. LEAVIS (essay date 1944)

[*An influential English educator and critic, Leavis articulated his views in lectures, in his many critical works, and in* Scrutiny, *a quarterly he cofounded and edited from 1932 to 1953. His critical methodology combines close textual analysis, predominantly moral and social concerns, and emphasis on the development of "the individual sensibility." Although Leavis's advocacy of a cultural elite, the vagueness of his moral assumptions, and his refusal to develop a systematic philosophy have alienated many scholars from his work, he remains an important, if controversial, force in literary criticism. In this excerpt from an essay first published in 1944 to celebrate the centenary of Hopkins's birth, Leavis examines the Victorian and religious context of Hopkins's writings in an attempt to define his place in English literature.*]

That Hopkins has a permanent place among the English poets may now be taken as established beyond challenge: academic scholarship has canonized him, and the love of 'a continuous literary decorum' has forgotten the terms in which it was apt to express itself only a decade ago. It is now timely to ask just what that place is. Perhaps, indeed, formal evaluation may be judged a needless formality, the nature and significance of

Hopkins's work, once it has been fairly looked at, not being very notably obscure. However, the centenary year of his birth seems a proper occasion for attempting a brief explicit summing-up.

A poet born in 1844 was a Victorian: if one finds oneself proffering this chronological truism to-day, when the current acceptance of Hopkins goes with a recognition that something has happened in English poetry since Bridges' taste was formed, it is less likely to be a note of irony, invoking a background contrast for Hopkins, than an insistence, or the preface to it, on the essential respects in which Hopkins was, even in his originality, *of* his time. His school poem, **"A Vision of Mermaids"**, shows him starting very happily in a Keatsian line, a normal young contemporary of Tennyson, Matthew Arnold and Rossetti—in the association of which three names, it will perhaps be granted, the idea of 'Victorian poet' takes on sufficient force and definition to give that 'normal' its point. The elements of Keats in Hopkins is radical and very striking:

> Palate, the hutch of tasty lust,
> Desire not to be rinsed with wine:
> The can must be so sweet, the crust
> So fresh that come in fasts divine!
>
> Nostrils, your careless breath that spend
> Upon the stir and keep of pride,
> What relish shall the censers send
> Along the sanctuary side!
>
> O feel-of-primrose hands, O feet
> That want the yield of plushy sward,
> But you shall walk the golden street
> And you unhouse and house the Lord.

These stanzas come from an 'Early Poem' printed by Bridges immediately before **"The Wreck of the Deutschland"**. A contemporary reader, if we can imagine it published at the time of writing, might very well have judged that this very decided young talent was to be distinguished from among his fellow Victorian poets by his unique possession, in an age pervaded by Keatsian aspirations and influences, of the essential Keatsian strength. Such a Victorian reader might very well have pronounced him, this strength clearly being native and inward, unmistakably a poet born—a poet incomparably more like Keats, the poet's poet (Keats was something like that for the Tennysonian age), than the derivatively Keatsian could make themselves. Actually, the body of the mature work—**"The Wreck of the Deutschland"** onwards—in which Hopkins's distinctive bent and his idiosyncrasy develop themselves, doesn't prompt us with Keats's name so obviously. Yet the same strength, in its developed manifestations, is there.

It is a strength that gives Hopkins notable advantages over Tennyson and Matthew Arnold as a 'nature poet'. This description is Mr Eliot's [see Additional Bibliography], . . . and it is applicable enough for one to accept it as a way of bringing out how much Hopkins belongs to the Victorian tradition. Nature, beauty, transience—with these he is characteristically preoccupied:

> Margaret, are you grieving
> Over Goldengrove unleaving?
> Leaves, like the things of man, you
> With your fresh thought care for, can you?
> Ah! as the heart grows older
> It will come to such sights colder
> By and by, nor spare a sigh
> Though worlds of wanwood leafmeal lie;

And yet you will weep and know why.
Now no matter, child, the name:
Sorrow's springs are the same.
Nor mouth had, no, nor mind, expressed
What heart heard of, ghost guessed:
It is the blight man was born for,
It is Margaret you mourn for.

Here the distinctiveness and the idiosyncrasy might seem hardly to qualify the Victorian normality of the whole. . . . In

What heart heard of, ghost guessed,

where the heart, wholly taken up in the hearing, becomes it, as the 'ghost' becomes the guessing, we have, of course, an example of a kind of poetic action or enactment that Hopkins developed into a staple habit of his art. As we have it, this use of assonantal progression, here, its relation to the sensibility and technique of

Palate, the hutch of tasty lust

is plain. So too is the affinity between this last-quoted line and the 'bend with apples the moss'd cottage trees' in which the robust vitality of Keats's sensuousness shows itself in so un-Tennysonian, and so essentially poetic, a strength of expressive texture.

Hopkins was born—and died—in the age of Tennyson. This fact has an obvious bearing on the deliberateness with which Hopkins, starting with that peculiar genius, set himself to develop and exploit the modes and qualities of expression illustrated—the distinctive expressive resources of the English language ('English must be kept up'). The age in poetry *was* Tennyson's; and an age for which the ambition 'to bring English as near the Italian as possible' seems a natural and essentially poetic one, is an age in which the genius conscious enough to form a contrary ambition is likely to be very conscious and very contrary. That he was consciously bent on bringing back into poetry the life and strength of the living, the spoken, language is explicit—the confirmation was pleasant to have, though hardly necessary—in the **Letters** [see excerpt dated August 14, 1879]: 'it seems to me that the poetical language of the age shd. be the current language heightened, to any degree heightened and unlike it, but not (I mean normally: passing freaks and graces are another thing) an obsolete one'. His praise of Dryden . . . , held by Bridges to be no poet, is well-known: 'His style and rhythms lay the strongest stress of all our literature on the naked thew and sinew of the English language'. This preoccupation, pursued by a Victorian poet intensely given to technical experiment, would go far to explain the triumphs of invention, the extravagance and the oddities of Hopkins's verse.

But this is not the whole story. His bent for technical experiment can be seen to have been inseparable from a special kind of interest in pattern—his own term was 'inscape'. Here we have a head of consideration that calls for some inquiry, though it can be left for the moment with this parenthetic recognition, to be taken up again in due course.

Meanwhile, demanding immediate notice there is a head the postponement of which till now may have surprised the reader. It is impossible to discuss for long the distinctive qualities of Hopkins's poetry without coming to his religion. In the matter of religion, of course, he differs notably from both Tennyson and Matthew Arnold, and the relevance of the differences to the business of the literary critic is best broached by noting

that they lead up to the complete and staring antithesis confronting us when we place Hopkins by Rossetti. (pp. 44-7)

[Religion] in Hopkins's poetry is something completely other than the religion of Beauty. Rossetti's shamelessly cheap evocation of a romantic and bogus Platonism—an evocation in which 'significance' is vagueness, and profundity an uninhibited proffer of large drafts on a merely nominal account ('Life', 'love', 'death', 'terror', 'mystery', 'Beauty'—it is a bankrupt's lavishness)—exemplifies in a gross form the consequences of that separation of feeling ('soul'—the source of 'genuine poetry') from thinking which the Victorian tradition, in its 'poetical' use of language, carries with it. (pp. 47-8)

Hopkins is the devotional poet of a dogmatic Christianity. For the literary critic there are consequent difficulties and delicacies. But there is something that can be seen, and said, at once: Hopkins's religious interests are bound up with the presence in his poetry of a vigour of mind that puts him in another poetic world from the other Victorians. It is a vitality of thought, a vigour of the thinking intelligence, that is at the same time a vitality of concreteness. The relation between this kind of poetic life and his religion manifests itself plainly in his addiction to Duns Scotus, whom, rather than St Thomas, traditionally indicated for a Jesuit, he significantly embraced as his own philosopher. Of the philosophy of Duns Scotus it must suffice to say here that it lays a peculiar stress on the particular and actual, in its full concreteness and individuality, as the focus of the real, and that its presence is felt whenever Hopkins uses the word 'self' (or some derivative verb) in his characteristic way. **"Binsey Poplars"** provides an instance where the significance for the literary critic is obvious. (p. 48)

All the beauties Hopkins renders in his poetry are 'sweet especial scenes', 'selves' in the poignant significance their particularity has for him. Time 'unselves' them;

Nor can you long be, what you now are, called fair,
Do what you may do, what, do what you may,
And wisdom is early to despair.

The Victorian-romantic addicts of beauty and transience cherish the pang as a kind of religiose-poetic sanction for defeatism in the face of an alien actual world—a defeatism offering itself as a spiritual superiority. Hopkins embraces transience as a necessary condition of any grasp of the real. The concern for such a grasp is there in the concrete qualities that give his poetry its vitality—which, we have seen, involves an energy of intelligence.

These qualities the literary critic notes and appraises, whether or not he knows any more about Duns Scotus than he can gather from the poetry. There is plainly a context of theological religion, and the devotional interest has plainly the kind of relation to the poetic qualities that has just been discussed. But the activities that go on within this context, even if they make Hopkins unlike Tennyson, Browning, Matthew Arnold, Rossetti, and Swinburne, don't do so by making him in any radical way like T. S. Eliot. It is a framework of the given, conditioning the system of tensions established within it, and these are those of a devotional poet. We can hardly imagine Hopkins entertaining, even in a remotely theoretical way, the kind of preoccupation conveyed by Eliot when he says:

. . . I cannot see that poetry can ever be separated from something which I should call belief, and to which I cannot see any reason for refusing the name of belief, unless we are to shuffle names altogether. It should hardly be needful to say that it will not inevitably be orthodox Christian belief, although that possibility can be entertained, since Christianity will probably continue to modify itself, as in the past, into something that can be believed in (I do not mean *conscious* modifications like modernism, etc., which always have the opposite effect). The majority of people live below the level of belief or doubt. It takes application and a kind of genius to believe anything, and to believe *anything* (I do *not* mean merely to believe in some "religion") will probably become more and more difficult as time goes on.

The stress of the 'terrible sonnets' hasn't this kind of context. And Hopkins's habit is utterly remote from Eliot's extreme discipline of continence in respect of affirmation—the discipline involving that constructive avoidance of the conceptual currency which has its exposition in "Burnt Norton". For Hopkins the truths are *there,* simply and irresistibly demanding allegiance; though it is no simple matter to make his allegiance real and complete (this seems at any rate a fair way of suggesting the difference).

His preoccupation with this frame is of a kind that leaves him in a certain obvious sense simple-minded:

> Here he knelt then in regimental red.
> Forth Christ from cupboard fetched, how fain I of feet
>   To his youngster take his treat!
> Low-latched in leaf-light housel his too huge godhead.

It is the simplicity of the single-minded and pure in heart. Its manifestations can be very disconcerting, and we are not surprised to learn that as a preacher he was apt, in his innocent unconsciousness, to put intolerable strains on the gravity of his congregation. It appears in the rime of the stanza immediately preceding that just quoted (it will be necessary, because of the run-over of the sense, to quote the two preceding):

> A bugler boy from barrack (it is over the hill
> There)—boy bugler, born, he tells me, of Irish
>   Mother to an English sire (he
> Shares their best gifts surely, fall how things will),
>
> This very very day came down to us after a boon he on
> My late being there begged of me, overflowing
>   Boon in my bestowing,
> Came, I say, this day to it—to a First Communion.

It takes a Bridges to find all, or most, of Hopkins's riming audacities unjustifiable; they are often triumphant successes in that, once the poem has been taken, they become inevitable, and, unlike Browning's ingenuities, cease to call attention to themselves (that in the first of these two stanzas is a passable ear-rime). Nevertheless there are a fair number of the order of *boon he on-communion,* and it has to be conceded more generally that the naïveté illustrated has some part in the elaborations of his technique.

To say this, of course, is not to endorse [the] view that Hopkins is difficult because of his difficult way of saying simple things. It is relevant, but hardly necessary, to remark that for Hopkins his use of words is not a matter of *saying* things with them; he is preoccupied with what seems to him the poetic use of them, and that is a matter of making them do and be. Even a poet describable as 'simple-minded' may justify some complexities of 'doing' and 'being'. And if we predicate simplicity of Hopkins, it must be with the recognition that he has at the same time a very subtle mind.

The subtlety is apparent in the tropes, conceits and metaphorical symbolism that gives his poetry qualities suggesting the seventeenth century rather than the nineteenth. He can be metaphysical in the full sense; as, for instance, he is, triumphantly, in the first part of **"The Wreck of the Deutschland"**, notably in stanzas 4 to 8. The radically metaphorical habit of mind and sensibility that, along with concrete strength from which it is inseparable, makes his 'nature poetry' so different from Tennyson's and Matthew Arnold's, relates him to Herbert rather than to Eliot—it goes with the 'frame' spoken of above. It is a habit of seeing things as charged with significance; 'significance' here being, not a romantic vagueness, but a matter of explicit and ordered conceptions regarding the relations between God, man and nature. It is an inveterate habit of his mind and being, finding its intellectual formulation in Duns Scotus.

Of course, to be seventeenth-century in the time of Tennyson is a different matter from being it in the time of Herbert, Hopkins's unlikeness to whom involves a great deal more than the obvious difference of temperament. He is still more unlike Crashaw: his 'metaphysical' audacity is the expression of a refined and disciplined spirit, and there is no temperamental reason why it shouldn't have been accompanied by something corresponding to Herbert's fine and poised *social* bearing. But behind Hopkins there is no Ben Jonson, and he has for contemporaries no constellation of courtly poets uniting the 'metaphysical' with the urbane. His distinctiveness develops itself even in his prose, which has a dignified oddity such as one might have taken for affectation if it hadn't been so obviously innocent and unconscious.

Of the development of 'distinctiveness' in verse he himself says, in a passage that gives us the word:

> But as air, melody, is what strikes me most of all in music and design in painting, so design, pattern, or what I am in the habit of calling *inscape* is what I above all aim at in poetry. Now it is the virtue of design, pattern, or inscape to be distinctive, and it is the vice of distinctiveness to become queer. This vice I cannot have escaped [see excerpt dated February 1879].

Isolation, he might have added, would favour the vice. But the peculiar development of the interest in pattern or 'inscape' has, it may be suggested, a significance not yet touched on. We can't help relating it to a certain restriction in the nourishing interests behind Hopkins's poetry. It is as if his intensity, for lack of adequately answering substance, expressed itself in a kind of hypertrophy of technique, and in an excessive imputation of significance to formal pattern.

It may be replied that his concern for pattern in verse is paralleled by a concern for pattern (or 'inscape' we had better say, since the word associates the idea of 'pattern' with Hopkins's distinctive stress on the individuality or 'self' of the object contemplated) in the sights—a tree, a waterfall, a disposition of clouds—that he renders from nature; renders in drawings as well as in verse and prose. But his interest in nature—to call attention to that is to make the same point again. In assenting, half-protestingly, to Mr Eliot's description of him as a 'nature poet' one is virtually recognizing that a significant limitation reveals itself when a poet of so remarkable a spiritual intensity, so intense a preoccupation with essential human problems, gives 'nature'—the 'nature' of the 'nature poets'—so large a place in his poetry. What is revealed as limited, it will be said, is Hopkins's power to transcend the poetic climate of his age: in spite of the force of his originality he is a Victorian poet. This seems an unanswerable point. But even here, in respect of his limitation, his distinctiveness comes out: the limitation goes with the peculiar limitation of experience attendant upon his early world-renouncing self-dedication. . . . (pp. 49-53)

The force of this last point is manifest in the ardent naïveté with which he idealizes his buglers, sailors, schoolboys and his England:

> England, whose honour O all my heart woos, wife
> To my creating thought . . .

Meeting him in 1882, his old schoolmaster, Dixon, says: 'In so far as I can remember you are very like the boy of Highgate'. But this unworldliness is of a different order from the normal other-worldliness of Victorian poetry. Addressing Hopkins, Matthew Arnold might, without the radical confusion symbolized in his Scholar-Gypsy, have said:

> For early didst thou leave the world, with powers
> Fresh, undiverted to the world without,
>   Firm to their mark, not spent on other things;
> Free from the sick fatigue, the languid doubt . . .

The 'firmness to the mark' is really there in Hopkins's poetry; the 'mark' is not a mere postulated something that, we are to grant, confers a spiritual superiority upon the eternal week-ender who, 'fluctuating idly without term or scope' among the attractions of the countryside, parallels in his indolent poetical way the strenuous aimlessness of the world where things are done. To Hopkins it might have been said with some point:

> Thou hadst *one* aim, *one* business, *one* desire.

Yet this unworldliness, different though it is from Victorian poetical other-worldliness, does unmistakably carry with it the limitation of experience. And in his bent for 'nature' there is after all in Hopkins something of the poetical Victorian. It is a bent away from urban civilization, in the midst of which he spends his life, and which, very naturally, he regards with repulsion:

> Is Generations have trod, have trod, have trod;
>   And all is seared with trade; bleared, smeared with
>   toil;
>   And wears man's smudge and shares man's smell:
>   the soil
> bare now, nor can foot feel, being shod.

> And for all this, nature is never spent;
>   There lives the dearest freshness deep down
>   things; . . .

And in **"The Sea and the Skylark"** he says:

> How these two shame this shallow and frail town!
>   How ring right out our sordid turbid time,
> Being pure! We, life's pride and cared-for crown,

> Have lost that cheer and charm of earth's past prime:
>   Our make and making break, are breaking, down
>   To man's last dust, drain fast towards man's first
>   slime.

Towards these aspects of human life his attitude—he is very much preoccupied with them—is plain. But they have little more actual presence in his poetry than 'this strange disease of modern life' has in Arnold's.

To come back now to his isolation—we have not yet taken full account of it. It is not merely a matter of his having had no support or countenance in accepted tradition, contemporary practice, and the climate of taste and ideas: he was isolated in a way peculiarly calculated to promote starvation of impulse, the overdeveloped and ingrown idiosyncrasy, and the sterile deadlock, lapsing into stagnation. As a convert he had with him a tide of the élite (he could feel); as a Catholic and a Jesuit he had his communities, the immediate and the wider. But from this all-important religious context he got no social endorsement as a poet: the episode of **"The Wreck of the Deutschland"**—'they dared not print it'—is all there is to tell, and it says everything; it came at the beginning and it was final. Robert Bridges, his life-long friend and correspondent, confidently and consistently discouraged him with 'water of the lower Isis': 'your criticism is . . . only a protest memorializing me against my whole policy and proceedings'. As against this we can point, for the last seven years of Hopkins's life, to the enthusiasm of Canon Dixon, a good and generous man, but hardly transmutable by Hopkins's kind of need (or Hopkins's kind of humility) into an impressive critical endorsement or an adequate substitute for a non-existent public.

To these conditions the reaction of so tense and disciplined an ascetic is the reverse of Blake's: he doesn't become careless, but—'Then again I have of myself made verse so laborious' [see excerpt dated February 15, 1879]. . . . With the laboriousness goes the anguish of sterility. . . . (pp. 53-6)

It seems reasonable to suppose that if he had had the encouragement he lacked he would have devoted to poetry a good deal of the energy that (for the last years of his life a painfully conscientious Professor of Greek) he distributed, in a strenuous dissipation that undoubtedly had something to do with his sense of being time's eunuch and never producing, between the study of music, musical composition, drawing, and such task-work as writing a 'popular account of Light and Ether'. For he was certainly a born writer. (pp. 56-7)

Actually, of course, Hopkins did 'produce': there is a substantial body of verse, a surprising preponderance of which—surprising, when we consider his situation and the difficulties in the way of success—deserves currency among the classics of the language. His supreme triumphs, unquestionably classical achievements, are the last sonnets—the 'terrible sonnets' together with **"Thou Art Indeed Just, Lord"** . . . and that inscribed **"To R. B."**. . . . These, in their achieved 'smoother style', triumphantly justify the oddest extravagances of his experimenting. Technique here is the completely unobtrusive and marvellously economical and efficient servant of the inner need, the pressure to be defined and conveyed. At the other extreme are such things as **"Tom's Garland"** and **"Harry Ploughman"**, where, in the absence of controlling pressure from within, the elaborations and ingenuities of 'inscape' and of expressive licence result in tangles of knots and strains that no amount of reading can reduce to satisfactory rhythm or justifiable complexity. In between come the indubitable successes of developed 'inscape': **"The Wreck of the Deutschland"** (which seems to me a great poem—at least for the first two-thirds of it), **"The Windhover"**, and, at a lower level, **"The Leaden Echo and the Golden Echo"**. **"Henry Purcell"** calls for mention as a curious special case. There can be few readers who have not found it strangely expressive, and few who could have elucidated it without extraneous help. It is not independent of the explanatory note by Hopkins that Bridges prints; yet when one approaches it with the note fresh in mind the intended meaning seems to be sufficiently *in* the poem to allay, at any rate, the dissatisfaction caused by baffled understanding. (p. 57)

F. R. Leavis, ''Gerard Manley Hopkins,'' *in his* The Common Pursuit, *Penguin Books, 1963, pp. 44-58.*

W. A. M. PETERS, S.J. (essay date 1948)

[*Peters's book-length critical study of Hopkins is highly regarded, particularly for his detailed discussion of inscape and its effect in the poems. In the excerpt below, Peters demonstrates the meaning and importance Hopkins ascribed to inscape and instress.*]

In a letter to Bridges dated 15 February 1879 Hopkins wrote: '. . . But as air, melody, is what strikes me most of all in music and design in painting, so design, pattern or what I am in the habit of calling ''inscape'' is what I above all aim at in poetry' [see excerpt above]. And in a letter to Patmore, written some seven years later, he criticizes the poetic talent of Sir Samuel Ferguson as follows: '. . . he was a poet as the Irish are—to judge by the little of his I have seen—full of feeling, high thoughts, flow of verse, point, often fine imagery and other virtues, but the essential and only lasting thing left out—what I call *inscape* . . .'. (p. 1)

From these two quotations it is already abundantly clear, how important it must be for the understanding of Hopkins's poetry to know what he meant by inscape and what inscape meant to him as a poet. Curiously enough, critics have almost all of them refrained from examining this notion. There is no excuse for such negligence, as Hopkins confessed inscape to be the very aim of his poetry. Those critics who have paid attention to inscape, which in another place Hopkins calls 'the very soul of art', have, in my opinion, not grasped its meaning, nor have they realized its far-reaching implications: their treatment of inscape has been too cursory and superficial and even incorrect. Nearly all of them have taken 'inscape' for little more than one of the many words which Hopkins coined because the English language did not contain any one word representing this objective fact or thing, or because he was dissatisfied with the existing word for reasons of euphony. They have failed to see that this word represented something that was not observed by other men, therefore caused a very personal experience, and so was to stand for something not experienced by others, for which consequently there existed no word, because the need for it was never felt. For 'inscape' is the unified complex of those sensible qualities of the object of perception that strike us as inseparably belonging to and most typical of it, so that through the knowledge of this unified complex of sense-data we may gain an insight into the individual essence of the object. We are ever inclined to compare and contrast objects and to put before us what is universal in them. Our minds turn unconsciously as it were and instinctively to what this object has in common with others: it needs special concentration of our faculties to bring before the mind an object's distinctiveness. Now Hopkins habitually looked at objects with the fixed determination to catch what was individually distinctive in them in order thus to arrive at some insight into their essence as individuals. To express this set of individuating characteristics in a suitable term he coined the word 'inscape'.

Hopkins has nowhere defined 'inscape'. I could only draw up the definition given above after a detailed study of the many places in which the word occurs. I shall now attempt to show that the above definition is right. The best starting point to arrive at a correct definition is the analogy on which the word 'inscape' has been formed. The suffix 'scape' in 'landscape' and 'seascape' posits the presence of a unifying principle which enables us to consider part of the countryside or sea as a unit and as an individual, but so that this part is perceived to carry the typical properties of the actually undivided whole. By placing special emphasis on this second aspect of 'scape': 'the part is perceived to carry the typical properties of the actually undivided whole', 'scape' comes to stand for that being which is an exact copy or reflection of the individual whole on which it is dependent for its existence. In this meaning 'scape' is frequently used by Hopkins in his notes on the *Spiritual Exercises* of St. Ignatius Loyola as the translation of the *species* of the scholastic theory of knowledge: the species being the reflection made by a sensible object in our senses and on our mind, which actualizes our power to know the object with a sensitive or intellectual knowledge repectively, and in which the object is known. Bearing in mind this aspect of the meaning of scape I infer that '*in*-scape' is the outward reflection of the *inner* nature of a thing, or a sensible copy or representation of its individual essence; and thus I define it as the unified complex of those sensible qualities of an object that strike us as inseparably belonging to and most typical of that object, so that through the knowledge of this unified complex of sense-data we may gain an insight into the individual essence of the object. The correctness of this definition is confirmed by the relation between inscape and beauty as expressed by Hopkins in the following quotation: 'But if it (*sc.* verse) has a meaning and is meant to be heard for its own sake it will be poetry if you take poetry to be a kind of composition and not the virtue or excellence of that kind, as eloquence is the virtue of oratory and not oratory only and *beauty the virtue of inscape and not inscape only*' (italics mine). For beauty, as Hopkins sees it, lies in the 'relation between the parts to each other and of the parts to the whole', or, as he expresses himself more carefully, in the 'apprehension of the presence in one of more than one thing' ('On the signs of health and decay in the arts' (unpublished)). Hence for Hopkins beauty presupposes unity in the object, just as it presupposes inscape, which is clear from the above quotation. The reason why he related beauty to inscape must consequently be that in inscape there is inherent unity, a unity, that is, proceeding from the nature of the object itself.

It is now not hard to understand why Hopkins compared inscape to design and pattern, yet could not be satisfied with either of them. These terms do, indeed, denote a principle which creates unity and order; but the unity and order brought about by them are imposed from without and they are in no way the necessary outward manifestation of an intrinsic principle of unity, while it is precisely the outward manifestation of this intrinsic principle of unity which is signified by inscape. Thus there may be pattern and design while no inscape can be discovered; this is made clear by the following quotation in which 'scaping' is synonymous with pattern:

> I saw also a good engraving of his *Vintage Festival*, which impressed the thought one would gather also from Rembrandt. . . . of a master of scaping rather than of inscape. For vigorous rhetorical but realistic and unaffected scaping holds everything but no arch-inscape is thought of.

A photograph of Robert Bridges, Hopkins's schoolmate and correspondent.

But from this quotation it is equally clear that inscape *can* be present in a picture. Provided that in the poet's artistic vision the object of art shows forth an intrinsic unity that extends further than a mere harmonious ordering of parts as designated by pattern, the poet will grasp its inscape. Hence not only an organic being, as a flower, tree or animal, each a *unum per se*, will present itself to Hopkins's vision as an individual, but also objects of art, and even nature-scenes, can in his perception display a marked individuality. It is well to bear this point in mind. For if individuality—and similarly inscape—is taken in its strict philosophical sense only, one will be frequently faced by inconsistencies in Hopkins's use of this word. (pp. 1-3)

Hopkins was sincere when he wrote these pathetic lines: 'The ashtree growing in the corner of the garden was felled. It was lopped first: I heard the sound and looking out and seeing it maimed there came at that moment a great pang and I wished to die and not to see the inscapes of the world destroyed any more'. In his short poem on Binsey Poplars he is grieved for the same reason: the poplars were felled and so the rural scene was 'unselved', its inscape was destroyed.

Such a profound admiration and love of the inscapes of the world is most striking and requires a closer study. Why did Hopkins consider the inscapes so precious that their destruction pained him so severely and acutely? When man contemplates an object, he usually does it to grasp the beauty of the thing and to rejoice in its perception; in the case of Hopkins this is not altogether true. Inscape is not primarily valuable because it is so closely related to beauty; for in the quotations given Hopkins entirely prescinds from beauty. Inscape is appreciated for its own sake, for a value entirely its own. It was his spiritual outlook on this world that made inscape so precious to Hopkins; the inscape of an object was, so to speak, more 'word of God', reminded him more of the Creator, than a superficial impression could have done.

How intense his awareness was of the actual presence of God in each individual thing and how he realized that each individual thing in its own peculiar way brought him news about the Creator appears from a careful reading of his writings. God's utterance of Himself outside Himself is this world, he writes, so that then this world is 'word, expression, news of God'.

> I do not think I have ever seen anything more beautiful than the bluebell I have been looking at. I know the beauty of our Lord by it. As we drove home the stars came out thick: I leant back to look at them and my heart opening more than usual praised our Lord to and in whom all that beauty comes home. . . .

> This busy working of nature wholly independent of the earth and seeming to go on in a strain of time not reckoned by our reckoning of days and years but simpler and as if correcting the preoccupation of the world by being preoccupied with and appealing to and dated to the day of judgment was like a new witness to God and filled me with delightful fear.

It is a theme which continually recurs in his poetry:

> I kiss my hand
> To the stars, lovely-asunder
> Starlight, wafting him out of it; . . .

I walk, I lift up, I lift up heart, eyes,
> Down all that glory in the heavens to glean our
> Saviour; . . .

The world is charged with the grandeur of God.
> It will flame out, like shining from shook foil;

Always and everywhere he is reminded of

> him that present and past,
> Heaven and earth are word of, worded by.

To this poet all things 'are charged with love, are charged with God and if we know how to touch them give off sparks and take fire, yield drops and flow, ring and tell of him'. But nowhere has he more emphatically spoken of the actual presence of God in things than in the following quotation:

> Neither do I deny that God is so deeply present to everything ('Tu autem, O bone omnipotens, eras superior summo meo et interior intimo meo') that it would be impossible for him but for his infinity not to be identified with them or, from the other side, impossible but for his infinity so to be present to them. This is oddly expressed, I see; I mean/a being so intimately present as God is to other things would be identified with them were it not for God's infinity or were it not for God's infinity he could not be so intimately present to things.

Quotations such as these fully justify our conclusion that Hopkins appreciated inscape so highly because in perceiving inscape he knew the individual well; and the better he knew the individual, the more sparks it threw off, to use his own words, 'sparks that rang of God'.... This consciousness of the presence of God in things markedly influenced his loving admiration of the inscapes of the world, for as his attention concentrated more and more intensely on the individual and on the individual as 'charged with love, charged with God', he came more and more to look upon the object as worthy of a *personal* love. There is evidence in his writings that Hopkins was acutely aware of the fact that, in spite of profound generic and specific differences, man and beast and inanimate nature were all alike 'selves', 'supposits', so that *from this angle of vision* there was between man and the rest of creation a difference of degree, not one of kind. In man the self was joined to a free nature, while in all other things the self was not so raised. Thus he writes: 'A person is defined a rational (that is/ intellectual) supposit, the supposit of a rational nature. A supposit is a self...'. 'Now if self begins to manifest its freedom with the rise from an irrational to a rational nature, it is...'. This most peculiar attitude towards the self—whether joined to a rational or to an irrational nature—immediately proceeding from his habitual search for the inscape of things, drove Hopkins instinctively to their *impersonation*, a personifying, that is, of the irrational selves on the level of sensitive perception, unconscious therefore, in so far as Hopkins neither reflected upon it nor intellectually accounted for it. I wish to stress the words 'on the level of sensitive perception'; this restriction implies that the impersonation did not take place by an explicit act of comparison by and in which the intellect presented the irrational object as a person. For this reason I have chosen the term 'impersonation', and I preserve the term 'personification' for that figure of speech which cannot exist without a conscious act of intellectual reasoning. As soon as the poet reflects on his perception and becomes thereby conscious of his impersonation, he at once opens the way to complete personfication. Personification is in Hopkins frequent enough:

> Some find me a sword; some
> The flange and the rail; flame,
> Fang, or flood' goes *Death* on drum....

> *Earth*, sweet *Earth*, sweet *landscape*...

> ... Natural heart's ivy, *Patience* masks,
> Our ruins of wrecked past purpose....

> *Fury* had shrieked 'No lingering!
> Let me be fell: force I must be brief'....

When will you ever, *Peace*, wild wooddove, shy wings shut,
Your round me roaming end, and under be my boughs?...

Not, I'll not, carrion comfort, *Despair*, not feast on thee....

I caught this morning morning's minon, kingdom of daylight's dauphin, dapple-dawn-drawn....

> *Hope* had grown grey hairs,
> *Hope* had mourning on,
> Trenched with tears, carved with cares,
> *Hope* was twelve hours gone....

> This, by *Despair*, bred Hangdog dull; by *Rage*, Manwolf, worse;...

These are some instances of complete personification and in most of them the use of the capital is ample proof of it. A proof so tangible as this in the case of impersonation cannot

of course be given, because the use of capitals would argue that Hopkins had reflected on his impersonations and so we should be back again to personification. But there are in his poetry indications enough that place the fact of impersonation beyond any reasonable doubt. Among these indications I mention in the first place the extremely frequent absence of the article. This absence has the effect of making the common noun into a kind of proper name. 'The omission of *the* is I think an extension of the way in which we say "Father", "government", etc.', so Hopkins remarked himself. But the use of such proper names surely points to the fact that in inescaping an irrational being its outstanding individuality impressed him so much that he unreflectingly looked upon this being as a person. Instances abound:

> ... For *earth* her being has unbound...

> ... while *moon* shall wear and wend...

> Bright *sun* lanced fire in the heavenly bay....

> Delightfully the bright wind... beats *earth* bare...

> *Earth* hears no hurtle then from fiercest fray....

Very striking is the very frequent absence of the article before parts of the body:

> ... *mind* has mountains...

> Nor *mouth* had, no nor *mind*, expressed
> What *heart* heard of, *ghost* guessed....

> Father and fondler of *heart* thou hast wrung...

> ... nor can *foot* feel, being shod....

> To what serves mortal beauty!—dangerous; does set
> dancing *blood*—

I have only given a selection of examples; a cursory reading of the poems will impress any reader with the frequency of the absence of the article. This scant use of the article cannot be explained or accounted for by the fact that the article 'took up room in the lines which [Hopkins] could not afford them'. Bridges in his preface to the notes to Hopkins's poetry has thus tried to account, not for the omission of the article explicitly, but for the omission of what he calls 'purely constructional syllables'. This explanation is most unconvincing; for while other poets had to fit their matter in closely defined 'room', the expanse of which was limited by the metre based on a certain fixed number of syllables to the line, Hopkins was free—though free within bounds, which he could not transgress with impunity—to increase or decrease the number of syllables; it was the elasticity of sprung rhythm. In maintaining that Hopkiins was free in fixing the length of the line I repudiate the false conclusion that he could therefore squeeze as many syllables into any one line as he liked, provided he took care not to exceed the fixed number of stressed syllables; even sprung rhythm has its rules and even strict rules, as he told Bridges more than once. 'Lack of room', however, yields no explanation of the many omissions in a poet like Hopkins, who even lengthened his lines by 'outrides', which are purely extrametrical syllables. Lack of room should be the last resource in our attempts to account for the omission of articles, conjunctions, pronouns, &c.

The omission of the article is not the only indication pointing to Hopkins's practice of impersonation; strongly in favour of it is his habit of addressing the objects he contemplates. For we do not ordinarily address inanimate objects unless we feel that there is present some ground for considering them as in sympathy with us and capable of responding to our sympathy towards them. Though by itself this practice does not strictly prove impersonation to the exclusion of personification proper, the fact that Hopkins does not use the capital, in my opinion makes impersonation the more likely explanation. It serves no purpose to give a complete list of all the lines in which Hopkins addresses the objects of his contemplation: some more striking instances may be given:

> My aspens dear, whose airy cages quelled. . . .

> . . . graceless growth, thou hast confounded
> Rural rural keeping . . .

> The heart's eye grieves
> Discovering you, dark tramplers, tyrant years. . . .

> Brute beauty and valour and act, oh, air, pride, plume,
> here Buckle! . . .

> My heart, but you were dovewinged, I can tell,
> Carrier-witted, I am bold to boast . . .

> Heart, you round me right
> With: Our evening is over us . . .

But in the examples given so far it is not only the omission of the article or the form of address that points to impersonation; through his keen awareness of the individuality of the objects of contemplation Hopkins was naturally led to attribute to them qualities which by right only belong to persons. Thus to repeat some quotations: 'earth her being has unbound', 'what heart heard', 'does set dancing blood', 'discovering you, dark tramplers, tyrant years'. Elsewhere Hopkins speaks of the 'behaviour' of clouds and again impersonation of the air and breakers and snowflakes is implied in the following lines:

> She to the black-about air, to the breaker, the thickly
> Falling flakes, to the throng that catches and quails
> Was calling 'O Christ, Christ, come quickly'

If we study the quotations more closely we find that frequently the object is seen in action: 'wind beats earth bare', 'bright sun lanced fire', the aspens 'quelled or quenched . . . the leaping sun', 'thrush . . . does so rinse and wring the ear', tempest 'carries the grain', &c. If Hopkins saw things as 'charged with love, charged with God', he saw them thereby also as charged with activity. His poetry teems with examples: he speaks of 'wild air', 'live air', a bird's 'wild nest', 'wild starlight', &c. Nature was to him 'a Heraclitean Fire'.

> The glassy peartree leaves and blooms, they brush
> The descending blue; that blue is all in a rush
> With richness; . . .

'The heart rears wings bold and bolder' and, to Hopkins's keen perception as a beholder 'hurls earth for him off under his feet'.

In the **"Deutschland"** there occur these lines:

> [they] fell to the deck
> (Crushed them)

It might sound strange that the deck 'crushed' the victims of the waves as if it were falling on top of them with its 'crushing' weight and not the other way about. To Hopkins the deck displayed an activity and actively took part in the ruin of the crew and the passengers as much as the storm-winds and the waves and the falling snow. Instances of this kind, not too obvious and easily overlooked in the reading, are by no means rare. In his poem **"God's Grandeur"** Hopkins wrote: 'There

lives the dearest freshness deep down things', where *lives* should receive its due emphasis; for once the inscape had been caught, the object began to be active and to live; each mortal thing 'Deals out that being indoors each one dwells'. This constant attribution of activity and life as a rule found its origin in Hopkins's impersonation of the object; this is the explanation which he himself has given to it in an essay written in his undergraduate days, entitled: **"On the Connexion between Mythology and Philosophy"**. . . . The following paragraph is relevant here:

> Those things which like the common chattels of the house are in the control of man entirely and offer no resistance except weight, become generalized, that is cease to have individuality or personality, but all things which by their freedom from man's control, their irregular and unaccountable sequence, and their influence on man himself most of all, look like persons and seem to have will of their own, these receive only personal names.

Though this paragraph was written when Hopkins was still at Oxford, it already shows his peculiar attitude towards the things of nature, which he developed as time went on. We need add nothing to it; only be it noticed how again Hopkins seems to identify individuality and personality.

I have mentioned only some of the more obvious indications of impersonation in Hopkins's poetry. Impersonation was the natural result of his having inscaped an object, of his perceiving the object as charged with God. Because of this impersonation he was grieved to see the inscapes of the world destroyed and because of it he regretted that the inscapes 'went unnoticed'.

Once Hopkins had inscaped an object and unreflectingly personified it, there was created the possibility of communication between the poet and the object as between two persons. The object is no longer passive, but is perceived to act independently of the poet. Hence the poet, who now unreflectingly looks upon the object as a person, will ascribe to it properties only applicable to man: examples of this we have seen. But inversely this object, this quasi-person, will impress the stamp of its own individuality, of its own 'self', on the poet. The impression thus made by inscape upon the poet, not by means of any poetic activity on the part of the poet but in virtue of its own individual essence, is interpreted by him in terms of human *affects*. But before further entering into this important but not easy question I must first turn to another coinage of Hopkins's, intimately bound up with inscape and as fundamental to a right understanding of the poet; we have arrived at the notion of *instress*.

As in the case of inscape, Hopkins has nowhere defined 'instress', although it is of no rare occurrence. The starting point in trying to get at its precise meaning will be the use of the noun 'stress', which in Hopkins's philosophical writings stands for the perfection of being, proper to a thing. He identifies it with the Greek [word] . . . , in scholastic terminology rendered by *actus*, which is the principle of actuality in a thing. The preference of 'stress' to 'act', the normal word in scholastic terminology, most likely finds its reason in the greater expressiveness of the Saxon word, 'stress' well marking the force which keeps a thing in existence and its strain after continued existence. The noun 'instress' adds little to this meaning of stress except in so far as the prefix emphasizes that this force is intrinsic to the thing. A good instance of its use is found in his notes on the *Spiritual Exercises* of St. Ignatius, which have been partly edited by House; the following quotation occurs among the unpublished notes: '. . . as in man all that energy or instress with which the soul animates and otherwise acts in the body is by death thrown back upon the soul itself; so . . .' The verb 'to instress' is oftener found; the following quotations all bear out the fundamental meaning of 'to come to stress', 'to actualize':

> And as a mere possibility, passive power, is not power proper and has no activity it cannot of itself come to stress, cannot instress itself. . . .

> . . . for the constant repetition, the continuity, of the bad thought is that actualising of it, that instressing of it. . . .

> This access is either of grace, which is 'super-nature', to nature or of more grace to grace already given, and it takes the form of instress-ing the affective will, of affecting the will to-wards the good which he proposes. . . .

> It is to be remarked that *choice* in the sense of taking of one and leaving of another real al-ternative is not what freedom of pitch really and strictly lies in. It is choice as when in En-glish we say 'because I choose', which means no more than . . . I instress my will to so-and-so.

In this sense the verb occurs twice in his poetry:

> What the heart is! which . . .
> To its own fine function, wild and self-instressed,
> Falls light as ten years long taught how to and why.

This example is clear enough, which, perhaps, cannot be said of the second, occurring in the **"Deutschland"**:

> Since tho' he is under the world's splendour and wonder,
>   His mystery must be instressed, stressed;

yet the same meaning should be attached to the verb here; 'actualized' as a translation would be clumsy, but 'realized', while preserving its original signification, hits the sense exactly.

It is most important that one should firmly grasp and continually bear in mind this fundamental meaning of 'instress' before turning to its use by Hopkins elsewhere, where it is not always employed with the same accuracy and well-defined meaning. The original meaning of instress then is that stress or energy of being by which 'all things are upheld', and strive after continued existence. Placing 'instress' by the side of 'inscape' we note that the instress will strike the poet as the force that holds the inscape together; it is for him the power that ever actualizes the inscape. Further, we observe that in the act of perception the inscape is known first and in this grasp of the inscape is felt the stress of being behind it, is felt its instress. I speak of 'feeling the instress' and I do so with good reason. Inscape, being a sensitive manifestation of a being's individ-uality, is perceived by the senses; but instress, though given in the perception of inscape, is not directly perceived by the senses, because it is not a primary sensible quality of the thing. Hence it follows that, while inscape can be described, however imperfectly, in terms of sense-impressions, instress cannot, but must be interpreted in terms of its impression on the soul, in terms, that is, of *affects* of the soul. We can now understand why and how it is that 'instress' in Hopkins's writings stands for two distinct and separate things, related to each other as cause and effect; as a cause 'instress' refers for Hopkins to that core of being or inherent energy which is the actuality of the object; as effect 'instress' stands for the specifically indi-vidual impression the object makes on man. The first meaning is illustrated by the following instances:

> [Description of Ely Cathedral] The all-power-fulness of instress in mode and the immediate-ness of its effect are very remarkable. . . .

> . . . a pair of plain three-light lancets in each clearstory of the S. transept, which dwell on the eye with simple direct instress of trinity. . . .

> Take a *few* primroses in a glass and the instress of—brilliancy, sort of starriness: I have not the right word—so simple a flower gives is remarkable. . . .

> To Westminster Abbey, where I went round the cloisters . . . took in the beautiful paired triforium-arcade with cinqfoiled wheels riding the arches (there is a simplicity of instress in the cinqfoil) etc. . . .

> Millais—*Scotch Firs: 'The silence that is in the lonely woods'*—No such thing, instress absent, firtrunks ungrouped, four or so pairing but not markedly.

In some of these quotations Hopkins tries to express the instress in some sensible form; but the lines about the primroses well show how difficult it was to give precisely the nature of that fugitive perfection of instress. In the following quotations there is an interesting mingling of the two senses of instress:

> Bluebells in Hodder wood, all hanging their heads one way. I caught as well as I could . . . the lovely / what people call / 'gracious' bid-ding one to another or all one way, the level or stage or shire of colour they make hanging in the air a foot above the grass, and a notable glare the eye may abstract and sever from the blue colour / of light beating up from so many glassy heads, which like water is good to float their deeper instress in upon the mind. . . .

> . . . the greatest stack of cloud, to call it one cloud, I ever can recall seeing . . . The instress of its size came from comparison not with what was visible but with the remembrance of other clouds. . . .

> Tall larches on slope of a hill near the lake and mill, also a wychelm, also a beech, both of these with ivory-white bark pied with green moss: there was an instress about this spot.

In the following examples 'instress' should be taken in its second sense and is nearly synonymous with impression:

> I saw the inscape though freshly, as if my eye were still growing, though with a companion the eye and the ear are for the most part shut and instress cannot come. . . .

> The comet—I have seen it at bedtime in the west, with head to the ground, white, a soft well-shaped tail, not big: I felt a certain awe and instress, a feeling of strangeness, flight (. . .), and of threatening. . . .

> We went up to the castle but not in: standing
> before the gateway I had an instress which only
> the true old work gives from the strong and
> noble inscape of the pointedarch.

In the second example we again feel that Hopkins is doing his best to find words to express the peculiar sensation which instress gives. But as instress is of necessity as distinctive as inscape, general terms will never crystallize its peculiar quality; the poet can only approach its nature by stating what it is like and what it recalls:

> The blue was charged with simple instress, the
> higher, zenith sky earnest and frowning, lower
> more light and sweet.

Very instructive in this respect is this following quotation:

> On this walk I came to a cross road I had been
> at in the morning carrying it in another 'running
> instress'. I was surprised to recognize it and
> the moment I did it lost its present instress,
> breaking off from what had immediately gone
> before, and fell into the morning's.... And
> what is this running instress, so independent of
> at least the immediate scape of the thing, which
> unmistakeably distinguishes and individualises
> things? Not imposed outwards from the mind
> as for instance by melancholy or strong feeling:
> I easily distinguish that instress. I think it is
> this same running instress by which we iden-
> tify, or, better, test and refuse to identify with
> our various suggestions / a thought which has
> just slipped from the mind at an interruption.

Hopkins is working out a problem here; on the one hand he is sure that the effect of instress has its origin in the object itself, is as distinctive of the object's individuality as inscape and consequently does not proceed from the onlooker's subjective mood, in terms of which something objective is interpreted; on the other hand he cannot describe this peculiar effect which the object causes in him except in terms of personal subjective impressions. These impressions, as he notices himself, being personal and subjective never touch the real essence of the instress, which in its objectivity is individually distinctive. And relevant is the last phrase: in trying to recover the thought that has just slipped from our mind we can turn to the impression it has left there and having grasped the instress of the thought in its distinctiveness we may thus be able to recover the inscape of the thought. It is in this passage more than anywhere else that we see Hopkins at work to disentangle the essentially twofold aspect of instress. Indeed, it is not improbable that as yet Hopkins had not reflected upon its precise nature; he felt what instress meant and not writing for any public he took no trouble sharply to distinguish its double meaning. It is only when he is engaged upon writing on philosophical and theological subjects—and he had great hopes that this work would be published—that he took care to delineate what precisely he meant by 'instress'. But in this exposition I have not followed the chronological order; the instances of 'instress' taken from his diary are all of them dated earlier than 1875, the first year that was completely devoted to the study of theology; and the instances from which I derived the fundamental meaning of 'instress' are all dated later than this year. Consequently we find that in his later letters he no longer wavers which meaning to attach to 'instress' and which meaning to put in the first place: if 'instress' is used in non-philosophical writings, he identifies it with the sensation or *affect* aroused in him by inscape. If he feels the need to try and describe this individually distinctive impression he has recourse to like impressions made on him by other inscapes. The first traces of this exclusive use of 'instress' as synonymous with feeling are found in the closing pages of his diary, written in 1875:

> Looking all around but most in looking far up
> the valley I felt an instress and charm of
> Wales....

> Then ... I looked into a lovely comb that gave
> me the instress of *Weeping Winifred,* which all
> the west country seems to me to have....

In his correspondence he mentions among the many beauties of Dixon's poetry 'the instress of feeling', and to Patmore he writes that in his [Patmore's] poems the intelligence is in excess of the 'instress or feeling'. And notice how Hopkins associates various instresses:

> His [i.e. William Barnes's] poems used to charm
> me by their Westcountry 'instress', a most pe
> culiar product of England, which I associate
> with airs like Weeping Winefred, Polly Oliver,
> or Poor Mary Ann, with Herrick and Herbert,
> with the Worcestershire, Herefordshire and
> Welsh landscape, and above all with the smell
> of oxeyes and applelofts: this instress is helped
> by particular rhythms and these Barnes employs.

At the risk of a slight digression I draw the reader's attention to the logical inference from the above section about 'instress'. If Hopkins is going to describe the individually distinctive aspect of an object, he can do so by giving a word-picture in terms of its inscape, or he can choose a second way and describe it in terms of instress, which, as we have shown, was to Hopkins as distinctive as inscape. Most of the passages quoted in this chapter establish Hopkins as a writer who takes great pains to describe things objectively in minutest detail. This is what we should expect; for most of the quotations I have so far given were taken from his prose writings, in which the emotional appeal is made subject to objective representation and so there is little room for instress. But the passages in which 'instress' occurs in its second sense already show that even in his diary the second way of representing things is not lacking; thus, for instance, he speaks of 'sad-coloured sky', 'pinings of snow', 'grave green', 'happy leaves'. It is to be expected that in his poetry this way of giving the essence of things should come more to the fore than in his prose writings: thus he describes the heavy boots of the ploughman as 'bluffhide', the ploughed unsown fields as 'surly mould', the iron tools and boot-nails of workmen as 'surly steel'; hail he calls 'grimstones', which was afterwards rejected for 'hailropes'; he speaks of 'proud fire', the 'shy wings' of the wooddove, the blacksmith's 'grim forge' &c. I single out two instances for full quotation:

> Flesh falls within sight of us, we, though our flower
>   the same,
>   Wave with the meadow, forget that there must
> The *sour scythe* cringe, and the *blear share* come.
>   **"Deutschland"**

A magnificent combination of these two forms of description is found in the opening lines of his poem **"Spelt from Sibyl's Leaves"**:

> Earnest, earthless, equal, attuneable, vaulty,
>   voluminous, ... stupendous
> Evening....

The pause marked by Hopkins himself indicates the transition from description by instress to that by inscape; in *stupendous* the two waves reach a common crest, for *stupendous* is expressive of both inscape and instress.

I must point to another inference from Hopkins's consciousness of instress: it serves him as a source of imagery. For just as things may be described in terms of another thing which visually or auditorily is like or unlike it, so this writer describes an object in terms of another because the instress that each possesses for him affords a ground for comparison or contrast. I am well aware that this is not peculiar to Hopkins nor do I hold that a good deal of imagery in other poets may not be explained in the same way. I only wish to point out that as a source of imagery, association of impressions, such as found in Hopkins, finds its logical explanation in the attention he was ever paying to the instress of things. We are not then surprised that in Hopkins there occur instances of *synaesthesia*, which is always based on association of impressions. Thus we read in his diary:

> Above the Breithorn Antares sparkled like a bright crabapple tingling in the wind. . . .

> But this sober grey darkness and pale light was happily broken through by the orange of the pealing of Mitton bells.

And in his poetry Hopkins speaks of the 'moth-soft Milky Way' (**"Deutschland"**), of 'bugle blue eggs', 'thunderpurple', 'very-violet-sweet'; the song of the thrush strikes the poet 'like lightnings'. Most interesting is the way in which Hopkins appears to have associated the sound of bells with flames of fire. Thus in the **"Deutschland"** he writes of 'belled fire', and in a quotation from his diary . . . , we read of '*sparks* that *ring* of God'. Similarly, an object displaying great activity recalls to him the flames of fire: poetic inspiration is 'live and lancing like the blowpipe flame'. We thus have the series: activity—flames of fire—the pealing of bells; the curious thing is that this series we find complete in his magnificent sonnet **"The Windhover"**. Having described how the bird rides and strides the steady air, he exclaims: 'how he rung upon the rein of a wimpling wing', where 'rung' very possibly might cause obscurity. In the sestet the poet bids the bird's 'beauty and valour and act', the 'air, pride, plume' join, and seeing the bird fly forth in its majesty he continues:

> . . . AND the fire that breaks from thee then, a billion
> Times told lovelier, more dangerous, O my chevalier!

The words 'fire' and 'tolled' show how the instresses of the bird in action, of fire and of tolling bells, are joined in one poetic experience. (pp. 9-19)

'Inscape' and 'instress' are two terms which well bring out Hopkins's preoccupation with the 'self' of things. These coinages clearly point to his intense awareness of what was individually distinctive in every object and to his consciousness of the object's independence in being and activity. This should be remembered in the reading of Hopkins's poetry, for in it is situated a characteristic and essential difference between Hopkins and other poets. It might, indeed, be objected that what I have put forward as typical of Hopkins is found in most poets. It does not, for instance, appear that Hopkins's reaction to the impressions received from external objects is so very different from that of other poets: they all interpret such impressions in terms of various *affects;* at the most it would seem to follow that, because Hopkins was more conscious of the individuality

of these objects and their effect upon man, his reaction following the contact with objects was more reasoned and less spontaneous than the reaction of other poets. But such a way of presenting things is superficial; the difference between Hopkins and other poets goes deeper. Hopkins contemplated objects separately, each with its own individuating characteristics, each independent in its existence and activity, even granted that he used 'individual' in a somewhat extended sense. Through his impersonation he was ever in communication with them as with persons, each with 'life' entirely its own. The result of this attitude was that the object appealed to the poet in virtue of its own emotional atmosphere; if any object stirred Hopkins emotionally, the appeal arose in and from the object as from a real person. The poet is passive, receptive; he has opened wide his heart the better to respond to this quasi-personal appeal of the object. There is no question of inferring from impressions received that the object possesses certain qualities; Hopkins cannot ascribe to an object qualities which to his mind it does not really and literally possess. Here Hopkins differs essentially from other poets. They may indeed be similarly affected by external reality, but they interpret those impressions altogether otherwise. Approaching nature through the imagination they interpret the emotions arising in themselves as due to a great poetic sensibility and not as due principally to any independent activity on the part of the object. Poetic fancy makes them attribute the emotion to a fancied, imagined, but unreal emotional appeal directly forthcoming from the object itself; they cast round it an emotional atmosphere which the object possesses only in virtue of the poet's imagination and of the poet's imaginative interpretation. In Hopkins there remains a clearly marked separation between the activity of the poet and the independent activity of the object; they do not become one in a poetic experience in which the subjective element and the objective element have been fused by the imagination. The emotional activity ascribed to an object by Hopkins is real to him and not fancied, as real as its inscape.

The importance of these remarks is not to be underestimated in the judging of Hopkins's poetry. It is this peculiar non-imaginative attitude towards the selves that gives his poems that severity, even rawness of tone which is the very opposite of, for example, Keats's luxuriousness. I do not discredit one method of approaching and interpreting external reality nor do I favour the other as more poetic, nor do I hold of course that Hopkins lacked poetic imagination. I only wish to stress the fact that Hopkins's living conviction that things were 'selves' prevented him from bestowing upon them imagined life and imagined activity; hence that breath of seriousness which blows through the whole of his small but exquisite poetic *œuvre.* (pp. 19-21)

> *W. A. M. Peters, S. J., in his* Gerard Manley Hopkins: A Critical Essay towards the Understanding of His Poetry, *Oxford University Press, Oxford, 1948, 213 p.*

W. H. GARDNER (essay date 1949)

[*In the following excerpt from the conclusion to his widely respected two volume study of Hopkins, Gardner demonstrates Hopkins's status as a major poet.*]

When this Epilogue was first written, some ten years ago, it included the following words:

> The best of the later, deeply-pondered critical studies of Hopkins . . . have all sought to es-

tablish the fact that Hopkins was not merely an interesting experimentalist and innovator in the technique of poetry; they have proved that he is entitled to be acknowledged as a complete and successful poet.

That it should still be necessary to enunciate this claim points to an unhealthy state of criticism, a tendency to pay too much attention either to the manner and technique of poetry or to the matter alone—an extraordinary inability to comprehend poetry as it really is, that almost mystical *compositum* of thought, emotion, and form.

The many pages we have ourselves devoted to the formal aspects of Hopkins's verse have been justified (in as many more pages) by the clear assumption that the importance of his new and striking manner is dependent upon the supreme value of the total poetic effect. Apart from the rare and exalted pleasure to be derived from his work, the attitudes evoked are undoubtedly conducive to the social and spiritual welfare of mankind.

Too many of the critics who have written articles on Hopkins the Revolutionary Poet, the Innovator, or the Pioneer have created a false standard of assessment; they have, in Fr. Lahey's odd but true phrase, "prescinded from the well-spring of Hopkins's poetry" [see Additional Bibliography]. But this wellspring was not solely his religious ideals: it was that region in the subconscious mind where all the hidden tributaries of sensory experience met and mingled with his deepest intellectual convictions. To a degree not realized by many who have deplored his "frustration" and "self-laceration", the aesthetic and purely poetic values of Hopkins were ontologically or mystically bound up with his strong religious emotions.

Hence the poetic *compositum* or total poetic effect of Hopkins's work can be known and felt only by those who acknowledge God and the supernatural basis of life, and who at the same time appreciate the natural and traditional foundations of Hopkins's rhythm and style. All other readers may hold and cherish some *part* of this poet, but they cannot claim to comprehend and expound his complete personality, experience, and significance.

Hopkins's great work as a rhythmist has a unique absolute and historical value. Its unique absolute value lies in a variety, a subtlety, and a power of rhythmical effect which have never been surpassed and have probably never been equalled in any other poetry of comparable bulk. Its historical importance is that it proved, once for all, that the old native and popular stress-rhythms are as worthy to be considered the traditional rhythms of English poetry as the Romance syllabic metres which date from Chaucer. It is unlikely, however, that syllabic metres will be finally superseded; for the sprung, expressional, and cumulative rhythms of Hopkins demand a greater share of "auditory imagination", a more delicate sense of musical tone and timing, than are given to most poets. Sprung rhythm either succeeds perfectly or fails lamentably. . . . [Hopkins] triumphantly avoided all the pitfalls by combining what was healthy and robust in the native rhythms with the finest graces of the Greek melic poetry and Welsh *cynghanedd*.

As a master of poetic diction and of poetic 'linguistics' Hopkins again occupies a unique historical position. In an age of diffused Romanticism, he broke through the hidebound literary tradition which, save for brief exceptions in Wordsworth, Keats, and Browning, had for nearly two hundred years divorced the diction and phrasing of poetry from the direct perceptions of everyday life and language. Carefully avoiding the prosaism

of Browning, the archaism of Swinburne, and (for the most part) the awkwardness of Doughty, Hopkins restored to poetry something like the fluidity and resourcefulness of Elizabethan English; by so doing he materially helped all later poets to reduce the gap which had always seemed to exist inevitably between the greatest master of poetic language, Shakespeare, and his successors.

Of almost equal importance is the mark left by Hopkins's powerful idiosyncrasy upon the *texture* of English poetry. The rich phonal qualities of his verse reinforce, and are themselves enhanced by, the flexible stress-rhythm; and all these auditory elements are at the same time skilfully modulated to suit the shifting phases of closely packed thought and developing emotion. Pre-eminently Hopkins's example has revived the tradition (long in partial abeyance) that poetry is to be read with the ear and not merely with the eye.

Hopkins, in fact, has set up a standard of poetic beauty which, for the many who now fully acknowledge its fascination, is profoundly disturbing. After an intensive reading of Hopkins, most other English poetry seems outwardly facile and in varying degrees inadequate: its harmonic pattern is too simple, too adventitious; it seems not to have advanced far enough along the road which leads from plain utilitarian prose to the purest of literary art-forms—to the "condition of music". This does not mean that the admirer of Hopkins can no longer enjoy other poets: his appreciation of Shakespeare, of Donne and the other early seventeenth-century poets, of Milton and Keats will probably be increased rather than diminished. It does mean, however, that the proportion of other poetry to which he can return with the old enjoyment will be noticeably smaller; his taste, sharpened and refined by Hopkins, will demand a more exquisite amalgam of thought and emotion, a more significant concentration and point, to make up for the lack of *inscape* and *instress* in the outward form.

Gathering and retwining so many straying strands of the European poetic tradition, Hopkins was a great eclectic who was also eminently creative and original. The total complex of his style is (to use his own expression) a poetic "species"; as such it can never recur—except by shameless imitation.

Our final estimate may in some measure be influenced by the answer we give to one outstanding question, namely, how far Hopkins can be said to reveal, through his poetry, a truly mystical vision. He knew the Purgative Life, and had glimpses of the Illuminative; but that last calm 'possession' of God was a consummation desired but never attained in this world. Nevertheless, his direct apprehension of the Infinite through the medium of His creation frequently assumes a mode of expression which is identical with that of the acknowledged mystics. . . . (pp. 368-70)

Current verdicts on Hopkins's ultimate status as a poet vary between the designations "minor" and "great". The former points to the relative smallness of his output,—for this, and this only, can provide reasonable grounds for calling him a *minor* poet. But the deficiency is more than compensated by the absolute merit and subsequent influence of those poems which will continue to be *read*, and not merely admired, as long as the English language endures. In some age not attuned to his peculiar music and message, his reputation may suffer temporary eclipse; but the re-emergence of his fame will be all the brighter.

Hopkins is already a 'classic'. In his poetry we recognize not only what he himself demanded—"a fine execution", but also what Joseph Warton rightly called the two chief nerves of all genuine poesy—the Sublime and the Pathetic. By both criteria Hopkins attains the heights, though not the long sustained flights, of the acknowledged great masters—of Dante, Shakespeare, Milton. It is this fact, coupled with his unique individuality, which sets him apart from and above the exquisite *minor* poets, like Herrick, Marvell, and Christina Rossetti.

We shall attempt to justify those critics who have already pronounced Hopkins a *major* poet. Firstly, the fact that a *Times* reviewer, in giving him this title, compared his achievement in "bulk and quality" with that of Matthew Arnold is significant: it would appear that Hopkins's fourteen hundred lines can make as deep an impression as the fourteen thousand of Matthew Arnold. Indeed, whether his work be considered from the point of view of matter, manner, or both, Hopkins is, for the present writer, the more important poet; though in saying this we do not call in question the *major* status usually assigned to Arnold, Swinburne, and D. G. Rossetti.

According to Dr. F. R. Leavis,

> Hopkins was one of the most remarkable technical inventors who ever wrote, and he was a major poet. . . . He is likely to prove, for our time and the future, the only influential poet of the Victorian age, and he seems to me the greatest.

An Australian critic, D. P. McGuire, writes:

> The genius of Hopkins comprehended, as none other has comprehended even to our own day, the characteristic features of the oncoming world: the still increasing tempo, the still increasing complexity of modern life. For the social philosopher as well as for the common reader he is the most important poet since Shelley.

Such judgments will not pass unchallenged; and it must be admitted in the best interests of Hopkins that each pronouncement contains an unfortunate touch of exaggeration. Surely Browning and Whitman cannot be dismissed as less influential than Hopkins; and surely those two very considerable poets, together with Tennyson, will in future times be of the highest importance to the social philosopher and probably also to the common reader.

D. P. McGuire's statement about the increasing tempo and complexity of modern life suggests a further relevant observation. The growing bulk of the best European literature makes it ever more difficult for people of culture to keep pace with it. If we must have specialization and ample scope for personal preferences, then Hopkins is certainly a major poet on the showing of the above representative critics; but if those who are to decide the value and status of a poet are to be conversant with all the best poetry of the modern world, then the significance of mere *quantity* in a poet's output must be held to be rapidly diminishing. For most readers, it is obviously more profitable to skim the cream of *two* famous poets than to imbibe all, good and indifferent, of either one. Even Hopkins, who urged Patmore to write more poetry for the sake of his fame, was slightly contemptuous of his laboriously prolific contemporaries: "Just think of the blank verse these people have exuded". And to-day Mr. T. S. Eliot is certainly not alone in thinking that the effect of some of the nineteenth-century poets was lessened by their bulk:

Who now, for the pleasure of it, reads Wordsworth, Shelley and Keats even, certainly Browning and Swinburne and most of the French poets of the century—entire?

Who, indeed? And why should Coleridge, Byron, Tennyson, and William Morris be excluded from the list? Stopford Brooke reduced Coleridge to "twenty pages of pure gold"; and if this sifting and refining process were extended to all the above poets, the result would be a series of selections each of which would be hardly larger (if not actually smaller) than the total output of Hopkins. Such selections are constantly being made, chiefly for educational purposes, and the editors show no great diversity of choice. It should therefore be frankly admitted that only by their best can the voluminous writers of the past be poetically and culturally active to-day. Such an admission would bring the self-winnowed Hopkins into line with most of the poets whose work now commands a much larger space in our libraries and academic literary manuals.

For some years to come the many alleged faults and errors of taste in Hopkins may seriously reduce the bulk of his 'active' poetry. Meanwhile, we may go back for reassurance to Longinus, who asked himself whether the greater number or the higher quality of excellences should bear the bell in literature. The higher natures, he said, are the least faultless. Major excellences, even if not uniformly present, should always carry the election; for their greatness of thought if for nothing else.

A manuscript copy of two sonnets that Hopkins included in a letter to his mother.

According to Wordsworth, however, the emphasis in any assessment of poetry is to be placed not on 'thought' but on 'sensibility'. Of genius in the fine arts, he says,

> the only infallible sign is *the widening the sphere of human sensibility*.... Genius is the introduction of a new element into the intellectual universe ... the application of powers to objects on which they had not before been exercised, or the employment of them *in such manner as to produce effects hitherto unknown*.

By this criterion, too, Hopkins was undoubtedly a genius, and is certainly a major poet.

After a century of poetry in which the purely intellectual element was, to say the least, uncertain, diffused or exiguous, it is not surprising that to-day poets and critics alike are trying to redress the balance. In this respect, the scope and quality of Hopkins's work has provoked some adverse comparisons. The late W. J. Turner, for instance, said that Hopkins did not show the intellectual powers of Keats—that he had not the power of philosophic thought as manifested by Shakespeare, Milton, Donne, Keats, and Shelley.

Now although this opinion is true as regards the greater intellectual range of Shakespeare, Donne, and Milton, it contains, we think, a serious fallacy. W. J. Turner, like Dr. Richards and other agnostic critics, assumes too readily a position which would require volumes to 'justify', namely, that Christian beliefs and principles are mere emotional vagaries having little to do with intellection. It would be extremely difficult to prove that the free play of intellect in agnostic poets like Shelley and Keats has produced ideas and attitudes which are *more valuable* than those arising from the play of an intensely original mind and imagination among and around the matured tenets of Christianity. (pp. 370-73)

In the exercise of a mature intellect upon the raw materials of poetry, as also in the underlying and unifying metaphysic of his finished work, Hopkins must be pronounced equal and in some ways superior to both these earlier poets. Where they are promising and sometimes successful (in the invention of character and fable), Hopkins makes no claim to excellence; where they are really strong (in the speculative and meditative lyric), he is, we think, even stronger.

No informed critic would nowadays deny the major status of Donne, Baudelaire, and Walt Whitman. They are still living forces; though their influence is largely refracted through the minds of other writers, they continue to modify thought and action. Now for the present writer at least, Hopkins, in the sheer power or stress of his genius, has a real claim to rank with these three poets.

His affinity with Donne derives from the play of intellect on the problems of faith and religious endeavour—the yearning of imperfection towards perfection, the desire to know and hold God more closely—together with the play of individual sensibility upon the materials of poetry and on the conventional standards of diction and rhythm. In Donne, the clash between the 'man of the world' temper and the claims of a pious and ascetic calling did not admit of a poetic reconciliation so clear and sharp as that of Hopkins; for Donne never found, as Hopkins did in Catholicism, an interpretation of life which could be so flushed with feeling as to become a complete and illuminating experience. Although Donne has the wider range of ideas, he is often fanciful, fantastic, and inconclusive; Hopkins,

though hardly less 'cerebral' and exciting and frequently far more troubled, expounds on the whole the more rational and realistic world-view.

Baudelaire, too, was a poet who looked at human life and the universe with almost the same eyes as Hopkins; but the two men differed fundamentally in their interpretations of what they saw. Not always, however, in their reading of life: at times it seems to be rather a difference in the degree of will-power or moral consistency of which each was capable—the gift of grace not only of seeing what is best but of holding only to that. For instance, Baudelaire's *L'Horloge* expresses the same high and strict morality as Hopkin's **"To His Watch"**; *L'Avertisseur* and many other poems show the French poet's constant preoccupation with sin and redemption. In *Le Gouffre* (where the link is Pascal) we find that overwhelming sense of the simultaneous presence and absence of God, that apprehension of 'le vide et le néant' which only the mind capable of the fullest realization of the numinous can experience. What could be more like Hopkins than

> et sur mon poil qui tout droit se relève
> Mainte fois de la Peur je sens passer le vent,

and

> Sur le fond de mes nuits Dieu de son doigt savant
> Dessine une cauchemar multiforme et sans trêve.
>
> J'ai peur du sommeil comme on a peur d'un grand trou,
> Tout plein de vague horreur, menant on ne sait où;
> Je ne vois qu'infini par toutes les fenêtres,
>
> Et mon esprit toujours du vertige hanté
> Jalouse du néant l'insensibilité.—

and again:

> J'implore to pitié, Toi, l'unique que j'aime,
> De fond du gouffre obscur ou mon cœur est tombé?

Nevertheless, one great difference cannot be overlooked: Baudelaire's physical and mental morbidity made him the poet of *Les Litanies de Satan* and other works which must be read (if read at all) with the strictest caution. However much we admire the artist and pity the man, the sheer diabolism of much of his verse lowers the value of his achievement. By contrast, Hopkin's moral healthiness more than compensates for his smallness of output and frequent obscurity.

In his essential sanity Hopkins was closer to Whitman, whose impetuous rhythms, dynamic style, and pervasive nature-mysticism are often so like his own. Both poets expressed the "pure wild volition and energy of nature". As Mr. Charles Madge once pointed out in an illuminating short essay, there is a Corybantic strain in each one, much as the inhibited and obedient Jesuit differed from the broad-minded and broad-tongued Democrat. Hopkins's sky "all in a rush with richness" and his ecstatic "What is all this juice and all this joy"? are paralleled by Whitman's

> Hefts of the moving world at innocent gambols silently
>   rising, freshly exuding,
> Scooting obliquely high and low....
> Seas of bright juice suffuse heaven.

Both were fascinated by the infinite variety and laciness of natural beauty; as Whitman said:

> I effuse my flesh in eddies, and drift in lacy jags;

and Whitman, like Hopkins, knew the value of a strict asceticism in his private life. Yet here again there is a fundamental difference: it will redound, we think, to the Christian poet's credit that he shows a more pronounced "chastity of mind", a strength to resist the glib emotional generalization. The great friendly Whitman-arm thrown indiscriminately round the shoulders of Humanity may prove, in the end, a Judas-kiss. Instead of singing:

None has begun to think how divine he himself is, and how certain the future is,

Hopkins was prophetically inclined to lament the fact that too many have arrogantly assumed divinity, while too few have begun to think how divine they might become and how desperately uncertain their souls' future may be.

We can agree with E. E. Phare [see Additional Bibliography] when she says that the mere prose substance of Hopkins's poetry has more value than that of most avowedly didactic and philosophic poetry. The same critic asserts too that if all their respective poetical works were turned into prose paraphrases, Hopkins would have the better of Browning and possibly, also, of Wordsworth. Her doubt as regards Wordsworth is reassuring; for Wordsworth is, of course, the greater poet. But Miss Phare's opinion will not seem extravagant to anyone who sets the highest value upon the Christian faith and philosophy. Moreover her choice of Wordsworth and Browning in this context is a more extraordinary tribute to Hopkins's merit than at first appears; for of all nineteenth-century English poets, these two have probably given an intellectual stimulus, a more constructive and hopeful orientation, to the greatest number of intelligent people.

Before drawing our final conclusion we must say a last word about Hopkins's faults. That he left so many poems unfinished was partly his misfortune and partly to his credit: he refused to substitute putty and rubble for genuine inspiration. The peculiar nature of his mind and inner experience made it necessary for him to fuse, adapt, twist and sometimes distort the elements of his native language; and at rare times idiosyncrasy led him into oddity or extravagance. Yet the truth of Erigena's saying, that 'a vice is but a spoilt virtue and can have no separate existence', is in this case so curiously demonstrated that the task of absolute critical discrimination becomes well-nigh impossible: what seems good to one reader may seem bad to another. All the critic can do is to expound the processes of thought and expression, indicate the general solipsist tendency, and leave the individual educated reader to form his own judgment on this word or that construction. We must repeat, however, that most of this poet's awkwardness and difficulty disappears when we have taken the trouble to master his idiom. His style is not for imitation, because it is doubtful whether the same combination of qualities will ever be found again in one man.

When the clamour of protest and approval has died down, these facts about our subject will, we believe, emerge clearly: that by his unique personality and character, merging good living with high thinking; by his interpretation of beauty and duty, touching man to the very quick of his being; by his power of speech at once sweet and strong, melodic and harmonic; by his skill in architectonic and execution; by the stimulus he gave to the ethical and creative purposes of poets yet to be—by these and other qualities Gerard Manley Hopkins has certainly earned the distinction of being called a *major poet:* and in his finest moments he is assuredly one of our greatest. (pp. 374-78)

W. H. Gardner, in his Gerard Manley Hopkins (1844-1889): A Study of Poetic Idiosyncrasy in Relation to Poetic Tradition, *Vol. II, revised edition, Yale University Press, 1949, 415 p.*

BABETTE DEUTSCH   (essay date 1952)

[Deutsch, a respected American critic and poet, focuses on "The Windhover" as she examines Hopkins's use of language both to convey insights into nature and to praise God.]

One is inclined to read multiple meanings into Hopkins' phrases, knowing from his own exposition of his poems how much he could make of a word. In **"Spring and Fall"** the language is unusually simple, except for the line, "Though worlds of wanwood leafmeal lie," and even there the neologisms need no glossing. Where the poet does make difficulties for the reader with words of his own coinage it is in the effort to render fully and immediately the "thisness" of a thing. For Hopkins it was at once a duty and a delight to praise the Creator in praising His creation. To do so was to lay a finger on the inscapes of flowers, skies, birds, faces, on those individualizing traits which were so hard to define, partly because of their uniqueness, partly because he saw them as intrinsic to the inexpressible pattern in the mind of God. Like his unknown contemporary, Emily Dickinson, with whom he had so much in common, he wrenched the language to convey a unique insight. Undeceived as to the obscurities that he found it impossible to avoid, he held that poems dark at first reading should explode. His own lyrics are seldom to be understood as rapidly as they are read, and though they may explode, are apt to yield more light the more carefully they are scrutinized. One of his own favorites among his lyrics is a case in point.

"The Windhover" is a poem to be read with the ears, surely, but there are far deeper implications than this windy music reveals at first hearing. The bird, kin to the American sparrowhawk, is the falcon or kestrel. While in the title Hopkins chose to give it the local name descriptive of its hovering flight, in the body of the poem he refers to it as a "Falcon," capitalizing the word to emphasize the symbolism, and he makes the most of the courtly associations of falconry. Dedicated "To Christ our Lord," the sonnet expresses the poet's central convictions. (pp. 294-95)

The octave presents the bird poised in mid-air, balancing, as it were, on the wind. The opening lines seem to say of the falcon what he wrote in his journal of the waters at Holywell, a place of pilgrimage on the Welsh coast: the bird, like the well spring, is "the sensible thing so naturally and gracefully uttering the spiritual reason of its being." The falcon does this too insofar as, in functioning thus perfectly, it exhibits its selfhood and reflects the Creator. At the same time the bird, as a "sensible thing," flying and rejoicing in its flight, the natural and graceful creature seen and rejoiced in, is placed in opposition to all that is above and beyond brute nature. Do not air and wind, breath and spirit, go back to the same root meanings? In a later lyric Hopkins compares the Blessed Virgin to the air we breathe, a comparison that one recalls in reading the lines of **"The Windhover"** where the "world-mothering" element seems something finer than the atmosphere of earth.

The words "valour" and "pride," though not opposed, are distinguishable. "Valour" suggests physical prowess; "pride" carries connotations of majesty and moral propriety. The noble purport of "air, pride, plume" is enhanced by the exclamation "O my chevalier!" The word "chevalier" held special significance for a poet who thought of himself as a soldier of Christ.

> Brute beauty and valour and act, oh, air, pride,
> plume, here
> Buckle!

This literally clinches the image. If the obvious meaning of "buckle" is to fasten on armor, the word has other meanings: to grapple, to crumple or bend to the breaking point, and also to grapple or engage, as, in Scottish or North of England dialect, it means "to marry." The falcon in its glorious motion is an instance of "brute beauty" everywhere, and here an image of spiritual beauty. In the person of Christ the two "buckle," being one. But since the world reflects God imperfectly, the falcon as a type of physical excellence is no match for the type of moral grandeur, and so in the contrary sense, the two, contending, "buckle." "AND" it is precisely when the image of "brute beauty" suggested by the bird weds, surrenders, "buckles," to the image of divine grace, that a fire breaks from him, far more resplendent than the gleam of his wings in the morning light. An infinitely "more dangerous" fire, too, the perils of the spiritual life being greater than those any soldier of fortune has to face.

The language is so highly charged that it asks for analysis, though the poem is so closely integrated that to dismember it is almost to destroy it. The octave of this sonnet cannot be appreciated without understanding of the sestet, although it is wholly different in tone and seemingly different in intention. The vision of the bird rebuffing the big wind in its mastery of the elements all but contradicts what the sestet says about the way in which the self, serving, *is* served by submission, obedience, sacrifice. Yet there are oblique hints of the conclusion at the start.

> how he rung upon the rein of a wimpling wing
> In his ecstasy!

The "wimpling wing" may suggest a nun's wimple. The word "rung" is more allusive. It recalls the term in falconry for the bird's upward spiraling, but the word used by Hopkins means rather to linger in the ear or the memory, or to sound, like a bell, perhaps rung in triumph, perhaps a summons to prayer; "rung" is also used in speaking of a coin thrown on a counter to test it, and so suggests the testing of a man's soul, an idea borne out by the sestet.

The windhover is called "morning's minion": the favorite child, the servant of the morning, as Christ is the son and servant of God. He is "daylight's dauphin" as Christ is, accepting the sun as the image of the Trinity, its substance representing God: the power that begets life, its light, Christ: the intelligence that sustains life, its warmth, the Holy Ghost: the love that beautifies and vivifies creation. However one interprets it, more can be read into the poem than its surface meaning.

> My heart in hiding
> Stirred for a bird,

What stirs the heart is not only "the achieve of, the mastery of the thing!": it is the hidden dread of the powers against which the bird contends. The watcher knows the brevity of any physical triumph. But one may also read into the lines a sense of this brutish world's threat to the understanding, and the thought that spiritual triumph may come of pain and loss.

A passage in a sermon by Hopkins the priest illumines more fully the work of Hopkins the poet. Speaking of Christ, he said: "Poor was his station, laborious his life, bitter his ending: through poverty, through labour, through crucifixion his majesty of nature more shines." This might be taken as the text of **"The Windhover,"** or as a prose gloss upon it. Elsewhere, commenting on the *Spiritual Exercises* of Ignatius Loyola, he declared that "a man with a dungfork in his hand, a woman with a sloppail" gives God glory, if the worker means to do so. The plow pushed steadily against the dark resistance of the soil it furrows, the crumbling ember among the ashes in consenting to extinction, just as the coarse work dutifully done, like the majesty of Christ's nature in the dark circumstances of his life and death, "more shines." The image of the sacrificed God seems implied in the last line of the poem, where the falling embers are said to "gall themselves, and gash gold-vermilion." Although "gall" is used as a verb and not as a noun, it carries shadowy suggestions of the bitter cup accepted in the Garden of Gethsemane, the cup of wine mixed with gall offered to the man on Golgotha. It is typical of Hopkins that he should turn a transitive verb into an intransitive one to suit his purposes. This use of "gash" underscores the passive nature of Christ's victimage. Not the least remarkable thing about the poem is the way in which it powerfully presents the bird exulting in sheer physical delight and makes that sensuous body function as an argument for the imitation of Christ, whose greatest degradation, the cross, was also, for the devout believer, his highest flight. Further, if one accepts the medieval symbolism of the Trinity, is it not true that the understanding is crucified anew in every age? Socrates, drinking the hemlock, Boethius, dying in prison, Huss, burning at the stake, Lauro de Bosis dropping from his lone plane, the numberless anonymous members of the Resistance, they too are exalted by their crucifixions. The savior returns, the race of man is redeemed, the sacrifice is renewed.

To examine separately either the substance or the pattern of this poem is of course to do it violence. Yet technically alone it repays study. Like so many of Hopkins' pieces, it takes extraordinary liberties with the form of which it remains a striking example. Here is that strict thing, a sonnet, written in sprung rhythm, with many "outriders," or extra, slack syllables not noted in scanning. The first line ends on a hyphen, so that perforce the reader rushes on without even so much of a pause as the line arrangement of poetry seems to require. Moreover, the predominant foot, rare in any English poem, is a long syllable followed by three short ones, as in the compound word: "dapple-dawn-drawn." The rhyme scheme too is unusual. It is apparently Petrarchan, with the conventional abbaabba octave and the sestet also on two rhymes: cdcdcd. But the octave is so arranged that the "b" rhyme is a weak version of the "a" rhyme: "king" chimes with "riding." The whole sonnet is a rich tissue of elaborate harmonies. This is evident even in the first two lines, broken off from the exuberant sentence that they introduce:

> I caught this morning morning's minion, kingdom
> of daylight's dauphin, dapple-dawn-drawn Falcon,
> in his riding . . .

The alliterative consonants are obvious enough, but the ear catches before the mind recognizes the vowel echoes in "caught" "dawn" "drawn," as well as in the initial syllables of "dauphin" and "falcon," latent in the first syllable of the repeated "morning." There are blunted echoes of the four "ings," and the short "i" of "minion" "dauphin" "in," recurs, ending with the same consonant, once voiceless, once voiced, in "this" and "his." So much, and it is only a fraction of what might be said, for the aural pattern of the poem.

The form demands notice not merely because of its intrinsic interest but also because it illustrates the give-and-take between freedom and discipline that is part of what this sonnet, in the common phrase, is "about." Of the less than sixty complete poems that compose Hopkins' literary legacy, thirty are sonnets, but it is characteristic of his dual allegiance that of these thirty, more than half were written with the large liberties that he took with **"The Windhover."** The first lines of a few should suffice to show this: "Look at the stars! look, look up at the skies!" or "Summer ends now; now, barbarous in beauty, the stooks arise" or "Yes. Why do we all, seeing of a soldier, bless him? bless," or again the longest sonnet ever made: **"Spelt from Sibyl's Leaves."**

"The Windhover" is also worthy of notice because, like the greater part of his work, it exemplifies the practice of the seventeenth-century men whose imagery implied their belief in an ordered universe with a recognized hierarchy of values, and who saw in the simplest and coarsest things instances of general truths. So Hopkins can compare the flaming out of God's grandeur to the "shining from shook foil," its gathering greatness to the ooze of oil, and therewith compose a sonnet that pharaphrases one of his comments on the *Spiritual Exercises.* His "curtal" sonnet, the simplest he wrote, **"Pied Beauty,"** is a variation on this theme.

A writer of metaphysical poetry, in every sense of the term, Hopkins seems nevertheless not to have been influenced by the members of that company. He was strongly attracted by the work of George Herbert, but his admirations sent him scurrying in the opposite direction from their object. His verse is closer to that of Thomas Traherne, who held that God may be known only through His creation; that the creation becomes most significant when perceived by the mind of man; that man's duty is continually to re-create the world in his mind and so give it back to the Creator. To love the world He made as He loves it is to arrive here and now "to the estate of immortality." Traherne's poetry is less remarkable than his prose writings, which, with the radiant delight of a child and the power of the Psalmist, declare the glory of God. Those glowing metaphors express the same sense of "the world's splendour and wonder" that one finds repeatedly in the poetry of Hopkins. Indeed, such was the poet-priest's relish of what appealed to ear and eye, nostril, palate, and sensitive fingertips, that even a lyric on the beauty of poverty and the excellence of renunciation has a Keatsian tinge. Sensuousness crops up in the most unexpected places, as in the unlikely image spilled out in the midst of **"The Wreck of the Deutschland"**:

> How a lush-kept plush-capped sloe
>   Will, mouthed to flesh-burst,
> Gush!—flush the man, the being, with it, sour or sweet,
>   Brim, in a flash, full!

Undeniably, however delicately, sensual delight suffuses the lyric comparing the Virgin to the air, and all naturally crowds the poems in praise of spring bloom and harvest weather, lark song and rushing stream, aspen or ash boughs taboring the skies. Yet with the fewest exceptions these poems illustrate the idea that mortal beauty serves to point to "God's better beauty, grace." Bridges deprecated the fact that Hopkins' poems displayed "the naked encounter between sensualism and asceticism" [see excerpt dated 1918]. The encounter is rather between the sensuous pantheist and the athlete of God, and it is as naked as the meeting of wrestlers or lovers. (pp. 296-301)

Babette Deutsch, "The Forgèd Feature," in her Poetry in Our Time, Henry Holt and Company, 1952, pp. 286-311.

GEOFFREY H. HARTMAN (essay date 1954)

[*An American critic, poet, and editor, Hartman champions the creative imagination in his critical writings, guarding it against what he sees as the twin dangers of formalism and reduction. Though he acknowledges that the mind continually seeks a sense of order, Hartman maintains that the role of imaginative literature is to confront and convey experience without classifying it or turning it into an abstraction. In the following excerpt, Hartman discusses "The Windhover," emphasizing that "whatever interpretation is given to Hopkins, in order to hold true, it must be based on his understanding of Christ."*]

One could examine [Hopkins'] psychology, his theory of cognition, the statement on revelation contained in his poetry. It would then be pointed out that Hopkins places great faith in the hard, direct, vision which tries to seize an object in its immediate and mind-unprejudiced beauty, and makes the act of mere attention a sine qua non for knowledge. This in turn could be related to the effort of impressionist painting, and perhaps to the phenomenological spirit in general, which tries to obtain the eyes' or the senses' "figura rasa." It could be linked to the historical development that, starting with Occam's and Duns Scotus' criticism of the *species intelligibilis,* leads to Hume's merging of impression, image, and idea and to Wordsworth's trust in what we have called imperceptible cognition. Hopkins differs, of course, from both Wordsworth and more modern philosophy by putting the unity of cognition not in the nature of event as process (very roughly, Whitehead), nor in the event as occasional awareness of the divine and subsistent ground of vision (Wordsworth), but in the event as Christ. No one has gone further than Hopkins in presenting Christ as the direct and omnipresent object of perception, so deeply ingrained in the eyes, the flesh, and the bone (and the personal sense of having eyes, flesh, and bone), that the sense of self and the sense of being in Christ can no longer be distinguished. This is surely the *agon* of the late sonnets:

> Cheer whom though? the hero whose heaven-handling
>   flung me, foot trod
> Me? or me that fought him? O which one? is it each
>   one?

It is possible; in Hopkins there is a viewpoint on cognition; but whatever faculty we choose for analysis we come squarely against the poet's conception of Christ, just as wherever we start in Wordsworth we return to the dialectic of love between man and nature. Whatever interpretation is given to Hopkins, in order to hold true it must be based on his understanding of Christ. . . . Hopkins is the most Christ-possessed of the modern Christian poets whose religious fervor is beyond doubt but who, like Wordsworth and Eliot, either do not mention Christ at all or introduce him under the strange, litotic and rather inconceivable figure of *Christus absconditus.* Though Hopkins actually names Christ infrequently, and though some critics have refused to consider him as a specifically Christian poet, it is precisely here that his interest lies. He attempts to conceive Christ as hardily and heartily as did the poets up to the time of Crashaw. It is Hopkins as modern poet dealing with Christ, Hopkins as celebrant of "the dense and the driven Passion," who must finally concern us.

In "**The Windhover**" some ideal of elegance is on the point of fading away, and this is more swiftly evident in the style than in the theme, as if on the creation of a new style everything depended. Hopkins is in revolt not only against a residual diction of generality but also against the diction of sweetness which at the time of his writing was uttering its swan-song in the work of Pater and the Pre-Raphaelites. Like Verlaine, Hopkins would wring the neck of eloquence. In this respect there are certain evident things to say: (1) he is a plosive and guttural more than a liquid and murmuring poet; (2) he prefers words of Anglo-Saxon and dialect coin; (3) he aims at an essentially asyndetic style; (4) he is not afraid of cacophonous repetition, seeks it even, whether in the chime of vowels—the *i*'s and *i*'s of "does so rinse and wring / The ear, it strikes like lightnings"—or in word repetition—"morning morning's" of "**The Windhover**"; (5) he cultivates a rhythm in which nothing hypnotic remains and which, as in the octave of "**The Windhover,**" may be used in description of physical movement.

These features militated against the half-way house of nineteenth century eloquence which, while admitting more and more the poetic values of the concrete, stubborn, irreducible material world, favored melic euphemism in religious and what Hopkins derides as "blethery bathos" in sensual poetry. Pater's awareness of physical beauty, while real, is nevertheless an ideal limited by Greek example and too soon exhausted by the delicacy of a rose. "Who would change the color or curve of a rose-leaf for that . . . colorless, formless, intangible being Plato put so high?" We are leagues away from the oil and foil of Hopkins' poetry which employs words with the avowed attempt to transcribe the full physicality of created things and created senses. Although Hebraic and Asiatic metaphor is often more audacious than his, no poet before Hopkins has made such a precise use in religious poetry of what Irving Babbitt, decrying post-romantic literature as illegitimately engaged in word-painting, calls in his *New Laocoon* "local impressions." Babbitt is scarcely wrong except in judgment; Hopkins does indeed use eye and sense as plot for, and not merely clothing of, subject or idea; and he differs from his contemporaries precisely in the entire and unrestrained acceptance of word-painting. "Word-painting," he writes in 1887, "is, in the verbal arts, the great success of our day."

If Hopkins placed such emphasis on local impressions and word-painting it was because he wished to restore to God physical compulsion, and this involved the use of words to render the immediacy of the senses as nerve and muscle and sensation. "**The Windhover**" tells not only of the passing of an ideal of eloquence but also of the passing of a concept of divine Grace. The love that goes from God to man and from man to God is not, for Hopkins, a human or yet an intellectual love, and if it be love at all it is hidden and conceived under the divine attribute of material immensity. "Thou mastering me / God!" begins his first great poem; two centuries before, Newton, to have God accord with his cosmology, suggested that *Dominus* be replaced by *Deus,* and even preferably by *Aeternus,* since the first and even the second implied a personal relationship as of master to servant inconceivable in a universe regulated by strict eternal law: the polemics against this by Blake and Wordsworth are well known. But Hopkins, whose persistent cry is *Dominus,* Master, has instinctively accepted the fact that the act of God's mastery over man is indistinguishable from the act of God's mastery over matter. And "**The Windhover**" shows that this is not mastery at all—for the control and "achieve" of the bird over the elements is rejected—but *an inexplicable law of sacrifice* given by God in Christ, evident

even in the inorganic world, yet lacking in man. For Hopkins, as for the modern poet, the compulsion to God is not through an evidence of the intellect or of the sweet-violent soul but through a mark left physically on man and his sensing, whereby he becomes, as Claudel has said of Rimbaud, a mystic in the savage state.

Therefore in Hopkins, against tradition, Christ the human and spiritual intermediary between man and God becomes Christ the supreme physical revelation and physical compulsion. This could be expressed better by saying that Hopkins views the world through the actual body of Christ, instead of through His spiritual body, which is the Church. Hence his relative indifference to theological questions, and his extreme sensitivity to physical media, whether word, air, or his own body, which at the end wrestles with itself as with Christ, not knowing any longer how to distinguish one from the other, or soul from self, Christ being but the supreme *haecceitas*. But Christ is such only by sacrifice, and Hopkins' attention is taken by the sacrificial body, his steady quest being to show man as fated in Christ as He was in man and the body of man:

> . . . How a lush-kept plush-capped sloe
> Will, mouthed to flesh-burst,
> Gush!—flush the man, the being with it, sour or
> sweet,
> Brim, in a flash, full!—Hither then, last or first,
> To hero of Calvary, Christ's feet—
> Never ask if meaning it, wanting it, warned of it—men
> go.

This passage from the eighth stanza of "**The Wreck of the Deutschland**" makes clear how Hopkins represents a wished-for fatality of the spirit as a possible compulsion of the body: like the ripe sloe (a kind of communion wafer!) which will burst beneath the stress of the mouth, man, entirely sensed and under divine stress, inevitably imitates the sacrificial action of Christ. We are reminded of "**The Windhover**" with its embers that fall and gash gold-vermilion: "gash" is a transitive verb made intransitive as if to suggest that the coal's wound like that of Christ is self-inflicted. For "**The Windhover**" also is haunted by the thought that the material world is nearer to Christ's Passion, Crucifixion and flaming Resurrection than free-willed man. (pp. 64-7)

> *Geoffrey H. Hartman, "Hopkins," in his* The Unmediated Vision: An Interpretation of Wordsworth, Hopkins, Rilke, and Valéry, *Yale University Press, 1954, pp. 47-67.*

ALAN HEUSER   (essay date 1958)

[*Heuser's* The Shaping Vision of Gerard Manley Hopkins *traces Hopkins's creative development. In the conclusion, excerpted below, the critic outlines the artistic and philosophical movements that influenced Hopkins's life and poetry.*]

In both art and religion Hopkins was closely linked with his times. The Oxford movement of Pusey and Newman overtook him in his pursuit of classical studies: he became first an Anglo-Catholic, then a Roman Catholic and a Jesuit. The Pre-Raphaelite movement of painters and poets, together with the critics Ruskin and Pater, gave him his artistic context: he became painter, poet, and critic too. Then, while the debate between science and religion was going on, Hopkins developed a theory of art using the best of both worlds—the laws of science and the life of religion—combining wild naturalism (type of Mary) with religious idealism (type of Christ). On the one hand, there was a Romantic return to primitive innocence of sensations; on the other, a Christian striving towards the perfect Manhood. Here was the peculiar Pre-Raphaelite tension between angelic heaven and fleshly earth, without any of its sickliness, for Hopkins' work was free from two Victorian diseases—subjective dream indulgence in vogues of escape and reverie, brooding exploitation of confused emotionalism and passive sensationalism. In Hopkins all had the immediacy and 'rash-fresh' clarity of authentic vision, the intensity of honest sensations and emotions.

The problem of the Victorian age was its divorce of ideal theory and practical vision, together with the substitution of ethical for religious and metaphysical values. In verse there was a double weakening: the blight of archaic diction (often pseudo-Elizabethan) and the effeminacy of exotic forms (French verse forms of the rondeliers). The triumph of Hopkins' achievement was a heightening of living language, a reinforcement of familiar forms by native stress, an illuminative integration of vision and theory, an exhilarating conquest of religious meaning, by which even failure (in the dark sonnets) was made victorious. Behind the vision of nature, under the wilderness and sufferings of the world, Hopkins discovered no dry theory but a lively one, echoing with the songs of creation and redemption. Nature rang with sympathetic analogies. As in George Herbert, all nature was seen in terms of a musical metaphor, and there was ultimate harmony, harmony of nature in grace where innocence and perfection were to be restored after the universal extension of sacrifice.

Beyond his fellow Victorians Hopkins was faithful to his poetic voice, sometimes denying it utterance, but never forcing it for the sake of mere writing, always relying upon genuine inspiration, always advancing in rhetorical technique. His lack of a reading public was an unforeseem advantage. Many other poets, writing on a par with prose writers, betrayed voice and vision to a mass audience, so that at the core of their works are found hesitancy and evaporation of meaning. The problem of private vision assuming public voice and aimed at a large, undefined audience made the longer works of Tennyson and Browning tedious (*Idylls*, the *Ring*) and actually put an end to the poet in Arnold. The problem of Hopkins was the reverse: public vision of creation and redemption revealed by private oracle and received by a very few, the audience widening only long after the death of the poet.

Placing Hopkins' poetry in the English poetic tradition has been found a difficult task. Various schools have been invoked along with his name—Wordsworthian, Miltonic, Keatsian or Pre-Raphaelite, the alliterative school of Middle English, the new metaphysical school of Patmore and Thompson. Each of these influenced Hopkins at some stage in his development; the Pre-Raphaelite school was the most significant. If a distinct label is needed, perhaps 'baroque' is almost satisfactory, expressing the vehement and fiery incarnation of idea in word-made-flesh, the word rendered sensational. Jesuit tradition in the baroque style links Hopkins directly to the seventeenth-century poetic experience of controlled violence and surprise, of Christian feeling infusing and commanding classical forms, and thus he recalls the poetry of Donne, Herbert, Crashaw, Quarles, and Benlowes. Yet how did this happen in the nineteenth century? It must not be forgotten that Pre-Raphaelite art arranged realistic detail of nature for ideal message-value, to tell a story or embody an idea, and that this technique carried on, in a new key, the old tradition of the baroque emblem-books. The verse-picture combination of the black and white emblem came

to coloured life in the poetry-painting association of Pre-Raphaelite art: not only were pictures painted to illustrate poems and vice versa, but book-illustration in art and word-painting in literature were widely popular. In Hopkins Pre-Raphaelite symbolism and Jesuit emblem-tradition met in a new baroque, independent and fresh, for Hopkins remained deliberately his own species, unique, as he thought all poets should be.

Hopkins' three great technical advances were in diction, rhythm, and texture. For him poetic diction meant 'current language heightened'. He sought out provincialisms and coinages native to the concrete and living roots of language, combining these specific marks into alogical, co-ordinated, and exclamatory periods. Sprung rhythm derived force and flow, not from haphazard accents, but from high stresses important to 'fetch out' the sense by emphasis. The style was declamatory, interpretive, and followed a free pattern fitting the individual phrase or line of thought—reminiscent of Purcell's bold liberties and surprises threaded on a continuous melodic line. But the new metre and the new language would have been frigid innovations without the entire expressional texture fused with them—chiming of consonants and alliteration of vowels—a concatenation of syllables similar to Welsh systems of lettering. Neglect of this rich overlay of textural echo would result in a loss, not of a mere ornament, but of the very nature of sprung rhythm.

Along with advances in language and rhetorical technique, Hopkins left to the poetic tradition significant contributions in lyric form, especially in sonnet and ode. Concentrating on the Petrarchan sonnet, with its careful balance of octave and sestet, Hopkins experimented in contracted and expanded modes . . . , always maintaining basic rhymes and proportions. . . . Expanded sonnets were the more important, in order to make the English sonnet equal in length to the Italian. Lines were lengthened by extra stresses (to six or eight feet), by extrametrical syllables (outrides), or by additional half-lines (codas and burden-lines); sometimes all three methods were used. In each case Hopkins gave his sonnet the orchestral fullness and impact of an ode. He turned to the ode proper in either of two modes—the Horatian or the Pindaric—often with an elegiac intent in view. For the Horatian ode he kept to a series of quatrains written in compressed style of simple tetrameter and/or trimeter. For the Pindaric he maintained a strophic or stanzaic manner in elaborate metric, frequently dividing the ode into two parts.

Beyond technical advances in versification and contributions in lyric form, Hopkins' poetry wrestled with a strong core of thought (Christian ideas infused with Gothic feeling into classical forms). The three notes of his nature verse—joy, pity, and fear—came to him from his religious life: the joy of creative light in sacramental sonnets of nature, the pity of the compassionate cloud in poems of the pastoral care for men, and the fear of redemptive night in the dark sonnets of personal desolation. Over these notes—the exaltation of joy, the catharsis of pity and fear towards a new joy—was woven his characteristic spiritual imagery: images of the soul as angelic voice or bird (winged *eros* or *psyche*), with its activities of affection as love-lace (organic growth, binding *philia*) and of election as battle-armour (military combat, sacrificial *agape*), based on the mystery of the self (naval or racing course of pitch). Under the poetry there lay the foundations of a life truly lived in honesty with acceptance. (pp. 95-8)

[Hopkins' creative vision moved] from naturalistic idealism through a philosophy of inscape and instress to a Scotist voluntarism and a Pythagorean Platonism of music, memory, and

number. Under the pressure of Greek and Pre-Raphaelite studies, Hopkins' concrete vision soon acquired an abstract theory.
Vision and theory interlocked in his pursuit of the three arts
of painting, music, and poetry. Principles learned from colour-
music, from Pre-Raphaelite art and art-criticism, from plain-
chant and counterpoint in music, from Greek and Welsh studies
in verse mutually enriched the poetry as well as the aesthetics
behind the poetry. Hopkins was for ever reaching behind vision
to theory. In his early years he turned from naturalistic idealism
to set up a new Realism in Platonist terms—fixed types in a
scale of nature—out of which emerged a philosophy of inscape
and instress. In his maturity he developed the philosophy into
a psychology, a verse theory, a theology, a moral idealism,
and a Scotist scheme of salvation. Finally he speculated in the
preconscious realm of memory and in number. In each case a
musical metaphor lay at the base of creative vision. And at
every stage of development there was renunciation and revival:
when Hopkins gave up painting, he cultivated word-painting
in journals; after he burnt his poetry, there was a long silence,
followed by the discovery of a new verse theory; when he
found poetry difficult in later years, he turned to musical composition. The death of an old art brought forth new life, and
death passed into resurrection.

Vision and theory met in the interaction of poetry and spirituality, in the relationship between aesthetics and religion.
Inspiration or desolation in Hopkins' prayer life gave in the
poetry corresponding ejaculations of comfort or distress. His
stylistic habit of invocation was the natural consequence of
vocation directing frequent aspirations to God. Hopkins' life-
long occupation with Greek scholarship maintained in him a
Platonist view of reality, not always caught up by Scotism into
a world of Christian truth, nor always turned into Christian
poetry. There remained the underworld of the preconscious and
primitive, ideal types and mirror images among pagan myths
and Pythagorean numbers. Here in the storehouse of memory
was the world of angelic possibles. It was in this way that
Hopkins pursued his speculations.

What was the vision, its theory, its applications? The vision
of creation was trinitarian—testifying to the fatherhood of being,
the sonship of inscape, the spirituality of stress—and unitive
through 'the stem of stress' or tangible finger of power in all
creation. The theory centred on three key terms: inscape, the
inward tongue-shape of the creature; instress, its inward stem-
pressure of feeling and will; pitch, its directed singularity. The
theory was extended to verse—'the inscape of spoken sound',
quaint margaretting based on chime pattern and stress curvature; to human nature—a moral inscape forged by instress of
will and fulfilled in the sacrificial Humanity of Christ; to psychic
experience of lower heart—stress and slack of feeling, instress
by association in the unconscious below reason; to the spiritual
world of higher heart with levels of instress—affective will
determined by nature, elective will free at pitch—and with
focus on correspondence to grace in the line or stem of sequence
of stress in the heart. Now, with the emergence of a doctrine
of the self, with the Scotist distinction between individuality
and nature, the developed theory elaborated echoes on levels
of being—sakes as reflexions of individual pitch, keepings as
reflexions of specific nature. Finally, the fixed points of Platonic Realism were defined in terms of Pythagorean numbers,
and mathematics held out promise for a philosophical basis to
metre and music. The Greek doctrine of music provided an
important basis for the theory of pitch (degree of tuning on the
string of being), stress (God's bow pressing on the string), and
instress (man's bow responding). Yet the theory, however far

abstracted, was ever brought home to the concrete through
Hopkins' strong senses, his interest in primitive sensation
breaking from the unconscious, in spiritualization of sensation.
Furthermore, it must be remembered that the vision passed
through four or five stages, that it was always in development.
(pp. 98-100)

> *Alan Heuser, in his* The Shaping Vision of Gerard
> Manley Hopkins, *1958. Reprint by Archon Books,
> 1968, 128 p.*

BRIGID BROPHY, MICHAEL LEVEY, AND CHARLES OSBORNE   (essay date 1967)

[*Brophy is an Anglo-Irish novelist, dramatist, and critic. She is
known for her provocative and acerbic remarks, particularly the
iconoclasm of* Fifty Works of English and American Literature
We Could Do Without, *in which she and coauthors Michael Levey
and Charles Osborne attack such works as* Hamlet, Wuthering
Heights, *and* Moby Dick. *In this excerpt from that work, the
authors denigrate Hopkins's poetry.*]

Hopkins's is the poetry of a mental cripple. Sympathize as one
might with his confusion, with the absurd struggle that went
on within him between priest and poet, it is impossible not to
end by feeling complete exasperated with the disastrous mess
he made of his life. The muscle-bound, determinedly 'difficult'
verse that he produced is really abhorrent. It may have a sentimental appeal to his co-religionists, but to others Hopkins is
surely the most unrewarding of the Victorian poets. The interior
war in his permanently bared breast between aesthetic and
ascetic is a blatantly uneven combat: the aesthete scarcely exists. The man is all metaphysics, mysticism and neurotic longing for the cross. Add to these disabilities the baleful influence
of Dante Gabriel and Christina Rossetti, and it is immediately
apparent that poor Hopkins hadn't a chance.

In his groping attempts to find his own mode of expression,
Hopkins is not unlike Browning, but he lacks completely
Browning's sudden illumination. Hopkins is at the mercy both
of his superstitions and of his theories. It was the theories
which proved the more dangerous to his verse. His meaningless
and arbitrary definitions of 'inscape' and 'instress' serve to
underline the almost Nihilist emptiness of his thought. In a
letter, Hopkins wrote: 'You know I once wanted to be a painter.
But even if I could I would not I think, now, for the fact is
that the higher and more attractive part of the art put a strain
on the passions which I shd think it unsafe to encounter.' No
wonder his poetry is so cringingly irrelevant. There is nothing
brave about his obscurity: it is that of weak-mindedness and
theology. (pp. 97-8)

> *Brigid Brophy, Michael Levey, and Charles Os-
> borne, "Poems of Gerard Manley Hopkins," in their*
> Fifty Works of English and American Literature We
> Could Do Without, *1967. Reprint by Stein and Day
> Publishers, 1968, pp. 97-8.*

PATRICIA M. BALL   (essay date 1968)

[*Ball argues against the tendency in critical circles to consider
Hopkins a modern poet, suggesting that both his subject matter
and system of values were firmly rooted in the Victorian age.*]

The attraction of Hopkins for poets and readers of the post-1918
world is often attributed to the originality of his technical
achievements, and his segregation from his age has been in
consequence much stressed. Yet in his work, the continuity of

modern and nineteenth-century preoccupations is really exhibited: he attracts because he is essentially of his time, and his vision is recognized for what it is by his twentieth-century reader, though it might well have been missed by his sincerity-blinded contemporaries.

His poetry feeds on the concept of self, and even more, of 'selving': that is, the process of consciously achieving identity. The fact that for him such a process is God-directed and God-initiated helps to demonstrate how distinct this kind of self-awareness is from any more superficial state of selfishness or merely sterile introspection. Although he is theologically unique among the poets of his century, Hopkins, in the nature of his creative drive and his goals, is representative not a maverick. He fuses a chameleon passion with an egotistical single-mindedness, seeking to realize all things inwardly and fully while discovering his own 'inscape' the more intensively, as his heart 'stirs' for what he contemplates and becomes. The immediacy of self-experience is to him the central wonder in the human universe, the starting point from which all must begin. That he speaks of his 'selfbeing' in terms that recall Keats in their sensuousness is no coincidence:

> . . . my selfbeing, my consciousness and feeling of myself, that taste of myself, of *I* and *me* above and in all things, which is more distinctive than the taste of ale or alum, more distinctive than the smell of walnut leaf or camphor, and is incommunicable by any means to another man (as when I was a child I used to ask myself: What must it be to be someone else?) Nothing else in nature comes near this unspeakable stress of pitch, distinctiveness, and selving, this selfbeing of my own . . . searching nature I taste *self* but at one tankard, that of my own being.

The child's question is the question of the Romantic chameleon temperament, and Hopkins's context shows how rooted it is in the keen apprehension of the unique self. The effort to communicate the incommunicable 'self-taste', the pondering on other selves, both lead to further realization of the central identity which quickens all else and to which all must be referred back again: Hopkins and his fellow nineteenth-century poets share this stimulus to creativity.

"The Wreck of the Deutschland" illustrates the link, in its refusal to be content with an objective narrative account of the nuns' drowning. Following Keats in his thinking on "Hyperion", Hopkins finds it imperative to be present in his poem as an experiencing consciousness. He erects a structure where his spiritual vision and psychological crises are related to the ship-wreck and its consequences, as Keats confronts his inner condition in witnessing the suffering gods. The poem is reflexive, an egotistical mirror-work. Action is modified by the mind beholding it and the coalescing of the two is part of the poem's nature, not merely of the circumstances of its genesis.

For the Jesuit poet, all leads beyond itself, the sense of the individual being to him inseparable from the 'infinite I AM'. Coleridge's phrase is particularly suitable, for Hopkins shares with him the beliefs that such an ultimate concept only confirms the pivotal role of the self-conscious mind, and that the search for the fullest possession of the latter is the route to the God-head, offering the sole experience of this which is humanly attainable. Hopkins has a clearer formula of given values than his fellow-poets, yet he too relies on the processes of imagi-

native self-experience as the means of vitalizing them and so making them wholly valid and potent. Systems of theology and philosophy react upon the hypersensitive membrane, 'that inmost self of mine', with its response that transforms all notions and actions to self-knowledge: 'what I do is me'. The enlightening extension of such subjective recognition is the touchstone for Hopkins as for his Romantic predecessors, his contemporaries, and those later poets whom he joins as a companion familiar for reasons which underlie and influence his 'modern' use of words.

Although, like Browning, Hopkins displays the vigour of his Romantic inheritance rather than its burdens, he is in some ways recognizably the fellow of Tennyson, Arnold and Clough—his kinship with the latter extending to their common fate of enjoying a twentieth-century instead of a contemporary esteem. The self-taste could turn sour for Hopkins as for other Victorians and he too has his black poetry:

> I am gall, I am heartburn. God's most deep decree
> Bitter would have me taste: my taste was me;
> Bones built in me, flesh filled, blood brimmed the curse.
> Selfyeast of spirit a dull dough sours. I see
> The lost are like this, and their scourge to be
> As I am mine, their sweating selves; but worse.
> **("I Wake and Feel the Fell of Dark . . .")**

Hopkins in the Terrible Sonnets articulates a specialized fear, self divorced from God. But the dread of such isolation is alien neither to the torment of Maud's lover enclosed in his own consciousness nor to the loneliness of islands in Arnold's sea. Therefore he is a poet of his time, despite all that marks him off. Behind him lies the same imaginative hinterland as that affecting all Victorian poets, and if he brings Romantic energies to work on Victorian despairs, he pursues the empirical path being beaten out by those around him.

These characteristics of Hopkins move his modern audience. Recent generations of readers have recognized not just his verbal freshness, but his passionate fidelity to the perceiving self and the 'exact curve' of his experience, with the intensity of his chameleon powers serving the quest—one of duty, as he saw it—for deeper self-realization. Identity was the concept that quickened him and his poetry strives to incarnate the idea. In acknowledging the stature of Hopkins's imagination, we in this century have acknowledged our own needs; we have also accepted the authentic Romantic tradition as a relevant and animate poetic force, however loud the voices crying its obituary. (pp. 223-26)

> *Patricia M. Ball, "Conclusion: Masks and Anti-Masks," in her* The Central Self: A Study in Romantic and Victorian Imagination, *The Athlone Press, 1968, pp. 221-29.*

WENDELL STACY JOHNSON (essay date 1968)

[*In his* Gerard Manley Hopkins: The Poet as Victorian, *Johnson considers Hopkins's themes of nature and the self in light of Victorian ideas. In the following excerpt from that work, Johnson explores the significance of light and darkness in Hopkins's poems, briefly comparing his imagery with that of other Victorian poets.*]

Images of light, of fiery sunlight, starlight, moonlight, are everywhere in Hopkins, contrasted with and complemented by the images of shadow and of night. The poet's love for painting, his early desire to emulate the Pre-Raphaelites in art, and Ruskin's influence on him may have something to do with his interest in precise description of light effects and visual phenomena. In fact, Hopkins can sometimes evoke a brightly lit and shaded landscape more vividly than the painter-poet Dante Rossetti does.

Of course, his concern for just how things are lit and how they look is by no means unique in his times; the criterion of exact fidelity to nature, applied to painter and poet alike, is generally accepted in Victorian criticism of the arts, and it is not only Ruskin who describes in words or represents in drawings how light and shadow define the forms of objects. It is a matter of visual accuracy, something that Tennyson, too, very much cares about.

While the imagery of light is literal for Hopkins and the poets of his century, it is also something more for them: for Wordsworth, the essence of nature is revealed in a glorious light seen clearly only by the young and innocent; and for Tennyson, Arnold, and Swinburne, daylight, nature's light, may be literally but also metaphorically both creative and destructive. The special quality of Hopkins' poems about light is their way of distinguishing a devotion beautifully illuminated, to nature, which is to be represented faithfully, from a sense of nature's being fallen and alien, its light partly darkness. These two attitudes toward nature, toward the world of sunlight and stars, might be said to alternate in other Victorian poets; in Hopkins they occur simultaneously. . . . [One] of his favorite adjectives is *dappled;* his world is double in a pictorial sense and in a metaphorical one, always being dappled with sun and shadow. In ocean, in landscape, and in all creatures he finds harsh, fleeting beauty and imperfectly reflected, echoed power and grace. (pp. 125-27)

Hopkins uses darkness to describe the dreary and sometimes dreadful sense of being only oneself, cut off from the glory of heaven:

> I wake and feel the fell of dark, not day.
> What hours, O what black hours we have spent
> This night!

So begin the most terrible of all his lines on being oneself. In **"Carrion Comfort,"** too, during inner tempest and suffering, the most the speaker can do is ''wish day come'' after the night ''Of now done darkness [when] I wretch lay wrestling with (my God!) my God.''

Yet, although man mourns his mortal self in darkness, as Margaret does in **"Spring and Fall,"** the darkness is ambiguous and intermittent. Light and darkness intertwined make up the major imagery of **"Spelt from Sibyl's Leaves,"** which is about the mixed nature of this mortal world. Heavy baroque lines describe the straining toward death of ''hearse-of-all-night,'' but also the stars in ''fire-featuring heaven.'' These lines concern the tendency of selves, of forms, to dissolve and be forgotten or dismembered—but also the oracular promise of something else. The dapple and the doubleness of earthly life seem to rush toward the singleness of night, of death; yet there remain two spools, two folds, two aspects of each reality, including self: light, white, right, as well as darkness, black, wrong. So ''Selfwrung, selfstrung, sheathe- and shelterless, thoughts against thoughts in groans grind.''

But behind the dappled world and its temporary darkness, and, at least in one sense, within the very darkness, Hopkins believes there is light. That is just the point that has been made by the language and imagery of **"The Deutschland."** In that poem there are three versions of light: the lovely light of nature represented by stars and the clear bright sky, sustained by the Holy Ghost; the fiery light of divine power represented by lightning and ''fire of stress,'' or flames of grace, the working of God the Father; and the light of virtue or grace incarnate represented perfectly in Christ, the kindly ''heart's light,'' but also reflected in Christ-like man seen as a ''beacon of light.'' It is necessary to pass from the first stage through the instress demanded by the second before reaching the third stage, which allows a full recognition of human—and Christ-imitating—inscape. And this means discovering that, just as in thunder there is lightning, so above and acting through the fact of mortal darkness there is still the light of divine power: ''Thou art above, thou Orion of light.'' Christ is re-born through darkness and drowning.

Because Hopkins is a poet of doubleness, a poet of Christian paradox, he is misread when these three stages are separated from each other, or when he is taken not to have a single and consistent imaginative scheme. There are urgent tensions within his art, and indeed there is at the center of it a seeming contradiction, because there is a seeming contradiction at the center of Christian thought. But the several elements are almost always present, at least implicitly, in his verse. Hopkins does not express the conflict between, and alternating of, priest and artist, or devotional writer and nature poet, or ascetic and aesthete; and he does not sometimes believe that the landscape in which men live is wholly dark, nor does he sometimes believe that it is wholly bright. (pp. 144-46)

The dappled imagery of light and darkness is, in fact, ubiquitous in Hopkins. For instance, ''the fire that breaks from'' the windhover relates that creature to the ploughed-down clods that shine and the galled embers that ''gash gold-vermillion.'' It seems clear, however, and important, that the poet can distinguish several sorts of light: the light of earthly nature, as in **"God's Grandeur,"** which turns to darkness as it dies; the light of mortal human selves, as in **"To What Serves Mortal Beauty?"** which becomes dark only insofar as it is mortal and removed from a divine source; the light of God himself, the flame of the Father in **"The Deutschland"** that makes use of deadly darkness to evoke men's own bright inner lights, but also the milder light of the Son, which contends with the darkness in men and which is reflected by those inner lights flashing from the heroic nun and from the windhover.

One question the light imagery in Hopkins' poetry might be taken to pose is whether these several sorts of light form an imaginative pattern, whether they are related accidentally or essentially. . . . Hopkins, like other Victorian poets, both appreciates the beauty of natural light and recognizes its harshness. This can be a matter of mood. He can alternately derive hope and joy from daylight, as Tennyson does from the dawn in ''The Two Voices,'' and see it as bafflingly irrelevant to his own inner darkness, as Tennyson does in the early lyrics of *In Memoriam,* where the dawn is ''blank.'' He can recognize the ambiguity of nature's light, its significance depending upon mood and point of view—as Tennyson perhaps does in ''The Vision of Sin,'' which ends, ''God made himself an awful rose of dawn,'' and as Arnold does in ''The New Sirens'' and Swinburne in ''The Lake of Gaube,'' for examples. But Hopkins' thought is more systematic, being founded on dogma, than that of most other Victorian writers, and for him a proper response to the light of nature must distinguish it from but also specifically relate it to the fire which is human inscape—and to God the ''Orion above.'' The problem is one of personal belief but also one of poetic imagery.

Victorian imaginations, still largely dominated by the grandeur and the difficulties of the Romantic temper, repeatedly brood upon the relation of man to external nature, of the human figure to the landscape. In Hopkins' scheme of imagery, this becomes specifically the problem of how the light of self, the flash of human inscape, is related to the natural lights and beauties of the world. Hopkins' answer can be given only by reference to the light of God in Christ. A relationship is definitely established in **"That Nature Is a Heraclitean Fire and of the Comfort of the Resurrection,"** the poem whose title both states a proposition and introduces a subject for contemplation. Joining the proposition about nature constantly inconstant and the contemplation of the fact of an unnatural or miraculous event breaking into the otherwise continuous natural flux, the poet can observe the supposed nature of men and assert the true state of mankind.

Like so many other lyrics about natural loveliness, this poem begins with a literal description of a scene. And, again characteristically, the poet is attracted by the sky and light effects. Clouds are like puff-balls, or pillows, or groups of roisterers thronging the heavens, gleaming "in marches." They sparkle as they march or move along, or they brighten up large areas, territories in the sky. Bright rays of sun make strips of light (shives, which are slices or threads) and ropes of shadow (if "tackle" means rope) under the arches of elm trees. The light and shadow produce stripes, lacy patterns with lances or lashes of brightness on the ground, and when the bright and dark "pair," the landscape is literally seen as pied or dappled, as spotted. For the moment this seems like a delightful dappling, as it has been in **"God's Grandeur."** Still, the evidence is that storms occur in this world: yesterday's tempest has left some marks. And, precisely as in **"God's Grandeur,"** man's treading down and marking natural beauty also flaws it—even though ministering winds erase the marks as natural grandeur renews itself.

> Delightfully the bright wind boisterous ropes, wrestles,
>   beats
>   earth bare
> Of yestertempest's creases; in pool and rutpeel parches
> Squandering ooze to squeezed dough, crust, dust;
>   stanches,
>   starches
> Squadroned masks and manmarks treadmire toil there
> Footfretted in it.

The boisterous wind moves in a current across the ground as if it were a rope pulled rapidly; in swaying things here and there it seems to be wrestling, and even to be beating against the earth in its playfulness, as it blows away or flattens out the litter left by yesterday's rain storm. The wind and sun dry up, or parch, into dusty peels the mud of pool and ditch (rut), making the ooze spend or squander its wetness and become damp earth like dough that can be kneaded—and, at last, become crisp dry dough, or crust, hard earth with a residue of dust. In fact, the wind appears not only to stanch wetness, as one would stop up a wound and dry it, but also, like an efficient servant, to starch and leave both clean and crisp the rumpled earth's very "masks and manmarks," those signs of human habitation that cover up the landscape. These are the artificially arranged (squadroned) signs of man's pedestrian toil on the boggy earth. "Treadmire toil" suggests also the futility of most human labor, the sense of man's being "bogged down." Man has "footfretted [marks] in it," has disturbed the earth, just as his tramping over any creature might "fret" it. The first

sentence of the poem, then, four lines long, describes the sheer delight of sky, light, and earth. The second, just over four lines long, again shows nature renewing itself after man has marred its beauty. The third sentence, marking the end of a primary stage in the poem, sums up these meanings and implies much more, using the imagery of fire from the ancient philosopher Heraclitus: "Million-fueled, nature's confire burns on." In spite of men, it would seem now, the world of lovely things continues to exist. But even more than the clouds, the sunlight and the parching, starching wind do, all of them images that hint of change, the philosopher's image of the bonfire poses difficulties. All things are burning, Heraclitus said, and constant change is the only reality. Fire has to feed on fuel that cannot literally, like the mythical phoenix, renew itself; so the fire of nature is constantly renewed only as the millions of inscaped, individual, parts of nature are constantly consumed and utterly destroyed. The life of nature, then, means the endless death of all its parts. And, after all, like the elm tree and its leaves, the body of man is a part of nature, one of the fuels in its burning. For all the delight of this first stage and for all the excitement of the phrase, "nature's bonfire burns on," there is an uneasy undertone heard in the qualifying words, "million-fueled."

Even so, the first nine lines of the poem are mainly a celebration of natural vitality. Appropriately, the second stage is introduced as a contrast. For once, Hopkins marks his transition with the adversative, "but." If the **"Heraclitean Fire"** begins as a nature poem comparable with **"God's Grandeur"** and **"Pied Beauty,"** it proceeds as a reflection on man's mortality, and thus becomes rather like **"Spring and Fall."** It proceeds in sober, clear, and shorter sentences, with little of the playful echoing and verbal delight of the first section, where the poet has teased, tricked, skipped, and poured out his joy until he and his reader are breathless; and he has in fact written in "gay-gangs" of words, repeating sounds constantly in alliteration and internal rhyme just as the very life of bonfire nature repeats, sustains, always varies and yet constantly restates itself. Now, instead, the words move heavily. "Both are in an unfathomable, all is in an enormous dark / Drowned." And Hopkins' imagery, rather than one of skies and brightness, is one of light quenched, darkness, drowning, blurring, and emptiness. For now his subject is not aesthetic but moral, and the point of view is not the artist's so much as the mortal realist's. Once more the idea of inscape, of unique selfhood, provides for this shift. Seen only as a part of nature, man has the most fully developed individual identity in the landscape. And so, even if he litters and frets the rest of nature with his trash, with his marks, he himself is the finest mortal thing in a world of mortal things, the pride of all nature.

> But quench her bonniest, dearest to her, her clearest-
>   selved spark
> Man, how fast his firedint, his mark on mind, is gone!

Man's mortal spark, his bodily beauty and natural grace, can be quenched by water, by tempest and wrecking, or merely by burning itself out. One way or another, it dies. And this fact is no less painful to Hopkins than it is to the Tennyson of *In Memoriam*. Now clearly, man's mark on mind is as dear as his mark on nature can be fretting: this "firedint" mark is his communicating of self to other selves, other minds. But, as **"The Lantern Out of Doors"** has put it, the bright mark of self is soon consumed by death or distance, as individual men soon die and are forgotten. The mortal brevity of nature's highest form makes both the form and all of nature seem now dark and melancholy:

Gerard Hopkins, reflected in a lake

Hopkins's sketch of himself reflected in a lake, dated 1864.

Both are in an unfathomable, all is in an enormous dark
Drowned. O pity and indignation! Manshape, that shone
Sheer off, disseveral, a star, death blots black out; nor
    mark
        Is any of him at all so stark
But vastness blurs and time beats level.

Again darkness and drowning are opposed to light and vitality.
But now manshape is merged into landshape, or landscape,
and all is darkened, all is dead, all shape is lost. For Hopkins,
life is defined by individual shape, by inscape, the unique shape
naturally evolving from an inner principle of being that is
precisely "disseveral" because it is one, not several, not general or typical. Like his much admired Duns Scotus, with his
individuating principle of *haecceitas,* or concrete separate being,
Hopkins can conceive of universal nature only as existing in
shapes. Ironically, however, the very constancy and self-
renewing of nature that the first stage of this poem celebrates—
the fact that "nature is never spent"—is what has to destroy
all forms, just as, biologically, birth has to imply death. Time
"beats level" the very mark or memory of any man just as
today's wind "beats earth bare" and stanches "manmark."
What the speaker now sees is what he saw at first, but he sees
with different eyes, from a different vantage point, or, one
might say, in a different season of the mind, the season not of
spring morning but of fall evening. He sees that life in space
and time must mean, for men as well as for everything else,
death in space and time. Seeing this, he imagines all space and
time not as a bonfire really but as a shapeless, chaotic, great
ocean of darkness: "Unfathomable," "enormous," vast.

The adverb "delightfully" gives a key to the first stage, the
phrase "pity and indignation" sets the mood of the second,
and the verb "to be" defines the sense of the third and final
stage, the resolution. This begins "Enough!" The exclamation
can be taken in the usual sense, "Enough of all this morbid
reflection," meaning that it is nonsense or wrong to dwell on
such melancholy thoughts. In fact, however, and the point is
relevant to Hopkins' dark "terrible sonnets" of his very late
period (this poem is, of course, one of his last), it can better
be read to mean no more than what it literally says. The reflections on mortality have gone on not too long but simply
long enough. It is good and necessary to think, even in pity
and indignation, of how natural beings die, but one can dwell

on such matters only so long. The first and second stages are
both necessary to lead one on to the final stage. And this final
reflection on what it means for man truly to *be* represents a
higher version of the subject with which the poem began. For
the subject now again is renewal, the renewal of life. First,
nature renews itself after storms and pollutions. Second, since
nature is like a great fire, in renewing itself it destroys all its
individual forms; and from man's point of view this fact makes
all of nature dark and terrible because within it shape, or specific being, is ephemeral. But, third, a man's shape, or being
can be renewed as a fire is, and yet not destroyed, because it
is more than natural. In nature's renewal of its fire there can
be no resurrection, for nature consumes shape; the supernatural
renewal restores and preserves shape, for it is precisely a resurrection of the body. So "the Resurrection" of Christ, which
sets the pattern for an ultimate resurrection of all men's bodies,
is a "heart's clarion" like the trumpet call of the angel Gabriel
on the last day.

    Away grief's gasping, joyless days, dejection,
        Across my foundering deck shone
    A beacon, an eternal beam. Flesh fade, and mortal trash
    Fall to the residuary worm; world's wildfire leave but
        ash:
            In a flash, at a trumpet crash,
    I am all at once what Christ is, since he was what I am,
        and
    This Jack, joke, poor potsherd, patch, matchwood,
                immortal
        diamond,
            Is immortal diamond.

"Grief's gasping," the dejection of "joyless days," is what
the darkest poems about the sense of self have expressed. But
now, in this great and almost final poem, the imagery is echoed,
and the themes are more succinctly developed, of Hopkins'
most ambitious earlier work, **"The Deutschland."** . . . And in
this final mood the poet is willing to let time and space blur,
to let the flesh fade, the mortal body be consumed by worms
and by the Heraclitean fire that leaves only ash, the literal dust
to which mortal bodies return. For the flash of light reveals an
inner shape that outlasts infinitely the splendid but brief natural
form. A man, for Hopkins, is like the windhover and any other
creature that reveals Christ's inscape, and yet he is much more
than any other creature can be: he is what Christ is "in a flash."
He is Christ-like when he flashes forth his own light all of a
sudden. And he is what Christ is "at a trumpet crash," at the
clarion call signalling the resurrection of all bodies on the day
of judgment. The tenses—what Christ was on earth, what I
am, what bodies will be at last—are all merged in an eternal
present, a being essentially out of time. "I am," this body
"is." Time is still kept in mind, as Christ "was what I am,"
a man incarnate in the flesh, at a point in history, but the
meaning of all human history since that time—and "since"
means both "because" and "ever since"—is eternal as well.
Everything in time belongs partly to nature, but what is wholly
natural is fuel in the temporal bonfire. Man exists not only in
time, as Christ has been not only of the mortal flesh. Thus, a
man, who appears to be and partly is common, "Jack" the
common man, and trivial, a "joke," who appears to be mere
clay, "potsherd," and fuel for the all-consuming fire of time,
"matchwood," is really more than all this. Hopkins has used
the term "Jack" several times before: in **"The Candle Indoors,"** in the lines (about "Jackself") **"My Own Heart Let
Me Have More Pity On,"** and in the fragment that begins,

"The Shepherd's Brow, Fronting Forked Lightning," in which "Man Jack the man is, just." In each place the name suggests an everyman, a common and a dull sort of creature. In the **"Heraclitean Fire"** Jack the ordinary self becomes a diamond. This last image carries the sense of infinite durability, for a diamond is the hardest of substances and is indestructible by fire. It also suggests the beauty of form that has been produced by stress, as the carbon of the jewel is like the earth and ember of **"The Windhover,"** flashing forth its brilliance only after having been submitted to intense pressure. And the diamond, for all its brilliance, is not so much the source as the reflector of light, catching it and flashing back. The immortal diamond is the creature and not the creator, even though at best it imitates and beautifully shows forth the divine and perfect light.

The **"Heraclitean Fire"** calls for such explication as this not because of its ambiguous phrasing and syntax, for it is less ambiguous than **"The Windhover"** and much of **"The Deutschland;"** and in fact the first part, its verbally most difficult one, has a total meaning extremely simple and obvious. Rather, the best of Hopkins' verse sustains a thinking-out of one's response to it, as the last part of this poem does, because for him art and thought are one. The rhyme, rhythm, and imagery *are* meaning, and it is as important in reading Hopkins to observe the ironic rhyming of "spark" and "dark," the change in speed of the sentences, from "all is in an enormous dark" to "a heart's clarion!" and the several implications of "dust," "bonfire," and "diamond," as it is to know the eschatology of the resurrection of the body.

In his thinking and feeling through images, often ambivalently, Hopkins is, again, as recognizably Victorian as Tennyson or Arnold. The difference is that his ambivalence is emotional but not, so to speak, intellectual; at best, his images both invite a double response and retain a single meaning. Men's inscapes are expressed in the observed lights of nature, as they are natural and mortal; yet the light that shapes an individual being is the reflection as well of divine light. And the image, of the body, the beacon, or the diamond, remains one. This is why, in spite of all his sufferings and anxieties—and he is quite as much in earnest about man's life, the beauty of nature, and the will of God as any other Victorian—Hopkins seems to have a more consistent imagination, in dealing with the largest of themes, than many of his contemporaries.

The danger of this consistency might be his striking the reader as narrow, as repetitive. Still, his imagery is specific and real, and his traditional response to Victorian questions about man and nature is as rich, complex, and personal as it is essentially paradoxical. He is more technically original and not much more limited by subject than George Herbert. Like Herbert and unlike the Tennyson of the *Idylls,* who is also deeply concerned with spiritual self and physical nature, Hopkins has full intellectual control of his imagery and plot. For Tennyson's attempted image of Christ, a King representing pure spirit in conflict with the senses, is actually a Manichean anti-Christ who can only demonstrate how sterility and death, not marriage and its promise of birth, result from this conflict. If Hopkins' intellectual control of image and action is more consistent than Tennyson's, his point of view toward self and nature—as distinct from mood—is more consistent than, for instance, Arnold's; in Arnold's poetry, the ocean of external nature is sometimes man's exemplar of natural virtue and sometimes wholly alien to man. And although it is not necessarily a fault when a poet shifts the sense of a metaphor or symbol from poem to poem—with certain writers, one might argue, the

result is freshness and variety—Arnold's shifting reveals an uncertainty about how to define or imagine man and nature, an uncertainty that makes the tone in his straightforward intellectual poems ring false by sounding either shrill or vague, as Hopkins' poetic statements of belief—even those that are relatively flat—virtually never do. Finally, Hopkins sustains his imagery within a poem much more consistently than Swinburne can, with his kaleidoscopic images of praise for freedom from all dogma and imposed forms. Tennyson writes poetry with more profoundly mysterious and more powerful symbolism; Arnold has a greater range and variety of mythic sources and ideas; and Browning has more dramatic force, more negative capability. Yet, compared with his major contemporaries, with whom he shares so many interests, Hopkins is more often able to concentrate into the brief lyric a clearly conceived, a coherently imagined, "philosophic" meaning. This is so because, as the consistency of his descriptive and metaphoric language from poem to poem may suggest, he maintains a central and single, if complex, idea of man and nature.

Not that Hopkins is in every respect superior to other Victorian poets. But within his range and at his best, his artist's imagination orders idea, plot, iconography, and tone in a way quite remarkable for his period, while using the themes of his period. Such poems, both personal and intellective or "objective," as **"The Windhover," "Spring and Fall,"** and, especially, **"That Nature Is a Heraclitean Fire"** are as luminous, as clear and whole, as any of the greatest English lyrics. (pp. 149-63)

> *Wendell Stacy Johnson, in his* Gerard Manley Hopkins: The Poet as Victorian, *Cornell University Press, 1968, 178 p.*

PAUL L. MARIANI (essay date 1970)

[Mariani provides a commentary on "Spelt from Sibyl's Leaves" in which he presents the poem as a meditation on hell.]

Sometime in the bleak twilight days of October 1884, Hopkins conceived and began **"Spelt from Sibyl's Leaves,"** for early drafts of the poem exist in his unpublished Dublin Notebook for this period. There is an appropriate shadowiness around the inception of this poem which stands at the threshold of the splendid series of sonnets of desolation written most probably between January and midsummer of 1885. (p. 197)

Hopkins' world [was dark] and wintry, and almost two years elapsed before he told Bridges about his sonnet. Even then he remarks only on its rhythm. "I have at last completed but not quite finished the longest sonnet ever made and no doubt the longest making," he wrote Bridges on November 26, 1886, from St. Stephen's, Dublin. "It is in eight-foot lines and essays effects almost musical." And two weeks later he finally sends off the sonnet to Bridges with the almost fond remark that this is indeed an exceptional child of which to be proud:

> I mean to enclose my long sonnet, the longest, I still say, ever made; longest by its own proper length, namely by the length of its lines; for anything can be made long by eking, by tacking, by trains, tails, and flounces. I shd. be glad however if you wd. explain what a *coda* is and how employed. Perhaps I shall enclose other sonnets. Of this long sonnet above all remember what applies to all my verse, that it is, as living art should be, made for performance and that its performance is not reading

with the eye but loud, leisurely, poetical (not rhetorical) recitation, with long rests, long dwells on the rhyme and other marked syllables, and so on. This sonnet shd. be almost sung: it is most carefully timed in tempo rubato. . . . I send tonight only one sonnet.

The music of the sprung eight-stress lines of this extraordinarily heavy sonnet is quite a departure from anything Hopkins had created before. The rhythm here is more percussive and owes something of its grounding to traditional Gregorian chant and the older classical heptachord, both of which allow for a wide range of modulation in the chanting voice. The accompaniment remains throughout a steady eight-stress line, marked by a strong caesura after the fourth foot. But the fluctuation of speed between lines is surprisingly great, and Hopkins has here rid himself of the metrical equivalence of the musical "tyranny of the bar." For example, there is the difference between the slow, stately, echoing bass of

> Earnest, earthless, equal, attuneable, | vaulty,
>   voluminous, . . . stupendous

of line 1, and the muffled drum-beat finality of the second half of line 8,

> whelms, whelms, and will end us,

whose six syllables receive (at least conceptually) the same metronomic time as either half of line 1, with ten and nine syllables respectively. The rhythm of the sonnet was given Hopkins' careful attention and, in fact, is indispensable to the understanding of the poem, as we shall see.

The lines may be very long, but they are not monotonous. And certainly the serious subject matter demands a solemn, meditative, almost chanting line. . . . "**Spelt from Sibyl's Leaves**" is his only sonnet to employ an eight-stress line, but the rhythmical experiment is a success because the thought demands such a line. After this sonnet Hopkins reverted to the Alexandrine line, perhaps because of the tendency of the eight-stress line with its pronounced caesura to break into two parts.

"**Spelt from Sibyl's Leaves**" has received close attention from several perceptive critics of Hopkins, including Leavis, Gardner, and Boyle. It has also received several quite different interpretations and some fine glosses. But that it is first of all an Ignatian meditation on the state of hell has not, to my knowledge, been adequately stated. Nevertheless, there are several notes made for a meditation on hell among Hopkins' spiritual writings which together offer a prose paraphrase of the sonnet.

The poem opens with a vivid Ignatian composition of place. Evening is overtaking day, straining to blend inexorably and irreversibly into night. This blending of evening into night is mimetically captured in the digraph and vowel chiming and smooth blending of word into word in "*Ear*nest, *ear*thless, *equal*, attune*a*ble." But the dental stops work against a too-easy blending. There is a pause and then a chiming at the other end of the alphabet with "*v*aulty, *v*olumin*ous*, . . . stupend*ous*." Hopkins uses seven epithets to inscape "Evening." Evening is radically different from the "dapple" of day, and the gay, pied complexity of the world of light gives way to somber, undifferentiated uniformity. The colorful mask of the world, which before seemed to be morally neutral, is peeled away to reveal its essentially "earnest" nature. Evening becomes strange and dark and must be judged by quite other than diurnal standards; it is attuneable, able to be harmonized, to

be blended into one indistinguishable mass, like matter returning to its primal chaotic state, like the waters of Genesis.

Evening "strains" to become the nighttime as well as the night, the end, of all time. Hopkins stresses that sense of vast interstellar emptiness with the last three epithets of evening and the description of night as "tíme's vást, womb-of-all, home-of-all, hearse-of-all night." All returns to its primordial home, to its original state (its "womb"), to its hearse. Everything moves inexorably toward its end, and the end is like the beginning. For we come from darkness, and we return to darkness. There is in the adjective "voluminous," besides the meaning of volume, the equally relevant meaning of foldings, coilings, and windings (*volumen*) as evening unrolls into night, like parchment leaves on which are inscribed the record of our life. The sense of awe and of terrifying isolation in a strange world where nothing of what we knew remains is captured in the muffled drum-beats of the first two lines. We are under the cavernous "vaulty" dome of evening, in the burial chamber of our life. And we are at the entrance to Virgil's hell in Book Six of the *Aeneid:*

> Dimly through the shadows and dark solitudes they
>   wended,
> Through the void domiciles of Dis, the bodiless regions:
> Just as, through fitful moonbeams, under the moon's
>   thin light,
> A path lies in a forest, when Jove has palled the sky
> With gloom, and the night's blackness has bled the
>   world of colour.

Those commentators who see this sonnet as dealing only with a pre-Christian world are partially correct in that hell for Hopkins means experiencing eternal separation from God, regardless of religion. But the *Dies Irae,* which is a traditional part of the Roman Catholic Burial Mass, also joins the pagan Sibyl's prophecies with those of the Bible. In the first tercet, David is linked with the Cumaean prophetess:

> Dies irae, dies illa,
> Solvet saeclum in favilla:
> Teste David cum Sibylla.
>
> (Day of wrath, that day
> Will unwind time into ashes:
> Both David and Sybil are witness.)

The receding "hornlight" of the sun, that opaque, horn-colored, serene twilight which is so pervasive after the sun has sunk below the horizon, continues to fade in the west. Above, the cold, flickering white points of the first stars begin to appear, showing their light but not altering the disposition of blackness on earth. The "fire-folk" of "**The Starlight Night**" now seem to sit in judgment, as they "overbend us," and show us God's anger in the "Fíre-féaturing heaven." The stars reveal themselves as having always been behind the dappled sky, and their progressive unfolding etched against the darkening heavens is caught in the unfolding of the words. "Earliest stars" elides into the more sharply focused "earl-stars," and is then more forcefully stressed in "stárs principal." One phrase literally unravels from the one before, as our life itself ravels off onto "twó spools." The heavens appear in all their terrifying vastness now that earth resolves herself into a world of shadows. There is a similar image of God's awesomeness in the heavens, eternally there, beyond the bright dapple of day, in "**The Blessed Virgin Compared to the Air We Breathe.**"

As evening becomes night and the light wanes, the complexity and variety which all things showed in the light now fade, and shapes (scapes) are forced to blend together, to lose all distinctiveness and selfhood. Only the most elementary outlines breaking against the dark skyline can be made out, and the skeletal selves seem "self ín self steepèd." Left to themselves, without the external light of the sun, the beauty of the trees fades and only the grotesque, frightening, gnarled outline remains. What is true of the trees is true of all things. Earth's unbinding is rapidly and "qúite / Disremembering, dísmémbering áll now." There has been no signaled shifting from the vividly pictured natural scene of the falling night to the spiritual vision of the Armageddon of the world and of the Last Judgment; the spiritual reality resides as by a sign in the natural, and any allegorical transition between the two would only water down the reality of both for Hopkins. The progression of the first six and one-half lines has been from evening to night, from the evening of a man's life to death itself, from judgment to hell.

The speaker turns inward now to make the logical application to himself, and addresses his innermost self, his heart:

> Heart, you round me right
> With: Our evening is over us; our night | whelms,
> whelms, and will end us.

There is a sense of drugged pain in the chiming of the diphthongs—in the *ow* of "round" and "our," which is repeated, in the Greek *aie* of "right," and in the repetition of the short *e* which ceases only in the finality of "end" and is percussively repeated on four stressed words within six syllables: "whélms, whélms, ánd will end us."

In line 9 the speaker, continuing to address his heart, remarks that in the dark night only the blacker outline of the leaves is etched against the sky:

> Only the beakleaved boughs dragonish | damask the
> tool-smooth bleak light; black,
> Ever so black on it.

"Damask" is a rich and complex verb. It suggests, together with "beakleaved" and "tool-smooth," the streaked metallic hardness of damascene steel. But it also suggests the weaving of damascene cloth in the images of two spools of thread, one black, one white, which follow. One type of damascene cloth is woven with a uniformly dark thread against a uniformly lighter background so that the contrast between the two is all the sharper and more distinctive, and the "twó tell, each off the óther." Both images are there in the straining and grinding of adamantine steel strands (permanence), and in the heightening of one color against the other, with no smooth transition between.

Hopkins insists on the centrality of this dark tree, for the speaker again turns to his heart with "Óur tale, O óur oracle!" Now he applies to himself what he has learned from the leaves by which the Sibyl, the ancient prophetess of Cumae, foretold the future. Life wanes as surely as does the day; it too winds to its west, and all of its multiplicity and multicolor, its "once skéined stained véined varíety" resolve into two final and eternal opposites for each of us. The scapes—the essential, moral meaning of all of our past actions—are like a mixed flock of sheep and goats which is to be separated into "twó flocks, twó folds—black, white; right, wrong." The biblical allusion is to Christ's coming to judge the world: "When the Son of Man comes in his glory, and all the angels with him, he will sit down upon the throne of his glory, and all nations will be gathered in his presence, where he will divide men one from the other, as the shepherd divides the sheep from the goats; he will set the sheep on his right, and the goats on his left" (Matthew 25:31-33). But here the application is rather to the multiplicity of our thoughts and our actions during our lifetime, which will be sorted out according to their underlying moral worth.

In line 12, the speaker makes the resolution to be more aware, to be more wary, of this final moral judgment. He must realize more fully that in the final reckoning only the moral nature of his life will count, that it is this which he must heed ("reck"). He must "mind," that is, regard this simple but difficult moral lesson; but the verb focuses on that total awareness to which he must turn his total mind. That world he must be "ware of" is hell, in which for all eternity he will be confronted with the scapes, the patterns, of his past actions. Now their real nature as displeasing to God will be revealed. Here in this inner hell, until the Final Judgment, the disembodied spirit will have to suffer the torture of tasting itself; here, what might have been and what is act on the consciousness like a "rack / Where, selfwrung, selfstrung, sheathe- and shelterless, thóughts agaínst thoughts ín groans grínd."

"The fall from heaven was for the rebel angels what death is for man," Hopkins writes in his meditation on hell. With death, the soul loses all extension and activity outward and is confined in upon itself.

> [In] man all that energy or instress with which
> the soul animates and otherwise acts in the body
> is by death thrown back upon the soul itself. . . .
> This throwing back or confinement of their energy is a dreadful constraint or imprisonment
> and, as intellectual action is spoken of under
> the figure of sight, it will in this case be an
> imprisonment in darkness, a being in the dark;
> for darkness is the phenomenon of foiled action
> in the sense of sight.

The world of **"Spelt from Sibyl's Leaves"** is this world of darkness and frustration.

It is within this dark world that we are confronted with our past actions, which leave "in our minds scapes or species, the extreme 'intention' or instressing of which would be painful and the pain would be that of fire, supposing fire to be the condition of a body . . . *texturally at stress.*" It is these dark scapes of a man's past life which are outlined against the blackness of hell and which Hopkins figures in the "beakleaved boughs dragonish" etched against the night. For "the understanding open wide like an eye, towards truth in God, towards light, is confronted by that scape, that act of its own, which blotted out God and so put blackness in the place of light." The dark background which highlights an even darker "self ín self steepèd" scape is a poetic rendition of St. Theresa's vision of hell, paraphrased by Hopkins: "'I know not how it is, but in spite of the darkness the eye sees there all that to see is most afflicting.' Against these acts of its own the lost spirit dashes itself like a caged bear and is in prison, violently instresses them and burns, stares into them and is the deeper darkened."

In hell, then, we are our thoughts, and the disparity between what *is* and what might have been is made absolutely and finally clear to us. And the two spools of right and wrong become a rack where our very self wrings against itself, where our thoughts, disembodied and unprotected scapes, are forced to grind against each other. This fiery friction of the two opposing threads rubbing against each other discharges its strain in groaning. And this violent action between what was expected and what is, is marvelously caught in the extreme muscular tension of Hopkins' tortuous rhythmic stressing of "thóughts agáinst thoughts ín groans grínd."

Of the underlying moral quality of all our actions, Hopkins stresses unequivocally that

> God is good[,] and the stamp, seal, or instress he sets on each scape is of *right, good,* or of *bad, wrong.* Now the sinner who has preferred his own good . . . to God's good, true good, and God, has that evil between him and God, by his attachment to which and God's rejection of it he is carried and swept away to an infinite distance from God; and the stress and strain of his removal is his eternity of punishment.

For with death, as he had remarked just before, "the soul is left to its own resources, with only the scapes and *species* [the instressed disembodied thoughts] of its past life; which being unsupplemented or undisplaced by a fresh continual current of experience, absorb and press upon its consciousness ['self ín self steepèd']." That a morally wrong but pleasurable act is repulsive in hell Hopkins insists upon. In hell, the awareness of a scape's repulsiveness is instressed upon us, continually burning itself into out consciousness or, in other terms, into our very self. Hell-fire, then, is explained by Hopkins as that terrible counterstress of the self as it is and as it might have been. And if there is a lack of brimstone in Hopkins' sonnet, it is replaced by a suffering all the more terrible because all the more philosophically and logically viable.

The "beakleaved boughs dragonish" means the essential evil of the scapes of the speaker's past actions; the dragon . . . is for Hopkins the devil, a "coil or spiral," a "thrower of things off the track." That the boughs are beakleaved inscapes the terror and insidiousness of the speaker's past actions; the beak belongs to the devil because he gathers "up the attributes of many creatures. . . . And therefore I suppose the dragon as a type of the Devil to express the universality of his powers . . . and the horror which the whole inspires. . . . [It] symbolizes one who aiming at every perfection ends by being a monster, a 'fright.'"

By meditating on the nature of judgment and hell, it is stressed in upon Hopkins that he must constantly be aware and be wary of a moral world, in which the beautiful dapple of creation is to be used for God's glory by giving it all back to Him. The sharpened agony of this realization of what essentially matters—right, wrong—evokes that bitter selftaste in himself, the frightening realization of his own unworthiness before the Judge of the Universe, and the pain of mastering himself. His meditation on hell evokes the hell within.

There is no consolation or hope to be found in this sonnet; it has been constructed carefully on Ignatian principles. David Downes comments that "the poetic colloquy ends with the admonishment to avoid trying to live a life, as it were, between right and wrong, for this is to be put on a frightful rack of suffering." But the poem does not say to give over contemplating a strictly moral universe. And the only resolution of the sonnet is the summoning of the speaker's will and understanding to be more aware that only right and wrong finally count. The sonnet is a sonnet of desolation, and in his comments on making the fifth exercise, the meditation on hell, St.

Ignatius writes, "here it will be to ask for a deep awareness of the pain suffered by the damned, so that if I should forget the love of the Eternal Lord, at least the fear of punishment will help me to avoid falling into sin." In meditating on a desolate subject, the exercitant is not to summon up images of consolation. And Hopkins does not.

The bitter fruit which Hopkins gleans from the meditation is the "spelt," the hard-grained wheat derived from the Sibyl's leaves. For in the grinding of thought against thought, in the excruciating self-scrutiny of the particular examen, Hopkins hoped, as he wrote some months later in **"Carrion Comfort,"** that "my chaff might fly; my grain lie, sheer and clear." "Make haste then," Hopkins urged in a sermon on death delivered sometime after his Liverpool ordeal, "work while it is day, and despair of any other chance than this: *the night is coming,* says your master, *when no man can work.*" (pp. 197-209)

Paul L. Mariani, in his A Commentary on the Complete Poems of Gerard Manley Hopkins, *Cornell University Press, 1970, 361 p.*

J. HILLIS MILLER   (lecture date 1975)

[*Miller is associated with the "Yale critics," a group generally considered the most influential critical circle in America today. Throughout his career he has applied several critical methods to literature, including New Criticism, the existential phenomenology of Georges Poulet, and deconstructionism. Miller's comments on "The Wreck of the Deutschland," first made in a 1975 lecture and excerpted below, center on Hopkins's use of language as a central theme and metaphor, as well as on the fundamental importance of various levels of rhyme as an organizing principle in the poem.*]

By linguistic moment I mean the moment when language as such, the means of representation in literature, becomes a matter to be interrogated, explored, thematized in itself. Such questioning may seem a special feature of literary criticism today, but in fact it has always been present in one way or another in literature itself. It may be that, in our tradition at least, literature is to be distinguished from other uses of language by its momentum toward such self-questioning, rather than by specific ethical or metaphysical themes. In any case, in the work of some writers among the Victorians, in spite of their overt commitment to a mimetic theory of literature, this linguistic moment becomes explicit enough and prolonged enough so that it displaces nature or human nature as the primary focus of imaginative activity. Examples would include the work of Meredith, of Ruskin, or of Pater.

A similar displacement from nature, from the self, and even from God may be observed in the poetic thought of Gerard Manley Hopkins. As I have elsewhere argued [see Additional Bibliography] and as is easy to see, there are in fact three apparently incompatible theories of poetry in Hopkins, each brilliantly worked out in theory and exemplified in practice. Poetry may be the representation of the interlocked chiming of created things in their relation to the Creation. This chiming makes the pied beauty of nature. Poetry may explore or express the solitary adventures of the self in its wrestles with God or in its fall into the abyss outside God. Poetry may explore the intricate relationships among words. These three seemingly diverse theories of poetry are harmonized by the application to all of them of a linguistic model. This model is based on the idea that all words rhyme because they are ultimately derived from the same Logos. Nature is "word, expression, news of God," and God has inscribed himself in nature. The structure of nature in its relation to God is like the structure of language in relation to the Logos, the divine Word; and Christ is the Logos of nature, as of words. The permutations of language, as in the final two lines of **"That Nature Is a Heraclitean Fire,"** correspond to or mime the permutations of the self as it is changed by grace from its Jackself, steeped in sin, turned from God, to a more Christ-like, Logosimilar, self:

> I am all at once what Christ is,   since he was what I
>   am, and
> This Jack, joke, poor potsherd,   patch, matchwood,
>   immortal diamond,
>   Is immortal diamond.

In all three realms the notion of rhyme, or the echoing at a distance of entities which are similar without being identical, is essential. Since the structure of language is the indispensable model or metaphor by means of which Hopkins describes nature or the self, the actual nature of language is a matter of fundamental importance to him. From the earliest writings of his (aside from juvenile letters) that are extant, the "Early Diaries," to the last poems, Hopkins shows his fascination with language as such. It is one theme of his masterwork, the poem which combines latently all the later poetry, both the poetry of nature and the poetry of the self—**"The Wreck of the Deutschland."** Language is not just admirably exploited by Hopkins in **"The Wreck"** to say what he wants to say. It is also interrogated for its own sake. One can see why, since everything else, his vision of nature and the self in their relations to God, hangs on the question of the nature of language and of the adequacy of the linguistic metaphor.

Everywhere in **"The Wreck of the Deutschland"** may be seen operating as its fundamental organizing principle the exploitation of rhyme in an extended sense—that is, as the echoing at a distance of elements which are similar without being identical. Rhyme operates in **"The Wreck"** both on the microscopic level of local poetical effect and on the macroscopic level of the large structural repetitions organizing the whole.

On the local level there are repetitions with a difference of word sounds, of word meanings, and of rhythmical patterns. As is indicated by the etymological speculations in Hopkins's early diaries, the basis of Hopkins's interest in the labyrinth of relations among the sounds of words is the assumption that if words sound the same they will be similar in meaning. Each sequence of words with the same consonant pattern but with different vowels—for example, *flick, fleck, flake,*—is assumed to be a variation on a single ur-meaning from which they are all derived. But all words whatsoever, all permutations of all the letters of the alphabet, are assumed to have a common source in the Word, "him that present and past, / Heaven and earth are word of, worded by," as Hopkins puts it in this poem. This attention to sound similarities in their relation to similarities of meaning is perhaps most apparent in the emphatic use of alliteration throughout the poem (breath/bread, strand/sway/sea, bound/bones in the first few lines); but there are many other forms of sound echo—assonance, end rhyme, internal rhyme, recurrences of vowel seqences, and so on—which the attentive reader will follow as threads of embodied meaning in the tapestry of the poem. In all these cases the underlying assumption is theological as well as technical. The fact that Christ is the Word, or Logos, of which all particular words are versions, variations, or metaphors allows Hopkins even to accommodate deliberately into his poem words which

are similar in sound though opposite in meaning. Christ underlies all words and thereby reconciles all oppositions in word sound and meaning: "Thou art lightning and love, I found it, a winter and warm."

The same assumptions are the grounds for the various forms of repetition with a difference of word meaning in the poem. The complex fabric of recurring metaphors is not mere verbal play to unify the poem. This fabric is based on the assumption that metaphorical comparisons reflect ontological correspondences in the world, correspondences placed there by the God whom heaven and earth are word of, worded by. Fire, water, sand, and wind are the primary elements of this "metaphorology." To the recurrence of metaphors may be added the repetition of metaphorical elements by thematic motifs which exist on the literal level of narrative in the poem. It is no accident that the poet's experience of grace in the first part of the poem is described in terms of fire, sand, and water which anticipate the elements literally present in the lightning, sandbar, and ocean waves of the **"The Wreck."**

In the same way Hopkins's frequent use of puns assumes that a single sound may be a meeting place, crossroads, or verbal "knot" where several distinct verbal strands converge. This convergence is once more evidence of ontological relations among the various meanings present in layers in a single word. Man's condition as sullenly fallen, stubbornly "tied to his turn" away from God (**"Ribblesdale"**), for example, may be expressed by calling him "dogged in den." Here "dogged" is a quadruple pun meaning sullenly determined, doglike, twisted down (as a "dog" is a kind of bolt), and hounded (as a wild animal is chased by dogs into its den and kept at bay there). There may also be an expression of the reciprocal or mirror-image relation between man and God in the fact that dog, man's epithet here, reverses the letters that spell God. This would give a fifth level of implication to the pun.

Hopkins's use of sprung rhythm, a distinctive feature of **"The Wreck of the Deutschland,"** is discussed briefly in the well-known letter of October 5, 1878, to R. W. Dixon [see excerpt above]. Hopkins's prosodic practice is a complex matter, since most of his verse combines sprung rhythm with elements from the ordinary accentual rhythm of English poetry; but the basic principle of sprung rhythm is simple enough. Each foot or measure has a single strong beat, but there may be "any number of weak or slack syllables" [see excerpt dated 1883(?)], so that a foot may have only one syllable or many, though the time length of all feet is the same. This gives the great effect of tension or "springing" to such verse. Moreover it should be remembered that Hopkins insisted that sprung rhythm is the "rhythm of common speech and of written prose, when rhythm is perceived in them." Hopkins expected his poetry to be recited aloud with the emphases and rhythms of common speech. (pp. 47-50)

The rhythmical complexities in **"The Wreck"** are not, however, merely experimental ends in themselves. They are another form of repetition with variation, another way to set down or to specify a given sound pattern which is then differentially echoed in later units of the poem, according to the fundamental principle of all poetry, which Hopkins identified in **"Poetry and Verse"** as "repetition, *oftening, over-and-overing, aftering.*"

Finally the sprung rhythm of **"The Wreck"** has as much a theological basis as any of the other forms of rhyme. As Hopkins says in the letter to Dixon of 1878, he "had long had haunting [his] ear the echo of a new rhythm which now [he] realized on paper.'' The strategic use of the metaphor of music in **"The Wreck"** makes it clear that the rhythm echoed in the poet's ear and then embodied in the words of the poem is no less than the fundamental rhythm or groundswell of the creation, the ratio, measure, or Logos which pervades all things as fundamental melody may be varied or echoed throughout a great symphony. The long Platonic and Christian tradition connecting the notion of rhythm to the Logos or underlying principle of things, ''Ground of being, and granite of it,'' as Hopkins calls it here, is subtly integrated into the texture of thought of this poem as well as into its rhythmical practice. When the poet is at the point of affirming attunement of the tall nun with the name of Christ, worded everywhere in the creation, he affirms that His name is ''her mind's'' ''measure'' and ''burden,'' where ''measure'' is musical measure and ''burden'' is fundamental melody, as in Shakespeare's ''Come Unto these Yellow Sands'': ''And, sweet sprites, the burden bear.'' The sprung rhythm of **"The Wreck"** is not merely a device for achieving a high degree of tension and patterning in the poem but is based on the belief that God himself is a rhythm which the poet may echo in his verse, his breath in its modulations and tempo answering God's ''arch and original Breath.''

To these small-scale forms of organization corresponds the way in which the large-scale dramatic or narrative structure of the poem is put together. Like ''Lycidas,'' ''Adonais,'' or *In Memoriam* **"The Wreck of the Deutschland"** is only nominally about the dead whom it memorializes. The poet's response to the death of another is the occasion for a highly personal poem about the poet's inner life and his sense of vocation. Once again repetition with variation is the basis of Hopkins's poetic practice.

The key to the overall structure of **"The Wreck of the Deutschland"** is given in stanza eighteen in which the poet describes his tears when he reads of the death of the nuns in his safe haven ''away in the loveable west, / On a pastoral forehead of Wales'': ''Why, tears! is it? tears; such a melting, a madrigal start!'' The poet's tears are a madrigal echo or rhyme of the nun's suffering—that is, an echo of the same melody on a different pitch, as in the basic musical structure of a Renaissance madrigal, canon, or round. This canonlike response leads the poet first to reenact in memory an earlier experience in which he felt God's grace, then, in the second part of the poem, to reenact in his imagination the death of the nuns. The doubling of this narrative, the memory of his own experience doubling his vivid picture of the shipwreck, causes a redoubling in a new experience of God's presence to the poet. This new experience of grace occurs within the poem itself and is in fact identical with the writing of it. The poem is addressed directly to God in the present tense, and this immediate relation of reciprocity between the poet and the God who ''masters'' him is the ''now'' of the poem generated by its doubling and redoubling of the two earlier ''nows'' which it reiterates.

All the various techniques of ''rhyme'' in **"The Wreck of the Deutschland,"** though perhaps based on methods Hopkins had learned from Pindar's odes, from Old English verse, or from the complex Welsh system of poetry called *cynghanedd*, are in fact a magnificent exploitation of the general properties of language as they may be put to the specifically poetic use. This use Roman Jakobson calls the set of language towards itself. This formulation occurs in an essay in which Jakobson quotes with approval Hopkins's expression of the same idea. In the passage in question Hopkins defines poetry as repetition. As

he puts it, ''poetry is in fact speech only employed to carry the inscape of speech for the inscape's sake,'' and ''in this light poetry is speech which afters and oftens its inscape, speech couched in a repeating figure.''

Hopkins's exploitation of the multiple possibilities of repetition in language is, however, based throughout on the theological notion that God is the Word. The divine Word is the basis of all words in their relations of similarity and difference. The play of phonic, verbal, and rhythmical texture in **"The Wreck of the Deutschland"** is controlled by the fixed idea of a creator, God, who has differentiated himself in the creation. The world is full of things which echo one another and rhyme. The same God is also the Word behind all words, the ''arch and original Breath.'' The branches and twigs of the tree of language are divided in derived forms of the initial Word. Word and world in this happily correspond because they have the same source.

This theory of poetic language is not merely exploited in **"The Wreck."** It is one of the chief thematic strands in the poem. Repeatedly, in one way or another throughout **"The Wreck,"** the question of language comes up, for example in ''I did say yes'' and ''truer than tongue'' in the second stanza. One main theme of the poem is its own possibility of being. **"The Wreck of the Deutschland,"** like many great poems of the nineteenth and twentieth centuries, is, in part at least, about poetry. In this, in spite of Hopkins's Catholicism, he may be seen as a poet in the romantic tradition, a poet who belongs in the great line leading from Wordsworth, Blake, and Hölderlin through Baudelaire, Tennyson, and Rimbaud to poets of our own century like Yeats, Rilke, and Stevens. Moreover, by exploring this aspect of the poem, the reader encounters what is most problematic about it, both in its form and in its meaning.

In a celebrated letter to Baillie of January 14, 1883, Hopkins develops a theory that in classical literature (for example in Greek tragedy) the overt narrative meaning may be matched by a covert sequence of figures or allusions constituting what he calls an ''underthought.'' This will be an ''echo or shadow of the overthought . . . an undercurrent of thought governing the choice of images used.'' . . . If the overthought of **"The Wreck of the Deutschland"** is the story of the tall nun's salvation and its musical echo both before and after by the poet's parallel experience of grace, the underthought of the poem is its constant covert attention to the problems of language. This linguistic theme is in a subversive relation of counterpoint to the theological overthought.

One important thematic element in **"The Wreck of the Deutschland"** is the image of a strand, rope, finger, vein, or stem. This image is Hopkins's way of expressing the link between creator and created. One form of this motif, however, is precisely ''tongue,'' present in the poem in ''truer than tongue,'' in ''past telling of tongue,'' with its reference to the gift of tongues which descended at Pentecost on the Apostle in tongues of flames (Acts, 2:1 ff.), in ''a virginal tongue told,'' and in the conflation of God's finger and the tongue of the bell which the tall nun rings (stanza 31). The creative stem of stress between God and his creatures is also a tongue that speaks by modulating the archoriginal breath, the undifferentiated word which is Christ, as the tongues of fire at Pentecost were ''cloven.''

Christ, the second person of the Trinity, the link between God the father and the creation, is both a principle of unity, the only means by which man may return to the singleness of the Godhead, and at the same time He is the principle of differentiation. Christ is the model for the multiplicity of individual

Three pages on which Hopkins recorded his observations of clouds, taken from one of his notebooks.

things in the world, including that most highly individuated creature, man. This is one meaning justifying Hopkins's epithet for Christ in stanza thirty-four: "double-naturèd name." Christ is both God and man, both one and many. If he is the avenue by which man loses his individuality in God, in imitating Christ or, like the tall nun, in reading Christ as the single word of the creation, at the same time Christ is the basis of puns in language. He is also the explanation of the fact that God manifests himself as both lightning and love, as winter and warm— that is, in words that sound alike but have opposite meanings. The devil is in this a diabolical imitation of Christ, as Abel and Cain are brothers, or as Deutschland is "double a desperate name," the name both of the ship and of a country, a country which is itself double. Germany has given birth both to a saint, Gertrude, lilylike in her purity, and to Luther, the "beast of the waste wood."

The theme of language in **"The Wreck"** moves toward the ambiguous vision of a God who is single but who can express himself in language and in his creation only in the multiple. Though it takes a "single eye" to "read the unshapeable shock night"—that is, to see the unitary presence of God in the storm—this insight must be expressed by the poem in multiple language. There is no masterword for the Word, only metaphors of it, for all words are metaphors, displaced from their proper reference by a primal bifurcation. When the tall nun "rears herself," like "a lioness . . . breasting the babble," she is moving back through the multiplicity of language (by way of the pun on Babel) to the Word—Christ. But what the nun says must be interpreted ("the majesty! What did she mean?"), ultimately moved back into the Babel or babble, the confusion of tongues introduced by Babel and confirmed by the gift of tongues at Pentecost.

In the same way the straightforward linear narrative of Hopkins's poem is continuously displaced by all the echoes and repetitions which turn the language of the poem back on itself in lateral movements of meaning. These lateral relationships proliferate endlessly in multitudinous echoes. If Hopkins's basic poetic strategy, as Geoffrey Hartman has noted, is a differentiation of language which attempts to say the Word by dividing the word, these divisions are controlled by no central word which could be enunciated in any language.

Striking evidences revealing Hopkins's awareness of this tragic eccentricity of the language of poetry appear in two crucial places in the poem where the poet presents an ornate series of terms or metaphors for the same thing. In one case, significantly enough, the series names the act of writing, that act whereby God's finger inscribes his own name on those he has chosen, "his own bespoken." The stanza (22) presents a series of metaphors for the act of stamping something with a sign, making it a representation or metaphor of something else, man a metaphor of Christ. These are metaphors for metaphor:

> Five! the finding and sake
> And cipher of suffering Christ,
> Mark, the mark is of man's make
> And the word of it Sacrificed.
> But he scores it in scarlet himself on his own
>   bespoken,
> Before-time-taken, dearest prizèd and priced—
>   Stigma, signal, cinquefoil token
> For lettering of the lamb's fleece, ruddying of the rose-
> flake.

"Finding," "sake," "cipher," "mark," "word," "score," "stigma, signal, cinquefoil token," "lettering"—each is only one more word. The series is controlled by no unmoving word in any human language which would be outside the play of differentiations.

The other such list appears at the climax of the poem, the appearance of Christ to the nun at the moment of her death.

It comes just after a passage in which the poet's syntactical control breaks down (the ellipses are Hopkins's): "But how shall I . . . make me room there: / Reach me a . . . fancy, come faster—." Then follows a list of names for Christ. Significantly, this is the only place in the poem, and one of the few places in all Hopkins's English poetry, where the poet speaks with tongues himself and inserts a word not in his native language: "There then! the Master, / *Ipse*, the only one, Christ, King, Head." The tragic limitation of poetic language lies in the fact that the Word itself cannot be said. Far from having a tendency to fall back into some undifferentiated ground of phonemic similarity . . . , a word by the very fact that it is just that pattern of vowels and consonants which it is, cannot be the Word. The words of human language, for Hopkins, seem to have been born of some primal division, a fall from the arch and original breath into the articulate. This fall has always already occurred as soon as there is any human speech. Words have therefore a tendency to proliferate endlessly their permutations by changes of vowel and consonant as if they were in search for the magic word that would be the Word. From this point of view it is surely significant that the original meaning lying behind most of the word lists in Hopkins's early diaries is one form or another of the gesture of dividing or marking. The sequence "flick, fleck, flake" is only one striking example of this. For Hopkins too the beginning is diacritical, an event of separation; and all word sequences may be followed back not to a primal unity but to a primal division or splitting. Even the intimate life of the Trinity, in which Hopkins was much interested, is characterized, for him, by the act whereby God divides himself from himself, goes outside himself, "as they say *ad extra*."

The metaphor of language has a peculiar status in Hopkins's poem. It seems to be one model among others for the relation of nature to Christ or for the relation of the soul to Christ. A chain of such metaphors exists in Hopkins's poems and prose writings: music, echo, visible pattern or shape for nature's interrelations of "rhyme" in the connection of one item in nature to another and of each item to its model, Christ; cleave, sex, threshing, pitch (with a triple pun) for the action of grace on the soul. Along with the other items in the first sequence is the metaphor that says nature is interrelated in the way the words in a language are interrelated. This is one reason why Hopkins is so insistent that words should be onomatopoeic in origin. In the second sequence is included the metaphor that says the transformations of grace are like the changes from one word to another in a chain that goes from Jack to diamond. Christ is the Word on which all other words are modelled.

The difficulty raised by these terms in the two sequences is double. In the first place there is something odd about using as a model what in other cases has to be taken for granted as a transparent means of naming. Language about language has a different status from language about pomegranates being cloven, about threshing, or about sexual intercourse. Insofar as language emerges as the underthought of **"The Wreck of the Deutschland,"** language in general and figure in particular are made problematical. They no longer can be taken for granted as adequate expressions of something extralinguistic. Second, this metaphor, like all the others, asks to be followed as far as it can be taken. When this happens in Hopkins's case, the whole structure of his thought and textual practice—theological, conceptual, or representational—is put in question by the fact that there is no master word, no word for the Word, only endless permutations. For Hopkins these permutations were not based on the emanation from a primal unity. The "origin"

of language was that nonorigin which is a bifurcatio furcation which, as soon as there is language at all, h already taken place. It is this split, not unity, that by a backward movement to the origin of language, etymological speculations in Hopkins's early diaries, is not "the Word" that is reached in **"The Wreck Deutschland"** or in **"That Nature Is a Heraclitean Fire,"** but only another word, or a tautology: "diamond is diamond" in **"That Nature Is a Heraclitean Fire,"** or the breakdown of language when Christ appears to the tall nun in **"The Wreck of the Deutschland"** or when the poet tries to describe the marking of man by Christ with the "stigma, signal, cinquefoil token."

There are indeed two texts in Hopkins, the overthought and the underthought. One text, the overthought, is a version (a particularly splendid version) of western metaphysics in its Catholic Christian form. In this text the Word governs all words, as it governs natural objects and selves. Like Father, like Son, and the sons are a way back to the Father. "No man cometh to the Father but by me" (John 14:6). On the other hand the underthought, if it is followed out, is a thought about language itself. It recognizes that there is no word for the Word, that all words are metaphors—that is, all are differentiated, differed, and deferred. Each leads to something of which it is the displacement in a movement without origin or end. Insofar as the play of language emerges as the basic model for the other two realms (nature and the effects of grace within the soul), it subverts both nature and supernature. The individual natural object and the individual self, by the fact of their individuality, are incapable of ever being more than a metaphor of Christ—that is, split off from Christ. They are incapable by whatever extravagant series of sideways transformations from ever becoming more than another metaphor. On the one hand, then, "No man cometh to the Father but by me," and on the other hand, "No one comes to the Father by imitating me, for I am the principle of distance and differentiation. I am a principle of splitting which is discovered to have always already occurred, however far back toward the primal unity one goes, even back within the bosom of the Trinity itself."

If the tragedy of language is its inability to say the Word, the mystery of the human situation, as Hopkins presents it, is parallel. The more a man affirms himself the more he affirms his eccentricity, his individuality, his failure to be Christ, or Christlike, an "AfterChrist," as Hopkins puts it. It is only by an unimaginable and, literally, unspeakable transformation, the transformation effected by grace, such as the nun's "conception" of Christ at the moment of her death in **"The Wreck of the Deutschland,"** that the individual human being can be turned into Christ. The fact that this transformation is "past telling of tongue" in any words that say directly what they mean is indicated not only by the fact that the action of grace (both in this poem and throughout Hopkins) is always described in metaphor, but also by the fact that such a large number of incompatible metaphors are used, forging, sexual reproduction, speaking, eating and being eaten, threshing, rope-twisting, armed combat, change of pitch or angle ("she rears herself"), the last itself a triple pun.

To put this in terms of the linguistic metaphor: if Hopkins's poetic theory and practice are everywhere dominated by word-play based on a recognition that the relation of rhyme is the echoing at a distance of entities which are similar but not identical, the change of man through grace into Christ is a transcendence of that distance and difference into identity, a change of play into reality in which the image becomes what it images: "It is as if a man said," writes Hopkins, "That is Christ playing at me and me playing at Christ, only that it is no play but truth; That is Christ *being me* and me being Christ." **"The Wreck of the Deutschland,"** like all the great poems of Hopkins's maturity, turns on a recognition of the ultimate failure of poetic language. Its failure is never to be able to express the inconceivable and unsayable mystery of how something which is as unique as a single word—that is, a created soul— may be transformed into the one Word, Christ, which is its model, without for all that ceasing to be a unique and individual self. (pp. 51-9)

> *J. Hillis Miller, "The Linguistic Moment in 'The Wreck of the Deutschland'," in* The New Criticism and After, *edited by Thomas Daniel Young, University Press of Virginia, 1976, pp. 47-60.*

JAMES MILROY   (essay date 1977)

[*In this excerpt from his book on the "general configuration of Hopkins's language," Milroy describes the main features of the poet's lexicon, considering the relationship between Hopkins's use of this vocabulary and its linguistic sources. Further, he details two beliefs central to Hopkins's language: that sound echoes sense and that language conforms to natural laws.*]

It is relatively easy to describe in a general way the main characteristics of Hopkins's lexicon, to note its differences from the usage of other poets, to point to the origin of much of it in dialect, trade usage and colloquial English, and even to show the development of this special 'enabling' language in his diaries and Journal. . . . [A] discussion of the formative influences on Hopkins's concept of 'current language', . . . [turns] considerable attention to the nature and sources of this vocabulary. Hopkins favours monosyllabic words of early English origin (usually Anglo-Saxon, Scandinavian or early Norman French), which are currently or potentially used in two or more parts-of-speech classes (*catch, coil, comb, ruck*). Many have phonaesthetic or etymological associations within connected series (*st-, sk-, fl-, gr-* series and others are listed in the diaries; *trod* and *trade* are etymologically connected; *dew: degged* is an etymological doublet). In their form, some of these words are not standard English (*pash, mammock, slogger*), but more often words which are standard in form are used in senses which are not the normal standard ones. Sometimes a dialectical sense must be invoked (*road*, [**"Felix Randal"**]), and this is often difficult to separate from the usage of traditional crafts and trades (*random* in [**"Felix Randal"**] is a localized usage, but it is also specific to masonry). Yet others (*pitch, sake, -scape*) have developed specific Hopkinsian usages, usually in the prose of the Journal. Like the others, these tend also to be words of early English origin, and they are part of [Hopkins's] linguistic purism and *in-earnestness*. . . . Sometimes Hopkins explains the meaning of these key terms in his prose writings, and other general terms developed for the craft of description (*siding, stall* and the like) are frequent in the Journal. Hopkins's exploitation of etymology (even though it sometimes becomes a language-game) is also part of his purism and *in-earnestness*. It is not undertaken for the sake of resuscitating obsolete meanings (any more than his dialectal uses are motivated by a desire to 'preserve' dialect), but because it enables him to exploit and draw attention to patterns and relationships that actually do exist in the language and to return to literal rather than metaphorical senses of many words (thus, *trade* implies the act of treading as well as the derived sense:

'commerce'). The rich semantic texture and suggestiveness of Hopkins's poetry are largely due to his exploitation of these various lexical and semantic patterns. As Norman MacKenzie has noted, many of these words and usages have been wrongly ascribed to the influence of English literary classics (*gear* for example has been ascribed to Spenser). Overwhelmingly, the sources of Hopkins's lexicon lie, not in the classics, but in his observation of the patterns of current language, aided by knowledge derived from dictionaries and language scholarship.

But the relation of Hopkins's poetic uses of this vocabulary to its sources in the language is complex and difficult to explain. Every reader of Hopkins experiences difficulty in knowing the precise meaning of a word in a given context. Some ordinary words, like *buckle* in **"The Windhover"**, are notorious cruxes, but many others which have been less often discussed, are equally troublesome. What precisely does the poet mean by *pied and peelèd May* or *belled fire* or *disseveral*? If we do not fully understand them, our understanding of his poetry is limited to that extent. When the word is not a normal standard word at all (*brandle, sloggering*), we may think we have found the answer by tracing a dialectal or historical origin, only to discover that the dialectal or 'original' meaning does not quite fit the use in context. There is also a set of favourite Hopkinsian words, which constitute his basic vocabulary for describing inscape (*skeined, rope, comb, rack, bow* and others). These stand out because they often depart from expected norms and, although we usually understand them in an obvious sense, we do not fully grasp or 'catch' them unless we are aware of a complex set of semantic associations which they usually carry. Their inscape 'must be dwelt on'.

We do not *explain* the special effect of this rich language by merely stating that individual words are of provincial or early English origin. We must also ask why he uses these words and not others, and consider them in relation to his methods of heightening language in context in the poetry. The word *doom* occurs three times in his completed mature poems (*doomfire* and *doomsday* once each); *comb(s)* four times; *coil* once (also *care-coiled*); *rack* five times. They stand out because they occur where we might expect a different word, and their choice is conditioned by Hopkins's ideas about language in general and the phonetic, grammatical or semantic effects he wants to achieve in given contexts. The kinds of example we must bear in mind as we discuss his lexical usage are these: why does the poet prefer *braids of thew* to, for example, 'cords of muscle'; or *of a fourth the doom to be drowned* to 'of a quarter the fate to be drowned'? It is less relevant to suggest that Hopkins might be conditioned by metre and rhythm than it would be to suggest it of other poets: sprung rhythm gives freedom. Other phonetic devices such as alliteration and vowelling may be more important, but they are only part of an explanation (*fate* is indeed a puny word beside *doom*), since semantic associations are relevant too. The obvious preference in these passages for Anglo-Saxon words (*braids, thew, fourth, doom*) is hardly more of an explanation, since we must further ask *why* Anglo-Saxon words should be preferable. The answer to this is broadly a semantic one. . . . [Native] English words contract much more complex, subtle and far-reaching networks of relationship within the language than do Classical borrowings, and that is so whether the relationships are grammatical, semantic or phonaesthetic. Such words can be said to have more 'meaning' in the sense that they have more associations, and one word from the set (e.g. *stalwart*, from the *stand, stall, stallion, stead, steady* set) suggests the 'meaning' of one or more of the others and partakes of some of their 'meanings' by association. *Doom* is a more sublime and magnificent word than *fate* partly because it belongs to a set that includes *doomsday.* Similarly, as some semanticists argue, a word commonly used in everyday speech (therefore usually Anglo-Saxon) may pick up associations from the collocations in which it is frequently used; thus, in a sense *dark* is part of the 'meaning' of *night* and *night* part of the 'meaning' of *dark.* Again, since they are more frequently used, it is Anglo-Saxon and other early English words that we are most likely to 'know' in this way by the company they keep. (pp. 154-56)

[It] is our task to explore how Hopkins employs and selects from the vocabulary of current language to heighten his language, to make us savour words for their own sake as he savours them, to give them richer meaning and association than they have in ordinary speech, and make them 'ring' or echo their whole beings. In this we must remember two things. Hopkins believed that sound could echo sense, and he also believed that language, like nature, conformed to natural laws in that it was organized and structured in consistent and systematic ways. We shall discuss these two points in order.

First, . . . modern linguistic scholars take perfectly seriously the idea of *phonaesthesia,* not to the extent of believing that there is necessarily universal phonetic symbolism and that languages are based on strict onomatopoeia, but they do agree that, within particular languages, certain phonetic structures may carry sense associations of various kinds. Hopkins's 'etymological' series are based on associations that are psychologically real for speakers of the language. . . . [Experiments have established] that people do tend to associate back vowels and open front vowels (e.g. *u* as in *doom, o* as in *road, a* as in *dance, bad*) with magnitude, and the other front vowels with smallness. Thus a *roll* is 'large', and a *reel* relatively 'small' . . . , *doom* is a 'large' word, *fate* a 'small' one. Similarly, consonants can be arranged along a scale of relative 'brightness'; voiceless consonants are 'brighter' than voiced, and of the voiced consonants dental-alveolars (*d*) are 'darkest', labials less 'dark' and palatal-velars (*g* as in *get*) least 'dark'. Plainly, on this scale *doom* is a 'dark' word whereas *fate* is 'bright'. These considerations, even if they are probably more language-specific than Hopkins thought, are plainly of the utmost relevance to his poetry, especially since he seems to have held these views himself.

They are most obviously relevant when Hopkins in his Journal or poems is trying to suggest the sound of something by the words he uses, for example the backdraught of the tide that *shrugged* the stones and *clocked* them together. *Click* is a 'small' sound; *clock* a 'large' one. And if Hopkins had coined *sliggering* rather than *sloggering* (of the *brine* in "**The Deutschland**"), the sound suggested would be less heavy and sharper. Most would accept that, in our general vocabulary of action, movement and sensation, such words as *thud, thump, bump* are heavier, larger, darker words than *hit, flip, kick* and so on. *Flint-flake* waves on a black-backed sea are light and sharp, *flecks* on a relatively dark, heavy, rolling background. It is clear that Hopkins is aware of such phonetic suggestiveness, and he often exploits it.

Important as it is to understand that Hopkins believed that many words 'rhyme' with the texture, shape and sense-impressions of the things they stand for, it is probably more important (because it is less obvious) to understand Hopkins's exploitation of structural patterns specific to and inherent in the English language. He was well aware that a language was organized in phonology and grammar and that there were systematic

relationships through derivation or phonetic similarity. . . . [His use of *-le* words is noticeable] in "**Pied Beauty**", but from his poetry in general many more may be added, including *brandle, buckle, cobble, dimple, nursle, throstle* (a thrush), *truckle, twindle, wimple.* For Hopkins this derivational sub-system was supremely productive. In his diary and Journal he can be seen collecting such provincial uses as *rickles, stickles* ('foamy tongues', i.e. the small 'sticks' of water in waterfalls), and *grindlestone* for 'grindstone'. But he also finds these *-le* words useful in the descriptive prose of the Journal. Clouds are frequently *curdled;* in colour they may be *ruddled* (*ruddle* is related to *red* and is ochre for marking sheep). Carnations are 'powdered with *spankled* red glister', mountains are 'shaped and *nippled'.* Water *wimples,* and the wavy markings in glaciers are *wimplings.* A tree is described 'rubbing and *ruffling* with the water', and other trees *dapple* their 'boles' with shadow. The wind also *dapples,* foam is *cobbled,* and waves are *scuppled.* Hopkins observes a *brindled* heaven, and the lightning streaks in veins of '*riddling* liquid white'. Some of these words are complex coinings (*scuppled, spankled* and others will be discussed later), but others can clearly be associated with root forms: *dapple* with *dab, brindled* with *brinded* and so on. In one case, Hopkins is kind enough to indicate his derivation by its context: *ruffle* is a derivative of *rub,* phonaesthetically if not etymologically (Onions: 'of unkn. origin'), and its further association with *rough* (and cf. *shuffle*) merely strengthens its meaning. The consonant changes (*b—p, b—f*) in these pairs would not trouble Hopkins at all; they are frequent historical changes, and, as he recognized in his lecture-notes, these consonants are closely related phonetically (in this case they belong to the *labial* series). Similarly, the *b* of *rub* is 'darker' and 'heavier' than the *f* of ruffle. In his poetry also, Hopkins frequently helps us to understand a word by placing it in a context where meaning can be 'carried over' from one neighbouring word to another, as with *rubbing* and *ruffling.*

Hopkins was acutely conscious of the interrelationship of pairs like *curd: curdle, brand: brandle* (cf. also *honeysuck* in ["**Epithalamion**"]), and it is prudent to remember this when we consider *buckle* in "**The Windhover**". He may have believed it to be in some way related to *buck* (which he applies to the leaping, rolling waves in "**The Deutschland**"), and . . . those critics who believe *buckle* to mean 'collapse' are probably nearly correct. Since Hopkins was fond of semantic blends as well as phonetic ones, we may suggest here that, taking into account his liking for imagery of violent motion and fluid substances, *buckle* may carry with it a suggestion of leaping, thrusting or quick movement (like the *buck* of the waves) together with the idea of *bending* (from a false etymology, OE *bugan:* bend) and collapsing (as the waves of "**The Deutschland**" collapse in a flood over the deck). But, however we may view this suggestion, it is undoubtedly important to bear in mind that Hopkins was keenly aware of derivational systems of this kind. (pp. 157-59)

Hopkins uses the normal grammatical resources of the language to derive words from one other by affixation and by compounding. In this way he can create new words not normally recognized as part of the language. Thus, *overvault* ["**The Loss of the Eurydice**"], *overbend* ["**Spelt from Sibyl's Leaves**"], *under be* ["**Peace**"], are modelled on *overthrow, underlie* and the like. They are always potential in the language, and their precise meaning is suggested by their membership of a derivational class. They differ in meaning from *bend over, be under* because they are systematically related to words which have a stative (almost permanent state) meaning, as *lie under* (temporarily) differs from *underlie* (with duration, even permanency and rest, implied). The *-le* and *-er* suffixes have a number of possible meanings. Apart from the agent-noun use of *-er* (*bake: baker*), they seem very often to have diminutive or frequentative force. Just as he favours prefixed or suffixed derivatives, so Hopkins is capable of back-formations: *encumbered* becomes *cumbered*, *overwhelms* becomes *whelms* (in "**Sibyl's Leaves**"); in "**Pied Beauty**" the 'normal' word *brindled* becomes *brinded*. Harry Ploughman's muscles, that 'onewhere *curded*, onewhere sucked or sank' are not only like stringy curds, but also *curdled*. Thus, even when such pairs or sets exist in standard usage with standard meanings, Hopkins is capable of using the words in new ways and suggesting new meanings and associations by exploiting the internal relationships in sub-systems which he has perceived in the language. At the level of morphology, this is analogous to the principle of rhyming that he exploits phonetically. Series which alliterate or partly rhyme phonetically are like these derivational series; to a certain extent the derivatives rhyme and have the same 'meaning' as the root forms; to a certain extent they differ. The language enthusiast derives pleasure from such controlled variation in the vocabulary.

The effects of Hopkins's exploitation of these grammatical-semantic relations are various. Words like *disremember* ("**Sibyl's Leaves**"), *disseveral* ("**Heraclitean Fire**"), *unchild, unfather* ("**Deutschland**"), *onewhere* ("**Harry Ploughman**"), *leafmeal* ("**Spring and Fall**"), *after-comers* ("**Binsey Poplars**") belong to derivational series. Most of these words require the context in which they occur for the full interpretation of their meaning (or better, *inscape*); but all are at least partly interpretable from their relationships within the language. The prefixes *un-* and *dis-* have various uses, of which Hopkins prefers the *privative* or *reversative* ones. God (in the "**Deutschland**") has made him and then almost *unmade* him; in "**Carrion Comfort**" he will not *untwist* 'these last strands of man'. To *disremember* is similarly reversative. Something *remembered* can quite logically be *disremembered* (*forgetting* is not necessarily a reversal of remembering, but rather its absence), and the word's exclusion from the general English lexicon is accidental. The meaning of *unchild* and *unfather* is privative—to deprive of children and fathers, or to do away with children and fathers, but the prefixes could potentially have different force; the verbal uses of *to child* (to give birth) and *to father* (to be, or act as, a father) are not parallel. Clearly, to *unfather* could mean 'to cause not to be a father'; to *unchild* someone could similarly mean 'to cause not to be a child'. That Hopkins does not intend these meanings is made obvious largely by the context: 'the widow-making, unchilding, unfathering deeps'. *Disremembering* and *disseveral* belong to contexts in the poems where etymological and phonetic association is important, and our understanding of them depends partly on this. Hopkins suggests relationships of meaning and grammar by using words in consecutive series in which the words concerned seem to have similar reference and by the device of *variation*. The contextual clues in 'Manshape that shone *sheer off, disseveral, a star*' suggest that Hopkins is alluding to the creation of Man in God's image and Christ in Man's shape. *Sheer off* and *disseveral* seem to refer to the *star*, which is Man. The star is distant (*sheer off*); *disseveral*, however, is difficult to interpret. It looks like an adjective formed from *dissever* ('to cut, separate': in this case *dis-* is an intensive, not a reversive, prefix), which would give the meaning *cut off* (and therefore at a distance), and this is reinforced by the pun on *sheer off* (also 'cut off'). But *disseveral* is also interpretable as *dis + several*, with *dis-* acting this time as a negative prefix. In this case, the

meaning is 'not several', therefore only *one*, 'unique'. On the semantic level, we can discern here the beginnings of a concatenation of the kind that we have called *gradience* on the phonetic level, in which the terms are linked by common properties: *sheer off* ('pure, clear, shining', and also 'cut off'); *disseveral* ('cut off', and also 'unique'); if a third term had been added, we may speculate that it would have maintained the notion of singularity and added something new. We may also see such a series as an instance of semantic 'rhyme', and note that each word in a series may also carry two or more clear meanings. They are semantic blends, of complex meaning.

The interpretation of Hopkins's coinings or special uses of words depends, therefore, on the relationships contracted by the words in two different dimensions of language: on the one hand, the underlying systems to which the words are made to belong, and on the other, the order in which Hopkins actually employs them—their contexts in the poems. Linguists distinguish these two kinds of relationships as *paradigmatic* (systematic relations within the language by which forms belonging to the same class or system can be substituted for one another in like environments) and *syntagmatic* (sequential relations). Thus, in a phrase such as *the big man*, the sequential relation of the items to one another is syntagmatic, whereas the relation of *big* to the class of adjectives that may be substituted for it is paradigmatic. In this way, word-classes (parts of speech) within the grammar of a language may be defined or delimited; if we further require that substitutable words belong to particular semantic sets (colour-words, adjectives of size, verbs of motion) we are defining particular *semantic fields*. In some of Hopkins's derivatives (*overbend, onewhere*), the paradigmatic relations of the words are alone sufficient to account for their meanings; in others the contexts are necessary, and sequential relations in the text must be invoked. Indeed, it may even be suggested that Hopkins *defines* many such words by his actual use of them in particular contexts, and even that it is one of his purposes to *define* words by *foregrounding* such relationships. . . . [The] disposition of words in their contexts can sometimes be a more decisive clue to the meaning of the less familiar words than their origins in dialect or elsewhere. (pp. 159-62)

James Milroy, in his The Language of Gerard Manley Hopkins, *Andre Deutsch, 1977, 264 p.*

MICHAEL SPRINKER   (essay date 1980)

[*In his poststructuralist study of Hopkins, Sprinker finds "harshness," "sterility," and "dogmatism" to be the most striking characteristics of the poems. He states, "My reading of Hopkins attempts to solicit [these aspects] of his texts and to liberate those texts from the weight of a critical tradition that has rendered them more or less innocuous—'sivilized' them, as Huck Finn would say." In the following excerpt, Sprinker presents his reading of "The Windhover" as an example of his proposed approach to Hopkins, arguing that the work is an allegorical representation of the process of composing poetry.*]

. . . a poem both takes its origin in a Scene of Instruction and finds its necessary aim or purpose there as well. It is only by repressing creative "freedom," through the initial fixation of influence, that a person can be reborn as a poet. And only by revising that repression can a poet become and remain strong. Poetry, revisionism, and repression verge upon a melancholy identity, an identity that is broken afresh

by every new strong poem, and mended afresh
by the same poem.
                          —Harold Bloom, *Poetry and Repression*

Among the innumerable commentaries on **"The Windhover,"** none, so far as I am aware, has recognized in this poem an allegory of the writing of poetry. There have been many elucidations of the poem's allegorical elements, and there have been almost as many readings of the poem as a representation of Hopkins's personal crisis as a poet. But no reading has brought together the two strains of interpretive strategy that would read the poem as a figural presentation of poetic figuration, a powerful rhetorical statement about the burden and the inevitability of rhetoric. Those commentators who have labeled the poem autobiographical do not go far enough, for the poem is indeed an autobiography, though less of the empirical, historical self of the poet than of the poetic identity that is and can only be realized in the writing of the poem itself. As he did even more grandiosely in **"The Wreck of the Deutschland,"** Hopkins creates himself as poet in this poem, though in the paradoxical, antithetical mode peculiar to poetry in which creation is inseparable from destruction. Hopkins becomes a poet in **"The Windhover"** by a phoenix-like act of self-immolation; from the ashes of the empirical self emerges the renewed self of the poet. (p. 4)

The separation of the poetic self from the empirical self is, Bloom argues, the dominant force in all poets since Milton, and in saying so Bloom is not alone. Compare, for example, Erich Heller's description (strongly influenced, as is Bloom's theory of poetry, by Nietzsche) of the "lyrical I" of the modern poet:

> The "I" of the successful lyrical poem is not identical with the empirico-biographical "I" of the poet. In the act of poetic creation it frees itself, Nietzsche writes, of his individual will and turns itself into a mere medium, in which and through which it finds its redemption by contemplating and uttering the *idea* of itself. . . . Through the poem the poet's self becomes an "aesthetic phenomenon," as Nietzsche calls it in *The Birth of Tragedy*, saying of it that it is the *only justification* of world and existence, and now, by implication, also of the human person. . . . The "I" of the poem, as subject *and* object of lyrical contemplation, begins to speak only when the "merely"-human "I" has come to an end.

This realization of poetic selfhood, for both Bloom and Heller, is perishable and must be renewed with each lyrical moment. As Bloom puts it, poetic identity "is broken afresh by every new strong poem, and mended afresh by the same poem." The more pronounced fragility of this identity among modern poets in comparison to their classical ancestors is the sad central motif of both Heller's and Bloom's work, and it is the increasing fragility of Hopkins's poetic identity as his career progressed that I wish to reveal.

"The Windhover" begins by posing this very problem, the meaning of the "lyrical I." Who or what is the "I" that announces itself in the poem's first word? And what is signified by "caught"? "Caught a glimpse of" seems an obvious reading, but the sense of "capture" lingers in the background. Perhaps seeing (perceiving) and possessing do not, as Geoffrey Hartman has suggested, entirely conflict: "So thing and perceiver, thing and actor, tend in the sight of Hopkins to be joined to each other as if by elecrical charge; they are connected like windhover and wind in terms of stress given and received." What is caught? The windhover, "morning's minion, king- / dom of daylight's dauphin, dapple-dawn-drawn Falcon." This would appear to resolve the ambiguity of "caught," since if we read the poem literally (as Paul Mariani commands us always to do with Hopkins), it would be unlikely that Hopkins meant he had physically captured a kestrel. As the poem continues, this becomes more clear, for Hopkins indicates that what he "caught" is not so much the bird itself as its actions. . . . It is almost as if the capturing were accomplished not by Hopkins but by the kestrel, whose flight caught and riveted the poet's attention, an experience which is recaptured in the representation of it in the poem. As Hartman argues, "thing and perceiver," bird and poet, are joined in the act of perception, so that the flight of the windhover is "caught" by Hopkins only when Hopkins is himself "caught" or arrested by the unusual form of the bird's flight.

To read the poem in this way is to take it, in the first instance, as the representation in language of a perceptual experience, a mimesis of the physical world inhabited by the poet. Though I would not deny that Hopkins had indeed observed the flight of the kestrel and that he could describe its peculiar manner of hovering in the wind very accurately, all this seems to me only the beginning of any reading of the poem. Strictly speaking, the poem is not about a bird at all, nor even about the transcriptions of a perceptual experience, though interpretation must begin with the elements and relationships posited by the poem as if it were about a physical bird and the sighting of its flight by the poet. If the bird in the poem has a referent outside the poem itself, it is not so much the kestrel as all those birds so preternaturally present in the Romantic lyric: Keats's nightingale, Shelley's skylark, Tennyson's eagle, Hardy's darkling thrush, Yeats's falcon and golden singing bird, and Stevens's blackbird. In each of these poems, the song or the flight of the bird becomes an emblem of the poet's own voice, of his vocation, in the original sense of a "calling or summons," as a poet. **"The Windhover,"** like two other of Hopkins's poems of this period, **"The Sea and the Skylark"** and **"The Caged Skylark,"** situates itself within this powerful tradition, which, along with running water, the tower of mountain peak, the wind, *et cetera,* is among the principal tropes of Romanticism. Hopkins's windhover is itself troped in the poem. The poem is thus a figurative response to the figures of Romanticism. . . . But Hopkins gives the further rhetorical twist, unusual among the major English Romantics, of religious orthodoxy. Keats wrote his "Ode to a Nightingale," Shelley addressed his poem "To a Skylark," but Hopkins addresses his poem "To Christ Our Lord."

All interpreters of **"The Windhover"** have recognized that its true subject is not the flight of the kestrel but the Incarnation and Redemption of Christ. Most have assumed that this "underthought" is the figurative meaning intended by the literal description of the bird's movements. W. H. Gardner's paraphrase of the poem is representative:

> I *inscape* this windhover as the symbol or analogue of Christ, Son of God, the supreme Chevalier. May the human equivalents of this bird's heroic graces and perfectly disciplined *physical* activity be combined and brought to a much higher *spiritual* activity in my own being, just as these attributes were once and for all so

transmuted in Christ. It is the law of things that characteristic natural action or "selving," however humble it may be, frequently gives off flashes of heart-stirring beauty; how much more then should characteristically Christ-like action (including conscientious toil and willing self-sacrifice) give glory and be pleasing to Christ our Lord!

Gardner's interpretation shows a characteristic confusion of the literal with the figurative. The bird's flight is "literally" represented in the poem; Christ is "figuratively" represented by "the symbol or analogue" of the windhover. But in what sense can the poem be said to represent the flight of the windhover? Obviously, the bird is not physically present on the page, nor can the reader actually behold its flight. What the reader perceives are the words of the poet, which are themselves already figural. Hopkins does not say simply that he saw a hawk, a falcon, a kestrel, or a windhover (the last word is already a figurative designation for this species of bird, a metonymy derived from the kestrel's peculiar manner of flying), but that he "caught this morning morning's minion, king- / dom of daylight's dauphin, dapple-dawn-drawn Falcon." Nor does he say that he beheld a bird in flight, but "caught" "his riding" and "striding," "how he rung upon the the rein of a wimpling wing," "the hurl and gliding." Whatever perceptual experience might have preceded the writing of the poem, the poem itself presents only language; the tropes and figures of the first eight lines are taken from language, not from nature. If the poem has a literal meaning it is simply this: "I am a poem."

To paraphrase Bloom, who claims that poems are psyches represented in texts, the poem is a self presented textually in the tropes of language structured by rhythm and rhyme. To write poetry was for Hopkins an act of self-creation, or, in Hopkins's own terminology, "selving." The best gloss on **"The Windhover"** is thus another poem by Hopkins in which the language of the poem foregrounds the activity of selving:

> As kingfishers catch fire, dragonflies draw flame;
>   As tumbled over rim in roundy wells
> Stones ring; like each tucked string tells, each hung bell's
> Bow swung finds tongue to fling out broad its name;
> Each mortal thing does one thing and the same:
>   Deals out that being indoors each one dwells;
>   Selves—goes itself, *myself* it speaks and spells,
> Crying *What I do is me: for that I came.*
>
> Í say more: the just man justices;
>   Keeps gráce: thát keeps all his goings graces;
> Acts in God's eye what in God's eye he is—
>   Christ. For Christ plays in ten thousand places,
> Lovely in limbs, and lovely in eyes not his
>   To the Father through the features of man's faces.

If each "mortal thing" "Selves—goes itself; *myself* it speaks and spells, / Crying What I do is me: for that I came,'" then each poem says no more than "I am a poem, this poem, 'As kingfishers catch fire.'" But the "lyrical I" who speaks this poem and identifies himself in the sestet says more. The poem not only proclaims its own existence but also its imitation of Christ. This is not at all the same thing as saying that the poem or the "I" *is* Christ. The poem's action, represented in the figure "the just man justices," is the representation of the self in the tropes of language, the transformation of self from existent to text. This action of the poem, its selving, is a me-

tonymy for Christ's Incarnation. Just as Christ is "worded," to take a figure from **"The Wreck of the Deutschland,"** in the *Logos,* so the poem attains being through rhetoric; just as Christ triumphally proclaims His being in the world by His death on the cross and His Resurrection, so the poem cries out its own being by revealing itself as language, and not just any language but the troped language we designate poetry. No poem can present itself except rhetorically; no poem can say more of itself than "I am a poem."

This brings us back to the question I first posed, and which the poem itself first raises: who or what is the "I" that announces its presence at the beginning of **"The Windhover"** and speaks what follows? And to whom is this "I" speaking? The poem is addressed or perhaps dedicated "To Christ Our Lord." Is it He, then, who is spoken to when the "I" exclaims "O my chevalier!" and "ah my dear"? If so, what is the point of the poem? To instruct Christ in the meaning of His own sacrifice? And is there not more than a little presumption in addressing Christ as "my dear"?

These are all challenging questions, and I believe the poem proposes them to any rigorous reading. To begin to answer them, we must return to my original claim about this poem, that it is an allegory of the writing of poetry. I understand allegory in the following way. Allegorical art originates in what we might today call an excess of the signified. This is to say that the allegorical sign is produced by a heterogeneity between sign and referent, between word and thing. The value of the allegorical sign arises in an act of interpretation in which the interpreter—the poet or the reader of the poem—relates one allegorical sign to another. The value of the sign is thus determined by its relationship to other signs rather than to anything outside the signifying structure of which it is a part. As Walter Benjamin instructs us concerning the allegorical art of the baroque German drama, the purpose of allegory "is not so much to unveil material objects as to strip them naked. The emblematist does not present the essence implicitly, 'behind the image.' He drags the essence of what is depicted out before the image, in writing, as a caption, such as, in the emblem-books, forms an intimate part of what is depicted." Allegorical art foregrounds the signifying process. It forces the signifying structure of the allegorical script upon the reader's attention and deflects any attempt by the reader to interpret the allegorical sign as a representation of something beyond the allegory itself. Allegory thus arises from and produces in the reader a "deep-rooted intuition of the problematic character of art."

The interpretive problems presented by **"The Windhover"** derive from its allegorical structure. As I have suggested, it simply will not do to refer the imagery of the poem back to some perceptual experience of the flight of the kestrel, for the language of the poem is irreducibly figural and does not originate in a physical event in nature. "Morning's minion, king- / dom of daylight's dauphin" and all the other representations of the windhover in the poem are tropes which cannot refer to or be interpreted by referring to any species of bird in nature. Neither does the figure of Christ which lurks in the background of the poem's imagery ("dauphin," "ecstasy," "chevalier," "gall," "gash") resolve the poem's language into a fixed and invariant system of meanings arranged in a hierarchy (as the reading of Gardner and most other allegorists seeks to establish). Each of the words reminding the reader of the presence of Christ in the poem is itself a figural, not a literal, image of the Redemption. Christ is the Prince of Peace, and thus the word "dauphin" in the second line can be assigned a value that inserts the figure of Christ into the poem's signifying structure, but this only by a metonymic substitution, since Prince of Peace is only one of Christ's attributes and not His true or complete being.

Moreover, much of the poem cannot be referred back to Christ as the interpretive key to the poem's significations. The word "chevalier," for instance, can be understood as an indication of Christ as soldier/knight, a commonplace in Jesuit spirituality instilled in Hopkins by his making the *Spiritual Exercises.* Its peculiar appropriateness to the poem, however, is determined by a series of equestrian figures that have no bearing on or particular reference to Christian iconography: "striding / High," "rung upon the rein," "shéer plód makes plough down sillion / Shine." The figure of Christ as chevalier does not determine the value of these phrases, any more than they determine the value of Christ's knighthood, but both taken together produce a signifying structure in which Christ, kestrel, poet, horse, and much else are elements whose value fluctuates with the differing juxtapositions that the poet and reader make among them. Any reader must make appeals to other signifying structures outside the poem, such as Christian iconography, particularly in its Jesuit form, Shakespeare's *Henry V*—which is where Gardner locates the origin of "dauphin" and the images of the horse, falconry, skating; but none of these structures can be designated as primary or absolutely determinate for the poem's meaning.

It is only within the poem itself, in the play of the various figures derived from these other signifying structures, that the signs taken from elsewhere can be assigned a determinate value, and then only in the sense that the value of each sign is determined by the signifying structure of the poem which the sign itself goes to produce. In other words, there can be no final, unchanging meaning for the poem. What the poem intends is an allegorical structure constituted by a repetition of signs in a relationship of temporal difference in which meaning is a perpetually deferred event, for any meaning that might be attached to the allegorical sign depends not only on those signs which precede and succeed the allegorical sign itself but also on the alteration in value it will effect in those other signs. As Paul de Man has correctly said, "allegory designates primarily a distance in relation to its own origin, and, renouncing the nostalgia and the desire to coincide, it establishes its language in the void of this temporal difference." An allegorical poem like **"The Windhover"** displays meaning as an historical event that is not part of a continuum but exists as a moment in a dispersion or field of events capable of being crystallized momentarily by the tracing of certain lines of force through the field. These lines of force are the interpretive strategies suggested by the text and deployed by the reader, but such strategies specifically lack any hierarchical principles by which one pattern can be said to control all the others. Allegory signifies the incapacity of the text to be controlled, dominated, or explained by any single reading or any synthesis of several readings; it is the dance or play of interpretation as unrestricted economy.

We are brought back once again to my original question: Who or what is the "I" that opens the poem, and what has this "I" "caught"? Briefly, the "I" is the poet, not the empirico-biographical person Gerard Manley Hopkins, but the "lyrical I." It is the poet as he creates himself as poet in the unfolding of the text. What the poet "catches" (the pun on the noun form—"catch" as song or tune—is, I believe, certainly submerged in the text . . .) is the figurative play of language achieved in the poem. In this way, the windhover *is* the poem; the figurative flight of the bird described in the first ten lines is an allegorical representation of the poet's own struggle with language in writing poetry. Insofar as the poem is realized, insofar as it becomes the poem that the poet is speaking, it achieves and masters the flight of figurative language. "The achieve of, the mastery of the thing!" is the poet's exclamation of his desire to create the poem, to master the tropes of language that are so admirable and seemingly inimitable in themselves. Having attained this plateau of self-consciousness, knowing that the object of his desire is the already achieved mastery of figure, the poet turns back upon himself to reflect upon the means of this mastery. Having "caught" the windhover in the octet, the poet reproduces the manner of his catching in the sestet. In these six lines, some of the most quoted and indeed most beautiful in modern poetry, Hopkins allegorizes his own poetic destiny by doubling the poem back upon itself to reflect the process of its own making:

> Brute beauty and valour and act, oh, air, pride, plume,
>   here
>   Buckle! AND the fire that breaks from thee then, a
>   billion
> Times told lovelier, more dangerous, O my chevalier!
>
>   No wonder of it: shéer plód makes plough down
>   sillion
> Shine, and blue-bleak embers, ah my dear,
>   Fall, gall themselves, and gash gold-vermilion.

All commentators agree that the interpretive crux of the poem is the word "Buckle," and many have noted that the poem does precisely what this word proclaims at the point where it occurs in the poem—it collapses only to rise again transfigured. . . . Gardner's commentary admirably summarizes the principal critical positions with respect to the poem, and he quite rightly tries to show that . . . three meanings of "Buckle!" can be sustained in a single interpretation.

But Gardner fails to recognize what for me remains the most compelling implication of his own reasoning, namely, that the "personal and vocational 'Imitation of Christ'" which he correctly identifies as the subject of the poem is accomplished only in the act of poetic creation. The poem is not a meditation, as silent prayer would be, but a textual realization on the mystery of Christ's suffering. The struggle of the poet with figurative language and the signifying structures bequeathed to him by tradition is dramatized in the figural representations of the flight of the windhover and the Crucifixion and Resurrection of Christ. The powerful *askesis* of Christ's Incarnation and Crucifixion is doubled in the image of the bird's apparent collapse in flight, and both are figural representations of the poet's own *askesis* necessary to the creation of the poem. The flight of the windhover does not present a forbidding image of physical grace antithetical to the poet's "hidden" spiritual crusade, but rather, by its figural hovering in the first nine lines and its fall in line ten, the poem brings forth the paradoxical triumph through limitation that is Christ's peculiar achievement and the poet's destiny. By an act of willed limitation, the poet, like Christ, blazes forth in greater glory, his poetic "fire" shines "a billion / Times told lovelier, more dangerous." Most of all, it is the diligent labor, the repetition over and over again of the familiar tropes and figures inherited from tradition that give this poem its special power to move us. Hopkins's "shéer plód" over the ground of conventional language and religious imagery, his stirring of the "blue-bleak embers" of English Romantic poetry and of the traditions of Catholic spirituality, makes his own poetic plough shine and

A portrait of Hopkins the year before he died.

cause those dying embers of tradition to "gash gold-vermilion." The fallen world of nineteenth-century poetry and post-medieval Catholicism gives impetus to this poem, but the poet himself produces the glorious burst of energy that precedes the utter collapse of tradition into complete skepticism and nihilism. As Benjamin has wisely remarked, allegory originates in the Fall of Man: "The triumph of subjectivity and the onset of an arbitrary rule over things, is the origin of all allegorical contemplation. In the very fall of man the unity of guilt and signifying emerges as an abstraction. The allegorical has its existence in abstractions; as an abstraction, as a faculty of the spirit of language itself, it is at home in the Fall."

Poised on the edge of the abyss, allegory maintains its precarious equilibrium at a severe price, for the poet's Christ-like resurrection in his poem is achieved only through the most strenuous linguistic somersaults. Finally, the strain of maintaining his balance became too great for Hopkins, as the increasingly evident despair in his late poems and letters shows. The glorious fire that breaks forth in **"The Windhover"** was gradually extinguished by the growing frigidity of Hopkins's poetic life, which ended with the mournful sestet of his last poem, **"To R. B."**:

> Sweet fire the sire of muse, my soul needs this;
> I want the one rapture of an inspiration.
> O then if in my lagging lines you miss
>
> The roll, the rise, the carol, the creation,
> My winter world, that scarcely breathes that bliss
> Now, yields you, with some sighs, our explanation.

(pp. 4-15)

Michael Sprinker, in his "A Counterpoint of Dissonance": The Aesthetics and Poetry of Gerard Man-

ley Hopkins, *The Johns Hopkins University Press, 1980, 149 p.*

DANIEL A. HARRIS   (essay date 1982)

[Harris's study of Hopkins's late works, the terrible sonnets, is concerned primarily with their imagery, structure, and textual difficulties. In the excerpted passages below, he compares Hopkins's final poems of failure and isolation with his earlier, celebratory sonnets, pointing to changes in Hopkins's use of nature imagery, in his poetic structure, and in his approach to his audience.]

Hopkins's "terrible sonnets" of 1885, the bitter fruit of his pained years in Dublin, culminate his sporadic career as a poet. These six sonnets have attracted more attention than any of his other works except **"The Wreck of the Deutschland"** and **"The Windhover."** In all their brevity, they command a respect accorded greatness that can scarcely be claimed of any comparably small group of poems in Victorian or modern British literature. It must therefore seem odd, if not perverse, to write of them, as I have done . . . , as failures. An explanation is in order.

By "failure" I do not intend a critical or aesthetic judgment about their ultimate poetic worth. Instead, I use the word in a comparative sense to suggest the differences—in imaginative temperament and religious vision—between the "terrible sonnets" and Hopkins's earlier poetry: these poems "fail" to embody the methods he had previously employed, the aims he had formulated. If this were all, however, a more neutral term might well have sufficed to describe these achievements of his late career. Yet Hopkins himself considered the poems failures, albeit of a subtle kind; and it is to his own perceptions that I adhere in using the word.

Hopkins saw in these poems the fragmentation of his capacity to represent his Christian vision adequately; he took their radical shift in imaginative procedure, as measured against his earlier work, to be the mark of his decline. As he wrote frankly to his lifelong friend Robert Bridges, the poems came to him "like inspirations unbidden and against my will." Hopkins's oxymoronic simile, loaded with nuance, is not only a religious confession but the implied statement of an aesthetic position. Although he derived his phrase from Shelley ("To a Skylark," stanza 8), he here winced at Shelley's delight in the spontaneity of "hymns unbidden." By "unbidden," Hopkins meant "unwanted." The six sonnets did not manifest that penetrating delineation, that inscaping of Christ in nature which had formerly been his joy; nor did they serve a communal function by implicitly ministering to an imagined congregation. The poems verged towards nightmare: they revealed a deformed image of his own humankind and a violation of Christ's body; they failed to enact the gradual attainment of colloquy with God which he had previously made the basis of his poetic structures. Certainly the "terrible sonnets" were a new kind of poetry, and Hopkins was uncomfortable with their heterodoxy. In the phrase "against my will," he judged himself by the strictest standards of Christian volition and acknowledged that he had been compelled by instincts merely natural into writing the "wrong" kind of poetry. He recognized that he could no longer generate the sole kind of poetry he cared to produce or felt justified in producing: poems in praise of God. He would later admit to Bridges that in his "lagging lines" Bridges would "miss / The roll, the rise, the carol, the creation" which had informed his earlier work. Private torment was no fit subject for poems, and particularly not for a man who honored obedience as much as Hopkins did.

Hopkins's attitude, however, was more complex than this. Although he construed the poems as failures in the terms just stated, he also named them "inspirations"—even if not divinely prompted. What the very occasion of *having* inspirations must have meant to a man who wrote Bridges of "that coffin of weakness and dejection in which I live" can only be surmised. He must have had some sense of their poetic merit, whatever their spiritual worth; for he subjected them neither to neglect nor to burning (as he had most of the poetry written prior to his conversion) but to extensive revision. And he had the courage to revise with an eye for literary excellence, not conformity with religious convention. If one or two muddled images mar the poems (notably in **"Patience"**), they are the minute but significant indications that the spiritual crisis which prompted the poems left its mark upon his craftsmanship. But there is precious little here that evinces any diminution in power of conception, diversity in technical skill, or emotional range in delineating the soul's operations. Indeed, the "terrible sonnets" show a sudden and darkly brilliant heightening in Hopkins's scope and linguistic incisiveness. It is an irony in his tragic life that the "inspirations unbidden" he could not entirely accept have generally achieved a fame far greater than the poems of which he approved. For the religious and aesthetic failures Hopkins saw mirrored *in* the poems—their deviations from his former designs—never became a failure *of* the poetry itself. (pp. xiii-xiv)

"To Seem the Stranger," the most barren of the "terrible sonnets," contains no images from nature at all. **"I Wake and Feel"** evokes the natural world only through a pun ("fell": animal pelt). These facts suggest a central poetic truth about the world of these sonnets: nature has virtually disappeared from Hopkins's ken. In contrast to the density of natural images in his preceding work, only seven images from nature appear in the "terrible sonnets." Three of these, however, have their source or analogue (appropriately) in Job: the whirlwind in **"No Worst"**; the tempest and the chaff and grain in **"Carrion Comfort."** They are, indeed, so traditionally Biblical that their very conventionality demonstrates the failure, in the entire group, of what Ruskin called the "penetrative imagination," the faculty through which the ideal artist "plunges into the very central fiery heart" of phenomena. Hopkins's loss of capacity, learned from Ruskin, to "catch" the inscapes of nature is equally evident in the remaining four images: the mountains in **"No Worst,"** the ivied tower and the beehive in **"Patience,"** and the dappled sky in **"My Own Heart."** ... [These] images exhibit a structure of metaphor wholly at variance from that of the earlier work. At best, they are decorations; they instance, too, Hopkins's solipsistic and uncontrolled self-projection upon things. In no case, though Ruskin had urged it as the suitable end of a properly Christian poetic language, do they reveal the powerful capability that "affirms from within" the phenomena themselves.

This radical cautery of images embodying God's manifested structure and beauty—and the altered form of those few natural images that remain—is the clearest possible index that Hopkins's universe has suffered a cataclysmic fragmentation, a crisis whose bereft aftermath seems a large-scale enactment of Shakespeare's "Bare ruin'd choirs, where late the sweet birds sang." (p. 19)

It is a bitter proof of Hopkins's creative integrity and wholeness of sensibility that his personal suffering of Christ's withdrawal should have manifested itself in the actual structure of the "terrible sonnets," as well as in the imagery rooted in pathetic fallacy and dehumanization. While it is ... difficult to establish the causal relations between religious disposition and poetic form, it is nevertheless plain that the structure of the "terrible sonnets" differs markedly from that of the earlier poems. This change correlates directly with Christ's disappearance, both from nature and from the self, and with the emergence of Hopkins's solipsism. As he had lost the sacramental reciprocity between himself and nature, so, too, he became estranged from God. ... The "terrible sonnets" show, formally, an explicit and unalleviated psychomachia, an inturning of design through which contact with exterior reality is blocked or evaded. ... In its most significant manifestation, ... this introversion of design eliminates, curtails, or distorts the climactic colloquy with Christ that is the center of the Ignatian meditative pattern: the poems are dismembered, theologically unfinished. Thus, although the "terrible sonnets" may be complete as sonnets (that is, as conventionally constructed *literary* artifacts), their structure is psychically and religiously incomplete when compared both with Hopkins's earlier work and with traditional Ignatian design. Their incompleteness, particularly because it is of so organic a kind, is telling evidence of Hopkins's inability to wrest free of the "fell of dark" that enshrouded him. (p. 75)

Because its speaker cannot bear or transmit Christ the Word, **"To Seem the Stranger"** enacts, intimately, Hopkins's failure in ministry; since the "woman clothed with the sun" is an allegorical type of the Catholic Church as well as of the Virgin, it broaches this theme from a broadly institutional, as well as personal, perspective. Yet although the poem is the only one of the "terrible sonnets" to engage this theme directly, the concern is common to them all. **"Carrion Comfort"** can speak *about* Hopkins's past conversion and reception into the priesthood, but it cannot actually perform a priestly function in the present. Though Hopkins may complain, in **"To Seem the Stranger,"** that England does not hear him, he himself makes no effort to breach the silence. None of these poems postulates, as part of its rhetorical form, an individual human audience, much less a society or congregation whom the speaker serves as priest through his poetic capacity; their isolated self-enclosure is too absolute to permit those priestly and ritual gestures towards an implied audience through which he had previously fulfilled his ministry. The poems thus render the disintegration of the Christian community and, in microcosmic form, the dissolution of the visible Catholic Church. Although commentators have attended exclusively to Hopkins's relationship with God, and sometimes to its breakdown, the collapse of his connection to the religious community—no less significant than the more obvious but more private disaster—is also enacted in these poems. It is frankly a spectacle of some pathos to consider this impotence in his public institutional capacity as the concluding episode, if only in the poetry, of a man who had repudiated the Anglicanism of his family and nation, converted to Catholicism, entered the most demanding of its orders, and striven, often under adverse conditions, to serve adequately in a social role for which he was not temperamentally suited. The separation between the priest and his community that the "terrible sonnets" mirrors is the earthly correlative, within the process of daily religious life, of Hopkins's inability to sustain his communication with Christ.

Because the "terrible sonnets" lack an implied audience, they contrast in the sharpest manner possible with Hopkins's earlier poetry. This sudden cancellation of religious activity in its social dimension, however, can only be defined through its antithesis, the fullness of ministry which Hopkins had previously incorporated into his poetry; for on this matter the "terrible sonnets" provide nothing but the evidence of negation. Yet even to propose the existence of an implied audience in the bulk of Hopkins's work (to say nothing of its disappearance in the "terrible sonnets") is seemingly to disregard some known facts of his biography and to open afresh the unresolved issue of Hopkins's complicated and disquietingly ambivalent attitudes towards writing and publishing. It is essential here to make the distinction between an actual reading public exterior to the poems and the hypothesized or fictive audience Hopkins came to envisage both *for* and *in* his work; this second audience—which Hopkins later saw vanish—is the one under discussion now. But the two kinds of audience were much entwined, however unconsciously, in his mind. Indeed, the second acted as surrogate for the first; its creation was necessitated, emotionally and artistically, by Hopkins's ascetic renunciation of an earthly fame which publication before an actual reading public might have conferred. (pp. 129-30)

From a religious perspective, the absence of the fictive human audience corresponds exactly with Hopkins's failure to achieve colloquy with God in the immediate present: the languages of prayer and of ministry are stopped simultaneously. The priest cannot serve his community: he cannot articulate their prayers, cannot give them counsel or encouragement, cannot bid them to participate in the supernatural life of the Church and the Ruskinian vision of nature's sanctity. So little can he administer the sacraments that he can only portray himself, in **"I Wake and Feel,"** as a parody of the Eucharist. Hopkins later acknowledged this failure in **"To R. B."**:

I want the one rapture of an inspiration.
O then if in my lagging lines you miss

The roll, the rise, the carol, the creation,
My winter world, that scarcely breathes that bliss
Now, yields you, with some sighs, our explanation.

The confessed loss of "the carol," communal song, touches by its plangent intimacy. Despite his attempts in **"Carrion Comfort"** and **"To Seem the Stranger"** to reclaim his weakened priestly identity, in the "terrible sonnets" his speaker is largely represented as a man divested of his ecclesiastical office. If the spectacle of that denuding endows the poems with some of their tragic power, it must be remembered that the deprivation of those functions for which he cared so deeply, even in the poetry, was for Hopkins a grievous torment unmitigated by any belief in heroic dignity gained from suffering. What mattered most to Hopkins, in the simultaneous dissolution of his priestly conversations with God and with the fictive community he served, was not the personal tribulation he endured; it was instead his anguished awareness of contributing to the fragmentation of the Church. Beyond his intuition that God may have withdrawn Himself from the world or that England would be deaf to his entreaties loomed his understanding that the primary elements in the *ecclesia*—God and Christ, Their priest, and his community—had become, like nature itself, atomized and disjunct. It is hardly to be questioned that Hopkins took responsibility for the disjunction, despite his believing in the Apocalypse as part of God's design, and that he conceived the central failure of his ministry to be his inability to mediate between humankind and divinity.

A priest without a congregation, a Jesuit blocked from colloquy with God, Hopkins was left with an exhibitionism he must have despised: poems whose motive seemed not the praise of

God but the personal catharsis of private anguish, an incoherent and sometimes animalized agony which he thought so little the model of Christian humiliation and so much the venial travesty of Christ's suffering that he could but represent his pain as parody. If he could see that "my asking to be raised to a higher degree of grace was asking also to be lifted on a higher cross," Hopkins could observe with equal clarity the contemptible puniness of his misery and could utter a self-mocking prayer addressed, significantly, to no one: "tame / My tempests there, my fire and fever fussy" (**"The Shepherd's Brow"**). His earlier capacity for amplifying his own experience so that it became an aspect of the public Christian consciousness had vanished. When he ordered the "terrible sonnets" as he did in fair copy, he exerted his last effort to make his suffering instructive. With the failure of that effort in the unexpected revisions of **"To Seem the Stranger,"** his earnest desire to communicate acceptable Christian truth to the only audience now left him—Bridges—was thwarted also. The poems were indeed written, as Hopkins insisted in language rife with an exact religious knowledge of his degree of failure, "against my will." (pp. 142-44)

> *Daniel A. Harris, in his* Inspirations Unbidden: The "Terrible Sonnets" of Gerard Manley Hopkins, *University of California Press, 1982, 174 p.*

ADDITIONAL BIBLIOGRAPHY

Andreach, Robert J. "Gerard Manley Hopkins." In his *Studies in Structure: The Stages of the Spiritual Life in Four Modern Authors*, pp. 12-39. New York: Fordham University Press, 1964.
    Traces Hopkins's spiritual development as evidenced in his poems.

Bender, Todd K. *Gerard Manley Hopkins: The Classical Background and Critical Reception of His Work*. Baltimore: Johns Hopkins Press, 1966, 172 p.
    Posits that Hopkins's poetic innovations were at least partly derived from his classical and religious training.

Borrello, Alfred, ed. *A Concordance of the Poetry in English of Gerard Manly Hopkins*. Metuchen, N.J.: Scarecrow Press, 1969, 780 p.
    A computer generated concordance of Hopkins's English-language poetry.

Bottrall, Margaret, ed. *Gerard Manley Hopkins, Poems: A Casebook*. Casebook Series, edited by A. E. Dyson. London: Macmillan Press, 1975, 256 p.
    Reprints selected criticism important to the growth of Hopkins's reputation.

Boyle, Robert, S. J. *Metaphor in Hopkins*. Chapel Hill: University of North Carolina Press, 1960, 231 p.
    A study of Hopkins's use of metaphor. Boyle includes rhythm among the metaphorical vehicles that Hopkins uses in his poetry.

Broadbent, J. B. "Religious Love Poetry." In his *Poetic Love*, pp. 88-128. London: Chatto & Windus, 1964.
    Contains a discussion of Hopkins as a poet of religious love. Broadbent compares Hopkins's approach with that of the English metaphysical poet John Donne.

Bump, Jerome. *Gerard Manley Hopkins*. Twayne's English Authors Series, edited by Herbert Sussman, no. 332. Boston: Twayne Publishers, 1982, 225 p.
    A biographical and critical survey.

Cotter, James Finn. *Inscape: The Christology and Poetry of Gerard Manley Hopkins*. Pittsburgh: University of Pittsburgh Press, 1972, 347 p.

Examines Hopkins's use of myth in his poetry and its relation to Roman Catholic theology.

Davie, Donald. "Hopkins as a Decadent Critic." In his *Purity of Diction in English Verse*, pp. 160-82. London: Chatto & Windus, 1952.
    Evaluates Hopkins's literary judgments through a study of his letters. Davie places Hopkins second to Matthew Arnold as the greatest Victorian critic.

Devlin, Christopher, S.J., ed. *The Sermons and Devotional Writings of Gerard Manley Hopkins,* by Gerard Manley Hopkins. London: Oxford University Press, 1959, 370 p.
    Includes Devlin's critical and explanatory introductions to selections of Hopkins's sermons, spiritual writings, and private notes.

Donoghue, Denis. "Hopkins, 'The World's Body'." In his *The Ordinary Universe: Soundings in Modern Literature*, pp. 78-89. New York: Macmillan Co., 1968.
    Discerns an ambiguity in Hopkins's works resulting from his invocation of nature "as the mediating term between Self and God."

Downes, David Anthony. *Gerard Manley Hopkins: A Study of His Ignatian Spirit*. New York: Bookman Associates, 1959, 195 p.
    Studies Hopkins's poetry as an expression of Jesuit spirituality.

————. *The Great Sacrifice: Studies in Hopkins*. Lanham, Md.: University Press of America, 1983, 120 p.
    Contains essays on Hopkins's life and surroundings, on his attempt to find a state of balance between his roles as poet and priest, and on his religious imagination.

Dunne, Tom. *Gerard Manley Hopkins: A Comprehensive Bibliography*. Oxford: Clarendon Press, 1976, 394 p.
    A bibliography of Hopkins scholarship through 1970.

Eliot, T.S. *After Strange Gods: A Primer of Modern Heresy*. New York: Harcourt, Brace and Co., 1934, 72 p.
    A reprint of a lecture in which Eliot briefly discusses Hopkins as a devotional poet and compares him with George Meredith.

Ellsberg, Margaret. *Created to Praise: The Language of Gerard Manley Hopkins*. London: Oxford University Press, 1987, 160 p.
    Studies Hopkins's use of language as a reflection of the tension between his vocations of poet and priest.

Empson, William. Chapters IV and VII. In his *Seven Types of Ambiguity*, pp. 133-54, pp. 192-233. New York: New Directions, 1947.
    Includes influential criticism on the language of "The Windhover."

Fausset, Hugh I'Anson. "Gerard Hopkins: A Centenary Tribute" and "The Conflict of Priest and Poet in Hopkins." In his *Poets and Pundits: Essays and Addresses*, pp. 96-103, pp. 104-13. London: Jonathan Cape, 1947.
    An appreciative essay and a discussion of Hopkins's roles as poet and priest.

Fulweiler, Howard W. *Letters from the Darkling Plain: Language and the Grounds of Knowledge in the Poetry of Arnold and Hopkins*. Columbia: University of Missouri Press, 1972, 173 p.
    A linguistic and epistemological study.

Graves, Robert, and Riding, Laura. "The Unpopularity of Modernist Poetry." In *The Common Asphodel: Collected Essays on Poetry, 1922-1949*, by Robert Graves, pp. 95-108. London: Hamish Hamilton, 1949.
    A discussion of Hopkins as a modern poet. Graves and Riding, themselves modern poets, find an affinity with Hopkins in his expression of feeling, use of language, and deviation from accepted "literary decorum."

Grigson, Geoffrey. *Gerard Manley Hopkins*. Edited by Ian Scott-Kilvert. London: Longman Group for the British Council, 1955, 34 p.
    A general introduction focusing on Hopkins as a nature poet.

Hartman, Geoffrey H., ed. *Hopkins: A Collection of Critical Essays*. Twentieth Century Views, edited by Maynard Mack. Englewood Cliffs, N.J.: Prentice-Hall, A Spectrum Book, 1966, 182 p.
    Includes essays on Hopkins's works by such critics as Hartman, Herbert Marshall McLuhan, J. Hillis Miller, and Walter J. Ong.

Holloway, Marcella Marie. *The Prosodic Theory of Gerard Manley Hopkins*. Washington, D.C.: Catholic University of America Press, 1947, 117 p.
    Examines time, measure, and stress in Hopkins's sprung rhythm.

The Hopkins Quarterly. Columbia, S.C. 1974-.
    A quarterly journal devoted to Hopkins studies.

House, Humphry. "Gerard Manley Hopkins I, II, III." In his *All in Due Time: The Collected Essays and Broadcast Talks of Humphry House*, pp. 159-74. London: Rupert Hart-Davis, 1955.
    Three essays on Hopkins: an appreciative review, a response to Phare's critique (see entry below), and a discussion of Hopkins's influence on later poets.

Hudson, Derek. "Lewis Carroll and G. M. Hopkins: Clergymen on a Victorian See-Saw." *The Dalhousie Review* 50, No. 1 (Spring 1970): 83-7.
    Explores linguistic affinities between Carroll and Hopkins.

The Kenyon Critics. *Gerard Manley Hopkins*. The Makers of Modern Literature Series. Norfolk, Conn.: New Directions Books, 1945, 144 p.
    Influential essays by Austin Warren, Herbert Marshall McLuhan, Harold Whitehall, Josephine Miles, Robert Lowell, Arthur Mizener, and F. R. Leavis. Most of these essays first appeared in the *Kenyon Review* in 1944.

Lahey, G. F., S.J. *Gerard Manley Hopkins*. London: Oxford University Press, 1930, 172 p.
    The first full-length biographical study of Hopkins.

Leavis, F. R. "Gerard Manley Hopkins." In his *New Bearings in English Poetry: A Study of the Contemporary Situation*, pp. 159-93. Ann Arbor: University of Michigan Press, Ann Arbor Paperbacks, 1960.
    Recognizes Hopkins as the greatest Victorian poet.

MacKenzie, Norman H. *Hopkins*. Writers and Critics, edited by A. Norman Jeffares and R. L. C. Lorimer. Edinburgh: Oliver and Boyd, 1968, 128 p.
    A general introduction to Hopkins's works with special attention given to textual difficulties.

Mariani, Paul. *A Usable Past: Essays on Modern and Contemporary Poetry*. Amherst: University of Massachusetts Press, 1984, 268 p.
    Includes essays on such topics as Hopkins's aesthetics, the meaning of "The Wreck of the Deutschland," and central metaphors in Hopkins's poems.

McChesney, Donald. *A Hopkins Commentary: An Explanatory Commentary on the Main Poems, 1876-89*. London: University of London Press, 1968, 195 p.
    Provides detailed explications of Hopkins's major works.

Miles, Josephine. "Hopkins: The Sweet and Lovely Language." In her *Eras and Modes in English Poetry*, 2d ed., pp. 164-77. Berkeley and Los Angeles: University of California Press, 1964.
    Studies Hopkins's use of language.

Miller, J. Hillis. "Gerard Manley Hopkins." In his *The Disappearance of God: Five Nineteenth-Century Writers*, pp. 270-359. Cambridge: Harvard University Press, Belknap Press, 1963.
    Explores Hopkins's spiritual development as revealed in his works.

Milward, Peter, S.J. *A Commentary on the Sonnets of G. M. Hopkins*. 1969. Reprint. Chicago: Loyola University Press, 1969, 200 p.
    Provides individual commentary on thirty-one Hopkins poems, most of them sonnets.

————. *Landscape and Inscape: Vision and Inspiration in Hopkins's Poetry*. Grand Rapids, Mich.: William B. Eerdmans Publishing Co., 1975, 126 p.

A detailed discussion of images evoked in Hopkins's poetry, illustrated by numerous color photographs.

————, ed. *Readings of "The Wreck": Essays in Commemoration of the Centenary of G. M. Hopkins' "The Wreck of the Deutschland."* Chicago: Loyola University Press, 1976, 172 p.
A selection of essays on "The Wreck of the Deutschland."

Motto, Marylou. *"Mined with a Motion": The Poetry of Gerard Manley Hopkins.* New Brunswick, N.J.: Rutgers University Press, 1984, 203 p.
Studies "the motions of voice" in the poetry of Hopkins.

Phare, Elsie Elizabeth. *The Poetry of Gerard Manley Hopkins: A Survey and Commentary.* Cambridge: Cambridge University Press, 1933, 150 p.
Deals with the form and meaning of several of Hopkins's poems, with emphasis on his use of imagery.

Read, Herbert. "Inscape and Gestalt: Hopkins." In his *The True Voice of Feeling: Studies in English Romantic Poetry,* pp. 76-86. New York: Pantheon Books, 1953.
Examines Hopkins's application of his theories of poetic diction to his writing.

Ritz, Jean-Georges. *Robert Bridges and Gerard Hopkins, 1863-1889: A Literary Friendship.* London: Oxford University Press, 1960, 182 p.
A biographical study chronicling the friendship between Bridges and Hopkins.

Robinson, John. *In Extremity: A Study of Gerard Manley Hopkins.* Cambridge: Cambridge University Press, 1978, 175 p.
Considers the importance of Hopkins's Jesuit priesthood to his poems.

Schneider, Elisabeth W. *The Dragon in the Gate: Studies in the Poetry of G. M. Hopkins.* Perspectives in Criticism, no. 20. Berkeley and Los Angeles: University of California Press, 1968, 224 p.
Commentary on important aspects of Hopkins's poetry, including rhythm and other elements of style.

Sitwell, Edith. "Three Eras of Modern Poetry (First Lecture)." In *Trio: Dissertations on Some Aspects of National Genius,* by Osbert Sitwell, Edith Sitwell, and Sacheverell Sitwell, pp. 97-139. 1938. Reprint. Essay Index Reprint Series. Freeport, N.Y.: Books for Libraries Press, 1970.
Discusses misuse of Hopkins's techniques by poets of the 1930s.

Spender, Stephen. "The Modern Necessity." In his *The Struggle of the Modern,* pp. 98-109. Berkeley and Los Angeles: University of California Press, 1963.

A comparison of Hopkins and D. H. Lawrence as writers employing a modern idiom in poetry of religious obsession.

Storey, Graham. *A Preface to Hopkins.* London: Longman, 1981, 150 p.
Provides biographical background and a critical survey of Hopkins's works.

Sulloway, Alison G. *Gerard Manley Hopkins and the Victorian Temper.* New York: Columbia University Press, 1972, 245 p.
Examines Hopkins in the context of the Victorian age.

Thomas, Alfred, S.J. *Hopkins the Jesuit: The Years of Training.* London: Oxford University Press, 1969, 283 p.
Details Hopkins's religious training after he joined the Society of Jesus.

Thornton, R. K. R., ed. *All My Eyes See: The Visual World of Gerard Manley Hopkins.* Sunderland, England: Ceolfrith Press, 1975, 148 p.
An illustrated study of Hopkins's sketches and his surroundings. This work includes a chapter on Hopkins as an art critic.

Treece, Henry. "Gerard Manley Hopkins and Dylan Thomas." In his *How I See Apocalypse,* pp. 129-39. London: Lindsay Drummond, 1946.
Discusses Hopkins's influence on Thomas.

Walhout, Donald. *Send My Roots Rain: A Study of Religious Experience in the Poetry of Gerard Manley Hopkins.* Athens: Ohio University Press, 1981, 203 p.
Examines "the structure of religious experience characteristically informing Hopkins's poetry."

Walsh, Elizabeth, R.S.C.J. "Gerard Manley Hopkins: A Study in Counterpoise." *The Southern Review* XII, No. 1 (January 1976): 64-82.
Suggests that the suffering Hopkins expressed in the terrible sonnets was related to his exploration of his own inscape.

Weyand, Norman, S.J., ed. *Immortal Diamond: Studies in Gerard Manley Hopkins.* New York: Sheed & Ward, 1949, 451 p.
A collection of essays by Jesuit scholars on various aspects of Hopkins's works.

Winters, Yvor. "The Poetry of Gerard Manley Hopkins." In his *The Function of Criticism: Problems and Exercises,* pp. 103-56. London: Routledge & Kegan Paul, 1962.
A reprint of Winters's attack on Hopkins that first appeared in the *Hudson Review* in 1949.

Mariano José de Larra (y Sánchez de Castro)

1809-1837

(Also wrote under pseudonyms of Fígaro, El bachiller Don Juan Pérez de Munguía, El pobrecito hablador, El duende satírico, Andrés Niporesas, and Ramón de Arriala) Spanish satirist, critic, journalist, dramatist, and novelist.

Larra is often considered the greatest Spanish satirist of the nineteenth century. Despite the political repression of his day, he criticized the religious intolerance, intellectual limitations, and conservatism of Spanish society in numerous *artículos de costumbres,* or sketches of customs. These humorous but virulently satirical depictions of everyday Spanish life, many of them written under the pseudonym of Fígaro, established Larra as a popular and powerful social critic. While Larra remains best known for his *artículos de costumbres,* he also wrote influential political and literary essays, as well as a verse drama, *Macías,* and a novel, *El doncel de don Enrique el Doliente,* which are regarded as seminal contributions to Spanish Romanticism.

Larra was born in Madrid shortly after the Napoleonic occupation of Spain. Upon the French withdrawal in 1813, Larra's father, a native Spaniard who served as a doctor in the French army, fled with his family to Bordeaux, France, where Larra attended school. The family returned to Madrid five years later when amnesty for French sympathizers was declared, and in 1824 Larra entered the University of Valladolid. After an unhappy love affair, however, Larra left the University and moved back to Madrid, where in 1828 he founded the periodical *El duende satírico del día.* Editor of the journal, as well as its chief contributor, Larra offered a highly satirical view of Spanish society, attacking political corruption, low standards of literary taste, and social stagnation. This publication was suppressed by the government after only five issues, and in 1832 Larra established another periodical, *El pobrecito hablador,* which met with a similar fate after fourteen issues. Despite these setbacks, Larra continued to write articles for various journals, and in 1833 he joined the staff of the periodical *La revista española* to which—as Fígaro—he contributed many of the bitterly satirical pieces that established him as one of Spain's most famous and powerful journalists. Larra's essays fall roughly into three categories: *artículos de costumbres,* political articles, and literary criticism. The first group has been consistently praised as best illustrating his mordant wit and keen observation. Following in the tradition of the Spanish *costumbrista* writers who sought to capture the manners and customs of a particular locale, Larra was unsparing in both the honesty and sarcasm of his observations. Eagerly read by Larra's contemporaries, these colorful essays cover a wide spectrum of Spanish life, ranging from descriptions of poor service in Madrid restaurants to depictions of such characteristically Spanish institutions as the bullfight and the masked ball. In contrast, Larra's political essays lacked the humorous appeal of his *artículos de costumbres,* revealing instead his strong desire for political justice and, at the same time, his cynicism regarding the prospects for reform. In the last category of his essays, his literary criticism, Larra espoused the principles of liberalism and progress, helping to establish the artistic ideals of Spanish

Romanticism. His critical commentary includes several notable articles on Spanish and French Romantic drama.

In addition to working as a journalist, Larra wrote dramas for the Madrid stage during the 1830s. Though they proved popular and lucrative, Larra's plays are for the most part close translations of the works of such contemporary French dramatists as Eugène Scribe, Victor Henri Joseph Brahain Ducange, and Casimir Delavigne, altered only slightly for Spanish audiences. One exception, however, is *Macías,* the original verse drama that is usually considered Larra's best play. Based upon the legend of the fifteenth-century Galician poet Macías O Namorado, *Macías* combines Romantic themes with the unities of Greek drama and was well received when it premiered in 1834. The tale of Macías also constitutes the plot of Larra's only novel, *El doncel.* A historical work that, according to scholars, shows the influence of Sir Walter Scott, *El doncel* is recognized as one of the first examples of Romanticism in Spanish fiction.

Despite Larra's literary success, the final years of his life were marred by tragedy. In 1829, he married Josefa Anacleta Wetoret y Martínez, but the marriage proved a failure and Larra eventually fell in love with another woman, Dolores Armijo, who did not return his affection. During the mid-1830s, he also experienced financial difficulties and grew increasingly pessimistic about the prospects for political reform in Spain, writing one of his bleakest satires, "El día de difuntos de 1836," in which he compares Madrid to a cemetery. In 1837, after repeated quarrels with Armijo, the twenty-seven-year-old Larra shot and killed himself.

During the 1800s, Larra's writings were largely unknown outside Spain, and even today few of them have been translated into English. Nevertheless, in the twentieth century his works have elicited a small body of appreciative English-language criticism. In studying Larra, twentieth-century critics lament the lack of a comprehensive biography and the scarcity of scholarly research on his life. In addition to attempting to fill this biographical void, modern commentators have examined such topics as his Romantic tendencies, political stance, and satiric technique. Today, *Macías* and *El doncel* are recognized for their impact upon the development of Spanish Romanticism, and Larra's political and literary articles are considered of interest as reflections of the social and political climate of nineteenth-century Spain. Yet Larra is best known for his *artículos de costumbres,* which continue to be admired as some of the best works in their genre. Although they have sometimes been censured for being anti-Spanish, these essays on what Larra viewed as Spanish backwardness and indolence have been interpreted by most critics as an appeal for widespread education and social reform. The *artículos de costumbres* have also been repeatedly praised for their perceptive observations and caustic humor, qualities that made Larra, as F. Courtney Tarr expressed it, "the most applauded, most dreaded, and most highly paid pen of his time."

PRINCIPAL WORKS

"A la exposición primera de las artes españolas" (poetry) 1827; published in newspaper *Diario de avisos de Madrid*
No más mostrador (drama) 1831
    [*Quitting Business* published in periodical *Poet Lore,* 1924]
El doncel de don Enrique el Doliente (novel) 1834
Macías (verse drama) 1834
*Fígaro: Colección de artículos dramaticos, literarios, políticos y de costumbres, publicados en los años 1832, 1833, y 1834. 5 vols. (essays) 1835-37
*Obras completas de Fígaro (essays) 1835
"El día de difuntos de 1836" (essay) 1836; published in periodical *El Español*
"La nochebuena de 1836" (essay) 1836; published in periodical *El Redactor general*
Obras completas de D. Mariano José de Larra ("Fígaro") (essays, poetry, dramas, and novel) 1886
Obras de D. Mariano José de Larra (Fígaro) (essays, poetry, dramas, and novel) 1960; published in *Biblioteca de autores españoles, second series*

*The essays in these collections were first published in various periodicals, including *El duende satírico del día, El pobrecito hablador, La revista española,* and *El Español.*

***

F. COURTNEY TARR (essay date 1928)

[*Tarr outlines the contents of* El duende satírico del día, *examining them both within the context of Larra's works as a whole and in*

relation to the literary movements of his day. For additional commentary by Tarr, see the excerpt dated 1937.]

The [*El duende satírico del día*], published at Larra's own expense, was issued irregularly by four successive printers during the year 1828—in January (or February), March, May, September, and December. Its author was only nineteen years of age and unknown in the field of letters save for his **"Oda a la exposición de la industria española del año 1827,"** a composition to which he later refers as "una mala oda que el demonio nos tentó a publicar." Yet this inexperienced youth not only wrote five numbers of a journal which contains, as we shall see, the best example of the *artículo de costumbres* prior to the *Cartas españolas,* but dared to deliver a crushing attack on the leading literary journal of the day, *El correo literario y mercantil,* and its editor, D. José María Carnerero, who was among the most prominent and influential men of letters of the time.

But Larra is by no means boldly blazing a new trail. The title and contents of his journal will show that, in the main, he is following the satirico-polemical *genre* so abundant in the Peninsula in the late eighteenth and early nineteenth centuries. Even in the choice of title, Larra is following a well-worn tradition. The demon, ghost, or goblin came into use as a satiric device with Luis Vélez de Guevara's *Diablo cojuelo.* That Larra was specifically influenced by Lesage's version of Guevara is shown in the fifth *cuaderno,* when the Duende's interlocutor, D. Ramón Arriala, says: "Es decir que de esta hecha Asmodeo se volverá a sepultar en el fondo de su botella; el *Duende* feneció." Asmodée is the name of the demon in the *Diable boiteux,* not in the *Diablo cojuelo.*

The use of the word *duende* in titles of satiric pamphlets and journals had been frequent in Spain since Manuel Freyre de Silva's "Duende crítico de Palacio," a weekly series of satiric poems circulated in manuscript and aimed at Patiño and other ministers of Philip V. (pp. 31-32)

Each number of Larra's journal bears on the title-page the following epigraph: "Des sotises du temps je compose mon fiel." After the heading of each *cuaderno,* except the first, comes this citation from Phaedrus: "Neque enim notare singulos mens est mihi, Verum ipsam vitam et mores hominum ostendere." In addition, each article in each issue, beginning with the second, is headed by two or more epigraphs indicating the contents, or purpose of the article. The authors quoted are: Horace, Virgil, Boileau (twice), Racine *fils,* Quevedo (three times), Padre Isla, Iriarte, and "Jorge Pitillas." These authorities, augmented by Calderón, Voltaire, Jovellanos, and Moratín (father and son), are also cited throughout the pages of the journal. (p. 33)

These epigraphs and citations afford specific information concerning some of the literary influences at work on Larra during his formative period. They reveal a serious-minded and somewhat pedantic youth, with a classical and eighteenth-century background, a preoccupation with correct diction, and a decided leaning toward the critical and the satiric. Our examination of the individual *cuadernos* will confirm these inferences.

The first issue contains two articles, the opening one serving as a short Introduction, not only to the second, but also to the series. It is cast in the already threadbare satiric form, the dialogue. The interlocutors are el duende and el librero. The latter comes to persuade the former to write a journal, suggesting as a theme "los abusos, los ridiculeces, en una palabra, lo mucho que hay que criticar," and asserting that the duende is especially fitted for the job "con ese genio que Dios le dió tan mordaz." The duende at first refuses, because of the danger of offending individuals who, not understanding that satire is general, would consider themselves attacked personally and demand satisfaction. Having thus defined his position, the duende finally consents, in these words:

> Sí, señor; por ultimo ha vencido usted, bien a mi pesar; ahí van esos borrones; póngalos usted en limpio, en la inteligencia de que no quiero que nadie sepa que yo soy el que los publico; póngalos usted cualquier título, que en el día no se repara mucho en eso, y mientras más desatinado, más gusta, es decir, más llama la atención, más se compra; de modo que ya eso del título es especulación del librero; pero entienda usted que no le doy licencia sino para anunciarlo pelado de toda alabanza; nada de prevención, que juzgue el público lo que quiera.
>
> (pp. 33-4)

The attack on absurd titles and dishonest advertising of books, indicated in these lines, will be developed at length in the succeeding article, **"El café."** At the very start we see suggested the keynote of the series: hatred of ignorance, pretense, and bad taste, especially in matters literary.

Although the dialogue is a traditional satiric form and one frequently used in pamphlets and journalistic literature since the eighteenth century, Larra here seems to be directly inspired by the *avant-propos* to the first volume of the collected articles of Jouy, a dialogue entitled "L'Hermite de la Chaussée d'Antin et le libraire." He takes from Jouy, however, only the idea indicated in the title, the contents of the article being his own. The direct, sharp, short sentences have little of the diffuse and involved quality that unfortunately characterize, in varying degree, the rest of the journal. Stylistically, it is the best composition in the series and the one which most clearly foreshadows the author of *No más mostrador* and *El pobrecito hablador*.

Following this dialogue is a long and loosely constructed article entitled **"El café."** The opening paragraphs are worth citing as a sample of Larra's method and style; note how his sentences grow more and more involved as he warms up to his subject:

> No sé en qué consiste que soy naturalmente curioso; es un deseo de saberlo todo que nació conmigo, que siento bullir en todas mis venas, y que me obliga más de cuatro veces al día a meterme en rincones excusados por escuchar caprichos ajenos, que luego me proporcionan materia de diversión para aquellos ratos que paso en mi cuarto y a veces en mi cama sin dormir; en ellos recapacito lo que he oído, y río como un loco de los locos que he escuchado.
>
> Este deseo, pues, de saberlo todo me metió no hace dos días en cierto café de esta corte, donde suelen acogerse a matar el tiempo y el fastidio dos o tres abogados que no podrían hablar sin sus anteojos puestos, un médico que no podría curar sin su bastón en la mano, cuatro chimeneas ambulantes que no podrían vivir antes del descubrimiento del tabaco: tan enlazada está su existencia con la nicociana, y varios de estos que apodan en el día con el tontísimo y chabacano nombre de lechuguinos, alias, botar-

ates, que no acertarían a alternar en sociedad si los desnudasen de dos o tres cajas de joyas que llevan, como si fueran tiendas de alhajas, en todo el frontispicio de su persona, y si les mandasen que pensaran como racionales, que accionaran y se movieran como hombres, y, sobre todo, si les echaran un poco más de sal en la mollera.

> Yo, pues, que no pertenecía a ninguno de estos partidos, me senté a la sombra de un sombrero hecho a manera de tejado que llevaba sobre sí, con no poco trabajo para mantener el equilibrio, otro loco cuya manía es pasar en Madrid por extranjero; seguro ya de que nadie podría echar de ver mi figura, que por fortuna no es de las mas abultadas, pedí un vaso de naranja, aunque veía a todos tomar ponch o cafe, y dijera lo que dijera el mozo, de cuya opinión se me da dos bledos, traté de dar a mi paladar lo que me pedía, subí mi capa hasta los ojos, bajé el ala de mi sombrero, y en esta conformidad me puse en estado de atrapar al vuelo cuanta necedad iba a salir de aquel bullicioso concurso.
>
> (pp. 34-5)

Here we see the duende playing the traditional rôle of the curious, solitary observer. Everything and everybody he sees and hears are grist to his satiric mill. The execution is wholesale and summary. A single stroke or two suffices to sketch in the caricature of the habitués of the café.

The bulk of the article is devoted to reporting two typical café conversations: one political, the other literary. The first, and shorter one, occurs between vain and ignorant persons who deliver opinions on world-politics as if they knew more than Talleyrand or Metternich. Ignorance and presumption are here flayed, as they are in the second conversation, which a petulant *literato* starts off with the following broadside:

> Los buenos espanoles, los hombres que amamos a nuestra patria, no podemos tolerar la ignominia de que la cubren hace muchísimo tiempo esas bandadas de seudoautores, este empeño de que todo el mundo ha de dar a luz, ¡maldita sea la luz! ¡Cuánto mejor viviríamos a obscuras que alumbrados por esos candiles de la literatura!

He then launches into a diatribe against a number of the insignificant productions of the moment, denouncing contents, style, titles, and the absurd posters advertising them. Considerations of space forbid the reproduction of any of his violent, verbose, and pedantic speeches, in which critical terms such as *indecencias, chocarrerías, necedades* rub shoulders with citations from Horace, Virgil and Boileau. One of his sentences occupies twenty-six lines of printed text!

But this critic, D. Marcelo, is revealed as a pretentious and insincere person. The duende ridicules his affectation of snuff and spectacles, his excited manner of speech, and his hypocritical patriotism. Thus, through him, Larra is able to satirize ignorance and sham both in the poor literature of the day and in the wordy café critics. Literary satire evidently lies very close to his heart, for this feature—to us the least interesting both in content and style—consumes one-half of the entire article.

D. Marcelo leaves and the duende turns again to the types represented in the café. A decided improvement over the rapid-fire method of the opening paragraphs is now visible. The figures are drawn with more detail, and even stock types are presented with touches of original observation and analysis. For example, of the fool who thinks to gain friends by lavish spending, Larra says: "El no conocía que nunca se granjea sino enemigos el que ofende el amor propio de los demás haciendo siempre el gasto." A dramatic contrast is provided by having this same spendthrift refuse alms to a poor old woman. An original, contemporary type is the hypocritical ticket speculator who uses the waiter as a catspaw. The well-dressed "beat" is, of course, a conventional figure, but he is presented in a new way: through the eyes of the waiter, who is one of his victims. Other characters depicted are the military Don Juan, the inveterate smoker, and the elderly devotee of billiards.

In this article Larra is apparently inspired, but only in a general way, by Jouy's "Les Restaurateurs," in which the Hermite describes the frequenters of a restaurant and reports snatches of their conversation. Instead of a literary discussion, there is a dispute over the merits of certain actresses. The types depicted—even the military gallants—are different in the two articles.

Despite the space devoted to literary satire, **"El café"** is essentially an *artículo de costumbres*. Furthermore, it represents, especially in the latter portion, the highest stage in the development of that *genre* prior to the articles of Estébanez Calderón and Mesonero Romanos in *Cartas españolas*. Its plan is not original, and many of the figures are stock satiric types; nevertheless, the wealth and variety of the characters, the extensive use of dialogue, the touches of real observation and analysis, the creation of original figures and a potentially dramatic scene—all these features make it superior to the juvenile attempts of Mesonero in *Mis ratos perdidos* and to the timid essays contained in *Minerva, El censor,* and the later *Correo literario y mercantil*. On the whole, it is a good example of one class of the *costumbrista* article: the presentation of a gallery of types. The thrifty *Curioso parlante* could have elaborated the types here outlined into a dozen of his later sketches.

But no more types appear in the *Duende*; the youthful satirist seems to have put all his slender stock into this one article. Add to this his evident bent for literary discussion, and we may account for the fact that the succeeding numbers of the journal show the following trends: (1) retrogression and disappearance of the *costumbrista* elements and (2) accentuation of literary satire and polemic.

The second *cuaderno* has as its leading article a long satiric review of Ducange's *Treinta años, o la vida de un jugador*. This melodrama is ridiculed at every turn, without the slightest attempt at impartiality, and is held up as a horrible example of the results of the French domination of the Madrid stage. Extreme and poorly written as this review is, it possesses an interest as showing Larra's adherence to the ideas of the neoclassic school and his intense literary patriotism. Horace and Moratin are his gods. Romanticism is ridiculed as an extravagant French innovation, to be coupled with such ephemeral crazes as hydrotherapy, hypnotic cures, and the Tilbury coach. He is elaborately sarcastic over the fact that the French are now doing what Boileau condemned the Spaniards of Lope's day for doing, namely, writing plays that do not conform to the rules. He is indignant that such a monstrosity as Ducange's play, worse than the worst of Lope and Calderón, should be successful in Madrid simply because it bears the Paris trade-

mark. After reading this article it is impossible to accuse Larra of being *afrancesado,* at least in his youth. The burden of his complaint is summed up in the following paragraph, the final one of the article:

> ¡Cómo ha de ser! Paciencia. El drama es malo; pero no se silbó. ¡Pues no faltaba otra cosa sino que se metieran los españoles a silbar lo que los franceses han aplaudido la primavera pasada en París! ¡Se guardarán muy bien de silbar sino cuando se les mande o cuando venga silbando algun figurín, en cuyo caso, buen cuidado tendrían de no comer, beber, dormir ni andar sino silbando, y más que un mozo de mulas, y aunque fuera en misa! ¡Silbar a un francés! ¡Se mirarían en ello! Que hagan los españoles dramas sin reglas, *mais nous,* nosotros, que no somos españoles, y que no sabemos, por consiguiente, hacer comedias malas. *Mais nous,* que hemos introducido en el Parnaso el melodrama anfibio y disparatado, lo que nunca hubieran hecho los españoles; *mais nous,* que tenemos más orgullo que literatura; *mais nous,* que en nuestro Centro tenemos a todo un Ducange, que nos envanecemos de haber producido *La huérfana de Bruselas, Los ladrones de Marsella, La cieguecita de Olbruck, Los dos sargentos franceses,* etc.; *mais nous,* por último, que somos franceses, que habitamos en París, que no somos españoles (gracias a Dios) también sabemos caer en todos los defectos que criticamos y sabemos hacer comedias, *ut nec pes nec caput uni redatur formae,* y sabemos, lo que es mas, hacer llorar en nuestra comedia melodramática, reír en nuestra tragedia monótona y sin acción, y bostezar en la cansada y tosca música de las óperas con que, a pesar de Euterpe, nos empeñamos en ensordecer los tímpanos mejor enseñados.

(pp. 35-9)

This is the first article entirely devoted to a literary subject. Carried away by his interest in literary theory and discussion, Larra is veering away from the satire of customs. He seems to realize this himself, for the second article of the second *cuaderno* consists of a letter to the *Duende* from a fictitious subscriber, H. W., gently upbraiding him for having devoted so much space to literary satire in **"El café,"** and urging him to continue the criticism of cafés and restaurants; this the correspondent himself proceeds to do under the guise of pointing out defects for the *Duende* to satirize. Attention is called to their silly pretentiousness in names and ornamentation, which stands out in ludicrous contrast to their real backwardness and lack of comfort, service, and cleanliness. Following is an extract from the indictment:

> A propósito: criticad los manjares, sobre todo aquel engrudo llamado crema, de que no saben salir en todo el año; aquella execrable mostaza, hecha a fuerza de vinagre; aquel cocido insipido y asqueroso, y, lo que es peor, aquel sacar los mozos los cubiertos del bolsillo, donde los tienen confundidos con las puntas de los cigarros o donde participan de elementos aun peores.

(pp. 39-40)

This letter appears under the heading **"Correspondencia de 'El Duende',"** a title probably suggested by the *Correspondance de l'Hermite* of Jouy. This journalistic device—satire and criticism in the form of letters from fictitious correspondents—was, however, a well-established feature in the periodical literature of the preceding era. It represents a natural adaptation to literary journals of the real correspondence of newspapers and of the epistolary form of criticism and satire in such widespread use throughout the period between the *Cartas marruecas* and the *Cartas españolas.*

In this letter Larra again reveals his dislike of pretense. In addition, it shows other characteristic traits of the later Fígaro: hatred of backwardness and love of the refinements of material existence.

The café theme having been exhausted, Larra opens the third *cuaderno* with an article called **"Corridas de toros,"** which is in a very different vein from the others in the series. The major portion consists of a long and serious sketch of the history of bullfighting, with a great display of erudition in the shape of dates, references, citations, and even a select Bibliography. This leads up to the real point of the article: some ironic observations on the public's love for such a vulgar, dirty, and ill-smelling place as the *plaza de toros.* Even the tender-hearted maiden who faints when she pricks her finger with a needle is an enthusiastic *aficionada*! Larra deplores the fact that the average citizen should spend his income first in the wineshops and then in the *plaza.* But there is not a word of description of the spectacle itself, no feeling for its drama, movement, and color. Larra has little pictoric sense, little love of concrete detail for its own sake; he is interested primarily in the historical and social implications of his subject. He seems more closely akin to the eighteenth century here than elsewhere in the journal, both in his erudition and his passion for social reform; it is significant that at the close of his article he sums up his own position with a citation from Jovellanos' *Pan y toros.*

> Venga a los toros el chino y aprenderá a decir
> mucho en pocas palabras de la perspicacia de
> los españoles; venga todo el mundo a unas fies-
> tas, en que, como dice Jovellanos, el "crudo
> majo hace alarde de la insolencia; donde el
> sucio chispero profiere palabras más indecentes
> que él mismo; donde la desgarrada manola hace
> gala de la impudencia; donde la continua gri-
> tería aturde la cabeza más bien organizada; donde
> la apretura, los empujones, el calor, el polvo
> y el asiento incomodan hasta sofocar, y donde
> se esparcen por el infectado viento los suaves
> aromas del tabaco, el vino y los orines."
>
> (pp. 40-1)

This is the last of the articles dealing with customs. Starting with **"El café"** there has been a steady retrogression. From a gallery of contemporary types directly presented we reverted, first, to the epistolary stage, and finally to the critical essay on manners and customs in the academic manner.

The remainder of the third *cuaderno,* under the heading of **"Correspondencia de 'El Duende',"** is taken up with Larra's answer to the attack of a pamphleteer of Madrid, who has successfully hidden his identity under the pseudonym of Guindilla. This polemic is not noteworthy except for showing Larra's preoccupation with correct syntax, his resentment that his journal should be called a *papel inútil,* and for the fact that he

here employs his favorite weapon, ironic praise, thus foreshadowing the *Carta panegírica a D. Clemente Díaz.*

The fourth and fifth *cuadernos* are entirely given over to literary criticism and polemic. The fourth contains a wholesale condemnation of the *Correo literario y mercantil* in the form of a detailed review of the first twenty numbers. It starts off in Larra's characteristic ironic vein: The *Correo* is praised for its utility as a soporific and for its remarkable gift of printing much without saying anything. Then each department of the paper is taken up in order: unclassified articles, *teatros, correspondencia, misceláneas críticas,* and *variedades.* The tone is irritatingly patronizing; minute faults are magnified, and at times there is obvious straining to make a point. Sarcasm and personalities are freely employed. Extreme and unfair as his method here is, Larra's basal idea is the same as that which animates the later Fígaro: love of truth and hatred of ignorance, superficiality, and sham. For example, the theatrical reviews in the *Correo* are branded as insufficient, ignorant, and presumptuous, and the articles on the "Costumbres de Madrid" are condemned as false and superficial. (pp. 41-2)

This attack on the *Correo,* which to us seems uncalled for, was in accord with the satirico-critical tradition established by the journals and pamphlets of the eighteenth century. Polemic was the rule rather than the exception, particularly during the fervid political upheavals in the periods 1808-14 and 1820-23. The *Correo* could not fail to reply, just as tradition compelled Larra to answer Guindilla. Numbers 34, 35, 36, 38, 40, and 41 contain replies and attacks on the *Duende.*

In the fifth *cuaderno* Larra returns to the attack in the form of a dialogue between the Duende and D. Ramón Arriala. The Duende affects surprise and pain at the *Correo's* reception of his benevolent criticism, but D. Ramón flays Carnerero and his paper pitilessly. The *Correo* is answered point by point and in the greatest detail. Twelve pages (in the Cotarelo text) are devoted to one item: the proper definition of *genio* and *ingenio.* Consequently, this *cuaderno* is the most lengthy and tiresome of the entire series. Although Larra easily has the better of the argument, his real critical powers are obscured by his insistence on *minutiae* and his extreme prolixity.

The details of Larra's dispute with the *Correo* are unimportant. These *cuadernos* are chiefly of value in showing (1) Larra's courage; (2) the great difference in style and method between the prolix, pedantic Duende and the direct, incisive Fígaro; and (3) the similarity of the Duende's ideals and those of the later Fígaro. Despite its extreme and carping tone, this polemic reveals Larra's fundamental characteristics: genuine patriotism and a love of truth, sincerity, and progress. The *Correo* is condemned because it does not live up to the program announced in its prospectus, and is branded as being neither *literario* nor *mercantil,* because it provides no real stimulus to the national renascence in letters and industry.

Larra closes his *cuaderno* with a defiant "'el *Duende* está ya en pie." But unfortunately he did not confine the dispute to the columns of his journal; it came to a climax when he almost precipitated in a café in a personal quarrel with one of the editors of the *Correo.* This hitherto-unrecorded incident in Larra's life comes to light in the following manner: The leading article in the *Correo* for January 9, 1829, is a long and dignified manifesto, signed by the publisher (Pedro, Ximénez de Haro) and both editors (José María de Carnerero and Juan López Peñalver de la Torre) to the effect that certain excesses recently committed compel them to serve notice that in the future they will prosecute to the limit of the law any person transgressing the bounds of propriety in conducting literary disputes with them or their journal. The succeeding issue of the *Correo* (January 12) contains the following characteristically frank and courageous communication from Larra:

> Sres, redactores del *Correo*. Muy Sres, míos; he leído el artículo que han insertado vmds., en el número anterior de su periódico, relativo al decoro que los escritores deben al publico y se deben a sí mismos; y como dicho artículo acaba por contraerse a la indicación de un lance ocurrido en la noche del 29 de diciembre ultimo en un café de esta capital, y yo fuí en él el que llevó la palabra contra uno de vmds., no puede quedarme duda que yo soy el objeto principal de los reflexiones que vmds., publican. Con este motivo, no creo comprometer los principios que me rigen, declarando, como declaro, que en el citado lance vertí frases que yo mismo he desaprobado, cuando vuelto de un primer momento de calor, a que todo hombre está sujeto, conocí evidentemente que la moderación del redactor a quien dirigí la palabra fué la que evitó las consecuencias desagradables que se hubieran de otro modo originado. Esta declaración pública me parece que honra mis sentimientos, y espero la aprueben todos los que (como vmds., observan) no quieren vivir en el *trastorno* y en la *licencia*.
>
> En cuanto a la parte literaria de las discusiones que sostengo con el *Correo*, no tengo que hacer retracción alguna; y tanto los redactores como yo sostendremos nuestra cuestión según los medios, el talento y la inspiración con que cada uno cuente para defender sus opiniones.
>
> (pp. 42-4)

But no more issues of the *Duende* appeared. The foregoing incident may be taken as supporting the traditional belief that it was suppressed by the censor on Carnerero's initiative. This belief has been based on the vague and somewhat inaccurate statement of Larra's uncle that

> a los diez y nueve años empezó a publicar un periódico muy erudito y muy mordaz satirizando las costumbres madrileñas, con el título de *Duende satírico*, que suspendió al año y medio de su publicación, porque algunas personas de valimiento que se creían satirizadas en él interpusieron su influjo con el gobierno para que mandase suspender su publicación, y lo lograron.

The matter is, however, by no means certain. The *Duende* may have perished because of Larra's inability to find a publisher willing to take the risk of issuing the journal. In any event, the quarrel with Carnerero was certainly patched up before October 2, 1829, when the *Correo* publishes a very eulogistic notice of Larra's ode, **"A los terremotos ocurridos en España en el presente año de 1829."**

Our conclusions may be summarized as follows: In the *Duende satírico del día*, Larra starts out to satirize contemporary types and customs and produces in **"El café"** the most highly developed *articulo de costumbres* prior to the *Cartas españolas*. But the *costumbrista* material deteriorates and disappears be-

fore the increasing emphasis given to literary satire and polemic in the traditional manner. The dispute with the *Correo literario y mercantil* ends a personal quarrel for which Larra apologizes in a characteristic letter. Uneven as they are in literary merit, the articles in this youthful journal throw considerable light on Larra's formative period. The courage, patriotism, and hatred of ignorance, backwardness, and pretense which Larra shows in his later works are foreshadowed here. His intellectual background is fundamentally classic and eighteenth century. This is revealed, not only in the numerous citations and in his literary doctrines, but also in the abstract and critical quality of his mind, his preoccupation with ideas, rather than things, and in his enthusiasm for reform and progress. The *Duende satírico del día* makes clear the fundamental nature of Larra's relationship to the generation of Jovellanos and Moratín. (pp. 44-5)

> *F. Courtney Tarr, "Larra's 'Duende Satírico Del Día'," in* Modern Philology, *Vol. XXVI, No. 1, August, 1928, pp. 31-45.*

L. A. WARREN   (essay date 1929)

[*Warren extols Larra as "the greatest author of Spanish Romanticism" and also discusses the realistic and satiric nature of his writings.*]

It was as a journalist that Larra was well known in his time, and it is his journalistic articles that give him his fame to-day and an assured position in literature. He managed to crowd much into his short life of twenty-eight years. The expenditure of his energy in the Bohemian atmosphere of Madrid cafés during the romantic decades is reflected in his articles. His other literary work was considerable; he was an admirable dramatic critic; he wrote several plays which were successful at the time, but are not praised by modern critics.

His novel *El doncel de Don Enrique el Doliente* is the only romantic historical novel in Spanish worth consideration, for if it does not show a thorough mastery of the culture and life of the Middle Ages, if it lacks imagination, yet the historical apparatus is adequate. The book, which treats of fifteenth-century court life and of a well-known legend, can be read with considerable interest. Its chief defect seems to be in the construction, which causes a shifting of interest in the middle of the work: one's attention has been roused and fixed upon the curious character of Don Enrique and his peculiar treatment of his wife, and then one is required to transfer it to his equerry, who develops a hopeless and passionate love affair into which Larra pours the fervours of his temperament.

The short articles are, however, his main work. Larra is the greatest author of Spanish Romanticism. He is not only a romanticist, however, for his most remarkable literary qualities are vivid realism and biting sarcasm. His is a powerful intellect united with a melancholy disposition. The chief characteristics of his works are wit, lucidity, observation, and a compact style. He expresses a great deal in a very little space and his matter always repays careful reading.

Larra is more Spanish than romantic; that is to say, he belongs more to his race than his period, and is one of the greatest satirists of a country famous for satire. The chance political events of 1833, the liberalism and freedom of the press during the ensuing years, the temper of the minds of that time, caused him to think and feel and enabled him to express himself just as he did express himself; but he is a leading fundamental Spanish type of all times and more than an ephemeral romanticist. If he had lived about 1630 he would have resembled Quevedo, in 1730 Torres Villaroel, in 1900 Baroja; and, although his manner is spontaneous, the closest resemblance is to Quevedo.

Larra is an observer and a realist. He has a wonderful eye for seeing, and a wonderful mind for condensing what he has seen into a short space. Condensation gives power and solidity to writing—the essays of Dean Inge, for example. But being a romanticist Larra is restless and unsettled; it is when travelling in Estremadura that his roving eye and active mind enable him to give a concise and admirable summary of the province full of facts condensed into short space: he notes the appearance of the country, its economic resources, its art, industries, way of life, the character of its inhabitants. All this is recorded as seen by a man of European civilization, but a Spaniard nevertheless. Larra is a Madrileño, and most of his best articles are about the social customs of Madrid. He is a first-rate *costumbrist,* he sharply notices the life, habits and talk of the town, and puts before the reader with sarcastic irony what he has seen; the jests and satires come thick and fast; he hits the mark every time. When at his best as in **"Las antiguedades de Merida,"** almost every sentence is a sarcasm; penetrating as is the satire, it is expressed with that verve, charm and good-humour which are of the manner of Spanish wit:

> The vehicle went slowly; nevertheless, it was not a government vehicle, and it took a long time to lose sight of the delicious pavement, the different cupolas of the numerous convents, which, like the spectre described by Virgil, plunge their feet into the depths and raise their heads into the clouds, occupying everything. From time to time I turned my head and looked backwards, not like Hector towards his Andromache, but because I still seemed to hear outside the gates the noise of lawyers and poets in the café del Príncipe; the monotonous singsong voice of our comic actors still resounded in my ears; I heard the hissing of our talented romantics and classics. Inner doubts pursued me like a remorse: reforms were the only things which did not pursue me, they, without doubt, were the persecuted.

> The noise finally died down and instead Castille unrolled before my sight the arid map of its sandy desert. . . . It was certainly not the towns which hindered my progress: travelling through Spain all the time one feels like Noah's dove going forth to see if the country was habitable; the vehicle wandered alone, like the ark, in an immense extension of bare horizons. Neither houses nor villages. Where is Spain?

> Three days we wandered on through emptiness: towards the end of a fourth a limitless plain unfolded itself before my eyes, and outlined against the pale depths of a misty sky stood up confusedly the signs of a splendid town. Were there men at last? I asked myself. No; but there have been. They were the ruins of the ancient Emerita-Augusta.

As a realist Larra is interested in what is going on around him and as a Spaniard, mainly in life; secondly as a romantic in ultimate values. As a man who has fully experienced life he

A depiction by Gustave Doré of the elegant Paseo del Prado, where Larra often strolled.

cares more for men than for things; as a romantic he is interested in what goes on in the mind. Consider, then, his eyes for accurate recording; his being a *madrileño;* his powerful mind; his romantic disposition; his restlessness; the liberal ideas which he held about progress and civilization and his Spanishness which regards a life of purpose as the thing that matters. It is the combination of all these influences which lead him to stress the absolute futility and emptiness of Madrid fashionable life and the amazing idleness and laziness of the Spanish people. 'En este pais no se hace nada.' 'Nothing is ever done in this country.' Nobody ever does anything is the *leitmotiv* of his articles:

> ¿Está malo el día? el capote de barragán: a casa de la marquesa hasta las dos; a casa de la condesa hasta las tres; a tal otra casa hasta las cuatro: en todas partes voy dejando la misma conversación, en donde entro oigo hablar mal de la casa de donde vengo, y de la otra adonde voy; ésta es toda la conversación de Madrid.

> Is the weather bad? A waterproof overcoat: to the marchioness' house till two; to the countess' house till three; to somebody else's house till four; wherever one goes the same conversation; when I enter a room I hear people speaking ill of the house I've just come from, and of the house I'm just going to: that is all the conversation in Madrid.

Unite the Spaniard's laziness with his realistic outlook that only the solid things of life have value and this is the result:

> 'Mineralogy will teach you the knowledge of metals, of—'

> 'Let us do nothing until it teaches us where to find a mine.'

> 'Study geography then.'

> 'Get along with you; if I've got to go a journey tomorrow, money will be what I shall want and

not geography; the postillion will know the road, it's his business, and the way to the town where I'm going.'

'Languages.'

'I'm not studying for an interpreter: if I'm going abroad and take money they'll understand that, it's the universal language.'

'Literature, letters.'

'Letters of credit. Any other kind is an absurdity.'

... Blessed be God, Andrés, blessed be God, who has seen fit to show pity upon us and enlighten our ideas on this point. These powerful reasons are the cause of our not studying, from not studying comes our not knowing anything, and from our ignorance follows the inevitable sequel of that loathing and boredom for books which we have, and which so much redounds to the honour and advantage, and above all of the repose of the country.

Laziness being the strongest trait in the character of the Spaniard, he does not take the trouble to procure those comforts of material life which he alone values. But Larra is not lazy; he wants to stir up his country to action. A Liberal in politics, he believes in progress; as a Spaniard he likes practical life and his aim is to introduce into Spain all the comforts and improvements of modern civilization.

Larra, considered in his day a brilliant jester, was in reality excessively serious. He saw no gaiety in the Spanish people, there being no gaiety in himself to reflect it. He is full of gall at the wretchedness of the world, he thinks deeply over it and his bitterness increases. He expresses his pessimism with cutting sarcasm and mordant irony, the expression of a melancholy, disillusioned temperament. (pp. 63-8)

In his reflected melancholy turned inwards upon himself Larra belongs to his own romantic period; as the brilliant satirist sharply observing and wittily criticizing manners and customs Larra is the objective, realistic, social Spaniard of all times. (p. 69)

> *L. A. Warren, "Modern Spanish Novelists: The Costumbristas, Descriptive Picture Writers," in his* Modern Spanish Literature: A Comprehensive Survey of the Novelists, Poets, Dramatists and Essayists from the Eighteenth Century to the Present Day, Vol. I, Brentano's Ltd., 1929, pp. 63-71.

F. M. KERCHEVILLE (essay date 1931)

[Kercheville discusses Larra's contribution to Spanish liberalism.]

The greatest liberal of the early nineteenth century in Spain is undoubtedly the justly famous "Fígaro" (Mariano José de Larra). In fact, Larra is the one truly great liberal between Cadalso in the eighteenth century and Galdós and his contemporaries of the nineteenth and twentieth centuries.

Conditions in Spain were certainly not favorable to the cause of liberalism during the first half of the nineteenth century. From 1809 to 1814 there was fought what has been termed the "War of Liberation" against Napoleon. During most of this time Joseph Bonaparte occupied the throne. After the overthrow of Napoleon there might have been some hope for a revival of the liberal spirit, but this hope was soon blasted by the restoration to the throne of Ferdinand VII, who turned out to be one of the most despotic of all Spanish kings. The constitution which had been gained by a bitter struggle was annulled, and the Inquisition was set into operation once more. This condition of affairs led to the exile of practically every liberal-minded Spaniard—and these were Spain's greatest patriots and deepest thinkers. In 1833, at the death of Ferdinand, most of these liberals returned. Then came revolutions, the brief Republic of Castelar, and in 1874 the restoration of the Bourbons to the throne in the person of Alfonso XII.

Larra lived and wrote during the worst part of these turbulent times, his dates being 1809 to 1837. It is no wonder that he was so thoroughly pessimistic, for Larra was a deep thinker, and had an extremely sensitive soul. His liberalism was no pose, and, although he wrote much bitter and biting satire, he never allowed it to degenerate into caricature and absurd ridiculousness.

Fígaro fought constantly and consistently for the following ideals (without, however, setting up any definite creed): the freedom of the press, political freedom, true justice, religious tolerance, a sane patriotism as opposed to excessive *"españolismo,"* a better system of education, tolerance as opposed to blind traditionalism in manners and customs, open-mindedness and reception of the best in foreign ideas, cleanliness and progress in sanitation and health, and industry and genuine effort as opposed to traditional Spanish sloth.

Larra is known chiefly for the brilliant and biting satire in which he couches his liberal ideas and must be read to be really appreciated. He is especially bitter in his denunciation of the tyranny which allowed no freedom of expression in Spain, and he openly satirizes the so-called "liberty" in his country. In writing about the freedom of the press he says: "Cada periódico dice que la tiene en su casa; pero en realidad el público es como la libertad, que todos dan en decir que la tenemos, y ninguno la ve."

Fígaro is a sworn enemy of *"españolismo"* and the traditional apathy and lack of ambition on the part of Spaniards. He wittily remarks: "Aquí [en España] nadie desea más de lo que tenemos; mira tú si nos contentamos con poco."

The terrible condition of Spanish politics in the early nineteenth century and the unstable economic basis for any progress in Spain are dealt severe blows by Fígaro's inimitable satire. He shows that the Spanish nation is gradually being bled of all its strength by corrupt practices and underhand dealing on the part of favorites.

Something of the actual conditions under which Spanish liberals were forced to live during those trying years of the first part of the nineteenth century may be gained from the following sincere lines: "Ahora nos hemos venido sin fecha [los liberales]: como ratones arrojados de la despensa por el gato [they were just coming back from exile] ... Ahora bien, nuestro gato es la anarquía, porque el otro que había en la casa se escaldó para siempre." (Fígaro could not know what would take place after 1837!)

No one realized better than Larra that true liberalism is neither anarchy nor radicalism. He hated anarchists and extreme radicals just as he did despots, because as a thinker he realized that fundamentally these are the same. Both soon develop into the direst tyranny, and so Larra can truthfully say: "Una clase aborrezco, pero de ganas, a saber, esos hombres naturalmente turbulentos que se alimentan de oposición, a quienes ningún gobierno les gusta.'' Some idea may be gained of Larra's hatred of tyranny and his utter sadness at Spain's terrible condition in the following concluding lines of his **"Dia de difuntos."** After exclaiming bitterly ''aquí yace el trono''—''aquí yace el valor castellano''—''aquí yace el crédito nacional''—''aquí yace la libertad de pensamiento,'' he looks deeply into his own heart and exclaims: ''Aquí yace la esperanza.''

Larra was not, however, always so pessimistic as the expression above seems to indicate, for he does manifest at times some faith in the regeneration of Spain, as can be seen in his conclusion to his translation of the *Dogma de los hombres libres*. In this connection, he has the courage to write:

> Religión pura, fuente de toda moral, y religión, como únicamente puede existir, acompañada de la tolerancia y de la libertad de consciencia; libertad civil; igualdad que abre la puerta a los cargos públicos para los hombres todos, según su idoneidad, y sin necesidad de otra aristocracia que la del talento, la virtud y el mérito; la libertad absoluta del pensamiento escrito. He aquí la profesión de fé del traductor de las ''Palabras de un Creyente.''

Such expressions as the above are the battle cries of tolerance, political and religious liberty, liberty of the press, and the true aristocracy of talent and merit. These have ever been heard and will continue to be heard in the conflicts between liberalism on the one side and despotism and intolerance on the other. Larra was a thorough pessimist, and yet it was the decree of fate that his writings were to become the inspiration for later liberals, and his tomb the mecca of those who love liberty.

There are those who are tempted to smile when any mention is made of liberal thought in Spanish literature. They sincerely believe that there could be no evidence of liberal ideas in the Spain of the Inquisition, the Spain who slew her Moors and expelled her Jews, the Spain of absolutism in both Church and State. But those who smile in this instance overlook two of the deepest and most fundamental elements of the Spanish genius: namely, its tendency toward paradox, and its almost fanatic love of independence and individualism.

Nowhere is the peculiar Spanish genius seen more clearly than in the liberalism of Larra [and in the expressions of liberalism by the outstanding Spanish writers of the previous centuries]. These writers stand as an eternal refutation to the popular belief that there is little, if any, liberal thought in Spanish literature. They give the lie to those who persist in viewing Spain and the Spaniards in the light of that ancient and misleading blackmail: ''Spain of the bloody Spanish Inquisition.'' Spain has had her Inquisition, her bloodsheds, and her bonfires of persecution, but there is also that other side of the picture, the side of liberalism so often overlooked. Romanticism is found side by side with realism in Spanish literature; idealism lights up the gloomiest corners of pessimism and materialism; and in the same way, liberalism is seen ever present even in the darkest days of despotism and fanaticism. This fact can hardly be overemphasized. (pp. 199-202)

[There] has been little political or religious liberalism in Spanish thought with an organized body marching in a unified movement with its banners, its platforms, and its creeds. For the Spaniards have an innate dislike for ''doctrinaires,'' ''parties,'' and ''schools.'' They insist on their ''personal liberty'' and independence, and conceive of liberalism largely in the light

of those terms. Spanish literature of the eighteenth, nineteenth, and twentieth centuries abounds in this spirit of liberty, but every liberal thinks in his own independent way. There are countless individual expressions of political, religious, social, ethical, and moral liberalism, but there is no one prescribed ''doctrine.''

An almost unlimited capacity for self-criticism seems to be a fundamental characteristic of the Spanish genius, and it is used to advantage when occasion presents itself. This is an outstanding quality in Larra. From Juan Ruíz to Unamuno the outstanding element in Spanish liberalism is satire. The Spaniards have ever been proficient in the use of satire and irony. Nowhere is this better illustrated than in that great series of rogue novels which are veritable mines of liberalism. This irony, this satire, flowed in the very life blood of Fígaro. (p. 202)

> *F. M. Kercheville, "Larra and Liberal Thought in Spain," in* Hispania, *Vol. XIV, No. 3, May, 1931, pp. 197-204.*

E. HERMAN HESPELT (essay date 1932)

[Hespelt appraises the originality of Larra's dramas.]

Larra's translated dramas are perhaps the least interesting of his writings; certainly they have been the most neglected. Only eight of the thirteen which he is known to have produced have ever found their way into his collected works, and these always appear apologetically in a sort of appendix at the end of the volume. The only critics who have granted the dramas any considerable amount of space and attention have been far less interested in them than in the more original phases of his work, and none of them has taken the trouble to inquire seriously into the sources of the plays or to make a conscientious comparison between Larra's versions and his originals. (p. 117)

It is a well-known fact that Larra undertook his first dramatic composition at the suggestion of the impresario Juan Grimaldi. Grimaldi was Larra's friend, a member of the Parnasillo, and the author of the very successful *Todo lo vence amor o la pata de cabra*, an arrangement of the fantastic French piece *Le pied de mouton*, by Martainville and Ribié, which was presented in Madrid in 1829 and continued to play for 123 performances.

On the advice, then, of his experienced friend, Larra decided to write for the theater. His first work, *No más mostrador*, was produced on April 29, 1831, in the Teatro de la Cruz, the theater which at that time, as Chaves tells us, was given over chiefly to ''comedias antiguas españolas, las óperas bufas de poco aparato y rara vez tragedias y dramas'' [see Additional Bibliography]. Larra called his work ''Comedia original,'' but as early as 1834 an anonymous writer in the *Diario de Comercio* called attention to the fact that it was rather a translation of Scribe and Mélesvilles' *comédie-vaudeville, Les adieux au comptoir*. Larra answered this objection on the following day (March 23, 1834) in *La Revista Española* in an article entitled **"Vindicación."** ... The most important sentences in Larra's statement are the following:

> Deseando probar mis fuerzas en el arte dramático hace algunos años, y a la sazón que buscaba asunto para una comedia, cayó en mis manos aquel *vaudeville* en *un acto corto* de Scribe. Presumiendo por mis limitados conocimientos que no podría ser de ningún efecto en los teatros de Madrid, apoderéme de la idea,

y haciéndola mía por derecho de conquista, es-
cribí el *No más mostrador, en cinco actos largos;*
hice más; habiendo encontrado en Scribe dos
o tres escenas que desconfié en escribir mejor,
las aproveché, llevado también de la poca im-
portancia que en mi cuadro iban a tener. Yo
no sé si esto se puede hacer, lo que sé es que
yo lo he hecho.

In the light of this defense of Larra's it is important to re-
examine the Spanish version in order to ascertain the extent of
the original material it contains. The theme of the play is a
very familiar one:

An honest bourgeois, who has made his fortune in business,
has planned to marry his daughter to the son of an old friend,
who is also a successful merchant. The girl's mother, however,
is socially ambitious and determined that her daughter shall
wed a count, at least. In order to overcome his wife's prejudices
the father persuades the young suitor to pose as a certain profligate nobleman. The ruse is successful; the mother is enchanted with the aristocratic deportment and elegant appearance of her prospective son-in-law; the young people find that
they have met at a party and are already in love. It remains,
then, only necessary for the father to find some way of reconciling his wife and daughter to the young man's plebeian origin.
Scribe brings this about by the use of a very simple expedient.
The father tells the girl that the "Count" has withdrawn his
offer and has decided to marry someone in his own class. The
girl, overcome with grief, declares that had their rôles been
reversed, she would never have treated him so; that, no matter
what his station in life, she would have chosen him before all
others. Since the parents have agreed in the beginning that the
girl is to be allowed her own choice of a husband, this confession nullifies any possible objections on the mother's part, the
father explains the true state of affairs, and they all "live
happily ever after."

Larra's solution is much more complex. He introduces a real
count, the rightful owner of the name which the young suitor
has assumed, who is also an applicant for the girl's hand. The
count learns that the girl's father favors another and, for his
own purposes, assumes his rival's name. Posing as the merchant's son, he incurs the enmity of both mother and daughter,
challenges the young suitor to a duel, loses some incriminating
letters, and then, as suddenly as he has appeared, withdraws
again, because he has fallen heir to the fortune of a rich aunt
and has no longer need to marry for money. The father, in the
meantime, has spread rumors that his house is ruined; the young
lover comes to the rescue of the family's affairs; the mother's
objections are overcome by his generosity; and so, once more,
"all's well that ends well."

The development of the situation, the part of the plot common
to both plays, takes up in Scribe's drama thirteen of the sixteen
scenes of which it is composed. Only the last three scenes are
concerned with the dénouement. Of these thirteen scenes,
twelve—not the "*dos o tres*" to which Larra confesses—have
their counterpart in *No más mostrador*. They are distributed
through the first two acts of the drama. These two acts contain,
in addition to the borrowed material, only six short scenes that
are Larra's own. The last three acts, however, which are taken
up with the solution of the situation, are entirely original.
Concerning the borrowed scenes it should be noted that none
of them are literal translations of their models, but in all of
them the situations are the same as in Scribe's play, the same
characters are on the stage together, they speak of the same

subjects and use here and there the same words. Almost every
one of the longer speeches in this part of Larra's play has some
echoes of Scribe in it. Yet, as all his commentators have noticed, Larra succeeded in transforming his characters into genuine Spanish types and his scene into the home and shop of a
Madrid draper. The language which his people speak, in spite
of his own frequently quoted criticism of the Gallicism "el
ridículo," is lively and vigorous Spanish. If we allow, then,
a very broad use of the adjective, we may consider Larra
justified in calling *No más mostrador* original.

With far less right he applied the term to his second play,
Felipe, which was produced in the Teatro del Príncipe on
February 28, 1832, and which purported to be a "*comedia
original en dos actos*" by "D. Ramón de Arriala." Actually
Felipe is a close adaptation of another of Scribe's *comédies-
vaudevilles, Philippe.* The argument of the play is briefly as
follows:

A young man, who believes himself to be an orphan, has been
brought up as the ward of a rich and noble lady who has an
inordinate amount of dignity and family pride. The young man
is threatened with the loss of his benefactress' good will because he has lost heavily at cards, but the lady's major-domo,
Philip, successfully cajoles and scolds his mistress into con-
doning this piece of folly. Then it is discovered that the youth,
Frederick, is guilty of a worse crime—that of falling in love
with Madame's niece, for whom she has been planning a brilliant marriage. This insult to her pride cannot be forgiven, and
Frederick is to be banished forever from her sight. Then once
more Philip intercedes for him, reproving the lady for her pride
and reminding her of her higher duty. For Frederick is his son,
and *hers,* born during a time of revolution when the lady had
taken refuge from the soldiers who were invading her home in
the tent of a poor sergeant, but unrecognized and unblessed by
a mother's affection—a sacrifice to family pride. Philip now
demands for their child his right to happiness. The lady's better
self triumphs and she receives Frederick with a tender embrace
and consents to his marriage with the girl he loves.

Scribe's play ends here. For Larra's more democratic Spanish
audience this would probably have seemed to be too slight a
reparation for the sacrifices which Philip had made to his wife's
family honor. In Larra's final scene the proud noblewoman
confesses the truth and publicly acknowledges Philip as her
husband. The confession comes as something of a shock to the
reader, for nothing in the lady's previous behavior has led him
to believe her capable of such magnanimity. Larra must have
felt this himself, for he has the lady say to the other characters
in her last speech in the play: "Más despacio podré explicaros
este arcano."

In addition to this important change in the conclusion of the
drama, Larra has made a few other modifications in his original
which are worth noting. He has divided his play into two acts,
whereas Scribe's play has only one. Larra's first act ends with
Scribe's scene x, and the second act begins with a short monologue by Frederick which Larra has inserted to explain how
the young man happens to be still in the same place where the
end of the first act left him. Frederick is anxious to speak once
more with the girl he loves, and in order to see if she is still
in her room he walks over to her door and *looks through the
key-hole!* Scribe's young lover has no need to be guilty of such
a breach of etiquette.

When the first scene of the French play opens, Madame's
young niece is discovered reading *Tom Jones* with sincere

emotion, because she finds the plight of that poor orphan analogous to her lover's. Larra doubtless thought that no charming Spanish girl would be reading such a novel and so has omitted these lines.

His other changes consist in superficialities, such as the Hispaniolizing of proper names or the substituting of ''una época tempestuosa en que el amor a la independencia de la España y la intrepidez bastaban para encontrar los grados y los honores en la trinchera enemiga'' for Scribe's brief reference to the revolution in France. Except for this, his work is a faithfully wrought translation of his original. (pp. 118-22)

[A careful study of all the dramas] which Larra borrowed from the French only confirms one in the belief that his interest in them was financial rather than artistic. Larra was first of all a journalist. He had the successful journalist's conception of literature as a salable commodity and the journalist's awareness of the likes and dislikes of his public. He chose to work only on such plays as had had more than average success in Paris. With the exception of the year 1833, he regularly presented two or three dramas each year. The theater thus became for him a fairly dependable source of supplementary income, though the sums which he received for the rights of production appear very small when compared with the amount he received as salary from *El Mundo* and *El Redactor General*.

Larra was an accomplished and a conscientious translator. He did not spare himself pains to reproduce the tone as well as the meaning of his original. The greater number of his changes . . . are dictated by a desire to bring his story nearer to his public and to respect their social, religious, or patriotic prejudices. Only in *Don Juan de Austria*, the last of his adaptations, does he make very much of an effort to improve upon the technique of his model. And much less often than one would expect does he insert into the plays critical comments of his own on society and literature.

The translated dramas are Larra's literary hack-work, but even the hack-work of a man of Larra's talents is worth studying if we wish to form a true estimate of his gifts. If Larra had lived longer, he might possibly have graduated from this theatrical apprenticeship to more exalted fields of dramatic art, but it is doubtful. One of his critical essays—his discussion of *Los amantes de Teruel*, for example—is worth far more than all his translated plays put together. (p. 134)

> E. Herman Hespelt, ''The Translated Dramas of Mariano Jose de Larra and Their French Originals,'' in Hispania, Vol. XV, No. 2, March, 1932, pp. 117-34.

F. COURTNEY TARR   (essay date 1937)

[*Here, Tarr offers a centennial tribute to Larra's life and works. For additional commentary by Tarr, see the excerpt dated 1928.*]

The most important centennial anniversary in Spanish letters falling in the present year is unquestionably that of the self-inflicted death, on February 13, 1937—less than six weeks before his twenty-eighth birthday (March 24)—of Mariano José de Larra, the precocious genius whose journalistic writings (critical essays and satirical sketches) constitute the outstanding achievement, the most enduring monument in Spanish prose literature of the first half of the nineteenth century. Of all the figures of his generation, Larra is the only one whose popularity and prestige has steadily increased with the passing of time, the only one whose literary art and personality is more genu-

inely and significantly alive today than when he wrote. This despite his early—though not premature—death and the opprobrium resulting from suicide (an opprobrium which clouded his reputation in official literary circles during almost the entire nineteenth century); and even despite—or, in a deeper sense, because of—the apparently ephemeral and intensely personal nature of his writings.

These seeming anomalies, so in keeping with Larra's paradoxical genius, need no explanation for those who are familiar with the articles and sketches of El Pobrecito Hablador and of Fígaro, the successive pseudonyms under which he wrote his best-known works: articles and sketches which have today a deeper appeal and significance than at the time and place for which they were written; articles and sketches which delight, amaze, and move by their lasting aptness of vision, of expression, of feeling; articles and sketches which lay bare in an ever increasing *crescendo* of sensitive wit, passionate irony, and despairing satire, the foibles of his times and those of mankind, the dilemma of his own soul and that of his country.

A bitter civil war was raging when Larra took his life in utter despair at what he conceived to be his own and his country's hopeless plight, a despair born of the inexorable logic of pessimism and the passion of frustrated ideals and ambitions, personal and patriotic. A bitter civil war—one in which the same historical and psychological forces are at grips, forces which he alone among his contemporaries felt as dolorous personal realities—is raging as the centenary of his death passes by. A coincidence, of course, but one as bitterly ironical and significant as those coincidences and paradoxes which so abound in Larra's own life and works, in his own art and soul, as to make of them one grim and glorious irony; a coincidence which bears the most striking and painful testimony to the uncanny insight of the author of **''El casarse pronto y mal,''** **''Ventajas de las cosas a medio hacer,''** **''Las palabras,''** to mention only a few of the sketches which, although arising from the circumstances and written for the public of one hundred years ago, have become the classic literary and personal embodiment of the historical and spiritual conflict that is Spain.

Larra, then, is no mere *costumbrista*, a writer of humorous sketches of once contemporary but now antique manners and customs, the pigeonhole usually assigned him, for convenience of classification, in the manuals of literature. The outmoded style and subject-matter of the *artículo de costumbres* as practiced by his contemporaries are the direct antithesis of the eternal timeliness—and timelessness—of thought, feeling, and expression to be found in the best work of Fígaro. To him manners and customs, events and phenomena, are of no interest *per se* (hence the minimum of description in his work), but intensely so as manifestations of underlying human verities, historical, social, and psychological. For Larra, the *artículo de costumbres* is a means, not an end: a convenient and popular form in which to cast his scrutiny, critical and emotional, of the social, political, and cultural panorama of his time and place; a form at once light in tone and serious in implication, partaking of all the advantages of the critical essay and the formal satire, but with none of their disabilities of limited public and of personal and intellectual responsibility. In times of strict censorship and high partisan passion, the very pretense of unpretentiousness was for Larra the *artículo's* most effective (and protective) arm. As the people's jester—for such, in effect, was Fígaro—he could permit himself liberties of critical expression impossible in any other form.

Such a position, at once humble and exalted, was, for these very reasons, Larra's joy and his torment. For at heart he desired earnestly, passionately, to be taken by his public as seriously as he took himself in his rôle of literary arbiter and political mentor. Hence his insistence on the social utility of literature in general and of satire in particular, his high conception of the mission of the poet-publicist, his anxiety to preserve—in appearance at least—an independence superior to parties and schools. He was as quick to insist on the dignity and objectivity of his satire and criticism as to seize upon the opportunities and immunities of his lowly *genre*. He was never satisfied to owe the fame that was his life's blood to his skill as a comic writer. (Hence his early and none too successful attempts—in comparison with his *artículos*—in other fields: poetry, theatre, novel.) As his literary reputation grew, it galled him more and more to owe it chiefly—despite his pride therein—to his talent for the burlesque. Hence his endeavor to raise the tone, scope, and aim of satire and criticism in Spain (especially after his trip—or flight—abroad in 1835), an attempt foredoomed to failure, because of the all-pervading preoccupation with politics and the refractoriness of Spanish artists and writers to dictatorial pretensions, no matter how justified or how disguised. Hence, too, his idea of the tragic lot of the satirist: applauded, but unheeded and misunderstood. Here lie—in part—the roots of that dilemma of pride and despair (all the more real because it was so largely imaginary) which drove him to his death, after the very independence and prestige which he had striven to maintain and to increase had been greatly (if only momentarily) impaired by his unpopular and equivocal political position before and after the revolution of August, 1836.

But posterity has granted him the sort of fame he craved, and because of the very *artículos* which were his pride and his cross, and which so completely fulfil the possibilities and transcend the limits of the *genre*. No one, before or since, has ever used it to such advantage as he, from the standpoint both of contemporary effect—Fígaro's was the most applauded, most dreaded, and most highly paid pen of his times—and of permanent literary result. For it was, of course, a form peculiarly, perfectly, suited to Larra's equivocal and paradoxical personality and genius, to his hyperlogical mind and supersensitive soul. It allowed the fullest play to his extraordinary rhetorical talent, to the inspiration and elaboration of verbal suggestion, to the ingenious and contrapuntal interplay of words and concepts. (In this Larra's genius—or rather *ingenio*—is as essentially Spanish as that of Seneca, Martial, or Quintilian, as that of Cervantes, Quevedo, or Unamuno.) For in Larra's best and most characteristic articles the point of departure often lies in a single happy phrase or concept—frequently the title—the implications of which are developed with amazing agility of wit and originality of application. Larra's creative gift lies in adaptation and in expression, rather than in innovation. To the traditional forms and devices of the satirist and the *costumbrista* he gives a turn at once personal and national, contemporary and universal, adapting them with gay wit and bitter irony (and with all the intermediate gradations) to his own temperament and times, to his own situation and that of his country.

Here lies the key to Larra's personality, literary and human—the two are inextricably intertwined—to that peculiarly rich interplay (and deep conflict) of the analytic and the subjective, of logic and passion, that is the soul and the art of Fígaro. He is, of course, primarily a satirist—the last great Spanish satirist—in direct line of succession from Cervantes and Quevedo, to whom he owes so much in style and in spirit (not to mention

Larra's tragic Spain, as interpreted by Gustave Doré.

his more tangible debt to his immediate predecessors Cadalso, Moratín, Miñano, as well as to Horace, Boileau, and Jouy). But—and this is the distinctive mark of his genius—a satirist whose insight into human nature in general and that of his countrymen in particular comes not so much from observation (despite the *costumbrista* pose) as from unceasing and increasing, pitiless and implacable introspection. His criticism and his satire are at bottom auto-criticism, self-satire. And under the impact of adverse circumstances, both for his country and for himself—it is curious to note the uncanny coincidences between the ups and downs of his personal affairs, his literary career, and the political situation—the conventional despair of the satirist becomes a living, intimate reality. Hence the sob in his satire, the bitter yet elegiac quality especially characteristic of his final—and finest—trilogy (**"El día de difuntos," "Horas de invierno," "La Nochebuena de 1836"**), in which, carried away by the suggestion of the theme and the circumstances, personal and political, of the moment, he identifies, like the genuine romantic he is, his own and his country's plight, fusing and confusing literature and life into original and authentic art.

In no writer, then, do the literary, the personal, and the circumstantial interact in a more complete fashion or with more compelling results than in Larra. In a broad sense all his original writings—even his verses, his plays, and his novel—are *obras de circunstancias,* personal or political. Yet his is an outstanding case of literary art transcending the limitations of ephemeral subject-matter and inconsequential form. No writer is more personal, even confessional, than Larra, despite the spurious objectivity of the *costumbrista;* no writer is more intensely preoccupied with his literary and personal reputation, as well as with the welfare and progress of his native land. (Hence his desperate need of self-justification and the baffling blend of sincerity and sophistry that mark his attempts, public and private, to that end.) A pessimist whose passion was progress, an impatient, easily disappointed idealist, Larra, like Don

Quixote, was the victim of his own logic and rationalizations, but, unlike Don Quixote, rebellious against them, erecting and dissecting them at one and the same time. His self-created dilemma, analyzed with merciless despair in that masterpiece, **"La Nochebuena de 1836,"** with the deliberately paradoxical sub-title of *delirio filosófico,* is summed up in that incomparably exact and poignant phrase *ebrio de deseos y de impotencia.*

His suicide, then, was no fortuitous occurrence, but the inevitable result of the play of circumstances—personal, political, and literary—on his temperament. The fatal interview with Dolores Armijo de Cambronero (the married woman with whom he had been hopelessly in love since May of 1831 and who called on him on the evening of February 13, 1837 to break with him for a second time) was merely the last straw, the occasion, not the cause.

Larra is, of course, a genuine romantic, the most authentic of his generation in Spain, and one of the most outstanding in the literary annals of the world. Not because of his death in the orthodox Wertherian fashion (the ultimate concordance, in his case, of literary example and inner urge). Nor—even less—because of any external romanticism in his writings. For he wrote little, if any, in that mode: even his play **Macías** and his historical novel on the same theme—the semi-legendary Galician troubador whose love for a married lady leads him to his death (again the combination of the literary and the personal)—are not romantic in form (unless the pseudo-archaeological historical novel be considered a romantic form). But they are intensely romantic in feeling, in the exaltation of love as superior to any moral law. Eclectic in his criticism, eclectic and even traditional in his literary forms, his romanticism is of the spirit, and, like that of Stendhal—the comparison can be carried much further—could not be appreciated in the Spain of his day. Not until the 1880's (note the coincidence) did he begin to occupy serious critical attention, and not until the rise of the generation of '98, which saw and felt as he did the problem of Spain and of the sensitive, intellectual Spaniard, did he really come into his own, did he really find the kind of public he longed for in life.

Thus it is that in recent times Larra the man, the romantic, rediscovered and put into circulation by a sympathetic generation, has really overshadowed Larra the writer, the poet (in the broad sense of the term). Yet, after all, Larra's greatest gift, that which makes him truly a classic (and not a mere classicist, despite his eighteenth-century education and rationalism, and his literary preceptism) is that of expression—adequate, original, enduring expression—that fusion of content and form, of thought and feeling that marks his best works. Just as Cervantes—in a far greater way, of course—made out of the antiquated romances the greatest of modern novels, so Larra has made out of the jocose sketch, the humorous commentary on the *trivia* of the immediate scene, a real minor work of art, of lasting intellectual, emotional, and esthetic appeal. (pp. 46-50)

> *F. Courtney Tarr, "Mariano José de Larra (1809-1837)," in* The Modern Language Journal, *Vol. XXII, No. 1, October, 1937, pp. 46-50.*

ROBERT KIRSNER (essay date 1951)

[*In the following excerpt from a comparative study of Larra and Benito Pérez Galdós, Kirsner differentiates between the authors' critical attitudes toward Spain, emphasizing the autobiographical nature of Larra's writings.*]

Galdós' intent to censure orthodox conformity with national customs and institutions, as manifested in his early novels, such as *Doña Perfecta* and *Gloria,* recalls the virulent criticisms directed against Spain by Mariano José de Larra (1809-1837). The latter, whose vision of Spain is intimately expressed in his *Artículos de Costumbres,* dedicated himself to probing into and portraying the defects of his country and countrymen. Sensitive to every aspect of Hispanic life, Larra experienced as a personal frustration Spain's inability to solve her problems. In essence, his attitude was one of self-criticism; as he destroyed Spain, so he destroyed himself.

The critical attitude of Galdós towards existing consuetudes resembles that of Larra inasmuch as both writers strive to direct attention to the shortcomings and failures of the Spanish people. Nonetheless, their approach to these problems, an expression of their innermost personal experiences, varies greatly. Whereas Larra cynically resigns himself to expatiate on social and moral values, Galdós seeks to oppose them. The latter, though pessimistic in his outlook, retains some faith in the future of Spain; he expresses his concept of values in the creation of characters. Larra, on the contrary, is unable to forge positive symbols because of his obliterative approach. He is intent on destroying prevalent modes of life, not on creating new ones.

The two essays which most effectively express Larra's anguished preoccupation with Spain are: **"La Nochebuena de 1836"** and **"Fígaro en el cementerio."** The former, in which the author maintains an imaginary dialogue with his servant, is principally an introspective analysis which reveals a spiritual state in harmony with the author's concept of Spain. The latter, an allegory written in epitaphic form, is a deprecative evaluation of prevalent institutions. Both abound with astringent observations which manifest Larra's disquieted state of mind. His pathetic attitude, permeated with a feeling of hopelessness, is paradoxical; it is one of militant acquiescence. At the same time that he is intellectually resigned to the shortcomings of his nation (depicted in his articles as inherent and perennial evils), he is emotionally struggling to overcome a vicarious feeling of contrition. Conscious of the incongruity that exists between the possibilities and the achievements of Spain, Larra experiences a personal sense of remorse when he considers his country's failure to exist in accordance with his dreams and aspirations.

The following passages, in which the mythical servant speaks to him, are expressive of Larra's perturbed spiritual state.

Maś de uno te he visto morder y despedazar. . . .

> Tú buscas la felicidad en el corazón humano,
> y para eso le destrozas, hozando en él, como
> quien remueve la tierra en busca de un tesoro.
> Yo nada busco, y el desengaño no me espera
> a la vuelta de la esperanza . . . Despedazado
> siempre por la sed de gloria . . . y eres también
> despedazado. . . .

The prevalence of words like "destrozar" and "despedazar" is indicative of Larra's harrowing position. Desirous of instituting reforms and conscious of his inability to achieve them, he undergoes a spiritual crisis which leads him to assume a destructive attitude towards himself and his society. His obloquies render imperceptible whatever merits might exist. Spain is constantly envisaged as a nation characterized by impotence and impoverishment.

Miré el termómetro y marcaba muchos grados
bajo cero; como el crédito del Estado.

Segunda comedia: un novio que no ve el logro
de su esperanza; ese novio es el pueblo español:
no se casa con un solo gobierno, con quien no
tenga que reñir al día siguiente. Es el matri-
monio repetido al infinito.

Larra is not oblivious to the fact that his vision of Spain is a
reflection of his inner life. He dramatically perceives the existing harmony upon discovering that he is the tomb of the vast
cemetery named Madrid.

El cementerio está dentro de Madrid. Madrid es el
cementerio.
Mi corazón no es más que otro sepulcro.

Larra's style cannot be dismissed as being characterized by
figures of speech. His metaphors are not vacuous expressions
of a literary tradition. His *Artículos* do not follow a pattern of
sentimentality or "sensiblerie." Larra's posture cannot be designated merely as romantic if it is to be clearly understood.
Though at times hyperbolized, the *Artículos,* unlike his romantic works, constitute an authentic revelation of the author's
anguished state.

Although not all of the *Artículos* are quite so subjective as "La
Nochebuena de 1836" and "Fígaro en el cementerio," none
contains any degree of objectivity. Whatever the subject is,
the treatment is always personal.

¿Qué quieres? ¡En la sociedad siempre triunfa
la hipocresía!

—Esa es la sociedad. Era mi amigo íntimo.
Desde entonces no tengo más que amigos; ín-
timos, estos pesos duros que traigo en el bol-
sillo: son los únicos que no venden: al revés,
compran.

Larra's approach is no less pungent when he describes individuals, who are effaced before they have an opportunity to
appear as positive creations.

. . . Braulio está muy lejos de pertenecer a lo
que se llama gran mundo y sociedad de buen
tuno . . . tiene una cintica atada al ojal, y una
crucecita a la sombra de la solapa . . . Es tal su
patriotismo, que dará todas las lindezas del ex-
tranjero por un dedo de su país.

Braulio does not even emerge as a typical character. Whereas
Galdós forges characters who are symbols of his concept of
good and evil, Larra seems unable to create living images of
his concepts because of his hostile and obliterative approach
to the society of his time. (pp. 210-12)

The works of Larra may be designated as the transition between
Cervantes and Galdós though Larra, himself, does not create
novels. The novel, a literary form which had not been cultivated
for more than two and one half centuries, becomes the vehicle
for Galdós' expressive power. Larra's composition of quasi-
novels, as manifested by some of his *Artículos,* such as "El
Castellano Viejo" and "El Casarse Pronto y Mal," represents
the intermedium between the two novelists. The aforemen-
tioned articles contain rudimentary characteristics of a novelistic style. The conflict between the individual and society,
inevitably culminating in the defeat of the former, is forcefully
expressed. Nonetheless, the would-be tragic character who brings

about his own vanquishment, is invariably the author himself.
Larra's writings, then, lack extrospection, which is as pertinent
to a novelistic style as introspection. He seems unable to ob-
jectivize his preoccupation with contemporary problems, and
thus his works acquire the character of an autobiography.
(pp. 212-13)

It is, of course, possible to conjecture on the ultimate form of
literary expression that Larra would have undertaken had he
lived beyond his twenty eight years of self destructive life.
After all, what were the literary achievements of Galdós before
the age of thirty? It is conceivable that, like Cervantes and
Galdós, he might have acquired a more sympathetic understanding of human frailties. On the other hand, like Quevedo
and Gracián, he might have become even more harsh in his
judgment of men as he grew older. However, it is on the basis
of their literary creations that authors must be evaluated, not
on hypotheses. It is on this baasis that Galdós emerges as the
Cervantes of his century, Larra as the modern Quevedo. (p. 213)

> *Robert Kirsner, "Galdós and Larra," in* The Mod-
> ern Language Journal, *Vol. XXXV, No. 3, March,
> 1951, pp. 210-13.*

GERALD BRENAN (essay date 1953)

[Brenan considers Larra's importance to Spanish literature.]

The articles that Larra scribbled in haste at night for his paper
are what we read of his today. It was the age of great journalists.
Paul Louis Courier had only a few years before been making
a name for himself in Paris. There was Leigh Hunt in England
and Heine in Germany. Larra's articles deal with literature and
the drama, with contemporary types and customs, with Madrid
society, but above all with Spain, her character, her place in
the world, her predicament—the Spain that 'like a new Penelope, spends her time in alternately weaving and unweaving
her dress'. Larra was one of those unhappy people who would
like to believe, but cannot. A romantic by inner conviction and
a Liberal because he hated tyranny, he saw no grounds for
romanticism or for optimism in the world about him. Unlike
his poet contemporaries, who suffered from all the false hopes
and easy expectations of men who have been exiles, he had
spent the dark days of the reaction in Spain. There the iron
had entered into his soul: he knew what conditions were, he
realized how desperate was the state and how unalterable the
character of his countrymen, and he felt a deep pessimism.
The failure of his play and of his marriage increased this. Where
divorce is impossible, love affairs outside the framework of
marriage are necessarily unstable and full of torment. What
we find therefore in his articles is the reporting of a very
intelligent and observant man who has lost all his illusions.
He writes in a style that is admirably direct and spontaneous;
since Quevedo, no one had written prose with such force and
economy and, though he lacks the great satirist's command of
the full resources of language as well as his powerful and
tormented imagination, his dry tone of understatement makes
an admirable background for his flashes of sardonic wit and
irony. Larra is not so witty as Heine, but he is nearly so: he
is more astringent and tonic and therefore more in keeping with
modern taste. Although his themes are too local and Spanish
to make a very general appeal (here painters such as Goya have
an advantage), there is no one, I think, except the great German, who can approach him as a journalist. His early death
was a tragedy for Spanish literature. (pp. 377-78)

Gerald Brenan, ''Nineteenth-Century Prose,'' in his The Literature of the Spanish People: From Roman Times to the Present Day, *second edition, Cambridge University Press, 1953, pp. 377-416.*

DONALD L. SHAW (essay date 1972)

[*Shaw surveys Larra's life and works, focusing on his contribution to early Spanish Romanticism.*]

The chief meeting-place of the Romantics in Madrid in the middle 1830s was the café of the Teatro del Príncipe (now the Español). Here publishers like Carnerero and Delgado and the manager of the Príncipe itself met Espronceda, Mesonero, Bretón, García Gutiérrez, and their fellow-Romantics in what came to be known as *El Parnasillo.* In 1838 this group formed the short-lived *Liceo Artístico y Literario* which for a time rivalled the *Ateneo* (founded 1820) as a centre for literary life, with debates, lectures, poetry readings, and other similar functions. Apart from Espronceda, the major figure of the *Parnasillo* was Mariano José de Larra. . . . In 1828, rebelling against his family background, he abandoned his studies and founded his first periodical, *El Duende Satírico del Día.* Only five numbers appeared, but the best of these already reveal extraordinary powers of observation and particularly mordant humour in a boy of nineteen. The following year, against parental opposition, he married Pepita Wetoret. The marriage, whose reflections can be seen in **"El casarse pronto y mal"**, was a disastrous failure and though the couple had three children, they separated in 1834, the year, ironically, of Larra's drama *Macías* with its exalted vision of the love-ideal. During the interval he had founded another short-lived satirical review, *El Pobrecito Hablador,* and translated a number of plays from the French, chiefly by Scribe, as well as staging his own full-length *No más mostrador,* based on a one-act piece by a French author. *El Conde Fernán González,* Larra's only other original play, though extant, was never performed.

Macías stands as an early monument in Spain to Romantic passion. In it Larra may be said to have invented the great Romantic formula for drama: love thwarted by fate leading to death. Again and again in the play Macías asserts that life without love is meaningless torment, and in the lyrical climax of Act III proclaims explicitly the Romantic love-ideal:

> Los amantes son solos los esposos
> su lazo es el amor ¿Cuál hay más santo?
> 　　　. . . ¿Qué otro asilo
> Pretendes más seguro que mis brazos?
> Los tuyos bastaránme, y si en la tierra
> asilo no encontramos, juntos ambos
> moriremos de amor. ¡Quién más dichoso
> que aquél que amando vive y muere amado!

Macías reveals a curiously hybrid technique, since it both attempts clumsily to observe the unities and to follow the fashion of imitating the Golden Age *comedia.* The imitation is of course doctored. There is significantly no *gracioso* and no sub-plot. The ending especially, with its loud Romantic overtones, contrasts completely with the sensibility of the Golden Age. The play as a whole is defective both as a work of art and of stagecraft. The verse-medium is stiff and the imitation of the Golden Age manner self-conscious. Macías, for all his exaltation, is something of a light-weight. Above all, not enough of the passion is expressed in action. But its influence on later plays, *El trovador* of Gutiérrez and *Los amantes de Teruel* of

Hartzenbusch in particular, compels us to regard it as a seminal work.

Apart from *Macías* and a historical novel, **El doncel de don Enrique el doliente,** Larra's major writings are the theatre criticism, literary and political satire, and *costumbrista* articles he published in his own two periodicals and a half a dozen others. They show him to have been at once the most intellectually analytic and the most unhappy of the Spanish Romantics. He struggled to believe in the triumph of truth over error, the inevitable progress of humanity, and in his own phrase, 'la regeneración de España'. But the consistent betrayal of Liberal ideas by successive Liberal ministries in the 1830s, which disillusioned Rivas and exasperated Espronceda, produced in Larra a cold and bitter despair. This combined with his own more abstract scepticism, his failure to get into parliament, and his break with his mistress, Dolores Armijo, to produce his suicide.

Larra's early articles in *El Duende* are very unequal, but they already illustrate some of his basic characteristics: his interest in ideas rather than things; the faith in the truth which underlies his biting exposure of shams and hypocrisy; and the deep, indignant, patriotism which kept him always among the opposition. **"El café"** above all, his first really memorable article, places him, while still in his teens, far ahead of the still feeble efforts of his fellow-*costumbristas.*

The characteristic of *costumbrismo* was its interest, not in observed reality as a whole, but in those aspects of reality which were both typical of a given region or area in Spain and at the same time pleasingly picturesque and amusing. The field of the *costumbrista* writers, that is to say, was deliberately limited. Their concern was not to describe popular life and behaviour as it really was. Their aim was to select only what gave a striking impression of 'local colour', especially if it represented a pleasant survival from the past. They helped to bring into being what we now call *la España de pandereta:* the peninsular equivalent of 'Merrie England', and just as artificial. The *costumbrista* movement has a long history in Spanish letters before the early nineteenth century. It was reinforced by the emergence of a general European interest in short visual descriptions of local types and customs, and especially by the 'historical' Romantics' attachment to what was intrinsically *castizo* and Spanish. A good example from Larra is **"La diligencia."** But while this is typical *costumbrismo*, it is not typical Larra—except in the brilliance of its technique. It is a piece of satirical description for its own sake. It lacks the outright social criticism and genuine reformist intention which are inseparable from Larra's best work. For it is not only that Larra portrays individuals while the *costumbristas* usually portray types; it is not only that he excels in neat construction, humorous dialogue, and irony, while their articles are so often replete with rambling description; what makes Larra a great writer, rather than merely a great *costumbrista*, is the deep personal involvement which brings the man constantly into his writings, and the courageous discussion of the problem of Spain which these writings contain.

The typical *costumbrista* article by Larra deals either with some specific aspect of *madrileño* life—cafés, housing, parks, a masked ball—or more usually of Spanish social life in general—education, cultural life, the class system, the public services. After an opening generalisation, Larra passes swiftly to concrete illustrations. His own participation and first-person description frequently add impact and conviction to his criticism. Observed detail, artfully humorous dialogue, and ironic asides combine with comic exaggeration to present recognisable people and situations in a satirical light. The result is usually amusing and sometimes hilarious, but in many of Larra's representative articles an undertone of despair is present at the close. Despite his opposition to negativism, defeatism, and self-deception by Spaniards, the picture which emerges from his *costumbrista* articles is that of a corrupt, empty society rotted by inefficiency, idleness, and apathy.

Larra's political articles have, with a few exceptions, proved less durable than his *costumbrista* social criticism, though he himself undoubtedly regarded them as more important. Indeed this is perhaps the reason. For in his political writings Larra often took his *papel de redentor* so seriously as to compromise his satirical manner. They present the rare spectacle of a young man who began as a moderate and became continuously more radical with age. But since Larra tends to attack attitudes of mind rather than socio-economic evils, and sees the remedy in education and enlightenment rather than in specific measures of reform, we see no very definite doctrinal content in his work.

As a literary critic Larra began conventionally in *El Duende* from a Neo-classic standpoint. But in his review of Martínez de la Rosa's *Poesías* in 1833 he took his stand firmly beside Alcalá Galiano in asserting a necessary connection between literature (which for him always meant literature of ideas) and the spirit of his own times. Early in 1836 he developed the idea into his major statement of opinion, **"Literatura. Rápida ojeada sobre la historia e índole de la nuestra"**, which ranks as a major Romantic manifesto. Attacking, with Mora and Galiano, the religious intolerance and ideological stagnation of the Golden Age, and hailing in the Reformation the origins of 'las innovaciones y el espíritu filosófico', Larra called for a literature which reflected recent intellectual progress 'rompiendo en todas partes antiguas cadenas, desgastando tradiciones caducas y derribando ídolos . . . una literatura nueva, expresión de la sociedad nueva que componemos'. Its guiding principles were to be liberty and truth.

Larra was able to identify this new literature largely with romanticism and his articles on major Romantic plays, Spanish and French, are of central importance. By far the most revealing of them, however, are the two in which he attacks Dumas's *Antony*. For here Larra suddenly found himself face to face with a truth which was neither 'útil', 'bueno', nor the 'expresión del progreso humano'. It was on the contrary Byron's 'fatal truth', Leopardi's 'infausta verità', Espronceda's 'verdad amarga': the Romantics' realisation that the truth about human existence might be in total disharmony with an optimistic interpretation of life. Larra states this, indeed, as a fact, which he not only does not attempt to deny, but even holds to be the inevitable discovery of the rest of mankind in the future. (pp. 18-22)

> *Donald L. Shaw, "Espronceda and Larra," in his*
> The Nineteenth Century, *Ernest Benn Limited, 1972,*
> *pp. 14-22.*

SUSAN KIRKPATRICK   (essay date 1977)

> [*Kirkpatrick views Larra as a representative of Spanish Romanticism, basing her observations upon a detailed analysis of his ideas concerning "the relation of individual to society, of private feeling to public reality."*]

The case of Mariano José de Larra is especially rich as an example of the particularity of Spanish Romanticism. Because he was a journalist and literary critic as well as a poet, dramatist, and satirist, his writing reveals the conjunctures of the political and literary preoccupations of his time and place with unusual clarity. His perspective was unique, partly because his trajectory was different from that of other Romantic liberals in that he did not share the experience of political exile and remained at a critical distance from the campaign to introduce Romanticism in Spain. The criteria with which he judged the movement led him to view it sympathetically as liberalism in art and as a means of creating a national literature, but at the same time to condemn those ultra-individualistic tendencies which undermined the social cohesion he regarded as essential to the liberal cause. Despite this position of critical detachment, however, the *crise de conscience* provoked by the failure of Larra's guiding mission—the consolidation of a liberal, middle-class public—produced a reorientation of his late work that was profoundly, if not self-consciously, Romantic. We shall see how his last essays not only question the validity of a liberal value system rooted in eighteenth-century thought, but also reveal a radical shift in the way he conceived the relation of individual to society, of private feeling to public reality.

From the very beginning of his career, the principal target of Larra's satirical articles was the obscurantism of the *ancien régime*, which he represented as permeating every aspect of Spanish society. *El Pobrecito Hablador*, a serial he began to publish in 1832 at the end of the reign of Ferdinand VII, was ingeniously subversive in its indictment of the intellectual, social, and economic backwardness fostered by the absolutist regime. This negative critique, attacked as purely destructive by Larra's opponents, was based nevertheless on long-range, constructive aims. Although the conditions of censorship made complete frankness impossible, in some of the *Pobrecito* articles Larra was relatively explicit about his objective: namely, to form a middle-class public whose common goals and assumptions were based on liberal ideology.

He specifically addressed the topic in **"Casarse pronto y mal,"** an article he published midway through the *Pobrecito* series in November 1832, by devoting the introduction and the conclusion to a discussion of the premises of his satire and his relation to his public. The piece begins with a sequence of brief dialogues which represent the conflicting reactions of his readers to previous articles. This image of a reading public so deeply divided in its opinions and attitudes that its contradictory expectations are impossible for any writer to meet is more than a rhetorical device for self-justification, since he returns to it from a different angle in the conclusion. Here, in a forthright effort ("Nosotros *declaramos* positivamente que nuestra intención . . .") to make explicit the aim of the little story which forms the main body of the essay, he emphasizes again the division of his public, this time into two sharply distinct groups— a majority still ignorant of the new lights of the age and a tiny elite, too precipitate in its eagerness to follow the latest trends emanating from France. It is to this latter group, he says, that he has directed the anecdote about a young couple who thought themselves progressive, but were in reality immature and foolish. He exhorts enlightened Spaniards not to try prematurely to catch up with more advanced nations, but to begin with the foundations of progress: "[E]mpiécese por el principio: educación, instrucción. Sobre estas grandes y sólidas bases se ha de levantar el edificio. Marche esa otra masa, esa immensa mayoría que se sentó hace tres siglos; deténgase para dirigirla la arrogante minoría, a quien engaña su corazón y sus grandes deseos, y entonces habrá alguna remota vislumbre de esperanza.'' That is, the progressive class, if it hopes to effect real change, must consolidate its base on two levels: it must lay down fully and solidly the intellectual foundations of the modern world view, and devote itself to the dissemination of the new consciousness in order to unify a major sector of Spanish society behind its projects.

"Entretanto, nuestra misión es bien peligrosa," he continues, at once identifying his own calling as a writer to the task of consolidation and emphasizing its difficulty in a nation whose deep fissures were to widen into civil war before the year was out. The mission Larra set himself obeyed the imperative of the times: if out of the crumbling structures of the *ancien régime* a new social and political order was to rise, one which would permit the development and expansion of modern capitalism, a new social formation must emerge, coalescing around a sense of common interests and a coherent program capable of promoting these interests. During the period of the *Pobrecito Hablador* a political coalition was developing among sectors of the middle classes and of the aristocracy which for various reasons opposed the succession of Ferdinand VII by his reactionary brother Charles. Yet the basis of unity was negative, a common enemy rather than shared interests or objectives; and in fact, once the crown was secured for the Infanta Isabel, this coalition was split apart by the problem of fashioning a system which would meet the divergent needs of its constituents.

Spain's fragmented economic base provided no grounds for an immediate program that could unify the various segments of the still rudimentary bourgeoisie. . . . The process of bourgeois revolution . . . was marked in Spain by the fragmentation and internal division of the socio-economic sectors which initiated and pushed it forward. Profound obstacles retarded the formation of a national bourgeoisie capable of consolidating broad popular support in its revolutionary struggle to transform the older structures of Spanish society.

The tenor of the *Pobrecito Hablador* indicates that Larra perceived this problem as primarily ideological and cultural in nature. He believed that only if the authority of reason were established as firmly among the majority of the public as it was among the liberal intellectual elite, could that elusive and urgent unity be achieved. Through education and instruction Spaniards could be shown the inherent rationality of nature and social processes, the necessity for critical examination of ideas and historical reality, and the validity of the universal principles which such examination brought to light. He was confident that once this was accomplished, broad-based agreement on liberal goals would follow naturally, for, to Larra as to the other Spanish liberals of the time, such concepts as the rights of man and the perfectibility of human society were the luminous truths which the new spirit of rationality revealed. The light of reason would eliminate the sources of division and conflict and bring the Spanish people together around common values, illuminating the way to social justice, progress, and prosperity.

Larra's belief that literature was a primary instrument in the task of propagating rational and progressive attitudes governed his understanding and acceptance of Romantic art as it was introduced by the liberals who returned from exile when Ferdinand died. In fact, it is he who expressed most clearly the close connection Spanish liberals saw between the new literary trend and their social program. In January 1836, when hopes were still high that the government of Mendizábal would produce substantive liberalization, Larra paused to formulate for

the new journal *El Español* his view of literature in general terms. Calling on his own generation to produce a literature which would correspond to the new society in the process of being formed, he described the ideal guiding the forces of change: "*Libertad* en literatura, como en las artes, como en la industria, como en el comercio, como en la conciencia. He aquí la divisa de la época, he aquí la nuestra, he aquí la medida con que mediremos.'' He thus declares the central demand of the Victor Hugo variety of Romanticism—artistic liberty—to be an integral aspect of a social movement to free the industrial and commercial classes from the constraints of the *ancien régime*.

It should be noted that in this article Larra does not advocate Romanticism as a specific literary school. However, in elaborating what he regards to be literature's proper function, he draws on those currents of European Romanticism most compatible with the goal of consolidating a liberal public. For example, he laments the dependence of Spanish writers on French models and the absence of a truly national literature since the eighteenth century:

> Muchos años hemos pasado de entonces acá sin podernos dar cuenta siquiera de nuestro estado, sin saber si tendríamos una literatura por fin nuestra o si seguiríamos siendo una postdata rezagada de la clásica literatura francesa del siglo pasado. En este estado estamos casi todavía: en verso, en prosa, dispuestos a recibirlo todo, porque nada tenemos. . . .

Thus, what Larra felt to be the immediate need to which Spain's young writers must respond coincided with the Romantic emphasis on national identity. He hoped for the emergence of an authentic national literature that would be part of the process of forging a new, progressive national class: ". . . esperemos que dentro de poco podamos echar los cimientos de una literatura *nueva*, expresión de la sociedad *nueva* que componemos, toda de *verdad*, como de *verdad* es nuestra sociedad." His conception of the truth which the new literature was to represent also incorporated the Romantic focus on subjectivity and emotion: "las pasiones en el hombre siempre serán verdades, porque la imaginación misma ¿qué es sino una *verdad* más hermosa?" But instead of isolating art's object, the truth of feeling, from other kinds of truth, he regards it as a corollary of politics: "En política el hombre no ve más que *intereses* y *derechos*, es decir, *verdades*. En literatura no puede buscar por consiguiente sino *verdades*." In establishing an equivalence between interests and rights as the substance of politics, on the one hand, and feeling and imagination as the substance of literature, on the other, Larra implies an essential unity. Passions, dreams, aspirations are another side of that basic social reality—the individual—which liberal political ideology treats in economic and legal terms. In this way Larra presents the artistic exploration of subjectivity as a valid and necessary component of the liberal project. These considerations are implicitly synthesized in the mission he urges on his fellow writers in the final paragraph: to express the new consciousness, national and personal, that accompanies the transformation of Spanish society, and, above all, to disseminate it to "la multitud ignorante aún." (pp. 456-61)

The confidence with which **"Literatura"** asserts the harmonious identity of public and private, of personal feeling and social goals, is deceptive. Disturbing insights had arisen from Larra's engagement, as an apostle of progressive consciousness, with the concrete developments of the liberal struggle for hegemony after 1833. As the unstable alliance which had formed to assure Isabel's succession to the throne began to split into quarreling factions, Larra came increasingly to feel that the ideological bases for unity were neither so self-evident nor so solid as he had at first thought. His uneasiness was registered in certain developments that took place in his writing between the summers of 1834 and 1836.

One indication of the process can be found in the satires on parliamentary rhetoric written in 1834-35. In these articles Fígaro ridicules the demagogic use of liberal terms and catchwords by revealing the absurdity, self-interest, or conservatism of the arguments they clothe. Although his attacks are directed against the strong moderate faction which supported Prime Minister Martínez de la Rosa in his refusal to institute substantive liberal reform, they gradually begin to reveal a critical attitude toward liberal generalizations themselves. Witty play upon terms such as "pueblo" or "representación" hints at their susceptibility to multiple, even contradictory, interpretations in different contexts and to rhetorical manipulation by political factions of diverse persuasions. This satirical treatment prefigures the skepticism of Larra's late articles with regard to the universal, objective value of liberal concepts and principles.

In particular, the divisions that so profoundly disrupted the period of transition following Ferdinand's death affected Larra's conception of society and nation as they were constituted in Spain. Initially, in the *Pobrecito Hablador,* he had conceived of Spanish society as a coherent whole whose weaknesses were reflected at all levels—in individuals, in the culture, in the various social groupings, in the rulers—and whose rifts, due to differences in "enlightenment," could be bridged by education. The experience of the succeeding years, however, forced him to probe more deeply for the sources of that disunity which must be overcome if the liberal ideal of "national sovereignty" were not to remain a term devoid of real content. The search led him toward a vision of his society as split into classes with distinct cultural, political, and economic characteristics. In **"Jardines públicos"** (June 1834) he describes the totally different recreational habits of the lower classes, the middle class, and the aristocracy; in **"El hombre-globo"** (March 1835) he

An illustration of "La diligencia" by Dibujo Pellicer.

analyzes their differences in political consciousness and revolutionary potential; and in **"Modos de vivir que no dan de vivir"** (June 1835) he attempts to acquaint his middle-class audience with the economic circumstances of the urban lower classes. A remark at the beginning of **"El album"** (May 1835) generalizes these perceptions:

> La cuna, la riqueza, el talento, la educación, a veces obrando separadamente, obrando otras de consuno, han subdividido siempre a los hombres hasta lo infinito, y lo que se llama en general la sociedad es un amalgama de mil sociedades colocadas en escalón, que sólo se rozan en sus fronteras respectivas unas con otras, y las cuales no reúne en un todo compacto en cada país sino el vínculo de una lengua común, y de lo que se llama entre los hombres patriotismo o nacionalismo.

By mid-1835, then, he had come to see "society" as essentially heterogeneous, "nation" as an idea linking groups with little else in common except a tongue and a geographical location. In this context we can better understand why **"Literatura"** holds up national consciousness as a goal to be achieved, rather than a reality.

Such preoccupation with the gaps between liberal rhetoric and reality, together with a more profound comprehension of social division, paved the way for the next phase of Larra's intellectual and political evolution. It was precipitated by the progressives' disillusionment with the government of Mendizábal. The hopeful tone of **"Literatura"** reflected the wide-spread liberal belief that the new prime minister, a man of impeccable progressive credentials, was the leader required to put down the Carlist rebellion, to straighten out the fiscal affairs of the state, and to give Spain a new Constitution that would provide for a truly representative government. Mendizábal, however, quickly became embroiled in the internal battles of the liberal factions. Some of his maneuvers with respect to the drafting of a new electoral law brought him sharp criticism from Fígaro in February 1836, because in an effort to preserve his faction's political control, he had abandoned the progressive principle of broadening the electoral base. In March, Mendizábal's plan for auctioning appropriated ecclesiastical land put into clear focus for Larra the tendency of the liberals in power to sacrifice principle to self-interest while clothing the transaction in progressive rhetoric. In a review of Espronceda's pamphlet against Mendizábal, Larra adopted his friend's position that instead of constituting agrarian reform and winning broader support for the liberal cause, the specific provisions of the program would worsen the economic situation of the rural lower classes while benefiting only those classes who already held land and capital. Other articles written in the spring of 1836 (**"Dios nos asista"** and **"Los barateros"**) are also critical of an elite which supported liberal measures only insofar as they strengthened its political hegemony and furthered its economic interests to the exclusion of the middle and lower classes.

By early summer of 1836, then, Larra's fervent advocacy of liberal ideals was tempered by awareness of how they became deeply problematic in their application to a real context of opposing class interests and of factional struggles for power. The symptoms of growing ambivalence are evident, curiously enough, in a two-part review of Alexandre Dumas' Romantic drama *Anthony.* In this review, written scarcely six months after **"Literatura,"** Larra attacks certain Romantic tendencies on the grounds that they are detrimental to the central task of

Spanish writers. He strongly objects to the extreme, anti-social individualism he finds in the drama, which glorifies the hero's total rejection of society in his pursuit of a blindly egotistical passion. Larra regards Romantic individualism of this sort as "la desorganización social . . . literaria y filosóficamente," immoral in any case, but dangerously disruptive in a Spain that lacks social cohesion, which is "un campo de batalla donde se chocan los elementos opuestos que han de constituir una sociedad." He argues that it is highly inappropriate to import from France a literature which will further divide the advanced elite from the mass of the public because it remains incomprehensible to the latter, while encouraging nihilistic irresponsibility in the former.

What is most striking about this denunciation of the cult of the latest French Romantic literature is the pessimistic perspective from which Larra reiterates those persistent themes—the need for unified progress among the public, and for social responsibility in the writer. If, on the one hand, he urges his compatriots to travel the road of progress together and at an appropriate pace in order to overcome any obstacles on the way, on the other hand he is hardly encouraging about what lies ahead: "*Antony,* como la mayor parte de las obras de la literatura moderna francesa, es el grito que lanza la humanidad que nos lleva delantera, grito de desesperación, al encontrar el caos y la nada al fin del viaje." He does not question the validity of the message, only its impact on those still at the beginning of the journey. He appears, then, to believe or to suspect that the liberal impulse he has so long defended in politics and art will inevitably lead to the destructive, disintegrative values he finds so objectionable in *Anthony.* "Libertad en política, sí, libertad en literatura, libertad por todas partes; si el destino de la humanidad es llegar a la nada por entre ríos de sangre,. . . no seamos nosotros los únicos privados del triste privilegio de la humanidad; libertad para recorrer ese camino que no conduce a ninguna parte. . . ." This negative vision of "liberty" and "progress" reveals to what extent the seeds of doubt were undermining Larra's liberal faith. Disturbing questions lie just under the surface of the troubled, sometimes self-contradictory essays on Dumas' drama. Might liberty mean the freedom not to be forced toward progress? Might it, interpreted as individual freedom from all conventional *mores,* destroy the very basis of human society? Might the cause of progress best be served by constraining the vanguard? Might progress itself be negative, leading to the destruction of the illusions and social conventions that make reality tolerable, to the unmitigated materialism of commerce, industry, and science? These doubts, which laid open to question the internal coherence of liberal ideals and the validity of the rational attitudes on which they were believed to rest, were immanent in Larra's work during the spring and early summer of 1836. The next convulsion of the Spanish body politic and its impact on Larra's personal life was to touch off in Fígaro an irreversible crisis of values which was similar in character to that of other European Romantics, even though its causes and consequences were firmly rooted in Spanish reality.

It is often said that the coup of August 1836, which disbanded the Parliament to which Larra had been elected in July, was an important factor in his morose state of mind in the autumn and ultimately in his suicide in February 1837. F. Courtney Tarr has unfolded in all its complexity the grain of truth embedded in this view by reconstructing Larra's involvement in the treacherous arena of Spanish politics between May and November [see Additional Bibliography]. What Tarr's fine literary detective work discloses is that, through a combination of sheer personal opportunism and real conviction about the needs of the moment, Larra compromised his progressive stand and his claim to journalistic independence. He suppressed his criticism of the Moderate government and wrote anonymously in its behalf, in exchange for its powerful backing of his candidacy to a seat in the new Parliament to be convened in August. This transaction brought the would-be politician nothing but disaster. The Mendizábal faction, certain to lose the elections and pushed further to the left in an endeavor to regain its political base, resorted to armed rebellion and forced the Queen-Regent to legitimize the Constitution of 1812. Members of this faction, of course, formed the cabinet. As a result, Larra not only lost his chance to be a member of Parliament, but, worse still, found himself in opposition to a government which promised to take all the measures he himself had strongly advocated during the preceding year. A mixture of perverse pride and honest conviction that the new government's rhetoric was a fraud made it impossible for him to realign himself with the progressive left wing, whose respect he did value. Yet if he criticized the new cabinet, as he had all the previous ones, few would believe that he was not motivated by personal disappointment, and Larra was extremely sensitive about his reputation for integrity and independence, already considerably tarnished as a result of the summer. This bind was the more excruciating in that he had only his ambition and his misreading of the course of Spanish history to blame.

Larra's plight forced him to reevaluate the connection between himself, both as a writer and as an individual subject, and his society. On the one hand, he felt alienated from former allies and misunderstood by friends and enemies alike; his sense of having a role in the ongoing process of public life had been seriously undermined. On the other hand, he had been forced to recognize that the conflicts, divisions, and paradoxical compromises which had once provoked him to describe the liberal movement as a "laberinto inextricable" were duplicated in his own internal contradictions. If political factions vacillated on matters of principle, used the rhetoric and sometimes the real momentum of revolution to promote their special interests, or confused rationalization with reason, Larra himself had rationalized personal ambition as disinterested public service, had vaunted the integrity of his principles to hide an expedient transaction, and now found it impossible to separate pride from intellectual independence, emotion from judgment, resentment from conviction. This new self-knowledge led back dialectically to a re-assessment of social reality.

One of the most striking signs of the crisis was the revision of his earlier view of the social function of the writer and literature. **"Horas de invierno"** (December 1836), a review of a collection of translated French works, constitutes a kind of disavowal of the profession of faith Larra had made in **"Literatura"** nearly twelve months before. Whereas in the earlier essay he had argued for the development of a national literature, at once expression and advocate of the consolidation of a progressive class, he now asserted that Spanish writers should resign themselves to translating what was written in the rest of Europe. His case is based on two main points: first, Spain's decadence and its inferior position in the hierarchy of European nations, and second, the lack of a public for original writing within Spain.

The latter observation occasions a lyrical outburst of anguish:

> Escribir como escribimos en Madrid es tomar
> una apuntación, es escribir en un libro de me-
> morias, es realizar un monólogo desesperante

y triste para uno solo. Escribir en Madrid es llorar, es buscar voz sin encontrarla, como en una pesadilla abrumadora y violenta. Porque no escribe uno siquiera para los suyos. ¿Quiénes son los suyos? ¿Quién oye aquí? ¿Son las academias, son los círculos literarios, son los corrillos noticieros de la Puerta del Sol, son las mesas de los cafés, son las divisiones expedicionarias, son las pandillas de Gómez, son los que despojan, o son los despojados?

This nightmarish image of the Spanish writer as rendered virtually aphonic by the lack of response from the surrounding social environment ("echo" is the term Larra uses earlier in the essay) clearly repudiates Larra's earlier hope of contributing through the press to the formation of a unified public consciousness. Fígaro's new picture of the situation suggests that his despair stems from his sense that what might have been a liberal public had dissolved into warring factions, further splintering a society rent by civil war and open to plunder from all sides. Whatever the subjective components of his anguish, it reflected a reality—namely, that the various sectors of the Spanish middle classes who sought change had not been able to unify as a bourgeoisie conscious of common interests and strengths, but, instead, remained divided, weak, and unreliable.

This assessment of the internal situation justifies the essay's pessimism regarding Spain's place among European powers, in that any prospect of catching up with England or France was diminished by the lack of cohesion. However, there is a more subtle connection between Larra's treatment of the European context and his view of Spanish reality that points to a new, deeply negative perception of the march of history itself. Just as Spain is divided into the plunderers and the plundered, so is the international scene, so is human society:

> [L]as naciones, como los individuos, sujetos a la gran ley del egoísmo, viven más que de su vida propia de la vida ajena que consumen, y ¡ay del pueblo que no desgasta diariamente con su roce superior y violento los pueblos immediatos, porque será desgastado por ellos! . . . Ley implacable de la naturaleza: o devorar, o ser devorado. Pueblos e individuos, o víctimas o verdugos.

The law of self-interest was, of course, the foundation of liberal political economy, the source of those interests and rights to which Larra twelve months before in **"Literatura"** had so complacently refered as the substance of social reality. What he then assumed to be capable of regulation and harmonious development through liberal institutions he now regards as an irremediably voracious and predatory struggle. Thus, the truth whose artistic expression he once believed to be part of a process of national cohesion has become in his eyes the insuperable obstacle to the formation of a community which the artist might address. The implacable law of power, not reason, governs world history, individual relations, and, of necessity, literary production. Hence the explicit message of the article: Spanish writers, isolated within their own nation, itself weak and dominated, are condemned simply to transmit the creative work of others.

In **"Horas de invierno"** it is evident that Larra's recent experience had not only shaken his previous faith in the public mission of his work, but had also affected his view of fundamental social order, which now seemed to him inherently divided, conflictive, shaped by the blind struggle for power. A satirical article he wrote during this period, **"El día de difuntos de 1836,"** further reflects a crisis in the values and assumptions that had formerly guided his writing. In this piece, his satirical references no longer imply an unequivocal correlation between justice and liberal programs. Using as his principal device the satiric epitaph, he expresses sardonic approval of the demise of the Inquisition and the Royal Statute which the Queen-Regent had imposed instead of a constitution, but at the same time he treats with elegiac mourning the appropriation of monastic lands which earlier he had certainly approved in principle. Whereas six months before he had asserted that he would not defend royal prerogatives, he now represents attacks on monarchical tradition as shameful and saddening. Indeed, in this article the passing of older traditions appears chaotic and frightening, rather than positive. What this suggests is a collapse of the categories of order and value which Larra had once assumed to be inherent in the processes of historical change. He suspects that the external world is void of human rational meaning.

His response to this sense of alienation from his social context is to turn inward. A new valuation of subjectivity is implicit in the tone and structure of **"Día de difuntos,"** where Fígaro's formerly acerbic, ironic commentary on the public scene becomes almost undisguisedly confessional and introspective. The references to current events are closely integrated with evocations of Fígaro's emotional state. He begins, for example, by describing his personal melancholy through a series of similes that allude to the disastrous state of the national economy and to recent political disturbances. This introduction prepares the ground for the central satirical structure of the piece—the projection of Fígaro's inner despondency upon external reality. The narrator goes out to observe the All Soul's Day rituals of Madrid and finds reflected in the city itself the morbid mood he had felt alone in his study: "Un vértigo espantoso se apoderó de mí y commencé a ver claro. El cementerio está dentro de Madrid. Madrid es el cementerio. Pero vasto cementerio donde cada casa es el nicho de una familia, cada calle el sepulcro de un acontecimiento, cada corazón la urna cineraria de una esperanza o de un deseo." The anguished perspective that transforms Madrid into a huge graveyard is validated as "seeing clearly," as if it were a lens that brought into focus what had before been obscure. The metaphorical vision reveals what is true, that Madrid *is* a cemetery, that in each of its public monuments can be read an epitaph commemorating a catastrophe: "Los ministerios: Aquí yace media España; murió de la otra media. . . . La Bolsa: Aquí yace el crédito español." (pp. 461-67)

But the true nature of external reality is not the only revelation to be gained by the projection of subjectivity. The conclusion of the article adds another level to the complex dialectic of self and other, as Fígaro reacts violently to the emotional tonality of his own, now objectified vision: "¡Fuera, exclamé, la horrible pesadilla, fuera!" Having projected his psychological life upon the external situation in order properly to evaluate and understand its underlying irrationality, the narrator then tries to separate himself from that horror, to cast it out totally, like a possessing demon, upon the outside world to which it corresponds. Then the feeling self may attempt to turn inward to find refuge from its alien, repellent context. "Una nube sombría lo envolvió todo. Era la noche. El frío de la noche helaba mis venas. Quise salir violentamente del horrible cementerio. Quise refugiarme en mi propio corazón, lleno no ha mucho de vida, de ilusiones, de deseos." Yet, fleeing the cold nocturnal nightmare of Madrid to the inner sanctuary of his own soul, he finds there only a corresponding despair: "¡Santo cielo! También otro cementerio. Mi corazón no es más que otro sepulcro. ¿Qué dice? Leamos. ¿Quién ha muerto en él? ¡Espantoso letrero! *¡Aquí yace la esperanza!''* Thus, the structure of **"Día de difuntos"** implies a circular process. Larra's intensified alienation, his perception of a rupture between the inner being and the social context, is expressed in Fígaro's despondent mood. The link between self and other is now seen as metaphorical, symbolic, rather than metonymic and contiguous, as the narrator finds in his own subjective response of rage, despair, and anguish the true measure of the situation of Spanish society as a whole. But this objectification of inner feelings, in turn, reveals with greater clarity his own condition.

The new insights gained by this reexamination of self and world are crystallized in an extraordinary essay written at the end of December, **"La nochebuena de 1836."** On the first page, the narrator's meditations lead him to the image of the relation between inner being and external world which informs both the structure and sense of the article as a whole.

> Ora volvía los ojos a los cristales de mi balcón; veíalos empañados y como llorosos por dentro; los vapores condensados se deslizaban a manera de lágrimas a lo largo del diáfano cristal; así se empaña la vida, pensaba; así el frío exterior del mundo condensa las penas en el interior del hombre, así caen gota a gota las lágrimas sobre el corazón. Los que ven de fuera los cristales los ven tersos y brillantes; los que ven sólo los rostros los ven alegres y serenos.

The inner and outer are distinct and opposed; in fact, the manifest thrust of the image is to emphasize the contrast between the exterior mask presented to the world and the intimate reality it conceals. At the same time, however, the simile sets up a symbolic correspondence between the window, an external object, and inner life. The cold exterior becomes perceptible as the mist within; outer reality both produces and is revealed by the inner condensation of feeling. The self, hermetically sealed off from the outside, is qualitatively different, yet reality can be read in the unique configurations it forms through mediated contact with the world.

In order to analyze the condensations of feeling and aspiration which reproduced in his own heart the condition of Spanish society, Larra adopted as his model the Horatian satire in which the slave speaks the truth to his master during the Saturnalia. The center of the article consists of a dialogue between Fígaro and his drunken servant. Because there is an unresolved ambiguity about the source of the voice that issues from the servant, the classical convention is made a vehicle of self-objectification; the words Fígaro hears are a projection of the accumulated self-knowledge which enables him to see himself as other. The voice of truth reveals the narrator's sense of guilt with regard to the hypocrisy, egotism, and vanity reflected in his personal life; it mercilessly dissects his inconsistencies as a writer who will sacrifice principles to please a public he despises, who claims fearless independence but spends sleepless nights worrying about enemies, disapproval, and retribution. A telling critique of Fígaro's political pretensions follows: "Te llamas liberal y despreocupado, y el día que te apoderes del látigo azotarás como te han azotado. Los hombres de mundo os llamáis hombres de honor y de carácter, y a cada suceso nuevo cambiáis de opinión, apostatáis de vuestros principios." Here we see that Larra's introspection has been one

of the sources of that changed view of the historical panorama found in the other essays of this period. The self-knowledge gained in the crises of the summer and fall has brought him to regard the liberal enterprise as the insubstantial mirage that hides from view the power struggle which is the substance of social reality. Thus, the process by which he casts his own intimate reflections upon his truth-telling servant, so that they can be known, also reveals the truth about Spanish society. Examining the contradictory patterns of his own feelings, ideals, and choices, he traces the conflicting pressure points of the surrounding reality. (pp. 468-69)

[It can be] argued that Romanticism was an artistic response to social transformations and their impact on the intellectual inheritance of the eighteenth century, and that this response pictured a profound break between the individual subject and the social or natural world, which it attempted to span in new ways. Larra's late works show that in some respects he conformed to this paradigm, even though Spanish reality did not duplicate the conditions of the countries where Romanticism first appeared. This coincidence was possible because the interaction of literary and political developments which we have examined in detail eventually caused Larra to doubt the internal consistency of rational, enlightened, liberal ideals as well as their correspondence to historical and even psychological reality. Increasingly alienated from a world which seemed hostile and irrational, he turned inward to discover paradoxically in subjectivity a new gauge of external reality and a more complex relation to it.

However, since the Romantic consciousness expressed in these last articles grows out of a specifically Spanish context, it takes a particular form. The dialectic of the "self" and the "other" provides Larra with a new cognitive model, but it does not help him to reconstitute value—the inner man provides no alternative to external chaos, it only reflects it. Consequently, in **"La nochebuena"** as Fígaro's confrontation with truth ends, he is left gazing sleeplessly at a yellow box labeled "Mañana." Two months later Larra shot himself with the pistol he kept in the yellow box at his bedside.

This point brings us [to the question of the] . . . particular character of Spanish Romanticism. In order to understand just how Larra's outlook shows the impress of the social realities confronting the Spanish writer, it is helpful to compare the desperate negativity of Larra's vision of the relation of self and society with that of the English Romantic poets, as it is characterized by Karl Kroeber:

> Wordsworth insists that only through celebration and sanctification "Of the individual Mind that keeps her own / Inviolate retirement" do we attain the possibility "Of joy in the widest commonalty spread." Or in his less famous phrasing, "Possessions have I that are solely mine, / Something within which yet is shared by none . . . I would impart it, I would / Spread it wide." Romantic individualism is thus double-edged. Individualism is also cultural, though not social, representativeness. From "This Lime Tree Bower My Prison" to the "Ode on a Grecian Urn" we find poetry directed toward the paradoxical unifying of solitude and commonalty defining individualism as basic humanness.

Larra, on the other hand, could find no source of joy in the cultural representativeness of the solitary individual mind; in fact, it was precisely the cause of his despair because in his situation he had no sense of being able to create and project value from within. The voice of self-knowledge describes his dilemma: "inventas palabras y haces de ellas sentimientos, ciencias, artes, objetos de existencia. . . . Y cuando descubres que son palabras, blasfemas y maldices." As the old structures crumble away, the search for new values upon which to base social life seemed to him to yield nothing solid—only a language which represented desires instead of reality. Aside from the futile projection of his hopes upon the quasi-world of words, his interior landscape offered with despairing lucidity only the image of the external disruption.

Unlike the English bourgeois poets who carried within them the confidence of a powerful new class that it could "spread wide" the values uniquely theirs, this Spanish bourgeois writer felt too strongly the weakness of a national class he once described as having "un alma de imitación." As he himself pointed out, "Escribir como Chateaubriand y Lamartine en la capital del mundo moderno es escribir para la humanidad." In contrast, to write as Larra did in Madrid was more on the order of a monologue. The audience he despaired of lacked the resources and cohesion to realize fully its aspiration to achieve national hegemony, much less world dominance. The final piercing words of the servant illuminate from Fígaro's internal window the dilemma of his public, liberal Spain: "Yo estoy ebrio de vino, es verdad; pero tú lo estás de deseos y de impotencia!" (pp. 469-71)

> Susan Kirkpatrick, *"Spanish Romanticism and the Liberal Project: The Crisis of Mariano José de Larra,"* in Studies in Romanticism, *Vol. 16, No. 4, Fall, 1977, pp. 451-71.*

ADDITIONAL BIBLIOGRAPHY

Adams, Nicholson B. "A Note on Larra's *El doncel.*" *Hispanic Review* IX, No. 1 (January 1941): 218-21.
Compares *El doncel* to the novels of Sir Walter Scott.

Brent, Albert. "Larra's Dramatic Works." *Romance Notes* VIII, No. 2 (Spring 1967): 207-11.
Lists the composition, performance, and publication dates of Larra's dramas.

Chaves y Rey, Manuel. *Don Mariano José de Larra (Fígaro): Su tiempo, su vida, sus obras.* Seville: Impr. de la Andalucia, 1898, 241 p.
An important Spanish-language biography. Critics regard this work as useful but sometimes factually inaccurate.

Hendrix, W. S. "Notes on Jouy's Influence on Larra." *The Romanic Review* IX, No. 1 (January-March 1920): 37-45.
Briefly examines Larra's debt to Étienne Jouy.

Ilie, Paul. "Larra's Nightmare." *Revista Hispánica moderna* XXXVIII, No. 4 (1974-75): 153-66.
Examines Larra's life and works in an attempt to present a "psychobiographical" sketch. Ilie contends that the modernity of Larra's writings is due less to his revolutionism than to the "incompatibility between his unconscious prejudices and his political ideas."

King, Lionel. "Larra and the Birth of Spanish Liberalism." *Contemporary Review* 228, No. 1321 (February 1976): 64-8.
An introductory study of Larra's life and works.

Lovett, Gabriel H. "About Larra's *Afrancesamiento.*" *Revista de estudios Hispánicos* IV, No. 1 (April 1970): 3-18.
A discussion of Larra's patriotism and his reaction to the Spanish war against Napoleon from 1808 to 1814.

Sánchez, Roberto G. "Between *Macías* and *Don Juan*: Spanish Romantic Drama and the Mythology of Love." *Hispanic Review* 44, No. 1 (Winter 1976): 27-44.
A comparison of Larra's *Macías* and José Zorrilla y Moral's *Don Juan Tenorio.* Sánchez explores the similarities between the two Spanish Romantic dramas and concludes that both works portray "the hidden fears and desires of the society of the time."

Tarr, F. Courtney. "Reconstruction of a Decisive Period in Larra's Life (May-November, 1836)." *Hispanic Review* V, No. 1 (January 1937): 1-24.
An account of the political events that may have precipitated Larra's suicide.

——. "Romanticism in Spain and Spanish Romanticism: A Critical Survey." *Bulletin of Spanish Studies* XVI, No. 61 (January 1939): 3-37.
An outline of the development of Spanish Romanticism with scattered references to Larra.

Ullman, Pierre L. *Mariano de Larra and Spanish Political Rhetoric.* Madison: University of Wisconsin Press, 1971, 428 p.
A biography that focuses on the political aspects of Larra's life and writings.

Vanderford, Kenneth H. "A Note on the Versification of Larra." *Philological Quarterly* XIII, No. 3 (July 1934): 306-09.
Examines the poetic style of *Macías.*

Karl (Heinrich) Marx

1818-1883

German philosopher, essayist, historian, and journalist.

Widely regarded as one of the most significant figures in the history of ideas, Marx is known as the father of modern communism. His beliefs—outlined most fully in *Manifest der kommunistschen Partei* (*The Communist Manifesto*) and *Das Kapital* (*Capital*)—provide the ideological basis for most communist and socialist governments and have had a profound effect on world politics in the twentieth century. Marx's philosophy, which involves a complex analysis of capitalism in the context of the economic evolution of human society, can be summarized in a single sentence from the *Manifesto:* ''All history is the history of class struggle.'' Marx's orientation was mainly that of a revolutionist who actively sought to bring about economic and political change in capitalist societies. Although the practical application of his ideas has been vigorously debated over the years, Marx remains one of the most influential thinkers of the modern era for his theoretical contributions to the fields of political science, economics, philosophy, and sociology.

Marx was born in Trier, Germany, to a Jewish attorney and his wife. Several years after Marx's birth, his father converted to Christianity and raised the children as Protestants; Marx, however, never affiliated himself with any religion. After attending secondary school in Trier, he studied history, law, and philosophy from 1835 to 1841 at the Universities of Bonn and Berlin. While a student in Berlin, Marx became acquainted with the works of the German philosopher Georg Wilhelm Friedrich Hegel, who interpreted history as a series of moral, social, and political problems for which there first arises a positive solution, or thesis, followed by a counter proposition, or antithesis. The combination of the thesis and antithesis, according to Hegel, in turn leads to a balanced compromise, or synthesis. Known as the Hegelian dialectic, this concept of unity through opposition profoundly influenced Marx's ideas about economics and history. Marx's thought during this period was also shaped by his association with the Young Hegelians, a radical group who espoused rationalist beliefs and the principles of the French Revolution and who denied the possibility of supernatural revelation. Upon leaving the University of Berlin, Marx attended the University of Jena, where he received a doctorate in philosophy in 1842. He intended to become a teacher, but his affiliation with the Young Hegelians had already marked him as a revolutionary thinker, and no university would hire him. Turning instead to journalism, Marx wrote essays on philosophical issues for a number of journals, and in 1843 he took an editorial position with the radical Cologne newspaper *Rheinische Zeitung*. Shortly afterwards, however, the paper was suppressed by government censors.

Seeking an environment that he felt would be better suited to intellectual growth and his interest in socialism, Marx moved to Paris in 1843; just before he left, he married Jenny von Westphalen, whom he had known since childhood. The most fortuitous consequence of Marx's move to Paris was his meeting with the German philosopher Friedrich Engels, the son of a wealthy manufacturer, who became Marx's closest friend as well as his collaborator and financial supporter. Engels shared Marx's contempt for the domination of the wealthy over the

poor, and the two eventually formulated the theory of historical materialism. According to this theory, history is guided by economics and evolves in stages. Capitalism, they argued, is the last phase of historical development prior to the emergence of communism and is marked by the exploitation of the individual worker and the prosperity of the landowners. They believed that the conflict between these two classes—the landowners, or capitalists, and the laborers, or proletariat—would produce communism, or self-government by the proletariat. Marx and Engels contended that all members of a communist society would be equal and that no one would be exploited since possessions and property would be shared. In addition, Marx and Engels considered religion incompatible with the goals of communist society. Marx once wrote, ''Religion is the opium of the people,'' and with Engels contended that any belief in a supernatural force, because of its traditional focus on submission to a higher power, would work against their revolutionary ideals.

Aside from his friendship with Engels, life in Paris quickly soured for Marx, largely because of the threat of censorship.

In 1845 he and his family moved to Brussels. Engels, too, moved to Brussels and together they soon published two philosophical works, *Die heilige Familie* (*The Holy Family*) and *Die deutsche Ideologie* (*The German Ideology*). In addition, Marx wrote *Misère de la philosophie* (*The Poverty of Philosophy*), a response to the French economist Pierre Joseph Proudhon and his book *Philosophie de la misère;* while Proudhon contended that society is controlled by moral values, Marx argued that it evolves as a result of historical forces that are not affected by morality. In 1848, Marx and Engels published the *Manifesto*, which was written to serve as the platform for the Communist League, a political organization of German workers. In this brief, passionate essay, they argued for the abolition of private property, urging the workers of the world to unite and revolt against the capitalists. Within the *Manifesto*, Marx and Engels first fully applied the concept of historical materialism and outlined their theory of class struggle. Marx's greatest desire was to create a classless society through socialism. Although the proletariat would initially rule after overthrowing the landowning class, Marx believed that eventually all class differentiation would disappear and that government would exist to monitor commodities and property, not individuals. Political strife, according to Marx, would then be replaced with peace.

After the publication of the *Manifesto*, Marx returned to Cologne, where he edited a communist newspaper, the *Neue rheinische Zeitung*. Because the paper encouraged the abolition of taxes, it was quickly suppressed and Marx was arrested and charged with treason. Though later acquitted, he was exiled from all land controlled by Prussia and he returned to Paris. However, political dissidents were viewed unfavorably in the city, which had just recovered from the French Revolution of 1848. Since the French government had no interest in harboring the controversial author of the *Manifesto*, Marx was offered the choice of moving to a remote area of France or leaving the country altogether. Once again, Marx and his family relocated, this time to London, where they remained for the rest of Marx's life.

Though the political climate proved more hospitable in London, Marx was unable to find employment, and his family lived in abject poverty. Engels, who had remained a loyal supporter throughout their friendship, provided some financial help until Marx found a position with the New York *Tribune* in 1852. As a foreign correspondent for the newspaper, he wrote vehement letters denouncing czarism in Russia and detailing his desire that Britain use its military might to crush the Russian regime. Despite his impoverished circumstances, Marx continued to write prolifically, producing historical studies in addition to his journalism. In the 1850s, he composed some of his most notable works, including *Der achtzehnte Brumaire des Louis Bonaparte* (*The Eighteenth Brumaire of Louis Bonaparte*), *Zur Kritik der politischen Ökonomie* (*A Contribution to the Critique of Political Economy*), and *Die Klassenkämpfe in Frankreich 1848 bis 1850* (*The Class Struggles in France, 1848-1850*). These writings, which discuss contemporary political events in light of his theories, are today considered insightful analyses of society and economics in nineteenth-century Europe. Around this time, Marx had also begun to accumulate material for what would be the culmination of his life's work, *Capital*. He spent most of every day writing and researching in the British Museum, where he first composed the *Critique of Political Economy*. This work was intended as the initial volume in a projected series that would explore several aspects of political economy. Though Marx never completed the project, he subsequently reworked the *Critique of Political Economy* and published it as *Capital*. Its entire publication was fraught with complications, and only one volume appeared in Marx's lifetime.

Capital is a vast work detailing the history of capitalism, its characteristics, and the events Marx believed would lead to its inevitable decline and destruction. The focal point of *Capital* is Marx's theory of surplus value. He posited that a product's actual value is determined by the amount of labor required to produce it. Since the individual laborer is not paid according to the product's market value, but according to a set wage, the capitalist landowner receives the surplus value of the individual's labor. Other topics discussed in *Capital* include fluctuations in the economy and the role of the individual in the marketplace. Marx commented, in addition, on the demeaning and alienating effects of rapid industrialization upon the working class. As in the *Manifesto*, he set forth his ideal of a world without social stratification where everyone shared equally in production, labor, and profits. Critics note that, as much as it is an economic study, *Capital* is a visionary work and an astute philosophical indictment of the times in which Marx lived. *Capital* brought Marx enduring fame but the years of strenuous research and poverty had taken their toll on his health, and he died in 1883.

Marx's writings have proved controversial since their publication. His ideas have inspired debate even among his followers, whose occasional excesses prompted Marx himself to declare "I am no Marxist." Most historians concur that his greatest contribution to sociological and economic thought is the call for revolution inherent in his philosophy. Since his death, Marx and his works have been acknowledged as the shaping force of international communism. Ironically, the social changes that Marx predicted would take place in the most typically capitalist countries, England and France, occurred instead in czarist Russia. Marx's ideas had their most profound effect during the late nineteenth and early twentieth centuries, when they formed the ideological basis of the Russian Revolution. While some commentators now hail Marx as a prophet, others consider him a fanatic who, in his efforts to promulgate his theories, oversimplified history and failed to consider the roles of morality, pride, and shared sympathy in human affairs. Many critics also question his vehement opposition to religion. On the other hand, critics have suggested that Marx's hatred of capitalism arose from his loathing of his own deprived conditions and that his desire to care for the poor stemmed from his loving feelings for his family. Critical estimations of his work, therefore, rarely fail to take into account the circumstances of his life.

Marx's philosophy has also had a lasting impact on the field of literary criticism. Though he had no specific theories about literature, a Marxist school of literary criticism arose in the late nineteenth century, when several critics attempted to infuse literary scholarship with socialist theory. In the twentieth century, the Hungarian writer Georg Lukács, considered the foremost Marxist critic, has successfully championed a critical method that measures an author's stature by his or her sensitivity to the struggles of the proletariat. The practices of Marxist critics have been faulted by a number of prominent commentators, among them Edmund Wilson and Stanley Edgar Hyman, who have contended that historical, economic, and political theories are not well suited to literary and artistic analysis. Nevertheless, Marxist literary evaluations have figured prominently in contemporary critical discourse and are often praised for their eclectic approach.

Despite the controversial nature of Marx and his writings, he is regarded as one of the most important philosophers of the modern era and it is impossible to deny his impact on the political development of many countries throughout the world. His *Capital* and *Manifesto*, two of the best-known works in world literature, constitute the underlying basis of communist theory in the twentieth century.

PRINCIPAL WORKS

*Die deutsche Ideologie: Kritik der neuesten deutschen
    Philosophie in ihren Reprasentanten Feuerbach, B.
    Bauer und Stirner, und des deutschen Sozialismus in
    seinen verschieden Propheten* [with Friedrich Engels]
    (essay) 1845-46
    [*The German Ideology*, 1938]
*Die heilige Familie; oder, Kritik der Kritischen Kritik,
    gegen Bruno Bauer und Konsorten* [with Friedrich
    Engels] (essay) 1845
    [*The Holy Family*, 1956]
*Misère de la philosophie: Réponse à la "Philosophie de la
    misère" de M. Proudhon* (essay) 1847
    [*The Poverty of Philosophy*, 1900]
Manifest der kommunistschen Partei [with Friedrich Engels]
    (manifesto) 1848
    [*The Manifesto of the Communist Party*, 1850; also
    published as *The Communist Manifesto*, 1930]
Der achtzehnte Brumaire des Louis Bonaparte (history)
    1852
    [*The Eighteenth Brumaire of Louis Bonaparte*, 1898]
Zur Kritik der politischen Ökonomie (history) 1859
    [*A Contribution to the Critique of Political Economy*,
    1904]
Das Kapital: Kritik der politischen Ökonomie. 3 vols. [with
    Friedrich Engels] (essay) 1867-94
    [*Capital: A Critical Analysis of Capitalist Production.* 3
    vols., 1887-1909]
**Die Klassenkämpfe in Frankreich 1848 bis 1850* (essay)
    1895
    [*The Class Struggles in France, 1848-1850*, 1924]
*Karl Marx, Friedrich Engels: Historich-kritische
    Gesamtausgabe* [with Friedrich Engels] (essays,
    histories, criticism, and letters) 1927-36?
***Ökonomisch-philosophische Manuskripte* (essays)
    1932
    [*Economic and Philosophic Manuscripts of 1844*, 1959]
Karl Marx: Early Writings (essays, histories, and
    criticism) 1963
Selected Letters: The Personal Correspondence, 1844-1877
    (letters) 1981

*Since the date of publication of this work is unknown, the date of composition has been used.

**This work was written between 1850 and 1859.

***This work was written in 1844.

KARL MARX (essay date 1867)

[*In the following excerpt from the preface to* Capital, *dated 1867, Marx describes the work as an examination of "the capitalist mode of production, and the relations of production and forms*

of intercourse . . . that correspond to it." For additional commentary by Marx, see the excerpt dated 1873.]

[*Capital*], whose first volume I now submit to the public, forms the continuation of my book *Zur Kritik der Politischen Ökonomie. . . .* (p. 89)

The substance of that earlier work is summarized in the first chapter of this volume. This is done not merely for the sake of connectedness and completeness. The presentation is improved. As far as circumstances in any way permit, many points only hinted at in the earlier book are here worked out more fully, while, conversely, points worked out fully there are only touched upon in this volume. The sections on the history of the theories of value and of money are now, of course, left out altogether. However, the reader of the earlier work will find new sources relating to the history of those theories in the notes to the first chapter.

Beginnings are always difficult in all sciences. The understanding of the first chapter, especially the section that contains the analysis of commodities, will therefore present the greatest difficulty. I have popularized the passages concerning the substance of value and the magnitude of value as much as possible. The value-form, whose fully developed shape is the money-form, is very simple and slight in content. Nevertheless, the human mind has sought in vain for more than 2,000 years to get to the bottom of it, while on the other hand there has been at least an approximation to a successful analysis of forms which are much richer in content and more complex. Why? Because the complete body is easier to study than its cells. Moreover, in the analysis of economic forms neither microscopes nor chemical reagents are of assistance. The power of abstraction must replace both. But for bourgeois society, the commodity-form of the product of labour, or the value-form of the commodity, is the economic cell-form. To the superficial observer, the analysis of these forms seems to turn upon minutiae. It does in fact deal with minutiae, but so similarly does microscopic anatomy.

With the exception of the section on the form of value, therefore, this volume cannot stand accused on the score of difficulty. I assume, of course, a reader who is willing to learn something new and therefore to think for himself.

The physicist either observes natural processes where they occur in their most significant form, and are least affected by disturbing influences, or, wherever possible, he makes experiments under conditions which ensure that the process will occur in its pure state. What I have to examine in this work is the capitalist mode of production, and the relations of production and forms of intercourse . . . that correspond to it. Until now, their *locus classicus* has been England. This is the reason why England is used as the main illustration of the theoretical developments I make. If, however, the German reader pharisaically shrugs his shoulders at the condition of the English industrial and agricultural workers, or optimistically comforts himself with the thought that in Germany things are not nearly so bad, I must plainly tell him: *De te fabula narratur!*

Intrinsically, it is not a question of the higher or lower degree of development of the social antagonisms that spring from the natural laws of capitalist production. It is a question of these laws themselves, of these tendencies winning their way through and working themselves out with iron necessity. The country that is more developed industrially only shows, to the less developed, the image of its own future.

But in any case, and apart from all this, where capitalist production has made itself fully at home amongst us, for instance in the factories properly so called, the situation is much worse than in England, because the counterpoise of the Factory Acts is absent. In all other spheres, and just like the rest of Continental Western Europe, we suffer not only from the development of capitalist production, but also from the incompleteness of that development. Alongside the modern evils, we are oppressed by a whole series of inherited evils, arising from the passive survival of archaic and outmoded modes of production, with their accompanying train of anachronistic social and political relations. We suffer not only from the living, but from the dead. (pp. 89-91)

The social statistics of Germany and the rest of Continental Western Europe are, in comparison with those of England, quite wretched. But they raise the veil just enough to let us catch a glimpse of the Medusa's head behind it. We should be appalled at our own circumstances if, as in England, our governments and parliaments periodically appointed commissions of inquiry into economic conditions; if these commissions were armed with the same plenary powers to get at the truth; if it were possible to find for this purpose men as competent, as free from partisanship and respect of persons as are England's factory inspectors, her medical reporters on public health, her commissioners of inquiry into the exploitation of women and children, into conditions of housing and nourishment, and so on. Perseus wore a magic cap so that the monsters he hunted down might not see him. We draw the magic cap down over our own eyes and ears so as to deny that there are any monsters.

Let us not deceive ourselves about this. Just as in the eighteenth century the American War of Independence sounded the tocsin for the European middle class, so in the nineteenth century the American Civil War did the same for the European working class. In England the process of transformation is palpably evident. When it has reached a certain point, it must react on the Continent. There it will take a form more brutal or more humane, according to the degree of development of the working class itself. Apart from any higher motives, then, the most basic interests of the present ruling classes dictate to them that they clear out of the way all the legally removable obstacles to the development of the working class. For this reason, among others, I have devoted a great deal of space in this volume to the history, the details, and the results of the English factory legislation. One nation can and should learn from others. Even when a society has begun to track down the natural laws of its movement—and it is the ultimate aim of this work to reveal the economic law of motion of modern society—it can neither leap over the natural phases of its development nor remove them by decree. But it can shorten and lessen the birth-pangs.

To prevent possible misunderstandings, let me say this. I do not by any means depict the capitalist and the landowner in rosy colours. But individuals are dealt with here only in so far as they are the personifications of economic categories, the bearers . . . of particular class-relations and interests. My standpoint, from which the development of the economic formation of society is viewed as a process of natural history, can less than any other make the individual responsible for relations whose creature he remains, socially speaking, however much he may subjectively raise himself above them.

In the domain of political economy, free scientific inquiry does not merely meet the same enemies as in all other domains. The peculiar nature of the material it deals with summons into the fray on the opposing side the most violent, sordid and malignant passions of the human breast, the Furies of private interest. The Established Church, for instance, will more readily pardon an attack on thirty-eight of its thirty-nine articles than on one thirty-ninth of its income. Nowadays atheism itself is a *culpa levis* [venial sin], as compared with the criticism of existing property relations. Nevertheless, even here there is an unmistakable advance. I refer, as an example, to the Blue Book published within the last few weeks: 'Correspondence with Her Majesty's Missions Abroad, Regarding Industrial Questions and Trades' Unions'. There the representatives of the English Crown in foreign countries declare in plain language that in Germany, in France, in short in all the civilized states of the European Continent, a radical change in the existing relations between capital and labour is as evident and inevitable as in England. At the same time, on the other side of the Atlantic Ocean, Mr Wade, Vice-President of the United States, has declared in public meetings that, after the abolition of slavery, a radical transformation in the existing relations of capital and landed property is on the agenda. These are signs of the times, not to be hidden by purple mantles or black cassocks. They do not signify that tomorrow a miracle will occur. They do show that, within the ruling classes themselves, the foreboding is emerging that the present society is no solid crystal, but an organism capable of change, and constantly engaged in a process of change. (pp. 91-3)

Karl Marx, "Preface to the First Edition," in his Capital: A Critique of Political Economy, Vol. I, *translated by Ben Fowkes, Vintage Books, 1977, pp. 89-93.*

MIKHAIL BAKUNIN   (essay date 1871)

[*Bakunin, considered by many historians the most prominent force in Russian revolutionary anarchism, was a vehement opponent of Marxism. However, the following excerpt from remarks written in 1871 indicates his admiration for Marx's scholarship.*]

Marx was . . . much more advanced than I was [in 1845], and he still remains today incomparably more advanced than I—as far as learning is concerned. I knew nothing at that time of political economy, I still had not got rid of metaphysical abstractions, and my Socialism was only instinctive. He, although younger than I, was already an Atheist, an instructed Materialist, and a conscious Socialist. It was precisely at this time that he elaborated the first bases of his system as it is today. We saw each other pretty often, for I greatly respected him for his learning and for his passionate and serious devotion—though it was always mingled with vanity—to the cause of the proletariat, and I eagerly sought his conversation, which was always instructive and witty, when it was not inspired by petty hate, which alas! was only too often the case. There was, however, never any frank intimacy between us—our temperaments did not permit. He called me a sentimental Idealist, and he was right; I called him vain, perfidious, and sly, and I was right too.

Mikhail Bakunin, "Bakunin's Reminiscence," translated by K. J. Kenafick, in The Portable Karl Marx, *edited and translated in part by Eugene Kamenka, The Viking Press, 1983, p. 26.*

KARL MARX   (essay date 1873)

[*In the following excerpt from his 1873 postface to the second edition of* Capital, *Marx offers a brief critique of the Hegelian dialectic. For additional commentary by Marx, see the excerpt dated 1867.]*

My dialectical method is, in its foundations, not only different from the Hegelian, but exactly opposite to it. For Hegel, the process of thinking, which he even transforms into an independent subject, under the name of 'the Idea', is the creator of the real world, and the real world is only the external appearance of the idea. With me the reverse is true: the ideal is nothing but the material world reflected in the mind of man, and translated into forms of thought.

I criticized the mystificatory side of the Hegelian dialectic nearly thirty years ago, at a time when it was still the fashion. But just when I was working at the first volume of **Capital,** the ill-humoured, arrogant and mediocre epigones who now talk large in educated German circles began to take pleasure in treating Hegel in the same way as the good Moses Mendelssohn treated Spinoza in Lessing's time, namely as a 'dead dog'. I therefore openly avowed myself the pupil of that mighty thinker, and even, here and there in the chapter on the theory of value, coquetted with the mode of expression peculiar to him. The mystification which the dialectic suffers in Hegel's hands by no means prevents him from being the first to present its general forms of motion in a comprehensive and conscious manner. With him it is standing on its head. It must be inverted, in order to discover the rational kernel within the mystical shell.

In its mystified form, the dialectic became the fashion in Germany, because it seemed to transfigure and glorify what exists. In its rational form it is a scandal and an abomination to the bourgeoisie and its doctrinaire spokesmen, because it includes in its positive understanding of what exists a simultaneous recognition of its negation, its inevitable destruction; because it regards every historically developed form as being in a fluid state, in motion, and therefore grasps its transient aspect as well; and because it does not let itself be impressed by anything, being in its very essence critical and revolutionary.

The fact that the movement of capitalist society is full of contradictions impresses itself most strikingly on the practical bourgeois in the changes of the periodic cycle through which modern industry passes, the summit of which is the general crisis. That crisis is once again approaching, although as yet it is only in its preliminary stages, and by the universality of its field of action and the intensity of its impact it will drum dialectics even into the heads of the upstarts in charge of the new Holy Prussian-German Empire. (pp. 102-03)

> *Karl Marx, "Postface to the Second Edition," in his* Capital: A Critique of Political Economy, Vol. I, *translated by Ben Fowkes, Vintage Books, 1977, pp. 94-103.*

PAVEL ANNENKOV   (essay date 1880)

[A liberal Russian tourist who met Marx in Paris, Annenkov here sums up his impressions of Marx's appearance and personality. Annenkov's comments were first published in Vestnik Evropy *in April 1880.]*

Marx himself was the type of man who is made up of energy, will and unshakable conviction. He was most remarkable in his appearance. He had a shock of deep black hair and hairy hands and his coat was buttoned wrong; but he looked like a man with the right and power to demand respect, no matter how he appeared before you and no matter what he did. His movements were clumsy but confident and self-reliant, his

ways defied the usual conventions in human relations, but they were dignified and somewhat disdainful; his sharp metallic voice was wonderfully adapted to the radical judgements that he passed on persons and things. He always spoke in imperative words that would brook no contradiction and were made all the sharper by the almost painful impression of the tone which ran through everything he said. This tone expressed the firm conviction of his mission to dominate men's minds and prescribe them their laws. Before me stood the embodiment of a democratic dictator such as one might imagine in a day dream. (p. 12)

> *Pavel Annenkov, in a recollection of Marx, in* Karl Marx: Interviews and Recollections, *edited by David McLellan, Barnes & Noble Books, 1981, pp. 11-14.*

FRIEDRICH ENGELS   (speech date 1883)

[Engels delivered a eulogy at Marx's burial in 1883. In the following excerpt from his speech, he assesses Marx's role in history. For additional commentary by Engels, see the excerpts dated 1886 and 1888.]

On the 14th of March, at a quarter to three in the afternoon, the greatest living thinker ceased to think. He had been left alone for scarcely two minutes, and when we came back we found him in his armchair, peacefully gone to sleep—forever.

An immeasurable loss has been sustained both by the militant proletariat of Europe and America, and by historical science, in the death of this man. The gap that has been left by the departure of this mighty spirit will soon enough make itself felt.

Just as Darwin discovered the law of development of organic nature, so Marx discovered the law of development of human history: the simple fact, hitherto concealed by an overgrowth of ideology, that mankind must first of all eat, drink, have shelter and clothing, before it can pursue politics, science, art, religion, etc.; that therefore the production of the immediate material means of subsistence and consequently the degree of economic development attained by a given people or during a given epoch form the foundation upon which the state institutions, the legal conceptions, the ideas on art, and even on religion, of the people concerned have been evolved, and in the light of which they must, therefore, be explained, instead of *vice versa*, as had hitherto been the case.

But that is not all. Marx also discovered the special law of motion governing the present-day capitalist mode of production and the bourgeois society that this mode of production has created. The discovery of surplus value suddenly threw light on the problem, in trying to solve which all previous investigations, of both bourgeois economists and socialist critics, had been groping in the dark.

Two such discoveries would be enough for one lifetime. Happy the man to whom it is granted to make even one such discovery. But in every single field which Marx investigated—and he investigated very many fields, none of them superficially—in every field, even in that of mathematics, he made independent discoveries.

Such was the man of science. But this was not even half the man. Science was for Marx a historically dynamic, revolutionary force. However great the joy with which he welcomed a new discovery in some theoretical science whose practical application perhaps it was as yet quite impossible to envisage, he experienced quite another kind of joy when the discovery involved immediate revolutionary changes in industry, and in historical development in general. (pp. 68-70)

For Marx was before all else a revolutionist. His real mission in life was to contribute, in one way or another, to the overthrow of capitalist society and of the state institutions which it had brought into being, to contribute to the liberation of the modern proletariat, which *he* was the first to make conscious of its own position and its needs, conscious of the conditions of its emancipation. Fighting was his element. And he fought with a passion, a tenacity and a success such as few could rival. (p. 70)

And, consequently, Marx was the best hated and most calumniated man of his time. Governments, both absolutist and republican, deported him from their territories. Bourgeois, whether conservative or ultra-democratic, vied with one another in heaping slanders upon him. All this he brushed aside as though it were cobweb, ignoring it, answering only when extreme necessity compelled him. And he died beloved, revered and mourned by millions of revolutionary fellow workers—from the mines of Siberia to California, in all parts of Europe and America—and I make bold to say that though he may have had many opponents he had hardly one personal enemy.

His name will endure through the ages, and so also will his work! (pp. 70-1)

> *Friedrich Engels, "Engels's Speech at the Graveside of Karl Marx," in* The Portable Karl Marx, *edited and translated in part by Eugene Kamenka, The Viking Press, 1983, pp. 68-71.*

G. B. S. LARKING [PSEUDONYM OF BERNARD SHAW] (letter date 1884)

[*Shaw is generally considered the greatest and best-known dramatist to write in the English language since William Shakespeare. An outspoken socialist, Shaw nevertheless disagreed heartily with some of Marx's concepts. In the following excerpt, Shaw points out the weaknesses of Marx's theory of surplus value. For additional commentary by Shaw, see the excerpt dated 1887.*]

I have read with much pain the opening numbers of the journal which you have put forth under the sacred name of *Justice*. Do you ever reflect, when you speak harshly of our "competitive," or *Bourgeois* civilisation, that we ourselves are products of that civilisation; that many of us are its triumphs; that our mothers and fathers are its honoured source, our wives and sisters its ornaments, and our sons and daughters its hope and its future? Civilisation is not the engine, the loom, or the pyramid; it is Man, the master of these things.

Let me put this matter to you more closely, and with economic precision. You have adopted the theory of "surplus value" put forward by the late Dr. Karl Marx, a man of great talent, but one who, with unexampled ingratitude, devoted his life to casting odium upon the civilisation whose culture he inherited, whose society he enjoyed, whose literature instructed him, whose labour supported him, whose inventions enabled him to survey the globe and to traverse its continents, in whose cradle his children slept, and in whose midst his own life was passed. His theory, as I understand it, is that the capitalist, having a monopoly of raw material and means of production, refuses to the labourers access to these materials and means until they agree to surrender to him the produce of their labour, minus

only the smallest sum upon which they can maintain themselves and their families. I need hardly point out the preposterous absurdity of a theory which assumes that the labourer is helplessly dependent on the capitalist in the face of the axiom that labour is the source of all wealth, an axiom which no political economist has ever denied, and which Marx himself insisted on as the foundation of Socialism. How can the labourer be at the mercy of the upper and middle classes when these are admittedly dependent on the labourer for their very subsistence? But let us pass by this contradiction, which underlies all the teaching of Marx, and proceed to consider the consequences of accepting his theory. Let us suppose that the labourer, by working for a day, produces a table worth a pound, ten shillings of which represents the value of the wood, wear and tear of tools, rent of workshop, lighting, &c., &c., and the remaining ten shillings the wear and tear of the man, or his labour. According to Marx, the capitalist who supplies the wood, tools, workshop, &c., does so on the condition that he shall, besides being reimbursed for them by receiving ten shillings out of the price of the table, receive also, out of the other ten shillings due solely to the labourer, as large a share as he can possibly screw out of him by the threat of putting the job up to auction among his starving competitors. Let us suppose that in this way he induces the labourer to content himself with three shillings out of the ten which he has earned, and pockets seven shillings as profit. (I may observe here that Marx, with all his ingenuity, could never explain why a labourer should make a present of more than half his earnings to an employer who was absolutely dependent on him for all his wealth.) Our imaginary capitalist then, selling the table for its value—one pound, makes a profit of seven shillings. But mark what must ensue. Some rival capitalist, trading in tables on the same principle, will content himself with six shillings profit for the sake of attracting custom. He will sell the table for nineteen shillings; that is, he will allow the purchaser one shilling out of his profit as a bribe to secure his custom. The first capitalist will thus be compelled to lower his price to nineteen shillings also, and presently the competition of brisk young traders, believing in small profits and quick returns, will bring the price of tables down to thirteen and sixpence, or even lower if the reduction in price can be used as a pretext for securing another sixpence out of the labourer's three shillings. Take the price at thirteen and sixpence. If the seven shillings be indeed robbed from the labourer, then the purchaser, getting a table worth a pound for thirteen and sixpence, gets six and sixpence of the plunder, and the capitalist only sixpence; that is, the buyer is thirteen times as great a thief as the seller. But who are the buyers? Editors of *Justice, we* are the buyers, we and our parents, our sisters and brothers, our wives and children. Do these dear ones commit theft whenever they enter a shop? Do you dare to assert that the many men of whose probity England is justly proud are systematic thieves? For this is what your theory of surplus value comes to.

I have only to add that one result, admitted by you, of the competitive system is cheapness. I think you will hardly deny that cheapness is an inestimable blessing. For a few shillings the workman can obtain, at the American Novelty Shop, domestic appliances which Louis XIV would have sought for in vain when furnishing Versailles or Marly. For a few pence he can taste the delights of Shakespeare's page, and unlock the treasures of our noble literature. When you tell us that such beneficent cheapness is but the cheapness of stolen goods, and that we, being the receivers, are worse than the thieves, you poison our prosperity at its source, and embitter those reflections on our national greatness which were once the pride and the solace of Englishmen. I dare avouch that you shall never persuade us that we are either slaves or thieves. Something within us gives you the lie. We have said that "Britons never will be slaves;" we have said that "An honest man's the noblest work of God," and we mean both. (pp. 1-8)

G. B. S. Larking [pseudonym of Bernard Shaw], in a letter to the editor of "Justice" on March 15, 1884, in Bernard Shaw & Karl Marx: A Symposium, 1884-1889, Random House, 1930, pp. 1-8.

FREDERICK ENGELS   (essay date 1886)

[In this excerpt from his 1886 preface to Capital, Engels outlines the economic conditions which, in his opinion, make England ripe for a "peaceful and legal revolution." For additional commentary by Engels, see the excerpts dated 1883 and 1888.]

Capital is often called, on the Continent, 'the Bible of the working class'. That the conclusions arrived at in this work are daily more and more becoming the fundamental principles of the great working-class movement, not only in Germany and Switzerland, but in France, in Holland and Belgium, in America, and even in Italy and Spain, that everywhere the working class more and more recognizes, in these conclusions, the most adequate expression of its condition and of its aspirations, nobody acquainted with that movement will deny. And in England, too, the theories of Marx, even at this moment, exercise a powerful influence upon the socialist movement which is spreading in the ranks of 'cultured' people no less than in those of the working class. But that is not all. The time is rapidly approaching when a thorough examination of England's economic position will impose itself as an irresistible national necessity. The working of the industrial system of this country, impossible without a constant and rapid extension of production, and therefore of markets, is coming to a dead stop. Free-trade has exhausted its resources; even Manchester doubts this its quondam economic gospel. Foreign industry, rapidly developing, stares English production in the face everywhere, not only in protected, but also in neutral markets, and even on this side of the Channel. While the productive power increases in a geometric ratio, the extension of markets proceeds at best in an arithmetic one. The decennial cycle of stagnation, prosperity, overproduction and crisis, ever recurrent from 1825 to 1867, seems indeed to have run its course; but only to land us in the slough of despond of a permanent and chronic depression. The sighed-for period of prosperity will not come; as often as we seem to perceive its heralding symptoms, so often do they again vanish into air. Meanwhile, each succeeding winter brings up afresh the great question, 'what to do with the unemployed'; but while the number of the unemployed keeps swelling from year to year, there is nobody to answer that question; and we can almost calculate the moment when the unemployed, losing patience, will take their own fate into their own hands. Surely, at such a moment, the voice ought to be heard of a man whose whole theory is the result of a life-long study of the economic history and condition of England, and whom that study led to the conclusion that, at least in Europe, England is the only country where the inevitable social revolution might be effected entirely by peaceful and legal means. He certainly never forgot to add that he hardly expected the English ruling classes to submit, without a 'pro-slavery rebellion', to this peaceful and legal revolution. (pp. 112-13)

Frederick Engels, "Preface to the English Edition," in Capital: A Critique of Political Economy, Vol. I

by Karl Marx, translated by Ben Fowkes, Vintage Books, 1977, pp. 109-13.

G. BERNARD SHAW   (essay date 1887)

[Writing about Capital in the National Reformer in August 1887, Shaw presents his arguments against Marx's theory of capitalism. For additional commentary by Shaw, see the excerpt dated 1884.]

Twenty years ago, when [the] first instalment of Karl Marx's now famous [Das Kapital] was published, arose the claim that Socialism, formerly a dream, had become a science. Thenceforth, Robert Owen, St. Simon, and Fourier were to be regarded as well-intentioned Utopists, and Lassalle as one who saved himself by plagiarizing Marx, whose book is revelation. Here is the authentic history of the past, and the sure prophecy of the future, of human society. Here is the first and last exhaustive analysis of the incidents of the ceaseless struggle of man with Nature for wealth, the all-inclusive synthesis of those incidents and consequently the completed science of Political Economy. Here, also, is the one infallible recipe for the Millennium. He that believeth is a true "scientific Socialist"; he that believeth not is a middle-class self-seeker, a bourgeois, an exploiter of labor, and most likely a police spy.

I may take it for granted by the readers of the National Reformer that no person of reasonable self-respect would have anything to say to any author on these terms. The evident grudge entertained against Marx by many of his shrewdest English critics may be accounted for much more conclusively by their well-founded mistrust of popes, prophets, and messiahs of all denominations, than by a savage hatred of the working class not discernible elsewhere in their writings, or by a ten pound note from Bismarck. On the other hand, the fact that such outrageous pretensions should be made on behalf of Marx, goes far to prove that he was an extraordinary man; for he himself was as innocent of the excesses of his devotees as an Indian idol of the self-torture of its worshippers. Nor was there anything in his personal career to kindle the imagination or stir the blood. He was no orator; he fought no duels, rescued no distressed matrons, nor figured in any causes célèbres; as a practical conspirator he seems to have been a failure; and there was nothing picturesque about his many years of research among the Blue Books at the British Museum reading-room. The wave of Socialism raised him on its crest, no doubt; but it raised him no higher than colleagues of his whose names are unknown. The charm of his conversation, admitted by those who knew him personally, would not alone account for his reputation, although it is true that his reputation must be measured by its intensity as much as by its width. Thus we get to the famous Communist Manifesto, and its huge amplification, Das Kapital, as the material of his celebrity. When the last word has been said about the book, no more will be needed about the man.

That last word, however, is still a long way off, since the entire book is not yet published; the volumes now in question being only a fragment, and that, too, a fragment which leaves unexplained a difficulty apparently fatal to the whole Marxian theory. (pp. 103-07)

The term "bourgeois" has often provoked well deserved ridicule when used by Socialist members of our bourgeoisie as a question-begging epithet to fling at an opponent of Socialism. They have taken it from Marx; but they have not taken it as they found it. By a "bourgeois economist" Marx means, not necessarily an economist who is wrong as far as he goes, but one who assumes that Capitalism, based on Individualism [or the settlement of a country by the allotment of its natural resources as private property to individuals], is the final and only possible social order. To Marx, capitalism, with its wage-slavery, is only a passing phase of social development, following primitive communism, chattel slavery, and feudal serfdom into the past. He never loses consciousness of this movement; and herein lies one of the secrets of the novelty and fascination of his treatment. He wrote of the nineteenth century as if it were a cloud passing down the wind, changing its shape and fading as it goes; whilst Ricardo the stockbroker, and De Quincey the high Tory, sat comfortably down before it in their office and study chairs, as if it were the great wall of China, safe to last until the Day of Judgment with an occasional coat of whitewash. Further, he writes as one in whom ''the notion of human equality has already acquired the fixity of a popular prejudice''. From title page to tail piece there is not one moment of ruth, not one passage of apologetics, for the system of privileges upon which we are at present working. He knows that weighty arguments can be brought forward in support of that system, just as weighty arguments can be brought forward in favor of flogging, duelling, and laws against blasphemy; but he only betrays consciousness of them by his unrelenting scorn for those who believe in their preponderance. In the class which sought to live at the expense of another class, and pretended to benefit it by doing so, he saw only thieves and hypocrites—vermin in the commonwealth, born in the estate of vermin through no fault of their own, but none the less to be unsparingly denounced and exposed with their apologists until such time as their expropriation might become feasible. This unsleeping sense of the transitory character of capitalism, and of the justice of equality, is the characteristic spirit of Marx, the absence of which so disgusts his pupils when they attempt to read the ordinary treatises, in spite of the facts that no economist of any eminence has ever defended things as they are, except from inability to conceive a rational alternative, and that De Quincey was the last economist of first-rate ability who was complacently *bourgeois* [for a ridiculous reason] in Marx's sense. (pp. 108-11)

There is, perhaps, a feeble reflexion of Marx's implacable contempt for the external aspect of capitalistic civilization in the petulant outcry against railways and machine-made goods, which may almost be described [and condemned] as fashionable; but its usual accompaniment is a proposal to escape by ''restoring'' mediævalism on much the same lines as those adopted by the architects who ''restore'' our cathedrals. There is none of this futile retrogressiveness in Marx. He never condescends to cast a glance of useless longing at the past: his cry to the present is always ''Pass by: we are waiting for the future''. Nor is the future at all mysterious, uncertain, or dreadful to him. There is not a word of hope or fear, nor appeal to chance or providence, nor vain remonstrance with nature, nor optimism, nor enthusiasm, nor pessimism, nor cynicism, nor any other familiar sign of the giddiness which seizes men when they climb to heights which command a view of the past, present, and future of human society. Marx keeps his head like a God. He has discovered the law of social development, and knows what must come. The thread of history is in his hand. . . . Marx, in this first book of his, treats of labor without reference to variations of skill between its parts; of raw material without reference to variations of fertility; and of the difference between the product of labor and the price [wage] of labor power, as ''surplus value'' without reference to its subdivision into rent, interest, and profits. This will explain to any student how it is that those who know nothing of economics except what they

have learned from this Marxian fragment, and who innocently believe that it covers the whole subject, are repeatedly betrayed into taking up absurd positions in economic discussions. Also how some economists, too confident in their own skill to do more with any new treatise than dip into it here and there, have supposed that Marx himself was ignorant of the considerations he purposely omitted, and have dismissed him with a contemptuously adverse decision, which they will some day, possibly, be glad to forget.

Whatever may be the ultimate verdict as to Marx, it must be borne in mind that the extraordinary impression he makes does not depend on the soundness of his views, but on their magnificent scope and on his own imperturbable conviction of their validity. (pp. 113-18)

> *G. Bernard Shaw, ''Karl Marx and 'Das Kapital' (First Notice),'' in* Bernard Shaw & Karl Marx: A Symposium, 1884-1889, *Random House, 1930, pp. 103-19.*

FREDERICK ENGELS (essay date 1888)

[*In the following excerpt from a preface to an 1888 edition of the* Manifesto, *Engels explains the genesis of the work and details the roles that he and Marx played in its composition. For additional commentary by Engels, see the excerpts dated 1883 and 1886.*]

[The history of the **Communist Manifesto**] reflects, to a great extent, the history of the modern working-class movement; at present it is undoubtedly the most wide-spread, the most international production of all socialist literature, the common platform acknowledged by millions of working men from Siberia to California.

Yet, when it was written, we could not have called it a 'Socialist' manifesto. By 'socialists', in 1847, were understood, on the one hand, the adherents of the various utopian systems: Owenites in England, Fourierists in France, both of them already reduced to the position of mere sects, and gradually dying out; on the other hand, the most multifarious social quacks, who, by all manners of tinkering, professed to redress, without any danger to capital and profit, all sorts of social grievances; in both cases men outside the working-class movement, and looking rather to the 'educated' classes for support. Whatever portion of the working class had become convinced of the insufficiency of mere political revolutions, and had proclaimed the necessity of a total social change, that portion then called itself communist. It was a crude, rough-hewn, purely instinctive sort of communism; still, it touched the cardinal point and was powerful enough amongst the working class to produce the utopian communism, in France, of Cabet, and in Germany, of Weitling. Thus, socialism was, in 1847, a middle-class movement, communism a working-class movement. Socialism was, on the Continent at least, 'respectable'; communism was the very opposite. And as our notion, from the very beginning, was that 'the emancipation of the working class must be the act of the working class itself', there could be no doubt as to which of the two names we must take. Moreover, we have, ever since, been far from repudiating it.

The **Manifesto** being our joint production, I consider myself bound to state that the fundamental proposition, which forms its nucleus, belongs to Marx. That proposition is: that in every historical epoch, the prevailing mode of economic production and exchange, and the social organization necessarily following from it, form the basis upon which is built up, and from which alone can be explained, the political and intellectual history of that epoch; that consequently the whole history of mankind (since the dissolution of primitive tribal society, holding land in common ownership) has been a history of class struggles, contests between exploiting and exploited, ruling and oppressed classes; that the history of these class struggles forms a series of evolutions in which, nowadays, a stage—the proletariat—cannot attain its emancipation from the sway of the exploiting and ruling class—the bourgeoisie—without, at the same time, and once and for all, emancipating society at large from all exploitation, oppression, class distinctions and class struggles.

This proposition which, in my opinion, is destined to do for history what Darwin's theory has done for biology, we, both of us, had been gradually approaching for some years before 1845. How far I had independently progressed towards it is best shown by my *Condition of the Working Class in England*. But when I again met Marx at Brussels, in spring 1845, he had it ready worked out, and put it before me, in terms almost as clear as those in which I have stated it here. (pp. 64-6)

> *Frederick Engels, "Preface to the English Edition of 1888," in* The Revolutions of 1848: Political Writings, Vol. I *by Karl Marx, edited by David Fernbach, Allen Lane, 1973, pp. 62-6.*

CHARLES J. LITTLE (essay date 1890)

[*Little here discusses Marx's personal attributes and critiques* Capital, *concluding that "he was an anatomist not a savior of society."*]

Marx though a Jew was no more like Spinoza and Mendelssohn than Saul of Tarsus was like Gamaliel. For his heart was full of fight and his brain was full of fire. He was the incarnate antithesis of existing ideas, with a nature dynamic and polemic. Dominant systems of thought and action challenged him to criticism and to warfare. Though capable of passionate affection, he was a bitter hater; he had no tribal, or race, feeling and no patriotism. He had an intense interest in humanity, but little interest in particular men. . . .

Heine speaks [of Marx] as "my stiff-necked friend." His power he discovered but he did not love him as he loved Lasalle. For there was no poetry, no romance, no chivalry in Marx. He was an anatomist of society, caring nothing for its beauties; absorbed completely in the study of its diseases. He saw in Germany nothing to admire but its philosophy. The national idea so potent with Lasalle, he deemed a useless and bewildering chimera. His heart full of hot Jewish blood, yet he despised the people of Israel, declaring all religions to be only the "opium of mankind."

The essays published by him in 1843 on "**Hegel**" and "**The Jews**" are more valuable as indices of character than as products of mind, but remarkable in either aspect. Here was an Ishmaelite with colossal brain and a heart of boiling lava, a revolutionist who summoned, not the citizens of a nation, but all men everywhere to the otherthrow of existing institutions, a powerful thinker who denied God, an economist who scoffed at the state, who arraigned progress at the bar of human misery, challenging capital to mortal combat and proclaiming the Republic of the Poor. Nevertheless, Marx would have little to do with the German communists of Paris. (p. 694)

In Marx, as in Heine, two spirits ruled by turns; the poet could in the twinkling of an eye exchange his garments of light for a cloak of darkness, the song of an angel for the ribaldry of an intellectual blackguard; so the great thinker Marx could leap in an instant from the height of a weighty argument to the dunghill of personal abuse and abandon the glory of his insight and the discoveries of reason, in order to provoke the passions of the ignorant to furious hatred and irrational hostility.

Marx himself admits in *Capital* that the individual capitalist is helpless, so long as the system lasts. In words serene and lofty he pictures him as the unconscious factor in a historical process from which there is no escape until the epoch of reconstruction shall begin. In him, therefore, the fury of the agitator was either mere spleen or a deliberate appeal to the baser nature of the lewder sort. For if he believed that only by the contagion of hate could the work of transformation be wrought, what became of his principle, that only knowledge of the laws of economic structure could be the permanent basis for an enduring and harmonious social activity? (p. 695)

Most criticism of Marx is shallow to disheartenment. For instance not a few of his critics think they are attacking Marx when they are pounding the doctrine of value held by Adam Smith, Benjamin Franklin, and James Stewart! Others think to discredit him by calling him a Hegelian fond of obscure terms, intricate formulas, and the dialectic method. Whereas *Capital* more than any political economy in existence is built upon facts. Darwin's *Origin of Species* surpasses it both as an argument and as an exposition of a theory. But in both the method of investigation was the same, observation and induction. Like Darwin, Marx had a clear-cut theory to expound and defend: a theory, too, at variance with the beliefs and wishes of the powerful. For the [first volume of *Capital*] as explained by him was every whit as offensive to society as our arboreal ancestors with pointed ears and a prehensile tail. (p. 697)

[The] discussion of surplus value is the life of *Capital*. Smith and Ricardo preceded Marx in its discovery. But neither of them showed precisely what it was that created surplus value, nor why, nor how. Marx, however, tried to show all three and that value is nothing but congealed labor of a particular kind, congealed human energy. He demonstrated an antithesis between money and commodity by which he showed how money became capital, and how capital lived upon the purchase and exploitation of potential labor. By dividing capital into constant and variable, he could study the process of creating surplus value in its minutest details. Surplus value he regarded as absolute or relative. Absolute surplus value is obtained by making the laborer work longer than the time necessary to equivalate his wages. Relative surplus value is obtained by improvement in machinery and in technical process; "by the intensification of labor."

Now, I repeat, Marx the thinker never blames the capitalist in the concrete. It is the system that is wrong; the species capitalist that he abhors. Once the character of the system and the genesis of the species are clearly understood, they are doomed. Production is already by the division and co-operation of labor socialistic. Distribution should be socialistic as logical sequence. Land is the birth-right of humanity, so are the energies of nature. Why are these not a blessing and a help to all that toil? In the struggles about the length of the working day; about child labor; for decency and safety in mines and factory; in the crises produced by credit and speculation; in the relatively surplus population and the appearance of the industrial reserve army; in combinations of capitalists and laborers against each other; in the catastrophes of commerce and of industry; in the concentration of money; in a plutocracy sordid, rapacious, tyrannical, without bowels of compassion and without culture, the seeds of disease are doing their fell work.

But though Marx discusses all these topics with immense knowledge and with reflections profound, subtitle, startling in number and in sagacity, he nowhere discusses the ethics of the question. How much the capitalist *ought to get,* he never asks. He tries to show *what* he gets, how and whence and why he gets it, and why he must continue to get it until the poisonous blood of the present system has wrought its final doom. If he proves severe upon "the abstinence theory" and pillories the defenders of existing conditions, that is only by the way.

It is often objected to Marx that he pays no attention to supply and demand, to the utilities of a commodity or of a service as elements of value. Now what Marx does is to deny that these have any thing to do with value. The value of a commodity or of a service is equivalent to the portion of the energy of society necessary to produce it or to perform it. But prices are fixed by ignorance and folly, by persuasion and caprice, by the compulsions of nature and social circumstance. The difference between price and value is precisely what Marx thinks scientific insight will abolish. He never dreamed of denying that prices are fixed by the competition and combinations of buyers and sellers. This is what he complains of as the vicious outcome of existing conditions; this is the chief cause of the workmen's slavery. (pp. 697-98)

That men suffer prices to be regulated by competition is a gloomy fact; they once suffered their lives to be regulated by the follies of astrology and called that a science.

Finally, Marx had a genius for the vivisection of the industrial system, not for the healing thereof; he was an anatomist not a savior of society. Collectivism . . . is only implied but nowhere fully delineated and scientifically established by him.

The working classes and humanity would owe him far more, if he had not spoken, so often so unadvisedly with his lips. He would not have been less loved, had he been more lovable. But he never swerved in his devotion to the working classes. For them he lived and thought, was poor and in exile, suffered reproach, obloquy, hatred, and contempt. Only the bitterness of his spirit and the fierceness of his heart perturbed the workings of his powerful mind, converted what might have been solar energy, into electric outburst, and thus prevented the perfection of his thought. And so *Capital* is a Cyclopean labor left forever incomplete. (p. 698)

> *Charles J. Little, "Karl Marx: 1818-1883," in The Chautauquan, Vol. X, No. 6, March, 1890, pp. 694-98.*

V. I. LENIN   (essay date 1913)

[*A staunch follower of Marx, Lenin was the chief leader of the 1917 Bolshevik Revolution and became premier of the Soviet Union. In the following excerpt from an essay first published in 1913, he explains the underlying philosophical structure of Marxism and the importance of Marxist teachings.*]

Throughout the whole civilized world Marxist teachings draw upon themselves the extreme hostility and hatred of all bourgeois science (both governmental and liberal). It sees in Marxism something in the nature of a harmful "sect." No other attitude could be expected, for an impartial social science is impossible in a society founded on class struggle. In one way

or another every governmental and liberal science defends wage slavery, and Marxism has declared ruthless war against this slavery. To expect impartial science in a wage-slave society is rather stupidly naïve—like expecting owners to be impartial on the question whether to raise the workers' wages at the expense of the profits of capital.

But never mind that. The history of philosophy and the history of social science offer abundantly clear proof that Marxism has nothing similar to "sectarianism" in the sense of a shut-in, ossified doctrine standing apart from the main road of development of world civilization. On the contrary, the very genius of Marx lay in the fact that he gave the answer to those questions which the most advanced thought of humanity had already raised. His teachings arose as a direct and immediate continuation of the teachings of the greatest representatives of philosophy, political economy and socialism.

The teaching of Marx is all-powerful because it is true. It is complete and symmetrical, offering an integrated view of the world, irreconcilable with any superstition, with any reactionism, or with any defense of bourgeois oppression. It is the legitimate inheritor of the best that humanity created in the 19th century in the form of German philosophy, English political economy, French socialism.

Let us dwell briefly upon these three sources and therefore constituent parts of Marxism.

The philosophy of Marxism is materialism. Throughout modern European history, and especially at the end of the 18th century in France, where a decisive battle was fought against all kinds of medieval rubbish, against serfdom in institutions and ideas, materialism proved to be the only consistent philosophy, true to all the teachings of the natural sciences, hostile to superstition, bigotry, etc. The enemies of democracy tried therefore with all their might to "refute," undermine and slander materialism, defending various forms of philosophic idealism, all of which come down one way or another to a defense or support of religion.

Marx and Engels defended philosophic materialism with the utmost determination, and many times explained the profound error of any departure from this foundation. Their views are expounded most clearly and in the greatest detail in the works of Engels, *Ludwig Feurebach,* and *Anti-Dühring,* works which, like the **Communist Manifesto,** are everyday books on the table of the class-conscious worker.

But Marx did not rest in the materialism of the 18th century. He made an advance in philosophy. He enriched materialism with the acquisitions of the German classic philosophy, especially the system of Hegel which had led in its turn to the materialism of Feuerbach. The chief of these acquisitions is the dialectic—that is, the understanding of evolution in its fullest, deepest and most universal aspect, the understanding of the relativity of human knowledge, which gives us a reflection of eternally evolving matter. The most recent discoveries of natural science, radium, the electron, the transmutation of elements, have admirably confirmed the dialectic materialism of Marx—all the teachings of the bourgeois philosophers, with their "new" ways of returning to an old and rotten idealism, to the contrary notwithstanding.

While deepening and developing philosophic materialism, Marx carried it through to the end, extending its mode of understanding nature to the understanding of human society. The historic materialism of Marx is one of the greatest achievements of scientific thought. The caprice and chaos reigning up to that time among opinions about history and politics were here replaced by a strikingly whole and symmetrical and scientific theory, showing how out of one set-up of social life, another higher one develops in consequence of a growth of the productive forces—capitalism for example out of feudalism.

Just exactly as a man's knowledge reflects a nature existing independently of him—matter, that is, in a state of development—so also the social understanding of man (that is, his various views and teachings, philosophical, religious, political, etc.) reflects the economic structure of society. Political institutions are a superstructure resting on an economic foundation. We see, for instance, how the various political forms of the contemporary European states serve as a reinforcement of the rulership of the bourgeoisie over the proletariat.

The philosophy of Marx is that finished philosophic materialism which has given humanity in general, and the working class in particular, the greatest of all instruments of understanding.

Having seen that the economic structure is the basis upon which the political superstructure arises, Marx gave most of his attention to the study of this economic structure. His chief work *Capital* is devoted to a study of the economic structure of contemporary—that is, capitalist—society.

The classic political economy up to Marx's time had been formed in England, the most highly developed capitalist country. Adam Smith and David Ricardo in their investigation of the economic structure had laid down the principle of the labor theory of value. Marx continued their work. He firmly established and consistently developed this theory. He showed that the value of any commodity is defined by the quantity of socially necessary labor time involved in its production.

Where the bourgeois economist had seen a relation between things (exchange of commodity for commodity) Marx discovered a relation between people. The exchange of goods expresses the connection formed between separate producers by means of the market. Money means that this connection is becoming closer, inseparably uniting in one unit the whole industrial life of the individual producers. Capital implies a further development of this connection. The labor power of man becomes a commodity. The wage-worker sells his labor power to the owner of land, factories and the instruments of labor. One part of the working day he spends in order to meet the cost of supporting himself and his family (wages), but another part of the day he spends working for nothing, creating for the capitalist surplus value, the source of profits, the source of the wealth of the class of capitalists.

The doctrine of surplus value is the keystone of the economic theory of Marx. (pp. xxi-xxiv)

From the first beginnings of commodity economy, from simple barter, Marx followed the development of capitalism to its highest forms, to large-scale production.

And the experience of all capitalist countries, both old and new, proves clearly every year to a larger and larger number of workers the truth of this doctrine of Marx.

Capitalism has conquered throughout the world, but its victory is only an earnest of the victory of labor over capital.

When serfdom was overthrown and the "free" capitalist society saw the light of day, it suddenly became clear that this freedom meant a new system of oppression and exploitation of the toilers. Various socialist doctrines began to emerge as a reflection of this oppression and a protest against it. But this original socialism was a utopian socialism. It criticized the capitalist society, condemned it, cursed it, dreamed of its destruction, drew fanciful pictures of a better structure, and tried to convince the rich of the immorality of exploitation.

But utopian socialism could not show a real way out. It was unable to explain the essence of wage labor under capitalism, to discover the laws of its development, or to find that social force capable of becoming the creator of a new society.

Meanwhile the tumultuous revolutions which accompanied the fall of feudalism, of serfdom—everywhere in Europe but especially in France—were making it more and more manifest that the foundation of the whole development and its motive force was the struggle of classes.

Not one single victory of political liberty over the feudal class was gained without overcoming a desperate resistance. Not one capitalist country has been formed on a more or less free democratic basis without a life-and-death struggle between the different classes of capitalist society.

The genius of Marx lay in the fact that he was able sooner than others to make and consistently carry out the inference to which the whole of world history leads. That inference is the doctrine of class struggle.

People always have been and they always will be the stupid victims of deceit and self-deception in politics, until they learn behind every kind of moral, religious, political, social phrase, declaration and promise to seek out the interests of this or that class or classes. The partisans of reform and betterment will always be fooled by the defenders of the old régime, until they understand that every old institution, no matter how savage and rotten it may seem, is sustained by the forces of this or that dominant class or classes. And there is only one way to break the resistance of these classes: namely, to find in the very society surrounding us, to find and educate and organize for the struggle, those forces which can—and owing to their social situation must—form a power capable of sweeping away the old and creating the new.

Only the philosophic materialism of Marx has shown the proletariat a way out of that spiritual slavery in which up to now all oppressed classes have been sleeping. Only the economic theory of Marx has explained the actual situation of the proletariat in the general structure of capitalism.

Throughout the whole world, from America to Japan and from Sweden to South Africa, independent organizations of the proletariat are multiplying. The proletariat is educating and enlightening itself by waging its class struggle. In casting loose from the prejudices of bourgeois society, uniting more and more closely, learning to take the measure of its successes, it is tempering its powers and growing irresistibly. (pp. xxiv-xxvi)

V. I. Lenin, "The Three Sources and Three Constituent Parts of Marxism," translated by Max Eastman, in Capital: The Communist Manifesto and Other Writings *by Karl Marx, edited by Max Eastman, The Modern Library, 1932, pp. xxi-xxvi.*

HAROLD J. LASKI (essay date 1927)

[*A noted English political scientist with strongly held Marxist views, Laski was also a popular lecturer and teacher. In addition, he was an outspoken and active participant in the British Labour Party, advocating labor reforms that were in line with his socialist thought. In the excerpt below, Laski offers an explication and balanced assessment of the materialist interpretation of history, focusing on Marx's prediction that a proletarian revolution would occur.*]

It is worth while to insist upon what the materialist interpretation of history is not, before discussing its general validity. It has no necessary connection, in the first place, with the metaphysical theory of materialism. That doctrine, though communists in general adopt it, is equally compatible with Buckle's view that climate is the decisive factor in historic events. Nor does it insist that economic conditions are the sole cause of change; it merely argues that they are its main cause. Roughly speaking, it is an argument to the effect that man's situation is the preceptor of his duty, and that in that situation economic elements are paramount simply because the means of life are the first thing to which men must pay attention.

In this simple form, it is impossible not to regard the theory as in the main true. It is clear, for example, that the substance of legal categories is largely determined by their economic context. Contract, tort, the law of husband and wife, are all of them set and altered by the system of production out of which they grow. More specifically, a rule like the "common employment" doctrine in English law could only have been born in a capitalist society; and the limitations upon the suability of the State in contract all bear upon them the marks of a business civilisation. The adjustment, moreover, of church practice to its economic environment has been very striking; the way, for example, in which the doctrine of grace received an interpretation which made business success a proof of God's favour, and poverty an index to His anger, is proof that ecclesiastical theory does not evade the general ambit of the doctrine. And anyone who considers the history of the interpretation of the American Constitution will find little difficulty in seeing in its attitude to problems like those of child labour, or the State regulation of wages and hours, a proof of the general truth of the materialist view. There is no department of human life in which the governing ideas and institutions will not be found, upon examination, to be largely a reflection of a given set of economic conditions.

We must be careful, indeed, not to push the theory too far. There are particular sets of facts in which it is not helpful as an explanation; and there are others where the obvious requirements of an economic environment cannot be met through the pressure of noneconomic factors. They will not wholly explain, even though they are often relevant to, the actions of an individual; as Lassalle, for example, or Robert Owen. Often enough, a man's political creed is born, not of an economic situation, but of an intense psychological dislike for the atmosphere of his family. Nor can either religious or nationalist movements be wholly explained in religious terms. The loyalty of Catholic working-men to their religion, the fierce separatism of the Balkans, both involve methods of explanation which have reference to a human nature not exclusively determined by material conditions. Possibly the Catholic working-man is unwise in preferring his Church to his class; and certainly the nationalism of the Balkans, with its perpetual recurrence of war, is the chief cause of its economic backwardness. But, in cases like these, the rational interest of men is overcome by distracting counter-currents of loyalty which afford them satisfaction superior to that which reason might afford.

Here, indeed, it may be argued, is the real weakness of materialism as a philosophy of history. It is too exclusively preoccupied with a rational theory of human action to remember how much of man's effort is nonrational in character. "The larger events in the political life of the world," writes Mr. Bertrand Russell, "are determined by the interaction of material conditions and human passions." Obviously the latter can be modified in their operation by intelligence; but obviously, also, the modification is at best but partial. When we estimate, therefore, the character of a social system we must measure not merely the effect upon men of the way in which they earn their bread, but of the wider total effect upon them of the chance in that system to satisfy their chief impulses. Men may choose a less advantageous economic order, even when its utility is obviously exhausted, because they prefer its psychological results to those of its antithesis. A state, for example, which did not afford adequate opportunity to energetic and determined men would rapidly change even if it satisfied the inert majority of its members.

All this, however, is merely a footnote to the general truth of the materialist interpretation; it does not destroy its general adequacy. The difficulties emerge less in this aspect than when we come to its communist application. Here, critics have naturally fastened upon two things. They deny the validity of class-antagonism as a permanent social fact; and they argue that there is no reason to accept the Marxian deductions therefrom as an accurate prevision of the future.

We are not for the moment concerned with the political or ethical results of the doctrine of class-war. . . . What is here important is the question whether it is true. Those who deny it usually do so upon two grounds. They argue, first, that there is an interdependence of social interests which makes it impossible for one class to be injured without all being injured; and, secondly, they argue that, in each social conflict that arises there is an objectively just solution which is the good of the community as a whole. A minor argument is sometimes employed to the effect that the class-consciousness of which Marx speaks is either non-existent or confined to an insignificant minority of society.

In fact, however, none of these views really touches the core of the communist position. The Marxian does not deny the interdependence of classes: what he insists upon is that in the relationship of this interdependence the interests of the capitalist class are considered superior to those of the working-class. It would certainly be difficult for any observer to urge with seriousness that this is not the case. Rarely, indeed, in history does a party or class in power deliberately sacrifice its own well-being to that of others. The history of things like the franchise, education, the administration of justice, the laws of inheritance, of, that is to say, privilege in general, is not the history of its voluntary surrender by its possessors; every concession won has been secured only after hard fighting, in which, very often, either the threat or fact of violence has been an integral part of the victory. "Had the people of England," said Mr. Gladstone, "obeyed the precept to eschew violence and maintain order, the liberties of this country would never have been obtained." The communist answer to a theory of social interdependence is an admission of its truth and an argument that, under the present scheme, its benefits are not justly divided between classes. This seems well within the facts.

Nor is the second argument much more tenable. It is true that in most social conflicts the parties demand more than they feel they ought to have, and that each is but little careful of the well-being of those indirectly affected by the dispute. But a theory which urges the existence of an objectively just decision in the dispute omits to declare who is to determine what that decision shall be. The communist, from his standpoint necessarily, denies that any such arbitrator can be found. For into his decision there will enter a stream of ideas and prejudices begotten of the special complex of interests to which he belongs, even if he be unconscious of their presence. Nor can a capitalist government be regarded, in any just sense, as an impartial judge. Its main purpose is, he argues, to uphold capitalism; and that makes it *a priori* inclined to favour one of the disputants. Anyone who examines, for instance, the series of disputes in the British coal industry since 1919 will find it difficult to maintain that the government of the day has acted impartially as between miners and mine owners. Whenever the interests of capitalism have required it, the results of inquiries have been evaded; and even when their tenor has been verbally accepted, care has been taken to deny their spirit in applying them.

To accept the materialist conception is not, of course, to say that it explains all historic phenomena. There are passages in Marx's works in which this claim seems to have been made; and some of his less cautious disciples have written—wrongly—as though this was the view that he took. In fact, Marx was himself, as a rule, insistent upon the limits within which the theory applies; and he was well aware that while productive systems act upon men, men also react upon productive systems. Criticism of the doctrine, indeed, should concentrate less upon its general outline than upon the communist prophecies which have grown out of it. It is difficult, in the first place, to see why the communist should be assured of the ultimate triumph of the proletariat. An observer of modern capitalism might well argue that the evidence points not to some single and universal solution, but to a variety of quite different results. What may occur, for instance, in a small and highly industrialised country like England, may bear little resemblance to the destiny of peasant civilisations like Roumania and Hungary; and the mere problem of size in America might well make the issue there qualitatively different from what it is in most European countries.

Nor is this all. A revolution that failed might easily lead to a Fascist dictatorship which would discover new forms of industrial organisation more nearly resembling feudalism than anything we have known under the régime of free contract. Marx's view, in short, that a given system of production is governed by inevitable ''laws'' which direct its outcome unduly simplifies the problem. For those ''laws'' are merely tendencies which are, at each instant of time, subject to a pressure which makes prophecy of their operation at best a hazardous adventure. The currents of fact and thought which the communist emphasises are undoubtedly there; but there are also counter-currents of fact and thought upon which sufficient stress is rarely laid.

It is worth while, here, to remember the circumstance under which Marx himself wrote. He knew well the two revolutionary periods of 1789 and 1848; his views were largely generalisations built upon them. The insight he displayed in their analysis was remarkable; but it is difficult not to believe that, at times, the agitator in him was victorious over the scientist. His view is obviously built upon a confidence in rationalism which most psychologists would now judge to be excessive. It has in it that optimistic temper which stamps him as the child of the Enlightenment. Tennyson's ''far-off divine event towards which the whole creation moves'' has just the same serene certainty. Wordsworth's view of evil as the parent of good has the same happy triumph of faith over doubt, as Marx's insistence that,

however often defeated, the proletariat emerges triumphant. He writes of a social system as though it were a species that must conform to the morphological tests of the naturalist. It has no function save to unfold the necessary stages of its evolution. But no social system is, in fact, of this kind. Its life is not merely an inevitable unfolding of inherent tendencies. There are always the novel and unexpected to give the lie to our predictions.

But the communist reliance upon a kind of natural law in social evolution leads him seriously to underestimate the power of forces which are of a non-economic kind. The degree to which nationalism, for instance, will resist economic necessity is remarkable. The mysterious nature of herd-impulse may be admitted; but our ignorance of its nature ought not to blind us to its significance. An English working-man ought, doubtless, to feel that he has more in common with the French or German worker than with the English capitalist. The fact remains that, in general, he gives no sign of such feeling. Some would add that Marx underestimated also the power of religion to influence the actions of men; though anyone who measures the substance of Christian doctrine with the achievement of Christian civilisation may well doubt whether, in this realm, Marx went very far astray.

Nor is it easy to see why his view of the communist state should be accepted. If the revolution he foresaw became universal, there is no inherent reason why the result should be the kind of society he desired. For, in the first place, the intensity of destruction now requisite to the overthrow of a social system might well make impossible a society in which generous impulses had opportunity; and, in the second place, while economic classes might, by hypothesis, disappear, another form of class-rule, that of a doctrinal aristocracy, for example, might take its place. The poison of power is notorious, and it is difficult to see why communists should be held immune from its toxins. It is, indeed, so much the most powerful of the factors by which men in politics are moved that there is no theoretical reason why those who make the communist revolution, or their successors, should abdicate from the pleasant task of exercising authority over their fellows. Ideologies produce economic systems, just as economic systems produce ideologies. The communist emphasises the second, but he is too little willing to see the possible consequences of the first.

We cannot, either, overlook the possibilities that better industrial organisation and the prospects of scientific discovery might easily make of capitalism a system able to satisfy the main wants of the workers. It might then be true of them, as it seems to be true of the American worker in our own day, that they would thereby be led to exchange political power for material comfort. Capitalism is not an unchanging phenomenon; and the margin of possible improvement, under its ægis, is larger than its critics like to admit. The intensity of production, for instance, which might follow a general level of high wages, might, so far from leading to revolution, prove a safeguard against it by the great increase it secured in the average standard of life. We may agree with Marx that, unless capitalism proves itself capable of large reforms, it is destined to perish; but that does not commit us to the theory that communism will take its place. For, in the first place, the breakdown of capitalism might result not in communism, but in anarchy from which there might emerge some dictatorship unrelated in principle to communist ideals; or, in the second, the victory of the working-class might lead to the discovery that the operation of a communist system is impossible. Neither Marx nor his disciples, that is to say, can predict of a revolution more than that a change in the system of production will be the precursor of a change in the habits of society. If that change means the social ownership of the means of production, it is possible to assume that the habits of society will be better, since, under the present system, these have but little relation to justice. But the assumption, however justified, still remains an act of faith.

There is, however, a defence for the Marxian view of inevitable revolution that must not be overlooked. Few of the great social changes with which history acquaints us but have been accompanied by violent upheaval; and even the prediction of its inevitability, as in the France of the *ancien régime,* has not moved those in power to make the concessions which might have avoided it. Why, it may be asked, should we assume that in this respect the future will be different from the past?

On any *a priori* ground, we have no reason to make any such assumption. Those who possess to-day the instruments of economic power are certainly not less anxious to preserve them than were their predecessors. We can only argue that the general democratisation of political institutions makes popular want more effective in securing response than at any previous time; and that the cost of revolution, even if unsuccessful, is now so immense that few Governments would be prepared to risk its coming if concession could purchase its avoidance. We can point, also, to the fact that whereas to Marx one of the root causes of revolution was the increasing misery of the working-class, the evidence seems to prove a genuine and important

improvement in their condition during the last hundred years. If that condition continues (a condition, however, which involves the maintenance of peace), the resultant prosperity might leave a margin within which changes of the necessary range might be secured.

It is, of course, impossible to say that they will be secured. Modern civilisation is, at best, a fragile thing; and while there are revolutionary forces at work which, in a period of war or similar crisis, might easily make for disaster, there are also counter-revolutionary forces the hostility of which to social change are not less dangerous. Lenin in Russia must be paralleled by Mussolini in Italy. Nor must we make too much of the view that the average worker has little thought of the class-relationship which Marxism postulates. In ordinary times this is true, and Marx himself both admitted and explained it. But revolutions always spring from the acts of a minority, and their power is enormous to educate rapidly into exactly that class-consciousness postulated by communists. The two outstanding facts before us are the inevitability of change, and the certainty that any serious attack upon the position of the workers will meet with resistance. Unless, that is to say, there is a considered and continuous effort after social improvement, their united influence might easily demonstrate the truth of the communist position.

We conclude, then, that the materialist interpretation of history is, as general doctrine, undeniable. In the context of communism, there is no necessary connection between its theses and the inferences and predictions made by Marx. A necessary connection may, however, be made. The only way to avoid its coming is to prove by social policy that it is unnecessary. We cannot urge with any profound conviction that this is being done. The invasion of human demands for the benefit of a few is still the rule rather than the exception in history. The strength of the communist position lies in its insistence that it will remain the rule. Thereby it draws the attention of the disinherited to the glaring disparities of our social order. History shows clearly that they will act upon their observation unless they are shown that they can obtain by other means the reasonable satisfaction of their desires. (pp. 77-90)

Harold J. Laski, "The Materialist Interpretation of History," in his Communism, *Henry Holt and Company, 1927, pp. 55-90.*

Marx's birthplace in Trier.

EDMUND WILSON   (essay date 1932)

[Wilson, one of the foremost men of letters in twentieth-century America, wrote widely on cultural, historical, and literary matters, producing several seminal critical studies. He is often credited with bringing an international perspective to American letters through his discussions of European literature. In the following excerpt, Wilson outlines what he considers the major flaws of Marxist literary criticism. For additional commentary by Wilson, see the excerpt dated 1940.]

The worst Marxist criticism has . . . a good deal in common with Humanism. Communist criticism has behind it a powerful living movement, whereas Humanism is feeble and effete; but Marxism at its worst is like Humanism in that both are in the position of trying to gauge the value of works of art on the basis of their literal conformity to a body of fixed moral dogma. The question is, does the work of art contribute toward a certain social end? The question itself is a proper one; but this does not mean that everybody who asks it is fitted to give an answer. What happens in the case of the Humanist or the academic type of Marxist is that he elaborates in a void, a sphere of sheer abstraction, a set of ideal specifications for advancing the end proposed. It is as if a business man, intent on the promotion of his business, who had never had any experience of either the materials or the tools of carpentry and who had never done any sitting, were to draw up careful designs for the construction of chairs for his office. The only difference is that the Humanist locates in the past, where as a matter of fact it never existed, his ideal theoretical chair, whereas the Marxist locates it in the future, where it has never existed yet. They cannot understand that art is something that has to grow out of the actual present substance of life to meet life's immediate needs. The artist, as I have said above, may see into his own future; but the Humanist or the non-artistic Marxist has no credentials whatever which should convince us that he can see into the future of art.

Thus Marxism at its most academic misjudges, it seems to me, the true roles of many of the elements of present bourgeois culture. In the case, for example, of all that department of contemporary literature which stems from French symbolism and of which the chief representative is Joyce, the Marxist assumes too easily that expressing, as to a great extent it does, the morbidity and introversion of bourgeois culture in its decline, it must be completely valueless to the future. This takes no account of its psychological or of its technical discoveries. Bound up as these unquestionably are with the sickness of bourgeois society, Joyce like Freud and Dostoevsky will probably continue to have something to teach us about understanding the mind of man even under communism, and hence in remolding it. And the literary devices of the neo-Symbolists may well turn out to be among the technological improvements made under capitalism which communism will be glad to take over. "The last word of capitalism, the Taylor Plan," wrote Lenin, "combined the refined cruelty of bourgeois exploitation with a certain number of scientific gains which are extremely valuable for the analysis of the mechanical movements necessary in working. . . . The Soviet Republic should take over every technical advance which is scientific in character and offers some advantage." It should be possible to convince Marxist critics of the importance of a work like *Ulysses* by telling them that it is a great piece of engineering—as it is. Henry Ford bought the Johannson gauges because they were true to the millionth of an inch, and the Soviets would be glad to have them. The Joyces and the Eliots and the Cummingses possess the Johannson gauges of consciousness. One of the principal achievements of these writers, furthermore, has been the invention of a literary shorthand which syncopates the syntax of the old literary language, and this shorthand is likely, I should say, to play its role in the creation of the language of the future.

The question of the difficulty of these works seems to me far less serious than it is sometimes assumed to be. Most working-class people at present would never be able to read Joyce; but then, not very many bourgeois do either. Yet his influence has filtered through the whole body of bourgeois literature, from the more popular serious novelists and dramatists who imitate him to the sketches in the barbershop weeklies. It is a question of technical education. Every Marxist assumes that proletarians will prove themselves equal—they do today—to mastering the mechanical techniques. Why should they not master the artistic ones as well? The difficulties of literary and artistic works are always being overadvertised by the mandarins who have an interest in keeping a monopoly of them and who usually don't understand them themselves. Art, like everything else, requires

study and practice; but there is no reason why proletarians, given the opportunities, should not learn all there is to be learnt about it and bring its benefits to the rest of society just as the chemist or the electrical engineer does. The tendency to reject works of art on the ground of their outlandishness or difficulty suggests on the part of the Marxist critic as it does on the part of the academic bourgeois a simple lack of competence in his calling.

It is true that the artists I speak of are occupied to a considerable extent in giving voice to the gaga state of mind of the contemporary cultivated bourgeois and that these developments of method and style are closely bound up with this. But a really first-rate book by an agonizing bourgeois may have more human value, more revolutionary power, than second-rate Marxists who attack it. A really great spirit does not lie even though its letter killeth. Personally I can testify that the writer who has made me feel most overwhelmingly that bourgeois society was ripe for burial was none of our American Marxist journalists but Proust.

I should add that all these mistaken views which unintelligent Marxists derive from Marxism are attributed to it even more frequently by bourgeois critics who want to discredit it by saddling it with absurdities. (pp. 322-23)

> Edmund Wilson, "The Literary Class War: I," in The New Republic, *Vol. LXX, No. 909, May 4, 1932, pp. 319-23.*

MAX EASTMAN   (essay date 1932)

[*An essayist, poet, and editor, Eastman was a commentator on American life and literature who greatly influenced American criticism after the first World War. In 1911 and 1917, respectively, he helped found two notable Marxist periodicals, the* Masses *and the* Liberator, *which he also edited. Here, Eastman explores* Capital *and the* Manifesto, *suggesting that the main obstacle to reading Marx for English and American audiences is his overly philosophical approach.*]

It took a revolution in Russia to wake up the English-speaking world to the importance of Karl Marx. Marx regarded England as a model of the mature workings of that capitalist system which he analyzed, and he would regard present-day America as a super-model. Nevertheless it is just in England and America that Marxism never found a home. It never took firm root among our radical minded intellectuals; it never became the official philosophy of our organizations of the working class, as it has almost everywhere else in the world. There must be some reason why in the countries most advanced economically this most advanced economic theory and program never took hold. I think the principal reason is that Marx was educated in the atmosphere of German metaphysics. He began life as a follower of Hegel, and he never recovered from that German philosophical way of going at things which is totally alien to our minds. (p. vii)

Marx gave the world as important a gift of scientific knowledge as any man of the modern era; he is one of the giants of science. Nevertheless, he did not have this mental attitude. His approach to his problems was philosophical. It was German-professorial in the very sense that seems unnatural to us more skeptical and positivistic Anglo-Saxons. He wanted to revolutionize human society and make it intelligent and decent, and he studied its history and its present constitution with that end in view, and drew up a plan by which the thing might be accomplished. But instead of presenting his thoughts in this simple and clear form as a specific plan for the solution of a specific problem, he started in by deciding in general what the universe is made of and how it operates, and then gradually worked down towards a demonstration that by the very nature of its being and laws of its operation this universe is inevitably going to revolutionize itself, and it is going to revolutionize itself in just the manner outlined in his plan, and therefore as intelligent parts of a universe of such a kind it behooves us to get to work on the job. That method of approaching a job is alien to the Anglo-Saxon mind—especially to the hard-headed and radical specimens of the Anglo-Saxon mind. That is surely one reason—and I think it is the main reason—why Marxism does not take firm root in our culture where its lessons are most directly applicable.

In this I do not mean to boast of any inherent superiority of the Anglo-Saxon brain cells. The more advanced simplicity of logic with which Englishmen like John Stuart Mill approached social problems, however tame their solution of them, was doubtless closely associated with that more advanced industrial development of which Marx himself was so clearly aware. It is important, however, that those young Americans who wish to approach Marx as a teacher—and they all ought to—should not be "buffaloed" by his philosophic mode of approach. They are very likely to in these days, because those most interested in propagating the ideas of Marx, the Russian Bolsheviks, have swallowed down his Hegelian philosophy along with his science of revolutionary engineering, and they look upon us irreverent peoples who presume to meditate social and even revolutionary problems without making our obeisance to the mysteries of Dialectic Materialism, as a species of unredeemed and well-nigh unredeemable barbarians. They are right in scorning our ignorance of the scientific ideas of Karl Marx and our indifference to them. They are wrong in scorning our distaste for having practical programs presented in the form of systems of philosophy. In that we simply represent a more progressive intellectual culture than that in which Marx received his education—a culture farther emerged from the dominance of religious attitudes.

For it is the relic of a religious attitude to attribute your plan for changing the world to the world itself, and endeavor to prove that the "inner law" of this world is engaged in realizing your ideals. Marx was an implacable enemy of religion, and he was also—or thought he was—in revolt against philosophy. He liked to repeat the saying of Ludwig Feuerbach that "the metaphysician is a priest in disguise"; and he expressed many times the desire to get philosophy out of the way of his revolutionary science. It was with this motive that he so vigorously insisted that the world consists of matter and not spirit. But the essence of philosophy in its kinship with religion is not to declare that the world is spirit, but to declare that this world of spirit is sympathetic to the ideals of the philosopher. Marx banished the spirit, but retained in his material world that now still more extraordinary gift of being in sympathy with his ideals. He retained, that is, the philosophic method and habit of thought. It was not that he wanted help from the universe, but he did not know how else to formulate his colossal plan for controlling social evolution except to implant it as "historic necessity" in evolution itself. The combination of affirmative and confident action in a given field with a general attitude of scientific scepticism was unknown to him. (pp. viii-x)

[Marx seeks] those aspects of society and those laws of its history which will guide him in the effort to transform it in the direction of his goal. And here the great work of his genius begins. It divides itself into two sections: first, an explanation of the dominant part played in all human culture and all its history by a gradual change and development of the technique of wealth production; and second, an analysis of our contemporary capitalist method of production. I call the first section "The Theory of History"; the second section is of course Marx's famous contribution to economics, [*Capital*]. (p. xii)

The theory of history was summarized in this way by Friedrich Engels, the close friend and co-creator of Marx's ideas:

> Marx discovered the simple fact (heretofore hidden beneath ideological overgrowths) that human beings must have food, drink, clothing and shelter first of all, before they can interest themselves in politics, science, art, religion and the like. This implies that the production of the immediately requisite material means of subsistence, and therewith the existing phase of development of a nation or an epoch, constitute the foundation upon which the state institutions, the legal outlooks, the artistic and even the religious ideas are built up. It implies that these latter must be explained out of the former, whereas the former have usually been explained as issuing from the latter.

It is impossible to exaggerate the influence of this simple idea upon the subsequent development of historic knowledge. All thoughtful men have profited by it and they will forever. It marks a turning point in the whole art of understanding history. Here again, however, the fact that Marx conceived himself to be writing a *philosophy* of history, an explanation of the whole thing as a single process, and one which was leading up to and with necessity including his proposed plan for the future, led him to state the case in a way that is unacceptable to a modern scientific mind. The fact that men have to eat and shelter and clothe themselves before they do other things, makes the productive forces a primary factor in explaining history, a factor *conditioning* all others. That is to say that no historic phenomenon can arise and endure which *runs counter* to the prevailing mode of production. This does not mean, however, that everything which arises and endures is *explained by* the prevailing mode of production. Again the idea of effective cause is confused with that of indispensable condition. It is confused with that of indispensable condition. It is confused by Engels in this most simple statement of the theory, and it is confused still more explicitly by Marx in his Introduction to the *Critique of Political Economy*—the classic passage. "The mode of production," he says, "*conditions* the social, political and spiritual life process. . . ," and in the very next sentence, as though but developing the same thought: "It is not the consciousness of men which *determines* their existence, but on the contrary their social existence *determines* their existence, but on the contrary their social existence *determines* their consciousness." There can be no doubt here that the limiting condition and the determining cause are being interchanged without discrimination, and if the reader will take my word that this is true throughout the entire Marxian system, he will find Marx infinitely easier to read.

In *Capital,* for instance . . . , Marx turns to the investigation of our present-day method of production. He does so because this conditions and limits the success of any efforts that social reformers may make to improve our society. They may talk about liberty, equality, fraternity, and so on, but if these aims are inconsistent with the mode of production, all their noble talk will merely expand in the air. Now Marx is . . . interested in liberty, equality, fraternity—in all that is implied by these abstract slogans, and more too. He is interested in forming a society in which wealth shall be distributed according to need, work demanded according to ability. He sees at a glance that our system of production renders such a dream impossible. Capitalist production involves economic classes and the exploitation of one class by another inherently and eternally. It involves class struggle inherently and eternally. But there is nothing inherently eternal about capitalist production itself. It was a product of change; it evolved out of feudalism; it may not necessarily be the end of that evolution. One need not, therefore, simply abandon one's plan for a better society as impractical, and fall back upon the sad enterprise of doctoring up in small ways the one we have. One may by further investigation and exercise of ingenuity devise a scheme by which the mode of production can again be changed, and thus new conditions created which will not be inconsistent with the ideal of a classless society. It was this latter step that Marx took, and that made him the intellectual father of the Russian revolution and one of the greatest men in human history. He devised the scheme—or the science, rather, for that is what it has become—of engineering with class forces. He pointed out that by organizing and directing the struggle of the working class against the capitalists and their associates, and by interlinking with this struggle in certain quite possible ways the struggle of the poor peasants and tenant-farmers against the landlords, and carrying it forward to a veritable "dictatorship" of these exploited classes, it would be possible to take possession of the instruments of production and change the system. It would be possible to change it in those ways necessary in order to make reasonable the effort to create a classless society in which men will receive according to need and work according to ability.

Marx saw clearly enough that this manœuvre would be possible only in a crisis, only at a moment when the system had broken down so badly that the dominant classes were unable to rule and the exploited classes were driven by suffering to forceful and imperious action—only at a moment of actual or potential civil war. He was therefore concerned to find out whether the capitalist system of production does not inevitably produce crises, any one of which may possibly become severe enough to make such action practical. There is little doubt that he did demonstrate the inevitability under a capitalist system of the recurrent crisis of overproduction, and bound up therewith the inevitability of imperialist wars. His contribution to the understanding of business crises and the causes of war will not often be denied today even by the most "bourgeois" economists. And thus he completed the scientific task set by his apparently utopian aims—the task of finding out how the existing system of wealth production might be changed in such a way as to make these utopian aims possible of attainment, and reasonable to strive after.

It was not necessary for him as an engineer to prove that this change is inevitable. It was not even necessary to prove that social evolution is tending in that direction. He might, indeed, have believed with Spengler that it is tending in an opposite direction, towards decay and disaster, and that this deliberate and informed action—this new economic engineering science—is the only thing that can save us from the fate of the older civilizations. All he had to prove was that in spite of the *limiting conditions* his method of action is practical, and the occasions for its application will arise.

That is the sum and substance of *Das Kapital* as a part of an engineering science. Owing to his philosophical mode of approach, however, his training in the school of Hegel, Marx felt obliged to prove that his whole scheme of salvation is involved with "historic necessity" in the very laws of the capitalist system which "work with iron necessity toward inevitable results." It was with this sense of his mission that he approached his studies in economics.

[He wrote to his friend Weydemeyer in 1852:]

> As far as I am concerned . . . I cannot claim to have discovered the existence of classes in modern society or their strife against one another. Petty bourgeois historians long ago described the evolution of class struggles, and political economists showed the economic physiology of the classes. I have added as a new contribution the following propositions: 1. That the existence of classes is bound up with certain phases of material production; 2. That the class struggle leads necessarily to the dictatorship of the proletariat; 3. That this dictatorship is but the transition to the abolition of all classes and to the creation of a society of the free and equal.

Or to put this mode of approach in the youthful words of his friend Engels: "With the same certainty with which from a given mathematical proposition a new one is deduced, with that same certainty can we deduce the social revolution from the existing social conditions and the principles of political economy."

Such words reveal the essence of what is unscientific and untrue in the Marxian system—the reading of the desired result into the limiting conditions, the failure to realize the central rôle played in all science by the working hypothesis. *Given* these conditions, *if* such and such action is taken, then the conceived result will follow: that is the language of science, and that is as far as the knowledge of man can reach. The attempt of Marx to know more than is possible to know, to prove more than he needed to prove, is what makes his great book, *Capital,* cumbersome and obscure and something of an affliction even upon the most willing. (pp. xv-xvi)

[The *Communist Manifesto* also] contains, to be sure, a good deal of the metaphysic of history. Its very first sentence—"The history of all hitherto existing society is a history of class struggles" shows that disposition to read one's own interests into the definition of facts, which distinguishes the philosopher from the scientist. "No hitherto existing society has ever been changed fundamentally except by way of a class struggle" is all that the authors needed to say. But on the whole the *Communist Manifesto,* being the program of a conspiratorial league of revolutionists who hoped it might be possible in the approaching revolutionary disturbances in Europe to overthrow the bourgeoisie and establish a communist state, contains little of the phraseology of the dialectic philosopher. Historic necessity and the logic of evolution, are here pretty well forgotten. The universe is dropped out of the picture. The Communist League declares concretely in the language of common sense and of practical science that such and such are their "views" and such their "aims," and that these aims can be attained only by such and such methods. (pp. xvi-xvii)

> *Max Eastman, in an introduction to* Capital: The Communist Manifesto and Other Writings *by Karl*

Marx, edited by Max Eastman, The Modern Library, 1932, pp. vii-xviii.

RALPH FOX (essay date 1937)

[*Fox explains the Marxist concept of artistic creation, denying the charge that in Marxism human beings are subordinate to economic processes.*]

Marxism is a materialist philosophy. It believes in the primacy of matter and that the world exists outside of us and independently of us. But Marxism also sees all matter as changing, as having a history, and accepts nothing as fixed and immutable. In the seventeenth century few English writers would have quarreled with a materialist view of life, though their view of materialism would not have been the same as that of Marx and Engels. To Shakespeare, drawing his philosophical views from Rabelais and Montaigne, there would have appeared nothing outrageous in the Marxian view of life. For the greater part of the eighteenth century a materialist view of life would have been accepted without question by many of the greatest British writers.

It is not so today. It has not been so for more than a century. Today the literary journalist protests that materialism and imagination cannot go to bed together. The result, they suggest, would not be creation, but simply an unholy row. It is a curiously perverted view, for it would appear to be the most natural thing in the world for the imaginative writer, and particularly the novelist, to adopt a materialist view of life.

"Being determines consciousness" is the Marxist definition of the ultimate relation between matter and spirit. Whether or not this is the actual view of the artist it must, in fact, be the basis of his creative work. For all imaginative creation is a reflection of the real world in which the creator lives. It is the result of his contact with that world and his love or hate for what he finds in that world.

It is the lights and colors, the forms and shapes, the breath of the winds, the scents of life, the physical beauty or the physical ugliness of animal life, including the lives of human beings, the acts, the thoughts, the dreams of actual men and women, including the creator himself, that form the stuff of art.

Milton demanded three things of poetry, that it be "simple, sensuous and passionate." Art that is not sensuous, that is not concerned with perception of the real world, with sensible objects, is not art at all, not even the shadow of art. The essence of the creative process is the struggle between the creator and external reality, the urgent demand to master and recreate that reality. "But does not Marxism claim that works of art are merely a reflection of economic needs and economic processes?" it will be objected.

No, this is not the view of Marxism, though it is the view of a number of materialists of the nineteenth century of the positivist school whose views have nothing in common with Marxian, dialectical materialism. Marx has clearly stated his ideas on the relationship between the spiritual processes of life, of which artistic creation is one, and the material basis of life, in the famous Preface to his *Critique of Political Economy*. Here is the passage:

> The mode of production of the material means of existence conditions the whole process of social, political and intellectual life. It is not the consciousness of men that determines their existence, but, on the contrary, their social existence determines their consciousness. At a certain stage of their development, the material forces of production in society come in conflict with the existing relations of production, or—what is but a legal expression for the same thing—with the property relations within which they had been at work before. From forms of development of the forces of production these relations turn into their fetters. Then opens an epoch of social revolution. With the change of the economic foundation the entire immense super-structure is more or less rapidly transformed. In considering such revolutions the distinction should always be between the material revolution in the economic conditions of production which can be determined with the precision of natural science, and the juridical, political, religious, aesthetic, or philosophic—in short, ideological forms—in which men become conscious of this conflict and fight it out.

Marx, then, certainly believed that the material mode of life in the end determined the intellectual. But he never for a moment considered the connection between the two was a direct one, easily observed and mechanically developing. He would have laughed to scorn the idea that because capitalism replaces feudalism, therefore a "capitalist" art immediately replaces "feudal" art, and that all great artists must in consequence directly reflect the needs of the new capitalist class. Nor . . . did he consider that because the capitalist mode of production was a more progressive one than the feudal, capitalist art must therefore always stand on a higher level than feudal art, while feudal art in turn must stand above the art of the slave States of Greece and Rome, or the ancient Eastern monarchies. Such crude and vulgar views are foreign to the whole spirit of Marxism.

Changes in the material basis of society, Marx rightly urged, can be determined by the economic historian with the precision of natural science (which, of course, is not the same thing as saying that these changes are scientifically determined). But no such scientific measurement of the resulting changes in the social and spiritual superstructure of life is possible. The changes take place, men become conscious of them, they "fight out" the conflict between old and new in their minds, but they do so unevenly, burdened by all kinds of past heritage, often unclearly, and always in such a way that it is not easy to trace the changes in men's minds. (pp. 21-4)

Marxism, therefore, while reserving the final and decisive factor in any change for economic causes, does not deny that "ideal" factors can also influence the course of history and may even preponderate in determining the *form* which changes will take (but only the form). It is only a caricature of Marxism to suggest that it underestimates the importance of such a spiritual factor in human consciousness as artistic creation, or to make the absurd claim that Marx considered works of art to be the direct reflexion of material and economic causes. He did not. He understood perfectly well that religion, or philosophy, or tradition can play a great part in the creation of a work of art, even that any one of these or other "ideal" factors may preponderate in determining the *form* of the work in question. Among all the elements which go to make a work of art it is, however, only the economic movement which asserts itself as *finally* necessary, for what Marx and Engels considered to be true of historical changes they also considered true of aesthetic creation.

It is often objected against Marxism that it denies the individual, who is merely the prey of abstract economic forces which drive him to his doom with the inevitability of a Greek fate. We will leave aside the question of whether or not the conception that man is driven by external fate to an inevitable end makes the creation of a work of art impossible. Perhaps Calvinism has never produced great art, but the idea of doom and fate has done so—in the Greek tragedies, in the works of Hardy, to mention only two instances. It is nevertheless possible that the objection, if it really represented the Marxian view, would be a valid one. At least this objection is prompted by the humanist tradition of the great art of the western world, and is therefore worthy of respect, even though it is based on a grave misunderstanding.

For Marxism does not deny the individual. It does not see only masses in the grip of inexorable economic forces. True, some Marxist literary works, particularly some ''proletarian'' novels, have given innocent critics cause to believe that this is the case, but here perhaps the weakness has been in the novelists who have failed to rise to the greatness of their theme of man changing himself through the process of changing nature and creating new economic forces. Marxism places man in the center of its philosophy, for while it claims that material forces may change man, it declares most emphatically that it is man who changes the material forces and that in the course of so doing he changes himself.

Man and his development is the center of the Marxist philosophy. How does man change? What are his relations with the external world? These are the questions to which the founders of Marxism have sought and found answers. I do not wish here to outline Marxist philosophy, for that is done more capably elsewhere, but let us examine for a moment this question of man as an active historical agent, man at work and struggling with life, for this is the man who is at once artistic creator and the object of art. This is the way in which Engels explained the part of the individual in history:

> History makes itself in such a way that the final result always arises from conflicts between many individual wills, of which each again has been made what it is by a host of particular conditions of life. Thus there are innumerable intersecting forces, an infinite series of parallelograms of forces which give rise to one resultant—the historical event. This again may itself be viewed as the product of a power which, taken as a whole, works *unconsciously* and without volition. For what each individual wills is obstructed by everyone else, and what emerges is something that no one willed. Thus past history proceeds in the manner of a natural process and is also essentially subject to the same laws of movement. But from the fact that individual wills—of which each desires what he is impelled to by his physical constitution and external, in the last resort economic, circumstances (either his own personal circumstances or those of society in general)—do not attain what they want, but are merged into a collective mean, a common resultant, it must not be concluded that their value = 0. On the contrary, each contributes to the resultant and is to this degree involved in it.

Here is not only a formula for the historian, but also for the novelist. For the one concern of the novelist is, or should be, this question of the individual will in its conflict with other wills on the battleground of life. It is the fate of man that his desires are never fulfilled, but it is also his glory, for in the effort to obtain their fulfillment he changes, be it ever so little, in ever so limited a degree, life itself. Not X = 0 is the Marxist formula for the fate of man, but ''on the contrary, each contributes to the resultant and is to this degree involved in it.''

The conflict of wills, of desires and passions, is not, however, a conflict of abstract human beings, for Engels is careful to emphasize that man's desires and actions are conditioned by his physical constitution and, finally, by economic circumstances, either his personal circumstances or those of society in general. In his social history it is, in the last resort, the class to which he belongs, the psychology of that class, with its contradictions and conflicts, which plays the determining part. So that each man has, as it were, a dual history, since he is at the same time a type, a man with a social history, and an individual, a man with a personal history. The two, of course, even though they may be in glaring conflict, are also one, a unity, in so far as the latter is eventually conditioned by the former, though this does not and should not imply that in art the social type must dominate the individual personality. Falstaff, Don Quixote, Tom Jones, Julien Sorel, Monsieur de Charlus are all types, but they are types in whom the social characteristics constantly reveal the individual, and in whom the personal hopes, hungers, loves, jealousies and ambitions in turn light up the social background.

The novelist cannot write this story of the individual fate unless he also has this steady vision of the whole. He must understand how his final result arises from the individual conflicts of his characters, he must in turn understand what are the manifold conditions of lives which have made each of those individuals what she or he is. ''What emerges is something that no one willed,'' how exactly that sums up each great work of art, and how well it expresses the pattern of life itself, since behind the event that no one willed a pattern does exist. Marxism gives to the creative artist the key to reality when it shows him how to discern that pattern and the place which each individual occupies in it. At the same time it consciously gives to man his full value, and in this sense is the most humanist of all the world outlooks. (pp. 25-8)

Ralph Fox, ''Marxism and Literature,'' in his The Novel and the People, *1937. Reprint by International Publishers, 1945, pp. 21-8.*

JOHN MIDDLETON MURRY (essay date 1938)

[*Murry was a noted English essayist, magazine editor, and literary critic during the first half of the twentieth century. In the following excerpt, he expounds on Marx's political and social theories, pointing out that they are limited by a ''bias . . . toward the elimination of the moral and religious processes from history.''*]

The fatal hiatus in Marx's theory was that it assumed an absolute discontinuity in the moral and political evolution of society. If all previous classes in Germany had failed to identify themselves with the demand of the nation as a whole, why and how could the proletariat succeed in doing so, when the spark required to transmute its economic demand into the political demand had to be far stronger and more stubborn than the spark required for the subordinate political revolutions, of which it had shown itself incapable? Because the political demand which the proletariat must make if it were to fulfill its historical mission was the supreme demand for economic and political equality together. How could a people which had never made, with the conviction of its own indefeasible sovereignty, *any* political demand, suddenly rise, out of sheer economic compulsion, to the height of making the supreme political demand? Ah! but the proletariat was not of the people; it was outside society; it was a new thing, a new *Unding*. Now that, with all respect to Marx, was visionary self-delusion as regards Germany. There could be no such absolute cleavage between the new class and existing society; and the possibility could have occurred only to a mind at once in desperation, and seeking consolation for its despair in the imaginary potentialities of an abstract economic man. There is an economic nexus in society, but there is a cultural, a moral and political nexus also. Marx was now ignoring it. His proletariat lived in a social vacuum, under a bell-jar as it were, filled with an unmitigated atmosphere of misery, oppression and complete social outlawry. This was impossible to imagine in Germany. Nevertheless, imagine it. The consequence would be a relapse to complete savagery. Out of that complete savagery how could the will to the supreme social and political purpose arise? It was inconceivable.

But let us admit that this moral, political, economic isolation of the Marxian proletariat is abstract—merely the general ground-plan of history to come; and let us suppose that a hunger-proletariat was actually conceivable in Germany. Then the new class partakes of the moral and political atmosphere of society as a whole, as it indubitably must. Inevitably, it assimilates the national tradition of political cowardice, of lack of political self-respect, of the absence of a sense of fundamental human equality, of that fatal Lutheran indifference of the *Biedermann* on which Marx had laid his finger when he wrote: "In France it is enough that a man should be something for him to demand to be everything; in Germany a man must be nothing in order not to resign all claim to be anything." How should a class reared in that moral atmosphere push its economic demand to a maximum? For the non-moral, non-political demand of the proletariat is the right to exist—nothing more—not in the least the demand for the right of economic *equality*. Is it not inevitable that a proletariat, reared in such an atmosphere, should make only the pure economic demand—for the means of subsistence? In other words, from the Marxian proletariat of Germany, as Marx himself conceived it, you could get only—precisely what you have got—namely, a readiness to revert to true slave-status: to be kept, fed, sent hither and thither under command, to be free of all individual responsibility. The proletariat which is to be capable of fulfilling its historical mission must needs be a proletariat kindled and inspired by moral enthusiasm—more explicitly, by a political tradition of the demand for equality, as a moral imperative.

It may be said that Marx overcame this difficulty by postulating that the proletariat should be "class-conscious." That tediously familiar phrase is an evasion of the difficulty, not a solution of it. For what is a "class-conscious" proletariat? Precisely a proletariat "conscious of its historical mission" and inspired by it. And what is its historical mission? To be the class that is the means of establishing a society of political and economic equality. But such a society is a moral ideal, and can be conceived only by the moral imagination. It is a moral mission of which the proletariat has to be conscious; and it is more than halfway toward a dangerous equivocation if you insist on disguising the real nature of this mission from yourself, and from other simpler people, by calling it simply an "historical mis-

sion," above all when the main emphasis of your theory of history is on the fact that history is, well-nigh exclusively, an economic and material process. You cannot, however much the particular circumstances of your case make you desire to do so, get a society of political and economic equality by pure economic and material process. At some point in the process, if it is to achieve the end you desire, the economic determinant *must be transmuted* into an overwhelming moral motive; and the longer that transmutation is delayed, the more difficult it will be to accomplish. There is, indubitably, a sheer economic necessity at work in the contradictions of capitalism; but that sheer economic necessity, untransmuted by the moral motive, unleavened by the political tradition of democracy, will carry the proletariat not into a society of freedom and equality, but into a society of acquiescent slavery.

In other words, the conception of a "class-conscious" proletariat is sufficient on one condition alone, namely, that the particular proletariat of whose historical mission the proletariat is to be conscious should have a real history of political struggle and sacrifice for the moral ideal of equality. Take that condition away and your "class-conscious proletariat" inevitably sinks "beneath the level of history." (pp. 329-31)

What it reduces to is this: that Marx's theory of the regeneration of society by the proletariat contains a fatal equivocation. The proletariat that is capable of establishing a classless society is not a proletariat in the Marxian sense, at all; that is to say, it is not a class morally and politically outside society. It is a class which has already conquered equality of political rights within extant society and therefore already to the highest degree of extant possibility has succeeded in incorporating itself in society. In so far as society is a moral entity, the proletariat that is capable of a creative function has already enforced its claim to belong to that moral entity. Henceforward the process of the moralization of society may be slow and laborious, but at every moment (if Marxist Socialism is to *mean* anything) the working-class must be in the van of that process. If for any considerable period it allows itself to fall "beneath the level of history" it cannot fulfill its historical mission; for then the necessary economic reorganization of society will come from above the working-class.

That may seem to be a cumbrous way of restating the proposition that there is absolutely no way to a society of true equality—that is to say, a society of political *and* economic equality—except through a society of political equality. Nor would Marx have directly repudiated that proposition; but I am certain that he would never have asserted it in the unequivocal fashion in which it is asserted here. He half-deliberately hedged on this vital point, and there is a good deal of theoretical justification for a particular and pernicious brand of Marxism which talks (or used to talk till Moscow gave it different orders) contemptuously of "capitalist democracy" and persuades itself that "democracy" and "capitalism" are interchangeable terms; so that it follows inevitably in the half-baked minds in which this brand of Marxism finds response that the way to the overthrow of "capitalism" must be through the overthrow of "democracy." And although Marx would probably have repudiated that fantastic extravagance, he cannot be acquitted of having sown the seed from which it grew. Moreover, we have suggested the true source of this dangerous ambiguity in his thinking—his own personal need as a politically conscious German, deeply and justly mistrustful of the moral and political inertia of his countrymen, to conceive a process by which the creation of a society of political and economic equality should not depend on the preliminary achievement of political equality. That personal, or national, need gave a tremendous bias to Marx's thought—a constantly operative unconscious tendency to minimize the efficacy and the necessity of the moral motive in history.

It is the duty of those who believe that Marx made a great contribution to man's understanding of his destiny, to understand the cause and nature of this bias in Marxism, and to correct it: not merely to maintain, quite clearly and unequivocally, the practical proposition that there is absolutely no way to a society of social justice except through the conquest of equal political rights and of the further right to exercise those rights to the full: that there is, in simple fact, no way to Socialism except through effective democracy. They have to understand, not merely instinctively that that proposition is true, but intellectually also, *why* that proposition is true, and how and why the seed of the dangerous heresy which either repudiates or whittles away that truth came to be planted in Socialist thought. And there is no more cogent and satisfying way of laying hold on that truth than by confronting Marx with Rousseau.

Marx has the apparent advantage that he seems more relevant to the actual condition of modern society than Rousseau; he is, as they say, more "contemporary." It appears to be obvious that a man who wrote definitely about the society of industrial capitalism should have more to tell us than a man who definitely warned mankind against entering the era of unrestricted capitalism at all. (pp. 332-34)

But, it may be said, Rousseau did not understand the class-struggle in history. Therefore he did not foresee the great historical mission of the working-class. That is literally true. But let us not delude ourselves. Whether the working-class will fulfill its "great historical mission" is still very much in question. History has not yet decided that it will. It is, assuredly, by no means inevitable that it will. And if our previous analysis of what the fulfillment of the historical mission of the working-class really involves is correct, its fulfillment depends upon the working-class being animated by a conviction of the dignity and equality and sanctity of human beings as such. Is it likely, is it even conceivable, that this conviction should ever become the *monopoly* of the working-class? Rousseau declared that the establishment of the classless society—which he conceived much more clearly and positively than Marx—depended on the existence of men with the imagination to conceive it and the moral will to achieve it. Does Marxism wish to deny that? In so far as it does, is not Marxism mistaken? Has that been really superseded by the theory that the working-class by pursuing its interests will bring us to the classless society? Everything depends upon what we mean by "interests"—a kind of discrimination at which Rousseau was a much better hand than Marx. Rousseau's vital distinction between *amour propre*—self-interest—and *amour de soi*—the true self-interest of Man—is completely ignored by Marx. It is in the *true* self-interest of every man that he should work to establish the classless society. Is it not, therefore, interest of that enlightened order that the Marxist means. Does he mean interest in the immediate sense, in which one might say: "It is to my interest that no one should enjoy a higher wage than I?" But interest of that kind will divide the working-class, not unite it. None the less, there is, of course, a real sense in which the working-man should be the apt disciple of the fundamental doctrine of human equality. It is obvious that the wage-slave of industrialism should see more clearly the inhuman deprivation of necessities and freedoms under which he labors, than the privileged man will ever

see how he, by existing in an unnatural society, is deprived of necessities and freedom of a different order. But did Rousseau dream of denying that? It was fundamental to his vision.

Where Marx added to Rousseau was not by the doctrine of the class-struggle, because Rousseau made no claim to be a historian, and the doctrine of the class-struggle, as we have seen, is a broken reed when it comes to making history, instead of interpreting it; nor by his doctrine that political power must correspond to economic power—a very doubtful doctrine as generally understood—but by his analysis of the actual economic working of Capitalism. Marx proved that uncontrolled Capitalism must break down. But he did not prove, because it cannot be proved, that Capitalism must be replaced by Socialism. That depends; and what it depends upon is how far men, and not the working-class alone, are responsive to the doctrines of Rousseau—and of a greater than he: moral and political doctrines, exceedingly profound and everlastingly true, and therefore capable of apprehension by truly simple minds.

Here is a crucial difference between Rousseauism and Marxism. Marxism is incomprehensible by the simple mind: and by the simple mind, I mean the mind which feels a profound and elemental distinction between right and wrong. It is fatal to our humanity if ever we lose the simple mind. Some of us are bound to lose it for a time; it is our destiny that education and experience in this epoch of economic contradiction and spiritual uncertainty should entangle us in a radical skepticism, but unless we regain the simple mind we are lost. The only way by which we can fight to retain or regain the simple mind is by resolutely refusing all merely intellectual conclusions which do violence to our deep, instinctive sense of ultimate right and wrong.

Marxism is a difficult doctrine, and for its true understanding requires a mind habituated to work simultaneously on many different levels—on three, certainly—on the economic, on the political, and on the moral; and I am impelled to add a fourth—namely, the religious. It is folly to indulge the belief that the mind of the average man is capable of this. Implant in the average man, if you can; the belief that history is in the main an economic process, and he is, in most cases, bound to believe it is a purely economic process: you cannot expect him to understand that it is simultaneously *also* a political process, *also* a moral process, *also* a religious process: still less that the political process, if it is to be regenerative, is precisely the process in which the economic and moral and religious processes are fused together.

The bias of Marxism is toward the elimination of the moral and religious processes from history. Once you have got them out, however, you cannot get them back again; yet you cannot do without them. For material forces do *not* create their political equivalents. There are no political *equivalents* to material forces. An army of 5,000 men may be either more than a match for twice, or less than a match for half, its number. God is not always on the side of the big battalions. (pp. 334-37)

Marx, to Rousseau, would have seemed like a curious, powerful and prophetic successor to the *philosophes*—just as confident a believer as they in automatic and inevitable Progress (though by the instrumentality of catastrophe), and just as reluctant as they "to interrogate the human heart" and to accept the facts of human nature. The means by which, in his analysis of the social macrocosm, Marx managed to avoid the necessity of moral criticism were very simple. He declared that the moral motive was impotent to change society. On the negative side, this is plausible enough, at least to the superficial observer; morality and religion have assuredly not accomplished very much. On the other hand it is probably true that they have accomplished all the enduring *good* that has been accomplished. Marx's simple mistake was to imagine that because morality and religion have done so little to change society for the better, they have done nothing to prevent it from lapsing back into the worse. Marx accepted the existence of an inherent tendency to social degeneration only as an eccentric episode in human history: the tendency was operative precisely as long as Marx desired that it should be operative, namely, from the moment that he wrote up to the point at which it produced an intolerable situation of open class-warfare. When that Armageddon was ended, the tendency miraculously ceased to exist.

The arbitrariness of this eschatological conception of an absolute hiatus in the moral history of mankind Marx concealed from himself by the doctrine that humanity, under capitalism, had passed into a condition where the only classes were economic classes—classes distinguished by more, or less, or no control over the instruments of production. Therefore, men had only to abolish *all* private control of the instruments of production to abolish classes altogether. This was positively naive. Economic classes are the means, in one particular form of society, of providing the raw material from which the functional classes necessary in all forms of society are recruited. Political power must be exercised by somebody. The abolition of the economic basis of class-distinction means merely that another way of recruiting the functional classes must be found. The new way may be a juster way of recruiting the functional classes; but they must be recruited. And nothing can prevent the abuse of their power by such classes except the moral will in individuals to which Rousseau appealed; either in the members of the superior functional classes themselves—to control themselves—or in those on whom their power is exercised—to control their rulers—or in both together. The problem of human society in fact begins where Marx believed in ended.

What Marx tried to do was to abolish the problem of human society, which is the problem of human nature, altogether. Society, he believed, would regenerate itself, and maintain itself in a condition of regeneration, both automatically. It is hardly to be wondered at that in practice this strange doctrine ends in legitimating a secular theocracy, which can admit no criticism of itself by the criterion of any absolute ideal outside and independent of itself. A condition is attained in which progress toward perfection is postulated to be inevitable. If the progress toward it involves falsehood, injustice, cruelty, tyranny and organized inhumanity, that is appearance only; for obviously the necessary means to an inevitable good are themselves necessary and inevitable and good. That is to say, Good and Evil are mere words. (pp. 339-41)

Marxism, like Rousseauism, is of positive value, that is to say, truly and enduringly creative of *good,* only when it is conceived as ancillary to the eternal truth of Christianity and the idea of the eternal Church. The difference, in this respect, between the two doctrines, is that Rousseau was conscious of this ancillary relation, whereas Marx was not. We may say that Marx reverted to the primitive Jewish-Christian eschatology which flourished while the expectation of the End was general, and that his doctrine is a completely secularized Jewish eschatology. Rousseau, on the other hand, was the inheritor of classical Christianity—that is, of the Christian faith which was slowly adjusted to the realization that the End was not to be: and in fact Rousseau was a convinced Christian all his life. But the

doctrines of both can be fully understood only when they are conceived as a prophetic summons to the visible Christian Church to wake from its cowardice and lethargy, of which the cause is human inertia, but of which the excuse is a specious insistence on other-worldliness: an actual surrender to this world by a total dissociation of the Kingdom of God from any condition of the world in time. The Church is *the* Church, only when it is in a condition of vital tension between the two realizations: that the Kingdom of God cannot be established in the world in time, and that the Kingdom of God *must* be established in the world in time. (pp. 342-43)

> *John Middleton Murry, "Karl Marx: Secular Messianism and Secular Theocracy," in his* Heroes of Thought, *Julian Messner, Inc., 1938, pp. 329-43.*

ISAIAH BERLIN (essay date 1939)

[*Berlin is a noted British philosopher and student of Marxism. In the following excerpt from a work first published in 1939, he explicates the economic theories detailed in* Capital *and the* Manifesto.]

[*Das Kapital*] was conceived as a comprehensive treatise on the laws and morphology of the economic organisation of modern society, seeking to describe the processes of production, exchange and distribution as they actually occur, to explain their present state as a particular stage in the development constituted by the movement of the class struggle, in Marx's own words, 'to discover the economic law of motion of modern society' by establishing the natural laws that govern the history of classes. The result was an original amalgam of economic theory, history, sociology and propaganda which fits none of the accepted categories. Marx certainly regarded it as primarily a treatise on economic science. The earlier economists, according to Marx, misunderstood the nature of economic laws when they compared them with the laws of physics and chemistry, and assumed that, although social conditions may change, the laws that govern them do not; with the result that their systems either apply to imaginary worlds, peopled by idealised economic men, modelled upon the writer's own contemporaries, and therefore usually compounded of selected characteristics which came into prominence only in the eighteenth and nineteenth centuries; or else describe societies which, if they were ever real, have long since vanished. He therefore conceived it as his task to create a new system of concepts and definitions which should have definite application to the contemporary world, and be so constructed as to reflect the changing structure of economic life in relation not only to its past, but also to its future. In the first volume Marx made an attempt at once to provide a systematic exposition of certain basic theorems of economic science, and more specifically to describe the rise of the new industrial system, as a consequence of the new relations between employers and labour created by the effect of technological progress on the methods of production.

The first volume therefore deals with the productive process; that is, on the one hand, the relations between machinery and labour, and on the other those between the actual producers, that is the workers and those who employ and direct them. The remaining volumes, published after his death by his executors, deal largely with the impact on the theory of value of the circulation of the finished product, which must obtain before its value can be realised, that is the system of exchange and the financial machinery which it involves, and with relations between producers and consumers, which determine prices, the rate of interest and profit.

The general thesis which runs through the entire work is that adumbrated in the **Communist Manifesto** and Marx's earlier economic writings. It rests on three fundamental assumptions: (a) that political economy seeks to explain who obtains what goods or services or status and why; (b) that it is therefore a science not of inanimate objects—commodities—but of persons and their activities, to be interpreted in terms of the rules which govern the capitalist market economy, and not pseudo-objective laws beyond human control, such as those of supply and demand, which govern the world of natural objects—objects whose behaviour is, as it were, external to the lives of men, who look upon this process as part of an eternal, natural order before which men must bow down, since they are impotent to alter it. This illusion, or 'false consciousness', is what he calls 'fetishism of commodities'; (c) that the decisive factor in social behaviour in modern times is that of industrialisation; with the rider that the earliest and fullest form of it—the industrial revolution in England—offers the student the best example of a process that will, in due course, take place everywhere. Marx traces the rise of the modern proletariat by correlating it with the general development of the technical means of production. When, in the course of their gradual evolution, these means can no longer be created by each man for his own use, and division of labour is born, certain individuals (as Saint-Simon had taught), owing to their superior skill, power and enterprise, acquire sole control of such instruments and tools, and thus find themselves in a position in which they can hire the labour of others by a combination of threats to withhold necessities of life from them and of offering them more in the form of a regular remuneration than they would receive as independent producers, vainly attempting to achieve the same results with the old and obsolete tools which alone they have in their possession. As a result of selling their labour to others, these men themselves become so many commodities in the economic market, and their labour power acquires a definite price which fluctuates precisely like that of other commodities.

A commodity is any object in a market economy embodying human labour for which there is a social demand. It is thus a concept which, Marx is careful to point out, can be applied only at a relatively late stage of social development: and is no more eternal than any other economic category. The commercial value of a commodity is asserted—this is the conclusion of his argument—to be directly constituted by the number of hours of socially necessary human labour, that is, how long it takes an average producer to create an average specimen of its kind (a view derived from a somewhat similar doctrine held by Ricardo and the classical economists). . . . Even after the reasonable reward of the employer's own work in his capacity as the organiser and manager of the processes of production and distribution is deducted, a definite residue of the social income remains, which in the form of rent, interest on investments, or commercial profit, is shared, according to Marx, not by society as a whole, but solely by those members of it who are called the capitalist or bourgeois class, distinguished from the rest by the fact that they alone, in their capacity as sole owners of the means of production, obtain and accumulate such unearned increment.

Whether Marx's concept of value be interpreted as meaning an average norm, round which the actual prices of commodities oscillate, or an ideal limit towards which they tend, or that

which in some unspecified sense prices 'ought' to be, or an element in the sociological explanation of what constitutes and satisfies the material interests of men in society, or something more metaphysical—an impalpable essence, infused into brute matter by the creativeness of human labour, or, as unsympathetic critics have maintained, a confusion of all these; and again whether the notion of a uniform entity called undifferentiated human labour (which according to the theory constitutes economic value), different manifestations of which can be compared in respect of quantity alone, is, or is not, valid—and it is not easy to defend Marx's use of either concept—the theory of exploitation based on them remains comparatively unaffected. The central thesis which made so powerful an appeal to workers, who did not for the most part begin to comprehend the intricacies of Marx's general argument about the relation of exchange value and actual prices, is that there is only one social class, their own, which produces more wealth than it consumes, and that this residue is appropriated by other men simply by virtue of their strategic position as the sole possessors of the means of production, that is, natural resources, machinery, means of transport, financial credit, and so forth, without which the workers cannot create, while control over them gives those who have it the power of starving the rest of mankind into capitulation on their own terms. (pp. 173-76)

Already Fourier, and after him Proudhon, had declaimed against the processes by which the great bankers and manufacturers, by means of their superior resources, tend to eliminate small traders and craftsmen from the economic market, creating a mass of discontented, *déclassé* individuals, who are automatically forced into the ranks of the proletariat. But the capitalist is, in his day, a historical necessity. He extracts surplus value and accumulates; this is indispensable to industrialisation and is history's agency of progress. 'Fanatically bent on increasing value, he ruthlessly forces the human race to produce for the sake of production.' He may do so brutally and for purely selfish motives; but in the course of this 'he creates those material conditions which alone can form the real foundations of a higher form of society, of which the full and free development of every man is the dominant principle'. He had already paid his tribute to the progressive role of industrialisation in the **Communist Manifesto**. 'The bourgeoisie', he wrote, 'cannot exist without constantly revolutionising the instruments of production, and thereby the relations of production and with them the entire relations of society . . . During its rule of scarcely one hundred years, it has created more massive and colossal productive forces than all the earlier generations taken together. Subjection of the forces of nature to man, application of chemistry and industry to agriculture, steam navigation, railways, the electric telegraph, clearing entire continents for cultivation, canalisation of rivers, whole populations conjured up out of the earth—what earlier age had even a presentiment of such gigantic social forces slumbering in the lap of socialised labour?' But the capitalist will have played his part, and will then be superseded. He will be 'liquidated' by his own essential characteristics as an accumulator. Ruthless competition between individual capitalists, seeking to increase the quantity of surplus value, and the natural necessity arising from this of lowering the cost of production and finding new markets, is bound to lead to greater and greater fusion of rival firms, that is to a ceaseless process of amalgamation, until only the largest and most powerful groups are left in existence, all others being forced into a position of dependence or semi-dependence, in the new centralised industrial hierarchy, ruling over a concentration of productive and distributive machinery, which grows, and will continue to grow, faster and faster. Centralisation is a direct product of rationalisation: of increased efficiency in production and transport secured by the pooling of resources, of the formation of great monopolistic trusts and combines which are capable of planned co-ordination. The workers previously scattered among many small enterprises, reinforced by continual influx of the sons and daughters of the ruined small traders and manufacturers, automatically become united into a single, ever-growing, proletarian army by the very processes of integration at work among their masters. Their power as a political and economic body, increasingly conscious of its historical role and resources, grows correspondingly greater. Already trade unions, developing in the shadow of the factory system, represent a far more powerful weapon in the hands of the proletariat than any that existed before. The process of industrial expansion will tend to organise society more and more into the shape of an immense pyramid, with fewer and increasingly powerful capitalists at its summit and a vast, discontented mass of exploited workers and colonial slaves forming its base. The more machinery replaces human labour, the lower the rate of profit is bound to fall, since the rate of 'surplus value' is determined solely by the latter. The struggle between competing capitalists and their countries, which are in effect controlled by them, will grow more deadly, being wedded to a system of unhampered competition, under which each can only survive by overreaching and destroying his rivals. (pp. 177-78)

[Marx did not] allow for the consequences of the growth of state control or democratic resistance, nor the development of political nationalism as a force cutting across and transforming the development of capitalism itself, either as an obstacle to unchecked exploitation or as a bulwark to the gradually impoverished section of the *bourgeoisie,* which would form an alliance with the reaction in its desperate anxiety to avoid its Marxist destiny of falling into the proletariat below it. In other words, he foresees neither Fascism nor the welfare state.

His classification of social strata into the obsolescent military-feudal aristocracy, the industrial *bourgeoisie,* the *petite bourgeoisie,* the proletariat, and that casual riff-raff on the edge of society which he called the *Lumpenproletariat*—a fruitful and original classification for its time—over-simplifies issues when it is too mechanically applied to the twentieth century. A more elaborate instrument is required, if only to deal with the independent behaviour of classes, like the semi-ruined *petite bourgeoisie,* the growing salaried lower middle class, and above all the vast agricultural population, classes which Marx regarded as naturally reactionary, but forced by their growing pauperisation either to sink to the level of the proletariat, or to offer their services as mercenaries to its protagonist, the industrial *bourgeoisie.* The history of post-war Europe, at any rate in the west, requires to be considerably distorted before it can be made to fit this hypothesis.

Marx prophesied that the periodic crises due to the absence of planned economies, and unchecked industrial strife, would necessarily grow more frequent and acute. Wars, on a hitherto unprecedented scale, would ravage the civilised world, until finally the Hegelian contradictions of a system whose continuance depends upon more and more destructive conflicts between its constituent parts would obtain a violent solution. (p. 179)

In a celebrated passage in the twenty-second chapter of the first volume of *Das Kapital* he declared:

While there is a progressive diminution in the number of capitalist magnates, there is of course a corresponding increase in the mass of poverty, enslavement, degeneration and exploitation, but at the same time there is a steady intensification of the role of the working class— a class which grows ever more numerous, and is disciplined, unified and organised by the very mechanism of the capitalist method of production which has flourished with it and under it. The centralisation of the means of production and the socialization of labour reach a point where they prove incompatible with their capitalist husk. This bursts asunder. The knell of private property sounds. The expropriators are expropriated.

The state, the instrument whereby the authority of the ruling class is artificially enforced, having lost its function, will disappear. He had, in the *Communist Manifesto* of 1847-8, and again in 1850 and 1852, made it clear that the state will not vanish immediately: there must occur a period of revolutionary transformation from capitalism to communism. In this transitional period the authority of the state must be preserved, and indeed enforced, but it will now be controlled entirely by the workers, once they have become the dominant class; indeed (to use the formula of one of his later writings), in this first phase of the revolution the state will be 'the revolutionary dictatorship of the proletariat'. In this period, before economic scarcity has been overcome, the reward of the workers must be proportional to the labour they supply. But once the 'all-round development of the individual' has created a society in which 'springs of co-operative wealth flow more abundantly', the communist goal will be reached. Then, and not before, the whole community, painted in colours at once too simple and too fantastic by the Utopians of the past, will at last be realised—a community in which there will be neither master nor slave, neither rich nor poor, in which the world's goods, being produced in accordance with social demand unhampered by the caprice of individuals, will be distributed not indeed equally— a notion so lamely borrowed by the workers from the liberal ideologists with their utilitarian concept of justice as arithmetical equality—but rationally. . . . (pp. 179-80)

The publication of *Das Kapital* had . . . provided a definite intellectual foundation for international socialism in the place of a scattered mass of vaguely defined and conflicting ideas. The interdependence of the historical, economic and political theses preached by Marx and Engels was revealed in this monumental compilation. It became the central objective of attack and defence. All subsequent forms of socialism hereafter defined themselves in terms of their attitude to the position taken in it, and were understood and classified by their resemblance to it. After a brief period of obscurity, its fame began to grow and reached an extraordinary height. It acquired a symbolic significance beyond anything written since the age of faith. It has been blindly worshipped, and blindly hated, by millions who have not read a line of it, or have read without understanding its, at times, obscure and tortuous prose. In its name revolutions were made (and are); counter-revolutions concentrated (and concentrate) upon its suppression as the most potent and insidious of the enemy's weapons. A new social order has been established which professes its principles and sees in it the final and unalterable expression of its faith. It has called into existence an army of interpreters and casuists, whose unceasing labours for nearly a century have buried it beneath a mountain of commentary which has outgrown in influence the sacred text itself.

In Marx's own life it marked a decisive moment. He intended it to be his greatest contribution to the emancipation of humanity, and had sacrificed to it fifteen years of his life and much of his public ambition. The labour which had gone towards it was truely prodigious. For its sake he endured poverty, illness and persecution both public and personal, suffering these not gladly indeed, but with a single-minded stoicism whose strength and harshness both moved and frightened those who came in contact with it. (p. 181)

> Isaiah Berlin, in his Karl Marx: His Life and Environment, *fourth edition, Oxford University Press, Oxford, 1978, 228 p.*

EDMUND WILSON (essay date 1940)

[*Wilson provides an analysis of rhetoric in* Capital, *focusing on its style, imagery, and thematic intent. For additional commentary by Wilson, see the excerpt dated 1932.*]

Karl Marx's great book *Das Kapital* is a unique and complex work, which demands a different kind of analysis from that which it usually gets. At the time when Marx was working on the first volume, he wrote Engels that whatever the shortcomings of his writings might be, they had "the merit of making an artistic whole"; and in his next letter to Engels he speaks of the book as a "'work of art,'" and mentions "artistic considerations" in connection with his delay in getting it finished. Certainly there went into the creation of *Das Kapital* as much of art as of science. The book is a welding-together of several quite diverse points of view, of several quite distinct techniques of thought. It contains a treatise on economics, a history of industrial development and an inspired tract for the times; and the morality, which is part of the time suspended in the interests of scientific objectivity, is no more self-consistent than the economics is consistently scientific or the history undistracted by the exaltation of apocalyptic vision. And outside the whole immense structure, dark and strong like the old Trier basilica, built by the Romans with brick walls and granite columns, swim the mists and the septentrional lights of German metaphysics and mysticism, always ready to leak in through the crevices.

But it is after all the poet in Marx who makes of all these things a whole—that same poet who had already shown his strength in the verses he had written as a student but whose equipment had not been appropriate to the art of romantic verse. Marx's subject is now human history; and that bleak inhuman side of his mind which disconcerts us in his earlier writings has been filled in with mathematics and logic. But it is the power of imagination as well as the cogency of argument which makes *Das Kapital* so compelling.

Let us, then, before we go behind *Das Kapital*, take into account the tremendous effect which it produces on us the first time we read it.

It is characteristic of Marx's work in general that there is more of the Hegelian interplay between opposites than of the Hegelian progression from the lower to the higher about his use of the dialectical method. His writings tend to lack formal development; we find it hard to get hold of a beginning or an end. But this is less true of the first volume of *Das Kapital*, as Marx finally got it into shape, than perhaps of any other of his

productions. Once we have worked through the abstractions of the opening, the book has the momentum of an epic.

It is a vision which fascinates and appals us, which strikes us with a kind of awe, this evolution of mechanical production and of the magnetic accumulation of capital, rising out of the feudal world, with its more primitive but more human handicrafts; wrecking it and overspreading it; accelerating, reorganizing, reassembling, in ever more ingenious complexity, ever more formidable proportions; breaking out of the old boundaries of nations; sending out the tracks and cranes of its commerce across countries and oceans and continents and bringing the people of distant cultures, at diverse stages of civilization, into its system, as it lays hold on the destinies of races, knocks new shapes out of their bodies and their minds, their personalities and their aspirations, without their really grasping what has happened to them and independently of any individual's will. Yet all this development is not merely technological; it is not actually the result of the operation on humanity of a remorseless non-human force. There is also a human principle at work—"those passions which are," as Marx says, "at once the most violent, the basest and the most abominable of which the human breast is capable: the furies of personal interest." For another element of Marx's genius is a peculiar psychological insight: no one has ever had so deadly a sense of the infinite capacity of human nature for remaining oblivious or indifferent to the pains we inflict on others when we have a chance to get something out of them for ourselves.

In dealing with this theme, Karl Marx became one of the great masters of satire. Marx is certainly the greatest ironist since Swift, and he has a good deal in common with him. Compare the logic of Swift's "modest proposal" for curing the misery of Ireland by inducing the starving people to eat their surplus babies with the argument in defense of crime which Marx urges on the bourgeois philosophers (in the so-called fourth volume of *Das Kapital*): crime, he suggests, is produced by the criminal just as "the philosopher produces ideas, the poet verses, the professor manuals," and practising it is useful to society because it takes care of the superfluous population at the same time that putting it down gives employment to many worthy citizens.

Marx has furthermore in common with Swift that he is able to get a certain poetry out of money. There is in Swift a kind of intellectual appetite for computations and accounts and a feeling almost sensuous for currency. In the *Drapier's Letters*, for example, we seem to see the coins, hear them, finger them. But with Marx the idea of money leads to something more philosophic. . . . Marx presents us with a picture of a world in which the commodities command the human beings.

These commodities have their own laws of movement; they seem to revolve in their orbits like electrons. Thus they keep the machinery moving, and they keep the people tending the machines. And the greatest of the commodities is money, because it represents all the others. Marx shows us the metal counters and the bank-notes, mere conventions for facilitating exchange, taking on the fetishistic character which is to make them appear ends in themselves, possessed of a value of their own, then acquiring a potency of their own, which seems to substitute itself for human potency. Marx had stated the whole theme in a sentence of an English speech of 1856: "All our invention and progress seem to result in endowing material forces with intellectual life, and in stultifying human life into a material force." Mankind is caught helpless in a web of wages and profits and credit. Marx's readiness to conjure up these visions of independent and unpetitionable fetishes, which, though inanimate, usurp the rights of the living, is evidently primarily derived from his own deficiency in personal feeling, which he projected into the outside world. Like other great satirists, he punished in others the faults he felt to be dangerous in himself; and it was precisely this blinded and paralyzed side of Karl Marx's peculiar personality which had made it possible for the active and perceptive side to grasp and to explain and to excoriate, as no one else had been able to do, that negation of personal relations, of the responsibility of man to man, that abstract and half-unconscious cruelty, which had afflicted the life of the age.

Marx, to be sure, loves his abstractions, too; he elaborates them at inordinate length. A good deal of this part of *Das Kapital* is gratuitous and simply for show; and one's interest in it is naturally proportionate to one's capacity for enjoying exercises in pure logic. Marx's method does possess a certain beauty: it enables him . . . to make distinctions infinitely subtle—though, if one looks at it the other way round, he may appear to be almost perversely turning concrete industrial processes into the slippery definitions of metaphysics. (Engels used to complain that it was difficult to recognize the historical processes behind the steps of the dialectical argument.) But the chief value of these abstract chapters which alternate with the chapters of history is—in the first volume, at any rate—an ironic one. It is a great trick of Marx's first to hypnotize us by the shuttling back and forth of his syllogisms, to elevate us to the contemplation of what appear to be metaphysical laws; and then, by dropping a single phrase, to sting us back to the realization that these pure economic principles that lend themselves to such elegant demonstration are derived simply from the laws of human selfishness, and that if they may be assumed to operate with such sureness, it is only because the acquisitive instinct is as unfailing as the force of gravitation. The meaning

A portrait of Marx's wife, Jenny von Westphalen.

of the impersonal-looking formulas which Marx produces with so scientific an air is, he reminds us from time to time as if casually, pennies withheld from the worker's pocket, sweat squeezed out of his body, and natural enjoyments denied his soul. In competing with the pundits of economics, Marx has written something in the nature of a parody; and, once we have read *Das Kapital,* the conventional works on economics never seem the same to us again: we can always see through their arguments and figures the realities of the crude human relations which it is their purpose or effect to mask.

For in Marx the exposition of the theory—the dance of commodities, the cross-stitch of logic—is always followed by a documented picture of the capitalist laws at work; and these chapters, with their piling-up of factory reports, their prosaic descriptions of misery and filth, their remorseless enumeration of the abnormal conditions to which the men and women and children of the working class have had to try to adjust themselves, their chronicle of the sordid expedients by which the employers had almost invariably won back, minute by minute and penny by penny, the profits that legislation, itself always inadequate and belated, had tried to shave down a little, and with their specimens of the complacent appeals to morality, religion and reason by which the employers and their economist apologists had had the hypocrisy to justify their practice—these at last become almost intolerable. We feel that we have been taken for the first time through the real structure of our civilization, and that it is the ugliest that has ever existed—a state of things where there is very little to choose between the physical degradation of the workers and the moral degradation of the masters.

From time to time, with telling effect, Marx will light up for a moment the memory of other societies which have been fired by other ideals. The disgrace of the institution of slavery on which the Greek system had been founded had at least, in debasing one set of persons, made possible the development of an aristocracy of marvelous taste and many-sided accomplishment, whereas the masses of the people in the industrial world had been enslaved to no more impressive purpose than "to transform a few vulgar and half-educated upstarts into 'eminent cotton spinners,' 'extensive sausage makers' and 'influential blacking dealers.'" The feudal system of the Middle Ages, before it had been thrown into disorder by the rebellion of the nobles against the king, had at least guaranteed certain rights in return for the discharge of certain duties. Everybody had in some sense been somebody; whereas when the industrial depression occurred and the mill closed its door on the factory worker, neither his employer nor the State was responsible for him. Where the baron had blown in his plunder in such a way as to give his dependents a good time, the great new virtue of the bourgeois was thrift, the saving of money in order to reinvest it. And though Marx has always kept our nose so close to the counting-house and the spindle and the steam hammer and the scutching-mill and the clay-pit and the mine, he always carries with him through the caverns and wastes of the modern industrial world, cold as those abysses of the sea which the mariner of his ballad spurned as godless, the commands of that "eternal God" who equips him with his undeviating standard for judging earthly things.

Something like this is our first impression of *Das Kapital.* It is only later, when we come to think about it coolly and after some further acquaintance with Marx's writings, that its basic inconsistencies become plain.

The most obvious of these is the discrepancy between the scientific point of view of the historian and the moral point of view of the prophet. (pp. 289-94)

On the one hand, Marx is telling you in *Das Kapital* that a certain "historic" development, indispensable for the progress of the race, could only have been carried out by capitalism; and, on the other hand, he is filling you with fury against the wickedness of the people who have performed it. It is as if Darwin had been a kind of Luther Burbank and had caused the blood of his readers to boil over the inadequacies, in the sight of the ideal, of the species produced by evolution and the wrongs of those animals and plants which had been eliminated in the struggle for life. Marx, the scientific historian, declares that the centralization required for socialism could have been provided in no other way than by the competitive processes of capitalism. (p. 295)

We may allow ourselves at first to be persuaded that Marx has somehow provided "scientifically" the turpitude of the capitalist class, that the triumph of the cause of the worker is somehow guaranteed by "economics." There is the Marxist Theory of Surplus Value.

The worker, according to Marx, has sold his capacity to labor like any other commodity on the market; and its value has been determined by the minimum amount required to keep him alive and capable of working and of procreating a fresh supply of workers—which is all the employer has an interest in enabling him to do. The worker, then, is hired for this minimum amount, which is due him for, say, six hours of labor, and is then compelled to work by the employer, on penalty of losing his job, for as long as eight or ten hours. The manufacturer thus robs the worker of from two to four hours of work and sells the product of this work at its value. This value of the stolen work is characterized as "surplus value" and said to constitute the manufacturer's profit. On this the manufacturer grows fat and insolent while the worker is kept down as close as possible to the necessaries of bare subsistence.

Now, certainly the manufacturer, left to himself, will tend to work his labor as hard as possible and to pay them the least possible wages. But what does it actually mean to say that labor determines value?—an idea which Marx had found in embryo in Ricardo and Adam Smith. It was easy to point out many things of which the value was obviously *not* determined by labor: old furniture, old masters, radium; and in the case of manufactured products themselves, it by no means held true that their value on the market was proportionate to the amount of work that had gone into them. It was not true that the profits of a manufacturer who employed a great many workers and spent relatively little on plant was larger than the profit of another manufacturer who spent a great deal on plant and employed relatively little labor—though on Marx's theory it seemed that it should be so. (pp. 295-96)

Marx did not attempt to deal with this problem in the only section of *Das Kapital* he published. The solution was put off till a later volume, which he never lived to complete; and it was not until 1894 that Engels was able to bring out the posthumous section (Volume III) of Marx's manuscript which contained it. It now turned out that Marx had frankly recognized that "as a general rule, profit and surplus value are really two different magnitudes." All profits did come out of surplus value; but the effect of the competition of the capitalists—since the pouring of capital into some lucrative line of industry tended to scale down the rate of profit, while its withdrawal from some less profitable line had the effect of bringing it up—was to level out this rate of profit so that everybody made about the same. The total amount of profit would correspond to the total amount of surplus value; but the individual surplus values had, as it were, been pooled by the individual capitalists, and the profits divided up in such a way that each one got a share which was proportionate to the amount of the capital he had invested. As for the merchant, he did not create value in the same way that the worker did; he merely saved money for the manufacturer in distributing the latter's product and he got a cut out of the latter's surplus value. The people who worked for the merchant did not really create value either; they, too, got a cut out of the manufacturer's profit, but they were cheated out of a part of what they had earned in the same way that the factory workers were cheated by the manufacturer. As for the landlord in capitalist society, he collected *his* cut of the surplus value in the shape of the rent which was paid him by the manufacturer and the merchant. (pp. 296-97)

But in the meantime, for more than a quarter of a century, from 1867 to 1894, the idea that all value was created by labor had been steadily marching on. It had been accepted by Marx's followers as one of the fundamental tenets of their faith, and they had been confidently looking forward to the day when the master would resolve all problems and give the irrefutable reply to their enemies. And now when the third volume of *Das Kapital* came out, even economists sympathetic to Marx expressed disillusion and disappointment.

One is almost inclined to conclude that there may have been something in the contention of the Italian economist Loria, who thought that Marx had never really wanted to face the world with the later developments of his theory but had purposely left it for Engels to deal with them after his death. Certainly the moral effect of the overwhelming first volume of *Das Kapital* is likely to be weakened by an acquaintance with its successors. If all value is created by labor only in some metaphysical sense, then there may be more in those utility theories of value which Marxists regard as capitalist frauds than we had formerly been willing to admit. If it is possible for values to be reckoned as Marx reckoned them, in units of an abstract labor power, why was it not possible—what Marx had denied—to reckon them in units of an abstract utility?—especially when the supposed value of labor seems to have nothing to do with fixing prices, whereas the demand of the consumer obviously has.

But the truth is that all such theories are incomplete: real prices are the results of situations much more complex than any of these formulas, and complicated by psychological factors which economists seldom take into account. The economist tends to imagine that value—and value in the sense of actual prices is easily confused with value in a moral or philosophical sense—is something mainly created by the group to which he belongs or whose apologist he aims to be. . . . Karl Marx, who was not only on the side of the worker but wanted to see him inherit the earth, asserted that all value was created by labor. His effort to support this assertion with a theoretical justification exhibits clearly—it is perhaps the most striking example—the inconsistency in Dialectical Materialism between the tendency to represent everything as relative, every system of economics as an ideology projected by special class interests, and the impulse to establish principles with some more general sort of validity, upon which one's own conduct may be based. (pp. 298-99)

[Let us also] note the crudity of the psychological motivation which underlies the world-view of Marx. It is the shortcoming of economists in general that each one understands as a rule only one or two human motivations: psychology and economics have never yet got together in such a way as really to supplement one another. Marx understood sordid self-interest and its capacity for self-delusion, and he understood the proud human spirit throwing off degradation and oppression. But he tended to regard these as exclusively the products of class specialization rather than as impulses more or less common to humanity which might be expected to show themselves, or to be latent, in people of any class.

Marx would have run up against more complicated questions of the motivation of economic groups if he had gone on with his class anatomy of society. What he shows us in the first volume of *Das Kapital* is always the factory worker immediately confronting the manufacturer, the peasant confronting the landowner; in this section it is always the direct exploiter who is meant when Marx speaks of the capitalist. But in the second and third instalments, which deal with the circulation of capital, Marx must reckon with the tradesmen and the bankers and with what we now call the white-collar class, who work for them; and the picture becomes much more complex. Marx did not, however, get around to discussing the interrelations between these class forces until the very last pages of his manuscript; and it seems significant that of the chapter called "The Classes" he should have written only a page and a half. Modern capitalist society, Marx says here, may be divided into three great classes: "the owners of mere labor-power, the owners of capital, and the landlords, whose respective sources of income are wages, profit and ground-rent." But there are also "middle and transition stages," which "obliterate all definite boundaries." The question is, What constitutes a class? "At first glance, it might seem that the identity of the revenues and of the sources of revenue" of each makes the basis of each of the three great classes. But from this point of view the physicians and the officials would constitute classes, too. (pp. 300-01)

Marx dropped the class analysis of society at the moment when he was approaching its real difficulties.

What Karl Marx, then, had really based his prophecies on . . . was the assumption that, though the employer had always shown himself to be grasping, the socialist worker of the future—having made what Engels describes in *Anti-Dühring* as the "leap from the realm of necessity into the realm of freedom"—would always act for the good of humanity. The dominant class of the capitalist era had never willingly done anything but rob the poor in the interests of the well-being of their own group; but the dominant class of the proletarian dictatorship would never dream of abusing its position.

It ought also to be noted at this point that Marx and Engels had come to believe that there had been an epoch in the prehistoric past when a different standard of morality had prevailed. Since writing the *Communist Manifesto,* they had had occasion to revise their opinion then expressed, that "the history of all human society, past and present, has been the history of class struggles.". . . Marx and Engels now looked back—and thereby nourished their faith in the future—to something in the nature of a Golden Age of communist ownership and brotherly relations. (pp. 301-02)

[There] remained with Marx and Engels, in spite of their priding themselves upon having developed a new socialism that

was "scientific" in contrast to the old "utopian" socialism, a certain amount of this very utopianism they had repudiated.

Let us consider why Marx should have assumed that the morality of the revolutionary proletariat would necessarily be more improving for humanity than the morality of the exploiting bourgeoisie. The moralities which people profess are, according to Marx's theory, inextricably tied up with their class interests; so that there are a morality of the bourgeoisie and a morality of the proletariat, and the two are antagonistic. The morality of the bourgeoisie has had for its purpose to cultivate those virtues which were necessary to build up its own position and to justify the crimes of which it has been guilty in dispossessing and destroying the workers; the morality of the proletariat consists in the loyalty, the self-sacrifice and the courage which will make it possible for it in turn to dispossess and destroy the bourgeoisie. Yet it is *right* for the proletariat to expropriate the bourgeoisie, and even to imprison them and kill them, in some sense in which it has *not* been right for the bourgeoisie to do the same things to them. Why? Because, the Marxist would answer, the proletariat represents the *antithesis,* which, in the course of the dialectical evolution from the lower to the higher, is coming to carry the *thesis* into the *synthesis.* But in what way is the revolutionary morality distinguishably superior to the morality with which it struggles and which it will ultimately supplant?

It is distinguished by its recognition of certain fundamental human rights. Karl Marx in his early writings has had a great deal to say about these rights. Later on, when he is writing *Das Kapital,* he no longer invokes them so explicitly. . . . [Marx] had ridiculed Proudhon for introducing into contemporary economics the eighteenth-century abstraction of a universal natural man endowed with a fundamental right to own property. But Marx himself was to be assuming throughout his life that every human being was entitled to what was described by another exponent of the eighteenth-century philosophy as "life, liberty and the pursuit of happiness." (pp. 303-05)

And now we have got to the real bottom of Marxism—to the assumption that class society is wrong because it destroys, as the *Communist Manifesto* says, the bonds between man and man and prevents the recognition of those rights which are common to all human beings. If no such human rights exist, what is wrong about exploitation? But there is no ultimate way of *proving* they exist any more than there is of proving that in the sight of God all souls are of equal value. You cannot reason an English Tory into a conviction that the lower classes are not unalterably inferior to the upper; and it would be useless to dispute with a Nazi over the innate inferiority of non-Nordics. . . . [Even] with the aid of historical evidence, you cannot necessarily convince people that the progress of human institutions involves a process of progressive democratization: you can only appeal to them by methods which, in the last analysis, are moral and emotional. And this Karl Marx knew magnificently how to do. The great importance of his book is not at all that it establishes an incomparable essence of value inherent in agricultural and factory work, but that it shows in a concrete way how the worker has been misused by the employer and that it makes the reader indignant about this. While Karl Marx is pretending to tell us that all these horrors have advanced human civilization and that all morality is a relative matter, he is really convincing us that a true civilization will be impossible without our putting an end to them and is filling us with fervor for a morality of his own. (pp. 305-06)

Now where does the animus behind *Das Kapital* come from? It is the bitterest of all Marx's bitter books. It has hardly a trace of the exhilaration which gives his earlier work a kind of fire. "Reading your book again," he wrote Engels April 9, 1863—the book was *The Condition of the English Working Class in 1844*—"has sadly made me feel my age. With what freshness and passion and boldness of vision and freedom from learned and scientific scruples you have handled the subject here! And the illusion that tomorrow or the day after tomorrow the result will spring to life as an historical reality before our eyes gives the whole a warm and spirited humor—with which the later 'gray on gray' makes a damnably unpleasant contrast."

But it is not only age which makes the difference between Engels' book and Marx's. It is impossible to read *Das Kapital* in the light of Marx's life during this period without concluding that the emotional motivation, partly or totally unconscious no doubt, behind Marx's excoriation of the capitalists and his grim parading of the afflictions of the poor is at once his outraged conviction of the indignity and injustice of his own fate and his bad conscience at having inflicted that fate on others. Marx himself is not only the victim, the dispossessed proletariat; he is also the exploiting employer.... In a letter to Siegfried Meyer, written April 30, 1867, when he has finally got *Das Kapital* off to the printer, he speaks of it as "the task to which I have sacrificed my health, my happiness in life and my family."

True—as he goes on to say—it has all been done for the ideal and for mankind: "I laugh at the so-called 'practical' men and their wisdom. If one had the hide of an ox, one could naturally turn one's back on the sufferings of humanity and look after one's own skin; but, as it is, I should have considered myself very unpractical if I had died without completing my book, at least in manuscript form." "To work for humanity," says Lafargue, "was one of his favorite phrases." For that science to which one sacrifices others "should not be," as Marx writes elsewhere, "an egoistic pleasure: those who are in a position to devote themselves to scientific studies should be also the first to put their knowledge at the service of humanity."

Yet if you choose to work for humanity, if you will not write for money, why then you must make other people earn it for you or suffer and let others suffer, because you haven't got it.

If it was true . . . that Marx and Engels in relation to one another were like the electrodes of the voltaic cell, it became more and more obvious as time went on that Marx was to play the part of the metal of the positive electrode, which gives out hydrogen and remains unchanged, while Engels was to be the negative electrode, which gradually gets used up. (pp. 308-09)

[The] better times to which Marx looked forward when the first volume of *Das Kapital* was finished, were never really to come. Engels had hoped, as he told him, that his outlook would now become less gloomy. But Marx's poverty and his dependence on others were permanent features of his life; and as their consequences had become more painful, he could only grow more bitter.... [Unlike] certain other aging men, he grew less tolerant instead of more. *Das Kapital* is the reflection of this period. He said that he had written the terrible chapter on the "Working Day" at a time when, as a result of his illness, his head had been too weak for theoretical work; and when he had finally finished this book, he wrote Engels: "I hope that the bourgeoisie as long as they live will have cause to remember my carbuncles." Thus, in attacking the industrial system, he is at the same time declaring his own tribulations, calling the Heavens—that is, History—to witness that he is a

just man wronged, and damning the hypocritical scoundrel who compels others to slave and suffer for him, who persists in remaining indifferent to the agony for which he is responsible, who even keeps himself in ignorance of it. The book has behind it the exalted purpose, it is a part of the noble accomplishment, of Karl Marx's devoted life; but the wrong and the hurt of that life have made the whole picture hateful or grievous. The lofty devotion and the wrong are inextricably involved with one another; and the more he asserts the will of his highest impulses, the blacker the situation becomes.

Marx may appear to have kept the two things apart when he has set the bad capitalist on one side and the good communist of the future on the other; but, after all, to arrive at that future, the communist must be cruel and repressive just as the capitalist has been; he, too, must do violence to that common humanity in whose service the prophet is supposed to be preaching. It is a serious misrepresentation of Marx to minimize the sadistic element in his writing. In his address to the Communist League of April, 1850, he had declared to the revolutionary working class that, "far from opposing so-called excesses, the vengeance of the people on hated individuals or attacks by the masses on buildings which arouse hateful memories, we must not only tolerate them, but even take the lead in them." Nor was this . . . a tendency which he reserved for politics. (pp. 312-13)

If we isolate the images in Marx—which are so powerful and vivid in themselves that they can sometimes persuade us to forget his lack of realistic observation and almost produce the illusion of a visible and tangible experience—if we isolate and examine these images, we can see through to the inner obsessions at the heart of the world-vision of Marx.

Here all is cruel discomfort, rape, repression, mutilation and massacre, premature burial, the stalking of corpses, the vampire that lives on another's blood, life in death and death in life:

> The Abbé Bonawita Blank . . . operated on magpies and starlings in such a way that, though they were free to fly about as they pleased, they would always come back to him again. He cut off the lower part of their beaks so that they were not able to get their food themselves and so were obliged to eat from his hand. The good little bourgeois who looked on from a distance and saw the birds perched on the shoulders of the good priest and apparently dining with him in a friendly fashion, admired his culture and his science. His biographer says that the birds loved him as their benefactor. And the Poles, enchained, mutilated, branded, refuse to love their Prussian benefactors!
>
> (pp. 313-14)

There is a German expression "*lasten wie ein Alp*," which means something like "weigh like an incubus," to which Marx was very much addicted. We find it on the first page of *The Eighteenth Brumaire*, where he says that, "The tradition of all the dead generations weighs like an incubus on the brain of the living." We [see] it in the letter . . . in which he tells Engels that the injury to his friend's career for which he feels himself responsible has weighed like an incubus on his conscience; and he had written to the Countess Hatzfeldt after Lassalle's death that this event—in a similar phrase—had weighted upon him "like a hideous and evil dream." In writing about *Das Kapital* to Engels, he says that the task weighs upon him like an incubus; and he complains that the Workers' International "and everything that it involves . . . weighs like an incubus on me, and I'd be glad to be able to shake it off." It is always the same oppression, whether Marx has objectified it and generalized it as the oppression of the living by the dead or felt it personally as his own oppression under the conviction of his own guilt or under the greatest of his own achievements. It is always the same wound, as to which it is never quite clear— as in the case of the Dialectic, which is now a fundamental truth of nature, now an action performed by human agents, as in the case of the development of the capitalist economy, which is now an inevitable and non-moral process, now the blackest of human crimes—whether the gods have inflicted it on man or man has inflicted it on himself. It is always the same burial alive, whether it is the past trying to stifle the present or the future putting away the past. (pp. 315-16)

Such is the trauma of which the anguish and the defiance reverberate through *Das Kapital.* To point it out is not to detract from the authority of Marx's work. On the contrary, in history as in other fields of writing, the importance of a book depends, not merely on the breadth of the view and the amount of information that has gone into it, but on the depths from which it has been drawn. The great crucial books of human thought— outside what are called the exact sciences, and perhaps something of the sort is true even here—always render articulate the results of fundamental new experiences to which human beings have had to adjust themselves. *Das Kapital* is such a book. Marx has found in his personal experience the key to the larger experience of society, and identifies himself with that society. His trauma reflects itself in *Das Kapital* as the trauma of mankind under industrialism; and only so sore and angry a spirit, so ill at ease in the world, could have recognized and seen into the causes of the whole-sale mutilation of humanity, the grim collisions, the uncomprehended convulsions, to which that age of great profits was doomed. (p. 317)

> Edmund Wilson, "Karl Marx: Poet of Commodities and Dictator of the Proletariat," in his To the Finland Station: A Study in the Writing and Acting of History, 1940. Reprint by Doubleday & Company, Inc., 1953, pp. 289-329.

JACQUES BARZUN (essay date 1941)

[*Barzun is a French-born American man of letters who has produced distinguished works in various fields, including history, culture, musicology, literary criticism, and biography. Among his important studies are* Darwin, Marx, Wagner, The House of the Intellect, Berlioz and the Romantic Century, *and* A Stroll with William James. *Barzun's style, both literary and intellectual, has been praised as elegant and unpretentious. In the following excerpt, Barzun evaluates Marx's ideas about class warfare, pointing out that in his scientific orientation, "Marx fell in line with all the cultural forces of his age and fastened his grip on the future."*]

Just as Marx's gift to sociology has been the materialistic conception of history, so his message to the masses has been the idea of the Class War. The *Communist Manifesto* of 1848 has remained for all popular and practical purposes the chief, the only, embodiment of Marx's thought. Overcharged with theory though it is in parts, its effective "nonscientific" rhetoric about struggle, chains, and the need of banding together to cast them off has proved to be the true "People's Marx." . . . *Capital* may still be called the Bible of the Working Class, but it is a

Bible that is seldom opened, being, like many a book of Revelations, too symbolical to apply.

Similarly, from the rest of the Marx-Engels writings, only what fits the simple idea of class war could help active socialists. The bare words "exploitation," "surplus value," "capitalist system," "labor-source-of-all-value," were enough by themselves to supply texts for inflammatory speeches and arouse proletarians to the meaning of their experience. In an age of social Darwinism, the combination of the ideas of struggle, of historical evolution and of progress, proved irresistible. The Marxists became simply a sect in the larger church, a sect whose special tenets ran somewhat as follows: The struggle for life is universal; human history shows that progress comes from the conflict of classes; since your masters exploit you, you are bound to fight them; if you do not, resistless evolution will take its course and leave you behind in its wreckage. Hence you must gird your loins and help bring it about, for the fight is to the strong and the race to the swift; and you are both, because, independently of your individual wills, the next stage in history is the abolition of capital ownership and the dominance of the proletariat. Workers of the world, unite! You have nothing to lose but your chains!

In urging these lessons, Marx and Engels set the pattern of all subsequent Marxist polemics by using what may be called the evolutionist's double standard: When you do it, it's wrong, because you are the past; when we do it, it's right, for we are the future. The mood—borrowed from science—is that of a mighty ruthlessness. History, like nature, is "tough." Thus, "during the conflict and right after the battle, the workers must to the fullest extent possible work against the bourgeois measures of pacification, and compel the democrats to carry into action their present terroristic phrases. They must work to prevent the immediate revolutionary excitement from being promptly suppressed after the victory. They must keep it going as long as possible. Far from setting themselves against so-called excesses, examples of popular revenge against hated individuals or public buildings with only hateful memories attached to them, they must not only tolerate these examples but take in hand their very leadership." At the same time, dealing with the Commune and looking back to the June Days of 1848, Engels wrote: "It was the first time that the bourgeoisie showed to what a mad ferocity of vengeance it can be stirred up, so soon as the proletariat dares to stand up against it as a separate class with its own interests and demands."

Marx wanted the proletariat to outdo the enemies in "mad ferocity," and then to build the new order which would end all class wars. But when the leaders of a revolution begin by sowing suspicion of mankind and imputing dastardly motives to an enemy whom they have just proved to be historically determined in his acts, they must expect the return of the boomerang sooner or later and be themselves ready to face the firing squad or the assassin's knife. That is to say, they must carry on a new class war for their own skins, now identified with the evolution of history.

As an historian of revolutions and *coups d'état,* Marx must have known this. One wonders, therefore, by what secret mechanism he expected that in *this* case men goaded to destruction and sadism would settle down into artisans of peace and order. His optimism ("Force is the midwife of Progress") tided him over the difficulty. The only guide to constructive action which he offers is, as we know, the ten points of the *Communist Manifesto,* revised, of course, in the light of changed conditions. The proletariat, having wreaked its vengeance on the exploiting classes, goes back upon its tracks and dispossesses them little by little through nationalization, the abolition of inheritance, and so forth. Nowhere does Marx's imaginative weakness and inconsequence appear more clearly than in this surrealist mixing of bloody revolution with reformism. The reform is carried out, to be sure, by a dictatorship of the proletariat, but here again we are never told whether it comprises the whole working class acting through democratic elections or only the compact minority of ruthless leaders who have just led the rest to final victory.

Meantime of course, the idea of class war is clear and simple enough to fit the obvious facts of life in a world of rich and poor. Mr. H. G. Wells, who never was a Marxist doctrinaire, who, on the contrary, finds Marx his *bête noire,* has given an excellent account of the state of feeling to which Marx in his popular incarnation appealed. "There would have been Marxists," says Wells, "if Marx had never lived. When I was a boy of fourteen I was a complete Marxist, long before I had heard of Marx. I had been cut off from education, caught in a detestable shop, and I was being broken in to a life of mean and dreary toil. I was worked too hard and for such long hours that all thoughts of self-improvement seemed hopeless. I would have set fire to the place if I had not been convinced it was over-insured."

Such a state of mind, born of economic exploitation, should indeed have made Marxists at the rate of mass production. The trouble was that when Utopia through fighting is preached to people whose condition inspires revolt, the result is not two groups of which one is the historically elect, but rather fifty groups of which none has any real chance of exterminating the rest in due theoretical form. Even in theory, Marx and Engels had to introduce distinctions in order to preserve the face-to-face antagonism of two classes from denial by facts. Besides the real proletariat they discerned a *Lumpenproletariat,* or rabble; and besides the real bourgeoisie, a petty bourgeoisie. Hence the need of propaganda to make all but the bourgeoisie, which is so by nature, class-conscious. And since the conflict between these two ultimate groups still leaves the peasants out of account, Marx is obliged to borrow an idea from that eminent bourgeois Macaulay, who had said that the middle class was the natural representative of the general interest. Marx merely changes the terms and says of the working classes that they are the "natural trustees" of the peasant interest. The principle of each class for itself, determined to war by its economic condition, has to be eked out with propaganda urging group solidarity and with mutual trust between two classes, one of which ceases to behave as a class and acts for another.

The result of this contradiction in practical politics is energy wasted in quibbles over dogma and the consequent splitting up of revolutionary parties over purity of intention and belief. You then find socialists and communists of every hue, some calling themselves nationalists, some racialists, some possibilitists, others anarchists or syndicalists, each group believing itself the only true embodiment of the future and each, in virtue of its own supreme principle, subdividing itself into a fine dust of agitated particles, ready to annihilate all the others if it could only find a point of vantage in the chaotic whirl. The small band of "self-appointed saviors" emerges by a process of Natural Selection which itself inspires an endless struggle for survival. The tactics by which Marx triumphed over Bakunin and Proudhon, by which later Lenin became head of the Bolshevik Party, and by which Stalin overthrew Trotsky, have indeed produced powerful survivors, but it would be hard to

show wherein the process differs from bourgeois politics, and how it produces any greater fitness for organizing, governing, and improving mankind.

Until late into the nineteenth century the Marxian socialists, even with converted Anarchists added, remained without influence on the masses of the European population. A good many intellectuals, particularly the Russian victims of Czarist oppression, like Lenin, Stalin, and others, found relief in the promise of wholesale and speedy revenge which Marx's creed held out to them. It is not for those who did not suffer their wrongs to judge them. But other intellectuals who seemed to adopt violence as a tonic—in complete ignorance of its effects—were really not contemplated in Marx's theory as forming anything more than the initial guides of a deep and resistless movement from below. And this movement predicted by Marx never manifested itself anywhere at any time under the banner of strict Marxism.

The truth is that the spread of socialism as a doctrine in prewar Europe was no more due to Marx's direct political efforts than to the persuasiveness of his abstractions. It was the followers of Proudhon, Louis Blanc, and Bakunin who, with a handful of Marxists, formed the First International. But if anyone can claim as his own handiwork the transformation of modern socialist ideas into a truly popular movement, it is the much-reviled Ferdinand Lassalle. It is usual nowadays to belittle his role in German history and to depreciate his mind and character. Marx, who could not bear rivalry, started the fashion. He always referred to Lassalle opprobriously and called him the Jewish Nigger. Except for the religious and social background which they had in common, Lassalle was everything that Marx was not—a scholar, an artist, and a man in whom, despite appearances, logic and enthusiasm combined with a rare degree of balance. He was above all a born leader of men and a natural master of politics. At the age of thirty-nine, after two years' campaigning, he had built up in the teeth of opposition by the government, the industrialists, and the humanitarian liberals, a German Workers' Party. In those two years of indefatigable activity—1862-1864—he spoke to thousands throughout the Germanies, he published twenty volumes, large and small, on political and social questions, carried on an enormous correspondence, and organized "sections" wherever his pen or his person could reach. His force, magnetism, ingenuity, oratorical power, knowledge of people and of history, were lavishly expended in a way ruinous to his health, but which created what had never existed before: a party of the Fourth Estate growing almost simultaneously with the industrialization of a great European power. It was this party which a decade after Lassalle's death joined the Marx-controlled International to form the great German Social Democratic Party. (pp. 202-09)

[Marx and Engels] kept an aloof silence while he spent his strength and resources upon the task. Lassalle dead, they collected the fruits of his labors and expressed their relief at his removal by insulting his memory and accusing him of plagiarism. Meanwhile the youth of the united Social-Democratic Party comforted Marx's last years—for he looked upon it as his handiwork—as well as those of his wife, who naturally shared that agreeable assumption.

The error of perspective in this picture is that the "Great Social-Democratic Party" which forced Bismarck and his successors to steal so much of its thunder worked presumably in the name of Marx, but actually on Lassallean principles. It was national, for, as Lassalle perceived, a German national state was the first demand of all Germans after the failure to unify in 1848, nor could economic problems be handled otherwise than nationally in the European system of sovereign states. It was political and not revolutionary, for the German working class wanted tangible benefits together with security of life and limb—another lesson remembered from 1848; and lastly, it always tended away from Marx's theoretical materialism to Lassalle's practical idealism. As a political party doing a political business, it could not overlook the part of mind and theory in action, and its leaders very soon replaced Marxian materialism by a neo-Kantian philosophy which Lenin was later to attack. Meanwhile, what remained of Marxian fatalism was throughout a hindrance to its natural development, and even contributed to its final downfall before the active anti-determinism of Hitler. (pp. 209-10)

As for Lassalle's plagiarism from Marx, the accusation comes malapropos from the upholders of a doctrine which combines none too harmoniously a collection of insights borrowed from others. Lassalle was seven years younger than Marx, but he had been brought up in the same Hegelian school of thought and had, independently of all Marxian influence, taken a somewhat similar path. When Marx published the stillborn *Critique of Political Economy* in 1859, Lassalle was giving to the world his extraordinary study of Heraclitus the Obscure. Lassalle's concern with the Greek philosopher who reduced the whole world to the motion of particles marks the practical materialistic tendency of the decade. But unlike Marx, Lassalle did not let materialism obscure the Hegelian insight into the function of mind. All three—Hegel, Marx, and Lassalle—stressed the historical mode of treating all social questions. But the dialectical process was not for Lassalle a piece of machinery embedded in history. It seemed to him rather the natural way of conceiving motion and change. Fully as early as Marx, he stressed the social and practical origins of legal systems and constitutions, but faithful to Hegelian thought, he never supposed that they were mere offprints of a self-existing material reality. "Long before barricades can be raised in the outer world," he told the Court of Assize in 1848, "the citizen in the world of mind must have dug the pit which will swallow up the forms of government." Consciousness was a logical and necessary part of his sociology, not an embarrassing illusion as in Marx.

Whether in the courtroom or on the platform, Lassalle's studies in law, history, government, and philosophy made him a formidable debater, but they appear at their fullest and maturest in his written works. In strong contrast to Marx's crabbed polemics and tortuous erudition, everything in Lassalle is lucid, generous, and orderly. There is but little oversimplification, yet simplicity is the result, unmarred by any attempt at original profundity if it happens that at this point he is neither original nor profound. In economics, Lassalle accepts the classical labor theory of value as reinterpreted by Rodbertus, and when borrowing from Marx the doctrine of surplus value to explain the formation of capital, he is careful to make full acknowledgment.

For the rest, Lassalle draws on the same general fund of socialist ideas which we know to be due in the first instance, not to Marx, but to Fourier, Saint-Simon, Hess, Sismondi, and other socialists of the first half of the century. The conclusion so often insinuated, that Lassalle was a hasty and incomplete popularizer of Marx, is thus groundless. And the even more plausible view that he was a forerunner of modern fascism overlooks his essentially aristocratic and artistic nature. Had he remained what he was, he might indeed have accepted for the benefit of the German workers a broader paternalism than Bismarck's; or he might have helped to establish an equalitarian

state based on universal manhood suffrage—a demand which he pressed from the very beginning—but he would never, one can safely surmise, have been a party to any anti-intellectual, lower-middle-class, boasting-and-cringing uniformitarian dictatorship whose use of socialist doctrine is to destroy above and below, warring on the aristocracy of talent and continuing to enslave the proletariat. (pp. 211-13)

[It can be said that the] failure of Marxism between 1890 and 1914 was due to the inherent sheeplikeness of men. But then what becomes of the inevitable evolution of history based on class antagonisms? Marx reserved the sheeplike qualities exclusively for the Christian bourgeoisie and made fun of its traditional religious symbol—the Lamb of God. The proletariat on the contrary was supposed to be fierce, atheistical, heroic, long-suffering, and infallible. It would not hesitate to strike when the hour itself had struck. Yet it did nothing of the kind.

The fact was that although popular Marxism sounded very much in tune with the Darwinian struggle for life, it overlooked two things. One, the irreducibly individual character of this struggle insofar as it exists, which means an unwillingness to risk life until the collective victory is reasonably sure; the other, the inheritance, by tradition, of a hundred different forms of association other than class. The scientific farmer joined cooperatives and made politics serve his needs. The backward peasant stuck to his wooden plow and hated the city laborer; the city laborer stuck to his bottle of gin and refused to be the heroic artisan of the future; the active, the intelligent, the political-minded among the workers, joined trade-unions and political parties that would give them immediate concrete benefits through social legislation—shorter hours and more pay—the materialistic conception of history expressed in consumers' goods. The religiously inclined followed the lead of their churches, all of them engaged in social betterment of one kind or another.

Moreover, as voting citizens who had been educated at public expense, and who were more and more sedulously courted by politicians, peasant and proletarian began to take an increasing interest in national destinies. Nationalism and imperialism became intense passions which the new yellow press was not slow to exploit and to satisfy. Fed on vicarious prestige, diplomacy, and power politics, the new masses often outstripped their leaders and did as much to foster the "New Imperialism" and the race for armaments as the sinister economic influences tending in the same direction. To these forms of partisanship, racialism lent a pseudo-scientific aura, its doctrines seemingly borne out by plain facts whenever war or the competition of cheap foreign labor piled its burdens upon existing evils of more local origin.

Whichever way the late nineteenth-century world is examined, Marx's single proletarian class waging a single combat against its hereditary enemy appears as a dimmer and dimmer abstraction. It was an idea which might have come true, if the masses who were to form the class and wage the war had been simply and directly taught by a leader of genius, very different in mind and temperament from the propounder of the theory: or again if the masses had remained illiterate as they were in 1850, or if, desperate and religiously inspired, they had had faith enough in progress through the Martyrdom of Man to sacrifice themselves and the present benefits of unionized bargaining to the Marxist Utopia; or if, getting poorer and poorer instead of becoming in so many cases "petty bourgeois" of the most unrepentant kind, they had begun a slave revolt against a mere handful of plutocrats.

Since none of these things happened, we are obviously left with too many if's for any one theory to withstand. Marx had without a doubt crushed Utopian socialism, he had poured scorn on the principle of co-operation to the right of him and on the anarchical ideal to the left; he ultimately had his name, his catchwords, his picture, and his books widely circulated among the political groups concerned with improving the lot of the worker. But neither the lightening of class bonds nor the concentration of capital in a few hands, nor international unions across frontiers, nor the "next step" in historical evolution, came as he predicted it, where he predicted it, or for the good of those to whom he predicted it. The hopeless splitting up of international socialism at the outbreak of the war of 1914; the occurrence of the communist revolution, not in Germany where it belonged, but in Russia, where a conspiratorial group of Marxian type, relying more on "ideas" than on "conditions," rose to dictatorship over an overwhelming agrarian country; finally, the mystical-nationalist form of "the revolution" in Germany and Italy—are as many witnesses to the failure of popular Marxism.

One thing only did Marx contribute to the revolt of the masses in our century. In insisting upon group violence for alleged economic ends under the aegis of complex and would-be scientific theories, Marx fell in line with all the cultural forces of his age and fastened his grip on the future. But this means that like many another religious success, his has been that of temperament expressed through scattered aphorisms, and not the working out of predictions based on scientific system. (pp. 213-16)

> *Jacques Barzun, "The Social Revolution: The People's Marx," in his* Darwin, Marx, Wagner: Critique of a Heritage, *Little, Brown and Company, 1941, pp. 202-16.*

BERTRAND RUSSELL (essay date 1945)

[*A respected and prolific author, Russell was an English philosopher and mathematician known for his support of humanistic concerns. In the following excerpt, he evaluates Marx as a philosopher.*]

Karl Marx is usually thought of as the man who claimed to have made Socialism scientific, and who did more than any one else to create the powerful movement which, by attraction and repulsion, has dominated the recent history of Europe. . . . [As a philosopher], he is difficult to classify. In one aspect, he is an outcome, like Hodgskin, of the Philosophical Radicals, continuing their rationalism and their opposition to the romantics. In another aspect he is a revivifier of materialism, giving it a new interpretation and a new connection with human history. In yet another aspect he is the last of the great system-builders, the successor of Hegel, a believer, like him, in a rational formula summing up the evolution of mankind. (p. 782)

Marx, like Bentham and James Mill, will have nothing to do with romanticism; it is always his intention to be scientific. His economics is an outcome of British classical economics, changing only the motive force. Classical economists, consciously or unconsciously, aimed at the welfare of the capitalist, as opposed both to the landowner and to the wage-earner; Marx, on the contrary, set to work to represent the interest of the wage-earner. He had in youth—as appears in the **Communist Manifesto** of 1848—the fire and passion appropriate to a new revolutionary movement, as liberalism had had in the

time of Milton. But he was always anxious to appeal to evidence, and never relied upon any extra-scientific intuition.

He called himself a materialist, but not of the eighteenth-century sort. His sort, which, under Hegelian influence, he called "dialectical," differed in an important way from traditional materialism, and was more akin to what is now called instrumentalism. The older materialism, he said, mistakenly regarded sensation as passive, and thus attributed activity primarily to the object. In Marx's view, all sensation or perception is an interaction between subject and object; the bare object, apart from the activity of the percipient, is a mere raw material, which is transformed in the process of becoming known. Knowledge in the old sense of passive contemplation is an unreal abstraction; the process that really takes place is one of *handling* things. "The question whether objective truth belongs to human thinking is not a question of theory, but a practical question," he says. "The truth, i.e., the reality and power, of thought must be demonstrated in practice. The contest as to the reality or non-reality of a thought which is isolated from practice, is a purely scholastic question. . . . Philosophers have only *interpreted* the world in various ways but the real task is to *alter* it."

I think we may interpret Marx as meaning that the process which philosophers have called the pursuit of knowledge is not, as has been thought, one in which the object is constant while all the adaptation is on the part of the knower. On the contrary, both subject and object, both the knower and the thing known, are in a continual process of mutual adaptation. He calls the process "dialectical" because it is never fully completed.

It is essential to this theory to deny the reality of "sensation" as conceived by British empiricists. What happens, when it is most nearly what they mean by "sensation," would be better called "noticing," which implies activity. In fact—so Marx would contend—we only notice things as part of the process of acting with reference to them, and any theory which leaves out action is a misleading abstraction.

So far as I know, Marx was the first philosopher who criticized the notion of "truth" from this activist point of view. In him this criticism was not much emphasized, and I shall therefore say no more about it here, leaving the examination of the theory to a later chapter.

Marx's philosophy of history is a blend of Hegel and British economics. Like Hegel, he thinks that the world develops according to a dialectical formula, but he totally disagrees with Hegel as to the motive force of this development. Hegel believed in a mystical entity called "Spirit," which causes human history to develop according to the stages of the dialectic as set forth in Hegel's *Logic*. Why Spirit has to go through these stages is not clear. One is tempted to suppose that Spirit is trying to understand Hegel, and at each stage rashly objectifies what it has been reading. Marx's dialectic has none of this quality except a certain inevitableness. For Marx, matter, not spirit is the driving force. But it is matter in the peculiar sense that we have been considering, not the wholly dehumanized matter of the atomists. This means that, for Marx, the driving force is really man's relation to matter, of which the most important part is his mode of production. In this way Marx's materialism, in practice, becomes economics.

The politics, religion, philosophy, and art of any epoch in human history are, according to Marx, an outcome of its methods of production, and, to a lesser extent, of distribution. I think he would not maintain that this applies to all the niceties of culture, but only to its broad outlines. The doctrine is called the "materialist conception of history." This is a very important thesis; in particular, it concerns the historian of philosophy. I do not myself accept the thesis as it stands, but I think that it contains very important elements of truth, and I am aware that it has influenced my own views of philosophical development as set forth in the present work. Let us, to begin with, consider the history of philosophy in relation to Marx's doctrine.

Subjectively, every philosopher appears to himself to be engaged in the pursuit of something which may be called "truth." Philosophers may differ as the definition of "truth," but at any rate it is something objective, something which, in some sense, everybody ought to accept. No man would engage in the pursuit of philosophy if he thought that *all* philosophy is *merely* an expression of irrational bias. But every philosopher will agree that many other philosophers have been actuated by bias, and have had extra-rational reasons, of which they were usually unconscious, for many of their opinions. Marx, like the rest, believes in the truth of his own doctrines; he does not regard them as nothing but an expression of the feelings natural to a rebellious middle-class German Jew in the middle of the nineteenth century. What can be said about this conflict between the subjective and objective views of a philosophy?

We may say, in a broad way, that Greek philosophy down to Aristotle expresses the mentality appropriate to the City State; that Stoicism is appropriate to a cosmopolitan despotism; that scholastic philosophy is an intellectual expression of the Church as an organization; that philosophy since Descartes, or at any rate since Locke, tends to embody the prejudices of the commercial middle class; and that Marxism and Fascism are philosophies appropriate to the modern industrial State. This, I think, is both true and important. I think, however, that Marx is wrong in two respects. First, the social circumstances of which account must be taken are quite as much political as economic; they have to do with power, of which wealth is only one form. Second, social causation largely ceases to apply as soon as a problem becomes detailed and technical. (pp. 783-86)

What is conventionally called "philosophy" consists of two very different elements. On the one hand, there are questions which are scientific or logical; these are amenable to methods as to which there is general agreement. On the other hand, there are questions of passionate interest to large numbers of people, as to which there is no solid evidence either way. Among the latter are practical questions, as to which it is impossible to remain aloof. When there is a war, I must support my own country or come into painful conflict both with friends and with the authorities. At many times there has been no middle course between supporting and opposing the official religion. For one reason or another, we all find it impossible to maintain an attitude of sceptical detachment on many issues as to which pure reason is silent. A "philosophy," in a very usual sense of the word, is an organic whole of such extra-rational decisions. It is in regard to "philosophy" in this sense that Marx's contention is largely true. But even in this sense a philosophy is determined by other social causes as well as by those that are economic. War, especially, has its share in historical causation; and victory in war does not always go to the side with the greatest economic resources.

Marx fitted his philosophy of history into a mould suggested by Hegelian dialectic, but in fact there was only one triad that concerned him: feudalism, represented by the landowner; capitalism, represented by the industrial employer; and Socialism, represented by the wage-earner. Hegel thought of nations as the vehicles of dialectic movement; Marx substituted classes. He disclaimed always all ethical or humanitarian reasons for preferring Socialism or taking the side of the wage-earner; he maintained, not that this side was ethically better, but that it was the side taken by the dialectic in its wholly deterministic movement. He might have said that he did not advocate Socialism, but only prophesied it. This, however, would not have been wholly true. He undoubtedly believed every dialectical movement to be, in some impersonal sense, a progress, and he certainly held that Socialism, once established, would minister to human happiness more than either feudalism or capitalism have done. These beliefs, though they must have controlled his life, remained largely in the background so far as his writings are concerned. Occasionally, however, he abandons calm prophecy for vigorous exhortation to rebellion, and the emotional basis of his ostensibly scientific prognostications is implicit in all he wrote.

Considered purely as a philosopher, Marx has grave shortcomings. He is too practical, too much wrapped up in the problems of his time. His purview is confined to this planet, and, within this planet, to Man. Since Copernicus, it has been evident that Man has not the cosmic importance which he formerly arrogated to himself. No man who has failed to assimilate this fact has a right to call his philosophy scientific.

There goes with this limitation to terrestrial affairs a readiness to believe in progress as a universal law. This readiness characterized the nineteenth century, and existed in Marx as much as in his contemporaries. It is only because of the belief in the inevitability of progress that Marx thought it possible to dispense with ethical considerations. If Socialism was coming, it must be an improvement. He would have readily admitted that it would not seem to be an improvement to landowners or capitalists, but that only showed that they were out of harmony with the dialectic movement of the time. Marx professed himself an atheist, but retained a cosmic optimism which only theism could justify.

Broadly speaking, all the elements in Marx's philosophy which are derived from Hegel are unscientific, in the sense that there is no reason whatever to suppose them true.

Perhaps the philosophic dress that Marx gave to his Socialism had really not much to do with the basis of his opinions. It is easy to restate the most important part of what he had to say without any reference to the dialectic. He was impressed by the appalling cruelty of the industrial system as it existed in England a hundred years ago, which he came to know thoroughly through Engels and the reports of Royal Commissions. He saw that the system was likely to develop from free competition towards monopoly, and that its injustice must produce a movement of revolt in the proletariat. He held that, in a thoroughly industrialized community, the only alternative to private capitalism is State ownership of land and capital. None of these propositions are matters for philosophy, and I shall therefore not consider their truth or falsehood. The point is that, if true, they suffice to establish what is practically important in his system. The Hegelian trappings might therefore be dropped with advantage. (pp. 787-89)

[There] are certain respects in which the rationalism of Marx is subject to limitations. Although he holds that his interpretation of the trend of development is true, and will be borne out by events, he believes that the argument will only appeal (apart from rare exceptions) to those whose class interest is in agreement with it. He hopes little from persuasion, everything from the class war. He is thus committed in practice to power politics, and to the doctrine of a master class, though not of a master race. (p. 790)

Bertrand Russell, "Karl Marx," in his A History of Western Philosophy, and Its Connection with Political and Social Circumstances from the Earliest Times to the Present Day, *Simon & Schuster, 1945, pp. 782-90.*

MARTIN BUBER   (essay date 1946)

[*Buber was an important Austrian-born Israeli religious philosopher, best known to theologians for his influential* I and Thou. *In the following excerpt from a work first published in 1946, Buber examines Marx's stance toward Utopian Socialism as it is reflected in his reactions to the Paris Commune, a proposed form of government for France.*]

Right from his earliest socialistic formulations up to the full maturity of his thought Marx conceived the end in a way that comes very close to "utopian" Socialism. As early as in August, 1844, he was writing: "Revolution as such—the overthrow of existing power and the dissolution of the old conditions—is a political act. But without Revolution socialism cannot carry on. Socialism needs this political act in so far as it needs destruction and dissolution. But when its organizing activity begins, when its ultimate purpose, its soul emerges, socialism will throw the political husk away." We must read this in conjunction with the following passage written earlier on in the same year: "Only when man has recognized and organized his 'forces propres' as *social* forces [it is therefore not necessary, as Rousseau thinks, to change man's nature, to deprive him of his 'forces propres' and give him new ones of a social character] and, consequently, no longer cuts off his social power from himself in the form of political power [i.e. no longer establishes the State as the sphere of organized rule] only then will the emancipation of mankind be achieved." Since Marx is known even in his early days to have regarded politics as obviously nothing but the expression and elaboration of class-rule, politics must accordingly be abolished with the abolition of the latter: the man who is no longer "sundered from his fellow-man and from the community" is no longer a political being. This, however, is not regarded as the first consequence of some post-revolutionary development. Rather, as is clearly stated in both the above passages, Revolution as such, i.e. Revolution in its purely negative, "dissolvent" capacity, is the last political act. As soon as the organizing activity begins on the terrain prepared by the overthrow, as soon as the positive function of socialism starts, the political principle will be superseded by the social. The sphere in which this function is exercised is no longer the sphere of the political rulership of man by man. Marx's dialectical formulation leaves no doubt as to what the sequence of events actually is in his opinion: first the political act of *social* revolution will annihilate not merely the Class State, but the State as a power-formation altogether, whereas the *political* revolution was the very thing that "constituted the state as a public concern, that is, as the real State". On the other hand, "the organizing activity" will begin, i.e. the reconstruction of society, only after the complete overthrow of existing power—whatever organizing activity preceded the Revolution was only organization for the struggle. From this we can see with the greatest clarity what it is that connects Marx with "utopian" socialism: the will to supersede the political principle by the social principle, and what divides

him from it: his opinion that this supersession can be effected by exclusively political means—hence by way of sheer suicide, so to speak, on the part of the political principle.

This opinion is rooted deep in Marx's dialectical view of history, which found classical formulation fifteen years later in the preface to his book *A Critique of Political Economy.*

Yet, in the concluding section of his polemic against Proudhon, we encounter what appears to be a not inconsiderable limitation. "The working-class," he says, "will, in the course of its development (dans le cours de son développement), replace the old bourgeois society by an association which will exclude classes and their antagonisms, and there will no longer be any political power in its proper sense (il n'y aura plus de pouvoir politique, proprement dit), since political power is nothing but the official sum (le résumé officiel) of the antagonisms obtaining in bourgeois society." "No political power in its proper sense"—that means: no political power in the sense of an expression and elaboration of class-rule, which is quite self-evident if class-rule really has been abolished. Let us leave aside for the moment the question which obviously never entered into Marx's field of vision, namely, whether in those circumstances the proletariat would really be the "last" class, with whose accession to power class-rule would collapse altogether, that is, whether a new social differentiation would not arise within the victorious proletariat itself, one which, even though the class-designation might not apply, might very well lead to a new system of domination. There still remains, however, the no less momentous question as to the nature and extent of political power in the "improper" sense, that is to say, the political power that no longer rests on class-rule but persists after the classes have been abolished. Might it not be possible for such power to make itself no less felt, indeed more felt, than that based on class-rule, especially so long as it was a matter of "defending the Revolution"—so long, in fact, as humanity as a whole had not abolished class-rule, or even, perhaps, so long as humanity had not adopted the view or the realization of socialism prevailing in that particular State in which the victory of the proletariat had been won? But the thing that concerns us most of all is this: so long, in such a State or States, as this fixed point of view prevails, and prevails with all the technique and instruments of power at the disposal of our age, how can that spontaneity, that free social form-seeking and form-giving, that unfettered power of social experimentation and decision so indispensable to the realization of socialism and the emergence of a socialist form of society—how can they possibly get to work? By omitting to draw a clear line of demarcation between power in its proper and improper senses Marx opens the door to a type of political principle which, in his opinion, does not and cannot exist: a type which is not the expression and elaboration of class-rule, but is rather the expression and elaboration of power-tendencies and power-struggles not characterized by class, on the part of groups and individuals. Political power in the improper sense would accordingly be "the official sum of antagonisms" either within the proletarian class itself or, more precisely, within the nation in which "class-rule has been abolished".

His impressions of the problematical revolution of 1848 served to sharpen Marx's critical attitude to experiments in social restructure. If the "little experiments, inevitably abortive" had already been censured in the *Manifesto,* now [in *The Class Struggles in France*] "doctrinaire socialism" was accused of "wishing away the revolutionary conflict of the classes and the need for it by means of petty artifices and gross sentimentalities'', and (in the *Eighteenth Brumaire* of 1852) the French proletariat was reprobated for having partly committed itself to ''doctrinaire experiments, exchange-banks and workers' associations'', and thus to a ''movement which, having given up the struggle to overthrow the old world despite all the means at its disposal, prefers to seek its own salvation behind society's back, privately, inside the narrow framework of its existence, and which will thus necessarily come to grief''. (pp. 82-4)

In one of his most significant writings, the address to the General Council of the International on the civil war in France, he sketched a picture of the growth, activities and aims of the [Paris] Commune. The historical reliability of this picture has been disputed, but that does not concern us here: the picture is a confession and one that is of great importance for our theme, which is the variations in Marx's views concerning the evolution of a new society.

What distinguished the Commune in Marx's eyes *toto genere* from all earlier endeavours, ''its true secret'', is that it was ''essentially a working-class government''. That is to be understood literally: Marx means a government not merely appointed by the working-class but also actually and factually exercised by it. The Commune is ''the self-government of the producers''. Born of universal suffrage and elected by the Parisians themselves, representation of this kind, consisting as it does of members who can be replaced at any time and who are bound by the definite instructions of their electors—such representation ''should not be a parliamentary but a working body, executive and legislative at the same time''. The same form of organization was to be provided for every commune in France right down to the smallest village. The provincial communes were to administer their common affairs in the district parliament and the district assemblies in their turn were to send deputies to the national delegation. In place of centralized State-power originating from the era of absolute monarchy, ''with its omnipresent organs'', there would consequently emerge a largely decentralized community. ''The few, but important, functions, still left over for a Central Government were to be transferred to communal, i.e. strictly answerable officials.'' The decentralization, however, would not be a fragmentation but a reconstitution of national unity on an organic basis, and would mean a reactivating of the nation's forces and therefore of the national organism as a whole. (pp. 86-7)

But the political structure of the Commune is, for Marx, only a prelude to the real and decisive thing—the great social transformation to which, with its plans and its dispositions, it would inevitably have led had it not been destroyed. He sees in the Commune ''the finally discovered political form, in whose sign the economic liberation of labour can march forward''. The Commune wanted ''to make individual property a truth, by converting the means of production, land and capital into the mere tools of free and associated labour'', and labour amalgamated in Producer Co-operatives at that. ''If Co-operative production,'' Marx cries, ''is not to remain a snare and a delusion, if it is to oust the capitalist system, if the Co-operatives as a whole are to regulate national production according to a common plan and thereby take it under their own control—what else would that be, gentlemen, but Communism, and a Communism that is *possible*?'' That is, a communism that proves its possibility in the teeth of the widespread notion of its ''impossibility''. A federalism of communes and Co-operatives—for that is precisely what this picture sketches—is thus acknowledged by Marx as genuine communism. To be sure, he still sets his face against all ''Utopianism''. The working-

class ''has no cut-and-dried Utopias to introduce by a plebiscite''. The communal and co-operative system which it wants to build up into a new community and a new society, is not a contrivance of the mind: only out of the reality of the association of old and new generations, the reality that is gradually emerging from the nation itself, out of these things alone can the working-class build its work and its house. ''It has no ideals to realize, it has only to set free those elements of the new society which have already developed in the womb of the collapsing bourgeois society.'' Here we have [a notion of development] dating from 1847; but this time it is completely unequivocal and indubitably meant in the sense of a pre-revolutionary process, one, moreover, whose nature consists in the formation of small, federable units of men's work and life together, of communes and Co-operatives, in respect to which it is the sole task of the Revolution to set them free, to unite them and endow them with authority. This certainly accords at all points with the famous formula given in the *Critique of Political Economy* twelve years previously, as regards the new and higher conditions of production which, however, will never supplant the old ''until the material conditions for their existence have been gestated in the womb of the old society itself''. But it is nowhere hinted in the report of the General Council that the Paris Commune miscarried because the gestation had not been completed. And the ''elements of the new society'' that had developed in the womb of the old, collapsing one—they were for the most part those very Co-operatives which had been formed in France under the influence of ''utopian'' socialism, just as the political federalism of the communes Marx described had been formed under the influence of Proudhon. These Co-operatives it was that were characterized as ''little experiments, inevitably abortive'' in the *Communist Manifesto*; but had the Commune triumphed—and everything in the Report indicates that it could have triumphed but for this or that particular circumstance—then they would have become the cell-substance of the new society.

From this standpoint—i.e. of Marxist *politics of revolution*—statements like the following one by Engels in 1873 can therefore be understood: ''Had the autonomists been content to say that the social organization of the future would admit authority only within the bounds unavoidably set by the conditions of production themselves, then we could have agreed with them.'' (pp. 87-8)

Marx always remained a centralist at heart. For him the communes were essentially political units, battle-organs of the revolution. Lenin asks, ''If the proletariat were to organize itself absolutely freely into communes, and were to unite the activities of these communes in a common front against Capital . . . would that not be . . . proletarian centralism?'' Of course it would, and to this extent Lenin . . . is Marx's faithful interpreter. But that is true merely of the revolution as such, which—in the sense of Marx's definition of the commune—is not a ''development'' spread out over several generations, but a coherent historical *act,* the act of smashing capitalism and placing the means of production in the hands of the proletariat. But in the French programme for the communes each individual commune with its ''local self-government'' is by no means a mere cog in the great apparatus of revolution, or, to put it less mechanically, not merely an isolated muscle within the revolutionary exertions of the body politic—on the contrary it is destined to outlast the upheaval as an independent unit equipped with the maximum of autonomy. During the act the commune's particular will merges spontaneously in the great impulse of the whole, but afterwards it is to acquire its own sphere of decision and action, so that the really vital functions are discharged "below" and the general administrative functions "at the top". Each commune is already invested in principle with its own proper powers and rights within the revolutionary process, but it is only after the accomplishment of the common act that they can come into actuality. Marx accepted these essential components of the commune-idea but without weighing them up against his own centralism and deciding between them. That he apparently did not see the profound problem that this opens out is due to the hegemony of the political point of view; a hegemony which persisted everywhere for him as far as concerned the revolution, its preparation and its effects. Of the three modes of thinking in public matters—the economic, the social and the political—Marx exercised the first with methodical mastery, devoted himself with passion to the third, but—absurd as it may sound in the ears of the unqualified Marxist—only very seldom did he come into more intimate contact with the second, and it never became a deciding factor for him.

To the question of the elements of social re-structure, a fateful question indeed, Marx and Engels never gave a positive answer, because they had no inner relation to this idea. Marx might occasionally allude to "the elements of the new society which have already developed in the womb of the collapsing bourgeois society", and which the Revolution had only "to set free"; but he could not make up his mind to foster these elements, to promote them and sponsor them. The political act of revolution remained the one thing worth striving for; the political preparation for it—at first the direct preparation, afterwards the parliamentary and trades unionist preparation—the one task worth doing, and thus the political principle became the supreme determinant; every concrete decision about the practical attitude to such re-structural elements as were actually present, in the process of formation or to be constituted anew, was reached only from the standpoint of political expediency. Natually, therefore, decisions in favour of a positive attitude were tepid, uncoordinated and ineffectual, and finally they were always cancelled out by negative ones. (pp. 95-6)

This zig-zag line may well serve as a symbol of the tragic misdevelopment of the Socialist Movement. With all the powerful forces of propaganda and planning it had gathered the proletariat about itself; in the political and economic field it had acted with great aggressive aplomb in attack and defence, but the very thing for which, ultimately, it had made propaganda and planned and fought—the evolution of the new social form—was neither the real object of its thought nor the real goal of its action. What Marx praised the Paris Commune for, the Marxist movement neither wanted nor achieved. It did not look to the lineaments of the new society which were there for all to see; it made no serious effort to promote, influence, direct, co-ordinate and federate the experiments that were in being or about to be; never by consistent work did it of its own accord call any cell-groups and associations of cell-groups of living community into existence. With all its great powers it lent no hand to shaping the new social life for mankind which was to be set free by the Revolution. (p. 98)

> *Martin Buber, "Marx and the Renewal of Society,"*
> *in his* Paths in Utopia, *translated by R. F. C. Hull,*
> *1949. Reprint by Beacon Hill, 1958, pp. 80-98.*

PAUL TILLICH (essay date 1948)

[*Tillich, a German-born American, was a leading theologian and philosopher whose writings on Christianity deal with the rela-*tionship between psychology and religion. Reevaluating the Man-ifesto *on its centennial, he explores "the lasting truths in the thought of a man whose ideas have changed the world as few other ideas have done."*]

In this year, 1948, a century after the appearance of that most passionate, profound and effective expression of his ideas, the **Communist Manifesto,** it is difficult and dangerous to write about Karl Marx—difficult because of the many divergent and often contradictory interpretations of his thought that have arisen inside as well as outside the Marxist movement, dangerous because his name has become so potent a political and semi-religious symbol, divine or demonic, that whatever you say about him will be used against you by fanatics on both sides. You will be called a pitiful misinterpreter of Marx by some, a reactionary by others, a Communist by many, especially by professional red-baiters. I take these risks because I believe that there is truth in Karl Marx. . . .

How much truth, then, is there in Marx? We may distinguish three aspects or kinds of truth: scientific truth, situational truth, ultimate truth. Let us ask the question on all three counts.

It is impossible for a non-economist to discuss the strictly economic doctrines of Marx, nor is it necessary for our purpose. Obviously everything merely scientific in Marx is subject to scientific criticism. Today, after a hundred years of research, most of his economic theories either have undergone great development or have been radically transformed if not completely rejected. His doctrines of work and value, his theories of accumulation and concentration, his interpretation of the proletarian situation, and so on, were important because of the questions they raised. But the answers he gave have been largely undercut.

There is, however, one aspect of Marx's work in this field which transcends the merely scientific problem, though it is a part of it; namely, his method. Marx's method is sociological, dialectical and materialistic. He puts the so-called economic laws into the context of man's total behavior as it develops under special sociological conditions. He does not believe in the abstract functioning of these laws, but shows that their validity depends on the structure of the society in which they operate. Thus his method is concrete, dynamic and critical, in contrast to the attempts, partly justified though they were, of theoretical economists to formulate economic laws according to the pattern of mathematical physics. The fact that the controversy between these two approaches is still far from being decided confirms the significance of Marx's sociological economics.

It is from this point of view that Marx's so-called dialectical materialism must be understood. Both "dialectical" and "materialism" are extremely ambiguous terms and require definition. As applied to Marx, "dialectical" means that he tries to reveal the driving forces in a social structure by pointing out the contradictory elements in it and describing them as necessary consequences of the structure itself. Life produces the contradictions by which it is driven onward; in other words, life is dialectical, and therefore must be described dialectically. Marx did not invent this method, and Marxians as well as non-Marxians apply it, often unconsciously; but Marx used it consciously and radically.

Proper understanding of the term "materialism" demands that we distinguish between Marx and Marxism. Marx's materialism was not a metaphysical idea but a theory about the influence of the economic factor in history. Hence his method has often been called "economic materialism" or "the economic interpretation of history." The latter term avoids the ambiguities of the word "materialism." But perhaps that word should not be avoided, because it best expresses Marx's anti-idealist bias.

According to Marx, the economic realm constitutes the "substructure" on the basis of which the cultural and spiritual "superstructure" arises. Movements in the superstructure are determined by movements in the substructure. As a methodological point of view, this idea has influenced most post-Marxian historians, especially those who deal with single aspects of man's cultural life, such as art, religion, morals. (p. 906)

But there is an ambiguity in Marx's conception of substructure and superstructure. It may be taken to mean that cultural forms and creations have a reality of their own, though their emergence is conditioned by material factors. This is the view that Marx himself took in regard to the independent truth of science. But his analogy may also be taken to mean that the superstructure is a mere projection or reflection of the substructure, without any independent truth. This is the interpretation that Marx used in his criticism of religion and metaphysics. He called them "ideologies" and denied any validity to their symbols and concepts. But in so doing he overleaped the frame of his own method and made assertions that are implicitly religious and implicitly as well as explicitly metaphysical. These statements of his were a bridge to the metaphysical materialism of later Marxists and the reason for the utter confusion about the meaning of "dialectical materialism."

So much for the scientific truth in Marx. We come now to the question of the situational truth in his work—more precisely, the truth of his analysis of bourgeois society, the forces that drive it, its pervading ideologies and its self-destructive contradictions. It is of the greatest importance here to distinguish three situations: that which Marx himself found, that which developed under the influence of his analysis, and that which exists today, after two world wars. It is in his study of the first of these situations—capitalism in its early stages as he observed it in England and other highly industrialized countries—that Marx made his permanent contribution to the understanding of bourgeois society.

It seems to me that the whole field of historiography offers very few pieces of structural analysis that can compare for profundity, scientific originality and prophetic insight with Marx's interpretation of the capitalistic system and its sociological implications. That is why his ideas have made world history. The ideas of every prophetic thinker can be cut to pieces by those who come after. But their power survives criticism and proves inexhaustible.

To be sure, Marx's analysis cannot be applied directly to the world of the mid-20th century. It does not fit Great Britain and continental Europe as they are now. The situation of labor, for example, has changed radically, owing in great degree to the influence of Marx himself. There is no proletariat in the strictly Marxian sense in the United States, nor in Asia. In Europe the proletariat is hopelessly split into democratic and totalitarian groups. Its advance guards have become functionaries or bureaucrats instead of the elected representatives that Marx conceived of. (pp. 906-07)

Marx had other limitations. He did not perceive the decisive impact of national power relations on all historical developments, and he did not realize the tenacity of religious traditions and the natural conservatism of the vast majority of people on

Engels, Marx, Marx's daughters Laura and Eleanor, and Jenny in 1864.

all levels. These limitations spring partly from his inadequate doctrine of man . . . ; but partly they were conditioned by the actual situation in Europe in the mid-19th century.

In this period the intelligentsia was still fighting on the side of the developing bourgeoisie in opposition to the powers of absolutistic reaction. The industrial proletariat—recruited in part from the disintegrating lower middle classes—was the only group that felt the full impact of rising capitalism. They alone were driven by destiny into revolutionary protest against this system. The gathering of absolute power into their own hands seemed the only way to justice. The churches did not comprehend the situation at all. Slowly and reluctantly they admitted liberal ideas, but they rejected completely the revolutionary tendencies of the proletariat. The international situation was relatively stable, owing to the balance-of-power politics played in masterly fashion by Great Britain.

No wonder that Marx was unable to foresee the utterly changed conditions of the 20th century, which were indeed to be brought about in large measure by his own ideas. The astonishing thing is that he saw as much as he did, and saw it in a way that makes even his erroneous prophecies significant. . . .

[Finally, there is the question of] the ultimate truth in Marx. Ultimate truth is truth about the human situation as such, about the meaning of our existence and all existence. If we call this the religious question, we must ask whether there is religious truth in Marx. It seems paradoxical to put such a query to a system which is outspokenly anti-religious. But the paradox disappears when we define religion in the larger sense as being concerned with ultimate or unconditional or infinite things, as distinguished from religion in the narrow sense; namely, the complex of symbols and institutions expressing an ultimate concern and centered around the idea of God. Religion in the latter sense can certainly not be found in Marx. In this regard, all the truth he offers is critical truth. Nevertheless, it is of lasting importance.

By calling religion an ideology, Marx implies that it provides a transcendent escape for the victims of the class struggle—that is, for the great masses of people—and thus deadens their revolutionary passion for changing the existing order. This is a challenge Christianity must meet. The church ought to scrutinize itself continually to see whether it is justified. Christian thought must ever be on guard lest it give grounds for the suspicion that it is cultivating an ideology which can be exploited by the ruling classes. This is simply a concrete application of the prophetic admonitions against idolatry. Idolatry and religious ideology have the same root; namely, the perversion of man's concern for ultimate things into a concern for the preliminary, conditional and finite—for example, power in one of its many forms.

Another of Marx's permanent contributions lies in his attack on idealism. The word "idealism" is almost as ambiguous as "materialism." Both can signify a moral attitude. In this sense, Marx is extremely idealistic. To call him materialistic in the moral sense is a sign either of ignorance or of propagandistic dishonesty. His criticism of idealism is carried by a tremendous moral passion.

The idealism Marx challenged was that which he encountered in German classical philosophy and in the general belief that modern society is in a state of harmonious progress. Powerfully he describes man's estrangement from himself in the bourgeois society. The proletarian is in a state of complete dehumanization. He has become an object, a thing, a mere tool. The idealism Marx opposed did not recognize that man had been dehumanized, and therefore he rejected it. This side of Marx's doctrine is much closer to classical Christianity than is the progressivistic idealism of many modern Protestant groups. It is a secular expression of Christian realism.

A third element of ultimate truth in Marx is his dynamic-prophetic interpretation of history. This obviously derives from Jewish tradition, more especially from prophetic tradition. It was a decisive challenge for a Christianity which had lost all capacity for historical thinking and spoke exclusively of "God and the soul." The Kingdom of God is not a static heaven into which individuals enter after death; it is the dynamic divine power in and above history which drives history toward ultimate fulfillment. It refers to groups as well as to individuals, and demands continuous efforts toward justice, which is basic in it. (p. 907)

As with every systematic thinker, it is possible to derive the various elements of ultimate truth in Marx from his doctrine of man, or more precisely from his interpretation of human existence. It could be said with some justification that Marx has no doctrine of man, if by this phrase is meant a systematic treatment of the nature of man. Marx certainly would have declined such an approach. For him, man is always man in society and history. But in order to make any meaningful criticism of man in the bourgeois period he had to presuppose man as he should be or potentially is. Every word of Marx's early writings, and large parts of his later ones, shows that there

was alive in him a rather clear intuitive perception of human potentialities, enabling him to set forth his passionate protest against the distorted existence which, as he saw it, began with the beginning of the class struggle—that is, with the beginning of history.

While Marx's picture of man as he might be is that of classical humanism, including the ideas of creative freedom and the equal dignity of all persons, he was keenly aware that man is a bodily and therefore a sense-determined being. This is his "anthropological materialism," the basis of his "historical materialism." It is the same paradox which the Bible sets forth in the dual statement that man is made in the image of God and that he is made of dust. Marx's combination of these two ideas—the humanist conception of man's potentialities and his own realistic conception of man's dependence on material conditions—has been responsible for many misunderstandings of his doctrine on the part of friends and foes alike, and has caused divergent developments and splits in the Marxist movement.

As against Christian and humanist idealism, Marx laid all the emphasis on the material side. Improvement of man's daily lot, he held, could alone create the conditions for fulfillment of the spiritual side. But his emphasis on the material has largely defeated his purpose. Wherever Marxist socialism has come to power it has been lacking in noble personalities and has placed its confidence chiefly in institutions and in the change of material conditions. Along with Marx's negation of religious transcendence, this development has brought about the perversion of his ideas, the catastrophes of Marxism and its antihumanist transformation into present-day communism. It has darkened the significance of Marx's prophetic analysis. It has buried the lasting truths in the thought of a man whose ideas have changed the world as few other ideas have done.

Marx is not Marxism and Marxism is not Stalinism. Only dishonest propaganda can identify them. We must approach Marx as he is, free from the connotations that have distorted his picture. Thus we shall find truth in him—scientific truth, situational truth, ultimate truth. (p. 908)

> *Paul Tillich, "How Much Truth Is There in Karl Marx?" in* The Christian Century, *September 8, 1948, pp. 906-08.*

KARL LÖWITH (essay date 1954)

[*Löwith outlines Marx's theory of self-alienation, whereby "products govern men, and not vice-versa," discussing it as a contributing factor in the rise of "revolutionary consciousness" among workers.*]

The specific concept that Marx uses in his analysis of the bourgeois-capitalist world is that of "human self-alienation," which expresses itself in the political economy as the "anatomy" of the bourgeoisie. "Political economy" includes, for Marx, man's economic existence as well as his human consciousness of it. Marx considers the material conditions of production to be the "skeleton" of society, and thus he transfers the emphasis from Hegel's "bourgeois society" to the "system of needs" as such. At the same time Marx's idea implies the specifically "materialist" thesis that the material conditions of life are of fundamental significance for all other conditions. This led eventually to the vulgar Marxist thesis: that the so-called material "basis" is the foundation on which, as on an independent stratum, the superstructure is to rise; this superstructure must therefore be interpreted ideologically as derived from the "foundation." It was chiefly in this vulgarized form that Marxist doctrine became subject to criticism. However strongly Marx himself supported this interpretation—and Engels even more strongly—the fact remains that Marx had come to terms with philosophy before his criticism of political economy began to dominate in his thinking.

In this respect Marx's development can be summed up as follows: at first he criticized religion philosophically, then he criticized religion and philosophy politically, and at last he criticized religion, philosophy, politics, and all other ideologies economically. According to Marx's own words, however, the economic interpretation of all manifestations of human life was but the "last result" into which his critical revision of Hegel's metaphysical and political philosophy developed—in Hegel's words, "a corpse which has left behind its living impulse." To rediscover this living impulse contained in Marx's analysis of man's self-alienation, we must turn from *Capital* to Marx's early philosophical writings; we can find, for example, the "living impulse" from which the first chapter of *Capital* resulted, in 1867, expressed as early as 1842 in a discussion of a theft of lumber, published in the *Rheinische Zeitung.*

The original form of Marx's critical analysis of the capitalist process of production is his analysis of the bourgeois world, which is characterized by the alienation of man from himself. To Marx, as an Hegelian, the bourgeois-capitalist world represents a specifically "irrational" reality, and a world that for rational man is inhuman, perverted, de-humanized. In the preface to his doctoral thesis and in a letter to Ruge in 1843, Marx called himself an "idealist" who had the "impertinence" to try "to make man a human being." Therefore we have first to show that man as such was Marx's primary concern, and that this remained true even after his discovery of the "new" man in the proletarian. For what Marx ultimately aimed at was a "human" emancipation of man, not merely a legal one—that is, at "real humanism." (pp. 204-05)

Marx's criticism develops as a criticism of modern society and economy—without losing, however, its basic anthropological, and thus its philosophical, meaning. "If man is social by nature, he develops his true nature only within society, and the power of his nature cannot be measured by the power of the single individual but only by the standard of society." Marx pursues the basic and universal alienation of man in all realms of reality, in its economic, political, and immediately social forms. The economic expression of this problem is the world of "commodities," its political expression is the contradiction between "state" and "society," and its immediate social expression is the existence of the "proletariat." (pp. 210-11)

The economic expression of man's self-alienation is the commodity. As Marx employs the term, "commodity" does not mean one special kind of object contrasted with other kinds, but the "commodity-form," a fundamental ontological character which, in the modern world, all kinds of objects have in common. It is the commodity-form or commodity-structure which characterizes the alienation or estrangement of man from himself as well as from things. Consequently, *Capital* begins with an analysis of the commodity. The fundamental meaning of this analysis lies in its criticism of a bourgeois society and bourgeois man. In *Capital* this criticism finds direct expression only in casual notes and marginal remarks; it is, however, one main theme in an early debate concerning the law about the theft of lumber (*Holzdiebstahlgesetz*) of 1842. Here Marx undertakes his first brilliant unmasking of the perversion of "means" and "ends," of "thing" and "man"—the perver-

sion that implies the self-estrangement of man, his externalization, his transformation from himself into a *thing*—lumber. This highest degree of externalization, to behave toward oneself in terms of something different and alien, is labeled by Marx, in his doctoral thesis, "materialism" or "positivism," and he calls himself, as one who aims to abolish this estrangement, an "idealist." The externalization of man into an object is alienation from himself because, in their proper sense, things are what they are for man, while man is man for himself.

What Marx wanted to make clear in this debate can be summed up as follows. Lumber, which belongs to a private owner (that is, to a capitalist), and which can therefore be stolen by a man who does not own it privately, is not mere lumber, but something of economic and social relevance and human significance, even though its significance is concealed in the lumber itself. Endowed with this human-social quality, lumber is not the same for its owner as it is for the man who owns nothing and steals the lumber. As long as one man is aware of himself solely or primarily as the owner of lumber, having only this narrow-minded, partial consciousness of himself, while the other man is accordingly regarded merely as a lumber-thief, but not as a human being—as long as these unphilosophical ideas prevail, no equitable punishment (equitable from a human viewpoint, that is—not merely "correct" from the legal viewpoint) can be imposed. Both humanly and legally a dead thing, an "objective power," something non-human, mere wood, determines man and "subsumes" him, unless he is capable of directing and controlling his material and objective relationships in a human-social way. The determination of man through mere lumber is possible, however, because lumber, like any other commodity, is itself an objectified expression of sociopolitical relationships. Like any other commodity, it has the character of a fetish. For this reason "wooden idols rise while human sacrifices fall." In the words of Marx's concluding passage:

> If, therefore, lumber and owners of lumber as such make laws, these laws will differ in nothing but the place where they are made and the language in which they are written. This depraved materialism, this mortal sin against the Holy Spirit of peoples and of mankind, is a direct consequence of the doctrine that the Preussische Staatszeitung preaches to the lawgivers: that when making a law about lumber, they are to think of nothing but wood and lumber, and are not to try to solve each material problem in a political way—that is, in connection with undivided civic reasoning and civic morality.

When something like lumber, this seeming "thing in itself," becomes the standard for the being and behavior of man, man will necessarily be reified and alienated from himself. (pp. 211-12)

In *German Ideology* Marx raises the same question as in the debate on lumber, though he no longer treats it in the same way. He asks again: Whence comes the strangeness with which men behave toward the products of their own labor, so that they no longer have power and control over their reciprocal relationships? Why, instead, do these products become independent forces, so that "the power of their lives overpowers their own makers"? How does it happen that the personal behavior of the individual has to reify itself and thereby estrange itself, while it exists at the same time as an independent power outside the individual?

Marx replies that this perversion is caused by the division of labor. Accordingly, the way in which men have worked up to the present time must be abandoned; it must be transformed into "total self-activity." This transformation will include not only abolition of the division of labor but also abolition of the separation between city and country—which is "the most striking expression of the subsumption of the individual under the division of labor." Abolition of the division of labor can be accomplished only on the basis of a universal communist order of society, which will not only make all property common property but will also make man's very being, in all of its self-expressions, a common—that is, a communist—matter. (pp. 213-14)

[*Capital*] is not simply a critique of political economy but a critique of the man of bourgeois society in terms of that society's economy. The "economic cell" of this economy is the commodity-form of the labor products; and the commodity, like the lumber in the lumber-theft debate, is an economic expression of self-alienation. Self-alienation consists of this: that a thing whose original purpose is to be useful is not manufactured and exchanged for anyone's actual needs, but appears on the commodity market as an object with an autonomous commodity-value, independent of its utility. This is true whether economic or intellectual products are traded, whether the commodities are cattle or books. Only through the salesman, for whom the commodity has merely exchange value, can the commodity reach its consumer, the buyer. The fact that an object intended for use becomes autonomous as a commodity offers another illustration of the general situation in modern bourgeois society, namely, that products govern men, and not vice versa.

To uncover this hidden perversion, Marx analyzes the "object-like appearance" (the German word *Schein* means both "appearance" and "disguise") of modern conditions of labor as expressed in the "fetish-character" of the commodity. As a commodity, a table or a chair is a "sensuous-supersensuous" thing—that is, an object whose qualities are at the same time perceptible and imperceptible to the senses. We perceive without difficulty exactly what a table means as an object for use; but what it means as a commodity—as an object that costs money because of the invested labor (that is, the invested working time) that it represents—is at first a hidden social phenomenon. As Marx expresses it in *Capital,* "The table no longer stands with its feet firmly on the ground, but stands on its head in front of all the other commodities, spinning whims from its wooden skull, far more wonderful than if it were to begin dancing of its own free will."

The commodity-form is mysterious because in it the social character of man's labor appears disguised as an objective character stamped upon the product of that labor; therefore the relation of the producers to the sum total of their own labor is presented to them as a social relation which exists not among themselves but among the products of their labor. (pp. 215-16)

At first the producers of commodities—that is, of any kind of objects in the ontological form of commodity—make their social contacts only by exchanging their products. As these contacts take place only through things, the social conditions that underlie the commodities do not appear to the producers as labor-conditions of men. On the one side, these social conditions appear as purely objective and material relations among the various producers of commodities. On the other side, because of the objective character of modern commodities, these social conditions acquire a quasi-personal character on the modern commodity market, which follows its own economic laws. At first, men are not aware of this perversion, their self-consciousness being reified at the same rate. Marx says that although this perversion had to come about, he does not consider it irrevocable. Like other social structures, it can be transformed through revolutionary action and theoretical criticism. (p. 217)

Thus it seems that only the price of a commodity can be changed, not its form as such. If we compare the economic order of our society with other social and economic epochs in history, however, we see at once the historical character of the present perversion of the economic order, by which the products of labor as commodities have acquired authority over their producers. Whatever else we may think about the so-called Dark Ages and Middle Ages, with their conditions of personal dependence, at least the social conditions of labor appear in these centuries as the personal conditions of the people, and not disguised as the social conditions of things. (pp. 217-18)

In the light of this historical perspective Marx develops the possibility of a future communist order of society, in order to contrast the "opaque" perversion of the modern world of commodities, its inhumanity, with the "transparency" in a communist society of men's social relations to the products of their own labor. The world of commodities cannot be abolished except through a fundamental revolution in all the concrete conditions under which men now live. Not only "decapitalization" is needed to change the commodity-form to the utility-form; it will also be necessary to reintegrate the particularity of a reified man into "natural man," whose human nature is, according to Marx, fundamentally social. Man is a *zöon politikon,* though not in an ancient Aristotelian *polis* but in a modern industrial *cosmopolis.* (p. 218)

In considering man's political self-alienation in terms of bourgeois society, Marx says: "The abstraction of the state as such belongs to modern times only, because the abstraction of private life belongs to modern times. . . . The *true* man [of modern times] is the private man of the present political constitution."

The political expression of man's self-alienation is found in the inner contradiction between the modern state and bourgeois society; in the contradiction, that is, that exists in a man of the bourgeois state and society because he is partly a private person and partly a public citizen but in no way a whole man—what Marx would call "a man without contradictions." Indirectly, Marx's critique of the principle of economy as "political" economy criticizes at the same time the social and political conditions of this particular society with its particular kind of economy. While his criticism of the commodity as the essential character, the ontological structure, of all our objects, is directed against the perversion of man into a thing, he now directs his criticism of the bourgeois state and society against the bourgeois way of life—its bourgeois humanity, which is essentially "privacy," a privation. This criticism is a main topic in [Marx's writings on Hegel] and also in his discussion of Bauer's essay on the Jewish problem. . . . [These] works give a systematic presentation of Marx's views about man's self-alienation in its social and political forms. . . . (p. 220)

Marx's purpose was to build a new world through theoretical criticism and practical destruction of the one that had grown old. Out of existing reality, with its specific forms of society and state (a state that is basically unpolitical because it is political in an abstract way), he wanted to develop the "true reality" in which essence and existence, or reason and reality, are one and the same. In 1852, ten years after he wrote *The Holy Family,* Marx gave an historical account of this world grown old in *The Eighteenth Brumaire* of Louis Bonaparte. He described that era of the bourgeois revolution as a caricature of the greater revolution of 1789. He contended that the passions of the later period were without truth, for its truth had no passion; that its reality was completely watered down and living on loans; that its development was merely a constant repetition of the same tensions and relaxations; that its conflicts inflamed each other only to end in dullness and collapse. Its history was a history without events, its heroes performed no heroic deeds, its supreme law was irresolution. His criticism may be compared with the contemporary analysis by Kierkegaard, *The Present Age;* both men turned against Hegel's philosophy of reconciliation, though in opposite directions.

According to Marx, the contradiction between private and public life must be resolved. The deficient private humanity of the man of bourgeois society is to be sublated in a commonwealth which embraces the whole existence of man—including his "theoretical" existence—shaping him from head to foot into a communistic, universally human being. (pp. 222-23)

In discussing the social expression of man's self-alienation in terms of the proletariat, Marx says: "If socialist writers attribute a world-historic role to the proletariat, their reason for doing so is not . . . that they consider the proletarians gods— but rather the opposite." And in the introduction to [Marx's writings on Hegel] we find the following statement: "The dissolution of the whole of modern society is represented in the particular class of the proletariat." In this group lies the positive possibility of a human emancipation, not because it is a class within bourgeois society but because it is itself a society outside of the established one. It is a society "which can no longer lay claim to any historical title but only to the human title, which does not stand in one-sided opposition to the actions of the German state but in absolute opposition to its fundamental principles. Finally, the proletariat is a sphere which cannot become emancipated without emancipating itself from all the remaining spheres of society, thereby in turn emancipating them; it is, in a word, the complete loss of man and therefore can regain itself only by completely regaining man."

Marx's philosophy, in which man is a "common essence," has found its weapon in the proletariat, just as the proletariat found its weapon in his philosophy. "The head of this emancipation is philosophy, its heart is the proletariat." The possessing class and the proletariat represent, fundamentally, the same kind of estrangement of man from himself; the difference is that one class feels itself healthy and fixed in this state of alienation—though without any critical consciousness of it— while the other class is a dehumanization that is conscious of being dehumanized and therefore strives to overcome it. The proletariat is, so to speak, the self-consciousness of the commodity. It is forced to alienate itself, to externalize itself like a commodity; but for this very reason it develops a critical and revolutionary consciousness, a class-consciousness. In one way, however, the proletarian is less dehumanized than the bourgeois, since his dehumanization is a manifest one, not the unconscious, hidden, and spiritualized dehumanization of the bourgeois. (pp. 227-28)

Marx does not attribute fundamental and universal importance to the proletariat because he considers that its members are

"gods," but because to him the proletariat embodies potentially universal humanity—man's common existence though he is now in the extremity of self-alienation. The fundamental importance of the proletariat corresponds exactly to the commodity-form of modern objects. The class of the wage-earner has a universal function because the wage-earner is completely externalized through "the earthly question in life size"; because he is merely a salesman of his own labor, a personified commodity and not a human being. In him the economic phase of life shows itself most clearly as human destiny and thus, with the proletariat as the nucleus of all social problems, the economy necessarily becomes the "anatomy" of bourgeois society. . . . (pp. 228-29)

Marx's investigations, unlike those of empirical sociology, are not concerned with mutual relations between single empirical fields, or with "factors" which are considered to be of equal significance and to represent, when added up, the whole of reality. He was no abstract empiricist, just as he was no abstract philosophical "materialist" who would deduce his theory from economic principles. Marx analyzes our entire self-contradictory human world in terms of man's self-alienation, of which the existence of the proletariat is the climax and the key to the whole. This self-alienation is investigated in terms of its possible abolition, and not—as in Hegel's work—in terms of its dialectical sublation. Marx intends no more and no less than the abolition of the contradiction of particularity and universality, of privacy and public life. (pp. 229-30)

It is true that man's self-alienation is conditioned by the type and degree of development of the material conditions of production, by the division of labor, and by the sum of the concrete conditions of his life. But these conditions are structurally united in the social nature of man, who is his own world and whose self-consciousness is a world-consciousness. The sum of conditions cannot be derived from abstract economic factors; the latter must be integrated into the concrete system of historic human conditions. "Real" man is not man "in the irrationality of his existence . . . as he walks and stands . . . as he is externalized . . . through the whole organization of our society," a semblance of himself. In his true reality man is an essence which has to be brought into existence through action. Marx was convinced that the reality that accounts for the problematic condition of our society drives with historic necessity toward the fulfillment of his views, just as his philosophy moves toward its historic realization. (p. 230)

Karl Löwith, "Man's Self-Alienation in the Early Writings of Marx," in Social Research, *Vol. 21, No. 2, Summer, 1954, pp. 204-30.*

ERICH FROMM (essay date 1961)

[*A German-born American psychoanalyst and philosopher, Fromm is best known for his psychological writings probing the nature of humanity's independence and quest for freedom. Here, Fromm points out some fundamental misconceptions about Marx's theories regarding materialism and the individual.*]

Among all the misunderstandings [about Karl Marx in the twentieth century] there is probably none more widespread than the idea of Marx's "materialism." Marx is supposed to have believed that the paramount psychological motive in man is his wish for monetary gain and comfort, and that this striving for maximum profit constitutes the main incentive in his personal life and in the life of the human race. Complementary to this idea is the equally widespread assumption that Marx neglected the importance of the individual; that he had neither respect nor understanding for the spiritual needs of man, and that his "ideal" was the well-fed and well-clad, but "soulless" person. Marx's criticism of religion was held to be identical with the denial of all spiritual values, and this seemed all the more apparent to those who assume that belief in God is the condition for a spiritual orientation.

This view of Marx then goes on to discuss his socialist paradise as one of millions of people who submit to an all-powerful state bureaucracy, people who have surrendered their freedom, even though they might have achieved equality; these materially satisfied "individuals" have lost their individuality and have been successfully transformed into millions of uniform robots and automatons, led by a small elite of better-fed leaders.

Suffice it to say at the outset that this popular picture of Marx's "materialism"—his anti-spiritual tendency, his wish for uniformity and subordination—is utterly false. Marx's aim was that of the spiritual emancipation of man, of his liberation from the chains of economic determination, of restituting him in his human wholeness, of enabling him to find unity and harmony with his fellow man and with nature. Marx's philosophy was, in secular, nontheistic language, a new and radical step forward in the tradition of prophetic Messianism; it was aimed at the full realization of individualism, the very aim which has guided Western thinking from the Renaissance and the Reformation far into the nineteenth century.

This picture undoubtedly must shock many readers because of its incompatibility with the ideas about Marx to which they have been exposed. But before proceeding to substantiate it, I want to emphasize the irony which lies in the fact that the description given of the aim of Marx and of the content of his vision of socialism, fits almost exactly the reality of present-day Western capitalist society. The majority of people are motivated by a wish for greater material gain, for comfort and gadgets, and this wish is restricted only by the desire for security and the avoidance of risks. They are increasingly satisfied with a life regulated and manipulated, both in the sphere of production and of consumption, by the state and the big corporations and their respective bureaucracies; they have reached a degree of conformity which has wiped out individuality to a remarkable extent. They are, to use Marx's term, impotent "commodity men" serving virile machines. They very picture of mid-twentieth century capitalism is hardly distinguishable from the caricature of Marxist socialism as drawn by its opponents.

What is even more surprising is the fact that the people who accuse Marx most bitterly of "materialism" attack socialism for being unrealistic because it does *not* recognize that the only efficient incentive for man to work lies in his desire for material gain. Man's unbounded capacity for negating blatant contradictions by rationalizations, if it suits him, could hardly be better illustrated. The very same reasons which can be said to be proof that Marx's ideas are incompatible with our religious and spiritual tradition and which are used *to defend* our present system *against* Marx, are at the same time employed by the same people to prove that capitalism corresponds to human nature and hence is far superior to an "unrealistic" socialism.

I shall try to demonstrate that this interpretation of Marx is completely false; that his theory does not assume that the main motive of man is one of material gain; that, furthermore, the very aim of Marx is to liberate man from the pressure of economic needs, so that he can be fully human; that Marx is

primarily concerned with the emancipation of man as an individual, the overcoming of alienation, the restoration of his capacity to relate himself fully to man and to nature; that Marx's philosophy constitutes a spiritual existentialism in secular language and because of this spiritual quality is opposed to the materialistic practice and thinly disguised materialistic philosophy of our age. Marx's aim, socialism, based on his theory of man, is essentially prophetic Messianism in the language of the nineteenth century.

How can it be, then, that Marx's philosophy is so completely misunderstood and distorted into its opposite? There are several reasons. The first and most obvious one is ignorance. It seems that these are matters which, not being taught at universities and hence not being subjects for examination, are "free" for everybody to think, talk, write about as he pleases, and without any knowledge. There are no properly acknowledged authorities who would insist on respect for the facts, and for truth. Hence everybody feels entitled to talk about Marx without having read him, or at least, without having read enough to get an idea of his very complex, intricate, and subtle system of thought. It did not help matters that Marx's ***Economic and Philosophical Manuscripts,*** his main philosophical work dealing with his concept of man, of alienation, of emancipation, etc., had not until now been translated into English, and hence that some of his ideas were unknown to the English-speaking world. This fact, however, is by no means sufficient to explain the prevailing ignorance, first, because the fact that this work of Marx's had never before been translated into English is in itself as much a symptom as a cause of the ignorance; secondly, because the main trend of Marx's philosophical thought is sufficiently clear in those writings previously published in English to have avoided the falsification which occurred.

Another reason lies in the fact that the Russian Communists appropriated Marx's theory and tried to convince the world that their practice and theory follow his ideas. Although the opposite is true, the West accepted their propagandistic claims and has come to assume that Marx's position corresponds to the Russian view and practice. However, the Russian Communists are not the only ones guilty of misinterpreting Marx. While the Russians' brutal contempt for individual dignity and humanistic values is, indeed, specific for them, the misinterpretation of Marx as the proponent of an economistic-hedonistic materialism has also been shared by many of the anti-Communist and reformist socialists. The reasons are not difficult to see. While Marx's theory was a critique of capitalism, many of his adherents were so deeply imbued with the spirit of capitalism that they interpreted Marx's thought in the economistic and materialistic categories that are prevalent in contemporary capitalism. Indeed, while the Soviet Communists as well as the reformist socialists, believed they were the enemies of capitalism, they conceived of communism—or socialism—in the spirit of capitalism. For them, socialism is not a society humanly different from capitalism, but rather, a form of capitalism in which the working class has achieved a higher status; it is, as Engels once remarked ironically, "the present-day society without its defects."

So far we have dealt with rational and realistic reasons for the distortion of Marx's theories. But, no doubt, there are also irrational reasons which help to produce this distortion. Soviet Russia has been looked upon as the very incarnation of all evil; hence her ideas have assumed the quality of the devilish. (pp. 2-7)

The first hurdle to be cleared in order to arrive at a proper understanding of Marx's philosophy is the misunderstanding of the concept of *materialism* and *historical materialism*. Those who believe this to be a philosophy claiming that man's material interest, his wish for ever-increasing material gain and comforts, are his main motivation, forget the simple fact that the words "idealism" and "materialism" as used by Marx and all other philosophers have nothing to do with psychic motivations of a higher, spiritual level as against those of a lower and baser kind. In philosophical terminology, "materialism" (or "naturalism") refers to a philosophic view which holds that matter in motion is the fundamental constituent of the universe. In this sense the Greek pre-Socratic philosophers were "materialists," although they were by no means materialists in the above-mentioned sense of the word as a value judgment or ethical principle. By idealism, on the contrary, a philosophy is understood in which it is not the everchanging world of the senses that constitutes reality, but incorporeal essences, or ideaas. Plato's system is the first philosophical system to which the name of "idealism" was applied. While Marx was, in the philosophical sense a materialist in ontology, he was not even really interested in such questions, and hardly ever dealt with them.

However, there are many kinds of materialist and idealist philosophies, and in order to understand Marx's "materialism" we have to go beyond the general definition just given. Marx actually took a firm position *against* a philosophical materialism which was current among many of the most progressive thinkers (especially natural scientists) of his time. This materialism claimed that "the" substratum of all mental and spiritual phenomena was to be found in matter and material processes. In its most vulgar and superficial form, this kind of materialism taught that feelings and ideas are sufficiently explained as results of chemical bodily processes, and "thought is to the brain what urine is to the kidneys."

Marx fought this type of mechanical, "bourgeois" materialism "the abstract materialism of natural science, that excludes history and its process," and postulated instead what he called in the *Economic and Philosophical Manuscripts* "naturalism or humanism [which] is distinguished from both idealism and materialism, and at the same time constitutes their unifying truth." In fact, Marx never used the terms "historical materialism" or "dialectic materialism"; he did speak of his own "dialectical method" in contrast with that of Hegel and of its "materialistic basis," by which he simply referred to the fundamental conditions of human existence.

This aspect of "materialism," Marx's "materialist method," which distinguishes his view from that of Hegel, involves the study of the real economic and social life of man and of the influence of man's actual way of life on this thinking and feeling. (pp. 8-9)

Marx described his own historical method very succinctly: "The way in which men produce their means of subsistence depends first of all on the nature of the actual means they find in existence and have to reproduce. This mode of production must not be considered simply as being the reproduction of the physical existence of the individuals. Rather, it is a definite form of activity of these individuals, a definite form of expressing their life, a definite *mode of life* on their part. As individuals express their life, so they are. What they are, therefore, coincides with their production, both with *what* they produce and with *how* they produce. The nature of individuals thus depends on the material conditions determining their production."

Marx made the difference between historical materialism and contemporary materialism very clear in his thesis on Feuerbach:

"The chief defect of all materialism up to now (including Feuerbach's) is that the object, reality, what we apprehend through our senses, is understood only in the form of the *object* or contemplation (Anschauung); but not as *sensuous human activity,* as *practice;* not subjectively. Hence in opposition to materialism, the active side was developed abstractly by idealism—which of course does not know real sensuous activity as such. Feuerbach wants sensuous objects really distinguished from the objects of thought; but he does not understand human activity itself as *objective* activity." Marx—like Hegel—looks at an object in its movement, in its becoming, and not as a static "object," which can be explained by discovering the physical "cause" of it. In contrast to Hegel, Marx studies man and history by beginning with the real man and the economic and social conditions under which he must live, and not primarily with his ideas. Marx was as far from bourgeois materialism as he was from Hegel's idealism—hence he could rightly say that his philosophy is neither idealism nor materialism but a synthesis: humanism and naturalism.

It should be clear by now why the popular idea of the nature of historical materialism is erroneous. The popular view assumes that in Marx's opinion the strongest psychological motive in man is to gain money and to have more material comfort; if this is the main force within man, so continues this "interpretation" of historical materialism, the key to the understanding of history is the material desires of men; hence, the key to the explanation of history is man's belly, and his greed for material satisfaction. The fundamental misunderstanding on which this interpretation rests is the assumption that historical materialism is a psychological theory which deals with man's drives and passions. But, in fact, historical materialism is not at all a *psychological* theory; it claims that *the way man produces determines his thinking and his desires,* and *not* that his main desires are those for maximal material gain. Economy in this context refers not to a psychic drive, but to the mode of production; not to a subjective, psychological, but to an objective, economic-sociological factor. The only quasi-psychological premise in the theory lies in the assumption that man needs food, shelter, etc., hence needs to produce; hence that the mode of production, which depends on a number of objective factors, comes first, as it were, and determines the other spheres of his activities. . . . Certain economic conditions, like those of capitalism, produce as a chief incentive the desire for money and property; other economic conditions can produce exactly the opposite desires, like those of asceticism and contempt for earthly riches, as we find them in many Eastern cultures and in the early stages of capitalism. The passion for money and property, according to Marx, is just as much economically conditioned as the opposite passions.

Marx's "materialistic" or "economic" interpretation of history has nothing whatsoever to do with an alleged "materialistic" or "economic" striving as the most fundamental drive in man. It does mean that man, the real and total man, the "real living individuals"—not the ideas produced by these "individuals"—are the subject matter of history and of the understanding of its laws. Marx's interpretation of history could be called an anthropological interpretation of history, if one wanted to avoid the ambiguities of the words "materialistic" and "economic"; it is the understanding of history based on the fact that men are "the authors *and* actors of their history."

In fact, it is one of the great differences between Marx and most writers of the eighteenth and nineteenth centuries that he does *not* consider capitalism to be the outcome of human nature and the motivation of man in capitalism to be the universal motivation within man. The absurdity of the view that Marx thought the drive for maximal profit was the deepest motive in man becomes all the more apparent when one takes into account that Marx made some very direct statements about human drives. He differentiated between constant or "fixed" drives "which exist under all circumstances and which can be changed by social conditions only as far as form and direction are concerned" and "relative" drives which "owe their origin only to a certain type of social organization." Marx assumed sex and hunger to fall under the category of "fixed" drives, but it never occurred to him to consider the drive for maximal economic gain as a *constant* drive.

But it hardly needs such proof from Marx's psychological ideas to show that the popular assumption about Marx's materialism is utterly wrong. Marx's whole criticism of capitalism is exactly that it has made interest in money and material gain the main motive in man, and his concept of socialism is precisely that of a society in which this material interest would cease to be the dominant one. (pp. 10-14)

It is very important to understand Marx's fundamental idea: man makes his own history; he is his own creator. As he put it many years later in *Capital:* "And would not such a history be easier to compile since, as Vico says, human history differs from natural history in this, that we have made the former, but not the latter." Man gives birth to himself in the process of history. The essential factor in this process of self-creation of the human race lies in its relationship to nature. Man, at the beginning of his history, is blindly bound or chained to nature. In the process of evolution he transforms his relationship to nature, and hence himself.

Marx has more to say in *Capital* about this dependence on nature:

> Those ancient social organisms of production are, as compared with bourgeois society, extremely simple and transparent. But they are founded either on the immature development of man individually, who has not yet severed the umbilical cord that unites him with his fellow men in a primitive tribal community, or upon direct relations of subjection. They can arise and exist only when the development of the productive power of labor has not risen beyond a low stage, and when, therefore, the social relations within the sphere of material life, between man and man, and between man and nature, are correspondingly narrow. This narrowness is reflected in the ancient worship of Nature, and in the other elements of the popular religions. The religious reflex of the real world can, in any case, only then finally vanish when the practical relations of everyday life offer to man none but perfectly intelligible and reasonable relations with regard to his fellow men and to nature. The life-process of society, which is based on the process of material production, does not strip off its mystical veil until it is treated as production by freely associated men, and is consciously regulated by them in accordance with a settled plan. This, however, demands for society a certain material groundwork or set of conditions of existence

> which in their turn are the spontaneous product of a long and painful process of development.

In this statement Marx speaks of an element which has a central role in his theory: *labor.* Labor is the factor which meditates between man and nature; labor is man's effort to regulate his metabolism with nature. Labor is the expression of human life and through labor man's relationship to nature is changed, hence through labor man changes himself. (pp. 15-16)

> *Erich Fromm, in his* Marx's Concept of Man, *Frederick Ungar Publishing Co., 1961, 260 p.*

STANLEY EDGAR HYMAN   (essay date 1962)

[*In the following excerpt, Hyman offers a detailed overview of the style and themes of Marx's works, focusing especially on their imaginative and dramatic aspects.*]

The Holy Family is . . . a negative preliminary work, a killing off of the "speculative idealism" of the Young Hegelians, Bruno and Edgar Bauer and their followers, and their master Hegel with them. It is an oddly schoolboyish polemic, and the wit is mostly ponderous. The Bauers called their movement "Critical Criticism," and Engels opposes to it "the base mass in all its massy massiness." . . . Marx, who wrote most of the book, indulges in a variety of comic devices. He creates Critical "idealistic intestines" to oppose to the "vulgar body," puns on the name "Bauer" ("peasant" in German), interrupts quotations with such asides as "Collect yourself, Reader," or wild calls for help, and creates antitheses on this order: "His art is not that of disclosing what is hidden, but of hiding what is disclosed."

Marx clubs the Bauers and their followers with French realistic socialism and the materialism of Ludwig Feuerbach. Edgar Bauer's translation of Proudhon is mercilessly mocked. Bauer does not understand: that Proudhon "first makes a real science of political economy possible"; that he proceeds not from the realm of ideas but "from the fact of poverty, of misery"; that "his work is a scientific manifesto of the French proletariat and therefore has quite a different historic significance than that of the literary bungling of a Critical Critic." Feuerbach is a hero because his *Theses on the Reform of Philosophy* were banned by the censor, as nothing by Critical Criticism would ever be. Charles Fourier's "masterly" remarks are quoted against Criticism's inanities.

Against the Bauers, and encouraged by Feuerbach's glorification of "love," Marx succeeds in defining (perhaps more eloquently than he ever did again) his own humanistic vision. He writes:

> Here Critical Criticism is not against love alone, but against everything living, everything which is immediate, every sensuous experience, any and every *real* experience.

The French Revolution, which the Bauers denigrate, was a "hammer" of freedom and enlightenment, and its slogans are still full of meaning:

> Equality is the French expression for the unity of human essence, for man's consciousness of his species and his attitude toward his species, for the practical identity of man with man, i.e., for the social or human relation of man to man.

Defending Proudhon's categories against Edgar Bauer, Marx writes:

> But Not To Have is not a mere category, it is a most disconsolate reality; today the man who has nothing is nothing, for he is cut off from existence in general and still more from a human existence.... Not To Have is the most desperate *spiritualism*, a complete unreality of the human, a complete reality of the dehumanized, a very positive To Have, a having of hunger, of cold, of disease, of crime, of debasement, of all inhumanity and monstrosity.

The importance of materialism, Marx explains, is that from the empirical world "man experiences and gets used to what is really human and that he becomes aware of himself as man." He sees the proverb "What's done is done" as "the *stoic* and at the same time *epicurean* human principle of a free and strong nature," and elsewhere affirms "human independence" against Christian "debasement."

Marxist editors have tended to scorn *The Holy Family* as "of little general interest today" or "a bit obsolete," ... but it is of great interest in foreshadowing most of Marx's later themes and imaginative designs. Its organizing metaphor is the blasphemous one of the title, that the Bauers are Jesus, Mary and Joseph. Criticism is "holy," "like God" it is almighty and all-wise, Bruno Bauer's treatises are "the annunciation of the Critical Saviour and Redeemer of the world" (the nasty comedy here is that Bauer had lost his teaching post for denying the historical reality of Jesus Christ). The group is endlessly called "the Holy Family of Charlottenburg" and "the Holy Critical Family," and Marx explains that it arose out of Bruno Bauer's divine freedom from all human passions:

> That is why he sets up for himself a *holy family*, just as the solitary God endeavours to do away with his boring isolation from society in the Holy Family.

Bauer can look forward to "the *Critical last judgment* like a second triumphant *Christ*, and, after defeating the dragon, ascend calmly to heaven." The last chapter of the book, "The Critical Last Judgment," is a wild parody of the Book of Revelation. (pp. 88-90)

As he attacks the Bauers and their followers, Marx attacks Eugène Sue's *Mysteries of Paris*, which they had praised, and for many pages he deserts the Bauers to go after the Sue directly. Sue writes to satisfy "his monkish, bestial lust" and is "the most wretched offal of socialist literature." His sin, like that of Critical Criticism, seems to lie in falsifying life, and thus denying it. Sue distorts love while Critical Criticism rejects it and "plays about with prostitutes." (p. 90)

Where *The Holy Family* had used Feuerbach's materialism to destroy the idealism of Hegel and the Young Hegelians, [*The German Ideology*] in turn kills off Feuerbach and the Left Hegelians and utopian "True" socialists he influenced, by all the former devices of mockery plus new charges of plagiarism and venality. The wild blasphemous outpouring of *The Holy Family* here is only a sacrilegious trickle: Stirner is "Saint Max" or "Blessed Max" and Bauer is "Saint Bruno"; "The bourgeois attitude towards the institutions of the bourgeois regime is like that of the Jew towards the Law"; True Socialism is founded and builds its Church on "the Rock of Ages," or uses a "stone which the builders have rejected" as its cornerstone, to find

it only "a stumbling-block"; Gruen is mocked with a parody of the Parable of the Talents.

Thinkers are now seen not as independent speculators, however misguided, but as spokesmen of a class, "ideologists," defined as those "who make the perfecting of the illusion of the class about itself their chief source of livelihood." They are thaumaturges and charlatans, and Marx and Engels continually expose "the whole trick" or "the following tricks" of their operations. They are again clubbed with the realistic French, with Fourier's "masterly observations" or "Gargantuan view of man," or the demonstration that Gruen has plagiarized from the French communist Cabet. The tone of anti-Germanism is now ferocious. (pp. 91-2)

Arid and quibbling as much of it is, *The German Ideology* nevertheless has the first bold imaginative designs in Marx's work. It opens in Marx's preface with a riot of metaphor. He paraphrases the view of the German ideologists: "The phantoms of their brains have gained the mastery" over men; "Let us liberate them from the chimeras, the ideas, dogmas, imaginary beings under the yoke of which they are pining away." Marx announces "the aim of uncloaking these sheep, who take themselves and are taken for wolves." Later Marx and Engels write: "They all imagine that they are weaving the web of history when, as a matter of fact, they are merely spinning the long yarn of their own imaginings"; or, "This great cock of the walk turns out, however, to be a perfectly ordinary capon." Sometimes the language is a fireworks of word-play, as when they write: "There must of necessity be one sacred head, the spearhead of all these philosophical and theological heads, in a word, the speculative unity of all these blockheads."

Behind the fireworks there are a number of comprehensive imaginative visions. One is of capitalism soiling and fouling everything it touches. The philosophers are "industrialists of philosophy," and "each with all possible zeal set about retailing his apportioned share." Trade, "as an English economist says, hovers over the earth like the Fate of the Ancients." Industrial capitalism "destroyed as far as possible ideology, religion, morality, etc., and where it could not do this, made them into a palpable lie." Bourgeois writers are "quacks and quill-drivers," "broken-down literary hacks." Wild nature has somehow been corrupted: there is "the bitterest competition among plants and animals"; tall and stately oaks are "tall and stately capitalists" consuming the nutriment of the tiny shrubs; parasites are "the ideologists of the vegetable world"; there is "open warfare" everywhere in nature. (pp. 92-3)

Opposed to [the] vision of universal war and corruption is an origin myth of Man Producing. Men become human only as producers: "They themselves begin to distinguish themselves from animals as soon as they begin to *produce* their means of subsistence, a step which is conditioned by their physical organization." (p. 93)

[*The Poverty of Philosophy*] is an attempt to demolish Proudhon and the French socialists, once so realistic compared with the woolly Germans, but now seeming equally utopian to Marx.... The only new device in Marx's bag of rhetorical tricks is that he corrects Proudhon's arithmetic and keeps reminding him of it. If the Germans are not social thinkers, they are the greatest scientists as well as the greatest musicians, and Marx says in the foreword that he writes as "both German and economist," that is, as a scientific economist. Treating Proudhon's idealism as he had earlier treated Hegel's, Marx stands every statement on its head, beginning with Proudhon's title....

The thinkers quoted against Proudhon are now the realistic English economists, and now Marx rather likes their bluntness. "Sophistication," he says wryly, "as the English call the adulteration of commercial goods." He writes approvingly of Adam Smith, but his particular hero is David Ricardo, the wealthy banker who expounded bourgeois society "scientifically," who "takes his starting point from present-day society," whose "theory of values is the scientific interpretation of actual economic life." (p. 95)

The only thing retained from German philosophy is the Hegelian dialectic, now purged of Hegel and his idealism. Marx explains and demonstrates the dialectic at length. Poor Proudhon is dismissed as some sort of social climber trying to be a Hegelian philosopher.... Instead of Hegel's "language of pure reason, separate from the individual," Marx's dialectic is now grounded in the real sensuous world. His constant appeal in the book is away from economic theory, abstraction, and category to observed economic behavior: "The old vine-growers of France in petitioning for a law to forbid the planting of new vines; the Dutch in burning Asiatic spices, in uprooting clove trees in the Moluccas," are source materials for studying the relation of scarcity to value. The consumer is not an abstraction but "the worker who buys potatoes" or "the kept woman who buys lace." History is seen as "a continuous transformation of human nature," the "idyll" of "the good old patriarchal life" on the soil has been "hurled into the movement of history," and the book ends with "the last word of social science," which turns out, surprisingly, to be George Sand's call to revolutionary action: "Combat or death, bloody struggle or extinction." (p. 96)

Few books, it seems to me, have based their economics more firmly on moral sentiment than *The Poverty of Philosophy,* and its characteristic tone is the strident voice of ethical outrage.... Some of the great moral themes of *Capital* are announced in miniature: Scottish economy is "the driving out of men by sheep"; the factory system is "children kept at work at the whip's end." Almost the only praise Marx had for Proudhon, when he wrote a memorial notice for him in 1865, is that Proudhon sometimes revealed "a deep and genuine feeling of indignation at the infamy of the existing order."

If this is the first hesitant voice of an Old Testament prophet, some of Marx's indignation with Proudhon in the book is directed at a rival, or false, prophet, a prophet of Baal.... "The actual Genesis," Marx snarls later in the book, "shows us God as the world's first manufacturer." The book's dominating metaphor, and one that from this time on distinguishes everything Marx writes, might be called, not "Secrets Wrested from the Bosom of God," but "Veils Stripped off Jezebel." Proudhon "rediscovers his first hypotheses in all their nakedness"; when he writes something, Marx must "tear the veil from this mystical language." Ricardo is reproached by the innocent French "because it annoys them to see economic relations exposed in all their crudity, to see the mysteries of the bourgeoisie unmasked." Proudhon disguises Society behind the "myth" of Prometheus, but Marx tears the mask away and exposes naked social relations. Most of Marx's mockery and parody of Proudhon's metaphors and "poetic images" stems from his conviction that they *conceal* and *hide,* whereas Marx's own metaphors and poetic images *reveal* and *expose.*

The other feature of the book that foreshadows the direction of Marx's future writing is a semi-dramatic form, not of the theatre, but voices perhaps in a lecture room or meeting hall. Even more than in *The Holy Family,* Marx interrupts quotations with asides, as though he were reading them aloud. He introduces authorities with "Let old Boisguillebert have the floor," or "Let us listen also to a modern economist." He asks and answers rhetorical questions, as though manipulating an audience.... In his *Address on the Question of Free Trade,* written at the same time, delivered at a public meeting, and printed as an appendix to the English translation of *The Poverty of Philosophy,* Marx goes directly into a playlet form to write speeches for manufacturers, workers, shopkeepers and farmers. From the dialogues of polemic, Marx was beginning to venture further afield into drama. (pp. 96-8)

In the revolutionary year of 1848, Marx's great masterpiece of rhetoric, *The Communist Manifesto,* appeared. The fog of polemical quibbling suddenly seems to clear, and the opening sentence is like a trumpet blast: "A spectre is haunting Europe—the spectre of communism." The spectral image had always fascinated Marx, and his early writings are full of it. What made this spectre different was that the others were illusions to be exorcised, whereas this concealed a reality that was, for the ruling class, worse than their phantoms. For the first time, Marx was in conformity with his last thesis on Feuerbach, he was no longer interpreting the world but directly attempting to change it. The last sentences of the *Manifesto* are a ringing call to action:

> The proletarians have nothing to lose but their chains. They have a world to win.
>
> Working men of all countries, unite!

Between this fierce opening and conclusion, a simple polarization of past and present history is offered. "The history of all hitherto existing society is the history of class struggles," Marx writes, and races through history documenting his generalization. The present struggle is sketched in with the same broad strokes: the bourgeoisie is not only wicked but inept, and "unfit any longer to be the ruling class in society," the proletariat is not only "the immense majority" but it has powerful allies like Marx and Engels, "a small section of the ruling class [that] cuts itself adrift, and joins the revolutionary class, the class that holds the future in its hands." Some of this is information addressed to the proletariat, some threats addressed to the bourgeoisie. (pp. 98-9)

The Communist Manifesto is almost an anthology of revolutionary rhetoric, and some of its most effective slogans are borrowed. Werner Sombart has shown that "The proletarians have nothing to lose but their chains" and "The workers have no country" are Marat's, and that "the exploitation of men by men" is from Bazard. The nexus of "cash payment" is Thomas Carlyle's, and had been quoted in Engels' *The Condition of the Working Class in England in 1844.* "The free development of each is the condition for the free development of all" is apparently modified from "the consumption of all," presupposes the consumption of all," a statement of Karl Gruen's mocked in *The German Ideology.* The *Manifesto* has this composite character because "Citizen Marx" had been directed to draw it up as an official statement by the central committee of the newly-formed Communist League, and had been given three earlier unsatisfactory drafts to work from, the last of them by Engels....

Engels' document, entitled *Principles of Communism,* is a question-and-answer catechism addressed to workers. It asks, and soberly answers, such questions as "What is the proletariat?," "What have been the later consequences of the industrial revolution?," "Will it be possible to abolish private property at one blow?'' Answers are lacking to such questions as ''How will the problem of nationalities be dealt with under a communist regime?'' and ''How will the various religions be dealt with under communism?'' as though Engels scrupulously recognized the difficulty of the questions. The tone is pacific, and Engels' characteristic answer to ''Will it be possible to bring about the abolition of private property by peaceful means?'' begins ''It is a thing greatly to be desired, and communists would be the last persons in the world to stand in the way of a peaceful solution.'' The list of a dozen recommended measures has a lot in common with Marx's list in the *Manifesto,* and is in fact somewhat bolder. (p. 100)

In other words, where Engels aimed at instructing the proletariat and reassuring the bourgeoisie, Marx sets out deliberately to incite the proletariat and provoke the bourgeoisie. This raises the interesting question of the audience for whom the *Manifesto* is written. *The Holy Family, The German Ideology,* and *The Poverty of Philosophy* do not really appear to be written with any audience in mind, or at best an audience of a few Hegel-reading radical intellectuals. Engels' draft is written to be read by every literate and serious working man, but Marx's text is written to be read by the world. Workers are to exult in it, but their enemies in chancelleries and bourses, in offices and clubs, are to read it too and shiver. . . . Anyone who had predicted that the next work by the author of *The Holy Family, The German Ideology,* and *The Poverty of Philosophy* would be a spectacular worldwide best seller could have gotten very good odds in the late months of 1847.

Perhaps the explanation is again not rhetorical effectiveness but imaginative design. The key metaphor in the work is the one of stripping away veils that made its first appearance in *The Poverty of Philosophy,* The *Manifesto*'s most powerful rhetorical passage is formally organized around that image. . . . (pp. 101-02)

It is the bourgeoisie, Marx says, that has pitilessly torn things asunder, drowned them in icy water, torn away the veil and left them naked, stripped them of their halo. In truth, Marx tears away these veils and halos in the bourgeoisie's name. *He* shows the naked reality behind the illusions, as Darwin showed the naked war behind the face of nature bright with gladness.

The other metaphors in the work similarly play on glamorous illusion and bitter reality: the aristocracy waved ''the proletarian almsbag,'' but the people ''saw on their hindquarters the old feudal coat of arms''; the aristocracy ''pick up the golden apples dropped from the tree of industry,'' which turn out to be wool, beet-sugar, and potato-spirits; ''Christian socialism is but the holy water with which the priest consecrates the heart-burnings of the aristocrat.'' The most elaborate mixed metaphor in the book is a peculiarly elaborate way of saying ''veiling nakedness.'' . . . The accompanying image of action is a fairy-tale one: as capitalism has transformed men into commodities, so communism will transform those commodities back into men. ''Laborers, who must sell themselves piecemeal, are a commodity, like every other article of commerce,'' but the revolution will break the spell and restore them as men, free to develop their human capacities. Marx had written in . . . 1844: ''One who compares the huge baby-shoes of the proletariat with the dwarfed and down-at-heel political shoes of the bourgeoisie, cannot but prophesy that Cinderella will grow to giant stature.''

Four years later, his Cinderella had become Jack the Giant Killer. The great historical drama, on the stage of the world,

was finally announced. No more closet dramas, concert readings on the lecture platform, or colloquies before the curtain of history. Marx swings into the last section of the *Manifesto* with impatience: ''But let us have done with the bourgeois objections to communism.'' He announces the great tragic drama of worldwide revolution, in which the proletariat will be bathed in blood, to wash off the bourgeois muck, and will rise in epiphany at the end, immaculate, transformed, glorious and all-powerful. Germany ''is on the eve of a bourgeois revolution'' which ''will be but the prelude to an immediately following proletarian revolution,'' universal and world-wide. *The Communist Manifesto* is in fact only a stage prologue to the greatest historical drama ever to be performed. (p. 103)

As a work of rhetoric [*The Class Struggles in France, 1848-1850*] is primarily, as its title suggests, an interpretation of contemporary history in terms of the conflict of classes. The classes are not the simple bourgeois-proletarian polarity of *Wage-Labor and Capital,* but a tangle of interrelating and opposing groups: the finance aristocracy, the landed aristocracy, the industrial bourgeoisie, the shopkeepers or petty bourgeoisie, the proletariat, the *lumpenproletariat* or declassed, and the peasantry. There is little direct economic analysis. . . .

Marx's rhetorical emphasis is not, as in *Wage-Labor and Capital,* on the permanent injustice of capitalism, but on the special and dramatic wickedness, luxuriance and immorality of the French ruling classes. (p. 107)

The thematic metaphor pervading *The Class Struggles in France* is that of a theatrical performance. What the declassed do surreptitiously, the ruling class does publicly and theatrically: ''On the most prominent stages of bourgeois society, the same scenes were publicly enacted which regularly lead the *lumpenproletariat* to brothels, to workhouses and lunatic asylums, before the Bench, to prisons, and to the scaffold.'' New classes of French society were suddenly ''forced to leave the boxes, the stalls and the gallery and to act in person upon the revolutionary stage!'' The Constituent Assembly ''played the principal and state role on the proscenium.'' The peasants, ''for a moment active heroes of the revolutionary drama, could no longer be forced back into the passive and spineless role of the chorus.'' ''With the proletariat removed for the time being from the stage,'' the bourgeoisie takes over. A period is characterized ''not by the phrase but by the accent and the gesture which enliven the phrase.'' This drama, however, is not the grand historical tragedy for which the *Manifesto* had raised the curtain. Marx tries a variety of theatrical identifications. At one point he calls it ''tragi-comic,'' at another ''a melodramatic scene''; at other times he describes it in terms of opera, ''many-voiced song'' from which ''the chest notes were missing,'' although loudly applauded by a claque.

What Marx finally identifies as his dramatic form is straight comedy. Events are a ''clumsily constructed comedy,'' the speeches of Barrot are ''worthy of a Beaumarchais,'' political jockeyings are ''this great comedy of intrigues'' and ''Thus the comedy was played.'' It is all ''an unutterable comedy.'' In this comedy ''the Bourse Jews'' or ''the Jews of finance'' are the stock comic Jew, sinister but harmless, ''Bourse wolves'' without any teeth. In the action, all the sections of the exploiting class have their masks torn off, ''the veil that shrouded the republic was torn to pieces,'' even the state deficit is rudely disrobed. It is Marx's old metaphor of stripping the veil from wicked Jezebel, but here closer to the throwing off of disguises at the end of the comedy. The party of the Mountain, Marx notes, ''instead of tearing his web of deceit to pieces, took the parliamentary comedy tragically''; but Marx knows that the real tragedy, the great historical drama, will come later. (pp. 108-09)

If *The Class Struggles in France* was high-level journalism, interested in pointing the moral of events for communist readers, *The Eighteenth Brumaire,* however close in time it is to the events it deals with, is history, primarily concerned with producing a meaningful and coherent organization of those events. Marx was testing his materialist theory by history, as his correspondence at the time shows he was similarly testing Ricardian economics. (p. 109)

There is a constant organic analogy for politics. ''These graded ministries constituted a sort of thermometer, on which parliament could read off the decline in its vital heat.'' Latent differences appear among the Party of Order ''much as when dried infusoria come into contact with water, exhibit renewed vital energy, and promptly undergo division.'' For the birth of Louis Bonaparte's dictatorship, Marx produces a particularly unlovely image: ''All that was needed was a bayonet thrust to burst the bladder, so that the monster could leap into the light of day.'' (p. 112)

In *The Class Struggles in France*, it had been ''the dung heap of history'' onto which repudiated parties were thrown. Here the same obsolescence is imaged in a book, ''Their page of history was closed,'' and it is obviously a playbook. Louis Bonaparte is trying to turn back to an earlier page, to revert to an earlier historical drama. ''From 1848 to 1851 there was nothing more than a walking ghost of the old revolution,'' Marx writes. Its present form is ''the adventurer who hid his commonplace and unpleasing physiognomy behind the iron deathmask of Napoleon.'' All sorts of ghosts walk the stage: rumors of a *coup d'etat* are a ''spook''; the ''Red Spectre'' is conjured up and exorcised; even Hamlet's ghost puts in its appearance. In his borrowed mask and costume and the lustre of his stage effects, Louis Bonaparte thinks to put on a brave historical pageant, but he is only the dead walking.

The drama finally performed on the stage, following the historical tragedy of the French Revolution, the prologue of 1848, and the comedy of the period covered in *The Class Struggle,* is farce, as the book's opening announces. With characteristic kindliness, Marx introduced Louis Bonaparte in *The Class Struggles in France* as the peasants' symbol. . . . In *The Eighteenth Brumaire*, Louis Bonaparte is the figure of the buffoon. He is ''this adventurer, goaded onward by his debts,'' whose ''long career as a vagabond adventurer had equipped him with sensitive feelers which enabled him to perceive the most favorable moment for extorting money.'' (pp. 112-13)

The Eighteenth Brumaire of Louis Bonaparte has little of Marx's familiar imagery of unmasking or tearing away the veil. The farce is all too nakedly visible on the stage. (p. 114)

A Contribution to the Critique of Political Economy, which appeared in 1859, is Marx's first ambitious publication as an economist. Written for his peers, it indulges in little rhetoric and keeps Marx's poetic imagination in check. . . . Much of its reputation comes from the official statement of the doctrine of historical materialism in the preface, an expansion of the briefer statement in *The Eighteenth Brumaire* about the economic foundation of society and the ideational superstructure. Marx announces the book's intention in the preface with the statement that ''the reader who wishes to follow me at all, must make up his mind to pass from the special to the general,'' and the first chapter explains that he will deal with a diamond

as a diamond, whether it is ''on the breast of a harlot, or in the hand of a glasscutter.''

Marx never regarded it as an easy, popular, or readable work. Much of the argument of the *Critique* is in the form of series of equations, and the style is that of a textbook: ''Let one ounce of gold, one ton of iron, one quarter of wheat and twenty yards of silk represent equal exchanges values''; or ''For the sake of simplicity gold is assumed throughout as the money commodity.'' Marx's ideal in the book is apparently the ''frivolous, rapacious and unprincipled adventurer'' Sir William Petty. . . . (pp. 116-17)

The *Critique* constantly suggests scriptural sinfulness: hoarders are searching for ''the eternal treasure, which neither moth nor rust can eat''; Luther is quoted against luxury and gluttony; there is even an odd joking reference to economics before Adam Smith as ''pre-Adamic,'' with its hint that bourgeois production is a Fall. (pp. 117-18)

A Contribution to the Critique of Political Economy was written by the first method, moving from concrete to abstract, but Marx's vision was of a work of economics that would move from the abstract to the concrete, ''a rich aggregate of many conceptions and relations,'' Darwin's tangled bank. It is the announcement of *Capital*. (p. 118)

[Aside from being a work of economy,] *Capital* is also a work of history. The first volume gives its subject a historical or genetic explanation in the penultimate section on ''The Accumulation of Capital'' and even a speculative prehistory in the final section on ''The So-Called Primitive Accumulation.'' Both turn out to be, as one might guess, histories of theft. The third volume is more traditionally historical, with Marx's dogged genetic concern, so that a chapter giving an account of the cotton crisis of 1861-1865 begins with a ''Preliminary History, 1845-1860.'' The fourth volume . . . is straight critical history of ideas. If the test of history is accurate prediction (as it is where history claims to be scientific), *Capital* does not come off as well as Marx's books on events in France, or even as well as his *Tribune* journalism. Marx sees a future of increased piece work, since ''piece-wage is the form of wages most in harmony with the capitalist mode of production''; of longer hours, since ''machinery is the surest means of lengthening the working day''; of lower wages, since ''The constant tendency is to force the cost of labor back towards zero''; of general worsening of conditions, since ''In proportion as capital accumulates, the lot of the laborer must grow worse.'' (pp. 128-29)

In some respects, like everything Marx wrote, *Capital* is a work of philosophy. Marx notes indignantly in the preface to the second edition that the Paris *Revue Positiviste* charged him with treating economics metaphysically. He replies that a Russian reviewer refutes the charge with the statement ''The method of Marx is the deductive method of the whole English school,'' although why a work cannot be both metaphysical and deductive he does not say. Sometimes, as Berlin notes [see excerpt dated 1939], Marx's concept of value seems very metaphysical, as when he writes: ''The value of commodities is the very opposite of the coarse materiality of their substance, not an atom of matter enters into its composition.'' Most of the philosophy in the book, however, is in the form of dialectics. In the preface to the second edition, goaded by his reviewers, Marx explains how his materialist dialectics (what Plekhanov later named ''dialectical materialism'') differs from Hegel's idealist and ''mystifying'' dialectics. . . .

The reversals and antinomies that so pleased Marx in *The Poverty of Philosophy* now lead to Hegelian paradoxes and ''reflex-categories'' in economics: ''Concrete labor becomes the form under which its opposite, abstract human labor, manifests itself''; ''The labor of private individuals takes the form of its opposite, labor directly social in its form''; ''It must have its origin both in circulation and yet not in circulation''; and so forth. Contradictions arise, interpenetrate, are reconciled, and provoke new contradictions. ''Relative surplus value is absolute,'' Marx announces like a good dialectician, ''Absolute surplus value is relative.'' (p. 130)

Whatever *Capital*'s field, Marx was interested in making the study of society scientific. He wanted ''the natural laws of capitalist production,'' defining ''laws'' as ''tendencies working with iron necessity towards inevitable results.'' It is these over-riding laws that forcibly assert themselves like gravity when a house collapses. The later part of the volume is full of them: ''the iron law of proportionality,'' ''the constant tendency to equilibrium,'' ''the law of capitalist production,'' ''the general law of capitalist accumulation,'' and so on endlessly. In this objective science, ''England is used as the chief illustration'' not because Marx is interested in the conditions of English life, he insists, but because for capitalist production, England is ''classic ground,'' or only in England has a phenomenon ''the classic form.'' . . .

More than any sort of social science, *Capital* is preachment, value judgment, moral exhortation, ethical protest and imperative. It seems amazing that this has been a matter of dispute. (p. 131)

Everywhere *Capital* reproaches the capitalists for their injustice, denounces the existing order as wicked, explodes with wrath or cries with pain. It is a Manichaean world in which the forces of good and evil are locked in eternal combat. . . . The book's vision, developing the Carlylean cash-nexus passage in the *Manifesto,* is of everything slimed and corrupted:

> Objects that in themselves are no commodities,
> such as conscience, honor, etc., are capable of
> being offered for sale by their holders, and of
> thus acquiring, through their price, the form of
> commodities.

As intangibles become commodities, man becomes ''a thing, although a living conscious thing.'' Women, of course, become prostitutes—what better symbol for turning flesh into commodity, people into things? Prostitution is everywhere in the book. ''Glasgow pigs together in its wynds and closes'' gallant Highlanders along with ''prostitutes and thieves.'' The factory relay-system ''drove the youths to the pot-house, and the girls to the brothel.'' With Australian unemployment, ''prostitution in some places there flourishes as wantonly as in the London Haymarket.'' The ruling class itself Marx divides into ''young whores and old nuns.'' The book quotes the cynical ''*Pecunia non olet*'' that one of the Roman emperors (Vespasian, I think) replied when charged with living off a tax on urinals. Marx keeps reminding us that in money we cannot smell ''a trace of surplus-value,'' but the final effect is to make the whole of capitalist production stink to heaven. *Capital* has little or nothing to say about communism or socialism, but a vision of the good life shines through it. . . . This good life is not only healthy, free, and spontaneous, but it is oddly primitive, rejecting the division of labor. It asks of men, with Goethe and Hegel, that they be able to do everything, that they be whole men. The capitalist world of cruelty, ruthlessness and horror

A drawing depicting Marx as Prometheus in chains, made after the banning of the Rheinische Zeitung.

is preparing the way for this better one with iron inevitability, and Marx walks before it with a lantern.

We get closer to the essential nature of *Capital* if we deal with it, not as science, social science, or exhortation, but as imaginative literature. In a letter to Engels in 1865, Marx wrote, ''Whatever shortcomings they may have, the merit of my writings is that they are an artistic whole.'' *Capital* is much more structured than its method of composition would suggest. Part I is brought to a climax with the Rabelaisian prose of Marx's old favorite Sir William Petty. . . . The book's periodic descents into the horrors of capitalism are spaced so that each comes as a fresh shock, and each is followed by a deliberate flatness, what Stendhal called ''benches for my readers to sit down on.'' Thus after the ghastliness of ''The Working-Day,'' Part III ends calmly on the bourgeois delusion ''that with the shortening of the working-day by 2 hours, the selling price of 12 spinning machines dwindles to that of 10!'' The book's effective finish comes at the end of the penultimate chapter, with the famous announcement about outgrown capitalism:

> This integument is burst asunder. The knell of
> capitalist private property sounds. The expro-
> priators are expropriated.

This is followed by a footnote quoting from *The Communist Manifesto.* The last chapter is a quiet coda, almost an appendix, the sort of anticlimax beloved of the Greek dramatists.

The poetic texture of *Capital* is an amazing richness of image, symbol, and metaphor. One of Marx's principal sources is classical mythology (he took a course in it at the university), which he uses with a surrealist freedom. . . . [In the preface, Marx talks of] ''the Furies of private interest''; to quote Petty's creation myth for material wealth, ''Labor is its father and the earth its mother''; to describe the ''Sisyphus-like labor'' of the hoarder; to reveal a law ''that rivets the laborer to capital more firmly than the wedges of Vulcan did Prometheus to the rock.''

If the laborer is Sisyphus and Prometheus, capital is not only Gorgon and Furies but a whole menagerie of supernatural horrors. It is a monster ''that vampire-like only lives by sucking living labor''; possessing a ''vampire-thirst for the living blood of labor''; and will not loose its hold, quoting Engels, ''so long as there is a muscle, a nerve, a drop of blood to be exploited.'' It has a ''werewolf's hunger for surplus-labor.'' *Capital*'s machines are giants and ogres: ''a mechanical monster whose body fills whole factories, and whose demon power, at first veiled under the slow and measured motions of his giant limbs, at length breaks out into the fast and furious whirl of his countless working organs.'' Two pages on machinery say ''cyclopean,'' ''stupendous,'' ''cyclopean,'' ''cyclopean,'' ''cyclopean,'' ''gigantic,'' ''monster,'' ''such a weight that not Thor himself could wield it.'' The capitalists are ghouls: ''coining children's blood into capital''; killing children in silk manufacture so that ''the children were slaughterd out-and-out for the sake of their delicate fingers''; exporting ''the capitalized blood of children.'' They are ''flesh agents,'' ''dealers in human flesh,'' and force workmen to become lesser slave dealers, and sell their own wives and children to the factories.

Accompanying these metaphoric myths are metaphoric rites. The most important are of birth and rebirth. Marx's aim, he says in the preface, is to ''shorten and lessen the birth-pangs'' of the new society. Capital is ''value big with value, a live monster that is fruitful and multiplies.'' ''Force is the midwife of every old society pregnant with a new one.'' Rebirth is a protean metamorphosis even in economics. . . . (pp. 132-34)

Marx's favorite metaphor in the early books, stripping away the veil, here finds its place as the ritual of exposing beautiful temptresses as the loathly hags they are. His preface announces not only raising the veil so we can see the Medusa head, but ''the ultimate aim of this work, to lay bare the economic law of motion of modern society.'' In a sense, it has already been done for him: ''Modern Industry rent the veil that concealed from men their own social process of production.'' Marx will expose the gods worshipped as things of wood and stone. In a section on ''The Fetishism of Commodities and the Secret Thereof,'' he explains that a commodity is ''something transcendent,'' that it has a ''mystical character,'' that it is ''a mysterious thing,'' and explains: ''In order, therefore, to find an analogy, we must have recourse to the mist-enveloped regions of the religious world.'' Marx then deals with commodities in terms of ''fetishism,'' ''magic,'' ''necromancy.'' The hoarder is a worshipper who ''makes a sacrifice of the lusts of the flesh to his gold fetish.'' (p. 135)

Like a poet, Marx strives to summon up an immediacy of sensation, to make the reader feel the experience itself. Adulteration is a good example. He begins with a footnote early in the book, remarking that those selling cheap bread below its value sell it ''adulterated with alum, soap, pearl ashes, chalk, Derbyshire stone-dust, and suchlike agreeable, nourishing, and wholesome ingredients.'' When he returns to the topic a few chapters later it is with increased fury. . . . Later in the book

Marx similarly forces the reader down into the filth and squalor of English workingclass life, into the choking factory room where ''it is exceptionally unpleasant to stand even 10 minutes,'' and children work 10 hours or more a day. He produces an oppressive sense of claustrophobia using nothing more than images based on statistics on the space workers are allotted: children working in a space of 12⅔ cubic feet, ''less space than the half of what a child would occupy if packed in a box measuring 3 feet in each direction,'' or bedrooms in which each adult had as much air as ''he would have if he were shut up in a box of 4 feet measuring each way, the whole night.''

Marx was somewhat defensive about the style of *Capital*. He writes in the preface to the second edition:

> The mealy-mouthed babblers of German vulgar economy fell foul of the style of my book. No one can feel the literary shortcomings in *Capital* more strongly than I myself.
>
> (pp. 135-36)

Along with the richness of imagery, the outstanding characteristics of Marx's style and language in the book are its polyglot and polymathic learning, and the vigor of its abuse. Besides the technical references to almost every science and branch of knowledge, the book is full of untranslated quotations in Greek and Latin, French and Italian, and English, as though Marx were writing not for an audience of workers but for German Ph.D.'s, as perhaps he was. (pp. 136-37)

The other barrier to the reader, Marx's polemic style, was natural to him and lifelong, if augmented during the composition of *Capital* by his miseries and physical ailments. . . . Marx's language is in fact restrained in the book, as compared to his correspondence with Engels, which crackles with invective and abuse. . . . In the first volume of *Capital,* invective and learning combine at times to produce an amazing rhetoric, as in a ferocious attack on ''the greed for gold.'' (p. 137)

The basic form of *Capital* is dramatic. Recommending that Engels study the Irish history of 1779 and 1780, Marx wrote to him: ''This period is of the highest interest, scientifically and dramatically.'' Although it was now balanced with science, his interest in the world stage of history remained as strong as it had ever been. Marx begins the book with an apology in the preface for making dramatic characters out of abstractions, like Darwin on Nature. . . . In fact, everything is personified in the book. Linen tells us things and ''betrays its thoughts,'' a table ''evolves out of its wooden brain grotesque ideas,'' any commodity is ''a born leveller and a cynic,'' ''commodities are in love with money, but 'the course of true love never did run smooth,''' prices are ''wooing glances cast at money by commodities,'' ''circulation sweats money from every pore.'' . . . The true dramatic hero of *Capital,* however, is the personified Proletariat, whose voice is suddenly heard addressing the Capitalist in the ''Working-Day'' chapter. . . . Elsewhere in the book, the Proletariat is silent victim rather than protesting voice, his role to suffer rather than act, and if the work is not a tragedy, its failure would seem to lie in the failure of its protagonist to be an active force.

The villainous real men in the book are rarely capitalists, almost always hireling political economists, and they tend to be rather ludicrous villains as Marx's invective heats up and begins to glow. (pp. 138-39)

The subsidiary personified villain in the book is the Jew. Marx loses few opportunities for a sneer or innuendo at Jews. The language spoken by commodities is Hebrew, and they are "inwardly circumcised Jews"; the quantity of precious metals in a country is not changed by "a Jew selling a Queen Ann's farthing for a guinea"; capital speaks in the voice of Shylock; "The chosen people bore in their features the sign manual of Jehovah." An old joke of Bruno Bauer's about the Jews, that they live "in the pores of Polish society" the way the gods of Epicurus live in the Intermundia, charmed Marx so much that he repeats it in every volume of the book. There are one or two sneers at Christians, on the order of "The sheep's nature of a Christian is shown in his resemblance to the Lamb of God," but the Jews are Marx's especial butt. (p. 141)

The dramatic movement of *Capital* consists of four descents into suffering and horror, which we might see as four acts of a drama. At first Marx writes as though he were taking the reader on a guided tour. . . . By the next page, we realize that we are actually being taken to the play. (p. 143)

The first act is "The Working-Day" chapter. Its theme is announced a few pages before it begins when Marx reminds the capitalists of "the boys and girls whom you employ," and its action is mostly the mistreatment of women and children. (pp. 143-44)

The next act is the "Machinery and Modern Industry" chapter, its theme announced in the preceding chapter with a footnote about "abnormal development of some muscles, curvature of bones, etc.," and the statement that manufacture "converts the laborer into a crippled monstrosity." Its dual preoccupation is the mutilation of men and the deaths of children. (p. 144)

The third act is the "The General Law of Capitalist Accumulation" chapter. Here working men are slain like the children, with the average life-span in Manchester 38 for the upper middle class and 17 for the workers, in Liverpool 35 for the upper middle class and 15 for the workers. The chapter sets its tone with a quotation from a Dr. Hunter: "It is not too much to say that life in parts of London and Newcastle is infernal." The Inferno we go down into is packed with the damned, a Bosch hell of bodies obscenely heaped together, where working people live up to 18 in a room, up to 10 in a cellar, 5 or 6 to a bed. "Adult persons of both sexes, married and unmarried," Marx writes, "are huddled together in single small sleeping rooms." "Decency must always be outraged, and morality almost of necessity must suffer," he concludes, adding a few choice details of bastardy and incest. (pp. 144-45)

The last act of Marx's drama is the book's final part, "The So-Called Primitive Accumulation." Here we go back into the origins of the capitalists' economic power: "In actual history it is notorious that conquest, enslavement, robbery, murder, briefly force, play the great part." . . . There are two sections of horrors. The first is a summary of the bloody legislation against vagabondage in England, concluding, "Thus were the agricultural poeple, first forcibly expropriated from the soil, driven from their homes, turned into vagabonds, and then whipped, branded, tortured by laws grotesquely terrible, into the discipline necessary for the wage system." The second is a recital of the crimes against the aboriginal peoples in the colonies. (p. 145)

All this is very far from the great historical tragedy Marx had been pursuing for twenty years. *Capital* has a pathetic rather than a tragic protagonist. Marx notes: "And just as in society, a general or a banker plays a great part, but mere man, on the other hand, a very shabby part, so here with mere human

labor." The dramatic form of *Capital*, I would submit, is Victorian melodrama. (p. 146)

Capital is a synthesis of many things. As Marx drew on a wide range of thinkers for his ideas, so he drew on many traditional forms in the culture besides drama. A comparison with scriptural form has frequently been made. Engels announces in his preface to the first English translation "*Das Kapital* is often called, on the Continent, 'the Bible of the working class,'" and it seems to have been so defined in a resolution at one of the congresses of the International. . . . In the sense that it could be quoted to all purposes and contains something for everybody, as the later history of communism and socialism shows, *Capital* is certainly a Bible. In terms of basic scriptural form, it is much less a Bible than *The Origin of Species*. Where scriptural form is a reenactment of creation followed by a fixing of destinies, or Genesis and Leviticus, Marx's laws arise out of the dynamic processes to which most of his book is devoted, with the myths and rites of Genesis appended in the history of accumulation at the end. (pp. 146-47)

Marx draws extensively on the Bible and Christian theology, but in a secularized and parodied form. He accepts as inevitable the consequences of the Fall in Genesis, Hegel's first negation, that labor is "the everlasting nature-imposed condition of human existence," but denies the Edenic myth, the negation of the negation, insisting that no human existence could or should be exempt from labor. Capitalism, he notes, has its own myth of original sin, the fable of the grasshopper and the ant. . . . Marx simply substitutes the story of Jacob and Esau, and dates man's fallen condition from the time one brother stole another's birthright. He mocks the theological vocabulary by using words like "incarnation" and "transubstantiation" for the embodiment of labor in commodities or money (with just a suggestion of seriousness in the sacrificial role of the working class). Marx takes a positive pleasure in blasphemy, parodying scriptural quotations: "As the hart pants after fresh water, so pants his soul after money, the only wealth"; "It is the old story: Abraham begat Isaac, Isaac begat Jacob, and so on. The original capital of £10,000 brings in a surplus-value of £2000, which is capitalized"; "Want of faith in the national debt takes the place of the sin against the Holy Ghost, which may not be forgiven"; "The birth of the latter [Modern Industry] is heralded by a great slaughter of the innocents"; "What then becomes of the ten commandments, of Moses and the prophets, of the law of supply and demand?"

In one of its aspects, *Capital* is sometimes quite funny, in a sardonic fashion. Marx remarks that Robinson Crusoe, as soon as he gets on the island, "commences, like a true-born Briton, to keep a set of books." He illustrates exchange with a Bible-seller who puts the proceeds into brandy, and comments "Our Hotspur is enabled to sell his Bible, and only because the latter has sold the water of everlasting life is the distiller enabled to sell his *eau-de-vie*." Marx characterizes the market economy: "There alone rule Freedom, Equality, Property, and Bentham." Of working women unemployed by a crisis: "They had time to learn to cook. Unfortunately, the acquisition of this art occurred at a time when they had nothing to cook." (pp. 147-48)

Capital is a tissue of puns and word-play, most of them untranslatable. An encounter between linen and a coat becomes a comic courtship because the German "*zugeknoepften*" means not only "buttoned-up" but "reserved," and because linen is a feminine word and coat a masculine. The few puns that can be translated come through without much distinction. . . . (p. 148)

The ultimate question about *Capital* is the one Engels asks in his preface to the second volume: "How is it that Marx's theory of surplus value struck home like a thunderbolt out of a clear sky, in all modern countries, while the theories of all his socialist predecessors, including Rodbertus, remained ineffective?" The poet Freiligrath thought that it was the book's appeal to businessmen, rather than economists "in sentiment" like himself, and wrote to Marx in 1868: "I know that in the Rhineland many young merchants and factory owners are enthusiastic about the book." Shaw's answer to Engels' question, in the preface of *Back to Methuselah,* is in terms of his own mystique: "Like Darwin, he had for the moment the World Will by the ear." I would submit that it was not Marx's theory but Marx's book as a powerful imaginative construct, like Darwin's, that struck home or seized the great ear. Perhaps the final irony was that of the Russian censorship, which permitted the publication of a Russian translation in 1872 on the ground that although the book showed a pronounced socialist tendency, it was not written in a popular style and was unlikely to find many readers. (p. 149)

> *Stanley Edgar Hyman, "Marx," in his* The Tangled Bank: Darwin, Marx, Frazer and Freud as Imaginative Writers, *1962. Reprint by Grosset & Dunlap, 1966, pp. 79-186.*

NATHAN ROTENSTREICH   (essay date 1965)

[*In his discussion of* The Poverty of Philosophy, *Rotenstreich explains Marx's antagonism toward Proudhon's philosophic abstractions, positing that Marx's arguments became exaggerated and refutable.*]

Marx's book, *The Poverty of Philosophy,* is without a doubt one of his most poignant works. It is important for the formulation of his own ideas, for the polemic carried on with his colleagues, and particularly for the determination of his own relation to philosophy. The title Marx gave to this book was derived from the title of a book by Proudhon, *The Philosophy of Poverty.* Nevertheless, Marx had some justification for using this title even though it approximated Proudhon's; beyond Marx's great love for acid language and for alliteration, it was his intention to show the poverty in the very nature of philosophical inquiry, as an inquiry involving contemplation and abstraction, and the poverty in the conclusions of the inquiry whenever they touch on the actual reality of man and his future. He found it necessary, therefore, to substitute for this inquiry something that would progress beyond philosophy and bring it to its realization, that is, an economic-intellectual inquiry arising in a Marxian theory to become the inheritor of a comprehensive philosophical world view. (pp. 105-06)

Marx's acidity in the polemic against Proudhon is of a relevant conceptual character. In addition, the polemic reveals a personal negative evaluation. As is well known, Marx was not an easy friend and a difficult adversary. He took advantage of the evident weaknesses of Proudhon, such as his ignorance of German, which he himself admits, and his lack of direct access to philosophical writings, especially those of Hegel, even though he felt himself influenced by these works. Marx argued that Proudhon used Hegelian-type phrases and did not in point of fact understand the method of the dialectic. In his typical mocking sarcasm, Marx said, "Let us for an instant take M. Proudhon himself as a category" and goes on to indicate that Proudhon did not use the dialectical manner. "It is not the category which poses and opposes itself by its contradictory nature; it

is M. Proudhon who disturbs himself, argues with himself, and strives and struggles between the two sides of the category." It is evident that Marx is engaging in a bitter personal criticism, when he says that the disturbance is to be attributed to the author and not to the content in front of him. (p. 106)

No doubt to a certain extent Marx was not fair to Proudhon, not because Marx argued against his philosophical importance, but because he argued against Proudhon's personal vacillation. . . . Proudhon's letter of 1846 in which he testified to his own condition as antidogmatic and said that he preferred to burn property in a small fire rather than spread new flames by a Bartholomean night turned against the owners of property. If Proudhon's weakness lay in deficient intellectual capacity, then Marx's criticism of Proudhon is a kind of exposure by the powerful of the weak. The weakness of Proudhon was the product of a conscious attitude, which showed awareness of the boundaries of dogmatism and led to arguments in the name of skepticism. In the violent polemic, Marx did not refer respectfully to the fully admitted conscious assumptions and limitations deriving from the attitude of his opponent. Marx himself did not prefer to burn his opponents in small fires. (pp. 106-07)

In his letter, Proudhon called Marx a philosopher and undoubtedly this name was in accord with the conceptual usage of the time. Marx in his book against Proudhon called him the "true philosopher." In this book, the fundamental position of Marx against philosophy as an engagement in abstractions becomes markedly clear. Hence, we must discuss the various terms and implications contained in Marx's argument. It is interesting to note that Marx did not direct his attack against abstraction as a general philosophical position. He objected to abstract inquiries into the matter of human reality in general and into matters of economic reality in particular. And he said, "What Hegel has done for religion, right, etc., M. Proudhon seeks to do for political economy."

What is this abstract occupation with matters of political economics? . . . Proudhon and others discussed economic exchange as personal exchange between two individuals, abstracting from the framework of society and history in which these exchanges take place. Marx pointed out two distinguishing characteristics of such abstract discussion. (1) This discussion isolates the individual man from his social surroundings and transforms him into an atomic creature. Abstraction means here the isolation of individuals from the social whole. (2) Abstraction takes place when the processes as they occur in actuality are not followed and when the creation of an artificial model, or the fabrication of processes in preferred; the argument being that this fabrication reflects or describes reality as it is. Marx wrote that, "He pushes abstraction to the farthest limits, in confounding all producers in a single producer, all consumers in a single consumer, and in establishing the struggle between these two chimerical personages. But in the real world matters go otherwise. The competition between those who offer and the competition between those who demand forms a necessary element in the struggle between buyers and sellers." The detachment of the individual from society and the concern with an imaginary model of society cause deviations from the dynamic nature of social reality. Marx's argument against the abstraction of Proudhon's inquiry, resulting from its philosophical nature, is also the substance of the Marxian argument against the socialist utopia. Utopia in general, and the socialist utopia in particular, are kinds of imaginary models. They represent the result and the manifestation of isolation from existing reality and the creation of another pattern of reality in its stead. Abstraction, therefore, is present in the foundation of utopia itself. Marx's argument against the abstract character of the economic analysis of Proudhon is thus but a detail of his arguments against abstraction in general, as in the first thesis on Feuerbach.

It can be urged that Marx exaggerated to such an extent in his arguments against abstraction that he began to become hyperbolic and that, at any rate, his conclusions are refutable. . . . Initially, Marx said that property developed in different historical periods and its nature was determined by the nature of the social relations. Therefore, the nature of a specific property in a specific historical period, such as bourgeois property, cannot be defined without referring to the period. It follows that the definition of a specific property is nothing but the description of the social and economic conditions of this particular society. Later, however, Marx exaggerated even more, saying that property cannot be defined at all without referring to a historical period. Marx did not want to deny that property exists in social reality. But does the *concept* "property" have no meaning at all? If it had no general reference, how could Marx use the concept property in referring to both the feudal and the capitalist periods? Does Marx want to assert that the use of the concept "property" is merely nominalistic? It would be difficult to hold that Marx was a nominalist in this matter. It is evident that there are constant factors in all property, independent of the actual historical scene, such as ownership and the actual legal sanction to use whatever the property owner has in his possession. Marx's emphasis on reality and history, dealt with later, caused him to exaggerate here. It appears not only in his nominalistic tone in whatever concerns concepts in general, but in his treatment of the constant factors in the historical evolution of property. In summary, the argument against abstraction is cogent in its proper place, that is, it is adequate against the substitution of a model for reality. The development of natural science in our time testifies to this. But the argument against abstraction does not apply to what is presented as essentially abstract, that is, to the concept; and the concept of property clearly is a *concept*. The argument does not apply to the relations existing in a complex reality, such as the relation of ownership, and the authority to exhibit ownership. This relation is not abstract, for it is a part of actual reality. Marx substituted the argument against the abstract for an argument against the constancy of features in a phenomenon like property, and these two are not one and the same thing. (pp. 107-10)

What led Marx to argue against Proudhon that, "We have now to talk metaphysics while speaking of political economy"? The debate with Proudhon on the question of the "established value" sheds light on this central topic. Marx understood Proudhon's treatment, and it seems that he understood it correctly, as the attempt to determine the absolute value of goods, a value independent of the circumstances in which the product is produced, in which it reaches exchange, and in which it is used by the consumer. To translate Marx's view into this language, it seems that he thought that Proudhon, as it were, sought to determine the *natural law*, as a law implied in the nature of reality, and thus hidden behind the *positive law*, connoting the law regulating the human conditions and social life here and now implemented by legal and political authorities governing and enforcing law. Proudhon thereby offered a solution to the socio-economic question whether the "established value" as the natural law should be the economic norm. Or, again, that the actual positive law should dominate society. The detach-

ment of the value of merchandise from the actual historical-social circumstances is merely an abstraction. Here Marx's statement is correct. This abstraction is not proper, since what is referred to is not the abstraction of concept or the detachment of the stable factor from surrounding circumstances. That to which reference is made is isolation of something that must not be isolated, that is, the actual value of merchandise or products. Marx was inclined to call all isolation of this kind "mystification." However, it seems that he was right when he argued that there is a kind of mystification in assuming the possibility of an established value. A mystification results if the attempt is made to discover a fundamental value separate from the merchandise. In opposition to this abstraction, Marx urges a return to reality. One of the distinguishing marks of this reality is that neither the producer nor the consumer have a free choice, and that a free buyer and a free producer are nonexistent when abstracted from circumstances, for they are actual and concrete agents. Since there is no absolute or established value beyond the economic circumstances, money is no longer viewed as a thing but as a social relation. The result of these considerations and analyses is not merely a new emphasis on actual reality in contradistinction to a model, but a further element is involved. When reality is approached abstractly, the relations between men (human relations as distinct from intermerging economic relations) cease to exist. On the abstract level, there are no concrete economic relations, only essences and categories. (pp. 110-11)

Has Marx shown that the power of reality reaches a point where all the relations existing within it become one and are no longer human relations but mere functional relations? Are they no longer relations between one individual and another, but only between workman and capitalist, for instance? Behind Marx's extreme analysis stands the concept of a comprehensive self-alienation within social reality. In order to gain the full import of the idea of this comprehensive and singular alienation of man from himself, it must first be determined that: (1) The power is inherent in all social relations to expropriate man completely from his essence and thus reduce him to an agent who only fulfills a function within social circumstances. (2) Man has no essence that can remain separate from and not eradicated by economic reality. Although in this particular book, Marx himself is inclined to the most extreme view that man has no constant essence, it is precisely this idea that is difficult to maintain or support from Marx's own analysis. For if man did not have an essence, the essence of a free creature not enslaved to its products, there would be no place for even a conceptual distinction between man as an individual and man as a self fulfilling an economic function, as is a workman or capitalist. Even though Marx was extreme in his formulations, we must adopt the idea that he assumed that man has a nature, even though it has become muddled and confused within economic reality. The more Marx attempted to clarify the power of reality factually, the more he tended to show the perversions that man undergoes in terms of his metaphysical essence ceasing to be man and becoming only an industrialist or worker. Thus Marx evaluated reality from the point of view of man's comprehensive nature, which became restricted and dismembered in the prevailing social conditions. To put it differently, Marx had no refuge from metaphysics when he criticized reality as having power over its own course of events, even though this reality is nothing but a perverted system when viewed in terms of the essential nature of man.

If the distinction between man as an individual and man in terms of an economic function is accepted, the question can be asked: Is a complete obfuscation of the human essence possible? Is it conceivable that man becomes merely an agent of an economic function? It seems that in the excitement of the polemic against utopian abstraction, Marx became caught up in what may be called *deterministic abstraction*, which caused him to attribute the decisive force of man to economic reality. It would have been enough if Marx had simply said that there is a contradiction between human relations and economic relations; or that there is a predominance of economic relations over human relations; for then he would not have been forced to such a radical statement as that human relations are completely nonexistent. He could have shown that economic relations are not human relations, and hence he would not have reached a level of abstraction at which he claimed that reality is nothing but economic relations. In summary, since the idea of the overwhelming force of economic relations could not stand on its own logic, Marx was led to the assumption or conclusion that economic relations are the comprehensive relations in human reality. When Marx said, ''The right is only the official recognition of the fact'' he wanted to make this include the economic right; but again, the argument of universality does not hold. It can be agreed that an economic right is the formulation of an economic fact, just as a physical law is the formulation of a fact, that is, the reality of nature. But when Marx broadened the formulation, saying, ''The same men who establish social relations conformable with their material productivity, produce also the principle, the ideas, the category, conformable with their social relations'', this was a broad formulation that included a great deal more than was necessary. It involved him in serious difficulties. What are the types of principles, ideas, and categories about which he spoke? If he was talking about economic principles, there is no quarrel. However, Marx did not formulate the matter solely on the basis of the relation between economic principles and the economic domain, but as a general statement based upon the use of the concept *category*. Is the category of reality, for example, determined by the realm of social relations? Marx referred to those individuals who establish economic relations and categories, as the same. Did he hold that, since the real man is the determined agent of economic relations, he is also the one who thinks up the categories of reality? This touches on the inner limitations of the philosophy of Marx. Precisely because he wanted to show the dependence of human reality on man, he was inclined to make an exaggerated interpretation of human reality. He placed in it everything that exists within the horizon of man, including principles and categories. Yet what is found within man's horizon is not as such the product of man *in* his social relations. That man lives in a changing reality does not transform all contents in this reality into a passing historical product. The Marxian attachment to actual social reality leads rather to radical historicist conclusions containing no internal necessity with respect to the issue under discussion, even if it is agreed with Marx that reality has a power of its own. Even assuming with Marx that work is a process occurring between man and nature and that man establishes his own metabolism with nature through his own act, it would not follow that there is no structure of physical nature that has to be comprehended and understood as such. Man's act may be related to changing historical conditions, but the structure of nature, thus in a way absorbed in history through the historical act, does not cease to have its own character, which has to be taken into consideration by human beings in their historical acts. Man changes nature, although within the limits of the structure of nature. It seems that Marx's radical historicism as exhibited here—even for the sake of polemic objectives—blurs the distinction between changing acts in nature, and nature as a structure of its own.

Another way to formulate the position of social reality is to emphasize the historicity of this reality, rather than the statements and the abstractions of Proudhon's theory. The subsequent discussion of the meaning of the Marxian concept of history shows that it is not at all univocal. One of the weak points of the entire system is that it uses the concept of history in its broad and hence ambiguous sense. (1) Marx stressed that, according to Proudhon, there is no room for *becoming*, because things did not come to be. Such factors as economic-social relations and economic laws are given a priori, according to Proudhon. Since there is no becoming, there is no dissolution. (2) Therefore, Marx felt entitled to identify history with flux. But this conclusion is not at all necessary. Even if it is believed that relations come about and are not given from the very beginning, it is not necessary to hold that these relations are in flux. At any rate, it is not implied that all that comes into being passes away again. In this matter, Marx seemed to accept as obvious certain cosmological assumptions, particularly those of the Middle Ages: since the world was created, it necessarily ends in time, it is transient. But Marx should have clarified the relation between what is coming to be and what is transitory and fleeting, as well as one other decisive matter—that knowledge may also come into being and pass away, so that there was a time when this or that phenomena was not known as it is known now. Did Marx want to say that what is known is in flux, for it was arrived at *through* an evolving process? It can be conjectured, for instance, that the idea of human rights came about in specific circumstances. First it was nonexistent, or was not considered valid, but now it is thought valid. Does the fact of the evolution of knowledge also imply the fact of the passing away of the content of what is known until it is no longer valid in any circumstance? In this decisive matter, Marx did not distinguish between coming to be and validity, and this failure is representative of his system in general. (3) Therefore, Marx opposed the position that the principle determines history and instead maintained the idea that history determines the principle. But, again, the meaning of this statement must be queried. Is the meaning simply neutral, namely, that any principle arises in specific historical circumstances, as does the principle of individualism, which, according to Marx, arose in specific circumstances? On the other hand, how does history as a process give rise to principles? Whence do principles come? Are not facts and events alone sufficient for history, without the formulation of principles at all? Is the very *realm* of principles determined by history? By not arguing through or clarifying the distinction between coming to be and validity, Marx failed to explain the relation between the spheres of principles and contents. He subsequently assumed in his famous statement, ''Existence determines consciousness,'' the unilateral dependence of principles upon history. (pp. 112-16)

Nathan Rotenstreich, "Poverty of Philosophical Speculation," in his Basic Problems of Marx's Philosophy, *The Bobbs-Merrill Company, Inc., 1965, pp. 105-43.*

GEORG LUKÁCS (essay date 1970)

[*Lukács, a Hungarian literary critic and philosopher, is acknowledged as one of the leading proponents of Marxist thought. In the following excerpt, Lukács discusses Marxist aesthetics, exploring its emphasis on realism, objectivity, and the role of the creative artist in society.*]

Marx's and Engels' studies in literature are in a peculiar literary form. The reader must understand first of all why they are as they are so that he can adopt a proper approach to reading and understanding them. Neither Marx nor Engels ever wrote a special book or even a particular essay on literary questions. In his maturity Marx constantly dreamed of expounding his views on his favourite author, Balzac, in an extensive critique. But this project, like so many others, remained only a dream. The great thinker was so completely involved in his fundamental work on economics until the day of his death that neither this work on Balzac nor one he planned on Hegel was ever realized. (p. 61)

[The] Marxist system—in contradistinction to modern bourgeois philosophy—never departs from the concept of a total historical process. According to Marx and Engels, there is only one comprehensive science: the science of history, which comprehends the evolution of nature, society and thought, etc. as an integrated historical process and aims at discovering its laws, both general and particular (that is, as they relate to individual periods). This view does not imply—and this is the second characteristic of their system—historical relativism under any circumstances. In this regard, too, Marxism is to be distinguished from bourgeois thinking. The essence of the dialectical method lies in its encompassing the indivisible unity of the absolute and the relative: absolute truth has its *relative* elements (depending on place, time and circumstances); relative truth, on the other hand, so far as it is really truth, so far as it reflects reality in a faithful approximation, has an *absolute* validity.

A consequence of this aspect of the Marxist view is that it does not admit the separation and isolation of individual branches of knowledge so fashionable in the bourgeois world. Neither science as a whole nor its individual branches nor art has an autonomous, immanent history arising exclusively from a peculiar inner dialectic. Their development is determined by the movement of the history of social production as a whole; changes and developments in individual areas are to be explained in a truly scientific manner only in relation to this base. Of course, this conception of Marx and Engels, which is in sharp opposition to many modern scientific preconceptions, is not to be introduced mechanically, as is customary among many pseudo-Marxists and vulgar Marxists.

We will return to this problem for further, close analysis. For the present, we merely want to emphasize that Marx and Engels never denied or misconstrued the relative autonomy existing in the development of particular areas of human activity (law, science, art, etc.). They recognized, for example, how an individual philosophic concept is linked to a preceding one, which it develops, combats and corrects. Marx and Engels deny only that it is possible to explain the development of science or art exclusively or even primarily within their own immanent contexts. These immanent contexts do undoubtedly exist in objective reality but merely as aspects of the historical context, of the totality of the historical process within which the primary role in a complex of interacting factors is played by the economic: the development of the means of production.

The existence, substance, rise and effect of literature can thus only be understood and explained within the total historical context of the entire system. The rise and development of literature are part of the total historical social process. The aesthetic essence and value of literary works and, accordingly, their effect, are part of that general and integrated social process in which man masters the world through his consciousness. In accordance with the first aspect of the Marxist system we dis-

cussed, Marxist aesthetics and literary and art history form part of historical materialism; and from the second aspect they represent an application of dialectical materialism. In both respects, of course, they form a special and peculiar part of *this whole,* with definite and specific laws and definite and specific aesthetic principles.

The generalized principles of Marxist aesthetics and literary history are to be found in the doctrines of historical materialism. Only with the aid of historical materialism can we understand the rise of art and literature, the laws of their development and the varied directions they follow in their advance and decline within the total process. That is why at the very outset we must examine certain general, basic questions regarding historical materialism. And not only to establish our scientific foundation but also to distinguish genuine Marxism, the genuine dialectical philosophic view, from its cheap vulgarization; for it is in this area that such vulgarization has perhaps most seriously discredited Marxist doctrine.

It is well known that historical materialism sees the directive principle, the basic determinant of historical development, in the economic base. The ideologies, including literature and art, figure merely as superstructure and thus as secondary factors in the process of development.

Misunderstanding this basic concept, vulgar materialism draws the mechanical, distorted and misleading conclusion that there exists a simple causal relationship between base and superstructure in which the former figures solely as cause and the latter as effect. In the view of vulgar Marxism the superstructure represents a mechanical, causal consequence of the development of the means of production. Such relationships are unknown to the dialectical method. Dialectics reject the existence of any purely one-sided, cause-and-effect relationships; it recognizes in the simplest facts a complicated interaction of causes and effects. And historical materialism insists that in a process so multilevelled and multifaceted as the evolution of society, the total process of the social and historical development emerges in the form of an intricate complex of interactions. Only with such an approach is it possible to confront the problem of ideologies. Anyone who sees ideologies as the mechanical, passive product of the economic process at their base simply understands nothing of their essence and their development and does not expound Marxism but a distortion and caricature of Marxism.

In one of his letters Engels says regarding this question: "Political, legal, philosophical, religious, literary and artistic development rest on the economic. But they also react on each other and on the economic base. It is not that the economic factor is the only active factor and everything else mere passive effect, but it is the interaction with the economic base which always proves decisive in the last analysis."

A consequence of this Marxist methodological orientation is the assignment of an extraordinarily important role in historical development to the creative energy and activity of the individual. According to the basic Marxist concept of historical development, man becomes differentiated from the animals through work. An individual's creative activity is an expression of man's creation of himself, of man's making himself into a man through work; the character, capacity and level of this development are determined by objective natural and social conditions. This conception of historical evolution runs through all Marxist social philosophy and consequently through Marxist aesthetics. Marx declares in one place that music creates a musical sense in men. This concept is again part of the total Marxist concept regarding the evolution of society. Marx concretizes this observation thus: ". . . only through the disclosure of the objective richness within man's natural being will the richness of the subjective human sensibility, an ear for music, an eye for artistic form, be trained for the first time or actually created: in brief, senses capable for the first time of human enjoyment, senses established as essential faculties of man as man."

This concept has great significance not only for understanding the historical and socially active role of the individual but also for understanding how Marxism views the individual periods of history, the evolution of culture, the limits, problems and perspectives of such an evolution. Marx concludes his statement as follows:

> The education of the five senses is the work of all previous history. A sense confined within harsh necessity has only restricted sensibility. For starving men civilized eating does not exist, only the mere abstraction: food. It can be absolutely raw and hardly distinguishable from animal fodder. The desperate or anxious man has no sensibility for the finest drama; the hawker of metals sees only the market value of a metal but not its beauty or special qualities. He has no mineralogical sense. Thus the objectivization of human nature, in theoretical as well as practical respects, is necessary for both humanizing man's mind and senses and for creating a human mind corresponding to the full richness present in man and nature.

Man's intellectual activity therefore enjoys a specific relative independence in every field, especially in art and literature. Any of these fields or spheres of activity evolves on its own—through the activity of the individual creative person—out of earlier achievements, which it carries to higher development, even if critically and polemically.

We have already noted that this autonomy is relative and that it does not mean a denial of the priority of the economic base. One is not to conclude, however, that the subjective conviction that every sphere of intellectual life evolves on its own is a mere illusion. This autonomy has its objective basis in the very nature of that evolution and in the social division of labour. Engels wrote in this connection: "People who are involved with this [ideological development, G. L.] belong to distinct spheres within the division of labour; thus they have the impression of cultivating an autonomous field, especially to the extent that they do form an independent group within the social division of labour, and their productions (including their mistakes) exert an influence on the entire social development, even on the economic. But in the last analysis, they remain under the dominant influence of the economic development." And in a further comment, Engels explains how he conceives the economic primacy methodologically:

> The ultimate supremacy of the economic development over these fields, too, is a certainty to me, but it takes place within the particular conditions of the individual field: in philosophy, for example, through the influence of economic factors operating primarily in a political guise on the philosophic material at hand, that furnished by the preceding philosophers. The

economy does not create anything *a novo,* but determines how the content of the earlier thought will be modified and advanced, accomplishing this indirectly for the most part since it is the political, legal and moral reflexes which exercise the greatest direct effect on philosophy.

What Engels says here about philosophy is fully pertinent to the basic principles of the development of literature. It goes without saying that considered in isolation every development has its own particular character, that one cannot mechanically generalize on an apparent parallelism in two developments and that the evolution of any particular sphere has its own peculiar character and its own laws within the laws of the total social development.

Now if we attempt to concretize the general principle in what we have discussed, we arrive at one of the important principles of the Marxist conception of history. In absolute opposition to vulgar Marxism, historical materialism recognizes that ideological development does not move in a mechanical and predetermined parallel with the economic progress of society. It has certainly never been inevitable in the history of primitive communism and of class societies (societies about which Marx and Engels wrote) that every economic and social upsurge be accompanied by a flourishing of literature, art and philosophy; it is certainly not inevitable that a society on a high social level have a literature, art and philosophy at a higher stage of evolution than a society on a lower level.

Marx and Engels repeatedly and emphatically pointed out this uneven development in the field of the history of ideologies. Engels illustrated this concept by noting that French philosophy in the eighteenth and German philosophy in the nineteenth century emerged in completely, or at least comparatively, backward nations; thus in philosophy these lands could exercise a leading role though economically backward in comparison to the countries surrounding them. Engels stated: "And so it happens that economically retarded nations can play first violin in philosophy: France in the eighteenth century as against England, on whose philosophy the French based their own; later Germany in regard to both."

Marx formulated this concept in general terms in regard to literature but perhaps even more acutely and decisively. He declared:

> In art it is recognized that specific flourishing periods hardly conform to the general development of society, that is, of the material base, the skeleton, so to speak, which produces them. For example, the Greeks compared with the moderns, or Shakespeare. People understand that certain forms in art, like the epic, for example, can no longer be produced in the classical form exemplifying an epoch of history, once art production as such emerges; thus within the realm of art itself certain genres are possible only at an underdeveloped stage of artistic evolution. If this is the case with particular art forms, then it is not at all surprising that it should be the case in the relationship of art as a whole to the general development of society.

For genuine Marxists such a conception of historical development precludes any schematic approach, any recourse to analogies and mechanical parallels. How the principle of uneven development is manifested in any field in the history of ideologies in any period is a concrete historical question which a Marxist can answer only on the basis of a concrete analysis of the concrete situation. That is why Marx concluded his statement by saying: "The difficulty lies only in the general formulation of these contradictions. As soon as they are made specific, they are immediately resolved."

Marx and Engels defended themselves during their entire careers against the oversimplification and vulgarization of their so-called disciples, who substituted for the concrete study of the concrete historical process a conception of history based on abstract deductions and analogies and sought to substitute mechanical relationships for complicated, concrete dialectical relationships. (pp. 61-8)

Although the historical investigations of Marx and Engels in the field of art and literature encompass the entire development of society, they directed their attention chiefly, as they did in their scientific investigations of economic development and social struggles, to analyzing the fundamental issues of their time, of modern developments. If we examine the Marxist approach to literature, we see what an important role is assigned to the principle of the uneven development in extrapolating the particularities of any period. Undoubtedly, capitalism represented the highest stage of economic production in the development of class societies. But Marx was also convinced that this mode of production was essentially unpropitious for the evolution of literature and art. Marx was not the first nor the only one to expose this fact. But he was the first to disclose the factors responsible for this state of affairs in their full scope. For one gains insight into such a situation only through a comprehensive, dynamic and dialectical approach. Of course we can merely touch on this question here.

It should now be clear to the reader that Marxist literary theory and history constitute only part of a comprehensive whole: historical materialism. Marxism does not define the fundamental hostility to art of the capitalist mode of production from an aesthetic point of view. Indeed if we were to make a quantitative or statistical study of Marx's comments, something which is impermissible, of course, we might say from the start that such questions hardly interested him. But anyone who has studied *Capital* and Marx's other writings attentively will see that (in context) some of his comments provide a more profound insight into the heart of the question than the writings of anti-capitalist romanticists who busied themselves with aesthetics all their lives. Marxist economics actually relates the categories of economics, the basis of social life, back to where they appear in reality, as human relationships and past these to the relationship of society to nature. Yet Marx simultaneously demonstrates that under capitalism all these categories appear absolutely reified so that their true essence, men's relationships, are obscured. It is this inversion of the fundamental categories of existence that produces the fetishizing of capitalist society. In men's consciousness, the world appears otherwise than it is, distorted in structure, divorced from its actual relationships. Under capitalism a special intellectual effort is required for a man to see through this fetishizing and grasp the actual substance—man's social relations—behind the reified terms which determine daily life (goods, gold, prices, etc.).

Now humanism, that is, the passionate study of man's nature, is essential to all literature and art; and good art and good literature are humanistic to the extent that they not only investigate man and the real essence of his nature with passion but also and simultaneously defend human integrity passionately against all attacks, degradation and distortion. Since such

tendencies (especially the oppression and exploitation of man by man) attain such a level of inhumanity in no other society as under capitalism just because of the objective reification we have mentioned, every true artist, every true writer as a creative individual is instinctively an enemy of this distortion of the principle of humanism, whether consciously or not.

It is obviously impossible to pursue this question further here. In an analysis of particular works of Goethe and Shakespeare, Marx emphasizes the dehumanizing effect of money, which deforms and corrupts mankind:

"Shakespeare emphasizes two aspects of money:

"1. It is the visible divinity, the transformation of all human and natural qualities into their opposite, the general distortion and inversion of things; it reconciles impossibilities;

"2. It is the universal whore, the universal procurer of men and nations.

"The distortion and inversion of all human and natural qualities, the reconciliation of impossibilities—the *divine* power—in money derives from its being essentially the alienated, alienating and self-alienating essence of the human species. It is the property of mankind alienated.

"What I cannot do as a *man,* what is beyond my innate capacities, I accomplish through money. Money thus transforms each of these essential capacities into something that it is not in itself, that is, into its opposite."

Marx's statement does not cover all the major ramifications of the question. The hostility toward art in the capitalist mode of production is exemplified in the capitalist division of labour. To understand this contention fully one must refer to the totality of the economy once again. We will investigate only one aspect of our problem, the principle of humanism again, which the proletarian struggle for freedom inherited from earlier democratic and revolutionary movements and evolved to a higher qualitative level: the demand for a free development of a many-sided, integrated man. Contrarily, the hostility to art and culture inherent in the capitalist mode of production brings a disintegration of man, a disintegration of the concrete totality into abstract specializations.

The anti-capitalist romantics also understood this fact. But viewing it simply as fate or misfortune, they sought refuge sentimentally and idealistically in primitive societies and inevitably ended as reactionaries. Marx and Engels never denied the progressive character of the capitalist mode of production, but they were relentless in exposing its inhumanity. They demonstrated that on this road mankind could only create the material bases for the final and real liberation, socialism. But though recognizing the economic, social and historical inevitability of the capitalist social order and decisively repudiating any nostalgia for epochs that had already had their day, Marx and Engels did not relax their criticism of capitalist culture but even intensified their attacks. If they refer to the past, they do not do so in any romantic flight into the past but merely to determine the origin of a struggle for freedom which advanced mankind out of a still more sordid and desperate period of exploitation and oppression, feudalism. Thus when Engels writes of the Renaissance, he directs his comments to the struggles for freedom, to the initial stages of the workers' struggles for freedom; and if he contrasts the mode of production with the later capitalist division of labour, he does not do so to exalt the former but rather to point the way to future liberation. (pp. 68-71)

Marx and Engels urged the writers of their time to take an effective stand through their characters against the destructiveness and degradation of the capitalist division of labour and to grasp man in his essence and totality. And because they missed in most of their contemporaries this attempt at viewing mankind individually and as a whole, they considered these writers insignificant epigones. (p. 71)

From the foregoing observations it should be clear how the economic base of the capitalist mode of production reacts upon literature—for the most part independently of the author's control. But Marx and Engels hardly underestimated the subjective aspect of creation. In the course of our further discussion we will return for a closer examination of this question. Now we will merely call attention to one particular. The average bourgeois writer, identifying with his class and its prejudices and with capitalist society in general, is fearful of attacking real problems and shrinks from doing so. In the course of the ideological and literary struggles of the late 1840s, the youthful Marx wrote a close critique of Eugene Sue's extraordinarily popular and influential novel then being widely read in Germany, *The Mysteries of Paris*. We will merely note that Marx lashed out at Sue for his cowardice in depicting only the surface of capitalist society and for his opportunism in distorting and falsifying reality. Of course, no one reads Sue any more. But in every decade fashionable writers appear who cater to bourgeois moods of the moment, writers for whom, with appropriate modifications, this critique is fully pertinent.

We have seen our analysis, which began with the origin and development of literature, shift almost imperceptibly to aesthetic questions in the narrower sense. And so we arrive at the second complex of questions in the Marxist view of art. Marx considered the investigation of historical and social conditions in the genesis and development of literature to be extraordinarily important, but he never contended that literary questions were thereby exhausted: ". . . the difficulty does not lie, however, in understanding how Greek art and epic are linked to certain social forms of development. The difficulty is in understanding why they still provide us with aesthetic pleasure and serve in certain measure as norms and unattainable examples."

Marx approaches the question which he poses himself from both contextual and historical points of view, noting the relevance of the Greek world, the normal childhood of humanity, to the spiritual life of later generations. The investigation thus does not return to the problem of the social origin but advances to the formulation of basic principles of aesthetics, again not from a formalistic point of view but within a comprehensive dialectical context. Marx's reply indeed evokes two great complexes of questions concerning the aesthetic essence of a work of art of any period: what is the significance of such a representation of the world within the evolution of mankind? And how does the artist represent a particular stage within this evolution?

Only with such an approach can we proceed to the question of artistic form. This question can, of course, be posed and answered only in closest relationship to the general principles of dialectical materialism. It is a fundamental thesis of dialectical materialism that any apperception of the external world is nothing but the reflection of a reality existing independently of the consciousness, in the thoughts, conceptions, perceptions, etc., of men. Though in the most general formulation of this thesis, dialectical materialism is in agreement with all other types of materialism and in sharp opposition to any variant of idealism, it is still to be decisively distinguished from mechanical materialism. Criticizing this outmoded materialism, Lenin insisted that it is not capable of conceiving the theory of reflection dialectically.

As a mode of reflection of the external world in human consciousness, artistic creation is subsumed under the general epistemology of dialectical materialism. However, because of the peculiar character of artistic creation, it is a particular, special part often with distinctive laws of its own. In the following remarks, we will touch on some of the particularities of the literary and artistic reflection without attempting, even in broad outline, any exhaustive treatment of this complex question.

The theory of reflection is nothing new in aesthetics. The image, the mirroring, to use the metaphor made famous in the play scene in *Hamlet*, where Shakespeare exposed his own literary theory and practice, is an ancient concept. It was central to Aristotle's aesthetics and has continued to dominate nearly every great aesthetic since—except for the periods of decadence. An account of this historical development is, of course, beyond the scope of this [essay]. We need merely point to the many idealistic aesthetics (Plato's, for example) which in their own way are based on this theory. More important is the fact that all great writers of world literature have instinctively or more or less consciously followed this theory of reflection in their work and have followed this orientation in seeking to clarify their own artistic principles. The aspiration of all great writers has been the artistic reproduction of reality; fidelity to reality, the unsparing effort to render reality comprehensively and realistically has been the real criterion of literary greatness for every great writer (Shakespeare, Goethe, Balzac, Tolstoy).

The fact that Marxist aesthetics approaches this key question without any pretension to radical innovation surprises only those who, without any basis or real knowledge, associate the ideology of the proletariat with the "radically new", with artistic avantgarde-ism, believing that the cultural liberation of the proletariat means the complete abandonment of the past. The classics and founders of Marxism never maintained such a view. In their judgment, the liberation struggles of the working class, the working-class ideology and culture to be created, are the heir to all mankind has produced of value over the millenia.

Lenin once declared that one of the superiorities of Marxism to bourgeois ideologies lay precisely in its capacity critically to accept the progressive cultural heritage and to absorb whatever was great in the past. Marxism does surpass its predecessors only insofar—but this "only" is of extraordinary significance for methodology and content—as it renders all their aspirations conscious, eliminating all idealistic and mechanistic deviations, relates these aspirations of their effective causes and includes them in a system of consciously defined laws of social development. In the field of aesthetics, literary theory and literary history, we can say in summary that Marxism raises to conceptual clarity those fundamental principles of creative activity which have been present in the philosophic outlook of the best thinkers and the works of the outstanding writers and artists over the centuries.

To clarify some of the more important problems involved here, we have to face the question: what is that reality of which literary creation must provide a faithful reflection? The negative response is required first of all: this reality does not consist simply of the immediately perceptible superfice of the external world, nor simply of accidental, ephemeral, contingent phenomena. While Marxist aesthetics makes realism the crux of its theory of art, it also combats vigorously any kind of naturalism and any direction which is satisfied with a photographic reproduction of the immediately perceptible superfice of the external world. Here again Marxist aesthetics does not propound anything radically new but merely raises to the highest level of consciousness and clarity what has been central to the theory and practice of great artists of the past.

Marxist aesthetics combats with equal vehemence another false extreme in the theory and practice of art, the conception which holds that since copying reality is to be rejected and artistic forms are independent of this superficial reality, artistic forms therefore possess their own autonomy, that perfection of form and striving after perfection are ends in themselves abstracted from reality and that artistic perfection is independent of reality; and thus the artist has the right to transform and stylize reality at will. In this struggle Marxism continues and expands the view of the truly great figures of world literature regarding the nature of art, according to which the task of art is the truthful and accurate representation of the totality of reality; art in this view is as far removed from the photographic copy as it is from what is ultimately mere dabbling with abstract forms.

With such a conception of art, a key question of the epistemology of dialectical materialism is posed: the question of appearance and reality, a question with which bourgeois thought and consequently bourgeois aesthetics has never been able to cope. Naturalistic theory and practice propounds a mechanical, anti-dialectical unity between appearance and reality; in this dubious hotch-potch, reality is inevitably obscured and generally even disappears. The idealistic philosophy of art and the artistic practice of formalist stylization sometimes recognize the contrast between reality and appearance, but through lack of dialectic or through incomplete idealist dialectic see only the antithesis between appearance and reality without recognizing the dialectical unity of opposites in this antithesis. (This problem is obvious in Schiller, both in his interesting and searching aesthetic studies and in his creative practice.) And the literature and theory of decadent periods generally combine both false tendencies: in place of a true investigation of reality, there is a dabbling with superficial analogies as much abstracted from reality as the theories of ideas in the classics of idealism; these empty constructions are then adorned with naturalistic, impressionistic, etc., details, and parts organically related are assembled into a pseudo-unity by means of some mystical ''conception of the world''.

The true dialectic of reality (Wesen) and appearance rests on their being equal aspects of objective reality (Wirklichkeit), products of reality and not just of consciousness. Yet—and this is an important axiom of dialectical apprehension—reality has various levels; there is the ephemeral reality of the superfice, never recurring, momentary; and there are the more profound elements and tendencies of reality which recur in accordance with definite laws and change according to changing circumstances. This dialectic pervades the whole of reality so that in this context appearance and reality constantly achieve new relationships; that which opposed appearance as reality, as we look beneath the superfice of immediate experience, figures upon renewed examination as appearance, behind which another, new reality arises. And so on to infinity.

True art thus aspires to maximum profundity and comprehensiveness, at grasping life in its all-embracing totality. That is, it examines in as much depth as possible the reality behind appearance and does not represent it abstractly, divorced from

phenomena and in opposition to phenomena, but represents instead and dynamic dialectical process in which reality is transformed into appearance and is manifested as a phenomenon and reveals the other side of the process in which phenomenon in motion discloses its own particular reality. Furthermore, these individual aspects not only contain a dialectical movement, a transference into each other, but also stand in continuous interaction as elements of a continuous process. Real art thus represents life in its totality, in motion, development and evolution.

Since the dialectical conception combines the universal, particular and individual into a dynamic unity, it is clear that this particular dialectics must also be manifested in specific art forms. For in contrast to science which dissolves this activity into its abstract elements and seeks to conceptualize the interaction of these elements, art renders this activity perceptually meaningful as movement in a dynamic unity. One of the most important categories of this artistic synthesis is the type. Thus Marx and Engels allude to this concept first in defining true realism. (pp. 72-7)

The type, according to Marx and Engels, is not the abstract type of classical tragedy, nor the idealized universality as in Schiller, still less what Zola and post-Zola literature and literary theory made of it: the average. What characterizes the type is the convergence and intersection of all the dominant aspects of that dynamic unity through which genuine literature reflects life in a vital and contradictory unity—all the most important social, moral and spiritual contradictions of a time. The representation of the average, on the other hand, inevitably results in diluting and deadening these contradictions, the reflection of the great problems of any age; by being represented in the mind and experiences of an average man, they lose their decisiveness. Through the representation of a type, the concrete, universal and essential qualities, what is enduring in man and what is historically determined and what is individual and what is socially universal, combine in typical art. Through the creation of the type and the discovery of typical characters and typical situations, the most significant directions of social development obtain adequate artistic expression.

We must add another observation to these general remarks. Marx and Engels saw in Shakespeare and Balzac (as against, we may note, Schiller and Zola respectively) the artistic, realistic direction which best conformed to their aesthetic. The choice of these particular outstanding figures reveals that the Marxist conception of realism is not to be confused with any photographic reproduction of daily life. Marxist aesthetics simply asks that the writer represent the reality he has captured not abstractly but as the reality of the pulsating life of pheomena of which it forms an organic part and out of whose particular experiences it evolves. But in our opinion it is not necessary that the phenomena delineated be derived from daily life or even from life at all. That is, free play of the creative imagination and unrestrained fantasy are compatible with the Marxist conception of realism. Among the literary achievements Marx expecially valued are the fantastic tales of Balzac and E. T. A. Hoffmann.

Of course there is imagination and imagination, and fantasy and fantasy. If we seek a criterion by which to judge them, we must return to the fundamental doctrine of dialectical materialism: the reflection of reality.

Marxist aesthetics, which denies the realism of a world depicted through naturalistic detail if it does not express the essential dynamic forces, accepts the fantastic tales of Hoffmann and Balzac as among the highest achievements of realistic literature, since these essential elements are exposed through the very fantasy. The Marxist conception of realism is realism in which the essence of reality is exposed perceptually and artistically. This represents the dialectical application of the theory of reflection to the field of aesthetics. It is not surprising therefore that the concept of the type should be emphasized in Marxist aesthetics. The type, on the one hand, permits a resolution of the dialectic between reality and appearance not to be found in any other field; on the other hand, it provides a link to the social and historical process of which the best realistic art provides an accurate reflection. This Marxist conception of realism represents a continuation of what great masters of realism like Fielding demanded of their own artistic practice. They called themselves historians of bourgeois reality, of the private life of their times. But Marx goes further in regard to the relation of great realistic art to historical reality, assessing the works of the realists even more highly than they did themselves. (pp. 78-9)

In posing such demands on art, Marxist aesthetics demonstrates its consequent, radical objectivity. In the Marxist view the definitive quality in great realism is the passionate and dedicated search to grasp and reproduce reality as it is objectively and essentially. There are many misconceptions in regard to this tenet of Marxist aesthetics. Many people claim it means underestimating the role of the creative artist and of the subjective factors in creative effort. People confuse Marx with the vulgarizers who pretend that the mechanistic and false objectivism of naturalism is Marxism. We have seen that one of the central problems of Marxist ideology is the dialectic of appearance and reality, the recognition and extrapolation of the reality from the network of contradictory phenomena. If we do not believe that the creative artist "creates" something radically new *ex nihilo* but recognize that he discovers a reality existing independently of himself and not accessible to everyone, eluding for a long time even the greatest artists, then the activity of the creative artist not only is not eliminated; it is not diminished in the slightest. If Marxist aesthetics views as the greatest achievement of the creative effort the artist's making us aware of the social process and making it meaningful and experientially accessible and in setting down in his work his own self-awareness and his own awakening to the social evolution—surely the result is no underestimation of the artist's activity but a just and lofty assessment, such as has never previously been accorded.

Here, as elsewhere, Marxism presents nothing "radically new". Platos's aesthetics, the doctrine of the aesthetic reflection of ideas, treats this question. But Marxism once again sets right side up the aesthetic truth which the great idealists had left standing on its head. On the one hand, as we have seen, Marxism does not admit an exclusive opposition between appearance and reality but seeks the reality in the appearance and the appearance in its organic relation to the reality. On the other hand, for Marxism the aesthetic capturing of the reality and of the idea is not a simple, definitive act but a process, an active, step-by-step approximation of essential reality, a recognition of the fact that the most profound essence of reality is never more than a part of the total reality to which the surface phenomena also belong.

If Marxism demands radical, extreme objectivity in aesthetic cognition and representation, it also emphasizes the indispensable role of the creative artist. For this process, this step-by-step approximation of the hidden reality, is accessible only to the greatest and most persevering genius. The objectivity of Marxist science extends even to recognizing the abstraction—the truly meaningful abstraction—not as a mere product of man's consciousness, but further to demonstrating how (especially with the primary forms of the social process, the economic forms) the abstraction is itself a product of social reality. Investigating this process of abstraction with clearsighted imagination, unravelling its intricacies and concentrating the full complexity within the general process into typical characters and situations is a task which only the greatest artistic genius can attempt.

We see then that the objectivity of Marxist aesthetics does not lead to a rejection of the subjective factor in art at all. However there is still another aspect of this question to be examined. We must note that the objectivity enunciated by Marxism does not imply non-partisanship toward social developments. Marxist aesthetics correctly recognizes that since the great artist does not represent static objects and situations but seeks to investigate the direction and tempo of a process, he must grasp in his art the character of such a process; and such understanding in itself presupposes taking a stand. The concept of the artist as an uncommitted observer above social movements (Flaubert's "impassibilité") is at best an illusion or self-deception; or, more generally, simply an evasion of the basic issues of life and art. There are no great artists who do not express their own attitudes, yearnings and aspirations in their representation of reality.

Does this contention contradict our previous statement that the essence of Marxist aesthetics is its objectivity?

We do not think so. And to eliminate confusion about any apparent contradiction, we will touch briefly on the Marxist interpretation of so-called tendentious art and seek to define the place of such art in Marxist aesthetics. What is tendentiousness? From a superficial point of view, it is the attempt of the artist to demonstrate, propagate or exemplify a political or social view. Interestingly and characteristically whenever discussing such artificial concoctions, Marx and Engels speak with especial irony, particularly when a writer distorts objective reality . . . in order to demonstrate the truth of some thesis or to justify some partisan policy. Marx protested against the attempts even of great artists to use their works or individual characters for immediate and direct expression of their personal opinions; he argued that they thereby prevented their characters from fully exposing their capacities in accordance with the inner and organic dialectic of their own existences. (pp. 79-82)

In the Marxist conception, the triumph of realism implies a complete break with that vulgar conception of literature and art which appraises creative works mechanically in terms of a writer's political attitudes, according to a so-called class psychology. The Marxist approach we are exploring is exceedingly well-adapted to illuminating complicated literary phenomena, but only when it is applied concretely, in an historical spirit, with genuine aesthetic and social insight. Anyone who imagines it to be a ready-made formula applicable to any literary phenomenon misinterprets the Marxist classics like the vulgar Marxists of the past. In order to eliminate any further misunderstanding in regard to this approach, let me simply add that the triumph of realism, as defined by Engels, does not mean either that the writer's explicit ideology is a matter of indifference or that any work in which a writer departs from his explicit ideology ipso facto represents a triumph of realism. There is a victory of realism only when great realist writers establish a profound and serious, if not fully conscious, association with a progressive current in the evolution of mankind. Thus, from a Marxist point of view, it is inadmissible to set bad or mediocre writers on the pedestal of the classics simply because of their political convictions.... (p. 85)

Earlier idealist thinkers had defended humanism much as did Marx and Engels, combating in the name of humanism the political, social and moral currents against which Marx and Engels struggled. Yet only the materialist viewpoint provided a key to understanding that the undermining of humanism in the disintegration and crippling of human integrity was an inevitable consequence of the material and economic structure of society. The division of labour of class societies, the separation of town from country and of physical from intellectual labour, the oppression and exploitation of man by man, the specialization of capitalist production (a major factor in the disintegration of the individual)—all are material and economic processes.

Regarding the cultural and artistic effects of these factors idealist thinkers had written with insight and wisdom, in elegiac and ironic tones, but with their materialist view Marx and Engels were able to probe to the root causes. And by probing to the roots, they were able to go beyond mere ironic criticism of the anti-humanism in the development and very existence of class societies and beyond mere nostalgic yearning for some imaginary idyllic past; they were able to demonstrate scientifically how this entire process originated and where it was going and how to defend man's integrity effectively, in actual life, in relation to actual men; how to change the material bases which cause the crippling and deformation of men; and how to awaken men to consciousness and to action as agents of this social and political consciousness—the revolutionary proletariat—in order to create material bases not only for preserving social and political, moral, intellectual and artistic achievements but also for raising them to new, unprecedented heights.

This radical objectivity provides the crux of Marx's thinking. He once contrasted the condition of men under capitalist society and under socialist society thus: ''Displacing *all* the physical and intellectual sensibilities, there is the simple alienation of all the senses—the sense of possession. Man must be reduced to this absolute impoverishment before he can again create a new personal richness out of himself....

''The elimination of private property thus represents the complete emancipation of all human sensibilities and qualities; but it is precisely through this emancipation that these sensibilities and qualities become *human,* both subjectively and objectively.''

Thus socialist humanism is the core of Marxist aesthetics and of the materialist conception of history. Contrary to bourgeois preconceptions reinforced by the gross, anti-dialectical conception of history of vulgar Marxism, this materialist conception, which probes universally to the roots, does not deny the aesthetic beauty of the blossoms. On the contrary, the materialist conception of history and Marxist aesthetics alone provide the key to an understanding of the unity and organic relationship of roots and blossoms.

On the other hand, the fact that historical materialism sees the real and ultimate liberation of humanity from the deformation of class society only under socialism does not at all imply a rigid, undialectical, schematic opposition to, or the summary rejection of, the culture of class societies or an indifference to their varied cultural achievements and their cultural and artistic influences (as is often the case with the vulgar simplifiers of

The title page of the first German edition of Capital.

Marxism). Though the true history of mankind will begin with socialism, pre-history provides the elements in the formation of socialism, and the steps in this evolution cannot be matters of indifference to champions of socialist humanism. Nor to Marxist aesthetics.

Socialist humanism accomplishes the unification of historical and purely artistic knowledge within Marxist aesthetics, the continuous convergence of historical and aesthetic evaluation. Thus Marxist aesthetics resolves the question with which men of stature have long been grappling (a question which eluded lesser men simply because they were lesser men): the integration of the enduring aesthetic value of a work of art into the historical process, the process from which the work in its very perfection and aesthetic value is inseparable. (pp. 86-8)

> *Georg Lukács, "Marx and Engels on Aesthetics,"
> in his* Writer and Critic and Other Essays, *edited and
> translated by Arthur Kahn, Merlin Press, 1970, pp.
> 61-88.*

S. S. PRAWER   (essay date 1976)

[*Prawer is a German-born English critic and educator specializing in German literature. In the following excerpt, he analyzes* The German Ideology *as a reflection of Marx's philosophical and aesthetic development. Prawer's commentary centers on Marx's concepts of "totality" and on his thoughts about art and the artist in society.*]

As its title suggests, [**The German Ideology**] is concerned with the cloud-cuckoo-land of post-Hegelian idealist philosophy, with a world in which *Geist* and *Idee* are the only ultimate realities. 'None of these philosophers', Marx and Engels complain, 'have thought of asking how German philosophy connects with the facts of German life or their own critique with their material surroundings.'

> In total contrast to German philosophy, which descends from heaven to earth, we here ascend from earth to heaven. That is to say, we do not set out from what men say, imagine, or conceive, nor from what has been said, thought, imagined, or conceived of men, in order to arrive at men in the flesh. We begin with real, active men, and from their real life-process show the development of the ideological reflexes and echoes of this life-process. The phantoms of the human brain also are necessary sublimates of men's material life-process, which can be empirically established and which is bound to material preconditions. Morality, religion, metaphysics, and other ideologies, and their corresponding forms of consciousness, no longer retain therefore their appearance of autonomous existence. They have no history, no development; it is men, who, in developing their material production and their material intercourse, change, along with this their real existence, their thinking and the products of their thinking. Life is not determined by consciousness, but consciousness by life. Those who adopt the first method of approach begin with consciousness, regarded as the living individual; those who adopt the second, which corresponds with real life, begin with the real living individuals themselves, and consider consciousness only as *their* consciousness.

This is indeed Hegelianism turned upside down—or right side up, as Marx and Engels would claim. Literature and the arts receive no specific mention in this uncompromising passage; but it should not be difficult to see what dangerous consequences might flow from an unimaginative extension of such principles. Critics might all too easily be tempted into overlooking that literary forms do, to some degree at least, have a history and development of their own, and that material life is, in not inconsiderable ways, affected by human consciousness. Would there not be a danger that the baby of observation and good sense might find itself thrown out with the Hegelian bathwater? To obviate dangers of this kind, Marx and Engels stress, in a later passage of *The German Ideology,* that a complete view of the relationship between material life and consciousness must include the principle of *interaction:*

> This conception of history therefore rests upon the development of the real process of production, taking its point of departure from the material production of immediate life, tracing the forms of social intercourse, bound up with, and produced by, this mode of production, and conceiving civil society in its various stages as the foundation of all history. It also describes civil society in its actions as state power, explains

the origins and follows out the developing processes, of all its various theoretical creations and forms of consciousness, religion, philosophy, morality, etc. In this way, of course, this whole matter may be presented in its totality....

'Totality' includes 'reciprocal interaction', *Wechselwirkung.* The notion of interaction significantly tempers that of one-sided dependence.

'Totality' is a key notion of *The German Ideology* ...; and Joachim Israel has usefully distinguished two of the ways in which Marx uses it. It may mean 'ideal totality' in the sense that man, as an ideal type, is 'endowed with all the characteristics which characterize the species and which can be increasingly manifested as society and its productive forces develop'. In this sense the term applies to 'society as thought and experienced'. In another sense, however, 'totality' may apply, not to mankind as a whole, but to individuals; and here its use is meant to raise questions about the chances given individuals or groups have of realizing their capacities and talents in a given social order. But, Israel rightly concludes, the two notions of 'totality' here distinguished are related. 'Total man as an ideal type, as the essence of the species' is 'approached by individual man in his historical process of development.' When he can 'appropriate his world' in the '"total" way' Marx thinks possible in the better society of the future, then the fully developed individual will approach, or coincide with, the ideal type.

The concept of 'totality' stands in dialectical relation to another key notion of *The German Ideology:* division of labour. The division of labour characteristic of modern society is said to have opposed 'abstract' individuals to a 'totality' of productive forces which confront them in reified form; and this is said to imply a stunting of individual development that can only be overcome by the abolition of private property, by a remoulding of society in such a way that every man will be able to develop his full human potential and thus produce a new kind of 'totality'. Marx and Engels concentrate particularly on one aspect of division of labour: the division between men busied with everyday material production, and men busy with the production of ideas. These latter, we are told, formulate or express for the most part the ideas, the ideology, of a dominant class. But, as the very existence of *The German Ideology* demonstrates, writers and thinkers can place themselves in opposition to dominant modes of thought. They are able to do this because there are already at work, at home or abroad, forces that contradict, forces that are destined to overthrow, the socio-economic system to which the ruling classes of a given society owe their superiority and hegemony.

In [his writings on Feuerbach] Marx had attacked 'mechanical materialists' for their one-sided stressing of human determination by external circumstances. What such materialists neglected, he believed, was the self-changing and liberating effect of *Praxis.* 'The coincidence of the changing of circumstances and of human activity or self-changing', the third Feuerbach thesis had proclaimed, 'can be conceived and rationally understood only as *revolutionary practice*'. *The German Ideology* develops this theme. While stressing that 'men are the producers of their conceptions, ideas, etc.—real active men, as they are conditioned by a definite development of their productive forces and the intercourse corresponding to these', Marx and Engels also proclaim unequivocally that 'under favourable circumstances individuals can rid themselves of their local narrow-mindedness', and that thinkers born into the bourgeoisie need not be confined, for the rest of their lives, in the ideology of that class. What *The German Ideology* terms 'communist consciousness' depends on the existence of the proletariat, to whose sufferings and aspirations it corresponds; but such consciousness may well 'arise among the other classes too through the contemplation of the situation [of the proletariat]'. Marx and Engels thus find room for doctrines that, like their own, go counter to the interests of the class to which their proponents belong. All men, Marx believes, are products of circumstances; but he believes no less firmly that all men are potentially able to change their circumstances, and that in their striving for such change they acquire insights denied to those who passively acquiesce.

Such qualifications and complexities must be kept in mind when we read the famous passage in which Marx and Engels attempt to describe the relationship of ideas to a 'dominant material force' and to 'dominant material relationships'. Read by itself the passage has an ominous reductional clarity ('The dominant ideas are nothing more than . . .') which its context in *The German Ideology* does something to counteract:

> The ideas of the ruling class are, in every age, the ruling ideas: i.e. the class which is the dominant *material* force in society is at the same time its dominant *intellectual* force. The class which has the means of material production at its disposal, has control at the same time over the means of mental production, so that in consequence the ideas of those who lack the means of mental production are, in general, subject to it. The dominant ideas are nothing more than the ideal expression of the dominant material relationships, the dominant material relationships grasped as ideas, and thus of the relationships which make one class the ruling one; they are consequently the ideas of its dominance. The individuals composing the ruling class possess, among other things, consciousness, and therefore think. In so far, therefore, as they rule as a class and determine the whole extent of an epoch, it is self-evident that they do this in their whole range and thus, among other things, rule also as thinkers, as producers of ideas, and regulate the production and distribution of the ideas of their age. Consequently their ideas are the ruling ideas of their age. For instance, in an age and in a country where royal power, aristocracy, and the bourgeoisie are contending for domination and where, therefore, domination is shared, the doctrine of the separation of powers appears as the dominant idea and is enunciated as an 'eternal law'. The division of labour, which we saw earlier as one of the principal forces of history up to the present time, manifests itself also in the ruling class, as the division of mental and material labour, so that within this class one part appears as the thinkers of the class (its active conceptualizing ideologists, who make it their chief source of livelihood to develop and perfect the illusions of the class about itself), while the others have a more passive and receptive attitude to these ideas and illusions, because they are in reality the active members of this class

and have less time to make up ideas and illusions about themselves.

Later on *The German Ideology* experiments with other ways of describing the same relationship. In a passage on the philosophy of Kant, Marx and Engels try out various terms connected with 'mirroring' and 'correspondence':

> The condition of Germany at the end of the last century is completely reflected [*spiegelt sich vollständig ab*] in Kant's *Critique of Pure Reason* . . . Kant's 'goodwill' wholly corresponds to [*entspricht vollständig*] the impotence, oppression, and wretchedness of the German bourgeoisie . . .

The same passage goes on to call Kant a 'palliating spokesman' (*beschönigender Wortführer*) of the German bourgeoisie, berates his alleged ignorance of the way in which ideas are conditioned and determined (*bedingt, bestimmt*) by the nature of material production, and speaks of the 'idealistic expression [*Ausdruck*] of the real interests' (which latter are economic and determined by class).

Not surprisingly, *The German Ideology* deals not only with 'complete reflections of the kind just illustrated, but also with the distortions such reflections may introduce. Ideologies are described as 'diffused reflections' (*Reflexe*) and as 'echoes' of the 'real processes of living'. In ideologies, men and the conditions of their life 'appear upside down, as in a camera obscura'. Such distortions and inversions may be explained by reference to the historical processes within which men have their being (*aus ihrem historischen Lebensprozess*). It has been noted, however, that the images of 'mirroring' and 'reflecting' which play so important a part in later Marxist theory are not *directly* applied to literature in any work in which Marx himself had a dominant share.

It is in *The German Ideology* too that Marx and Engels first unveil their famous model of 'base' and 'superstructure'. They speak of 'the social organization which develops directly out of production and social intercourse and which at all times forms the basis [*die Basis*] of the state and the rest of the idealist superstructure [*Superstruktur*]'; and they deplore the development of capitalism in so far as it converts everything into money relationships and thus destroys, for the worker, 'all natural and inherited family and political conditions, for instance, together with their whole ideological superstructure [*Uberbau*]'. . . . (pp. 106-11)

[In the *Economic and Philosophic Manuscripts*] Marx had already turned his attention to 'the element of thought itself—the element of thought's living expression—*language*' and had insisted that this was of a 'sensuous' nature. *The German Ideology* expands on this theme in an aside on the physical basis of language:

> From the start the 'spirit' is afflicted with the curse of being 'burdened' with matter, which here makes its appearance in the form of agitated layers of air, sounds, in short, of language. Language is as old as consciousness—language *is* practical consciousness that exists also for other men, and for that reason alone it really exists for me personally as well; language, like consciousness, only arises from the need, the necessity, of intercourse with other men . . .

This points to something constantly in evidence in Marx's response to literature: his sensitive awareness of its sound and movement (like his wife, and later his children, Marx loved to declaim and read aloud); and also his feeling that works of literature, linguistic artefacts, answered a specific human need, that in doing so they created new needs for which other works of art would provide new satisfactions.

Among the passages of *The German Ideology* dealing explicitly with literature and the arts there are some which are likely to be viewed with some scepticism by those for whom the writings of Marx and Engels are not canonical texts. Marx and Engels react sharply against Max Stirner's overstressing of the role individuals play in the production of art. They cite the example of Mozart, some of whose works were scored or completed by others, and that of Raphael, who left to his pupils the execution of many details in important paintings. This leads them to take a hopeful view of the part 'organization' might play in the production of not just more but *better* literature—a view they try to support by pointing to the popular stage in contemporary France, and by dubious analogies from historiography and the sciences. . . . 'It goes without saying', Marx and Engels add, 'that all such organization based on modern division of labour leads to very limited results'; and they point forward to a future communist society in which the artist and poet as a specialist, a full-time expert, will be entirely superseded by the all-round man who is an artist amongst other things. . . . One doubts if Marx and Engels could have found many grounds, in the history of the fine arts up to their own time, for a belief that the future of painting lay with part-timers rather than professionals. They are looking forward to an era from whose vantage-point all previous history would appear as mere pre-history. It remains curious, nevertheless . . . , that Marx should propose the life of the dilettante as the model of the good life in the liberated society of the future—a life where men 'hunt in the morning, fish in the afternoon, rear cattle in the evening, just as they have a mind, without ever becoming hunter, fisherman, shepherd or critic'.

Two principles enunciated in this book will, however, command more general assent. Neither was new; both, indeed, had been proclaimed, and brilliantly demonstrated, by Herder; but their restatement was none the less timely. 'Great nations like the French, the North Americans, and the English', Marx and Engels write, 'constantly compare one another, in practice and in theory', and they call for an application of historically based comparative methods to the arts, both in an international and a national context. In such researches, they stress, the study of *Verkehr*—material and intellectual intercourse and interaction between individuals, social groups, and countries; international communications—will play an essential part. . . . Comparison shows up the uniqueness, the individuality of an artist like Raphael; but it must also show to what extent the development of his talent was conditioned by time and place. Marx and Engels add that such development was conditioned by *demand* too, by the calls the artist's society makes on him, by the need it shows for his art—and that such demand 'depends, in its turn, on the division of labour and state of education [*Bildungsverhältnisse*] which results from it'.

What may be called the 'comparative' principle restated in *The German Ideology* is supplemented by renewed stress on the 'historical' principle: by an insistence that valid criticism of literature, no less than criticism of the visual arts, must be based on historical understanding. What a strange notion of 'uniqueness' and 'individuality' Max Stirner exhibited, Marx

and Engels exclaim, when he complained of Klopstock's failure to take an 'original' view of the Christian religion!

> Klopstock's attitude to religion, Stirner tells us, was not 'unique and individual', although it was a particular attitude to religion, namely that which made Klopstock what he was, which made Klopstock Klopstock. His attitude would, one supposes, have been 'unique and individual' only if he had adopted, not that of Klopstock, but that of a modern German philosopher!

The authors of *The German Ideology* make no secret of their personal distaste for Klopstock—'blessedly forgotten' they call him. . . . They insist, however, that he must be understood on his own terms and in his own setting; they insist that no literary critic is worth his salt if he lacks historical imagination.

The approach to literature characteristic of *The German Ideology* is resolutely historical in Hegel's sense: in the sense, that is, which sees recurring themes (the family, for instance, or the state, and the conflicts engendered by and within them) treated differently in each great epoch. There is a difference, however, that comes out clearly in the passage in which *The German Ideology* tries to trace the history of hedonism in modern Europe:

> The philosophy of pleasure emerged in modern times with the decline of feudalism and the transformation of the feudal landed nobility into the lusty, pleasure-loving and extravagant court nobility of the absolute monarchy. Among this nobility it still takes the form, primarily, of *an immediate, naïve view of life which is given expression in memoirs, poems, novels* and so on [my italics]. It becomes a real philosophy only in the hands of several writers of the revolutionary bourgeoisie who participated, on the one hand, in the education and mode of life of the court nobility and who shared, on the other, the more general outlook upon affairs of the bourgeoisie—an outlook based on the more general conditions of existence of the bourgeoisie. It was therefore accepted by both classes, although from quite different points of view. Among the nobility the language of pleasure was understood to be restricted to the confines of the first estate and its conditions of life; by the bourgeoisie it was generalized and applied to all individuals, without distinction; this meant abstracting from the actual conditions of life characteristic of such individuals, and the theory became transformed, therefore, into a stale and hypocritical moral doctrine. As the further course of development overthrew the nobility and brought the nobility into conflict with its opposite, the proletariat, the nobility became devoutly religious and the bourgeoisie solemnly moral and strict in its theories; although in practice the nobility did not in the least renounce pleasure while the bourgeoisie even made of pleasure an official economic category— *luxury*.

Hegel would not have been surprised at this depiction of rococo or anacreontic literature as more 'immediate' and 'naïve' than the philosophy which grew up around it. What is specifically

Marxian, however, in this passage from *The German Ideology*, is its stress (constant, from now on, in Marx's work) on the class-origins of both literature and philosophy and the class-conflicts of whose history their history is part.

[The *Economic and Philosophic Manuscripts*] had deplored German concentration on 'history in its abstract-general character—as politics, art, literature, etc.' In *The German Ideology* Marx and Engels return to this charge. They pour scorn on the so-called 'true' socialists because of their absorption in books rather than life: 'The lack of any *real,* passionate, practical party conflict in Germany meant that even the social movement was at first a *merely* literary one. "True socialism" is a perfect example of a social literary movement that has come into being without any real party interests . . .', and they constantly voice their suspicion of any culture that is merely belletristic. The creations of a novelist, Jean Paul Richter, are cited to illustrate the intermingling of 'petty huckstering and large illusions' in the mind of Germans who lived under Napoleonic occupation—and the authors add scornfully that this is evidence their butt Max Stirner will accept because belletristic sources are the only ones he knows. The same charge recurs over and over again. . . . To characterize Stirner and other theorizers and philosophers in post-Hegelian Germany Marx and Engels constantly quote, therefore, or allude to, contemporary writers like Willibald Alexis, Friedrich Halm, Karl von Holtei, Nicolaus Becker, Hoffmann von Fallersleben. Such allusions are clearly intended to convey the cultural ambience—stuffy and philistine, in the opinion of Marx and Engels—in which German philosophers live and move and do their thinking. In such an ambience, *The German Ideology* goes on to allege, the whole of history begins to take on, for a thinker like Stirner, the guise of the crudest contents of German lending libraries, while 'the *theatrum mundi* shrinks to the Leipzig book-fair'. . . . To see life in the image of sub-literature: that is the nemesis of those who fail to come to terms with modern politics, economics, and science. Their fate (a dreadful one in Marx's eyes!) will be to be read by no one but *literati* just like themselves. Germany's 'true socialists', *The German Ideology* prophesies, 'will concentrate more and more on a petty-bourgeois public and on impotent and ragged *Literaten* as representatives of that public'.

Yet Marx and Engels clearly enjoy demonstrating, throughout *The German Ideology,* that they can cite literary sources with the best of them. The Bible, as in *The Holy Family,* is ubiquitous, sometimes quoted 'straight', more often in riotous parody: 'Yes, consider the lilies of the field, how they are eaten by goats, transplanted by man into his buttonhole, how they are crushed beneath the immodest embraces of the dairymaid and the donkey-driver!' Shakespeare's Timon is brought on once more, to show how much more clearly an Elizabethan dramatist could convey an essential function of money than a modern German philosopher. . . . (pp. 112-18)

As *The German Ideology* proceeds, we find the satiric poems of Heine being quoted, with increasing frequency, to characterize and knock down German opponents. Marx and Engels do not shrink, however, from treating these poems as *Gebrauchslyrik,* verse meant for use, verse whose original wording is not sacrosanct but may be altered and adapted to suit its new context. (p. 119)

The author who dominates *The German Ideology,* however, is not Heine but Cervantes. The whole work is shot through with allusions to, quotations from, and parodies of *Don Quixote*. . . . Such allusions perform a patent structural function. They transform *The German Ideology* into a mock-epic, in which the

characters invented by Cervantes prefigure the German butts of Marx and Engels. 'Supported by these sayings of Feuerbach, Sancho begins a fight . . . already patterned out in the nineteenth chapter of Cervantes'; or again, in a passage which characteristically merges Cervantes and the Bible: 'The battle "for man" is the fulfilment of the word that stands chronicled in Cervantes xix . . .' At the same time Cervantes provides a standard: how much more heroic is the Knight of La Mancha, we are meant to think, how much more sensible his squire, than their later counterparts! And last but not least: Cervantes provides, in this new context, occasion for a game of inversions, of changing roles and sides, of permutations, which Marx was always glad to play. (pp. 119-20)

Similar use of the Bible, throughout *The German Ideology,* serves similar purposes—with the additional advantage, from the polemicist's point of view, that it might startle the pious reader into attention and response through the still potent shock of blasphemy. This purpose has also prompted Marx and Engels to quote chapter and verse of *Don Quixote* in the manner, and in the archaic style of vocabulary and syntax, in which pious German writers and speakers were wont to quote their Bible. (p. 120)

The German Ideology continues the close scrutiny, begun in *The Holy Family,* of the way German writers use their language. Metaphors, grammatical constructions, even prose-rhythms are examined in an effort to demonstrate an opponent's incompetence, illogicality, or lack of imagination. (p. 122)

In [his writings on Feuerbach] and *The German Ideology* the concepts of 'Praxis' and 'Ideology' first assume the important place they will ever afterwards retain in Marx's thinking. . . . This clearly affects Marx's approach to literature too—from the [*Economic and Philosophic Manuscripts*] onwards he sees all the arts as part of that universal creative activity through which man 'transforms and creates his world and himself'. And though there is a good deal in *The German Ideology* which non-Marxists cannot easily accept, its central notion, that of 'ideology' itself, remains a useful one. It implies, as Karl Mannheim has notably demonstrated, that 'opinions, statements, propositions and systems of ideas are not taken at their face value but are interpreted in the light of the life-situation of the one who expresses them'. It has made men more ready to look behind opinions, perceptions, and interpretations in order to discover life-situations with which they may be connected. It has made critics and theorists try to discover . . . the 'ideological field' into which an author is born, within which he has his formative intellectual experiences, and against which he has to define his own developing world-view. It has made them ask questions about the internal unity of given systems of thinking and feeling, their special *problématique* marked by the absence of certain problems as much as by the presence of others. It has led to inquiries into the relation of particular works or particular systems to larger 'ideological fields' and, of course, into the relation of both to the economic, social, and political organization characteristic of given countries and periods. To find such questions relevant and important we do not have to share Marx's . . . political convictions; and we have cause to be grateful to Marxist critics for keeping them steadfastly before us. (pp. 123-24)

S. S. Prawer, "Praxis and Ideology," in his Karl Marx and World Literature, *Oxford at the Clarendon Press, 1976, pp. 103-24.*

HAYDEN WHITE (essay date 1979)

[*In the following excerpt, White analyzes the style of* The Eighteenth Brumaire, *drawing conclusions about Marx's theories regarding "the form and the content" of social phenomena.*]

Marx opens the **Eighteenth Brumaire** with a signal that he is about to unfold a "farce." The farcical nature of the events to be depicted is manifested in their outcome: the elevation of the charlatan "Crapulinski," the roué, opportunist, and fool—the original Napoleon the Great's nephew—Louis Bonaparte, to the imperial purple by a coalition of criminals, lumpenproletariat, peasants, and high bourgeois property owners. But, Marx reminds us a number of times throughout the discourse, this grotesque and absurd outcome of events—in which the least admirable man in France is hailed as the representative and defender of the interests of all classes of French society—was already implicitly present in the first, or February, phase of the Revolution of 1848, which had swept Louis Philippe from the throne and proclaimed the Second Republic.

How had this transformation, so remarkable and unforeseen by most of the actors in the spectacle, come about? Marx's answer to this question consists of an explication of the relationship between what he calls the true content of the "modern revolution" and the forms which specific revolutions take as a result of the conflict of interests which a class-divided society engenders.

The relation between the form and the content of any social phenomenon in any specific historical situation, Marx argues here and elsewhere, is a product of a conflict between specific class interests as these are envisaged and lived by a given class, on the one side, and general or universal human interests, which derive from the system of needs, primary and secondary, that are peculiar to mankind, on the other. Ideals are always formulated in terms of putatively universal human values, but since social perceptions are limited to the range of experiences of a given social class, the universally shared common interests of living men everywhere are always interpreted in a situation in which goods and political power are unevenly distributed in terms of the immediately envisaged *material* interests of the dominant class. This is why the political program of 1848, designed to establish a republic, quickly got transformed into a program designed to undermine this republic in the interest of protecting private property. The bourgeoisie in power says "Republic," against the old regime of inherited privilege and despotism, but it means "aristocracy of wealth." It says: "Justice," when it seeks to enlist the lower classes in its struggle against the old regime; but it means "Law and Order" when the aristocracy of wealth is established. It says, "Liberty, Equality, and Fraternity," when it is at the barricades or sending the lower classes to them; but it invokes "infantry, cavalry, and artillery," when the lower classes try to claim these rights in concrete terms. It comports itself on the historical stage like a tragic hero in its early phases of development, but its avarice and fetishism of commodities soon force it to abandon in practice every ideal it continues to preach in theory, and to reveal itself as the "monster" which any human being who conceives of life as an epic of production for profit alone must become.

So much is commonplace for Marxists, but exists only as a judgment still to be demonstrated. Part of the demonstration must be historical, since the process being analyzed is construed as a historical process. Marx chooses the events in France between 1848 and 1852 as a microcosm of the plot which every bourgeoisie must ultimately play out. And his demonstration of the adequacy of this judgment to the events themselves consists of a dialectical explication of those events as products of an interplay between forms and their actual contents, on the one side, and the form of the whole and its obscured universal meaning, on the other.

On the surface of the events, Marx discerns a succession of four formal incarnations of the revolutionary impulse. Each of these incarnations is simultaneously a response to socioeconomic reality (here construed as class interests) and an attempt to deny the universal meaning of the revolution in relation to ideal human aspiration. He divides the drama into four phases, each of which is signalled by a change in the form of government established on the political level. But the form of government established is itself a projection of a form of political consciousness, itself a product of either a coalition of classes, more or less self-consciously contrived, or of a specific class.

The real protagonist of Marx's narrative is neither the proletariat (its Dussardier) nor Louis Bonaparte (its Sénécal), but rather the bourgeoisie as it lives through the longings, sufferings, and contradictions of its existence. . . . (pp. 224-25)

[The] bourgeoisie and the revolution in which it will achieve its "absurd" triumph passes through four stages of consciousness: February 1848 is metaphoric; political aspiration and social ideals are entertained in the euphoric spirit of unspecified desires and glimpsed in the image of "a social republic." Marx says of this period: "Nothing and nobody ventured to lay claim to the right of existence and of real action. All the elements that had prepared or determined the Revolution, the dynastic opposition, the republican bourgeoisie, the democratic-republican petty bourgeoisie and the social-democratic workers, provisionally found their place in the February *government*". "It could not be otherwise," Marx continues; "Every party construed [the republic] in its own sense". Although the proletariat proclaimed a "social republic," and thereby "indicated the general content of the modern revolution," the proclamation was both naive and premature, given the interests and powers of other social groups. And this accounts for the "confused mixture of high-flown phrases and actual uncertainty and clumsiness, of more enthusiastic striving for innovation and more deeply rooted domination of the old routine, of more apparent harmony of the whole society and more profound estrangement of its elements," which characterized this phase of the whole revolutionary process.

Phase two of the Revolution, the period of the Constituent National Assembly, 4 May 1848 to 29 May 1849, represents the period of dispersion of the revolutionary impulse across a series of contending parties and groups, a period of strife and specification of contents, emblematized by the bloody street warfare of the June Days (23-26 June 1848) and the progressive betrayal of one group by another until the bourgeois republicans accede to dictatorial power in the Legislative National Assembly, an accession which demonstrated to every observer of the event that "in Europe there are other questions involved than that of 'republic or monarchy.' It had revealed," Marx says, "that here [in Europe] *bourgeois republic* signifies the unlimited despotism of one class over other classes." Under the sign of the motto, "property, family, religion, order," every alternative party is crushed. "Society is saved just as often as the circle of its rulers contracts, as a more exclusive interest is maintained against a wider one. Every demand of the simplest bourgeois social reform, of the most ordinary liberalism, of the most formal republicanism, of the most insipid democracy, is simultaneously castigated as an 'attempt on society' and stigmatised as 'socialism'.''

With the dictatorship of the bourgeoisie, we have passed into the third phrase of the Revolution, the synecdochic phase in which the interests of a specific segment of society are identified with the interest of society as a whole. This pseudo-universalization of the interests of the bourgeoisie, this incarnation of the universal in the particular, this fetishism by a class of itself, is a preparation for the absurdity represented by Bonaparte's claims to be ''the savior of society'' and the irony of his use of the motto ''property, family, religion, order'' to justify his suppression of the *political* power of the bourgeoisie.

In this, the last phase of the Revolution, bourgeois

> high priests of 'religion and order' themselves are driven with kicks from their Pythian tripods, hauled out of their beds in the darkness of night, put in prison vans, thrown into dungeons or sent into exile; their temple is razed to the ground, their mouths are sealed, their pens broken, their law torn to pieces in the name of religion, of property, of family, of order. Bourgeois fanatics for order are shot down on their balconies by mobs of drunken soldiers, their domestic sanctuaries profaned, their houses bombarded for amusement—in the name of property, of family, of religion, and of order. Finally the scum of bourgeois society forms *the holy phalanx of order* and the hero Crapulinski [from Fr. *crapule* 'gluttony'] installs himself in the Tuileries as the 'savior of society'.

What justification do I have for calling the modes of relationship among the elements of society represented in Marx's characterization of the phases of the Revolution by the names of the tropes of figurative language? The best reason is that Marx himself provides us with schematic representations of the modes of figuration by which to characterize the relation between the forms of value and their contents in his analysis of the ''language of commodities'' in chapter 1 of *Capital*. Most of this chapter consists of an adaptation of the traditional conception of the rhetorical tropes to the method of dialectical analysis. Here the problem, Marx says, is to understand the Money Form of Value, the ''absurd'' notion that the value of a commodity is equivalent to the amount of money it is worth in a given system of exchange. And just as the explanation of the ''absurd'' spectacle of Bonaparte's posing as the ''savior of society''—while unleashing all of the criminal elements of society to an orgy of a consumption ungoverned by any respect for human values or the persons who produced by their labor the commodities being consumed—is contained in the understanding of the first phase of the Revolution which brought him to power, the February phase; so too the absurd form of value is explained by reference to the structure of the Elementary or Original Form of value, the form contained in the simple metaphorical *identification* of ''x amount of Commodity A'' with ''y amount of Commodity B.'' Once the purely figurative nature of this statement of equivalency is grasped, once it is seen that, like any metaphor, it both contains a deep truth (regarding the similarity of any two commodities by virtue of their nature as products of human labor) and at the same time masks this truth (by remaining on the superficial level of an apprehension of their manifest similarity as commodities), the secret of men's capacity to bewitch themselves into believing that the value of anything equals its exchange, rather than its

use, value is revealed for everyone to see. Just as irony is implicitly present in any original, primitive or naive characterization of reality in a metaphor, so too the absurdity of equating the value of a product of human labor with its money value is contained implicitly in the equating of any given commodity with any other as a basis of exchange. And so too with the other two forms of value, the Extended and the Generalized forms, which Marx analyzes in this chapter of *Capital*. They are to *metonymy* and *synecdoche,* the relationships by contiguity and putative essential identity, respectively, as the second and third phases of the Revolution are to the same tropes.

To be sure, Marx's analysis of the forms of social phenomena, whether of commodity values or of political systems, is carried forth on the assumption that he has perceived their true contents, which the forms simultaneously figure forth and conceal from clear view. The true value-content of all commodities is for him the amount of human labor expended in their production, which is precisely equivalent to their use value, whatever their apparent value in a given system of exchange. The true content of all political and social forms, similarly, is the universal human needs which they at once manifest and obscure. Marx's aim as a writer was to clarify this relation of content to form in a way which he thought, correctly I believe, was consistent with Hegel's dialectical method of analysis, although—in his view—Hegel had got the form-content distinction wrong way about. But he carried forward the method of Hegel's *Phenomenology* and *Logic* by divining the element of consciousness which was the basis and bane of humanity's efforts to grasp reality and turn it to its service. This element was man's capacity for what Vico called ''creative error,'' a capacity of the figurative imagination without which reason itself would be inconceivable, just as prose without poetry would be unthinkable. More: he divined clearly what Hegel only in passing glimpses and in his pursuit of the secret of Being-in-General too quickly passes over; namely, that the secret of human consciousness is to be found in its most original product, which is not reason, but figurative language, without which reason could never have arisen.

What does the discernment of a common pattern of tropological representations of the modes of consciousness imply with respect to the project of ''realistic representation,'' on the one side, and the problem of style, on the other? With respect to the former, I would suggest, it permits us to identify the ''allegorical'' element in realistic discourse, the secondary meaning of the events depicted on the surface of the narrative which mediates between those events and the judgment rendered on them, launched from the consciously held ideological position of the writer. The progression of these structures of consciousness permits the encoding of the process through which the protagonist is passing in his/its ''education,'' in terms which allow the writer a judgment on its end phase as a stage of cognitive awareness. This quite apart from whatever archetypal schema may be revealed in the literary encoding of the events in generic terms, i.e., as comedy, tragedy, romance, satire or farce. (pp. 225-28)

With respect to the problem of style, our analysis of the [discourse of Marx] . . . suggests that we should regard style, at least in realistic discourse, as the process of this transcoding operation. When we speak of the style of a discourse, we should not feel compelled to limit ourselves to a consideration of either the linguistic-rhetorical features of a text or to its discernible ideological posture, but should seek rather to characterize the moves made, on the axes of both selection and combination, by which a form is identified with a content and the reverse. (pp. 228-29)

Hayden White, *"The Problem of Style in Realistic Representation: Marx and Flaubert," in* The Concept of Style, *edited by Berel Lang, University of Pennsylvania Press, 1979, pp. 213-29.*

AMIRI BARAKA (essay date 1980)

[*Baraka, an acclaimed American author in several genres, was an important voice in the black nationalist movement of the 1960s and is now a proponent of Marxist-Leninist ideas. Here, Baraka comments on* The Letters of Karl Marx, *which he considers unrepresentative of Marx's genius because it "never goes beyond the fragmented, personal, and therefore superficial."*]

Karl Marx speaks in [*The Letters of Karl Marx*] out of these letters, in fragments. We see an enormously erudite mind in action—on the street, in the house, in a day-to-day struggle with deadly capitalism and its supporters, even with those calling themselves "Communists." What is heady about this is that Marx, the fundamental scientific socialist, philosopher and activist is shown facing real life under capitalism.

The Letters of Karl Marx, though truncated, offers us exposure to the man's sweep and depth. Some of the letters are study guides in themselves. Some are a workingman's deep lament to be so trapped by a primitive economic system.

But the 366 letters of Marx that this editor and publisher choose to print are also problematic in that we obviously do not have the full context of the correspondence. The editor, Saul Padover, says, "The criteria for the selection of the letters in this book were personality, biography and ideas. Purely political communications as well as technical economic discussions, have been omitted as ephemeral and without enduring qualities"!

Padover, apparently, has cut the deepest intellectual heart out of the correspondence: "The personal letters, however, a true reflection of Marx the man and the thinker, continue to have an abiding freshness and significance." You see what has happened. The editor-translator has tried to "DeMarx" the collection by removing its real political significance and reducing it to "At Home With The Artist." . . .

This selection from the 1,523 letters extant tends to reduce Marx just to the level of the radical scholar struggling to pay the rent and laying the hand hard and regular on Engels. Of course this should be known—the grim life of poverty the ruling class sentences any revolutionary thinker to—but the immense scope, historical impact and scientific importance of Marx's work are consequently limited and obscured.

In the end, *The Letters of Karl Marx* merely shows us a harried radical given to outbursts of chauvinism both national and sexual, a little of which is tinged with "anti-Jewish" drollery, especially relating to Ferdinand LaSalle (even though Marx's father was a converted Jew), which is a little like Blacks calling other Blacks "Nigger." With Padover the emphasis *must* be on personality, a *People* magazine profile approach to a collection of letters, rather than the collection a serious person would make, which would of necessity try to emphasize the development of Marx's thought and political works. Marx is not remembered for his arguments with butchers and bakers, or complaints about his health (though these things are of some interest *secondarily*), he is remembered for constructing a basic scientific Communist philosophy as a method of analysis and a means of action, in real life!

Dealing exclusively with Marx's private life rather than with his work is futile. However, the life-shaking, stompdown poverty undergone by this great revolutionary intellectual, as he tries to give working and oppressed people a fundamental weapon with which to struggle, is immensely humbling and, not so strangely, inspiring. The repeated loss of their children, the ravaging illness suffered by Marx and his wife, Jenny, which grew more destructive as they aged, and against which Marx, unyielding and determined, goes on with his research and writing and political work—all this makes one put in some useful perspective the hostile attacks and circumstances in one's own life.

For, even in this collection, Marx's brilliance cannot be covered completely. From the earliest letter to his father, in which we see the 19-year-old Marx's visionary and highly critical mind and fantastic learning, we are aware that we are in the presence of a stunning erudition and an irrepressible determination. We *can* also see that his is a life of struggle. He struggles with the various versions of utopian socialism that flooded Europe at the time—with Feuerbach, the young Hegelians, Proudhon, LaSalle. He struggles with the reactionary governments of Europe and we see the succession of his many exiles, as he is thrown out of one country after another not only because of his thought, but also because of his activism.

In *The Letters* there is some discussion included on the excruciating effort (even physical pain) that was necessary, for instance, to write *Das Kapital.* We glean something of Marx's incisive analysis of the American Civil War and his cogent analysis of the world international situation. . . . We even come to understand how Marx could "predict" the Commune. He says in letter 204 to Engels, "If you look at the last chapter of my *Eighteenth Brumaire,* you will find that I say that the next attempt of the French Revolution will be no longer, as before, to transfer the bureaucratic-military machinery from one hand to another, but to *smash* it, and this is the prerequisite for every real peoples' revolution on the Continent." A prescription as true today as it was then. . . .

But *The Letters of Karl Marx* never goes beyond the fragmented, personal and therefore superficial. For instance, Padover omits the letters from Engels, and Engels in all ways must be seen as the *cofounder* of scientific socialism. He is not just Marx's Angel (Engel). But Marx's frequent plea for money and an occasional Engels' reply are about all we get of Engels.

Lenin once said of the Marx-Engels correspondence, "If one were to attempt to define in a single word the focus, so to speak, of the whole correspondence, the central point at which the whole body of ideas expressed and discussed converges—that word would be *dialectics.*"

But *The Letters of Karl Marx* is anything but dialectical. It is not whole-sided but one-sided, and therefore it misses the essence of Marxism. This "collection" is merely a bourgeois comment on Marx, extremely unfortunate since it interferes with our understanding of Marx himself. One awaits then a collection in English of the Marx-Engels correspondence made by a Marxist, or at least by someone not committed to making Marx un-Marx-like.

Amiri Baraka, "The Domesticated Marx," in Book World—The Washington Post, *January 13, 1980, p. 8.*

GEORGE A. PANICHAS   (essay date 1980)

[*Panichas discusses* The Collected Letters of Karl Marx *and concludes that they depict Marx as "first, last, and always a professional revolutionary." This essay was first published in the Fall 1980 issue of the* Modern Age.]

The personal side of Marx disclosed in [*The Letters of Karl Marx*] is not especially sympathetic. The softer, gentler elements that lend themselves to hagiography are precisely those that in Marx transpose into rancor, abrasiveness, pugnacity, self-righteousness; into a consuming aggressiveness that helps to explain why, for their books, biographers of Marx have used such subtitles as "a study in fanaticism," "the passionate logician," and "man and fighter." Here it is worth noting that Marx was an admiring student of Epicurus, the materialist Greek philosopher; his doctoral thesis sought to show the differences between Democritus and Epicurus. Yet, even the little we know of Epicurus's life, as reported by a third-century Greek biographer, Diogenes Laertius, gives a picture of a man of "unsurpassed good will," gentleness, reasonableness. For these qualities one will look in vain in Marx's letters, most of them written to his intimate friend and collaborator, Friedrich Engels, . . . from whom, as Marx said, he kept no secrets. These letters help to delineate Marx's outer and inner terrain; the public man and the private man emerge monogenically, despite some scholars' insistence that there are "many Marxes." Such insistence tends not only to rationalize the flaws in Marx's character but also to disregard his brutal intellectuality. No matter how eclectic or protective his apologists may be, the Marx who reveals himself in these letters is precisely the Marx perceived with astonishing insight by Carl Schurz, . . . the German-American statesman and writer. In his autobiography Schurz recalled being present at a congress of democratic associations, held in Cologne in the summer of 1848, and went on to pen this memorable sketch of Marx, one of the participants:

> The somewhat thick-set man, with his broad forehead, his very black hair and beard and his dark sparkling eyes, at once attracted general attention. He enjoyed the reputation of having acquired great learning, and as I knew very little of his discoveries and theories, I was all the more eager to gather words of wisdom from the lips of that famous man. This expectation was disappointed in a peculiar way. Marx's utterances were indeed full of meaning, logical and clear, but I have never seen a man whose bearing was so provoking and intolerable. To no opinion, which differed from his, he accorded the honor of even a condescending consideration. Everyone who contradicted him he treated with abject contempt; every argument that he did not like he answered either with biting scorn at the unfathomable ignorance that had prompted it, or with opprobrious aspersions upon the motives of him who had advanced it. I remember most distinctly the cutting disdain with which he pronounced the word "bourgeois"; and as a "bourgeois," that is as a detestable example of the deepest mental and moral degeneracy he denounced everyone that dared to oppose his opinion.

Schurz's impression of Marx correlates with the overall impression of the letters in this volume. Neither apologetics, nor critical or biographical eclecticism, nor a psychohistorical approach can alter the traits that shaped Marx's character and defined his sensibility. Engels himself, in a short eulogy delivered at Marx's burial in unconsecrated ground at Highgate Cemetery, London, on March 17, 1883 [see excerpt dated 1883], helps us to penetrate that character and to measure that sensibility when he asserts that fighting was Marx's element (*Der Kampf war sein Element*). Any perusal of his letters corroborates this belligerent aspect of Marx's life. Marx's was a life without felicity or refining grace, without *humanitas;* a life that lacked appreciation of music, sun, beauty, poetry. To be sure, in a letter dated November 10, 1837, which has been preserved from his youth and which begins this collection, a nineteen-year-old Marx, then studying at Berlin University, writes at length to his father of his ambition to be a poet who wants to find "the dances of the Muses and the music of Satyrs." But he goes on to explain in this remarkable letter of self-examination and self-advertisement that his ambition "was purely idealistic," poetry "to be merely a companion." (pp. 193-95)

Cocksureness marks even his earliest letters, as does also a condescending and a choleric attitude. During his stay in Bonn he particularly vented his disdain on the theologians of Bonn University, singling out Friedrich Rudolf Hasse for special abuse: "`. . . I never saw anything more in him than a big, booted provincial parson . . . [who] speaks of religiosity as a product of life experience, by which he probably means his flourishing pedagogy and his fat belly, for fat bellies undergo all kinds of experiences and as Kant says, when it's behind it's an *F.*, and if above, a religious inspiration. The pious Hasse with his religious constipations!" Early on in these letters, in fact, Marx's scatological orientation takes hold and becomes at times as embarrassing as his anti-semitism. . . . Indeed, as one repeatedly encounters mean attitudes in Marx's letters, the reasons why he did not become a lyric poet or a *Dozent* ("rotten and rotting others") explain themselves without much difficulty. In Marx some, like Amiri Baraka, hear the voice of "the new Moses." But the voice of Marx is unvaryingly grim, oppressive, unyielding, harsh. The so-called "many Marxes" speak in one voice, homogenous rather than resilient, strident rather than compassionate. To read Marx's letters is to be reminded of how far he is removed from, how much he is antagonistic to, the serene counsel of a Baruch Spinoza: "With regard to human affairs, not to laugh, not to cry, not to become indignant, but to understand." It is not understanding that one finds in Marx's letters; nor is it the virtue of equanimity, what Marx's "worthy Epicurus" spoke of as imperturbability, that informs his thought. Rather, it is the voice of a driven and possessed man that speaks with shrill intransigence, the voice of one who delighted in struggle. "It is bad to perform menial services even for freedom and to fight with needles instead of clubs," we hear Marx screaming in one letter. And again we recall the words in Engels's funeral oration: "Battle was his element."

The early 1840s were to signal the beginning of Marx's lifelong journalistic efforts, invariably revolving around his radical social criticism of political questions. His letters during this period provide an ardent revolutionary view of "the old world [which] belongs to the philistines." In a letter written in September 1843, while he still lived in Cologne, Marx spoke of the need to discover the new world from a critique of the old one, pleading for a "ruthless criticism of all that exists, ruthless also in the sense that criticism does not fear its results and even less so a struggle with the existing powers." The chief function of the critic should be the creation of a criticism of and a participation in politics, "in *real* conflicts, and in identifying with them." "The reform of consciousness consists *only* in making the world aware of its perception, waking up from its own dream, *explaining* its own actions," he wrote with a Promethean defiance that anticipated *The Manifesto of the Communist Party*. . . . One of his most important letters [written in Brussels] is that of December 28, 1846, in which he discussed Pierre-Joseph Proudhon's book *The Philosophy of Poverty*. This long letter speaks volumes in communicating Marx's violent polemical manners, as well as showing his materialist concept of history, it also looks ahead to Marx's destructive criticism of Proudhon, a libertarian socialist, in *La Misère de la philosophie*. . . . Contempt and controlled rage are evident throughout this letter; Marx, as Engels so well described his friend's intellectual weaponry, "battled with a passion and a tenacity which few could rival."

Marx judged Proudhon's book as being "on the whole bad, very bad." He accuses his socialist contemporary of failing to understand "the present social conditions in their concatenation" and of being incapable of comprehending economic development. Emphasizing that man's material relationships form the basis of all his relationships, Marx charges that Proudhon confuses ideas with things and that, "incapable of following the real movement of history, gives you a phantasmagoria which has the presumption of being a dialectical phantasmagoria." As such Proudhon's is "Hegelian rubbish." . . . Proudhon, as an unforgiving Marx knew, distrusted the latter's authoritarian and centralist ideas, no less than he distrusted the Communism that destroys freedom by taking away from the individual control over his means of production. Marx posits his arguments with savage force in order to paint Proudhon as a socialist political theorist who sought to equilibrate his radical, realist, and moralist orientations. For Marx, then, Proudhon accepts and even deifies economic categories which, as motive forces, express bourgeois relationships in the form of thought. (pp. 195-97)

Undoubtedly there are those who prefer to explain away the paradoxes in Marx's personal attitudes as being the derivatives of a normative-Victorian character or as the manifestations of a day-to-day struggle with, in Baraka's words "deadly capitalism and its supporters, even with those who count themselves 'Communists.'" But that Marx could also be at once a bourgeois and a revolutionary prophet is corroborated by some of the letters. He speaks, for instance, of his need for the "absolute quiet" that he finds in family life: "Under 'quiet,' I understand 'family life,' the 'noise of children'—this 'microscopic world' that is much more interesting than the 'macroscopic' one." At the very same time he thrills to the severe consequences of the economic crisis which began in Europe in 1857. To Ferdinand Lassalle, the leading spokesman for German socialism, whom Marx distrusted and repeatedly mocked as a "Nigger-Jew," he wrote on May 31, 1858: "On the whole, the present period is agreeable. History has patently in mind to take again a new start, and the signs of dissolution everywhere are delightful for every mind not bent upon the conservation of things as they are." Marx's words here support Baraka's belief that picturing Marx as "the domesticated Marx" is an untruth. They also remind us that Marx was first, last, and always a professional revolutionary, pitilessly preoccupied with the collectivist society of the future. His was a materialist sensibility, rooted in the cult of science and utopian socialism, that makes so devastatingly pertinent Albert Camus' charge that Marx "found any form of beauty under the sun completely alien." In essence, then, Marx affirmed a system that is me-

chanistic and ruthless: a philosophical destructiveness. Whatever generosity of spirit he may have had was to be readily sacrificed to the laws of social necessity and to the phenomenon of Marx himself. (pp. 199-200)

Not unexpectedly the letters underline the absence of an aesthetic sense. Neither paintings nor music appealed to Marx. And though he admired Aeschylus, Shakespeare, and Goethe, his admiration was unremarkable in enthusiasm and ultimately subordinated to *primum vivere* as his first principle of determination. . . . "Bookworming" was, as he said, his most enjoyable occupation, but he lacked any aesthetic response to books or fondness for them, as he was the first to admit: "I am a machine, condemned to devour them and then, throw them, in a changed form, on the dunghill of history." . . . In the end Marx's own explanations of himself, given in the Victorian parlor game of "Confessions," serve as the best way of presenting a man who sometimes signed his letters as the "Moor." His favorite virtue, he said, was Strength; his favorite characteristic, Singleness of Purpose; his idea of happiness, To Fight; his favorite heroes, Spartacus and Kepler; his favorite color, Red; his favorite motto: *De omnibus dubitandum* (You must have doubts about everything). (pp. 200-01)

Whether one is presenting or conferring with Marx, he remains inescapable. "His name will live through the centuries and so also will his work." Engels was absolutely right in the last sentence of his eulogy at Marx's gravesite. (p. 202)

> *George A. Panichas, "Presenting Mr. Marx," in his* The Courage of Judgment: Essays in Criticism, Culture, and Society, *The University of Tennessee Press, Knoxville, 1982, pp. 193-202.*

ROY EDGLEY (essay date 1983)

[*Edgley explores "the relation between the work of Marx and of Marxism on the one hand, and philosophy on the other."*]

Marxism did not spring complete from Marx's head. It developed, through his own life, in relation to the European culture that was the historical antecedent and contemporary context of his work; and since his death it has continued to develop in the real movement in which Marx's work has survived and grown in the work of others. Marxism is a contemporary reality. In Marx's own day communism haunted Europe. Today Marxism haunts the whole globe.

What then is the relation between the work of Marx and of Marxism on the one hand, and philosophy on the other? How did his work respond to the European philosophical tradition as it had developed up to and into his own lifetime, and how has Marxism responded since? In particular, how does Marxism relate to philosophy today, in our own time and place? It goes without saying that in relation to the richness and diversity of the material my account will necessarily be highly selective and schematic. My main purpose is to identify significant continuities and discontinuities between Marxism and philosophy in ways that will enable me to bring them to focus in a Marxist critique both of some dominant themes in contemporary English philosophy and of some recent Marxist philosophy.

Marxist philosophy? The chief question to be raised is: is there any such thing? The reality of Marxism is most obviously and centrally political. It is a form of socialism, the political movement of working-class struggle for emancipation from capitalism. But what distinguishes Marxism as a type of socialism is its commitment to both scientific theory and a comprehensive radicality in practice and theory: the radical practice of revolutionary politics united with the radical theory of a science of society. The nature of that relation, that unity of theory and practice, is itself a key problem for Marxist practice and theory. Marx himself both exemplified this unity in his own life's work and theorized its necessity in the massive corpus of theory transmitted to us in his writing. It is for that theoretical work that Marx is distinguished. But that theory is centrally science, social science. Though science is a feature of bourgeois and pre-bourgeois culture, in its modern dominant form arising with the birth and growth of capitalism itself, Marx and Engels are firmly committed to the scientific mode of investigating and understanding reality, and indeed regard their type of socialism as superior to other types chiefly on the ground of its scientificity: Engels identifies it as 'scientific socialism'. As such, Marxist theory raises the question raised by the establishment of science in general in European culture: the question whether science supersedes philosophy as a form of thought, as it seems to supersede religion; and if not, what the place and role of philosophy is in Marxism, in particular its relation to Marxist science; and thus the relation of both to political practice, especially the Marxist practice of revolutionary politics. The question is not simply that of the relation of Marxist science to a possible Marxist philosophy, but also the question of the relation of Marxist theory, including its philosophy if any, to philosophy in general, including non-Marxist and specifically bourgeois philosophy. Marx and Marxism, as Marx himself frequently acknowledges, are heavily indebted to the European philosophical tradition, especially to Aristotle, to the materialism of the Scientific Revolution and the Enlightenment, and to Hegel. Nevertheless, Marxism radically transforms this inheritance and in crucial ways opposes it. Just as Marxist political practice opposes bourgeois political practice, so Marxist theory in general opposes bourgeois theory. If Marxist social science opposes bourgeois forms of thought and theory in economics, politics, sociology and historiography, is there a Marxist philosophy that opposes bourgeois philosophy?

There seem to be three general possibilities. Either there is a distinctive Marxist philosophy that opposes bourgeois philosophy, perhaps as Marxist social science opposes the bourgeois social sciences. Or there is a philosophy in Marxism that is not distinctively Marxist, a philosophy Marxism shares with bourgeois thought, the opposition between Marxist and bourgeois theory being at the scientific level. Or there is no such thing as philosophy of any kind in Marxism because Marxism opposes bourgeois philosophy by opposing philosophy as such. Only the first possibility would allow us to claim clearly and unequivocally that Marx and Marxism make a contribution to philosophy. The second would deny that. The third might allow the claim, but only in a Pickwickian sense: it would imply that Marx's contribution to philosophy was a contribution to its supersession.

The existence of a Marxist philosophy, it must be admitted, is more doubtful than the existence of a Marxist social science. Nevertheless, Marxist social science does not exist as a Marxist form of the special social sciences, of economics, political science, sociology and history; and it does not oppose these bourgeois social sciences in a straightforward way. Thus there is no Marxist economics in the sense in which there is bourgeois economics, and that for a general reason that divides into two, namely the specialization of intellectual labour in our class-divided society. This specialization is, on the one hand, a division not only between intellectual and manual labour but also between theory and practice, particularly political practice;

and on the other hand a multiple division within the field of intellectual labour or theory, the division in which the various 'subjects' or 'disciplines' are constituted. Thus bourgeois economics is an academic subject, an intellectual discipline on its own understanding sharply separated both from other subjects, such as political science and history, and also from political practice. The opposition of Marxism to the bourgeois forms of thought in these specialist subjects is partly opposition to their very form as specialist subjects. Marxism thus does not oppose these disciplines on their very own ground, establishing an alternative set of such specialisms. That ground, this specialist form, is itself, according to Marxism, mystificatory. At the theoretical level Marxism develops a unified theory in which the real relations between the economic, the political and the historical are made explicit and understood. It is for this reason that the subjects most hospitable to Marxism under capitalism have been sociology and history. Sociology aims to be a social science that is general and comprehensive. History studies the specific and concrete, and when it resists its consequent anti-theoretical tendencies finds an application for ideas from any of the special sciences. But even these subjects standardly remain academically theoretical, remote from acknowledged and explicit involvement in practical politics.

Oddly enough, there is here, arising from that original doubt about the existence of a Marxist philosophy, the beginning of an argument for a significant and positive relation between Marxism and philosophy, and one that has in it some truth about the actual relation between them as it occurs both historically and within Marx's own development. (pp. 239-42)

In opposing the divided specialisms of bourgeois social science Marxism has a 'philosophical' character. . . . It seeks unity, both within theory and between theory and practice, and in doing so it opposes the bourgeois social sciences at a fundamental or radical intellectual level. Specifically Marxist theory opposes bourgeois economics, for example, not, or not only or centrally, at the level of observed fact, but at the deeper conceptual level, the level of the concepts or language in terms of which those observations are interpreted and theoretically appropriated. Thus, for instance, whereas bourgeois thought separates the economic from the political, Marxism reveals their internal interconnection, and in the process develops a conceptual framework very different from that of bourgeois economics and political science. This conceptual differentiation may extend down to those theoretically basic categories that philosophy has taken as *a priori* and thus as its own object of inquiry, such as knowledge and reason. Would it follow that Marxism, in opposing the bourgeois social sciences at the scientific level, opposes the philosophy embedded in those bourgeois sciences by incorporating its own distinctive philosophy? Or could it be the case that just as Marxism opposes the bourgeois social sciences not on their own ground but on some other, so it opposes bourgeois philosophy, both within and outside social science, not on its own ground, as philosophy, but on some other?

Within the Marxist movement itself the latter option, with its implication that there is no Marxist philosophy, Marxism opposing philosophy as such, has maintained a fairly constant if sometimes shadowy presence. It has been explicitly and enthusiastically seized by various types of 'vulgar Marxism', more or less anti-intellectual, which have tended to portray all abstract ideas, or perhaps all non-scientific ideas, as pejoratively ideological. But it also occurs in more respected versions of Marxism in uneasy partnership with the former option, with its claim that there is a distinctive Marxist philosophy. Indeed, in Marxism since Marx's death it is this view that has been dominant, and it moreover provides us with a widely accepted way of classifying historically the main phases of the Marxist movement. At a very general level, there have been two influential forms that this Marxist philosophy has taken, the earlier more closely connected with the later work of Engels, the later with the earlier work of Marx.

The earliest view to develop and become influential in the Marxist movement was that Marxist philosophy is dialectical materialism ('diamat') and that this philosophy is related to Marxist science, namely historical materialism, in one or more ways, as the philosophy of that science: as a 'world-view' generalized from and supported by that science, or as an ontology on which that science is based, or as an epistemological foundation or methodology of that science. The first generation of Marxism after Marx's death, up to the Russian Revolution, was dominated by the two most famous and influential books of the founders, Marx's *Capital* and Engels' *Anti-Dühring,* and these two books were widely thought of in accordance with that division of labour, the former the basic science of Marxist economics, the latter the related philosophy of Marxism.

Dialectical materialism is the union of the two main streams of philosophy that Marx inherits and transforms: the materialism of the Scientific Revolution, especially in its English and French Enlightenment forms, and the dialectics of Hegel. The combination of these in dialectical materialism involves Marx's rejection both of traditional scientific and Enlightenment materialism as non-dialectical, i.e., as 'metaphysical' or 'mechanical', and of Hegel's dialectics as idealist. The element of scientific materialism claims that reality is wholly or basically material, not basically, or constituted by, thought or ideas, as Hegel holds, and is governed by natural laws that science seeks to discover. The element of dialectics claims that this reality is neither a static substance, nor a mass of atoms or subsystems that are related to one another purely externally, nor a process of cyclical or repetitive change, nor a process of merely gradual evolutionary change; on the contrary, it is a causally interconnected totality, both internally unified and contradictory, driven by its contradictions in a process of inevitable developmental change, revolutionary as well as evolutionary, and in its revolutionary changes bringing forth genuine qualitative novelty. The laws governing nature, society and human thought are dialectical in that sense, and science is the attempt to discover them. As a scientific study of capitalism, *Capital,* for instance, discloses that bourgeois society has a material base, its economy, which is subject to irreconcilable contradictions, and that the gradual intensification of these contradictions will inevitably produce a revolutionary transformation of the whole society from capitalism to socialism. *Capital* is an attempt to formulate the laws of such development.

This account raises many problems. The most relevant one here is whether, and if so how, it sustains the claim that there is a distinctive Marxist philosophy. It's clear that the formulation of diamat as a unique combination of materialism and dialectic was first put forward and argued for in Marxism, and that it has remained more or less peculiar to the Marxist tradition. However, there is a way in which the very content of diamat itself both resists the claim that it is distinctively philosophical and suggests that its confinement to Marxism is a historical contingency. For the laws of dialectical materialism are said to characterize the whole of reality and thus to be validated by science in general, including the natural sciences,

at least as they advance from their earlier 'mechanical' and ahistorical phase into their mature modern forms. Dialectical materialism is consequently not a philosophy in any sense in which philosophy is distinct from science, nor is it distinctive even of Marxist science. (pp. 245-48)

Roy Edgley, "Philosophy," in Marx: The First Hundred Years, *edited by David McLellan, Frances Pinter (Publishers) London in Association with Fontana Books, 1983, pp. 239-302.*

MARGARET A. ROSE   (essay date 1986)

[In the following excerpt, Rose analyzes Marx's view of nature as it is reflected in his attitude toward German Nazarene and Russian Social Realist art, concluding that he defined nature "neither as the objectification of 'Spirit', nor as the ideal subject-matter of art, but that to which productive man was tied by economic needs and interests."]

Writing in opposition to both the cultural and political policies of the Prussian monarchy, as also in opposition to the orthodox Hegelian interpretation of Hegel as a legitimator of those policies, the young Karl Marx was both to read Hegel's aesthetics in the context of early nineteenth-century Prussian political history and to reject the defence of the latter which conservative readings of Hegel had seen him as giving. Marx was of course also to differ from Hegel in his concept of what Nature was. Defining Nature neither as the objectification of 'Spirit', nor as the ideal subject-matter of art, but that to which productive man was tied by economic needs and interests, Marx was, however, and contrary to Socialist Realist art history, never to invert explicitly Hegel's preference for Idealist art into one for the naturalist or realist art of his time in which rural Nature and its populace were celebrated. Though inverting Hegel's claim . . . that the 'universal class' mediating between public and private interests would best be made up of a bureaucracy of permanent land owners (i.e., Prussian Junker class), by arguing in his [writings on Hegel] that the universal class was, by virtue of the process of dialectic inversion, the opposite to the propertied, Marx did not at the same time raise Hegel's contrastingly low opinion of landscape in art to any higher level, or designate it as the art most appropriate to the needs of the new 'Universal' class of the unpropertied. Perhaps because this was defined in *The Communist Manifesto* and other later works as the proletariat, this new 'universal class' was one which was also to become much more closely associated with the city than the country in Marx's works, and one which was for him to have little to do with the romanticization of the rural landscape.

Given that claims like this may also lead some to wonder about the relationship of Marx's own thought to the recent rehabilitation and re-evaluation of the rural pre-industrial landscape as subject-matter for a critically realistic art, this paper will attempt to give some background history both to Marx's reactions to the Hegelian relegation of nature and landscape to the objectifications of Spirit, and to the Social and Socialist Realist development of a 'Marxist Aesthetic' (not necessarily based in Marx) which is sympathetic rather than antipathetic to the depiction of the rural landscape.

With regard to Marx's views on Hegel's aesthetics, and their characterization of Nature, one work which must be mentioned, if only briefly, is Marx's much ignored research in Bonn in early 1842 for a thesis on 'Hegel's hatred of religious and Christian art'. (pp. 152-53)

Research into the art of Marx's time shows clearly enough . . . that one explanation for the title of Marx's planned treatise on Hegel's 'hatred of Christian and Romantic art' is that the Christian and Romantic art defended in Hegel's *Aesthetics* as best expressing Spirit was also the art given patronage and protection by Prussian authorities to whose own 'Romanticism' Marx was already clearly antipathetic by 1842.

Apart from collecting the works of old Christian masters praised explicitly by Hegel, both Friedrich Wilhelm III and Friedrich Wilhelm IV had given patronage to the groups of neo-Christian artists known as the German Nazarenes or Brethren of St. Luke. (p. 154)

While the extracts for Marx's unpublished treatise on 'Hegel's hatred of religious and Christian art' show Marx to have been interested in using Carl von Rumohr, Grund and Böttiger to argue for a sensualistic and even Hellenistic base to the Christian art favoured by both Hegel and the Prussian court of Marx's time, articles actually published by Marx in early 1842 explicitly attack both the Romanticism and religious and political ultramontanism of the then new monarch Friedrich Wilhelm. In all, Marx's rejection of the Hegelian aesthetic's justification of the art of Raphael and his like as the highest representations of Spirit can be seen to be based not only in a rejection of the primacy of Spirit in history, but also in a rejection of the politics of the patronage given the neo-Christian artists of his own time—one of his most trenchant criticisms of Friedrich Wilhelm IV in 1842 being that that monarch had not only given patronage to Romantic and Christian art, but protected it by new censorship instructions explicitly directed towards the blandishment of those like Marx who might dare to criticize either the State or its Church.

Putting aesthetic questions aside for more clearly political and economic ones in his later works, Marx also went on to describe more closely in those texts what he meant by material nature. Defining this in his *Economic and Philosophic Manuscripts* of 1844 not only as the 'species-being' of man spoken of by Feuerbach in his *Essence of Christianity* of 1841 as having been alienated by Christian art and religion, but also as the productive power of the worker, Marx had gone on the *The German Ideology* . . . to describe the way in which the divisions of labour of particular ages had served to produce particular forms of art, including that of the Raphael so admired by the German Nazarenes, as also by both Hegel and the Prussian court. Following this, Marx gave yet another defence of Greek art [in 1857, when] . . . he argued that Greek art was great because it could show man the way in which history had been changed by way of material production. Though accused by some recent critics for idealizing Greek art here, Marx may be seen as using it again (as in the 1840s) against the Christian art which had been popular in his native Prussia, and which was now also popular in his adopted London thanks to the patronage given it by another Bonn pupil of Eduard d'Alton, Prince Albert, the Prince Consort.

Without digressing into the many fascinating links between the German Nazarenes and the Prince Consort or into the lesser known links between the latter and Marx's teacher Eduard d'Alton, it is also relevant to the present subject to point out that Marx was to break with the Hegelian and Idealist aesthetic in general in his [emphasis on] . . . the importance of understanding the primacy of material production over the reflection of Spirit in nature which Hegel had described as the basis of human cultural and social life. (pp. 154-55)

[Other] comments made by Marx in works published in the nineteenth century could also have formed the basis of an aesthetic antipathetic to the reflectionist and populist theories offered by Social and Socialist Realists in the 1930s as alternatives to the 'productivist' aesthetic ideas of the avant-garde Constructivists of the 1920s. Where these Constructivists had, like Marx himself, emphasized the importance of linking the arts to material production, Socialist Realists of the Thirties both rejected the concept of an avant-garde of artists free from Government control and turned back to Social Realist traditions condemned by the Constructivists. Amongst those traditions was that which saw the function of art as being to reflect the social reality around it and that which had led to the rural life of Russia being made the primary subject-matter of its art. (p. 155)

[Given] the links between German Nazarene and Russian Social Realist art of the nineteenth century, we may now ask whether the attribution of sympathy for both a Realist and populist tradition of painting to Marx himself in Socialist Realist aesthetics has been an imposition of a view ironically all too closely related to the populist and often sentimental Nazarene art against which Marx's 1842 treatise and other works had earlier been directed.

Looking again at what Marx understood by Nature in the majority of his works, and, that is, at a concept concerned with modern man's post-industrial production of his environment, it would seem that he himself would have had no brief for the Populist 'sacralization' of the countryside and of its inhabitants as it occurred in both German Nazarene and the Russian social realist art of his own time, and which was, to some extent at least, to be echoed in the subject-matter of some Socialist Realist works of the 1930s, from works showing Stalin against a backdrop of cheerful agricultural workers, to industrial workers outlined against dramatic mountain backdrops, or to Lenin shown talking with imagined peasant delegations in the Smolny. Breaking with Hegel's view of nature as the objectification of Spirit, and never explicitly expressing the Russo-Hegelian view that art should primarily reflect social reality, Marx, by contrast, appears to have had little time for the German artists of his own time who had either imbued the landscape with religious symbolism, or depicted it in naïve harmony with its peasant populace.

In summary it may be said that while Hegel had seen Nature as but an objectification of Spirit, and Marx begun from the premiss that material nature was not only the subject of history but one defined by its relationship to human production, more recent rehabilitations of the rural landscape in art have looked to a world in which Nature, though no longer totally idyllic, is still essentially pre-industrial and non-productive. Though the assumption of Socialist Realism that Marx was a defender of 'realism' appears to have persisted, and been joined by an implication that his name may also be associated with the populist preference for rural subjects, the connection of both of these 'aesthetics' with that of the Nazarenes of his time must also give us pause to question the validity (on both historical and philosophical grounds) of their assumed connection with Marx.

Even an application of Marx's own principles of demythologization to the appropriation of his name by these aesthetics would have shown them to have little in common with his own early nineteenth-century ideas. Though these included a rejection of Hegel's expressed preference for the Romantic Christian art of Raphael as well as a rejection of his relegation of Nature to an objectification of 'Spirit', they cannot be seen to have included a rehabilitation of landscape art or of the crude realism of rural genre painting which Hegel had relegated below Raphael. Given these facts it would seem that there is still room for more critical (and historical) studies of Marx's own ideas on aesthetics, as well of what has come to be known as 'the Marxist aesthetic'. (pp. 156-57)

> *Margaret A. Rose, "Theories of Nature from Hegel to Marx," in* The British Journal of Aesthetics, *Vol. 26, No. 2, Spring, 1986, pp. 150-60.*

ADDITIONAL BIBLIOGRAPHY

Acton, H. B. *What Marx Really Said*. New York: Schocken Books, 1967, 148 p.
    A discussion of the basic tenets of Marxism.

Adams, H. P. *Karl Marx in His Earlier Writings*. London: Frank Cass & Co., 1965, 221 p.
    An analysis of Marx's early philosophical works.

Avineri, Shlomo. *The Social and Political Thought of Karl Marx*. Cambridge: Cambridge University Press, 1969, 268 p.
    An assessment of Marx's life and career. Avineri's goal is to "emancipate the study of Marx's thought from the historical circumstances through which we have become acquainted with the various stages of Marx's intellectual development."

Ball, Terence, and Farr, James, eds. *After Marx*. Cambridge: Cambridge University Press, 1984, 287 p.
    A collection of essays written in honor of the centenary of Marx's death.

Beer, M. *The Life and Teaching of Karl Marx*. Rev. ed. Translated by T. C. Partington and H. J. Stenning. London: George Allen & Unwin, 1925, 159 p.
    A biographical study that focuses on Marx's significance as a historical figure.

Bloch, Ernst. *On Karl Marx*. Translated by John Maxwell. New York: Herder and Herder, An Azimuth Book, 1971, 173 p.
    A detailed study of Marx's philosophical development.

Blumenberg, Werner. *Portrait of Marx: An Illustrated Biography*. Translated by Douglas Scott. New York: Herder and Herder, 1972, 196 p.
    A detailed biography.

Bottomore, Tom, ed. *Karl Marx*. Makers of Modern Social Science. Englewood Cliffs, N.J.: Prentice-Hall, A Spectrum Book, 1973, 188 p.
    A diverse collection of essays on Marx by prominent scholars, including Berlin, Lukács, and Benedetto Croce.

Boudin, Louis B. *The Theoretical System of Karl Marx in the Light of Recent Criticism*. Chicago: Charles H. Kerr & Co., 1907, 286 p.
    An explication of Marx's theories with reference to the Revisionist movement.

Cameron, J. M. *Scrutiny of Marxism*. Viewpoints, no. 3. London: SCM Press, 1948, 128 p.
    An analysis of Marxist philosophy and its role in history.

Cole, G. D. H. *What Marx Really Meant*. New York: Alfred A. Knopf, 1934, 309 p.
    A detailed explication of several aspects of Marx's thought.

Croce, Benedetto. *Historical Materialism and the Economics of Karl Marx*. Translated by C. M. Meredith. 1914. Reprint. London: Frank Cass & Co., 1966, 188 p.
    A detailed analysis of the form, methods, application, and interpretations of historical materialism. Croce also delineates the respective boundaries of scientific, philosophical, social, historical, and economic appraisals of Marxism.

Demetz, Peter. *Marx, Engels, and the Poets: Origins of Marxist Literary Criticism*. Rev. ed. Translated by Jeffrey L. Sammons. Chicago: University of Chicago Press, 1967, 278 p.
    A discussion of the genesis and development of Marxist critical analysis.

Dupré, Louis. *The Philosophical Foundations of Marxism*. New York: Harcourt, Brace & World, 1966, 240 p.
    Examines Marx's early works in light of his theoretical development.

Eastman, Max. *Marx, Lenin, and the Science of Revolution*. 1926. Reprint. Westport, Conn.: Hyperion Press, 1973, 266 p.
    Analyzes Marx's philosophy and its application in "revolutionary engineering."

Elster, Jon. *Making Sense of Marx*. Studies in Marxism and Social Theory, edited by G. A. Cohen, Jon Elster, and John Roemer. Cambridge: Cambridge University Press, 1985, 556 p.
    A scholarly explication of Marx's economic, historical, and philosophical theories.

Eubanks, Cecil L. *Karl Marx and Friedrich Engels: An Analytical Bibliography*. Garland Reference Library of Social Science, vol. 100. New York: Garland Publishing, 1984, 299 p.
    A comprehensive bibliography of writings on Marx and Engels and a list of their individual and collected works.

Evans, Michael. *Karl Marx*. Bloomington: Indiana University Press, 1975, 215 p.
    An overview of Marx's life, work, and theoretical development.

Hook, Sidney. *Marx and the Marxists: The Ambiguous Legacy*. An Anvil Original, edited by Louis L. Snyder, no. 7. Princeton, N.J.: D. Van Nostrand Co., 1955, 254 p.
    A general treatment of Marxism and its influence.

Hyman, Stanley Edgar. "The Marxist Criticism of Literature." *The Antioch Review* 7, No. 4 (Winter 1947-48): 541-68.
    Discusses Marx's own literary criticism as the basis of Marxist criticism.

Koren, Henry J. *Marx and the Authentic Man: A First Introduction to the Philosophy of Karl Marx*. Pittsburgh: Duquesne University Press, 1967, 150 p.
    A brief introduction to Marxism.

Korsch, Karl. *Karl Marx*. Modern Sociologists. London: Chapman & Hall, 1938, 247 p.
    Surveys Marx's views on society, political economy, and history.

———. *Marxism and Philosophy*. Translated by Fred Halliday. London: NLB, 1970, 159 p.
    Reprints of essays on Marxist philosophy that were originally published in the 1920s and 1930s.

Lachs, John. *Marxist Philosophy: A Bibliographical Guide*. Chapel Hill: University of North Carolina Press, 1967, 166 p.
    A detailed bibliography of writings on Marx arranged according to subject matter. Each chapter is prefaced by an overview of the most significant writings on that topic.

Laski, Harold J. "The Communist Manifesto." In *Essays in the History of Political Thought*, edited by Isaac Kramnick, pp. 323-37. Englewood Cliffs, N.J.: Prentice-Hall.
    An explication of the *Manifesto* by an eminent Marxist critic.

Lewis, John. *The Life and Teaching of Karl Marx*. New York: International Publishers, 1965, 286 p.
    A biographical and critical study of Marx.

Lifshitz, Mikhail. *The Philosophy of Art of Karl Marx*. Translated by Ralph B. Winn. 1938. Reprint. London: Pluto Press, 1973, 186 p.
    Traces "some crucial aesthetic themes in Marx's work in terms of their integral relations to the developing totality of his thought."

Maguire, John. *Marx's Paris Writings: An Analysis.* Dublin: Gill and Macmillan, 1972, 170 p.
    Studies the work done by Marx during his stay in Paris, focusing on the *Economic and Philosophic Manuscripts.*

McLellan, David. *The Young Hegelians and Karl Marx.* Books That Matter. New York: Frederick A. Praeger, Publishers, 1969, 170 p.
    Points out the influence of Hegel as well as a number of other German philosophers upon Marx's theoretical development.

———. *Marx Before Marxism.* New York: Harper & Row, Publishers, 1970, 233 p.
    Examines the historical context in which Marx's early writings were composed.

———. *The Thought of Karl Marx: An Introduction.* London: Macmillan, 1971, 237 p.
    A chronologically arranged description of Marx's works followed by excerpts from his writings and a discussion of their themes.

———. *Karl Marx: His Life and Thought.* New York: Harper & Row, Publishers, 1973, 498 p.
    A detailed biographical study of Marx.

———. *Marxism After Marx: An Introduction.* New York: Harper & Row, Publishers, 1979, 355 p.
    A comprehensive analysis of the evolution of Marxist doctrine.

———, ed. *Karl Marx: Interviews and Recollections.* London: Macmillan Press, 1981, 118 p.
    A collection of interviews and personal recollections that provide a portrait of Marx as he appeared to his contemporaries.

Mehring, Franz. *Karl Marx: The Story of His Life.* Translated by Edward Fitzgerald. London: George Allen & Unwin, 1936, 575 p.
    The classic biography, now considered by many scholars to be out-of-date and biased.

Mészáros, István. *Marx's Theory of Alienation.* 1970. Reprint. New York: Harper & Row, Publishers, Harper Torchbooks, 1972, 356 p.
    Discusses various features of Marx's theory of alienation, including its conceptual structure, its economic, political, moral, and aesthetic aspects, and its contemporary significance.

Meynell, Hugo. "Corrupt Society: Marx." In his *Freud, Marx and Morals,* pp. 64-103. Totowa, N.J.: Barnes & Noble Books, 1981.
    Discusses Marx's perception of human nature and his description of its actual and ideal state.

Miller, James. *History and Human Existence: From Marx to Merleau-Ponty.* Berkeley and Los Angeles: University of California Press, 1979, 287 p.
    A reading of Marx based on his treatment of subjectivity and its interpretation by existentialists.

Miller, Richard W. *Analyzing Marx: Morality, Power and History.* Princeton, N.J.: Princeton University Press, 1984, 319 p.
    A detailed analysis of Marx's ideas regarding morality, power, and history.

Nicolaievsky, Boris, and Maenchen-Helfen, Otto. *Karl Marx: Man and Fighter.* Rev. ed. Translated by Gwenda David and Eric Mosbacher. London: Allen Lane, Penguin Press, 1973, 492 p.
    A historically based biography, first published in 1933, that focuses on political events occurring during Marx's life.

Padover, Saul K. *Karl Marx: An Intimate Biography.* New York: McGraw-Hill Book Co., 1978, 667 p.
    An extensive biography based on Marx's works, correspondence, and personal writings.

Payne, Robert. *Marx.* New York: Simon and Schuster, 1968, 582 p.
    A biographical study of Marx that attempts "to draw a portrait of the man as he was, with his family and friends, and to present him for the first time as a living human being."

———, ed. *The Unknown Karl Marx: Documents concerning Karl Marx.* New York: New York University Press, 1971, 339 p.
    A collection of writings about Marx previously unpublished in the United States. These documents include several youthful essays by Marx, pieces by his daughters, and several letters.

Rühle, Otto. *Karl Marx: His Life and Work.* Translated by Eden Paul and Cedar Paul. New York: Viking Press, 1929, 419 p.
    An early biography that is now considered unreliable.

Schmidt, Alfred. *The Concept of Nature in Marx.* Translated by Ben Fowkes. London: NLB, 1971, 251 p.
    Analyzes Marx's concept of philosophical materialism and the relationship between nature and society in his works.

Schumpeter, Joseph A. *Capitalism, Socialism, and Democracy.* New York: Harper & Brothers Publishers, 1942, 381 p.
    Discusses Marxism as the basis of contemporary socialism.

Solomon, Maynard, ed. *Marxism and Art: Essays Classic and Contemporary.* New York: Alfred A. Knopf, 1973, 649 p.
    A collection of essays about various aesthetic theories stemming from Marxism.

Steiner, George. "Marxism and the Literary Critic." *Encounter* XI, No. 5 (November 1958): 33-43.
    A discussion of the genesis and development of Marxist literary criticism.

Trotsky, Leon. "*The Communist Manifesto* Today." In *The Communist Manifesto,* by Karl Marx and Friedrich Engels, pp. 3-11. New York: Pathfinder Press, 1970.
    An assessment of the *Manifesto* pointing out the relevance of the work in modern times. Trotsky dated his essay 1937.

Tucker, Robert C. *Philosophy and Myth in Karl Marx.* 2d ed. Cambridge: Cambridge University Press, 1972, 263 p.
    A critique of the philosophy of Marx.

Untermeyer, Louis. "Karl Marx." In his *Makers of the Modern World: The Lives of Ninety-Two Writers, Artists, Scientists, Statesmen, Inventors, Philosophers, Composers, and Other Creators Who Formed the Pattern of Our Century,* pp. 26-33. New York: Simon and Schuster, 1955.
    A general overview of Marx's life and thought.

Williams, Raymond. *Marxism and Literature.* Oxford: Oxford University Press, 1977, 217 p.
    An evaluation of the development of Marxist literary criticism in the twentieth century.

Wilson, Edmund. "Marxism and Literature." In his *The Triple Thinkers: Twelve Essays on Literary Subjects,* rev. ed., pp. 197-212. New York: Oxford University Press, 1948.
    Assesses the role of literature and art in Marx's philosophy and its interpretation by other critics.

Cyprian Kamil Norwid

1821-1883

Polish poet, dramatist, short story writer, and essayist.

Norwid is considered one of the most innovative nineteenth-century Polish poets. Shunning many of the conventions of Romantic poetry, he employed a consciously difficult style and meticulous methods of construction to express his artistic and philosophical beliefs. Rebuked, and at times ridiculed, by his contemporaries for the idiosyncratic nature of his writings, Norwid retained an unshakable belief in his poetic calling and intended for his most ambitious work, a collection of poems entitled *Vade-Mecum,* to serve as a handbook of verse forms for future generations. Although Norwid received little recognition in the nineteenth century, early twentieth-century critics rediscovered his works, praising both his creativity and artistic integrity. Norwid is now remembered not only for his contributions to Polish poetry, but also for the modernity and originality of his aesthetic philosophy, expounded in his verse, short stories, prose works, and dramas.

Born in Laskowo-Głuchy near Warsaw, Norwid was orphaned at the age of nine and subsequently raised by relatives. He spent his adolescence in the atmosphere of political turbulence following the 1830 Polish uprising against Russia and received only a few years of high school education. He began studying art in Warsaw in 1837 and three years later published his first verses, gaining recognition in Warsaw literary circles as a talented young poet. Following in the steps of earlier Polish intellectuals who had fled Russian-ruled Poland in search of political and artistic freedom, Norwid left his homeland in 1842 and traveled through Germany and Italy, composing poetry and studying sculpture, art history, and archaeology. In 1848, while living in Rome, he wrote his first version of *Wanda,* a verse drama based upon the popular Polish legend of Princess Wanda, and began developing an artistic philosophy that countered the popular tenets of Romanticism. As his works came to reflect these beliefs, Norwid experienced increasing critical hostility and had problems finding a publisher. In Italy, he also met and fell in love with Maria Kalergis, a celebrated beauty of Russian-Polish origin, who failed to return his affection. Financial difficulties and Kalergis's indifference led Norwid to move in 1849 to Paris. There, in the early 1850s, he published *Promethidion,* a statement of his aesthetic beliefs in the form of two verse dialogues and a prose epilogue, and *Zwolon,* an experimental drama about young Polish émigrés in France. During this period, he also completed *Krakus,* a verse drama about the legendary dragon-killer Prince Krakus, as well as the second version of *Wanda.* With the exception of an unhappy sojourn in New York from 1852 to 1854, Norwid remained in Paris for the rest of his life, struggling to support himself as a sculptor, draftsman, and, at times, manual laborer. Although he came into contact with Frédéric François Chopin, Adam Mickiewicz, Juliusz Słowacki, and other influential Polish figures, Norwid's poor health and unusual artistic theories eventually caused him to become isolated from Paris émigré society. He wrote prolifically, however, producing verse dramas, short stories, and poems, most of which remained unpublished during his lifetime. Although one collection of his poetry, *Poezje,* was printed in 1863, Norwid was unable to find a publisher

for what is today considered his most important work, *Vade-Mecum,* which was completed in 1865 but did not appear until after his death. Deaf and suffering from tuberculosis, he moved in 1877 to a Paris home for poor and elderly Polish émigrés. Norwid died there in 1883 after spending the final years of his life in artistic obscurity and worsening health.

Norwid's unique aesthetic philosophy strongly affected his writings, which differ markedly from those of his Romantic contemporaries in terms of style, themes, and structure. Norwid's highly individual style displays his interest in the literary significance of *przemilczenie,* or that which remains unstated. He was often deliberately ambiguous, using both irony and the intentional omission of words and phrases to evoke a creative response from the reader. Biographers have suggested that early nineteenth-century censorship of the Polish press as well as Norwid's hearing problems may have contributed to this fascination with the artistic uses of silence. Norwid's works also differ thematically from those of the popular Romantic writers of his day; unlike the Romantics, who celebrated individual heroism, Norwid believed in social progress through meaningful labor and collective sacrifice. Silent, socially-minded leaders—rather than active, heroic types—tend to be the protagonists of his dramas and the objects of admiration in his poetry. Furthermore, in contrast to the emphasis in most Romantic literature upon passionate emotions and spontaneous forms, Norwid's works generally are philosophic in tone and painstakingly constructed.

Norwid's literary output comprises several genres, including poetry, dramas, short stories, and essays, but critics generally praise his lyric poetry as his greatest accomplishment. The best of these works, collected in *Vade-Mecum,* exhibit a variety of stylistic innovations, notably the introduction of free verse to the Polish language. Thematically, Norwid often treats such urban problems as alienation, boredom, and poverty, and many of his poems are based upon actual events. Two poems that commentators frequently single out for particular approbation are ''Fortepjan Szopena'' (''Chopin's Piano''), a free verse account of the destruction of the famous composer's piano in the Warsaw Rising of 1863, and ''Bema pamięci żałobny rapsod'' (''Funeral Rhapsody in Bem's Memory''), in which a contemporary war hero is given the funeral of an ancient warrior. Norwid's most frequently discussed plays, the verse dramas *Wanda* and *Krakus,* are also concerned with Poland's political fortunes. In both of these works, Norwid adapted Polish folklore to present protagonists who sacrifice themselves for their country. In addition to his writings in verse form, Norwid wrote many prose works, including short stories, literary reviews, essays, and a published series of lectures on Słowacki. Among the most acclaimed of his short stories are ''Stygmat,'' ''Ad leones,'' and ''Tajemnica Lorda Singlewortha'' (''Lord Singleworth's Secret''). Written with allegorical overtones, these stories explore such issues as the effect of one's past upon one's behavior and the influence of capitalism upon art. Norwid's most popular prose work was *Czarne kwiaty,* a series of recollections of literary and artistic people whom he visited shortly before their deaths. *Białe kwiaty,* which Norwid conceived as a counterpart to *Czarne kwiaty,* is a set of anecdotal observations upon the effects of silence in different settings.

In accordance with his own prediction that ''The son will pass this writing by, / but you, grandson, will recall / What vanishes today,'' Norwid's work was, for the most part, neglected until the early twentieth century. Although he was praised in Warsaw for his early poems, Norwid was soon dismissed by contemporaries as a cryptic writer and an eccentric. It was not until 1901, when Zenon Przesmycki began publishing Norwid's works in the magazine *Chimera,* that a revival of scholarly interest occurred and Norwid became the object of critical admiration in Poland. Despite his high reputation in his native country, few of his works have been translated into English. Nonetheless, in the twentieth century Norwid has received increasing attention from English-language critics, who generally agree that his poor contemporary reception was due to ideological differences from his readers. Recent critical studies of Norwid often focus on his aesthetic philosophy, particularly as expressed in *Promethidion* and his lyric poetry. In addition to examining such topics as Norwid's influence upon modern Polish writers through his experimentation with language and meter, commentators have explored how Norwid used his poetic innovations to convey his philosophical beliefs. Today, for his unique artistic philosophy, Norwid is remembered as one of Poland's most original nineteenth-century poets.

*PRINCIPAL WORKS

Promethidion (verse dialogues and essay) 1851
Zwolon [first publication] (verse drama) 1851

Czarne kwiaty (reminiscences) 1856; published in periodical *Czas*
Białe kwiaty (essays) 1857
O. Juliuszu Słowackim; w sześciu publicznych posiedzeniach (lectures) 1860
Krakus [first publication] (verse drama) 1863; published in *Poezje*
Poezje (poetry, verse dramas, verse dialogues, and essay) 1863
Wanda [first publication] (verse drama) 1863; published in *Poezje*
Pisma zebrane. 4 vols. (poetry, verse dramas, drama, and prose) 1911-46
**Vade-Mecum* (poetry) 1947
Pisma wszystkie. 11 vols. (poetry, verse dramas, drama, short stories, prose, lectures, and letters) 1971-74

*Most of Norwid's early poems first appeared in Warsaw periodicals, including *Przeglad Warszawski* and *Biblioteka Warszawska*. Many of his works, however, were not published until the twentieth century.

**This work was completed in 1865.

Selections of Norwid's poetry in English translation have appeared in the following publications: *Botteghe oscure, Five Centuries of Polish Poetry, Golden Treasury of Polish Lyrics, The Modern Polish Short Story, A Polish Anthology,* and *Slavic and East European Review.*

JULIAN KRZYZANOWSKI (essay date 1931)

[*Krzyzanowski examines Norwid's ideological differences from the Romantics as expressed in his poetry and verse dramas.*]

[Norwid,] who was so unhappy in his life, was equally lacking in fortune in his versatile artistic activity. He was a gifted painter and sculptor; his plastic works, however, scattered as they were all over Europe, did not supply him with the means of livelihood. It is even impossible to appreciate them justly to-day, because only a small part of them is known and has been preserved.

He was a poet and a playwright above all; but his fortunes in this field were similar to his fortunes in the field of sculpture. He sent his writings to the publishers and editors of periodicals; many of them were discovered, in time, among the papers of the editorial offices, but a considerable amount of them were lost. Moreover, as he was not understood by his contemporaries, even the few of his works published in his lifetime became a target for fierce attacks on the part of the critics, and the victim of discouraging indifference on the part of the readers. All these circumstances could not compel Norwid to renounce his work; he considered his activity a lofty mission, and he found comfort in the hope that his time would come, though long after his death. ''The son will pass by my writing, but thou, my grandson, wilt remember it, because I shall not exist any more,'' was his prophetic consolation.

He was quite aware of his ill-luck, and he reconciled himself to it. He ascribed it to the unlucky star under which he was born. He declared this in fact in his autobiographical elegy [**''The People's Hands Were Swollen with Applause''**], from which the lines above are quoted. He expressed his views on his own life in a poetic figure of a dark land covered with gigantic laurels, overshadowing with its branches all who came too late. The inhabitants of this mysterious country, satiated with poetry, had no palms for further applause nor ears for the songs of the late-comers; therefore a poet who was born too late could have no audience. And yet he did not leave his path, because he was initiated into it, and anointed for it by God's finger; he would run his course to its end, though alone and forlorn. In other words, it was the poet's profound belief in the value of what he had to tell his readers that supported him at the hardest moments of his life.

The real cause, however, of the indifference with which Norwid met from his contemporaries, rested on the fact that he was of another type from the recognized poets of his period, and that, expressing this difference in his works, he opposed the views generally accepted by his generation. His position and his failures were dictated by his mentality and its constituents, which, for the most part, had nothing in common with the composition of the Romantic mind.

Amongst the characteristic features of the Romantic outlook was the high esteem given to the individualist and the egocentric; in Polish literature, as we know, these two elements combined to create the idea of a heroic leader of the nation saving it at the cost of his own happiness or even his life. Norwid, though he never underrated the true greatness of any outstanding individual, was free from the exaggerated appreciation of individuality; his views on greatness approached rather the Christian ideal of humility, while it was the social element of life which he considered the most important basis of national prosperity. No wonder, then, that readers who could not find in his works that which they were accustomed to receive from Mickiewicz and his compeers, remained indifferent to Norwid's opinions.

The idea of the heroic leader was a part of the general views on Poland's future and her attitude towards other European nations. All the emigrant writers believed in the philosophic system called Messianism. Norwid, alone, did not seem to have shared these views; his works, consequently, did not answer the demands of the period which sought for the solution of the political problems in poetry.

Both the peculiarly Polish hero-worship and Messianism had their common source in the high appreciation of feeling which was considered the essential and only worthy element of the human soul. Norwid was of a different opinion. He maintained the necessity of the equal development and importance of all the qualities of our consciousness, therefore he was against the contemptuous treatment of the rational and reasonable.

Finally, whilst Mickiewicz's dream had been to live to see his masterpiece, *Pan Tadeusz,* in the hands of the peasant readers, in which desire were mirrored the democratic tendencies of the period, Norwid deliberately accentuated his aristocracy; he destined his labours for a chosen few, for the qualified lovers of great art and great poetry. He addressed in his works "the chosen ten thousand" readers, although in his lifetime he could find barely ten.

Literary formulas seem at times to be misleading, or, at least, to make the problems for the explanation of which they were invented darker. Therefore I should prefer to avoid introducing the term "classicism" with respect to Norwid, though undoubtedly the classicist ideals were familiar to the Polish poet, and though they often found in his writings perfect expression. His preference for some ancient themes, his love of the form of the Platonic dialogue and, finally, his style, have a great deal more in common with the classicist aesthetic ideals than with those proclaimed by the Romantics.

The last of these attributes, Norwid's style, perhaps brings us nearest to the explanation of his lack of popularity with his contemporaries. It is certain that he liked to go his own way, and this applies not only to his modes of thought, but also to his style, which differs from that of the Romantic poets. Whilst the Romantics neglected their literary forms and sacrificed them to the abundance of their matter, Norwid paid great attention to his carefully thought out form. He sought for adequate harmony between both these essential qualities of any work of art, and never sacrificed the form to the demands of the matter. But this method entailed a serious danger which he was not always able to avoid, or overcome. In order to express his ideas as perfectly as possible, he was often compelled to create new modes of expression, a new vocabulary and a new syntax; these often lacked necessary clearness, and proved to be above the readers' abilities or, at least, their patience. They demanded as much effort as did the works of the ancient writers. But any reader who is able to break the back of these preliminary difficulties may enjoy fully the beauty of the peculiar world created by the poetic recluse within these difficult forms.

That world is very rich both in subject and form. Its greatest treasure is in Norwid's lyric poetry; but it contains as well many dramatic works and short stories.

Norwid's lyrics are as difficult to criticize as any other. A large collection called **Vade Mecum** forms the poet's memoir in which he notes all his thoughts and feelings. He was aware of this, and in the elegy quoted earlier he described his verses as "letters sent via Babylon to Jerusalem, and yet reaching their destination, an artist's memoir, crossed out and scribbled over and smudged, and yet quite real". This lyric memoir is marked with melancholy, in accordance with the author's soul. From his earliest work, Norwid saw in his poems a "black thread of sadness", which accompanied him always and everywhere.

Sometimes its source was the poet's homesickness and loneliness. So, in a short poem, called **"My Song"**, he gave voice to his nostalgia. He yearned for his country because it was a blessed land, a paradise of his childish memories; it was a country where people picked up crumbs of bread because they were considered a gift of Heaven; they did not harm the storks' nests because these birds are friends of men. He longed for the people who answered "yea" and "nay", and who had the Gospel simplicity in their hearts; but he clearly knew that he would not see it again with his mortal eyes because he was destined to wander all over the foreign world.

Sometimes his melancholy originated in the realization that the world and man are mean and shallow, that there is no room on earth for real greatness of spirit and character. When the famous General Bem died, who had fought for Poland in the Rising of 1830, and later played an eminent part in the Hungarian Revolution in 1849, Norwid celebrated his memory in a marvellous poem which St. Zeromski considered one of the highest revelations of modern poetry. Nowhere, indeed, were the plastic abilities of Norwid manifested to such an extent as in this short **"Funeral Rhapsody"**, as he called it. The dead hero became an ancient warrior carried to his pyre by a suite of soldiers, preceded by groups of lamenting women and accompanied by his faithful horse and his trusty armour. The poet was equally susceptible to the greatness of character of the departed; he saw in him a forerunner of the new era, that of the universal freedom for which the heroic warrior had fought under many colours. Finally, he did not shut his eyes to the deep gulf separating his own day from the much-dreamt-of future, to the realization of which the brave General had devoted his life.

The poet who had resisted all the temptations of everyday and commonplace feelings, whose poetic lyre never sounded with the love of woman, willingly portrayed the great manifestations of human greatness and human sorrow, the love of ideals, and his attempts to adapt them to earthly life.

The same subjects which had inspired him in his lyrics found an equally fine expression in his plays, which were also stamped with his personality. For that reason, though some of them are based on a clear and definite plot, they would hardly prove successful on the stage. They are symbolic and full of deep significance, but, at the same time, their essential meaning is so deeply concealed that they need collaboration and even some effort on the part of the reader.

The first of them, called *Vanda,* is written in a series of short scenes reproducing the well-known mediaeval legend of the fabulous Princess of Kracow who refused the proposal of a German Prince and, besieged by him, preferred death to marriage with the invader. She drowned herself in the Vistula, and her subjects raised to her memory a tumulus near Cracow. Norwid took this subject, but he transformed it according to his idea of its inner and hidden meaning.

Vanda's subjects, the peasants, come to the royal residence with gifts which will help the Princess to recover. They have been told of Vanda's dangerous disease. She is dumb, and there is no medicine that can assist her to utter a single word or cry by which her life may be saved. With them comes the disguised German suitor; Vanda recognizes him, but she cannot accept his proposal. The Prince cannot understand her; he sees her tears and hears her answer that she must be left an orphan and in solitude because she cannot betray the confidence and belief of her subjects who see in her something unearthly, lofty and untouched by human vice and passion. The Prince leaves her, and Vanda bids a pyre be built of the gifts brought to her by her people. This having been kindled, she enters it and dies in the flames.

Norwid, who had his definite aesthetic views, formed a theory which he considered very important for the explanation of any artistic phenomenon. It was the theory of Silence as a means of poetic expression. According to it no artist, particularly a poet, is able to express the whole of his idea. There remains always something that must be left unspoken, unexpressed in words; it must be expressed by means of silence, which is, however, sometimes more eloquent than words could be. And it is just in his plays that he employs silence to put forward the very depths of the mysterious powers of the human soul.

Accordingly, instead of the mediaeval tradition which saw in Vanda an ordinary woman, acting on the impulse of an exclusively patriotic nature, Norwid introduced into the story a later *motif,* invented by the earlier Polish playwrights, that of love. In his play Vanda loves the German suitor, and yet she cannot achieve her wishes; she refuses to marry him, for she knows that her union with an alien consort will bring misfortune on her subjects. They cannot live together with the robbers who do not appreciate the "sacred laws of neighbourliness", and who often violate them. Consequently she must renounce any idea of her personal happiness, and sacrifice herself for the sake of the welfare of her subjects. But this conflict between her lofty appreciation of her royal duties and the feelings of a girl's heart, is given voice only in a dozen lines, and it is shown rather as a psychological necessity than as a dramatic and living

picture. Thus Vanda becomes rather a marble statue, called to life by the poet's dream, than a girl-queen of a primitive and savage nation. This does not mean that the dramatic poem is a failure, that there is in it a want of harmony between the poet's intentions and their artistic realization. Norwid wished to produce a dramatic and tragic dream, and he achieved it. But it is hardly possible to find a dramatic poem elsewhere in which its corner-stone, the conflict of love and duty, could have been expressed so economically, and in such few words, as in *Vanda.*

Still, Norwid did not confine himself to the merely traditional *motifs* leading Vanda to her sacrifice. At the moment of her death there appears in the sky a strange portent; it is the shadow of a mighty hand, pierced through and through. The poet who quotes on the title-page of the play a stanza from the religious song of Kochowski, the seventeenth-century poet, telling how Christ turned his martyred head northwards and looked on distant Poland, attaches this pious view to the subject of his dramatic poem. Accordingly, he makes the fabulous Polish Princess an unconscious precursor of the later Christianity, a national saint, who anticipates the divine teaching of the Gospel and fulfils it in her short life. In this way the "mystery play", as Norwid called it, embraced in its four hundred lines a vast subject fit for a full-length tragedy.

And perhaps nowhere in Norwid's poetical works has the difficult art of masterly simplicity been so successfully accomplished as in *Vanda.* He avoided all poetic ornaments; his laconic style, however, perfectly expressed all the poet wished to have expressed. Its precise eloquence appeals strongly to the reader's imagination, but, as a matter of fact, it demands an intelligent and attentive reader, one of the "chosen ten thousand", to whom Norwid addressed his poem.

The poet, who proved so successful in his dramatic miniature, as *Vanda* may rightly be called, created another masterpiece in *Krakus.* Its subject may be found in the same cycle of the mediaeval legends as *Vanda.* According to the chronicles, Vanda was the daughter of an old prince who became famous, after he had killed a terrible dragon who had his den underneath the Prince's castle. His deed was immortalized by his subjects as was that of Vanda. They set up a mound which was called after the Prince's name, Krakus. But the last years of the brave Prince were darkened by disasters. His two sons began to quarrel over his legacy, and one of them was slain by his brother-rival. Then, the legend says, the royal murderer was banished, and Vanda adorned her forehead with her father's crown.

In Norwid's play all these events are given a special and particular meaning. The old Prince, broken by age and disease, sends his two sons into the country to seek remedies against the monster living beneath the castle. He who will destroy the dragon will be proclaimed the sovereign. Rakus and Krakus, the two youthful heirs, take leave of the father and come to an old hermit, whom they ask for help. The old man bids them find an enchanted spring; he who drinks its sacred water will save his country. As the horse of Krakus, the younger prince, has lost a shoe, Krakus is compelled to remain in the forest while his happier brother, deaf to his entreaties, goes on. Instead of seeking for the spring, he comes to Kracow at the very moment of his father's death. He declares his readiness to fight against the monster, and appoints the day. Then he rides in full armour, but not against the serpent. He meets his brother in disguise, who thus attempts to avoid the inevitable fight, and he kills him. The basic element of the poem centres in the history of the silent victim. Krakus, left behind in the forest, discovers the secret fountain, and learns from its murmurings the truth about the nature of the dragon; he understands that the monster lives in his brother's breast, filled with jealousy and thirst for power. He resolves then to sacrifice himself, to die unknown, instead of arousing domestic war. (pp. 268-77)

It is easy to point out the affinity of both plays. It is evident not only in the fact that both **Vanda** and **Krakus** are bound up with the parts of the same legend, but in the method of dealing with what the poet considered its essence.

Vanda dies, covered with the shadow of the hand of the Saviour; the pagan Krakus becomes a symbol of self-sacrifice, trying to conquer the evil embodied in his brother's feelings. The old hermit, when asked by the princes for advice, tells them in mysterious terms that in the distant lands the Chaste Maiden has overwhelmed Satan, but he has escaped and found refuge in their country. He can be conquered only by sanctity and sacrifice; and it is Krakus who followed the hermit's suggestion, and so, unconsciously, performed the work of Christ in the land to which the dying Lord turned his eyes of agony.

The play of **Krakus,** in consequence of its subject and the necessity of introducing other characters, is more complex than **Vanda.** Moreover, the poet handles in it themes which remind us of the Romantic love of the fantastic. Thus Prince Krakus arrives in his dream at the wonderful fountain; he understands its warnings; he enjoys the hospitality of the marble threshold on which he lays his weary head. But, as in dealing with the dragon, here also Norwid avoids the fantastic; his fountain and threshold symbolize the sisterly relationship of Nature with the forlorn youth; Nature gives to him what he cannot find amongst men.

Finally, the terrible sensation of hopelessness and spiritual loneliness, gentle in **Vanda** and more acute in **Krakus,** but peculiar to the whole of Norwid's literary work, nowhere finds better expression than in these two poems.

Silent heroes, like Vanda and Krakus, one finds also in other plays of his, in **Zwolon,** [**Noc tysiączna druga**], [**Kleopatria i Cezar**] and others. They arrest the reader's attention when, like shadows, they appear and disappear before his eyes, and in a few words express the poet's views on the most complex problems of human nature. An intimate and initiated lover of Norwid watches their gestures and movements, and is really able to enjoy the mysterious eloquence of the poet. Norwid, who in one of his poems said that lyrics must be stamped with asceticism, introduced the same feature into his plays—and anyone who cannot resist the charm of books like *The Little Flowers of St. Francis,* with their simplicity and naïvety, may discover both these elements in Norwid's dramatic poems. For, despite all outward appearance, they are as simple and, at the same time, profound as some of the mediaeval miracle-plays. (pp. 278-79)

> *Julian Krzyzanowski, "Lyric and Dramatic Poetry of Norwid," in his* Polish Romantic Literature, *E. P. Dutton and Company Inc., 1931, pp. 265-79.*

MANFRED KRIDL (essay date 1956)

[Kridl provides a broad overview of Norwid's poetry, noting his artistic skill and his importance in Polish literary history.]

First place among Norwid's rich and many-sided poetic works goes to his lyric poems. Simple lyrics, such as **"Moja piosnka"**

("My song"), are relatively rare. But even in poems of this kind Norwid's typical devices may be found in the crystalization of things and emotions, as, for instance, in the second stanza, where a symbolic 'black thread' becomes an equally symbolic 'book mark,' 'a string' to tie flowers, and reappears on the meadows in 'autumnal weavings.' **"Pielgrzym"** (**"The Pilgrim"**) requires a deeper reading because of the greater concentration of artistic expression, which cannot be translated, much less paraphrased in prose. The picture of a pilgrim exile, deprived of home and land in the material sense, but proud of extending his soul to the skies ('I dwell in the womb of heaven') and of owning as much land as he can cover in moving forward, is conceived, with an unusual economy, in four expressive and forceful images. This kind of poetic conception is seen in many of Norwid's lyric works. One of his most characteristic poems is **"Bema pamięci żałobny rapsod"** (**"To the Memory of Bem, A Funeral Rhapsody"**). . . . According to Norwid, Bem was one of those talented Polish officers who in exile attained the stature of true knights, champions of an idea. It is to this symbol of a knight that the poet pays tribute in the poem. The poem takes the form of a poetic-symbolic vision of the burial of ancient heroes. The armor, sword, torches, wax candles, falcon, war-horse, banners, women in mourning and boys drumming on axes and shields—these images carry us back to the days of Scandinavian heroes. The imagery is changed in the second part of the poem as the funeral procession becomes a symbolic procession of knights (in the meaning explained above) who go out into the world with the body of a hero as their leader, in order to awaken slumbering cities, to revive 'fainting hearts,' and to open the blind eyes of nations. The verse of the poem flows in a hexameter of its own, unequaled in its majestic and evocative rhythm. The language is in harmony with the entire vision, giving images of such force, expressiveness and originality as 'broken hands' on the armor, the horse which lifts its feet up like a 'dancer,' the axes 'grown bluish from sky,' the shield 'red from the lights,' etc. (pp. 307-08)

Norwid felt the genius of Chopin . . . and memorialized him in the poem **"Fortepjan Szopena"** (**"The Piano of Chopin"**). . . . He considered Chopin 'our foremost artist,' and in the poem *Promethidion* described his art as 'raising the inspirations of simple folk to a power which touches to the core and encompasses all of humanity.' In an obituary on Chopin he wrote: He knew how to gather wild flowers without shedding either their dew or their lightest down. And he knew how to transform them with the radiance of art into stars and meteors and comets that shine upon all Europe. In **"The Piano of Chopin"** the same thought is expressed in poetic images and formulations. The beginning of the poem speaks of the artist's 'days before his last' which mark the dawn of a new life. Death will not 'tear asunder' this life, on the contrary, it will 'emphasize it' and give it new meaning. The essence of Chopin's art is described in stanzas IV and V. One essential trait is its simplicity, a simplicity found in artistic perfection that is achieved only on the highest level of art. A second trait is its national quality, symbolized in the image of a country house built of larch wood, into which enters 'ancient virtue'. This is the future, ideal Poland 'taken at the zenith of absolute perfection of its history,' but still the same Poland in spite of every change, still in the Piast tradition of 'transfigured wheelwrights,' rural and agricultural, preserving the traditional features of its national character.

The ninth stanza describes an incident based on actual facts. In 1863, at the time of the Insurrection, an attempt was made in Warsaw on the life of the then Russian governor-general of

Poland, Count Berg. From the windows of the Zamoyski palace shots were fired at him. The Cossacks were called to the scene; they set fire to the palace and ransacked it. While doing this, the soldiers flung Chopin's piano, which had been kept in the palace, out of the window into the street. In the poem this fact is turned into a stirring symbol. The poet first depicts the Old City of Warsaw, where Chopin was brought up, with the Cathedral of St. John, the 'patrician houses' in the Old Square, and the column of King Sigismund on the Castle Square. Then follows a description of the arrival of the Cossacks, the fire in the building, and at last the vision of sacrilegious hands seizing and hurling to destruction the piano, the symbol of Chopin's art. 'The Ideal fell to the Pavement,' exclaims the poet; the great artist's instrument, which had expressed his inspiration, is destroyed and desecrated. The symbol of Chopin's art shared the fate of so many other symbols and ideas. It is the fate of everything which arouses men from slumber, provokes their anger and their will to destroy what disturbs them.

This poem, like the rhapsody about Bem, reveals in its extraordinary force and fullness some basic characteristics of Norwid's poetry: it compresses a universal meaning within particular facts, conceiving them in condensed and crystallized poetic visions so that almost every word opens up limitless perspectives; it creates a new poetic language and a new versification to encompass in them the most immaterial elements. Norwid's poetic accomplishment reaches beyond the direct expression of simple things. The reader must work hard to penetrate the essence of Norwid's poetic world, but the labor is rewarding because it affords artistic experiences of a kind rarely offered by Polish poetry.

Let us take a few examples of Norwid's ability to transpose material facts on to the level of universal symbols. He tells, for instance, of a Polish exile, Jan Gajewski, who perished in the explosion of a steam engine. This provides Norwid with the occasion for a short poem, **"Na śmierć ś.p. Jana Gajewskiego"** . . . , in which this man's death symbolizes the spiritual redemption of contemporary materialistic civilization, represented by a steam engine. At the same time it furnishes a symbol of brotherhood between a reborn nobleman and the workers who died with him in the explosion. The following is a summary of one of the stanzas:

> He did not die for profit.
> One body composed of many bodies revealed one
> common face when it was buried on foreign land—
> a simple laborer with a nobleman, the Son of
> Sacrifice with the Sons of Oppression.

Another event used by Norwid was a massacre of Christians which took place in Syria. Hearing about this, the Emir Abdel-Kader, a Moslem, hastened on his own initiative to the aid of the Christians whom he defended for eight days before the European armies arrived. This event inspired Norwid's poem (**"To Emir Abdel-Kader"**), which builds up to these lines of great poetic impact and effect in the last two stanzas:

> And if in the tears of persecuted people, and
> in the innocent blood of virgins, and in the
> awakening child, the same God lives, then your
> tent should be larger than the forests of David
> because of the three Magi you were the first to
> mount your horse in time!

We see here the same process as in Norwid's other works: particular events or facts are sublimated into universal symbols. The Christian army was late in coming to the rescue of a

A self-portrait by Norwid at age twenty-two.

Christian people, who were defended by a Moslem, a man of chivalrous and humanitarian spirit. The poet compares him to the foreign Magi when they came to Bethlehem, while his deed is expressed in the suggestive metaphor 'you mounted your horse in time.' (pp. 308-10)

One of the most beautiful love poems in Polish forms a part of Norwid's **"A Dorio ad Phrygium."** It is impossible to summarize it, because it contains untranslatable images and phrases of purest poetry. Its structure consists of a series of comparisons, interrupted suddenly and left without the corresponding part. In the same poem Norwid displays a true clairvoyance of the Polish countryside. The age-old existence of the country is condensed into eight lines, its very essence, its philosophy, and the biological significance of farming life. These lines are filled with the charm and beauty of the land, its life conceived in terms only of today and tomorrow (the past is simply yesterday, the future no more than tomorrow; all days are alike, occupied by the same toil which admits neither of interruption nor change, or of any dreams about the past and the future). And finally there is its slow, stately, considered rhythm, like that of nature itself, having a fit time for everything and a spiritual balance and calm without haste or feverishness.

Among Norwid's longer poetical works we must mention *Promethidion.* In the introduction we read the poet's artistic credo and a kind of poetic definition of art. This definition has nothing in common with the classical conception of poetry as being both *dulce et utile,* both 'play and pedagogy.' It comes closer to romantic conceptions, but differs from them in its heavier emphasis on the social element in art. If we translate the poetic images into prose, we obtain the following outline of Norwid's position: in epochs of peace ('calm,' as the poet calls them) art is an 'arc of covenant,' a rainbow which connects the earth with the sky after 'the deluge of history.' In times of storms and thunderbolts art cannot act directly, but sets the tone of action, awaiting the moment when conscience is transformed into deed, 'assumes the form and concreteness of marble,' and leads the victors home to decorate with laurels the tombs of those who have fallen. The social element is expressed more forcefully in the following lines which may be considered complementary to the preceding images:

> And this is how I see the art of future Poland:
> as a *banner atop the tower of human work,* not
> as a plaything or a moral lesson.

Promethidion is written entirely in the form of a conversation between several persons on the subject of art, its essence, significance, and its role. The poem thus becomes a discussion on esthetics, and the predominantly discursive tone is emphasized by numerous footnotes and a long epilogue in prose. It is not merely a rhymed treatise, of the type seen in Krasiński, for it is interspersed with magnificent poetic visions. The larger part, however, undoubtedly possesses a didactic character with many obscure and difficult points. This is unfortunately true of many other long poems by Norwid: *Quidam, Niewola . . . , Rzecz o wolności słowa . . .* , of the plays, [*Kleopatria i Cezar*], *Krakus, Wanda,* and of other works besides. They treat historical, social, philosophical and esthetic problems, frequently all of them together; they often contain very original and profound opinions and beautiful lyrical passages, but they do not form organic unities as works of art. Even the most beautiful individual passages cannot save the whole when it is overburdened with abstract reasoning, arguments, or specific 'philosophical theses' which attempt to prove some truth and thus provoke a logical discussion, which is not the natural reaction to poetry. (pp. 311-12)

Norwid takes his place in the history of Polish literature primarily as one of its most distinguished lyric poets. . . . [His poetry] is unique, original, always seeking an individual mode of expression, and owing little or nothing to the great contemporary writers. One of its fundamental traits, we repeat, is that it renders concrete facts as symbols of universal significance, and does this to a higher degree than can be found in other Polish poets. Another equally rare trait consists in its condensation and fusion of artistic devices, the opening of unexpected and far-reaching perspectives on problems of the highest importance, and the rediscovery of a completely fresh form of expression for even the most ordinary and common feelings. To achieve this intellectual and emotional atmosphere, Norwid created a poetic language capable of operating just as masterfully with abstract as with concrete terms, interchanging them one with another in the most unusual combinations, a language full of neologisms and the strangest etymologies. His poetry is further characterized by the use of meters of such variety as can only be compared with the metrical forms of Słowacki's last works, or with works dating much later in the development of Polish poetry. (p. 315)

> *Manfred Kridl, "Polish Romanticism after 1831,"
> in his A Survey of Polish Literature and Culture,
> translated by Olga Scherer-Virski, Mouton, 1956,
> pp. 241-320.*

ZBIGNIEW FOLEJEWSKI (essay date 1963)

[*Folejewski considers Norwid's unconventional approach to the short story form as exemplified in "Bransoletka."*]

In the work of the Polish poet, Cyprian Kamil Norwid . . . , artistic prose occupies an important place. He is also one of the first Slavic writers who all through their creative career showed serious and unceasing preoccupation with theoretical and technical problems of such modern literary forms as the novel and especially the short story. The confrontation of Norwid's theoretical views in this respect and his practice as demonstrated in a number of prose works is a problem of considerable literary interest both in its historical and in its structural aspects. . . . (p. 115)

In his views on the most popular form of artistic prose, i.e., on the novel, Norwid always occupied a rather arbitrary position of superiority if not of scorn. This was not so much a mark of respect for poetry typical of the romantic period as it was Norwid's characteristic resistance to the danger of intellectual and artistic conformity in following conventions superimposed by the rules of novel writing. How much of a pioneer of modern art and how much of a Don Quixote there was in this lonely Polish artist fighting the windmills of both Polish and Western literary conventions is a matter which cannot be exhausted here. Quite characteristic are the following lines from Norwid's dedication of ["**Bransoletka**"] to his friend Antoni Zaleski, which is a poetic interpretation of his theory in this respect.

> Remember how we walked together, saying
> Things that had no concrete meaning,
> But nonetheless made sense and moved us deeply.
> Nor human will nor time effaces them
> Indeed, they willy-nilly stir our memory,
> And in our mind they seek fulfillment
> And seem familiar like bells we heard in childhood.

What was alluded to here in sketchy poetic form is further pursued in many instances both in theoretical comments and also incorporated in stories themselves.

Especially significant are Norwid's remarks in one of his stories, "**The Secret of Lord Singleworth**", in which the author outlines the difference between the novel and the short story genres. In the latter he emphasizes as essential the moment of internal unity of motif achieved by concentrating on some significant observation in its deeper philosophical sense. After having refused to go into the usual antecedents of his hero, Norwid elaborates on his personal aesthetic goal as a short story writer, stating very emphatically:

> To answer all these questions and also many
> others which would result from them, one would
> have to write not a short story which aims at a
> faithful presentation of a *unique observation*
> [italics mine. Z. F.], one would have to be a
> novel writer experienced in this craft and well
> trained in art.

This stress on unity and uniqueness of motif ("unique observation") is in full agreement with the structural requirements of short story technique, but in the writer's practice the emphasis on reflection and the element of subjective lyrical symbolism differentiate Norwid's stories from the typical short story. (pp. 115-17)

["**Bransoletka**"] constitutes, in my opinion, an excellent illustration of the problem of compromise between Norwid's theoretical attitude, alien to all popular conventions of artistic prose, and his practice, which unavoidably had to lead him to following certain conventional requirements. (p. 117)

Although Norwid often voiced his opposition to such canons of literary technique as dramatic plot, the presence of a hero, etc., in his actual work he was of course not entirely free of the very literary conventions against which he so vigorously protested. It is true that he never wrote a novel, but in his short stories and especially in his plays we can see many technical devices typical of the prose writing of this period, especially in Germany and France.

As said before, ["**Bransoletka**"] is probably the best example of Norwid's short story technique. It may be said to be based on a conventional short story pattern. The "plot" can be summarized in a few words:

The writer-narrator, after having heard of the ensuing wedding of Edgar and Eulalia, accidentally finds Edgar's present to Eulalia, a golden bracelet, lying on the street. He gives the bracelet to the family of a little boy whom he had seen picking up rubbish and to whose house he is led, as if by Providence, idly following a priest bearing the Holy Eucharist. The narrator informs Edgar of his find and Edgar rushes to regain the bracelet, but the "loss of a pre-wedding present never occurs without reason". Thus the story ends with the information that Eulalia has married a banker.

These are the external events forming the plot of the story. One can easily see how conventional and insignificant this bare pattern is. One must remember, of course, that such an account is not much different from the summary of any purely lyrical poem. What is important here is the deeper significance of the related events in the story in which these seemingly incidental details play the key role from the functional point of view and in the final analysis decide the course of action and the fate of the heroes. It is in the first place the lost bracelet that predestines the mutual relationship of both the two principal figures, Edgar and Eulalia, and also influences the fate of the secondary characters. Thus one of the basic requirements of short story composition—unity of motif—is fulfilled by the author. On the other hand, Norwid clearly disregards another important requirement of short story technique, namely, the requirement of speed of action. . . . (pp. 117-18)

It does not seem probable that Norwid was simply incapable of constructing a story based on conventional principles of a tight plot and a reasonably speedy action leading to a dramatic conclusion. On the contrary, it appears that the author's conscious efforts were concentrated on avoiding conventional patterns. As for the matter of being capable of devising a regular short story based on conventional rules, it had been sufficiently demonstrated at an earlier stage; among Norwid's juvenilia we find . . . **"The Benevolent Protector, or Bartholomew as Alphonse"**, which fulfills the basic structural requirements of short story writing while remaining at the same time a wholly mediocre work.

As we have seen, the basic structural motif in ["**Bransoletka**"] is entirely conventional. What makes the story unique is the degree of the author's personal engagement, his double participation in both the course of events and in their philosophical interpretation. This participation, though very discreet and hidden under the mask of a narrator, adds to the authenticity of the story. The intense lyricism of the author's reactions to the scenery and to the related events, blended on the one hand with objective, detached philosophical reflections and, on the other, with sharply outlined realistic details, strikes a peculiar balance between literary convention and an almost modernistic "anti-novelistic" technique.

The story begins in accordance with all the typical nineteenth century requirements. Without preamble, the author confronts the reader through a few fragments of a seemingly loose and insignificant conversation with the main characters of the story. Again, in accordance with the generally accepted technical requirements, only certain selected aspects of their character are revealed, aspects that are relevant to the presentation of the main motif. The interplay of these bare elements of plot, and the freely applied philosophical observations account for the final effect of the story, which in spite of the fragmentary technique makes the impression of a completed structure. Where the author economizes with direct information, he makes up for it by way of poetic reflection that becomes a functional part of the structure. There is no doubt that this is a conscious literary device, determined by the author's awareness of the necessity of accepting certain basic laws of literary fiction and at the same time trying not to follow them too closely. As is usual in such cases, a compromise was unavoidable.

This method is quite consistently used in almost all of Norwid's short stories, but ["**Bransoletka**"] is the best example of its application. Each of the seemingly marginal impressions of the narrator, who is walking through the streets after the ball, has its organic function in the work, a function whose full significance can be fully realized only retrospectively at the conclusion. This certainly increases the final effect of the story. The interplay of lyricism and realism, typical also for his poetry, creates a specific aura in Norwid's prose works; certain details realistically observed and described acquire a different symbolic significance in the light of the lyrical and philosophical reflections.

The narrator walking the streets, deeply absorbed by his thoughts, displays an almost suspiciously keen sense of observation, noticing the most minute details of the surroundings. Some of these details, such as the little boy picking up rubbish with a hooked stick ("bigger than the child") or the humble procession following the priest on his way to the sick, have both their philosophical sense and also their functional part in the course of action.

These contrastive images—of a golden bracelet in a gutter or "the holiest of all the tangible and untangible things in the world" escorted by a few poor servant women to the home of an ailing ragpicker—are closely related to Norwid's poetic search for "diamonds in the ashes", a search that reflects his entire artistic attitude—romantic and anti-romantic at the same time.

A somewhat similar interplay of elements of realistic though poetically sublime observation and lyric mood can be observed in the detailed description of the Venetian gondolas appearing in the moonlight in **"Menego"** or of the sudden storm in Norwid's last story, ["**Stygmat**"].

In accordance with the line of evolution in Norwid's concept of style, one can observe a certain shift in stress as far as the function of the realistic element is concerned. However, his awareness of the constant interaction of the "important and the futile" in all observable elements of life, however insignificant they may seem, never lets the writer lose touch completely with realistic observation.

> How strange is life, and how [strange it is that]
> we can see that everything in life is impor-
> tant . . . and futile.

It is not easy to classify Norwid's short stories from the point of view of the typology of this genre and to determine whether they are "stories of action" or "stories of character" or of something else again. It seems that most of Norwid's short stories are neither typical stories of action nor of character. One can see that in them both events and characters are presented in a very sketchy way; the emphasis is put rather on the element of setting and philosophical reflection for which the plot and the conflict of characters often seem only pretexts. Perhaps the term "stories of setting" would define the type closer. I mentioned before that this shift in stress is obviously not so much a result of Norwid's inability to use the classical short story pattern as his conscious striving towards greater artistic freedom. This led him to seek forms of composition in which the stress on reflection would not be felt as being merely the ballast of superfluous digressions. (pp. 118-21)

[A] recurrent note in Norwid's general aesthetic attitude [is] a note of opposition to conventional forms. In a letter to Konstancya Górska he remarks:

> Take all the writers of love stories, novel writers, *feuilletonists,* reporters, and ask them the following question—
>
> A quoi se réduiront tous les sentiments intimes comme l'amour, l'amitié, l'affection de coeur, etc . . . après avoir été élaborés *publiquement* avec leur détails les plus subtiles pendant tout un siècle?

It is easy to see how this unwillingness to compromise with any conventions led the writer to a position which can almost be termed as *avant la lettre* an "anti-novel" and "anti-short story" type of prose writing. His entire notion of style often borders on the concept of "anti-style"—by which Norwid means lack of any artificiality, any concessions to stylistic conventions. In his [*Czarne Kwiaty*] he argues the necessity of "avoiding style out of respect for things for which there exists no stylistic formulae". He often repeated the claim that he himself wrote exactly as he spoke, i.e., without any artificial stylization, using words and phrases as they normally came in natural spontaneous conversation. This idea of a "natural style" (Norwid claimed that the saying, "le style c'est l'homme" applied to him better than to any other writer) is, of course, pure theory; in practice Norwid chiseled his words and sentences with great care, and one can always see how much labor this ideal of "natural" style cost the writer. Nevertheless, works like the above mentioned [*Czarne Kwiaty*] and especially [*Białe Kwiaty*] belong to a group of Norwid's prose writings which could be classified as an attempt to create a special type of "anti-short story" story. Based on actual events and observations, these sketches are an attempt to uncover a deeper significance in fragmentarily related events, words, coincidences. The actual subject matter here is consciously shifted to the background while the deeper aspects, often of seemingly secondary significance and usually disregarded in conventional stories, assume special importance.

Speaking of Norwid's search for less conventional and more personal form and trying to explain the sketchy, fragmentary character of his narrative, we must recall also his theory of "silence" or "omission" (*przemilczenie*) as an essential element of speech and art. This theory was finally formulated (in an exaggerated form, to be sure, but not without some quite suggestive factual arguments) in one of Norwid's last essays, ["**Milczenie**"], and characteristically enough there is also an almost direct reference to it in his last short story, namely in the ["**Stygmat**"]. What is especially important in this theory is the awareness of the existence of significant and insignificant, *obvious* elements in speech and writing, the latter ones being only an echo of the external reality. Economy, suppression of the obvious, is one of the conditions of communicating something meaningful. (pp. 124-26)

> *Zbigniew Folejewski, "C. K. Norwid's Prose and the Poetics of the Short Story," in* American Contributions to the Fifth International Congress of Slavists, *Vol. 2, September, 1963, pp. 115-26.*

JERZY PIETRKIEWICZ (essay date 1966)

[*Pietrkiewicz discusses Norwid's didactic methods in* Vade-Mecum.]

In the sixties of the last century, a young practitioner of verse would certainly have needed some guidance to steer between the doldrums of post-romantic poetry and the exciting possibilities of prose, which was gaining more and more ground in literature. Baudelaire's *Les Fleurs du Mal* of 1857 offered a new direction, but the scandal aroused by the court prosecution obscured and also delayed its literary impact. Swinburne in 1865 had *Atalanta in Calydon* to his credit, though this promise and his later lyrical poems gradually gave way to superficial experiments with form.

For the poet Cyprian Norwid who, without any success, had challenged the Polish romantic convention, the prospects in the sixties seemed more hopeful. After the deaths of Mickiewicz in 1855 and of Krasiński in 1859, the grand manner that had sustained writing in exile was over, and the literary scene seemed empty enough for a bold poet to assert himself. Norwid possessed a strong inner conviction of his talent and had already voiced his authority, both as a poet and a moralist, in the play *Zwolon* and the verse dialogue *Promethidion*. Slighted, misunderstood and ignored he certainly was, but this did not alter his high claims or diminish his desire to guide those who were prepared to 'go with him': *vade mecum*, he had in effect been repeating, in a quiet but persuasive tone, from the beginning of his haphazard career.

Now a mature man of forty-four, he declared himself more openly than ever. His carefully planned collection of example-poems was intended to serve as a handbook of living new verse, a hundred pieces with a prologue and epilogue, justifying the overall title of *Vade-mecum*. During 1865 he worked on the final arrangement and early next year the Leipzig publisher Brockhaus received the manuscript. From that time on, the story of the collection is typical of Norwid's ill-fated projects: he could not get it printed, though he tried again and again. . . . (p. 66)

In 1962, a hundred years after the first drafts, the collection *Vade-mecum* finally appeared in a reliable edition of ten thousand copies. (p. 67)

What are we then to do with a handbook which was not used by those for whom it was devised? Does a delayed example remain valid, and can it ever be directly understood, without some hindsight? Here, I think, the loss of a few poems from *Vade-mecum* matters less than the loss in our appreciation of the experimental didacticism that guided the concept of the book. After all, nearly ninety poems and some fragments have survived; the arrangement is clearly visible; the prose address to the reader ("**Do czytelnika**") declares the passing of the romantic pronouncements on wide historical issues and the nation's rights. Polish poetry, Norwid says in his address, has come to a critical moment, and certain public duties, once readily accepted by poets, must be taken over by journalists and social reformers. We are moving towards a more normal epoch. But the moral denominator has to be recognised in the norm of things. Throughout *Vade-mecum* it is this moral denominator that holds the structure of the verse, poem after poem. 'One must not bow to Circumstances and ask the Truths to stand behind the door'—a typical remark from a poem significantly entitled . . . **"Początek broszury politycznej"**.

A detailed examination of content might perhaps reveal the wrong sort of didacticism, for the inner consistency of *Vademecum* and its obvious intellectual purpose are the very qualities which make the lyrical poise look like a withdrawal from poetry. It is therefore important to discuss Norwid's didactic experiment as an achievement in form rather than in subject matter. Moreover, this should be done without resorting to the most striking novelty in the volume, free verse, which naturally enough still fascinates modern critics. Thus the poem about Chopin's pianoforte, deservedly famous for its metrical originality, may be taken as an example of the didactic technique which the poet consciously heightens to give the final abstraction ('ideal') its extraordinary physical strength. The musical instrument thrown by the Russian soldiers on to a Warsaw street touches a moral reality with its dying sounds. An ideal has reached the cobbles: 'ideał sięgnął bruku'. Every section, and there are ten of them in **"Fortepian Szopena"**, carries some didactic point, subtly enveloped in the language of metaphors, until the whole concept literally crashes against a physical obstacle ('bruk'), releasing simultaneously both a poetic surprise and the surprise of a moral truth.

Norwid used his memories of Chopin on more than one occasion but here as in a much earlier work, *Promethidion*, the opening lines have the same colloquial ease: 'Byłem u Ciebie w te dni przedostatnie' (in **"Fortepian"**) and 'Taka rozmowa była o Chopinie' (in *Promethidion*). The colloquial tone affects the metre as much as it helps the didactic intention to emerge, almost unnoticed, and then it suddenly asserts itself by means of a paradox when we think we have just accepted an argument:

> I—oto—jak ciało Orfeja,
> Tysiąc Pasji rozdziera go w części;
> A każda wyje: *'Nie ja!'* . . .
> *Nie ja'*—zębami chrzęści—
>
> Lecz Ty?—lecz ja?—uderzmy w sądne pienie,
> Nawołując: *'Ciesz się, późny wnuku!'* . . .
> Jękły—głuche kamienie:
> Ideał—sięgnął bruku'—

In Norwid's ironic comedies, colloquialisms of this double function can be interpreted as a result of his familiarity with the code and style of sophisticated salons. However poor and embittered he was, the art of polite conversation would always provide him with aesthetic examples. And it was not only the high comedy of contrasts; he found excellent examples in those conversational half-statements, evasive idioms and silences that also belonged to the pattern of social discourse.

All this, in my view, he exploited best in lyrical verse, especially when a moral is not spoken but shown like a silent pitfall under the comfortable cadences of speech:

> Cóż? powiem jej . . .
> Zwierciadło pęknie,
> Kandelabry się skrzywią na *realizm*,

> I wymalowane papugi
> Na plafonie—jak długi—
> Z dzioba w dziób zawołają: *'Socjalizm!'*

Hence the impression that a lyrical poem like **"Nerwy"** is closer in tone to our day than the dialogue of his plays, which at times seems too stilted and remote. The reason is simple. His poetic theatre had to depend more on conversational sequences which he tried to recapture for the atmosphere of his social scenes, the language echoing with phrases that have since become typical of mid-19th-century Polish. By contrast, Norwid's use of colloquial elements in lyrical poetry was fragmentary, in the nature of meaningful asides, and serving a concealed didactic argument. Beware of secret traps in stock phrases, in idiomatic prattle, in the very fluency of your words; if you want to go with me, *vade mecum* at the risk of falling into the truth which once was the Word and is being covered up by language. Such is Norwid's warning, implied by his consistent exploration of the surfaces of speech. A view from above has its risks also, for 'at the height of thinking there is a sphere from which the view is steep'.

> Na wysokościach myślenia jest sfera,
> Skąd widok stromy—
> Mąci się w głowie i na zawrót zbiera,
> W chmurach—na gromy.

The colloquial extension of 'zbiera się' from the giddy head to the clouds before thunder illustrates the technique which appears to be effortless because of the casual passage of the metaphor from sentence to sentence.

Sometimes such passage is due to a grammatical device. In **"Nerwy"** the nervous oscillation of mood happens, so to speak, on two levels of tenses: in the past (imperfective and perfec-

A manuscript page from "Chopin's Piano."

tive), and in the future (mainly perfective). The poet has seen the hungry poverty of Parisian slums, his thoughts still clinging to the banister of a dilapidated staircase from which he has escaped; and against this shocked recollection he imagines himself paying a visit to a baroness, she seated on a satin sofa, and the painted parrots on the ceiling crying from beak to beak: 'socialism!' There will be another cowardly escape from truth: the visitor's polite silence, the mockery of a social decorum. The nervous anxiety, however, up to the last line of the poem if built not on a fact but on a possibility—the visit may or may not take place. The perfective aspects of verbs in the final phrases *cóż powiem jej, kandelabry się skrzywią na realizm, usiądę z kapeluszem w ręku,* intensify one after another the moral realisation which is now stronger than the possible occurrence of an event. This, in fact, creates a lyrical aura around the realistic details and around the eloquent silence of the didactic ending.

At this point perhaps it is permissible to remove the derogatory meaning from didacticism as practised by Norwid in his experimental *Vade-mecum.* A didactic bias in a work of art almost invariably compromises either the honesty or the craft of its maker; but Norwid is curiously incapable of turning a didactic intention into a biased argument or a compromised form. The charge of obscurity which his contemporaries perpetuated was directed as much against his idiosyncratic style as against his religious thought, although he himself saw it rooted in the simple questions and answers of the catechism. It seems that a great deal of misunderstanding was caused by his new presentation of moral problems through the idiom of a poetry not dressed with customary embellishments, but on the contrary denuded of all prettiness and pious pretence. Nothing mechanically devotional could ever muffle his desire to repeat the old truths which he knew were at variance with language as it had become. 'There is no need to take the Gospel through a glove'.

Experiment apart, there is in *Vade-mecum* a strangely archaic vein running through poems with titles like **"Gadki"** (Chatter), **"Litość"** (Pity), **"Czułość"** (Tenderness), **"Historyk"** (The Historian), **"Zagadka"** (A Riddle). They are succinct yet somewhat rugged in structure, all going back to the very old tradition of apophthegms and riddles. This gnomic type of verse passed from Greek and Latin to the vernacular literatures of Europe and established itself as an independent genre. It appealed to mediaeval and humanist moralists alike, found favour with the baroque seekers of conceit and paradox, left its distinct mark on the mystical revelations of Angelus Silesius . . . , and in a cryptic way travelled via the romantic visionaries to the symbolists, to be finally revitalised by Ezra Pound in *Lustra.*

Gnomic writing in Polish literature alone occupies a considerable place, though it seems to be treated as an inferior by-product of poets. Sixteenth-century apophthegms in Rej's *Zwierciadło* may look too mediaeval next to the epigrammatic *fraszki* of Kochanowski, but they are in the same stream of didactic verse, whether anecdotal or sententious. Besides, Rej can be surprising, as in "Niecnota" where his rhyme literally coils an abstraction into a venomous serpent:

> Niecnota wąż jadowity,
> Co leży na drodze zwity.

In Potocki's *Moralia* the same tradition flourishes abundantly and emerges again in the parables and fables of the classicist Krasicki who brings anecdotal moralising to perfection by ex-

tending the function of dialogue within the shortest possible form.

Among Norwid's titles, the word *fraszka* occurs a few times, no doubt as an acknowledgement of his admiration for Kochanowski, but in *Vade-mecum* we witness a truly experimental fusion of all the gnomic characteristics, from *sententia* and apophthegm to fable and parable. Both classical sources and the native vernacular tradition are used with skill and reverence so that the result is never stylistic pastiche.

"Posąg i obuwie", with its apposition of sculpture and footwear, consists almost entirely of dialogue, in which it recalls the manner of Krasicki, yet the moral is spread over the whole length of the poem through Norwid's technique of meaningful probing into speech. Thus the phrase 'zabija czas' links with 'wieczność', then with 'zwieczniają się chwile' and the repeated 'trwa'. On the other hand, 'Ostatni despotyzm' is constructed out of brisk snippets of dialogue, more after the fashion of satires, and the function of direct speech here is to register the jumpy rhythm of conversation, as well as to build a narrative sequence without any anecdotal matter. The word 'mekintosze' makes its entry into Polish poetry accompanied by a sound effect, 'chrzęszczą' ('mackintoshes clanking in the hall'), becoming immediately memorable. Other short poems, like **"Wakacje"**, **"Echa-czasu"** or **"Język-ojczysty"**, reveal a similar treatment of direct speech.

"Fatum", a masterpiece of brevity, stands out against these experiments with form, because its apophthegmatic equation, i.e. Misfortune—a wild beast facing man, operates within a lyrical emotion so imaginable that the equation soon dissolves and it is the man in the end who reduces the beast back to a mere abstraction. The question arises what exactly makes **"Fatum"** translatable—its apophthegm or its precise emotion? For it seems to demand attention when transferred into another language. The whole poem is here quoted in an English version:

> *Mischance,* ferocious, shaggy, fixed its look
> On man, gazed at him, deathly grey,
> And waited for the time it knew he took
> To turn away.
>
> But man, who is an artist measuring
> The angle of his model's elbow joint,
> Returned that look and made the churlish thing
> Serve his aesthetic point.
> Mischance, the brawny, when the dust had cleared
> Had disappeared.

"Ruszaj z Bogiem" can be described as a set of variations on the phrase 'God speed', which should never have lost its cardinal meaning, and the exegetist in Norwid restores it by letting the colloquial carelessness fall into his ironic traps. A man does speed after God when he follows a priest with the host (stanza three). Superficially, each stanza is harnessed to an example, suggesting a rational argument as in traditional verse of this moral type, and yet the comment at the end breaks off into a lyrical paradox: 'I can't say more; no poet has thought it up, it is too beautiful'.

A parallel exposure of a meaning bleared through repeated usage gives a precise tone to 'our circle' in the poem **"Kółko"** and to 'Siberias' in the poem **"Syberie"**.

A moralist who happens to be a genuine innovator in his medium of expression must surely possess a sophistication which from the start protects him against naïvety and didactic boredom. Norwid lets his sophistication shift meanings about, a biblical quotation merging with a proverbial saying, a collo-quial twist ready to confound our habits of association. The habits are often inherited, each word has its past. If *Vade-mecum* is taken to be a guide to future poetry, it is also a guide to the poetic diction of the past. It would be a simplification of Norwid's achievement a hundred years ago to keep pre-senting him as a precursor only. His seeing ahead was not of the prophetic kind in the romantic sense. He saw through rather than ahead. His preoccupation with speech, both ordinary and heightened, made him distrust our media of communication and fear propaganda. He registered the first signs of that grow-ing separation between words and reality which afflicts our contemporary perception. His interest in semantics sprang from the same realisation, though it could at times result in idio-syncratic lapses. When moralising towards the future, he pre-ferred to speak through parables, for which as a devout Chris-tian he had a most perfect example.

'You complain about the darkness of my speech; have you at least lit the candle yourself?' ("Ciemność"). Elsewhere in *Vade-mecum* Norwid speaks bitterly of his supposed obscurity and compares it with the lucid semblance of manufactured literature and manufactured folklore. "Ciemność", **"Ironia"** and **"Klaskaniem mając obrzękłe prawice"** (the most personal poem in the collection) pose this perennial dilemma of the writer, while **"Powieść",** a sample of mock-novelistic plot, and **"Kolebka pieśni",** about the debasement of peasant poetry, point to the pollution of literary sources, showing how much sham passes under the 'genuine-native' label. Like other ex-perimental artists, he wants to find for himself whether par-ticular forms or genres represent what they are supposed to represent. Hence a number of conversational pieces in which he really talks shop (e.g. **"Czas i prawda", "Wielkie-słowa", "Cacka", "Krytyka"**), but he knows about self-betrayal in the process of writing, and 'closes his notebook quietly, like the door of a cell'.

There is admittedly some inherent obscurity in Norwid's work which the passage of time and posthumous recognition have not altogether removed. It results not so much from the allusive and metaphoric congestions of his style, but rather from the didactic emphasis which, aiming inward, almost ceases to be didactic. Norwid's contemporaries missed it completely; today his experiments within the gnomic tradition still seem to be puzzling.

What he did, in fact, was to reverse the usual didactic practices by imposing a poetic sequence on a moral and not *vice-versa*. In **"Nerwy"** and **"Fatum",** for instance, the imposition is such that the reader has no alternative but to accept the hidden message, whereas one merely acknowledges with a nod a moral tag attached to an 18th-century fable, satire or verse letter. With Norwid we only too often get his points wrong, because we expect to follow a logical sequence leading to *one* conclu-sion, preferably at the end of the poem. Instead, he gives us poetic premises, seemingly disconnected. In other words, Nor-wid breaks up the didactic bias within a lyrical pattern and allows poetry to convince directly. His 'moralising' has there-fore something of an appeal to faith, poetic faith perhaps, and only in this personal sense does he promise self-revelation after the experience of his poetry. Norwid never presumes to convert us to some communal vision.

In 1860, at the beginning of his great decade, he delivered six lectures on the poet Słowacki, in which he said:

> Man comes upon this planet to bear witness to
> the truth. . . . The truth embraces life and is

therefore obscure, because it embraces a dark thing. If I took away life from the truth, I would take away that which verifies it, and then it would become a clear falsehood.

Vade-mecum will remain a dark manual, because it is verified against life. (pp. 68-75)

> *Jerzy Pietrkiewicz, "Cyprian Norwid's 'Vade-Mecum': An Experiment in Didactic Verse," in* The Slavonic and East European Review, *Vol. 44, No. 102, January, 1966, pp. 66-75.*

GEORGE GÖMÖRI (essay date 1967)

[*Gömöri analyzes* "Funeral Rhapsody," *focusing on how the poem reflects Norwid's concept of heroism. For further com-mentary by this critic, see the excerpt dated 1974.*]

The nineteenth century was an age unprecedented in its enthu-siasm for heroes and heroism; since the Renaissance no inter-nationally shared "cult of the personality" had reached the proportions of the cult of Napoleon or of the elegant poet and adventurer Lord Byron. This hero-worship had its origins in the Romantic concept of the individual, especially of the out-standing individual whose tragic destiny was to lead mankind and defy society at the same time. In the first half of the nineteenth century no Romantic poet could help being fasci-nated, at least for a while, by the world-shaking career of Bonaparte or the "Satanic" laughter of Byron, or both. The triad of great Polish Romantic poets, Mickiewicz, Słowacki and Krasiński, shared pro-Napoleon sentiments to an amazing degree and each of them glorified Napoleon in verse or prose. They also paid tribute to native heroes, soldiers or generals whose feats were performed during the national uprising and revolutionary war of 1830-1831 . . . and they admired Byron both as a poet and a social rebel who finally gave his life for the freedom of a foreign nation. In this respect there was but little difference between Mickiewicz and Cyprian Norwid who honored Byron with these words: "Byron was the Socrates of poets, since he was able to realize the poetic element in his life and deed, knowing what he was doing . . ."

The young Norwid's views on greatness and heroism have a definitely Romantic coloring. It was only after 1848 that he consciously began developing a new and "un-Romantic" model. Some of the young Norwid's heroes were, like those of many Polish students who had been educated in the gymnasium, selected from the gallery of Plutarch and of antiquity in general; others were chosen from national history. In all likelihood his admiration for Caesar and Alexander the Great, for Kościuszko and Napoleon dates from his childhood and adolescence— Napoleon, as a champion of free Poland, occupying the place of a national hero in his heart. Later on, during his *Wanderjahre* in Western Europe he learned to respect a new set of heroes whose names were not unknown to him before, but whose greatness he realized only in these years: great artists and schol-ars, such as Dante, Michelangelo, Copernicus and Chopin. And last but not least, he admired many great men venerated by the Church: apostles, saints, martyrs. Norwid, a staunch believer, was not only attracted to these Christian or crypto-Christian heroes—as years went by he became increasingly certain that, if the heroic element existed in his life, it was to be realized through such a silent and humble Christian sacrifice.

What were Norwid's criteria of heroism? The dedicated service of God, mankind, nation and individual man, or in a word, the service of Truth. Truth for Norwid could be historical or religious, aesthetic or social, but it would be more to the point to say that for him all truths appeared interdependent; bearing witness for a historical truth could bring the world closer to the final victory of Christ (through human freedom to liberation through God's freedom) and the uncompromising creativity of the artist would change the concepts and indirectly the life of the society. (pp. 145-46)

The most personal and in some ways the most unconventional element in Norwid's concept of heroism was his reverence for the "silent heroes" of duty, devotion and self-sacrifice whose chief medium of self-realization was work. In 1849 he wrote in a note to **Promethidion**: *"Bohaterstwo* jest półogniwem ksie-życowym na chorągwi prac ludzkich, to jest, sztuce . . .'' (*Heroism* is a crescent-like link at the top of the banner of human labor, that is, art . . .)

Another poem of Norwid's, **"Bohater,"** equates heroism with creative work. First, the heroes of the legendary past are evoked (for example, Jason who sailed off for the Golden Fleece, the dragon-killers of folk-tales) but they only serve to contrast the new hero whose deeds are less spectacular but whose patience and endurance are almost infinite. The hero of the industrial age is not aided by miracles; his victory is won through work and suffering. This kind of introverted heroism suited Norwid's temperament better than direct action, so often premature:

> Niechże więc Kolchów wiek sobie nie wraca,
> Współczesność w równej mam cenie:
> Heroizm będzie trwał, dopóki praca;
> Praca!—dopóki stworzenie!

Heroism in this new epoch is then realized in the creative act of the individual. Ever since he recognized its validity, Norwid had been working toward this model, while continuing to appreciate and sometimes glorify the ancient and Romantic models. Martyrs of a noble cause, soldiers fighting for and in the name of freedom were for Norwid heroes whose historical moment had arrived, who lived up to their mission.

Amongst Cyprian Norwid's Polish heroes, General Józef Bem occupies a special place. He praised Bem in articles and correspondence and devoted one of his most popular, and most beautiful poems to the General's memory. (pp. 147-48)

It is hard to tell exactly when Norwid thought for the first time of writing a poem to, or about, Bem, but it can be taken for granted that he had been meditating on the General's life and example for months before he actually wrote the **"Funeral Rhapsody."** This is clear from Norwid's article entitled **"Z pamiętnika (O zemście)"**, published for the first time in Bent-kowski's *Goniec Polski* on February 5, 1851. The article begins with an interesting comparison, Norwid's contrast between the two generations of emigrés. He does not deny the merits of the older generation, or its excellence in soldierly virtues. However: "Our generals and officers have become knights in exile. First, they were soldiers, full of excellent qualities and talents . . . but [the transformation] of the nature of fighting spirit in General Chłopicki into the nature of power which directed Bem's frail arm is that of the soldierly into the knightly."

Norwid makes a clear distinction here between the professional soldier-like spirit and "the holy heroism" which is the privilege of knights, that is, soldiers fighting for higher ideals. . . . If anyone was, Bem was certainly fighting for an ideal, not for money or out of a sense of professional duty. If Napoleon was called (ironically, or in all seriousness?) "the World-Spirit on

horseback,'' the frail and sickly-looking little general could have appeared to Norwid as the Spirit of Freedom embodied. In another article, which remained unpublished in his lifetime, the author of **Promethidion** wrote about Bem with unreserved admiration, ranking him together with Czartoryski, Mickiewicz and Chopin: "Bem, w bohaterstwie, na czele wieku stawa." (In heroism Bem takes the lead of the age.) Years later, when, in a letter to Karol Ruprecht, Norwid listed all the injuries suffered by the best Poles of his age for their outspokenness or non-conformist attitudes ("everybody was a traitor who uttered even a shade of truth"), he did not forget to mention Józef Bem: "General Bem (a man equal to Hannibal) twice miraculously missed by a pistol bullet . . ." This was an obvious reference to the attempts on Bem's life in France and in Hungary, in both cases by compatriots—by fanatical young Poles of democratic convictions.

The remark which we have just quoted from Norwid's letter to Ruprecht helps us to a better understanding of his relationship to Bem. The General became Norwid's hero, not merely on account of his objective merits, such as his undeniable courage and sangfroid manifested on the battlefield, but partly because the poet found him psychologically more to his taste than any other general or distinguished soldier. In 1846 Bem stood above the squabble of the parties; he ceased to be a close associate of the *Hôtel Lambert*, but did not join the *Towarzystwo Demokratyczne*. This could not have failed to appeal to Norwid since he also refused to identify himself with either the Conservatives or the Democrats. Moreover, Bem was misunderstood, hated and slighted by many of his contemporaries. This factor probably enhanced Norwid's predilection for the General: Bem must have appeared to him as a tragic hero whom neither his Romantic and extravagant deeds nor his classical virtues could make wholly acceptable to many Poles who measured "greatness" by party loyalties. . . . (pp. 150-52)

"Bema Pamięci Żałobny-Rapsod" was written in December, 1851, approximately a year after Bem's death, at a time when C. K. Norwid was living in Paris in constant material difficulties and in a state of increasing alienation from Polish society. . . . (p. 153)

[It] is a poem born out of a synthesis of different styles, moods, and ages. It is not eclectic but its poetic material is heterogeneous. It is a eulogy for a *romantic* hero whose deeds and sacrifices elevated him to the rank of *classical* kings and demigods, who, moreover, became the central figure of a legend, a popular and *national* legend. If a real synthesis was to be achieved all these elements had to be fused together in the style and the mood of the poem. We shall never know whether it was a result of a conscious or an intuitive concentration that Norwid succeeded in creating this synthesis, but it is certainly the fruit of a unique creative effort.

The title itself is interesting: it is a funeral rhapsody, not a threnody. Threnodies, mourning poems, are usually defined as "songs of lamentation for the dead." Poems of this type, in Polish *treny,* have a well-known pattern: they enumerate the merits of the deceased, bemoan his premature or untimely death, lament about the loss suffered by the living. The word *rhapsody,* on the other hand, means a variety of things. It comes from the Greek *rhaptein* and *adein,* meaning literally "songs stitched together." It could also mean "emotional utterance"—in music a rhapsody is an emotionally colored piece of work. For the Polish Romantics, however, a rhapsody was part of an epic poem, usually on an historical subject. . . . Norwid's **"Funeral Rhapsody"** does not fit into this scheme;

though it can be regarded as part of an epic "work" (the epic of history), it is more likely that the author knew both the etymology of the word and its musical usage. The **"Funeral Rhapsody"** is, in fact, stitched together from six homogenous parts which create a heterogeneous, yet poetically coherent, entity. Also, this is one of Norwid's most musical poems: the music of the language is used to amplify thought and imagery. (pp. 155-56)

[It] is almost impossible to reproduce the "content" of the **"Funeral Rhapsody"** in prose; it is the mood and the images that make the poem, not the narrative. On the other hand, it is wrongly assumed by some critics that the **"Funeral Rhapsody"** could appeal only to the ear and the eye, and not to the intellect. Our imagination, when reading the poem, should not be merely visual—it has to be also historical.

The poem is centered around the vision of a majestic funeral. Kridl describes it the following way: "The image of the funeral has nothing in common with reality. It is a poetic-symbolical vision of the burial of ancient heroes' remains. Armor, sword, torch . . .—all these [objects] bring us back into the prehistoric age of some kind of Scandinavian heroes" [see excerpt dated 1956]. The last sentence points to a misunderstanding. Norwid's vision of the funeral had nothing to do with the Vikings; rather, it has grown out of the poet's image of Bem as a *knight* and a *national hero*. Bem's legend cuts across history; it is based on a poetic synthesis of ages and cultures, not so much prehistoric as supra-historic.

The poem opens with a rhetorical question addressed to the hero: "Why do you leave us, Shade, with hands crossed over your armor . . ."—an image that recalls some medieval tombstones which depict the dead prince or warrior in a lying position, hands joined together in prayer, or just crossed in a peaceful gesture. The next lines confirm the impression given by the opening line, namely that Norwid is speaking to and about a great knight, a military commander. It is the funeral of a "lord"; not only the armor and the torches but the presence of the dead man's horse and falcon testify to his high rank. (The falcon is regarded as a symbol of feudal excellence.) From Part I, then, it is quite clear that a great soldier's funeral is taking place—somewhat similar to the final scene of *Hamlet*, where the hero is carried out on a shield, with flags and banners fluttering against the sky in the background. The transition to the mood of Part II is subtly prepared from the fifth line onwards; it is here that the striking image of drooping flags is introduced. The flags are mourning with their wings dropped like "dragons, salamanders and birds pierced through by spears." This simile . . . associates Bem with Krakus, the dragon-killer, and fuses the mood of Part I into that of Part II, transforming the funeral of a knight into the funeral of an old Slavic hero. Part I is finished with a further elaboration of the "dragonlike flags" idea; the fallen monsters are compared to "the many ideas which you were ever pursuing with your spear." Since this sentence is addressed to Bem, by implication he is ranked together with Krakus and the archetypal dragon-killer, St. George. Struggle for freedom is symbolic dragon-killing.

Part II shows strong similarities with the final (funeral) scene of the second version of *Krakus*. Norwid has studied the funeral habits of the old Slavs, but he also took the liberty of stylizing them: in both *Krakus* and **"Bema Pamięci Żałobny-Rapsod"** the mourners, instead of depositing into the open grave vessels full of food and drink, destroy them before the grave as a sign of their grief. The young women in the mourning procession (*panny żałobne*) correspond to different modes of mourning—

A scene from a 1967 Warsaw production of Kleopatra i Cezar. *From* Cypriana Norwida Teatr Bez, *by Kazimierz Braun. Panstwowy Instytut Wydawniczy.*

some, according to the old Slavic habit, carry "fragrant sheaves" of wheat or hay to the grave, while others are gathering their tears into shells (an image suggestive of Greek mythology), and still others are looking for a road *even if it was built centuries ago*. It was the poet who italicised this last phrase— it is a fairly clear allusion to Christianity. For Norwid, only through the Christian understanding of history is the meaning of a national hero's sacrifice revealed.

The "old Slavic mood" is maintained throughout Part III. The armed retinue taking part in the procession is, in fact, an army from the times of the Piasts. The soldiers carry axes and shields, spears and bows as well as a huge banner. All these weapons could be found in the armory of the Polish army in those days when people marched to the battlefield singing "Bogurodzica" and other religious hymns. The banner swaying in the smoke (which might be the smoke of a battle) is perhaps a symbol of Poland, torn and tattered by history but reaching into the sky. In Part IV a historiosophic metaphor is introduced. The procession disappears in a ravine to reappear soon afterwards, the chorus of the mourners dies down to return suddenly with undiminishing force. It resembles a powerful wave; and if we regard the procession as the continuous march of history throughout the ages, Part IV can be regarded as a symbolic representation of *the ebb and flow of history*.

This is the voice of Norwid, the student of history. Norwid, the metaphysician, dictates the following four lines (Part V)—

the funeral procession halts and the body is placed in the grave. The precipice "that Mankind finds no way to leap" is probably Death: historically right or wrong, when his time comes, no mortal can escape it. The image of Bem as an "old Slavic" leader is reasserted in the last line of Part V, when his horse is killed and follows his master into the grave.

In the concluding part of the poem the vision of the imaginary funeral opens a vista into the future, onto the long march of generations into Canaan or God's Kingdom: the living carry on the struggle of the Hero until final victory. Although from other works, such as *Niewola*, we know that Norwid believed in a transcendental liberation, he saw the complete emancipation and social liberation of mankind as a prerequisite to God's Kingdom. The struggle has to go on, until "mury Jerycha porozwalają jak kłody," the walls of Jericho tumble down like logs. Finally, all nations will rise from their historical slumber and realize themselves in history. The poem ends in an expressive half-line. There is no mark of exclamation after the concluding words; what they attempt to reproduce is the slow, momentous movements of history: "Dalej—dalej—(On . . . on . . .)."

What gives the poem, built of elements and images at the first sight seemingly unrelated, its peculiar unity? Apart from the formal coherence (the whole poem is written in hexameters) and a certain, though not at all self-evident, logic inherent in Norwid's thinking that pervades the **"Funeral Rhapsody,"** there is a unifying continuity in the poem. It is the *continuity of motion*. As Kazimierz Wyka noted, the technique of the **"Funeral Rhapsody"** is cinematographic, anticipating moving pictures by half a century. This is why the poem makes such a lasting impression on most modern readers, many of whom do not care for other, philosophically deeper poems of Norwid. Verbs play an important role in keeping the poem "in motion"—in three of the six unit-opening lines the first stress falls on a verb (*Idą, Wchodzą, I powleczem*) and in another case on verb-substitute (*Dalej*). In Part VI, the most dynamic part of the poem, there are not less than seven verbs or verbal nouns in four lines. (pp. 157-60)

All in all, the **"Funeral Rhapsody"** is a unique stylistic feat of a poet who, thanks to his intelligence and inspiration, succeeded in overcoming the resistance of the language. . . .

It is a moving and beautiful poem, and, in spite of its historical optimism, a poem written in grief. In a way it was Norwid's poetic tribute to an age, the funeral of which he had to attend in 1849-1850—the age of Romantic deeds and expectations. Bem represented the best this age could offer to mankind; he was the last Hero of an army of fanatic freedom-lovers who lived in a constant expectation of the revolutionary day of judgement and whose last hopes were buried together with him and with the fall of the French Republic. Norwid mourned the epoch that could never be again, knowing that the march of history continues, that history will call forth new heroes, a new kind of heroism. In his **"Funeral Rhapsody"** human and national tragedy are pitted against historical hope. (p. 161)

> George Gömöri, "The Poet and the Hero: Genesis and Analysis of Norwid's 'Bema Pamięci Załobny-Rapsod'," in *California Slavic Studies, Vol. IV, 1967, pp. 145-61.*

CZESŁAW MIŁOSZ (essay date 1969)

[*Miłosz provides an overview of Norwid's works, examining his place in Polish literary history and the nature of his aesthetic philosophy.*]

Though he was well-read in Western European literature, [Norwid] preserved complete independence from the literary currents of the day. Even though some of his poems bring to mind works of Théophile Gautier and the budding French symbolists, basically he was against aestheticism. As a man and as a poet, Norwid aspired to be like Don Quixote, a knight of truth (his poem on Don Quixote is one of his best). His weapon was a subtle irony so hidden within symbols and parables that his first readers hardly noticed it. To break the monotony of regularly repeated "feet" within the syllabic pattern, he deliberately made his verse sound roughhewn; often he would just abandon the syllabic system for free verse. In a letter (to Bronisław Zaleski) of November 1867, he revealed that he was completely aware of what he was doing:

> What Karol says about the number of syllables is *the most hideous barbarism* and *shows complete ignorance of even Horace himself.*
>
> When my **Vade-Mecum** comes out in print, they will see, they will recognize what the true lyric of the Polish language is like because as yet they do not know it at all, nor have they the flimsiest notion about it.
>
> There is no prose; there was never any prose in the world—all that is complete nonsense. *What is a Period in Prosody?* There never was any prose—and number, which the writer cannot hide in long-and-round-sounding words, is nothing but a total *destruction of the nature of rhythm.*
>
> Perfect lyric poetry should be like a cast in plaster; the slashes where form passes form, leaving crevices, must be preserved and not smoothed out with a knife. Only the barbarian takes all this off of the plaster with his knife and destroys the whole, but I swear before you that what Poles call lyric poetry is just *a pounding and a mazurka.*

Norwid's imagery also put him on the opposite shore from the current fashion. His training as a sculptor and as a draftsman inclined him to flee the colorful and the picturesque. He uses subdued colors, a chiaroscuro transfixed with shafts of light (he particularly admired Rembrandt), but this is not an art for art's sake. Every line serves to bring the reader closer to the philosophical goal of the poem, and Norwid, undoubtedly, is the most "intellectual" poet ever to write in Polish.

Norwid's encounter with industrial civilization somewhat recalls the experiences of his American contemporaries, writers with a rural background. When Emerson, formulating the program of the transcendentalists, said, "It is better to be alone than in bad company"; or, "All that is clearly due today is not to lie"; or, "This is not a time for gaiety and grace. His [the transcendentalist's] strength and spirits are wasted in rejection"—Norwid could have accepted these maxims as his own. But an even more striking analogy can be found with Herman Melville. Both writers made similar use of irony. In the world which the industrious white man created and which he called a Christian world, Melville saw nothing but brutality, callousness, greed, and misery. He was an Ishmael, wandering over the face of the earth in search of primeval innocence, and he seemed to locate that innocence beyond the pale of the materialistic civilization of the nineteenth century. Norwid, as a newcomer, from a preindustrial society, thrown into the jungle of Western Europe, was alien to all the bustle of buying and selling. Images of ghastly London and Paris streets which appear in some of Norwid's poems parallel the American writer's descriptions in prose. Although Norwid probably never read Melville, in one of his short stories, entitled ["**Cywilizacja**"], he employed the symbol of a ship similarly to the way Melville handled it in his *Confidence Man.* But Norwid's solutions were not Melville's. If we were to search for the reason, we might make conjectures about the collectivist tradition in Poland versus the isolation of the individual in America or about Roman Catholicism versus Protestantism. Whatever the reason, Norwid could not simply reject civilization, hypocritical and pharisaical though it may be, in the name of an innocent, natural pre-Christian man. While Melville was mainly concerned with the problem of Man and Nature (an obsession for many American writers), Norwid concentrated upon the problem of Man and History. He has been called a "poet of ruins" because he went to the sources of European history in the Mediterranean region and listened to the echoes of its past. For Norwid, History was a continuity, a process tending in a certain direction, a constant accomplishment of God's hidden plan through mankind. A given civilization was just a phase between the past and the future; the present could not simply be cast aside, because it was the place where the future was being engendered. The materialistic civilization of the nineteenth century worshiped financial and political power, condemning those who were true to the conscience of history, be they individuals or groups, to martyrdom. The goal of history, according to Norwid, was "to make martyrdom unnecessary on the earth," and the achievement of this was, therefore, the only criterion of progress. As he said himself:

> A man is born on this planet to give testimony to the truth. He should, therefore, know and remember that every civilization should be considered as a means and not as an aim—thus, to sell one's soul to a civilization and at the same time to pray in church is to be a pharisee.

Because he was convinced that Christ had led man out of the realm of fatality and into the realm of freedom, Norwid's attention constantly turned to early Christianity both in verse and in prose. His long poem *Quidam* is, for instance, a vision of Rome in the second century. Historical meditation cannot be separated from Norwid's poetry. It is its very core. And some of his views are striking: his stress on the role of "peripheries"—Samaria for Judea, Gaul for the Roman Empire, America for Europe—and the gradual movement from the centers toward the peripheries; or his theory of "stumbling blocks": for America—the Negro, for England—Ireland, for the old Polish *Respublica*—the Ukraine, for Russia, Prussia, and Austria—Poland, for France—continuous revolutions; or his principle of "things passed over in silence": every epoch passes over something in silence, and that which remains beneath the surface, inadmissible to the consciousness of one era, becomes a motive power in the next.

Norwid was not a politician, and he maintained his distance from all the political groupings of the Great Emigration. He believed that an artist participates in history through his art. His conception of art is closely connected with his respect for human labor. While he elaborated his philosophy of labor and art independently from Ruskin and Morris in England, he resembled them in some respects. He was not a socialist, though some of the writings of French socialists combined with his own life experience as an artisan may have gone toward shaping

his pious approach to human toil. His theory of art is set forth in the long poem *Promethidion,* written in the form of a conversation among a few characters and provided with footnotes in prose. The title means "Prometheus' child." To Norwid, Prometheus was more a giver of crafts to mankind than a rebel; thus, labor, whether a peasant's, a sailor's, or an artist's—or that very poem—is Prometheus' child. As a Christian, Norwid saw in labor the result of original sin. Before his Fall, man lived in harmony with God and the universe. Through sin, he entered the path of history, and to redeem himself, man must work throughout innumerable millennia. But work is redeeming only if it is accepted with love and not as a scourge imposed by the fear of starvation or punishment. Work accepted with love is the highest manifestation of human freedom. However, in modern times manual labor has become a scourge, and the only work performed with love and joy is that of the artist. This means that a complete cleavage exists between the work of "the people" and the work of the creative and educated circles. Only if these two branches of human endeavor are united will it be possible for toiling people to share the joy known by the artist. If the highest forms of art were to be united with the humblest objects of everyday life, the chasm separating those who live *by spirit alone* from those who live *only by their hands* would disappear. The artist should be an "organizer of the national imagination." Norwid was drawing upon his observations of his native country when he said:

> Those nations which forgot about the uplifting function of art, which failed to establish *their own* art, and so failed to bring forth a chain of handicrafts—either lost their real existence or are just toiling; their work, disconnected from the *work* of the *spirit,* is not more than a fatality and a penance imposed upon one social layer. The "people," whose very souls are shaped by *manual* work, must, by necessity, grow further and further from those higher circles of the nation who perform only mental work. For the *contents of thought* obtained through manual work are different from those obtained by *pure thinking.* The result is that abstract thought, deprived by degrees of its ties with humble labors, returns in difficult moments (i.e., politically difficult) to folk wisdom, peasant motifs, proverbs, legends, or songs—and even technological folk traditions. Often, it is too late, and the backbone with its marrow uniting the total sum of work in a given nation disintegrates into *remembrances of the past* and *longings for the future.*

Art must come from a dialogue between the popular imagination and the "learned" imagination of an artist. To quote Norwid again: "The best musician is the People, but the composer is their fiery tongue." This means that the composer transforms his native music into an art that is more than national, and, in fact, it is universal. Frédéric Chopin (a personal friend) was for Norwid an ideal example of such a composer. Norwid's revolt against mazurkas in poetry is, therefore, nothing other than a revolt against a shallow interpretation of folk tradition. As for his negative opinion of "art for art's sake," it can be summed up in one line from his *Promethidion:* "Art is a banner on the tower of human labors."

Because of his forward-looking treatment of Polish verse, Norwid's role has sometimes been compared to Mallarmé's in

French poetry. It would be a mistake, however, to draw analogies with French symbolists. On the one hand, Norwid was rooted in the Romantic preoccupation with History. On the other, he overcame his isolation as an individual through an understanding of the complex links between a work of art and the collectivity; unlike Mallarmé, he did not limit himself to "purifying the language of the tribe," but always strove to convey a message. One is tempted to say that the social orientation, which is so noticeable in Polish literature from Kochanowski on, culminated in Norwid, and his influence in the twentieth century has been to act as a counterbalance to the overbearing presence of the French symbolists.

Norwid is not an impeccable poet. The nearly complete absence of an audience, and thus, the lack of any controls, permitted him to indulge in such a torturing of the language that some of his lines are hopelessly obscure. But his poems are never just a translation of philosophy into verse. His philosophy seems to grow organically with his images, although the weight of intellectual contents is so great that sometimes it threatens to break the artistic structure. Several of Norwid's poems put him on a level with Mickiewicz and have become part of Poland's classical heritage. One of the most famous, **"To the Memory of Bem, A Funeral Rhapsody"** (**"Bema pamięci rapsod żałobny"**), honored a Polish hero—an insurrectionist in 1830-1831, and a leader of the revolutionary Hungarian army in 1848-1849. Under Norwid's pen, Bem's funeral takes on features of an old Slavic pre-Christian rite, and this march of primitive tribesmen and women is itself transformed into a march of all humanity over the obstacles of tyranny toward the future. The poem has a very intricate metrical pattern and is one of the examples of the "Polish hexameter." But what proved to be most fruitful for modern Polish poetry was Norwid's collection of short poems, *Vade-Mecum,* which remained unpublished in his lifetime and dates probably from before 1866. . . . Norwid, in attaching so much importance to *Vade-Mecum* (as seen from his letter, quoted above, to Zaleski), was not mistaken. That collection gives us a sampling of his qualities at their best. And today's readers may see in his controlled irony a foreshadowing of the kind of poetry Jules Laforgue or T. S. Eliot were to write.

The long poem *Quidam,* already noted in connection with Norwid's philosophy, analyzes the interplay between three basic societal factors in second-century Rome under the rule of the Emperor Hadrian—the Jews, the Greeks, and the Romans. It can be placed beside those versified dramas in which Norwid reconstructs the life of ancient Egypt [*Kleopatria i Cezar*] or harks back to the era when pre-Christian folk myths were born in Poland (*Krakus, Wanda, Zwolon*). In an unfinished play bearing a double title, . . . [*Za kulisami: Tyrtej*], he effectively uses the device of a "play within a play": at a masquerade ball, contemporary "good society" is prattling in a salon; simultaneously in another room a tragedy is performed about a Greek hero. The tragedy is a flop; the salon is insensitive to heroism. Norwid's play was meant to highlight the decay of the nineteenth century; heroism, not the garish, obvious kind but rather a silent and concealed virtue, was really his concern as a dramatist. The same applies to his comedies with a strong satirical bent: . . . [*Pierścień wielkiej damy*], . . . [*Miłość czysta u kąpieli morskich*]. In the first of these, the main character, Mak-Yks, is a poor young man who lives in a garret provided for him by his relative, a countess. He is not unlike Norwid himself: proud, wounded, pure-hearted, living in the company of his books. Barely tolerated by his aristocratic benefactress,

Mak-Yks is the only true human being in the surrounding display of vanity and frivolity.

Norwid's plays are sometimes performed in Poland, but they are difficult to stage on account of their reliance upon innuendos and their deliberate avoidance of blatant effects. They could more aptly be called dramatic poems.

Norwid also left several prose studies on art and a few short stories. There is nothing about the latter that recalls the realistic stories of the nineteenth century, and, indeed, they are modern parables. In **"The Secret of Lord Singleworth"** (**"Tajemnica Lorda Singleworth"**), for instance, a rich Englishman travels around Europe—which is nothing extraordinary, except that in every city he goes up in a balloon. We learn at the end that he suffers from an obsession with impurity, intensified by what he sees in various capitals. In . . . [**"Stygmat"**] the central motif is our lack of independence due to a "stigma" imprinted on us by a convention, or by civilization, or by a circumstance, so that we act a role and are not ourselves. In . . . [**"Cywilizacja"**] the line between reality and dream is blurred, and a journey in a ship across the Atlantic gradually takes on the aspect of an expedition of civilized but half-crazy mankind into the unknown and toward shipwreck. Perhaps the best single piece of Norwid's prose is **"Ad Leones,"** written at the end of his life in 1881. This is a story of a dignified, healthy, highly talented sculptor in Rome. He spends every evening at the Café Greco, attracting admiring glances because of his nonchalant elegance, his beard, and his beautiful greyhound bitch. He is working on a huge group sculpture representing Christians being thrown to the lions, hence the title "Ad Leones." The work happens to attract an American banker, who wishes to buy it immediately, under one condition: that some details be changed and that it be renamed "Capitalization." The sculptor readily complies and, with a few movements of his chisel, transforms the central figure of the lion into a coffer. This story, one of Norwid's most biting satires, grew out of his reaction to current exhibitions of art in Paris.

Norwid's extant correspondence, painstakingly gathered by Zenon Miriam Przesmycki at the beginning of our century, not only elucidates his artistic work, but, taken together, forms a kind of philosophical diary. The correctness of his judgments on events and, in particular, his negative appraisals of the Polish mentality, which he regarded as warped by political oppression, have been corroborated by subsequent developments, and today he sounds astonishingly up-to-date.

Norwid's intense historicism, his refusal to practice a narrowly utilitarian poetry, and, at the same time, his rejection of "art for art's sake" paved the way for a specific kind of literature that meditates on history and art and that is, perhaps, uniquely Polish. His reflections on work inspired one of the most original Polish thinkers of the twentieth century, Stanisław Brzozowski. Let us notice, too, that Norwid marks the transition from the concept of the writer or artist as a purely spiritual creature to one which sees him as a good craftsman whose labor should be recompensed by society. Thus, Norwid left his imprint upon the Polish literary scene both as a poet and as a philosopher; but as one of our contemporaries, Mieczysław Jastrun, justly stressed in his introduction to the *Selected Poems* of Norwid:

> It is being said that Norwid is first of all a thinker, a philosopher. This is incorrect. Norwid is, first of all, an artist, but an artist for whom the most interesting material is thought, reflection, the cultural experience of mankind.

An 1861 drawing by Norwid entitled "Solo."

Or, to put it another way, one may use the words of an eminent literary critic, Kazimierz Wyka, according to whom "the poetic world that is natural to Norwid is the objective world of culture." (pp. 271-80)

> *Czesław Miłosz, "Romanticism," in his* The History of Polish Literature, *1969. Reprint, second edition, by University of California Press, 1983, pp. 195-280.*

REUEL K. WILSON   (essay date 1973)

[Wilson surveys Norwid's short stories, discussing such topics as narrative technique, characterization, theme, and style.]

Norwid practised a number of different literary genres. He is best known (and justly so) for his "intellectual" lyrics; yet a long discursive poem, the *Promethidion,* written in dialogue form, contains perhaps the most eloquent statement of the poet's unique artistic credo. (p. 143)

Norwid also penned some dramas in verse (mostly on legendary or historical themes) as well as numerous treatises on a variety of subjects—artistic, political and religious. Curiously enough, however, his ideas are more dramatically and succinctly embodied in the short story than in any other genre outside of his poetry. These little stories (the author called some of them "legends" or "fables"), almost invariably provide poignant

illustrations of the clash between reality and illusion. The author-narrator remains an aloof observer, a commentator upon those often trite or trivial events which so often have tragic reverberations in the lives of the participants and spectators. Our exile's view of Western European civilization seems strikingly modern, even present-day. A brief analysis of a few of the stories will perhaps convey some concrete idea of Norwid's literary imagination.

In the first place, the stories (in contrast to the predominantly solemn poetry) reveal a sense of that delicate dry humour which the French call *esprit.* Occasionally the tone resembles that of Mallarmé's poems in prose. (There is, however, no evidence to show that Norwid knew the work of his younger French contemporary.) Both poets approach their subjects through the use of circumlocutions and highly-polished baroque imagery. Everyday objects, apparently insignificant details, are "disguised" by complicated syntax and unconventional metaphor; shapes and colours taken directly from the outside world are subjected to impressionistic distortions. And yet, despite their innovative techniques, both poets have been clearly influenced by the elegant language of the *salon.*

Norwid, unlike Mallarmé, considered that art should have a moral function, and perhaps this serves as an indication of his "Easternness." The poets, novelists and critics of nineteenth-century Russia and Poland thought it their responsibility to educate and improve their countrymen; they seek out and comment upon the most burning issues of their day. The didactic, "patriotic" current still dominates Russian literature, as is evidenced by the longevity of the baneful doctrines of socialist realism.

Norwid's concern with history, recent political events, his travels, his ability passionately to sympathize with the sufferings of others, strongly contrast with Mallarmé's herculean but tranquil labours in the midst of semi-bourgeois seclusion.

At first glance Norwid's sometimes anecdotal, sometimes theoretical prose technique seems tortuous, even "romantically-hazy"—a style that he wished to eschew. Here is the lyrical evocation of a sailing-ship from the story ["**Cywilizacja**"]:

> 'And so you see,' I said to my young acquaintance, 'that these things are not totally alien to me; of course, from the great beams of the sailing vessel which recall the structure of an ark and which rest on the very bottom of the ship's hold; having then walked through dark places where the anchor chains, rusty from the salt water, are coiled or stretched out lengthwise in careless repose on the planking; having walked yet higher to the cabin passage-ways, and higher onto the ship's deck where every board has been washed white and soft and all together they are beautifully curved like the lid of a violin case; and, having lifted your eyes thither, where the unshakeable nets of many lines criss-cross in the heavens, or where the air strikes its tents with broad sails, or where the three towering crosses of the masts resemble some mystical trinity when they expire in the morning mists, in lees of opal chiaroscuro and warm and salty moisture, lees once penetrated by the lost rays of a departing sun—all this, as you see, is familiar to me.'

Despite the eccentricities of language and syntax, the poetic style conveys a vivid impression of rapid movement in space. Here, in one sentence-paragraph (intentionally lacking a main verb) the narrator has conducted us through the universe, made archetypal, of the sailing-ship—from the underworld of its nether regions to the promise of salvation on the tallest cross-bars of its masts.

There can be no question about the primarily visual quality of Norwid's literary imagination, and when dealing with such potentially dramatic themes as the corrupting power of civilization, exile and the Slavs, or human misunderstanding, he was convinced that the highest effect could and should result from understatement and intentionally neutral, unemotive language. A chance pose, a gesture, a random platitude, acquire depth and significance because of the associations they evoke in the author's imagination. He approaches life directly, always striving for essentials, whether they be banal or exalted.

In order to delineate character, Norwid in his prose employs a kind of double vision: we first see the person from a lofty or romantic point of view—which is forthwith qualified by some factual observation or prosaic detail. Norwid, to be sure, understood the dangers and absurdities implicit in the Romantic *weltanschauung;* still, a not unromantic air of nostalgic self-irony surrounds his protagonists.

The resolution of the stories is usually tragi-comic. The two young lovers in ["**Stygmat**"] Rose and Oscar, are prevented from marrying happily by a mutual understanding displayed towards each others' defects. The setting is, ironically, a health spa. . . . Rose ("a lush Ukrainian beauty for those who know how to look, or 'a comely' or 'not bad looking lass' for those who see things in the ordinary way") suffers from an inability to modulate her speaking voice. She acquired this unfortunate defect during childhood when she was obliged to take care of her father, a deaf ex-army officer. Oscar, a widowed violinist who is in love with Rose, has had to care for a neurasthenic wife over a period of years and therefore he overreacts to the most trifling annoyances. Since neither suspects the secret of the other's "stigma," when Rose loudly avows her feelings for Oscar in the midst of an assembled company, the latter takes umbrage and breaks with her forever. A thunderstorm echoes the lovers' rift, and shortly thereafter the heroine dies. On taking leave of the narrator, to whom he has confided his misfortunes, the desperate Oscar sheds a tear, which, having joined with a drop of cold sweat, "ran its course, dividing his entire face in two." (Here is an excellent illustration of Norwid's twofold aesthetic which fuses the sentimental and the prosaic—often with tragi-comic results.) The narrator and Rose's guardian, a general's widow, discuss the lovers' tragedy. The latter observes: "From the moment we begin to become suspicious of our ideal for any reason, our relationship with it is already finished. There are no mistakes in this domain, only betrayals."—An astute commentary on human nature in general and the Romantic sensibility in particular.

In the second part of the story the author digresses in order to expound his ideas on the stigma as a factor determining historical events and national characteristics. He attributes, for example, the Viking Normans' ability for ruthless organization to their contact with the sea and their experience in weathering storms; the Teutons have brought to history the "stigma" of the forest—the Mongols, the "stigma" of the steppe. In developing this rather naive and far-fetched historicism (he sees in Gothic art a subconscious effort by the Germans (sic) to recreate the intricate forms and shapes of the virgin forest), the poet attempts to convey an encyclopaedic panorama. Indeed, this tendency to interpret history in a far-reaching philosophical manner characterizes much of Norwid's work. (It is perhaps his artistic Achilles' heel.) In this story these passages reflect the author's preoccupation with linking the most trivial, albeit potentially tragic, aspects of everyday life (the events of Part I) with broad theoretical concepts (the view of history presented as the narrator's dream in Part II).

The story ends with a characteristically double view of human nature. A local newspaper editor (Norwid felt that journalism represented the ultimate prostitution of literature and he inevitably casts editors into the role of vulgar and mercenary servers of Mammon) intrudes upon the narrator, in whom he awakens feelings of profound loathing. The narrator finds an antidote to the crushingly depressing impression left by the editor's banal inquisitiveness, when, a few days later, a young peasant girl presents him with an iris and a feather, thereby restoring his faith in literature.

The Polish painter Byczkowski in "**Menego**," who drowns while swimming on the Lido near Venice, is another unfortunate victim of excessive romanticism coupled with circumstances beyond his control. The theme of this story could well be described as Norwid's poignant artistic portrayal of the Slavs in the role of slaves. Byczkowski (who appears, after the first reference, as simply ''B''), an emigré who has followed the teaching of his academic German masters Kaulbach and Cornelius with truly Slavic submissiveness and obedience, has been brought to Italy by some wealthy German aristocrats. The discussions on art between the narrator and B contain passages of great eloquence and beauty. The narrator expounds to B a neoclassical conception very dear to the author's own heart: because of its simplicity, classical architecture represents one of Man's greatest artistic achievements—the ruins are as beautiful as the original structures, for they reflect the harmony of the first idea (The legend)—nothing begun in love will perish: ''Roma quanta fuit, ipsa ruina docet.'' B and the narrator also agree that the masters of the Renaissance must have been inspired by the life they saw in the street as well as by a funded perception of their own personal thoughts and experiences. A conception of art which the (then-fashionable) Munich academics would never have allowed, remarks B.

B is portrayed as the victim of Romantic ideas. He has come to an *impasse* in his career as an artist and this is reflected in his unrealized ambition: to paint a *chef d'oeuvre* portraying a fisherman holding an empty shell—his day's catch. (B wants the fisherman's silent pose to reveal the whole story of his miserable life.) B, in fact, cannot save himself from ludicrousness (and tragedy). In the café he summons the waiter, (whose name is Domenico, Ménego for short) by shouting ''Menégo,'' inadvertently using the Polish penultimate accent. Since in Venetian dialect this means ''I am drowning,'' the waiter makes a joke at the Pole's expense. The irony is, of course, that B does finally drown and we are left with the suspicion that he has probably committed suicide. He leaves behind ''as a keepsake'' a handkerchief given to him by ''our great Lord Byron'' (i.e., J. Słowacki) in Dresden. Moreover, he makes the fateful trip to the Lido knowing that ''Lord Byron, while riding on horseback, had described Mazeppa'' there.

Another important story set in Venice is **''The Secret of Lord Singleworth.''** The author announces in the very first paragraphs that literal truth is unimportant to the story. It is irrelevant whether or not the Singleworths were a long-established English noble family, and even whether they existed at all. The author's purpose is to ''record an exceptional psychological observation.'' Norwid, in point of fact, had the greatest contempt for professional writers of fiction, and, as we shall see, this story illustrates his finesse at rendering low subjects in elevated, poetic language. His aim is to draw symbolic implications from everyday objects; to deduce moral and artistic truth from a superficially amusing parable.

Unlike **''Menego,''** in which the city plays a highly visual role, **''The Secret of Lord Singleworth''** dramatizes the political implications of the situation in Venice during the tyrannical Austrian domination. Norwid makes several acute observations on popular reactions to the police-state with its ''double-think'' psychology. Because of the restrictions on free speech, the Venetian people express their resentment in a multitude of subtle ways.

> The despotism of the foreign government of that time had to take the necessary precautions (since it had no natural boundaries) lest the slightest whisper should, gaining ground, reach its own natural boundaries and that, the more abhorred the liberty of freely and openly expressed opinion, the stronger, the more profound, and more striking would be the force of meaningful silences, unfinished sentences, the

blinking of eyes, the clearing of throats and sneezes.

There is an interesting similarity between this quotation and Norwid's views on the need for art to be allusive, full of meaningful silences. These remarks also apply to the situation in the Poland of today, or, for that matter, that of a hundred years ago. Norwid was, furthermore, aware that Venice, like Poland, had enjoyed democratic traditions until a foreign take-over at the end of the eighteenth century.

The main subject of the story is the eccentric, controversial Lord Singleworth, whose daily balloon-voyages mystify public opinion all over Europe. The Tsar's governor in Odessa, General Kutasov (the word *kutas* has most unflattering implications in Polish), we are told, even sent a police agent up in another balloon to observe Singleworth during his stay in Russia. The agent ascertains that Singleworth is not engaged in subversive activities; moreover, the carefully handled box (actually a privy, although the Russian authorities had suspected that it contained gunpowder) which he carries along, looks as though it might contain ''a round Etruscan or porcelain vase.''

Singleworth's trips awaken three kinds of speculation: ''deep conjecture,'' ''sharp witticism,'' and ''trivial anecdotes.'' A Heidelberg professor proposes the theory that Singleworth is engaged in making meteorological observations. Another, more popular view, advanced by a French journalist, holds that the lord's balloon-ascents are devoted to the demands of personal hygiene.

Upon the lord's arrival in Venice, a popular street bard, Tony di Grazia (''public figure and historical personage'') delivers a lengthy humourous discourse on the implications of Singleworth's voyages. Tony speaks with histrionic talent, modulating his tone to emphasize the transition from one speaking voice to another; all the while maintaining a mock-solemn rhetorical style. Ostensibly chiding the assembled bystanders for giving credence to the personal hygiene theory (rumour had it that a scrap of soiled paper had floated to earth in the main square on Murano), Tony argues both for and against aesthetic contemplation as Lord Singleton's governing motivation. Seen from the ground, the edifices and monuments of the past are stained by ''a rain of blood and tears,'' i.e., unhappy suicides. (Tony's reference here to human suffering contains an oblique allusion to the current atmosphere of political repression under the Austrians.) Nonetheless these monuments *are* worthy objects for the aesthetic sensibility—even from the sky; although, Tony speculates, the four gold chargers atop St. Mark's Cathedral (''when their golden lungs are inflamed and they shake their manes gilded by Corinthian bronze in the sunlight'') must appear from the Englishman's lofty perspective as merely ''a disappearing exception among grey masses.'' (One notes the poet's fondness for light-dark contrast.)

Tony then goes on slyly to plead for the soiled paper thesis, but on aesthetic grounds (!). For him the rubbish heap is a repository of poetic objects, each of which suggests a story of its own. ''Who knows, if my Muse was not a commode?'' Through his character, Norwid is proclaiming (like a Baudelaire) the potential for beauty in objects conventionally thought to be sordid or ugly. The ''improvisator'' ends his ''rhapsodies'' with a jibe at the Austrian police: if it is a question of smelling out Lord Singleworth's secret, their noses are ''so handsome'' that a Neapolitan would envy them.

At the beginning of Part II, the narrator relates that a scandalized mother removed her child from a restaurant where the assembled patrons had started to discuss the telltale scrap of paper. (The child, meanwhile, has been completely absorbed in the contemplation of some oranges.) The author uses this incident to stress that he is not going to follow the example of that censorious mother: the artist should be free to choose whatever theme he wishes (i.e., free from self-imposed or external censorship), even if this means sullying the "whiteness," the "fragrance," or the "newness" of the paper.

In the final scene, a delegation comprised of the narrator and several fashionable Italians visit the lord to ascertain the true reason for his aerial voyages. They have made a wager on this subject and appointed the narrator to be their spokesman. Singleworth, who receives them politely, turns out to be a Promethean figure, a purist in the literal sense of the word. Well-aware that his idealism will seem ridiculous to the continental mind, he offers, nevertheless, an impassioned explanation for his bizarre flights. His real motive is an uncontrollable urge to escape the filth and impurity of everyday life (although, he implies with subtle irony, he obviously cannot resist the demands of physical necessity). He cannot endure social injustice, the terrible contrast between an appearance of order and prosperity on the one hand, and misery and exploitation on the other. His flights are a protest, a step towards truth. "People are not clean . . ." he says, "they are merely perfumed." At the end, Tony, the earthly counterpart (and antithesis) of the lord, hails Singleworth as the harbinger of a new epoch that will bring purification to all humanity—"something similar to an American religious revival."

Lord Singleworth (who is motivated by a strange mixture of scientific and romantic notions) protests against the existing order on both philosophical and aesthetic grounds. He refuses to accept the idea that cleanness equals the opposite of dirt, a standard widely accepted in a world where men's nervous systems have become accustomed to pungent perfumes as an antidote to foetidness. The lord's moving speech can easily be closely identified with the poet's own view of the artist's role in society.

The artist's motives too are commonly misunderstood and ridiculed. His search for the absolute ideal causes him to flee the society of men, yet the rewards are great. From the high atmosphere above the earth, says the lord, "Cast down whatever you will, and then watch the falling meteor in a sapphire summer sky. . . . How beautiful it is!" In other words, having risen to a certain elevation above society, the artist may create something of beauty out of any object. Tony, who is not an escapist like the lord, has proclaimed a similar aesthetic, "at street level." Singleworth's situation, no matter how exalted, will (unlike Tony's) always be bitterly lonely, doomed as he is to a sterile heroism that evokes only incomprehension from the world below.

From the vantage point of his own Promethean isolation, Norwid had little use for "scientific" materialism. In most of these tales of contemporary life the villains are the newspaper editors, the commercially motivated artists, the would-be progressive intellectuals, the capitalists. He condemns these products of modern society with a satiric irony worthy of Dostoevsky.

The "legend" ["**Cywilizacja**"] is an eloquent fable on the empty and sterile philistinism of contemporary life. In sombre language often reminiscent of Conrad the narrator describes his sea voyage on the steamship *Civilization*. The ship's passengers are an incongruous assortment of humanity: among them are some nuns, a Capuchin monk, a few princes from the South Seas, an Archeologist, a cavalry officer, an atheistic "Emigrant," and an editor. As the *Civilization* founders in the midst of a sinister mass of icebergs, we sense how cold, vulgar, and empty the pursuits of its "civilized" passengers have been. If, in the poet's view, sailing-ships afford man the possibility for valiant and dignified struggle with Nature, as well as an opportunity for the serene contemplation of his own insignificance, that triumph of technology, the steamboat, is a sign of man's arrogant conception of himself as master of a universe without God. The wreck of the *Civilization* must be interpreted in terms of a divine punishment wherein innocent and guilty alike perish. At the very end the narrator awakens propped up on the arm of a nun who informs him that she has just held a candle at his wake. This touch of surrealistic ambiguity underlines the dreamlike quality of this ship of fools' journey to annihilation—beyond the limits of time and space.

In one of his last stories "**Ad Leones**" Norwid takes up a similar theme: the moral bankruptcy of nineteenth-century "scientific" materialism. The rationale of nineteenth-century progress can, moreover, exert a corrupting and debilitating influence on the artist. The cast of characters—a fashionable sculptor and his admirers—seem very familiar to us today, although the story is set in Rome a hundred years ago. The shallow posturing of the *dilettanti* who foregather daily in the Café Greco is nothing, however, in comparison with the bland cynicism of their cronies, a newspaper editor and a tutor. The irony of the piece lies in the fact that the sculptor, called "Ad Leones" by his friends because he is working on a group representing the Christians being thrown to the lions, willingly changes the conception of his work to please a wealthy American (a newspaper man) who has been scouted out as a prospective buyer. Responding to the promptings of the editor and the tutor, the sculptor changes the cross carried by one of the figures into an enormous key.

When the American arrives, he interprets the group as a depiction of thriftiness (he mistakes the mass of clay meant to be a lion for a coffer, and agrees to buy it on condition that the sculptor design the group so that it clearly represents "Capitalization." The narrator, a modest, idealistic artist, has, in the meantime, been ignored when he expressed his own opinions about the "group's" artistic and religious implications. His long-winded speech on the difficulties involved in executing the original (to him) deeply religious scene has struck a dissonant note in this assemblage of philistines. The narrator finally departs, a saddened witness to the ridiculous folly of his selfish, materialistic companions.

While he was always quick to turn a bitterly satirical arsenal against intellectual or artistic meretriciousness, Norwid was deeply sensitive to human frailty. The ironic tone is, for example, highly sympathetic when dealing with Byczkowski (in "**Menego**"), that dedicated but ungifted failure. Indeed, one of Norwid's main themes is the tragic (or comic) distance between our hopes and our achievements.

Nor does Norwid ever strike a note of self-pity, or make capital out of his tragic position as an exile. He expresses the view . . . that the main obstacle depriving Polish writers of universal appeal is precisely their obsession (natural enough in a country under such long domination by powerful neighbours whose objectives towards Poland have involved stifling free expression of the Polish national identity) with parochial themes. Norwid strove manfully for universality. His heroes are general human types; their tragedies are usually the result of an inimical world order, not a local catastrophe.

Norwid at age sixty-one, by Pantaleona Szyndlera.

Norwid always kept aloof from established literary conventions. In his own view, his style, to which little justice can be done in translation, aims for suggestiveness, realism (i.e., that which is inspired directly by life) and subtle drama. Many of his best effects are achieved through imagery and detail which contrast light and shadow, silence and noise, becoming and being, absence and fulfillment. It is this last fulfillment to which his heroes aspire, but the chasm between the reality and the ideal is too great. In his tragic aspect, then, Norwid is a Romantic; but on the technical side he is both a precursor and an anachronism. In fact he was more influenced by Shakespeare, Calderon and the Bible, than by contemporary trends. If his work suffers from too many *ex cathedra* pronouncements, the beauty and originality of his imagery as well as the finesse of his psychological insights render the short stories which I have discussed unique in the history of Polish literature. (pp. 144-52)

> Reuel K. Wilson, "Cyprian Norwid: A Tribute to the Storyteller," in MOSAIC: A Journal for the Comparative Study of Literature and Ideas, *Special Issue: The Eastern European Imagination in Literature, Vol. VI, No. 4, Summer, 1973. pp. 141-52.*

GEORGE GÖMÖRI (essay date 1974)

[*Gömöri elaborates on the importance of* Promethidion *as an expression of Norwid's artistic beliefs. For additional commentary by this critic, see the excerpt dated 1967.*]

Promethidion is a very ambitious undertaking. In this versed poetic treatise in two dialogues with an epilogue, Norwid tried to pose *and* answer all the esthetic and broadly philosophical questions which he thought were relevant to most educated Poles of the nineteenth century. In its form the poem resembles the Platonic dialogues, and the nature of the discussion between Norwid's protagonists, the challengers or mouthpieces of his ideas, shows the author's familiarity with not only the Platonic but also the Neoplatonic schools of esthetics. Winckelmann, the great German art critic who rediscovered Greek art for his contemporaries, was another, rather obvious influence. Some critics pointed out borrowings from, or parallels with, the esthetic theories of Lamennais and the Polish philosopher and reformer Libelt. The whole work, nevertheless, blends these different influences in such a way as to create the impression of novelty and originality.

The very title of the epic poem is a neologism coined from the name of Prometheus and the Greek suffix *eidon*, meaning "the son" or descendant of Prometheus. Prometheus, who presented mankind with fire, is an archetypal figure from Hesiod and Aeschylus onwards. He was interpreted by such different writers as Goethe, Shelley, and Victor Hugo, and for the Romantics he symbolized a satanic-humanist revolt against tyranny. He was seen as an un-Christian teacher and savior of mankind. Polish critics emphasized that Norwid was obviously more attracted to Aeschylus's interpretation than that of Shelley; others pointed to Michelet's interest in the myth of Prometheus as a possible influence on Norwid. It seems to me that Norwid's models should be sought elsewhere. His ambition in *Promethidion* was to discuss universal problems from a Polish angle. It is therefore not impossible that the title originates from the striking lines of Słowacki's *Agamemnon's Grave*:

> Poland! . . .
> . . . you are the only son of Prometheus:
> But the vulture devours not your heart—your brains.

Yet the key to Norwid's general and in some ways un-Romantic concept of *Promethidion* lies in the *Palingénésie* of the French philosopher P. S. Ballanche, whose work (and this can, and perhaps will, be proved by further research) exerted an overriding influence on Norwid's thought and work. Ballanche mentioned the name of Prometheus more than once in his long and seminal philosophical treatise, characterizing the hero of the Greek myth at one point in the following manner: *"Prométhée c'est l'homme se faisant lui-même par l'énergie de sa pensée."* Prometheus is the man who creates himself through the energy of his thought, and, Ballanche continues, the conflict symbolized in his myth is the eternal conflict between the general "laws of history" and man's "existential will." Norwid regarded man as master of his own destiny. For him man was not a lonely rebel against a tyrannical God, but rather a rebel against the indifferent determinism of nature, social routine and historical stagnation. Prometheus's act of *rebellion* was less important for Norwid than his act of *creation*—the gift of fire that he gave mankind, the gift of tools for work and self-expression. "Fire" here stands for "word," for according to Ballanche (and Norwid) Prometheus awakened mankind from its semidormant state and made it conscious of its supreme task: to reach God through self-perfection. It is this Prometheus, the speech-giver, the patron saint of arts, that captured Norwid's imagination.

Yet in the poetic treatise itself the original myth of Prometheus is not discussed. Most of the poem is devoted to arguments and monologues on the nature or, even more ambitiously, on the essence of art. The first dialogue titled "Bogumił" is about *form* or the notion of beauty; whereas the second titled "Wiesław" is concerned with *content,* which is in Norwid's view goodness—and both principles are united in the light of truth. Bogumił's dialogue opens with a discussion in a salon on the merits of Chopin's music. It soon becomes a controversy about the aims and correct definition of beauty. Someone expresses the flippant view that beautiful is what "pleases everybody," whereupon Maurycy, a participant of the debate, ripostes with words that could be Norwid's own: "*Beautiful* is not . . . what *pleases* people at present or had pleased them in the past / *But what ought to please* . . . what *improves*" (italics in the original). Beauty is not and cannot be the privilege of a caste or the leisured few, but there is something aristocratic in it and therefore not everyone can grasp beauty immediately. A Count declares that for him "order is beauty." This class-motivated view is challenged by Ambrozy, another member of the group. Subsequently, Bogumił, the main character of this part of *Promethidion,* expresses his view in an inspired monologue. He calls upon "the eternal man" to define the essence of beauty, uncontaminated by sectarian or political interests, independent of the whims of fashion. The answer is: beauty is "the Form of Love." Every person has the capacity to partake in this divine gift, either as a creator of things of beauty or as a recipient.

Between beauty and work there is a close connection. Bogumił, or rather his "Eternal Man," connects the two in a passage vital to Norwid's esthetic theory and quoted in most commentaries on this subject:

> Because beauty exists—to enchant
> and rouse to work—and work: to bring resurrection

Bogumił-Norwid's interest in beauty is not confined to esthetics: it has an ethical aspect as well. The upper classes tend to subjectivize beauty, to equate it with the comfortably integrated, the convenient. This "subjectivism," argues Norwid, is a distortion of truth and leads, among other things, to social upheavals which then restore the "objective" meaning of beauty. As for the poet and the artist who creates beauty, he is also serving his community. This is the link between Bogumił's "ethical" interpretation of beauty and the statement that "the greatest poet is the simple people." Almost a Romantic-populist commonplace, it nevertheless reflects Norwid's admiration for popular art and folk-poetry, for he believed that genuine national art should arise and evolve from folk-art. This did not mean an imitation of folk-art *forms* (in which many lesser Romantics, including Lenartowicz, did indulge) but an openness to the inspiration of the people, an absorption of elements such as those that enriched Chopin's music. Folk-art should not be imitated but elevated to the level of high art. Here lies a striking similarity between Norwid's and Libelt's views, the latter writing in his *Aesthetics:* "The best example of how to create great art from folk-motifs was given to us by Chopin in his music."

Bogumił's monologue ends with a detailed exposé of his concept of "national art." In Norwid's opinion Poland has not yet found its "form," its true artistic self-expression. Artistic taste is underdeveloped; the fine arts are hardly appreciated. Artists in Poland are martyrs: art "grows out of their ashes"—a theme which often recurs in Norwid's correspondence in later years. Now he dreams of something genuine and organic, a great "national chapel" growing out of the combined efforts of Polish artists—a feat of architecture in which the "Polish soul" would express itself. This vision, incidentally, shows

that Norwid at this period was still more interested in painting than in literature. From this fragment of *Promethidion* it appears that he still regards fine arts as the highest form of artistic expression. But the art-theoretician changes into an apostle of future art in the often quoted passage that connects the fundamental (for Norwid) ideas of art and work:

> And I see art in the Poland of the future
> As a *banner at the tower of human works*
> Neither as a plaything nor as a kind of *science*
> But like *the highest craft of an apostle*
> And *the humblest prayer of an angel.*

Work has a double meaning and function for Norwid. Although he accepts the traditional Catholic idea that work is God's punishment inflicted on mankind for "the loss of Eden," he also believes that it is a means, if not *the* means, to human self-emancipation, in man's (Adam's) Promethean effort to reach God. Man's gradual perfection, on the other hand, is impossible without the humanization, or without a more Norwidian concept of the "spiritualization," of labor. Norwid is convinced that "unnecessary work has to vanish" and in fact will vanish, though not entirely, due to mechanization. He puts his faith into the possibility that "work [will be] *increasingly lightened by love,*" for neither unbounded technological progress nor radical social reforms can change the basic nature of work which for Norwid is expiation.

This view involved more love than economic investment—a somewhat unrealistic program for 1851. But Norwid is aware of this: in a lengthy footnote he discusses the Great Industrial Exhibition just held in London in that year, expressing the hope that with this huge show of industrial might "industrial idolatry will reach its apogee" and a new kind of practical estheticism will develop. The main problem is that work is alienated from creativity, the artifact is merely useful, instead of satisfying man's innate sense of beauty. Norwid reflects upon this in the work's prose "Epilogue" which is a collection of thoughts and comments loosely connected with the treatise itself. The gap between beauty and usefulness can be bridged, he argues, through "the circulation of the idea of beauty"—not only should art be a continuation and triumphant culmination of work, but products of work should also be permeated by beauty through the production of esthetically pleasing artifacts. In Part XVIII of the "Epilogue" Norwid deplores the rigid barrier separating art galleries from industrial exhibitions: they should, ideally, constitute one organic entity! This is a modern idea which shows Norwid's foresight and affinity with such antiindustrial reformers as Ruskin and Morris. (pp. 29-33)

Whereas the first dialogue is mainly about art, the second one concentrates on a search to define truth. Wiesław, the main protagonist, describes the evolution of public opinion as the evolution of "mankind's conscience." The more man is permeated by conscience, the closer is he to God. Konstanty, another partner in the dialogue, calls this "mysticism, Schelling or Plato." Wiesław retorts with a somewhat cryptic remark about the nature of "mysticism," Norwid adding in a footnote that some people explain everything that is *beyond* reason as unreasonable; rejecting "mysticism" out of hand is plain superficiality or lack of humility toward things not yet understood. This is, by the way, an unveiled criticism of Positivism; but some following passages indicate that Norwid's hero is also at odds with the Romantics.

To be sure, he acknowledges the legitimacy of the "prophetic mission": the true prophet has to fulfill two conditions only—

to believe in the God of his Fathers and to fight *"for truth by truth"* (an implicit rejection of "Wallenrodism," a form of Romantic nihilism maintaining that a ruthless enemy may be fought with unethical methods based on Mickiewicz's poem *Konrad Wallenrod*). Furthermore, the prophet has to be disinterested and prepared to speak the truth *for its own sake*, not in the service of a cause however sublime. While the prophet is preoccupied with truth, the bard (*wieszcz*) fixes his sight on beauty. Both see only one side of the Essence and so they complement each other, neither of them having a monopoly of revelation. Poland also has its share of prophets, but autocracy and "stupidity" stifles their voice; their place is taken by politicians, charlatans and "fortune-tellers," for whom Norwid has but little respect. They represent only the superficial "outward" truth of the historical situation; they are play acting in mouthing ultranationalistic, ultraspiritual or simply loyalistic "truths," which are in fact self-justifications. Norwid is convinced that as long as people refuse to internalize truth, the resurrection of independent Poland is impossible; it will not happen before "Poland wins *the war of truth* with herself." Prophetic words, recalling Słowacki at his most pessimistic. Truthfulness is more essential than will power and determination to defeat the enemy.

Some of the ideas expressed in a more or less elliptic fashion appear in the prose "Epilogue" once again. Each nation has its own particular contribution to the development of art. The starting point in the development of new Polish art is, symbolically, "Chopin's grave." Here the argument of the "Bogumił dialogue" is reiterated: through an internal evolution of the spirit the "popular" (*ludowy*) element could be elevated to the level of the "universal." In this the task of the Polish artist is enormous since "he has *to organize the national imagination*" in the same way as the statesman organizes the political forces of the nation. Norwid's ideal is clearly a healthy and organic society, which lives in harmony, honors its critics, and listens to its prophets. Yet he feels that there is a terrifying gap between the patriarchal, agrarian past and the free, industrial but esthetically organized future—especially in the case of Poland where the gap between the desperately poor peasant tilling the land and the property-owning classes is almost unbridgeable. While he does not advocate any concrete plan of reform in the "Epilogue" to *Promethidion,* his real, overriding concern is to rechannel Polish thinking into new categories. Instead of directing most attention to such "outward" problems as diplomatic or political ways and means of liberating Poland, he stresses the necessity of a greater "turning inwards," national self-analysis, and organic social work in the spirit of complete truthfulness. He is among the first Polish writers to defy "martyrology": *"the victory over one's own nation . . .* should lead to making martyrdom unnecessary: and that is PROGRESS" (original emphasis retained). This last sentence sums up Norwid's rejection of Wallenrodian Romanticism, the ideology of exalted self-sacrifice that had mesmerized a whole generation since 1830-1831. For the author of *Promethidion,* a nation exists only inasmuch as it is conscious of its own problems. Without a dialogue between the constituent parts of the nation (what Norwid calls the "word of the people" and "the written word") no such consciousness can arise. The answer is work in the spirit of love; work, instead of armed insurrections, and the development of an art which is capable of "ennobling" and harmonizing Polish society into a single entity. The Norwid of *Promethidion* eschewed political action. After the revolutionary twilight of 1849-1851, he is disillusioned with politics and states with axiomatic brevity in the "Epilogue": "Only to art, perceived in its full truth and dignity, can a Pole today devote his life." Note the word "devote." From now on Norwid regards his creative work as a service not only to Poland but to mankind. He appears alternately in two roles—as philosopher unraveling the secrets of the past and as prophet foretelling the doom of the industrial civilization built on "money and blood." (pp. 33-5)

What makes the enjoyment of *Promethidion* as poetry difficult is not so much its didactic character but its heterogeneity. The language of the poem oscillates between the discursive prose of the salon and a philosophically inclined lyrical rhapsody. Along with striking *poetic* formulations of ideas or impressive metaphors, there are thickets of lines puzzling in their deliberate (though perhaps only seeming) impenetrability. In other words, while *Promethidion* is a challenge to the explorer of Norwid's thought, one is left with the feeling that he has not yet found the golden mean between discreet didacticism and imaginative allusiveness which characterizes some of his best lyrics, especially the bulk of the *Vade-Mecum* cycle. *Promethidion* is an experimental piece of poetry. While parts of it stand by themselves as good pieces of descriptive or lyrical verse, the work as a whole is so obviously organized around the exposition of certain esthetic and ethical values that it is almost impossible to judge it from a purely literary viewpoint. One of Norwid's most sensitive critics, Tadeusz Makowiecki, sees the significance of this work precisely in terms of its ideas. As Norwid was the first Polish poet to realize that the Romantic Era had come to an end, he made a special effort to create a "synthetic antithesis": a kind of realism which does not reject Romanticism in its entirety but rather transcends it, while incorporating certain elements of the Romantic consciousness. *Promethidion* is the result of this effort, and it is important and valuable in spite of its minor shortcomings. (p. 36)

George Gömöri, in his Cyprian Norwid, *Twayne Publishers, Inc., 1974, 162 p.*

ADDITIONAL BIBLIOGRAPHY

Corliss, Frank J., Jr. "Time and the Crucifixion in Norwid's *Vade-Mecum.*" *Slavic and East European Journal* XI, No. 3 (1967): 284-95.
  An examination of Norwid's conception of time that focuses on the image of the crucifixion in *Vade-Mecum*.

Czerniawski, Adam. "A 'Flawed' Master." *Oficyna Poetow* VIII, No. 2 (May 1973): 5-7.
  An introduction to Norwid's life and works.

Gömöri, George. "The Myth of Byron in Norwid's Life and Work." *The Slavic and East European Review* 51, No. 123 (April 1973): 231-42.
  Notes the admiration for Lord Byron evidenced in Norwid's works and correspondence.

Jauss, Hans Robert. "Norwid and Baudelaire as Contemporaries: A Notable Case of Overdue Concretization," translated by Manfred Jacobson. In *The Structure of the Literary Process: Studies Dedicated to the Memory of Felix Vodička*, edited by P. Steiner, M. Červenka, and R. Vroon, pp. 285-96. Linguistic and Literary Studies in Eastern Europe, vol. 8. Amsterdam: John Benjamins Publishing Co., 1982.
  Explores the affinity between Norwid's and Charles Baudelaire's works and poetic theories.

Kliger, George, and Albrecht, Robert C. "A Polish Poet on John Brown." *The Polish Review* VIII, No. 3 (Summer 1963): 80-5.
  Comments on Norwid's views on abolitionism in America and translates two poems by Norwid written in tribute to John Brown.

Krzyzanowski, Julian. "Polish Romantic Literature: Zygmunt Krasinski and Cyprian Kamil Norwid." In his *A History of Polish Literature*, translated by Doris Ronowicz, pp. 287-307. Warsaw: Polish Scientific Publishers, 1978.

    An introduction to the lives and works of the two poets.

Pietrkiewicz, Jerzy. "Introducing Norwid." *The Slavic and East European Review* 27, No. 68 (December 1948): 228-49.

    Compares Norwid with Gerard Manley Hopkins.

————. "Patriotic Irritability." *The Twentieth Century* 162, No. 970 (December 1957): 545-57.

    A discussion of the patriotism of Joseph Conrad with a brief comparison drawn between Conrad, Chopin, and Norwid. The critic predicts that Norwid "may still prove to be the greatest artist of the three."

Sławińska, Irnea. "Two Concepts of Time in Dramatic Structure: Turgenev and Norwid." In *For Wiktor Weintraub: Essays in Polish Literature, Language, and History Presented on the Occasion of His 65th Birthday*, edited by Victor Erlich and others, pp. 479-92. The Hague: Mouton, 1975.

    A comparison of the works of Norwid and Ivan Turgenev that focuses on the authors' depiction of time.

Weintraub, Wiktor. "Norwid-Pŭskin: Norwid's 'Spartacus' and the *Onegin* Stanza." *Harvard Slavic Studies* 2 (1954): 271-85.

    A detailed study of the metrical structure of Norwid's poem "Spartacus."

Wilcher, A. "The Bible in the Poetry of Cyprian Norwid." *Slavic and East-European Studies* XV (1970): 120-24.

    Gives a brief analysis of biblical elements in "Prayer of Moses."

Christoph Martin Wieland

1733-1813

German poet, novelist, editor, translator, essayist, and dramatist.

A versatile and influential German writer, Wieland composed pioneering works in several genres. He is primarily known for his epic poem *Oberon,* which is noted for its introduction of new styles of poetic expression, and for his novel *Geschichte des Agathon (The History of Agathon),* regarded as the first work in the tradition of the German *Bildungsroman,* or novel of psychological development. Wieland is also remembered as the author of the first German translation of William Shakespeare's plays and as the editor of the *Teutsche Merkur,* one of the leading German periodicals of the eighteenth century. Although he founded no literary school and stood apart from the emerging literary movements of his day, *Sturm und Drang* and Romanticism, Wieland's innovations had a profound effect upon the writings of his contemporaries. During much of his lifetime, Wieland was considered one of Germany's most important authors. However, his reputation declined toward the end of the eighteenth century, and it was not until the early 1900s that critics began to reassess his contribution to German literature.

Wieland was born in Oberholzheim, a small village near Biberach, Germany. As a youth, his education was largely directed by his father, a clergyman who exposed him to pietistic teachings at an early age. When he was fourteen, Wieland was sent to a boarding school in Klosterberge. There, he developed an interest in classical literature that he retained throughout his life. In 1750, at his family's urging, Wieland went to the University of Tübingen to study law, but within a few months he dropped out to pursue a writing career. Remaining in Tübingen, he composed a number of pietistic poems, including *Anti-Ovid, Hermann, Die Natur der Dinge,* and *Zwölf moralische Briefe.* These works attracted the attention of the famous Swiss critic Johann Jakob Bodmer, and from 1752 to 1754 Wieland lived with him in Zurich under his tutelage. After leaving Bodmer's household, Wieland stayed in Switzerland for several years, spending most of his time tutoring and writing. During this period, his works gradually became less spiritual in nature, prompting the German author Gotthold Ephraim Lessing to remark in 1759 that Wieland had forsaken the "ethereal spheres to wander again among the sons of men."

The change in Wieland's philosophical outlook became more marked in his writings after 1760, when he returned to Biberach. Now a well-known author, he was quickly welcomed into the aristocratic circle that was headed by Count Anton Heinrich Friedrich Stadion in nearby Warthausen. Under Stadion's influence, as well as that of Christine Hagel, a young woman with whom he had a passionate affair between 1762 and 1764, Wieland adopted an epicurean philosophy of life. This liberalization in his thought is evident in his works of the 1760s, which are characterized by whimsicality and eroticism. Though many of Wieland's contemporaries denounced his new philosophy as "frivolous," he composed some of his most popular works during this decade, among them the novel *Die Abenteuer des Don Sylvio von Rosalva (The Adventures of Don Sylvio),* the first of three versions of *Agathon,* a collection of verse tales entitled *Comische Erzählungen,* and the comic poem *Mu-*

sarion. In addition, he published prose translations of twenty-two Shakespeare plays, thus introducing German readers to the dramatist's works.

With the support of various members of the Warthausen circle, Wieland was elected to a professorship in philosophy at the University of Erfurt in 1769. He published a number of works while teaching there, notably *Der goldene Spiegel,* a didactic political novel containing an enthusiastic defense of government by constitutional monarchy. This work gained the admiration of Duchess Anna Amalia of Saxe-Weimar, and in 1772 she appointed Wieland tutor to her sons. Wieland, who had married Dorothea von Hillenbrand in 1765 and was now the father of several children, welcomed the position partly because it ensured him a sizable income for the rest of his life; in addition, he anticipated that the post would allow him ample time to pursue his writing career. Until his death in 1813, Wieland lived in or near Weimar and, along with such other literary luminaries as Johann Wolfgang von Goethe and Johann Christoph Friedrich von Schiller, he helped raise the town to a position of cultural eminence. One of his greatest accomplishments during these years was his establishment of *Merkur.* Founded in 1773 and edited by Wieland until 1796, *Merkur* became the most influential literary review in Germany. Not only did many of Wieland's writings first appear in the journal, but the works of other leading authors, including Goethe, Schiller, and Novalis, were also featured. Of Wieland's contributions to *Merkur*, the satiric novel *Die Geschichte der Abderiten (The Republic of Fools)* and *Oberon* have been singled out as his most significant. Critics often note that both of these works exemplify the successful balance between humor and seriousness that Wieland achieved in his writings of the 1770s and 1780s. Following this period, Wieland turned his attention almost exclusively to prose, composing increasingly didactic works that failed to achieve the popularity of his earlier writings.

Although Wieland published a variety of types of works, including translations, novellas, fairy tales, and essays, commentators generally agree that he made his most important contributions to German literature as a novelist and poet. He is frequently credited with introducing the modern novel into Germany with *Don Sylvio* and *Agathon*. In *Don Sylvio*, a romance written in imitation of Miguel de Cervantes's *Don Quixote*, Wieland displayed an interest in the psychological growth of his main character that was new to German fiction. Wieland's fascination with psychology became even more apparent in *Agathon*, a semiautobiographical work set in ancient Greece in which the hero's intellectual and spiritual development closely parallels Wieland's own. Wieland was unsatisfied with *Agathon* when it was first published in 1766-67, and he subsequently published revised versions in 1773 and 1794. To the second version he added, among other sections, an introductory essay describing the concept of history as he used it in the work; he augmented the conclusion of the third version in order to round out Agathon's story. *Agathon* has been repeatedly acclaimed as a psychological masterpiece, and scholars agree that it initiated the important literary tradition of the *Bildungsroman*. In addition, critics have praised Wieland's complex narrative technique in the novel, examining in detail his method of involving readers in the story.

Of Wieland's many poetic works, *Oberon* and *Musarion* have received the most attention. *Oberon*, widely regarded as Wieland's finest achievement, is a fanciful epic that he adapted from a variety of literary sources, including the anonymous chivalric romance *Histoire de Huon de Bordeaux*, Shakespeare's *A Midsummer Night's Dream*, and Geoffrey Chaucer's "A Merchant's Tale." Since its publication, *Oberon* has been commended for its graceful rhythms. Indeed, several critics have argued that Wieland's innovations in meter helped to make the German language less rigid, thus establishing it as a more effective vehicle of poetic expression. *Musarion*, too, has been praised for its fluent verses. However, it is most often admired as the finest example of the rococo style in German literature, and several studies have been devoted to analyzing its rococo elements, including its sensuous pastoral settings and voluptuous descriptions of the human body.

Wieland's works were praised by some of the most important writers of his time, including Goethe, Lessing, and Friedrich Gottlieb Klopstock. Yet several of Wieland's contemporaries denounced his conversion from pietism to epicureanism and charged him with lax morality. During the late eighteenth century, the number of attacks on Wieland's alleged immorality proliferated, and his popularity with the public declined as well. The view of Wieland as a licentious writer persisted throughout the 1800s, and his works were overshadowed by those of Goethe and Schiller. In the twentieth century, scholars have reassessed Wieland's accomplishments. In addition to exploring such specific aspects of his thought as his social and political views, attitude toward women, and relationship to the intellectual cur-

rents of his time, critics have emphasized his pioneering achievement as a novelist, poet, translator, and editor. Today, *Agathon* is recognized for its historical importance as the first German *Bildungsroman*, and *Oberon* continues to be admired as a significant contribution to the development of the German language. Wieland is also credited with helping to shape the reading tastes of the German public through his translations of Shakespeare's plays and his work as editor of *Merkur*. In assessing the importance of Wieland's many innovations, most modern commentators agree with John A. McCarthy, who recently concluded that Wieland "was one of the few men of genius who truly deserve to be known as a *praeceptor Germaniae* (educator of Germany)."

PRINCIPAL WORKS

Anti-Ovid (poetry) 1752
Hermann (poetry) 1752
Die Natur der Dinge (poetry) 1752
Zwölf moralische Briefe (poetry) 1752
Der geprüfte Abraham (poetry) 1753
   [*The Trial of Abraham*, 1764]
Lady Johanna Gray (drama) 1758
Araspes und Panthea (dialogues) 1760
   [*Araspes and Panthea; or, The Effects of Love*; published in *Dialogues from the German of M. Wieland*, 1775]
Clementina von Porretta (drama) 1760
Shakespeares theatralische Werke. 8 vols. [translator; from Shakespeare] (dramas) 1762-66
Der Sieg der Natur über die Schwärmerei; oder, Die Abenteuer des Don Sylvio von Rosalva (novel) 1764
   [*The Adventures of Don Sylvio de Rosalva*, 1773]
Comische Erzählungen (poetry) 1765
Geschichte des Agathon (novel) 1766-67; also published in revised form, 1773, 1794
   [*The History of Agathon*, 1773]
Idris und Zenide (poem fragment) 1768
Musarion; oder, Die Philosophie der Grazien (poetry) 1768
Die Grazien (poetry) 1770
   [*The Graces*, 1823]
Sokrates Mainomenos; oder, Die Dialogen des Diogenes von Sinope (novel) 1770
   [*Socrates Out of His Senses; or, Dialogues of Diogenes of Sinope*, 1771]
Der neue Amadis (poetry) 1771
Der goldene Spiegel; oder, Die Könige von Scheschian (novel) 1772
Ein das Wintermärchen (poetry) 1776
Das Sommermärchen (poetry) 1777
Oberon (poetry) 1780
   [*Oberon*, 1798]
Die Geschichte der Abderiten (novel) 1781
   [*The Republic of Fools: Being the History of the State and People of Abdera, in Thrace*, 1861]
Die geheime Geschichte des Philosophen Peregrinus Proteus (novel) 1791
   [*Private History of Peregrinus Proteus, the Philosopher*, 1796]
C. M. Wielands sämmtliche Werke. 39 vols. (poetry, novels, dialogues, fairy tales, novellas, dramas, and essays) 1794-1811
Agathodämon (novel) 1799
Aristipp und einige seiner Zeitgenossen. 4 vols. (epistolary novel) 1801-02

Menander und Glycerion   (epistolary novel)   1804
Das Hexameron von Rosenhain   (fairy tales and novellas)
    1805
Krates und Hipparchia   (epistolary novel)   1805
    [*Crates and Hipparchia,* 1823]
Briefe. 5 vols.   (letters)   1812
***Christoph Martin Wieland: Werke.* 5 vols.   (poetry,
    novels, dramas, dialogues, translations, and essays)
    1964-68

*This work was first published serially, 1774-80, in the periodical the
Teutsche Merkur under the title *Die Abderiten.*

**This collection includes commentary by Fritz Martini and Hans
Werner Seiffert.

THE CRITICAL REVIEW   (essay date 1764)

[*This critic praises the beautiful imagery in Wieland's poem* Der
geprüfte Abraham (The Trial of Abraham). *This essay was first
published in the* Critical Review *in 1764.*]

The German muses, who, in the last age, were remarkable for
their awkward carriage, are, in the present, as distinguishable
for elegance and grace: we have already endeavoured to do
justice to the ingenious Gesner, and allowed Mr. Klopstock
that degree of merit which he seemed intitled to: the author of
The Trial of Abraham, whoever he is, seems by no means
inferior to his cotemporaries, with regard to his poetical excellency, as every impartial reader will acknowledge, on perusal of the little work now before us, which, even through
the medium of but an indifferent translation, abounds with
many striking beauties. The history of Abraham's intended
sacrifice, as related in holy writ, of itself a most interesting
event, is here illustrated by some natural circumstances, and
adorned with poetical imagery. In the first canto Abraham
receives the command from God to sacrifice his son: he resolves, after many doubts and struggles with himself, to conceal the dreadful news from Sarah his wife, but imparts it to
his friend Eliezer. Two guardian angels are introduced, who
converse about this important event, and admire the goodness
and resignation of Abraham. In the second canto, Isaac is
supposed to return from the house of Nahor to his father's; the
joy and festivity on this occasion are described, and artfully
contrived to form a striking contrast to the melancholy scene
that is to follow, when Abraham acquaints his son that he must
attend him to Moriah, to sacrifice to the Lord. Isaac prepares
to attend him. The third canto gives us an account of the
patriarch's journey to Moriah, where he discovers to Isaac the
command which he had received from God. The tenderness,
reluctance, and piety, of the father, the son's duty, resignation
and obedience, are happily and pathetically described. . . .

[The] composition is truly dramatic, and such as, in good
hands, might form an excellent oratorio, or sacred tragedy.
(p. 425)

We wish the nature of our work would permit us to insert
Abraham's reflections on his journey to Moriah, which the
reader will meet with in the third canto, as they are remarkably
beautiful, though not more so than his address to the Almighty,
just before he is going to sacrifice his son. Sarah's dream, in
the fourth book, is . . . finely imagined, and . . . poetically described. . . . (p. 426)

A review of ''The Trial of Abraham,'' *in* The Reception of Classical German Literature in England,
1760-1860: A Documentary History from Contemporary Periodicals, Vol. 4, *edited by John Boening,
Garland Publishing, Inc., 1977, pp. 425-26.*

G. E. LESSING   (essay date 1769)

[*Called ''the founder of the German theater,'' Lessing was one
of the most acute intelligences of the eighteenth century. Through
his dramatic and critical works he helped free German literature
from the French classical school's narrow conventions. His* Ham-
burgische Dramaturgie, *a revolutionary plea for a dramatic form
developed not from rules but from observation and inspiration,
is acknowledged as the first European handbook of dramatic technique. In the following excerpt from an English translation of that
work, Lessing commends Wieland's Shakespeare translations. This
essay was first published in German in 1769.*]

Critics have spoken ill of [Wieland's collection of Shakespeare
translations]. I have a mind to speak very well of it. Not in
order to contradict these learned men, nor to defend the faults
they have discovered, but because I believe there is no need
to make so much ado about these faults. The undertaking was
a difficult one, and any other person than Herr Wieland would
have made other slips in their haste, or have passed over more
passages from ignorance or laziness and what parts he has done
well few will do better. Any way his rendering of Shakespeare
is a book that cannot be enough commended among us. We
have much to learn yet from the beauties he has given to us,
before the blemishes wherewith he has marred them offend us
so greatly that we require a new translation. (p. 42)

G. E. Lessing, in a chapter in his Hamburg Dramaturgy, *Dover Publications, Inc., 1962, pp. 40-3.*

THE CRITICAL REVIEW   (essay date 1773)

[*This anonymous critic views* Don Sylvio *as a poor imitation of
Cervantes's* Don Quixote. *This essay first appeared in the* Critical
Review *in 1773.*]

The reputation which Cervantes acquired by that excellent satire, *The History of Don Quixote de la Mancha,* has prompted
sundry authors to attempt performances of a similar kind, all
of which have, however, fallen short of the merit of that truly
original production. [**Don Sylvio de Rosalva**] is a fresh instance
of the difficulty, we had almost said the impossibility, of ri-
valling the work of Cervantes, although that author's manner
is in some places not unhappily imitated. The madness of Don
Quixote has indeed, the advantage of being in itself much more
diverting than that of Don Sylvio de Rosalva, as the latter had
conceived notions that the absurdities related in fairy tales were
real and indisputable facts; absurdities far more repugnant to
common sense than the chimerical notions of chivalry entertained by Don Quixote, and which are therefore not so easily
imagined by the reader. (p. 431)

A review of ''Reason Triumphant over Fancy. . . .
'Don Sylvio de Rosalva','' *in* The Reception of Classical German Literature in England, 1760-1860: A
Documentary History from Contemporary Periodicals, Vol. 4, *edited by John Boening, Garland Publishing, Inc., 1977, pp. 431-32.*

RALPH GRIFFITHS (essay date 1774)

[*Griffiths praises Wieland's realistic depiction of ancient Greece in* Agathon *but censures the immoral ending of the novel. This essay was originally published in March 1774 in the* Monthly Review.]

Mr. Wieland has already been introduced to the acquaintance of our Readers. . . . In [previous] articles we asserted the *originality* of this German genius, and allowed his talent for delicate humour, and pointed satire. We observed, nevertheless, that we thought, in some instances, he kept the manner of Sterne, the English Rabelais, in view; and we still consider him as in some measure a disciple of that eminent master: yet he follows no leader with so much servility as to incur the reproach of being an *imitator*.

It seems to be the peculiar fancy of this Writer, to spirit his readers back into the remote ages of ancient Greece, when Greece was in the zenith of her glory; when Plato, Socrates, Xenophon, and other venerable sages flourished: to walk with them in the academic grove, to converse with them in the scientific portico, to tread over again the steps of Time, and to join the wisdom and the manners of antiquity with the knowledge and the improvements of later ages. Nor is the assemblage at all unnatural. The art of the Writer, in a great measure, prevents us from seeing where the mixture takes place; so that it is not every ordinary reader who can mark the point where Attic science unites with German wit; and where the Grecian moralist deviates into the hero of a feigned history.

Nor is it only the wisdom and the virtue of ancient Greece that are . . . revived [in *Agathon*] and produced as objects of our contemplation and esteem. This various Writer introduces us, likewise, to the luxurious scenes, the *convivial banquets,* of the polite and elegant, as well as the sage and philosophic, Athenians; who were equally disposed to the enjoyment of mental and corporeal pleasures. We share with them the gratifications of the table, the raptures of music, and all the delights of the most refined and voluptuous love.

But here the graver part of Mr. W.'s readers may be apt to raise some objections to the morality of his present performance. They may enquire whether he has not painted sensual enjoyments in colours that are too seductive to young minds, and persons of warm feelings; and whether his work will not, therefore, prove dangerous to those readers who do not always sufficiently discriminate the luxurious description and the moral inference.

Our Author is, indeed, aware of this objection; to which, however, he does not admit that his work is justly amenable. He seems to think that if we would give virtue a real advantage over vice, the encounter should be strictly conformable to the laws of honour; that each side should have fair play; that both parties should be allowed room to exert their full strength, in order to render the superiority of the conqueror the more conspicuous, and the victory more complete and decisive. And here let the Author defend his own cause [in an extract from his preface to *Agathon*].

> In several places of this work . . . we have given our reasons why we have not made Agathon the model of a perfectly virtuous character. The world is already sufficiently stocked with copious treatises of morality, and every one may freely indulge his fancy (for nothing is easier) in forming a hero, who shall from his cradle to his grave, in every circumstance and relation

of life, always perceive, think, and act as a perfect moralist. But as Agathon was intended to represent a real character, in which others might discover their own likeness, we maintain that the author could not, consistently with this design, make him more virtuous than he is; but if others are of a contrary opinion (for it is certain that the best character is that which has the greatest qualities with the fewest faults) we only desire that they would, among all mankind, fix upon any one, who, in a similar situation, would have been more virtuous than Agathon.

(p. 437)

[In a preface to the English version of *Agathon,* the translator censures] his Author for certain careless expressions, and an indelicacy in some of his allusions, which, as he observes, we should not have expected in so elegant a Writer; but we think there is, in this work, a defect of more importance than any of those which he has noticed. A romance, or a novel, like other fables, usually ends with a moral deduction; and it is proper that this should always be the case, not only because the moral is the main object and end of the piece, but because the farewell impression left on the Reader's mind when he closes the book, is generally that which strikes the deepest, and lasts the longest. Now, although the balance obviously inclines in favour of morality, throughout the whole of Agathon's history, there is no exemplary inference of this kind at the conclusion of the work; for, there, the hero of the tale relapses (after his return to virtue, in the third volume) into his misplaced love for a beautiful and highly accomplished courtezan, who had deluded and fascinated him in the early part of his youth, and of his adventures. This, in the Author, is criminal; but he has also grossly violated the laws of female delicacy and decorum, by introducing this courtezan to the acquaintance and friendship of an amiable and virtuous lady, who certainly could not, consistently, at least, with our modern notions of honour, attach herself to such a person, without relinquishing all pretentions to reputation.

In justice to Mr. W. we must not, however, omit to acquaint our Readers, that he does not, in fact, appear to have intended the close of the fourth volume for the final completion of his design. On the contrary, he there talks of certain 'supplements and additions' to the History; which may not be unworthy the attention of the public, and which will give us a view of the opinions and conduct of the amiable Agathon, at fifty years old. (p. 439)

> *Ralph Griffiths, in a review of "The History of Agathon," in* The Reception of Classical German Literature in England, 1760-1860: A Documentary History from Contemporary Periodicals, Vol. 4, *edited by John Boening, Garland Publishing, Inc., 1977, pp. 437-39.*

THE MONTHLY REVIEW, LONDON (essay date 1796)

[*In the following excerpt from a review of Wieland's collected works, volumes V-X, the critic examines Wieland's method of characterization. This essay was first published in the* Monthly Review, *London, in 1796.*]

Wieland is distinguished for ductility of imagination. His fancy, endowed with intuitive ubiquity, is alike at home in every place and every age, and knows how to invest the costume, and to think within the range of idea appropriate to its peculiar situation. Like the Dervis-friend of Fadlallah, he seems able to shoot his soul into the body of man or woman, libertine or sage, of antient or modern, of Persian, Greek, or Goth; and, by a voluntary metempsychosis, to animate each with characteristic expression. Yet still it is *his* soul which pierces through every disguise; it is with him the effect of art and skill to substitute himself for another: an observing eye discovers that the alteration is assumed. It is by means of his varied knowledge of every thing relating to the manners, superstitions, and history of different nations, that he contrives to personate all with so classical a propriety. It is Larive in Orestes, Larive in Orosman, always accurate, always admirable,—but still Larive. His characters are less the creation of a plastic genius than the mouldings of an accomplished artist: he does not animate his figures, like Prometheus, by putting fire within, but, like Pygmalion, by external touches of the chisel. Nor are his personages so varied as at first sight they appear. He imitates general, not individual, nature: with him every character is a species; and it is with a very limited number of these, that he has undertaken the variegated list of his dramatizations. (p. 459)

> *A review of "Sämmtliche Werke," in* The Reception of Classical German Literature in England, 1760-1860: A Documentary History from Contemporary Periodicals, *Vol. 4, edited by John Boening, Garland Publishing, Inc., 1977, pp. 459-62.*

[WILLIAM TAYLOR] (essay date 1797)

[*Calling* Oberon *Wieland's "masterpiece," Taylor focuses on the poem's sources, unity, and style. For additional criticism by Taylor, see the excerpt dated 1804.*]

On the twenty-second and twenty-third volumes [of Wieland's *Sämmtliche Werke*] it will be proper to expatiate a little: they contain the master-piece of Wieland—the child of his genius in moments of its purest converse with the all-beauteous forms of ideal excellence;—the darling of his fancy, born in the sweetest of her excursions amid the ambrosial bowers of fairy-land;—the *Oberon*—an epic poem, popular beyond example, yet as dear to the philosopher as to the multitude; which, during the author's life-time, has attained in its native country all the honors of a sacred book; and to the evolution of the beauties of which, a Professor in a distinguished university has repeatedly consecrated an entire course of patronized lectures.

To an English ear, the mere name of Oberon attracts curiosity; and fictions grafted on the tales of Chaucer, and connected with the *fablings* of our Shakspeare, would naturally be secure of some partiality of attention:—but it is not from English sources alone that the outline of this poem is derived. Its fable is triune. The first main action, consisting in the adventure undertaken by the hero at the command of Charlemagne, is almost wholly derived from an old story-book of chivalry, entitled *Histoire de Huon de Bordeaux;* one of the romances which the fair of Troyes in Champagne distributed among the reading world, in the first century of printing. . . . The second main action, consisting in the adventures of Huon and Rezia after their union, is more scantily borrowed from the French romancer, and more freely new-modelled by pruning away redundant adventures, and inserting new incidents.—The third main action passes wholly in the machinery of the poem, among its mythological personages, and consists in the reconciliation of Oberon and Titania; whom a rash oath, sworn on the occasion of their quarrel in the garden of January and May,

unwillingly separates,—until some mortal pair should set such an example of insuperable fidelity as Huon and Rezia at length realize. By means of this over-plot, (for we may not call the adventures of the *gods* an *underplot,*) these three distinct actions are completely braided into one main knot; so that neither could subsist nor succeed without each of the other;—and so that all are happily unwound together by a cotemporary solution. Huon could not have executed Charlemagne's order to fetch the beard of the Caliph of Bagdad, without Oberon's assistance; without this order, Huon's passion for Rezia would not have arisen; and without the hope which Oberon builds on their constancy, the Elfen king and queen would have had no motive for interfering with their fortunes. From this reciprocal importance, this mutual dependence of the heroes and of the gods, a peculiar species of unity arises, which has not merely the merit of novelty, but forms the peculiar and characteristic source of the perpetual interest of this poem. In other epopœas, the supernatural characters seem introduced merely "to elevate and surprise;" as if they belonged, like turgid phrases and long-tailed similes, to the arts of style: they interfere, only that the action may acquire strangeness and importance; they split into factions without a reasonable ground of discord; and, with the mischievous fidelity of subordinate partisans, are made to adhere to their champions through perfidy and guilt. In the *Oberon,* it is for interests of their own that they intervene; and the mechanism of their providence, while it guides by an irresistible necessity the conduct of the human agents, has still a motive for every interposition, and never stoops from heaven either to inflict or to reward from capricious tyranny or vague curiosity. The gods of Homer have no obvious and intelligible interest in either the demolition or the preservation of Troy; and Virgil preserves with almost as slight a pretext the traditional distribution of their factions. Tasso has scrupled to make use of those personages of the Christian mythology, to whom a natural interest might have been ascribed in the liberation of Jerusalem; and thus his machinery is nearly as capricious as the wizardry of Ariosto. Milton, indeed, has planted hostility between his angels on the sufficient provocation of the apotheosis of Jesus: but there is a bathos in passing from the war of Heaven to a contest about an apple. Wieland alone has annexed his machinery by an adequate link; while he preserves to his Elves that "diminutive agency, powerful but ludicrous, that humorous and frolic controlment of nature," and that care of chastity, which their received character among the fathers of song required them to sustain. (pp. 576-78)

[*Oberon* is a] well-rounded fable. . . . It were difficult to suggest a blemish in it. Yet, as the author has thought fit to convert the heroine to a religion which peculiarly enforces the duty of chastity; and as the turn of the whole story, not less than the law of France, sets a considerable value on the marriage-ceremony;—we have sometimes been tempted to think that this conversion should have been reserved until the sojournment on the island; and that the nuptial benediction should there have been pronounced by the hermit, previously to the interposition of Titania.

In the whole poem we discover but few similes: they belong, no doubt, to the exhausted class of ornaments. The style is less diffuse and trailing, less exuberant of circumstances and particulars, than in most productions of Wieland. It abounds, as in all his works, with sensible imagery and picturesque decoration: it studiously avoids the English fault of substituting general terms, and allegoric personification, for specific description and individual example. It does not habitually aspire at elevation, at grandiloquence, at pomposity; and, by this apparent easy negligence, it obtains *a wider arc of oscillation,* and can with less discrepancy descend to the comic or ascend to the sublime. Milton and Klopstock habitually assume the highest tone of diction which language admits: they have seldom resources in reserve when they wish to soar above their usual level of diction, but become affected, bloated, unintelligible. Milton's war of heaven is tame, and Klopstock's ascension is tedious: they have continually been on the stretch; and on great occasions they sink, as if unequal to their subject. Virgil and Tasso excel in the next degree of exaltation, and probably maintain the highest tone of style which is really prudent in the solemn epopœa. Homer, Ariosto, and Camoëns, have chosen a humbler but more flexile manner, which can adapt itself without effort or disparagement to a greater diversity of emotion and incident; which is more capacious of variety, and more accommodating to circumstance. In this respect they have served as models to the author of **Oberon,** who describes with equal felicity a palace in uproar, or a ridiculous dance; the hostilities of a tournament, or the conflicts of concupiscence. To the delineation of great passions, or the contrast of complex character, his subject did not invite: he is naturally equal to the tender and the beautiful; and no where disappoints the tiptoe expectation which he rouzes. His characters, if few, are consistent and distinct. His learned attention to the minutiæ of costume, whether Gothic or Oriental, may encounter without shrinking the armed eye of even microscopic criticism. The adventures of heroes are by him brought home to the affairs of ordinary life, to the bosoms of common men, and are thus secure of a sympathy coeternal with human nature. The busy life of his narrative, and the felicitous structure of his story, farther contribute to his unrelenting power of fascination. The reader clings to his book by a magnetism which a more sublime genius is often unable to emanate; and he returns to it with increased attraction. If there be an European poem likely to obtain, on perusal, the applause of eastern nations by its voluptuous beauties of imagery and magic magnificence of fancy, it is this.—In a good Persian translation, it would less surprise by its singularity than enrapture by its perfection. (pp. 583-84)

[*William Taylor*], *"Wieland's Works, Vols. XXI-XXIII," in* The Monthly Review, *London, Vol. 23, 1797, pp. 575-84.*

WILLIAM WORDSWORTH   (conversation date 1798)

[*An English poet and critic, Wordsworth was central to English Romanticism. Wordsworth's literary criticism reflects his belief that neither the language nor the content of poetry should be stylized or elaborate and that the aim of a poet is to feel and express the relation between humankind and nature. In the following excerpt, Wordsworth recounts a conversation he had with Klopstock in 1798 concerning Wieland's Oberon.*]

[Klopstock] said Wieland was a charming author, and a sovereign master of his own language: that in this respect Goethe could not be compared to him, or indeed could any body else. He said that his fault was to be fertile to exuberance. I told him the **Oberon** had just been translated into English. He asked me, if I was not delighted with the poem. I answered, that I thought the story began to flag about the seventh or eighth book; and observed that it was unworthy of a man of genius to make the interest of a long poem turn entirely upon animal gratification. He seemed at first disposed to excuse this by saying, that there are different subjects for poetry, and that poets are not willing to be restricted in their choice. I answered, that I thought the *passion* of love as well suited to the purposes

of poetry as any other passion; but that it was a cheap way of pleasing to fix the attention of the reader through a long poem on the mere *appetite*. Well! but, said he, you see, that such poems please every body. I answered, that it was the province of a great poet to raise people up to his own level, not to descend to theirs. He agreed, and confessed, that on no account whatsoever would he have written a work like the **Oberon**. He spoke in raptures of Wieland's style, and pointed out the passage where Retzia is delivered of her child, as exquisitely beautiful. I said that I did not perceive any very striking passages; but that I made allowance for the imperfections of a translation. Of the thefts of Wieland, he said, they were so exquisitely managed, that the greatest writers might be proud to steal as he did. (pp. 202-03)

William Wordsworth, in an extract from The Collected Works of Samuel Taylor Coleridge: Biographia Literaria, *Vol. 7 by Samuel Taylor Coleridge, edited by James Engell and W. Jackson Bate, Bollingen Series LXXV, Princeton University Press, 1984, pp. 202-03.*

HENRY CRABB ROBINSON   (diary date 1801)

[*A nineteenth-century English journalist, Robinson is remembered for his voluminous correspondence and diaries, which chronicle London's social and intellectual history. In the following diary notation made during a trip to Germany, Robinson compares Wieland's works with those of Voltaire.*]

Our first call was at the house of the aged Wieland. The course of my late reading had not led me to form terrifying ideas of his mental greatness, though as a *littérateur* he is one of the first writers of his country. He is not less universally read and admired in Germany than Voltaire was in France. His works amount to more than fifty volumes, all written for the many. He resembles the French wit in the lightness of his philosophy, in the wantonness of his muse (though it is by no means so gross), and in the exquisite felicity of his style. But he surpasses Voltaire in learning, if not in philosophy; for Wieland is no school-philosopher,—he belongs to the sensual school of Locke. And his favourite opinions are those of the common-sense, sceptical school. He is a sworn foe to the Kantian metaphysics, and indeed to all others. In his writings, as in his person and manners, he is a perfect gentleman.

Henry Crabb Robinson, in a diary entry of 1801, in his Diary, Reminiscences, and Correspondence of Henry Crabb Robinson, *Vol. I, edited by Thomas Sadler, third edition, 1872. Reprint by AMS Press, Inc., 1967, p. 58.*

WILLIAM TAYLOR   (essay date 1804)

[*Taylor comments on the nature and merit of the political opinions expressed in Wieland's* Dialogues between a Pair of Tongues. *He also briefly assesses the literary value of the dialogues. Taylor's essay was first published in the* Critical Review *in 1804. For additional criticism by Taylor, see the excerpt dated 1797.*]

The thirty-first volume [of Wieland's **Sämmtliche Werke**] contains twelve **Dialogues between a Pair of Tongues;** such, we believe, is the idiomatic rendering of what the Germans call *dialogues under four eyes,* and the French, more neatly, *tête-à-têtes.* They relate to phænomena of the French revolution: among them, in the second dialogue on the French oath of hatred to royalty, occurs the proposal, afterwards acted upon by the French, for investing Bonaparte with dictatorial power, as the most tried and efficient remedy for anarchy. This proposal; however natural and obvious a consequence of the known opinions and leaning of Wieland, appeared, after its realisation, like the inspired dictate of supernatural prescience;

> For old experience can attain
> To something like prophetic strain.

In order to destroy the merit of this guess, or counsel, the enemies of Wieland's sentiments attributed it to secret intelligence, conveyed through supposed confederacies of the illuminati. The vulgar (ambassadors belong sometimes to the vulgar) weakly credited this imputation; the curs of anti-jacobinism were hallooed throughout Europe upon the sage of Osmanstadt: he was reviled and insulted as the hired mouthpiece of Parisian conspirators.

The most important of these dialogues is the tenth, entitled **"Dreams Awake."** . . . It unfolds a project for reconstituting the German empire. It points out the practicability of assimilating the German constitution to the British; recommends bestowing on the imperial cities, and on the circles, or shires, a representation analogous to our house of commons; proposes to the petty sovereigns to accept a sort of peerage, under the name of dukes and athelings; and to the emperor, to assume an all-pervading sovereignty, and an efficacious executive power. (p. 509)

The opinion of Wieland is in nothing a solitary opinion: he is rather an eclectic philosopher, than an original thinker; and collects, from the whole surface of Europe, the results of the best discussions, with an equity which makes him in a remarkable degree the herald of public opinion, the representative of disinterested and instructed judges. He makes his political pamphlets, like his poems, by the process of inlaying; he veneers not with autochthonous wood, but with the finest of foreign growth; and he gives that exquisite fashion to his work, which secures its presence in the apartments of luxury and the palaces of sovereigns. His advice therefore is sure to be weighed by such as are within reach of those interior seats of political volition, which communicate to the practical world the critical and decisive impulse. The statesman reads Wieland to know what the world expects from his beneficence. The consolidation of Germany is now the favourite project of the country; and whichever of the two courts, the Austrian or the Prussian, first offers to carry through the design on conditions favourable to the liberty of the subject, will accomplish the conquest or absorption of all Germany.

As works of art, these dialogues are not excellent: they abound with common-places and needless interlocutions: a great deal of conversation seems to have been introduced only to increase the number of sheets for the printer: the talkers assert often, reason sometimes, and demonstrate rarely: their drift is vague; their excursions rather resemble an airing, than a stage on a journey. There is not enough of dramatic distinction: both speakers are too voluble; both select their decorations and allusions with far-fetched appositeness; both have information and urbanity. The concluding dialogue between Geron and a stranger (that is, between Wieland and the young sovereign whom he aspires to counsel) has more dramatic merit than the rest: it holds up Marcus Antoninus, the author of the *Meditations,* as the very attainable model of a highly praise-worthy sway; and treats the art of reigning as one of the liberal pursuits, to excel in which is quite within reach of a gentleman of good taste, common attention, and appropriate ambition. (p. 510)

William Taylor, in a review of "C. M. Wieland's Collective Works," in The Reception of Classical German Literature in England, 1760-1860: A Documentary History from Contemporary Periodicals, Vol. 4, *edited by John Boening, Garland Publishing, Inc., 1977, pp. 509-10.*

JOHANN WOLFGANG VON GOETHE (essay date 1811-14)

[*Goethe was a German writer who is considered one of the greatest figures in world literature. A genius of the highest order, he distinguished himself as a botanist, physicist, and biologist; he was an artist, musician, and philosopher; and he had successful careers as a theater director and court administrator. Above all, he contributed richly to his nation's literature. Excelling in all genres, Goethe was a shaping force in the major literary movements of the late eighteenth and early nineteenth centuries in Germany. In the excerpt below, Goethe castigates German critics for failing to recognize Wieland's genius. This essay was first published sometime between 1811 and 1814. For additional commentary by Goethe, see the excerpt dated 1813.*]

[Wieland] had developed early in those ideal regions in which youth loves to linger; but when so-called experience, contact with the world and women, spoilt his delight in those realms, he turned to the actual, and derived pleasure for himself and others from the conflict between the two worlds, where, in light encounters, half in earnest, half in jest, his talent found fullest scope. How many of his brilliant productions appeared during my student days! *Musarion* had the greatest effect upon me, and I can yet remember the place and the very spot where I looked at the first proof-sheet. . . . It was here that I seemed to see antiquity living anew before me. Everything that is plastic in Wieland's genius showed itself here in the highest perfection; and since the Timon-like hero Phanias, after being condemned to unhappy abstinence, is finally reconciled to his mistress and to the world, we may be content to live through the misanthropic epoch with him. For the rest, we were not sorry to recognize in these works a cheerful aversion to exalted sentiments, which are apt to be wrongly applied to life, and then frequently fall under the suspicion of fanaticism. We pardoned the author for pursuing with ridicule what we held to be true and venerable, the more readily, as he thereby showed that he was unable to disregard it.

What a miserable reception was accorded such efforts by the criticism of the time may be seen from the first volumes of the *Universal German Library.* Honorable mention is made there of the [*Comische Erzählungen*], but there is no trace of any insight into the character of the literary species. The reviewer, like every one at that time, had formed his taste on examples. He never takes into consideration that in criticizing such parodistical works, it is necessary first of all to have the noble, beautiful original before one's eyes, in order to see whether the parodist has really discovered in it a weak and comical side, whether he has borrowed anything from it, or whether, under the pretense of imitation, he has given us an excellent invention of his own. Of all this there is not a word, but isolated passages in the poems are praised or blamed. The reviewer, as he himself confesses, has marked so much that pleased him, that he cannot quote it all in print. When they go so far as to greet the exceedingly meritorious translation of Shakespeare with the exclamation: "By rights, a man like Shakespeare should not have been translated at all!" it will be understood, without further remark, how immeasurably the *Universal German Library* was behindhand in matters of taste. . . . (pp. 237-39)

Johann Wolfgang von Goethe, "German Literature in Goethe's Youth," translated by John Oxenford and Miss M. S. Smith, in his Goethe's Literary Essays, *edited by J. E. Spingarn, Harcourt Brace Jovanovich, 1921, pp. 226-48.*

JOHANN WOLFGANG VON GOETHE (AS REPORTED BY JOHANNES DANIEL FALK)   (conversation date 1813)

[*In this excerpt, Goethe praises Wieland's graceful, fluent, and humorous style. Goethe's remarks were made in a conversation with Johannes Daniel Falk shortly after Wieland's death in January 1813. For additional commentary by Goethe, see the excerpt dated 1811-14.*]

[Wieland] possessed an incomparable nature: in him all was fluency, spirit and taste! It is a cheerful plain, where there is nothing to stumble over, threaded by the stream of a comical wit, which winds capriciously in all directions, and sometimes even turns against its author. There is not the slightest trace in him of that deliberate, laborious technical quality, which sometimes spoils for us the best ideas and feelings, by making their expression seem artificial. This natural ease and freedom is the reason why I always prefer to read Shakespeare in Wieland's translation. He handled rhyme as a master. I believe, if one had poured upon his desk a composing-case full of words, he would have arranged them, in a little while, into a charming poem. (pp. 254-55)

Johann Wolfgang von Goethe, as reported by Johannes Daniel Falk, in an extract from Studies in German Literature *by Bayard Taylor, G. P. Putnam's Sons, 1879, pp. 254-55.*

[ROBERT FERGUSON]   (essay date 1825)

[*In this excerpt from a positive review of* Aristipp und einige seiner Zeitgenossen, *Ferguson discusses Wieland's changing philosophical views.*]

[During Wieland's 28th year], a most extraordinary revolution took place in his character, totally unexpected by his friends, and by the world. The Poet of Religion and of Virtue, it was now said, had become the advocate of infidelity and sensual feeling. Volume upon volume, work upon work, teemed from his prolific pen, in rapid succession; and the astonished public knew not whether to admire the grace and genius of the author, or to reprobate the inconsistency and levity of the man.

Little is known of the causes of this change. It originated most probably in the very nature of his studies. That high-wrought enthusiastic pitch to which he had elevated his imagination, had placed him beyond the sympathies and the affections of humanity. The follies, the vices, and the weaknesses, of our nature, were not a subject of commiseration, or even of contemplation, to one who could only look upon things in the abstract, and Wieland soon learned that the philosophy of Plato was not the philosophy of life. Perhaps, too, he deemed it dangerous to soar so high. (p. 673)

Be the cause what it may—whether owing to some palpable circumstance, or arising from the irksomeness of that melancholy, which is almost invariably an attendant on highly-excited imaginations and speculative minds, the change was sudden, and deeply rooted. The stern and gloomy bigot, the man who regarded the innocent jests of the poet Gleim, as reprehensible—now laid open the weaknesses of our nature with the light hand of a master. A vein of the keenest satire, worthy

of the translator of Horace—a playful grace, which procured him the title of the German Voltaire, and a brilliant voluptuousness of style, such as few could boast of, pervaded his writings, and impressed them with immortality. It must be confessed, however, that the works which were made the medium of his new philosophy, did not always inculcate the purest morality, or the soundest views of Christianity. Neither, on the other hand, was their immediate tendency so strongly marked as to have called forth such animadversion as they have met with. In this respect, none of them can be compared with the works of Schiller, or even of Goëthe. (pp. 673-74)

[Wieland's work *Aristipp*] is one of those which he wrote after he had renounced the Platonic Philosophy, and the moroseness of his former opinions. Of all his novels, [*Aristipp*] is perhaps the best written. The characters are drawn with consummate art; every trait is minutely marked, and yet, like a highly-finished engraving, the minuteness and the number of the lines never obtruding, serve only to present us with a beautiful and harmonious whole. The hero of the story is that Aristippus who founded the Cyrenaic sect—a character which was exactly suited to be the vehicle of the author's new opinions. Accordingly, we find Wieland taking every opportunity of introducing them, yet so elegantly, so mixed up with poetical descriptions and classical allusions, that the interest overwhelms us as we proceed. The work supposes a knowledge of the travels of Anacharsis. The object of the author is to develope motives, and depict character, not to give information on topographical subjects. Socrates, Plato, Aristophanes, and Xenophon, are presented to the reader by Wieland, by a man, be it remembered, who is numbered among the profoundest critics, and the most elegant poets, of his own or of any age. With such material, and such a hand to form it, who does not anticipate the interest of the production? It is the attribute of genius to be subservient to no time. The past and the future do not exist with respect to it; it is an emanation from the Divinity; and the deeds of centuries elapsed, or the anticipations of centuries to come, are grasped by it at the same moment, and are truly ever present. Not only do we see Socrates, but we hear him as he leads us from proposition to proposition, to the contemplation of the sublimest truths. We feel all the excitement that the works of the enthusiastic Plato must have created, when, as a young man, he *first* gave the reins to his boundless imagination, and his fame overshadowed his country. The freshness of feeling imparted by genius, makes us almost imagine that the treasures of antiquity have been laid open now, for the first time. The dream of Socrates is realized, and we hear the notes of the young swan at the very moment he bursts from the bosom of the sage, and fills the heavens with the melody of his song.

Although few writers have the power of elevating our thoughts, by presenting such beautiful imagery before us as Wieland, yet it must be confessed, that there is no one who seems to delight more in asserting the powers of *passion* over every faculty of the soul. There is not a tale of his, whether in prose or in poetry, which will not afford abundant proofs of the remark. His exquisite taste would not permit him to detail the grossness of sense; but the allusions, which are but half concealed in the voluptuous turns of his teeming style, are too striking not to be felt by all. We seldom can *only quit* a habit—but we generally detest what we renounce. This seems to have been Wieland's case: he was not contented with rejecting bigotry and stoicism, but he advocates looseness of thought and Epicurism. He considered Virtue, in the sensual application of the term, as a species of moral knight-errantry; and no one, he thought, was obliged to be a knight-errant. These feelings and opinions are certainly to be censured; but it must be re- membered, that they were not so much Wieland's own, as the result of the age in which he lived. The French philosophy, at this period, was the lord of the ascendant in the intellectual horoscope of Europe, and its baleful rays have not even now been obscured by the purer and more extensive emanations of a higher one. Wieland's views were too often but a reflection of this.

There is, at least, one advantage on our author's side, over the *Naturalismus* of Goëthe and Schiller, that his object is im- mediately seen—all his views are put argumentatively, and the mind thus avoids being surprised. (pp. 674-75)

> [*Robert Ferguson*], "Wieland's 'Aristippus'," in Blackwood's Edinburgh Magazine, *Vol. XVII, No. CI, June, 1825, pp. 673-81.*

AUGUST WILHELM von SCHLEGEL   (lecture date 1833)

[*A prominent figure in the German Romantic movement, Schlegel distinguished himself as an influential exponent of Romantic aes- thetic theory and as an illustrious translator of William Shake- speare's plays. As a critic, Schlegel was instrumental in advancing the philosophy formulated by his brother Friedrich von Schlegel and other members of the Romantic circle at Jena. In the following excerpt, Schlegel decries Wieland's philosophic conversion and condemns as immoral the works he wrote from the mid-1760s until the end of his career. This excerpt is from an 1833 lecture that Schlegel delivered at the University of Bonn.*]

[Early in his career, Wieland was] a zealous cultivator of the biblical epic; but about 1765 his character underwent a com- plete transition; he now appeared as the author of comic stories, and of romances, as *Agathon, Musarion,* and [*Der neue Amadis*]. The philosophy which he here inculcated was a kind of eclectic epicureanism; he was afraid of virtue running into excess, and would fain deprive her of even the semblance of enthusiasm. His grand problem seems to have been to combine sensuality with grace. That he was a tasteful writer no one can deny, but as a moral teacher he was decidedly reprehensible. The exalted efforts of our nature he always affected to view with scrupulous suspicion; any love, except the sensual passion, he decried as deceit or an illusion. Wieland, it would almost seem, wished to make a treaty with virtue and to allow her certain rights, on condition that she should desist from the persecution of vice.

As a prose writer, Wieland must be contented to take a much lower station than as a poet: his diffuseness is perhaps his least fault, for it is generally graceful; but his style is complex and full of parentheses. Greece in its bright period between Pericles and Alexander is his scene and subject; but his heroes, instead of being Greeks, are moderns, and of the French School. His light and humorous manner he chiefly owed to the study of Cervantes, Sterne, and La Fontaine; his disposition to philos- ophize is his own. In his prose works he has an unhappy method of betraying his erudition too consciously by recondite allusions and, what is worse, by foreign words. It is somewhat remark- able that his moral laxity and slippery descriptions should have been received favourably by a public then so unaccustomed to such liberties as the German; certainly they would have been tolerated in no other than a Grecian garb, and in no form except that of a philosophic romance; though here we must observe that Wieland's philosophy is far more dangerous than his el- egant licentiousness; the latter addresses itself only to the sen- ses, whilst the former strikes at the very basis of our moral nature.

The last great work of Wieland was his *Oberon,* a story in verse, on which his poetic fame is greatly grounded. It is an arbitrary, and far from harmonious, mixture of the fairy tale and the heroic legend. Then, again, even in the distant age of which it treats, and in the land of fairy, Wieland never forgets his philosophy and himself. How differently Ariosto, whose imitator he once announced himself to be, pictures the same period, displaying all the depth, clearness, and childlike, but healthy, simplicity of the epic poet!

The repose of Wieland's declining years was somewhat dis- turbed by the anxiety of his old friends to remind him of his desertion of the severe morality which he had formerly pro- fessed; but his conciliatory character had its effect even on the most violent of these. In private life, we must do him the justice to say, he was one of the most amiable of mankind; and it is his evident benevolence which has, doubtless, greatly contributed to hide from every eye except that of the critic the prejudicial effects which his works are calculated to produce. (pp. 32-3)

> August Wilhelm von Schlegel, "Schlegel's Lec- tures," in his A. W. Schlegel's Lectures on German Literature from Gottsched to Goethe, *edited by H. G. Fielder, Basil Blackwell, 1944, pp. 13-45.*

ALEXANDER TOLHAUSEN   (essay date 1848)

[*In the following survey of Wieland's works, Tolhausen briefly discusses such topics as the literary influences on the author, his style, and his moral teachings.*]

By manners a Frenchman, by feelings a German, by the spirit of his writings a Greek, Wieland won an audience that was far beyond the average of general readers. He trod a path quite distinct from that of Klopstock and Lessing, and his works belong to a province yet little explored by the mind of a Ger- man. Knowing the great art of appropriating without imitating, he stands conspicuous amongst that class of writers whose works embrace Universality. The school to which Wieland seemed to profess himself, at least in the second period of his life, was that of Epicur; yet a strong inclination to Eclectism is always perceptible in him, inasmuch as he casts the spirit, customs and manners of different countries and ages into one mould, which in spite of a seeming heterogeneity bears always the stamp of a certain originality and refinement of taste. He is—si *magna* licet componere *parvis*—an ingenious perfumer who, combining several essences, produces a sweet delightful scent, and as a French Academician [Hugo] has it: "Le parfum est la musique de l'odorat."—"If I have to make a certain way," says [Wieland] in his *Aristipp,* . . . "on which one may easily go astray, I am glad to find an expert guide; I walk at his side, sometimes even a little before or behind him, without stepping in his traces, or giving up the liberty to make now and then a little circuitous way, or perhaps to listen to a night- ingale in the bushes, to rejoice at a pretty view, or to find out by spelling the inscription of a ruined monument. Philosophy, I think, shares the fate of the noses. What essentially constitutes a nose is generally alike, and yet everybody has a particular one."

Among his earlier poems the epic one: *Arminius,* which he submitted to the inspection of the representative of the Swiss school, Bodmer, shews that he at first was inspired by the muse of Klopstock. Yet naturally prone to the more enticing and sweeter voice of Cupid, he abandoned the heroic line of poetry and devoted himself entirely to the lighter species of composition. It is from this time that may be traced the influence of the writings of Voltaire, Lucian, Shakspeare and Anacreon . . . upon the mind of this poet; for, however much the Messiad, Young and Bodmer were his ideals at first, the spirit of these writers was less adapted to his riper genius, and only made him resort with greater predilection to his more homely department. (pp. 53-6)

The mode of thinking [among German writers] at that time may be divided into three classes, that of the ideal and utter sublime; that which participated of both the ideal and physical in an equal degree; and lastly, that of the entire sensual. Wieland but seldom indulged himself in the latter, he never had the ambition of entering his name in the first class. Whatever Klopstock had conceived of the lofty idea of poetry, Wieland reduced to an earthly shape; he brought his angels and etherial beings within the touch of men, at the risk of dragging them into deformities. (pp. 56-7)

[What], in Wieland, must before all be upheld to admiration, is his fluency of language. His style unites generally to the richness of a scholar, the elegance and laisser-aller of a man who knows the world. Far from becoming pedantic, he moulds his philosophy, sprung from his taste of discrimination, into an expressive and at once charming language. His intuitive spirit of observation enabled him to have a deep insight into the leading principles of the human heart, and his genius rendered those impressions in a shape that bore the stamp of his own views, uncovering at the same time the weakness of human nature and allowing him to indulge in the pleasure of flagellating the "travers" of society with the scourge of his overflowing and unrelenting, but good-natured witticism. This general judgment of both the spirit and style of Wieland may appear somewhat lenient to those who, far from carrying themselves back in history, know of no other scale than that of their time. But as one of his biographers [Gruber] well says: "We must not forget that Wieland lived at a time when it was the custom to wear bag-wigs and stiffened skirts, and to walk with ladies dressed in farthingales, through alleys that were as stiff as the gossiping societies, where the young girls were sitting tightly laced under a towered hair-dress, whilst the old aunts had the exclusive right to let their tongues domineer with Gottschedian broadness and tediousness."

From among his numerous poetical works we distinguish above all his *Oberon.* This poem possesses the happy charm (whatever may be its moral estimate, in the strict sense of the word) to flow in a strain of poetic ease as yet unequalled in its genre. The blooming language of the Orient with the romantic sentiments of the Occident, the stern steel-clad manners of the Europeans with the pompous and effeminate customs of the East, are so happily blended in this poem that the reader's imagination is at once led back to the chivalric age, and becomes acquainted with the customs of a people, with whom the Christian nations stand in so opposite a direction in the mode of thinking. The harmony of versification Wieland exhibited in this poem, and the talent he displayed in describing sceneries of nature, are delighting to the senses, and sink deep into the bosom of him who is an admirer of the beauties of rural life. It is only to be regretted that Wieland did not continue in that department of poetry; for however great the merit of his prosaic works may be, the pre-eminence of his *Oberon* will not be questioned.

Wieland was also a moral writer. By his *Don Sylvio von Rosalva,* the plan of which is borrowed from Cervantes, he endeavours to shew how a misled imagination can fall into extra-

vagancies and even absurdities. At the same time he points out the means of restoring the mind to its natural vigour. His [*Die Geschichte der Abderiten* represents], with an inexhaustible wit and good humour, the folly of petty governments, follies which scarcely in our days can be interpreted without the aid of Clio. [*Der goldene Spiegel*] was composed for the instruction of the Princes of Weimar, who were entrusted to his care; though abounding in wise and moral precepts, this work has but the merit of the then "actualité." On the other hand, *Agathon,* a sort of autobiography, ranks with his most spirited romances, nor did Lessing fail, in his *Dramaturgy,* to bestow great praise upon its author. The idea which pervades it, is to shew how far virtue and spiritual excellence may be attained by the mere powers of nature, how far the character of man is formed by outward circumstances, how much experience, errors, unrelenting exertions and *frequent changes in our mode of thinking,* and before all, good society and good examples, may contribute both to our physical and moral welfare.

Yet with all those brilliant faculties of the mind, Wieland could not win the title of a national poet. He shared the fate of Klopstock, without having imbibed the spirit of that writer. There exists too vast a divergency between these two writers, as to allow to either of them to claim the honour of being the representative of the national feelings: for a poet can only become national when his compositions are imbued with those principles which partake of the leading characteristics of his nation. Neither Klopstock with his worlds above *the* world, nor Wieland with his writings breathing the voluptuous ease of an "homme du monde" were able to dig to their countrymen a well at which they could fling in time of thirst after intellectual refreshment. In short, neither of them became a Homer nor a Virgil. (pp. 57-62)

> *Alexander Tolhausen, "Wieland," in his* Klopstock, Lessing, and Wieland: A Treatise on German Literature, *Williams and Norgate, 1848, pp. 47-63.*

BAYARD TAYLOR (essay date 1879)

[Taylor was a minor American poet, novelist, and travel writer. Here, he points to Wieland's playful and delicate style, particularly as evidenced in Oberon, *in claiming that the author was one of the founders of the Romantic school in German literature.]*

[*Oberon*] is an admirable specimen of what Goethe calls the *naïve* in literature—the free, graceful play of the imagination. Indeed, as a specimen of poetic story-telling, it has not often been excelled in any language. We have, at present, such a story-teller in England—Mr. William Morris—the graces of whose metrical narratives are now delighting us; but their tone, even when he chooses a bright Greek subject, is grave almost to sadness. They are chanted in the minor key, and a sky of gray cloud, or, when brightest, veiled by a hazy mist, hangs over all the landscapes of his verse. Change this tone and atmosphere: let them be clear, fresh and joyous: add sunshine, and pleasant airs, and the multitudinous dance of the waves, and you have the character of Wieland's poetry. His *Oberon* is as charming now as when it was first written. It has all the grace and the melody and the easy movement of Ariosto. The severe critic may say that the poem teaches nothing; that many of the incidents are simply grotesque; that the plot is awkwardly constructed; that the hero exhibits no real heroism, and the fairy king and queen are borrowed from Shakespeare: the reader will always answer—"All this may be true, but the poem is delightful." The secret of *Oberon* seems to me, that Wieland has combined the joyousness and the freedom of the Greek nature, with the form and the manner of the romantic school in literature. . . . [A] light and rapid movement characterizes the whole poem, which seems to have been written only in holidays of the mind. The reading of it, therefore, is not a task, but a pure recreation. Wieland, in this respect, was an unconscious and unintentional reformer. Goethe . . . was led by Lessing to seek for the true principles of literary art; but it is equally certain that he learned of Wieland to relieve and lighten the gravity of his style—to add grace to proportion, and give a playful character to earnest thought.

Wieland must be considered as one of the chief founders of the romantic school. The "Storm and Stress" period, which was simply a fermentation of the conflicting elements—a struggle by means of which the new era of literature grew into existence—commenced about the year 1770, and continued for twenty years. During its existence the Romantic School was developed, separating itself from the classic school, by its freedom of form, its unrestrained sentiment, and its seeking after startling effects. It was a natural retaliation, that France, forty years later, should have borrowed this school from Germany. Wieland was not a partisan in the struggle; neither was he drawn into it, and forced to work his way out again, as were Goethe and Schiller. He belonged to the Romantic school by his nature, and to the classic school by his culture, but the former gave the distinguishing character to his works. (pp. 249-53)

Perhaps ten per cent. of the thirty-six volumes which he left behind him, are now read. The winnowing-mill of Time makes sad havoc with works considered immortal in their day. A great deal of Wieland's productiveness has been blown away as chaff, but enough sound grain remains to account for his influence, and to justify our honorable recognition of his genius. If he did not follow truth with the unselfish devotion of Lessing—if he was not animated by a lofty patriotic purpose, like Klopstock—we nevertheless do not feel inclined to judge him too rigidly. His grace, his humor, his delicate irony and refined though rather shallow appreciation of the element of beauty, disarm us in advance. We cannot escape a hearty friendly feeling for the man who was always so cheerful and amiable, and whose works, light as they may seem in comparison, form a counterpoise for so many of the "heavy weights" in German Literature. (pp. 253-54)

Just such an intellectual temperament as Wieland possessed was needed in his time. The language as well as the literature was in the process of development: there were enough of thoughtful and earnest minds engaged in the work, and they would have fallen too exclusively into the serious, brooding habit of the race, had they not been interrupted by Wieland's playful fancy and his delicate satire. Our English language found all these qualities combined in the one man, Shakespeare, but other countries have not been so fortunate. It required three men—Lessing, Wieland and Goethe—to perform a similar service for the German language. In this respect, the sportive element in Wieland's mind was as valuable as genius. It is certainly rarer. Much of our modern literature lacks the same quality. It betrays the grave labored purpose of the author, as if expression were a stern duty, instead of seeming, as it should seem, free, inevitable and joyous. Goethe says that Wieland was the only member of the Weimar circle who could publish his works in the monthly *Mercury* by instalments, as they were written, without being at all affected by the misconception of the public or the hostile criticism of his rivals. It is pleasant

to contemplate the activity of so serene and cheerful a mind. He never had a following of enthusiastic admirers, like Klopstock or Schiller, but the public regarded him always with a kindly good-will. It was for a time fashionable, in Germany, to depreciate his literary achievements. He has been accused of being governed by French influences, because of his light and volatile nature; but the influence, so far as it existed, soon wore off, and left only the natural resemblance, which was no fault. On the contrary, it was his good fortune and that of his contemporaries. (pp. 255-56)

*Bayard Taylor, "Klopstock, Wieland and Herder,"
in his* Studies in German Literature, *G. P. Putnam's
Sons, 1879, pp. 234-65.*

JOSEPH GOSTWICK (essay date 1882)

[*Gostwick focuses on the moral tone of Wieland's writings.*]

Wieland was a man, comparatively speaking, insignificant. His mind was for the most part imitative. It is not to be understood that he began any new æsthetic movement in literature; the transition most noticeable in his time was made by younger men. Yet it is true that, in his early life, and with deliberate intention, he renounced the old faith and declared himself a teacher of the new. "All the evils of society," said he, "have arisen out of tyranny and superstition." He next went on to show, that neither faith nor authority was now required for the true education of mankind; on the contrary, what was most needed was freedom—a freedom so wide that narrow-minded men would, no doubt, call it licence.

The younger poetical men of his time did not accept generally Wieland's artistic notions of poetry. To suppose that they did so would be far from the truth. But it is true, that Wieland was almost the earliest of those who proposed that, for the future, all connection of general literature with Christianity should be severed; it was determined in his day that poetry and art should be "non-Christian." The general character of the time, when "æsthetic culture" claimed supremacy, was first indicated—so far as religion and morality were concerned—when Wieland—renouncing his early pietism—suddenly changed the moral tone of his writings. (pp. 249-50)

The name of Wieland still holds a place in literary history, while his works, excepting his epic poem *Oberon,* are almost forgotten. They have been praised mostly on account of an easy and fluent style; while their purport has been censured by all critics who believe that true poetry and pure moral culture should be united. (pp. 260-61)

The personal character of Wieland was morally respectable; and he was mostly regarded as an amiable man. These facts make the more remarkable the licentious traits of his stories. In several of his writings he makes such a free use of irony that we are left in doubt respecting his intention. If we accept as serious many passages in his stories, we must come to the conclusion that a singular fixed idea had possession of his mind. He seems to have believed that a tendency to ascetic doctrine and practice was the prevalent error of his own times! To counteract that supposed tendency, he deliberately recommends doctrine and practice that may be called "epicurean" in the worst sense of the word. If he is ever earnest, it is in warning his readers of the unhappy tendencies of strict piety. He cannot forgive the teachers who led him to study in a severe school during his youth; and the object of several of his works is to expose the error of that school. In his poems, *Musarion* and the *Graces,* he repeats, again and again, his censure of ascetic notions of virtue. *Musarion* tells the story of a youth who, by severe early discipline, is led to retire from society, but soon finds out that he is not well qualified for a hermit's life. In [*Der neue Amadis*] the difficulty of finding wisdom and beauty united in one person is playfully described, and the hero, after a vain search for such perfection, marries a plain and intelligent wife. This conclusion, however dull, is the most edifying part of the story, of which some details are treated with great licence. In *Agathon,* a romance in prose, the writer is severe, but only against severity, and again denounces the stern doctrines impressed on his memory in early life. These are now represented by the teachings of an antique philosophy. Agathon, a Greek youth, is educated at Delphi, and afterwards lives at the court of Dionysius, where he learns to regard as impracticable all the moral theories of his early teachers. (pp. 262-63)

Wieland was inspired by no lofty ideas of a poet's mission. The duty of a poet, as he understood it, was to amuse his readers, and to fulfil it he must be, in the first place, conciliatory; he must adapt both his subject and his style to the fashion of his times. The taste of readers in the higher classes of society was still French when he began to write fictions. German literature must be changed, in order that it might be introduced to courts and to the higher circles. Wieland saw the necessity of this change, and while he wrote with gracefulness and vivacity, he extended greatly the range of topics found in light literature, and treated them in a style adapted to the tastes of the upper classes. For them the pious enthusiasm of Klopstock was tiresome, and they complained, not without cause, of his pompous and intricate style. No fault could be found in Lessing's style; but the great critic was a close thinker and wished to make his readers think also. This was in itself intolerable, and, moreover, he had the fault of refusing to write on such topics as the aristocracy cared for. Wieland understood their prejudices, and wrote to suit them. He had been educated under the influence of pietism; but he liberated himself from its restraints, and became as free in the treatment as in the choice of his subjects. This change in both style and purport took place so suddenly that it excited surprise. To use Lessing's words—"Wieland's muse made a sudden descent from heaven to earth!" It may be added, that his literary success was chiefly won by this bold transition. (pp. 264-65)

> *Joseph Gostwick, "Poetry: Klopstock—Wieland,"*
> *in his* German Culture and Christianity: Their Controversy in the Time 1770-1880, *Frederic Norgate,*
> *1882, pp. 248-66.*

KUNO FRANCKE   (essay date 1896)

[*Francke, a German-born American historian and educator, compares Wieland with Klopstock and emphasizes Wieland's role as an interpreter of rationalistic philosophy. This essay was originally published in 1896.*]

While Klopstock leaned to the English taste, Wieland inclined to the French. While Klopstock was an ardent and uncompromising republican, Wieland was in turn an advocate of enlightened absolutism, an admirer of the French Revolution of 1789, and again, after the declaration of the republic, a spokesman of German paternalism. While Klopstock, with a tenacity which came near being stubbornness, clung throughout his life to the spiritual ideals of his youth, Wieland constantly passed from one mental state to another, from pietism to cynicism,

from supernaturalism to materialism, from Platonic to Epicurean views, until at last he persuaded himself that he had found the solution of all moral problems in a *juste milieu* between pleasure and virtue, instinct and duty.

But in spite of this personal contrast between the two men, or rather because of it, Wieland performed a task for German culture closely allied to that performed by Klopstock. He, no less than the latter, helped to prepare the ground for that perfect intellectual freedom and equipoise, that universality of human interest and endeavour which was to be the signal feature of cultivated German society toward the end of the eighteenth century. Klopstock did his part by expanding and elevating the moral sentiment, Wieland did his by fostering a refined sensuality. Klopstock drew his strength from Pietism, Wieland was rooted in Rationalism. He endeavoured to quicken and broaden the realistic current of German literature . . . while Klopstock endeavoured to give a new and stronger impetus to the idealistic current. . . . Both men seem more remarkable to us for their aspirations than for their attainments. Klopstock often soared too high, Wieland still oftener sunk too low. The absence even in the Friderician age of truly national tasks and of a firmly established public opinion imparted to both an eccentric individualism, which in Klopstock appeared as a disregard for the limitations of reality, in Wieland as a capricious delight in its superficial appearances. And yet it is an injustice to both Klopstock and Wieland to speak of their works in a manner which is now only too common, as though they had no message to deliver to our own time, as though the spiritual ardour of the former, the serene sensuousness of the latter had lost their meaning for us moderns.

The first work in which Wieland showed his true fibre was the novel *Agathon.* . . . Up to that time he had been oscillating between weak attempts in the seraphic manner of Klopstock and Young, and equally weak imitations of French rococo literature. Now for the first time he struck a theme which brought out his own literary individuality and which at the same time put him into contact with the strongest intellectual current of the age, the rationalistic movement. To quote his own testimony about the intentions followed out in this novel, he chose the Horatian line: '*Quid virtus et quid sapientia possit*' for its motto, "not as though he wished to show in the character of Agathon what wisdom and virtue are by themselves, but how far a human being through natural power may advance in both; how large a part external circumstances have in our way of thinking, in our good and evil acts, in our wisdom and folly; and how only through experience, mistakes, incessant self-improvement, frequent changes in our mode of thought and, above all, through the example and friendship of wise and good men, we may become wise and good ourselves." In other words, he wished to point out in an object-lesson what the rationalistic philosophy of the time tried to point out theoretically—the true way toward individual perfection; and if this object-lesson appears less convincing to us than it appeared to Lessing when he called *Agathon* "the only novel for thinking men," this much is certain, that in the whole period between the *Simplicissimus* and *Wilhelm Meister* there is no German novel dealing with as broad phases of life in as successful a manner as Wieland's *Agathon.* (pp. 251-53)

Artistically, some of Wieland's later works are superior to *Agathon.* His *Die Abderiten* . . . will forever be the classic representation of German provincial town life in the eighteenth century, with all its insipidity, self-importance, and involuntary humour. (p. 261)

Among Wieland's poetical works, **Musarion** . . . is undoubtedly one of the most graceful and delicate impersonations of his imperturbable serenity and optimism, and of the "charming philosophy" of enlightenment and toleration. . . . (p. 262)

And in all later Romanticism, there is no work which in brilliancy of imagination, in lightness of movement, in crystalline clearness of action, and in golden worth of sentiment surpasses the ever youthful romance of **Oberon** . . . with its changing pictures "of rustic simplicity and oriental splendour, of city tumult and hermit life, of fearful deserts and elysian meadows, of knightly combats and magic dances, of joyful feasts and miserable shipwreck," of delight and grief, hope and despair, of heroism, constancy, friendship, and the final triumph of a stout and trusting heart.

And yet, with all the fuller development of literary skill and artistic finish which later years ripened in Wieland, the true inwardness of his activity, his peculiar significance as a typical representative of his time, was never more clearly brought to the front than in **Agathon.** It is impossible not to see here the first blossoming out of that spirit which was to mature its finest fruit in Goethe's *Faust.* A supreme interest in the problems of inner experience, a supreme faith in the inviolability and sacredness of the individual soul, a supreme desire for harmonious cultivation of all its faculties, an ever ready sympathy even with the wayward and the sinner, an unwavering trust in the intrinsic goodness of human character, and a sublime indifference to passing defects and temporary veilings of its true self,—these are the elements from which the highest and best in the work of Schiller and Goethe sprang, and all of them we find at least foreshadowed in this early work of Wieland.

It is the faithfulness to these principles which gave dignity and purpose to a life which otherwise might have spent itself in trifling levity. It is this which made Wieland one of the foremost shapers of cultivated German opinion toward the end of the eighteenth century. It is this which, with all his peacefulness of temper and adaptability of manner, forced him, too, into the front rank of fighters for popular justice and natural rights. For it is clear that what Wieland considers as the normal, natural, complete man cannot develop in the sphere of autocratic encroachments; and the hope of the race therefore must, according to his own premises, lie, for him, in the establishment and gradual expansion of legitimate freedom. (pp. 262-64)

> *Kuno Francke, "The Age of Frederick the Great and the Height of Enlightenment," in his* A History of German Literature as Determined by Social Forces, *fourth edition, Henry Holt and Company, 1901, pp. 228-300.*

MATTHEW G. BACH (essay date 1922)

[Bach studies Wieland's views on the role of women in society.]

[The] ideas of English and French enlightenment helped to improve the condition of women. The numerous publications and periodicals which dealt with . . . their spiritual and ethical development did not fail to impress the age with the nobility of woman's mission in human society. Though the old sex ideal of woman as a breeder and housekeeper still held sway, a new ethical ideal of womanhood slowly began to assert itself, the ideal of a woman with an individuality of her own, conscious of the dignity of her sex and anxious to be master of her body and soul.

Even those who in practice still clung to the old point of view, owing to the established custom and tradition, in theory at least could not help showing interest and enthusiasm for the new ideal and giving it their moral support.

We shall probably not go amiss in counting also Wieland in this latter class. His very nature made him unfit to become a radical in anything, no matter how advanced his ideas on a subject may have been. His whole philosophy was that of the calm, reasoning thinker, who strives for peace and harmony in everything. Consequently, in the feminist question also, he would never venture with his views into the extremes of the Storm and Stress or of Romanticism, which were esthetically as well as morally uncongenial to his type of mind.

Wieland felt the social injustice that woman had been subjected to as keenly perhaps as many of his contemporaries, and he really devoted the energies of a lifetime toward helping to right this wrong. But his temperament being what it was, he voiced his protest and suggested his remedies as a compromising mediator rather than as a drastic innovator. (pp. 53-4)

To be sure, some of his female characters, like Danae, Lais, Glycerion, Hipparchia profess extremely radical views on love and marriage, but this does not at all mean that the author subscribes to them heart and soul. The fact is, he is using them only as a mouthpiece to express the tendencies of the time or to reflect the influences which were working on him. No doubt Wieland's relations with Julie Bondeli, who . . . expressed a dislike for married life, or his acquaintance with Julie's friend, Marianne Fels, who was a sworn enemy of man, induced him to create characters representing the radical views of those two exceptional women.

What then are Wieland's liberal views on woman's social rights? Aside from occasional references to this matter in most of his writings, four works may be considered as the chief exponents of his theory of woman's subordinate position in human society. Aspasia in **Agathon,** Lais in **Aristipp,** Glycerion in **Menander und Glycerion,** and Hipparchia in **Krates und Hipparchia** advance more or less the same convincing argument in one form or another; if everything is true, Wieland thinks, which misogynists of the different centuries have said about the defects and shortcomings of the female sex, no one else can be blamed for it but man alone. Not by the superiority of his mind but by the brutal force of his muscles, he has usurped all the rights and privileges and reduced woman to a condition little better than that of slavery. Men call themselves the stronger and women the weaker sex. Granted this, woman's weakness is again the result of man's cruelty. By crafty devices and narrow-minded laws he has succeeded in excluding her from all spheres of social, economic and cultural activities and thus prevents her from developing her natural talents and robs her of all opportunity to perfect her individuality.

But Aspasia scorns the idea of woman's being weaker. Is there a man, she asks, no matter how great the strength he may boast of, who in an emergency could go through the same ordeal of suffering as a woman? Cannot the weakest woman often rule the strongest man by a mere look? Woman is by no means inferior to man with regard to intellect and understanding and is even superior to him in matters relating to delicacy of feeling, excellence of taste and judgment and the just appreciation of all things beautiful.

All through these centuries man has tried to keep woman in subjection, for fear he might sometime lose his prerogatives and power if she ever succeeded in rising from her humiliating position. Therefore he deprived her of all means of perfection and confined her to the small and petty circle of domesticity, thus degrading her as the mere toy of his pleasure.

It happens occasionally that some women overcome the obstacle laid in their way and rise above their sisters, but unfortunately they are too powerless to undertake anything for the liberation of their sex. Lais in *Aristipp,* for instance, is such an exceptional woman, combining with all the charms of external beauty the rare qualities of a highly cultured and refined personality. For this very reason she feels all the more the humiliation to which woman is subjected and her entire nature revolts against this man-made system. It is through her mouth that Wieland criticizes the conditions of his time. She is not a woman of Sappho's type, who would plunge to death from the Leucadian rocks for the love of a Phaon, and yet she is fully aware of the fact that the association with a man was a thousand times more agreeable to her than the company of Greek sisters. And she can see the reason for it in nothing else than the very low level of woman's intellectual equipment.

Greek education—and one might as well substitute ''German'' for the word ''Greek,''—says Lais, is little concerned in the development of woman's soul. Women are raised to become housewives. The Greek man expects from his wife no other qualification than the ability to bear beautiful children, to manage her servants, and to attend to her spinning-wheel. If she happens to be chaste and modest, avoids looking at other men, and thinks that the sun rises and sets with her husband, then he is very happy and thanks the gods for having granted him so virtuous a wife. But why should he not be satisfied? asks Lais. He does not have to see his wife much and can easily escape the boredom of her highly uninteresting company. Should he feel a desire for more attractive association with women, he can either keep a companion outside of wedlock or spend his free time in the house of hetairas. And one really must not wonder why man should seek his diversion outside his home and family. How can one expect him to find interest in the prattle of a wife who outside of her associations with ignorant servants or gossipy cousins and neighbors has no other contact with the world? (pp. 54-7)

But what of the woman whom Mother Nature had endowed with all the gifts to please, the woman whose mind does not allow itself to be wedged into the limited sphere of domestic routine? Shall she sacrifice her life's happiness to the demands of a time-worn custom of the land, or shall she purchase her freedom of will and independence of action at the price of being classed as an outcast? Lais does not hesitate to choose the fate of a hetaira, because only as such has she the opportunity to develop her individuality. And, in Aristipp's opinion, Lais makes no mistake; for it is not the class that lends dignity to the individual, but the individual that ennobles the class. Besides, no class is immune, maintains Lais, against certain preconceived opinions and prejudices. Why, even the honorable and worthy matrons are generally spoken of as stupid geese and magpies; or if they happen to be clever enough, they are considered hypocrites who spend their days and nights in doing nothing but seeking ways and means of deceiving their husbands and thus enjoying both the free privileges of the despised hetairas and the respect which is due the married woman.

A woman who wants to maintain her independence must look upon the male sex as upon a hostile power with which she must never enter into peaceful and sincere relations unless she be prepared to sacrifice her welfare. The reason why woman

should adopt this hostile attitude toward man is clear enough when one considers the shameful treatment accorded her by him all through the ages of history.

Social conventions have brought about a truce between the sexes, but in reality this apparent peace offers men only another way of continuing warfare. Since laws prohibit men the use of their muscles in the subjugation of women, they succeed in ensnaring them by their mendacious flattery and caresses. A very sensitive nature, a vivid imagination, and a too sympathetic heart are on the one side the noblest part of woman's character; but on the other they are the very things that cause her undoing. Through their tenderness and magnanimity they fall an easy prey to men's wiles.

Nature has endowed every creature with a weapon for defence. Woman's only protection in this struggle of the sexes is her beauty, but unfortunately it has proved to be a two-edged sword because it is never granted with the understanding how to use it advantageously. In order to regain her independence and at the same time retain her influence over man, woman must first of all conceive an exalted opinion of the dignity of her own sex and then devote all her energies to the development of her spiritual faculties. To attempt the liberation of the entire female sex is out of the question, but every woman should try at least individually to contribute to the uplift of as many of her sisters as she is able to reach. The woman who in addition to her external charms possesses also a superior mind, the woman who can appeal not only to the sensuous but also to the spiritual side of man, the woman who can assist him in his daily occupation by her excellent judgment and cheer him in his distress by her wit and humor, such a woman is destined to rule over hearts in human society. ''Slave or free, a beautiful woman who knows her power and also how to use it is a queen wherever she happens to be.'' (pp. 58-60)

Wieland fell in line with those of his contemporaries who advocated an education for woman as a necessary means for her social and moral uplift. He demanded equal rights with men ''for that sex which nature and our social constitution have brought into the tenderest and closest relationship with us . . . so that half of humanity . . . may be freed from a humiliating and oppressive condition of slavery and reinstated into the whole dignity which is due it.''

Wieland attacked the problem of woman's education as early as 1758 in his *Theages.* But here he still sees the achievement of perfection for woman in the beauty of her soul and the charm of her character. He thinks it a great misfortune that these ''Grazien,'' which are an inherent part of woman's nature, are being destroyed by the force of a wrong bringing-up. . . . (p. 61)

Gradually, however, Wieland comes to the conclusion that beauty and grace are not the prime requisites for perfection and he lays all the emphasis on culture and education. (p. 62)

Wieland combatted the old fashioned idea of woman's education which forbade her going beyond the mechanical knowledge of the catechism, a few Aesopian fables, and the ability to scribble a few necessary items in her daily marketing list. In *Krates und Hipparchia* he introduces with very subtle sarcasm the heroine's aunt Leokonoe as the representative of this conservative view. She strenuously opposes her niece's assertion of her independence by saying:

> I never liked to see you find more pleasure in
> books, which we women do not understand,
> than in working at the spinning wheel. In our

grandmothers' time, girls had enough education when they knew half a dozen Aesopian fables from memory and could write in a legible hand their daily marketing memorandum. The less a girl saw and heard, the less she asked, the better she was thought to have been brought up; and no honorable matron in the whole of Attica ever dared to dream of being on an equal footing with her husband or to complain about subjugation, because law and customary tradition have since time immemorial granted us a separate gynaeceon, where we alone rule.

Wieland missed no opportunity of contributing to what might raise the educational standards of women, and he lent full support to any undertaking which had in view the improvement of woman's condition. In his preface to the *Damenbibliothek,* written in Weimar, September 30, 1785, he says that he is happy to help the editor in his undertaking for the moral and cultural uplift of woman, "since nothing could be more pleasant to me than to devote part of my time to the sex which I shall honor and love as long as I am capable of loving anything and whose service has been my most ardent desire from my earliest youth."

When he made Sophie La Roche's first novel public, though she had enjoined upon him the strictest secrecy about it, he apologized to her "for not having been able to resist the desire to present all virtuous mothers and all amiable daughters of our nation with such a work: for it seemed to me best suited to promote among your sex, and even among my own, wisdom and virtue, the sole great merits of mankind, the only sources of true happiness."

According to Wieland an enlightened and civilized nation ought not to question whether women, "our mothers, wives, sisters, and daughters," are entitled to share in the national culture and to derive the benefits therefrom the same as man. Nor should it be a question of woman's capacity to vie with man, for it has been proven time and again that women are not inferior to men in reasoning power and understanding.

Already in the preface to his works of 1759 he has gone so far as to assert the superior critical judgment of women with regard to literary productions. Scholars, he thinks, are rarely good and reliable judges of poetical works. He prefers the opinion of men of the world and of experience, but more particularly that of the "fair sex," many of whom are called upon to decide what should please, for nature itself has made them the model of everything that is beautiful and charming. . . . Their delicacy of feeling, vividness of imagination, and fine grasp of what is beautiful, sublime and great makes them capable of enjoying the works of genius and of determining their actual value.

The real question is how far woman should go in her search after knowledge and education. Wieland thinks that the very nature of woman, together with her sphere of activity, points out the limits beyond which her desire for culture and knowledge should not go. He would rather have no line drawn restricting woman's entry into the realm of learning, particularly when she feels herself fitted for it and has no domestic duties to attend to. But on the whole he would like to see her take up those studies which would tend directly to make her "wiser, lovelier, and happier."

[Wieland asserts that woman] is by nature called upon to become a wife and mother. Her ability to educate her children grows naturally enough in the same proportion as her enlight-

enment, practical knowledge, and nobility of sentiment increase. Since woman really gives her sons their start in education she ought not to be ignorant of the national and political conditions of her country. Otherwise, how is she to inculcate in her child the noble feelings of patriotism and love for the nation of which he is a part?

Following the general tendency of his time, to diffuse knowledge among the female sex by providing woman with the corresponding educational means, Wieland also encouraged special publications for women, like the *Allegemeine Damenbibliothek,* edited by K. L. Reinhold, . . . and the *Historischer Kalender für Damen* under the editorship of Schiller.

In introducing the second annual number of Schiller's historical almanac to the reading public, Wieland emphasizes its unique importance and foremost place among the publications of its kind. The purpose of it, he argues, is not to entertain women by frivolities, but to enlighten them, to improve their understanding, and to ennoble their character. He maintains that at a time when woman is admitted to share unrestrictedly in the national culture, she should not be merely satisfied with cultivating her domestic virtues and social qualifications. The perfection of her soul also gives her the right to share with man the interest in and love for the fatherland. Women are, therefore, to learn to consider themselves as partners in the national association and as members of the political body of which they form a part. The poet is indignant at the fact that so many women, even of the higher classes, are completely ignorant of the history of their own country, while they are well informed on that of other lands. What makes the disgrace still greater is that German women are ashamed of being called Germans and look down upon everything that German literature, art or industry have produced. He therefore calls upon the representative men of the nation to unite their efforts towards the promotion of a more patriotic spirit among women by emphasizing above all the great national affairs and by making German themes such as language and history the object of their literary discussion. (pp. 62-6)

> *Matthew G. Bach, in his* Wieland's Attitude toward Woman and Her Cultural and Social Relations, *Columbia University Press, 1922, 100 p.*

JOHN C. BLANKENAGEL   (essay date 1926)

[*Blankenagel discusses the island scene in* Oberon, *contrasting this section of the poem with the rest of the work and analyzing Wieland's attitude toward nature.*]

That part of Wieland's *Oberon* which depicts the life of Hüon and Rezia on the island where they have been shipwrecked differs so essentially in tone, background, motivation, and thought from the rest of the poem as to constitute almost a separate entity. The ideas which the author here expresses may seem inconsistent with the spirit of romantic adventure which characterizes this work in general. Nevertheless, this episode, covering a period of about three years, makes a distinct break in the succession of outward adventures, and turns the reader's attention to the development of the inward qualities of the castaways. This affords the author a fitting opportunity to introduce ideas dealing with man's return to a state of nature, with nature herself, and with the mystic merging of heaven and earth in the soul of man. It is with these ideas and the contrast which they present to the rest of the poem that this paper is concerned.

It should be noted at the outset that the superior, playfully ironic tone which Wieland frequently employs toward his characters and themes is noticeably absent when the misfortunes of Hüon and Rezia begin. Moreover, his fondness for clever, salacious allusions gives way to a serious note in which ethical and spiritual values are stressed. The usual stilted reference to mythological characters is entirely lacking in this episode. The absence of such mannerisms and conventional artificialities marks the author's more intimate and personal approach to his subject and is indicative of the warmer sympathy he manifests.

The supernatural elements that play so prominent a part in *Oberon* are almost wholly wanting in the island episode. Gone are the magic horn, giants, dwarfs, hobgoblins, elves and ghosts, the carriages drawn by leopards or propelled through the air by swans, the lions with flames of fire darting forth from their eyes, the magic cup, the voices speaking out of the storm, and other fanciful inventions of fairy legend. Only the magic ring remains, and its supernatural influence ends with the rescue of Hüon and Rezia from death in the angry waters. Apart from the ring, it is largely the unobtrusive presence of Titania on the island that serves as an incidental reminder of a fairy myth. Her rôle is here limited to appearing to Rezia like a dream-vision at the birth of Hüonnet, to the abduction of the latter, and to the sudden transformation of the island into a desert waste at the death of the hermit. The liberation of Hüon, who had been abandoned on the island lashed to a tree, is the remaining vestige of the supernatural in this scene. Obviously, therefore, this element is reduced to a minimum and is of slight importance. It has given way to a scene and to events of rather concrete, realistic aspect, and of natural motivation. Here the lovers have an opportunity to manifest their truly human qualities under severely trying circumstances and without supernatural means to aid them. This brings them much closer to the reader by lending them a human interest which heroes of a supernatural type can scarcely inspire.

The island scene is characterized further by its kinship with the many "Robinsonaden" that followed in the wake of Defoe's *Robinson Crusoe*. Here is another repetition of the experiences of people who have been washed ashore on an apparently uninhabited island and forced to shift for themselves. Hüon and Rezia, however, are temporarily in a worse plight, since they are without supplies and implements rescued from shipwreck, having escaped with their lives alone. At some length Wieland portrays their first attempts at finding shelter, food and drink, and the difficulties attendant upon eking out a scant existence in a desert region where dates, roots, berries, eggs, and an occasional half-devoured fish snatched from a bird of prey are their sole food. But the very fact that Wieland allows these troubles to end with Hüon's subsequent discovery of the hermit is an indication that he is less concerned with all those details that mark the progress of the ordinary "Robinsonade." He is interested primarily in picturing the development of sterner human qualities in the lovers under most trying conditions. It is here that such virtues as fortitude, constancy, and continence are tested and strengthened. In this manner the genuineness of their affection, which is of fundamental importance in ultimately solving the Oberon-Titania plot, is clearly demonstrated. (pp. 161-63)

Another significant aspect of Hüon's and Rezia's sojourn on the island is the fact that they and the old hermit, Alfonso, whose habitation they eventually share, live virtually in a state of nature. In spite of his protests against Rousseau's views on the corruption of mankind through civilization, Wieland stages the crucial testing of the steadfastness of the lovers against a primitive background and in utter isolation from society. Moreover, as if to stress the virtues born and developed in simple life close to nature and far away from the over-refinements of civilization, Wieland emphasizes the character of the hermit and its influence upon Hüon and Rezia. With much detail the author portrays the striking contrast between the vanity of the artificial court life formerly led by Alfonso and the serene peacefulness of his present natural existence. (p. 163)

In the island episode, Wieland becomes spontaneous in his treatment of nature. Just as he warms up here to his theme and to his characters, so he also divests himself of a stilted mode of describing nature. She no longer serves as an artificial embellishment of conventional design. Instead of being drawn merely as a picturesque background or as an arabesque border, nature here plays a significant, a personal part. She is a companion, an associate in joys and sorrows, a living element which inspires mood and sentiment, and his sympathy with the human soul. Alfonso's soul is characterized as open only to truth, as open only to nature and clearly attuned to her, the magic power of the sunlight often bringing him back from a grave of melancholy. Contact with nature frees him from all grief; in her he sees the image of the creator, and in her contemplation lies the source of his peacefulness and happiness. Furthermore, nature is depicted as having a profound effect upon Hüon and Rezia. When the spirit of gloom prevails, when the fields mourn in dull silence, and melancholy hovers in the snow cloud, Hüon plays the harp and Rezia sings to dispel this brooding shadow. In contrast herewith Wieland pictures the bright winter which entices them forth, the stern cold rising like mist from the sea, the gleaming white snow on the mountains, and the evening sun setting in a purple glow. Here nature is their companion, inviting them to bathe in the pure stream of cold air surrounded by marvels of beauty and splendor. She is their benefactor, the source of their vigor, cheering them through and through, and freeing them from grief.

But nature is shown also in relation to the mood of the fairy queen Titania. While abandoned by the wrathful Oberon she hates the jesting of the elves, the dance in the moonlight and even beautiful May with her garment of roses. She flies through the empty airy spaces in the stormwind, finds rest nowhere and sadly seeks a place suited to her melancholy. This she finally discovers on a barren island in the great ocean. Towering up out of black, monstrous, volcanic ruins, it attracts her by its bleakness and impels her to direct her aimless flight toward it. Reeling down out of the air, she plunges into a black cave to weep undisturbed over her existence and, if possible, to turn into a lifeless stone among these very boulders. For a time her mood is not at all affected by the beautiful sun which comes to charm the rocks about her with magic light. Lying on a stone as on a sacrificial hearth she craves death. But in due time her heart responds, hope reawakens, and what had seemed unbearable fades away like a dream. As soon as her despondency ends she feels a sense of horror at the dark abysses in which she had been content to imprison herself. Quickly she causes some of the barren cliffs to disappear and an Elysium to stand before her. Thus nature and mood are not merely in accord, but mood refashions nature in accord with itself.

Mood as induced by nature is pictured as follows: In the evening, when their day's work has been completed, the hermit, Hüon, Rezia and their child are refreshed by the glory and splendor of the starry heaven; yet they are submerged into this sea of wonders with an awe tinged with ominous forebodings.

These presentiments of impending evil are fulfilled, for during the night the hermit dies, Hüonnet is abducted by Titania and the entire island soon resumes its former air of desolation and ruin, thereby reflecting the dismay and despair of the unhappy parents. No blade of grass remains; grove, garden and flowers have disappeared, leaving only a black, inhospitable scene of inaccessible cliffs and black, misshapen rocks.

Nature is endowed by Wieland with a moral sense, for as soon as Hüon and Rezia had been faithless to the command of chastity, the heavens turned black, all the stars became extinct, fierce winds were unleashed, the thunder rolled, and with fearful roaring an unparalleled storm broke loose. The earth's axis cracked, black clouds poured forth streams of fire, the sea raged and waves rose up like mountains. These details, it is true, are not given in the island scene itself, yet they immediately precede it and help give rise to it. Moreover, in the island episode reference is made to this outraged sensibility in the significant statement that all nature revolted against Hüon as soon as he yielded to the forbidden impulse of love. At the end of the eighth canto Wieland addresses his readers directly on the moral aspect of nature, declaring that the greatest gift nature can bestow, a treasure which is not lost but which follows man into a better life beyond, is a feeling heart and a pure mind.

Strangely enough, Wieland, who is generally regarded as a pronounced rationalist, enters the realm of mysticism in his characterization of Alfonso's soul life. Alfonso, says he, already belongs more to the next world than to this. At night, when he is half wrapped in slumber, his ears hear voices like those of angels wafted gently from the forest. Then it seems to him that the thin wall which separates him from his beloved ones falls. His inmost being unfolds, a sacred flame shines from his breast, and in the pure light of the invisible world his soul beholds heavenly visions. These endure even when his mildly bewildered eyes have closed in slumber. And when the morning sun again reveals nature's scene about him this state still continues. A gleam of heavenly bliss transfigures rock and grove, shines through and completely fills them; everywhere and in all creatures Alfonso then sees the image of the great, uncreated being, just as the image of the sun is visible floating in the dewdrop. Thus, in his spirit, heaven and earth finally merge imperceptibly into one. His very being seems to be aroused. And with it, at this vast distance from the turmoil of passion, in the sacredness that surrounds him, there awakens the purest of all senses. (pp. 163-66)

After the hermit's death the island episode is soon brought to a close. By dint of contrast with the rest of the poem, this scene serves to bring out in bold relief the inconsistency and the duality of Wieland's character. The master of playful irony manifests a warm, human interest; detached superiority yields to spontaneity; the antagonist of Rousseau depicts society as a corrupting influence and portrays nature as the undefiled source of goodness; the rationalist reverts to his earlier mystic tendency. (p. 166)

> *John C. Blankenagel, "The Island Scene in Wieland's 'Oberon'," in* PMLA, *41, Vol. XLI, No. 1, March, 1926, pp. 161-66.*

R. PASCAL   (essay date 1937)

[*Pascal discusses Wieland's attitude toward Shakespeare's works.*]

Wieland's translation of twenty-two [Shakespeare] plays appeared from 1762 to 1766, and from this time Shakespeare became the affair of all educated Germans.

The translation was carried through in a spirit of admiration and disgust, amused interest and boredom—in the end an affair of Wieland's leisure hours ("ein guter Teil der Arbeit ist fast mechanisch"). The first play tackled, *A Midsummer Night's Dream,* was translated into verse (with the exception, of course, of Shakespeare's prose passages); afterwards Wieland lacked the patience and the reverence for this, and even short lyrics are sometimes given in prose. The translations become more and more inaccurate and poor; Wieland shows himself, in the notes, more and more vexed with Shakespeare's coarseness, bad taste, etc.; he sees in Shakespeare's characters only eccentrics of a peculiarly British type—Hamlet is a "humorist"—Wieland is as condescending to the dramatist as was Voltaire in the *Lettres sur les Anglais* of 1734. For his critical notes Wieland used only Voltaire's criticism and the bad Pope-Warburton edition of 1747. As Preface Wieland translated Pope's Preface of 1725.

It seems at first sight curious that a man with so unstable and inadequate an appreciation of Shakespeare should have been the agent for the passionate Shakespeare cult of the following years. The reason lies very largely in the relationship between Wieland and the public. He was just emancipating himself from the intense and burdensome pietism in which his pious colleague Bodmer indulged. Shakespeare was a step on the way to the aristocratic, man-of-the-world manner of his later years. In strong contrast to the feeling of moral responsibility among the majority of his contemporaries, Wieland was attracted by the individualism of Shakespeare—and particularly by Shakespeare's fancifulness in such comedies as *A Midsummer Night's Dream, The Tempest,* etc. Wieland did not oppose the normal morality with the individualism of Shakespeare—this was reserved for the younger generation; he found in Shakespeare's fancy a preliminary stage of opposition, a flight into an unreal world. Thus Wieland's first Shakespearean production at Biberach, 1761, was a mixture of *The Tempest* and *A Midsummer Night's Dream;* and where Shakespearean elements are traceable in Wieland's work, as in **Don Sylvio von Rosalva** and **Oberon,** they belong to this world of fancy. Thus it was that, in an age of moral earnestness, it was the hedonist who translated Shakespeare. (pp. 7-8)

> *R. Pascal, in an introduction to his* Shakespeare in Germany: 1740-1815, *Cambridge at the University Press, 1937, pp. 1-36.*

GUY STERN   (essay date 1954)

[*Stern argues that the Jacinte episode of* Don Sylvio *is a satiric attack on the works of Samuel Richardson that does not, as some critics have contended, impair the unity of the novel.*]

Most German novels of the eighteenth century suffer from a common malady: a formlessness of structure and a rambling mode of narration which often detract from any artistic merit the novel may possess. Wieland's satiric novel, **Don Sylvio von Rosalva,** one of the striking exceptions to this general rule, has therefore justly been praised for its tightly knit structure and carefully planned plot development. Yet, frequently, this praise has been qualified by some critical comments aimed at Wieland's inclusion of two, at first glance, completely discursive episodes, which in the opinion of some, seriously impair the hard-won cohesiveness of the work. Is this really the case? Further study, I believe, especially of the functions of these episodes, will show that both, even the oft-condemned story of Jacinte, play an essential role in furthering the novel's polemic intent and are therefore integral parts of the work. Far from impairing the structure, Wieland achieved in this work, in a manner reminiscent of Henry Fielding's concentrated story management, a dramatic unity and technical polish not duplicated by him in any other novel, not even in *Agathon,* a work characterized by the author as "approaching, in some aspects, the manner of Fielding."

The fairy tale of Prince Biribinker, the other episode, can be (and has been) defended on rather obvious functional grounds: it provides the author with an additional weapon for his attack on fairy tales. By relating a tale even more fantastic than the eighteenth-century French inventions, he scores and accentuates their weaknesses.

Wieland's inclusion of Jacinte's life story, has, on the other hand, often been considered a major aesthetic flaw of the novel, seemingly forming a long-winded subplot which reflects a spirit directly opposed to that of the rest of the novel. Victor Michel believes that the Jacinte episode is no more an integral part of *Don Sylvio* than the Danae story is of *Agathon,* while an excellent work on the eighteenth-century German novel, among others, states that the "History of Jacinte" marks the author's temporary return to an earlier phase of his creative life, when he, very much influenced by Samuel Richardson, wrote numerous works interwoven with moralizing observations. Although this work by Margot Wesly shows a clear insight into Wieland's development as a writer (Wieland frequently did revert to the moralistic approach of his early period), her hypothesis seems scarcely adequate in explaining the presence of an apparently straightforward Richardsonian moralizing narrative in a novel described in such a standard reference work as Merker-Stammler as "hostile to Richardson."

Why then did Wieland add this panegyric to feminine virtue to a novel featuring otherwise no characters of prudish disposition, a narrative which includes (in the Biribinker episode) some who are downright wanton, and which lampoons all prudes in the person of Donna Mencia? Granted that Wieland was never averse to pointing a moral in his works, it still seems incongruous that he should choose in *Don Sylvio* one running directly counter to his avowed intention of "hurting certain prudes."

Wieland himself calls attention to this obvious incongruity; in a paragraph added to the second edition of *Don Sylvio,* he shows apparent agreement with Musäus' unfavorable review of this episode. Yet he also states that more than *one* (italics Wieland's) reason prevented him from presenting it more vividly and with more wit. . . . This seems to suggest that the episode's rather pedestrian mode of narration was deliberate. Analysis of the episode heightens the impression that Wieland could easily have changed it in a variety of ways, had he wished to do so. He could have reduced Jacinte's history to a few pages, without materially affecting the main plot, or else, among other possibilities, have enlivened it by giving even greater prominence to the erotic scenes. Why was Wieland unwilling to avail himself of these or other possibilities?

The not unreasonable assumption that an identical purpose underlies the two different episodes would at once solve one of the puzzles: Wieland's tongue-in-cheek attitude to Jacinte. An ironic intent would explain the purpose of such lines as: "We are very much afraid that the quick and half-open glance with which our readers have, yawning, hurried over this narrative has only too well borne out the judgment of this critic [Musäus], so that it would not be advisable to say anything in defense or

extenuation of the young lady. We conclude from the boredom which we ourselves experienced when, after seven years, we were forced to reread this story what is likely to happen to other people." . . . Elsewhere, Wieland does "not blame the readers, if they wish to see it [Jacinte's story] come to an end." . . . His sarcasm suggests a similarity between the two episodes not only in intent but also in method: as "Biribinker" led the whole genre of fairy tales to the point of absurdity by extravagance, the tedious moralizing of Jacinte's tale might well be designed to point up, by a similar exaggeration, the boredom characteristic of moral narratives of the Richardsonian type.

Does Wieland, in *Don Sylvio,* designate any literary works as boring? He indeed speaks of a multitude of "poor and mediocre, earnestly moralizing books of all forms, which disguised by promising titles depress the whole world with commonplace observations, distorted, hasty, and undigested thoughts, frosty declamations, and pious wishes of their boring authors." . . . Obviously Wieland is attacking the moralizing type of novel, a fact further borne out by several such attacks in *Agathon.* "Before you know it a book is finished which by its strict moral tone, its sparkling maxims, its actions and characters, each one a model, startles into applause all those good people who think every work excellent which praises virtue. . . . In vain may a suspicious literary critic shout himself hoarse that such a work demonstrates the ability of its author as little as it benefits the world." . . . But Wieland, not content with leaving his satire on such general terms, at one point interrupts the narrative of Jacinte to remark that "even the world-famous Pamela herself could not have acted more irreproachably, more nobly than she." . . . Wieland, by this time a violent foe of Richardson's moral heroes, did not mean this comparison as a compliment, but intended it as an ironic jibe, thus providing a key to the entire episode. It is, though more subtle and devious than Fielding's *Shamela* and *Joseph Andrews,* nonetheless a tangible satire on Richardson's *Pamela.*

Further evidence for this rests on two foundations: direct parallels with Richardson's original and with other previous satires attacking it. Jacinte's imprisonment in the house of the marquis, under guard of an elderly virago not unlike the ill-reputed Mrs. Jewkes, is reminiscent of Pamela's "Babylonian captivity" on Mr. B's estate; her pursuits and hair-breadth escapes in the marquis' bedroom have a strong Richardsonian flavor. Like Pamela, Jacinte threatens to commit suicide rather than surrender her virtue, giving Wieland the opportunity to have one of the bystanders say, sarcastically "Oh, this is beginning to become tragic . . . did anyone ever see anything like it: This is even more than Lucretia; for she at least wanted to test first whether it was worthwhile to stab herself." . . . Pamela's coquettish tricks of "putting off" her importunate lover by various artifices are emulated by Jacinte, who frankly admits having "displayed no small gift for coquetry" upon one occasion. . . . The steadfastness and virtue of both young ladies is fortified by thoughts of their parents, a rather far-fetched sentiment in the case of Jacinte, who, in Richardsonian style, invokes parents completely unknown to her. "Oh ye, whose blood animates this heart . . . whoever you may be, my heart tells me that you deserve to have a daughter whom you some day may acknowledge as such without blushing." . . . Jacinte, like Pamela, is addicted to fainting, provoking Wieland's remark that "the fainting of beautiful Jacinte was as harmless as those of all young ladies usually are, whether they have their basis in an excess of pain or pleasure." . . . Finally, Pamela and Jacinte constantly bandy about the words "virtue" and "innocence": both ladies, it would seem, protest too much.

Wieland further reveals the true character of the apparently virtuous maiden by using the same weapons as Fielding, the bludgeon of *Shamela* and the rapier of *Joseph Andrews*. The relation to the latter work becomes immediately apparent in some external similarities between the figures of Fielding's Pamela and Jacinte: both girls are the sisters of the hero; in both families the true relationship is obscured because one of the children has been abducted by gypsies before the story opens. More important is the internal resemblance. The sisters of both heroes have one thing in common: neither is quite what she seems. For example, Don Gabriel, during his narration of the Biribinker story, speaks cryptically of a talisman, used as a chastity belt. Don Sylvio, in his naïveté, understanding neither the function nor the position of the object, asks for a fuller explanation; Jacinte is obviously not as innocent as her brother: "The whole company, *the beautiful Jacinte not excepted,* smiled at this [Sylvio's] remark" (italics mine). Does not Wieland, by singling out Jacinte at this occasion, clearly show his satiric intent?

More decisive to my case is the scene in which Jacinte is revealed as a hypocrite. Like Fielding's Pamela, she is actually far less good-hearted than she appears at first glance. When her friend Estella, answering her call for help, is in turn attacked by a would-be ravisher, Jacinte terms this merely an "unhoped-for (or unexpected) change" ("unverhoffte Veränderung"), leaves her hard-pressed friend to shift for herself, and flees the scene of battle.... As long as she can preserve her jealously guarded virtue, she is little concerned whether or not her friend is raped.

Wieland employs still blunter methods to unmask the young lady, especially the traditional device of making a character convict himself: she herself plants the first doubts of her credibility. Fielding used this method in *Shamela*: Wieland lets Jacinte unconsciously convict herself. No one in her audience has expressed the slightest doubt of her story when she, for no reason, offers the following apologia: "The world, which always judges without knowing [the facts] or making the effort to investigate, has attributed artful intentions to me, of which the uprightness of my soul would never have been capable. However, I have placated myself with the fact that Don Eugenio knows me better. And when I carry out a resolution of long standing, I hope that even my severest critics will become reconciled to the respect he has shown me." ... Her resolution, significantly never carried out, is to enter a cloister. *Qui s'excuse, s'accuse.* Jacinte gives us even more precise information as to the charges against her. "He [the marquis] got very enraged at me, made the charge that my prudery was nothing but an artifice, whereby I intended to drive him to the folly of sacrificing his honor to me, and swore that he would have me at a cheaper price...." As it turns out, the marquis, though mistaken as to the object of her designs, does correctly predict her course of action. Her prim behavior eventually leads to a marriage with Don Eugenio. If the accusations of the marquis can be still further substantiated, then it can safely be said that Jacinte's behavior closely parallels the duplicity of *Shamela*'s heroine: She artfully plays the prude with a wedding ring as her incentive. Let us call another witness. Aside from the young lady herself, there are two other persons acquainted with her story, her lover, Don Eugenio, and Teresilla, her chambermaid. The former, as might be expected, is a "friendly witness"; Teresilla, however, provides her mistress with a

completely different character. To be sure, we are warned (otherwise the satire would become obvious) that her story, "*except for the chief circumstances* (italics mine) is probably as apocryphal as most maids' ... anecdotes about their mistresses." ... The reader himself must decide where "the chief circumstances" begin and end, where Teresilla tells truth and where falsehood.

> Pedrillo learned in this manner that Donna Jacinte was neither more nor less a Donna than any woman who hangs her washing on a fence.... For some time now she had caused quite a stir on the Granada stage and had had no fewer lovers ... than every man she encountered. Among these, no one had, however, exerted greater effort to conquer her heart than Don Fernand of Zamor, a very rich, young cavalier, who had gone to terrific trouble and expense for her, without, as far as people knew, having been able to receive the least thing from her. In short, among so many who had sighed for her, Don Eugenio of Lirias had been the only one whose passion—as virtuous as it was violent—she had apparently, if not encouraged, at least tolerated. However, no one who knew Donna Jacinte was so stupid as to be deceived by the appearance of strict virtue. It was an established fact that she was in love with Don Eugenio to excess and that she would not have been long cruel to him, if she had not had it in mind to bring him to a point where he would even commit the folly of marrying her....

As far as the reader can tell, Teresilla, despite her treachery toward her mistress (she assists in furthering the designs of Don Ferdinand upon Jacinte), is telling the truth according to her lights. Her assertion that Jacinte is no donna is made in good faith: only later does it emerge that Jacinte is Don Sylvio's long-lost sister. Therefore, if we take Wieland at his word and accept the salient facts of Teresilla's testimony, then we may, with a great deal of certitude, conclude that Wieland, in the character of Jacinte, set up a target for himself, at which he slyly but repeatedly fires as Fielding did at Richardon's heroine.

There is one major objection to such an assumption: in the main body of the novel Jacinte is highly regarded by all characters; the hero, upon first seeing her, feels at once brotherly affection toward her. However, Fielding also has Joseph treat his sister with cordiality and affection. In the descriptions of her no unkind word is said; all her inherent cunning and wickedness are shown by what she *does*. Besides, since both Fielding and Wieland deliberately avoided characters of a completely black or white hue, it is scarcely surprising that even persons serving as targets for their satiric barbs should have some good qualities.

It has often been said that the Jacinte story does not quite fit into the over-all tendency of **Don Sylvio**. "The life story of Jacinte has been put together ("zusammengeschrieben") acccording to old recipes and shows how even an innovator cannot free himself from old habits." Indeed, taken at face value, the Jacinte episode would cancel out much of the novel's satire: the attack on Donna Mencia is dulled by eulogizing her niece's virtue. The inner bond of the work, a reckoning with *Schwärmerei*, would seem to be weakened by Jacinte's story.

My hypothesis, on the other hand, would remove all objections of that nature. The Jacinte story, by its satiric intent a parallel to the narrative as a whole, could no longer be considered an extraneous element. Don Sylvio is the tool by which the stories of Madame d'Aulnoy and her likes are ridiculed; his sister is the means for mocking Richardson. Seen as a parodistic satire, the story of Jacinte assumes in Wieland's works a place similar to *Joseph Andrews* and *Shamela* in those of Fielding's. (pp. 96-101)

Guy Stern, ''Saint or Hypocrite? Study of Wieland's 'Jacinte Episode','' in The Germanic Review, Vol. XXIX, No. 2, Spring, 1954, pp. 96-101.

JAMES A. McNEELY (essay date 1961)

[*McNeely delineates the elements of historicism and rationalism in Wieland's social and political thought.*]

In contrast to most prominent writers of the German Enlightenment, Christoph Martin Wieland had a profound, intrinsic interest in the problems of society and government. At the same time, he was endowed with a vivid sense of historical perspective, which enabled him to achieve a considerable degree of objectivity in his social and political thought. Wieland himself was not unaware of the objective element in his writings. He was, in fact, extremely proud of it, and he often wrote—with characteristic self-irony—as if he alone had the secret key by means of which the events and personages of history could be properly evaluated. The words ''geheime Geschichte'' which he sometimes uses to describe his writings are to be interpreted in this sense—as if he is passing on to his readers the secrets of history which no one before him has been able to discover. (p. 269)

That Wieland was indeed highly competent to view the course of history objectively is nowhere more evident than in the series of essays on Rousseau, which Wieland published under the significant title of *Beyträge zur geheimen Geschichte des menschlichen Verstandes und Herzens.* (p. 270)

[In his analysis of Rousseau's first treatise, Wieland] recognizes quite clearly that Rousseau's so-called system was the result not of calm reflection, but rather of a bitter emotional reaction to the social injustices and political abuses which prevailed in eighteenth-century France. Only from such a direct emotional attitude could a philosopher come to the conclusion that moral decadence and social inequality were too high a price to pay for the arts and sciences or, in short, for the entire civilization of modern society. What Wieland means to convey by this successful attempt to expose the psychology underlying Rousseau's savage philippic is that the observer who, like Wieland himself, regards the situation with the calm reflection which is derived from a sense of historical perspective will not allow himself to be misled into such an exaggerated view.

This revelation of the psychological motives which gave rise to Rousseau's system does not, of course, constitute a refutation of the system itself, and it was not intended to be understood as such. What prompted Wieland's interest in the psychological motivation of the first discourse was his need to explain to himself and to his readers how a philosopher of such obvious genius could have reached such an erroneous conclusion. Although Wieland is unable to accept Rousseau's system itself, he admires its brilliance and is willing to concede the validity of two of its main premises: that the primitive state may have been a happy one and that the arts and sciences have always constituted a threat to human happiness. He maintains, nevertheless, that it is neither possible nor desirable to keep a nation in the precarious state of cultural ignorance.

Accounts of primitive peoples abound in Wieland's writings. These accounts are frequently so idyllic that one is tempted to conclude that Wieland shares with Rousseau the rationalist concept that the simple, uncivilized peoples are much happier and better than their civilized fellows. Wieland's description of the valley of Jemal in the novel *Danischmend,* for example, follows completely in the tradition of the exotic paradise: ''Es war ein langes, zwischen fruchtbaren Hügeln und waldigen Bergen sich hinziehendes Thal, Jemal genannt, von tausend Bächen und Quellen aus dem Gebirge bewässert, und von den glücklichsten Menschen bewohnt, die vielleicht damals auf dem ganzen Erdboden anzutreffen waren.'' . . . (pp. 270-71)

Wieland does not enlighten his readers concerning the exact nature and the causes of this happiness. Only from the description of the corruption which occurs later is one able to draw conclusions about the original conditions. The first blow against happiness in Jemal is struck by three fakirs who introduce the *Lingam.* According to Wieland, the *Lingam* is a kind of amulet to which a certain sect of Hindus pay idolatrous honors. It is meant as a symbol of corruption, for with it superstition and ornamentation are introduced into the valley. The superstition, i.e., the belief that one can achieve happiness through the means of civilized society, undermines the instinctively happy way of life in Jemal. The ornamentation leads to envy, rivalry, and animosity among the women. (p. 271)

Despite the appreciation which Wieland shows for rural simplicity in his description of life in Jemal, it is not in such a life that his ideal is to be found. It is not by chance that he provides us with so little information about the original conditions in Jemal. He is less concerned with detailing the nature and the causes of the original happiness than with demonstrating how quickly and easily it can disappear. In this connection, the obvious contrast between the native inhabitants of the valley and Danischmend, the philosopher-landholder who lives among them, is of crucial significance. The former succumb to the corrupting influence of the *Lingam* almost immediately, whereas Danischmend is not affected by it at all, except in so far as it changes his environment. (p. 272)

The people of Jemal are, after all, little more than children. Danischmend would not wish to purchase the kind of happiness they enjoy at the cost of his enlightened condition. He is content with his life among them, but it would be wrong to maintain that he has become one of these simple people. The figure of Danischmend in Jemal follows completely in the bucolic tradition. He is a landholder, but everything seems to thrive so well that he needs to devote only a very small part of his time to the land, and for the rest can give himself up to philosophical contemplation. Like Danischmend, Wieland himself might have a certain feeling of well-being among such people, but only if permitted to devote most of his time to his humanistic pursuits, to the acquisition of culture in an attempt to become happy and to make others happy.

Wieland's most valid argument against accepting the conclusions of Rousseau's system is to be found in an episode from the *Beyträge* in which Tlantlaquacapatli, an ''eminent Mexican philosopher,'' traces the development of Mexican civilization back to its earliest origins. Koxkox and Kikequetzal, the hero and heroine of Tlantlaquacapatli's history, are discovered at the beginning of the episode in a presocial state of nature. Their life is depicted with the glowing colors of the idyl, as a mixture of pleasure, innocence, and love. This idyl, however, does not last long. Only one change is enough to transform happiness into unhappiness, namely, the association with others. When the two are joined by a third, their little community is soon destroyed by jealousy and violence. When later a few more women join the group, the restoring of the balance does not restore the former happy state. Promiscuous behavior results, signifying the end of love and thus of happiness in the community. It becomes entirely corrupt, and supreme happiness has been distorted into utter misery. (pp. 272-73)

Although he may often allow himself to indulge in dreams of a golden age, [Wieland] is by no means convinced that there ever was a period of perfect primitive happiness. His descriptions of primitive peoples frequently give one the impression of conscious irony. Thus even Tlantlaquacapatli refers to the idyllic existence enjoyed by Koxkox and Kikequetzal as a "beautiful dream." . . . Wieland is willing, on the other hand, to concede the existence of a period of primitive happiness, but only to point out, at the same time, that what was experienced in this period of mankind's development could not have been perfect happiness, for the simple pleasures enjoyed by the primitive community are more than outweighed by the possibilities for happiness in the civilized state. . . . (pp. 273-74)

[Opposition] to Rousseau was not necessarily the most important factor in developing Wieland's tendency to think in historical terms. One possible direct source for such ideas is Adam Ferguson's *Essay on the History of Civil Society* . . . , which was familiar to Wieland at least by 1770 and which is also considered to have influenced Herder's historical thought. Like Ferguson, Wieland is aware that every individual historical period must be considered as a unity in itself and can be evaluated only by its own standards, that new values which are continually emerging in the course of the development of mankind cannot be measured against the values of older societies. Wieland may not always manage to carry these ideas to their logical conclusion and to refrain from comparing conditions in different epochs of human development, but the element of historicism in his writings is nevertheless sufficiently emphasized to forestall all attacks on his ideal of civilized man.

A supplementary aspect of Wieland's attitude toward the primitive state may be observed in the episode in *Der goldene Spiegel* of the "children of Nature," whose lawgiver Psammis has made the following principle into a fundamental law of the community: "Die Natur hat alle eure Sinne, hat jedes Fäserchen des wundervollen Gewebes eures Wesens, hat euer Gehirn und euer Herz zu Werkzeugen des Vergnügens gemacht." . . . The Children of Nature may be described as a nation of epicureans, who enjoy both freedom and equality. Their way of life is successful, however, partly because they practice moderation in their devotion to sensual pleasures and partly because a good deal of their pleasure is derived from making others happy. The Children of Nature represent for Wieland a valuable personal ideal, but it is not his intention to set up their community as either a desirable or a possible political ideal. On the contrary, he ridicules those who dream of an original state of natural happiness and maintains, quite in the spirit of Ferguson, that the proper concern of man is to live in and for his own times. . . . (pp. 274-75)

Despite the element of historicism in his thought, Wieland is not able to free himself from the rationalist tendency to think in terms of moral decline. He continually returns to the idea that civilized man is always in danger of succumbing to moral

corruption—unless, like Danischmend-Wieland, he has attained a high degree of spiritual and intellectual perfection. Since this will never be true for mankind as a whole, the state must attempt to minimize the harmful aspects of culture without eliminating its beneficial effects. Wieland's ideas concerning the achievement of this goal may be discerned in *Agathon* and, his major political writing, *Der goldene Spiegel*.

Agathon is essentially a philosophical novel. Its purpose is to demonstrate the development in the hero of a practical philosophy of life. According to Wieland, the supreme wish of man is happiness. But, since the richest sources of happiness are love and benevolence, man's capacity to enjoy life is greatest when he identifies his own interests with those of the common good. One of the chief aims of education, then, is training in the virtues of political life. *Agathon* thus becomes a political novel, and the education of Agathon himself includes initiation into the practical problems of society and its institutions.

The first of the three major episodes which contribute to the development of Agathon's political perception delineates his rise and fall as a popular leader in the Republic of Athens. The significance of this experience is twofold. In the first place, his failure inspires in him a violent antipathy to all forms of popular sovereignty. On leaving Athens, he is convinced that republican government, no matter what its specific constitution, will always result in tyranny. There can be little doubt that Wieland himself shares this derogatory attitude toward any form of popular sovereignty, for he emphasizes that Agathon's criticism is based on a profound and exact knowledge of the faults inherent in such states. Wieland is willing to concede, however, that in the case of extremely small states a republican constitution can sometimes be quite effective.

A more significant aspect of Agathon's experience in Athens is that it reveals his naïve idealism in matters of political and social reform. His program is based on an ideal of man as he should be according to metaphysical speculation and does not take into account the particular character of the Athenian people with their complicated social and political motives. At least in this period of his career, Agathon has no sense of historical perspective. He seems to believe in the existence of a social optimum which is valid for all peoples and all times. According to Wieland, this inability to think in historical terms is a weakness which is to be found all too frequently in those concerned with political and social reform, in idealists such as Algernon Sidney, Brutus, and, above all, Cato the Elder. (pp. 275-76)

When Agathon takes up the role of political reformer at the court of Dionysius the Younger in Syracuse, he attempts to base his program of reform on political realities, and for a time he is successful. In the end, however, he fails once more, which indicates an extreme pessimism on the part of Wieland concerning the possibility of any lasting measure of benevolent and equitable government under an absolute regime. Reflecting on his failure, Agathon himself becomes bitterly despondent and seems to have lost all faith in mankind. Then he is transported by the author to the Republic of Tarentum, which, as Wieland points out in a chapter entitled "Apologie des griechischen Autors," is a utopian republic existing only in the realm of ideas. . . . (p. 276)

Under the guidance of Archytas, the wise ruler of the Republic, Agathon regains his faith in human nature, his desire to serve once more his fellow men, and even his willingness to take on another task similar to the one he had attempted in Syracuse, but only in the case of extreme necessity. Despite this attempt to restore to Agathon his faith in mankind, it seems clear that Wieland does not believe it possible to create the ideal state except in what he calls the "Land of Ideas." A consideration of *Der goldene Spiegel* will offer a more definitive answer to this question.

Der goldene Spiegel demonstrates Wieland's general agreement with the belief held by the majority of Enlightenment political thinkers that the key to the kind of government which prevails under any particular regime is to be discovered in the character of the monarch himself. During the reign of Azor, who is weak, as well as that of Isfandiar, who is despotic, corruption and exploitation prevail in Scheschian, while under Tifan, who is benevolent and wise, the state flourishes. When the theories of government which are developed in the novel are examined more closely, however, it becomes evident that Wieland's political theories are by no means identical with those of his predecessors. It is the constitution which Tifan gives to his state that is of significance in this connection, for the governments of the other monarchs in the novel are described only in a negative way. What happens to Scheschian under Azor and under Isfandiar merely demonstrates the disastrous results of a government which has no principles other than those derived from royal caprice. Into his description of Tifan's regime, however, Wieland incorporates positive suggestions for the improvement of government, some of which are entirely new in concept.

The little state in which Tifan is brought up by the sincere and honest Dschengis is regulated entirely according to natural laws. The inhabitants enjoy absolute equality. All matters affecting the general welfare are decided by a court made up of the elders of the individual households. These communistic measures are, of course, typical of many small utopian communities, including those described by Wieland elsewhere in his writings. (pp. 277-78)

Wieland does not intend this ideal community to have political significance in itself. He is too much an empiricist to believe that political equality is possible except, perhaps, in a very small political unit. It had been one of Agathon's major failings that he had ignored political realities and had attempted to force a theoretically ideal form of government on people who were neither socially nor morally mature enough to support it. Dschengis' state is created for the sole purpose of establishing an environment suitable for the education of a prince who would otherwise have grown up amid the moral corruption of an extremely dissolute court.

After he has learned in this ideal environment how society should be governed according to the true concepts of nature and the destiny of man, Tifan is taken on a trip through the world, where he sees men and governments as they really are. He learns that the sublime concepts of innocent men and golden ages with which he had grown up are nothing more than golden dreams. . . . He now realizes—as had Agathon before him—that laws must be made to deal with men not as they should be, but as they are, and that the legislator must take particular care to prevent the conflict of individual interests and the contagion of moral corruption, the twin evils of the civilized state.

It is not surprising, therefore, that the total effect of Tifan's program of legislation . . . is to make Scheschian into a welfare state. The meticulous government control which he introduces is justified by the argument that the people lack the maturity to be trusted with any measure of social or political responsibility. (p. 278)

Although Wieland is a firm believer in absolute monarchy, he is by no means blind to the faults of this form of government. He knows that absolutism can easily become pure despotism, as is shown by the regimes of Azor and Isfandiar. It is the task of government to prevent corruption, but not to degrade the people to abject slavery. It is a question of finding a form of government which permits the king to do good, but does not leave him the power to do evil. In this respect, absolute power requires a limitation, and Wieland finds this limitation in the principle that the king shall not govern through the law, but the law through the king . . . , that is to say, the king must restrict himself merely to interpreting the law of nature or, as Wieland himself puts it, to discovering the will of the supreme lawgiver. . . . This is not a new idea, of course, but the way in which Wieland attempts to realize it is new.

In Wieland's ideal state, the constitution which prescribes the duties of the king is not simply a friendly warning to preserve the welfare of the people, but it is provided with *vis coactiva* in the fullest sense of the word. Before any ordinance of the crown can have the force of law, the leaders of the estates must test it for conformity with the constitution. If they discover a discrepancy, they must point it out to the ruler, together with the reasons for their disagreement. If the crown still insists on the validity of its decree, then the heads are required to convene the estates. Once a three-quarters majority of the estates have given their support to the leaders' objections, the law in question is considered to be invalid. Its publication can be prevented, if need be, by force. The competence to judge whether a particular law is in harmony with the constitution has thus been removed from the legislator, that is, from the king himself, and transferred to the estates.

From the standpoint of the German Enlightenment, that is a truly incredible measure, for it gives the estates the function of a supreme court with control over the legislative power. The practical impossibility of such a court in the absolute state is obvious. Wieland is writing, however, not so much to endorse a particular program of political action as to stimulate thought. That he himself is aware of the impractical nature of such constitutional limitations is evident from the objections which he has Sultan Gebal make to these innovations. . . . (pp. 279-80)

The important thing about Wieland's proposals in this matter is not so much their specific content as their intent. The dignity of man as the bearer of humanistic ideals is not consistent with lawless oppression. Wieland is so conscious of this discrepancy that he suggests changes which would incorporate constitutional limitations into the absolute state. This concession to constitutionalism seems to be purely nominal, however. Wieland has, in fact, very little faith in constitutional guarantees as deterrents to oppression. Even the best constitutions, he maintains, will not be able to prevent a monarch from oppressing his people: "die weiseste Staatsverfassung kann dem Monarchen nicht verwehren, durch einen unruhigen Geist, oder durch Trägheit und Schwäche der Seele, oder irgend eine ausschweifende Leidenschaft seine Völker unglücklich zu machen." . . . (p. 280)

This general statement is borne out in the case of Scheschian itself. The constitution which Tifan gives to Scheschian does not prevent that ideal state from degenerating into tyranny after his death. This degeneration is not, as the above quotation might lead one to suspect, simply the result of a series of unsatisfactory rulers. The cause of the decline is a gradual moral corruption which spreads slowly but inevitably through the entire population. Wieland does not share the naïve belief of Enlightenment thinkers before him that, if the monarch is good, all will be well in the state. The decline of Scheschian is an implicit repudiation by Wieland of the belief which the Enlightenment shared with Rousseau in the power of man to bring about lasting improvement in society by education or by constitutional change.

In the final analysis, then, the real cause of Scheschian's decline is the imperfectibility of man. Wieland evidently believes that the tendency to moral decline in man is so strong that it cannot be entirely eliminated by any human means. Once more we see Wieland on the border between rationalism and historicism. His concept of moral decline presupposes an absolute standard and therefore belongs to rationalist thought. But, by opposing to the rationalist striving for an ideal society the pessimistic thought that no state, not even the best possible, can last, he is again giving expression to an idea which has its roots in historical-relativistic thought. (pp. 280-81)

As we have seen, one of Wieland's major concerns was the problem of how to construct a form of government which would not degenerate into tyranny and how to establish a society governed by laws which would effectively check man's inherent tendency to moral decline. Whereas Herder and the *Sturm und Drang* insist that all men in all historical periods must have richness of experience and the greatest possible development of human capacities, Wieland still maintains—for pragmatic reasons—that equitable social institutions should be considered the sublime purpose of history. Admittedly, Wieland's approach to historicism is not always consistent. It signifies, nevertheless, the end of the period of Enlightenment political thought. Wieland's implicit denial of the perfectibility of man and, through him, of society points clearly to Herder and the *Sturm und Drang,* a period which expresses a new human situation and new political values and in which men no longer indulged in dreams of a future golden age. (p. 282)

> James A. McNeely, *"Historical Relativism in Wieland's Concept of the Ideal State,"* in Modern Language Quarterly, *Vol. XXII, No. 3, September, 1961, pp. 269-82.*

A. MENHENNET   (essay date 1964-65)

[*Menhennet points to the rococo and romantic qualities of* Idris und Zenide *in calling for a broader definition of the concept of the "literary Enlightenment."*]

Wieland's epic fragment *Idris und Zenide* . . . poses an interesting problem for the literary historian. It is, in my view, manifestly a product of the Enlightenment, yet the terms 'rococo' and 'romantic', which can also be applied to it, seem to stand in direct contradiction to this. The aim of the present essay is to resolve that contradiction and to suggest a corresponding adjustment in our understanding of the literary Enlightenment.

The tendency today is to draw a sharp distinction between Rococo and Enlightenment. Friedrich Sengle does this [see Additional Bibliography], and assigns *Idris* to the Rococo, more or less disregarding the Enlightenment as a factor. In fact, he calls the poem 'die bezeichnendste Nahtstelle zwischen Rokoko und Romantik'. And whenever he touches on Wieland's handling of the world of fairy-tale and romance, one senses his conviction of the incompatibility of that world with the Enlightenment. When elements of the latter are clearly present, he regards them as alien intrusions. Thus, in his com-

ments on the prose 'Märchen' *Die Salamandrin und die Bildsäule* . . . , he objects to Wieland's '. . . sehr flüchtige, ja widerwärtige Vermischung von Vernünftigkeit und Illusion' and to the 'platte . . . und ganz unkünstlerische Aufklärung' which, in his view, characterizes the work. I would contest the narrow concept of the Enlightenment which underlies such judgments.

It was Wieland himself who first applied the term 'romantisch' to *Idris*, subtitling the poem 'ein romantisches Gedicht'. This is the first of a whole series of poems by him which deal with 'romantic' material and it is here that one has to seek the theoretical basis on which his poetry in this vein rests. The first eight stanzas constitute a veritable romantic manifesto, which can be supplemented by the original preface and by some remarks in a letter to Gessner of 1766.

In stanza three, Wieland exhorts his muse:

> . . . wage dich in Welten,
> Worin die Phantasie als Königin befiehlt.

Here is the first of the romantic elements to be mentioned, and the most important. The others are folly and absurdity—i.e. elements which in themselves run counter to strict reason and common sense—sheer play, disorder (or at least complication), and finally the 'unnatural', the wondrous and the fairy-tale. The two features which stand out are the free(er) play of the imagination and the use of the wondrous.

But interwoven with this romantic thread is another, consisting entirely of features which stamp the poem as a conscious product of the Enlightenment. These are the rational, the serious (morality, metaphysics and human emotions 'under this frivolous exterior', as the letter referred to puts it), satire, the combination of entertainment with instruction, planning, nature, and truth.

The theoretical programme advanced is a pairing, an alliance (Wieland's own terms) of two sides which, while they are not incompatible, are also, for Wieland, not immediately harmonious. He writes with a sense of risk . . . which cannot be ascribed entirely to his (no doubt largely assumed) fear of the critics . . . and his attitude to the romantic is a gingerly one: compare the emphasis of such phrases as 'Vernunft sich *auch mit Torheit* paart' (stanza three, line eight), 'Natur *sogar in Märchen* rührt' (stanza five, line five) and 'Geschmack und Witz *mit Allem* sich verbinde' (stanza five, line six: my italics in each case). A similar defensive spirit is evident in this phrase from the preface:

> Es giebt Märchen, in denen bey allem Ansehen
> von Ungereimtheit und Frivolität mehr gesunde
> Vernunft steckt als in hundert sehr ernsten
> Folianten.

Wieland does not go into such theoretical detail elsewhere in his poetry. He probably considered that the case had been made in and by *Idris,* and when he used the word 'romantisch' in connexion with *Oberon* he was fairly clearly looking back and is likely to have had very much the same theoretical basis in mind. In the introduction to *Clelia und Sinibald* . . . we find him still canvassing the problem of 'nature' and the wondrous, certainly with typical grace and irony, but without giving the impression that the old rationalistic bastions of the Enlightenment have been abandoned. (pp. 91-2)

Even in the *Hexameron vom Rosenhain* . . . , where Wieland tries to draw support for the fairy-tale from the Romantic Movement itself, the 'Aufklärer' shows through. A fairy-tale should have the quality of a dream, but combined with 'as much truth as is necessary to deceive the imagination, to involve the heart and to lull the intellect to sleep'. The poet 'weaves the natural and the unnatural so cunningly together that the latter slips by unchallenged under the protection of the former'. . . .

The gulf between Wieland and the Romantic Movement is evident. His work in this field has to be seen in a different context, one which falls within the general field of the Enlightenment. The world of the romantic was by no means closed to the 'Aufklärer', even before Wieland. The word 'romantisch' was in use, though not primarily as a literary term. Adelung, in fact, would have liked to restrict it to its application to landscape. But it did acquire wider associations, particularly with the free ranging of the imagination, with the wondrous, and with the genre 'Roman'. Adelung himself emphasizes, as the principal characteristics of this genre, 'Verwirrungen' and 'das Wunderbare'. The wondrous plays an important part in the literary theory of the earlier Enlightenment. Even the fairy-tale had received attention before Wieland: Gottsched comments on it under the rubric of the wondrous and collections of fairy-tales had already been published. (p. 93)

The basic structure of *Idris* is not unlike that of the contemporaneous *Musarion*. We are shown two extremes, and a *via media* which fairly clearly represents Wieland's own position. Idris, the idealist, has impossibly lofty concepts of love and virtue and is not unreminiscent of the young Agathon. Balancing him is Itiphall, the cynical sensualist, who recalls Hippias and holding the centre, Zerbin and Lila, who have found a proper harmony in their love. Idris, the main hero, loves Zenide, a fairy princess who lacks only the ability to love: to win her, he must bring her statue to life with his embrace. Itiphall also seeks Zenide's hand. After a brush with his rival, Idris rescues Lila from the clutches of a centaur and is entertained by her and Zerbin, who tells him part of the story of his and Lila's love. Itiphall meanwhile reaches Zenide's realm, but mistakes the beauteous Rahimu for her and swears eternal fidelity before he discovers his error. Idris, unable to sleep after Zerbin's narrative, embarks on a magic boat and after landing, finds Zenide's statue and embraces it. It is, in fact, occupied by the female salamander Amöne, who becomes enamoured of him and spirits him away, determined to alienate his affections from Zenide in honourable combat, without the aid of deception. He escapes just in time and finds the statue once more. Again, it warms under his embrace, but on this occasion, it is an amorous nymph, from whom he has already had one narrow escape, who is inside it. She is less scrupulous than Amöne and Idris's virtue is in deadly danger—and at precisely this point, Wieland breaks off the narrative.

What would, or rather could have happened to Idris? The answer we give depends on our interpretation of his character and the nature of his love. That some degree of the disillusionment which is such a constant theme in Wieland's work in this period was to have been his lot seems certain. His naive concepts could hardly have escaped unscathed: the warning in III:120 ('Der Stärkste reize nicht die Rache der Natur') is unmistakable. Even Zerbin stumbles once, as do Hüon and Amanda in *Oberon*. But is Idris a chronic 'Schwärmer', along the lines of Don Sylvio and Amadis? True, the word 'Schwärmerei' occurs in connexion with him once or twice, but each time as the effects of love, from which no one is free: even Zerbin suffers from 'verliebte Schwärmerei'. . . . But true love is, in its *essence,* free from this clouding of the reason. It has a positive moral and ideal content which would clearly come,

for Wieland, under the heading of 'Enthusiasmus' i.e. inspiration by the true, the good, the beautiful as against the illusory object of 'Schwärmerei'. (The distinction is made by Wieland in the essay *Enthusiasmus und Schwärmerei* . . .). Don Sylvio's passion for a butterfly-princess is a 'Schwärmerei', from which he has to be cured; is the same true of Idris's love for Zenide? Amöne certainly thinks so, but then, she is an interested party. For another possibility, we can take a line through *Die Salamandrin und die Bildsäule,* which has several points in common with *Idris,* the most important being the statue-motif. Osmandyas falls in love with a statue but his passion has, in spite of its apparent absurdity, 'all the qualities of the truest, tenderest love . . . that ever fired a human breast'. Eventually, he receives the 'reward of his constancy' in the arms, not of the statue itself, but of its original. There is a mild disillusionment, but Osmandyas's love, while ridiculous in its *object,* is good and true in its *essence.* . . . Zerbin and Lila prove themselves in a similar way, by remaining true to what appears to be an illusion in spite of pressures and blandishments.

While there is exaggeration in Idris's idealism, there is also solid heroic virtue, shown particularly in the episode (V: 3-7) in which he is confronted by a horde of gruesome monsters. Here is a case of 'Natur im Märchen'. . .: Idris has left his magic sword behind, just as Zerbin loses his talisman and has to face his perils and trials a man, alone. The 'naturalness' of Idris's constancy here is proved by the fact that he does feel fear (stanza five) and in spite of touches of Wielandian irony, his heroism 'moves' us ('Natur im Märchen rührt', I: 5), as it does not, for example, in Canto Two, where he fights with magical means and walks coolly through walls.

Nor is it certain that his love is pure aberration. His rejection of the importunate nymph in Canto One arises, Wieland suggests, not out of 'Tugend oder Wahn' but out of 'Liebe selbst, und von der schönsten Art' . . . and the calling out of his beloved's name in Canto Five dispels the terrors which have assailed him.

So that we have a measure of satire and of the serious, moral, heroic element (both of which also fulfil the function of instruction and improvement). Satire, while not perhaps incompatible with Rococo, is more firmly rooted in the ethos of the Enlightenment. The heroic lies completely outside the accepted scheme of rococo. . . . But it was not foreign to the Enlightenment, as is witnessed by such works as Gottsched's *Der sterbende Cato,* Ewald von Kleist's *Cissides und Paches* . . . , Gellert's *Calliste,* Cronegk's *Codrus* or Lessing's *Philotas.* From his early epics through into the 'eighties, Wieland shows, *pace* Sengle, a strong heroic streak, one noticed by, among others, Schiller, in *Über naive und sentimentalische Dichtung,* and which can co-exist even with the rococo.

For there is much in *Idris* that can be called rococo: the light and playful tone of many passages (e.g. the Itiphall-passages, or the Dejanire-episode in Canto Two, in which the rococo mood does overcome the heroic), the mellifluous grace of the whole, the handling in many parts of the erotic and of nature, and stock motifs and situations such as the bathing-scene (*Idris* has three such, none without its rococo suggestiveness).

The romantiic, wondrous and fantastic is, of course, all around us. Sprites abound at every turn and even the human characters have access to magical powers. At times, Wieland does seem simply to be enjoying the free play of the imagination; freeing himself, as it were, from the law of gravity. W. Preisendanz . . . has laid great stress on this element of play. . . . But he overestimates its importance and independence: it is doubtful, indeed, whether the imagination is ever out of the control of the reason. Sometimes, this even manifests itself in a certain uneasiness about the fantastic nature of what is described, as when Idris comes to himself in the Wonderland to which Amöne has spirited him away:

> Er starrt erstaunt die neuen Wunder an.
> Zählt sich die wunderbarsten Fälle,
> Die ihm begegnet, vor und muss sich selbst gestehn,
> Er habe nichts unglaublichers gesehn.

(pp. 94-7)

At other times, Wieland's irony acts as a corrective. This irony does not detract at all from the morally positive parts of the action, which have their roots in nature, in eternal human characteristics. But it does ensure that we keep in touch with the real world and its values, as in V:9, where Wieland explains why, although Idris has been caught in a storm, his garment has remained dry:

> Ihr Herrn, erinnert euch, wir sind im Feenland:
> Der Sturm, der ihn so ungeneigt empfangen. . . .
> War lauter Zauberwerk, das keine Spuren lässt.

'Strange things may happen in Fairyland', implies Wieland, 'but you and I, dear reader, are rational beings and live in a world where one *does* get wet if one goes out in the rain.'

The reason is everywhere at work, ensuring that nature is not robbed of her birthright, that true enthusiasm is not confused with 'Schwärmerei' and that the imagination, which is ridden on a light rein, does not slip the rein altogether. It is the very sureness of Wieland's rational control which enables him to produce such an impression of freedom in his handling of the romantic.

The latter can appear in many functions—as an attraction in its own right, as a whetstone for heroic virtue (notably in Zerbin's struggle against his magician-rival Astramond in Canto Three), as a vehicle through which Wieland can indulge his taste for the sensuous and sumptuous . . . or the rather baroque streak in his imagination which is also reflected in his fondness for the conceit. We remember, in *Don Sylvio von Rosalva*, the semi-serious idea of a garment made of 'dry water'. In *Idris* we have, without apparent irony, garments made of 'heavenly azure woven through with sunshine'. . . . But whatever the form in which the romantic appears, it is never out of the control of the reason, however remote that control may at times appear to be.

Idris, then, is a work which is both rococo and, in our particular, eighteenth-century sense, romantic. But it is also consistently a work of the Enlightenment: an Enlightenment graceful and balanced enough to allow of the rococo tone, liberal enough to be able to take in the romantic, but basically still Enlightenment. (pp. 97-8)

What historical conclusions can be drawn from all this? Firstly, we see that it is possible to talk of a 'romanticism of the Enlightenment', which has a certain amount in common with, but must be clearly distinguished from the Romantic Movement of the late eighteenth and early nineteenth centuries. Secondly, we have the question of the relation of Enlightenment to Rococo. The latter has its place in historical terminology. It can render a certain style and mood, and their attendant themes and motifs better than any other term available. But it cannot be set up as a period-term on its own. Its scope is too limited for it to be able to stand on an equal footing with Enlighten-

ment. It cannot hope to contain all that is in *Idris*, let alone Wieland's work as a whole, or all that is in Gellert, Gleim or Uz. Nor does it really stand in contradiction to the Enlightenment. It is not irrationalistic and while it does reject mere drab utilitarianism, there is no sound warrant for assuming the latter to be the hallmark of the Enlightenment. The proper function of 'rococo' is as one component within a more liberal and a more just concept of the Enlightenment, a concept that has room for the Rococo and the romantic, for Lichtenberg as well as Gottsched and, for that matter, for 'Empfindsamkeit', which is by no means incompatible with Enlightenment and rubs shoulders with it quite happily in many authors and works, including *Idris* itself (cf. the account of the reuniting of Zerbin and Lila in Canto Two). The flexibility which has recently been introduced, largely through the work of Sengle, into our appreciation of eighteenth-century German literature before Goethe is welcome, but it should be flexibility within a unifying framework, one that does justice to the broad unity of German literature in this period. And for this, I do not believe that there is any alternative to a properly liberal and broadly based concept of the Enlightenment. (p. 99)

A. Menhennet, "Wieland's 'Idris und Zenide': The 'Aufklärer' as Romantic," in German Life & Letters, *Vol. 18, 1964-65, pp. 91-100.*

ELIZABETH BOA (essay date 1966)

[Boa describes rococo literary conventions and the way Wieland used them in Musarion. *For additional commentary by Boa, see the excerpt dated 1980.]*

In many ways we are still living in a post-Romantic and post-realist age. A work based on quite different literary conventions, such as Wieland's *Musarion*, may seem rather alien to the modern reader. For this reason alone, it is useful to look at *Musarion* not in isolation, but as a work written within a particular mode. A true judgement of the poem becomes possible if we realize the Rococo conventions within which it moves. (p. 23)

Rococo is not primarily a literary term at all, but one borrowed from architecture and the visual arts. . . . [As] a literary term, it is associated initially with the court literature of France under the *ancien régime*. If the term is to have any useful application to German literature, it is necessary to avoid definitions based too rigidly on the visual arts or on French literature, as such definitions inevitably force the conclusion that few or no German works conform to them. On the other hand, if no common features can be found in the multifarious works to which the term is applied, it ceases to be of much critical use and leads only to confusion. On all counts, it seems reasonable to attempt a fairly general characterization of Rococo, without aiming at an exact definition. We can then consider *Musarion* not only in order to determine why it is Rococo, but also to deepen and widen our understanding of the mode through detailed consideration of one work. The general term is after all abstracted from individual works.

The attributes which spring to mind when one thinks of Rococo works—elegance, charm, grace, lightness—all suggest aesthetic rather than emotional or intellectual qualities. More than many other literary terms, Rococo refers simply to a certain style. While this is true, it is perhaps misleading, since in literature this particular style becomes an end in itself. Rococo implies not just a style, but a mode in which all else is subordinate to style, or more generally to aesthetic considerations.

It must also be asked what the "all else" of Rococo is. Here perhaps three elements from which this style is compounded can be distinguished—an emotional, an intellectual and a sensual appeal. The intellectual and emotional qualities of Rococo are closely connected with the social background against which it flourished. It is essentially a secular mode of social rather than religious inspiration. It addresses itself to a fairly limited public, be it the aristocracy of the court of Louis XV or, in Germany, the small courts and the cultivated bourgeoisie of a few towns such as Dresden and Leipzig. The assumption of a cultivated, urbane public leads to a familiar tone of irony and humour dependent on mutual understanding between author and public. From one point of view, this worldly, frivolous mode could be considered an effete aristocracy's flight from the approaching deluge. More positively, it may be seen as the product of a society at last far enough removed from the upheavals of religious wars to turn from religious preoccupations and fanaticisms to social and secular themes. Compared with the baroque mode, Rococo tends to look at man in purely human terms. Human life is accepted as it is, rather than judged by religious categories. Pessimistic emphasis on the transience of life gives way to optimism and acceptance of man's sensual nature. Frivolity perhaps, but also common sense and realistic psychological insight are the marks of the mode. (pp. 23-4)

This is the background also of the Enlightenment with which Rococo has much in common. The distinctive feature of Rococo might be sought in its emotional appeal. Both have a humanistic rather than a religious approach to man. Both are optimistic. But where the Enlightenment emphasizes more typically the dignity and the self-sufficiency of man as a rational creature, Rococo is more concerned with the pleasures of earthly life and with man as a sensual being. As such, the predominant note is anti-heroic and common-sensical, gay and lighthearted. (p. 24)

The third, perhaps most essential element of Rococo, is a strong sensuous appeal, the logical outcome of a view of man as a rational, but also as a sensual, being. It is here that the analogy between literature and the visual arts is clearest. Bosoms and buttocks abound. The curving shape of the *rocaille*, from which the term Rococo is probably derived, is echoed in the curving shape of the female form, whether a Boucher nude or a Dresden shepherdess. It is a sensuality expressed through graceful formalism rather than harsh realism: *Fanny Hill*, not *Tropic of Cancer*. Colour, movement and decorative detail replace the grandeur and massiveness of the baroque style. The fluid rhythms of free verse replace stricter metres. The frozen flourish of a porcelain hunting group, the swirling movement and shifting colour of a Rococo interior, the all-pervasive decorative detail of a Mozart opera or an anacreontic poem: all these are manifestations of the sensuous and sensual appeal which is the hallmark of Rococo in whatever medium. (pp. 24-5)

Musarion was published in 1768 at the height of the Rococo fashion in German literature. It comes in the same period as the author's Rococo **Comische Erzählungen** and the novel **Agathon**. In the 1760s Wieland, after eight years in Switzerland, had returned to Biberach in his native Swabia. The nearby Schloß Warthausen provided a centre of intellectual and social activity under the patronage of Graf Stadion. In this atmosphere Wieland's conversion from the pietistic and sentimental tendency of his Swiss period was completed. In Swabia and in South Germany as a whole, Rococo culture found a more fertile soil than in Switzerland, and it is here that Wieland's first Rococo works were written, principal among them **Musarion**. (p. 26)

The poem is above all striking for the harmony it achieves between aesthetic and didactic intent. The dominant formal principle of irony fulfils the double function of creating the distance necessary both for aesthetic pleasure and for critical judgement. A philosophy which teaches the unity of ethics and aesthetics is expressed in a form which combines the didactic with the beautiful. We shall see how in a variety of ways—in the treatment of setting, situation and character, narrative technique, details of style and metre—Wieland exploits to the full both the formal beauty and the ironic wit of the Rococo mode with combined didactic and aesthetic effect.

Rococo has a marked tendency towards the miniature form. *Musarion* with almost fifteen hundred lines might seem rather long, but its length is mitigated by its structure. It falls into three sections, each of which forms a typically Rococo scene or tableau. (pp. 26-7)

The situation and setting of [the] first section are a charming example of Rococo art. With a few light strokes Wieland sketches an Arcadian-setting—we could easily imagine an embarcation to Cythera. We see a woodland slope with rough path, a glimpse of the nearby sea and close at hand a cottage with its inevitable linden tree, that archetypal symbol of all German idylls. A nightingale sings. True it is not yet night, but the nightingale is there in his formal rather than his zoological persona. We are in Arcadia, a highly formalized Arcadia robbed of all but the faintest memory of panic terror. As Musarion implies, in venturing into the wilderness, the main risk has been to her coiffure rather than her safety. . . . Her fear of cloven-hoofed satyrs is simply an excuse for accompanying Phanias to his cottage. . . . The setting then is not so much pastoral as mock-pastoral. In Wieland's irony, however, there is no satiric intent. Nature is not being mocked by a man of urban culture. His irony serves simply to preserve the pre-eminence of the human in this natural setting. The landscape he paints is neither completely formalized, as in a baroque garden, nor yet shown to be in opposition to culture, as in a wild romantic landscape. It might be compared to the landscape gardening of a Capability Brown in which art and nature produce a gentle harmony neither dominated by, nor yet threatening to man. The mythical age is remote, we are in a thinly disguised eighteenth century.

The same irony marks the treatment of the situation. The conventional meeting of nymph and hero or god suffers a comic reversal. As Musarion remarks, the old order is reversed and it is the hero, Phanias, who flees before the pursuing nymph. . . . The motif is ancient, but the psychology is eighteenth century. A variety of individual motifs contribute to the Rococo atmosphere, such as the nightingale, the gathering twilight, the rosy cheeks and graceful movements of Musarion. The flashback to the moment of Phanias' awakening love for Musarion is a perfect Rococo miniature. . . . He gazes with adoration at the nymph asleep in a grove after her bath. This sensual image is lightened by the comic counter-image of what Musarion saw when she awoke: "Something half way between faun and Eros!" . . . A typical Rococo blend, then, of Arcadian motifs, sensuality and an underlying humorous appeal to common sense. The comic lack of one typical motif—the garland of roses which Phanias is *not* wearing . . .—adds another of the ironic touches which transforms the general Arcadian setting into a Rococo Arcadia. (pp. 27-8)

The setting and situation of [the] second section form a second Rococo tableau, this time of a feast by candle-light. Here wine, music and love, the anacreontic themes, are united in a scene which begins with cultivated table talk, but ends as an orgy: a Rococo orgy, however, for it is only a "little Bacchanal".... The canvas is more richly painted than in the opening, coolly elegant, pastoral scene. Decorative motifs abound—the serving youth with his tangled hair, the bowls of fruit, the six jugs of nectar, the lyre and curling beard of Theophron, and the wreath of flowers which completes his transformation into amorous satyr. The strongly pictorial qualities of the poem, which would justify the use of the term Rococo even if it had no accepted literary usage, are splendidly exemplified in the lines describing the entrance of Chloe.... Her round head, crowned by the round shape of a basket with its rounded fruits, her curving breast and shapely calves, her knee, white as wax, glimpsed through shifting veils, what could be more Rococo? The curving decorative shapes, the movement, the grace, the sensuous and sensual appeal are all there to a high degree. The comparison with Hebe and Aurora add the literary touch of classical reference. The wit of the literary Rococo is present too in the reactions of the two philosophers—Theophron immediately inflamed, Kleanth more interested in the fruit. It is in this last detail of Kleanth's indifference to all but the culinary aspect of this feast of beauty that the subtlety of Wieland's art is most evident. Though the poet directs the barb initially against the coarse greediness of the self-confessed stoic, he also achieves a certain comic deflation of what might otherwise have been too cloyingly sweet or oppressively sensual in the description of Chloe. Wieland is no eighteenth-century D. H. Lawrence. Even the taste of sensual pleasure is improved by a grain of salt. This scene, like the first, is typically Rococo in setting, situation and individual motifs, though here we see the more rumbustious side of the mode, as compared with the delicate elegance of the first scene. Both combine the conscious formalism, the wit, the decorativeness and the lightedhearted sensuality which are the general marks of the mode. (pp. 28-9)

The third scene completes the Rococo tryptich. We enter that pre-eminent Rococo setting—a moonlit bed. The situation too is very Rococo—the persistent lover and the reluctant but finally yielding mistress. Once more details of presentation transform a classical motif into eighteenth-century Rococo. This love scene is not one of pagan nakedness nor of Roman self-abandonment in physical passion.... Wieland, in his bedroom scene, concentrates rather on the sighs and pleadings which are the preliminaries to love. It is the struggle of the nymph which we see, rather than her final abandonment, a prolonged titillation of the reader's senses rather than a frontal attack on his sensibilities. This is in line with countless anacreontic poems where lovers plead outside moonlit casements or are surprised in dalliance rather than in the act. The generally playful nature of Rococo is evident in this concentration on the preliminary play of love. Similarly Rococo offers not nakedness but indiscreet glimpses. In the preceding scene Chloe's veils and Musarions' slipped kerchief allow only momentary glimpses of knee or breast. Here too, a carnation-coloured nightgown allows Phanias to sense rather than see a youthfully swelling breast.... Even in the visual arts hints and glimpses are more typical than nakedness. The sensuous appeal of a Bustelli figurine lies in the curve of the whole figure, the typical coquettish backward look and perhaps the glimpse of an ankle. Much is left to the imagination as in pictures of young men watching young ladies on swings and even Boucher's most celebrated nude lies on her face.

In setting and situation this scene, like the others, makes full use of Rococo convention. Once more wit and humour prevent

the convention from becoming too sweet. Wieland's ironic use of convention is perhaps most evident in his treatment of the struggling nymph motif.... This motif in Rococo art is already highly formalized. The nymph struggles because it is the convention that she should, but the lover (and the author and reader) are perfectly aware that the flailing fists and clawing nails are a literary rather than a psychological manifestation.... Chloe declares she will scream if her lover kisses her—"And did she scream? Of course she did—But not till it was all over". Wieland takes this literary self-consciousness a step further. Since to scratch is the conventional preface to surrender, Musarion, therefore does not scratch since she is not going to surrender, at least until she is sure of Phanias' love. This is rather similar to the absent rose wreath in the first scene. Wieland adds an extra layer of irony to an already consciously artificial motif. He artificializes the artifice. The scene, then, is a daring combination of extreme sensual appeal with an extreme of witty distance from that very appeal.

The three sections of *Musarion* are three Rococo tableaux and in each we find the elegance, sensuality and wit characteristic of the mode. The Rococo spirit of the poem is evident also in details of style. Recurring anacreontic images and metaphors emphasize the pastoral setting. The joys and pains of love are conveyed through images of wine, dew, flowers, breezes, butterflies, bee-stings and honey. Flatterers and false friends are compared with swarms of flies.... Philosophy has true and false friends, just as the bee and the caterpillar suck honey or poison, respectively, from the same rose.... The minor deities of Arcadia, the gods of Olympus and the heroes of classical mythology are constant points of reference. Countless allusions to classical philosophy are decorative and meaningful. They underline the Greek setting; they contribute to the urbane tone of the poem which takes for granted a cultivated public; they express in classical terms a modern philosophy. The conventional, decorative vocabulary of Rococo, to which R. H. Samuel refers [see Additional Bibliography], is all-pervasive. But to concentrate simply on the conventional vocabulary and the principle of decorative detail would be to miss the essence of the style in *Musarion*. This is the blending of decoration and convention with a more familiar, colloquial style. As a result, we find at the level of language the same sort of witty play with convention as we remarked at the level of situation and setting. The conventionality of a phrase or an image is deliberately underlined through ironic juxtaposition with more familiar language. We are not invited to enter the convention, but are asked to contemplate it from outside, to admire artifice as artifice and to smile at it.

Other aspects of Wieland's style and technique in *Musarion* are the conversational tone of the narrator, his stance towards the characters and the reader, rhythmic and syntactical effects, the use of narrative suspense and so on. Though aphoristic and incisive verbal wit plays a rôle in *Musarion,* the main charm of the poem lies in a warmer overall humour produced by the chatty, familiar tone and leisurely pace at which the poem progresses. Wieland's main affinities in English "Rococo" are with Fielding, not Pope. (pp. 29-31)

The shifts in tone from the conventional and poetic to the familiar and down-to-earth distance us from the convention, cause us to look, admire and smile from the outside. The poet uses other techniques with a similar tendency. There is above all the ever-present voice of the narrator, pointing out to us aspects of his own art, addressing himself to the reader over the heads of his characters. There is the intrusion of a fictive

reader, expressing interest in the course of events and reminding us that this is fiction, not reality. As K. H. Kausch points
out, this also draws the reader into community with the author
and fellow-readers, so adding to the intimate, social tone typical of the Rococo *Verserzählung.* Equally ironic in effect is
the use of dramatic, or rather undramatic, suspense, since it
so often takes the form of the narrator inviting us to wonder
what will happen next, when this is quite obvious. Metre and
punctuation also create false suspense, as in the frequent use
of a dash in mid-line: "He leapt up from the ground, and—
stood a moment still". . . . Indeed the obviousness of the plot
as a whole, on which Emil Staiger comments, contributes to
the predominance of form. A plot is necessary, but we are not
absorbed by it, we are made aware by its very obviousness
that it is a formal device. We have seen how Wieland emphasises the formal quality of the Arcadian setting. This is true
also of his treatment of time, as Staiger points out in his analysis
of the Greek background which is really a timeless sphere.
That it is intended as timeless is evident from the way anachronism takes on the force of a formal principle. The casual
appearance of Hogarth, Goldoni or Cervantes in this classical
world is another example of Wieland's witty play with the
conventions he is using.

In a great variety of ways Wieland both exploits and ironizes
the poetic conventions on which **Musarion** is based. The final
effect is of a consciously beautiful, consciously artificial creation. Artificial is used here with no pejorative undertone, since
Wieland's irony is in no way destructive. He ironizes without
intent to invalidate, but rather to create the distance and awareness essential to aesthetic experience. The mirror of art is here
very much a magic mirror enframing a world of heightened
beauty and perfection. The strong aesthetic intent of Rococo
as a whole is very evident in **Musarion.** This non-mimetic,
formal approach points not only to an aesthetic but also to a
didactic intent. We are held at a distance not only that we may
admire, but also that we may learn. We have seen many incidental felicities in **Musarion,** but the success of the poem as
a whole must depend on how far Wieland has succeeded in
integrating didacticism and Rococo form. This question is of
peculiar significance, since Wieland's "philosophy of the
Graces" propounds the unity of ethics and aesthetics. A unified
form, at once didactic and beautiful, will convey with all the
greater conviction, indeed will exemplify, such a doctrine.

Musarion herself is intended as the very embodiment of the
"philosophy of the Graces". Her attributes are a combination
of physical and moral grace, the beauty of her mind being
manifest in the beauty of her form. The spirits hovering round
her, like cherubs round any Rococo beauty, are the Muses, the
Graces, and Love himself. . . . These deities are not merely
decorative but convey the attributes of Musarion: wisdom, charm,
beauty, and warmth. The Graces in particular convey the double meaning of physical and moral grace. The grace of Musarion is her essence and is manifest in her graciousness to
others. This is analogous to the religious use of grace which
is a gift of God to be bestowed on others. Musarion's perfection
is human, however, not God-given. Yet even Musarion does
not escape the veil of humour which envelops the poem since,
as we saw, we are invited to regard her simultaneously as poetic
ideal and ordinary desirable girl. Musarion's double nature as
poetic ideal and desirable girl expresses in itself the philosophy
of the poem which teaches a high ideal and yet takes account
of human nature. It also allows Wieland to express his philosophy while preserving the humour and sensuous appeal of
Rococo.

Phanias is treated even more ironically than Musarion. None
of his feelings is taken seriously, neither his misery at the
beginning, manifest in his unkempt beard and missing rose
wreath, nor his illusory devotion to stoic wisdom. We do not
identify with Phanias. His psychology is not presented from
within, as an end in itself, to allow the reader insight into a
complex individual. He serves rather as a vessel for certain
types of emotion which we are invited to judge from a combined
moral and aesthetic standpoint. This is reminiscent of the treatment of Hans Castorp in *The Magic Mountain,* as is the use
of an irony which brings both enlightenment and aesthetic
pleasure. There is a general affinity between formal irony to
create aesthetic distance and didactic irony used as critique,
and Wieland's didactic presentation of his characters in no way
conflicts with the Rococo form of the poem. He merely takes
the inherent comic tendencies of the mode and uses Rococo
humour to a didactic end.

The grace of Musarion is bestowed on Phanias through what
amounts to an educative process. Wieland, whose novels represent the first great examples of the German *Bildungsroman,*
follows in this Rococo poem too the development of a young
man towards maturity. Musarion's philosophy is largely expounded through her attempts to counter the extremes into
which Phanias falls. By a neat irony, the last step consists of
Phanias drawing Musarion away from momentary exaggeration
when he finally persuades her to accept his love. . . . The educative process is complete and the pupil has become an equal
partner in the dialogue.

In the excesses of Phanias and the doctrines of his two mentors,
Wieland criticizes major tendencies of his own age. In the
arguments of the stoic Kleanth, Wieland attacks the still surviving aspect of baroque thought which preaches the vanity of
all life and the mortification of the flesh as the source of all
evil. Musarion, and Wieland, partially accept the view that life
is governed by fortune or fate, a fate which includes human
nature itself. Kleanth's mistake is double: his conclusion that
all is therefore vanity is too pessimistic; his belief in his own
power of rational control over the "baser" side of his nature
is too rationalistic and takes no account of human psychology.
Wieland's strongest argument is the psychological insight that
an excess of asceticism and a too blind belief in the powers of
reason turn man not into sage or saint, but into beast. Kleanth
ends up appropriately in the pig-sty. Wieland teaches, as does
Shaftesbury, that true humanity is achieved not through the
suppression but through the cultivation of human nature.

In Theophron, the poet castigates another form of contemporary
excess. Theophron, unlike Kleanth, is a worshipper of beauty,
but of beauty freed from the "filth of sensuality". . . . His
discourse is pursued in tones of high enthusiasm. He too, though
in a different way, seeks to transcend the human condition and
so falls into various extravagant postures, symbolized in his
refusal to eat beans, a ludicrous aspect of pythagorean doctrine.
Wieland is criticizing all the various excesses of emotional
idealism where the overheated imagination loses all touch with
reality. *Empfindsamkeit* and *Schwärmerei* or sentimentality and
enthusiasm are the terms applied to the various types of irrational, at times anti-rational, cult of spirituality and feeling
current in the eighteenth century. (pp. 33-6)

Has Wieland succeeded in integrating the philosophy and the
Rococo form of the poem? Occasionally a certain strain is
evident. In the last section Musarion's need for reassurance
concerning Phanias' intentions seems more typical of a well-
brought-up, middle-class young lady than of a Greek hetaira

or a Rococo beauty. Overemphasis on humble acceptance of one's lot occasionally disturbs. For the most part, however, the wit with which the philosophy is presented, and indeed the nature of the philosophy itself, allow for perfect formal integration. This is achieved in a variety of ways. One way, as we have seen, was the presentation of the characters. Another is the parallelism of intellectual and physical, or moral and aesthetic qualities which is set up, so that physical description implies moral or intellectual judgement. A striking example of the mingling of the sensual and the philosophical is the glance of Musarion (described with Popean brilliance), to which the poet devotes no less than thirty-three lines. . . . The effect of this glance on Phanias is to arouse his love again, but also to demolish his argument in favour of stoic asceticism by actively proving its emptiness. Similarly Phanias' wild beard and Theophron's refusal to eat beans are both signs of extravagance and do as much to discredit their intellectual attitudes as any argument. Musarion's beauty and the wrinkled ugliness of Kleanth imply a moral and intellectual judgement on their respective attitudes.

A similar mingling of the sensuous and aesthetic with the ethical and intellectual extends also into details of style. A sensuous adjective qualifies an abstract noun, a verb conveying a physical effect is used to suggest moral or emotional effects, and so on. (pp. 36-7)

Above all it is the "mischievously gentle tone of irony" . . . of Musarion, and of the narrator, which allows so much philosophy to be tempered with wit in Rococo form. The typical conversational tone of the Rococo *Verserzählung*, taken over from Lafontaine and first exploited in German by Hagedorn, is used by Wieland with great mastery. As Preisendanz points out, this technique owes much also to Fielding and the English novel and brings *Musarion* close to Wieland's novels. It serves a similar purpose here to that in the novels. It allows the author to interpret his material, to illuminate it from as many angles as possible, so that the process of interpretation becomes more important than the action itself. . . . The voice of the narrator in Musarion serves as much to create the poetic form as to express a philosophy and the one cannot be separated from the other. Indeed *Musarion* is valuable as a work of art rather than as a potted version of Shaftesbury's moral philosophy, because that philosophy has been transformed into eloquent and elegant Rococo form. The end of the poem provides a brilliant example of Wieland's irony. . . . A typical Rococo intrusion of reader and narrator breaks into the idyllic vision of Phanias' and Musarion's wise and peaceful life together. The reader, no doubt exhausted by all the philosophy, catches the poet before he closes to ask about Theophron and Kleanth. The former has learnt to eat beans, says the narrator, and the latter emerged the next day from the pig-sty and was never heard of again. Thus the poem closes on a comic anti-climax in a typical Rococo play with the convention of the pastoral idyll. Yet this comic close does not invalidate the ideal of the "philosophic idyll", but simply underlines that it is an ideal. The comic twist is a humorous expression of Wieland's rueful insight into human limitation, an insight which informs his whole philosophy. Thus philosophic import and Rococo formal wit are fused here as in the poem as a whole.

Musarion is very much a central work of its age. Formally it is indebted to the literary conventions of the mid-eighteenth century. The "philosophy of the Graces" is compounded of the moral and aesthetic philosophy of Shaftesbury, the rational and optimistic humanism of the Enlightenment, and a concern

with nature and the imaginative powers of man which might be called pre-romantic. A final evaluation of the poem must surely rest on its nature as a complex unity. It is complex through its variety of appeal to the senses, the mind and the emotions, through the balance it holds between so many currents of thought. It is a unity by virtue of its complete integration of form and content, or rather of aesthetic and didactic intent, since both "form" and "content" combine these two elements. Is it exemplification or transcendence of the Rococo mode? Preisendanz argues that its seriousness lifts it above the frivolity of Rococo. Huizinga, on the other hand, writes of Rococo as a whole words which certainly apply to *Musarion:* "Few ages in the history of art have held such a perfect balance between the serious and the playful as Rococo". Does it matter in the end? A literary generalization is a step-ladder to approach the individual work and can be left behind when its purpose is accomplished. (pp. 37-9)

> *Elizabeth Boa, "Wieland's 'Musarion' and the Rococo Verse Narrative," in* Periods in German Literature: Texts and Contexts, Vol. II, *edited by J. M. Ritchie, 1966. Reprint by Dufour, 1970, pp. 23-41.*

LIESELOTTE E. KURTH-VOIGT (essay date 1974)

[Kurth-Voigt examines the development of Wieland's narrative technique, focusing on the multiple points of view in his early writings.]

The phenomenon of different or contrasting evaluations of all aspects of life, as they are observed from diverse points of view, evidently fascinated Wieland; it was to become one of his favorite literary topics and importantly influenced his artistic method of representation. As in his critical writings, so in his earliest creative works, his consideration and inclusion of multiple points of view affirms for him the significance of each perspective as a component part of reality. Beyond that there are subtle or probing allusions reaching over the frame of the individual work and bringing adjoining perspectives into focus; dramatic scenes and intimate dialogues demonstrate the partial accuracy of dissenting opinions or biased judgments; and the subjective narration of human experiences by fictive figures reveals the circumscribed range of man's vision or expresses the limits of his mental capacity.

Very few of Wieland's early works have been analyzed or interpreted with adequate care, none exhaustively, and there is no comprehensive study that treats them as a unit with sufficient attention to artistic detail. (p. 89)

Some of Wieland's youthful works are modest in scope and undistinguished in their artistic qualities, to be sure; others, however, warrant more attention than they have hitherto received. The following discussion of a select group of these writings does not try to rectify the omission. Its aim is more specific: the analysis of typical sections from the more important works is for the purpose of demonstrating the presence of perspectivism and indicating the skilful utilization of the point-of-view technique even in Wieland's earliest writings. Such an approach cannot do full justice to the aesthetic values of these works, but it may show that their meaningful inclusion in more comprehensive studies will lead to new and clearer insights.

The very first of the larger works, the didactic poem *Die Natur der Dinge,* published in 1752 (when Wieland was only nineteen), and in substance a vindication of Leibniz' *Theodicée,* introduces perspectivistic traits. The model for the poem, grate-fully acknowledged by Wieland, was Lucretius' *De Rerum Natura,* and the poet intended the reader to notice many par-allels in content, form, and style. Both men attempt to prove a specific philosophical thesis and chose to do so in poetry. Each poem comprises six books, is composed in verse, and incorporates essential elements of classical rhetoric. Strikingly similar is the predominance of a vocabulary that stimulates the sense of sight; and the extensive use of visual images that are transformed into symbols or function as metaphors and similes is a common characteristic of both works.

Yet more revealing than these similarities are Wieland's de-partures from the model, particularly in the presentation of conflicting arguments and the ordering of supporting details. At the beginning of the poem he invokes the muses as Lucretius had done, but he requests a different kind of guidance. Inspired with divine enthusiasm by Minerva he hopes to rise above the common earthlings and plans to observe the universe from "heavenly heights":

> Ein ungewohnter Flug
> Hebt mich den Himmeln zu; von Millionen Sternen
> Umringt, lernt sich mein Blick vom niedern Pol
> entfernen. . . .

The superior point of view announced in these lines is, how-ever, not consistently maintained, and the perspective of the poet is intermittently augmented by the views of eminent philosophers.

In the first book of the poem man is initially represented as a weary wanderer who has lost his way. Darkness and the dim-ness of his vision blunt his mental perception and cause him to go astray; passion, vice, and sensuousness shroud his mind, and prejudices obstruct his outlook. At times his mental range is even more narrowly circumscribed, and his image of God's universe is clouded by a deceptive haze. This deplorable con-dition is depicted in an almost facetious manner that may seem inappropriate in a serious poem; man is compared to a tiny fly being attached to a statue of gigantic size. . . . [The] extended simile, although perhaps unwittingly humorous, nevertheless reveals young Wieland's sense of the comic. At this early stage in his career, however, he did not permit his ironies to range widely, possibly because he considered the resulting mood unsuitably frivolous for a poet whose serious intention it was to edify and instruct the discriminating reader.

In his attempts to judge the entire universe by the small frag-ment he is able to observe, man has often fallen into error. But he does not seem wholly responsible for his mistaken beliefs, for unreliable philosophers and false prophets have often misled him, sometimes even deliberately. Both poets therefore present a *refutatio* of delusive concepts; yet whereas Lucretius reports fallacious arguments in indirect discourse, Wieland, perhaps recollecting Cicero's method in the *De Na-tura Deorum,* offers deceptive opinions in such a manner that they reveal more immediately the bias of their advocates. The precepts of Zoroaster, for example, are advanced in direct speech, rather conspicuously exposing their rigid limitations. Living in a dark forest, his mind filled with frightening images, the Persian contemplates the cause and nature of evil in the world; and from a dismal *Anblickspunct*—in a later edition Wieland uses the term *Augenpunkt*—he views the misery of mankind:

> Ein boshaft Wesen ists, das uns das Seyn misgönnet,
> Sein Herz ist stetes Feur, wo Zorn und Rache brennet
> Und dunkle Flammen speyt; es nährt mit unserm Blut,
> Gleich einem fetten Oel, die unglückselge Glut. . . .

The personal experiences of the ancient prophet are necessarily limited; but Zoroaster finds his distressing visions of man's life on earth affirmed in the writings of the past, and the works of poets constitute a meaningful extension of his limited knowl-edge of empirical reality. . . . (pp. 93-5)

The fifth book of the poem takes up, directly and explicitly, questions of viewpoint, perspective, and relativity. A prefatory statement expresses the poet's convictions and attempts to guide the reader's interpretation of subsequent sections:

> Die Form der Dinge ist so mannichfaltig, als
> die Gesichtspuncte, woraus sie gesehen wer-
> den. Die Grösse, der Raum, die Zeit, die Qual-
> itäten der Körper usw, sind bloß relative Dinge.

A major part of the book is designed to exemplify this notion and support the poet's contention that man's perception of reality is utterly subjective and depends inevitably on the po-sition from which an object or occurrence is viewed. Although *Die Natur der Dinge* foreshadows, technically and thematically, comparable features of later works, it contains a notable con-trast to the writings of the mature Wieland. In this early poem the author does not remain neutral; instead, he challenges con-testable philosophic views and presents counter-arguments in which he eloquently refutes the ideas of those whom he opposes.

The next larger work, also published in 1752, is the collection of *Zwölf moralische Briefe.* The preface, virtually a formal *exordium,* announces the poet's intention to portray virtue in its most pleasing form, to acquaint the reader with its beauties and commend to him an easy manner by which he can find happiness, "Glückseligkeit." The defense of his ambitious undertaking concludes with a thoroughly confident assertion: "So sehe ich die Sache an, und ich bin gewiß, daß viele hierinn eben so denken wie ich."

The self-confidence expressed in these lines and a first super-ficial reading of the epistles may create the impression that the events depicted in the *Moralische Briefe* are observed exclu-sively from the poet's point of view, by artistic design a firmly established superior standpoint. To be sure, the idealistic first-person speaker is easily identified with the young Wieland, and the interpolated moralizing reflections unquestionably ad-vance his own values; yet a closer examination of the text reveals that the poet supports his opinions by a clever manip-ulation of authoritative views, for almost every one of the conclusions reached in these letters is reinforced by historic and literary perspectives. The method, employed by Wieland with remarkable skill, reflects his acquaintance with classical rhetoric and foreshadows the principles of his own *Theorie . . . der Red-Kunst* (1757), the summary of lectures which he pre-sented when he was a tutor in Zurich. Confirming a traditional dictum of oration, he recommends that every narration be sub-stantially supported by external proof to achieve the highest degree of probability. Convincing evidence to be incorporated in the *confirmatio* should be extracted "*a testimonio,* da man seinen Satz durch Zeugnisse, die eine große Autorität haben, und *ab exemplo,* da man ihn durch historische Beyspiele be-stätigt." (pp. 95-6)

A second didactic poem of the early period, the *Anti-Ovid* of 1752, . . . treats questions of love, sex, and eroticism. The popularity of Ovid and the contemporary approbation of anac-reontic poetry afforded the stimulus for the work, which was ostensibly intended as a counter-perspective to the *Ars Ama-*

toria. The first lines of the poem announce the poet's intention, somewhat awkwardly in the earliest version:

> Erzehl, o Lied, die seltne Kunst zu lieben,
> Die Kunst der goldnen Zeit, da jedes weiche Hertz
> Von zärtlichen der Tugend werthen Trieben
> Noch überfloß. . . ,

more explicitly in the last version of the poem:

> Die Kunst zu lieben sangst du uns, Ovid:
> Die wahre Art zu lieben sey mein Lied!

Although these lines seem to indicate that the poet will portray virtuous, perhaps even Platonic love, and at the same time relegate Ovid and his followers to a position of little importance, he does not at all silence the "singers of sensuous love." On the contrary, throughout his work he presents a double perspective: the images of pure love, affectionately delineated by the idealistic young poet, alternate with the portrayal of lusty eroticism in scenes that are borrowed from literature and are intended to serve as *exempla negativa.*

The deplorable weakness of man in permitting himself to be seduced by the evil tempter Ariman, by the wanton songs of Anacreon, or by the sinful teachings of Ovid, the "Meister loser Künste," rouses the poet's indignation. Yet he is even more perturbed when he discovers that these literary representations are imitations of reality and that, for example, Juvenal and Petronius, who in their satires ridiculed the outrageously sordid behavior of their contemporaries, actually took their models from life. Although man should perhaps be held responsible for all his acts, extenuating circumstances relieve him of part of his guilt, for personified voluptuousness, that is *Wollust,* dulls his awareness of evil with flattery and deceives him by creating a favorable image of herself:

> Sie borgt die Farbe der Natur.
> Sich uns gefälliger zu schmücken;
> Verbirgt, was sie entehrt, den aufgehaltnen Blicken,
> Und zeigt uns schlau die schöne Seite nur. . . .

A searching and critical scrutiny of her entire domain is not possible from the poet's superior vantage point; he may have to change his position, a necessity he seems to resent:

> Doch wie? soll ich dann von den Höhen
> . . . . . .
> In deinen Staub herunter steigen,
> O Pöbel! . . .

Despite his indignation, however, he descends and cannot help but mock the acts of folly he now must observe. Although it was certainly not his intention to write satire, it is literally forced out of him by the deplorable behavior of man, and with cutting sarcasm he portrays the fate of those who are enslaved by sensual pleasures and passion. (pp. 99-100)

The sketches of human folly in the *Anti-Ovid* clearly reveal the talent for satire which Wieland developed to perfection in his later writings. At this early stage, however, the young poet seems rather shocked by his inclination to expose man's weaknesses in this fashion. He suddenly realizes that he has temporarily lost sight of his intentions to panegyrize virtue; fortunately, however, love herself restrains the "Juvenalean hand" from boldly painting more scornful pictures of this sort and leads him back to his nobler task. The mediated negative perspective of the satire is again balanced by idealistic portrayals also selected from literature. Uz, Gleim, and Hagedorn are offset by Gellert, Klopstock, Haller, and Lange, who through

their depiction of pure emotions encourage man to rise above the lowlands of sexual desires and physical involvement.

During the first year of his diversified literary activity Wieland also began to experiment with narrative techniques that were to become characteristic features of his later writings. The fourth larger work, the collection of *Erzählungen* (1752), introduces several significantly new modes of presentation. In contrast to the didactic poems, these verse tales belong to the genre of fiction. Although for the most part the poet enacts the role of omniscient narrator, he occasionally tries—as Henry James would much later describe such an attempt—"to get into the skin of the creature." The point of view from which events and emotions are intermittently seen approximates that of the title heroes, for example Balsora, Zenim, and Gulhindy, or Melinde; in two other tales the poet's perspective sporadically converges with that of representative characters, "Die Unglycklichen" of the third story, and "Der Unzufriedene" of the fourth tale. In the earliest works, *Die Natur der Dinge, Moralische Briefe,* and *Anti-Ovid,* the voices of other authorities, that is philosophers, writers, and historians, were occasionally heard, but the poet himself was the dominant speaker. The *Erzählungen,* by contrast, present monologues and dialogues of purely fictive characters, sparingly in the first tale, most extensively in **"Selim,"** the last of the six stories, in which at times the poet only provides stage directions and has his figures carry on an almost dramatic dialogue. Although there are three voices at work here: that of the narrator, that of Selim, the hero of the tale, and that of Selima, his beloved companion, they are not yet distinctive enough to characterize the individual speakers as being basically different from each other; all three use the same poetic and stylized language reflecting their common idealizing enthusiasm for the beauty and pleasures of nature. (pp. 100-01)

A second collection of letters, the nine **Briefe von Verstorbenen an hinterlassene Freunde** (1753) reveals—as the title indicates—a unique perspective which was actually prefigured in an earlier English work of 1728, *Friendship in Death* by Elizabeth Singer Rowe. The method of presentation is technically different from that of the *Moralische Briefe* in that the events are subjectively reported by fictive figures without the overt intrusion of the poet. Unquestionably, however, the correspondents are made to share the author's superior point of view; they obviously sanction his ideal conception of the function of literature and tacitly confirm his views on the moral obligations of writers as Wieland had expressed them in a personal letter of March 1752: "—ich habe von der Dichtkunst keinen kleinern Begrif, als daß Sie die *Sängerin* Gottes, seiner Werke, und der Tugend sevn soll." (pp. 102-03)

The collections of fictive letters were succeeded by a series of *Gespräche,* formal dialogues invariably characterized by the subtle manipulation of multiple perspectives. Wieland considered the first of these dialogues, the **"Gespräch des Socrates mit Timoclea von der scheinbaren und wahren Schönheit"** (1754), of seminal importance, and it appeared in every edition of his collected works because it was "der erste Versuch des Verfassers in der dialogistischen Kunst." As the title indicates, the topic of the dialogue is beauty, and many aspects of it, particular and general, physical and spiritual, are viewed from multiple points of view. The mirror image of Timoclea presents her beauty in a favorable light, and the slave girl attending her expresses an equally flattering opinion, yet Timoclea mistrusts both mirror and slave. Her concept of beauty has been influenced by literature, and the ideal images portrayed in poetry serve her as a means to measure her own physical qualities. The possibility that diverging evaluations of her external beauty could exist, and the seeming lack of absolute standards, puzzle the young girl. She therefore implores Socrates to tell her truthfully whether or not she is beautiful. . . . He promises to grant her request but before he can do so he must express a word of caution: beauty is relative, and its appreciation depends on the beholder. . . . An envious woman will naturally find her less attractive than a man who admires her. The dialogue soon reaches beyond the limited subject of Timoclea's appearance. Socrates develops his theory of physical and spiritual beauty, interprets the body as the mirror of the soul, and touches upon Wieland's perennial topic, the nature of man. In typical socratic fashion he guides Timoclea into philosophical dialogue by asking leading questions and extracting the only possible, predictable answers. It is not by chance that at the end of their conversation their intellectual vantage points coincide and their perspectives converge.

More complex in construction is a later group of dialogues, *Theages oder Unterredungen von Schönheit und Liebe* of 1755. Conversations treating the topics of beauty and love are presented in a letter addressed to a fictitious recipient written by an equally fictitious figure who willingly admits the limits of his objectivity and frankly betrays the bias of his personal views. Although the work remained a fragment, the published parts do reveal the variety of views that would have been offered in the completed work. A major section of the epistle is the reproduction of a dialogue between the correspondent and his friend Nicias, an enthusiastic Platonist. Interpolated into the conversation, reported partly in direct speech, are several other dialogues, the most extensive one between Nicias and the hermit Theages, and an unusually intriguing exchange of opinions between Theages, also a Platonist, and Aspasia, who does not fully subscribe to his idealistic visions of love. Viewpoints are thus enfolded within one another and several individual perspectives are offered, even if they are not widely separated or contrasting. (pp. 104-05)

The early development of the point-of-view technique reaches its culmination in *Araspes und Panthea* . . . (1760). It was written during the time of Wieland's "metamorphosis" and testifies to the author's descent from his *Adlerflug* to earth. In contrast to the former idealizing depiction of love, the theme of the dialogues is the question of whether the mastery of passion depends on man's free will or if there are forces at work that disable his reason when sensual desire takes possession of him. Araspes' love for Panthea is the central event, and the psychological discussion of the hero's involvement by every one of the interlocutors produces a complex pattern of analytical perspectives. The initial dialogue between Cyrus and Araspes, still a rather theoretical discourse, reveals their contrasting views. Cyrus believes that man is often helplessly enslaved by his passion for a woman and is therefore unable to control his emotions or the ultimate consequences of his action. Araspes does not agree, but is convinced that he has the capability to check his desires of his own volition. Experience, however, was to teach him differently. His admiration for Panthea, the wife of Abradates, turns into love, and he is seized with an uncontrollable desire to possess her, a development which is observed and interpreted from diverse points of view.

The first one to notice the profound change in his attitude is Araspes himself; the progression of his entanglement is intermittently accompanied by monologues of searching self-analysis and, as Shaftesbury had described the technique, Araspes becomes his own subject and undergoes a process of "self-dissection." The soliloquies are at first meant to help him understand his conflicting emotions; later, however, they serve to rationalize and vindicate his questionable behavior. Araspes is also permitted to verbalize his feelings in intimate conversations with Arasambes, who basically shares the views of Cyrus: there is no escape from passion unless the lover removes himself from the object of his desire; Arasambes therefore implores Araspes to renounce his appointment as the guardian of Panthea.

A diverging double perspective is provided through the dialogue between Panthea and her wise old servant Mandane. Whereas the young woman idealizes the feelings of Araspes and interprets them as unselfish and virtuous love, Mandane sees his infatuation as an illness which can only be cured by severe measures, at best perhaps the betrayal of his passion to Cyrus.

Still another perspective develops when the slave girls, virtually enacting the role of the chorus in Greek tragedy, voice their views and predictions. In their earthy approach to questions of love and sex they correctly analyze Araspes' behavior as typical of a man ardently desiring the woman he adores; and they interpret Panthea's obvious concern for his welfare as an expression of her own erotic feelings. It is only a question of time, they actually hope, before the lovers will gratify their desire and commit adultery. Not only has their own experience led to these insights, literature, too, portrays the fate of women pursued by passionate lovers, and at the very moment when Araspes attempts, though unsuccessfully, to seduce Panthea, they perform an antiphony of love and temptation, guilt and atonement. In the concluding dialogue with Cyrus, Araspes reveals that the experience has deepened his understanding of the nature of man. He is not any more the idealist who expects to master his passions with superior self-control; he now is aware of the complex character of human beings and concludes that man must have two souls which are responsible for his actions. . . . (pp. 111-12)

The story of Araspes and Panthea is presented without the intervention of a personal of fictive narrator, and the excellence of the work testifies to the success of Wieland's experimentation with philosophic and dramatic dialogue. His predilection for this artistic method also found expression in the two tragedies of the early period, *Lady Johanna Gray* (1758) and *Clementina von Porretta* (1760). Although both plays reveal Wieland's persistent and attentive study of man, their major characters are still idealized and their depiction does not yet manifest the poet's descent from his superior point of view, nor does it demonstrate the irrevocable return from his *Adlerflug*. Wieland's presentation of perfect figures should not be censured as a misinterpretation of human nature; on the contrary, he was sensitively aware that this manner of portrayal essentially constituted a glorification of man and did not at all conform to the principles of psychological realism in literature that were so very earnestly advocated by many of his contemporaries; he therefore repeatedly explained his reasons for the adherence to a tradition that was much debated at the time when his plays were performed in Germany and Switzerland. His theoretical discussion of tragedy contained in the *Theorie und Geschichte der Red-Kunst und Dicht-Kunst* . . . supports the poetic creation of perfect characters . . . and the preface to *Lady Johanna Gray* affirms his conception that tragedy should present noble, heroic, and virtuous figures. . . . Reiterating these views in his personal correspondence, he asserted his privilege to portray equally idealized figures in his second tragedy and defiantly disregarded the criticism to which *Lady Johanna Gray* had been subjected by well-known men of letters in Berlin, among them Lessing. (pp. 112-13)

Lessing's criticism of *Lady Johanna Gray* was indeed severe. He ridiculed Wieland's principles as expressed in the preface of the published work and, cuttingly sarcastic, rejected the presentation of perfect characters on the stage. (pp. 113-14)

Lessing was nevertheless convinced that Wieland would abandon the deceptive idealization of man at his return to earth from the "etherial regions" and recognize the true nature of a being that participates in good and evil. "Und alsdenn," Lessing predicts, "wenn er diese innere Mischung des Guten und Bösen in dem Menschen wird erkannt, wird studiret haben, alsdenn geben Sie Acht, was für vortreffliche Trauerspiele er uns liefern wird!"

Not much later Wieland did indeed explicitly renounce the ideals of his youth, and it was perhaps no coincidence that in his personal correspondence he spoke of the change in his perspective, his "Herabsteigen auf die Erde," in a language that recalls Lessing's formulations. He also revealed more frankly than his contemporaries would appreciate that he was well acquainted with the complexities of human nature. Yet Lessing's prediction did not come true; Wieland delivered no splendid tragedies but preferred to portray man in all his inglorious imperfection less seriously and in different genres. (p. 114)

> *Lieselotte E. Kurth-Voigt, in her* Perspectives and Points of View: The Early Works of Wieland and Their Background, *The Johns Hopkins University Press, 1974, 189 p.*

MARTIN SWALES (essay date 1978)

[*Swales discusses Wieland's complex narrative technique in* Agathon, *concentrating on his frequent and seemingly inconsistent statements regarding the hero's character and the factual authenticity of the novel.*]

For readers of English novels, *Agathon* might, I suspect, prove a somewhat forbidding prospect. It is a daunting novel, not just because of its length, but also because of its profuse digressions, digressions that are not mitigated by the exhilarating zaniness of, say *Tristram Shandy*. We have an abundance of narrative commentary and discursive reflections on moral and epistemological questions that threatens to swamp the slender and not exactly gripping plot. Moreover, this wealth of narrative rumination is not only bulky, it is also curiously paradoxical and inconsistent. For this reason it can be nothing short of infuriating. One obvious example is the first few sentences of the Preface with which the novel opens: "The editor of this present story sees so little likelihood of persuading the public that it is in fact derived from an old Greek manuscript that he believes it is his best course of action to say nothing about this matter and to leave it up to the reader to think what he pleases." . . . We begin, in other words, with a statement that is immediately withdrawn as pointless, which cannot but make us wonder why the statement should have been made in the first place. We may already suspect what in fact proves to be the case: the narrator does not abandon his references to the original manuscript, they recur frequently throughout the novel.

Having left the question of authenticity of source behind him, our narrator proceeds to raise the issue of why we should be interested in such a person as Agathon. It is suggested to us that the truth of any fictional work resides in its naturalness, in that it is conceived in accordance with and shows respect for the "ways of the world," that its characters "are not capriciously invented by the imagination or design of the author, but have been taken from the inexhaustible storehouse of nature herself." . . . The human heart is portrayed truthfully, naturally; the passions of which it is capable are shown as arising from specific characteristics, from precisely documented circumstances. Our narrator—or rather, "editor," as he continues to designate himself despite the conclusion he has reached in the opening paragraph—informs us that his chief aim is to render the manifold nature of Agathon's being in all its complexity, and that he has chosen this young man to be his center of interest because of his intimate acquaintance with the details of Agathon's life. He blandly continues:

> For this reason he can reliably assert that Agathon and most of the other characters who are part of his story are real people. They are the sort of people who have existed in great numbers from time immemorial, and they exist to this very day. Moreover, he can say that—with the exception of some trifling circumstances, of certain consequences and specific details of chance events, and of whatever else belongs to the decorative embroidering of the story—everything that is essential to this story is as historically true and perhaps even a shade more authentic than anything written by the most reliable political historians which we at present possess. . . .

(pp. 38-40)

At this point the reader may be forgiven if his head begins to spin slightly. Although we have already been told that credibility in a work of art is not a question of authenticated facts but of the reader's sense that the story could happen, we are now faced with special pleading to the effect that most of the characters had real-life originals. (*Most* of them, we ask ourselves, why not all?) We learn that some features of the story are not part of this authenticated reality. Well, which are they? Will we be able to distinguish them from the verifiable truth? And, to compound the confusion, we are told that the essence of the story is probably truer than anything written by the most scrupulous historians. It would seem, therefore, that the essential part will be essential whether it can be authenticated or not; indeed, it is the measure of its essentialness that it is more convincing than any verifiable facts. Of course, our narrator-editor continues, reality itself can be highly improbable (as even conscientious historians have attested), and for this reason "the author believes he has the right to expect that his readers will believe him absolutely when he positively asserts that Agathon did actually think or behave in a certain way." . . . Two comments seem to me appropriate here: first, the narrator, who has been the "editor" so far, now becomes the "author," which somewhat removes the note of special pleading for the authenticity of source material; second, at precisely the point when the "authenticity principle" seems to be on the wane we are most urgently requested to believe the writer when he strenuously asserts the factual accuracy of what he recounts.

The Preface concludes with some remarks on the character of Agathon himself. We are told that he is not a paragon of all the virtues, not a model of constancy and principle, and that this is the measure of his plausibility as a character. Moreover, we learn that our hero must be put to the test in the course of his journey through life and that only those readers who are themselves inclined to dishonesty and wickedness will be led astray by what they read (by the sophistry of Hippias, for example). We are assured that it is the narrator's plan that Agathon will learn from his various experiences, that he will end the novel as a wise and virtuous man. All this sounds very admirable, even though such assertions seem to contradict the early remarks to the effect that the truth (and value) of such a novel as this is to be found in its naturalness, "that the characters are not capriciously invented by the imagination or design of the author." . . . We are now assured that there is a "set of moral intentions which we have had in mind in composing this work." . . . (pp. 40-2)

I have summarized the arguments of the Preface in such length and detail because the Preface quite clearly establishes a whole set of narrative intimations which are sustained throughout the novel. Moreover, the Preface initiates precisely that narrative discursiveness of which I have spoken, a discursiveness that takes many forms. There are a number of features of the novel as a whole which I wish to highlight here. First, in the debate about the nature and validity of the story the reader is asked to bear in mind considerations of fictional truth and factual authenticity, of *Agathon* as a novel and as an edited diary. Second, the reader finds himself engaged in a debate about the nature of human experience, about that human potentiality within himself which allows him to identify as valid and to identify with fictional models of human behavior. Third, the reader is engaged in a discussion about morals, about the dialectic of general principles and specific cases, of norms and the intractably individual, relative context to which they must be related. Fourth, the reader is invited to reflect on human character, to ask to what extent an intact, coherent self can be said to realize itself with a kind of cumulative consistency, and to what extent the personality is constantly in flux, a self-renewing complex of contradictory and compensatory energies and potentialities. These and other concerns are mediated through a carefully activated narrative field of reference: we have an original text and its modern fictive reworking, an original narrator and a present editor-cum-narrator, and, above all else, the reader as notional presence, apostrophized, cajoled, and buttonholed as part of the overall fiction. Indeed, it is carefully suggested that there is a plurality of possible reader responses, and insofar as we are engaged in a debate with the narrator, we also find ourselves disputing our reading with notional fellow readers.

Two particular aspects of the complex of problems outlined above demand further consideration, largely because they highlight the interaction of discursive narrative fireworks and the overall import of the work. I have in mind the questions of Agathon's character and status as novel hero, and of the fiction of the original manuscript on which the novel is purportedly based. (pp. 42-3)

[Agathon] is a man who oscillates between the active and the contemplative life, between public and private activity, between senses and spirit. He is a cluster of complementary energies: when he tries to be idealistic, he finds that the responses of his senses cloud his certainties; when he feels attracted toward Hippias and all he stands for, his idealism reasserts itself; when he is living a secluded life, he is attracted by politics; when he is in politics he feels the appeal of a life withdrawn from the turmoil of social living. At any given point in Agathon's story, we feel that there are more aspects to his personality than he is able to realize in any one pursuit or course of action. Moreover, he is not an unthinking person. Yet over and over again we sense that his self-examinations, his analyses of his situation, are too simple, are too much a flight into convenient labels and principles to do justice to the lability of his experiential capacities. Agathon is much less a known quantity, a manageable entity than any given activity, any given attempt at self-explication would suggest. So what is Agathon? In an attempt to deal with this question I shall look at one particularly crucial passage at the end of Book IX, Chapter 5. The narrator's invitation to his readers here to reflect on the persona of his hero is a concentrated example of the kinds of statements that are very much part of the narrator's running commentary throughout the novel.

Characteristically, the narrator begins, "We make a brief pause here, in order to give the reader time to consider what he at this point may have to say for or against our hero." . . . The primary issue, then, is how to evaluate Agathon's behavior. We have just learned that in a debating contest our hero has spoken out against the republican form of government; the narrator immediately suggests that in this context (as elsewhere) we must bear in mind that Agathon's views are of necessity affected by the specific experiences he has undergone (here, the ingratitude of the Athenians). He goes on to argue that those readers who uphold constancy of character and attitude as the supreme virtue must ask themselves whether this is not a totally unreal demand to make on a human being: given that everything around us changes, how should we be the one immovable, consistent entity? The narrator gives point to his general reflections by referring us to certain kinds of novel fiction: "In moral novels we do admittedly find heroes who remain true to themselves in everything—and who are to be praised for this. . . . But in life we find matters very different." . . . The criterion invoked is that of experience, of "life." It tells us that we only grow and develop by undertaking activities which change us, mislead us, and alienate us from ourselves: "We have already seen our hero in various situations; and in each, through the force of circumstance, a little different from what he really is." . . . Implicit here is the notion that the reality of Agathon is a complex, elusive self not fully expressed by any specific activity in which he is engaged. The idea is clarified in the following passage: "He seemed by turns . . . a pious idealist, a platonist, a republican, a hero, a stoic, a voluptuary; and he was none of these things, although he at various times passed through all these phases and always a little of each rubbed off on him. It will probably continue like this for quite some time." . . . To observe the course of Agathon's life up to this point is to observe a series of events in linear sequence, a *Nacheinander*. Yet, potentially, he is all of those personae at one and the same time; his self is a *Nebeneinander* which can never be enacted in linear realization. The narrator is careful to add a further point: it might be tempting to conclude that this complex self can be apprehended as the sum total of all his past actions, but this would be to presuppose that Agathon's life is over and done with, that he is a known quantity to himself and to the readers, that there is no room for further change, for further activation of potential selves. The narrator advises caution here: what Agathon has been up to the present is not an exhaustive living out of his potentiality. Rather, his self is the result of chance; a contingent sequence of occurrences has activated him to various kinds of response. We must not judge prematurely, because we cannot claim premature certainty about him:

> But of his character, of what he really was and
> of what remained constant about him under all

these disguises . . . of all this we cannot yet speak. Hence, without passing premature judgment—a thing we are accustomed to do time and time again in everyday life—we will continue to observe him . . . and to refrain from evaluating the totality of his moral being until such time as we are acquainted with it. . . .

Interestingly, the narrator here reverses the emphasis in the comparison between literature (the novel) and life. In our everyday experience we are forced by pragmatic considerations into premature judgments (both epistemological and moral). But in terms of our interpretative relationship to this novel fiction before us, we can afford the luxury of scrupulousness, we can admit to complexities, to the vital dimension of that which has not yet become reality, of futurity as an abiding factor which must condition our response to a human being. Thus the narrator dismantles whatever clarity we think we may have attained about the protagonist (or indeed, whatever clarity the protagonist may think he has achieved about himself). The security of our cognitive and evaluative relationship to Agathon's character is disturbed by a two-pronged attack which criticizes a certain kind of novel fiction for its crude model of human behavior, and which also criticizes the realm of everyday human interaction for its adherence to simplistic, pragmatic judgments.

The implications of these narrative reflections are many and complex. Most obviously, they would appear to call into question any straightforward, cumulatively linear teleology in the novel. One begins to wonder whether there will ever be a watershed in Agathon's life from which point on we will know him reliably, fully, consistently. We also wonder whether Agathon himself will ever achieve such clarity, whether there is a set of insights which can be possessed once and for all. Moreover, one wonders whether such perfect cognition would automatically entail a particular kind of practical behavior (a certain career or activity). The import of the narrator's running commentary serves to suggest that such certainty is impossible because it could only be attained as a kind of Archimedean point located outside the self, outside the context of its living and functioning. And yet, in total disregard of such considerations, our narrator at times writes with a kind of sovereign assurance—both epistemological and moral—which seems to make nonsense of his earlier statements. One can, for example, find passages of evaluative commentary which seem curiously simplistic. This is particularly noticeable in the narrator's treatment of the Agathon-Danae relationship. At times he shows himself fully able to suggest the complexity of what is involved here, the process of mutual enrichment and transformation, the volatile interplay of reality and erotic illusion. At other times, however, he manifests a curious censoriousness and unproblematic, even self-righteous, certainty. For example, he describes Agathon and Danae as being "happy in this sweet infatuation" . . . and later insists that Agathon's involvement with Danae is a kind of abberation, "a lengthy progression along those mistaken paths on to which he had strayed." . . . Particularly significant is the end of Book VII, Chapter 9, where Agathon abandons Danae: "But as soon as it had come to the point where he believed himself deceived in his opinion of her character and moral worth, as soon as he found himself compelled to despise her—then she ceased to be Danae for him. And by a completely natural sequence of events, he again became Agathon in that same moment." . . . Of course, there is an element of doubt inherent in these remarks (one notes that Agathon *believes* himself to have been deceived), but even

so, the statement betrays a certainty about the hero's selfhood which is in marked contradistinction to the narrator's tentativeness about the nature of his protagonist. In part, such a certainty is shared by Agathon himself. When he set off for Syracuse, "he felt again that he was Agathon." . . . Later, when Agathon is overcome with longing for his pure, beloved Psyche, the narrator affirms that "all these symptoms vouch for the fact that he is still Agathon." . . . Such remarks set up a sustained implication that there *is* a known quantity Agathon, a constant individual whose life grows with necessity and coherence out of that childhood self raised in the temple environment. And that constant self would appear to be none other than Agathon the idealist, the *Schwärmer*. The reasons for this curiously disingenuous view of the main character are, in my view, bound up with the whole fiction of the original manuscript, to which I shall return.

I have already referred to the fact that the debate about character is channeled through a debate about novel fiction, about the reader's response to this present story and to other kinds of novels he has met. Part of the narrator's constant barrage of criticism is mounted against those who always know how to interpret a situation, how to evaluate a character. The narrator's long-windedness and all-pervading uncertainty become crystallized in his frequent assertions of the unnovellike quality of his intrusiveness. Indeed, he is prepared on occasion to suggest that the alienated reader who finds such digressions inappropriate in a novel may wish to skip the discursive interludes. *Agathon* is, then, a novel which makes traditional novel fiction (and its attendant expectations) explicitly thematic and challenges them. One might almost say that it is a novel which proclaims itself unreadable by the criteria of the traditional novel—but goes on to ask whether the traditional novel is worth reading in the first place. Particularly significant is the passage where we are explicitly told that Agathon is not really a novel hero:

> What we are essentially after with these remarks is simply that the kind of novel heroes we have been talking about are even less to be found within the realm of nature than are lions with wings or fish with girls' bodies . . . and that therefore the hero of our story, as a result of the changes and weaknesses to which we have seen him prone, is of course—we admit it—less of a hero, but the more so is he a man. And the more is he able to instruct us by his experience—even by his faults. . . .

It is the measure of the human probability of the figure of Agathon that he is precisely *not* a traditional novel hero, that morally and psychologically he is not a constant.

This brings me to a final point about narration in this novel: the constant references to the original manuscript. Here, of course, we are confronted by an ironic tension of assertions and intimations. On the one hand, we are asked to believe that the original manuscript is based on Agathon's own account of his life; hence it is authentic, and therefore, unchangeable. On the other hand, we are made clearly aware that the original manuscript reports a wildly providential story. Our narrator is able to use this story as a cipher for a mode of unsophisticated narration, for unsophisticated portrayal of the self as a known quantity—and can criticize it in terms of his own (modern) awareness of psychological (and hence, narrative) complexity. The opening of Chapter 5 of Book X is a sustained example of what I mean: "The author of the old manuscript from which we admit to having taken the greater part of this story, is, as we have seen, triumphant because he has managed to get his hero away from a court with his virtue entirely intact.'' . . . But this is followed by an enormous digression on the nature of human virtue and integrity. It concludes: ''Our thoughtful readers will quite clearly understand why we have scruples about applauding the original author of the Greek manuscript in his all too favorable assessment of the present moral state of our hero.'' . . . The suggestion is, of course, that we as modern readers have to be infinitely more cautious in our judgments than was the original writer.

The ironic fiction of the original manuscript allows Wieland to have his cake and eat it. But one still wonders why he should have bothered to incorporate this further strand of narrative intimation into his novel. The observations about verisimilitude and authenticity, about the complexity of modern reader responses vis-à-vis narratively naive fictional modes, have already been made with sufficient thoroughness. One must ask quite simply why Wieland bothered with the fiction of the original manuscript. There is, I think, one significant answer which is part and parcel of the whole problem of character and plot with which I have been concerned. The particular function I have in mind asserts itself with greatest clarity toward the end of the novel. Book XI begins with a criticism of the original author for having betrayed all concern for verisimilitude in order to furnish his readers with a resounding happy ending to the story: ''In this, the eleventh, book, we must admit that our author appears to have strayed somewhat from this our world . . . into the land of ideas, of miracles, of events which turn out exactly as one might have wished, into, to say it all over again, the land of Beautiful Souls and utopian republics.'' . . . It would appear that the temptation has proved too great: the original author decided ''to test and cleanse his [Agathon's] virtue, and to bring it to the required consistency,'' . . . so that the novel could end with a worthily climactic conclusion. This narrative teleology strikes the narrator (and his readers) as patently improbable, ''but what is a poor author to do?'' . . . The author's solution resides in a further polarization of the irony: the original manuscript is scrupulously adhered to but is called relentlessly into question at every turn. Indeed, our narrator goes so far as to turn this critical method on himself:

> The intentions which led him to publish the old manuscript, which came into his hands by chance, in a version whose form and character has been sufficiently illustrated by the previous ten books, have already been fulfilled. It is, we trust, unnecessary that we go into greater detail here. Yet this much we can say: that we have never intended to write a novel—although many may not have got this into their heads despite the title and the preface—and as this book, insofar as the editor has had a hand in it, is no novel, nor is intended to be one, he, the editor, can summon up little interest in the so-called tying of the knot—in the question whether the author of the manuscript has unraveled or cut the knot skillfully or clumsily. . . .

Despite all appearances to the contrary (appearances, we should add, which the narrator has most carefully exploited), the book we have been reading is apparently no novel. For this reason it does not matter whether the original has a felicitous or awkward conclusion: either way, it remains ''novel material,'' and our narrator has so far distanced himself from such fictions

that any tinkering with the original would be utterly superfluous. Book XI is, accordingly, allowed to proceed on its triumphant way as it chronicles the reunion of Agathon, Psyche, and Danae. ''And why not?'' asks the narrator, ''now that we all know how happy we can make our friend Agathon in the process.'' . . . Psyche, we are told, has been saved from the hands of pirates by a storm, and the narrator adds a heavily ironic defense of the stock-in-trade of the providential novel ending: ''You really have no cause to complain, gentlemen, for it is, to the best of our knowledge, the first storm in this story.'' . . . (pp. 44-53)

The concluding book of the novel reveals the full import of Wieland's irony, the extent to which he enabled himself to have his cake and eat it. At one level, novel convention is serenely allowed to take its course—because, one is tempted to add, Wieland would otherwise have denied himself the possibility of ending the enterprise on which he had embarked. In other words, he can both mount a critique of the novel genre and tell a novel at the same time. But this is not to be seen simply as some kind of urbane in-joke with the reader. For the discussion of novel expectations, of expectations about plot and character, is the principal channel by which Wieland brings into focus a much larger debate about issues of human cognition and value judgments, about moral norms and principles, about epistemological certainties. In order to initiate and to sustain this debate, Wieland had to intimate not only critique, but also the object of his critique. That is, he had to bounce his questioning off the stability and the simplistic human and narrative *donnée* of the traditional novel form. Without that ironic undertaking, without that ''critical-analytical relationship to the narratable,'' without that obstinate remnant of traditional novel plot, Wieland's *Agathon* would cease to be a work of narrative fiction. At that point, of course, one asks why Wieland should have wished to write any kind of novel in the first place. Why should he not have written some kind of philosophical or epistemological tract? Why did he not have the strength of his discursive convictions, of his *Essayismus, avant la lettre?* The answer must surely be—and this is the profoundest legitimation of the ironic stance adopted in *Agathon*—that there is an essential truth about even the most rudimentary of novel fictions. However much human character, for example, may be infinitely more complex than the traditional novel allows, may be a vitally interacting *Nebeneinander*, yet man, whether he likes it or not, does live and move within the *Nacheinander* of linear time. His life does have a plot, and, in part at least, he must conceive of himself in terms of a kind of personal and general historicity if he is to have any workable sense of his own identity, of those activities which are more rather than less appropriate to that self. Hence the narrator's curiously simplistic comments about Agathon as a character. They have a legitimate role to play in the whole debate about the protagonist's character because they are one pole of the dialectic which informs the novel. They constitute the stability which defines the volatility and flux of Agathon's character.

In one sense, the truth about Agathon is unknowable, is more than he can realize (in both senses of the word) at any one time. In another sense, he does have a story, a sequence of experiences which are inalienably his. And if he has a story, then the novel can have a plot. But the story is only part of the truth. Wieland's difficulties about concluding his story were real enough, as he revealed in a letter of July 1766: ''What do you say to *Agathon*? How do you believe it will end? And how would you like it to end? Be so kind and give me a fairly detailed answer: you can take as much time as you need.''

This could be the narrator addressing his readers. The difficulty about ending the novel was not artistic incapacity on Wieland's part but grew of necessity from his perception of human and fictional affairs. Because of the intractability of the problem, the first version of *Agathon* has an ending which the narrator relentlessly calls into question. Friedrich Sengle is surely right to stress that this first version has "the truth of the fragment" [see Additional Bibliography], an argument reinforced by Fritz Martini: "in its fragmentary character resided the personal and historical truthfulness of this book." For this reason I have devoted my attention throughout this chapter to the first version of *Agathon* and not to those subsequent editions in which Wieland strove increasingly to round off the novel. The truth of the conclusion to the first version is that it shows how at one level and within one set of terms Agathon's life so far can be brought to a conclusion, while at another level and within another set of terms his life cannot possibly be declared, even provisionally, closed.

Agathon is a difficult novel, but it is surely one that speaks with particular urgency to modern readers. We are, after all, used to reading novels about the impossibility (or, more accurately, the inauthenticity) of writing traditional novels. But such considerations are not the exclusive preserve of the twentieth-century novel. It is noteworthy that in a recent book on novel theory Gerhart von Graevenitz insists that many novels operate with a kind of "essayism" whereby they relativize their own referential intactness as texts. And it is hardly surprising that the examples he uses to illustrate his thesis are such works as *Wilhelm Meister's Apprenticeship*, *Indian Summer*, and *The Magic Mountain*, novels which critical consensus has so often dubbed Bildungsromane. If I may allow myself a polemical formulation, *Agathon* achieves its modernity because of, not in spite of, its historical significance as the first of the great Bildungsromane. (pp. 53-6)

> Martin Swales, "Wieland: 'Agathon' (1767)," in his *The German Bildungsroman from Wieland to Hesse*, Princeton University Press, 1978, pp. 38-56.

JOHN A. McCARTHY   (essay date 1979)

[*In the excerpt below, McCarthy summarizes Wieland's achievements.*]

A remarkable writer in several ways, Wieland occupies a prominent position in German letters. For one thing, he made remarkable contributions to the evolution of the German language as a vehicle of poetic expression, anticipating in his writing the lucidity of form and sublimity of sentiment which distinguish the Classical period. His prefiguring of the Romanticists' pantheistic appraisal of life is also remarkable. As a versatile writer, Wieland is again noteworthy, for he wrote everything from erotic Rococo verse poems to instructive essays, hilarious satires, and antiquarian novels. The range of this versatility is also expressed in his roles as teacher, translator, and journalist. As a teacher, he interpreted the humanistic idealism of past ages to younger generations (e.g., the concepts of *die schöne Seele*, virtuoso) and waged a battle against all kinds of prejudice and superstition. As a translator of Shakespeare, he ushered in a wave of poetic fervor among his countrymen; as a translator of Horace and Lucian, he provided German-speaking peoples with classical renditions of classical authors. Finally, as a journalist, he educated whole generations of Germans to aesthetic taste and to an appreciation of opposing points of view. His *Teutscher Merkur* was one of the longest-running and most influential periodicals of the eighteenth century. All in all, Wieland was one of the few men of genius who truly deserve to be known as a *praeceptor Germaniae* (educator of Germany).

Furthermore, Wieland was a receptive and innovative writer. Perhaps no other German writer except Heinrich von Kleist was so consciously responsive to epistemological debates in the eighteenth century or allowed them to shape both the content and the form of his works so extensively. Of the classical German authors, Wieland was the most politically and socially engaged, taking his lead from such French thinkers as Bonnet, Helvetius, Montesquieu, and Rousseau. Not only did he have rare insights into the mechanisms of society, but he also anticipated the results of later research in the areas of anthropology and depth psychology—disciplines which did not exist in his day—and all this because he took the maxim "know thyself" seriously.

That he was an innovative writer would seem to be astounding when we consider that he imitated such writers as Ariosto, Boccaccio, Cervantes, Euripides, Fielding, Lucian, Ovid, Shakespeare, Sterne, Tasso, Xenophon, and others. Yet precisely because of his openness to other cultures and styles, the Swabian learned early to experiment with form and meter, to adapt the best of other cultures to his own. As a result, he helped usher in the modern novel with its personal narrator and reader, producing in *Don Sylvio* the best German imitation of *Don Quixote* and in *Agathon* the first *Bildungsroman* in the eighteenth century. In *Der Neue Amadis*, Wieland unconsciously recreated the epyllion (short epic) and introduced the Italian *ottava rima* into German. With *Die Abderiten*, he introduced the first comprehensive social critique of bourgeois society. The ironic interplay between author and reader in these works required the reader to become an active participant in the narrative process and to gain independence from both self and fiction. As for his essays in the *Merkur* and elsewhere, they point forward to the classical nineteenth century type. Last, Wieland's thoughts on the dangers of a strictly nationalistic literature, as opposed to the intellectual and social advantages of a world literature, look forward to Goethe's celebrated idea of a *Weltliteratur*.

Obviously, Christoph Martin Wieland's many-faceted significance for German literary history cannot be summed up in a word. Yet Fritz Martini came close when he wrote: "Wieland's importance does not lie so much in the individual poetic find or even in the particular momentous thought, but rather in the totality of the impulses which he imparted right up into his old age to German culture, to the broad reading public as well as occasionally to intellectual giants such as Goethe, Schiller, even Novalis and Kleist." Wieland recognized very early the talent of younger authors and encouraged them to excel, to surpass even his own achievements. . . . [He was unselfish] in his praise of Goethe's genius, even before their friendship. Friedrich von Hardenberg and Heinrich von Kleist also gained his respect. For example, when the other giants of the German parnassus spurned Kleist as eccentric, Wieland opened his arms to the tortured youth as to a son and gave him encouragement, seeing in him a great dramatic talent capable of unifying the genius of Aeschylus, Sophocles, and Shakespeare.

Yet despite the author's contributions and stimuli—or perhaps because of them—few writers were as harshly treated by his countrymen as he. In the nineteenth century he was overshadowed by Goethe and Schiller—a paradox, since Wieland had had a substantial hand in preparing the *Bildungsmasse* (broad public) for an appreciation of the two. When Wieland was remembered, it was mostly for his supposed licentiousness, plagiarism, and desultoriness. With foreign critics during the nineteenth century Wieland fared better, for to them he appeared as an instigator of "both the Hellenic and the Romantic revival" and as "one of the most fertile and most profound of modern thinkers." Not until our own century has the public image of Wieland undergone radical change in Germany. (pp. 156-58)

Wieland lived in an age of extremes, of hope, and of uncertainty. Reason had liberated man from the bonds of orthodox belief, science had opened up new frontiers, and philosophy had interpreted the world in increasingly anthropologic terms. It was an exciting—and unnerving—age which culminated in a paradox: politically it led eventually to the new adventure of democracy; philosophically it peaked in Romantic solipsism. The former resulted from an optimistic rationalism which felt that reason could solve all of man's problems; the latter issued from a growing disillusionment with the powers of reason to answer all of man's questions and from the realization that life cannot be equated with logic. The paradox was unavoidable, since man himself is a composite of paradoxes: spirit and flesh, head and heart, capable of the best logic and the worst fanaticism. (p. 158)

Wieland confronted this dilemma of human nature by suggesting self-knowledge as the basis for improving mankind's lot. Because he realized that life is bigger than logic, he approached the Cartesian thinking of his epoch skeptically. Because his study of himself revealed the fraternity of mankind in its relationship to a higher order, he cajoled his reader through compassionate irony to recognize the folly of pursuing transitory goods to the neglect of the only permanent good. Because of the insights into his own nature, he could better understand others. This perception made him tolerant and made him a great educator. (p. 159)

> *John A. McCarthy, in his* Christoph Martin Wieland, *Twayne Publishers, 1979, 192 p.*

ELIZABETH BOA (essay date 1980)

[*Boa examines Wieland's depiction of women and their relationships with men in* Comische Erzählungen, Agathon, *and* Musarion. *She also considers Wieland's attitude toward women in the context of the moral and social values of his era. For additional commentary by Boa, see the excerpt dated 1966.*]

Addressing one of his fair readers in the first version of *Agathon* Wieland asks rhetorically: "Sie werden doch nicht wollen, daß ein Agathon sein ganzes Leben wie ein Veneris Passerculus (lassen Sie sich das von Ihrem Liebhaber verdeutschen) am Busen der zärtlichen Danae hätte hinwegbuhlen sollen?"... The fair reader is clearly expected to disapprove of Agathon's unmanly dallying like a sparrow of Venus, and knows no Latin. Such a passage is liable to provoke awkward double vision in a female reader of today: a simper at the teasing irony so characteristic of 18th-century fiction, but irritation at the apparent assumption of female ignorance. A refocussing of such contradictory reactions to do justice to Wieland as a man of his times requires some understanding of where he stood in the context of 18th-century mores and attitudes in his portrayal of women and relations between the sexes.

At the beginning of the 18th century women played only a small role in German literary life. By the end educated women of the prosperous bourgeoisie and lower aristocracy formed a significant sector of the reading public, while the topic of women—their nature, their social role, their spiritual influence—was a central theme in Weimar classicism and the Romantic movement. This development was a facet of a wider social change, the emergence of a middle class reading public and the associated rapid growth of literary and journalistic activity. (p. 189)

The moral weeklies did much to encourage the broadening of education for women beyond purely domestic skills. To be sure, women's education was conceived overwhelmingly as a preparation for marriage, the only path to security and status open to most women. But if women were to become understanding companions to their husbands, competent overseers of the household and skilled and loving educators of their children, their personal and intellectual development had to be fostered....

From the sixties, debate on educational matters was complicated by the advent of Rousseau and his German and Swiss disciples. If the founding father of liberal education had radical plans for boys, his views on girls as set forth in Book 5 of *Émile* . . . are quite different. Whereas boys are encouraged to be active and independent, girls are to be passive and subservient. No limits are set on male intellectual curiosity, but women are only granted some skills and a little social training that they may attract men and initiate the education of male children.... What mattered were woman's "natural" charm, her high moral calling, her feeling heart and her practical domestic duties. (p. 190)

Wieland's views on education make interesting comparison with Rousseau's. In an essay of 1785 on the education of women Wieland writes quite in the spirit of his works of the 1760s. First comes a glowing picture of sexual equality among the ancient Germanic peoples. It would be foolish, however, to take the excellent but untutored Germanic woman as a model for all times. The refinement and knowledge of later cultures should be open to both sexes. Women are by nature as gifted as men. Social circumstance alone determines the appropriate education for both sexes. From this social argument Wieland reverts to the argument from nature. Woman's "angeborene Bestimmung" and her own special sphere of action free her to be a consumer rather than a cultivator of the fruits of science. The latter function often imposes on men much wearisome toil, as does men's wider sphere of action. Women need do nothing that does not make them "weiser, liebenswürdiger und glücklicher." Their task is one of self-improvement rather than the active search for new knowledge or the pursuit of utilitarian ends. Wieland does not here state explicitly what woman's "angeborene Bestimmung" is, which is furthered by her self-improvement, nor does he say where her "eigener Wirkungskreis" lies, but he is presumably referring to motherhood and the family: the opening of the essay lists the sub-categories of womankind, defined through women's relations to men, as mothers, wives, sisters and daughters. A further essay of 1791 explicitly links woman's calling to her role as mother. But the argument from nature is incomplete on its own since, as Wieland has already suggested, social and historical factors shape the field in which human beings realise their "Bestimmung" and so determine the kind and level of culture appropriate to men and women alike. Moreover he goes on to grant to the few women who have the drive and the leisure the right to pursue knowledge for its own sake in all spheres of thought however remote from the practical duties that fall to most women.... The qualification hardly accords with the earlier praise of Germanic equality, but it is surely only a mildly ironic sop to male vanity. (p. 191)

The core of Wieland's argument is his subtle definition of the concepts of nature and culture where he comes close to Rousseau's profoundest insights. Human nature cannot be simple defined, Wieland suggests, since human capacities and dispositions are potentially boundless. They are realised and develop in an endless variety of cultural forms. Women are as fully human as men, their potential as unbounded. Rousseau shares this view of human nature as far as men are concerned, but seems to assume that woman's biological function must delimit her potential in a roughly similar way in all cultures. . . . (p. 192)

A selection of Wieland's Biberach works—three of the *Comische Erzählungen, Agathon* and *Musarion*—may illuminate Wieland's attitude to women in the turbulent sixties.

The *Comische Erzählungen, Agathon* and *Musarion* form thesis, antithesis and synthesis in Wieland's treatment of relations between the sexes. (The scheme is overneat, but may perhaps be forgiven by way of introduction.) The thesis of the *Comische Erzählungen* is the central value of sexual pleasure to men and women alike. With their mythical setting the poems have an abstract simplicity. *Agathon* is a much more social work. Though the setting is classical, it models social and political conditions in 18th-century Europe or perhaps, as Wolfgang Paulsen suggests, offers a parable of society as such, abstracted from any specific historical context. Human relations in society are ncessarily more complex than in a myth. The simple centrality of sex becomes complicated by social morality and politics. *Agathon* raises many questions. Its fascination lies in its uncertainty of answer. Tensions remain at the end. *Musarion,* less purely mythical than the *Comische Erzählungen,* is less realistic than *Agathon.* An idyll with realistic undertones, its conclusion is perfect as *Agathon's* is not. Musarion is a much richer figure than the goddesses and nymphs of the *Comische Erzählungen:* she is more ideally perfect than any character in *Agathon.* In her a synthesis of all the female qualities is achieved. A perfect woman, she is also the model of a perfect human being.

The first *Comische Erzählung . . . ,* "**Endymion**" tells how the goddess of chastity succumbs to the beauty of the sleeping Endymion. Wieland's mythical world is pre-social and pre-economic. No division of labour separates the sexes into economic categories. Class differences and the necessities of production do not exist. Nor does morality, for morality arises from social corruption. (pp. 195-96)

Wieland strips away, in true 18th-century fashion, the conditioning forces of society to discover what is truly natural, and hence—following Epicurus rather than the stoic Seneca—what is truly good. Joyful sensuality, the highest good enjoyed by mankind, is innocent in this prelapsarian paradise. The mythical age might be dismissed as simply unreal. Procreation results from sex, a fact untouched on in this magical world, and human beings are necessarily social. But Wieland's myth is a kind of thought-experiment, a psychological enquiry. How would people behave were they not constrained by economic need and conventional thinking? The criticism is less of society as such, than of conventions held to be necessary, but in fact historical and so open to change.

Sexual pleasure, the poem suggests, is natural and universal in both sexes. In the introduction before the appearance of Diana, Wieland describes the love games of the nymphs and the beautiful shepherd Endymion: "Der Schäfer war vernügt,

das Nymphenvolk nicht minder; / In Unschuld lebten sie beisammen wie die Kinder." . . . Most appealing in this sexual romp is the equal pleasure in both sexes. The nymphs are as quick to initiate love-making as the shepherds or satyrs, and are as open in their enjoyment. To make his point Wieland reverses traditional motifs. Generally beautiful women are glimpsed naked while bathing. Here it is the beautiful boy Endymion. . . . Clearly, members of either sex may be, to use the current ugly expression, sex objects to the other. Women as much as men enjoy the physical beauty of the opposite sex. The veil, traditional symbol of female modesty, has not been very effective in this Arcadia. When the enraged Diana arrives to scold the nymphs, she orders all who have been guilty to confess their immodesty visibly. . . . (pp. 196-97)

Diana, goddess of chastity and the hunt, presents a faintly military appearance. . . . She metes out punishment like a military commander—a curfew is imposed! Her view of love is warlike too. She issues a challenge to Cupid:

> Die Siege die dir noch gelungen
> Hat man dir leicht genug gemacht.
> Wer selbst die Waffen streckt, wird ohne Ruhm
>   bezwungen.
> Auf mich, auf mich, die deine Macht verlacht,
> Auf meine Brust laß deine Pfeile zielen! . . .

A battle between the sexes rages in these images of weapons and submission, wounds and conquest. How perverse compared with the mutual pleasure in the love games of Endymion and the nymphs! Cupid ungallantly refuses the challenge, for he knows that Diana will lower her weapons of her own volition.

The main psychological argument in the poem appears frequently in Wieland's work: puritanism rests at best on lack of self-knowledge, at worst on self-deception or simple hypocrisy. Ideals such as Platonic purity of Christian virtue or the mere feminine pride of Diana are the rationalisations of those afraid of their own nature. Dionysian desires rise into the dreams of even the innocent sleeping nun. . . . Diana is overcome not by arrows and violence or even gallant persuasion, but by her own sexual desires. The reversal of conventional roles reaches a comic climax as the young boy lies passively dreaming of the obscene and holy mysteries under the kisses of the all too active goddess. The bounds of delicacy are not quite crossed, but we are left in no doubt as to the pleasure even goddesses of chastity may enjoy. . . . (pp. 197-98)

In this poem Wieland finally threw off the dreamy idealism of his youth. The poem has been seen as a comic satire of *faux dévotes* or of courtly immorality, or even as a cynical attack on all womankind. . . . But like Mozart's opera, the poem is rather a liberation of women from the one-sided burden of morality imposed on them by society. There are barbs. The nymph Damalis gazing at her image in the water is a comic picture of feminine vanity: "O fände mich / Endymion nur halb so schön als ich!" . . . This catches beautifully the self-regarding silliness of feminine preoccupation with appearance. It also echoes, of course, the male vanity of Narcissus. Any feminist would agree with such criticism. More objectionable perhaps is the narrow definition of womankind as Diana first feels the stirrings of desire: "Sie kennt sich selbst nicht mehr, und fühlt in ihrem Leben / Sich izt zum erstenmal ein Weib." . . . But the poem is specifically about sex, not what else women may be. Wieland's humanity lies in his robust celebration of sexuality in men and women alike. The picture of sexual pleasure covers a wide gamut from teasing ceremonies, the inner sensations of desire to the Dionysian dreams and final extremity of passion. Sex is not reduced to Rococo flirtation though the games of love are savoured. This is surely more generous than Rousseau's defence of shame and sexual manipulation. (pp. 198-99)

"Aspasia oder die platonische Liebe" . . . takes up the theme of self-deception. The beautiful Aspasia is banished from the arms of her lover Cyrus to become high priestess to the virgin goddess Diana. She forgets the joys of ordinary human love and turns to visions of a spiritual world under the guidance of her mentor Alkahest, a wise man of the East who initiates her into the mysteries. But the only spirits she sees are the figments of her own fantasy: amoretti heads with little wings which gradually acquire beautiful male bodies—a telling insight into Aspasia's real desires. The couple's spiritual communion ends as one might expect. The moral? "Auch, wenn ihr je bei Mondenlicht im Grünen / *Platonisieren* wollt, platonisiert *allein!*" . . . The poem is interesting as a variation on a theme developed with more depth in *Agathon* and more wit in *Musarion*. Platonic communion and religious enthusiasm give way to the demands of the senses. The idiom of this poem is very much of the time. The terms of reference are today so unfamiliar that the poem is scarcely comprehensible without a fair amount of background knowledge.

On the other hand, the idiom of **"Das Urteil des Paris"** . . . is all too familiar as we plunge into the atmosphere of beauty competitions and strip shows. The poem tells how Paris awarded the golden apple to Aphrodite, goddess of love, rather than Juno, queen of the gods, or Pallas, goddess of war and wisdom. Juno tries to bribe him with power, Pallas with military glory. Aphrodite offers him Helen—and herself. The three goddesses strip off and submit to a connoisseur's detailed inspection. Significant features of female anatomy are listed. One is reminded reluctantly of the Miss World Competition. Indeed in *Agathon* Wieland imagines just such an international gathering. . . . He comments sensibly on the cultural relativity of beauty: the African ideal is very different from the Chinese. This surely invalidates the whole undertaking. But oddly he concludes that, nevertheless, Miss Persia would win. Kant too favoured Persian women of whom there cannot have been many in Königsberg. Can Montesquieu be to blame? Wieland, as always even-handed, awards the palm to Mr. Sparta in the male event. Such an involuntary association is perhaps mere feminist touchiness, but the humour in this poem is surely coarser, the mood more lubricious than in the other two. To be fair, Wieland concludes that sexual attraction is not simply a matter of anatomy. All three goddesses are perfect, each in her way as beautiful as the other. What attracts is the whole personality. Aphrodite wins by her smile and by that mysterious quality we now call sex-appeal. Aphrodite's sex-appeal comes from her own randiness, to put it crudely. Once more Wieland suggests that women may feel desire as strongly and freely as men, hardly an objectionable conclusion.

But before reaching his conclusion Wieland makes great play of the titillating strip show. From the start a voyeuristic mood prevails as Wieland addresses his poem, with a knowing nod and wink, to a male friend: "Ein Kenner, Ihr, Herr Doktor," . . . who like the author knows all about "Weiberseelen." Though the goddesses are unabashed (like the Miss World participants) the male reader is invited to enjoy their submission of their bodies to the superior judgement of the mortal male umpire. One notes that the losers are associated with various qualities, Juno with power, majesty and dignity, Pallas with

wisdom, learning and martial nobility. Women who go in for that sort of thing clearly risk losing their sex-appeal. (pp. 199-200)

The *Comische Erzählungen* celebrate sexual pleasure in men and women alike. Here at least the sexes are equal, for Wieland does not deny women's sexuality in the name of morality. Sex emerges victorious over idealism. The outcome is clear from the start. Chastity, virtue, heroism, honour do not stand a chance. In *Agathon* the forces are more evenly balanced, the tension sustained. If there is a solution it is not a clear-cut victory, but an ambiguous coming to terms. *Agathon* has a backbone of philosophical argument which may be outlined in abstraction. The hero is in love with the idea of virtue. His idea at first is puritanical and idealistic: goodness pertains to the spirit, imprisoned in its fleshly house. Sensual pleasure comes from our animal nature, not our spiritual essence. The highest love is pure and independent of sexual passion. Agathon learns by experience to reject such dualism as untrue and inhumane. Ideas and experience, Wieland suggests, are inextricably entwined in the human psyche. Pure rationalism or idealism ignores how sense experience determines our ideas and feelings. Pure sensualism or empiricism ignores how our imagination shapes and interprets the material of sense experience. . . . As a theory of perception Wieland's position dimly prefigures the integrative unity of Kant's epistemology. But unlike Kant, Wieland extends his integrated vision of the psyche into the sphere of ethics. An ethical theory, Wieland suggests, which sharply divides human beings into soul, spirit or seat of imagination on the one hand, and body, senses, register of experience on the other is unrealistic. The vivid ideas of the imagination, notably love, seek realisation and the body is our prime means of expressing love. Conversely, the great pleasure Agathon receives through his senses causes him to ennoble and heighten in his imagination the woman who so delights him. Both tendencies conflict with an overly spiritual conception of the good: Agathon's most altruistic impulses have been strengthened by his sensual experience. His initial idea of virtue was not only false, it was also inhumane for it had made him self-righteously cruel to Danaë who fell short of an inhuman perfection. (p. 203)

Wieland has nothing of Kant's harsh separation between inclination and virtue. He rejects Platonic ideas, but follows Plato in the *Symposium* in stressing love of the good as an emotional motivation or inclination. Inclination, however, may attach to lower or higher ends. True happiness comes from acting on the best inclinations. Wieland is sceptical of, yet perhaps tempted by, the Epicurean view, put so convincingly by Hippias: man is by nature good, and so must simply follow his inclinations to realise the good. Yet Wieland, a man of the Enlightenment, parts company with any vulgarised Rousseauistic cult of nature. Human nature, he suggests, is modified by the personal history of the individual, a history lived out in society. Such a view is closer to Rousseau at his most subtle. Wieland rejects the hedonist answer of Hippias, the cruder physicalist versions of moral sense theory, and Platonic or religious mysticism. But no clear counter definition emerges. (pp. 203-04)

The plot [of *Agathon*] follows the tug-of-war between virtue and pleasure. Agathon's love of Danaë, rooted in a blend of sensuous pleasure and unconscious association between her and his ideal Psyche, softens his harsh morality first in Smyrna and once more in Tarentum when he recognises that what matters is loving understanding of how she came to live as she did. Danaë, originally innocent, now mature and sophisticated, comes to recognise the value of independence and self-esteem. Her moral growth stems from her love of Agathon, a love which engages her whole personality, not just her senses. In the *Comische Erzählungen* pleasure was victorious over ideals such as chastity and honour. *Agathon* so defines virtue that it is compatible with pleasure. Love which is virtuous *and* pleasurable is the way to true Socratic happiness. But as the twists and turns of the plot and the open ending show such a resolution is not easily achieved.

The novel offers a psychological explanation of Agathon's love of virtue. It is rooted in his childhood and adolescent experience. The full story of Agathon's past comes well on in a long flashback. The time-structure of the novel is a masterstroke of wit and psychological subtlety. Agathon, in the midst of his affair with Danaë, tells her the story of his first love for the virginal Psyche and the awful business of the elderly Pythia. The situation is piquant. Danaë listens, hardly with delight, . . . to Agathon's vivid evocation of his feelings for the incomparable Psyche. As the reader listens along with her, a complex texture of interwoven emotions unfolds. Agathon recalls the emotions of someone in love for the first time, as memory heightens them into the aching nostalgia of the adult man for the intensity of his youth. In Danaë we sense the pang of bitterness—explicit in the subsequent account of her reactions . . .—of a mature woman a little older than Agathon who has loved freely and generously, who can never again be the virginal love of a young man. A cruel note is struck in the picture of the ageing Pythia's lust, so abhorrent to the young lovers, yet so pitiful. Another strand is Agathon's loving confidence in Danaë, his need to tell her of these experiences. The reader is vividly aware of the precarious balance of feeling in Agathon as he tells of his great love of Psyche to his beloved Danaë. This complex weave traces changing sexual feeling at different stages in life. Virginal purity may turn to the sour frustration of the aging priestess. Youthful idealistic love may give way to mature sexual fulfilment. These stages are not shown in linear succession, but juxtaposed directly, a structure illuminatingly described by Paulsen as a spiral. The flashback technique conveys the idea of personality as continuously evolving. Past experience affects present emotions; later events colour interpretation of the past. Agathon can now recognise the element of self-deception, the "Blendwerk seiner Phantasie," . . . in his idealism because of what he has learned from Danaë.

But ironically Agathon's confession and self-analysis are a first step towards his desertion of Danaë. Despite his rational understanding, Agathon is emotionally still in the grip of memories powerful enough to make him act irrationally and unfairly towards his mistress. Agathon's ostensible reason for leaving Danaë is his discovery of her past. The narrator seems to approve. But the reader can easily see through this ironic approval of uncompromising virtue. The cruelty of Agathon's behaviour discredits his justification. In any case his self-righteous indignation is mere rationalisation. His real motivation, the deep effect of an adolescent experience, is unconscious. Before he found out about Danaë's past, he was already dreaming of Psyche. As Paulsen suggests, the two women are intimately associated in Agathon's emotions: Danaë danced as Psyche before becoming Agathon's mistress. His love for both women is coloured by his feelings for the other, in neither case entirely non-sensual. Agathon, lover of the good, puts the whole moral burden on the object of his love, Danaë. She must embody the good or else she is not worthy of him. Yet Agathon, while claiming to act in the name of virtue, is in fact moved by the unslaked desire of an unconsummated love for Psyche and simple jealousy of Danaë.

Such a mixture of conscious moral and unconscious sexual motivation must strike the post-Freudian reader as familiar. Id and super-ego are secretly linked, though Wieland's explanation is rather different from Freud's. Adolescent rather than infantile experience accounts for Agathon's behaviour. His abhorrence of sexual license comes from the shock of the Pythia's approach. Until then, as his guardian, she had seemed more of a mother than a potential mistress. Under her care he had been taught to love virtue. The shock was all the greater because it coincided with his first idealistic love for Psyche, an unconsummated love, but with more sexual feeling in it than he was aware of. (pp. 205-07)

Wieland does go back beyond adolescence to Agathon's childhood as the original source of his idealistic imagination, but here too his account of childhood conditioning differs from Freud's in stressing social and cultural circumstances, not oedipal mythology, as the forces which shape Agathon's emotions and moral ideas. . . . Agathon and Psyche were brought up in the unworldly religious environment of the temple. Cultural models—platonic philosophy, mythology, the beautiful pictures and statuary of the temple—powerfully affected the imagination of the two young people. Though the models are different a similar pattern of romantic idealism as Wieland describes is still widespread, especially among girls. Wieland's model of childhood conditioning is interestingly lacking in sex-typing, and Psyche and Agathon are brought up parentless. Unlike Freud, Wieland makes no sharp sexual distinction in his picture of childhood. Of course Freud's theories were extrapolations from real social observation. Wieland's picture is more abstract. But just because of that he does not fall into Freud's error of universalising from a particular social environment. Wieland makes with sharp clarity the essential point: the adult personality is decisively and often unconsciously influenced by childhood experiences. This is also the prime argument in feminist attacks on sexual stereotypes. Social conditioning, not eternal nature, determines psychology. And social conditioning can change. Wieland is less fatalistic than Freud in another way. Though he recognises the continuing, often unconscious effect of childhood, he shows that later experience may modify implanted conditioning. Men and women are not doomed to play out an unconscious pattern. Adult experience can bring self-knowledge. Reason based on self-knowledge can modify if not banish the primary emotions.

Wieland's largely humane view of women flows from these psychological insights. He rejects the view that women should be more moral than men or that women are by nature more shameful or less passionate than men. He does remark that women have more need than men to feel trust in a sexual partner. But this is only to recognise that pregnancy is woman's lot. Wieland avoids all trace of the double morality which divides women into good, dull, marriage partners and bad exciting mistresses. Danaë is a hetaera, an experienced woman who is good and sexy! Her goodness is not the ignorant, vulnerable innocence of a young girl who has been protected from the world. Her virtue is founded on experience and critical judgement of society. Danaë, as we last see her, has become independent, determined to preserve her freedom of decision. Her behaviour is no longer governed by the wish to please men, even Agathon. She is no longer at the mercy of social conventions or her own sexual feelings. Her love for Agathon is as great as ever, but she is now in control of her fate, determined to act in the long-term interests of her lover and herself. Middle class emphasis on sexual morality in the 18th century was essentially progressive. It sought to raise the status of women by stressing cooperation between the sexes for their mutual benefit and the good of their children. But such moral concern was often marred by narrow-minded puritanism. All too frequently women's intellectual and sexual needs were ignored. All that counted was her virtue. Wieland shares the moral concern of his age, but does justice to the whole person. (pp. 207-09)

The question remains as to whether Agathon . . . married his Danaë. It . . . is unanswerable, or answerable as one wishes, for Wieland leaves it to the reader to decide. Agathon's feelings remain those of a lover not a brother so that Psyche pities his sufferings. Yet Danaë refuses to revert to the role of mistress. What will Agathon do? . . . Agathon and Danaë might find a way of living together more convenable than impure concubinage, but more satisfying than as pure brother and sister. If the lovers went on living in Tarentum Agathon must surely have found happiness with his Danaë; if they moved to Biberach he surely did not. But, to answer the last question, perhaps he ought to have. The close, for all its joking tone, is a sad recognition of the gulf between literary utopia and 18th-century reality.

In *Musarion* Utopia prevails and all sadness is banished. (p. 211)

Unlike the Cytheria or Pallas of **"Das Urteil des Paris,"** Musarion is not simply divine, but complexly human. The goddesses embodied qualities in allegorical isolation. Charm, beauty, wit, intellect, a loving heart and an independent spirit blend in Musarion. "Nie scherzte die Vernunft aus einem schönern Mund"—Such a line brilliantly expresses Wieland's integrative intention.

The poem tells how Musarion saves Phanias from religious enthusiasm and puritanical pessimism. Phanias's devotion to this unholy mixture came from disillusion. At once romantic and frivolous, he had fallen in love with Musarion and became jealous when she tired of his exaggerated protestations. Though he lived a life of pleasure himself, he would neither grant her the same freedom nor satisfy her that his love was more than infatuation. After losing his money in a bout of petulant debauchery he has retired to the country to devote himself to philosophy. But on the arrival of Musarion and the beautiful serving girl Chloe, his two mentors, Theophron, the Pythagorean enthusiast, and the stoic Cleanthes are shown up as false philosophers. Musarion teaches him that the good life is founded on pleasure and love. Virtue arises from the refinement and cultivation of the senses and the passions, not from their suppression.

The conflict between virtue and pleasure is resolved in the third section of the poem. Musarion and Phanias philosophise together—in bed, a comically practical demonstration of mental, physical and spiritual union. (pp. 212-13)

Will Musarion dwindle into a wife? One cannot quite picture her in the kitchen. None of the Biberach works copes with the domestic factor in the male-female equation. Nor does *Musarion* bridge the gap between private and public affairs. In *Agathon* private life and love are uneasily balanced against public life and politics. Here there is total separation. Musarion and Phanias will live out their idyll in isolation from the world. But in reality human beings cannot escape from society. The comic ending breaks into the idyllic mood, perhaps a hint that Wieland knew it was but a dream. The listener, no doubt bored

by the highminded prospect of the philosophic marriage, interrupts to ask about the other characters. Theophron, we hear, converted from the heavenly spheres by the spherical breasts of Chloe, has spent the night as one may imagine. Cleanthes, devotee of superhuman virtue, has ended up in the pig-sty in a sub-human drunken stupor. The listener's simple curiosity and the comic anti-climax remind us that we are reading a piece of literature, an idyllic dream.

The unresolved tensions in Wieland's work are as appealing as the ideals. His personality, responding to the world he lived in with all its contradictions, speaks vividly through his work. The full irony of the quotation at the start of this essay should now be clear: "Denn Sie werden doch nicht wollen, daß ein Agathon sein ganzes leben wie ein Veneris Passerculus (lassen Sie sich das von Ihrem Liebhaber verdeutschen) am Busen der zärtlichen Danae hätte hinwegbuhlen sollen?" This is a sly dig at frivolous women, women who *do* know Latin, and at soft, unheroic men. But it is also a delicate barb against a society which encouraged ignorance in women, lack of feeling in men and divided the spheres of private relations and social commitment.

Wieland shows much greater understanding of sexual relations and of women than many of his contemporaries. A man of literary sensibilities, he compares well with the philosophers whose abstractions do violence to the real complexities of human life. It would be interesting to compare Wieland's women with those of his literary contemporaries and successors. Musarion's sister Minna and her distant cousin Iphigenie continue the good work of civilising their menfolk. Women provide sex and salvation in *Faust*. There they do not merely dwindle into wives, but disappear altogether into the grand *ewig Weibliche* collective. Lenz is as understanding as Wieland on women's sexuality and more radical on their social deprivation. But such comparisons would take us too far here. How does Wieland look in a European context? His Danaë and Musarion do not shine quite as brightly as a Rosalind, a Millimant or a Célimène. The robust Fielding is more vividly realistic, Beaumarchais more political radical. But Wieland stands out as a psychologist of exceptional subtlety, and he certainly belongs in the mainstream of European comic writing. His humanity breaks through the sexual stereotypes, as great comedy through the ages has always done. (pp. 213-14)

> *Elizabeth Boa, "Sex and Sensibility: Wieland's Portrayal of Relationships between the Sexes in the 'Comische Erzählungen,' 'Agathon,' and 'Musarion'," in* Lessing Yearbook, Vol. XII, 1980, pp. 189-218.

MICHAEL BEDDOW (essay date 1982)

[*Contrasting* Agathon *with Henry Fielding's* Tom Jones, *Beddow underscores the originality of Wieland's conception of the novel as a genre.*]

[There is] a general affinity between the plot of *Tom Jones* and the pattern of events in [*Agathon*]. Both works employ a garrulous and discursive narrator to relate the story of an abundantly well-intentioned but initially somewhat naive and gullible young man, who is forcefully taught to understand the ways of the world he inhabits by a sequence of occasionally pleasant but mostly painful experiences. But this similarity is really only worth remarking upon in order to throw into relief the enormous differences between the two novels. The most obvious of these differences is probably the contrast betweeen the colourful and vigorous breadth of Fielding's depiction of contemporary England and the relatively small and thinly populated stage which Wieland's text sets before us, with its not particularly convincing Greek costumes and scenery. But this immediately apparent difference is subordinate to a more important one, which we need to appreciate if we are to pursue successfully the distinctive *generic* divergence between Wieland's novel and those of other contemporary writers, Fielding included. It is not just the setting or the detailed course of Agathon's represented education which differ from those we encounter in *Tom Jones,* but the kind of significance we are invited to see in that representation. Where Fielding portrays the education of Tom Jones as the fruit of a varied series of decidedly worldly encounters and mishaps that teach him the extremely practical virtue of prudence, Wieland makes the education of Agathon proceed via a sequence of emotional and intellectual crises which are calculated to raise philosophical problems of a high order of generality. Whereas Fielding is concerned, among other things, with the question of what constitutes right conduct and judgment in a variety of specifically rendered situations in which certain basic moral and epistemological principles are taken wholly for granted, Wieland has, by contrast, written a novel in which what is essentially at stake from beginning to end is, not so much what the hero should do in particular situations, but rather what view he—and beyond him the reader—should hold about the nature of man, the specific characteristics of humaniity and its place in the universe. That is a question which plays no part in Fielding's concerns; yet in *Agathon* it is the issue which shapes the novel as a whole and in all its parts.

It is in the light of this fundamental difference in kind between Wieland's fiction and the type of novel represented by Fielding that we should view and evaluate the rather colourless sham Greek setting and the sparseness of the plot by comparison with the length of the text in *Agathon.* It is of course quite true that, had he wanted to write a novel similar to Fielding's in setting and texture, Wieland would have been at a loss to find a suitable location, unless he had followed some of his artistically less scrupulous German contemporaries and written a novel set in an 'England' that would have rung even falser than his chosen 'Greek' world. Although . . . Wieland was far from being a blinkered provincial, he had simply never experienced the kind of social reality on which Fielding was able to draw so abundantly for the stuff of his fiction. But it would be a mistake to think that the mock-antique setting of *Agathon* was simply a makeshift remedy: behind Wieland's choice of a setting which has no genuinely historical character is the belief that his theme is one to which specifically historical factors are irrelevant. It would be a still more serious mistake to assume that this very choice of theme is in itself no more than a compensation for social deprivation. The very lack of a social world of sufficient weight and complexity to engage his powers of intellect and imagination left Wieland free to bring imaginative literature to bear upon questions of a depth and generality far beyond anything to be found in the prose fiction of eighteenth-century England, questions whose importance is established by their rootedness in the essential intellectual issues engaging thinkers in contemporary Europe. Obviously, *Agathon* is in one sense the story of the development of the principal character. But that story is not told as a study in psychology for its own sake: it is told in order to raise and illuminate issues concerning the nature and status of humanity. The question to which the narrator initially alerts us, namely: what kind of person is Agathon? is handled in a way that makes the represented answer decisively relevant to a further question which

the narrative contrives to ask with sustained insistence: what kind of a creature is man? This certainly does not mean that *Agathon* is just a set of philosophical meditations clothed in fictional garb. The fictional mode is not just a convenient but essentially dispensable vehicle for a 'message' that could be equally well conveyed in discursive fashion: it is an intrinsic part of an approach to the understanding of human nature which cannot be undertaken in any other way, which cannot, in particular, be rendered or defended by discursive argument alone.

For Wieland, 'reality' is more than the sum total of existent states of affairs in the observable world, since it includes human consciousness. This means that human nature cannot be 'read off' from the observable behaviour of human beings: a truly adequate description of that nature would have to take account of the whole range of human aspirations and ideals, especially insofar as they are in some degree at odds with external reality. Wieland's originality lay in perceiving that prose fiction was uniquely fitted to explore the full reality of human nature, because it was capable of conveying at one and the same time both imaginative aspirations and empirical reality, thus occupying a mediating position between purely imaginative art and purely factual history. As Defoe, Fielding and Richardson had all shown in their different ways, the novel was capable of embracing the breadth and variety of empirical reality to a degree that was simply not attainable within the formally much more circumscribed epic, lyrical and dramatic genres. At the same time, as the highly unlikely fictions of various kinds which were particularly popular with the German book-buying public demonstrated, prose fiction was as capable as any other literary medium of bodying forth images generated by the imagination which had no empirical correlative. Wieland realised that the novel could become the meeting place of private imagination and public reality, that it could depict and explore the interaction of the human imagination and the physical world in a way that aspired to do equal justice to the two components, one spiritual, the other factual, which together constituted in his view the fullness of human reality. The novel was, in other words, a peculiarly fitting medium for the rendering of the truth about human nature, since unlike other forms of discourse, it was capable of uniting in one and the same representation the realm of facticity and the realm of aspiration, of presenting in combination with empirical evidence of how human beings behave the imaginative evidence of their values and ideals. (pp. 21-5)

> *Michael Beddow, ''Negations: 'Geschichte des Aga-thon','' in his* The Fiction of Humanity: Studies in the Bildungsroman from Wieland to Thomas Mann, *Cambridge University Press, 1982, pp. 8-62.*

ADDITIONAL BIBLIOGRAPHY

Baker, Ernest A. Introduction to *The Adventures of Don Sylvio de Rosalva,* by Christoph Martin Wieland, pp. v-xxxiii. Library of Early Novelists. London: George Routledge and Sons, 1904.

> An overview of Wieland's life and works that concludes with a brief appraisal of *Don Sylvio.*

Beyer, Werner W. Introduction to his *Keats and the Daemon King,* pp. 3-52. New York: Oxford University Press, 1947.

> A detailed discussion of *Oberon.* In addition to summarizing the plot of the poem, Beyer comments upon its critical reception and

the extent to which Wieland relied on earlier sources in composing the work.

Bruford, W. H. "Duchess Anna Amalia and Wieland, 1756-1775" and "Weimar's Cultural Institutions and Their Creators: Wieland's Work." In his *Culture and Society in Classical Weimar, 1775-1806*, pp. 12-52, pp. 294-97. London: Cambridge University Press, 1962.
    Discusses Duchess Anna Amalia's introduction of the middle-class Wieland into the aristocratic world at Weimar and the author's role in the development of "Weimar classicism."

Clark, William H. "Wieland and Winckelmann: Saul and the Prophet." *Modern Language Quarterly* 17, No. 1 (March 1956): 1-16.
    Traces the influence of Johann Joachim Winckelmann on Wieland's works.

Craig, Charlotte. *Christoph Martin Wieland as the Originator of the Modern Travesty in German Literature*. University of North Carolina Studies in the Germanic Languages and Literatures, edited by Siegfried Mews, no. 64. Chapel Hill: University of North Carolina Press, 1970, 146 p.
    A study intended "to establish the extent to which Wieland contributed to the area of travesty, to investigate the poet's approach to his sources, the nature and quality of his innovations, and to appraise the level and distribution of his travesties in relationship to the sum total of his literary work."

Elson, Charles. *Wieland and Shaftesbury*. Columbia University Germanic Studies. New York: Columbia University Press, 1913, 143 p.
    Examines the influence on Wieland of Anthony Ashley Cooper, third earl of Shaftesbury.

Fitzell, John. "The Island Episode in Wieland's *Oberon*." *The German Quarterly* 30, No. 1 (January 1957): 6-14.
    An analysis of the island episode in *Oberon*. Exploring Wieland's philosophy concerning the relationship between humankind and nature, Fitzell claims that Wieland is a "forerunner of Romanticism."

Gooch, G. P. "Wieland and Herder." In his *Germany and the French Revolution*, pp. 142-73. London: Longmans, Green and Co., 1927.
    A biographical sketch of Wieland and a comparison of his works with those of Johann Gottfried von Herder.

Ilgner, Richard M. "The Development of the Epic within the Context of the Eighteenth-Century Background" and "Christoph Martin Wieland." In his *The Romantic Chivalrous Epic as a Phenomenon of the German Rococo*, pp. 13-30, pp. 31-54. European University Studies, Series I: German Language and Literature, vol. 275. Bern: Peter Lang, 1979.
    A detailed discussion of Wieland's use of the rococo and romantic styles.

Kistler, Mark O. "Dionysian Elements in Wieland." *The Germanic Review* 35, No. 2 (April 1960): 83-92.
    Examines the influence of Wieland's studies of Greek culture on his philosophy and writings.

Kurth-Voigt, Lieselotte. "Wieland and the French Revolution: The Writings of the First Year." *Studies in Eighteenth-Century Culture* 7 (1978): 79-103.
    Analyzes Wieland's works in which he comments on the French Revolution.

Leuca, George. "Wieland and the Introduction of Shakespeare into Germany." *The German Quarterly* 28, No. 4 (November 1955): 247-55.
    Faults critics for failing to recognize the historical importance of Wieland's translations of Shakespeare's plays.

McCarthy, John. *Fantasy and Reality: An Epistemological Approach to Wieland*. European University Papers, Series I: German Language and Literature, vol. 97. Bern: Herbert Lang, 1974, 166 p.
    An extensive examination of Wieland's theory of knowledge. McCarthy focuses on *Don Sylvio*, *Agathon*, and *Die geheime Geschichte des Philosophen Peregrinus Proteus (Private History of Peregrinus Proteus, the Philosopher)*.

———. "Shaftesbury and Wieland: The Question of Enthusiasm." In *Studies in Eighteenth-Century Culture*, Vol. 6, edited by Ronald C. Rosbottom, pp. 79-95. Madison: University of Wisconsin Press, 1977.
    A comparison of the works of the two authors.

Menhennet, Alan. "Rococo: C. M. Wieland." In his *Order and Freedom: Literature and Society in Germany from 1720 to 1805*, pp. 88-101. Literature and Society, edited by Herbert Tint. London: Weidenfeld and Nicolson, 1973.
    Discusses the rococo elements in *Don Sylvio*, *Musarion*, and *Agathon*.

———. "The 'Romanticism' of a Rationalist: Wieland and the Aeronauts." *Lessing Yearbook* XIII (1981): 229-51.
    Analyzes the relationship between Wieland's response to scientific advancement and his attitude toward Romanticism. Menhennet's argument is based on two essays on the subject of ballooning that Wieland contributed to *Merkur*.

———. "Wieland as Armchair Traveller." *Modern Language Notes* 99, No. 3 (April 1984): 522-38.
    Assesses Wieland's reviews of travel literature, particularly Georg Forster's *Reise um die Welt*, and examines Wieland's attitude toward both the dichotomy between nature and civilization and that between dreams and reality.

Minden, M. R. "The Place of Inheritance in the *Bildungsroman*." *Deutsche Vierteljahrsschrift für Literaturwissenschaft und Geistesgeschichte* 57, No. 1 (March 1983): 33-63.
    Maintains that the process of inheritance is a factor in the education of Agathon.

Parker, L. John. "Wieland's Musical Play *Die Wahl des Herkules* and Goethe." *German Life and Letters* n.s. XV, No. 3 (April 1962): 175-80.
    Draws parallels between the language of Wieland's play *Die Wahl des Herkules* and that of Goethe's drama *Faust*.

Rogan, Richard G. *The Reader in the Novels of C. M. Wieland*. European University Studies, Series I: German Language and Literature, vol. 433. Las Vegas: Peter Lang, 1981, 87 p.
    A study of narrative technique in *Don Sylvio*, *Agathon*, and *Abderiten*. Rogan examines the relationship in each novel betweeen Wieland's narrator, "fictional" readers, and "real" readers.

Samuel, R. H. "Rococo." In *Periods in German Literature*, edited by J. M. Ritchie, pp. 43-64. London: Oswald Wolff, 1966.
    Concentrates on Wieland's rococo works. Samuel calls *Musarion* "the artistic climax of what Rococo could achieve."

Schrader, Rebecca E. *A Method of Stylistic Analysis Exemplified on C. M. Wieland's "Geschichte des Agathon."* Germanic Studies in America, edited by Katharina Mommsen, no. 39. Berne: Peter Lang, 1980, 242 p.
    Examines the style of the fifth chapter in Book VI of *Agathon*. Schrader's purpose is twofold: to reach some conclusions about the language of the entire novel and to develop a method of stylistic analysis that can be applied to other literary works.

Sengle, Friedrich. *Wieland*. Stuttgart: J. B. Metzler, 1949, 610 p.
    An important German-language biography.

Stamm, Israel S. "Wieland and Sceptical Rationalism." *The Germanic Review* 33, No. 1 (February 1958): 15-29.
    Discusses both Wieland's skeptical view of human perfectibility and the distinctions between his works and those of the Romantics.

Thomas, Calvin. "Klopstock and Wieland." In his *A History of German Literature*, pp. 205-25. 1909. Reprint. Port Washington, N. Y.: Kennikat Press, 1970.
    An overview of Wieland's writings in which Thomas traces the development of Wieland's style and philosophy.

Van Abbé, Derek Maurice. *Christoph Martin Wieland (1733-1813): A Literary Biography.* London: George G. Harrap & Co., 1961, 191 p.
    A well-regarded biographical and critical study.

————. "Wieland and the 'Stately Homes' of Faëry: The Rococo Substructure of *Don Sylvio de Rosalva." Publications of the English Goethe Society* n.s. XLVII (1977): 28-46.
    Analyzes the rococo elements of *Don Sylvio.*

Whiton, John. "Sacrifice and Society in Wieland's *Abderiten." Lessing Yearbook* 2 (1970): 213-34.
    Focuses on the scene in Book IV of *Abderiten* in which the Abderites kill and eat a donkey. Whiton argues that the "symbolic implications of this eating . . . may be connected with Wieland's satiric intent" and that "there is an element of social redemption inherent in the collective consuming of the donkey."

Appendix

The following is a listing of all sources used in Volume 17 of *Nineteenth-Century Literature Criticism*. Included in this list are all copyright and reprint rights and acknowledgments for those essays for which permission was obtained. Every effort has been made to trace copyright, but if omissions have been made, please let us know.

THE EXCERPTS IN NCLC, VOLUME 17, WERE REPRINTED FROM THE FOLLOWING PERIODICALS:

American Contributions to the Fifth International Congress of Slavists, v. 2, September, 1963. © copyright 1963 Mouton & Co., Publishers. Reprinted by permission of the publisher.

American Literature, v. 11, May, 1939./ v. XL, March, 1968; v. XLVII, March, 1975. Copyright © 1968, 1975 Duke University Press, Durham, NC. Both reprinted by permission of the publisher.

The American Whig Review, v. XVI, November, 1852.

The Athenaeum, n. 1289, July 10, 1852.

Blackwood's Edinburgh Magazine, v. XVII, June, 1825; v. XVIII, August, 1825; v. LXXVII, May, 1855.

Book World—The Washington Post, January 13, 1980. © 1980, *The Washington Post*. Reprinted by permission of the publisher.

The Bookman, London, v. 49, January, 1916.

The British Journal of Aesthetics, v. 26, Spring, 1986. © Oxford University Press 1986. Reprinted by permission of the publisher.

California Slavic Studies, v. IV, 1967. © 1967 by the Regents of the University of California. Reprinted by permission of the publisher.

The Catholic World, v. LXXXVIII, January, 1909.

The Chautauquan, v. X, March, 1890.

The Christian Century, September 8, 1948.

The Christian Examiner and Religious Miscellany, v. 53, September, 1852.

CLA Journal, v. XXVI, September, 1982. Copyright, 1982 by The College Language Association. Used by permission of The College Language Association.

The Critical Review, London, v. 17, March, 1764; v. 35, 1773; n. 1688, 1804.

The Dial, v. 81, September, 1926.

The Dublin Review, v. 159, July, 1916.

The Edinburgh Review, v. L, October, 1829; v. LXIX, April, 1839.

The Fortnightly Review, n.s. v. XVI, September 1, 1874.

Fraser's Magazine for Town & Country, v. CI, May, 1838; v. LXXII, November, 1865.

German Life & Letters, v. 18, 1964-65. Reprinted by permission of the publisher.

The Germanic Review, v. XXIX, Spring, 1954.

Graham's Magazine, v. XLI, September, 1852.

Harvard Theological Review, v. 74, April, 1981 for ''The Legacy of Channing: Culture as a Religious Category in New England Thought'' by David Robinson. © 1981 by the President and Fellows of Harvard College. Reprinted by permission of the publisher and the author.

Hispania, v. XIV, May, 1931; v. XV, March, 1932./ v. L, September, 1967 for '' 'Martín Fierro' as Orphic Poetry'' by Lewis H. Rubman. © 1967 The American Association of Teachers of Spanish and Portuguese, Inc. Reprinted by permission of the publisher and the author.

The Journal of English and Germanic Philology, v. LXVII, October, 1968 for '' 'The Blithedale Romance': A Radical Reading'' by Nina Baym. © 1968 by the Board of Trustees of the University of Illinois. Reprinted by permission of the publisher and the author.

Justice, v. I, March 15, 1884.

Lessing Yearbook, v. XII, 1980. Copyright © 1980 by Wayne State University Press, Detroit, MI 48202. Reprinted by permission of the publisher.

The Liberator, v. 18, 1848.

Literary and Theological Review, v. I, June, 1834.

Macmillan's Magazine, v. XLII, May, 1880.

Modern Age, v. 24, Fall, 1980. Copyright © 1980 by the Intercollegiate Studies Institute, Inc. Reprinted by permission of the publisher.

The Modern Language Journal, v. XXII, October, 1937; v. XXXV, March, 1951; v. XXXVII, January, 1953.

Modern Language Quarterly, v. 18, June, 1957./ v. 22, September, 1961. © 1961 University of Washington. Reprinted by permission of the publisher.

Modern Philology, v. XXVI, August, 1928.

The Monthly Review, London, v. 50, 1774; n.s. v. 19, 1796; v. 23, 1797.

MOSAIC: A Journal for the Comparative Study of Literature and Ideas, v. VI, Summer, 1973. Copyright © *MOSAIC,* 1973. Acknowledgment of previous publication is herewith made.

The Nation, New York, v. XXIII, December 7, 1876; v. CXXX, April 16, 1930.

The National Reformer, August 7, 1887.

The New England Quarterly, v. III, January, 1930; v. XXXV, March, 1932./ v. XXXVIII, September, 1965. Copyright 1965 by *The New England Quarterly.* Reprinted by permission of the publisher.

The New Monthly Magazine, v. XCVIII, June, 1853.

The New Republic, v. LXX, May 4, 1932.

The Nineteenth Century and After, v. 73, May, 1913.

THE EXCERPTS IN NCLC, VOLUME 17, WERE REPRINTED FROM THE FOLLOWING BOOKS:

Addison, Daniel Dulany. From *The Clergy in American Life and Letters*. The Macmillan Company, 1900.

Anderson-Imbert, Enrique. From *Spanish-American Literature: A History, Vol. I*. Edited by Elaine Malley, translated by John V. Falconieri and Elaine Malley. Revised edition. Wayne State University Press, 1969. Copyright © by Wayne State University Press. All rights reserved. Reprinted by permission of the publisher.

Annenkov, Pavel. From a recollection of Marx, in *Karl Marx: Interviews and Recollections*. Edited by David McLellan. Barnes & Noble Books, 1981, The Macmillan Press Ltd., 1981. © David McLellan 1981. All rights reserved. Reprinted by permission of Rowman & Littlefield. In Canada by Macmillan, London and Basingstoke.

Arendt, Hannah. From *The Origins of Totalitarianism*. First edition. Harcourt Brace Jovanovich, 1951. Copyright 1951 by Hannah Arendt. Renewed 1979 by Mary McCarthy West. Reprinted by permission of Harcourt Brace Jovanovich, Inc.

Bach, Matthew G. From *Wieland's Attitude toward Woman and Her Cultural and Social Relations*. Columbia University Press, 1922.

Bakunin, Mikhail. From *Michael Bakunin and Karl Marx*. Translated by K. J. Kenafick. N.p., 1948.

Ball, Patricia M. From *The Central Self: A Study in Romantic and Victorian Imagination*. Athlone Press, 1968. © Patricia M. Ball, 1968. Reprinted by permission of The Athlone Press.

Barzun, Jacques. From *Darwin, Marx, Wagner: Critique of a Heritage*. Little, Brown and Company, 1941. Copyright 1941 by Jacques Barzun. All rights reserved. Reprinted by permission of the author.

Barzun, Jacques. From *Race: A Study in Superstition*. Revised edition. Harper & Row, 1965. Copyright 1937, 1965 by Jacques Barzun. All rights reserved. Reprinted by permission of Harper & Row, Publishers, Inc.

Beddow, Michael. From *The Fiction of Humanity: Studies in the Bildungsroman from Wieland to Thomas Mann*. Cambridge University Press, 1982. © Cambridge University Press 1982. Reprinted with permission of the publisher.

Bell, Michael Davitt. From *The Development of American Romance: The Sacrifice of Relation*. University of Chicago Press, 1980. © 1980 by The University of Chicago. All rights reserved. Reprinted by permission of the publisher and the author.

Berlin, Isaiah. From *Karl Marx: His Life and Environment*. Fourth edition. Oxford University Press, Oxford, 1978. © Isaiah Berlin 1978. All rights reserved. Reprinted by permission of Oxford University Press.

Biddiss, Michael D. From "Introduction: Human Inequality and Racial Crisis," in *Gobineau: Selected Political Writings*. By Joseph Arthur Gobineau, edited by Michael D. Biddiss. Cape, 1970. Introduction and compilation © 1970 by M. D. Biddiss. Reprinted by permission of Jonathan Cape Ltd.

Boa, Elizabeth. From "Wieland's 'Musarion' and the Rococo Verse Narrative," in *Periods in German Literature: Texts and Contexts, Vol. II*. Edited by J. M. Ritchie. Wolff, 1966. © 1966 Oswald Wolff (Publishers) Ltd. Reprinted by permission of Berg Publishers Ltd.

Brenan, Gerald. From *The Literature of the Spanish People: From Roman Times to the Present Day*. Second edition. Cambridge University Press, 1953.

Bridges, Robert. From *Poems of Gerard Manley Hopkins*. Edited by Robert Bridges. Oxford University Press, London, 1918.

Bridges, Robert. From an introduction in *The Poets and Poetry of the Century, Vol. 8*. Edited by A. H. Miles. Hutchinson & Co., 1894.

Brophy, Brigid, Michael Levey, and Charles Osborne. From *Fifty Works of English and American Literature We Could Do Without*. Stein and Day, 1968. Copyright © 1967 Brigid Brophy, Michael Levey, Charles Osborne. All rights reserved. Reprinted with permission of Stein and Day Publishers.

Brown, Arthur W. From *William Ellery Channing*. Twayne, 1962. Copyright © 1961 by Twayne Publishers. Reprinted with the permission of Twayne Publishers, Inc., a division of G. K. Hall & Co., Boston.

Buber, Martin. From *Paths in Utopia*. Translated by R. F. C. Hull. Routledge & Kegan Paul, 1949.

Carabine, Keith. From " 'Bitter Honey': Miles Coverdale as Narrator in 'The Blithedale Romance'," in *Nathaniel Hawthorne: New Critical Essays*. Edited by A. Robert Lee. Barnes and Noble, 1982. © 1982 by Vision Press Ltd. All rights reserved. Reprinted by permission of the publisher.

Cassirer, Ernst. From *The Myth of the State*. Yale University Press, 1946. Copyright 1946 by Yale University Press. Renewed 1974 by Henry Cassirer and Anne Applebaum. All rights reserved. Reprinted by permission of the publisher.

Chamberlain, Houston Stewart. From *Foundations of the Nineteenth Century, Vol. I*. Translated by John Lees. John Lane, 1910.

Champneys, Basil. From *Memoirs and Correspondence of Coventry Patmore, Vol. 2*. G. Bell & Sons, 1900.

Daiches, David. From *New Literary Values: Studies in Modern Literature*. Oliver and Boyd, 1936.

Deutsch, Babette. From *Poetry in Our Time*. Henry Holt and Company, 1952.

Dixon, R. W. From a letter in *The Correspondence of Gerard Manley Hopkins and Richard Watson Dixon*. Edited by Claude Colleer Abbott. Oxford University Press, London, 1935.

Eastman, Max. From an introduction to *Capital: The Communist Manifesto and Other Writings*. By Karl Marx, edited by Max Eastman. Modern Library, 1932. Copyright 1932 and renewed 1960 by The Modern Library, Inc. Reprinted by permission of Alfred A. Knopf, Inc.

Edgell, David P. From *William Ellery Channing: An Intellectual Portrait*. Beacon Press, 1955. Copyright 1955 The Beacon Press. Renewed 1983 by David Palmer Edgell. Reprinted by permission of the publisher.

Edgley, Roy. From ''Philosophy,'' in *Marx: The First Hundred Years*. Edited by David McLellan. Frances Pinter (Publishers) London in association with Fontana Books, 1983. Copyright © Roy Edgley 1983. Reprinted by permission of the publisher.

Emerson, Ralph Waldo. From *Journals of Ralph Waldo Emerson: 1820-1824, Vol. I*. Edited by Edward Waldo Emerson and Waldo Emerson Forbes. Houghton Mifflin Company, 1909.

Emerson, Ralph Waldo. From *Lectures and Biographical Sketches*. Houghton, Mifflin and Company, 1884.

Engels, Frederick. From a preface to *Capital: A Critique of Political Economy, Vol. I*. By Karl Marx, edited by Frederick Engels, translated by Samuel Moore and Edward Aveling. S. Sonnenschein, Lowrey, & Co., 1887.

Engels, Frederick. From a preface to *Manifesto of the Communist Party*. By Karl Marx, edited by Frederick Engels, translated by Samuel Moore. William Reeves, 1888.

Engels, Friedrich. From a speech at the graveside of Karl Marx in *The Portable Karl Marx*. Edited and translated in part by Eugene Kamenka. The Viking Press, 1983. Copyright © 1983 by Viking Penguin Inc. All rights reserved. Reprinted by permission of the publisher.

Fox, Ralph. From *The Novel and the People*. International Publishers, 1937.

Francke, Kuno. From *Social Forces in German Literature: A Study in the History of Civilization*. Henry Holt and Company, 1896.

Fromm, Erich. From *Marx's Concept of Man*. Frederick Ungar Publishing Co., 1961. Copyright © 1961 by Erich Fromm. Reprinted by permission of the publisher.

Gardner, W. H. From *Gerard Manley Hopkins (1844-1889): A Study of Poetic Idiosyncrasy in Relation to Poetic Tradition, Vol. II*. Revised edition. Yale University Press, 1949.

From an extract in *The Gaucho Martín Fierro*. By José Hernández. Translated by Frank G. Carrino, Alberto J. Carlos, and Norman Mangouni. State University of New York Press, 1974. Translation © 1974 by the translators. All rights reserved. Reprinted by permission of the publisher.

Gobineau, Arthur Joseph. From *The Inequality of Human Races*. Translated by Adrian Collins. William Heinemann, 1915.

Gobineau, Joseph Arthur. From an introduction to *Romances of the East*. D. Appleton and Co., 1878.

Goethe, Johann Wolfgang von. From ''German Literature in Goethe's Youth,'' translated by John Oxenford and Miss M. S. Smith, in *Goethe's Literary Essays*. Edited by J. E. Spingarn. Harcourt Brace Jovanovich, 1921.

Goethe, Johann Wolfgang von, as reported by Johannes Daniel Falk. From an extract in *Studies in German Literature*. By Bayard Taylor. G. P. Putnam's Sons, 1879.

Gömöri, George. From *Cyprian Norwid*. Twayne, 1974. Copyright 1974 by Twayne Publishers, Inc. All rights reserved. Reprinted with the permission of Twayne Publishers, Inc., a division of G. K. Hall & Co., Boston.

Gostwick, Joseph. From *German Culture and Christianity: Their Controversey in the Time 1770-1880*. Frederic Norgate, 1882.

Harris, Daniel A. From *Inspirations Unbidden: The "Terrible Sonnets" of Gerard Manley Hopkins*. University of California Press, 1982. Copyright © 1982 by The Regents of the University of California. Reprinted by permission of the publisher.

Hartman, Geoffrey H. From *The Unmediated Vision: An Interpretation of Wordsworth, Hopkins, Rilke, and Valéry*. Yale University Press, 1954 Copyright, 1954, by Yale University Press. Renewed 1982 by Geoffrey H. Hartman. All rights reserved. Reprinted by permission of the author.

Hawthorne, Nathaniel. From *The Blithedale Romance*. Ticknor, Reed, and Fields, 1852.

Hawthorne, Nathaniel. From *Love Letters of Nathaniel Hawthorne: 1839-1863*. The Society of the Dofobs, 1907.

Henderson, Philip. From *The Poet and Society*. Secker & Warburg, 1939.

Heuser, Alan. From *The Shaping Vision of Gerard Manley Hopkins*. Oxford University Press, London, 1958.

Holmes, Henry A. From *"Martin Fierro": An Epic of the Argentine*. Instituto de las Españas en los Estados Unidos, 1923.

Holmes, Henry Alfred. From "Fundamental Identifications in 'Martín Fierro'," in *"Martín Fierro": The Argentine Gaucho Epic*. By José Hernández, translated by Henry Alfred Holmes. Hispanic Institute in the United States, 1948.

Hopkins, Gerard Manley. From *The Correspondence of Gerard Manley Hopkins and Richard Watson Dixon*. Edited by Claude Colleer Abbott. Oxford University Press, London, 1935.

Hopkins, Gerard Manley. From *The Letters of Gerald Manley Hopkins to Robert Bridges*. Edited by Claude Colleer Abbott. Oxford University Press, London, 1935.

Hopkins, Gerard Manley. From *The Poems of Gerard Manley Hopkins*. Edited by Robert Bridges. Oxford University Press, London, 1918.

Hotz, H. From "Analytical Introduction," in *The Moral and Intellectual Diversity of Races*. By Count A. de Gobineau. J. B. Lippincott & Co., 1856.

Howe, Irving. From *Politics and the Novel*. Horizon Press, 1957.

Hyman, Stanley Edgar. From *The Tangled Bank: Darwin, Marx, Frazer and Freud as Imaginative Writers*. Atheneum Publishers, Inc., 1962. Copyright © 1959, 1960, 1961, 1962 by Stanley Edgar Hyman. All rights reserved. Reprinted with the permission of Atheneum Publishers, a division of Macmillan, Inc.

James, Henry. From "Nathaniel Hawthorne (1804-1864)," in *Library of the World's Best Literature Ancient and Modern, Vol. XII*. Edited by Charles Dudley Warner. R. S. Peale and J. A. Hill, 1896.

Johnson, Wendell Stacy. From *Gerard Manley Hopkins: The Poet as Victorian*. Cornell University Press, 1968. Copyright © 1968 by Cornell University. All rights reserved. Used by permission of the publisher, Cornell University Press.

Kaul, A. N. From *The American Vision: Actual and Ideal Society in Nineteenth-Century Fiction*. Yale University Press, 1963. Copyright © 1963 by Yale University. All rights reserved. Reprinted by permission of the publisher.

Kelly, Bernard. From *The Mind & Poetry of Gerard Manley Hopkins, S. J.* Pepler & Sewell, 1935.

Kridl, Manfred. From *A Survey of Polish Literature and Culture*. Translated by Olga Scherer-Virski. Mouton, 1956.

Krzyzanowski, Julian. From *Polish Romantic Literature*. E. P. Dutton and Company, Inc., 1931.

Kurth-Voigt, Lieselotte E. From *Perspectives and Points of View: The Early Works of Wieland and Their Background*. Johns Hopkins University Press, 1974. Copyright © 1974 by The Johns Hopkins University Press. All rights reserved. Reprinted by permission of the publisher.

Laski, Harold J. From *Communism*. Henry Holt and Company, 1927.

Lathrop, George Parsons. From *A Study of Hawthorne*. J. R. Osgood and Company, 1876.

Lawrence, D. H. From *Studies in Classic American Literature*. Thomas Seltzer, 1923, The Viking Press, 1964. Copyright 1923 by Thomas Seltzer, Inc. Renewed 1950 by Frieda Lawrence. Copyright © 1961 by The Estate of the late Mrs. Frieda Lawrence. All rights reserved. Reprinted by permission of Viking Penguin Inc.

Lee, D. C. J. From an introduction to *Gobineau*. By Ludwig Schemann. Arno Press, 1979. Reprinted by permission of the author.

Lenin, V. I. From "The Three Sources and Three Constituent Parts of Marxism," translated by Max Eastman, in *Capital: The Communist Manifesto and Other Writings*. By Karl Marx, edited by Max Eastman. Modern Library, 1932. Copyright 1932 and renewed 1960 by The Modern Library, Inc. Reprinted by permission of Alfred A. Knopf, Inc.

Lessing, G. E. From *The Dramatic Works of G. E. Lessing*. Edited by E. Bell. H. G. Bohn, 1878.

Levy, Oscar. From an introduction to *The Renaissance: Savonarola, Cesare Borgia, Julius II, Leo X, Michael Angelo*. By Arthur, Count Gobineau, edited by Oscar Levy, translated by Paul V. Cohn. G. P. Putnam's Sons, 1913.

Lewis, C. Day. From *Collected Poems: 1929-1933 & A Hope for Poetry*. Random House, 1935. Copyright 1935 by The Modern Library, Inc. Renewed 1962 by C. Day Lewis. Reprinted by permission of the Estate of C. Day Lewis and Sterling Lord Literistic, Inc.

Lukács, Georg. From *Writer and Critic and Other Essays*. Edited and translated by Arthur Kahn. Merlin Press, 1970. © The Merlin Press Ltd. 1970. Reprinted by permission of the publisher.

Male, Roy R. From *Hawthorne's Tragic Vision*. University of Texas Press, 1957.

Mariani, Paul L. From *A Commentary on the Complete Poems of Gerard Manley Hopkins*. Cornell University Press, 1970. Copyright © 1970 by Cornell University. All rights reserved. Reprinted by permission of the author.

Marx, Karl. From *Capital: A Critique of Political Economy, Vol. I*. Translated by Ben Fowkes. Vintage Books, 1977. Translation Copyright © 1976 by Ben Fowkes. All rights reserved. Reprinted by permission of Random House, Inc.

McCarthy, John A. From *Christoph Martin Wieland*. Twayne, 1979. Copyright 1979 by Twayne Publishers. All rights reserved. Reprinted with the permission of Twayne Publishers, a division of G. K. Hall & Co., Boston.

McGovern, William Montgomery. From *From Luther to Hitler: The History of Fascist-Nazi Political Philosophy*. Houghton Mifflin Company, 1941. Copyright, 1941 by William Montgomery McGovern. Renewed 1968 by Margaret M. McGovern. All rights reserved. Reprinted by permission of Houghton Mifflin Company.

Miller, J. Hillis. From "The Linguistic Moment in 'The Wreck of the Deutschland'," in *The New Criticism and After*. Edited by Thomas Daniel Young. University Press of Virginia, 1976. Copyright © 1976 by the Rector and Visitors of the University of Virginia. Reprinted by permission of the publisher.

Miłosz, Czesław. From *The History of Polish Literature*. Second edition. University of California Press, 1983. Copyright © 1969, 1983 by Czesław Miłosz. Reprinted by permission of the University of California Press.

Milroy, James. From *The Language of Gerard Manley Hopkins*. Deutsch, 1977. Copyright © 1977 by James Milroy. All rights reserved. Reprinted by permission of the author.

Murry, John Middleton. From *Heroes of Thought*. Julian Messner, Inc., 1938. Copyright 1938 by John Middleton Murry. Renewed © 1966 by Mary Middleton Murry. Reprinted by permission of Simon & Schuster, Inc.

Parker, Theodore. From a journal entry in *Life and Correspondence of Theodore Parker, Vol. I*. By John Weiss. Longman, Green, Longman, Roberts, and Green, 1863.

Parmée, Douglas. From an introduction to *Sons of Kings*. By Joseph-Arthur Gobineau, translated by Douglas Parmée. Oxford University Press, London, 1966. English translation, introduction, and notes © Oxford University Press, 1966. Reprinted by permission of Oxford University Press.

Parrington, Vernon Louis. From *Main Currents in American Thought: The Romantic Revolution in America, 1800-1860, Vol. 2*. Harcourt Brace Jovanovich, 1927. Copyright 1927, 1930 by Harcourt Brace Jovanovich, Inc. Renewed 1955, 1958 by Vernon L. Parrington, Jr., Louise P. Tucker, Elizabeth P. Thomas. Reprinted by permission of the publisher.

Pascal, R. From *Shakespeare in Germany: 1740-1815*. Cambridge at the University Press, 1937.

Patmore, Coventry. From a letter in *Further Letters of Gerard Manley Hopkins: Including His Correspondence with Coventry Patmore*. Edited by Claude Colleer Abbott. Revised edition. Oxford University Press, London, 1956.

Patterson, Robert Leet. From *The Philosophy of William Ellery Channing*. Bookman Associates, 1952.

Pearce, Roy Harvey. From "Day-Dream and Fact: The Import of 'The Blithedale Romance'," in *Individual and Community: Variations on a Theme in American Fiction*. Edited by Kenneth H. Baldwin and David K. Kirby. Duke University Press, 1975. Copyright © 1975 by Duke University Press, Durham, NC. Reprinted by permission of the publisher.

Pelliza, Mariano A. From an extract of a letter in *The Gaucho Martín Fierro*. By José Hernández, translated by Frank G. Carrino, Alberto J. Carlos, and Norman Mangouni. State University of New York Press, 1974. Translation © 1974 by the translators. All rights reserved. Reprinted by permission of the publisher.

Peters, W. A. M., S.J. From *Gerard Manley Hopkins: A Critical Essay towards the Understanding of His Poetry*. Oxford University Press, Oxford, 1948.

Pick, John. From *Gerard Manley Hopkins: Priest and Poet*. Oxford University Press, London, 1942.

Prawer, S. S. From *Karl Marx and World Literature*. Oxford at the Clarendon Press, 1976. © Oxford University Press, 1976. All rights reserved. Reprinted by permission of Oxford University Press.

Read, Herbert. From *Form in Modern Poetry*. Sheed & Ward, 1933. Reprinted by permission of the publisher.

Robinson, Henry Crabb. From *Diary, Reminiscences, and Correspondence of Henry Crabb Robinson, Vol. I*. Edited by Thomas Sadler. Third edition. Macmillan and Co., 1872.

Rotenstreich, Nathan. From *Basic Problems of Marx's Philosophy*. The Bobbs-Merrill Company, Inc., 1965. Copyright © 1965 by Macmillan Publishing Company. Reprinted with permission of Macmillan Publishing Company.

Russell, Bertrand. From *A History of Western Philosophy, and Its Connection with Political and Social Circumstances from the Earliest Times to the Present Day*. Simon & Schuster, 1945, G. Allen and Unwin Ltd., 1946. Copyright 1945, 1972, by Bertrand Russell. Reprinted by permission of Simon & Schuster, Inc. In Canada by Unwin Hyman Ltd.

Schlegel, August Wilhelm von. From *A. W. Schlegel's Lectures on German Literature from Gottsched to Goethe*. Edited by H. G. Fiedler. Basil Blackwell, 1944.

Shaw, Donald L. From *The Nineteenth Century*. Ernest Benn Limited, 1972. © Donald L. Shaw, 1972. Reprinted by permission of the author.

Sitwell, Edith. From *Aspects of Modern Poetry*. Duckworth, 1934.

Sprinker, Michael. From *"A Counterpoint of Dissonance": The Aesthetics and Poetry of Gerard Manley Hopkins*. Johns Hopkins University Press, 1980. Copyright © 1980 by The Johns Hopkins University Press. All rights reserved. Reprinted by permission of the publisher.

Swales, Martin. From *The German Bildungsroman from Wieland to Hesse*. Princeton University Press, 1978. Copyright © 1978 by Princeton University Press. All rights reserved. Reprinted with permission of the publisher.

Taylor, Bayard. From *Studies in German Literature*. G. P. Putnam's Sons, 1879.

Tinker, Edward Larocque. From *Life and Literature of the Pampas*. University of Florida Press, 1961. Copyright, 1961, by the Pan American Foundation, Inc. Reprinted by permission of the publisher.

Tocqueville, Alexis de. From extracts of six of his letters in *"The European Revolution" & Correspondence with Gobineau*. Edited and translated by John Lukacs. Doubleday & Company, Inc. Copyright © 1959 by John Lukacs. All rights reserved. Reprinted by permission of Doubleday, a division of Bantam, Doubleday, Dell Publishing Group, Inc.

Tolhausen, Alexander. From *Klopstock, Lessing, and Wieland: A Treatise on German Literature*. Williams and Norgate, 1848.

Torres-Ríoseco, Arturo. From *The Epic of Latin American Literature*. Oxford University Press, 1942.

Trattner, Ernest R. From *Architects of Ideas: The Story of the Great Theories of Mankind*. Carrick & Evans, Inc., 1938. Copyright, 1938, by Carrick & Evans, Inc. Renewed 1966 by Johanna Trattner.

Van Doren, Mark. From *Nathaniel Hawthorne*. Sloane, 1949. Copyright 1949 by William Sloane Associates, Inc. Renewed 1976 by Mark Van Doren. Reprinted by permission of William Morrow & Company, Inc.

Warren, L. A. From *Modern Spanish Literature: A Comprehensive Survey of the Novelists, Poets, Dramatists and Essayists from the Eighteenth Century to the Present Day, Vol. I*. Brentano's Ltd., 1929.

White, Hayden. From "The Problem of Style in Realistic Representation: Marx and Flaubert," in *The Concept of Style*. Edited by Berel Lang. University of Pennsylvania Press, 1979. Copyright © 1979 by Berel Lang. All rights reserved. Reprinted by permission of the publisher.

Whittier, John Greenleaf. From *The Complete Poetical Works of John Greenleaf Whittier*. Houghton Mifflin Company, 1894.

Williams, Raymond. From *Marxism and Literature*. Oxford University Press, Oxford, 1977. © Oxford University Press 1977. All rights reserved. Reprinted by permission of Oxford University Press.

Wilson, Edmund. From *To the Findland Station: A Study in the Writing and Acting of History*. Harcourt Brace Jovanovich, 1940. Copyright 1940, renewed 1968 by Edmund Wilson. Copyright © 1972 by Edmund Wilson. Reprinted by permission of Farrar, Straus and Giroux, Inc.

Woodberry, George E. From *Nathaniel Hawthorne*. Houghton, Mifflin and Company, 1902.

Woodberry, George Edward. From *Studies in Letters and Life*. Houghton, Mifflin and Company, 1891.

Wordsworth, William. From an extract in *Biographia Literaria*. By Samuel Taylor Coleridge. Rest Fenner, 1817.

Literary Criticism Series
Cumulative Author Index

This index lists all author entries in the Gale Literary Criticism Series and includes cross-references to other Gale sources. For the convenience of the reader, references to the *Yearbook* in the *Contemporary Literary Criticism* series include the page number (in parentheses) after the volume number. References in the index are identified as follows:

Audiberti, Jacques 1899-1965 ......CLC 38
  See also obituary CA 25-28R

Auel, Jean M(arie) 1936- ....CLC 31
  See also CA 103

Austen, Jane 1775-1817 ....NCLC 1, 13

Austin, Mary (Hunter)
  1868-1934.................. TCLC 25

Avison, Margaret 1918- .... CLC 2, 4
  See also CA 17-20R
  See also DLB 53

Ayckbourn, Alan
  1939-................CLC 5, 8, 18, 33
  See also CA 21-24R
  See also DLB 13

Aymé, Marcel (Andre)
  1902-1967....................CLC 11
  See also CA 89-92

Ayrton, Michael 1921-1975 ....CLC 7
  See also CANR 9
  See also CA 5-8R
  See also obituary CA 61-64

Azorín 1874-1967.................CLC 11
  See also Martínez Ruiz, José

Azuela, Mariano 1873-1952 .... TCLC 3
  See also CA 104

"Bab" 1836-1911
  See Gilbert, (Sir) W(illiam) S(chwenck)

Babel, Isaak (Emmanuilovich)
  1894-1941.............TCLC 2, 13
  See also CA 104

Babits, Mihály 1883-1941........ TCLC 14
  See also CA 114

Bacchelli, Riccardo 1891-1985......CLC 19
  See also obituary CA 117
  See also CA 29-32R

Bach, Richard (David) 1936-......CLC 14
  See also CANR 18
  See also CA 9-12R
  See also SATA 13
  See also AITN 1

Bachman, Richard 1947-
  See King, Stephen (Edwin)

Bacovia, George 1881-1957 ...... TCLC 24

Bagehot, Walter 1826-1877 ......NCLC 10

Bagnold, Enid 1889-1981 ....CLC 25
  See also CANR 5
  See also CA 5-8R
  See also obituary CA 103
  See also SATA 1, 25
  See also DLB 13

Bagryana, Elisaveta 1893- ....CLC 10

Bailey, Paul 1937- ....CLC 45
  See also CANR 16
  See also CA 21-24R
  See also DLB 14

Baillie, Joanna 1762-1851 .... NCLC 2

Bainbridge, Beryl
  1933-......CLC 4, 5, 8, 10, 14, 18, 22
  See also CA 21-24R
  See also DLB 14

Baker, Elliott 1922-.................CLC 8
  See also CANR 2
  See also CA 45-48

Baker, Russell (Wayne) 1925-......CLC 31
  See also CANR 11
  See also CA 57-60

Bakshi, Ralph 1938-..............CLC 26
  See also CA 112

Baldwin, James (Arthur)
  1924-......CLC 1, 2, 3, 4, 5, 8, 13, 15,
                         17, 42
  See also CANR 3
  See also CA 1-4R
  See also CABS 1
  See also SATA 9
  See also DLB 2, 7, 33
  See also CDALB 1941-1968

Ballard, J(ames) G(raham)
  1930-................CLC 3, 6, 14, 36
  See also SSC 1
  See also CANR 15
  See also CA 5-8R
  See also DLB 14

Balmont, Konstantin Dmitriyevich
  1867-1943.................. TCLC 11
  See also CA 109

Balzac, Honoré de 1799-1850 ..... NCLC 5

Bambara, Toni Cade 1939- ....CLC 19
  See also CA 29-32R
  See also DLB 38

Banim, John 1798-1842
  See Banim, John and Banim, Michael

Banim, John 1798-1842 and **Banim,
  Michael** 1796-1874 .... NCLC 13

Banim, Michael 1796-1874
  See Banim, John and Banim, Michael

Banim, Michael 1796-1874 and **Banim,
  John** 1798-1842
  See Banim, John and Banim, Michael

Banks, Iain 1954-........... CLC 34 (29)

Banks, Lynne Reid 1929-..........CLC 23
  See also Reid Banks, Lynne

Banks, Russell 1940-..............CLC 37
  See also CA 65-68
  See also CANR 19

Banville, John 1945- ....CLC 46
  See also CA 117
  See also DLB 14

Banville, Théodore (Faullain) de
  1832-1891.................. NCLC 9

Baraka, Amiri
  1934-........CLC 1, 2, 3, 5, 10, 14, 33
  See also Baraka, Imamu Amiri
  See also Jones, (Everett) LeRoi
  See also DLB 5, 7, 16, 38

Baraka, Imamu Amiri
  1934-........CLC 1, 2, 3, 5, 10, 14, 33
  See also Baraka, Amiri
  See also Jones, (Everett) LeRoi
  See also DLB 5, 7, 16, 38
  See also CDALB 1941-1968

Barbellion, W. N. P.
  1889-1919.................. TCLC 24

Barbera, Jack 1945- .... CLC 44 (431)

Barbey d'Aurevilly, Jules Amédée
  1808-1889.................. NCLC 1

Barbusse, Henri 1873-1935 .... TCLC 5
  See also CA 105

Barea, Arturo 1897-1957 .... TCLC 14
  See also CA 111

Barfoot, Joan 1946-...............CLC 18
  See also CA 105

Baring, Maurice 1874-1945 .... TCLC 8
  See also CA 105
  See also DLB 34

Barker, George (Granville)
  1913-........................CLC 8
  See also CANR 7
  See also CA 9-12R
  See also DLB 20

Barker, Howard 1946- ....CLC 37
  See also CA 102
  See also DLB 13

Barker, Pat 1943- ....CLC 32
  See also CA 117

Barnes, Djuna
  1892-1982........ CLC 3, 4, 8, 11, 29
  See also CANR 16
  See also CA 9-12R
  See also obituary CA 107
  See also DLB 4, 9, 45

Barnes, Julian 1946-..............CLC 42
  See also CANR 19
  See also CA 102

Barnes, Peter 1931-.................CLC 5
  See also CA 65-68
  See also DLB 13

Baroja (y Nessi), Pío
  1872-1956.................. TCLC 8
  See also CA 104

Barondess, Sue K(aufman) 1926-1977
  See Kaufman, Sue
  See also CANR 1
  See also CA 1-4R
  See also obituary CA 69-72

Barrett, (Roger) Syd 1946-
  See Pink Floyd

Barrett, William (Christopher)
  1913-........................CLC 27
  See also CANR 11
  See also CA 13-16R

Barrie, (Sir) J(ames) M(atthew)
  1860-1937.................. TCLC 2
  See also CA 104
  See also YABC 1
  See also DLB 10

Barrol, Grady 1953-
  See Bograd, Larry

Barry, Philip (James Quinn)
  1896-1949.................. TCLC 11
  See also CA 109
  See also DLB 7

Barth, John (Simmons)
  1930-......CLC 1, 2, 3, 5, 7, 9, 10, 14,
                         27
  See also CANR 5
  See also CA 1-4R
  See also CABS 1
  See also DLB 2
  See also AITN 1, 2

Blish, James (Benjamin)
    1921-1975..................CLC 14
    See also CANR 3
    See also CA 1-4R
    See also obituary CA 57-60
    See also DLB 8

Blixen, Karen (Christentze Dinesen)
    1885-1962
    See Dinesen, Isak
    See also CAP 2
    See also CA 25-28
    See also SATA 44

Bloch, Robert (Albert) 1917-.......CLC 33
    See also CANR 5
    See also CA 5-8R
    See also DLB 44
    See also SATA 12

Blok, Aleksandr (Aleksandrovich)
    1880-1921.................. TCLC 5
    See also CA 104

Bloom, Harold 1930-..............CLC 24
    See also CA 13-16R

Blount, Roy (Alton), Jr. 1941- .....CLC 38
    See also CANR 10
    See also CA 53-56

Bloy, Léon 1846-1917.......... TCLC 22

Blume, Judy (Sussman Kitchens)
    1938-.................. CLC 12, 30
    See also CLR 2
    See also CANR 13
    See also CA 29-32R
    See also SATA 2, 31
    See also DLB 52

Blunden, Edmund (Charles)
    1896-1974....................CLC 2
    See also CAP 2
    See also CA 17-18
    See also obituary CA 45-48
    See also DLB 20

Bly, Robert (Elwood)
    1926-.......... CLC 1, 2, 5, 10, 15, 38
    See also CA 5-8R
    See also DLB 5

Bochco, Steven 1944?-
    See Bochco, Steven and Kozoll, Michael

Bochco, Steven 1944?- and
    Kozoll, Michael 1940?- ....CLC 35

Bødker, Cecil 1927-..............CLC 21
    See also CANR 13
    See also CA 73-76
    See also SATA 14

Boell, Heinrich (Theodor) 1917-1985
    See Böll, Heinrich
    See also CA 21-24R
    See also obituary CA 116

Bogan, Louise
    1897-1970........CLC 4, 39 (383), 46
    See also CA 73-76
    See also obituary CA 25-28R
    See also DLB 45

Bogarde, Dirk 1921-..............CLC 19
    See also Van Den Bogarde, Derek (Jules
        Gaspard Ulric) Niven
    See also DLB 14

Bogosian, Eric 1953-..............CLC 45

Bograd, Larry 1953-..............CLC 35
    See also CA 93-96
    See also SATA 33

Böhl de Faber, Cecilia 1796-1877
    See Caballero, Fernán

Boiardo, Matteo Maria
    1441-1494.................... LC 6

Boileau-Despréaux, Nicolas
    1636-1711.................... LC 3

Boland, Eavan (Aisling) 1944-......CLC 40
    See also DLB 40

Böll, Heinrich (Theodor)
    1917-1985..... CLC 2, 3, 6, 9, 11, 15,
                        27, 39 (291)
    See also DLB-Y 85
    See also Boell, Heinrich (Theodor)

Bolt, Robert (Oxton) 1924- ....CLC 14
    See also CA 17-20R
    See also DLB 13

Bond, Edward 1934-......CLC 4, 6, 13, 23
    See also CA 25-28R
    See also DLB 13

Bonham, Frank 1914-..............CLC 12
    See also CANR 4
    See also CA 9-12R
    See also SAAS 3
    See also SATA 1

Bonnefoy, Yves 1923- .... CLC 9, 15
    See also CA 85-88

Bontemps, Arna (Wendell)
    1902-1973................ CLC 1, 18
    See also CLR 6
    See also CANR 4
    See also CA 1-4R
    See also obituary CA 41-44R
    See also SATA 2, 44
    See also obituary SATA 24
    See also DLB 48

Booth, Martin 1944-..............CLC 13
    See also CAAS 2
    See also CA 93-96

Booth, Philip 1925-..............CLC 23
    See also CANR 5
    See also CA 5-8R
    See also DLB-Y 82

Booth, Wayne C(layson) 1921- .....CLC 24
    See also CAAS 5
    See also CANR 3
    See also CA 1-4R

Borchert, Wolfgang 1921-1947 .... TCLC 5
    See also CA 104

Borges, Jorge Luis
    1899-1986...... CLC 1, 2, 3, 4, 6, 8, 9,
                        10, 13, 19, 44 (352)
    See also CANR 19
    See also CA 21-24R
    See also DLB-Y 86

Borowski, Tadeusz 1922-1951 ..... TCLC 9
    See also CA 106

Borrow, George (Henry)
    1803-1881.................. NCLC 9
    See also DLB 21

Bosschère, Jean de
    1878-1953................. TCLC 19
    See also CA 115

Boswell, James 1740-1795 .... LC 4

Bourget, Paul (Charles Joseph)
    1852-1935................. TCLC 12
    See also CA 107

Bourjaily, Vance (Nye) 1922-........CLC 8
    See also CAAS 1
    See also CANR 2
    See also CA 1-4R
    See also DLB 2

Bourne, Randolph S(illiman)
    1886-1918................. TCLC 16
    See also CA 117

Bova, Ben(jamin William)
    1932-........................CLC 45
    See also CLR 3
    See also CANR 11
    See also CA 5-8R
    See also SATA 6
    See also DLB-Y 81

Bowen, Elizabeth (Dorothea Cole)
    1899-1973...... CLC 1, 3, 6, 11, 15, 22
    See also CAP 2
    See also CA 17-18
    See also obituary CA 41-44R
    See also DLB 15

Bowering, George 1935-...........CLC 15
    See also CANR 10
    See also CA 21-24R
    See also DLB 53

Bowering, Marilyn R(uthe)
    1949-........................CLC 32
    See also CA 101

Bowers, Edgar 1924-..............CLC 9
    See also CA 5-8R
    See also DLB 5

Bowie, David 1947-..............CLC 17
    See also Jones, David Robert

Bowles, Jane (Sydney)
    1917-1973....................CLC 3
    See also CAP 2
    See also CA 19-20
    See also obituary CA 41-44R

Bowles, Paul (Frederick)
    1910-.................. CLC 1, 2, 19
    See also CAAS 1
    See also CANR 1, 19
    See also CA 1-4R
    See also DLB 5, 6

Box, Edgar 1925-
    See Vidal, Gore

Boyd, William 1952-..............CLC 28
    See also CA 114

Boyle, Kay 1903-............. CLC 1, 5, 19
    See also CAAS 1
    See also CA 13-16R
    See also DLB 4, 9, 48

Boyle, Patrick 19??- ....CLC 19

Boyle, T. Coraghessan 1948-.......CLC 36
    See also CA 120
    See also DLB-Y 86

Brackenridge, Hugh Henry
    1748-1816................... NCLC 7
    See also DLB 11, 37

Bradbury, Edward P. 1939-
    See Moorcock, Michael

Bradbury, Malcolm (Stanley)
    1932-........................CLC 32
    See also CANR 1
    See also CA 1-4R
    See also DLB 14

Author Index

Dagerman, Stig (Halvard)
1923-1954.................. TCLC 17
See also CA 117

Dahl, Roald 1916-.......... CLC 1, 6, 18
See also CLR 1, 7
See also CANR 6
See also CA 1-4R
See also SATA 1, 26

Dahlberg, Edward
1900-1977.............. CLC 1, 7, 14
See also CA 9-12R
See also obituary CA 69-72
See also DLB 48

Daly, Maureen 1921-.............CLC 17
See also McGivern, Maureen Daly
See also SAAS 1
See also SATA 2

Däniken, Erich von 1935-
See Von Däniken, Erich

Dannay, Frederic 1905-1982
See Queen, Ellery
See also CANR 1
See also CA 1-4R
See also obituary CA 107

D'Annunzio, Gabriele
1863-1938.................. TCLC 6
See also CA 104

Danziger, Paula 1944-.............CLC 21
See also CA 112, 115
See also SATA 30, 36

Darío, Rubén 1867-1916......... TCLC 4
See also Sarmiento, Felix Ruben Garcia
See also CA 104

Darley, George 1795-1846........ NCLC 2

Daryush, Elizabeth
1887-1977................ CLC 6, 19
See also CANR 3
See also CA 49-52
See also DLB 20

Daudet, (Louis Marie) Alphonse
1840-1897.................... NCLC 1

Daumal, René 1908-1944........ TCLC 14
See also CA 114

Davenport, Guy (Mattison, Jr.)
1927-................... CLC 6, 14, 38
See also CA 33-36R

Davidson, Donald (Grady)
1893-1968............. CLC 2, 13, 19
See also CANR 4
See also CA 5-8R
See also obituary CA 25-28R
See also DLB 45

Davidson, John 1857-1909...... TCLC 24
See also CA 118
See also DLB 19

Davidson, Sara 1943- ....CLC 9
See also CA 81-84

Davie, Donald (Alfred)
1922-...................CLC 5, 8, 10, 31
See also CAAS 3
See also CANR 1
See also CA 1-4R
See also DLB 27

Davies, Ray(mond Douglas)
1944-.......................CLC 21
See also CA 116

Davies, Rhys 1903-1978 ....CLC 23
See also CANR 4
See also CA 9-12R
See also obituary CA 81-84

Davies, (William) Robertson
1913-............ CLC 2, 7, 13, 25, 42
See also CANR 17
See also CA 33-36R

Davies, W(illiam) H(enry)
1871-1940.................. TCLC 5
See also CA 104
See also DLB 19

Davis, Rebecca (Blaine) Harding
1831-1910.................. TCLC 6
See also CA 104

Davis, Richard Harding
1864-1916.................. TCLC 24
See also CA 114
See also DLB 12, 23

Davison, Frank Dalby
1893-1970....................CLC 15
See also obituary CA 116

Davison, Peter 1928-..............CLC 28
See also CAAS 4
See also CANR 3
See also CA 9-12R
See also DLB 5

Davys, Mary 1674-1732 .... LC 1
See also DLB 39

Dawson, Fielding 1930-.............CLC 6
See also CA 85-88

Day, Clarence (Shepard, Jr.)
1874-1935.................. TCLC 25
See also CA 108
See also DLB 11

Day Lewis, C(ecil)
1904-1972............... CLC 1, 6, 10
See also CAP 1
See also CA 15-16
See also obituary CA 33-36R
See also DLB 15, 20

Day, Thomas 1748-1789............ LC 1
See also YABC 1
See also DLB 39

Dazai Osamu 1909-1948........ TCLC 11
See also Tsushima Shūji

De Crayencour, Marguerite 1903-
See Yourcenar, Marguerite

Deer, Sandra 1940- ....CLC 45

Defoe, Daniel 1660?-1731............ LC 1
See also SATA 22
See also DLB 39

De Hartog, Jan 1914-..............CLC 19
See also CANR 1
See also CA 1-4R

Deighton, Len 1929- ......CLC 4, 7, 22, 46
See also Deighton, Leonard Cyril

Deighton, Leonard Cyril 1929-
See Deighton, Len
See also CANR 19
See also CA 9-12R

De la Mare, Walter (John)
1873-1956.................. TCLC 4
See also CA 110
See also SATA 16
See also DLB 19

Delaney, Shelagh 1939-.............CLC 29
See also CA 17-20R
See also DLB 13

Delany, Samuel R(ay, Jr.)
1942-................... CLC 8, 14, 38
See also CA 81-84
See also DLB 8, 33

De la Roche, Mazo 1885-1961......CLC 14
See also CA 85-88

Delbanco, Nicholas (Franklin)
1942-.................... CLC 6, 13
See also CAAS 2
See also CA 17-20R
See also DLB 6

Del Castillo, Michel 1933- ....CLC 38
See also CA 109

Deledda, Grazia 1875-1936 ...... TCLC 23

Delibes (Setien), Miguel
1920-.................... CLC 8, 18
See also CANR 1
See also CA 45-48

DeLillo, Don
1936-...... CLC 8, 10, 13, 27, 39 (115)
See also CA 81-84
See also DLB 6

De Lisser, H(erbert) G(eorge)
1878-1944.................. TCLC 12
See also CA 109

Deloria, Vine (Victor), Jr.
1933-....................CLC 21
See also CANR 5, 20
See also CA 53-56
See also SATA 21

Del Vecchio, John M(ichael)
1947-......................CLC 29
See also CA 110

Dennis, Nigel (Forbes) 1912-........CLC 8
See also CA 25-28R
See also DLB 13, 15

De Palma, Brian 1940-............CLC 20
See also CA 109

De Quincey, Thomas
1785-1859.................. NCLC 4

Deren, Eleanora 1908-1961
See Deren, Maya
See also obituary CA 111

Deren, Maya 1908-1961 ....CLC 16
See also Deren, Eleanora

Derleth, August (William)
1909-1971....................CLC 31
See also CANR 4
See also CA 1-4R
See also obituary CA 29-32R
See also SATA 5
See also DLB 9

Derrida, Jacques 1930-............CLC 24

Desai, Anita 1937-............ CLC 19, 37
See also CA 81-84

De Saint-Luc, Jean 1909-1981
See Glassco, John

De Sica, Vittorio 1902-1974........CLC 20
See also obituary CA 117

Desnos, Robert 1900-1945 .... TCLC 22

Destouches, Louis Ferdinand 1894-1961
See Céline, Louis-Ferdinand
See also CA 85-88

Eliade, Mircea 1907-.............CLC **19**
See also CA 65-68
See also obituary CA 119

Eliot, George 1819-1880.......NCLC **4, 13**
See also DLB 21, 35

Eliot, John 1604-1690..............LC **5**
See also DLB 24

Eliot, T(homas) S(tearns)
1888-1965...... CLC **1, 2, 3, 6, 9, 10,
13, 15, 24, 34** (387; 523), **41**
See also CA 5-8R
See also obituary CA 25-28R
See also DLB 7, 10, 45

Elkin, Stanley (Lawrence)
1930-............. CLC **4, 6, 9, 14, 27**
See also CANR 8
See also CA 9-12R
See also DLB 2, 28
See also DLB-Y 80

Elledge, Scott 19??-......... CLC **34** (425)

Elliott, George P(aul)
1918-1980....................CLC **2**
See also CANR 2
See also CA 1-4R
See also obituary CA 97-100

Elliott, Sumner Locke 1917- ....CLC **38**
See also CANR 2
See also CA 5-8R

Ellis, A. E. 19??-...................CLC **7**

Ellis, Alice Thomas 19??-..........CLC **40**

Ellis, Bret Easton 1964- ...... CLC **39** (55)
See also CA 118

Ellis, (Henry) Havelock
1859-1939.................. TCLC **14**
See also CA 109

Ellison, Harlan (Jay)
1934-.................. CLC **1, 13, 42**
See also CANR 5
See also CA 5-8R
See also DLB 8

Ellison, Ralph (Waldo)
1914-.................. CLC **1, 3, 11**
See also CA 9-12R
See also DLB 2
See also CDALB 1941-1968

Elman, Richard 1934-.............CLC **19**
See also CAAS 3
See also CA 17-20R

Éluard, Paul 1895-1952 .... TCLC **7**
See also Grindel, Eugene

Elvin, Anne Katharine Stevenson 1933-
See Stevenson, Anne (Katharine)
See also CA 17-20R

Elytis, Odysseus 1911- ....CLC **15**
See also CA 102

Emecheta, (Florence Onye) Buchi
1944-......................CLC **14**
See also CA 81-84

Emerson, Ralph Waldo
1803-1882................... NCLC **1**
See also DLB 1

Empson, William
1906-1984.......... CLC **3, 8, 19, 33,
34** (335; 538)
See also CA 17-20R
See also obituary CA 112
See also DLB 20

Enchi, Fumiko 1905-.............CLC **31**

Ende, Michael 1930- ....CLC **31**
See also CLR 14
See also CA 118
See also SATA 42

Endo, Shusaku 1923- ...... CLC **7, 14, 19**
See also CA 29-32R

Engel, Marian 1933-1985..........CLC **36**
See also CANR 12
See also CA 25-28R
See also DLB 53

Engelhardt, Frederick 1911-1986
See Hubbard, L(afayette) Ron(ald)

Enright, D(ennis) J(oseph)
1920-...................CLC **4, 8, 31**
See also CANR 1
See also CA 1-4R
See also SATA 25
See also DLB 27

Enzensberger, Hans Magnus
1929-........................CLC **43**
See also CA 116, 119

Ephron, Nora 1941- .... CLC **17, 31**
See also CANR 12
See also CA 65-68
See also AITN 2

Epstein, Daniel Mark 1948-.........CLC **7**
See also CANR 2
See also CA 49-52

Epstein, Jacob 1956-..............CLC **19**
See also CA 114

Epstein, Joseph 1937-....... CLC **39** (463)
See also CA 112, 119

Epstein, Leslie 1938-..............CLC **27**
See also CA 73-76

Erdman, Paul E(mil) 1932- ....CLC **25**
See also CANR 13
See also CA 61-64
See also AITN 1

Erdrich, Louise 1954-....... CLC **39** (128)
See also CA 114

Erenburg, Ilya (Grigoryevich) 1891-1967
See Ehrenburg, Ilya (Grigoryevich)

Eseki, Bruno 1919-
See Mphahlele, Ezekiel

Esenin, Sergei (Aleksandrovich)
1895-1925.................. TCLC **4**
See also CA 104

Eshleman, Clayton 1935-...........CLC **7**
See also CA 33-36R
See also DLB 5

Espriu, Salvador 1913-1985........CLC **9**
See also obituary CA 115

Evans, Marian 1819-1880
See Eliot, George

Evans, Mary Ann 1819-1880
See Eliot, George

Evarts, Esther 1900-1972
See Benson, Sally

Everson, Ronald G(ilmour)
1903-......................CLC **27**
See also CA 17-20R

Everson, William (Oliver)
1912-...................CLC **1, 5, 14**
See also CANR 20
See also CA 9-12R
See also DLB 5, 16

Evtushenko, Evgenii (Aleksandrovich) 1933-
See Yevtushenko, Yevgeny

Ewart, Gavin (Buchanan)
1916-.................... CLC **13, 46**
See also CANR 17
See also CA 89-92
See also DLB 40

Ewers, Hanns Heinz
1871-1943.................. TCLC **12**
See also CA 109

Ewing, Frederick R. 1918-
See Sturgeon, Theodore (Hamilton)

Exley, Frederick (Earl)
1929-.................... CLC **6, 11**
See also CA 81-84
See also DLB-Y 81
See also AITN 2

Ezekiel, Tish O'Dowd
1943-................... CLC **34** (46)

Fagen, Donald 1948-
See Becker, Walter and Fagen, Donald

Fagen, Donald 1948- and
Becker, Walter 1950-
See Becker, Walter and Fagen, Donald

Fair, Ronald L. 1932-.............CLC **18**
See also CA 69-72
See also DLB 33

Fairbairns, Zoë (Ann) 1948- ....CLC **32**
See also CA 103

Fairfield, Cicily Isabel 1892-1983
See West, Rebecca

Fallaci, Oriana 1930- ....CLC **11**
See also CANR 15
See also CA 77-80

Faludy, George 1913-..............CLC **42**
See also CA 21-24R

Fargue, Léon-Paul 1876-1947 .... TCLC **11**
See also CA 109

Farigoule, Louis 1885-1972
See Romains, Jules

Fariña, Richard 1937?-1966 ....CLC **9**
See also CA 81-84
See also obituary CA 25-28R

Farley, Walter 1920-..............CLC **17**
See also CANR 8
See also CA 17-20R
See also SATA 2, 43
See also DLB 22

Farmer, Philip José 1918- ...... CLC **1, 19**
See also CANR 4
See also CA 1-4R
See also DLB 8

Farrell, J(ames) G(ordon)
1935-1979....................CLC **6**
See also CA 73-76
See also obituary CA 89-92
See also DLB 14

Farrell, James T(homas)
1904-1979............CLC **1, 4, 8, 11**
See also CANR 9
See also CA 5-8R
See also obituary CA 89-92
See also DLB 4, 9
See also DLB-DS 2

Farrell, M. J. 1904-
See Keane, Molly

Fassbinder, Rainer Werner
1946-1982....................CLC **20**
See also CA 93-96
See also obituary CA 106

Fast, Howard (Melvin) 1914-.......CLC **23**
See also CANR 1
See also CA 1-4R
See also SATA 7
See also DLB 9

Faulkner, William (Cuthbert)
1897-1962....... CLC **1, 3, 6, 8, 9, 11,**
14, 18, 28
See also SSC 1
See also CA 81-84
See also DLB 9, 11, 44
See also DLB-Y 86
See also DLB-DS 2
See also AITN 1

Fauset, Jessie Redmon
1884?-1961..................CLC **19**
See also CA 109

Faust, Irvin 1924- ....CLC **8**
See also CA 33-36R
See also DLB 2, 28
See also DLB-Y 80

Federman, Raymond 1928- ....CLC **6**
See also CANR 10
See also CA 17-20R
See also DLB-Y 80

Federspiel, J(ürg) F. 1931-........CLC **42**

Feiffer, Jules 1929- .... CLC **2, 8**
See also CA 17-20R
See also SATA 8
See also DLB 7, 44

Feinstein, Elaine 1930- ....CLC **36**
See also CA 69-72
See also CAAS 1
See also DLB 14, 40

Feldman, Irving (Mordecai)
1928-........................CLC **7**
See also CANR 1
See also CA 1-4R

Fellini, Federico 1920- ....CLC **16**
See also CA 65-68

Felsen, Gregor 1916-
See Felsen, Henry Gregor

Felsen, Henry Gregor 1916-........CLC **17**
See also CANR 1
See also CA 1-4R
See also SAAS 2
See also SATA 1

Fenton, James (Martin) 1949-......CLC **32**
See also CA 102
See also DLB 40

Ferber, Edna 1887-1968..........CLC **18**
See also CA 5-8R
See also obituary CA 25-28R
See also SATA 7
See also DLB 9, 28
See also AITN 1

Ferlinghetti, Lawrence (Monsanto)
1919?-...............CLC **2, 6, 10, 27**
See also CANR 3
See also CA 5-8R
See also DLB 5, 16
See also CDALB 1941-1968

Ferrier, Susan (Edmonstone)
1782-1854.................. NCLC **8**

Feuchtwanger, Lion
1884-1958 .... TCLC **3**
See also CA 104

Feydeau, Georges 1862-1921..... TCLC **22**
See also CA 113

Fiedler, Leslie A(aron)
1917-................. CLC **4, 13, 24**
See also CANR 7
See also CA 9-12R
See also DLB 28

Field, Andrew 1938- .... CLC **44** (463)
Field, Eugene 1850-1895 .... NCLC **3**
See also SATA 16
See also DLB 21, 23, 42

Fielding, Henry 1707-1754.......... LC **1**
See also DLB 39

Fielding, Sarah 1710-1768 .... LC **1**
See also DLB 39

Fierstein, Harvey 1954- ....CLC **33**
Figes, Eva 1932-.................CLC **31**
See also CANR 4
See also CA 53-56
See also DLB 14

Finch, Robert (Duer Claydon)
1900-........................CLC **18**
See also CANR 9
See also CA 57-60

Findley, Timothy 1930-............CLC **27**
See also CANR 12
See also CA 25-28R
See also DLB 53

Fink, Janis 1951-
See Ian, Janis

Firbank, (Arthur Annesley) Ronald
1886-1926.................. TCLC **1**
See also CA 104
See also DLB 36

Firbank, Louis 1944-
See Reed, Lou

Fisher, Roy 1930- ....CLC **25**
See also CANR 16
See also CA 81-84
See also DLB 40

Fisher, Rudolph 1897-1934 ...... TCLC **11**
See also CA 107

Fisher, Vardis (Alvero)
1895-1968....................CLC **7**
See also CA 5-8R
See also obituary CA 25-28R
See also DLB 9

FitzGerald, Edward
1809-1883.................. NCLC **9**
See also DLB 32

Fitzgerald, F(rancis) Scott (Key)
1896-1940.............TCLC **1, 6, 14**
See also CA 110
See also DLB 4, 9
See also DLB-Y 81
See also DLB-DS 1
See also AITN 1

Fitzgerald, Penelope 1916-........CLC **19**
See also CA 85-88
See also DLB 14

Fitzgerald, Robert (Stuart)
1910-1985......... CLC **39** (318; 470)
See also CANR 1
See also CA 2R
See also obituary CA 114
See also DLB-Y 80

FitzGerald, Robert D(avid)
1902-........................CLC **19**
See also CA 17-20R

Flanagan, Thomas (James Bonner)
1923-........................CLC **25**
See also CA 108
See also DLB-Y 80

Flaubert, Gustave
1821-1880................NCLC **2, 10**

Fleming, Ian (Lancaster)
1908-1964 .... CLC **3, 30**
See also CA 5-8R
See also SATA 9

Fleming, Thomas J(ames)
1927-........................CLC **37**
See also CANR 10
See also CA 5-8R
See also SATA 8

Flieg, Hellmuth
See also Heym, Stefan

Flying Officer X 1905-1974
See Bates, H(erbert) E(rnest)

Fo, Dario 1929- ....CLC **32**
See also CA 116

Follett, Ken(neth Martin)
1949-........................CLC **18**
See also CANR 13
See also CA 81-84
See also DLB-Y 81

Forbes, Esther 1891-1967.........CLC **12**
See also CAP 1
See also CA 13-14
See also obituary CA 25-28R
See also DLB 22
See also SATA 2

Forché, Carolyn 1950- ....CLC **25**
See also CA 109, 117
See also DLB 5

Ford, Ford Madox
1873-1939............... TCLC **1, 15**
See also CA 104
See also DLB 34

Ford, John 1895-1973............CLC **16**
See also obituary CA 45-48

Ford, Richard 1944- ....CLC **46**
See also CANR 11
See also CA 69-72

Forester, C(ecil) S(cott)
1899-1966....................CLC **35**
See also CA 73-76
See also obituary CA 25-28R
See also SATA 13

Forman, James D(ouglas)
1932-........................CLC **21**
See also CANR 4, 19
See also CA 9-12R
See also SATA 8, 21

Author Index

Gallant, Mavis 1922-........ **CLC 7, 18, 38**
See also CA 69-72
See also DLB 53

Gallant, Roy A(rthur) 1924- ....**CLC 17**
See also CANR 4
See also CA 5-8R
See also SATA 4

Gallico, Paul (William)
1897-1976.....................**CLC 2**
See also CA 5-8R
See also obituary CA 69-72
See also SATA 13
See also DLB 9
See also AITN 1

Galsworthy, John 1867-1933...... **TCLC 1**
See also CA 104
See also DLB 10, 34

Galt, John 1779-1839 .... **NCLC 1**

Galvin, James 1951-.............**CLC 38**
See also CA 108

Gann, Ernest K(ellogg) 1910- ......**CLC 23**
See also CANR 1
See also CA 1-4R
See also AITN 1

García Lorca, Federico
1899-1936................. **TCLC 1, 7**
See also CA 104

García Márquez, Gabriel
1928-.........**CLC 2, 3, 8, 10, 15, 27**
See also CANR 10
See also CA 33-36R

Gardam, Jane 1928-..............**CLC 43**
See also CLR 12
See also CANR 2, 18
See also CA 49-52
See also SATA 28, 39
See also DLB 14

Gardner, Herb 1934- .... **CLC 44 (208)**

Gardner, John (Champlin, Jr.)
1933-1982....... **CLC 2, 3, 5, 7, 8, 10,
18, 28, 34 (547)**
See also CA 65-68
See also obituary CA 107
See also obituary SATA 31, 40
See also DLB 2
See also DLB-Y 82
See also AITN 1

Gardner, John (Edmund)
1926-......................**CLC 30**
See also CANR 15
See also CA 103
See also AITN 1

Garfield, Leon 1921-..............**CLC 12**
See also CA 17-20R
See also SATA 1, 32

Garland, (Hannibal) Hamlin
1860-1940.................. **TCLC 3**
See also CA 104
See also DLB 12

Garneau, Hector (de) Saint Denys
1912-1943................. **TCLC 13**
See also CA 111

Garner, Alan 1935-..............**CLC 17**
See also CANR 15
See also CA 73-76
See also SATA 18

Garner, Hugh 1913-1979 ....**CLC 13**
See also CA 69-72

Garnett, David 1892-1981 ....**CLC 3**
See also CANR 17
See also CA 5-8R
See also obituary CA 103
See also DLB 34

Garrett, George (Palmer)
1929-.................... **CLC 3, 11**
See also CAAS 5
See also CANR 1
See also CA 1-4R
See also DLB 2, 5
See also DLB-Y 83

Garrigue, Jean 1914-1972 .... **CLC 2, 8**
See also CA 5-8R
See also obituary CA 37-40R

Gary, Romain 1914-1980.........**CLC 25**
See also Kacew, Romain

Gascoyne, David (Emery)
1916-.....................**CLC 45**
See also CANR 10
See also CA 65-68
See also DLB 20

Gascar, Pierre 1916-.............**CLC 11**
See also Fournier, Pierre

Gaskell, Elizabeth Cleghorn
1810-1865................... **NCLC 5**
See also DLB 21

Gass, William H(oward)
1924-.....**CLC 1, 2, 8, 11, 15, 39 (477)**
See also CA 17-20R
See also DLB 2

Gautier, Théophile 1811-1872..... **NCLC 1**

Gaye, Marvin (Pentz)
1939-1984....................**CLC 26**
See also obituary CA 112

Gébler, Carlo (Ernest)
1954-................... **CLC 39 (60)**
See also CA 119

Gee, Maurice (Gough) 1931-.......**CLC 29**
See also CA 97-100
See also SATA 46

Gelbart, Larry (Simon) 1923-......**CLC 21**
See also CA 73-76

Gelber, Jack 1932- ....**CLC 1, 6, 14**
See also CANR 2
See also CA 1-4R
See also DLB 7

Gellhorn, Martha (Ellis) 1908- .....**CLC 14**
See also CA 77-80
See also DLB-Y 82

Genet, Jean
1910-1986........**CLC 1, 2, 5, 10, 14,
44 (385), 46**
See also CANR 18
See also CA 13-16R
See also DLB-Y 86

Gent, Peter 1942-................**CLC 29**
See also CA 89-92
See also DLB-Y 82
See also AITN 1

George, Jean Craighead 1919- .....**CLC 35**
See also CLR 1
See also CA 5-8R
See also SATA 2
See also DLB 52

George, Stefan (Anton)
1868-1933............... **TCLC 2, 14**
See also CA 104

Gerhardi, William (Alexander) 1895-1977
See Gerhardie, William (Alexander)

Gerhardie, William (Alexander)
1895-1977.....................**CLC 5**
See also CANR 18
See also CA 25-28R
See also obituary CA 73-76
See also DLB 36

Gertler, T(rudy) 1946?- ...... **CLC 34 (49)**
See also CA 116

Gessner, Friedrike Victoria 1910-1980
See Adamson, Joy(-Friederike Victoria)

Ghelderode, Michel de
1898-1962................. **CLC 6, 11**
See also CA 85-88

Ghiselin, Brewster 1903- ....**CLC 23**
See also CANR 13
See also CA 13-16R

Ghose, Zulfikar 1935-.............**CLC 42**
See also CA 65-68

Ghosh, Amitav 1943- .... **CLC 44 (44)**

Giacosa, Giuseppe 1847-1906 ..... **TCLC 7**
See also CA 104

Gibbon, Lewis Grassic
1901-1935.................. **TCLC 4**
See also Mitchell, James Leslie

Gibran, (Gibran) Kahlil
1883-1931................. **TCLC 1, 9**
See also CA 104

Gibson, William 1914-............**CLC 23**
See also CANR 9
See also CA 9-12R
See also DLB 7

Gibson, William 1948- ...... **CLC 39 (139)**

Gide, André (Paul Guillaume)
1869-1951............... **TCLC 5, 12**
See also CA 104

Gifford, Barry (Colby)
1946-................... **CLC 34 (457)**
See also CANR 9
See also CA 65-68

Gilbert, (Sir) W(illiam) S(chwenck)
1836-1911.................. **TCLC 3**
See also CA 104
See also SATA 36

Gilbreth, Ernestine 1908-
See Carey, Ernestine Gilbreth

Gilbreth, Frank B(unker), Jr. 1911-
See Gilbreth, Frank B(unker), Jr. and
Carey, Ernestine Gilbreth
See also CA 9-12R
See also SATA 2

Gilbreth, Frank B(unker), Jr. 1911- and
Carey, Ernestine Gilbreth
1908-.....................**CLC 17**

Gilchrist, Ellen 1935- .... **CLC 34 (164)**
See also CA 113, 116

Giles, Molly 1942-........... **CLC 39 (64)**

Gilliam, Terry (Vance) 1940-
See Monty Python
See also CA 108, 113

Goyen, (Charles) William
    1915-1983............CLC **5, 8, 14, 40**
  See also CANR 6
  See also CA 5-8R
  See also obituary CA 110
  See also DLB 2
  See also DLB-Y 83
  See also AITN 2

Goytisolo, Juan 1931-.......CLC **5, 10, 23**
  See also CA 85-88

Grabbe, Christian Dietrich
    1801-1836..................NCLC **2**

Gracq, Julien 1910-..............CLC **11**

Grade, Chaim 1910-1982.........CLC **10**
  See also CA 93-96
  See also obituary CA 107

Graham, R(obert) B(ontine) Cunninghame
    1852-1936.................TCLC **19**

Graham, W(illiam) S(ydney)
    1918-......................CLC **29**
  See also CA 73-76
  See also DLB 20

Graham, Winston (Mawdsley)
    1910-......................CLC **23**
  See also CANR 2
  See also CA 49-52
  See also obituary CA 118

Granville-Barker, Harley
    1877-1946.................TCLC **2**
  See also CA 104

Grass, Günter (Wilhelm)
    1927-.......CLC **1, 2, 4, 6, 11, 15, 22,**
                           32
  See also CANR 20
  See also CA 13-16R

Grau, Shirley Ann 1929- .... CLC **4, 9**
  See also CA 89-92
  See also DLB 2
  See also AITN 2

Graves, Richard Perceval
    19??- .... CLC **44 (474)**

Graves, Robert (von Ranke)
    1895-1985...........CLC **1, 2, 6, 11,**
              39 (320), 44 (474), 45
  See also CANR 5
  See also CA 5-8R
  See also obituary CA 117
  See also SATA 45
  See also DLB 20
  See also DLB-Y 85

Gray, Alasdair 1934-..............CLC **41**

Gray, Amlin 1946-................CLC **29**

Gray, Francine du Plessix
    1930-......................CLC **22**
  See also CAAS 2
  See also CANR 11
  See also CA 61-64

Gray, John (Henry)
    1866-1934.................TCLC **19**
  See also CA 119

Gray, Simon (James Holliday)
    1936-.................CLC **9, 14, 36**
  See also CAAS 3
  See also CA 21-24R
  See also DLB 13
  See also AITN 1

Gray, Thomas 1716-1771...........LC **4**

Grayson, Richard (A.) 1951-.......CLC **38**
  See also CANR 14
  See also CA 85-88

Greeley, Andrew M(oran)
    1928-......................CLC **28**
  See also CANR 7
  See also CA 5-8R

Green, Hannah 1932-........CLC **3, 7, 30**
  See also Greenberg, Joanne
  See also CA 73-76

Green, Henry 1905-1974 ...... CLC **2, 13**
  See also Yorke, Henry Vincent
  See also DLB 15

Green, Julien (Hartridge)
    1900-................. CLC **3, 11**
  See also CA 21-24R
  See also DLB 4

Green, Paul (Eliot) 1894-1981......CLC **25**
  See also CANR 3
  See also CA 5-8R
  See also obituary CA 103
  See also DLB 7, 9
  See also DLB-Y 81
  See also AITN 1

Greenberg, Ivan 1908-1973
  See Rahv, Philip
  See also CA 85-88

Greenberg, Joanne (Goldenberg)
    1932-..................CLC **3, 7, 30**
  See also Green, Hannah
  See also CANR 14
  See also CA 5-8R
  See also SATA 25

Greene, Bette 1934-...............CLC **30**
  See also CLR 2
  See also CANR 4
  See also CA 53-56
  See also SATA 8

Greene, Gael 19??-.................CLC **8**
  See also CANR 10
  See also CA 13-16R

Greene, Graham (Henry)
    1904-.......CLC **1, 3, 6, 9, 14, 18, 27,**
                          37
  See also CA 13-16R
  See also SATA 20
  See also DLB 13, 15
  See also DLB-Y 85
  See also AITN 2

Gregor, Arthur 1923-..............CLC **9**
  See also CANR 11
  See also CA 25-28R
  See also SATA 36

Gregory, Lady (Isabella Augusta Persse)
    1852-1932.................TCLC **1**
  See also CA 104
  See also DLB 10

Grendon, Stephen 1909-1971
  See Derleth, August (William)

Greve, Felix Paul Berthold Friedrich
    1879-1948

Grey, (Pearl) Zane
    1872?-1939.................TCLC **6**
  See also CA 104
  See also DLB 9

Grieg, (Johan) Nordahl (Brun)
    1902-1943.................TCLC **10**
  See also CA 107

Grieve, C(hristopher) M(urray) 1892-1978
  See MacDiarmid, Hugh
  See also CA 5-8R
  See also obituary CA 85-88

Griffin, Gerald 1803-1840 .... NCLC **7**

Griffin, Peter 1942-.........CLC **39 (398)**

Griffiths, Trevor 1935-...........CLC **13**
  See also CA 97-100
  See also DLB 13

Grigson, Geoffrey (Edward Harvey)
    1905-1985...........CLC **7, 39 (330)**
  See also CANR 20
  See also CA 25-28R
  See also obituary CA 118
  See also DLB 27

Grillparzer, Franz 1791-1872 ..... NCLC **1**

Grimm, Jakob (Ludwig) Karl 1785-1863
  See Grimm, Jakob (Ludwig) Karl and
    Grimm, Wilhelm Karl

Grimm, Jakob (Ludwig) Karl 1785-1863
  and Grimm, Wilhelm Karl
    1786-1859..................NCLC **3**
  See also SATA 22

Grimm, Wilhelm Karl 1786-1859
  See Grimm, Jakob (Ludwig) Karl and
    Grimm, Wilhelm Karl

Grimm, Wilhelm Karl 1786-1859 and
  Grimm, Jakob (Ludwig) Karl
    1785-1863
  See Grimm, Jakob (Ludwig) Karl and
    Grimm, Wilhelm Karl

Grimmelshausen, Johann Jakob Christoffel
  von 1621-1676.................LC **6**

Grindel, Eugene 1895-1952
  See also CA 104

Grossman, Vasily (Semënovich)
    1905-1964..................CLC **41**

Grove, Frederick Philip
    1879-1948..................TCLC **4**
  See also Greve, Felix Paul Berthold
    Friedrich

Grumbach, Doris (Isaac)
    1918-...................CLC **13, 22**
  See also CAAS 2
  See also CANR 9
  See also CA 5-8R

Grundtvig, Nicolai Frederik Severin
    1783-1872..................NCLC **1**

Grunwald, Lisa 1959-........ CLC **44 (49)**

Guare, John 1938-..........CLC **8, 14, 29**
  See also CA 73-76
  See also DLB 7

Gudjonsson, Halldór Kiljan 1902-
  See Laxness, Halldór (Kiljan)
  See also CA 103

Guest, Barbara 1920-....... CLC **34 (441)**
  See also CANR 11
  See also CA 25-28R
  See also DLB 5

Guest, Judith (Ann) 1936-...... CLC **8, 30**
  See also CANR 15
  See also CA 77-80

Guild, Nicholas M. 1944-..........CLC **33**
  See also CA 93-96

Author Index

Hyde, Margaret O(ldroyd)
  1917-.....................CLC 21
  See also CANR 1
  See also CA 1-4R
  See also SATA 1, 42

Ian, Janis 1951-.................CLC 21
  See also CA 105

Ibargüengoitia, Jorge
  1928-1983.....................CLC 37
  See also obituary CA 113

Ibsen, Henrik (Johan)
  1828-1906............TCLC 2, 8, 16
  See also CA 104

Ibuse, Masuji 1898-..............CLC 22

Ichikawa, Kon 1915-.............CLC 20

Idle, Eric 1943-
  See Monty Python
  See also CA 116

Ignatow, David 1914-.....CLC 4, 7, 14, 40
  See also CAAS 3
  See also CA 9-12R
  See also DLB 5

Ihimaera, Witi (Tame) 1944-.......CLC 46
  See also CA 77-80

Ilf, Ilya 1897-1937 **and Petrov, Evgeny**
  1902-1942.................TCLC 21

Immermann, Karl (Lebrecht)
  1796-1840...................NCLC 4

Ingalls, Rachel 19??-..............CLC 42

Inge, William (Motter)
  1913-1973..............CLC 1, 8, 19
  See also CA 9-12R
  See also DLB 7
  See also CDALB 1941-1968

Innaurato, Albert 1948-...........CLC 21
  See also CA 115

Innes, Michael 1906-
  See Stewart, J(ohn) I(nnes) M(ackintosh)

Ionesco, Eugène
  1912-........CLC 1, 4, 6, 9, 11, 15, 41
  See also CA 9-12R
  See also SATA 7

Irving, John (Winslow)
  1942-............CLC 13, 23, 38
  See also CA 25-28R
  See also DLB 6
  See also DLB-Y 82

Irving, Washington 1783-1859 .... NCLC 2
  See also YABC 2
  See also DLB 3, 11, 30

Isaacs, Susan 1943-...............CLC 32
  See also CANR 20
  See also CA 89-92

Isherwood, Christopher (William Bradshaw)
  1904-1986..........CLC 1, 9, 11, 14,
                              44 (396)
  See also CA 13-16R
  See also obituary CA 117
  See also DLB 15
  See also DLB-Y 86

Ishiguro, Kazuo 1954?-............CLC 27
  See also CA 120

Ishikawa Takuboku
  1885-1912.................TCLC 15
  See also CA 113

Ivask, Ivar (Vidrik) 1927-.........CLC 14
  See also CA 37-40R

Jackson, Jesse 1908-1983..........CLC 12
  See also CA 25-28R
  See also obituary CA 109
  See also SATA 2, 29, 48

Jackson, Laura (Riding) 1901-
  See Riding, Laura
  See also CA 65-68
  See also DLB 48

Jackson, Shirley 1919-1965 ....CLC 11
  See also CANR 4
  See also CA 1-4R
  See also obituary CA 25-28R
  See also SATA 2
  See also DLB 6
  See also CDALB 1941-1968

Jacob, (Cyprien) Max
  1876-1944.................. TCLC 6
  See also CA 104

Jacob, Piers A(nthony) D(illingham) 1934-
  See Anthony (Jacob), Piers
  See also CA 21-24R

Jacobs, Jim 1942-
  See Jacobs, Jim and Casey, Warren
  See also CA 97-100

Jacobs, Jim 1942- **and**
  Casey, Warren 1935-..........CLC 12

Jacobs, W(illiam) W(ymark)
  1863-1943.................. TCLC 22

Jacobson, Dan 1929-........... CLC 4, 14
  See also CANR 2
  See also CA 1-4R
  See also DLB 14

Jagger, Mick 1944-
  See Jagger, Mick and Richard, Keith

Jagger, Mick 1944- **and**
  Richard, Keith 1943-.........CLC 17

Jakes, John (William) 1932- ....CLC 29
  See also CANR 10
  See also CA 57-60
  See also DLB-Y 83

James, C(yril) L(ionel) R(obert)
  1901-........................CLC 33
  See also CA 117

James, Daniel 1911-
  See Santiago, Danny

James, Henry (Jr.)
  1843-1916............TCLC 2, 11, 24
  See also CA 104
  See also DLB 12

James, M(ontague) R(hodes)
  1862-1936.................. TCLC 6
  See also CA 104

James, P(hyllis) D(orothy)
  1920-................ CLC 18, 46
  See also CANR 17
  See also CA 21-24R

James, William 1842-1910...... TCLC 15
  See also CA 109

Jandl, Ernst 1925-......... CLC 34 (194)

Janowitz, Tama 1957-.............CLC 43
  See also CA 106

Jarrell, Randall
  1914-1965......... CLC 1, 2, 6, 9, 13
  See also CLR 6
  See also CANR 6
  See also CA 5-8R
  See also obituary CA 25-28R
  See also CABS 2
  See also SATA 7
  See also DLB 48, 52
  See also CDALB 1941-1968

Jarry, Alfred 1873-1907....... TCLC 2, 14
  See also CA 104

Jean Paul 1763-1825............. NCLC 7

Jeffers, (John) Robinson
  1887-1962...........CLC 2, 3, 11, 15
  See also CA 85-88
  See also DLB 45

Jefferson, Thomas 1743-1826 .... NCLC 11
  See also DLB 31

Jellicoe, (Patricia) Ann 1927-.......CLC 27
  See also CA 85-88
  See also DLB 13

Jennings, Elizabeth (Joan)
  1926-.................... CLC 5, 14
  See also CAAS 5
  See also CANR 8
  See also CA 61-64
  See also DLB 27

Jennings, Waylon 1937-...........CLC 21

Jensen, Laura (Linnea) 1948-......CLC 37
  See also CA 103

Jerrold, Douglas William
  1803-1857................... NCLC 2

Jerome, Jerome K.
  1859-1927................. TCLC 23
  See also CA 119
  See also DLB 10, 34

Jewett, (Theodora) Sarah Orne
  1849-1909................TCLC 1, 22
  See also CA 108
  See also SATA 15
  See also DLB 12

Jhabvala, Ruth Prawer
  1927-................... CLC 4, 8, 29
  See also CANR 2
  See also CA 1-4R

Jiles, Paulette 1943-...............CLC 13
  See also CA 101

Jiménez (Mantecón), Juan Ramón
  1881-1958................. TCLC 4
  See also CA 104

Joel, Billy 1949-..................CLC 26
  See also Joel, William Martin

Joel, William Martin 1949-
  See Joel, Billy
  See also CA 108

Johnson, B(ryan) S(tanley William)
  1933-1973................. CLC 6, 9
  See also CANR 9
  See also CA 9-12R
  See also obituary CA 53-56
  See also DLB 14, 40

Johnson, Charles 1948-.............CLC 7
  See also CA 116
  See also DLB 33

Author Index

Author Index

Mistral, Gabriela 1889-1957 . . . . . . TCLC 2
See also CA 104

Mitchell, James Leslie 1901-1935
See Gibbon, Lewis Grassic
See also CA 104
See also DLB 15

Mitchell, Joni 1943- . . . . CLC 12
See also CA 112

Mitchell (Marsh), Margaret (Munnerlyn)
1900-1949 . . . . TCLC 11
See also CA 109
See also DLB 9

Mitchell, W(illiam) O(rmond)
1914- . . . . CLC 25
See also CANR 15
See also CA 77-80

Mitford, Mary Russell
1787-1855 . . . . NCLC 4

Mitford, Nancy
1904-1973 . . . . CLC 44 (482)

Mo, Timothy 1950- . . . . CLC 46
See also CA 117

Modiano, Patrick (Jean) 1945- . . . . . CLC 18
See also CANR 17
See also CA 85-88

Modarressi, Taghi 1931- . . . . . . CLC 44 (82)

Mofolo, Thomas (Mokopu)
1876-1948 . . . . TCLC 22

Mohr, Nicholasa 1935- . . . . CLC 12
See also CANR 1
See also CA 49-52
See also SATA 8

Mojtabai, A(nn) G(race)
1938- . . . . CLC 5, 9, 15, 29
See also CA 85-88

Molnár, Ferenc 1878-1952 . . . . . . TCLC 20
See also CA 109

Momaday, N(avarre) Scott
1934- . . . . CLC 2, 19
See also CANR 14
See also CA 25-28R
See also SATA 30, 48

Monroe, Harriet 1860-1936 . . . . . . TCLC 12
See also CA 109
See also DLB 54

Montagu, Elizabeth 1720-1800 . . . . NCLC 7

Montague, John (Patrick)
1929- . . . . CLC 13, 46
See also CANR 9
See also CA 9-12R
See also DLB 40

Montale, Eugenio
1896-1981 . . . . CLC 7, 9, 18
See also CA 17-20R
See also obituary CA 104

Montgomery, Marion (H., Jr.)
1925- . . . . CLC 7
See also CANR 3
See also CA 1-4R
See also DLB 6
See also AITN 1

Montgomery, Robert Bruce 1921-1978
See Crispin, Edmund
See also CA 104

Montherlant, Henri (Milon) de
1896-1972 . . . . CLC 8, 19
See also CA 85-88
See also obituary CA 37-40R

Montisquieu, Charles-Louis de Secondat
1689-1755 . . . . LC 7

Monty Python . . . . CLC 21
See also Cleese, John

Moodie, Susanna (Strickland)
1803-1885 . . . . NCLC 14

Mooney, Ted 1951- . . . . CLC 25

Moorcock, Michael (John)
1939- . . . . CLC 5, 27
See also CAAS 5
See also CANR 2, 17
See also CA 45-48
See also DLB 14

Moore, Brian
1921- . . . . CLC 1, 3, 5, 7, 8, 19, 32
See also CANR 1
See also CA 1-4R

Moore, George (Augustus)
1852-1933 . . . . TCLC 7
See also CA 104
See also DLB 10, 18, 57

Moore, Lorrie 1957- . . . . . . CLC 39 (82), 45
See also Moore, Marie Lorena

Moore, Marianne (Craig)
1887-1972 . . . . . . CLC 1, 2, 4, 8, 10, 13,
　　　　　　　　　　　　　　　　　　　　　　19
See also CANR 3
See also CA 1-4R
See also obituary CA 33-36R
See also DLB 45
See also SATA 20

Moore, Marie Lorena 1957-
See Moore, Lorrie
See also CA 116

Moore, Thomas 1779-1852 . . . . NCLC 6

Morand, Paul 1888-1976 . . . . CLC 41
See also obituary CA 69-72

Morante, Elsa 1918-1985 . . . . CLC 8
See also CA 85-88
See also obituary CA 117

Moravia, Alberto
1907- . . . . CLC 2, 7, 11, 18, 27, 46
See also Pincherle, Alberto

Moréas, Jean 1856-1910 . . . . TCLC 18

Morgan, Berry 1919- . . . . CLC 6
See also CA 49-52
See also DLB 6

Morgan, Edwin (George)
1920- . . . . CLC 31
See also CANR 3
See also CA 7-8R
See also DLB 27

Morgan, Frederick 1922- . . . . CLC 23
See also CA 17-20R

Morgan, Janet 1945- . . . . CLC 39 (436)
See also CA 65-68

Morgan, Robin 1941- . . . . CLC 2
See also CA 69-72

Morgenstern, Christian (Otto Josef Wolfgang)
1871-1914 . . . . TCLC 8
See also CA 105

Mori Ōgai 1862-1922 . . . . TCLC 14
See also Mori Rintaro

Mori Rintaro 1862-1922
See Mori Ōgai
See also CA 110

Mörike, Eduard (Friedrich)
1804-1875 . . . . NCLC 10

Moritz, Karl Philipp 1756-1793 . . . . . LC 2

Morris, Julian 1916-
See West, Morris L.

Morris, Steveland Judkins 1950-
See Wonder, Stevie
See also CA 111

Morris, William 1834-1896 . . . . . . NCLC 4
See also DLB 18, 35, 57

Morris, Wright (Marion)
1910- . . . . CLC 1, 3, 7, 18, 37
See also CA 9-12R
See also DLB 2
See also DLB-Y 81

Morrison, James Douglas 1943-1971
See Morrison, Jim
See also CA 73-76

Morrison, Jim 1943-1971 . . . . CLC 17
See also Morrison, James Douglas

Morrison, Toni 1931- . . . . CLC 4, 10, 22
See also CA 29-32R
See also DLB 6, 33
See also DLB-Y 81

Morrison, Van 1945- . . . . CLC 21
See also CA 116

Mortimer, John (Clifford)
1923- . . . . CLC 28, 43
See also CA 13-16R
See also DLB 13

Mortimer, Penelope (Ruth)
1918- . . . . CLC 5
See also CA 57-60

Mosley, Nicholas 1923- . . . . CLC 43
See also CA 69-72
See also DLB 14

Moss, Howard 1922- . . . . CLC 7, 14, 45
See also CANR 1
See also CA 1-4R
See also DLB 5

Motley, Willard (Francis)
1912-1965 . . . . CLC 18
See also obituary CA 106
See also CA 117

Mott, Michael (Charles Alston)
1930- . . . . CLC 15, 34 (460)
See also CANR 7
See also CA 5-8R

Mowat, Farley (McGill) 1921- . . . . . . CLC 26
See also CANR 4
See also CA 1-4R
See also SATA 3

Mphahlele, Es'kia 1919-
See Mphahlele, Ezekiel

Mphahlele, Ezekiel 1919- . . . . CLC 25
See also CA 81-84

Mqhayi, S(amuel) E(dward) K(rune Loliwe)
1875-1945 . . . . TCLC 25

Mrożek, Sławomir 1930- . . . . CLC 3, 13
See also CA 13-16R

Quiroga, Horacio (Sylvestre)
1878-1937.................. TCLC 20
See also CA 117

Quoirez, Françoise 1935-
See Sagan, Françoise
See also CANR 6
See also CA 49-52

Rabelais, François 1494?-1553 ...... LC 5

Rabe, David (William)
1940-.................. CLC 4, 8, 33
See also CA 85-88
See also DLB 7

Rabinovitch, Sholem 1859-1916
See Aleichem, Sholom
See also CA 104

Rachen, Kurt von 1911-1986
See Hubbard, L(afayette) Ron(ald)

Radcliffe, Ann (Ward)
1764-1823.................. NCLC 6
See also DLB 39

Radnóti, Miklós 1909-1944 ...... TCLC 16
See also CA 118

Rado, James 1939-
See Ragni, Gerome and
Rado, James
See also CA 105

Radomski, James 1932-
See Rado, James

Radvanyi, Netty Reiling 1900-1983
See Seghers, Anna
See also CA 85-88
See also obituary CA 110

Raeburn, John 1941-....... CLC 34 (477)
See also CA 57-60

Ragni, Gerome 1942-
See Ragni, Gerome and Rado, James
See also CA 105

Ragni, Gerome 1942- and
Rado, James 1939-.......... CLC 17

Rahv, Philip 1908-1973 .... CLC 24
See also Greenberg, Ivan

Raine, Craig 1944- .... CLC 32
See also CA 108
See also DLB 40

Raine, Kathleen (Jessie)
1908-.................. CLC 7, 45
See also CA 85-88
See also DLB 20

Rampersad, Arnold
19??-.................. CLC 44 (506)

Rand, Ayn
1905-1982........CLC 3, 30, 44 (447)
See also CA 13-16R
See also obituary CA 105

Randall, Dudley (Felker) 1914-......CLC 1
See also CA 25-28R
See also DLB 41

Ransom, John Crowe
1888-1974........ CLC 2, 4, 5, 11, 24
See also CANR 6
See also CA 5-8R
See also obituary CA 49-52
See also DLB 45

Rao, Raja 1909-.................CLC 25
See also CA 73-76

Raphael, Frederic (Michael)
1931-.................... CLC 2, 14
See also CANR 1
See also CA 1-4R
See also DLB 14

Rathbone, Julian 1935-............CLC 41
See also CA 101

Rattigan, Terence (Mervyn)
1911-1977....................CLC 7
See also CA 85-88
See also obituary CA 73-76
See also DLB 13

Raven, Simon (Arthur Noel)
1927-....................CLC 14
See also CA 81-84

Rawlings, Marjorie Kinnan
1896-1953.................. TCLC 4
See also CA 104
See also YABC 1
See also DLB 9, 22

Ray, Satyajit 1921- ....CLC 16
See also CA 114

Read, Herbert (Edward)
1893-1968....................CLC 4
See also CA 85-88
See also obituary CA 25-28R
See also DLB 20

Read, Piers Paul 1941-...... CLC 4, 10, 25
See also CA 21-24R
See also SATA 21
See also DLB 14

Reade, Charles 1814-1884 .... NCLC 2
See also DLB 21

Reade, Hamish 1936-
See Gray, Simon (James Holliday)

Reaney, James 1926-..............CLC 13
See also CA 41-44R
See also SATA 43

Rechy, John (Francisco)
1934-................CLC 1, 7, 14, 18
See also CAAS 4
See also CANR 6
See also CA 5-8R
See also DLB-Y 82

Redcam, Tom 1870-1933 .... TCLC 25

Redgrove, Peter (William)
1932-.................... CLC 6, 41
See also CANR 3
See also CA 1-4R
See also DLB 40

Redmon (Nightingale), Anne
1943-.......................CLC 22
See also Nightingale, Anne Redmon
See also DLB-Y 86

Reed, Ishmael
1938-.......... CLC 2, 3, 5, 6, 13, 32
See also CA 21-24R
See also DLB 2, 5, 33

Reed, John (Silas) 1887-1920...... TCLC 9
See also CA 106

Reed, Lou 1944-....................CLC 21

Reid, Christopher 1949-..........CLC 33
See also DLB 40

Reid Banks, Lynne 1929-
See Banks, Lynne Reid
See also CANR 6
See also CA 1-4R
See also SATA 22

Reiner, Max 1900-
See Caldwell, (Janet Miriam) Taylor
(Holland)

Remark, Erich Paul 1898-1970
See Remarque, Erich Maria

Remarque, Erich Maria
1898-1970....................CLC 21
See also CA 77-80
See also obituary CA 29-32R

Remizov, Alexey (Mikhailovich)
1877-1957.................. TCLC 27

Renard, Jules 1864-1910 .... TCLC 17
See also CA 117

Renault, Mary
1905-1983.............. CLC 3, 11, 17
See also Challans, Mary
See also DLB-Y 83

Rendell, Ruth 1930- ....CLC 28
See also CA 109

Renoir, Jean 1894-1979 ....CLC 20
See also obituary CA 85-88

Resnais, Alain 1922-..............CLC 16

Rexroth, Kenneth
1905-1982........ CLC 1, 2, 6, 11, 22
See also CANR 14
See also CA 5-8R
See also obituary CA 107
See also DLB 16, 48
See also DLB-Y 82
See also CDALB 1941-1968

Reyes y Basoalto, Ricardo Eliecer Neftali
1904-1973
See Neruda, Pablo

Reymont, Władysław Stanisław
1867-1925.................. TCLC 5
See also CA 104

Reynolds, Jonathan 1942?- ..... CLC 6, 38
See also CA 65-68

Reynolds, Michael (Shane)
1937-.................. CLC 44 (514)

Reznikoff, Charles 1894-1976.......CLC 9
See also CAP 2
See also CA 33-36
See also obituary CA 61-64
See also DLB 28, 45

Rezzori, Gregor von 1914-........CLC 25

Rhys, Jean
1894-1979........ CLC 2, 4, 6, 14, 19
See also CA 25-28R
See also obituary CA 85-88
See also DLB 36

Ribeiro, Darcy 1922-........ CLC 34 (102)
See also CA 33-36R

Ribeiro, João Ubaldo (Osorio Pimentel)
1941-.......................CLC 10
See also CA 81-84

Ribman, Ronald (Burt) 1932- ....CLC 7
See also CA 21-24R

Rice, Anne 1941-.................CLC 41
See also CANR 12
See also CA 65-68

Rice, Elmer 1892-1967 ....CLC 7
See also CAP 2
See also CA 21-22
See also obituary CA 25-28R
See also DLB 4, 7

Rostand, Edmond (Eugène Alexis)
    1868-1918................. **TCLC 6**
    See also CA 104

Roth, Henry 1906-.......... **CLC 2, 6, 11**
    See also CAP 1
    See also CA 11-12
    See also DLB 28

Roth, Philip (Milton)
    1933-......**CLC 1, 2, 3, 4, 6, 9, 15, 22, 31**
    See also CANR 1
    See also CA 1-4R
    See also DLB 2, 28
    See also DLB-Y 82

Rothenberg, Jerome 1931-..........**CLC 6**
    See also CANR 1
    See also CA 45-48
    See also DLB 5

Roumain, Jacques 1907-1944 .... **TCLC 19**
    See also CA 117

Rourke, Constance (Mayfield)
    1885-1941................. **TCLC 12**
    See also CA 107
    See also YABC 1

Roussel, Raymond 1877-1933 .... **TCLC 20**
    See also CA 117

Rovit, Earl (Herbert) 1927-.........**CLC 7**
    See also CA 5-8R
    See also CANR 12

Rowson, Susanna Haswell
    1762-1824.................. **NCLC 5**
    See also DLB 37

Roy, Gabrielle 1909-1983...... **CLC 10, 14**
    See also CANR 5
    See also CA 53-56
    See also obituary CA 110

Różewicz, Tadeusz 1921- .... **CLC 9, 23**
    See also CA 108

Ruark, Gibbons 1941-..............**CLC 3**
    See also CANR 14
    See also CA 33-36R

Rubens, Bernice 192?- .... **CLC 19, 31**
    See also CA 25-28R
    See also DLB 14

Rudkin, (James) David 1936- ......**CLC 14**
    See also CA 89-92
    See also DLB 13

Rudnik, Raphael 1933-............**CLC 7**
    See also CA 29-32R

Ruiz, José Martínez 1874-1967
    See Azorín

Rukeyser, Muriel
    1913-1980..........**CLC 6, 10, 15, 27**
    See also CA 5-8R
    See also obituary CA 93-96
    See also obituary SATA 22
    See also DLB 48

Rule, Jane (Vance) 1931-..........**CLC 27**
    See also CANR 12
    See also CA 25-28R

Rulfo, Juan 1918-1986 ....**CLC 8**
    See also CA 85-88
    See also obituary CA 118

Runyon, (Alfred) Damon
    1880-1946................. **TCLC 10**
    See also CA 107
    See also DLB 11

Rush, Norman 1933-......... **CLC 44 (91)**

Rushdie, (Ahmed) Salman
    1947-................... **CLC 23, 31**
    See also CA 108, 111

Rushforth, Peter (Scott) 1945-......**CLC 19**
    See also CA 101

Ruskin, John 1819-1900........ **TCLC 20**
    See also CA 114
    See also SATA 24

Russ, Joanna 1937-..............**CLC 15**
    See also CANR 11
    See also CA 25-28R
    See also DLB 8

Russell, George William 1867-1935
    See A. E.
    See also CA 104

Russell, (Henry) Ken(neth Alfred)
    1927-.....................**CLC 16**
    See also CA 105

Rutherford, Mark 1831-1913 .... **TCLC 25**
    See also DLB 18

Ruyslinck, Ward 1929-............**CLC 14**

Ryan, Cornelius (John)
    1920-1974....................**CLC 7**
    See also CA 69-72
    See also obituary CA 53-56

Rybakov, Anatoli 1911?- ....**CLC 23**

Ryder, Jonathan 1927-
    See Ludlum, Robert

Ryga, George 1932-..............**CLC 14**
    See also CA 101

Sabato, Ernesto 1911-........ **CLC 10, 23**
    See also CA 97-100

Sachs, Marilyn (Stickle) 1927-......**CLC 35**
    See also CLR 2
    See also CANR 13
    See also CA 17-20R
    See also SAAS 2
    See also SATA 3

Sachs, Nelly 1891-1970............**CLC 14**
    See also CAP 2
    See also CA 17-18
    See also obituary CA 25-28R

Sackler, Howard (Oliver)
    1929-1982....................**CLC 14**
    See also CA 61-64
    See also obituary CA 108
    See also DLB 7

Sade, Donatien Alphonse François, Comte de
    1740-1814.................. **NCLC 3**

Sadoff, Ira 1945-.................**CLC 9**
    See also CANR 5
    See also CA 53-56

Safire, William 1929- ....**CLC 10**
    See also CA 17-20R

Sagan, Carl (Edward) 1934- ....**CLC 30**
    See also CANR 11
    See also CA 25-28R

Sagan, Françoise
    1935-............. **CLC 3, 6, 9, 17, 36**
    See also Quoirez, Françoise

Sahgal, Nayantara (Pandit)
    1927-.....................**CLC 41**
    See also CANR 11
    See also CA 9-12R

Sainte-Beuve, Charles Augustin
    1804-1869................. **NCLC 5**

Sainte-Marie, Beverly 1941-
    See Sainte-Marie, Buffy
    See also CA 107

Sainte-Marie, Buffy 1941- ....**CLC 17**
    See also Sainte-Marie, Beverly

Saint-Exupéry, Antoine (Jean Baptiste Marie Roger) de 1900-1944 .... **TCLC 2**
    See also CLR 10
    See also CA 108
    See also SATA 20

Sait Faik (Abasıyanık)
    1906-1954................. **TCLC 23**

Saki 1870-1916................. **TCLC 3**
    See also Munro, H(ector) H(ugh)

Salama, Hannu 1936-.............**CLC 18**

Salamanca, J(ack) R(ichard)
    1922-.................... **CLC 4, 15**
    See also CA 25-28R

Salinas, Pedro 1891-1951........ **TCLC 17**
    See also CA 117

Salinger, J(erome) D(avid)
    1919-.................**CLC 1, 3, 8, 12**
    See also CA 5-8R
    See also DLB 2
    See also CDALB 1941-1968

Salter, James 1925-...............**CLC 7**
    See also CA 73-76

Saltus, Edgar (Evertson)
    1855-1921.................. **TCLC 8**
    See also CA 105

Saltykov, Mikhail Evgrafovich
    1826-1889................. **NCLC 16**

Samarakis, Antonis 1919-..........**CLC 5**
    See also CA 25-28R

Sánchez, Luis Rafael 1936- ....**CLC 23**

Sanchez, Sonia 1934-..............**CLC 5**
    See also CA 33-36R
    See also SATA 22
    See also DLB 41

Sand, George 1804-1876.......... **NCLC 2**

Sandburg, Carl (August)
    1878-1967...... **CLC 1, 4, 10, 15, 35**
    See also CA 5-8R
    See also obituary CA 25-28R
    See also SATA 8
    See also DLB 17

Sandburg, Charles August 1878-1967
    See Sandburg, Carl (August)

Sanders, Lawrence 1920-..........**CLC 41**
    See also CA 81-84

Sandoz, Mari (Susette)
    1896-1966....................**CLC 28**
    See also CANR 17
    See also CA 1-4R
    See also obituary CA 25-28R
    See also SATA 5
    See also DLB 9

Saner, Reg(inald Anthony)
    1931-.......................**CLC 9**
    See also CA 65-68

Sansom, William 1912-1976...... **CLC 2, 6**
    See also CA 5-8R
    See also obituary CA 65-68

Smith, Lee 1944- . . . . .CLC 25
See also CA 114, 119
See also DLB-Y 83

Smith, Martin Cruz 1942- . . . . .CLC 25
See also CANR 6
See also CA 85-88

Smith, Martin William 1942-
See Smith, Martin Cruz

Smith, Mary-Ann Tirone
1944- . . . . CLC 39 (97)
See also CA 118

Smith, Patti 1946- . . . . .CLC 12
See also CA 93-96

Smith, Pauline (Urmson)
1882-1959. . . . . TCLC 25
See also CA 29-32R
See also SATA 27

Smith, Sara Mahala Redway 1900-1972
See Benson, Sally

Smith, Stevie
1902-1971. . . . . CLC 3, 8, 25, 44 (431)
See also Smith, Florence Margaret
See also DLB 20

Smith, Wilbur (Addison) 1933- . . . . .CLC 33
See also CANR 7
See also CA 13-16R

Smith, William Jay 1918- . . . . .CLC 6
See also CA 5-8R
See also SATA 2
See also DLB 5

Smollett, Tobias (George)
1721-1771. . . . . LC 2
See also DLB 39

Snodgrass, W(illiam) D(e Witt)
1926- . . . . .CLC 2, 6, 10, 18
See also CANR 6
See also CA 1-4R
See also DLB 5

Snow, C(harles) P(ercy)
1905-1980. . . . . . CLC 1, 4, 6, 9, 13, 19
See also CA 5-8R
See also obituary CA 101
See also DLB 15

Snyder, Gary (Sherman)
1930- . . . . CLC 1, 2, 5, 9, 32
See also CA 17-20R
See also DLB 5, 16

Snyder, Zilpha Keatley 1927- . . . . . .CLC 17
See also CA 9-12R
See also SAAS 2
See also SATA 1, 28

Sokolov, Raymond 1941- . . . . .CLC 7
See also CA 85-88

Sologub, Fyodor 1863-1927 . . . . TCLC 9
See also Teternikov, Fyodor Kuzmich

Solomos, Dionysios
1798-1857. . . . . NCLC 15

Solwoska, Mara 1929-
See French, Marilyn

Solzhenitsyn, Aleksandr I(sayevich)
1918- . . . . .CLC 1, 2, 4, 7, 9, 10, 18, 26,
34 (480)

See also CA 69-72
See also AITN 1

Somers, Jane 1919-
See Lessing, Doris (May)

Sommer, Scott 1951- . . . . .CLC 25
See also CA 106

Sondheim, Stephen (Joshua)
1930- . . . . CLC 30, 39 (172)
See also CA 103

Sontag, Susan
1933- . . . . CLC 1, 2, 10, 13, 31
See also CA 17-20R
See also DLB 2

Sorrentino, Gilbert
1929- . . . . CLC 3, 7, 14, 22, 40
See also CANR 14
See also CA 77-80
See also DLB 5
See also DLB-Y 80

Soto, Gary 1952- . . . . .CLC 32
See also CA 119

Souster, (Holmes) Raymond
1921- . . . . CLC 5, 14
See also CANR 13
See also CA 13-16R

Southern, Terry 1926- . . . . .CLC 7
See also CANR 1
See also CA 1-4R
See also DLB 2

Southey, Robert 1774-1843 . . . . NCLC 8

Soyinka, Akinwande Oluwole 1934-
See Soyinka, Wole

Soyinka, Wole
1934- . . . . CLC 3, 5, 14, 36, 44 (276)
See also CA 13-16R
See also DLB-Y 1986

Spackman, W(illiam) M(ode)
1905- . . . . .CLC 46
See also CA 81-84

Spacks, Barry 1931- . . . . .CLC 14
See also CA 29-32R

Spanidou, Irini 1946- . . . . CLC 44 (104)

Spark, Muriel (Sarah)
1918- . . . . .CLC 2, 3, 5, 8, 13, 18, 40
See also CANR 12
See also CA 5-8R
See also DLB 15

Spencer, Elizabeth 1921- . . . . .CLC 22
See also CA 13-16R
See also SATA 14
See also DLB 6

Spencer, Scott 1945- . . . . .CLC 30
See also CA 113
See also DLB-Y 86

Spender, Stephen (Harold)
1909- . . . . CLC 1, 2, 5, 10, 41
See also CA 9-12R
See also DLB 20

Spengler, Oswald 1880-1936 . . . . . TCLC 25
See also CA 118

Spenser, Edmund 1552?-1599 . . . . LC 5

Spicer, Jack 1925-1965 . . . . CLC 8, 18
See also CA 85-88
See also DLB 5, 16

Spielberg, Peter 1929- . . . . .CLC 6
See also CANR 4
See also CA 5-8R
See also DLB-Y 81

Spielberg, Steven 1947- . . . . .CLC 20
See also CA 77-80
See also SATA 32

Spillane, Frank Morrison 1918-
See Spillane, Mickey
See also CA 25-28R

Spillane, Mickey 1918- . . . . CLC 3, 13
See also Spillane, Frank Morrison

Spinrad, Norman (Richard)
1940- . . . . .CLC 46
See also CANR 20
See also CA 37-40R
See also DLB 8

Spitteler, Carl (Friedrich Georg)
1845-1924. . . . . TCLC 12
See also CA 109

Spivack, Kathleen (Romola Drucker)
1938- . . . . .CLC 6
See also CA 49-52

Spoto, Donald 1941- . . . . CLC 39 (444)
See also CANR 11
See also CA 65-68

Springsteen, Bruce 1949- . . . . .CLC 17
See also CA 111

Spurling, Hilary 1940- . . . . . . CLC 34 (494)
See also CA 104

Staël-Holstein, Anne Louise Germaine
Necker, Baronne de
1766-1817. . . . . NCLC 3

Stafford, Jean 1915-1979 . . . . . CLC 4, 7, 19
See also CANR 3
See also CA 1-4R
See also obituary CA 85-88
See also obituary SATA 22
See also DLB 2

Stafford, William (Edgar)
1914- . . . . CLC 4, 7, 29
See also CAAS 3
See also CANR 5
See also CA 5-8R
See also DLB 5

Stannard, Martin 1947- . . . . . CLC 44 (520)

Stanton, Maura 1946- . . . . .CLC 9
See also CANR 15
See also CA 89-92

Stapledon, (William) Olaf
1886-1950. . . . . TCLC 22
See also CA 111
See also DLB 15

Stark, Richard 1933-
See Westlake, Donald E(dwin)

Stead, Christina (Ellen)
1902-1983. . . . . .CLC 2, 5, 8, 32
See also CA 13-16R
See also obituary CA 109

Steele, Timothy (Reid) 1948- . . . . . . .CLC 45
See also CANR 16
See also CA 93-96

Steffens, (Joseph) Lincoln
1866-1936. . . . . TCLC 20
See also CA 117
See also SAAS 1

Stegner, Wallace (Earle) 1909- . . . . . .CLC 9
See also CANR 1
See also CA 1-4R
See also DLB 9
See also AITN 1

Stein, Gertrude 1874-1946......**TCLC 1, 6**
  See also CA 104
  See also DLB 4

Steinbeck, John (Ernst)
  1902-1968........**CLC 1, 5, 9, 13, 21,**
                              34 (404), 45
  See also CANR 1
  See also CA 1-4R
  See also obituary CA 25-28R
  See also SATA 9
  See also DLB 7, 9
  See also DLB-DS 2

Steiner, George 1929-.............**CLC 24**
  See also CA 73-76

Steiner, Rudolf(us Josephus Laurentius)
  1861-1925.................**TCLC 13**
  See also CA 107

Stephen, Leslie 1832-1904 ....**TCLC 23**
  See also CANR 9
  See also CA 21-24R
  See also DLB 57

Stephens, James 1882?-1950 ......**TCLC 4**
  See also CA 104
  See also DLB 19

Stephens, Reed
  See Donaldson, Stephen R.

Steptoe, Lydia 1892-1982
  See Barnes, Djuna

Sterling, George 1869-1926 ......**TCLC 20**
  See also CA 117
  See also DLB 54

Stern, Gerald 1925-.............**CLC 40**
  See also CA 81-84

Stern, Richard G(ustave)
  1928-................ **CLC 4, 39 (234)**
  See also CANR 1
  See also CA 1-4R

Sternberg, Jonas 1894-1969
  See Sternberg, Josef von

Sternberg, Josef von
  1894-1969...................**CLC 20**
  See also CA 81-84

Sterne, Laurence 1713-1768 ....**LC 2**
  See also DLB 39

Sternheim, (William Adolf) Carl
  1878-1942.................**TCLC 8**
  See also CA 105

Stevens, Mark 19??- .... **CLC 34 (111)**

Stevens, Wallace
  1879-1955...............**TCLC 3, 12**
  See also CA 104
  See also DLB 54

Stevenson, Anne (Katharine)
  1933-................**CLC 7, 33**
  See also Elvin, Anne Katharine Stevenson
  See also CANR 9
  See also DLB 40

Stevenson, Robert Louis
  1850-1894...............**NCLC 5, 14**
  See also CLR 10, 11
  See also YABC 2
  See also DLB 18, 57

Stewart, J(ohn) I(nnes) M(ackintosh)
  1906-.................**CLC 7, 14, 32**
  See also CAAS 3
  See also CA 85-88

Stewart, Mary (Florence Elinor)
  1916-....................**CLC 7, 35**
  See also CANR 1
  See also CA 1-4R
  See also SATA 12

Stewart, Will 1908-
  See Williamson, Jack

Sting 1951-
  See The Police

Stitt, Milan 1941-.................**CLC 29**
  See also CA 69-72

Stoker, Bram (Abraham)
  1847-1912.................. **TCLC 8**
  See also CA 105
  See also SATA 29
  See also DLB 36

Stolz, Mary (Slattery) 1920-.......**CLC 12**
  See also CANR 13
  See also CA 5-8R
  See also SAAS 3
  See also SATA 10
  See also AITN 1

Stone, Irving 1903- ....**CLC 7**
  See also CAAS 3
  See also CANR 1
  See also CA 1-4R
  See also SATA 3
  See also AITN 1

Stone, Robert (Anthony)
  1937?-................ **CLC 5, 23, 42**
  See also CA 85-88

Stoppard, Tom
  1937-........ **CLC 1, 3, 4, 5, 8, 15, 29,**
                              34 (272)
  See also CA 81-84
  See also DLB 13
  See also DLB-Y 85

Storey, David (Malcolm)
  1933-.................**CLC 2, 4, 5, 8**
  See also CA 81-84
  See also DLB 13, 14

Storm, Hyemeyohsts 1935-.........**CLC 3**
  See also CA 81-84

Storm, (Hans) Theodor (Woldsen)
  1817-1888.................**NCLC 1**

Storni, Alfonsina 1892-1938.......**TCLC 5**
  See also CA 104

Stout, Rex (Todhunter)
  1886-1975....................**CLC 3**
  See also CA 61-64
  See also AITN 2

Stow, (Julian) Randolph 1935- .....**CLC 23**
  See also CA 13-16R

Stowe, Harriet (Elizabeth) Beecher
  1811-1896.................**NCLC 3**
  See also YABC 1
  See also DLB 1, 12, 42

Strachey, (Giles) Lytton
  1880-1932.................**TCLC 12**
  See also CA 110

Strand, Mark 1934-........ **CLC 6, 18, 41**
  See also CA 21-24R
  See also SATA 41
  See also DLB 5

Straub, Peter (Francis) 1943- ......**CLC 28**
  See also CA 85-88
  See also DLB-Y 84

Strauss, Botho 1944-..............**CLC 22**

Straussler, Tomas 1937-
  See Stoppard, Tom

Streatfeild, (Mary) Noel 1897-......**CLC 21**
  See also CA 81-84
  See also obituary CA 120
  See also SATA 20, 48

Stribling, T(homas) S(igismund)
  1881-1965..................**CLC 23**
  See also obituary CA 107
  See also DLB 9

Strindberg, (Johan) August
  1849-1912..............**TCLC 1, 8, 21**
  See also CA 104

Strugatskii, Arkadii (Natanovich) 1925-
  See Strugatskii, Arkadii (Natanovich) and
    Strugatskii, Boris (Natanovich)
  See also CA 106

Strugatskii, Arkadii (Natanovich) 1925-
    and **Strugatskii, Boris**
    (Natanovich) 1933- ....**CLC 27**

Strugatskii, Boris (Natanovich) 1933-
  See Strugatskii, Arkadii (Natanovich) and
    Strugatskii, Boris (Natanovich)
  See also CA 106

Strugatskii, Boris (Natanovich) 1933- and
    Strugatskii, Arkadii (Natanovich) 1925-
  See Strugatskii, Arkadii (Natanovich) and
    Strugatskii, Boris (Natanovich)

Strummer, Joe 1953?-
  See The Clash

Stuart, (Hilton) Jesse
  1906-1984..........**CLC 1, 8, 11, 14,**
                              34 (372)
  See also CA 5-8R
  See also obituary CA 112
  See also SATA 2
  See also obituary SATA 36
  See also DLB 9, 48
  See also DLB-Y 84

Sturgeon, Theodore (Hamilton)
  1918-1985........ **CLC 22, 39 (360)**
  See also CA 81-84
  See also obituary CA 116
  See also DLB 8
  See also DLB-Y 85

Styron, William
  1925-............. **CLC 1, 3, 5, 11, 15**
  See also CANR 6
  See also CA 5-8R
  See also DLB 2
  See also DLB-Y 80

Su Man-shu 1884-1918......... **TCLC 24**

Sudermann, Hermann
  1857-1928.................**TCLC 15**
  See also CA 107

Sue, Eugène 1804-1857..........**NCLC 1**

Sukenick, Ronald 1932- .... **CLC 3, 4, 6**
  See also CA 25-28R
  See also DLB-Y 81

Suknaski, Andrew 1942-...........**CLC 19**
  See also CA 101
  See also DLB 53

Summers, Andrew James 1942-
  See The Police

Summers, Andy 1942-
  See The Police

Summers, Hollis (Spurgeon, Jr.)
1916-.........................CLC **10**
See also CANR 3
See also CA 5-8R
See also DLB 6

Summers, (Alphonsus Joseph-Mary Augustus)
Montague 1880-1948 .... TCLC **16**

Sumner, Gordon Matthew 1951-
See The Police

Surtees, Robert Smith
1805-1864.................. NCLC **14**
See also DLB 21

Susann, Jacqueline 1921-1974......CLC **3**
See also CA 65-68
See also obituary CA 53-56
See also AITN 1

Süskind, Patrick 1949-...... CLC **44** (111)

Sutcliff, Rosemary 1920- ....CLC **26**
See also CLR 1
See also CA 5-8R
See also SATA 6, 44

Sutro, Alfred 1863-1933......... TCLC **6**
See also CA 105
See also DLB 10

Sutton, Henry 1935-
See Slavitt, David (R.)

Svevo, Italo 1861-1928 .... TCLC **2**
See also Schmitz, Ettore

Swados, Elizabeth 1951-..........CLC **12**
See also CA 97-100

Swados, Harvey 1920-1972 ....CLC **5**
See also CANR 6
See also CA 5-8R
See also obituary CA 37-40R
See also DLB 2

Swarthout, Glendon (Fred)
1918-........................CLC **35**
See also CANR 1
See also CA 1-4R
See also SATA 26

Swenson, May 1919- .... CLC **4, 14**
See also CA 5-8R
See also SATA 15
See also DLB 5

Swift, Graham 1949-.............CLC **41**
See also CA 117

Swift, Jonathan 1667-1745.......... LC **1**
See also SATA 19
See also DLB 39

Swinburne, Algernon Charles
1837-1909.................. TCLC **8**
See also CA 105
See also DLB 35, 57

Swinfen, Ann 19??-......... CLC **34** (576)

Swinnerton, Frank (Arthur)
1884-1982....................CLC **31**
See also obituary CA 108
See also DLB 34

Symons, Arthur (William)
1865-1945 .... TCLC **11**
See also CA 107
See also DLB 19, 57

Symons, Julian (Gustave)
1912-.................. CLC **2, 14, 32**
See also CAAS 3
See also CANR 3
See also CA 49-52

Synge, (Edmund) John Millington
1871-1909.................. TCLC **6**
See also CA 104
See also DLB 10, 19

Syruc, J. 1911-
See Miłosz, Czesław

Szirtes, George 1948- ....CLC **46**
See also CA 109

Tabori, George 1914- ....CLC **19**
See also CANR 4
See also CA 49-52

Tagore, (Sir) Rabindranath
1861-1941.................. TCLC **3**
See also Thakura, Ravindranatha

Taine, Hippolyte Adolphe
1828-1893.................. NCLC **15**

Talese, Gaetano 1932-
See Talese, Gay

Talese, Gay 1932- ....CLC **37**
See also CANR 9
See also CA 1-4R
See also AITN 1

Tallent, Elizabeth (Ann) 1954- .....CLC **45**
See also CA 117

Tally, Ted 1952-...................CLC **42**
See also CA 120

Tamayo y Baus, Manuel
1829-1898.................. NCLC **1**

Tammsaare, A(nton) H(ansen)
1878-1940.................. TCLC **27**

Tanizaki, Jun'ichirō
1886-1965..............CLC **8, 14, 28**
See also CA 93-96
See also obituary CA 25-28R

Tarkington, (Newton) Booth
1869-1946.................. TCLC **9**
See also CA 110
See also SATA 17
See also DLB 9

Tasso, Torquato 1544-1595 .... LC **5**

Tate, (John Orley) Allen
1899-1979...... CLC **2, 4, 6, 9, 11, 14,
24**
See also CA 5-8R
See also obituary CA 85-88
See also DLB 4, 45

Tate, James 1943- ....CLC **2, 6, 25**
See also CA 21-24R
See also DLB 5

Tavel, Ronald 1940- ....CLC **6**
See also CA 21-24R

Taylor, C(ecil) P(hillip)
1929-1981....................CLC **27**
See also CA 25-28R
See also obituary CA 105

Taylor, Eleanor Ross 1920- ....CLC **5**
See also CA 81-84

Taylor, Elizabeth
1912-1975..............CLC **2, 4, 29**
See also CANR 9
See also CA 13-16R
See also SATA 13

Taylor, Henry (Splawn)
1917-.................. CLC **44** (300)

Taylor, Kamala (Purnaiya) 1924-
See Markandaya, Kamala
See also CA 77-80

Taylor, Mildred D(elois) 1943- .....CLC **21**
See also CLR 9
See also CA 85-88
See also SATA 15
See also DLB 52

Taylor, Peter (Hillsman)
1917-...... CLC **1, 4, 18, 37, 44** (304)
See also CANR 9
See also CA 13-16R
See also DLB-Y 81

Taylor, Robert Lewis 1912-........CLC **14**
See also CANR 3
See also CA 1-4R
See also SATA 10

Teasdale, Sara 1884-1933........ TCLC **4**
See also CA 104
See also DLB 45
See also SATA 32

Tegnér, Esaias 1782-1846........ NCLC **2**

Teilhard de Chardin, (Marie Joseph) Pierre
1881-1955.................. TCLC **9**
See also CA 105

Tennant, Emma 1937- ....CLC **13**
See also CANR 10
See also CA 65-68
See also DLB 14

Teran, Lisa St. Aubin de 19??-.....CLC **36**

Terkel, Louis 1912-
See Terkel, Studs
See also CANR 18
See also CA 57-60

Terkel, Studs 1912-................CLC **38**
See also Terkel, Louis
See also AITN 1

Terry, Megan 1932- ....CLC **19**
See also CA 77-80
See also DLB 7

Tesich, Steve 1943?- ....CLC **40**
See also CA 105
See also DLB-Y 83

Tesich, Stoyan 1943?-
See Tesich, Steve

Tertz, Abram 1925-
See Sinyavsky, Andrei (Donatevich)

Teternikov, Fyodor Kuzmich 1863-1927
See Sologub, Fyodor
See also CA 104

Tevis, Walter 1928-1984..........CLC **42**
See also CA 113

Tey, Josephine 1897-1952 .... TCLC **14**
See also Mackintosh, Elizabeth

Thackeray, William Makepeace
1811-1863...............NCLC **5, 14**
See also SATA 23
See also DLB 21

Thakura, Ravindranatha 1861-1941
See Tagore, (Sir) Rabindranath
See also CA 104

Thelwell, Michael (Miles)
1939-........................CLC **22**
See also CA 101

Author Index

Author Index

Wodehouse, (Sir) P(elham) G(renville)
1881-1975........ **CLC 1, 2, 5, 10, 22**
See also CANR 3
See also CA 45-48
See also obituary CA 57-60
See also SATA 22
See also DLB 34
See also AITN 2

Woiwode, Larry (Alfred)
1941-...................... **CLC 6, 10**
See also CANR 16
See also CA 73-76
See also DLB 6

Wojciechowska, Maia (Teresa)
1927-..........................**CLC 26**
See also CLR 1
See also CANR 4
See also CA 9-12R
See also SAAS 1
See also SATA 1, 28

Wolf, Christa 1929-.......... **CLC 14, 29**
See also CA 85-88

Wolfe, Gene (Rodman) 1931- ......**CLC 25**
See also CANR 6
See also CA 57-60
See also DLB 8

Wolfe, Thomas (Clayton)
1900-1938............... **TCLC 4, 13**
See also CA 104
See also DLB 9
See also DLB-Y 85
See also DLB-DS 2

Wolfe, Thomas Kennerly, Jr. 1931-
See Wolfe, Tom
See also CANR 9
See also CA 13-16R

Wolfe, Tom 1931- ..... **CLC 1, 2, 9, 15, 35**
See also Wolfe, Thomas Kennerly, Jr.
See also AITN 2

Wolff, Geoffrey (Ansell) 1937-......**CLC 41**
See also CA 29-32R

Wolff, Tobias (Jonathan Ansell)
1945-................... **CLC 39 (283)**
See also CA 114, 117

Wolitzer, Hilma 1930-.............**CLC 17**
See also CANR 18
See also CA 65-68
See also SATA 31

Wollstonecraft (Godwin), Mary
1759-1797......................**LC 5**
See also DLB 39

Wonder, Stevie 1950- ....**CLC 12**
See also Morris, Steveland Judkins

Wong, Jade Snow 1922-..........**CLC 17**
See also CA 109

Woodcott, Keith 1934-
See Brunner, John (Kilian Houston)

Woolf, (Adeline) Virginia
1882-1941.............**TCLC 1, 5, 20**
See also CA 104
See also DLB 36

Woollcott, Alexander (Humphreys)
1887-1943.................**TCLC 5**
See also CA 105
See also DLB 29

Wordsworth, William
1770-1850.................. **NCLC 12**

Wouk, Herman 1915-........ **CLC 1, 9, 38**
See also CANR 6
See also CA 5-8R
See also DLB-Y 82

Wright, Charles 1935- ...... **CLC 6, 13, 28**
See also CA 29-32R
See also DLB-Y 82

Wright, James (Arlington)
1927-1980...........**CLC 3, 5, 10, 28**
See also CANR 4
See also CA 49-52
See also obituary CA 97-100
See also DLB 5
See also AITN 2

Wright, Judith 1915-.............**CLC 11**
See also CA 13-16R
See also SATA 14

Wright, L(aurali) R.
1939-.................. **CLC 44 (334)**

Wright, Richard (Nathaniel)
1908-1960...... **CLC 1, 3, 4, 9, 14, 21**
See also CA 108
See also DLB-DS 2

Wright, Richard B(ruce) 1937-......**CLC 6**
See also CA 85-88
See also DLB 53

Wright, Rick 1945-
See Pink Floyd

Wright, Stephen 1946- ....**CLC 33**

Wright, Willard Huntington 1888-1939
See Van Dine, S. S.
See also CA 115

Wright, William 1930- ...... **CLC 44 (526)**

Wu Ch'eng-en 1500?-1582?.......... **LC 7**

Wu Ching-tzu 1701-1754 .... **LC 2**

Wurlitzer, Rudolph
1938?-................. **CLC 2, 4, 15**
See also CA 85-88

Wylie (Benét), Elinor (Morton Hoyt)
1885-1928................... **TCLC 8**
See also CA 105
See also DLB 9, 45

Wylie, Philip (Gordon)
1902-1971...................**CLC 43**
See also CAP 2
See also obituary CA 33-36R
See also CA 21-22
See also DLB 9

Wyndham, John 1903-1969 ....**CLC 19**
See also Harris, John (Wyndham Parkes
Lucas) Beynon

Wyss, Johann David
1743-1818.................. **NCLC 10**
See also SATA 27, 29

Yanovsky, Vassily S(emenovich)
1906-..................... **CLC 2, 18**
See also CA 97-100

Yates, Richard 1926-......... **CLC 7, 8, 23**
See also CANR 10
See also CA 5-8R
See also DLB 2
See also DLB-Y 81

Yeats, William Butler
1865-1939............**TCLC 1, 11, 18**
See also CANR 10
See also CA 104
See also DLB 10, 19

Yehoshua, A(braham) B.
1936-.................... **CLC 13, 31**
See also CA 33-36R

Yep, Laurence (Michael) 1948-.....**CLC 35**
See also CLR 3
See also CANR 1
See also CA 49-52
See also SATA 7
See also DLB 52

Yerby, Frank G(arvin)
1916-.................. **CLC 1, 7, 22**
See also CANR 16
See also CA 9-12R

Yevtushenko, Yevgeny (Aleksandrovich)
1933-.................**CLC 1, 3, 13, 26**
See also CA 81-84

Yezierska, Anzia 1885?-1970.......**CLC 46**
See also obituary CA 89-92
See also DLB 28

Yglesias, Helen 1915- .... **CLC 7, 22**
See also CANR 15
See also CA 37-40R

Yorke, Henry Vincent 1905-1974
See Green, Henry
See also CA 85-88
See also obituary CA 49-52

Young, Al 1939-..................**CLC 19**
See also CA 29-32R
See also DLB 33

Young, Andrew 1885-1971.........**CLC 5**
See also CANR 7
See also CA 5-8R

Young, Edward 1683-1765..........**LC 3**

Young, Neil 1945- ....**CLC 17**
See also CA 110

Yourcenar, Marguerite
1903-.................... **CLC 19, 38**
See also CA 69-72

Yurick, Sol 1925-..................**CLC 6**
See also CA 13-16R

Zamyatin, Yevgeny Ivanovich
1884-1937................... **TCLC 8**
See also CA 105

Zangwill, Israel 1864-1926...... **TCLC 16**
See also CA 109
See also DLB 10

Zappa, Francis Vincent, Jr. 1940-
See Zappa, Frank
See also CA 108

Zappa, Frank 1940- ....**CLC 17**
See also Zappa, Francis Vincent, Jr.

Zaturenska, Marya
1902-1982................. **CLC 6, 11**
See also CA 13-16R
See also obituary CA 105

Zelazny, Roger 1937- ....**CLC 21**
See also CA 21-24R
See also SATA 39
See also DLB 8

Author Index

NCLC Cumulative Nationality Index

NCLC Cumulative Title Index

Title Index

Title Index

Title Index

Title Index

Title Index

Title Index

Title Index

Title Index

Title Index

Title Index

Title Index

Title Index

Title Index

Title Index